D1560089

The
ALASKA
WILDERNESS
MILEPOST®

Alaska Northwest Books™
A division of GTE Discovery Publications, Inc.
P.O. Box 3007, Bothell, WA 98041-3007

Barrow

Prudhoe Bay

Point Hope

**BROOKS RANGE
AND THE ARCTIC**

Kotzebue   BROOKS   RANGE

Arctic   Circle

**Seward
Peninsula**

BERING   Saint Lawrence
                    Island

Nome

Yukon   River

INTERIOR

SEA

Fairbanks

COAST   Saint Mathew
                   Island

River

RANGE

Mt. McKinley

Nunivak
Island

Bethel

ALASKA

Kuskokwim

Anchorage

Kenai   Valdez

Homer Seward   Cordova

Dillingham

Prince William
Sound

Yakutat   Haines   Skagway

Pribilof
Islands

Bristol Bay

Mt.
Katmai

**ALASKA PENINSULA/
ALEUTIANS**

Kodiak
Island

**SOUTHCENTRAL/
GULF COAST**

Juneau

Sitka

Petersburg
Wrangell

SOUTHEAST

Ketchikan

CONTENTS

(Continues on next page)

COVER — Photo by Fred Hirschmann ©1989

EDITORIAL: Publisher, Peter L. Green. General Manager, Gary C. Tranter. Publishing/Production Director, Kathleen M. Gammon. Editor, Virginia McKinney. Managing Editor, Sara Juday. MILEPOST Publications Editor, Kris Valencia. Editorial Assistance: Fay Bartels, Laurie Thompson.

ADVERTISING: National Advertising Sales Manager, Thomas G. Murphy. Alaska Sales Coordinator, Sara Juday. Traffic Manager, Victoria Snyder. Alaska Sales: Lynn Lausterer, Jerrianne Lowther, Kent Sturgis. National Sales: Elaine J. Corry, Pacific N.W. Media.

PRODUCTION: Production Manager, Nancy Deahl. Production Supervisor, Louise Helmick. Designer, Alyson Hallberg. Illustrations, Carol Haffar.

BUSINESS: Fulfillment Manager, Cherryl Benson. Fulfillment Supervisor, Georgia Boyd.

ISBN 0-88240-289-7   ISSN 0888-8884
Key title: The Alaska Wilderness Milepost

PRINTED IN U.S.A.
Alaska Norhwest Books
22026 20th Ave. S.E., Bothell, WA 98021
137 East 7th Ave., Anchorage, AK 99501

Publishers of:
The MILEPOST®
The ALASKA WILDERNESS MILEPOST®
NORTHWEST MILEPOSTS®
Books about the North Country

INTRODUCTION

From the Editors

Where the roads end is where Alaska begins. The folks who only see the metropolitan centers, the supermarkets and the super-highways, don't even get a good smell of the real Alaska. That's a compounding of berries and Hudson's Bay tea on untrammeled tundra, kelp and popweed and clams and decaying driftwood on a thousand beaches.

It's the sound of harsh and cold Bering Sea breakers dumping on the lonely western shore. It's the sound of waterfalls tumbling a thousand feet from Southeast snowfields and marmots whistling from the heights. It's clamoring geese, kreeking eagles and whirring hummingbird wings.

It's the endless expanses of sea where the waves march backward in great heaving swells to the Orient . . . where the peaks rise vertically from your feet to the heavens . . . everywhere things growing . . . browns, red, shiny black and a myriad shades of green.

To know this land is to love it. In this book we have put together some useful facts on how to get there, what to expect when you arrive and answered a lot of questions that you'll be glad somebody finally put together in one book.

Traveling Alaska with *The ALASKA WILDERNESS MILEPOST*®

The ALASKA WILDERNESS MILEPOST® has been designed to help you get the most out of your travels in the North. It is a guide not only to accommodations, services and what to see and do, but also to the people, history, land and wildlife of Alaska. If you find during your travels that we've left out information which would have been helpful to you, let us know! Use the Field Editor

Report in the back of the book or just drop us a note.

Information in *The ALASKA WILDERNESS MILEPOST*® is organized by geographical regions, starting with the most southerly, Southeast, and moving north to South-central/Gulf Coast, Alaska Peninsula/Aleutians, Bering Sea Coast, Brooks Range and the Arctic and the Interior. (Additionally, Southcentral/Gulf Coast is broken down into 6 subregions: Anchorage and the Mat-Su Valley; Copper River/Wrangell-St. Elias; Prince William Sound; Kenai Peninsula; Western Cook Inlet; and Kodiak. And the huge Bering Sea Coast region is also broken down into subregions: Bristol Bay, Yukon-Kuskokwim Delta and Seward Peninsula/Norton Sound.)

Each of the 6 regional sections begins with an introduction to the region and a map. The introduction section is followed by a section on the region's communities, listed alphabetically and including information on transportation, climate, airstrips, visitor facilities and other data, along with details on history, geography and lifestyle. The communities section is followed by a section on the attractions of the region. The attractions section covers national and state parks, forests, wildlife refuges and sanctuaries, river running, sportfishing, recreation cabins and hiking trails. Special features of each region, such as lighthouses, hot springs, landforms and historic sites, are also included for each region.

At the back of the book, a special BUYERS GUIDE section lists transportation, accommodations and guide services for each region.

Use the Contents, the Index at the front of

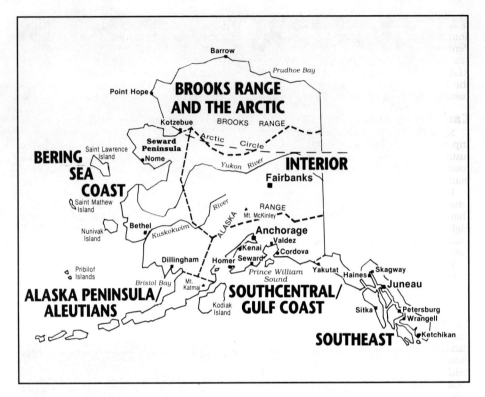

the book and the regional maps to locate communities and other destinations.

Other information helpful to anyone traveling off the beaten path in Alaska is included in the GENERAL INFORMATION section. For information on access points and other locations along Alaska's road system, refer to *The MILEPOST*®, the complete guide to North Country travel. For information on ordering *The MILEPOST*® and other books on the North, see the ALASKA NORTHWEST LIBRARY section at the back of the book.

Welcome to Alaska
Population: 531,000
Area: 586,412 square miles

Alaska is the most sparsely populated state in the Union, with about 1.1 square miles for every person. It is bounded on the north by the Arctic Ocean and on the south by the Pacific Ocean. To the east is the land mass of northern Canada and to the west the Bering Sea separates Alaska from Siberia.

Two extensive mountain systems span the Alaska mainland, and 17 of the 20 highest mountains in the United States are in the 49th state. Above the Arctic Circle is the Brooks Range, a northern extension of the Rocky Mountains, which was the last major mountain system in North America to be mapped and explored. More massive than the Brooks Range is the Alaska Range, which curves around southcentral Alaska and continues south through southeastern Alaska and Canada as the Pacific Coast ranges. Crown jewel of the Alaska Range is Mount McKinley (also known as Denali), the highest peak in North America and one of the tallest mountains in the world at 20,320 feet.

Alaska is one-fifth the size of the rest of the United States. From Ketchikan, on the southern end of the Southeast Panhandle, to Barrow, on the northernmost tip of the Arctic Slope, is as great a distance as from Florida to Minnesota. And despite the common notion of Alaska as one unbroken land of ice and snow, the regional variations in our largest state are dramatic. The maritime climate of the far-flung Aleutian Islands, which stretch a thousand miles across the North Pacific, is a world apart from the bitter cold winters and hot summers of the continental climate in the Interior.

There are 6 distinct natural regions that make up the state of Alaska: Southeast, Southcentral and the Gulf Coast, the Alaska Peninsula and the Aleutian Chain, the Bering Sea Coast, the Arctic and the Interior. *The ALASKA WILDERNESS MILEPOST®* describes the climate, geography, history, industries, communities and attractions of each region.

Caution to Travelers

Some facilities you may encounter on your trip to the Bush may be considerably more rustic than what you're used to. This is frontier country. You'll get lots of smiles, but not many of the frills of city travel.

Between the time our questionnaires were returned to us and the time of your trip, changes may have taken place. Costs may be higher, hours of operation may change and businesses may close. In all such cases the publisher will not be held responsible.

Readers are requested to inform us of any changes they encounter in their travels. Write to: *The ALASKA WILDERNESS MILEPOST®*, P.O. Box 3007, Bothell, WA 98041-3007.

A sincere effort has been made to give you a complete, accurate and up-to-date guidebook for this immense state. Your understanding of the reasons for the unavoidable exceptions described will be appreciated. The Field Editor Report form in the back of the book gives you an opportunity to let us know about any changes you may find, new attractions and the like.

Thanks

The ALASKA WILDERNESS MILEPOST® appreciates the assistance of the following in putting together this issue:

The U.S. National Park Service; U.S. Postal Service; U.S. Forest Service; U.S. Bureau of Land Management; U.S. Bureau of Customs; U.S. Coast Guard, 17th District; U.S. Fish and Wildlife Service; U.S. Geological Survey; U.S. Bureau of Indian Affairs; U.S. National Oceanic and Atmospheric Administration.

State of Alaska — Division of Tourism; Dept. of Community and Regional Affairs; Office of Enterprise; Division of Marine Highway Systems; Dept. of Transportation and Public Facilities; Dept. of Fish and Game; Division of Forestry; Division of Mining; Division of Parks and Outdoor Recreation; Office of History and Archaeology; Alaska State Troopers; Division of Fire Prevention; Alaska Court System; Dept. of Education; Division of Occupational Licensing; Dept. of Health and Social Services; Dept. of Revenue, Division of Public Services and Alcoholic

Beverage Control Board; Alaska State Museum; University of Alaska Museum; Dept. of Environmental Conservation; Dept. of Labor, Division of Research and Analysis; Division of State Libraries; University of Alaska, Arctic Environmental Information and Data Center, Cooperative Extension Service and the Alaska Wilderness Studies program.

The Alaska Municipal League; Anchorage Telephone Utility; Rural Alaska Community Action Program; Alaska Professional Hunters Assoc.; Alaska Air Carriers Assoc.; Museums Alaska, Inc.; Nova Riverrunners of Alaska; Tanana Chiefs Conference; Alaska Wilderness Guides Assoc.; Channel Flying Inc.; Exploration Holidays and Cruises; Kodiak Area Chamber of Commerce; Valdez Chamber of Commerce; Alaska Wilderness Sailing Safaris; Kodiak Island Borough; City of Cordova; Alaska Discovery Inc.

And the Native corporations, postmasters, teachers and hundreds of other individuals who provided information on community questionnaires.

Dramatic summit of Mount McKinley is often obscured by clouds. (Sharon Nault)

Air Travel

Alaska is the "flyingest" state in the Union; the only practical way to reach many parts of rural Alaska is by airplane. According to the Federal Aviation Administration, in 1989 there were 9,682 registered pilots — 1 out of every 56 Alaskans — and 9,414 registered aircraft — 1 for every 57 Alaskans. This figure is approximately 6 times as many pilots per capita and 12 times as many airplanes per capita as in the other states.

Alaska has about 475 airports. Information on some of these airfields is included in the community listings of *The ALASKA WILDERNESS MILEPOST®*. These brief descriptions are not intended as a guide for pilots flying in the North. Up-to-date information on airstrips, fuel and service, and radio facilities is published every 8 weeks in accordance with specifications and agreements by the U.S. Dept. of Defense, the Federal Aviation Administration and the Dept. of Commerce. Pilots planning to fly their own planes to Alaska should have the latest United States government flight information publication *Alaska Supplement*, and the free booklet, *Flight Tips for Alaskan Tourists*, available from the NOAA, 701 C St., Box 14, Anchorage, AK 99513.

There are at least 17 national and international airlines serving Alaska's major cities. At least 32 others provide scheduled service to other communities within Alaska. Consult a travel agent for current schedules and fares.

Air taxi operators are found in most Alaskan communities and aircraft can be chartered to fly you to a wilderness spot and pick you up later at a prearranged time and location. (Many charter services charge an hourly standby fee if the customer is not on time at the pickup point.) Most charter operators charge an hourly rate either per plane load or per passenger (sometimes with a minimum passenger requirement), others may charge on a per mile basis. Flightseeing trips to area attractions often are available at a fixed price per passenger. Multiengine planes are generally more expensive to charter than single-engine planes.

Sample fares: Cessna 206 wheel plane with 5 passengers, limited luggage, $200 an hour; Cessna 206 amphibious with 4 passengers, limited luggage, $225 an hour; Cessna 185 wheel plane with 3 to 5 passengers, $200 an hour; Cessna 185 floatplane with 5 passengers, $200 an hour; Grumman Goose amphibious with 9 passengers and luggage, $370 an hour; Bellanca Scout with 1 passenger, $120 an hour.

In general, the cheapest way to get to an out-of-the-way location is to take a commercial flight or scheduled mail plane to the closest community that has an air taxi service, then charter a flight to your destination.

Lists of air taxi services operating in the various regions of the state are included in the BUYERS GUIDE.

Alcoholic Beverages

The legal drinking age in Alaska is 21. Children may enter licensed premises, but only with a parent or guardian. There are several types of licensed premises in Alaska, including bars, restaurants, roadhouses and clubs. Consumption regulations are generally very broad, except that in some restaurants you may not be able to purchase beer or wine without also purchasing food. Closing hours are 5 a.m. at the latest; opening hours are 8 a.m. at the earliest. However, some cities have imposed tighter regulations. Packaged liquor, beer and wine are sold by licensed retailers rather than in state liquor stores.

Some villages are "dry" to varying degrees, and visitors should know this in advance to avoid breaking the law inadvertently. Bethel, Barrow and Kotzebue, among others, ban the *sale* of liquor, though importation for personal consumption is permitted. Other villages ban both *sale and importation*. And 18 villages have an even stricter law which bans *possession* of an alcoholic beverage. Do not bring even a hip flask into a village which bans importation or possession. Information on whether a village prohibits the sale, sale and importation, or possession of liquor is included in the community listings.

Antiquities Laws

State and federal laws prohibit excavation or removal of historic and prehistoric cultural materials without a permit. Nearly all 50 states have historic preservation laws; Alaska's extends even to tidal lands, thereby making it illegal to pick up artifacts on the beach. Penalties range from a $1,000 fine to 6 months in jail, or both.

It sometimes is difficult to distinguish between historic sites and abandoned property. Old gold mining towns and cabins, plus areas such as the Chilkoot and Iditarod trails, should always be considered historic sites or private property. Also, cabins that appear to be abandoned may in fact be seasonally used trapping cabins where the structure and possessions are vital to the survival of the owner.

Alaska law also prohibits the disturbance of fossils, including prehistoric animals such as mammoths.

Arctic Circle

This is an imaginary line that lies in an arc across the upper third of Alaska at approximately 66°33' north from the equator. (We say "approximately" because the Arctic Circle varies a few seconds in latitude from year to year.)

During the summer solstice, June 20 or 21, the sun does not set at the Arctic Circle (it appears not to set for 4 days because of refraction). Farther north, at Barrow, the sun does not set from May 10 to Aug. 2. At winter solstice, Dec. 21 or 22, the sun does not rise for 1 day at the Arctic Circle. At Barrow, the sun does not rise above the horizon for 67 days — daytime is more like twilight during that time.

You can cross the Arctic Circle with any of several airline and air taxi-operated arctic tours to such places as Fort Yukon, Prudhoe Bay,

Barrow and Kotzebue. These firms may give you a certificate commemorating your crossing.

Aurora Borealis

The aurora borealis, or northern lights, is produced by charged electrons and protons striking gas particles in the earth's upper atmosphere. The electrons and protons are released through sun spot activity and emanate into space. A few drift the 1- to 2-day course to Earth where they are pulled to the most northern and southern latitudes by the planet's magnetic forces.

Auroras can range from simple arcs to draperylike forms in green, red, blue and purple. The color depends on how hard the gas particles are being struck.

In northern latitudes auroras most often occur in the spring and fall months because of the tilt of the planet in relationship to the sun's plane. But displays may occur on dark nights throughout the winter.

Some observers claim the northern lights make a noise similar to the rustle of taffeta, but scientists say the displays cannot be heard in the audible frequency range.

To photograph the northern lights, you will need a sturdy tripod, a locking-type cable release (some 35mm cameras have both time and bulb settings, but most have bulb only, which calls for use of the locking-type cable release), and a camera with an f/3.5 lens or faster.

It is best to photograph the lights on a night when they are not moving too rapidly. And, as a general rule, photos improve if you manage to include recognizable subjects in the foreground — trees and lighted cabins being the favorites of many photographers. Set your camera up at least 75 feet back from the foreground objects to make sure that both the foreground and aurora are in sharp focus.

Normal and wide-angle lenses are best. Try to keep your exposures under a minute — 10 to 30 seconds are generally best. The following lens openings and exposure times are only a starting point, since the amount of light generated by the aurora is inconsistent. (For best results bracket exposures widely.) At f/1.2, 3 seconds for ASA 200, 2 seconds for ASA 400; at f/1.4, 5 seconds for ASA 200, 3 seconds for ASA 400; at f/1.8, 7 seconds for ASA 200, 4 seconds for ASA 400; at f/2, 20 seconds for ASA 200, 10 seconds for ASA 400; at f/2.8, 40 seconds for ASA 200, 20 seconds for ASA 400; at f/3.5, 60 seconds for ASA 200, 30 seconds for ASA 400.

Be sure to protect your camera from low temperatures until you are ready to make your

exposures. Some newer cameras have electri-
cally controlled shutters that will not function properly at low temperatures. Also, wind
the film slowly to reduce the possibility of
static electricity, which can cause streaks on
the film.

Avalanches

Anytime you put snow, mountains, and
backcountry travel together, you've got avalanche danger. Whether you're hiking, skiing,
snowshoeing, driving a dog team or a snowmobile, or even, in certain locations, driving a
car, you should know about avalanches and
how to avoid them.

Before you venture out, take an avalanche
awareness course. They are available in
Anchorage, Fairbanks, Juneau, Valdez, the
Kenai Peninsula, and the Matanuska Valley.
Then on the morning before your trip, call
the nearest avalanche hotline (check the
phone book under local information) for a
recorded message on snow conditions.

Once you are out on your own, there are a
few general rules to follow:

• Stay on the windward side of snowy
ridges. In other words, keep yourself between
the wind and the slope. If you do find yourself
with a snow-covered slope between you and
the wind, travel well away from the slope
itself.

• Choose routes through dense forests, on
level ground, or rocky ledges. Keep away from
slopes steeper than 15° and obvious avalanche
areas, such as paths cleared of trees by previous slides.

• If you do find yourself being swept away,
jettison your equipment and "swim" to try to
stay on top of the snow. Yell to your companions and try to push an arm or a leg upwards
so rescuers can find you.

Most of the land management agencies
have information on which of their summer
hiking trails are safe for cross-country skiing
in winter. Be smart: avoid the trails that the
experts rate unsafe. If you have any doubts
about your route, wear a locator beacon around
your neck. Make sure it is switched on, and
that you and your companions are trained in
its use.

Bears

Most of Alaska qualifies as bear country.
Although bears may be more abundant in
some places like Katmai National Park and
Preserve, Kodiak Island or Admiralty Island
National Monument, you're likely to encounter a black bear or brown bear on a hike just
about anywhere.

The Alaska Department of Fish and Game
publishes *The Bears and You,* recommended
reading for hikers in bear country. The pamphlet is available from ADF&G offices and
government information centers.

To minimize confrontations with bears:

Be aware when you are in prime bear
habitat, such as near salmon streams, in
willow or berry thickets, or areas with lots of
bear trails, prints or droppings. If you do spot
a bear, travel in a direction that will avoid it.

Feeding bears is illegal, dangerous and
encourages them to hang around campgrounds. Don't do it.

Keep a clean camp. Cook and eat well away
from your tent and do not keep food in your
tent. Wash dishes immediately after eating.
Set up a "food cache" out of reach of bears,
such as in a tree, or well away from your camp
if there are no trees. Pack out all garbage that
is not burnable to avoid attracting bears. Clean
all fish into the stream or river, being sure the
current carries away the offal.

Travel with others and make noise. Do not
let children travel separately from the group.
Whistle, sing, ring a bell or shake a can with a
few pebbles in it. Most bears would just as
soon not run into you either; let them know
you're coming and they will get out of the
way.

Do not camp on a bear trail. This is asking
for trouble. Bear trails often are located along
salmon streams, near berry patches and in
saddles on ridgetops. These trails often have
staggered oval depressions because bears
commonly step in the same places.

Never approach a bear cub or get between
a sow and her cubs. Cubs are curious and may
approach you. Back away; the sow will defend
them ferociously from any perceived threat.

Use a telephoto lens. Do not approach a
bear for a close-up shot.

Avoid game carcasses. If it is partially
concealed with branches and leaves, this may
be a bear's food cache. The bear may be nearby
and will defend its food.

Leave your dog at home. When hard
pressed, your dog may run to you and bring a
bear along, too.

Berry-picking

As if heading out into Alaska's backcountry were not reward enough in itself, this
beautiful state has been blessed with an abundance of wild berries. You may want to browse
on red currants as you hike along, or steer your
kayak toward the bank and grab a handful of
highbush cranberries as you float by. Or you
may be one of those serious gatherers who sets

out with special containers and won't come home until you have your quota of blueberries or lowbush cranberries or beach strawberries. Berries and other edible plants have long been an important source of roughage and vitamins for Alaska Natives and homesteaders. Whichever category of berry-picker you fall into, Alaska has the berries for you.

A helpful source to consult before you go is *Alaska Wild Berry Guide and Cookbook,* published by Alaska Northwest Books and available in bookstores. (See the ALASKA NORTHWEST LIBRARY in the back of this book for information on ordering.) Also useful is *Wild Edible and Poisonous Plants of Alaska,* put out by the University of Alaska Cooperative Extension Service, 2221 E. Northern Lights, Suite 240, Anchorage, AK 99508-4143; phone 279-5582. The latter book gives a rundown on other edible plants such as fiddlehead ferns and young fireweed shoots.

A couple of important cautions: Alaska does have a few poisonous plants, including one berry, the baneberry. Others are: narcissus-flowered anemone, poison water hemlock (very similar to wild celery), wild sweetpea, Nootka lupine, vetch, false hellebore, and death camas, a lily. *Be sure* you can identify these and know exactly what you are putting into your mouth.

The second danger comes with teeth and claws. Bears eat berries as an important part of their diet, and these creatures should definitely be given the right-of-way. Remember, there *are* no undiscovered berry patches in Alaska. The bears know them all.

Bicycling

In the 1890s men rode thousands of miles across the Alaska wilderness in the winter on their bicycles and lived to tell about it. With the growing popularity of the "mountain bike", Alaska has experienced a new surge of interest in "wilderness" bicycling opportunities.

Some improved trails are closed to the fat-tire mountain bikes year-round or in the early summer to protect the condition of the trail and the experience of those who wish to hike without fear of collisions. Other trails and backcountry roads are open to bicyclists. Mountain Bikers of Alaska, an Anchorage-based group, offers seminars on trail usage, advice for trip planning and safety and sponsors the annual Iditabike, 200-mile and 125-mile races held each February.

Favorite routes for Alaskan bikers include the trails in the Chugach National Forest on the Kenai Peninsula, the old mining roads near Chickaloon, and the road to McCarthy. Roads out of Nome, Ruby and Dillingham offer opportunities for more remote trips. The Milepost, the mile-by-mile guide to the road system in Alaska, provides an excellent guide for road bicyclists. It includes a log of the McCarthy road, the Denali Highway, the Denali Park Road and the Petersville Road, all favorites of those seeking dirt road excursions. See also *Wheels on Ice,* for a historical perspective of wilderness bicycling in Alaska. To order, see ALASKA NORTHWEST LIBRARY at the back of the book.

Bird-watching

With a good pair of binoculars and a bird guide, you are ready to spot some of the 424 species of birds that have been recorded for Alaska.

Alaska's varied habitats offer unparalleled opportunities to view North American and Asian species, some of which are found only in remote corners of Alaska's Bush.

Millions of shorebirds and waterfowl gather on the Yukon-Kuskokwim delta. A bush flight out from Bethel, headquarters for Yukon Delta National Wildlife Refuge, offers views of swans, brant, cackling Canada geese, emperor geese and numerous other species. Boaters and hikers are likely to flush lesser golden plovers, snipe, jaegers, godwits, sandpipers and sandhill cranes.

Offshore, in the Pribilof Islands, and to the south in the Aleutian Islands, seabirds mass in great colonies, their cries penetrating the fog. Red- and black-legged kittiwakes; horned and tufted puffins; crested, least, parakeet and whiskered auklets; northern fulmars; common and thick-billed murres; pigeon guillemots . . . the parade seems endless. Just as the daytime feeders return to their island burrows or ledges, the nighttime feeders take to the skies. Tours are offered to St. Paul Island or to St. George. (See the Pribilof Islands and community listings in the ALASKA PENINSULA/ALEUTIANS section.) Individual bird-watchers are also welcome. Another tour operator charters a flight each spring to Attu, westernmost of the Aleutian Islands, and can arrange for visitors to stop over in the Pribilofs.

Back on the mainland, fall visitors to Izembek National Wildlife Refuge can view virtually the world's population of brant geese as they feed on eelgrass prior to their flight to wintering grounds farther south on the continent.

Kenai National Wildlife Refuge lures waterfowl to its many lakes and ponds. The outlet to Skilak Lake offers prime habitat for swans. And just outside the refuge, near the mouth of the Kenai River, snow geese, and some white-fronted geese, rest each spring on their long flight north.

Chickaloon Flats serves as a staging area for waterfowl and nesting area for ducks. Sandhill cranes can be spotted from off Marathon Road, a good place also to view one of the peninsula's caribou herds. Cranes use the marshes along the Swanson River and Beaver Creek, while common and Pacific loons prefer the lakes of the Swanson River and Swan Lakes canoe systems. Look for three-toed woodpeckers near Upper Skilak Lake and for great horned owls throughout the refuge.

Islands just off the rugged outer coast of the Kenai Peninsula shelter puffins, black-legged kittiwakes, cormorants, murres and numerous other species. These areas, partly within Alaska Maritime National Wildlife Refuge or Kenai Fjords National Park, are easily reached from Seward or by a more strenuous trip from Homer.

Prince William Sound affords views of more seabird colonies, beginning with the kittiwake colony on the cliffs above Passage Canal, just across from Whittier. Farther east, the Copper River Delta and bays near Cordova sit astride a major flyway for shorebirds. While tiny dunlins, western sandpipers and sanderlings probe the muddy beaches for their next meal, trumpeter swans incubating their eggs stand out in the green delta. This is home, also, for the world's population of dusky Canada geese.

Bald eagles top the bird-watching attractions of Southeast. But the region's forests and rocky exposed seacoasts shelter numerous species. Try the Mendenhall and Stikine wetlands for Canada geese, swans, cranes, ducks and shorebirds. Great blue herons fish the region's lagoons, while raucous Steller's jays and belted kingfishers bring a flash of blue to the forests.

Late each fall, bald eagles gather along the banks of the Chilkat River near Haines, fishing on a late run of salmon. The Alaska Chilkat Bald Eagle Preserve has been established in recognition of this habitat's critical importance to the country's national symbol.

Alaska's Interior and Arctic offer abundant habitat for waterfowl and shorebirds. Sandhill cranes and numerous duck and geese species gather at Minto Flats, north of the Tanana River. The watery maze of Yukon Flats, along the Yukon River, nourishes some of the largest concentrations of waterfowl in the country. The high country of Denali National Park offers abundant raptors, ptarmigan and

several species of perching birds.

Hikers in the Brooks Range and on the North Slope should keep an eye out for raptors including several owl species and peregrine falcons. Closer to the Arctic Ocean look for shorebirds and waterfowl species such as king and spectacled eiders, brant and snow geese.

This brief account gives bush travelers an idea of what to look for in particular regions, but Alaska's bird list contains a number of rare species and changes frequently as new birds are reported. Check with one of the state's 5 chapters of the National Audubon Society for the latest information on bird sightings: Anchorage Audubon Society, Inc., 308 G St., Anchorage 99501; Juneau Audubon Society, P.O. Box 1725, Juneau 99802; Arctic Audubon Society, P.O. Box 82098, Fairbanks 99708; Kenai Audubon Society, P.O. Box 3371, Soldotna 99669; and Kodiak Audubon Society, Box 1756, Kodiak 99615. Call Anchorage Audubon Society's hotline, 248-2473, for updates on birding in Southcentral.

Boating, Canoeing and Kayaking

Whether traveling by sailboat, cruiser, rowboat, canoe, inflatable raft or kayak, Alaska offers thousands of miles of challenging and scenic waterways. Coastal waters provide not only a main transportation route but miles and miles of spectacular recreational boating opportunities. Inland it is possible to travel great distances on a seemingly limitless number of river and lake systems throughout the state.

For marine sailors, southeastern Alaska's Inside Passage and southcentral Alaska's Prince William Sound provide a sheltered transportation route and scenic recreational boating opportunities. (See also Sea Kayaking information in SOUTHEAST and SOUTHCENTRAL sections). There are numerous marine charter services throughout Southeast and in Southcentral, most offering sportfishing or sightseeing tours, others with marine craft for charter (most skippered, some bare-boat).

Boaters wishing to sail their own craft north should have appropriate nautical charts and pilot guides. For U.S. waters, check locally for authorized nautical chart dealers or contact the National Oceanic and Atmospheric Administration (NOAA). Local offices should be listed in the phone book under United States Government, Dept. of Commerce, or write the National Ocean Survey Distribution Division (C44), 5601 Lafayette Ave., Riverdale, MD 20840. (To order nautical charts by mail see Maps this section.) For Washington and Alaska waters you need the *United States Coast Pilot* (Books 8 and 9). For British Columbia waters, see the *British Columbia Coast Pilot* (Volumes I and II), available from authorized dealers or the Government of Canada Fisheries & Oceans Scientific Information and Publications Branch, Ottawa. Charts of Canadian coastal waters are available from authorized dealers or from the Chart Distribution Office, Dept. of the Environment, Box 8080, 1675 Russel Road, Ottawa, ON, Canada K1G 3H6.

Marine travelers may also check local bookstores for the following: *Marine Atlas* (Volumes I and II), by Frank Morris and W.R. Heath, published by Bayless Enterprises Inc., Seattle, WA, a compilation of charts from Olympia, WA, to Skagway, AK; and *Captain Farwell's Hansen Handbook*, by Captain R.F. Farwell, USNR, L&H Printing Co., Seattle, WA. Coastal travelers should have current NOAA Tidal Current Tables. Also helpful is *Marine Recreation, Southeast & Southcentral Alaska,* Forest Service leaflet number 175. Both are available from the U.S. Forest Service Information Office, P.O. Box 21628, Juneau, AK 99802.

Contact the Alaska Dept. of Transportation and Public Facilities (Box 3-1000, Juneau, AK 99802) for a directory of harbor facilities. USGS Topographic maps are useful for kayakers or other marine sailors who wish to camp or explore the coastal lands. These maps are available from USGS, 4230 University Dr., Anchorage, AK 99508 or 701 C. St., Anchorage, AK 99513.

Remember that U.S. visitors entering Canada by private boat must report to Canadian customs on arrival.

Inland boaters will find hundreds of river and lake systems suitable for traveling by boat, raft, kayak or canoe. Canoe trails have been established on rivers and lakes near Fairbanks, Anchorage, on the Kenai Peninsula, and on Admiralty Island in Southeast. Float trips for all skill levels can be arranged in nearly any part of the state.

Rivers included in *The ALASKA WILDERNESS MILEPOST®* are rated according to the International Scale of River Difficulty, obtained from the Bureau of Land Management, which administers some of Alaska's wild and scenic rivers.

Calm seas and sunny skies in Prince William Sound are heaven for kayakers. But the weather can change quickly for the worse, and it's wise to stay on shore when the waves kick up. Alaskan waters are cold and help is often far away. (J.H. Juday)

Class I: Moving water with a few riffles and small waves. Few or no obstructions.

Class II: Easy rapids with waves up to 3 feet and wide, clear channels that are obvious without scouting. Some maneuvering required.

Class III: Rapids with high, irregular waves often capable of swamping an open canoe. Narrow passages that often require complex maneuvering. May require scouting from shore.

Class IV: Long, difficult rapids with constricted passages that often require precise maneuvering in very turbulent waters. Scouting from shore is often necessary and conditions make rescue difficult. Generally not possible for open canoes. Boaters in covered canoes and kayaks should be able to Eskimo roll.

Class V: Extremely difficult, long and very violent rapids with highly congested routes which nearly always must be scouted from the shore. Rescue conditions are difficult and there is significant hazard to life in the event of an accident. Ability to Eskimo roll is essential for kayakers.

Class VI: Difficulties of Class V carried to the extreme of navigability. Nearly impossible and very dangerous. For teams of experts only after close study and with all precautions taken.

Alaska's rivers pass through wild country for the most part. Be extremely careful because help is often far away. BLM cautions that anyone planning a river trip in Alaska should prepare a "float plan" telling the number and ages of those in your party, number and type of craft you are using, what route you are taking and approximately how long the trip should take. Leave the plan with friends or relatives who will contact authorities after a specific time. Be sure to inform them of your safe arrival to avoid unnecessary searches.

BLM further advises the following:

Every member of your party should wear a U.S. Coast Guard-approved "white-water" life jacket. Alaskan waters are extremely cold and safe immersion time is short. Even the best swimmers should wear life vests at all times because the cold quickly saps strength, along with the will and ability to save yourself. Dress to protect yourself from the cold water and weather extremes. If you overturn, stay with your craft.

Never travel alone; a minimum of 2 to 3 craft is recommended. Have honest knowledge of your boating abilities. Be in good physical condition and equipped with adequate clothing. Be practiced in escape from an overturned craft, self-rescue and artificial respiration. Know first aid. At least 1 member of your party should be trained in cardio-pulmonary resuscitation.

River difficulty ratings may change drastically during high water or low water. Exercise good judgement. Have reasonable knowledge of the difficult parts of the trip. Equipment should be in good repair. Never get broadside of the current in fast water. Keep weight low in the craft. Overloading can be dangerous. Be careful of trees hanging in the water — go around, not under. For more information on floating Alaska's rivers and lakes, see *Alaska Paddling Guide* by Jack Mosby and David Dapkus (J & R Enterprises, 1982).

Sea kayakers from around the world are drawn to Alaska to paddle its sheltered waterways and challenge its open coast. Kayakers in Alaska can visit tidewater glaciers and natural hot springs, meeting whales and sea otters along the way. Finding a campsite is generally no problem in the popular kayaking regions of Southeast and Prince William Sound, because so much of the land is managed by the U.S. Forest Service or the State of Alaska. (More information on kayaking in specific areas is provided in the regional descriptions for Southeast and Southcentral/Gulf Coast)

The sea kayak with a spray cover (or the closed-deck canoe) is well-suited to exploring the labyrinth of channels and fjords found along much of Alaska's coast. Kayaks can slip through channels where the water is just inches deep at high tide. They can take refuge on tiny islands when the weather kicks up, or tie up to public docks in town.

The boats can be carried aboard Alaska ferries. Arrangements should be made in advance. Operators of key sightseeing vessels and many small boat operators offer drop-off service for kayakers, and folding boats can be flown into remote spots.

June, July and August are prime months for kayaking, as shirtsleeve weather alternates with rain. Knee-high rubber boots and foul-weather gear (including a sou'wester) are essential on the water, in camp and in town. A good-sized tarp and tent with plenty of headroom makes life in camp much more pleasant on rainy days.

Fast-drying polypropylene and pile clothing serve Alaska kayakers better than cotton or wool outdoor wear. Gore-tex is not the fabric of choice for kayak touring and camping in this environment; salt water and soil clog the pores and Alaska generates more than its share of reports of problems with leaking seams.

Kayakers do not agree on the best kind of sleeping bag. Down is more compressible and easier to stow, but synthetic fibers retain warmth much better when wet. A bag designed for use at 20°F and above is an appropriate choice.

Tides and tidal currents are forces to be reckoned with. A campsite close to the water may be under it — or a mile away on the opposite tide. Tidal currents limit the times that ferries can reach their docks. Those same currents can give a kayaker a welcome lift, an upstream struggle, or a real white-knuckle trip.

The water is cold — between 50° and 60°F. Capsizing can quickly lead to hypothermia, which can cause death in just over an hour. Rescue and self-rescue skills are critical. Many kayakers wear wetsuits when making long crossings. Others simply choose protected routes and stay ashore when paddling conditions are hazardous.

The other major hazard is Alaska's bears, found on the mainland in Southeast and Southcentral regions as well as on Admiralty, Baranof, Chichagof, Kodiak islands and on most of the islands in Prince William Sound. Campers in bear country should try to avoid encounters by making plenty of noise so bears know they are there and be especially careful not to attract them with food.

The wildness of Alaska's environment sets it apart from other places popular for sea kayaking. That same wildness (and distance from help in case of trouble) makes it important to go equipped with all of the standard safety gear recommended for outdoor recreationists and kayakers. It would be foolhardy not to take the appropriate nautical charts and tide and current tables. USGS Topographic maps are also useful for scouting the shoreline and possible campsites. All marine travelers should leave a copy of a planned itinerary with a responsible person. Marine radios are also useful.

For more information on kayaking in Alaska, see *The Coastal Kayaker* by Randel Washburne (Globe Pequot, 1983), and *Sea Kayaker* magazine, Vol. 2 No. 4 (Spring 1986).

The Bush

Originally used to describe large expanses of wilderness beyond the fringes of civilization inhabited by trappers and miners, "the Bush" has come to stand for any part of Alaska not accessible by road. Now a community accessed only by air, water, sled or snow machine transportation is considered a bush village, and anyone living there is someone from the Bush.

The Bush is home to most of Alaska's Native people and to many individualists who live on homesteads, operate mines or work as guides, pilots, trappers or fishermen.

The term Bush has been adapted to the small planes and their pilots who service areas that lack roads or elaborately developed airports. Bush planes are commonly equipped with floats or skis, depending on the terrain and season. For their oftentimes courageous air service, bush pilots have become the modern frontier hero.

Cabins

If you've ever wanted to get away from it all in a wilderness cabin, the U.S. Forest Service, the Bureau of Land Management, the Fish and Wildlife Service and the State of Alaska Division of Parks and Outdoor Recreation give you nearly 200 opportunities in Alaska.

Forest Service public-use recreational cabins are available by advance reservation. Cost is $15 per party per night (after July 1, 1990, cost will be $20). A computer cabin reservation system now enables any Forest Service office to process a cabin reservation for any cabin the Forest Service manages.

Anyone who is at least 18 years old may apply for a cabin permit for noncommercial use. Applications may be made in writing up to 180 days in advance of required times. *Payment must accompany the cabin application.* If there is more than 1 applicant for a specific cabin and time, a drawing will determine the permittee. Special drawings are held for certain Kenai Peninsula and Cordova area cabins during high-use periods; drawing times and rules are available from the Forest Service office. Fees will be refunded to unsuccessful applicants; refunds also are made upon written notice and return of permit at least 10 days prior to intended use. Only 1 change in reservations will be granted. Permits must be carried along to the cabin.

Cabins have tables, benches, bunks (without mattresses), wood or oil heating stoves, brooms and pit toilets. You must bring your own bedding and cooking utensils. An ax or maul is provided at cabins with wood stoves, but bring a small ax or hatchet in case the tools are not there. Be sure to check which kind of stove is provided. The Forest Service does not provide stove oil; only #1 diesel oil will work properly and 5 to 10 gallons per week are required, depending on weather conditions. Almost all cabins located on lakes have skiffs (bring your own life preservers and motor).

Bring extra supplies in case bad weather prolongs your stay.

For information contact: Chugach National Forest, 201 E. 9th Ave., Suite 206, Anchorage, AK 99501; phone 271-2599. Or, one of the Tongass National Forest area offices: Federal Building, Ketchikan, AK 99901, phone 225-3101; 204 Siginaka Way, Sitka, AK 99835, phone 747-6671; or P.O. Box 309, Petersburg, AK 99833, phone 772-3871.

BLM has 5 recreational cabins within 100 miles of Fairbanks available to the public by advance reservation for $15 per night. For reservations or information contact the BLM Fairbanks Support Center, 1541 Gaffney Road, Fairbanks, AK 99703-1399; phone 356-5345.

The Fish and Wildlife Service maintains 9 public-use recreational cabins on Kodiak National Wildlife Refuge available by advance reservation for $15 per night. For information or a reservation application contact: Refuge Manager, Kodiak National Wildlife Refuge, 1390 Buskin River Road, Kodiak, AK 99615; phone 487-2600

The Division of Parks and Outdoor Recreation rents public-use recreational cabins in Southeast, Southcentral and the Interior for $20 to $25 per night. For reservations or information in Southcentral contact: Alaska Division of Parks and Outdoor Recreation, P.O. Box 107001, Anchorage, AK 99510; in Southeast contact Alaska Division or Parks and Outdoor Recreation, 400 Willoughby Center, Juneau, AK 99801; in the Interior, contact the Division of Parks at 4418 Airport Way, Fairbanks, AK 99709.

Camping

Federal and state agencies maintain campgrounds in many areas of Alaska. Reservations are not accepted at any of them.

Fees are charged at some developed Alaska state campgrounds and waysides. For information and a brochure, contact the Alaska State Division of Parks, Pouch 107001, Anchorage, AK 99510.

The U.S. Forest Service provides numerous camping areas in Chugach and Tongass national forests; most of these campgrounds charge a fee of from $4 to $8 per night, depending on facilities. There is a 14-day limit at most campgrounds; this regulation is enforced and citations for overstaying the limit may result in a fine. For further information write the Public Affairs Office, U.S.D.A. Forest Service, P.O. Box 1628, Juneau, AK 99802. Walk-in services are available at the Chugach Forest Supervisor's office at 201 E. 9th Ave., Suite 206, Anchorage, AK 99501 and at offices

in Craig, Yakutat, Sitka, Wrangell, Ketchikan, Petersburg, Juneau, Thorne Bay, Girdwood, Seward and Cordova.

BLM maintains about 25 camping areas for which there is no charge, with the exception of the Delta BLM campground on the Alaska Highway. Write to the Bureau of Land Management, 701 C St., Box 13, Anchorage, AK 99513.

The National Park Service maintains 7 campgrounds in Denali National Park and Preserve. Camping fees are either not charged (3 campgrounds) or are $10 (4 campgrounds). There are established campgrounds at Glacier Bay and Katmai national parks and preserves; wilderness camping only in other national parks and preserves in Alaska. For further information, write the National Park Service, 2525 Gambell St., Anchorage, AK 99503; phone 271-2643.

The U.S. Fish and Wildlife Service manages several camping areas within Kenai National Wildlife Refuge. Contact the Refuge Manager, Kenai National Wildlife Refuge, P.O. Box 2139, Soldotna, AK 99669.

Most of the developed campgrounds in Alaska are located on the road systems. In the remainder of the state, there is wilderness camping only.

State and federal agencies that manage Alaska's public lands request that campers exercise minimum impact camping and hiking techniques to reduce damage to fragile wilderness areas. These techniques include the following:

Plan ahead to avoid impact: Travel and camp in small groups. Repackage food to reduce containers. Take a litterbag to carry out trash. Carry a stove and foods that require little cooking. Check with park, national forest and refuge offices for low-use areas.

Travel to avoid impact: Walk single file in the center of the trail. Stay on the main trail even if it is wet or snow-covered. Never shortcut switchbacks. Travel cross-country only on rocky or timbered areas, not on fragile vegetation. Look at and photograph, never pick or collect. In many areas no man-made trails exist. To minimize impact when in these areas, groups should travel in a fan pattern whenever possible. Use game trails, but be aware that you may surprise wildlife when hiking in brushy areas.

Make no-trace camps: Seek ridgetop, beach or timbered campsites. Camp away from the main trail, lakeshores and fragile plant communities. Choose well-drained, rocky or sandy campsites. Never cut standing trees, use only fallen dead wood. Avoid leveling or digging

9

CALENDAR OF EVENTS

JANUARY
ANCHORAGE ▪ Nastar Ski Races, Alyeska Ski Resort.
BETHEL ▪ Kuskokwim 300 Sled Dog Race.
HAINES ▪ Alcan 200 Snowmachine Rally.
JUNEAU ▪ Rainier Downhill Challenge Cup; Alascom Ski Challenge.
SOLDOTNA ▪ Clark Memorial Sled Dog Race to Hope.
WILLOW ▪ Willow Winter Carnival Race.

FEBRUARY
ANCHORAGE ▪ Gold Rush Classic Snowmachine Race to Nome; Fur Rendezvous; Women's World Championship Sled Dog Race (sprint); World Championship Sled Dog Race (sprint); Iditaski Nordic Ski Race; Master Giant Slalom, Alyeska Ski Resort.
CORDOVA ▪ Ice Worm Festival.
FAIRBANKS ▪ Yukon Quest International Sled Dog Race.
HOMER ▪ Winter Carnival.
JUNEAU ▪ Taku Rendezvous.
KENAI-SOLDOTNA ▪ Alaska State Championship Sled Dog Race (sprint).
KETCHIKAN ▪ Festival of the North.

NOME ▪ Iron Dog Gold Rush Classic Snow Machine Race to Big Lake via Iditarod Trail; Dexter Creek Classic Sled Dog Race.
VALDEZ ▪ Ice Climbing Festival.
WRANGELL ▪ Tent City Days.

MARCH
ANCHORAGE ▪ Iditarod Trail Sled Dog Race to Nome; Big Lake 500 Spring Classic Snowmobile Race; Iditabike.
ANDREAFSKY ▪ Andreafsky 90 Sled Dog Race.
DILLINGHAM ▪ Beaver Roundup.
FAIRBANKS ▪ Arctic Winter Games; Curling Bonspiel; Ice Festival; Open and Limited Class North American Sled Dog Race.
GALENA ▪ Winter Carnival.
JUNEAU ▪ Sourdough Pro/Am Ski Race; Southeast Championships.
KODIAK ▪ Pillar Mountain Golf Classic.
NOME ▪ Salmon Lake Derby Sled Dog Race; Bering Sea Ice Classic Golf Tournament; Nome to Golovin Snowmachine Race; Iditarod Sled Dog Race Finish & Events; Alaska Sweepstakes Sled Dog Race to Candle and back.
PEDRO BAY ▪ Winter Carnival.
SKAGWAY ▪ Windfest.
TOK ▪ Tok Race of Champions Sled Dog Race.

APRIL
ANCHORAGE ▪ Junior World Ski Championship and Spring Carnival, Alyeska Ski Resort; Native Youth Olympics.
BARROW ▪ Piuraagiaqta (Spring Festival).
COLDFOOT ▪ Coldfoot Classic Sled Dog Race, (350 miles).

JUNEAU ▪ Ski to Sea Race.
KOTZEBUE ▪ Archie Ferguson-Willy Goodwin Memorial Snow Machine Race (250 miles).
NOME ▪ Nome to Kotzebue Sled Dog Race.
SHISHMAREF ▪ Seward Peninsula Open-Class Championship Sled Dog Races.

MAY
HAINES ▪ King Salmon Derby.
HOMER ▪ Jackpot Halibut Derby.
KETCHIKAN ▪ King Salmon Derby.
KODIAK ▪ Crab Festival; Salt Water Fishing Derby.
NOME ▪ Stroak and Cloak Triathlon; Polar Bear Swim.
PETERSBURG ▪ Little Norway Festival; Salmon Derby.
SAVOONGA ▪ Walrus Festival.
SEWARD ▪ Exit Glacier Run.
SITKA ▪ Salmon Derby.
VALDEZ ▪ Halibut Derby.
WRANGELL ▪ Salmon Derby.

SEWARD ▪ Mount Marathon Race Jackpot Halibut Derby.
TALKEETNA ▪ Mountain Bike Rush.
VALDEZ ▪ Pink Salmon Derby.

JUNE
BARROW ▪ Nalukatag (Whaling Feast).
FAIRBANKS ▪ Yukon 800 Marathon River Boat Race.
KETCHIKAN ▪ Salmon Derby. Nome — Festival and Raft Race; ARCO-Jesse Owens Games.
SITKA ▪ All Alaska Logging Championship.
TANANA ▪ Nuchalawoya Festival.
VALDEZ ▪ Whitewater Weekend.

AUGUST
CORDOVA ▪ Silver Salmon Derby.
CRAIG ▪ Prince of Wales Island Fair and Logging Show.
FAIRBANKS ▪ Idita-foot Race.
GIRDWOOD ▪ Crow Pass Crossing, 26.5-mile foot race to Eagle River.
JUNEAU ▪ Golden North Salmon Derby.
KODIAK ▪ Rodeo and State Fair.
SEWARD ▪ Silver Salmon Derby.
VALDEZ ▪ Silver Salmon Derby.

JULY
Fourth of July celebrations take place in many towns and villages.
FAIRBANKS ▪ World Eskimo-Indian Olympics.
HATCHER PASS ▪ Rock Climbing Festival.
HOMER ▪ Halibut Derby.
NOME ▪ Anvil Mountain Run.

SEPTEMBER
FAIRBANKS ▪ Equinox Marathon.
WHITTIER ▪ Silver Salmon Derby.
WRANGELL ▪ Silver Salmon Derby.

OCTOBER
KETCHIKAN ▪ Chief Johnson Pole Potlatch (raising of a newly carved totem pole).
SITKA ▪ Alaska Day Celebration.
WRANGELL ▪ Winter Fishing Derby.

NOVEMBER
FAIRBANKS ▪ Northern Invitational Curling Spiel.

DECEMBER
KOTZEBUE ▪ Preliminaries for the Eskimo-Indian Olympics.

hip holes and drainage trenches. Make only small campfires in safe areas. Carry small firewood from timbered areas outside camp. Take lightweight, soft shoes for around camp. Avoid trampling vegetation. Use biodegradable soaps and wash well away from water sources (at least 100 feet). Bury human waste 6 to 8 inches deep and at least 150 feet from all potential water sources. On tundra, remove a fist-full of vegetation, scoop out a small depression and replace the tundra when finished. Mosses, leaves and snow are natural toilet paper. If you do use paper, burn it or pack it out. Don't bury other waste or trash (pack it out). Stay as quiet as possible and enjoy the quietness. Leave radios and tape players at home.

Leave a no-trace campsite: Pick up and pack out every trace of litter (including cigarette filters). Erase all signs of a fire. Replace rocks and logs where they were.

Customs Requirements

U.S. residents do not need passports or visas to visit Canada, or to travel through Canada on their way to Alaska, but they should carry some form of identification, such as a driver's license or voter registration card. Social Security cards are not positive identification. Birth certificates of children are sometimes required. Permanent residents of the U.S. who are not American citizens are advised to have their Alien Registration Receipt Card (U.S. Form 1-151 or I-551).

All persons other than U.S. citizens or legal residents and Canadians require a valid passport or an acceptable travel document.

Visitors to the U.S. who have a single entry visa should check with an office of the U.S. Immigration and Naturalization Service to make sure that they have all the papers they need to get back into the U.S. after traveling through Canada.

Persons temporarily in the U.S. who would require visas if coming to Canada directly from their countries of origin should contact the Canadian Embassy, Consulate or Office of Tourism in their home country before departure for the U.S.

Persons under age 18 who are not accompanied by an adult should bring a letter with them from a parent or guardian giving them permission to travel into Canada.

Although there is no set standard of monies required for entrance into Canada, the visitor must have sufficient funds to cover his cost of living per day for the planned length of stay. Consideration in assessing "sufficient funds" includes the locale in which the visitor plans to stay and whether he will be staying with a friend or relative. There have been reports of visitors being turned back for lacking $150 in cash. The visitor also must have return transportation fare to his country of origin.

Visitors planning to enter Canada by private boat should contact customs in advance for a list of ports of entry that provide customs facilities and their hours of operation. Immediately upon arrival, visitors must report to customs and complete all documentation. In emergency situations, visitors must report their arrival to the nearest regional customs office or office of the Royal Canadian Mounted Police.

Private pilots are required to give advance notice of arrival to both U.S. and Canadian customs services. Customs officers at most Alaskan airports request that calls be made during regular business hours, no matter when the service is to be required. For customs service at Fort Yukon, advance arrangements must be made through Fairbanks.

If you plan to cross the border into Canada in a remote area, such as on the Chilkoot Trail, you must contact the nearest Canadian Customs and Excise Office in advance, either at Fraser, BC, phone (403) 821-4111, or Whitehorse, YT, phone (403) 667-6471. For those planning a trip that will involve crossing the border from Canada into Alaska in a remote area, U.S. customs advises that they write or call ahead of time to the U.S. Customs Service, District Office, 620 E. 10th Ave., Suite 101, Anchorage, AK 99501; phone 271-5029. Tell that office where you plan to cross and customs will advise you where and how to check in. (Yukon River floaters should be aware that there are U.S. customs offices in Eagle and Fort Yukon.) Customs officers are also available at the following ports of entry: Ketchikan, Skagway, Haines, Alcan; and in the summer, Pokee Creek (Taylor Highway).

Canadian law prohibits transporting a pistol, and airline passengers must declare their firearms and check them as baggage. "Long guns" or hunting rifles may be taken into and through Canada.

Pets are allowed, as long as you have papers showing it has had a rabies vaccination within the preceding 36 months.

Endangered species laws prohibit crossing into Canada with animals or certain by-products made of their bone, skin, fur, etc. This also applies to carved ivory. Travelers wanting to take such items with them from Alaska through Canada must purchase a permit from the U.S. Fish and Wildlife Service (available at

DAYLIGHT HOURS

SUMMER MAXIMUM

	Sunrise	Sunset	Hours of daylight
Barrow	May 10	Aug. 2	84 days
Fairbanks	1:59 a.m.	11:48 p.m.	21:49 hours
Anchorage	3:21 a.m.	10:42 p.m.	19:21 hours
Juneau	3:51 a.m.	10:09 p.m.	18:18 hours
Ketchikan	4:04 a.m.	9:33 p.m.	17:29 hours
Adak	6:27 a.m.	11:10 p.m.	16:43 hours

WINTER MINIMUM

	Sunrise	Sunset	Hours of daylight
Barrow	Jan. 24 noon	Nov. 18 noon	None
Fairbanks	10:59 a.m.	2:41 p.m.	3:42 hours
Anchorage	10:14 a.m.	3:42 p.m.	5:28 hours
Juneau	9:46 a.m.	4:07 p.m .	6:21 hours
Ketchikan	9:12 a.m.	4:18 p.m .	7:06 hours
Adak	10:52 a.m.	6:38 p.m.	7:46 hours

1412 Airport Way in Fairbanks or at any U.S. Fish and Wildlife refuge office) before leaving Alaska, or you can mail the items and avoid the permit process. (Experienced travelers mail their ivory.) A list of restricted items can be obtained from Convention Administrator, Canadian Wildlife Service, Environment Canada, Ottawa, ON, K1A 0E7. For further Canadian customs information write: Regional Collector of Customs, 1001 W. Pender St., Vancouver, BC, V6E 2M8.

Visitors to the North should be aware that the import of the following into the U.S. from Canada is restricted except by special permit: Products made from sealskin, whalebone and whale and walrus ivory, sea otter or polar bear, and most wild bird feathers, mounted birds and skins. For a complete list of restricted items and information on import permits, contact the nearest U.S. Fish and Wildlife Service office.

For further U.S. customs information, including the free booklet, *Know Before You Go*, write: U.S. Customs Service, Washington, D.C. 20229.

Disabled Visitor Services

Alaska offers a variety of vacation experiences for disabled visitors. Every outdoor adventure from skiing and dog sledding to kayaking and camping are available to those with limited mobility. Many accommodations are equipped for the disabled traveler. (At least 1 Forest Service wilderness recreation cabin is equipped with a cantilevered dock for wheelchair access, as well as boardwalks and ramps.)

Two statewide groups offer assistance: Access Alaska, 3710 Woodland Park, Suite 900, Anchorage, AK 99517; phone 248-4777. And, Challenge Alaska, P.O. Box 110065, Anchorage, AK 99511; phone 563-2658.

Dog Mushing

Some years back, snow machines had virtually replaced the working dog team, but the sled dog has made a comeback which is due in part to the resurgence of interest in racing and a rekindled appreciation of the reliability of nonmechanical transportation. More than one bush traveler has survived an unexpected winter storm by curling up with several of the team dogs for warmth. (The expression "three dog night" refers to a very cold night in which 3 dogs are needed to keep warm.)

In addition to working and racing dog teams, many Alaskans keep 2 to 10 sled dogs for recreational mushing. And more and more winter visitors are experiencing the unique thrill of riding (or driving!) behind a team of dogs over a beautiful snow landscape.

Sled dog racing is Alaska's official state sport. It represents the state's rich history and frontier tradition. Races ranging from local club meets to world-class championships are held throughout the winter.

The sprint or championship races are

usually run over 2 or 3 days with the cumulative time for the heats deciding the winner. Distances for the heats range from about 12 to 30 miles. The size of the dog team also varies, with mushers using anywhere from 7 to 16 dogs per team. Since racers are not allowed to replace dogs during the race, most finish with fewer dogs than they started with. Injuries, sore muscles, or tender feet are just a few of the reasons dogs are dropped from the team.

Long-distance racing (the Kusko 300, the Yukon Quest, and the Iditarod) pits racers not only against each other, but also against the elements. Sheer survival can quickly take precedence over winning when a winter storm catches a dog team in an exposed area. Stories abound of racers giving up their own chance to finish "in the money" to help out a fellow musher who has gotten into trouble. Besides the weather, long-distance racers also have to contend with moose scares or attacks on the dogs; overflows on frozen rivers; sudden illness among the dogs; straying off the trail in poorly marked stretches (or when traveling in whiteout conditions); and sheer exhaustion of dogs and driver. With these and other threats to overcome, the eventual winners have truly persevered against all odds.

Race winners may take home a trophy for their club race or up to $50,000 for first place finish in the Iditarod Trail Sled Dog Race.

From January through March, it is possible to watch any number of world-class sled dog races. The major races are:

Clark Memorial Sled Dog Race, Soldotna to Hope; January.

Kusko 300, Bethel to Aniak; January.

Willow Winter Carnival Race, Willow; January.

Alaska State Championship Race, Kenai-Soldotna; February.

Women's World Championship Race, Anchorage; February.

World Championship Sled Dog Race, Anchorage; February.

Yukon Quest International Sled Dog Race, Fairbanks to Whitehorse in even-numbered years, with trail reversing in odd-numbered years; February.

Alaska Sweepstakes, Nome to Candle and back; March.

Iditarod Trail Sled Dog Race, Anchorage to Home; March (see Iditarod this section).

Open North American Sled Dog Championship, Fairbanks; March.

Tok Race of Champions, Tok; March.

But you need not own a dog team to get in on the fun of dog mushing. During their winter carnivals many communities have at least 1 dog team operator offering brief sled rides and photo opportunities. Several tour operators also offer customized backcountry sled dog tours, lasting from an hour to several days. Some guided cross-country ski treks offer dog team freight service to ferry skiers' backpacks between wilderness cabins. (See BUYERS GUIDE)

A variation of dog mushing, ski joring, is becoming a popular winter pastime. Instead of pulling a rider on a sled, in ski joring the dogs pull a skier.

Emergency Medical Services

Phone numbers of emergency medical services (if available) such as ambulance, clinic or hospital, are listed along with police and fire departments at the beginning of each community description. CB Channels 9 and 11 are monitored for emergencies in many areas; Channels 14 and 19 in some areas.

Employment

A popular misconception about Alaska is that high paying jobs go begging. Work in many industries is seasonal, with long periods of inactivity. The construction industry, where jobs are traditionally the highest paid, seems to have bottomed out at 60 percent below the 1983-84 peak. Cleanup jobs created by the Prince William Sound oil spill lured workers from throughout the state and created summertime shortages of low paid, unskilled labor. The temporary cleanup jobs, plus a slight rebound in the shrunken construction industry, led to the lowest unemployment rate (6.1 percent in July 1989) that the state has enjoyed since construction of the trans-Alaska oil pipeline in the mid-1970s. Looking over the job situation during a vacation is a good approach. For more information write to the Alaska Dept. of Labor, P.O. Box 3-7000, Juneau, AK 99802.

Ferries

Vessels of the Alaska Marine Highway System carry vehicles as well as passengers. There are 2 different systems serving 2 different areas: Southeast and Southcentral. These 2 systems DO NOT connect with each other.

The Southeastern system connects Bellingham, WA, and Prince Rupert, BC, with southeastern Alaska cities from Ketchikan to Hyder to Skagway. Its vessels include the *Columbia, Matanuska, Malaspina* and *Taku,* and the smaller *Aurora, LeConte* and *Chilkat.* Only 3 southeastern cities are connected to the Alaska Highway: Haines, via the Haines Highway, Hyder, via the Cassiar Highway, and Skagway, via Klondike Highway 2. All other communities in southeastern Alaska are accessible only by ferry or by air. In Southeast, ferries call at Ketchikan, Wrangell, Petersburg, Sitka, Juneau, Haines and Skagway. (Feeder vessels serve the smaller communities of Kake, Angoon, Tenakee, Hoonah, Pelican, Hollis, Metlakatla and Hyder/Stewart, BC.) The summer schedule, in effect from mid-May to late September, provides 1 sailing per week from Bellingham and 6 per week from Prince Rupert, with additional shuttle service between Ketchikan and Hyder/Stewart, BC, as well as between Ketchikan and Prince Rupert. During fall, winter and spring there is 1 sailing per week from Bellingham and 2 per week from Prince Rupert.

In southcentral Alaska, 1 ferryliner, the *Tustumena*, travels to Kodiak, Port Lions, Homer, Seldovia and Seward year-round, except for January and February. Another, the *Bartlett*, operates between Valdez and Cordova throughout the winter, then in late May extends its run to Whittier every day during the summer season except Thursday. There also is limited service during the summer to Chignik, Sand Point, King Cove and Cold Bay on the Alaska Peninsula and Unalaska/Dutch Harbor in the Aleutians.

BRINGING HOME YOUR ALASKAN FISH

Proper packaging is the key to transporting prize Alaska seafood to the Lower 48. To assure that your fish arrives in good condition, follow these steps:

■ Shippers should wrap fish in a 2.2 mil or 1.4 mil polyethylene bag tied to prevent leakage. Place bag in a sturdy, multiwalled, waxed fiberboard box that is leakproof (available from sporting goods dealers or Alaska Airlines for $6). Styrofoam panels lining the box will provide better protection and temperature control.

■ Pack the fish with no more than 5 lbs. of dry ice or gel pack ice. Regular wet ice will melt, and wet packages will be refused shipment. Seal boxes with at least 2 nylon or metal bands, duct tape or glass-fiber strapping tape (NOT masking tape).

■ Label box with name and address. Use "THIS SIDE UP" labels and place "KEEP COOL" or "KEEP FROZEN" labels on all sides of box.

■ Boxes must not weigh more than 100 lbs. for king salmon, 80 lbs. for all other fish. Packages should be able to withstand 275 lbs. of stress from the bottom and 200 lbs. on top. Additional shipping charges may be added.

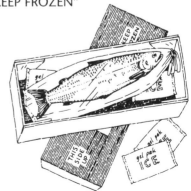

Courtesy of Alaska Airlines

Travel on the Alaska ferries is at a leisurely pace, with observation decks, food service and vehicle decks on all ferries. Cabins are available only on the 4 larger Southeast ferries and 1 Southcentral ferry. Travelers may schedule stopovers at any port on either route. Short local tours are available in many communities to coincide with ferry stopovers.

Keep in mind that the state ferries are not cruise ships: They do not have beauty salons, deck games and the like. The small stores on the larger ferries are open limited hours and sell a limited selection of items. The cafeteria-style food service is open only for meals. Cocktail lounges on board the larger vessels are open from late morning to midnight. It's a good idea to bring your own snacks, books, games and toiletries, since these are not always available on board.

The state ferries are popular in summer, so make reservations as far in advance as possible to get the sailing dates you want; cabin space is often sold out by mid-January on the Bellingham sailings. (Fares are normally reduced during the winter months and crowds are virtually nonexistent.) Cabin and/or vehicle reservations are required on all vessels. Passenger reservations are required on all sailings.

If cabin space is filled, you may go deck passage (walk-on) with reservations. This means you'll be sleeping on lounge chairs or on the deck itself. A limited number of lockers are available for walk-on passengers.

If you do not have reservations, or wish to sail on a different date, check with the Marine Highway office for space. Generally, walk-on passenger space is available except for Bellingham sailings and cabin and vehicle space is at a premium all year. You may go standby, which is literally standing by in the ferry traffic lanes until all reserved passengers and vehicles are on board: if there is space, standbys may board. However, as a standby you may not get guaranteed through-passage to your destination as standby passengers are subject to off-loading at each port of call! Make sure you understand how standby works before giving up your reservation.

Passenger fares are charged as follows: Adults and children 12 and over, full fare; children 6 to 11, half fare; children under 6, free. Passenger fares do not include cabins or meals. Senior citizens (over 65) may travel free within Alaska on a space-available basis on all vessels between Oct. 1 and May 15. Between May 16 and Sept. 30, senior citizens may travel free on all vessels except the *Columbia*, *Malaspina*, *Matanuska* and *Taku*. Cabins and

vehicle space are charged as usual. Cabin and vehicle space reservations are allowed 30 days prior to sailing if you are traveling on a senior citizen pass. Full payment is due for confirmed reservations at least 45 days prior to departure. Personal checks are not accepted unless written on an Alaska bank. Payment may be made with certified or cashier's checks or money orders. All major credit cards are accepted at all terminals and by phone. The 45 days assures time for your check to clear and your tickets to reach you in the mail. You can pick up prepaid tickets at your departure point, but you must pay for the tickets in advance and arrange with the Alaska Marine Highway office to hold your tickets at your departure point. From June 1 through Labor Day each year, U.S. Forest Service interpreters staff the Columbia, Malaspina, Matanuska and Taku ferries through waters bordering the Tongass National Forest in Southeast Alaska and they also serve on portions of the trips by the Bartlett and Tustumena in Prince William South near Chugach National Forest in Southcentral. Programs vary according to each ship's activities and include: narrative talks, films, slides, children's activities and brochures about the natural and cultural resources of Alaska's national forests.

For additional information, schedules, fares and reservations, write the Alaska Marine Highway, Box R, Juneau, AK 99811 or phone (toll free) 1-800-642-0066.

Firearms

In Alaska you are permitted to carry firearms for personal protection or sport hunting, but concealed weapons are illegal. Airline passengers must check their weapons as baggage. Or you may mail a firearm to Alaska through the U.S. Postal Service.

Fishing

The perfect fishing trip awaits you in Alaska, whether your idea of perfection is a sparkling little freshwater lake, a hidden saltwater cove, a family float down a salmon-filled river, or a marine charter in search of halibut. The possiblities are endless, and the fishing, excellent.

Salmon, of course, is the Alaska fish that comes to mind first when anglers dream their dreams. Who can forget that first taste of firm, pink meat from a freshly caught salmon? Besides the aptly named kings, there are also red salmon, pink, silver, and chum — which make for fine sport and fine eating.

Beyond the delights and varieties of salmon, Alaska offers trout (rainbow, steelhead, cutthroat), char (arctic, brook, lake, and Dolly

Varden), grayling, burbot, smelt, hooligan, whitefish, halibut, pike, herring and sheefish.

If this list overwhelms you, and you're wondering how to start planning your Alaska fishing adventure, the Alaska Dept. of Fish and Game has a very helpful publication. It's the March-April 1987 issue of *Alaska Fish and Game* magazine, *Recreational Fishing Guide.* Fishery biologists from throughout the state offer tips from their region on fishing holes, gear, and strategies for outwitting your wily prey. Maps and charts spell out good fishing locations and provide data on the available species, access to the spots, and the type of facilities, if any, that an angler might expect to find. Timing charts will put you in the right place at the right time.

The *Recreational Fishing Guide* costs $5 and is available from the Alaska Dept. of Fish and Game, P.O. Box 3-2000, Juneau, AK 99802-2000. If you wish to use VISA or MasterCard, call: inside Alaska (800) 478-4286; outside Alaska (collect) (907) 465-4286, 8 a.m. to 5 p.m. Alaska time. The department publishes a variety of materials including the bimonthly magazine *Alaska Fish & Game,* the *Wildlife Notebook Series,* a game fish poster, maps, and an award winning videotape featuring Alaska game sanctuaries. The department also provides free of charge the booklet Sport Fishing Predictions, designed to forecast when and where the best recreational fishing can be found. For price lists and the free Annual Sport Fishing Regulations Summary booklet, write the above address, call 465-4110, or contact any Dept. of Fish and Game office. Be sure you have the most recent information on bag limits and special permits for the year you are fishing.

A nonresident fishing license, valid for the calendar year issued, costs $36. A special 3-day nonresident license costs $10, or $20 for 14 days. Nonresidents under age 16 do not need a fishing license.

Resident sportfishing licenses cost $10. A resident is a person who has maintained a permanent place of abode within the state for 12 consecutive months and has continuously maintained his or her voting residence in the state, and any member of the military service who is on active duty and is permanently stationed in Alaska.

Nearly all sporting goods stores in Alaska sell fishing licenses. But because of irregular hours of operation sometimes found in the Bush and the possibility of unexpected fishing opportunities, it is advisable to buy your license in one of the larger communities before you head for the backcountry.

Once you've caught your fish, taken the photos to show family and friends, and are heading back to civilization, you may wonder what in the world to do with your catch. If you plan to take it back Outside, Alaska Airlines has important tips for you. (See box, page 15.) The University of Alaska Cooperative Extension Service also has booklets and brochures that will help, including *The Fisherman Returns* and *Pressure Canning Alaska Fish at Home.* For a complete list of their publications, available free or at low cost, write: University of Alaska, Cooperative Extension Service, 2221 E. Northern Lights, Suite 240, Anchorage, AK 99508-5582; phone 279-5582.

Finally, no discussion of fishing would be complete without mention of catch-and-release — for the simple reason that anglers in Alaska catch so many fish. Even if the logistics of your trip allow you to get back to town before your catch spoils, think twice before you fill your freezer with fish. How much, realistically, will your family consume over the next 3 to 6 months, before freezer burn spoils the delicate flesh? Especially for the slower growing species such as trout, catch-and-release makes sense. As state biologists point out in their *Recreational Fishing Guide:*

"Most Alaskan seasons and bag limits are generous, but even unguided and inexperienced anglers can find fishing so good that the limits would easily be exceeded if all fish were kept. Catch-and-release provides a method to continue fishing, stay within the law, and derive the greatest enjoyment from the recreational angling experience."

A brochure produced by the University of Alaska Sea Grant College Program, the Alaska Dept. of Fish and Game, the National Park Service and the U.S. Fish and Wildlife Service tells how to practice catch-and-release fishing:

• Use artificial flies and lures and a barbless hook appropriately sized for the size of fish you will be catching. Pliers can be used to pinch down barbs on conventional hooks.

• Play and release your fish as quickly as possible. A fish played to the point of exhaustion may not survive.

• When you are about to land the fish, try to keep it in the water. Don't let it flop in shallow water over rocks and never on dry land. When fishing from a boat, use a net, preferably a knotless nylon.

• Cradle the fish gently with 2 hands, one supporting the belly, the other just ahead of and underneath the tail. Keep your fingers out of and away from the gills. Use soft, wet gloves or wet your hands before handling the fish.

• Don't remove the fish from the water to take photographs; have your fishing buddy take the photos while you hold the fish just at the surface of the water.

• Try to remove the hook gently and quickly, keeping the fish underwater. If the fish is hooked deeply, cut the leader as close to the eye of the hook as possible.

• Revive the fish, if it is in a stream, by pointing its head into the current. In slow and still water, you may need to "walk" it for a few minutes — cradling it gently, moving up stream. As the fish recuperates, its gills will begin to work strongly. This may take some time, especially for larger fish. When the fish pulls against your hand, release it.

Copies of the brochure, *Catch and Release Fishing,* are available from resource agencies and at many locations where fishing licenses are sold.

Giardiasis

Alaska's many crystal-clear rivers and streams give the false impression that the water is pure and safe to drink. However, that pristine-looking water may contain a hidden hazard — a microscopic organism called *Giardia lamblia,* which causes an intestinal disorder called giardiasis. *Giardia* are carried in the intestinal waste of humans and some domestic and wild animals. The cysts of *Giardia* may contaminate surface water supplies such as lakes, streams and rivers. The organisms can survive in water for at least 2 months, so the problem is not limited to a particular time of year or sections of streams.

Giardiasis can cause severe discomfort. After ingestion by humans *Giardia* attach themselves to the walls of the small intestine. Disease symptoms usually include diarrhea, increased gas, loss of appetite, abdominal cramps and bloating. Weight loss may occur from nausea and loss of appetite. These discomforts may first appear a few days to a few weeks after ingestion of *Giardia,* and may last up to 6 weeks. Most people are unaware they have been infected and often have returned home from vacations before the onset of symptoms. If not treated, the symptoms may disappear on their own, only to recur intermittently during a period of many months. Other diseases can have similar symptoms, but if you have drunk untreated water you should suspect giardiasis and so inform your doctor. The disease is curable when treated with a prescribed medication.

To avoid this problem altogether, purify all surface water that is to be used for drinking or cooking.

The most certain method to destroy *Giardia* is to boil water (bring it to a full rolling boil, not simply steaming) for at least 1 minute. Boiling also will destroy other organisms that cause waterborne diseases. At high altitudes, you should boil the water for 3 to 5 minutes for an added margin of safety. If the water has a flat taste, pour it back and forth between clean containers 2 or 3 times.

Chemical disinfectants such as iodine or chlorine tablets work well against most waterborne bacteria and viruses that can cause disease, but they may not be totally reliable against *Giardia,* according to the U.S. Forest Service. The amount of iodine or chlorine necessary to kill *Giardia* depends on water temperature, pH, turbidity and contact time between the chemical and parasite. Research to determine the amount of chemical and duration of contact time is under way. In an emergency, it is recommended that you use an iodine-based water purification product, since iodine is often more effective than chlorine. If possible, filter or strain the water first, then allow the iodine to work at least 30 minutes before you drink the water. If the water is cold or cloudy, wait at least an hour, or use more iodine.

Glaciers

These sparkling rivers of ice that crack and moan and move around have long attracted visitors to Alaska. Some are tourists, curious just to see what a glacier looks like. Others are scientists, eager to study the glaciers' complex dynamics. Still others are adventurers, who venture onto these dangerous formations to camp and climb and ski.

Glaciers are an accumulation of ice, snow, rock, sediment, and water that moves under the influence of its own weight and gravity. Their spectacular blue color is caused by the fact that water molecules absorb every color except blue, which is reflected. Almost 5 percent or 300,000 square miles of Alaska are covered by active, moving glaciers. Most glaciers are found on the perimeter of the Gulf of Alaska in the St. Elias and Chugach mountains, and in the Wrangells and the Alaska Range to the north.

At tidewater, glaciers calve (chunks break off from the terminus) in spectacular displays of crashing ice. While the calving on land is usually less dramatic, it can be equally dangerous and should be appreciated from a distance. *CAUTION: Never approach the face of a glacier, either on foot or in a kayak. It could calve at any moment and crush or swamp anything in its path.*

For those who want to get a close look at a glacier, several are accessible by road or tour boat. (For complete information on how to get to these glaciers, consult *The MILEPOST®*.) But for the truly adventurous, merely looking at a glacier is not enough. And if you fall into this category, take heed: travel *on* a glacier is not for the uninitiated. It is a dangerous, sometimes fatal, undertaking that requires experience and skill. (See Wilderness Classes in this section.) If you are planning a trip in a glacier environment, the following safety tips could save your life:

• Do not travel alone, but always with an experienced companion.

• Know the symptoms of hypothermia and how to treat it.

• In crevasse areas, always rope up and always probe for snow bridges.

• Avoid icefalls, *seracs* (jagged pinnacles where crevasses sometimes intersect), and avalanche areas.

• Always carry emergency shelter, dry clothing and extra food.

• Know how to use crampons, ice ax and rope.

• Whenever possible, travel on skis or snowshoes to distribute body weight over a greater area.

• Do not travel in whiteout conditions. Make camp and wait for the weather to clear.

Among the most popular wilderness glaciers are the Ruth and Kahiltna glaciers in the Alaska Range a short plane ride from Talkeetna. (See the BUYERS GUIDE for details.) Kahiltna serves as the 7,200-foot base camp for Mount McKinley climbing expeditions.

NOTE: This information is excerpted from Alaska's Glaciers, published by The Alaska Geographic Society. For information on ordering, see the ALASKA NORTHWEST LIBRARY at the back of this book.

Gold Panning

Have you ever felt the urge to try your hand at striking it rich? After all, if early day prospectors could do it, why couldn't you? Gold has been luring adventurers north for more than a hundred years now, and the big strikes helped open up vast expanses of wilderness known before that only to Native Americans: Juneau in 1880; Circle City in 1893; the Klondike in 1896; Nome in 1898; Fairbanks in 1902.

Chances are slim that a little recreational gold panning will bring you an instant fortune. But it will get you out into the backcountry for an adventure the whole family can enjoy. All you need is a gold pan (sold in most Alaskan hardware stores), a small shovel, and a vial with a tight stopper (for keeping your gold!)

Before you head out, though, you *must* do a little homework. Recreational gold panning permitted, with some restrictions, on most public lands. But check with the region's federal Bureau of Land Management (BLM) or state Division of Mining to make sure there are no legal claims. If you want to mine on private land or on someone else's claim, you must get permission in advance.

Next, check with the regional office of the Alaska Dept. of Fish and Game to make sure the stream you have chosen is open to gold panning. Some of the more ambitious recreational prospectors use small suction dredges and sluice boxes, which can do considerable damage, especially in salmon spawning streams.

A few general guidelines will help you minimize the environmental impacts of your gold panning:

• Work only in active stream channels or unvegetated gravel bars.

• Excavating or digging in streambanks is prohibited.

• Do not wash soil and vegetation directly into the streamflow because silt and decay of organic matter can cut off the oxygen supply to fish eggs buried in spawning beds.

• Do not dig in, excavate, disturb, destroy, or remove archaeological, paleontological, or historical objects.

As for the panning itself, a few basic principles can help you end up with those precious golden flecks in the bottom of your pan. These tips were prepared by the Parks and Recreation Dept., City and Bureau of Juneau.

Once you choose a stream, look for a natural depression or other spot that might collect heavy material washing down during spring floods. Dig here with your shovel and put about a shovelful of the dirt and gravel into your pan. The panning operation consists of uniform agitation and washing. Hold the pan under water and use your hands to remove large stones and break up lumps of clay. Carefully pour off the muddy water and repeat the process a time or two.

While the pan is covered with water, shake and rotate it in a slightly circular motion, about 2 inches in any direction, keeping the surface horizontal. The action should be vigorous but not violent. This agitation causes the gold to settle and the light material to rise to the surface. Once the surface is composed of light minerals only (indicated by the unchanging appearance of the top portion), wash this part away by dipping the pan into the water then tipping it backward. Repeat this action until the material is washed forward out of the pan, first from one side then the other. Do this smoothly and quickly. The entire process of agitating and washing repeatedly is what settles the gold into the bottom of the pan.

Finally, nothing remains in the pan except the gold and heavy sands. For this last task of separation, you can use mercury, a magnet, or the wet tip of your finger. Good luck! And if you do strike it rich and want to file a claim, you'll need to pay another visit to the nearest office of BLM or Division of Mining.

Guides

Choosing the right guide for your hunting or fishing trip, your float down a remote river, that glacier climbing or bird-watching expedition calls for research, planning and luck.

If you don't know anyone who has taken a trip similar to the one you're planning and can personally recommend a guide, several resources can help you pull together a list of prospective guides to interview. You have one important source in your hand, the BUYERS GUIDE at the back of The ALASKA WILDER-NESS MILEPOST® is a good place to start. Check out advertisements Alaskan guides place in national magazines and The MILEPOST®. Write for the current Official State Vacation Planner, (Alaska Division of Tourism, P.O. Box E-301, Juneau, AK 99811; phone 465-2010). Also many state and national parks and and refuges in Alaska provides lists of approved guides and concessionaires.

Other sources: Alaska Wilderness Guides Assoc., Box 141061-W, Anchorage, AK 99514, phone 276-6634; Alaska Professional Hunters Assoc., Box 451-W, Talkeetna, AK 99676, phone 733-2688; Alaska Sportfishing Lodge Assoc., 500 Wall St., Suite 401, Seattle, WA 98121, phone (206) 352-2003. A complete list of registered guide-outfitters for hunting and freshwater fishing guides in Southeast is available for $5 from the Dept. of Commerce, Division of Occupational Licensing, Box D-Lic, Juneau, AK 99811-0800, or from the same office at 3601 C St., Anchorage, AK 99503. The Juneau office, phone 465-2453, can also provide information on how long a hunting guide has been in business and whether any complaints have been lodged against the guide.

Some guides, particularly the fishing and hunting guides, set up information booths at travel and sporting shows held in the Lower 48. If you can get to one of these show, you may have the opportunity to interview your prospective guide in person.

In lieu of a personal interview, once you have a list of prospective guides, write for information and after you have received the brochures, call each guide. Ask how long the guide has been in business and ask for the names and addresses of 2 or 3 clients from the previous year. Then contact those clients and get a report.

Also find out the details about the trip you have chosen, advises Babbie Jacobs of St. Elias Alpine Guides in McCarthy. What will be the maximum number of people allowed in the group? The minimum? Who will be your guide(s), and what are their age(s), experience, and number of years with the guide service? Do they guide as a full time occupation, or only as a sideline?

Traditionally, only big game hunting guides were licensed by the state, though beginning in 1989 freshwater fishing guides in Southeast (except Yakutat) must now be registered too. Some observers predict that the 1990 Alaska Legislature will enact a law regulating all fishing guides. The 1989 legislature revamped the big game guiding statutes and placed much stiffer requirements on anyone wishing to become a guide. In addition to a 3 year apprenticeship as assistant guide, oral and written exams and a demonstrated knowledge of first aid and CPR are required. Registered guides are now called guide-outfitters.

Prices of big game guiding services as well as other adventure trips vary greatly depending on the services offered and the logistics involved. With big game guides, the species hunted also influences the price.

Remember, the more questions you ask, the more confident you can be in your choice of guide. After all, you will be paying a considerable sum of money and entrusting not only your vacation but perhaps your life as well to this guide. It pays to choose carefully.

Hiking

There is a lot of wilderness in the Northland, so there is plenty of room to hike. Every kind of trail is available — from the one between your cabin and the outhouse to one that traverses a mountain range.

But the overwhelming majority of back-country regions have no trails at all, except the ones made by animals.

Except for Denali National Park and Preserve, Kenai Fjords National Park, the periphery of Wrangell-St. Elias National Park and Preserve, and the Kenai and Tetlin national wildlife refuges, there is no improved highway access to Alaska's national parks, preserves, monuments and refuges. Transportation is limited to small chartered aircraft and boats. Landing areas for the former are usually lakes or sand bars. In southeastern Alaska, access to wilderness areas is generally by small boat or floatplane from transportation centers served by the Alaska Marine Highway System or commercial, scheduled airlines.

Within the parks and refuges, there are few man-made trails or signposts. Knowledge of the use of topographical maps and a compass is essential. (See Wilderness Classes, this section.) No footbridges or cable cars exist to carry travelers over the many streams and rivers that crisscross the country. A heavy downpour of rain or glacial runoff from high summer temperatures can cause a stream that is ankle deep in the early morning to be a hip-deep torrent in the afternoon. Streams will be the most shallow and usually have less current where they are the broadest or most braided. Always wear shoes when fording streams as waters are excruciatingly cold and a rock rolled on a bare foot can result in a bad bruise or fracture. (See River Crossing, this section.)

Alaska's tree line is erratic: all of the Aleutians, the greater part of the Alaska Peninsula, the Bering Sea coastal plain, as well as the north slope of the Brooks Range are devoid of trees. Timberline ranges from 1,500 to 2,500 feet in the Interior; above that altitude is tundra. In Southeast and southcentral, tree line varies from about 3,000 feet near Ketchikan to about 1,500 feet along Prince William Sound near Valdez. Beyond tree line, firewood is limited to clumps of willows and alders, which cannot sustain heavy backcountry use. Primus stoves using gasoline or kerosene (not butane or propane because the empty containers must be packed out) are a necessity. *NOTE: Primus fuel is not allowed on scheduled airlines, so make arrangements with your bush pilot, who can transport it, to have a supply available when you are flown in.*

Where dead wood is plentiful (never cut a slow-growing tree in this country), campfires should be restricted to gravel bars or mineral soil. Even though the tundra is damp to the touch, it is a veritable peat bog and once ignited it can burn underground, even under the snow, for several years. Lichens, essential for caribou sustenance, can take up to 100 years to regrow.

Always expect the unexpected, as far as weather is concerned. Be equipped with good lightweight rain gear and hope that it won't be needed too often. Hypothermia (see below) can strike even in temperatures above freezing, when combined with wind, exhaustion and damp clothing. Don't forget sunglasses and sunscreen lotion.

Tents should be of good quality and able to withstand strong winds, especially above tree line. As frozen ground is quite often found a few feet below the surface, especially in the Interior and the Arctic, take a foam pad for insulation under a sleeping bag.

Be prepared to wait out the weather when depending on small bush planes for transportation. The terrain is rugged and there are no navigational aids to facilitate landing in remote areas. Take extra food, fuel and other necessary supplies and keep your schedule flexible. In Interior and northern Alaska, a flashlight is unnecessary from May to mid-August.

The northern environment is fragile. Trampled tundra plants take much longer to recover than flora found in more temperate climates. Tin cans, plastics and aluminum foil become embalmed rather than decaying. Frost will heave up any refuse that is buried, so pack out anything except paper, which can be burned. Plan menus accordingly; think about what you'll have to carry back out. Fishing can vary from mediocre to fantastic, but do not plan to live off the land.

The USDA Forest Service has developed Recreational Oppor-tunity Guides for most of the trails in the Tongass and Chugach National Forests. Some of these trails are described in the sections on these forests. Copies of the Forest Service publications may be obtained from the Forest Service field office near the trails you plan to hike.

Further information and details about routes, plane charters, outfitters and guides in any particular area can be obtained by contacting offices of the Alaska Public Lands Information Centers, National Park Service, U.S. Fish and Wildlife Service, the U.S. Forest Service, and the Alaska Division of Parks; see Information Sources this section for addresses. Addresses for particular units are included with the descriptions of those units (see INDEX). For a list of guides and outfitters offering a variety of guided trips into Alaska's wilderness, see the BUYERS GUIDE, or contact the Alaska Wilderness Guides Assoc., P.O. Box 89061, Anchorage, AK 99508; phone 276-6634.

Holidays

The following list of observed holidays in Alaska can help you plan your trip. Keep in mind that banks and other agencies may be closed on these holidays.

New Year's Day ....Jan. 1
Martin Luther King Day ......3rd Mon. in Jan.
Presidents' Day ....3rd Mon. in Feb.
Sewards' Day* ....Last Mon. in March
Memorial Day ....Last Mon. in May
Independence Day ....July 4
Labor Day...........................1st Mon. in Sept.
Columbus Day ....2nd Mon. in Oct.
Alaska Day* ....Oct. 18
Veterans Day......................................Nov. 11
Thanksgiving Day ....4th Thurs. in Nov.
Christmas Day ....Dec. 25

*Seward's Day commemorates the signing of the treaty by which the United States bought Alaska from Russia, signed on March 30, 1867. Alaska Day is the anniversary of the formal transfer of the territory and the raising of the U.S. flag at Sitka on Oct. 18, 1867.

Homesteading

There is no "free" land in Alaska. The state's 365 million acres of land are owned by the federal government (Bureau of Land Management, National Park Service, etc.), the state, Native claims and private individuals. The easiest and fastest way to acquire land for private use is by purchase from the private sector, through real estate agencies or directly from individuals. However, the state does have a homesteading program for *U.S. citizens* who have been residents of Alaska at least 1 year and are 18 years or older. (Federal homesteading laws were repealed in 1986.)

Under the state homestead program, residents have a chance to receive up to 40 acres of nonagricultural land or up to 160 acres of agricultural land without paying for the acreage itself. The homesteader, however, must survey, occupy and improve the land in certain ways, and within specific times frames to receive title.

The homestead act also allows homesteaders to purchase parcels at fair market value without occupying or improving the land. This option requires only that nonagricultural land be staked, brushed and surveyed, and that parcels designed for agricultural use also meet clearing requirements.

Other state programs available for acquiring land include lottery sales scheduled in the spring and fall and public auction (1-year residency required and participants must be 18 years or older).

Details on these programs are available from Alaska Division of Land and Water Management offices: Northern Region, 3700 Airport Way, Fairbanks, AK 99709; Southcentral Region, P.O. Box 107005, Anchorage, AK 99510-7005; and Southeastern Region, 400 Willoughby Ave., Suite 400, Juneau, AK 99801.

Horseback Riding

Adventures on horseback are available in Alaska, though they are sometimes difficult to find. Outfitters operate from several population centers (Anchorage, Fairbanks, the Mat-Su Valley, Seward, Homer, McCarthy and Kodiak), and a few hunting guides who use horses for their remote hunts will occasionally rent them out before the hunting season begins.

To locate an outfitter with horses to rent, check in our BUYERS GUIDE under Guides & Outfitters in both the adventure and hunting sections, and also check *The MILEPOST®* or contact the nearest chamber of commerce or convention and visitors bureau.

Hot Springs

The U.S. Geological Survey identifies 79 thermal springs in Alaska. Almost half of these hot springs occur along the volcanic Alaska Peninsula and Aleutian chain. The second greatest regional concentration of springs is in southeastern Alaska. Hot springs are scattered throughout the Interior and western Alaska as far north as the Brooks Range and as far west as the Seward Peninsula.

Early miners and trappers were quick to use the naturally occurring warm waters for baths. Today approximately 25 percent of the recorded thermal springs are used for bathing, irrigation or domestic use. Only a handful of the known hot springs can be considered developed and these are found in Southeast, Interior and the Bering Sea Coast/Seward Peninsula regions. Facilities can range from full resorts to simple changing shacks at crude dams to create sitting pools. (See also Special Features in the appropriate regions.)

Hunting

Sportsmen from all over the world travel thousands of miles to experience the excitement and rewards of a big game hunt in Alaska. And many Alaskans take full advantage of their proximity to the backcountry to fill their freezer full of meat and add a trophy to their walls. Whether the object is a large brown bear or a fleet-footed caribou, the hunting is great.

All nonresident aliens must be accompanied by a guide for any big game hunt.

Brown bear *(Ursus arctos)* are found throughout the state, though they are commonly called grizzlies when they live inland, away from coastal areas. Kodiak and the Alaska Peninsula are traditionally prime areas for hunting these large, dangerous omnivores, but other parts of the state also boast excellent sport. Nonresident hunters must be accompanied by a registered guide or a close relative over 19 who is an Alaska resident.

Black bear *(Ursus americanus)* occur over most of the forested areas of the state excluding Kodiak and major islands in Southeast and Prince William Sound. In many areas they are less common than browns. The best hunting is probably from the tidal areas in Prince William Sound, the Kenai Peninsula, the Susitna River drainages, and throughout Southeast, in late May, early June, and September.

Caribou *(Rangifer tarandus)*, the most nomadic of Alaska's mammals, range throughout the state except for Southeast and most offshore islands. The adult bull is one of the most impressive trophy animals in the North, and the hunt for them attracts several thousand nonresident sportsmen aa year. Caribou also serve as a major food source for Alaska Natives and other rural Alaskans.

A guide (or an Alaska first blood relative) is also required to hunt Dall sheep and mountain goats. (This new requirement for mountain goat hunting was enacted by the Alaska Legislature in the spring of 1989.)

Dall sheep *(Ovis dalli dalli)* are the only sheep native to Alaska and are found in the Brooks, Alaska, Chugach and Kenai ranges, the Talkeetnas, and the Wrangells. Stalking one of these proud white rams with the massive curling horns requires stamina and skill.

Mountain goat *(Oreamnos americanus)* hunting can be even tougher. It should be attempted only by properly equipped hunters in good physical condition. Goats occur from Southeast north and west along the coastal mountains in Cook Inlet and north into the Talkeetnas and the southern drainages of the Wrangells. They have also been transplanted to Kodiak, Chichagof, and Baranof islands, though they did not survive on Chichagof.

Moose *(Alces alces)*, the world's largest member of the deer family, occur throughout most of Alaska, except for the major islands of Southeast. They are most abundant in second-growth birch forests, timberline plateaus, and along the major rivers of Southcentral and the Interior. Trophy-class bulls are found through-

out the state, but the largest come from the Alaska Peninsula, the Susitna Valley, and Westcentral Alaska.

Sitka black-tailed deer *(Odocoileus hemionus sitkensis)* inhabit the wet, coastal rainforests of Southeast and Prince William Sound, and also occur on Kodiak and Afognak islands. Populations fluctuate with the severity of the winters. Because most winters in their range are mild and deer have a high reproductive potential, bag limits are generous, with the season open from August through December. Early season hunters climb to alpine areas, where they enjoy not only the hunt but unsurpassed scenery as well. Most deer, however, are taken in November, when the blacktails are on lower ranges.

Other big game species include the wolf, bison, elk, musk-ox and wolverine, while small game animals include grouse, ptarmigan and hares. Fur animals that might be hunted are the coyote, fox and lynx. At present there is no recreational hunting of polar bear, walrus or other marine animals.

Waterfowl are also abundant and the bag limits usually generous in seasons that often begin on Sept. 1. Taking of brant, geese, cranes, ducks, snipe and swans (the latter with only 300 permits issued and only for the Bering Sea region) requires both a state and federal duck stamp.

With such an enticing variety of animals to hunt — and tens of thousands of acres over which to hunt them — sportsmen can choose from any number of world-class hunts. Decisions of time and money to be spent, allied with preferred species and region of the state, will culminate in the experience of a lifetime.

Regulations: Hunters in Alaska must be aware of the rules and regulations BEFORE entering the field. The intricacies of licenses, tags, reports, stamps, seals, permits, tickets and guiding contracts should be worked out well in advance. Be sure your guide explains pertinent rules to you. (See Guides this section.) Failure to comply can result in substantial monetary fines, loss of trophies and property and even imprisonment. Several undercover "sting" operations in recent years have resulted in convictions of both guides and clients.

In general, the rules of common sense and fair chase apply: no shooting from or across a highway; no use of a helicopter (except for emergency rescue); no shooting from a moving motorboat; no driving or herding game with a plane, boat, or ATV; no fully automated weapons (machine guns); no land-

and-shoot (except for 1 or 2 species in certain areas); no radio communications or artificial lights.

The Alaska Dept. of Fish and Game has a small, no-nonsense brochure entitled *Help for the Nonresident Hunter*, which lays out what hunters must do before, during, and after their hunt. Acquiring one could prove advantageous.

One other note from ADF&G: Hunters who kill game, and who may not use all the meat legally required to be salvaged, are urged to contact the village council of the nearest town or village to offer the meat for their use. Wild game is important to many rural Alaskans. When giving game meat away, be sure to get a written receipt of it.

Copies of *Help for the Nonresident Hunter* are available from the Alaska Dept. of Fish and Game, P.O. Box 3-2000, Juneau, AK 99802. That office can also supply copies of the complete hunting regulations, which may also be obtained from any of the many department offices throughout the state.

Licenses are available from any designated licensing agent. (See information in the Community sections, though it's a good idea to get your license before you head into the backcountry.) Licenses may be obtained by mail from ADF&G, Licensing Section, 1107 W. 8th St., Juneau, AK 99801. They are also available at the major Dept. of Fish and Game offices in Anchorage, Fairbanks and Juneau.

A complete list of registered Alaskan guides is available for $5 from the Dept. of Commerce, Box D, Juneau, AK 99811 or 3601 C St., Anchorage, AK 99503.

There are 26 game management units in Alaska and a wide variation in both seasons and bag limits for various species. Check for special regulations in each unit.

Licenses and Tag Fees: Residents and nonresidents must submit a $5 fee with each application for a game species involved in a limited drawing. The musk-ox drawing requires a $10 fee.

Big game tags are required for residents hunting musk-ox and brown/grizzly bear and for nonresidents hunting any big game animal. These nonrefundable, nontransferable metal locking tags (valid for the calendar year) must be purchased prior to the taking of the animal. A tag may be used for any species for which the tag fee is of equal or less value.

Resident License Fees: No hunting or trapping licenses are required of residents of Alaska under age 16 or residents age 60 or older who have resided in the state for 1 year. A special identification card is issued for the senior citizen exemption.

Trapping license, $10; hunting license, $12; hunting and trapping license, $22; hunting and sportfishing license, $22; hunting, trapping and sportfishing license, $32.

Resident Tag Fees: Brown/grizzly bear, $25; musk-ox (bull), $500 on Nunivak Island and in Arctic National Wildlife Refuge, $25 from Nelson Island, and musk-ox (cow), $25.

Nonresident License Fees: Hunting license, $60; hunting and sportfishing license, $96; hunting and trapping license, $200.

Nonresident Tag Fees: Brown/grizzly bear, $350; black bear, $200; bison, $350; moose or caribou, $300; sheep, $400; elk or goat, $250; deer, $135; wolf, $150; wolverine, $150; musk-ox, $1,100.

Hypothermia

Exposure to wet, cold and windy conditions can lead to hypothermia, the number one killer of outdoor recreationists. Hypothermia is the body's reaction when it is exposed to cold and cannot maintain normal temperatures. In an automatic survival reaction, blood flow to the extremities is shut down in favor of preserving warmth in the vital organs. As internal temperature drops, judgment and coordination become impaired. Allowed to continue, hypothermia leads to stupor, collapse and possibly death. Most hypothermia cases develop in air temperatures between 30° and 50°F.

Any of the following are symptoms of hypothermia: Severe shivering; vague, slow, slurred speech; memory lapses, incoherence; clumsiness, lack of control of hands and feet; drowsiness, exhaustion.

The victim may deny any problem. Believe the symptoms, not the victim. Even mild symptoms require immediate treatment. Get the victim out of the wind and rain. Remove all wet clothes. If the victim is only mildly impaired, give him warm drinks (nonalcoholic) to raise his body temperature. Get the person into dry clothes and a warm sleeping bag. Well-wrapped, warm (not hot) rocks or canteens will help.

If the victim is badly impaired, attempt to keep him awake. Put the victim in a sleeping bag with another person — both stripped. If you have a double bag, put the victim between 2 warm people. Build a fire to warm the camp.

To prevent hypothermia, the U.S. Forest Service advises the following: Stay dry. When clothes get wet, they lose about 90 percent of their insulating value. Wool loses less heat than cotton, down and some synthetics. Choose rain gear that covers the head, neck, body and legs, and provides good protection against wind-driven rain. Polyurethane-coated nylon is best.

Ice Fishing

Many Alaskan fishing enthusiasts say fish caught in winter actually tastes better than those caught in summer. And, anyone at any age can enjoy ice fishing. It takes no major investment in new equipment, no specialized skills and can be done anytime after the water freezes. However, be sure to consult the Alaska Fishing Regulations for season openings and familiarize yourself with the regulations for the area you wish to fish. (See Fishing this section.)

Burbot, char, trout, land-locked salmon, grayling and whitefish are favorite prey for the ice fishermen. Burbot generally feed close to the bottom so try for them in not more than 20 feet of water. Many burbot are taken in only 1 or 2 feet of water. Burbot also hit best at night and fish heads and entrails are good bait. Don't fish too deep for trout or land-locked salmon either and use lures and spin-

ners for bait. Grayling are probably the most difficult fish to catch in winter but they can be taken using small spinners or bait. Whitefish are often hard to land because of their soft mouth but they are delicious, easy to fillet and you can use the head and tail for burbot bait.

Use common sense when out ice fishing. As you venture onto the ice, especially just after freezeup, drill a few test holes to determine the thickness and condition of the ice. Five or 6 inches of good ice is recommended for safe ice fishing. Be especially cautious in the spring. Even though the ice is thick, it can be rotten from the underside. Rotten ice can give way without a sound. Overflow is another potential danger because it can get you wet, so always take along extra warm clothes, especially dry socks, boots and gloves. Change immediately if you get wet!

The only specialized equipment you need is a good auger or ice chisel, a sharpening stone, and an ice skimmer. Don't bring your best rod and reel because a wet line freezes quickly and can foul your gear. Other items that make ice fishing safer and more comfort-

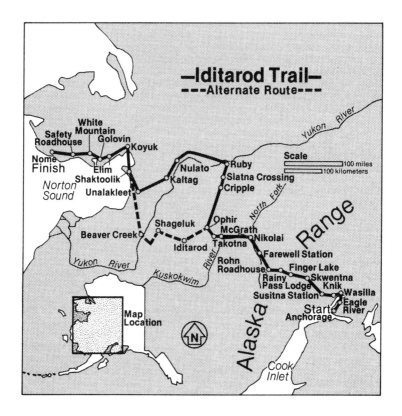

able include a long safety rope, a flask of hot refreshment, extra warm clothes, a tarp for sitting on or using as a wind shield and hauling gear, a gas lantern, snow machine, snowshoes and a power auger.

NOTE: This information was excerpted from Ice Fishing by Fred T. Williams, a pamphlet available from the Alaska Dept. of Fish and Game, P.O. Box 3-2000, Juneau, AK 99802-2000.

Ice Fog

This is a fog of tiny, spherical ice crystals formed when air just above the ground becomes so cold it can no longer retain water vapor. It is most common in arctic and subarctic regions in winter when clear skies create a temperature inversion. Surface heat radiates into space, forming a warm-air cap that contains cold air at low elevations. Ice fog is most noticeable when man-made pollutants also are trapped at low levels by the inversion.

Iceworm

Although generally regarded as a hoax, iceworms actually exist. These small, segmented black or brown worms — usually less than 1 inch long — thrive at temperatures just above freezing. Observers as far back as the 1880s have reported that at dawn, dusk or on overcast days, the tiny worms, all belonging to the genus *Mesenchytraeus*, may literally carpet the surface of glaciers. When sunlight strikes them, they burrow back down into the ice. The tiny worms feed on pollen and other windblown organic matter.

The Iditarod

The Iditarod Trail Sled Dog Race is a major annual sporting event in Alaska. The first race, conceived and organized by musher Joe Redington, Sr., of Knik, and historian Dorothy Page of Wasilla, was run in 1967 and covered only 56 miles. The race was lengthened in 1973, and the first-ever 1,100-mile sled dog race began in Anchorage on March 3, 1973, and ended April 3 in Nome. Of the 34 who started the race, 22 finished. The Iditarod has been run every year since its inception, and in 1976 Congress designated the Iditarod as a National Historic Trail.

Following the old dog team mail route blazed in 1910 from Knik to Nome, the trail crosses 2 mountain ranges, follows the Yukon River for about 150 miles, runs through several bush villages and crosses the pack ice of Norton Sound. It is strictly a winter trail because the ground is mostly spongy muskeg swamp.

The route attracted national attention in 1925, when sled dog mushers, including the famous Leonhard Seppala, relayed 300,000 units of life-saving diphtheria serum to epidemic-threatened Nome. In later years, as the airplane and snowmobile replaced the dog team, the trail fell into disuse. Through Redington's efforts, the trail has been assured a place in Alaska history.

From the starting line on Fourth Avenue in Anchorage, mushers race their teams to Eagle River, where they load the dogs onto trucks to Settler's Bay in Wasilla, where the race oficially begins. It heads out into the Bush, then, 1,000 miles later, to the finish line at Nome. In odd-numbered years, the race takes an alternate route south. While the route is traditionally described at 1,049 miles long (a figure that was selected because Alaska is the 49th state), actual distance is close to 1,100 miles. (See map on page 25.)

For more information contact the Iditarod Trail Committee, Pouch X, Wasilla, AK 99687; phone 376-5155.

Igloos

Also known as snowhouses, these ingenious domes of snow blocks provided temporary, often emergency, shelter for the Arctic Eskimos of Alaska. (Canadian Eskimos traditionally spent more time in their igloos.) Igloos are built in a spiral with each tier leaning inward at a greater angle than the tier below. The entrance passage consists of a tunnel and a cold trap in front of the sleeping platform. A small vent at the top of the dome allows for ventilation; and a window made of freshwater ice and situated above the entrance tunnel lets in light.

Information Sources

Agriculture: State Division of Agriculture, P.O. Box 949, Palmer, AK 99645; Cooperative Extension Service, University of Alaska, Fairbanks, AK 99701.

Alaska Natives: Alaska Federation of Natives, 411 W. 4th Ave., Anchorage, AK 99501.

Business: Alaska Dept. of Commerce and Economic Development, P.O. Box D, Juneau, AK 99811; Alaska State Chamber of Commerce, 310 2nd St., Juneau, AK 99801.

Camping and Hiking: Alaska Division of Parks, P.O. Box 107001, Anchorage, AK 99510; Alaska Public Lands Information Center, 605 W. 4th Ave., Suite 105, Anchorage, AK 99501; 250 Cushman, Suite 1A, Fairbanks, AK 99701; P.O. Box 359, Tok, AK 99780; Bureau of Land

Management, 701 C St., P.O. Box 13, Anchorage, AK 99513; Supervisor, Chugach National Forest, 201 E. 9th Ave., Anchorage, AK 99501; Tongass National Forest, P.O. Box 21628, Juneau, AK 99802, phone 586-8863; 3031 Tongass Ave., Ketchikan, AK 99901, phone 225-2148; 204 Siginaka Way, Sitka, AK 99835, phone 747-6671; or P.O. Box 309, Petersburg, AK 99833, phone 772-3871. National Park Service, 2525 Gambell St., Anchorage, AK 99503; U.S. Fish and Wildlife Service, 1011 E. Tudor Road, Anchorage, AK 99503.

Education: Alaska Dept. of Education, P.O. Box GA, Juneau, AK 99811; Alaska Wilderness Studies, College of Community and Continuing Education, University of Alaska Anchorage, 3211 Providence Dr., Anchorage, AK 99508; phone 786-1468.

Gold Panning: State Division of Geological and Geophysical Surveys, Mines Information Office, 3601 C St., Anchorage, AK 99503; Bureau of Land Management, 701 C St., P.O. Box 13, Anchorage, AK 99513.

Hunting and Fishing Regulations: Alaska Dept. of Fish and Game, P.O. Box 3-2000, Juneau, AK 99802.

Land: State Division of Land and Water Management, P.O. Box 107005, Anchorage, AK 99510; Bureau of Land Management, 701 C St., P.O. Box 13, Anchorage, AK 99513.

Military: Dept. of the Air Force, Headquarters, Alaskan Air Command, Elmendorf Air Force Base, AK 99506; Dept. of the Army, Headquarters, 6th Infantry Brigade (Alaska), Fort Richardson, AK 99505; State Dept. of Military Affairs, Office of the Adjutant General, 3601 C St., Anchorage, AK 99503; Dept. of Transportation, U.S. Coast Guard, 17th Coast Guard District, P.O. Box 3-5000, Juneau, AK 99802.

Mines and Petroleum: Dept. of Natural Resources, Division of Mining Information Office, P.O. Box 107005, Anchorage, AK 99510; Alaska Oil & Gas Conservation Commission, 3001 Porcupine Dr., Anchorage, AK 99501; Alaska Miners Assoc., 509 W. 3rd Ave., Suite 17, Anchorage, AK 99501; Alaska Oil and Gas Assoc., 121 W. Fireweed, Suite 207, Anchorage, AK 99503.

Outdoor and Environmental Assocs.: Alaska Bowhunters Assoc., P.O. Box 454, Girdwood, AK 99587; Alaska Center for the Environment, 700 H. St. #4, Anchorage, AK 99501; Alaska Dog Mushers Assoc., P.O. Box 662, Fairbanks, AK 99707; Alaska Sled Dog & Racing Assoc., P.O. Box 110569, Anchorage, AK 99511; American Alpine Club, Alaska Section, P.O. Box 335, Girdwood, AK 99587; Knik Kanoers & Kayakers, P.O. Box 101935, Anchorage, AK 99510; Mountain Bikers of Alaska, 20900 Boniface, #657, Anchorage, AK 99504; Mountaineering Club of Alaska, P.O. Box 102037, Anchorage, AK 99510; National Audubon Society, 308 G St., Suite 219, Anchorage, AK 99501; National Wildlife Federation, 750 W. 2nd Ave., Anchorage, AK 99501; Nordic Ski Club, P.O. Box 103504, Anchorage, AK 99510; Northern Alaska Environmental Center, 218 Driveway, Fairbanks, AK 99701; Sierra Club, Alaska Chapter, 241 E. 5th Ave., #205, Anchorage, AK 99501; Southeast Alaska Conservation Council, P.O. Box 021692, Juneau, AK 99802; Wilderness Society, 529 W. 8th, Suite 205, Anchorage, AK 99501; Women of the Wilderness, P.O. Box 775226, Eagle River, AK 99577; phone 688-2226.

Public Lands: Alaska Public Lands Information Center, 605 W. 4th Ave., Suite 105, Anchorage, AK 99501; 250 Cushman St., Suite 1A, Fairbanks, AK 99701; P.O. Box 359, Tok, AK 99780.

Travel and Visitor Information: Alaska State Division of Tourism, P.O. Box E, Juneau, AK 99811; Alaska State Marine Highway System, P.O. Box R, Juneau, AK 99811; Alaska Visitors Assoc., P.O. Box 102220, Anchorage, AK 99510.

See also the BUYERS GUIDE at the back of the book.

Insect Pests

An often asked question about travel to Alaska is "When's the best time to avoid mosquitoes?" The answer is probably midwinter. Summer is bug season and you will run into mosquitoes, black flies (also called whitesox, simulids and buffalo gnats), no-see-ums (also called punkies) and snipe flies.

Mosquitoes emerge from hibernation before the snow has entirely disappeared. They peak in about June, but continue to harass humans through the fall. Mosquitoes are especially active in the early morning and at dusk. Mosquito eggs hatch in water, so Alaska — with its many square miles of marshy tundra and lakes — is prime breeding ground.

The female mosquito penetrates the skin with a hollow snout to draw blood to nourish her eggs. Mosquito saliva, injected into the wound, is what causes the itch, redness and swelling. Mosquitoes are attracted to warmth, moisture, carbon dioxide and dark colors, among other things. Mosquitoes fly into the wind, relying on their antennae to sense a potential meal. They then home in to within a few inches to determine if it is a good meal. Insect repellents work by jamming mosquitoes' sensors so they can't tell if you are a meal.

Government sources recommend that you wear a lightweight hooded parka, tight fitting at the wrists, with a drawstring hood so it fits snugly around the face, and trousers tucked securely into socks, to reduce your chances of getting bitten. Mosquitoes can bite through thin material (such as a cotton shirt), so wear some heavier protection where mosquitoes are active. You may also want to wear a head net when mosquitoes are numerous. Choose a campsite away from mosquito-breeding areas. A 5-mph wind velocity grounds most mosquitoes, so locating your campsite where you'll catch a breeze also helps. Tents should be well-screened against bugs. Cooking outdoors also attracts mosquitoes, so keep food covered.

Many Alaskan hikers minimize the mosquito problem by selecting alpine hikes well above tree line in June and early July, when these pests are at their worst. The woodsy trails they use in May, August or even after the first frost in the fall.

The **black fly** biting season starts in May and lasts until freezeup. Activity may be quite localized, depending on your proximity to streams from which the adults are emerging. The reaction to a black fly bite is usually pronounced, and the swelling and itching may last a week or more. Unlike mosquitoes, black flies crawl on the skin under loose clothing and into the hair and ears to bite. The lightweight parka with drawstring hood and trousers tucked into socks will reduce black fly biting.

In some locations along the coast, **no-see-ums** are the major biting insect pest. The swarms of this tiny, gray-black, silver-winged gnat can be extremely bothersome. The no-see-um season extends from June through August. Their bite is a most annoying prolonged prick, after which the surrounding skin becomes inflamed, producing a small red spot that itches intermittently. No-see-ums bite exposed parts of the body. Clothing that covers as much of the body as possible gives the best protection.

Snipe flies are a troublesome pest in certain mountainous localities as far north as the Alaska Range. The pest season extends from late June to early August. The bite stings and is decidedly painful, but shortly afterward there may be little, if any, trace of the bite. These insects retire at sunset. Snipe flies can bite through thin clothing. Tightly woven outer garments that do not directly contact the body help to prevent biting.

According to government sources, mosquito repellents containing diethyl-meta-toluamide (DEET) are most effective. Folk wisdom has it that moisturizer made by a cosmetics firm (Avon's Skin-So-Soft) does the best job. It needs to be applied more frequently, but it does not melt plastics and fishing lines as the repellents high in DEET will. Make sure you apply repellent to all exposed skin, including hands, ears and feet. Repellent is less effective for black flies, no-see-ums and snipe flies. However, these pests are deterred by low humidity and wind.

Language

English is the primary language in Alaska. Many Native languages are still spoken, however, and the majority of Native people are bilingual in English and their own tongue.

Alaskans use several terms that visitors will hear constantly. "Outside" refers to anywhere outside of Alaska, most commonly the contiguous 48 states, which are also called the "Lower 48." "Cheechakos" (chee-CHAH-kos) are newcomers, while "sourdoughs" have lived in the North Country for a long time. "Freezeup" comes in the fall, when the rivers and lakes freeze for the winter. This is followed in the spring by "breakup," when the ice breaks up.

Lifeline to the Bush

Alaska's radio stations broadcast a wide variety of music, talk shows, religious and educational programs. Several stations also broadcast personal messages, long a popular and necessary form of communication in bush Alaska. These programs bring news of weddings, births and deaths, but also provide a quick way of telling Auntie at Brevig Mission, for instance, that her groceries will be on the next mailplane.

Stations with personal message programs include the following:

Anchorage, KYAK 650 kHz; 2800 Dowling, 99507. "Bush Pipeline" 8 p.m., transmitting within a 300-mile radius of Anchorage.

Barrow, KBRW-AM 680 kHz; P.O. Box 109, 99723. "Tundra Drums," ongoing 6 a.m. to midnight.

Bethel, KYUK 640 kHz; Pouch 468, 99559. "Tundra Drums," 8:30 and 11:30 a.m., 3:30 and 8:30 p.m.

Dillingham, KDLG 670 kHz; P.O. Box 670, 99576. "Bay Messenger," 10:25 a.m., 12:25, 2:25, 4:25 and 8:25 p.m.

Fairbanks, KIAK 970 kHz; P.O. Box 73410, 99707. "Pipeline of the North," 6:45 and 8:45 p.m. Monday through Saturday.

Galena, KIYU-AM 910 kHz; P.O. Box 165,

99741. "Yukon Wireless" 8 a.m., 12:05 and 6:35 p.m.

Glennallen, KCAM 790 kHz; P.O. Box 249, 99588. "Caribou Clatter," 7:20 a.m. and 12:20, 5:50 and 9:20 p.m.

Haines, KHNS-FM 102.3 MHz; P.O. Box 1109, 99827. "Listener Personals," 8:40 and 11:40 a.m., 1:40, 4:40 and 10:40 p.m.

Homer, KBBI-AM 890 kHz; 215 E. Main Court, 99603. "The Bay Bush Lines," at 7:20 and 9:55 a.m., and 2, 6 and 9 p.m.

Ketchikan, KRBD-FM 105.9 MHz; 716 Totem Way, 99901. Also received in Metlakatla, Hollis and Thorne Bay. Translator service to Klawock and Hydaburg, 90.1 MHz; Craig, 101.7 MHz. "Muskeg Messenger," 8:30 a.m., 1:30 and 7:30 p.m.

Kodiak, KVOK-AM 560 kHz and KJJZ-FM 101 MHz; P.O. Box 708, 99615. "Highliner Crabbers," 6:15 and 9:15 a.m., 12:25, 7:10 and 11:50 p.m. daily.

McGrath, KSKO 870 kHz; P.O. Box 70, 99627. "KSKO Messages," 58 minutes past the hour.

Nome, KICY 850 kHz; P.O. Box 820, 99762. "Ptarmigan Telegraph," 12:25 and 6:25 p.m.

Nome, KNOM 780 kHz; P.O. Box 988, 99762. "Hot Lines," 12:15 and 5:15 p.m. daily.

North Pole, KJNP 1170 kHz; P.O. Box 0, 99705. "Trapline Chatter," 9:20 p.m. Monday through Friday, 9:30 p.m. Saturday, 9:35 p.m. Sunday. Emergency messages any time.

Petersburg, KFSK-FM 100.9 MHz; P.O. Box 149, 99833. "Muskeg Messages," 5:19, 6:19, 7:19, 8 a.m., noon, 5:45 and 10 p.m.

Petersburg, KRSA 580 kHz; P.O. Box 650, 99833. "Channel Chatters," 6:15 and 7:15 a.m., 12:30, 5:15 and 9:15 p.m.

Sitka, KCAW-FM 104.7 MHz; 102 B. Lincoln St., 99835. Translator service to Angoon, 105.5 MHz; Kake, 107.1 MHz; Pelican, 91.7 MHz; Port Alexander and Tenakee Springs, 91.9 MHz. "Muskeg Messages" 6:55, 7:55 and 8:55 a.m.; 1 and 6:15 p.m. weekdays; 6:59 and 7:59 a.m., 1 and 5 p.m. on weekends. P.O. Box 520, 99835. "Muskeg Messages," 6:55, 7:55 and 8:55 a.m. and 1:15 and 6:15 p.m.

Soldotna, KSRM 920 kHz; SR2, Box 852, 99669. "Tundra Tom Tom," 6:30 p.m. daily.

Wrangell, KSTK-FM 101.7 MHz; P.O. Box 1141, 99929. Radiograms, 7:30 and 11:30 a.m., 5:30 and 9:30 p.m.

Maps

Alaska Maps: The best source for maps is the U.S. Geological Survey. USGS topographic maps are available in scales from 1:24 to 1:500. Maps of Alaska are available by mail from the USGS Western Distribution Branch, Federal Center, Bldg. 81, Box 25286, Denver, CO 80225. Write for an index of maps for Alaska; the index shows published topographic maps available, quadrangle location, name and survey date. (The index and a booklet describing topographic maps are free.)

Sales counters are maintained at USGS offices throughout the country; check the phone book to see if there's an office near you. In Alaska, USGS maps may be purchased over the counter (no mail order) at USGS offices located at 4230 University Dr., Room 101, Anchorage, AK 99508; and 701 C St., Room F-146, Anchorage, AK 99513; and Room 126, Federal Bldg., 101 12th Ave., Fairbanks, AK 99701. Residents of Alaska may order maps by mail from the Alaska Distribution Section, Federal Bldg., Box 12, Room 126, 101 12th Ave., Fairbanks, AK 99701. Many commercial dealers also sell USGS maps.

Chugach National Forest maps are available for a small fee from the U.S. Forest Service, 201 E. 9th Ave., Anchorage, AK 99501. Tongass National Forest maps are available from the U.S. Forest Service, P.O. Box 21628-P.A.O. Juneau, AK 99802.

Much of the travel in Southeast and Southcentral/Gulf Coast is by boat, and nautical charts are required for safe navigation. Contact local sporting goods or boat supply stores for charts of your route. For nautical charts through the mail, write: National Ocean Survey, Chart Sales and Control Data, 632 6th Ave., Room 405, Anchorage, AK 99501. Ask for a copy of Nautical Chart Catalog 3 for Alaska.

Canada Maps: Topographic maps of Canada are available from the Canada Map Office, 615 Booth St., Ottawa, ON, K1A 0E9. For western Canada, request a free copy of Index 2; the index shows published topographic maps available and gives an order number. Also available from the Canada Map Office is a list of authorized topographic map dealers.

Money/Credit Cards

Alaska uses American currency. Major bank and credit cards are widely accepted in the larger communities. The larger communities also have at least 1 bank (hours are generally from 10 a.m. to 3 p.m. weekdays; open until 6 p.m. Friday). However the majority of small communities have no banking facilities. Availability of cash may be limited, so even cashing a traveler's check may be difficult. It's a good idea to carry cash with you when traveling to remote areas.

Mountain Climbing

Seeking the heights in Alaska can take you anywhere from 20,320-foot summit of Mount McKinley to the 3,000-foot peak of an unnamed mountain in the Chugach Range. If there's one thing Alaska has plenty of, it's mountains. And the climbing is superb.

McKinley, North America's tallest peak, attracts some 900 climbers a year, with about half that number actually making the summit. The climb requires years of preparation, planning, and training, with time on the mountain averaging 21 days. Only the strongest and most experienced climbers should attempt McKinley, and even then tragedies occur. Each year the mountain claims an average of 2 climbers, though one terrible year (1967) saw 7 climbers die.

Because of Mount McKinley's popularity and the brief climbing season (April to July), serious trash and sanitation problems have developed along the heavily traveled West Buttress. Expeditions have been mounted for the sole purpose of cleanup, and National Park Service regulations require that all trash be packed out, though human wastes may be collected and disposed of into a deep crevasse. (For more on climbing Mount McKinley, see Attractions in the INTERIOR section.)

Seven authorized guide services offer climbs up McKinley. A handful of air services based in Talkeetna specialize in the glacier landings necessary to ferry climbers and their equipment to and from the mountain. (For more information, see BUYERS GUIDE.) An information packet available from the Park Service lists the guides, plus air taxis and dog teams for shuttling climbers' gear. The packet also contains information for foreign climbers, a bibliography, tips on radio, photography, equipment, and the like.

The National Park Service rangers based in Talkeetna are experienced climbers and take turns patrolling the mountain to help collect trash, provide emergency rescues, and assist at the 14,000-foot medical camp. Rangers estimate a McKinley climb to cost between $2,000 and $5,000, depending on whether the climb is guided. The estimates do not include the cost of transportation to Alaska.

Many serious climbers head for Alaska's lesser known but more difficult peaks. For ice climbs there is Mount Hunter or Mount Huntington (14,573 feet and 12,240 feet, respectively, both in the Alaska Range). Those interested in steep rock faces might choose peaks near Ruth Glacier, also in the Alaska Range. The Mooses Tooth, a 10,335-foot mountain 15 miles southeast of McKinley, offers steep rock and is itself a prominent peak. The Ruth Gorge is said to closely resemble Yosemite Valley.

To receive an information packet on climbs in Denali National Park, write: Denali National Park and Preserve, Talkeetna Ranger Station, P.O. Box 588, Talkeetna, AK 99676; phone 733-2231.

Those wishing to escape the crowds on McKinley might opt for 18,008-foot Mount St. Elias, Alaska's second-highest peak. (Mount Logan, second-tallest mountain in North America, lies across the border in Canada's Kluane National Park and is usually access through the Yukon.) The Wrangell and St. Elias mountain peaks have been attracting climbers for more than a century, and each year about a dozen international expeditions head into this mountain wilderness.

The Wrangell-St. Elias National Park and Preserve rangers are headquartered at Glennallen, and like the rangers at Talkeetna will send out information packets upon request. But unlike the McKinley rangers, those at Glennallen are just building their mountaineering program. They ask that climbers who have attempted one of the park's mountains stop into their office and report on the climb, the route used, the difficulties encountered, etc. This information, in spiral notebooks, is available in the office and is a rich source of last-minute advice for expeditions heading out. That address is: Superintendent, Wrangell-St. Elias National Park and Preserve, P.O. Box 29, Glennallen, AK 99588; phone 822-5235.

Climbs in the Brooks Range, on sedimentary rock, are less technically difficult and without so much ice and snow. These appeal to climbers seeking real solitude in high tundra country with the opportunity for considerable wildlife viewing. Technical climbs on granite abound in the Arrigetch Peaks in Gates of the Arctic National Park. Check with guides and air taxi operators in Bettles for specific climbs and logistical support. (See Bettles in BROOKS RANGE and the ARCTIC section; also the BUYERS GUIDE.) Check too with park officials: Superintendent, Gates of the Arctic National Park and Preserve, P.O. Box 74680, Fairbanks, AK 99707; phone 456-0281.

The Mountaineering Club of Alaska (P.O. Box 102037, Anchorage, AK 99510; recorded message phone 337-6679) is another rich sourch of information, particularly about ranges outside the national parks such as the Talkeetnas and the Chugach Range. For those of you who don't turn up your nose to a 7,000-

foot mountain, Alaska has thousands, for rock climbers and ice climbers alike. Information on these peaks and on mountain climbing in general, is readily available from the Mountaineering Club. One day in the summer of 1989 the club's trip hotline message phone was offering names and phone numbers for more information about the following: a basic rock climbing class; Mystery Mountain climb; McCarthy bike trip; Homicide Peak climb; Hidden Peak climb; Katmai traverse; Harding Icefield traverse (an annual trip).

Paralytic Shellfish Poisoning

Alaska has a significant problem with poisonous shellfish. This problem is commonly referred to as Paralytic Shellfish Poisoning or PSP, a serious illness caused by poisons concentrated in tiny organisms called *dinoflagellates*. Clams, mussels, geoducks, oysters, snails and scallops filter these food organisms from the water, absorb and store the toxin. Razor clams appear to accumulate toxin less readily than do hardshell clams; in Cook Inlet there has never been a documented case of PSP from properly cleaned razor clams. However, in southeastern Alaska there have been numerous poisonings from other types of clams. Toxin levels may be extremely high — death has occurred after ingestion of only 1 mussel. You cannot use the presence or absence of a red tide — caused by the rapid growth of certain kinds of planktons which may or may not produce toxins — to determine whether a beach is safe for clamming. In the case of butter clams and mussels, it does not matter whether there has been a red tide within the past 2 weeks or the past 2 years; there is no guarantee that they will be free of PSP. The organisms that cause PSP may be present at any time during the year. Neither cooking nor freezing eliminates the toxin.

Alaska clams may be poisonous unless they have been harvested from an approved beach. Commercial harvesting areas are tested for this poisoning and require approval from the Dept. of Environmental Conservation. Visitors to most beaches cannot be assured that the shellfish is safe; therefore it is wise to use caution when collecting shellfish for consumption. In general, avoid eating shellfish from recreational beaches and areas where shellfish could be infected by sewage from homes or campgrounds. All clams should be eviscerated (the gut and dark-colored parts removed) before eating. Discard clams with cracked shells, if the animal is discolored or if it appears to be dead.

When toxin is present, symptoms usually occur within 10 to 30 minutes of eating a clam or its broth. The first sign is tingling or burning of the lips, gums, tongue and face, gradually progressing to the neck, arms, fingertips, legs and toes. If a lot of toxin has been ingested, symptoms may extend to dryness of the mouth, nausea and vomiting, shortness of breath, loss of coordination, a choking sensation in the throat, dizziness, weakness and confused or slurred speech.

While death seldom occurs, it can result from respiratory muscle paralysis in 3 to 12 hours after the clams are eaten. Anyone who has eaten clams and has begun to experience symptoms like those above should promptly get medical care. An emetic to empty the stomach and a rapid acting laxative are current treatment. Artificial respiration applied when breathing becomes difficult or ceases may prove effective. Leftover clams should be saved for laboratory tests.

The latest information on which beaches are approved is available through the following agencies: Alaska Division of Agriculture, P.O. Box 1088, Palmer, AK 99645; phone 745-3236. Also, Southeast Regional Laboratory, Alaska Dept. of Health and Social Services, P.O. Box H, Juneau, AK 99811; phone 586-3586.

Permafrost

Permafrost, perennially frozen ground, is defined as ground which remains frozen for 2 or more years. In its continuous form, permafrost underlies the entire arctic region to depths of 2,000 feet. In broad terms, continuous permafrost occurs north of the Brooks Range and in the alpine regions of mountains (including those of the Lower 48).

Discontinuous permafrost occurs south of the Brooks Range and north of the Alaska Range. Much of the Interior and some of Southcentral are underlain by discontinuous permafrost.

Permafrost affects many man-made structures and natural features. It influences construction in the Arctic because building on it may cause the ground to thaw, and if the ground is ice-rich, structures will sink. Arctic and subarctic rivers typically carry 55 to 65 percent of precipitation falling onto their watersheds, roughly 30 to 40 percent more than rivers of more temperate areas. Consequently, northern streams are prone to flooding and have high silt loads. Permafrost is responsible for the thousands of lakes dotting the arctic tundra because ground water is held on the surface.

Poisonous Plants

There are poisonous plants in Alaska, but not many considering the total number of plant species growing in the state. Baneberry *(Actaea rubra)*, water hemlock *(Cicuta douglasii* and *C. mackenzieana)* and fly agaric mushroom *(Amanita muscaria)* are the most dangerous. Be sure you have properly identified plants before harvesting for food. Alaska has no plants that are poisonous to the touch such as poison ivy or poison oak, although some people develop allergic reactions from coming in contact with such plants as Indian rhubarb and nettles.

For more information on plants, read *Wild Edible and Poisonous Plants of Alaska*, available for $2 from Alaska bookstores or from the Cooperative Extension Service, University of Alaska, Fairbanks, AK 99701. Information on poisonous plants also is contained in *Plant Lore of an Alaskan Island, Alaska-Yukon Wild Flowers Guide, Alaska Wild Berry Guide and Cookbook,* and *Alaskan Mushroom Hunter's Guide.* see the ALASKA NORTHWEST LIBRARY section at the back of the book.

Postal Service

Just like currency, American postal rates apply in Alaska. Most communities have a post office and regular, although maybe not daily, mail delivery service. Overnight mail services are available between the Lower 48 and most major Alaskan communities. For fast service, send things first class. Surface mail, although cheaper, tends to take a long time.

Prices

The cost of living in Anchorage is about the same as in New York or San Francisco. As a general rule, it is cheaper in the larger, more accessible Alaskan communities. The smaller and more remote the community, the higher the prices.

According to a 1986 economic study, the cost of living in Anchorage was 21 percent higher than in Seattle. The most expensive areas of the state to live in were McGrath (62 percent higher than Anchorage), Kotzebue (54 percent higher) and Bethel (45 percent higher).

Railroads

The Alaska Railroad offers service between Fairbanks, Anchorage, Whittier and Seward. The railroad provides express service between Anchorage and Denali National Park from May to September. Local service stops anywhere along the line between Anchorage and Hurricane Gulch. Schedules vary depending on the season. For information contact the Alaska Railroad, P.O. Box 107500, Anchorage, AK 99510; phone 265-2494 or 800-544-0552.

The White Pass & Yukon Railroad, the historic route between Skagway and Whitehorse, resumed service in 1988 after a 5-year suspension. The railroad now offers daily summer service between Skagway and Fraser, British Columbia where passengers may connect with buses bound for Whitehorse. A tracked vehicle runs twice daily from Lake Bennett to service those hiking the Chilkoot Trail. Contact the railroad for current information at White Pass Depot, P.O. Box 435, Skagway, AK 99840; phone 983-2217 or 800-343-7373.

Religious Services

Nearly every Alaska community has at least 1 church, and often several denominations are represented. Information on churches is included in the community listings in this book.

Reptiles

For years it was said that Alaska had no snakes. However a University of Alaska zoologist confirmed that a species of (nonpoisonous) garter snake, *Thamnophis sirtalis,* has been seen on the banks of the Taku and Stikine rivers in southeastern Alaska.

River Crossing

Never take a river crossing lightly. Rivers are deceptively treacherous, especially cold glacial streams, and often represent the greatest hazard on a trip into the wilderness. Below are a few tips for safer crossings.

Where to cross: The secret of a safe crossing is being able to recognize a good ford. In general, look for a smooth, firm, gravel bottom with smooth, slow-moving water. Avoid boulders, smooth slabs, sand, mud, snags and logs, and don't underestimate shallow, fast-moving water. Sand or silt at the edge of a glacial stream might be quicksand.

Good fords are most often found:

• Where the river is wide, since the water in wide spots is usually more shallow and flows more slowly.

• Above rapids where a shallow stretch of water with a good bottom often can be found.

• Where the river runs in several channels since it is easier to cross several small streams

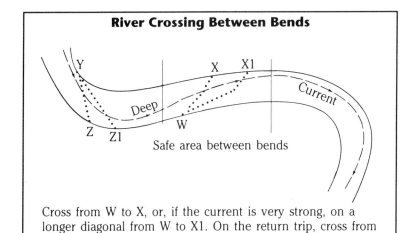

River Crossing Between Bends

Safe area between bends

Cross from W to X, or, if the current is very strong, on a longer diagonal from W to X1. On the return trip, cross from Y to Z or Z1. Note how current helps.

than one big one.

• Between bends where the water is shallower and quieter. Water tends to be deep on the outside bank of a curve and the current strong.

When to cross: If the river is up, the crossing is bad and there is no other route, camp until the river goes down even if it may mean being a day late. If heavy rain is coming and the river must be crossed, do so before it rises. Note that short, steep streams rise quickly but fall quickly and a stream in the Bush will rise and fall more slowly than one off bare hills. Glacial streams are deeper from about midday to midnight and lowest in the morning.

Clothing: Never attempt a crossing in bare feet. Wear your boots (you may remove your socks).

Trousers increase resistance to the current and impede movement. Therefore, wear shorts during the crossing or close-fitting woolen or synthetic long underwear. Immersion in a cold glacial stream for longer than 5 minutes can decrease all sensation and make it more difficult to maintain stable footing.

Packs: Except on the most difficult crossings, packs should be kept on. The weight can help you keep your footing. It is best to undo the waistband of your pack and loosen the shoulder straps, so the pack can be slipped off easily if you should be swept off your feet.

Plotting a course: Once you have determined where you will cross, take note of some marker on the other side where you want to emerge so downriver movement is not mistaken for progress across.

Making the Crossing:
• Move side-on to the current to reduce resistance.

• Steps should be short and shuffling to reduce risk of loss of balance when lifting your feet.

• Move steadily and do not stare at the water rushing at you but at your goal.

• Even in easy crossings, use of an ice ax or pole for a third leg will give greater stability and provide a way to test the bottom and the depth ahead. Place the "third leg" upstream, and move only one foot at a time.

• With more difficult crossings, group members can team up with body grips to increase stability, use a long pole as a type of handrail held parallel to the current or use a long rope to belay members across the stream.

NOTE: This information was excerpted from Wilderness Survival Guide *by Monty Alford which provides more information on tackling more difficult crossing, and other important survival tips. To order see ALASKA NORTHWEST LIBRARY at the back of the book.*

Skiing

For alpine skiers, Juneau, Fairbanks and Anchorage all boast resorts that feature gorgeous scenery, challenging runs and charming, rustic facilities. Three resorts lie within a short drive of Anchorage.

But for the more adventurous, the real skiing is done on narrow, lightweight cross-country skis across virgin snow deep in the backcountry. Opportunities for nordic skiing are limitless. Even in Southeast, helicopter skiing has opened up many areas for nordic skiing. Throughout the state many hiking trails are transformed into ski trails within the state's parks and forests, and U.S. Forest Service cabins are favorite destinations for many backcountry skiers. Before heading to the backcountry it is possible to practice on many ski trails within the major cities. And for nordic skiers seeking a less rugged experience, more and more wilderness lodges are developing groomed trails.

Most schools in Alaska teach cross-country skiing beginning at an early age, and classes for adults are offered through local parks departments and ski organizations. (See Wilderness Class, this section.) But very little instruction is necessary for cross-country skiing, just practice. Once you master the rhythmic kick and glide, the sidestep and herringbone for going up hills, then you're ready to try your hand at going downhill.

A fine way to hone your backcountry skiing skills is to take a few trips with your local ski club. Organized trips will put you in the company of new friends who are already expert at winter camping, avalanche safety and other important skills, as well as cross-country sking.

Backcountry skiers must take special pre-

Skier heads toward unnamed glacier in Ruth Ampitheater, Alaska Range. (Bill Sherwonit)

cautions, particularly when the temperatures are very cold. Remember, the body heat generated while skiing will dissipate rapidly in case of an immobilizing injury, and even a short trek can quickly become a survival ordeal. (See Hypothermia, this section.)

Dress in layers that you can shed and put back on as your activity level dictates. Wool on top of polypropylene long underwear works well, along with a warm hat and mittens. A wool scarf or ski mask will help protect your face, and gaiters, your legs and feet.

Never head out without an extra cable (if you have cable bindings) plus an extra tip in case you break a ski. These precautions can make the difference between an arduous "limp" back to shelter or a quick repair that puts you back on the trail.

Plan your route carefully. Just because a hiking trail is a summer favorite, don't assume it will be enjoyable — or safe — to ski. Many mountainous trails pose extreme avalanche danger and should never be approached in winter. Check with the appropriate land management agency for information on which trails are safe for winter use. (See Avalanches this section.)

Make sure you take into account Alaska's shortened hours of winter daylight. If you have a considerable distance to ski to your destination, make sure you're actually on the trail at first light, not "burning daylight" still making your preparations. Of course, for spring ski trips in late March and April, you'll enjoy the bonus of extra hours of daylight.

Please leave your dog at home. A swift kick from a moose's powerful hoof can kill or maim the family pet, and a moose being harassed by a dog can suddenly turn and charge skiers. Besides the danger to you and your pet, such a confrontation can prove fatal to the moose as well. In wintertime moose, along with much of Alaska's wildlife, live on the edge of survival. Energy depleted in a stressful encounter with a dog can push them over the edge toward exhaustion and starvation.

A final word, about skiing in extremely cold temperatures. Some people claim that Alaska is at its most beautiful when hoarfrost builds up thick on top of the frozen, snowy landscape. Skiing under these conditions, when the cold literally takes your breath away, can be an unforgettable experience. But exercise extreme caution: Batteries die, stoves refuse to light, equipment grows brittle and snaps. Nose, ears, fingers and toes can fall victim to frostbite more quickly than you'd believe possible. And as if all that weren't enough, the food and drink you carry in your pack can freeze solid. Start off with *hot* water in your thermos, not cold. And remember to allow for plenty of extra food, because you'll be burning calories like mad as you're out enjoying Alaska's winter.

Snow Machining

In bush villages, which have few if any roads and cars, snow machines provide winter transportation and freight hauling as well as winter fun. Many trappers use snow machines on their traplines, and homesteaders rely on them as well.

Recreational snow machining by both bush and urban Alaskans has grown into one of Alaska's most popular wintertime activities, though backcountry travelers must take special precautions. (See Avalanches, and Hypothermia, this section.) Each spring more than one snowmobiler is lost when rider and machine break through ice that is too thin to support their almost 600-pound combined weight. Monty Alford in his *Wilderness Survival Guide* advises that for safety you need a bare minimum of 3 inches of ice on a lake — provided that it is black ice totally supported by water and that the snow machine speed is kept below 10 mph. River ice, he advises is 15 percent weaker than lake ice; and sea ice, 50 percent weaker. Temperatures should be no higher than 20°F/-7°C.

Public lands have varying rules about where snow machines are allowed, so before you head out, check with local land managers to make sure you will be riding legally. Historic conflicts between cross-country skiers and snowmobilers have resulted in strict divisions of popular trails and areas between mechanized and nonmechanized use. Alaska has no publically developed trail system specifically for snowmobilers.

Snow machine races are scattered throughout the state from November into April. (See Calendar of Events, this section.) The third weekend in February sees the world's longest cross-country snow machine race, the Iron Dog Gold Rush Classic, from Nome to Big Lake along the historic, 1,049-mile Iditarod Trail. Two-racer teams are mandatory, as are lengthy layovers, and the winner usually reaches the final checkpoint in 2-1/2 to 3 days. By comparison, the record-setting winner of the Iditarod Trail Sled Dog Race reached Nome in just over 11 days. (See Iditarod, this section.) Snowmobilers making this 1,000-mile Iron Dog run need not actually compete, and most entrants sign up merely for the rewards

and adventures of the trail.

Western Alaska takes its snow machining seriously, and the 2 biggest money races among the regional competitions are held there each year. The winner of last year's 220-mile Nome to Golovin race took home close to $10,000. Kotzebue's Archie Ferguson-Willy Goodwin Memorial Race (250 miles from Kotzebue to Noorvik, Kiana, Selawik, back to Noorvik then Kotzebue) paid its winner $15,000.

For snowmobilers not interested in racing but in getting out to explore backcountry Alaska, a useful source is *Alaska Wilderness Trails* (S&R Publishing, P.O. Box 871213, Wasilla, AK 99687). This large format paperback details 23 trails accessible from Anchorage, Fairbanks, Glennallen, Tok, Delta Junction and from the highways, including the Denali Highway. The emphasis is on trails (many of them abandoned roads) for wildlife viewing, fishing and travel through old gold mining areas created around the turn of the century.

Telephone, Telegraph, Money Orders

All of Alaska uses the 907 telephone area code.

Telegrams, cablegrams, mailgrams, telex and FAX can be sent by telephone from anywhere in Alaska through Western Union. Major credit cards are accepted. Money orders by wire can also be arranged through Western Union, which is located at 3605 Arctic Blvd., Anchorage, AK 99503; phone 563-3131. (Banks can also wire money, but bank wires take considerably longer.) The Western Union office in Anchorage is open Monday through Saturday from 8 a.m. to 8 p.m. and Sunday from 10 a.m. to 4 p.m. except on national holidays. Western Union branch offices are located throughout the state. Information about branch offices may be obtained by calling 1-800-325-6000.

Television

Television in Alaska's larger communities, such as Anchorage and Fairbanks, was available years before satellites. Television reached the Bush in the late 1970s with the construction of telephone earth stations which could receive television programming via satellite transmissions. Same day broadcasts to the Bush, arriving via satellite, of news and sports events are subsidized in part by state revenues. The state also funds Satellite Television Project to nearly 250 rural communities with general and educational programming.

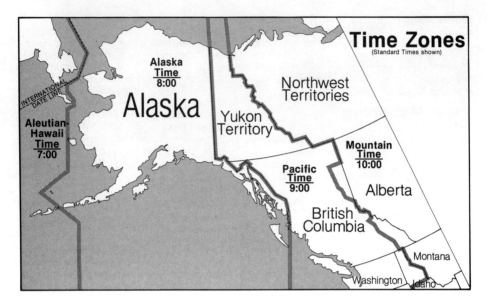

Time Zones

At Alaska's request, the federal government reduced the state's time zones from 4 to 2, effective Oct. 30, 1983. The state now is operating on Alaska time, or 1 hour earlier than Pacific time. The only residents of the state not setting their clocks on Alaska time are in the 4 small western Aleutian communities of Atka, Adak, Shemya and Attu and on St. Lawrence Island, which moved to Aleutian-Hawaii time, 1 hour earlier than Alaska time.

Tips for Survival

1. Stay put, you'll be easier to locate — if you've left your itinerary with a friend.

2. Make your site as conspicuous as possible from the air.

3. Know ground-to-air codes and other standard distress signals.

4. Always be equipped for emergencies and carry in your pocket: wooden matches in a waterproof container, a pocketknife and toilet tissue which can be used as fire-starter.

5. Shelters can be built from brush or snow. Snow is nature's insulator. With a little care, a trench, snow cave or igloo can be made. Of the 3, the snow trench requires the least effort, minimizing perspiration and contact with snow so clothing stays drier.

6. To be wet and then exposed to wind is the worst possible condition; the body loses heat 200 times faster with wet clothing than with dry.

7. A group can conserve heat by huddling together.

8. You can do without food for an extended time, but you can do without water for only a few days. This emphasizes the importance of having a water container and suggests there is little need to gather food immediately, which takes energy.

9. Don't try to sleep until all extremities are warm.

10. In winter, you can survive many hours if you lie on your back in a fetal position in a depression in the snow out of the wind with arms and knees drawn across your body, and adopt a running motion only when cold.

Recognized Distress Signals:

• Three fires in a triangle 100 feet apart.

• SOS tramped in the snow; trenches filled with boughs in a large open area.

• Any large conspicuous object, preferably one that is fluorescent orange, or something that will glisten in the sun to call attention to the area.

• Canoe being paddled in tight circles.

• Signaling with mirror.

• Flares from a pocket flare gun.

• Three gun shots at 10-second intervals.

• Whistling to attract a ground party.

• Tree cleared of all branches except top part (called a lobstick).

EDITOR'S NOTE: This information is excepted from Wilderness Survival Guide *by Monty Alford. To order, see ALASKA NORTHWEST LIBRARY at the back of the book.*

Tours

Tours have become so popular in recent years that tour companies have designed packages to meet the requirements of almost anyone, including those who wish to experience Alaska's wilderness areas. A packaged tour does not mean that you are bound by an itinerary that includes areas of little interest to you, nor by a time schedule that does not allow you to see and do the things of greatest interest to you.

There is such a wide variety of tours offered that chances are you can find one that includes areas you wish to see, your preference for mode of travel and one that will fit your pocketbook and calendar. The trip may be a complete air-travel tour, a cruise through the Inside Passage, a motorcoach tour from Seattle to Fairbanks, or a combination of air, sea and land travel. Tour companies offer escorted tours, independent tours or a combination.

You may select an escorted tour which is overseen by a competent director who accompanies the group on the entire journey, takes care of all luggage, tickets, hotel check-ins and alleviates all cares and anxieties, leaving the traveler free to enjoy the trip.

You may select an independent tour where you are completely by yourself, although there may be others traveling on the same itinerary. You would handle your own tickets, luggage, hotel check-ins and personal activities. The service companies are alerted to your arrival and arrangements are prepaid so you merely present a voucher for each requirement. At the larger transfer points, a company representative is available to answer questions and make possible changes so you are not left completely on your own; assistance is always nearby.

For more information about tours to Alaska, contact your travel agent or Alaska Northwest Travel Service Inc., 130 2nd Ave. S., Edmonds, WA 98020; phone (206) 775-4504 or toll free 1-800-533-7381.

Trichinosis

Trichinosis is a serious disease commonly associated with eating improperly cooked pork. However, the same parasite infects Alaska's bears, foxes, wolves, mink, walrus and seals; therefore, thorough cooking is necessary for the safe preparation of these meats.

Tularemia

The Dept. of Environmental Conservation advises visitors to Alaska to exercise caution in handling the snowshoe hare, which is often infected with tularemia, a disease transmissable to humans. The bacteria causing the disease are present in the blood and body fluids of infected hares. Humans usually acquire the disease during skinning and cleaning of the animals. The bacteria enter through cuts and breaks in a person's skin. Normal cooking kills the bacteria. Ticks transmit the disease from animal to animal and could expose humans to the disease if crushed while handling the hare, although these ticks do not feed on humans. Greatest risk is from May through September when ticks are present; the disease falls to low levels after freezing weather. Another, less virulent, variety of tularemia occurs in rodents and can be contracted by drinking improperly disinfected surface water.

Visiting Native Villages

If you're going to the Bush you probably will be visiting at least 1 village. You will encounter different languages and customs and a different, more leisurely sense of time. You may see racks of salmon drying during the summer season, or a whale being butchered in the spring. You likely will meet some wonderful people. But the village phone may not work and you may not have a flush toilet. If you are flexible and can cope without all the urban amenities you may be accustomed to, you can have a memorable trip.

Accommodations may be scarce. Hotels are available in larger communities such as Bethel, Kotzebue or Barrow. Smaller villages may have a community-operated lodge, but then again they may not. Most villages have general stores, but their stocks can be limited and many do not have regular hours. It's best to be prepared to be self-sufficient. Bring a sleeping bag (a tent may be a good idea, too) and your own groceries. Also, camera film may not be available, so bring your own. Laundromats and showers are available in some, but not all, communities.

Following are a few guidelines for visiting a village from the Tanana Chiefs Conference, Fairbanks, and the National Park Service.

Visitors should treat the village as they would a private home, where people respect local lifestyles, customs and the privacy of others. The village or city chief or the community council office is the best place to get general information. Information about accommodations and other conditions in villages also may be available from the bush airlines that serve them. *The ALASKA WILDERNESS MILEPOST®* includes information on accommodations in the community listings, but it is a good idea to write to a village leader before your trip for permission and/or to make arrangements for accommodations. (Some villages do not encourage visitors, while others do.) Advance reservations are recommended, particularly during the summer construction season. During winter months it is wise to call ahead to be sure lodges and facilities are open. Many operate only seasonally. If there is no lodge, visitors may be able to pay a local family or the school teachers for room and board. Be sure to ask permission before setting up a tent in or near a village; a few villages have campgrounds, but most do not. Visitors should always be courteous and never impose on the residents. Again, it's best to be prepared to be self-sufficient.

Visitors to bush villages should be aware of local ordinances concerning firearms, importation and use of alcoholic beverages, vehicles and pets. Photography is generally acceptable if done with consideration for the local residents; ask permission.

English is spoken in villages throughout the Bush. Translation should not be required except with elderly people. Sensitivity is the key to communicating in a cross-cultural setting. Visitors should avoid asking too many questions and making comparisons with "how we do it back home." It is important to speak slowly, listen intently and avoid intensely serious tones.

Local transportation is usually by snow machine, boat or 3-wheeler, but larger communities have a few cars and trucks. Visitors should be willing to pay local people for rides to and from the airport or for other transportation. Informal guiding for fishing is generally available; make arrangements in advance or ask around.

Gasoline is available for about $2 a gallon from local vendors in nearly all communities. Special camp fuels may not be available. Travelers should expect irregular hours at all service facilities.

Be aware that much of the land around bush communities is owned by Native corporations and you may need their permission to camp, hike, fish or hunt. Some village corporations are now charging user fees. Addresses of village corporations are included in the community listings in The ALASKA WILDERNESS MILEPOST®. Also, there may be public easements across Native lands to provide access to national parks or wildlife refuges. Contact the park or refuge office for information concerning your planned route.

Wilderness travelers may encounter local residents engaged in hunting, trapping or other subsistence activities. These activities are permitted on national park and refuge lands, and can include free-ranging activities, as well as stationary fishing and hunting camps or traplines. Your presence can influence game movements and thus disrupt subsistence uses. You may need to change your trip route to avoid interfering with subsistence activities. While a camp may look abandoned, chances are it is used periodically and should not be disturbed. Also, never touch fish nets, traps or other subsistence gear. This equipment is crucial to the livelihood of local residents.

When to Go/ What to Wear

One of the most often asked questions is "When is the best time to travel?" The high season is June through August, which are generally the sunniest months in Alaska, although July is often one of the wettest months in some regions.

In general, dress is casual. Comfortable shoes and easy-care clothes are best, although dressy clothes are certainly appropriate for a night out in the larger cities. If you forget something, there are stores in the larger communities where you can buy what you need.

In southeastern Alaska it's best to keep this in mind: If you can't see the tops of the mountains, it's raining. If you can see the mountaintops, it's going to rain. Southeast summers average nearly 60°F in July, with an occasional heat wave pushing temperatures into the 70s and 80s. Winters mean snow, more rain and sunshine, with a relatively warm January average in Juneau of about 29°F.

In Southeast, dressing in layers is the best plan throughout the year. Spring through fall, start with short sleeves, add a sweater or wool shirt and top it off with a light, waterproof jacket. When you're out in misty weather on the water, or near a glacier, gloves and hat are useful. In winter, just add another sweater or fiberfill jacket, plus light long underwear. Walking shoes like the moccasin style with rubber bottoms and low leather tops work well all year in Southeast.

Southcentral has a mixture of weather patterns. Prince William Sound has a mild, maritime climate, while Anchorage and inland areas have less precipitation and greater temperature ranges. July temperatures in Anchorage average nearly 60°F, with highs in the 70s. Snow stays on the ground generally from late October through mid-April.

To dress for a Southcentral summer of 50° to 70°F with low humidity, bring light clothing with a sweater or light jacket for cooler days. Light rain gear is advisable. For fall or spring, add a layer of wool or down, plus a light hat and gloves. For winter, wear a down jacket, wool hat and gloves, warm slacks and lined boots.

On the Alaska Peninsula and Aleutian Islands, arctic weather clashes with the more temperate climate of the North Pacific. The weather can change hourly. The Aleutians have an annual temperature variation of only 25 degrees, from 30° to 55°F. Clothing in several light layers, topped by water- and windproof outer layers works best. In mainland areas, dress warmly for winter with fiberfill and wool, with windproof outer garments. Wool hat and gloves, plus lined boots, are essential for snowy months.

In general the same type of clothing will suffice throughout the Bering Sea coast region: Several light layers in summer, and warmer layers in winter. Waterproof boots are advisable during break up season when the ground is soggy.

The arctic region gets little precipitation; its humidity is comparable to the world's deserts. Light, dry snow stays on the ground from September to May. Ice masses remain in the ocean through the summer. Only the top several inches of earth thaw for a few months.

The year-round rule for clothing is warm and windproof. In summer, wear a windproof jacket with a warm shirt or sweater underneath for the 40°F days. Again, layers allow for the most flexibility if the temperature changes. Rubber-soled footwear is useful. For fall, winter and spring, bring long underwear, warm slacks and shirt, wool sweater and thick down jacket. Warm, windproof covering for head and hands is essential.

The Interior experiences the greatest temperature variations in the state. You may see clear summer days in the 90s, and winter nights in the -50s. Total annual precipitation is low, but there are occasional thunderstorms in summer. Snow is on the ground from October through April. Winds are light.

Summer clothing means light slacks or shorts, light blouses or shirts, and a sweater for cloudy days. Add a couple of layers for spring and fall. The extremely low winter temperatures require layers of wool and down clothing, with warm hats, mittens and lined boots.

Wilderness Classes

If you've always wanted to get out and explore Alaska's backcountry but don't know how to go about it, consider taking a class. There are all sorts of courses offered that will teach you the fundamentals of backpacking, cross-country skiing, dog mushing, glacier climbing, canoeing, kayaking, or just about anything else that people do out of doors in the Great Land.

Imagine getting college credits for a course entitled "Wilderness Adventures and Natural History of Alaska." Or one called "Backpacking"; or "Ski Mountaineering: Ruth Glacier"; or "Tracking," "Canoeing," or "Family Camping." This is not a fantasy curriculum dreamed up by some desperate city-bound worker longing for the beauty and freedom of Alaska. It is a sampling of the courses offered for credit by the Alaska Wilderness Studies program within the College of Community and Continuing Education, University of Alaska Anchorage, 3211 Providence Dr., Anchorage, AK 99508; phone 786-1468.

The Alaska Wilderness Studies program teaches outdoor skills to almost a thousand people a year in its summer, fall and winter classes. Winter classes include skiing, telemarking, ice climbing, winter survival, map and compass reading, wilderness emergency care, dog mushing (the Anchorage Sled Dog Assoc. supplies the dogs and sleds), and ski joring (you bring the family mutt).

Winter classes usually cost less than $100; summer courses can be more expensive when they include travel. "Advanced Backpacking" in the Wrangells or Lake Clark, for example, cost $350 in 1989, including charter and transportation. In the past only a few non-Alaskans have taken these courses, but Alaska Wilderness School Director Todd Miner is hoping to attract out-of-state visitors for the summer classes beginning in 1990. All classes include weekend field days; and group, safety, and camping equipment are provided. Anyone interested in learning a new skill and experiencing Alaska on an intimate level is encouraged to apply.

The program's noncredit courses offer an even wider variety of topics: fly-fishing, rock climbing, ocean kayaking, expedition rafting, wildflowers, glacier travel and crevasses rescue, mountaineering for hunters, and others.

The wilderness school curriculum is not, unfortunately, duplicated throughout the state, though university branches elsewhere offer a few similar courses from time to time. But the university system is only one option for those seeking to acquire or improve on wilderness skills.

The Alaska Mountain Safety Center (9140 Brewster Dr., Anchorage, AK 99516; phone

VOLUNTEERS ARE NEEDED

If you like people, are concerned about the environment and have some time to spare, then Alaska's parks and forests have an opportunity for you. Volunteers are depended upon to assist in a variety of tasks, a few of which are listed below.

Backcountry Hosts: Monitor backcountry use and provide information about the area.

Campground Hosts: Welcome campers, provide information about the area and do minor maintenance.

Information Service: Provide information at visitor centers on what to do and see, and on the local natural and cultural history. Explain safety precautions and regulations regarding resource protection .

Research: Increase understanding of natural and historic resources, and of public outdoor recreation use.

Resource Management: Work on wildlife and fisheries surveys, erosion control, fire prevention, plant and insect projects, and water quality monitoring.

Trail Improvements: Maintain existing and construct new trails. For information contact: Volunteer Coordinator, Alaska State Parks, P.O. Box 107001, Anchorage, AK 99510, phone 762-2617; Volunteer Coordinator, U.S. Forest Service — Alaska Region, P.O. Box 21628, Juneau, AK 99802; Volunteer Coordinator, National Park Service, 2525 Gambell St., Room 107, Anchorage AK 99503, phone 271-2468; or Volunteer Coordinator, USDA — Chugach National Forest, 201 E. 9th Ave., Suite 206, Anchorage, AK 99501.

345-3566) offers training in avalanche avoidance and survival, skills crucial for anyone doing much backcountry travel in winter. And dozens of private organizations sponsor classes, trips and workshops. Check the list of outdoor and environmental associations under Information Sources in this section. The groups listed there, if they don't offer their own classes, will be able to steer you in the right direction. Also check the community calendar in local newspapers.

Be persistent. Chances are, if you don't find exactly the class you want, you'll find others interested in the same subject, and probably an expert who will be glad to teach you in a class you organize yourself.

Wildlife Watching

Alaska has a well-deserved reputation for abundant wildlife. Observing and photographing birds and mammals in their natural habitat can add immensely to your visit. However, wildlife observers may unintentionally harm wildlife, ruin opportunities for others to enjoy wildlife and occasionally endanger themselves. Following are some guidelines from the Alaska Dept. of Fish and Game for observing or photographing wildlife.

Observe animals from a distance. Use binoculars, spotting scopes or telephoto lenses to get a closer look. If an animal shows signs of being crowed or disturbed, sit quietly or move slowly away. Signs you are too close include the following:

From a mammal: Raises head high with ears pointed in your direction; is skittish, jumps at sounds or movements; moves away or lowers head, ears back in preparation for a charge, has erect hairs on neck and shoulders; displays aggressive or nervous behavior.

From a bird: Raises head, looks at you; is skittish; preens excessively or pecks at dirt or food; wipes bill; makes alarm calls, repeatedly chirps or chips; performs distraction display— broken wing, or tail spread.

Move slowly. Let the animal keep you in view. Avoid sneaking up on or surprising animals.

Limit the time you spend at or near a nest to 5 or 10 minutes. Do not disturb the plants around the nest or handle the eggs or young. Keep far enough away from nesting colonies that you don't flush the birds.

Never chase, repeatedly flush or harass animals on foot, in an auto, boat, plane, ATV, snowmachine or any other vehicle. Harassing animals is against state law and punishable by a $1,000 fine and up to 6 months in jail. Never allow your pets to harass wildlife.

Do not use tape recorded calls or other attraction devices except in areas people visit infrequently and then use them only sparingly. Bears attracted by predator calls can be extremely dangerous.

Never approach an animal when other people are observing it. Inconsiderate observers who approach too closely ruin their own wildlife photos and those of others. Frightened or nervous animals are less interesting to watch, and experienced wildlife observers can easily tell if the animal in a photo was alarmed or harassed.

Stop on roadsides to view wildlife only if a safe pullout area is available. Remain quiet and in your car. If you frighten the animal, you deny other people the chance to see it.

Always obtain permission from landowners before traveling on private property, even if you just want to look at the plants or wildlife. (Thousands of acres of land in the state have become the private property of Alaska Native corporations under the Alaska Native Claims Settlement Act.)

Never litter or deface property or the natural environment. Trespassing signs and regulations that limit everyone's opportunities to enjoy wildlife.

Always keep a good distance between you and a cow moose with calves. A cow may charge on little provocation, and her flying hooves can seriously injure a person.

For a good overview of wildlife observation in Alaska, consult A Guide to Wildlife Viewing in Alaska, a color-coded guide to the state's regions and habitats. This 170-page photo-illustrated book is available for $12.95 from the Nongame Wildlife Program, Alaska Dept. of Fish and Game, Div. of Wildlife Conservation, 333 Raspberry Road, Juneau, AK 99818.

Winds

Winds abound in Alaska, from the eastern fringes of Southeast to the western islands of the Aleutian Chain where some of the windiest weather has been recorded. A few of these winds occur often and significantly enough to be given the following colorful regional names: chinook, taku and williwaw.

Chinook: Old-timers describe these winds as unseasonably warm winds that can cause a thaw in the middle of winter. They also cause power outages and property damage, especially in the Anchorage bowl, where in recent years hundreds of homes have been built on the Chugach Mountain hillsides over which the chinook winds howl. (One such wind on April 1, 1980, caused $25 million in property damage, qualifying the city as a disaster area. Parts of Anchorage were without power for 60 hours.)

Until recently it was not possible to predict chinook winds. Today, however, meteorologists can tell if these winds are gathering, when they will arrive and their relative strength. Scientists determinded that such a warm wind could only originate in Prince William Sound and that its strength had to be at least 55 mph or faster just to cross the 3,500-foot Chugach Mountains. Other factors that need to be present are a storm near Bethel and relatively stable air over Anchorage. Chinook winds now can be predicted 55 percent of the time.

Taku: Taku winds are the sudden, fierce gales that sweep down from the ice cap behind Juneau and plague residents there. Takus are shivering cold winds capable of reaching 100 mph. They have been known to send a 2-by-4 timber flying through the wall of a frame house.

Williwaws: Williwaws are sudden gusts of wind that can reach 110 mph after the wind builds up on one side of a mountain and suddenly spills over into what may appear to be a relatively protected area. Williwaws are common in the Aleutians and are considered the bane of Alaska mariners. The term was originally applied to a strong wind in the Strait of Magellan.

Winter Travel

By far the most popular time to visit Alaska is during June, July and August, but gradually more and more people are discovering the delights of visiting the state between October and May.

Visitors to Alaska in winter generally find temperatures comparable to those of other winter travel destinations, fewer crowds and even bargains on some transportation and lodging costs.

Alaskans are noted for their devotion to winter sports and visitors are learning why. Skiing (alpine and nordic), dog mushing and snow machining offer tremendous opportunities to get out and enjoy the winters. (For more on these sports, see Skiing, Dog Mushing and Snow Machining, this section. And for a list of winter races and events, see Calendar of Events, also in this section.) Besides these major sports, Alaskans love ice hockey, ice skating, ice fishing, snowshoeing, sledding, wildlife viewing and watching the Northern Lights. Visitors receive a warm welcome and a friendly invitation to join in the fun.

Rough-hewn footbridge crosses Canyon Creek on the Chilkoot Trail about 8 miles from Dyea. The historic trail follows the route taken by gold-hungry adventurers in the Klondike gold rush of 1898. (George Wuerthner)

SOUTHEAST

The Region

A lush northern rain forest of incomparable beauty, Alaska's Southeast is a land where eagles soar, whales frolic and brown bear roam at will. Where dramatic tidewater glaciers, spectacular fjords, massive ice fields and rugged mountains bear the imprint of the last ice age. Where the rich cultural mix of Indians, Russians and gold prospectors enlivens the more recent history of the communities.

Amid the breathtaking beauty and the rich history of Southeast, opportunities for outdoor adventures abound. The protected waterways offer a lifetime of bays, fjords and channels to explore and some of the finest fishing in Alaska. Watching whales, rafting rivers, hiking and hunting, skiing the ice fields or retreating to a snug lodge in a secluded cove are other popular pursuits.

Location: Southeast stretches 560 miles from Dixon Entrance at the United States-Canada border south of Ketchikan to Icy Bay northwest of Yakutat.

Physical Description: Geological activity has sculpted more than a thousand islands in Southeast, including Prince of Wales, third largest in the country at 2,231 square miles. The region's narrow strip of mainland is isolated from the rest of North America by the St. Elias and Coast mountains. The St. Elias, topping out at 18,008 feet at the summit of Mount St. Elias, is the highest coastal range in the world.

Rivers: Numerous rivers drain this wet, steep land. Among the more important are the Stikine and Taku which breach the mountain barrier and provide some access into the Interior.

Climate

Warmed by ocean currents, Southeast experiences mild, warm temperatures averaging around 60°F in the summer. Winters are cool, alternating snow, rain and sunshine; January temperatures average 20° to 40°F. Subzero winter temperatures are uncommon.

The region experiences considerable annual rainfall, from 80 to more than 200 inches, with the heaviest rains in late fall and the lightest in summer. Populated areas receive from 30 to 200 inches of snow annually; the high mountains get more than 400 inches a year.

Vegetation

Heavy rainfall and a mild climate encourage timber growth. Three-quarters of Southeast is covered with dense forests, primarily western hemlock and Sitka spruce interspersed with red cedar and Alaska yellow cedar. Ground cover is luxuriant and includes devil's club, blueberries, huckleberries, mosses and ferns.

Wildlife

Big Game: Southeast has prime habitat for Sitka black-tailed deer, bears and wolves. Brown bears inhabit Admiralty, Baranof and Chichagof islands, and portions of the mainland. Black bears occur on other forested islands and the mainland. Moose browse in scattered populations and mountain goats stick to steep cliffs in Glacier Bay and other mountainous areas.

Furbearers and Nongame Species: Lynx, wolverines, foxes, mink, river otters, marten, porcupines and an assortment of small mammals range throughout Southeast.

Icy Bay
Wrangell-St. Elias
National Park and Preserve
Malaspina Glacier
Yakutat Bay
Yakutat■

Gulf of Alaska

Haines Highway ←

Skagway■

Klukwan■

Haines■

Alsek R.

Haines

Glacier Bay National
Park and Preserve

Glacier Bay

Excursion Inlet■
Gustavus■

Icy Strait

Cape Spencer
Light Station■
Cross
Sound
■Elfin Cove

Hoonah■

Pelican■

Eight
Fathom
Bight
Chichagof
Island

Kruzof
Island

Mt. Edgecumbe▲
St. Lazaria Island

Alaska Maritime
National Wildlife
Refuge

Sitka Sound

Biorka
Island

Pacific
Ocean

Wilderness Areas of Tongass National Forest

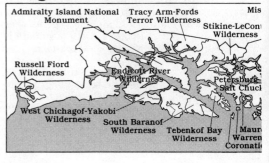

Admiralty Island National
Monument

Tracy Arm-Fords
Terror Wilderness

Mis

Stikine-LeCon
Wilderness

Russell Fiord
Wilderness

Endicott River
Wilderness

Petersburg
Salt Chuck

West Chichagof-Yakobi
Wilderness

South Baranof
Wilderness

Tebenkof Bay
Wilderness

Maur
Warren
Coronatic

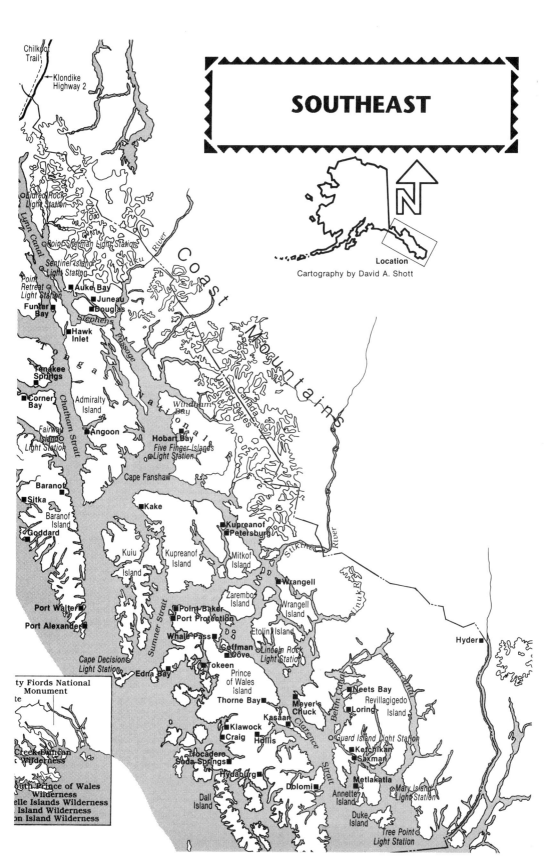

SOUTHEAST

Cartography by David A. Shott

Location

N

Chilkoot Trail

Klondike Highway 2

Eldred Rock Light Station

Point Sherman Light Station

Sentinel Island Light Station

Point Retreat Light Station

■Auke Bay

Funter Bay■

■Juneau

■Douglas

■Hawk Inlet

Tenakee Springs

■Corner Bay

Admiralty Island

Fairway Island Light Station

■Angoon

Windham Bay

Hobart Bay

Five Finger Islands Light Station

Cape Fanshaw

Baranof

■Sitka

Baranof Island

Goddard

■Kake

Kuiu

Kupreanof Island

■Kupreanof
Petersburg

Mitkof Island

Coast Mountains

Canada
United States

Taku River

Lynn Canal

Chatham Strait

Stephens Passage

Tongass National

Stikine River

■Wrangell

Zarembo Island

Wrangell Island

Port Walter

Port Alexander■

Point Baker
Port Protection

Whale Pass■

Coffman Cove

Etolin Island

Lincoln Rock Light Station

Inuk R.

Hyder■

Cape Decision Light Station

Edna Bay

Tokeen

Prince of Wales Island

Thorne Bay■

Meyer's Chuck

Neets Bay

Revillagigedo Island

Loring

Behm Canal

Kasaan

Guard Island Light Station

■Klawock

■Craig

Hollis

Trocadero
Soda Springs

Ketchikan
Saxman

Hydaburg

Dolomi

Metlakatla

Mary Island Light Station

Clarence Strait

Sumner Strait

ty Fiords National
Monument

Creek Duncan
Wilderness

outh Prince of Wales
Wilderness
elle Islands Wilderness
Island Wilderness
on Island Wilderness

Dall Island

Annette Island

Duke Island

Tree Point Light Station

Marine mammals abound in the region. Humpback and killer whales, sea lions and seals are easily seen in season in many waterways.

Birds: Southeast boasts the largest bald eagle population in the world. Thousands congregate each fall at the Alaska Chilkat Bald Eagle Preserve near Haines. Thousands of waterfowl pass through the area during migration, with huge flocks staging on the Stikine Flats and near other estuaries.

Fish: Salmon, halibut, black cod, shellfish, herring, steelhead, trout, grayling — the list goes on, for Southeast has some of the finest fishing, both sport and commercial, in the world.

Minerals

Gold brought the first non-Native settlers to the area beginning with the strike along the Stikine River in 1861. Juneau, largest city in the region, was founded because of a gold find. The region played a major role in the rush to the Klondike in 1898.

Mining in the Juneau Gold Belt mineral area north of Juneau continues today with several new mines being evaluated and opened on historical mining areas of the Tongass National Forest.

Other minerals have been mined during past decades, and today miners are proceeding to production at the base metals prospect on northern Admiralty Island and at the giant molybdenum find in Misty Fiords.

Public Lands

National Forests, Parks and Preserves: More than 95 percent of the land is under federal jurisdiction with about 73 percent within Tongass National Forest, largest in the country. Admiralty Island and Misty Fiords national monuments are also under Forest Service jurisdiction.

Glacier Bay National Park and Preserve shows off its icy wonderland northwest of Juneau. At extreme northern Southeast a portion of Wrangell-St. Elias National Park and Preserve protects another icy wilderness.

Historic buildings and other gold rush era remains are protected within Klondike Gold Rush National Historical Park at Skagway, and Tlingit and Russian history is preserved at Sitka National Historical Park.

National Wildlife Refuges: Some of Southeast's islands, rich with marine and bird life, are included in Alaska Maritime National Wildlife Refuge.

State Game Refuges and Preserves: Mendenhall Wetlands State Game Refuge protects critical habitat for a variety of bird species. Alaska Chilkat Bald Eagle Preserve ensures continued habitat for wintering eagles. And Dude Creek Critical Habitat Area at Gustavus protects a wet meadow rest stop for migrating lesser sandhill cranes.

State Recreation Areas and Parks: Of the state's 19 marine parks, 12 are located in Southeast. Chilkat State Park, which includes the Chilkat Islands Marine Park, provides excellent recreational opportunities just minutes from the city of Haines. Baranof Castle Hill State Historic Site and Old Sitka State Historic Site in Sitka, Totem Bight State Historic Park in Ketchikan and Wickersham House in Juneau offer examples of life and culture and early southeastern Alaska. In addition to these parks the state also maintains several recreation sites with picnic and camping facilities.

History

Southeast's mighty Indian cultures ruled the region when the first white men, the Russians, came to the area. After several skirmishes, the Russians won a foothold in the area and made Sitka the capital of Russian America. After the Americans took over in 1867, mining, fishing and timber provided the economic base.

Southeast remained Alaska's dominant region until WWII, when military activity and construction of the Alaska Highway shifted the emphasis to Anchorage and Fairbanks.

Today fishing, government, tourism and timber fuel Southeast's economy. Seven population centers and hundreds of little settlements dot the region's shoreline. About 20 percent of the region's population is Native, predominantly Tlingit, Haida and Tsimshian. Haida concentrate at Hydaburg and Tsimshian make their home at Metlakatla.

RIVER CROSSING

Never try to cross a river barefoot; the water is always too cold and the bottom may be rough. Undo the waistband of your pack but leave it on to help you keep your footing.

▼ C O M M U N I T I E S ▼

Angoon

Located on the west coast of Admiralty Island on Chatham Strait, at the mouth of Kootznahoo Inlet, 55 miles southwest of Juneau, 41 miles northeast of Sitka. **Transportation:** Scheduled ferry service via Alaska Marine Highway; scheduled seaplane service from Juneau. **Population:** 639. **Zip code:** 99820. **Emergency Services:** Police, Volunteer Fire Department, phone 788-3631; Clinic, phone 788-3633.

Elevation: Sea level. **Climate:** Moderate maritime weather, with monthly mean temperatures of 28°F in January and 55°F in July. Annual rainfall is 40 inches.

Private Aircraft: Angoon seaplane base; 0.9 mile southeast.

Visitor Facilities: Angoon has 1 motel and 1 bed-and-breakfast. Groceries and supplies are available. The Angoon Community Assoc. operates a laundry. No banking services. Fishing/hunting licenses may be purchased locally. Charter fishing boats and canoes are available; no other rental transportation. Fuel service (gas and diesel) and transient moorage are available at boat harbor.

Angoon is a long established Tlingit Indian settlement at the entrance to Kootznahoo Inlet. It is the only permanent community on Admiralty Island. On Killisnoo Island, across the harbor from the state ferry landing, a community of mostly summer homes has grown up along the island beaches. The lifestyle of the primarily Tlingit town is heavily subsistence: fish, clams, seaweed, berries and venison. Fishing, mostly hand trolling for king and coho salmon, is the principal industry. Unemployment in Angoon is high throughout the year.

The scenery of Admiralty Island draws many visitors to Angoon. The island boasts the largest nesting population of eagles anywhere. Angoon and vicinity offer exceptional feeding areas for killer and humpback whales and excellent saltwater and freshwater fishing. All but the northern portion of the island was declared a national monument and is managed by the U.S. Forest Service.

Kootznahoo Inlet and Mitchell Bay near Angoon offer a network of small wooded islands, reefs and channels for kayaking. Wildlife includes many brown bears (Admiralty Island's Indian name means "Fortress of Bears"), Sitka black-tailed deer and bald eagles.

Local residents can provide directions to the interesting old Killisnoo graveyards, located both on the island and on the Angoon shore of the old Killisnoo settlement, which once was one of the larger communities in southeastern Alaska.

Communications include phones in most households (and CB radios for local communication), daily mail service by plane, good radio reception and TV via satellite and cable. There are churches and a school with grades kindergarten through 12. Angoon prohibits the possession of alcoholic beverages. Community electric power, water and sewage systems are available. Freight comes in by barge and ferry. Government address: City of Angoon, P.O. Box 189, Angoon, AK 99820; phone 788-3653. Village corporation address: Kootznoowoo Inc., P.O. Box 116, Angoon, AK 99820.

Coffman Cove

Located on the northeast coast of Prince of Wales Island, 53 miles north of Klawock, 42 miles southeast of Wrangell, and 73 miles northeast of Ketchikan. **Transportation:** Accessible via Prince of Wales Island road system and by boat; daily floatplane service from Ketchikan; weekly service from Wrangell. **Population:** 272. **Zip code:** 99950. **Emergency Services:** Alaska State Troopers in Klawock, phone 755-2955; Craig medical clinic, Wrangell and Ketchikan hospitals.

Elevation: 10 feet. **Climate:** Cool and rainy, with average temperatures of 32°F in winter, 55°F in summer.

Private Aircraft: Floatplane landings only.

Nearest airstrip is in Klawock.

Visitor Facilities: Overnight accommodations are available at a bunkhouse; meals can be purchased at the cafe. Convenience foods, sporting goods, clothing, film, tapes and movies are available. There is a laundromat, but no banking services. Arts and crafts and gift items, including wood carvings, paintings, Indian beadwork, leather work and jewelry made by local artists, may be purchased. Fishing/hunting licenses and fishing charters are available. Diesel and regular gas and propane are available, as are tire repair and skiff rental. There is a state dock.

Coffman Cove is a family logging community, one of the largest independent camps in Southeast. Formerly owned and operated by Mike and Leta Valentine, the camp has been in operation in this area for about 15 years. Housing is in mobile homes. Recreation includes hunting (deer and bear), good fishing in area lakes and streams, boating, hiking, and also TV and VCRs. Coffman Cove's pioneer lifestyle and clean, safe environment were featured on ABC's *20/20* program in 1984, prompting a deluge of mail from around the country from people wishing to move here. While Coffman Cove does have fresh air, clean water and other advantages, residents point out the disadvantages of seasonal work, a faltering timber industry, and a lack of some conveniences taken for granted by people in larger communities. The Prince of Wales Island road system connected Coffman Cove to other island communities in 1985.

Coffman Cove is unincorporated. Communications include phones, mail plane, radio and TV. There is a Catholic church and a Protestant church here, both served by itinerant ministers from Wrangell. Coffman Cove's school has 5 teachers and grades 1 through 12 for its 66 pupils. The community has electrical power, water and sewage systems. Freight arrives by cargo plane, barge, ship and by road from Craig.

Craig

Located on the west side of Prince of Wales Island, 31 road miles west of Hollis, 60 air miles west of Ketchikan, at the south end of Klawock Inlet across from Fish Egg Island. **Transportation:** Air taxi service from Ketchikan; ferry from Ketchikan to Hollis and by road from Hollis to Craig. **Population:** 1,231. **Zip code:** 99921. **Emergency Services:** Police, Fire Department, phone 911; Public health nurse, phone 826-3433 or Health Clinic, phone 826-3257.

Elevation: 10 feet. **Climate:** Maritime with cool, moist, cloudy weather. Average temperature in January is 34°F; in July it is 56°F. Mean monthly precipitation ranges from 3.62 inches in June to 14.88 inches in October. Annual precipitation is 120 inches, including 40 inches of snow.

Private Aircraft: Seaplane base adjacent north; fuel 80. Airstrip located 7 miles north at Klawock; transportation to Craig provided by airlines.

Visitor Facilities: A full range of goods and services are available in Craig including overnight accommodations, restaurants and bars, 2 supermarkets, a general store, liquor store, gift shop, a laundromat, clothing and hardware stores, gas stations and beauty salons. Banking services available. Fishing/hunting licenses may be purchased at Classy Corner. Fishing and hunting trips can be arranged locally. Marine repair at the marina, and other major repair services available in town. Marine gas, diesel, propane, regular and unleaded gasoline also available. Rental transportation is not available. It is possible to arrange for rental cars in Klawock to be delivered to Craig. Transient moorage available at the city harbor.

Craig was once a temporary fish camp for the Tlingit and Haida people of this region. In 1907, with the help of local Haidas, Craig Millar established a saltery at Fish Egg Island. A permanent saltery and cold storage facility and about 2 dozen homes were built between 1908 and 1911 at the city's present location and the settlement was named for its founder. In 1912, the year the post office was established, E.M. Streeter opened a sawmill and Craig constructed a salmon cannery, both of which peaked during WWI. Craig was incorporated in 1922, and continued to grow throughout the 1930s, with some families from the Dust Bowl relocating to this Prince of Wales Island community. Although the salmon industry has both prospered and foundered over the years, fishing still accounts for about half of the employment in Craig today. In recent years, increased timber harvesting on the island has contributed jobs in logging and timber processing and there is also employment in government and construction.

Craig has become a service center for Prince of Wales Island, which is drawing an increasing number of visitors each year for its sportfishing and wildlife, both made more accessible by the expanding island road system.

Fishing on the island includes steelhead

in spring and midwinter; rainbow, Dolly Varden and cutthroat trout from spring through fall; pink salmon, July through August; silver and chum salmon, August to October; king salmon, May to October; and rockfish, halibut and cod all season.

Wildlife — particularly black bear and deer — is abundant on Prince of Wales Island. Crab Bay, within the Craig city limits, is one of the major resting and feeding areas for migratory waterfowl and shorebirds in southeastern Alaska. At low tide, visitors can hike around Cemetery Island, beachcomb and explore tide pools.

Prince of Wales Island has more of a road system than anywhere else in Southeast, so there is good access to remote locations for fishing, hiking, berry-picking, hunting and the like.

Communications in Craig include phones, mail plane, radio and TV. The community has 5 churches; an elementary school and high school; a library; and public electric power, water and sewage systems. Freight arrives by cargo plane, barge and by ferry to Hollis. Government address: City of Craig, P.O. Box 23, Craig, AK 99921; phone 826-3275. Village corporation address: Shaan-Seet Inc., P.O. Box 90, Craig, AK 99921.

Cube Cove

Located in Cube Cove, on northwest coast of Admiralty Island, 20 miles southwest of Juneau. **Transportation:** Boat or seaplane. **Population:** 200. **Zip code:** NA. **Emergency Services:** Alaska State Troopers in Juneau.

Elevation: Sea level.
Private Aircraft: Floatplane landings only.
Visitor Facilities: A privately operated logging camp. Formerly Eight Fathom Bight. No accommodations or visitor services.

Dolomi

Located in Port Johnson on the southeast side of Prince of Wales Island, 20 miles from Metlakatla, 27 miles from Ketchikan, due east of Hydaburg. **Transportation:** Charter seaplane from Metlakatla or Ketchikan; by boat. **Population:** 200. **Zip code:** 99926. **Emergency Services:** Alaska State Troopers and hospital in Ketchikan; emergency aid available at Camp Dolomi.

Elevation: Sea level. **Climate:** Typical Southeast weather: cool and rainy.
Private Aircraft: Floatplane landings on Port Johnson.
Visitor Facilities: Originally a mining town established around the turn of the century, Dolomi is now a floating logging camp

owned by Long Island Development, which provides a bunkhouse and cookhouse for residents. There are no visitor accommodations or services. Emergency accommodations, meals and diesel fuel may be available. Supplies are obtained in Ketchikan. There are no tourist attractions, but excellent fishing and deer hunting in the area is reported. Communications at the camp are provided by mail plane and radio. There is a school with grades 1 through 8.

Dora Bay

Located on Moira Sound, southeast side of Prince of Wales Island, 40 miles southeast of Craig. **Transportation:** Charter plane or private boat. **Population:** 10. **Zip code:** via Ketchikan. **Emergency Services:** Police and hospital in Ketchikan.

Elevation: Sea level. **Climate:** Typical Southeast, cool and rainy.
Private Aircraft: Floatplane landings only.
Visitor Facilities: This floating logging camp, previously located at Neets Bay, is operated by J.R. Gildersleeve Logging Co. The camp has no visitor facilities except for a radiophone.

Edna Bay

Located on Edna Bay at the southeast end of Kosciusko Island off the northwest coast of Prince of Wales Island, 45 miles north of Craig, 90 miles northwest of Ketchikan. **Transportation:** By boat or floatplane. **Population:** 68. **Zip code:** 99825. **Emergency Services:** For medical emergencies contact the U.S. Coast Guard, VHF radio channel 16; Alaska State Troopers in Ketchikan, contact by VHF radio.

Elevation: Sea level. **Climate:** Cool and wet. Private Aircraft: Floatplane landings only.
Visitor Facilities: Edna Bay is primarily a logging community with no visitor facilities or services. (A fish buyer is located in the bay in the summer.) Supplies are brought in by cargo plane or boat from Craig, Ketchikan or Petersburg. Communications are by mail plane and radio. The Edna Bay school has 13 students enrolled and offers grades 1 through 12.

Eight Fathom Bight
(See **Cube Cove**.)

Elfin Cove

Located at the northern tip of Chichagof Island, 70 miles west of Juneau, 33 miles northwest of Hoonah. **Transportation:** By seaplane or boat. **Population:** 47. **Zip code:** 99825. **Emergency Services:** EMT in Elfin

Cove, physician's assistant in Pelican, hospital in Juneau; Alaska State Troopers in Juneau, phone 789-2161, and Hoonah, phone 945-3655.

Elevation: 20 feet. **Climate:** Cool and wet in summer, with a mean monthly temperature in July of 54°F and 4.98 inches of precipitation. Precipitation averages 9.54 inches in January, with low temperatures to 28°F.

Private Aircraft: Floatplane dock; emergency fuel (100) available.

Visitor Facilities: A seasonal community which serves as fish buying and supply center for fishermen, Elfin Cove has 1 hotel and a cafe. Louie's Place (rental cabin) accommodates 6. Three lodges offer food, lodging and sportfishing during the summer. Groceries, fishing gear, public laundry, showers, liquor, gifts, stationery, boat electronics and marine hardware are available. Marine repair available in Pelican. All services are seasonal. No banking services. Boats may be rented and marine gas, diesel and propane are available at the fuel dock. Fishing/hunting licenses are available, and hunting and fishing charters may be arranged. Transient moorage available at Elfin Cove community dock.

This protected, flask-shaped harbor was originally called "Gunkhole" by fishermen anchoring here. Its safe anchorage and proximity to the Fairweather fishing grounds made this a natural spot for fish buyers and as a supply point for fishermen. Ernie Swanson built a store, restaurant and dock here in the late 1920s and renamed it Elfin Cove after his boat, the *Elfin.* John Lowell, another fish buyer, arrived in the 1940s and built a second dock, warehouse, store and a restaurant.

Everything at Elfin Cove is connected by boardwalks and most structures are built over the water on pilings. It is still a seasonal community, active during the fishing season when local businesses serve the commercial fishing fleet. Most of the residents migrate south or to Juneau for the winter. While most local people are fishermen or depend on the commercial fishing industry for a living, the area's scenery, sportfishing and other recreation are drawing an increasing number of tourists, and 3 lodges have been established in recent years. There is year-round bottom fish and halibut fishing and clamming. There is also salmon fishing in season. Local activities include berry-picking, mushrooming, hiking and cross-country skiing. Several attractions are within an hour's boat ride. Glacier Bay National Park is an hour's skiff ride; Port Althorp Bear Preserve is 40 minutes away by boat, and the abandoned Port

Althorp cannery is a 20-minute skiff ride as is the WWII George Island Coastal Rifle Station.

Communications at Elfin Cove, which is unincorporated, include phones, mail plane and VHF radio. Messages may be phoned in at 239-2202. There is a community water system. Electric power by private generators. Freight comes in by plane or by boat.

Excursion Inlet

Located 38 miles northwest of Juneau, due east of Gustavus, at the mouth of Excursion Inlet off Icy Strait. **Transportation:** By boat or plane. **Population:** 350 in summer, 2 in winter. **Zip code:** 99850. **Emergency Services:** Hospital and Alaska State Troopers in Juneau.

Elevation: Sea level. **Climate:** Cool and wet.

Private Aircraft: Seaplane base. Dirt road near cannery serves as airstrip.

Visitor Facilities: Excursion Inlet Packing Co. camp operates here in summer, and the company store (also known as Coho Mercantile) stocks clothing, first-aid supplies, hardware, film and sporting goods. Fishing/hunting licenses may be purchased. No overnight accommodations or food service for visitors. Marine gas, diesel, propane and regular gasoline are available in summer. Transient moorage available at Excursion Inlet Dock; fuel available at Excursion Inlet Cannery dock. Communications in summer include phones, mail plane, radio and TV. Freight comes in by barge and ship.

Funter Bay

Located 19 miles southwest of Juneau at the north end of Admiralty Island. **Transportation:** By boat or plane. **Population:** 10 to 20. **Zip code:** 99850. **Emergency Services:** Hospital and Alaska State Troopers in Juneau.

Elevation: Sea level. **Climate:** Cool and wet.

Private Aircraft: Floatplane landings only with dock.

Visitor Facilities: Food and lodging for 6 guests from mid-May to September available at local wilderness lodge which also offers fishing charters (advance reservations required). Fishing/hunting licenses may be purchased at the lodge in summer. There are 2 public dock facilities and 2 coves in the bay for anchoring small boats.

An important anchorage and the site of an abandoned cannery and gold mine, this area is the site of a state marine park. There are some summer cabins at Funter Bay. Most of the permanent residents are commercial fishermen. Excellent area fishing for salmon and halibut. There is a 3-mile trail to Bear Creek and about a 7-mile trail to Mount Robert Barron; both are unmaintained. Residents provide their own power, water and sewage disposal. Communications include radio and a weekly mail plane. Freight comes in by cargo plane and private boat.

Gustavus

Located at the mouth of the Salmon River on the north shore of Icy Passage off Icy Strait, near the entrance to Glacier Bay, 48 miles northwest of Juneau and 10 miles from Bartlett Cove, headquarters of Glacier Bay National Park. **Transportation:** Year-round charter air service from Juneau; scheduled boat and jet service in summer; private boat. **Population:** 219. **Zip code:** 99826. **Emergency Services:** Volunteer Emergency Response, phone 697-2222; Alaska State Troopers in Hoonah.

Elevation: 20 feet. **Climate:** Cool and rainy with average temperatures in January of 27°F and in July of 55°F. Mean precipitation ranges from 9.14 inches in October to 2.40 inches in June.

Private Aircraft: Gustavus airport 0.5 mile northeast; elev. 36 feet; length 6,800 feet; asphalt. Passenger terminal, ticket counter and public phone; air taxi offices; transient tie-downs; travel center; arts and crafts shop; fish products shop. Taxi and bus service available.

Visitor Facilities: As the gateway to Glacier Bay National Park and Preserve, Gustavus offers most visitor services, including several lodges, inns, bed-and-breakfast homes and cabin rentals which also serve meals. One lodge and a campground are located within the park at Bartlett Cove, approximately 12 sea miles from Gustavus. There are restaurants and a bakery. Groceries, hardware, fishing licenses and some fishing supplies may be purchased; no freeze-dried food is available. Gift shops are located in Gustavus and Bartlett Cove. Travel services are available. Boats and planes may be chartered for sightseeing, photography or fishing trips. Kayak and bicycle rentals and guided trips may be arranged. Propane and white gas for camping are available. Marine fuel can be purchased at Bartlett Cove. Public moorage at the state-operated dock and float; phone near the dock; no facilities.

Surrounded on three sides by the snow-covered peaks of the Chilkat Range and the Fairweather Mountains, Gustavus offers miles of level land with expansive sandy beaches, farmland and forest. Homesteaded in 1914 as a small agricultural community, the area was once named Strawberry Point because it produced abundant wild strawberries along the beach and in the meadows. Today, local residents and visitors still enjoy strawberries, blueberries, nagoonberries, huckleberries and other berries and flowers and a variety of animals and birds. Most residents maintain gardens and make their living by fishing, processing fish, supplying services, creating arts and crafts and working for the National Park Service. Gustavus caters to fishermen, sightseers and park visitors. Local residents recommend fishing for salmon, halibut and trout as well as beachcombing, hiking, kayaking, bird-watching and photography. The Gustavus Arts Council and National Park Service sponsor activities including folk dancing and concerts throughout the summer. The community enjoys an old-fashioned Fourth of July celebration with a greased pole hung horizontally over the Salmon River at the bridge. Contestants try to remove money tucked into the pole's end before they slide off into the chilly waters of the river below.

The Dude Creek Critical Habitat Area, adjacent to Gustavus and Glacier Bay National Park, offers the awesome sight of thousands of lesser sandhill cranes as they stop briefly in the wet meadows during the spring and especially in September during their fall migration. The open wet meadow bisected by forest-fringed Dude Creek is the largest such complex of its kind in the region and is enjoyed by local residents for recreation year-round. Primary access is gained via a section line extension of the Good River Road to the west of town. There are no public-use facilities.

Communications include phones, mail plane, radio and TV. The community has a church, fire station, library, community park and a school for grades kindergarten through 12. Heavy freight arrives by barge. For more information write, Gustavus Visitors Assoc., Box 167, Gustavus, AK 99826.

Haines

Located on Portage Cove, Chilkoot Inlet, on the upper arm of Lynn Canal, 80 air miles northwest of Juneau, 13 nautical miles southwest of Skagway, 155 road miles south of Haines Junction, YT. **Transportation:** Scheduled air service from Juneau; mainline port on the Alaska Marine Highway's Southeast ferry system; connected to the Alaska Highway by the Haines Highway. **Population:**

1,160. **Zip code:** 99827. **Emergency Services:** City Police, phone 766-2121; Alaska State Troopers, Fire Department and Ambulance, emergency only phone 911; Doctor, phone 766-2521.

Elevation: Sea level. **Climate:** Average daily maximum temperature in July, 66°F; average daily minimum in January, 17°F. Average annual precipitation 61 inches. Snow on ground usually from October through April.

Private Aircraft: Haines airport, 3.5 miles west, elev. 16 feet; length 4,600 feet; asphalt/gravel; unattended; fuel 100. Passenger terminal with restroom. Commercial airlines provide transportation to and from motels and some motels offer courtesy car pickup.

Visitor Facilities: Haines has all visitor facilities. There are 5 hotels/motels, 2 bed-and-breakfast accommodations, a lodge and 4 public campgrounds, 4 private camper parks and bunk-style accommodations. All supplies are available from local hardware and grocery stores. Fishing/hunting licenses may be purchased in Haines; there are 2 registered hunting guides and local charter boat operators offer fishing trips. There are several restaurants, cafes and taverns, a dry cleaner and laundromat, bank, car and motorhome rentals, automotive and marine repair, and gas stations. Propane, diesel, regular gasoline and marine gas are available. Transient moorage at the city small-boat harbor 1 block from city center.

The Chilkat Valley was first inhabited by Tlingit Indians, who jealously guarded fur trading routes from the coast into the Interior. A Presbyterian missionary named S. Hall Young established a mission at the present site of Haines in 1881. By 1884 there was a post office here and as placer gold mining began in the Porcupine District, about 36 miles upriver from Haines, the town became an important outlet. The Klondike gold rush of 1898 brought an influx of gold seekers, who opened up the Chilkat mountain pass to the Interior. In 1904, the U.S. government established Fort William H. Seward, which was renamed Chilkoot Barracks in 1922 and deactivated in 1946. The fort is a popular tourist attraction today. Haines was incorporated in 1910.

As a mainline port on the state ferry system and 1 of 3 Southeast communities connected to the Alaska Highway (the others are Hyder and Skagway), Haines remains an important route to the Interior for today's travelers. The Haines Highway, which connects the port of Haines with the Alaska Highway at Haines Junction, YT, is open year-round. The majority of employment in Haines is in service trades, followed by fishing, timber, government and construction. Fishing was one of the initial industries in Haines' early days, and remains a commercial industry and a visitor attraction. A sawmill owned by Chilkoot Lumber Co. began operation in November 1987, at the site of the former, idle sawmill along Lutak Inlet.

Along with sportfishing, visitors may explore the town's early history at Fort Seward, where the Chilkat Dancers interpret ancient Tlingit Indian legends and a local melodrama is performed. The Southeast Alaska State Fair is held in Haines in August. From October through January, the world's greatest concentration of American bald eagles takes place on the Chilkat River near Haines. The Chilkat Valley is the annual home of more than 3,000 bald eagles, which gather to feed on the late run of chum salmon in the Chilkat River. The 48,000-acre Alaska Chilkat Bald Eagle Preserve was established in 1982. Several custom and group tour operators offer trips to the preserve, including trips on snow machines, snowshoes and cross-country skis and photographic blinds for serious wildlife photographers. Raft trips are also available.

Other attractions include Sheldon Museum and Cultural Center, located at the corner of Front and Main streets. The museum features the art, history, ethnology and geology of the Haines area. The museum has special exhibits, guided tours, workshops and films, including the Audubon Society's *Last Stronghold of the Eagles* about the annual congregation of bald eagles near Haines, the largest such gathering in the world. Summer hours are 1-4 p.m. daily; morning hours are posted. Winter hours are 1-4 p.m. on days the state ferry arrives; open by appointment at other times. Admission is $2 for adults; children are free if accompanied by an adult. Another popular attraction is Alaska Indian Arts Inc., an arts center and gallery located in Building 23 on Fort Seward Drive. The center features the arts and crafts of southeastern Alaska's Tlingit and Haida Indians; the museum has guided tours, workshops and demonstrations. Year-round hours are 9 a.m. to 5 p.m. Monday through Friday. There is no charge to visit the carving shop; admission to watch Indian dancers is $5 for adults. A local business has bikes to rent and bicycle tours, and another offers glacier walks.

Communications include phones (most households have phones), a local newspaper *(Chilkat Valley News)*, radio (2 stations from

Juneau and local FM) and numerous TV channels provided by satellite and cable. There are churches and kindergarten, elementary, junior and senior high schools. The city operates water and sewage systems and a private utility supplies electricity. Freight arrives by ship, barge, plane or truck. Government address: City of Haines, P.O. Box 1049, Haines, AK 99827; phone 766-2231.

Hobart Bay

Located 70 miles south of Juneau and 40 miles north of Petersburg on the east shore of Stephens Passage. **Transportation:** Boat or seaplane. **Population:** 250. **Zip code:** 99850. **Emergency Services:** None available.

Elevation: Sea level.

Private Aircraft: No facilities.

Visitor Facilities: No visitor accommodations. There is a public dock.

Hobart Bay is a logging camp for Long Island Development Co. The land is owned by Goldbelt, Inc., the Juneau-based Native corporation which owns nearly 23,000 acres in the area. The camp has electricity, phone service and satellite TV reception. There is a public school with grades kindergarten through 12.

Hollis

Located on the east coast of Prince of Wales Island on Twelvemile Arm, 25 road miles east of Klawock, 35 miles west of Ketchikan. **Transportation:** By ferry from Ketchikan; on the Prince of Wales Island road system. **Population:** est. 125. **Zip code:** 99950. **Emergency Services:** Alaska State Troopers in Klawock; hospital in Ketchikan.

Elevation: 20 feet. **Climate:** Mean monthly temperature in January is 32°F and in July, 58°F. Mean monthly precipitation ranges from 3.28 inches in July to 18.14 inches in October.

Private Aircraft: Seaplane base with aircraft float and sheltered anchorage.

Visitor Facilities: There are no stores, restaurants, gas stations or other visitor facilities here. The ferry from Ketchikan that serves Prince of Wales Island docks at Hollis. There are a boat ramp, dock and floats for moorage, and there is a community phone at the school, 530-9001.

Hollis was a mining town with a population of 1,000 from about 1900 to 1915. In the 1950s, Hollis became the site of Ketchikan Pulp Co.'s logging camp, and served as the base for timber operations on Prince of Wales Island until 1962, when the camp was moved to Thorne Bay. Recent state land sales have

spurred the growth of a small residential community here, the subdivisions built in thick second-growth timber with trees 40 to 60 feet tall. A school with grades 1 through 12, the ferry terminal, and a U.S. Forest Service office are located here.

Hollis has no public utilities and in lieu of a local government has the nonprofit Hollis Community Council. A letter addressed to the Hollis Community Council, Hollis, AK 99950, will eventually find its way there after going through Ketchikan then coming over by pouch. Hollis itself has no post office.

Hoonah

Located on the northeast shore of Chichagof Island, about 40 miles west of Juneau and 20 miles south across Icy Strait from the entrance to Glacier Bay. **Transportation:** Scheduled and charter air service from Juneau; twice weekly state ferry service in summer. **Population:** 895. **Zip code:** 99829. **Emergency Services:** Alaska State Troopers and city police, phone 945-3655; Volunteer Fire Department; Clinic, phone 945-3235 or 945-3386; emergencies, phone 911.

Elevation: 30 feet. **Climate:** Typical southeastern Alaska climate, with considerable rainfall (100 inches annually). Summer temperatures in the 50s; winter lows to 14°F in February.

Private Aircraft: Hoonah airport, adjacent southeast; elev. 30 feet; length 3,100 feet; gravel; unattended, prior visual inspection recommended. Seaplane base with sheltered anchorage and dock.

Visitor Facilities: Accommodations and restaurants available. Hoonah has grocery and general stores, a gift shop, bank and laundromat. Fishing/hunting licenses may be purchased here. Guided hunting and fishing trips may be arranged locally. Major marine repair and marine gas, diesel and regular gasoline are available. Transient moorage available at the city harbor; the marina, which has showers and a laundromat, is a popular layover for boaters awaiting permits to enter Glacier Bay.

Hoonah is a small coastal community with a quiet harbor for the seining and trolling fleets. The most prominent structures are a cold storage facility, the lodge, bank, post office and public school. The village has been occupied since prehistory by the Tlingit people. In the late 1800s, missionaries settled here. Canneries established in the area in the early 1900s spurred the growth of commercial fishing, which remains the mainstay of Hoonah's economy. During the summer fishing season, residents work for nearby Excursion Inlet Packing Co. or Thomson Fish Co. in town. Halibut season begins in May and salmon season opens in midsummer and runs through September. Some logging also contributes to the economy. Subsistence hunting and fishing remain an important lifestyle here, and many families gather food in the traditional way: Catching salmon and halibut in summer, shellfish and bottom fish year-round; hunting deer, geese and ducks; and berry-picking in late summer and fall.

Hoonah Cultural Center, operated by the Hoonah Indian Assoc., features the history and culture of the local Tlingit Indians. Displays show Tlingit art and artifacts; a highlight is a large mural depicting the origins of the 2 original clans, who were forced by advancing glaciers to abandon their ancestral homes in Glacier Bay. The exhibits also interpret 3 8-foot-tall totem poles. The museum has special exhibits and guided tours. Hours are 9 a.m. to 4:30 p.m. Monday through Friday; open weekends by request. Admission is $2.

Communications include phones in most households (residents also use CB radios for local communication), mail plane, radio and TV via satellite and cable. There are several churches and both an elementary school and high school. There are community water and sewage systems and electricity is provided by a public utility. Freight arrives by plane or barge. Government address: City of Hoonah, P.O. Box 360, Hoonah, AK 99829; phone 945-3663. Village corporation address: Huna Totem Corp., 5245 Glacier Highway, Juneau, AK 99801.

Hydaburg

Located on the southwest coast of Prince of Wales Island, 36 road miles from Hollis, 45 road miles from Craig, 50 air miles west of Ketchikan. **Transportation:** Scheduled air service from Ketchikan; state ferry service to Hollis; private boat. **Population:** 475. **Zip code:** 99922. **Emergency Services:** State Troopers in Klawock, phone 755-2918; Village Public Safety Officer, phone 285-3321; Clinic, phone 285-3462; Volunteer Fire Department.

Elevation: 30 feet. **Climate:** Cool, moist, maritime climate with complete cloud cover about 60 percent of the time. Summer temperatures from 46° to 70°F. June and July are the driest months with an average of 5 inches of precipitation. Mild winter temperatures, range from 32°F to the low 40s. October and November are the wettest months with up to 18 inches of precipitation. Annual average precipitation is 120 inches

Private Aircraft: Seaplane base with sheltered anchorage and dock; watch for boat traffic.

Visitor Facilities: A boarding house provides rooms and meals. Meals are also available at a local inn. Groceries, hardware and sundry items are available. Crafts, such as Haida Indian carvings and baskets, may be purchased from residents. There are no public laundry facilities, banking services or rental transportation. Fishing/hunting licenses and guide services are not available. Marine machine shop and fuel available at harbor. Diesel and regular gasoline are available in town. Moorage at city of Hydaburg floats, 0.5 mile north of town.

Hydaburg was founded in 1911 and combined the populations of 3 Haida villages: Sukkwan, Howkan and Klinkwan. President William Howard Taft established an Indian reservation on the surrounding land in 1912, but, at the residents' request, most of the land was restored to its former status as part of Tongass National Forest in 1926. Hydaburg was incorporated in 1927, 3 years after its people had become citizens of the United States.

Most of the residents are commercial fishermen, although there are some jobs in construction and the timber industry. Subsistence is also a traditional and necessary part of life here. Hydaburg has an excellent collection of restored Haida totems. The totem park was developed in the 1930s by the Civilian Conservation Corps. There is also good salmon fishing here in the fall.

Communications include phones and TV. There are Assembly of God and Presbyterian churches here. Hydaburg has both elementary and high schools. There are community water, sewage and electrical power systems. No alcoholic beverages are sold in Hydaburg. Freight arrives by plane, barge and truck. Government address: City of Hydaburg, P.O. Box 49, Hydaburg, AK 99922; phone 285-3761. Village corporation address: Haida Corp., P.O. Box 89, Hydaburg, AK 99922.

Hyder

Located at the head of Portland Canal, 2 miles west of Stewart, BC. **Transportation:** By road via a spur of the Cassiar Highway; once-a-week state ferry service from Ketchikan in summer; charter air service and mail plane. **Population:** 73. **Zip code:** 99923. **Emergency Services:** Hospital and RCMP in Stewart, BC.

Elevation: Sea level. **Climate:** Maritime,

with warm winters and cool, rainy summers. Slightly less summer rain than other southeastern communities, but heavy snowfall in winter. Summer temperatures range from 41° to 57°F; winter temperatures range from 25° to 43°F.

Private Aircraft: Seaplane base at Hyder; airstrip at Stewart.

Visitor Facilities: Hyder has gift shops, a post office, 3 cafes, 2 bars and 1 inn, which offers rooms, cocktail lounge and restaurant. Hardware and sporting goods available. Nearby Stewart has 3 hotels/motels, 3 restaurants, 2 grocery stores, service stations, a bank, liquor store and other shops.

Hyder and Stewart, on either side of the U.S.-Canada border, share commerce and history. Captain D.D. Gaillard explored Portland Canal in 1896 for the U.S. Army Corps of Engineers. In the late 1890s, gold and silver were discovered in the hills near Hyder, attracting some prospectors. With the discovery in 1917 and 1918 of rich silver veins in the upper Salmon River basin, Hyder boomed. Few of the structures from this boom period survive, although many of the pilings which supported the buildings are still visible on the tidal flats. Hyder became an access and supply point for the mines, while Stewart served as the center for Canadian mining activity. Mining ceased in 1956, with the exception of the Granduc copper mine, which operated until 1984.

Today's economy is based on local trade and tourism. Some Hyder residents supplement their incomes by fishing, hunting and gardening.

Attractions in the Hyder/Stewart area include the stone storehouse built by Capt. D.D. Gaillard in 1896; it is the oldest masonry building in Alaska. Sightseeing tours of Salmon Glacier are available out of Stewart and charter small-boat trips on Portland Canal are available at the Hyder marina. Five species of Pacific salmon are found in waters near Hyder, with Salmon River and Fish Creek supporting one of Southeast's largest chum salmon runs. A new viewing platform on Fish Creek provides safe views of the chum salmon spawning area and the many black bears that come to feed each summer.

The U.S. Forest Service operates a visitor information center for Misty Fiords National Monument during the summer months (June to Labor Day). The office is located in the Hyder post office and fire hall.

Communications include phones, mail plane, radio and TV. Hyder has no public schools; students attend school in Stewart.

The community has electricity provided by a public utility. Wood and diesel are used to heat most homes. Residents rely on individual wells for water and septic tanks for sewage waste disposal. Freight arrives by barge, plane or truck. Government address: Hyder Community Assoc. Inc., Box 149, Hyder, AK 99923.

Icy Bay

Located 66 miles northwest of Yakutat, 150 miles southeast of Cordova, at the terminus of Guyot and Malaspina glaciers on the Gulf of Alaska coast. **Transportation:** Charter plane. **Population:** Varies. **Zip code:** 99850. **Emergency Services:** Alaska State Troopers in Cordova; medical facilities in Cordova and Yakutat.

Elevation: 50 feet. **Climate:** Cool and rainy in summer, with rain and snow in winter. Some below zero days in winter.

Private Aircraft: Icy Bay airstrip, 0.3 mile from camp; elev. 50 feet; length 4,000 feet; gravel; unattended and unmaintained.

Visitor Facilities: This is a privately operated logging camp; there are no visitor facilities or services here. The camp obtains supplies from Cordova and freight arrives by cargo plane or barge. Communications include mail plane, radio and TV. Icy Bay school has grades kindergarten through 12.

Juneau

Located on Gastineau Channel opposite Douglas Island, 91 nautical miles south of Haines, 577 air miles southeast of Anchorage, 900 air miles north of Seattle, WA. **Transportation:** Daily scheduled jet service from Seattle and from Alaska communities; commuter air service from Haines, Skagway and other Southeast points; year-round state ferry service. **Population:** 29,946. **Zip code:** 99801, 99802, 99803, 99811. **Emergency Services:** Alaska State Troopers, Police, Fire Department and Ambulance, phone 911; Bartlett Memorial Hospital, phone 586-2611.

Elevation: Sea level. **Climate:** Mild and wet. Average daily maximum temperature in July is 63°F; daily minimum in January is 20°F. Record high was 90°F in July of 1975; record low, -22°F in January 1972. Average annual precipitation 92 inches. Snow on ground intermittently from mid-November to mid-April.

Private Aircraft: Juneau International Airport, 9 miles northwest of downtown; elev. 18 feet; length 8,400 feet; asphalt; fuel 80, 100, JP4. Full-service passenger terminal. Bus service to downtown. Juneau Harbor Seaplane, adjacent north; unattended; watch for harbor boat traffic; fuel 80, 100 and A1. Juneau International Seaplane Basin, 7 miles northwest of downtown, dock and ramp available for public use.

Visitor Facilities: As capital of Alaska and the largest city in Southeast, Juneau has all services. This includes 13 hotels/motels, several bed-and-breakfasts, dozens of restaurants and gift shops, a few major shopping centers, laundries, banks, major repair service and rental transportation. Many fishing charter services operate out of Juneau and hunting/fishing licenses may be purchased at numerous outlets. All types of fuel are available. The City and Borough of Juneau operates several harbors. Transient moorage is available at the Juneau City Float, 2 blocks from city center; at Harris Harbor, 1 mile from city center; at the Douglas Boat Harbor, across the channel from Juneau; and at the Auke Bay float facilities, 12 miles north of Juneau.

Juneau got its start with the discovery of gold in 1880 by Joe Juneau and Dick Harris and the town boomed with the ensuing gold rush. By 1900, given Juneau's growth, mining activity, location on the water route to Skagway and the Klondike, along with the

Helicopters bring visitors to the Juneau Icefield for firsthand look at this huge remnant of the Ice Age. (Rollo Pool, staff)

decline of Sitka after the Russians left and whaling and fur trade fell off, it was decided to move Alaska's capital to Juneau. Transfer of government functions occurred in 1906. Today, government (federal, state and local) comprises an estimated half of the total basic industry, with tourism, construction and some mining making up the total. Dubbed "a little San Francisco," Juneau is a picturesque city, backed by the steep slopes of Mount Juneau (elev. 3,819 feet) and looking over Gastineau Channel. The city has an attractive waterfront park, a good spot to watch the floatplanes and ships in the channel. Juneau's skyline is dominated by several government buildings, including the Federal Building, the massive State Office Building, and the older brick and marble-columned Capitol Building.

The city and surrounding area offer a number of attractions. Boat and plane operators offer charter sightseeing and fishing. There is downtown shopping and self-guided walking tours to see the government buildings and Governor's Mansion. The Alaska State Museum, located just off Egan Drive at 395 Whittier St. features the archeology, art, botany, history, ethnology, geology and paleontology of the state. The museum offers special exhibits, guided tours, workshops, lectures, film presentations and demonstrations. More than 150 exhibits depict wildlife and habitats, Native culture, Russian America, pioneer days and industrial history. Hours from mid-May to mid-September are 9 a.m. to 7 p.m. Monday through Friday and 10 a.m. to 6 p.m. Saturday and Sunday. Hours from October through mid-May are 10 a.m. to 4 p.m. Tuesday through Saturday. The $1 admission was expected to go up in 1990. Another popular attraction is the Juneau Douglas City Museum, 114 W. 4th. It features Juneau's mining history from a personal viewpoint. Persons visiting the museum receive a postcard and 4 walking tour maps of Juneau. Summer hours are 9 a.m. to 5 p.m. Monday through Friday and 11 a.m. to 5 p.m. Saturday and Sunday. Open winters at reduced hours. Donations are requested.

There are several hiking trails accessible from downtown: Perseverance trail, 3.5 miles, begins at the end of Basin Road and leads to the old Perseverance Mine; Mount Juneau trail, steep and rugged, begins 0.5 mile up Perseverance trail; Granite Creek Basin trail begins about 1.8 miles up Perseverance trail and leads 1.5 miles along Granite Creek to a scenic basin; Mount Roberts trail begins at the top of Starr Hill (the east end of 6th Street) and leads 3.7 miles to Mount Roberts.

For bicyclists there are intermittent bike paths to Douglas and to Mendenhall Glacier. The glacier bike path begins at the intersection of 12th Street and Glacier Avenue and leads 13 miles north to Mendenhall Glacier. This magnificent glacier is about 13 miles by car from downtown Juneau. The U.S. Forest Service visitor center at the glacier has audio-visual displays, daily slide and film programs and guided hikes from early June through Labor Day and on weekends during the winter months. In the other direction from Juneau, on Douglas Island, is Eaglecrest ski area. Eaglecrest has downhill and cross-country skiing in winter.

Juneau has all the amenities of city life. There are many churches here, ranging from Apostolic to United Methodist. Juneau Borough Schools enroll more than 4,400 students in 5 elementary schools, 2 middle schools and 1 high school. Freight arrives by cargo plane or water. Government address: City and Borough of Juneau, City and Borough Manager, 155 S. Seward St., Juneau, AK 99801; phone 586-5240.

Kake

Located on the northwest coast of Kupreanof Island, 40 air miles and 65 nautical miles northwest of Petersburg, 95 air miles southwest of Juneau. **Transportation:** Scheduled airline from Petersburg or Juneau; state ferry from Petersburg and Sitka. **Population:** 665. **Zip code:** 99830. **Emergency Services:** Police, phone 785-3393; Health Center, phone 785-3333; Volunteer Fire Department, phone 785-3464.

Elevation: 10 feet. **Climate:** Temperate, with summer temperatures in the 50s, occasional highs in the 80s. Moderate rainfall most months, very little snow in winter.

Private Aircraft: Seaplane base southwest of town with dock. Airstrip 1 mile west of town; elev. 148 feet; length 4,000 feet; gravel; unattended, prior visual inspection recommended.

Visitor Facilities: Accommodations and meals available. There is also a coffee shop. Some hardware, clothing and other supplies available at the 3 local grocery stores. Fishing/hunting licenses are sold locally. No banking services. Laundromat available. There is a car mechanic and all types of fuel are available (marine, diesel, propane, unleaded and regular). Public moorage at City of Kake floats.

The town is a permanent village of the Kake tribe of the Tlingit Indians. The Tlingits from Kake had a well-earned reputation for aggression in the 18th and 19th centuries. In 1869, the Kakes murdered 2 Sitka traders in revenge for the shooting of a Native by a Sitka sentry. Reprisals taken by the U.S. resulted in the shelling and destruction of 3 Kake villages. The tribe eventually settled at the present-day site of Kake, where the government established a school in 1891. Residents have historically drawn ample subsistence from the sea. However, with the advent of a cash economy, the community has come to depend on commercial fishing, fish processing (there is a cannery) and logging. The post office was established in 1904 and the city was incorporated in 1952. The city's claim to fame is its totem, reputedly the world's tallest at 132 feet, 6 inches. It was carved for the 1967 Alaska Purchase Centennial Celebration.

Kake has phones, radio, TV and mail plane service. Church groups include Baptist, Salvation Army, Presbyterian and Assembly of God. Schools include an elementary school and a high school. Community electrical power, water and sewage systems are available. Freight comes in on the airlines or by barge. Government address: City of Kake, P.O. Box 500, Kake, AK 99830; phone 785-3804. Village corporation address: Kake Tribal Corp., P.O. Box 263, Kake, AK 99830.

Kasaan

Located on the east side of Prince of Wales Island, southest of Thorne Bay, on Kasaan Bay on the Kasaan Peninsula. **Transportation:** Charter plane or private boat. **Population:** 75. **Zip code:** 99924. **Emergency Services:** Alaska State Troopers and hospital in Ketchikan; Volunteer Fire Department.

Elevation: Sea level. **Climate:** Typical Southeast, cool and rainy, with average temperatures of 55°F in summer. Precipitation ranges from 3.89 inches in June to 11.30 inches in November.

Private Aircraft: Seaplane base, dock.

Visitor Facilities: Overnight accommodations with cooking and laundry facilities are maintained by Kavilco Inc., the local Native corporation, in remodeled buildings that were originally used as bunkhouses by the salmon cannery until 1953. There are no stores; supplies are flown in from Ketchikan or Craig. Diesel and regular gasoline are available at the public floats and dock.

Kasaan was founded by a group of businessmen from Outside Alaska as a copper mine site. A sawmill and general store were established around 1900 and a salmon cannery was built in 1902. Members of the tribe of Haidas living at Old Kasaan, located south of Kasaan on Skowl Arm, eventually relocated at New Kasaan, site of the mine and cannery. The copper mining company went bankrupt after 4 years, but the cannery continued to operate sporadically — with a half-dozen different owners — until 1953. Kasaan incorporated in 1976 under the Alaska Native Claims Settlement Act. The community has revitalized somewhat in recent years with the incorporation, but jobs are still scarce. Residents depend heavily on the subsistence lifestyle: fishing for salmon, halibut and bottom fish (in July, the whole village goes up to Karta Bay for subsistence fishing); hunting for deer; trapping for mink and marten; going out for black seaweed in April and May; and gathering clams (which are plentiful), some shrimp and Dungeness crab. The valuable timberland owned by Kavilco holds promise for economic improvement, and the community is hoping for a connecting road system to the rest of the island. There are a few jobs with the city, power plant and a Bureau of Indian Affairs road project currently under way, but as one resident puts it, "most people fish or are retired."

A 1,300-foot boardwalk leads from the harbor to a gravel footpath, which leads another half mile through the village to a totem park. The Kasaan Totem Park, part of a government-sponsored totem restoration program begun in 1937, contains a number of totems from Old Kasaan. Kasaan is only a few miles away from the Karta River, a favorite of sportsmen. The village corporation, however, does not allow camping on its land for fear of forest fires. Residents also fish in front of the village; watch for killer whales going up the bay; and watch the great numbers of eagles that soar overhead. The village has a community house and hosts a number of community dinners.

Communications include phones, mail plane, radio and TV. Kasaan's one-room schoolhouse has an enrollment of 12 students and a kindergarten through grade 12 curriculum. The community has electric power and water systems; sewage system is individual septic tanks. Freight is brought in by barge or cargo plane. Government address: City of Kasaan, General Delivery, Kasaan, AK 99924; phone 542-2212. Village corporation address: Kavilco Inc., General Delivery, Kasaan, AK 99924.

Ketchikan

Located on the southwest side of Revillagigedo Island on Tongass Narrows opposite Gravina Island, 235 miles south of Juneau, 90 miles north of Prince Rupert, BC. Transportation: Scheduled jet service, commuter and charter flights; state ferry service. Population: 12,982 (Borough). Zip code: 99901. Emergency Services: Alaska State Troopers, phone 225-5118; Police, phone 225-6634; Hospital, phone 225-5171; Fire Department/Ambulance, phone 225-9611 or 225-9616 or 911.

Elevation: Sea level. Climate: Rainy. Average yearly rainfall 162 inches and snowfall of 32 inches. July high temperatures average 65°F, minimum 51°F. Daily maximum in January 39°F; minimum 29°F.

Private Aircraft: Ketchikan International Airport on Gravina Island; elev. 88 feet; length 7,500 feet; asphalt; fuel 80, 100, jet A. All facilities at airport. Ketchikan Harbor seaplane base downtown; fuel 80, 100.

Visitor Facilities: Ketchikan has 5 hotels/motels. There is also bed-and-breakfast accommodations, a youth hostel (open May 31 through Labor Day), an area lodge and 2 resorts. This is a full-service community with restaurants, laundromats, banks, 2 shopping centers, gift shops and all types of fuel. Fishing/hunting licenses are available. There are 2 registered hunting guides (deer and bear hunting season begin in August) and several charter boat operators offer fishing and sightseeing trips. Rental cars are available at the airport and downtown. Rental boats are also available. Transient moorage is available at Thomas Basin, Ryus Float and the City Float downtown, and at Bar Harbor north of downtown.

Ketchikan's history is highlighted in several local attractions, including Creek Street, a former red-light district; Dolly's House one-time brothel; a local theater production of *The Fish Pirate's Daughter*, which portrays Ketchikan's earlier history; Totem Heritage Center; Tongass Historical Museum; and Totem Bight State Park, 10 miles north of town; and Saxman Totem Park, 2.5 miles south of town.

Ketchikan celebrates a 3-day Rainbreak Festival in May, a Blueberry Festival in August and in (some) Octobers a Chief Johnson Pole Potlatch to celebrate in the Tlingit Indian tradition the raising of a newly carved totem pole. The July 4 celebration includes the famous Logging Carnival.

Ketchikan is the gateway to Misty Fiords National Monument located 30 miles east of town and accessible only by boat or floatplane. A number of tour operators in Ketchikan offer a variety of trips into this scenic area.

Ketchikan has all the amenities of a

medium sized city. The area supports many churches, 4 public elementary schools, a junior high school, 2 high schools and a community college. Freight arrives by cargo plane and barge. Government addresses: Ketchikan Gateway Borough, 344 Front St., Ketchikan, AK 99901; phone 225-6151; City of Ketchikan, 334 Front St., Ketchikan, AK 99901; phone 225-3111.

For more information see *The MILEPOST®*, a complete guide to communities on Alaska's road and ferry systems, and *South/Southeast Alaska*, Vol. 14, No. 2 of the *ALASKA GEOGRAPHIC®*. To order see the ALASKA NORTHWEST LIBRARY section at the back of the book.

Klawock

Located on the west coast of Prince of Wales Island on Klawock Inlet, 24 road miles west of Hollis, 7 road miles north of Craig, 55 air miles west of Ketchikan. **Transportation:** Scheduled air service from Ketchikan; private boat; state ferry to Hollis. **Population:** 760. **Zip code:** 99925. **Emergency Services:** Alaska State Troopers, phone 755-2918; Police, phone 755-2261; Clinic, phone 755-2900; Fire and Rescue, phone 755-2222.

Elevation: Sea level. **Climate:** Maritime with cool, moist, cloudy weather; mild winters. Average temperature in January is 34°F, in July it is 56°F. Mean monthly precipitation ranges from 3.62 inches in June to 14.88 inches in October. Annual precipitation is 120 inches, including 40 inches of snow.

Private Aircraft: Klawock airstrip, 2 miles northeast; elev. 50 feet; length 5,000 feet; gravel; fuel 80; unattended; air service provides courtesy bus to town. Klawock seaplane base, sheltered anchorage, dock, fuel 80.

Visitor Facilities: Accommodations and meals at 2 area lodges. Rental cabins and RV spaces available. Gas, groceries, laundromat, film and first-aid supplies, sporting goods, clothing and some Native arts and crafts are available. Banking services are available. Fishing/hunting licenses may be purchased locally. Guided hunting and fishing trips and equipment available. Major repair services include marine engines, boats and cars. Automobiles and boats may be rented in Klawock. All types of fuel are available. Transient moorage available at public floats and public dock.

Klawock originally was a Tlingit Indian summer fishing village; a trading post and salmon saltery were established here in 1868. Ten years later a salmon cannery was built —

the first cannery in Alaska and the first of several cannery operations in the area. Over the years the population of Klawock, like other Southeast communities, grew and then declined with the salmon harvest. The local economy is still dependent on fishing and cannery operations, along with timber cutting and sawmilling. A state fish hatchery is located on Klawock Lake, very near the site of a salmon hatchery that operated from 1897 until 1917. Klawock Lake offers good canoeing and boating.

Recreation here includes good fishing for salmon and steelhead in Klawock River, salmon and halibut fishing in Big Salt Lake, and deer and bear hunting. Klawock's totem park contains 21 totems — both replicas and originals — from the abandoned Indian village of Tuxekan.

Klawock is a first-class city, incorporated in 1929. Communications include phones, mail plane, radio and cable TV. Churches include Baha'i and Assembly of God. Schools include an elementary school, junior high school and high school. Public electric power, water and sewage systems are available. No alcoholic beverages are sold in Klawock. (An ordinance which goes back to the Wheeler Howard Act of 1934 required — among other things — that Klawock be kept free of liquor before receiving federal funding for cannery operations.) Freight arrives by cargo plane, barge and truck. Government address: City of Klawock, P.O. Box 113, Klawock, AK 99925; phone 755-2261. Village corporation address: Klawock Heenya Corp., P.O. Box 25, Klawock, AK 99925.

Klukwan

Located along the Haines Highway, 21 miles north of Haines, on the north shore of the Chilkat River and near the junction of Klehini and Tsirku rivers, 22 miles west of Skagway and 100 miles northeast of Juneau. **Transportation:** Road from Haines. **Population:** 153. **Zip code:** 99827. **Emergency Services:** Alaska State Troppers and Clinic in Haines; Fire Department, phone 767-5555; Klukwan Village Safety Officer, phone 767-5588; Klukwan Health Aide, phone 767-5505.

Elevation: Less than 500 feet above sea level.

Private Aircraft: No facilities. See Haines this section.

Visitor Facilities: No visitor accommodations or services. Virtually all facilities are available in nearby Haines.

Klukwan is the only surviving village of 4 Tlingit villages in the Chilkat Valley. A survey in the late 1800s showed a population of more than 500 persons in Klukwan. It is the only inland settlement in southeastern Alaska. Klukwan has a strong sense of identity. Although the town has electricity, phone service and a modern school with grades kindergarten through 12, many residents continue a lifestyle based, in part, on subsistence activities. They fish for salmon and eulachon in the Chilkat River and use berries, trees and animals of the Tongass National Forest. The area also borders the Alaska Chilkat Bald Eagle Preserve.

Kupreanof

Located on Lindenberg Peninsula, on the northeast shore of Kupreanof Island, across from Petersburg. **Transportation:** Primarily by small boat from Petersburg. **Population:** 43. **Zip code:** 99833. **Emergency Services:** Alaska State Troopers and hospital in Petersburg; Volunteer Fire Department.

Elevation: Sea level. **Climate:** Summer temperatures range from 40° to 76°F, winter temperatures from 0° to 43°F. Average annual precipitation 105 inches, with mean monthly snowfall in winter from 0.9 to 29.2 inches.

Private Aircraft: Floatplane landings only, public dock.

Visitor Facilities: There are no facilities or services here for visitors. Residents obtain services and supplies in Petersburg, which is accessible by skiff.

Formerly known as West Petersburg, Kupreanof incorporated as a second-class city in 1975, mostly to avoid annexation by the City of Petersburg and preserve its independent and rustic lifestyle.

"We are secretive and grouchy," one resident bragged, and added that what he likes best about Kupreanof is "the privacy."

A small sawmill was started here in 1911 by the Knudsen brothers, and in the 1920s the Yukon Fur Farm began raising foxes, then mink; both the mill and fur farm operated into the 1960s. Today, Kupreanof has no industrial base or commercial activities. Most residents are self-employed or work outside the community. Subsistence activities also contribute to each household.

Boardwalks and trails connect some of Kupreanof, although locals use skiffs to travel around the community. Kupreanof is adjacent to Petersburg Creek-Duncan Salt Chuck Wilderness Area. A planked trail runs behind private property toward the Petersburg Mountain Trail and another trail which leads 1 mile to Petersburg Creek. (See also Southeast Trails, Petersburg Area.)

Communications include radio and 3 households have phones. Mail is received in Petersburg. Children also attend school in Petersburg. Less than half the residents have electricity supplied by individual diesel or gasoline-powered generators. Most homes use wood stoves for heating. Residents also provide their own water (from wells or creeks) and sewage systems (septic tanks or privies). Freight is transported by private skiff from Petersburg to Kupreanof. Government address: City of Kupreanof, P.O. Box 50, Petersburg, AK 99833; phone 772-3660 or 772-4548.

Labouchere Bay

Located on the northwest tip of Prince of Wales Island, 2 miles south of Point Baker, 50 air miles west of Wrangell, 121 road miles from Hollis ferry terminal. **Transportation:** Private boat or by road.

Elevation: Sea level.

This is a logging camp operated by Louisiana-Pacific Corp. No visitor facilities, stores or gas available. Radiophone available for emergencies.

Long Island

Located 50 miles southwest of Ketchikan and 42 miles south of Craig. **Transportation:** Boat or floatplane; mail plane. **Population:** 150. **Zip code:** NA.

Elevation: Sea level.

Private Aircraft: Floatplane landings only.

Visitor Facilities: This is a logging camp operated by Klukwan Inc. No visitor services or supplies available.

Loring

Located on Revillagigedo Island, 20 miles north of Ketchikan, at the northeast corner of Naha Bay on the east side of Behm Canal. **Transportation:** Accessible by boat or floatplane only.

Visitor Facilities: Open moorage available at state float; no other services or facilities here.

A small group of residents lives at this former cannery site. Established in 1885, the cannery closed in 1930 and the post office was discontinued in 1936.

In 1889, the side-paddle steamer *Ancon,* which carried mail, freight and passengers between the West Coast and southeastern Alaska, was wrecked at Loring. A cannery hand cast off the lines as the ship prepared to depart, but no one was in control of the vessel. The ship drifted onto a reef, a rock punctured the hull and the ship sank (no lives were lost). Today, pieces of the *Ancon's* rusted boiler can be seen at Loring at low tide.

Metlakatla

Located on the west coast of Annette Island, 15 miles south of Ketchikan. **Transportation:** Charter air service; state ferry from Ketchikan. **Population:** 1,056. **Zip code:** 99926. **Emergency Services:** Police, phone 886-4011; Clinic, phone 886-4741; Fire Department, phone 886-7922. Police, Fire and Ambulance, emergency only phone 911.

Elevation: Sea level. **Climate:** Mild and moist. Summer temperatures range from 36° to 65°F, winter temperatures from 28° to 44°F. Average annual precipitation is 115 inches; October is the wettest month with a maximum of 35 inches of rainfall. Annual snowfall averages 61 inches.

Private Aircraft: Floatplane landings only at seaplane base. Annette Island airstrip, length 7,500 feet, asphalt. Not maintained. Request permission to land from Metlakatla Indian Community.

Visitor Facilities: Permit required for long-term visits to Metlakatla; contact the tourism department, phone 886-1216. Overnight accommodations and restaurant service are available. Groceries and other supplies and banking services are available. Transient moorage available at Metlakatla boat harbor; marine gas at Union fuel dock, marine repairs available at cannery in season.

Metlakatla was founded in 1887 by William Duncan, a Scottish-born lay minister, who moved here with several hundred Tsimshian Indians from a settlement in British Columbia after a falling out with church authorities. Congress granted reservation status and title to the entire island in 1891 and the new settlement prospered under Duncan, who built a salmon cannery and sawmill. Today, fishing and lumber continue to be the main economic base of Metlakatla. The community and island also retain the status of a federal Indian reservation, which is why Metlakatla is allowed to have fish traps.

This well-planned community has a town hall, a recreation center with an Olympic-size swimming pool, well-maintained wood-frame homes, a post office, the mill and cannery. The Metlakatla Indian Community is the largest employer in town, with retail and service trades the second largest. Many residents also are commercial fishermen. Subsistence activities remain an important source of food for residents, who harvest seaweed, salmon, halibut, cod, clams and waterfowl.

Attractions include the Duncan Museum, the original cottage occupied by Father William Duncan until his death in 1918. A replica of the turn-of-the-century William Duncan Memorial Church, built after the original was destroyed by fire in 1948, is also open to the public.

Communications include phones, daily mail plane from Ketchikan, radio and TV. There are several churches and both elementary and high schools. The City of Metlakatla provides electric power, water and sewage systems. Freight arrives by barge. Government address: City of Metlakatla, P.O. Box 8, Metlakatla, AK 99926; phone 886-4868.

Meyers Chuck

Located on the northwest tip of Cleveland Peninsula off Clarence Strait, 40 miles northwest of Ketchikan. **Transportation:** Floatplane or private boat. **Population:** 52. **Zip code:** 99903. **Emergency Services:** Police and hospital in Ketchikan; Volunteer Fire Department.

Elevation: Sea level. **Climate:** No official records exist for Meyers Chuck. Residents say it's cool and rainy, with temperatures usually ranging from 20° to 40°F, with a few weeks of 0° to 20°F weather in winter.

Private Aircraft: Seaplane base with sheltered anchorage and dock.

Visitor Facilities: Accommodations at local lodge, or visitors may arrange for food and lodging in private homes. Some general merchandise and marine gas, diesel and regular gasoline are available. Fishing/hunting licenses may be purchased at the market. Banking services, laundromat and rental transportation are not available. Open moorage available at the community dock.

The early history of Meyers Chuck is a bit hazy, although records suggest that white settlers began living here in the late 1800s, and the community was probably named after one of these early residents. (The name, too, is a bit hazy; there has been some argument whether it was Meyer, Myer, Myers or Meyers. Longtime resident Leo C. "Lone Wolf" Smith favored Myers Chuck. "Chuck" is a Chinook jargon word, usually applied to a saltwater body that fills at high tide.)

The natural harbor and the large Union Bay cannery nearby — which operated from 1916 to 1945 — attracted fishermen to the townsite in the 1920s and postal service began in 1922. Today, most residents make their living fishing and supplement their income by working outside the community or depend on subsistence. There is good fishing for salmon, crab, clams, red snapper and halibut. There is deer and duck hunting and also trapping. Several retired people also make their homes here. There is not much here in the way of traditional tourist attractions. The chief attractions, according to Robert Meyer, are "the lovely sunsets and scenery."

Communications include phones, mail plane, radio and TV (via satellite dish). The Meyers Chuck School, which also serves as a community center, has approximately 9 students enrolled in grades kindergarten through 12. Most households have their own electrical generators and heat with wood. There is a community water system but no public sewage disposal; households are either on septic tanks or pipe sewage into the bay. Freight comes in by ship or plane. The village phone is 946-1234.

Pelican

Located on Lisianski Inlet on the northwest coast of Chichagof Island, 70 miles west of Juneau, 80 miles north of Sitka. **Transportation:** Scheduled air service from Juneau; charter air service available from other points; state ferry service in summer. **Population:** 247. **Zip code:** 99832. **Emergency Services:** Public Safety Officer, phone 735-2212; Clinic, phone 735-2250; Fire Department, phone 735-2212.

Elevation: Sea level. **Climate:** Winter temperatures range from 21° to 39°F, summer temperature from 51° to 62°F. Total average annual precipitation is 127 inches, with 120 inches of snow.

Private Aircraft: Seaplane base with sheltered anchorage and dock; fuel 80, 100.

Visitor Facilities: There are 2 bar-and-grills. One has 4 rooms to rent. The Corbins, who run fishing trips on their ketch, the *Demijohn,* have a fishing lodge rental cabin near Pelican. Groceries, hardware, first-aid supplies, camera film and fishing licenses are available, as are a laundry, showers and diesel, marine gas, propane and regular gasoline. Marine engine repair is available. No rental transportation available. Fishing guide service available. Transient moorage available at city harbor.

Established in 1938 by Kalle (Charley) Raataikainen, and named for his fish packer, *The Pelican,* Pelican's economy relies on commercial fishing and seafood processing. The cold storage plant processes salmon, halibut, crab, herring and black cod, and is the primary year-round employer. Pelican has dubbed itself "closest to the fish," a reference to its proximity to the rich Fairweather salmon grounds. Nonresident fishermen swell the population during the salmon trolling season, from about June to mid-September, and the king salmon winter season, from October through April. Pelican was incorporated in 1943. Most of Pelican is built on pilings over tidelands. A wooden boardwalk extends the length of the community and there are about 2 miles of gravel road.

Local recreation includes kayaking, hiking, fishing and watching birds and marine mammals. According to a local wag, special events here include the arrival and departure of the state ferry, the tide change, sunny days and a woman in a dress.

Chichagof Island boasts several attractions, such as abandoned mines and White Sulphur Hot Springs, where there is a Forest Service cabin. Across Lisianski Inlet from Pelican is the West Chichagof-Yakobi Wilderness of Tongass National Forest, a 265,000-acre area encompassing a 65-mile stretch of rugged Pacific Ocean coastline, a paradise for powerboat, sailboat and kayak enthusiasts.

Communications include phones, mail plane, radio courtesy of Raven Radio, Sitka 91-AM and TV. There is one church and a school with grades kindergarten through 12. Public electric power and water systems are available, but there is no public sewage system. Freight arrives by barge or on the state ferry in summer. Government address: City of Pelican, P.O. Box 757, Pelican, AK 99832; phone 735-2202.

Petersburg

Located on the northwest tip of Mitkof Island at the northern end of Wrangell Narrows, midway between Juneau and Ketchikan. **Transportation:** Daily scheduled jet service from major Southeast cities; local flights and charter air service; scheduled state ferry service. **Population:** 3,282. **Zip code:** 99833. **Emergency Services:** Alaska State Troopers, phone 772-3100; City Police, Ambulance and Fire Department, phone 772-3838; Hospital, phone 722-4291.

Elevation: Sea level. **Climate:** Maritime, wet and cool.

Private Aircraft: Petersburg airport, 1 mile southeast; elev. 107 feet; length 6,000 feet; asphalt; fuel 100, jet A; ticket counter and waiting room. Petersburg seaplane base has sheltered anchorage, dock, and fuel 80, 100.

Visitor Facilities: Accommodations available at downtown and area hotel, motel and inns, a bed-and-breakfast and at local campgrounds. Petersburg has several restaurants, a laundromat, public bathhouse, 2 banks, grocery stores, marine and fishing supply stores, hardware stores, drugstores, gas stations and gift shops. Fishing/hunting licenses are sold at several outlets and charter fishing trips are available locally. Major engine repair and all types of fuel are also available. There are 3 car rental agencies, 4 air charters, and several outfits offering boat rentals. Transient moorage available at city harbor.

Petersburg's attractions include the Sons of Norway Hall, built in 1912 and on the National Register of Historic Places; Clausen Memorial Museum, with its collections of local historical items; its busy waterfront, Scandinavian decorations, neatly laid-out streets and spectacular scenery. The big event of the year is the Little Norway Festival, held usually on the weekend closest to Norwegian Independence Day (May 17), when residents and visitors celebrate the community's heritage with costumes, dancing, contests and a big fish bake.

The community has all communications and public utilities. There are more than a dozen churches in Petersburg and both elementary and high schools. Freight arrives by barge, ferry or cargo plane. Government address: City of Petersburg, P.O. Box 329, Petersburg, AK 99833; phone 772-4511.

For more information see *The MILEPOST®*, a complete guide to communities on Alaska's road and marine highway systems. To order, see the ALASKA NORTHWEST LIBRARY section at the back of the book.

Point Baker

Located at the northwest tip of Prince of Wales Island, 50 miles west of Wrangell. **Transportation:** Private boat or charter plane. **Population:** 108. **Zip code:** 99927. **Emergency Services:** Alaska State Troopers in Petersburg; hospital in Wrangell; trained emergency technicians in Point Baker.

Elevation: Sea level. **Climate:** Like other Prince of Wales Island communities, a maritime climate with cool, wet, cloudy weather.

Private Aircraft: Seaplane float in harbor.

Visitor Facilities: No accommodations and limited services for visitors. There are a bar, restaurant and laundry. Groceries, liquor, ice, gas and diesel are available. Fishing/hunting licenses and rental boats are available at the trading post. Transient moorage at the state-operated floats.

Point Baker was named by Capt. George Vancouver in 1793 for the second lieutenant on his ship Discovery. Fish buyers operated here from about 1919 through the 1930s. The Forest Service opened the area for homesites, then in 1955 withdrew the townsite from Tongass National Forest. Most of Point

Early morning look outside the tent shows a clear, sunny day in Glacier Bay National Park and Preserve. Visitors to Glacier Bay often see brown and black bears along gravel beaches as well as the rare glacier bear, bluish in color. (George Wuerthner)

Baker's year-round residents are fishermen, and the population increases in summer with visiting fishermen. Halibut and salmon fishing is excellent in the area and residents also hunt for deer. Humpback whales pass by Point Baker and the bird life here includes eagles and blue herons.

Communications include mail plane, radio and TV. The trading post has the only phone. Residents take care of their own electric power and sewage, and get their water either from collecting rain water or from streams, although there is a freshwater hose at the dock. Freight arrives by plane or barge.

Port Alexander

Located on the south end of Baranof Island, 5 miles northeast of Cape Ommaney on the west side of Chatham Strait, 65 miles south of Sitka, 90 miles west of Wrangell. **Transportation:** Private boat or charter plane. **Population:** 128. **Zip code:** 99836. **Emergency Services:** Alaska State Troopers and hospital in Sitka; emergency technicians in Port Alexander.

Elevation: 20 feet. **Climate:** Average summer temperatures range from 41° to 55°F; winter temperatures from 32° to 45°F. Record high was 80°F in June 1958; record low 4°F in January 1953. Average annual precipitation is 172 inches, with October the wettest month.

Private Aircraft: Seaplane base. Sheltered anchorage and dock.

Visitor Facilities: Limited groceries, gas and diesel, and fishing/hunting licenses are available. One bed-and-breakfast offers lodging, but there are no other visitor accommodations or services here. Residents purchase supplies cooperatively from either Wrangell or Sitka. Public moorage at state floats (inner and outer harbors).

Port Alexander evolved into a year-round fishing community in the 1920s, settled by fishermen who trolled the Chatham Strait fishing grounds. In its heyday, Port Alexander's protected harbor was filled with up to 1,000 fishing boats at a time. The community prospered until the late 1930s, when the decline in salmon and herring stocks and the outbreak of WWII knocked the bottom out of fish buying, packing and processing at Port Alexander. Today, the majority of residents are commercial fishermen who choose to live here for the independent and subsistence lifestyle the area offers. Port Alexander was incorporated in 1974.

Communications include phones, a twice-weekly mail plane and radio. Port Alexander has a community water system, but electrical power and sewage systems are provided by individual households. The school, located next to Bear Hall community center, has grades kindergarten through 9. Port Alexander prohibits the sale of alcoholic beverages. Freight arrives by plane or barge. Government address: City of Port Alexander, P.O. Box 8725, Port Alexander, AK 99836; phone 568-2211.

Port Protection

Located at the northwest tip of Prince of Wales Island near Point Baker, 50 miles west of Wrangell and southwest of Petersburg. **Transportation:** Private boat or charter plane. **Population:** 55. **Zip code:** 99950. **Emergency Services:** Alaska State Troopers in Petersburg; hospital in Wrangell; emergency technicians in Port Protection.

Elevation: Sea level. **Climate:** Like other Prince of Wales Island communities, a maritime climate with cool, wet, cloudy weather. According to one resident, "the summers are nice and the winters are not."

Private Aircraft: Floatplane landings only.

Visitor Facilities: Food and lodging available in a private home, call 489-2212. Groceries, some clothing, first-aid supplies, hardware, film and sporting goods, along with gas and diesel are available. No banking services. Laundromat, public showers are available. Limited boat repair and boat rentals are available. Fishing/hunting licenses are available. Guide service may be arranged. Transient moorage at public float.

Like its neighbor, Point Baker, Port Protection was used as a fish-buying station and later settled by fishermen who had long used the cove for shelter from southeast storms. Credit for its "discovery" is given to a man named Johnson, who came ashore in the early 1900s to replace a wooden wheel lost off his boat and gave the spot its first name — Wooden Wheel Cove. In the late 1940s, Laurel "Buckshot" Woolery established a trading post and fish-buying station. The residents are either fishermen or retirees. Each household has at least one small boat, in addition to fishing vessels, to travel between homes in Port Protection and to Point Baker to pick up mail.

Excellent fishing in the immediate area in summer for salmon, halibut and rockfish. Boaters, kayakers and canoeists can make Port Protection their starting point for circumnavigating Prince of Wales Island. The community's 2 big local events are Fourth of July and the end-of-fishing-season barbecue.

Communications include phones; CB radios are used by most households. Port Protection also receives radio and TV reception. A school offers grades kindergarten through 12. Residents have their own generators for power or use kerosene for lighting. Wood-burning stoves provide heat. Springs, streams and rain water are the water supply, with some residents using individual gravity-flow water systems to pipe in water from uphill streams. Sewage system is outdoor privies or outfall pipes into the cove. Freight comes in by barge.

Saxman

Located 2 miles south of Ketchikan. **Transportation:** Road from Ketchikan. **Population:** 309. **Zip code:** 99901. **Emergency Services:** Alaska State Troopers and hospital in Ketchikan; Fire Department, phone 225-1981.
Elevation: Sea level.
Visitor Facilities: Virtually all facilities are available in nearby Ketchikan. Saxman has a fast-food restaurant, gas station and seasonal gift shop. There is no public boat dock or boat gas; no seaplane dock. There is a city-owned seaport.

The town's major attraction is Saxman Totem Park, which contains the largest collection of totem poles in the world. Saxman is also home to the Beaver Clan House which is the only clan house built in Alaska in the last 50 years. Constructed of hand adzed cedar, it features artwork by Tlingit artist Nathan Jackson. The local gift store specializes in Native and Alaskan handmade goods. The park is open year-round. Admission is charged. Also in summer, Native artists can usually be seen in various parts of Saxman, carving totems, weaving spruce baskets, or doing beadwork. Government address: City of Saxman, Route 2, Box 1, Saxman, AK 99901; phone 225-4166.

Sitka

Located on the west side of Baranof Island, 95 miles southwest of Juneau. **Transportation:** Scheduled jet service, commuter and charter flights; state ferry service. **Population:** 8,102. **Zip code:** 99835. **Emergency Services:** Alaska State Troopers, police, ambulance and fire department, phone 911; Hospital, phone 747-3241.
Elevation: Sea level. **Climate:** Maritime, with cool summers (55°F daily temperature in July) and mild winters (33°F in January). Annual precipitation, 96 inches.
Private Aircraft: Sitka airport on Japonski Island; elev. 21 feet; length 6,500 feet; asphalt;

fuel 80, 100, jet A-50. Sitka seaplane base adjacent; fuel 80, 100. Passenger terminal at airport.
Visitor Facilities: Overnight accommodations available at 5 hotels, 3 lodges, 7 bed-and-breakfasts, a youth hostel in town and a U.S. Forest Service campground 8 miles north of town. The downtown area has an array of businesses, including restaurants, laundromats, banks, drugstore, clothing and grocery stores and gift shops. Fishing/hunting licenses are sold at several outlets. Local charter operators offer sportfishing trips and there are 2 registered hunting guides. Major engine repair, rental transportation and all types of fuel available. Transient moorage available at the city float.

Sitka's Russian and Tlingit past is the major attraction for visitors. Replicas of the old Russian Blockhouse and St. Michael's Cathedral (rebuilt from original plans after a fire in 1966), and the original Russian Bishop's House (built in 1842), are open to the public. Sitka National Historical Park preserves the community's Russian and Tlingit heritage. Here a fine collection of totem poles is set among majestic spruce and hemlocks on a trail to the fort site. In mid- and late summer blueberries and huckleberries ripen along this trail. Museums in town include the Sheldon Jackson Museum on the campus of Sheldon Jackson College and the Isabel Miller Museum located in the Centennial Building.

The city has all communications and public utilities. There are more than a dozen churches, 3 elementary schools, a junior high school and high school. Freight comes in by barge and cargo plane. For visitor information contact: Sitka Convention and Visitors Bureau, P.O. Box 1226, Sitka, AK 99835; phone 747-5940. Government address: City and Borough of Sitka, 304 Lake St., Room 104, Sitka, AK 99835; phone 747-3294. Native corporation address: Shee-Atika, Inc., P.O. Box 1949, Sitka, AK 99835; phone 747-3534.

For more information see *The MILEPOST®*, a complete guide to communities on Alaska's road and marine highway systems, and *Sitka and Its Ocean/Island World*, Vol. 9 No. 2 of the *ALASKA GEOGRAPHIC®*. To order, see the ALASKA NORTHWEST LIBRARY section at the back of the book.

Skagway

Located at the north end of Taiya Inlet on Lynn Canal, 90 air miles northwest of Juneau, 13 nautical miles from Haines, 100 road miles from the Alaska Highway. **Transportation:** Daily scheduled flights from Juneau and

Haines via local commuter services; charter air service; scheduled state ferry service; connected to the Alaska Highway by Klondike Highway 2. **Population:** 712. **Zip code:** 99840. **Emergency Services:** Police, phone 983-2301; Clinic, phone 983-2255; Fire Department and ambulance, phone 983-2300.

Elevation: Sea level.

Private Aircraft: Skagway airport adjacent west; elev. 44 feet; length 3,500 feet; asphalt, fuel 80, 100.

Visitor Facilities: There are 6 hotels/motels, 2 bed-and-breakfasts, several restaurants, cafes and bars, grocery, hardware and clothing stores, a laundromat, a bank, and many gift and novelty shops. City-owned RV park on waterfront. Rental cars are available. Propane, marine and automobile gas are available, as are major repair services. Transient boat moorage available at the city harbor.

A 6-block area of downtown Skagway is included in Klondike Gold Rush National Historical Park. The main street, Broadway, is lined with false-fronted buildings and boardwalks. Park Service rangers lead daily guided walks through downtown in summer, and a film and slide shows are offered at the visitor center. The Trail of '98 Museum, owned and operated by the citizens of Skagway, has an interesting collection of gold rush memorabilia. Also included in the historical park is the 33-mile-long Chilkoot Trail, the old gold rush route over the mountains to Lake Bennett, where early gold seekers built boats to take them down the Yukon River to the Klondike. The Chilkoot Trail attracts more than 2,000 hardy souls each summer.

The historic White Pass & Yukon Route Railroad provided train service between Skagway and Whitehorse until 1982 when it shut down operations. In the spring of 1988 it renewed operation as an excursion train to the summit of White Pass and back. The three-hour trip departs daily from Skagway during the summer. (See Railroads in the GENERAL INFORMATION section.)

Special events in the community include the annual Windfest held the third weekend in March; a large Fourth of July celebration; Hugs and Kisses, a 3.5-mile race held the last Saturday in August; and the Klondike Trail of '98 Road Relay from Skagway to Whitehorse held the third weekend in September.

Communications include phones, mail plane, radio and TV. There are 4 churches, an elementary school and a high school. There are community electric power, water and sewage systems. Freight arrives by ferry or barge and by road. Government address: City of Skagway, P.O. Box 415, Skagway, AK 99840; phone 983-2297.

For more information order *The MILEPOST®*, a complete guide to communities on Alaska's road and marine highway systems. To order, see the ALASKA NORTHWEST LIBRARY section at the back of the book.

Tenakee Springs

Located on the north shore of Tenakee Inlet on the east side of Chichagof Island, 50 miles northeast of Sitka. **Transportation:** Scheduled and charter air service; state ferry service. **Population:** 123. **Zip code:** 99841. **Emergency Services:** Alaska State Troopers in Juneau; Health aide, phone 736-2206; Volunteer Fire Department; Village Public Safety Officer, phone 736-2211.

Elevation: Sea level. **Climate:** Maritime, with cool summers (45° to 65°F) and mild winters (24° to 39°F). Total precipitation averages 69 inches a year.

Private Aircraft: Seaplane base with dock.

Visitor Facilities: Food and lodging available. Groceries, first-aid supplies, hardware, camera film, sporting goods, fishing/hunting licenses and laundromat available. No banking services. Fuel available includes marine gas, diesel and propane. There is a boat mechanic in town. There is no rental transportation. Tenakee Springs has one street — Tenakee Avenue — which is about 2 miles long and 4 to 12 feet wide. There are only 2 vehicles in town. Residents walk or use bicycles or 3-wheel motorbikes for transportation. Public moorage available at state-operated floats.

Tenakee's natural hot springs first drew early prospectors and miners, and by 1895 the springs were enlarged to accommodate the increasing number of visitors. Ed Snyder built a general store here in 1899 and a post office was established in 1903. A cannery operated sporadically at Tenakee from 1916 to the 1960s. Some residents still make their living fishing commercially, although most year-round residents are retirees. The community also sees an influx of summer visitors: tourists, commercial fishermen and pleasure boaters, and Juneau and Sitka residents who have summer homes here. Tenakee Springs was incorporated as a second-class city in 1971.

Tenakee's major attractions are its quiet isolation and its hot springs. The bathhouse is located on the waterfront and has posted times of use by men and women. There is a U.S. Forest Service trail that runs east 7.8

miles from Tenakee Springs along the shoreline of Tenakee Inlet to Coffee Cove. The area also offers beachcombing and hunting and fishing.

Communications include a few phones, daily mail plane, radio and TV. A new school offers grades kindergarten through 12. A large generator plant provides electrical service to most households. There are no water or sewage systems. Residents haul water from streams and households have their own privies. Freight comes in by seaplane, ferry and barge. Government address: City of Tenakee Springs, P.O. Box 52, Tenakee Springs, AK 99841; phone 736-2221.

Thorne Bay

Located on the east coast of Prince of Wales Island, 47 air miles northwest of Ketchikan, 42 road miles east of Craig. **Transportation:** Scheduled air service from Ketchikan; 60 road miles from Hollis (ferry port); private boat. **Population:** 525. **Zip code:** 99919. **Emergency Services:** Village Public Safety Officer, phone 828-3905; Alaska State Troopers in Klawock; Clinic, phone 828-3906; doctor in Craig; Volunteer Fire Department, phone 911. **Elevation:** Sea level. **Climate:** Maritime, with cool, moist weather and mild temperatures.

Private Aircraft: Seaplane base with sheltered anchorage and dock.

Visitor Facilities: Accommodations available at a 1-room motel, a floatel, 5 rental log cabins, and a bed-and-breakfast. Stores and services include a restaurant; auto and boat repair; grocery, liquor, sporting goods, gift and hardware stores; and fuel supply outlets (marine gas, diesel, propane, unleaded and regular gasoline available). Gifts include pine needle raffia baskets made locally. No banking services. Fishing/hunting licenses and charter trips available.

Thorne Bay was incorporated in 1982, making it one of Alaska's newest cities. The settlement began as a logging camp in 1962, when Ketchikan Pulp Co. (now Louisiana-Pacific) moved its operations from Hollis. Thorne Bay was connected to the island road system in 1974. Camp residents created the community — and gained city status from the state — as private ownership of the land was made possible under the Alaska Statehood Act. Employment here depends mainly on the lumber company and the U.S. Forest Service, with assorted jobs in local trades and services. The area has good access to hunting and saltwater and freshwater sportfishing.

Communications include phones, regular mail service, radio and cable TV. A new dock serves private boats and commercial fishing vessels, and a new concrete boat launch is slated for construction in 1990. The project will also include a fish cleaning station. There is 1 church and a school with grades kindergarten through 12. The community has electric power, water and sewage systems. Freight comes in by plane, barge, ship and truck. Government address: City of Thorne Bay, P.O. Box 19110, Thorne Bay, AK 99919.

Tokeen

Located on the west coast of El Capitan Island off Sea Otter Sound, 60 miles southwest of Wrangell, 30 miles northwest of Craig, 80 miles northwest of Ketchikan. **Transportation:** Charter air service or private boat. **Population:** 3. **Zip code:** 99950. **Emergency Services:** Alaska State Troopers in Klawock; hospital in Ketchikan.

Private Aircraft: Seaplane base, unattended.

Visitor Facilities: A store here carries some groceries, first-aid supplies, hardware, film, sporting goods and liquor. Limited emergency fuel available includes marine gas, diesel, and regular gasoline. No other visitor services or facilities available. Public moorage at float.

Tokeen once had a mink farm and a cold storage plant. Tokeen is now privately owned and operated as a store and commercial fishermen's stop. The settlement likely was established by the former residents of Old Tokeen in the late 1930s or early 1940s.

Old Tokeen, located on the northwest end of Marble Island, 7 miles to the northwest, once had Alaska's largest marble quarry. Nearly $2 million worth of marble was taken out between 1905 and 1932. Tokeen marble was used in the Federal Building in Fairbanks, the Capitol Building in Juneau, Washington's state capitol in Olympia, WA, and in various other buildings around the country. Little remains of the mining operation except piles of waste marble.

Whale Pass

Located on the northeast cost of Prince of Wales Island on Whale Passage, 64 road miles north of Klawock. **Transportation:** By road from other Prince of Wales Island communities; floatplane or private boat. **Population:** 93. **Zip code:** 99950. **Emergency Services:** Alaska State Troopers. Physician in Klawock. **Elevation:** Sea level. **Climate:** Maritime, with cool, moist weather and mild temperatures.

Private Aircraft: Floatplane landings only.

Visitor Facilities: Accommodations are available and there is a small grocery store and a gas pump.

Whale Pass was the site of a floating logging camp. The camp moved out in the early 1980s, but new residents moved in after a state land sale. The community was connected to the Prince of Wales Island road system in 1985.

Wrangell

Located at the northwest tip of Wrangell Island on Zimovia Strait near the Stikine River delta, 154 miles south of Juneau and 90 miles north of Ketchikan. **Transportation:** Daily scheduled jet service from major Southeast cities and Seattle; daily commuter service to Ketchikan and Petersburg; air charter services; state ferry service. **Population:** 3,112. **Zip code:** 99929. **Emergency Services:** Alaska State Trooper, phone 874-3215; Police, phone 874-3304; Hospital, phone 874-3356; Ambulance, Rescue Squad and Fire Department, phone 874-2000.

Elevation: Sea level. **Climate:** Mild and moist with slightly less rain than other Southeast communities. Mean annual precipitation is 79.16 inches, with 63.9 inches of snow. Average daily maximum temperature in July is 61°F; daily minimum in January is 21°F.

Private Aircraft: Wrangell airport adjacent northeast; elev. 44 feet; length 6,000 feet; lighted asphalt runway; fuel 80, 100, A. Seaplane base adjacent south.

Visitor Facilities: There are 4 motels, a municipal campground and RV park; 7 restaurants, 2 fast-food outlets, gas stations, hardware, drugstore, grocery, clothing and sporting goods stores, gift shops, banks and a laundromat. Car rental, major repair service and all types of fuel are available. Fishing/hunting licenses may be purchased locally and there are several charter operations for fishing, hunting, Stikine River trips and glacier flightseeing. Transient moorage is available at the city harbor downtown and at Shoemaker Bay, 4.5 miles south of the city. A visitor information center is open during the summer.

Wrangell's history is featured at 3 local museums: Our Collections, Tribal House of the Bear on Chief Shakes Island and Wrangell Museum, housed in the oldest building in Wrangell.

Wrangell is home of Wrangell Forest Products, and the mill is open for tours each Friday during the summer season.

Celebrations and events include a salmon derby, held mid-May to early June; a big Fourth of July celebration; annual Coho and Halibut Derby on Labor Day weekend and Tent City Days, the first weekend in February which commemorates Wrangell's 3 gold rushes.

A variety of U.S. Forest Service roads lead to hiking trails, trout and steelhead streams and scenic overlooks. There are 23 Forest Service cabins available for public use by reservation in the Wrangell area. The most popular, the Anan cabin has plank trails to excellent black and brown bear observation posts during the pink salmon run from July through August.

For more information see Tongass National Forest Cabins, this section, or contact the Wrangell District Rangers office. The Forest Service has a courtesy phone at the Alaska Marine Highway ferry terminal to help facilitate visitor inquiries. The entire area has excellent salmon and halibut fishing, a large bald eagle population and outstanding scenery.

Wrangell has all communications and public utilities. There are a dozen churches, an elementary school and a high school. Freight arrives by ship, barge, ferry and cargo plane. Government address: City of Wrangell, P.O. Box 531, Wrangell, AK 99929; phone 874-2381.

For more information, see *The MILEPOST®*, a complete guide to communities on Alaska's road and marine highway systems. To order, see the ALASKA NORTHWEST LIBRARY section at the back of the book.

Yakutat

Located on Yakutat Bay on the Gulf of Alaska coast, where southeastern Alaska joins the major body of Alaska to the west; 225 miles northwest of Juneau, 220 miles southeast of Cordova. **Transportation:** Daily scheduled jet service; air charter; private boat. **Population:** 476. **Zip code:** 99689. **Emergency Services:** Alaska State Troopers, Police or Fire Department, phone 911; Clinic, phone 784-3391.

Elevation: Sea level. **Climate:** Maritime, with mild rainy weather. Average summer temperatures 42° to 60°F, with a record high of 86°F. Average winter temperatures 17° to 39°F, with a record low of -24°F. "Cloudiness is abundant," says one resident.

Private Aircraft: Yakutat airport, 3 miles southeast; elev. 33 feet; length 7,800 feet; asphalt; fuel 80, 100, A1+. Passenger and freight terminals; transportation to town available. Seaplane base 1 mile northwest; sheltered anchorage and dock.

Visitor Facilities: Meals and lodging available at 3 lodges and a bed-and-breakfast.

One lodge has kitchen units and a washer and dryer in the rooms. There also is a cafe and bar in town. All supplies are available at local businesses. There is a bank, but no public laundry. Fishing/hunting licenses may be purchased locally. Fishing guide services are available through local lodges and there are 5 registered hunting guides. Rental cars and charter aircraft are available. Marine gas, diesel, unleaded and regular gasoline are sold locally. Transient moorage at city harbor.

Yakutat Bay is one of the few refuges for vessels along this long stretch of coast in the Gulf of Alaska. The site was originally the principal winter village of the local Tlingit Indian tribe. Sea otter pelts brought Russians to the area in the 19th century. Fur traders were followed by gold seekers, who came to work the black sand beaches. Commercial salmon fishing developed in this century and the first cannery was built here in 1904. Today's economy is based primarily on fishing and fish processing. Salmon, black cod, halibut and crab make up the fishery. Government and local businesses employ most people. Timber harvesting is under way in the area. Subsistence activities are primarily fishing (salmon and shellfish), hunting (moose, bear, goats, ducks and small game) and gathering seaweed and berries. The soil is not suitable for agriculture and a vegetable garden requires a great deal of preparation to produce even small quantities.

The Yakutat City School District's infor-mation sheet for teacher applicants describes Yakutat's primary attraction as outdoor recreation. "If you enjoy the outdoors, there is plenty for you to do, including cross-country skiing, snowmobiling, hunting, fishing, hiking, biking and berry-picking in the late summer and early fall." Hunting and fishing in particular draw visitors. Steelhead fishing is considered among the finest anywhere, and king and silver salmon run in abundance in Yakutat area salt water, rivers and streams May through September. The Situk River, 12 miles south of Yakutat by road, is one of Alaska's top fishing spots. (See Sportfishing, this section.)

The surrounding scenery is also spectacular. Some Lower 48 travelers flying to Anchorage pick a flight with a Yakutat stop, hoping for a clear day and a clear view from the air of Malaspina Glacier northwest of town. Some cruise ships include Hubbard Glacier and Yakutat Bay in their itineraries. Nearer to town, Cannon Beach has good beachcombing and a picnic area.

Communications include phones in most households, a local radio station and 1 TV channel via satellite. Mail and newspapers are delivered daily by plane. There are 3 churches, an elementary school and a high school. Freight comes in by cargo plane or barge. Government address: City of Yakutat, P.O. Box 6, Yakutat, AK 99689; phone 784-3323. Native corporation address: Yak-tat Kwaan, Inc., P.O. Box 416, Yakutat, AK 99689.

Wide, smooth boardwalks make this Forest Service cabin accessible to the handicapped. At Lake Eva near Sitka, the cabin is reached via floatplane or skiff. (U.S. Forest Service)

▼ **A T T R A C T I O N S** ▼

National and State Parks, Forests, Etc.

Alaska Chilkat
Bald Eagle Preserve

This 48,000-acre state park located in the Chilkat River valley northwest of Haines was created in 1982 to protect the largest known congregation of bald eagles in North America. Each year, thousands of bald eagles come to this 5-mile stretch of the Chilkat River from October through January to feed on spawned-out chum salmon.

An upwelling of warm water usually prevents the Chilkat River from freezing over at its confluence with the Tsirku River near the village of Klukwan. The open water and the late salmon run draw eagles from throughout southeastern Alaska and western Canada, and provide abundant food when other sources are low. As many as 3,500 eagles have gathered here during peak times in November and hundreds stay into January. Extremely cold weather, which will freeze the open water, may force the eagles to leave at any time.

Alaskan bald eagles are slightly larger than those found in the continental United States. Adults have the characteristic white head and tail feathers and piercing yellow eyes; immature birds usually are mottled brown and white and sometimes are confused with golden eagles. Wingspan of these birds is 66 to 80 inches; average weight is 12-1/2 pounds, with females slightly larger than the males.

Bald eagles can fly at 30 mph and dive at 100 mph. They can see fish in the water at a distance of more than half a mile. Their basic diet consists of fish, although they do feed on waterfowl, small mammals and carrion when food is in short supply. Preferred habitat for these birds is in old-growth stands of timber along coastal shorelines. It is easy to spot them perched high in trees, sitting on rocks on beaches or soaring on the winds.

The gathering of eagles takes place within sight of the Haines Highway, which parallels the river. The heaviest concentration of eagles occurs between Milepost 17 from Haines and Milepost 22. This core area was set aside in 1972 as the Chilkat River Critical Habitat Area, 10 years before the protective area was enlarged and the larger area designated a preserve. Activities permitted within the preserve include hunting, fishing, trapping, berry-picking and picnicking — as long as the eagles are not disturbed. The eagles have adjusted to the noise along the highway, but they become greatly agitated and will take flight if approached too closely and without cover of trees and bushes. State land surrounding the preserve is part of the Haines State Forest Resource Management Area, in which logging, mining and other development is permitted. In the vicinity of Klukwan, much of the easily accessible land is Native-owned and should be treated as private property.

There are no visitor facilities in the perserve. The park office provides a list of commercial guides for permitted activities in the area, including river raft trips, photography and natural history tours. Rental cars and bus transportation, all other visitor facilities and guide services are available in Haines. There are pullouts along the highway from which to view and photograph eagles (telephoto lenses are recommended; best light between 10 a.m. and 2 p.m.); heavy truck traffic makes it unsafe to park or walk along the roadway. Visitors should also avoid walking out on the mud flats for their own safety and to avoid disturbing the eagles. Visitors should note that weather during the peak gathering times can be rainy, windy and/or snowy. Permits are required to build temporary blinds and other activities in the preserve.

Haines is accessible via the Haines Highway from the north, the Alaska Marine

Highway System from the south, and scheduled airlines from Juneau. For additional information on the park contact: Alaska State Parks, 400 Willoughby Ave., Juneau, AK 99801; phone 465-4563.

Chilkat State Park

Located south of Haines on the Chilkat Peninsula, Chilkat State Park offers spectacular views and excellent recreational opportunities. The 6,045-acre park consists of 2 sections. The northern unit, about 3,000 acres, includes Battery Point which was known as the Battery Point State Recreation Area until 1975 when the legislature added the 3,090-acre southern part and changed the name to Chilkat State Park.

Climate: In general, area weather is clearer and drier than in other areas of Southeast with warmer summers and colder winters. Average annual precipitation at Haines is 53 inches compared to 91 inches in Juneau. In winter, the coldest temperature recorded in Haines was -17°F but on sunny summer days, it is not uncommon for temperatures to rise to 80°F.

Wildlife: Within the park boundaries, animal populations include black bear, moose, eagles, grouse, coyotes and wolverine. On occasion, a brown bear may be encountered. In the waters surrounding the park, visitors are likely to see humpback whale, seals, sea lions, porpoises, and occasionally killer whales. There is also an abundance of waterfowl, and anglers will find 5 species of salmon and Dolly Varden, char and cutthroat trout.

Access: Chilkat State Park is one of the few road-accessible parks in Southeast, located just 7 miles south of Haines on the Mud Bay Road. A small dock and concrete boat launch provide boat access to the park.

Accommodations: The park offers both developed and undeveloped campsites. Facilities include 32 units for RV campers with a 15-day camping limit. A $5 fee per night is charged for overnight camping. Annual decals may be purchased from the Alaska Division of Parks for $50. Picnic sites, toilets with handicap access, water and a shelter are also found in the park. Deeper into the park, one will find remote camping sites.

Activities: Several trails in the park offer scenic views of mountain peaks and glaciers or glimpses of passing humpback whales. Fishing, boating, beachcombing and camping are also popular as well as cross-country skiing and snowshoeing in winter. (See Southeast Trails in this section for more information on trails in the park.)

Hikers and campers are cautioned to be prepared for changes in weather, especially if hiking above tree line. Take extra food, warm clothing, map, compass, first-aid kit, knife, matches and sunglasses even on day hikes.

For more information contact Alaska Division of Parks and Outdoor Recreation, Southeast Region, 400 Willoughby, Juneau, AK 99801; phone 465-4563; or Haines District Office, phone 766-2292.

Glacier Bay National Park and Preserve

This 3.3-million-acre park is located 50 air miles west of Juneau near the northern end of the Alaska Panhandle. It is bordered by Icy Strait and Cross Sound on the south, the Pacific Ocean on the west and Canada on the north. The park contains some of the world's most impressive examples of tide water glaciers. Other major attractions are the bay itself, whales and other wildlife, the massive Fairweather Range and the vast, unspoiled outer coast.

According to legend, Tlingit Indians — ancestors of present-day residents of Hoonah — camped along the shores of Glacier Bay before the glaciers advanced. Captain James Cook sighted and named 15,300-foot Mount Fairweather in 1778. A French explorer, Jean Francois de la Perouse, made the first recorded landing in what is now the park at Lituya Bay on the outer coast in 1786.

Russians and Aleuts pursuing sea otters and prospectors looking for gold were the only visitors to the vast wilderness until the late 19th century. In 1879 naturalist John Muir, with a group of Indian companions, paddled a canoe into Glacier Bay from Wrangell. Muir returned in 1880 and again in 1890 when he built a cabin at what is now called Muir Point. Other scientists followed, and a few settlers homesteaded at nearby Gustavus.

In 1794, when Capt. George Vancouver sailed through Icy Strait, he charted but did not enter Glacier Bay. The bay then was just a slight indentation in a 4,000-foot-thick wall of ice which marked the terminus of a massive glacier flowing down 100 miles from the St. Elias Range. Almost 100 years later, when Muir built his cabin at Muir Point just north of Mount Wright, the terminus of Muir Glacier was just to the north, 35 miles from where Vancouver had seen it. Now the terminus has retreated more than 25 additional miles, leaving a broad bay and a long, narrow inlet.

Glacier Bay is an invaluable outdoor laboratory for scientists seeking to understand the dynamics of glaciers. It is possible to travel from the "little ice age" across 2 centuries of plant succession, seeing how ice-scoured land evolves by stages into mature coastal forest.

For summer visitors the boat excursion from park headquarters at Bartlett Cove up Glacier Bay to calving Margerie Glacier is like watching a time-lapse movie which condenses the centuries of glaciation and plant succession into a day. Leaving the dock, passengers watch vegetation along the shoreline change from moss-laden coastal hemlock forests to spruce forests as the boat chugs along. Spruce trees, in turn, give way to thickets of willow and alder in Muir Inlet, which is often full of floating pan ice and icebergs higher than the boat itself. Here and there the stumps of huge trees, buried by moraines centuries ago then exposed by erosion, stick out along a barren beach.

Glacier Bay National Park and Preserve encompasses 16 active tidewater glaciers, including several on the remote and seldom-visited western edge of the park along the Gulf of Alaska and Lituya Bay. Icebergs calved off the glaciers float in the waters of the bay.

Wildlife: A trip by water into the park's many fjords offers sightings of humpback and killer whales cutting the water with their tall dorsal fins, or hair seals poking their heads up to stare at passing boats. During late spring hundreds of seals haul out on floating ice to give birth to their pups.

A decline in the number of humpback whales using Glacier Bay for feeding and calf-rearing led the National Park Service to limit the number of boats visiting the bay between June and September. These regulations apply to all commercial fishing boats, private craft, cruise ships and excursion boats. Check with the National Park Service office for current regulations. *NOTE: The whales come to Glacier Bay for only one reason; to eat enough to store the fat needed to see them through the winter. They do not feed year-round. Do not disturb them.*

Along gravel beaches, brown/grizzly, black and occasionally rare glacier bears (the bluish color phase of the black bear) forage for food. On high rocky ledges mountain goats are often sighted. *CAUTION: Wildlife in the park is protected and hunting is not allowed. Firearms are prohibited within the park.* Backcountry users should be careful to avoid encounters with bears.

More than 225 bird species have been reported in the park. Among the more common are black oystercatchers, cormorants, guillemots, puffins, gulls and terns. Fishing for silver and king salmon, Dolly Varden, cutthroat trout and halibut is excellent in the bay. An Alaska fishing license is required; charter fishing trips are available in Gustavus.

Climate: The Glacier Bay visitor season runs from mid-May through mid-September. (The park is not closed the remainder of the year, but most visitor facilities and transportation are closed.) Gray days are typical, although rain usually is light and intermittent. May and June usually have the most sunshine. Rainfall generally increases as the summer progresses. Summer temperatures average 50°F, but can vary to extremes. Visitors should bring clothing for possible below-freezing temperatures no matter what the month. Also bring full rain gear — from head to foot. Layer clothing, with shirts and sweaters worn under a windproof, rainproof parka or jacket, so you can withstand a range of temperatures when outdoors. Alaska's infamous biting insects are very much in evidence at Glacier Bay; gnats and flies are generally worse than mosquitoes. Bring plenty of insect repellent.

Activities: Glacier Bay offers many opportunities for exploration by kayak, canoe or motorboat (caution is advised because storms are sudden and floating ice can overturn or fracture off without warning). Kayaks may be rented at Gustavus. Certain areas of the park offer excellent cross-country hiking and backpacking possibilities. Many peaks more than 10,000 feet high challenge the experienced mountaineer. There are few established trails, but camping and hiking are generally permitted throughout the park. (Some areas may have camping restrictions because of bear activity. Be sure to check for safe areas with park service personnel.)

Campers and kayakers can arrange to be dropped off by concession vessels originating in Bartlett Cove or Juneau. All campers arriving at Bartlett Cove are provided with an orientation on safety and camping procedures by a park naturalist. A campground with 25 sites is located near the lodge and park headquarters at Bartlett Cove; the campground is free and no reservations are required. Two nature trails radiate from Bartlett Cove.

Park naturalists lead hikes daily and board cruise ships and tour boats to answer questions and interpret the scenery and wildlife. There are exhibits at the lodge, the dock and the Gustavus airfield; films and slide-illustrated talks are scheduled daily. In the summer rangers are stationed up the bay and elsewhere in the park.

Access: No roads lead to Glacier Bay. Access is by scheduled airline or air charter to Gustavus, cruise ships and charter boats, private boats and kayak tours. Packaged tours to the park also are available.

Accommodations: Meals and lodging are available by advance reservation at Glacier Bay Lodge. The concessionaire operates a tour boat; a list of other charter operators can be obtained from the Park Service. Accommodations and meals also are available in Gustavus (see the BUYERS GUIDE at the back of the book). Gasoline and diesel fuel may be purchased at Bartlett Cove, where a good anchorage is available for boats. There are no other public facilities for boats within the park; Gustavus has a dock and small-boat harbor. *CAUTION: Do not attempt to navigate Glacier Bay without appropriate charts, tide tables and local knowledge.*

Selected books, maps, charts, guides and other publications are offered for sale at the park or through the mail by the Alaska Natural History Assoc., Glacier Bay National Park and Preserve, Gustavus, AK 99826. Write for a free price list. For additional information contact: Superintendent, Glacier Bay National Park and Preserve, Gustavus, AK 99826; phone 697-2230.

Related USGS Topographic Series maps: Mount Fairweather, Skagway and Yakutat.

Klondike Gold Rush National Historical Park

This park was authorized in 1976 by the United States and Canada to commemorate the Klondike Gold Rush of 1897-98. Highlight of this park is the 33-mile-long Chilkoot Trail, over which 20,000 to 30,000 hopeful gold seekers struggled during the gold rush. Parks Canada is creating a Chilkoot Trail National Historic Park. The park also includes a visitors center in Seattle (jumping-off point for the gold rush throngs), the 8-block historical district in Skagway, the townsite of Dyea (dai-YEE) and the White Pass trail.

The Chilkoot Trail had long been used by Indians as a trading route, then by explorers, prospectors and surveyors. By the time of the major Klondike gold strike, nearly 2,000 prospectors had already crossed into the Yukon River drainage.

In August 1896, George Washington Carmack and 2 Indian companions, Skookum Jim and Tagish Charlie, found gold in a tributary of the Klondike River, setting off one of the greatest gold rushes in history. Although most of the good claims were already staked by the time the rush got under way, that

didn't stop a horde of gold seekers, disheartened and out of work because of a severe, nationwide economic depression, from streaming to Seattle and other West Coast ports to book passage North.

In July 1897, the first boatloads of stampeders landed at Skagway and nearby Dyea. One year later, the population of Skagway had ballooned from a handful of homesteaders to approximately 15,000. The stampeders each spent an average of 3 months hauling their year's supply of goods over either the Chilkoot Trail or the longer White Pass trail to Lake Bennett, where they built boats to float the remaining 560 miles downriver to Dawson, the Klondike and (they hoped) their fortunes. The frenzied parade lasted until the newly built White Pass & Yukon Route reached Lake Bennett in the summer of 1899, supplanting the Chilkoot Trail. Then, it was over. The Chilkoot Trail was all but abandoned. Dyea became a ghost town; its post office closed in 1902 and its population in 1903 consisted of 1 settler. Skagway's population plummeted to 1,000 by 1905. But the memories, the relics and the historic buildings of those exciting days still remain.

Many buildings in Skagway have been restored. Boardwalks, false-fronted buildings and horse-drawn wagons help evoke the atmosphere of the town during the gold rush. The Skagway Convention and Visitors Bureau (P.O. Box 415, Skagway, AK 99840) is located in the city hall. The building, completed in 1899, is the first granite building in Alaska and was built originally as the McCabe College for women. The Arctic Brotherhood Hall has a much-photographed facade, made up of some 20,000 pieces of driftwood assembled in an intricate pattern. The park's visitor center is located in the refurbished railroad depot on 2nd Avenue and Broadway. It is open from 8 a.m. to 8 p.m. in the summer, when park rangers are on duty to provide information about the park. Anyone intending to hike the Chilkoot Trail should stop at this center to find out about such things as current trail conditions and customs requirements. Walking tours and other programs are presented by the center from mid-May through mid-September. Commercial tours are available by bus, taxi, aircraft and horse-drawn buggy.

In Seattle, an interpretative center (117 S. Main St., Seattle, WA 98104) has been established in Pioneer Square. This unit of the park explains the role of Seattle in the Klondike gold rush, and has exhibits of supplies sold to stampeders and newspaper stories of the day. A mannequin surrounded by food and equipment depicts the "ton of goods" each stampeder was required to have before he was allowed to enter Canada. (The so-called "ton of goods" actually amounted to roughly 1,150 pounds of food and about 400 pounds of other necessities for survival.) This center also has information to help in planning a trip on the Chilkoot Trail, including lists of recommended equipment and maps.

Chilkoot Trail. The trail was used primarily by men — hauling their goods on their backs until tramways were built — because it was too steep for pack animals. The White Pass trail, parts of which parallel the White Pass & Yukon Route and the Klondike Highway connecting Skagway with the Alaska Highway, was an animal killer. Prospectors overloaded and beat their pack animals and forced them over the rocky trail until they dropped. More than 3,000 animals died on this trail, many at the place called Dead Horse Gulch. This trail is not accessible by foot today.

The Chilkoot Trail begins above Dyea, about 8 miles from Skagway. Little is left of Dyea, which once rivaled Skagway as the largest town in Alaska, except some foundation ruins and several rows of piling stubs, remains of a 1.3-mile-long wharf that once extended to salt water. Most of the buildings were torn down and the lumber used elsewhere. Of more interest is the Slide Cemetery where some 60 victims of an avalanche in April 1898 lay buried, poignant reminders of the hardships and tragedies of the gold rush.

To reach the trailhead, drive out Dyea Road 6.7 miles. The trail begins at a bridge over the Taiya River across from the Dyea townsite. Cab service is available in Skagway to and from the trailhead. The 40-mile trail is marked and has several campsites and shelters. The hike is arduous — usually taking 3 to 5 days. This is not a trail that offers wilderness solitude. More than 2,000 hikers make the trip each year; the heaviest concentrations of visitors occur within several days after the arrival of an Alaska Marine Highway ferry at Skagway. Detailed information, brochures and maps of the trail are available from the National Park Service visitor center in Skagway (address below). Information is also available from the ranger station on Dyea Road near the trailhead.

The Chilkoot Trail is managed as a historic backcountry trail and follows the original trail where feasible. It is an outdoor museum. Do not disturb or remove any historical artifacts. All artifacts are protected under state, federal and provincial laws. The National Park Service requests you "leave nothing but footprints and take nothing but photographs."

The Park Service cautions that hikers must be properly equipped and prepared to be self-sufficient on this trail. Weather conditions can change rapidly from hour to hour, especially in the summit area. You must be prepared for cold temperatures, snow, rain, fog and wind. An inch of rain in 24 hours is not uncommon. Trail conditions below tree line are often rough, with deep mud, standing water, slick rocks and roots making footing tricky. Conditions along the 8 miles of trail above tree line are even more severe. High winds, driving rain, low temperatures, heavy fog and rocky terrain may make hiking this section extremely difficult. The Park Service recommends that hiking gear include, among other items, a tent with waterproof rain fly, sturdy hiking boots, rain gear, wool clothing, sunglasses, glacier cream and a small stove with adequate fuel (there is no wood in the summit area and campfires are not allowed on the Canadian portion). Camping gear and supplies are available in Skagway (Skagway Sports Emporium). Camping is permitted only in the 11 designated areas. If you bring a dog, it must be on a leash. If there are bears in any of the areas you travel, you do not want your dog chasing them . . . or bringing them back to you. Bear sightings should be reported to rangers at Sheep Camp (on the trail), or at Dyea or Skagway.

Current trail conditions are available from the ranger stations in Skagway, Dyea or Sheep Camp. Parks Canada wardens are available for assistance at Lindeman. Hikers must pre-clear Canadian customs by calling (403) 821-4111 prior to leaving Skagway. If returning to Skagway after hiking the trail, be sure to check in with U.S. customs. Contact the Park Service for more information.

The White Pass & Yukon Route Railroad offers twice daily service for Chilkoot Trail hikers from Lake Bennett to the customs office at Fraser. For $67 apiece hikers get to ride in a small casey car, a tracked vehicle normally used for repairs. From Fraser hikers can travel the 28 miles back to Skagway on the regular train. The casey car leaves Lake Bennett at 8:30 a.m. and 1:15 p.m. Hikers may also walk out. They can leave the trail just north of Bare Loon Lake at Mile 29 on the trail and walk to the railroad tracks, then follow the tracks out to the Klondike Highway and the Log Cabin. For information on the White Pass & Yukon Railroad, contact the White Pass Depot, P.O. Box 435, Skagway, AK 99840; phone 983-2217 or 800-343-7373.

The Chilkoot Trail has been called "the longest museum in the world." Along the way you'll see historic ruins and artifacts from the gold rush. Among the highlights are the following:

Finnegan's Point at Mile 4.9. This is reputed to be the site of a bridge across a creek built by Pat Finnegan and his 2 sons. The Finnegans charged a toll for use of the bridge until they were overwhelmed by the hordes of gold seekers. A restaurant operated intermittently at the site.

Canyon City at Mile 7.8. In 1897 and 1898 this was the fourth-largest settlement along the trail after Dyea, Lindeman and Sheep Camp. A year later it was gone.

Pleasant Camp at Mile 10.5. Site of a toll bridge (long since washed out) and a restaurant in 1897. As the best level spot north of Canyon City, it was a popular campsite.

Sheep Camp at Mile 13. In the summer and fall of 1897 some stampeders cached their goods here before ascending the final leg over the pass. A half-dozen businesses served the transient population.

The Scales at Mile 16. This was a weighing place for goods hoisted or packed over the pass. It is said that packers reweighed their loads here and charged a higher rate for the steep climb over the summit. Restaurants, saloons and bunkhouses served the stampeders, who cached or discarded their goods here for the final push across the pass.

The "Golden Stairs." This was the name by which the 45-degree climb from The Scales to the 3,739-foot summit became known. In the winter, steps were chopped into the snow; in late summer the snow melted and the route crossed large boulders. It took the stampeders approximately an hour per trip; some took as many as 30 trips to get their outfits across the pass.

At the summit, Mile 16.5, hikers crossed the border into Canada. In February 1898 the Royal Northwest Mounted Police established a customs station near here. They levied a duty on goods going into Canada and enforced a new rule requiring each person to carry a year's supply of food and supplies into the Yukon. The rule later prevented many stampeders from starving once they reached Dawson.

Stone Crib at Mile 17. Just above the shores of Crater Lake are the remains of the northern terminus of the Chilkoot Railroad and Transportation Co.'s aerial tramway. When it was completed in May 1898 this tramway looped 45 miles of metal cables along the 9 miles between Canyon City and Crater Lake, enabling stampeders to have their goods hauled for 7¢ per pound from Dyea to Lindeman City via wagon road and tramway. Within a year after its completion the tram system was purchased by the White Pass & Yukon Route and dismantled to avoid competition with the new railroad. The tramway towers have collapsed and their remains can be seen along the trail. The stone crib that anchored the end of the cable continues to crumble. Sections of the wagon road are followed by today's hikers.

Deep Lake at Mile 23. This was the site of a major freight transfer point. Goods were ferried across Long Lake in the summer, then transferred to horses at Deep Lake for the trip to Lindeman City.

Lindeman City at Mile 26. By the spring of 1898, this was a tent town of 10,000. Here stampeders built boats and prepared for their water journey through Lake Lindeman and Lake Bennett and down to Dawson. In a cemetery on a hillside, 11 stampeders are buried.

Bennett at Mile 33. Stampeders from both the White Pass and Chilkoot trails gathered here during the gold rush. The town's population swelled to 20,000 as they built boats along the shore of Lake Bennett and waited for the ice to leave the lake. There isn't much left at Bennett except some cabin sites and the shell of St. Andrews Presbyterian Church on the hill. The church was built during the winter and spring of 1899.

For additional information contact: Superintendent, Klondike Gold Rush National Historical Park, P.O. Box 517, Skagway, AK 99840; phone 983-2921. Also, Superintendent, Yukon National Historic Sites, 119-204 Rense Road, Whitehorse, YT, Y1A 3V1; phone (403) 668-2116.

Related USGS Topographic maps for Dyea to Chilkoot Pass: Skagway B-1 and C-1. Related Canadian topographic maps for Chilkoot Pass to Lake Bennett: White Pass 104M/11 East and Homan Lake 104M/14 East (for sale from Canada Map Office, Dept. of Energy, Mines and Resources, 615 Booth St., Ottawa, ON, Canada K1A 0E9.

Marine Parks

The state of Alaska has established 19 marine parks as part of an international system of shoreline parks and recreation areas stretching from near Olympia, WA, up through British Columbia, Canada, and as far north as Prince William Sound. Eventually there may be more than 150 of these parks, most a 1-day boat trip from each other. The majority of these parks have no developed facilities. Following is a list of the 12 marine parks located in southeastern Alaska; for more information contact Alaska Division of Parks, Southeast Region, 400 Willoughby Center, Juneau, AK 99801.

Chilkat Islands. Located 13 miles south of Haines, directly off the tip of the Chilkat Peninsula, which is part of Chilkat State Park. This 503-acre marine park includes 4 small, forested islands with several reasonably well-protected anchorages. The islands offer excellent kayaking, boating, fishing, beachcombing and camping.

Sullivan Island. Located in Lynn Canal approximately 19 miles south of Haines and 6 miles south of the Chilkat Islands. The park is on a 3-mile-long peninsula at the southern tip of the island. There is protected moorage within the area. Recreational activities include salmon and halibut fishing, picnicking, beachcombing and camping. The area also is popular for deer hunting.

St. James Bay. Located on the west side of Lynn Canal, 12 miles northwest of Tee Harbor (Juneau) and approximately 42 miles south of Haines. This bay is a recreational destination as well as an overnight stop for boaters traveling between Haines and Juneau. There are many protected beaches and tidal flats. Activities include boating, kayaking, fishing, beachcombing, hiking, camping and picnicking. The Alaska Dept. of Fish and Game has identified this bay as the best waterfowl habitat and hunting area on Lynn Canal. Black and brown bear and mountain goats occur in the area.

Shelter Island. Located 6 miles west of Tee Harbor and approximately 20 miles northwest of downtown Juneau. The park, located on the northcentral portion of the island, offers kayaking, boating, fishing, diving, beachcombing, picnicking, hiking and fall hunting for Sitka black-tailed deer.

Funter Bay. Located 30 miles from Juneau on the west side of Admiralty Island. The park offers one of the best protected anchorages in the area and is popular for hunting and fishing.

Oliver Inlet. Located 12 miles south of Juneau on Admiralty Island between Seymour Canal and Stephens Passage. Good protected moorages are available in both Oliver Inlet and Seymour Canal. Oliver Inlet is one end of an overland portage route for boaters entering Seymour Canal from Juneau and provides access to Admiralty Island National Monument. The area has a State Parks Division recreation cabin, a 1-mile narrow gauge

tramway and a registration/information station for the monument. Recreational activities include hunting, fishing, boating, kayaking, beachcombing and wildlife viewing and photography. Humpback and killer whales, seals, sea lions, porpoise, salmon, halibut, rock fish, Sitka black-tailed deer and brown bear inhabit this area.

The state public-use cabin may be rented for $15 per night. Reservations are required for the cabin and may be made by writing the Alaska Division of Parks and Outdoor Recreation, 400 Willoughby Ave., Juneau, AK 99801; phone 465-4563.

Taku Harbor. Located 19 miles south of Juneau. The 700-acre park provides a well-protected anchorage and is a popular weekend boating destination.

Security Bay. Located on Kuiu Island, 20 miles southwest of Kake, near the junction of Chatham Strait and Frederick Sound. This is an island-filled bay which offers protected anchorage.

Beecher Pass. Located 15 miles south of Petersburg at the junction of Duncan Canal and Wrangell Narrows. The 740-acre marine park is filled with inlets and reefs.

Joe Mace Island. Located near the community of Point Baker on the northern tip of Prince of Wales Island. Activities at the 62-acre marine park, which is surrounded by old-growth forest, include boating and fishing.

Thoms Place. Located in a cove 22 miles south of Wrangell, off Zimovia Strait. A trail leads from the 1,400-acre marine park to Thoms Lake, site of a state parks division cabin. The cabin may be rented for $20 per night. Reservations may be made by writing the Alaska Division of Parks and Outdoor Recreation, 400 Willoughby Ave., Juneau, AK 99801; phone 465-4563.

Dall Bay. Located 14 miles south of Ketchikan. The 850-acre marine park provides boaters a protected anchorage before venturing out of Nichols Passage into Clarence Strait.

Tongass National Forest

This national forest encompasses 16.8 million acres, or more than 73 percent of all the land in southeastern Alaska. Created in 1907 by President Theodore Roosevelt to protect the timber resources, wildlife and fisheries of Southeast, this is the largest national forest in the United States. Its name comes from the Tongass clan of Tlingit Indians, who lived on an island at the southern end of the forest.

The forest lies west of the U.S.-Canada border and stretches from Ketchikan north to

Cross Sound and up the eastern side of Lynn Canal. Excluded from the forest are Glacier Bay National Park and the general area around Haines and Skagway. Another section of the forest surrounds Yakutat. Like all national forests, this is managed as a working forest, with logging and mining activities taking place along with recreational pursuits and fishery management.

Tree line usually extends from sea level to about 3,000 feet in the southern part of the forest and to 1,800 feet farther north around Icy Strait. In the south, the forests are primarily western hemlock and Sitka spruce, with scattered red cedar and Alaska yellow cedar. In the north the percentage of hemlock increases and mountain hemlock becomes more abundant. Red cedar extends only to the northern shore of Frederick Sound and Alaska yellow cedar often is found only as a small tree in swamps or muskeg. Other common species are red alder, black cottonwood and lodgepole pine.

Beneath the towering conifers are young evergreens and shrubs such as devil's club, blueberry and huckleberry. Moss and ferns cover the ground, and lichens drape many trees. The dense forest is broken by muskeg bogs, glacial outwash plains and marshlands in river valleys and deltas. Wildflowers splash color against a variegated green background.

Wildlife: Sitka black-tailed deer and its 2 main predators, the wolf and the bear are found in the forest. Wolves and black bears range throughout the mainland and most islands, except Baranof, Chichagof and Admiralty. These 3 islands, plus the mainland, are home for enormous brown/grizzly bears. The blue, or glacier, bear (a color phase of the black bear) is seen occasionally near Yakutat. Mountain goats have been transplanted to Baranof and Revillagigedo islands, but their natural range is the alpine area of the mainland. Some moose inhabit the larger river drainages and the Yakutat area. A limited number of lynx, wolverines, foxes, mink and land otters range widely through the area. The forest also is home for smaller mammals, including shrews, red squirrels, brown bats, flying squirrels, deer mice, red-backed voles, porcupines and pine marten.

Blue grouse, great horned owls, woodpeckers, Steller's jays and thrushes are some of the common birds in the forests. Robins, fox sparrows, hummingbirds and swallows can be seen along the forest edge. More bald eagles live in this region than in any other place in the world. Large numbers of waterfowl, such as diving ducks, mallards, mergansers and Canada geese, and more than 50 species of seabirds, including terns, gulls, kittiwakes, auklets and murres, can be seen here.

Marine mammals found along the shores of the forest include Dall and harbor porpoises, hair seals and humpback, minke, sei and Pacific killer whales. Gray whales and northern fur seals pass by during migrations and an occasional elephant seal has been spotted. Waters of the region teem with fish, including halibut and 5 species of salmon. Also present are Dungeness, tanner and king crab, shrimp and butter clams.

Activities and Accommodations: Camping is permitted anywhere in the national forest unless it is a day-use area or there is a sign specifically prohibiting it, such as at an archaeological site. No permits or fees are required for wilderness camping. Fees are charged for some developed campgrounds. Contact any Forest Service field office for information. Practice minimum impact camping techniques. Because of the wet climate, backpacking stoves are recommended. If campfires are made, use only dead or down wood and make sure that any campfires are extinguished; forest fires can occur even in this rainy region. Pack out all unburnable trash. Much of the forest is bear country. Be alert and cautious. Do not camp on bear trails or near salmon streams, wear a bell or make noise when hiking and do not leave food in or near your tent. But bells and other noises are not guarantees against encounters. Avoid salmon streams during spawning and do not approach such areas from downwind. It is legal to carry firearms in the national forest for bear protection but you should be familiar with safe operation of the weapon. Rifles with a caliber larger than .30-06 are recommended.

Gathering forest resources was once a necessity. Today it is enjoyed as a recreational activity and can lead to understanding the forest ecosystem, as well as the region's pioneer heritage.

Opportunities for obtaining berries, firewood, Christmas trees, and other forest resources are found throughout Tongass National Forest and local communities. Some resources are best captured through photography, and plant and wildflowers throughout Southeast offer excellent opportunities for the photographer.

Visitors should exercise discretion in gathering plants, the Forest Service advises. Fragile alpine and meadow areas may harbor rare and possibly endangered species, and plant regeneraton may be very slow, if not impossible once the plants are gathered. A general rule of thumb is to leave 6 plants for every 1 plant picked and pick plants 100 feet or more from all roadways.

Good berry-picking is usually found in areas that do not have thick timber growth. Clear-cut units from previous logging activity are generally good locations.

The local Forest Service office should be contacted prior to gathering firewood or cutting Christmas trees to show the areas where these activities are permitted.

You should know edible plants well before picking. There are at least 2 poisonous plants in Southeast (baneberry and poison hemlock) and visitors gather wild plants at their own risk. Permits are not required for Forest Service managed lands.

Two guidebooks that are helpful in the gathering of wild plants are *Alaska's Wilderness Medicines* — A natural history guide to Alaskan plants which can be used to promoted health and healing, for first-aid emergency care or to maintain wellness. More than 50 plant species are covered in this thorough guide; and *Discovering Wild Plants* — with 190 color photos and detailed black-and-white drawings of 147 plants (including wildflowers, trees, shrubs, berries, lichens, mosses, algae and fungi). Includes historical facts and legends, and explanations for plant use as medicinal remedies, massages, baths, rubs, and includes delicious recipes for wild foods. Both guidebooks are available from Alaska Northwest Books, see ALASKA NORTHWEST LIBRARY section at the back of the book.

The U.S. Forest Service maintains some 150 cabins (see chart, page 85) in Southeast which are available by advance reservation. The current fee is $15 per party per night. The fee increases to $20 July 1, 1990. Check with any Forest Service office for exact costs. Many Southeast communities have Forest Service offices which will provide information on local places to camp and hike (a list of trails follows). The Forest Service operates road-accessible campgrounds for tents and trailers at Juneau, Ketchikan, Sitka and Petersburg. For additional information contact: Tongass National Forest, Regional Office, P.O. Box 21628, PAO, Juneau, AK 99802; phone 586-8806.

Timber harvest has taken place in this region since before the Tongass National Forest was established. All but a small percentage has occurred since 1950. Out of the 16.8 million acres encompassed by the national forest, about 5 million acres have been identified as commercial forest, with about 2 million acres of that considered available for harvesting. Another 5.3 million acres has been set aside as wilderness in 2 national monuments and 12 designated wilderness areas, most of which are remote and accessible only by boat or aircraft.

Wilderness areas within Tongass National Forest were established by President Jimmy Carter on Dec. 2, 1980, under the Alaska National Interest Lands Conservation Act, which set aside nearly 103 million acres throughout the state as national parks, wildlife refuges, wilderness areas, wild and scenic rivers and other conservation areas.

Wilderness classification directs that these areas be managed to retain their natural qualities, unmarked by works of man. However, there are some exceptions because of Alaska's terrain: Motorized vehicles such as airplanes, boats and snow machines may be used for access to and within some of the wilderness areas. Also, because of the climate, existing shelter cabins were allowed to remain and others may be built for public safety. Fishing, hunting and trapping are allowed, subject to state regulations. Check with the local Forest Service office for the most up-to-date regulations.

Descriptions of the 14 wilderness areas within the Tongass National Forest, from north to south, follow:

Russell Fiord Wilderness. Located 25 miles northeast of Yakutat between the rugged Fairweather Range and the Brabazon Range. The most dramatic features of this 348,701-acre area are the heavily glaciated Russell Fiord, which extends more than 35 miles inland from Disenchantment Bay, and Nunatak Fjord, a narrow, 15-mile channel off Russell Fiord to the southeast.

Russell Fiord made headlines in 1986 when it was dammed by advancing Hubbard Glacier. The ice dam eventually weakened and broke, but scientists predict the glacier will close off the fjord again soon. There are numerous active glaciers above the fjords and the area is scientifically important for its record of recent geological events, post-glacial ecological succession and the effects of frequent earthquakes. Vegetation ranges from heavily forested river channels to alpine meadows. Situk Lake and the headwaters of the Situk Wild and Scenic River Study Area are within the wilderness area.

Wildlife includes mountain goats, wolves, brown and black bear, numerous furbearers, harbor seals, sea lions, shorebirds, songbirds, waterfowl and bald eagles. Fisheries are fairly limited, with the exception of lower Russell

Fiord and the headwaters of the Ahrnklin River.

Access is by floatplane from Juneau, 200 miles to the southeast, or by plane or boat from Yakutat, which has overnight accommodations and scheduled commercial air service. There also is limited access to within 2 miles of the area by road from Yakutat. There are 2 Forest Service cabins within this wilderness.

For information contact: Tongass National Forest, Chatham Area, 204 Siginaka Way, Sitka, AK 99835; phone 747-6671. Related USGS Topographic maps: Yakutat, Mount St. Elias.

Endicott River Wilderness. Located on the Chilkat Peninsula, on the west side of Lynn Canal, 45 miles northwest of Juneau and 30 miles south of Haines. The western alpine portion of this 98,729-acre area abuts Glacier Bay National Park for about 40 miles. This area is rugged, extending from sea level to elevations up to 5,280 feet. The Endicott River is the central feature of this wilderness area. It heads in broad, brush-covered flats within the Chilkat Mountains and flows easterly through a deep, glacially carved canyon. Glaciers cover the highlands of the upper valley. The vegetation is typical southeastern Alaska spruce and hemlock rain forest at lower elevations, and brush, small trees and alpine plants higher up. Average annual precipitation is 92 inches, highest in the fall and lowest April through June.

Wildlife includes black and brown bears, mountain goats and a limited number of moose. Hundreds of bald eagles may be seen along the river during salmon runs; a high number of eagles nest here also. Some deer may be present. Fish in the Endicott River include chum, coho and pink salmon.

Access is primarily by boat from Juneau or Haines to the confluence of the Endicott River and Lynn Canal, then by foot 2.5 miles to the eastern boundary of the wilderness. Boat access is best in spring and summer due to winter storms in Lynn Canal. There is limited wheel plane access near the headwaters of the Endicott River. There are no facilities in this wilderness.

For more information contact: Tongass National Forest, Chatham Area, 204 Siginaka Way, Sitka, AK 99835; phone 747-6671. Related USGS Topographic maps: Juneau.

West Chichagof-Yakobi Wilderness. This 264,747-acre wilderness occupies the western portions of Chichagof and Yakobi islands in the extreme northwest portion of the Alexander Archipelago of southeastern Alaska. It is a few miles west of Pelican and 30 miles north of Sitka.

The most dramatic feature of this area is the 65-mile-long stretch of rugged Pacific coastline, with exposed offshore islands and rocky highlands. Behind the barrier islands, rocks and reefs of the outer coast lie the quiet waters of a scenic inside passage, honeycombed with bays, inlets and lagoons. There are quiet tidal meadows and estuaries and steep mountains with peaks to 3,600 feet that rise out of the ocean. Western hemlock and Sitka spruce forests cover about one-third of the area and there are scattered lodgepole pines and cedar. Offshore islands support savanna glades under open spruce cover, and there is scattered alpin terrain, muskeg and estuaries. Hiking can be difficult in upland meadows because of downed logs, holes and hidden streams.

Wildlife includes Sitka black-tailed deer, brown bear, numerous furbearers, sea otters, sea lions and seals. The area is wonderful for boaters and kayakers. Strong winds off the Pacific Ocean can be dangerous in exposed stretches.

Access is by charter boat from Pelican or Sitka or chartered floatplane from Sitka or Juneau. The coastal area has excellent moorage and landing sites for boats and planes. There are 3 very popular Forest Service cabins, located at Goulding Lake, Lake Suloia and White Sulphur Springs, which also has a bathhouse overlooking Bertha Bay. (See Tongass National Forest Cabins in this section.)

For additional information contact: Tongass National Forest, Chatham Area, 204 Siginaka Way, Sitka, AK 99835; phone 747-6671. Related USGS Topographic maps: Sitka, Mount Fairweather.

Admiralty Island National Monument. Located about 15 miles west of Juneau, this monument encompasses 937,396 acres, or 90 percent of Admiralty Island. The island is bounded on the east and north by Stephens Passage, on the west by Chatham Strait and on the south by Frederick Sound.

The predominantly Tlingit Indian village of Angoon lies at the mouth of Mitchell Bay on the west side of Admiralty Island, adjacent to the wilderness. Excluded from the monument are mining interests at the north end of the island and east of Angoon. The terrain of most of the island is gentle and rolling, with spruce-hemlock forest interspersed with small areas of muskeg. Tree line generally is at 1,500 to 2,000 feet. Above timberline the forest changes to alpine-tundra with rock outcrops and ice fields. Annual precipitation is 100 inches over most of the island, although Angoon, in the rain shadow of Baranof Island, is drier.

Wildlife on the island includes giant brown bears (the Indians referred to the area as the "Fortress of Bears"), Sitka black-tailed deer, bald eagles, harbor seals, whales and sea lions.

Outstanding areas are the numerous bays and inlets. Seymour Canal, the major inlet on the east side of the island supports one of the largest concentrations of bald eagles in southeastern Alaska. Mitchell Bay and Admiralty Lakes Recreational Area are the 2 major recreational attractions within the monument. A 25-mile trail system links the 8 major lakes on the island and is part of the Cross-Admiralty canoe trail, which consists of a series of lakes, streams and portages across the island from Mole Harbor on the east to Mitchell Bay. Kayaking and canoeing around the island is popular, as is hunting, fishing, bird-watching, nature study and photography.

Primary access to the monument is by boat from Juneau or Angoon or floatplane from Juneau. Wheeled planes are allowed to land on beaches. There are overnight accommodations at Angoon. Facilities in the monument include 1 commercial lodge on Thayer Lake, and 7 trail cabins and 12 recreation cabins maintained by the Forest Service. (See Tongass National Forest Cabins in this section.)

For additional information contact: Admiralty Island National Monument, P.O. Box 2097, Juneau, AK 99803; phone 789-3111. Related USGS Topographic maps: Juneau, Sitka, Sumdum.

Tracy Arm-Fords Terror Wilderness. Located 50 miles southeast of Juneau and 70 miles north of Petersburg adjacent to Stephens Passage and bordered on the east by Canada.

Tracy and Endicott arms are the major features of this 653,179-acre wilderness. Both are long, deep and narrow fjords that extend more than 30 miles into the heavily glaciated Coast Mountain Range. At the head of these fjords are active tidewater glaciers, which continually calve icebergs into the fjords. During the summer, both fjords have quantities of floating ice ranging from the size of a 3-story building to hand-sized chunks, often obstructing small-boat travel. Fords Terror, off of Endicott Arm, is an area of sheer rock walls enclosing a narrow entrance into a small fjord. The fjord was named for a crew member of a naval vessel who rowed into the narrow canyon at slack tide in 1889 and was caught in turbulent, iceberg-laden currents for 6 "terrifying" hours when the tide changed. Most of the area is rugged snow- and glacier-covered mountains with steeply walled valleys dotted with high, cascading waterfalls. The lower slopes are covered with typical southeastern

Alaska spruce-hemlock rain forest; tree line is about 1,500 feet elevation. There are a few muskeg bogs with sedges, grass and sphagnum moss.

Wildlife includes mountain goats, wolverines, brown and black bears, numerous furbearers, a few Sitka black-tailed deer, bald eagles, shorebirds, sea lions, whales and harbor seals.

Access is primarily by boat or floatplane from Juneau or Petersburg. Large cruise ships and small charter boats include Tracy and Endicott arms on their itineraries. There are no facilities in this area. Camping may be difficult because of the steep terrain; a boat with sleeping accommodations is the best means of visiting this wilderness.

For additional information contact: Tongass National Forest, Chatham Area, 204 Siginaka Way, Sitka, AK 99835; phone 747-6671. Related USGS Topographic maps: Sumdum, Taku River.

South Baranof Wilderness. This 319,568-acre wilderness is located on the southern portion of Baranof Island, bounded by the open Gulf of Alaska on the west and Chatham Strait on the east. It is 50 miles south of Sitka and 20 miles north of Port Alexander.

High mountains rise sharply from sea level to more than 4,000 feet in less than 2 miles from the beach. Much of the higher areas have permanent ice fields and numerous active glaciers. Many valleys are U-shaped, carved by recent glacial activity with amphitheaterlike cirques at their sources, hanging valleys along their walls and dramatic waterfalls. Most of the valleys empty into long, deep fjords. Rainfall in portions of this area is among the highest in Southeast; up to 200 inches a year at Little Port Walter, just south of the wilderness, has been recorded. Storms from September through December can generate winds exceeding 100 mph.

Wildlife in the area includes Sitka black-tailed deer, brown bears, hair seals, mink, marten, land otters, bald eagles and a variety of other birds. There are major steelhead producing lakes and streams in this wilderness; other fish available include coho, red, pink and chum salmon, cutthroat and rainbow trout and Dolly Varden. Marine species include Dungeness and tanner crab, shrimp, herring and halibut.

Recreational activities include boating, kayaking, fishing and hunting. Access is primarily by floatplane or boat from Sitka, which has commercial air service and is on the Alaska Marine Highway System route. Many sheltered bays and fjords provide safe anchorage and sheltered floatplane landings. The Forest Service maintains 3 recreation cabins, located at Avoss, Davidoff and North Plotnikof lakes. (See Tongass National Forest Cabins in this section.)

For additional information contact: Tongass National Forest, Chatham Area, 204 Siginaka Way, Sitka, AK 99835; phone 747-6671. Related USGS Topographic map: Port Alexander.

Petersburg Creek-Duncan Salt Chuck Wilderness. This 46,777-acre area is located on the northeast portion of Kupreanof Island. The eastern boundary is near the unincorporated community of Kupreanof, directly across Wrangell Narrows from the city of Petersburg. The area continues west through the Petersburg Creek drainage to the salt chuck at the north end of Duncan Canal.

The Petersburg Creek drainage is a typical U-shaped glacier-carved valley. Its walls are steep in some areas, with visible rock outcroppings. The valley sides are forested with spruce and hemlock; muskeg bogs are common below.

Wildlife includes black bears, Sitka black-tailed deer, wolves, numerous furbearers and a variety of waterfowl. All species of salmon (except kings), Dolly Varden and cutthroat trout are found in Petersburg Creek and Petersburg Lake and its tributaries.

Recreational activities include hiking, backpacking, kayaking, fishing, wildlife observation and photography, as well as hunting in season. The wilderness area is reached primarily by boat at high tide from Petersburg to Petersburg Creek or to Duncan Canal and Duncan Salt Chuck. Floatplanes can land in Duncan Canal, on the Salt Chuck at high tide, and on Petersburg Lake. Petersburg Lake National Recreation Trail leads from salt water to Petersburg Lake. The Forest Service maintains 3 recreation cabins in the area, located at Petersburg Lake, and in the vicinity of Duncan Canal and Salt Chuck. (See Tongass National Forest Cabins in this section.)

For additional information contact: Tongass National Forest, Stikine Area, P.O. Box 309, Petersburg, AK 99833; phone 772-3841. Related USGS Topographic map: Petersburg.

Stikine-LeConte Wilderness. Located on the mainland of southeastern Alaska 6 miles east of Petersburg and 7 miles north of Wrangell. Its boundary extends from Frederick Sound on the west to the Alaska-Canada border on the east.

The most prominent feature of this 448,841-acre area is the powerful Stikine River. The river valley is narrow, surrounded by steep, rugged peaks, many of them glaciated. The river is heavily laden with silt from the numerous glaciers. The delta at the mouth of the river is 17 miles wide, formed from numerous slow-moving braided channels (3 of which are navigable). One hot and 2 warm springs are found along the river. The vicinity of LeConte Glacier — southernmost glacier in North America to empty directly into salt water — is mountainous, with numerous ice fields that extend into Canada. Alpine vegetation, including mosses, lichens and other small plants, grows above 2,000 feet. The lower slopes near salt water support typical Southeast spruce-hemlock rain forest. In the east, rainfall decreases and cottonwoods appear.

This is an important fish and wildlife area. Moose, mountain goats, brown and black bears, Sitka black-tailed deer and wolves inhabit the area. The delta of the Stikine is a major resting area for migratory birds. The lower Stikine has the second-largest seasonal concentration of bald eagles in southeastern Alaska when the birds gather to feed on hooligan (also called eulachon or smelt) runs in April. Several varieties of salmon, including kings, are found in the area.

Recreational activities include fishing and hunting in season, as well as kayak, canoe and raft trips down the Stikine. Thick brush along the river makes hiking difficult. Access is primarily by small boat from Petersburg or Wrangell; there also is limited access by floatplane. Air taxis in Petersburg and Wrangell offer scenic tours. There are no commercial lodges. The Forest Service maintains a number of recreational cabins in the area and 2 bathhouses at Chief Shakes Hot Springs. (See Tongass National Forest Cabins in this section.)

For additional information contact: Tongass National Forest, Stikine Area, P.O. Box 309, Petersburg, AK 99833; phone 772-3841. Related USGS Topographic maps: Petersburg, Bradfield Canal, Sumdum.

Tebenkof Bay Wilderness. This 66,839-acre wilderness is located on the west side of Kuiu (CUE-you) Island 50 miles southwest of Petersburg, bordered on the west by Chatham Strait.

This expansive and complex system of bays includes many small islands, islets and coves. Kayaking is excellent in the protected waters of Tebenkof Bay. The area has spruce-hemlock forest up to about the 2,000-foot elevation, where alpine plants take over. There is some muskeg and many small lakes and creeks.

Wildlife includes black bears, wolves and some smaller furbearers. Marine mammals are abundant. The area is on the migration route of many waterfowl. Trumpeter swans and bald eagles also occur here. The area is rich in fish and shellfish, including coho, red, pink and chum salmon, rainbow and steelhead trout, Dolly Varden, Dungeness and tanner crab, shrimp and halibut. The remains of Tlingit villages and camps as well as fur farms may be seen.

Recreational activities include kayaking and exploring the many streams, bays and coves. Access is by boat or floatplane from Petersburg or Wrangell. Many coves provide good anchorage. Chatham Strait can be hazardous at times because of swells and strong winds from the Pacific Ocean. There are 4 kayak portage trails which provide access to this wilderness from the town of Kake, which is a ferry stop on the Alaska Marine Highway System.

For additional information contact: Tongass National Forest, Stikine Area, P.O. Box 309, Petersburg, AK 99833; phone 772-3841. Related USGS Topographic maps: Port Alexander.

Coronation Island Wilderness, Warren Island Wilderness, Maurelle Islands Wilderness. All 3 of these island wildernesses are located off the northwest coast of Prince of Wales Island, south of Kuiu Island and north of Noyes Island. By air from Ketchikan it is 73 miles to the Maurelle Islands, 75 miles to Warren Island, and 110 miles to Coronation Island.

The Coronation Island Wilderness encompasses 19,232 acres; the Maurelle Islands Wilderness, 4,937 acres; and the Warren Island Wilderness, 11,181 acres. Warren Peak is a prominent feature of the Warren Island Wilderness, rising abruptly from sea level to 2,329 feet. The Coronation Island Wilderness includes the Spanish Island group as well as Coronation Island, which has numerous peaks rising sharply to nearly 2,000 feet. Maurelle Islands Wilderness is a group of nearly 30 small islands rising less than 400 feet above sea level. A number of islets, pinnacles and rocky shoals are found in surrounding waters. These island wildernesses have rocky, wind-swept beaches with steep cliffs. Trees near the shoreline are often wind sculpted. Tall stands of spruce are found in more sheltered portions of the islands.

Wildlife includes wolves, black bears, Sitka black-tailed deer, bald eagles, whales, seals, sea lions and sea otters. The cliffs and rocks are important seabird nesting and perching

areas. Some streams contain trout and salmon.

Kayaking among the Maurelle Islands is possible, although rugged. On the 2 larger islands, principal activities are beachcombing, wildlife observation and photography. There is a protected harbor at Hole-in-the-wall in the San Lorenzo Islands, which form the southern point of the Maurelle group. Access to these islands is by boat or floatplane from Ketchikan, Craig or Klawock.

Access to many of the islands is difficult as there is a lack of boat anchorage and plane landing sites and the islands are exposed to the winds and surf of the Pacific Ocean. Warren Island is so exposed to the prevailing southeast winds that it is inaccessible much of the year. The leeward sides of some of the islands do have some protected coves and beaches. There are no facilities on any of these islands.

For additional information contact: Tongass National Forest, Ketchikan Area, Federal Bldg., Ketchikan, AK 99901; phone 259-3101. Related USGS Topographic map: Craig.

Misty Fiords National Monument. Located at the southern end of the national forest adjacent to the Canadian border on the east and south, extending northward from Dixon Entrance to beyond the Unuk River. Its western boundary is about 22 air miles east of Ketchikan.

Misty Fiords National Monument encompasses 2.3 million acres (of which only 142,757 acres is nonwilderness), making it the largest wilderness in Alaska's national forests and the second largest in the nation. In the nonwilderness portion at Quartz Hill, U.S. Borax and Chemical Corp. is acquiring permits to develop and mine a deposit of molybdenum estimated to be one of the largest in the world. Fort Tongass, occupied from 1868 to 1870 as Alaska's first U.S. Army post, was located within this monument.

Taking its name from the almost constant precipitation characteristic of the area, Misty Fiords is covered with thick forests which grow on nearly vertical slopes from sea level to mountain tops. Dramatic waterfalls plunge into the salt water through narrow clefts or course over great rounded granite shoulders, fed by lakes and streams which absorb the annual rainfall of more than 14 feet. The major waterway cutting through the monument, Behm Canal, is more than 100 miles long and extraordinary among natural canals for its length and depth. Active glaciers along the Canadian border are remnants of massive ice sheets that covered the region as recently as 10,000 years ago. Periodic lava flows have occurred for the last several thousand years in an area near the Blue River in the eastern portion of the wilderness. The latest of these flows was in the early 1900s and is an attractive and unusual geologic feature.

Forested areas consist of Sitka spruce, western hemlock and cedar. Some Pacific silver fir, subalpine and black cottonwood are found. Beneath these trees grow huckleberry, alder, willow and other brush creating impenetrable thickets.

Few areas of the United States contain as many unusual wildlife species: mountain goats, brown bears, black bears, moose, martens, wolves, wolverines, river otters, sea lions, harbor seals, killer whales and Dall porpoises. A large number of birds, ranging from humming birds and trumpeter swans to herons and bald eagles, are found in the area. Misty Fiords is a major producer of coho, sockeye, pink and chum salmon and is especially important for king salmon. Numerous other saltwater and freshwater fish and shellfish also occur.

This monument offers magnificent scenery. Inlets, bays, arms and coves — some long and narrow, some short and broad — are variations on the fjords for which the area is named. The highlands are dotted with thousands of lakes, large and small, and innumerable streams. The Walker Cove-Rudyerd Bay Scenic Area, with its vertical granite cliffs topped by snowy peaks, has been protected for many years and is now part of the monument.

Kayak trips are popular, despite the rainy weather. Campsites, however, are difficult. Tides of up to 18 feet may be encountered; often the only safe campsite is up among the trees above high tide line. Firewood is plentiful, but usually wet. Behm Canal has few suitable campsites. In the summer of 1989 the Tongass Conservation Society and U.S. Forest Service began work on a sea kayak camping trail that was to include a map of the best camping sites. Check with the Forest Service in Ketchikan for progress on this project.

The most comfortable way to visit Misty Fiords is by cabin cruiser or some other sleep-aboard boat. Good moorages can be found; fresh water is plentiful ashore. The monument also is readily accessible by floatplane from Ketchikan or any other Southeast community. Tours are available on charter boats out of Ketchikan and large cruise ships often sail the deep waters of Behm Canal. There are 3 commercial lodges near the monument at Yes Bay and within the monu-

ment at Hidden Inlet and Humpback Lake. The Forest Service maintains a number of recreational cabins on freshwater lakes and on salt water (see Tongass National Forest Cabins this section), as well as several saltwater mooring buoys and some 20 miles of trails.

For additional information contact: Misty Fiords National Monument, 3031 Tongass Ave., Ketchikan, AK 99901; phone 225-2148. Related USGS Topographic maps: Prince Rupert, Ketchikan, Bradfield Canal.

South Prince of Wales Wilderness. This 90,996-acre wilderness is located at the southern tip of Prince of Wales Island, about 40 miles southwest of Ketchikan and a few miles south of Hydaburg. The area fronts on Dixon Entrance and on Cordova Bay, extending north to take in all of Klakas Inlet.

The first Haida Indian village in southeastern Alaska, Klinkwan, is within the South Prince of Wales Wilderness. This historic village site was established in the 19th century and abandoned in 1911. The sea coast is deeply indented with numerous bays and inlets. The Barrier Islands, a collection of more than 75 islets ranging in size from a few acres up to 500 acres, jut out into Cordova Bay. They are exposed to fierce ocean storms and their trees are stunted and sculpted by the wind. Topography on Prince of Wales Island ranges from lowlands containing many streams, lakes and wetlands to the sheer, 2,000-foot rock walls of Klakas Inlet, which extends 12 miles inland from Cordova Bay. Precipitation usually exceeds 100 inches per year and vegetation includes dense stands of large old-growth Sitka spruce, western hemlock, Alaska cedar and western red cedar, as well as numerous shrubs, wildflowers and grasses.

Wildlife includes black bears, wolves, Sitka black-tailed deer, small furbearers, land and shorebirds and bald eagles. This is one of the better sea otter habitats in southeastern Alaska. Many species of waterfowl migrate along the coastline. Coho, red, pink and chum salmon, cutthroat and rainbow trout and Dolly Varden occur in waters of this area. Also, Dungeness and tanner crab, shrimp, herring, halibut, abalone, giant barnacles, clams, mussels, octopus, sea urchins, sea anemones and starfish.

Access to this area is by floatplane or boat. Small boats can negotiate the area during the summer; however, Dixon Entrance is exposed to the ocean and can be extremely stormy and rough during other seasons. There are no facilities in this wilderness area.

For more information contact: Tongass National Forest, Ketchikan Area, Federal Bldg., Ketchikan, AK 99901; phone 225-3101. Related USGS Topographic maps: Dixon Entrance, Craig.

Tongass National Forest Cabins

The more than 150 Tongass National Forest recreational cabins are among the best lodging bargains in the state. Current cost is $15 per night for these rustic, but comfortable cabins which are accessible only by boat, floatplane, helicopter or hiking trail.

The fee may increase slightly. Check with any local Forest Service office for current fees. Use is limited to 7 consecutive days between April 1 and Oct. 31 and 10 consecutive days between Nov. 1 and March 31. Hike-in cabins have a 2-night limit. Permit days begin and end at noon.

Anyone who is at least 18 years of age may apply for a cabin permit. Applications may be made in person or in writing up to 180 days in advance of requested times. Fee must be included with application. Permits are issued on a first-come basis and must be carried along to the cabin. Cancellations and requests for refunds must be made in writing and mailed or brought to a Forest Service office with the original permit at least 10 days prior to intended use.

Cabins have tables, benches, bunks (without mattresses), wood or oil stoves, brooms and pit toilets. You must bring your own bedding and cooking utensils. An ax or maul is provided at cabins with wood stoves, but bring a small ax or hatchet in case the tools are not there. Be sure to check which kind of stove is provided. The Forest Service does not provide stove oil. Only #1 diesel oil will work properly and 5 to 10 gallons per week are required, depending on weather conditions. It is advisable to bring a gas camp stove for cooking. Most cabins located on lakes have skiffs with oars. You must bring your own life preservers and motor. Be sure to pull the boat above the high-water mark and tie it. Also, turn it over so it does not fill with rain water. Bring good rain gear, waterproof boots and plenty of warm clothing. Also bring extra food and other supplies in case bad weather prolongs your stay. Insect repellent is a must during the summer. Those traveling in bear country may want to carry a .30-06 or larger caliber rifle as a safety precaution if you know how to use the weapon. Burn all combustible trash and pack out all other garbage to avoid attracting bears. The Forest Service cautions

that you are "on your own" at these remote cabins. Be prepared to be self-sufficient and bring emergency equipment such as maps, compass, waterproof matches, a strong knife, first-aid kit and a space blanket. A detailed list of suggested items to take along is available from the Forest Service on request.

The accompanying chart provides basic information on each cabin within Tongass National Forest. Obtain additional information or make reservations through any ranger district office: **Juneau area** (including Admiralty Island): Tongass National Forest, Juneau Ranger District, 8465 Old Dairy Road, Juneau, AK 99801; phone 789-3111 or Centennial Hall Visitors Information Center, 101 Egan Dr., Juneau, AK 99801. **Ketchikan area** (including Prince of Wales Island and Misty Fiords): Tongass National Forest, Ketchikan Area, Federal Bldg., Ketchikan, AK 99901; phone 225-3101. **Petersburg area:** Tongass National Forest, Petersburg Ranger District, P.O. Box 1328, Petersburg, AK 99833; phone 772-3841. **Sitka area:** Tongass National Forest, Sitka Ranger District, 204 Siginaka Way, Sitka, AK 99835; phone 747-6671. **Wrangell area:** Tongass National Forest, Wrangell Ranger District, P.O. Box 51, Wrangell, AK 99929; phone 874-2323.

The charts on pages 85 through 89 list cabins alphabetically within each of the 9 major areas of Tongass National Forest. The charts show how many people the cabin sleeps; if the cabin is accessible by air, boat or trail; if hunting, fishing or beachcombing are available; and if the cabin has a skiff or stove. Special features or restrictions are also noted. (Check Southeast Trails for details on trails to cabins with trail access.)

Southeast Trails

Beginning on page 90 is a partial list of Southeast trails maintained by the U.S. Forest Service. The trails detailed here are in the Craig, Haines, Juneau, Ketchikan, Petersburg, Sitka and Wrangell areas. For more information, contact the Forest Service, P.O. Box 21628-PAO, Juneau, AK 99802-1628.

Most trails in Southeast are more difficult than trails with similar ratings in the Lower 48. This is because oversteepened slopes caused by glacial action, and high seasonal and daily variations in rainfall, can drastically alter trail conditions. Waterproof footwear such as knee-high rubber boots with good traction soles are often the best choice. Trail crews may be working on some trails; check with the local Forest Service or Alaska State Parks office for current trail conditions. Space limitations

TONGASS NATIONAL FOREST CABINS

	SLEEPS	AIR ACCESS	BOAT ACCESS	TRAIL ACCESS	HUNTING	FISHING	BEACHCOMB	SKIFF	STOVE
YAKUTAT AREA									
Alsek River *(High winds common in fall and winter)*	4	•			•	•			O
Harlequin Lake North *(Bring water)*	4	•		•	•				OH
Harlequin Lake South *(Bring water)*	4	•		•	•				OH
Italio River *(Area affected by tidal changes, storms and high winds)*	4	•			•	•	•		O
Lower Dangerous River *(Bring water)*	4	•			•			•	O
Middle Dangerous River *(Trail can be flooded; bring water)*	4			•	•				O
Middle Situk River North	6	•	•	•	•	•			OH
Middle Situk River South	6	•	•	•	•	•			OH
Situk Lake *(Available after July 15)*	4	•		•	•	•		•	W
Situk River Weir *(Trail can be muddy)*	6	•	•	•	•	•			W
Square Lake *(Nesting swans at head of lake)*	4	•			•	•		•	O
Tanis Mesa North *(Bring water; creek may be dry; high winds in fall)*	4	•			•				O
Tanis Mesa South *(Bring water; creek may be dry; high winds in fall)*	4	•			•				O
ADMIRALTY ISLAND									
Admiralty Cove *(Cove dry at low tide)*	6	•	•		•	•			W
Big Shaheen *(Bring gas for cooking)*	8	•	•		•	•		•	W
Church Bight *(Gambler Bay)*	8	•	•		•	•			W
Distin Lake *(Cabin in poor condition)*	4	•	•		•	•		•	W
East Florence	8	•			•	•		•	W
Hasselborg River *(cabin in poor condition)*	2	•	•			•		•	W
Jim's Lake	6	•			•	•		•	W
Lake Alexander	6	•			•	•		•	W
Lake Kathleen	5	•			•	•		•	W
Little Shaheen *(200 yards from Big Shaheen)*	8	•	•		•	•		•	W
North Young Lake	6	•	•	•	•	•		•	W
Pybus Bay	10	•	•		•				W
South Young Lake	6	•			•			•	W
Sportsman	4	•			•	•		•	W
West Florence	4	•			•	•		•	W

Type of stove provided is indicated as follows: O=oil stove, W=wood stove, G=outdoor grill, OH=oil heater.

TONGASS NATIONAL FOREST CABINS CONTINUED

	SLEEPS	AIR ACCESS	BOAT ACCESS	TRAIL ACCESS	HUNTING	FISHING	BEACHCOMB	SKIFF	STOVE
JUNEAU AREA									
Dan Moller (X-C skiing)	12			•					W
East Turner (Bears in area)	6	•				•		•	W
John Muir (Winter sports area)	16			•					W
Katzehin (Wheel plane access)	8	•	•		•	•			W
Peterson Lake (X-C skiing)	6			•		•			W
Spruce (Shallow draft river boat access at high tide)	6	•	•		•	•			W
West Turner (Boat and trail access required. Bears in area)	8	•		•		•		•	W
SITKA AREA									
Avoss Lake	10	•			•	•		•	OH
Baranof Lake	6	•			•	•		•	W
Breents Beach	6	•	•		•	•	•	•	W
Davidoff Lkae (Trail to Plotnikof Lake)	10	•				•		•	W
Fred Creek (Trail to Mt. Edgecumbe Crater)	6		•			•			W
Glolding Lakes	8	•				•		•	W
Kook Lake (Trail to Basket Bay)	10	•				•		•	W
Lake Eva (Handicap access)	6	•				•		•	W
Plotnikof Lake (Trails to Davidof Lake)	6	•			•	•		•	O
Redoubt Lake (Trails ro Lucky Chance Mine)	10	•	•	•	•	•		•	W
Shelikof (Large sandy beach)	8	•		•		•	•		W
Sitkoh Lake (4.3-mile trail from bay)	6	•				•		•	W
Suloia Lake	6	•			•	•		•	W
White Sulphur Spring (Hot springs bathouse)	4	•	•		•	•	•		W
PETERSBERG AREA									
Beecher Pass (Salmon fishing; need boat)	4	•	•		•	•			O&W
Big John Bay (Road access from Kate to 1.5-mile trail in)	4	•		•	•				O
Breiland Slough	7	•	•		•	•			O
Cascade Creek (Salmon and hailbut fishing; need boat)	6	•	•		•	•			O&W
Castle Flats (On mudflats; 13-to 15-foot tide needed for access)	5	•	•		•	•		•	O&W
Castle River (16-foot tide needed for access)	7	•	•		•	•		•	W
DeBoer Lake (Carry extra supplies; may weather in)	6	•			•	•		•	O

Type of stove provided is indicated as follows: O=oil stove, W=wood stove, G=outdoor grill, OH=oil heater.

TONGASS NATIONAL FOREST CABINS CONTINUED

	SLEEPS	AIR ACCESS	BOAT ACCESS	TRAIL ACCESS	HUNTING	FISHING	BEACHCOMB	SKIFF	STOVE
Devil's Elbow (16-foot tide needed for plane access)	7	•	•		•	•			O
Harvey Lake (Easy 1-mile trail from salt water)	7	•	•		•	•		•	W
Kadake Bay (18-foot tide needed for boat access)	6	•	•		•	•			O&W
Kah Sheets Bay (14-foot tide needed for access)	4	•	•		•	•			O&W
Kah Sheets Lake (2.7-mile hike from bay to cabin; renovated to accept wheelchairs)	4	•	•		•	•		•	O
Petersburg Lake (Ice fishing, X-C skiing)	4	•	•	•	•	•		•	O&W
Potrage Bay	6	•	•		•	•			O
Ravens Roost (Bring dry kinding)	8		•	•					W
Salt Chuck East (14-foot tide needed for access)	7	•	•	•	•	•		•	W
Salt Chuck West (14- to 17-foot tide needed for access)	4	•	•		•	•		•	W
Spurt Cove (Boat needed for fishing)	4	•	•		•	•			O&W
Swan Lake (Carry extra supplies; may weather in)	7	•			•	•		•	O
Towers Arm (16-foot tide needed for access)	4	•	•		•				W

WRANGELL AREA

	SLEEPS	AIR ACCESS	BOAT ACCESS	TRAIL ACCESS	HUNTING	FISHING	BEACHCOMB	SKIFF	STOVE
Anan Bay (No black or brown bear hunting. Trail to bear observation point)	7	•	•			•			O
Berg Bay (Mooring buoy provided)	7	•	•		•	•			O
Binkley Slough (No access at low tide; bring water)	6		•		•				O
Eagle Lake	4	•			•	•		•	W
Garnet Ledge (15-foot tide needed for access; rock hounding)	7		•						W
Gut Island #1 (15-to 17-foot tide needed for access; bring water)	6	•	•		•				O
Gut Island #2 (15-to 17-foot tide needed for access; bring water)	4	•	•		•				O
Harding River	6	•	•		•	•			O
Koknut (16-foot tide needed for access. Carry water)	4		•		•				O
Little Dry Island (15-to 17-foot tide needed for access. Carry water)	7	•	•		•				W
Mallard Slough (14-to 16-foot tide needed for access; bring water)	7	•	•		•				W
Marten Lake	4	•			•	•		•	W
Mount Flemer (Boat needed for hunting)	7		•		•				O

Type of stove provided is indicated as follows: O=oil stove, W=wood stove, G=outdoor grill, OH=oil heater.

TONGASS NATIONAL FOREST CABINS CONTINUED

	SLEEPS	AIR ACCESS	BOAT ACCESS	TRAIL ACCESS	HUNTING	FISHING	BEACHCOMB	SKIFF	STOVE
Mount Rynda (High river needed for plane or boat access)	7	•	•		•	•			O
Serief Island (15-to 17-foot tide needed for access. Carry water)	4	•	•		•				O
Shake Slough #1 (Boat needed for fishing; bring water)	4	•	•		•	•			O
Shake Slough #2 (Bring water)	7	•	•		•	•			O
Streamer Bay (Carry water)	5	•	•		•	•	•		O
Twin Lakes (Bring water)	7	•	•		•	•			O
Virgina Lake	4	•			•	•		•	O
PRINCE OF WALES ISLAND									
Barnes Lake	6	•	•		•	•		•	W
Black Bear Lake (Good weather required for access)	6	•			•	•		•	W
Control Lake (Road access)	8		•	•	•	•		•	W
Essowah	6	•			•	•		•	W
Grindall Island (Good salmon fishing)	6	•		•			•	•	W
Honker Lake	6	•		•	•	•		•	W
Josephine Lake	6	•			•			•	OH
Karta Lake (Boat to Karta Bay, 1.5-mile trail to cabin)	6	•	•	•	•	•		•	W
Karta River	6	•	•	•	•	•			O
Kegan Cove	6	•	•		•	•			W
Kegan Creek (Boat and trail access from Kegan Cove)	6	•	•	•	•	•		•	W
McGilvery Creek	6	•			•	•		•	W
Point Amargura	6	•	•		•	•			W
Red Bay Lake (1-mile hike from salt water)	2-3	•		•	•	•		•	W
Salmon Bay Lake (Sandy beach)	6	•	•	•	•	•		•	W
Salmon Lake (Old cabin with hand-hewn beams and shake floor)	6	•	•	•	•	•		•	W
Sarker Lake (Road access; bring motor for boat if arriving by road, there are no oars)	6	•	•	•	•	•		•	W
Shipley Bay (Skiff 0.8 mile from cabin at Shipley Lake outlet)	6	•	•		•	•		•	W
Staney Creek (Road access)	6	•	•	•	•	•			OH
Sweetwater Lake (Road access)	4	•	•	•	•	•		•	W
Trollers Cove	6	•	•		•	•			W

Type of stove provided is indicated as follows: O=oil stove, W=wood stove, G=outdoor grill, OH=oil heater.

TONGASS NATIONAL FOREST CABINS CONTINUED

	SLEEPS	AIR ACCESS	BOAT ACCESS	TRAIL ACCESS	HUNTING	FISHING	BEACHCOMB	SKIFF	STOVE
KETCHIKAN AREA									
Anchor Pass	6	•	•		•	•	•		W
Blind Pass	6	•	•		•	•	•		W
Fish Creek	6	•	•		•	•			OH
Fisheries	6	•			•	•		•	W
Heckman Lake *(Boat to Naha Bay, 6.3-mile trail to cabin)*	6	•		•	•	•		•	W
Helm Bay	8	•	•		•	•	•		W
Helm Creek	6	•	•		•	•	•		W
Jordan Lake *(Hike from Heckman Lake or Naha Bay)*	6		•	•	•	•		•	W
McDonald Lake *(Boat to Yes Bay, 1.5-mile trail to cabin)*	6	•	•	•	•	•		•	W
Orchard Lake	6	•			•	•		•	OH
Patching Lake	6	•			•	•		•	W
Phocena	6	•	•		•	•	•		W
Plenty Cutthroat *(Boat to Shtrimp Bay, 0.5-mile trail to cabin)*	4	•			•	•		•	W
Portage	6	•			•	•		•	W
Rainbow Lake	6	•			•	•		•	W
Reflection Lake *(Boat to Short Bay, 2-mile trail to cabin)*	6	•	•	•	•	•		•	W
MISTY FIORDS AREA									
Alava Bay	6	•	•		•	•	•		W
Bakewell Lake	6	•			•	•		•	W
Beaver Camp	6	•			•	•		•	W
Big Goat Lake	6	•			•	•		•	OH
Checats Lake	6	•			•	•		•	W
Ella Narrows	6	•			•	•		•	W
Hugh Smith Lake	6	•			•	•		•	W
Humpback Lake	6	•			•	•		•	W
Manzanita Lake	6	•			•	•		•	OH
Red Alders	6	•			•	•		•	W
Wilson Narrows	6	•			•	•		•	W
Wilson View	6	•			•	•		•	W
Winstanley Island	6	•	•		•	•			W
Winstanley Lake	6	•			•	•		•	W

Type of stove provided is indicated as follows: O=oil stove, W=wood stove, G=outdoor grill, OH=oil heater.

prohibit listing all of Southeast's fine hiking trails, so check locally for others.

Craig Area Trails

Kegan Lake Trail. This easy 0.5-mile trail begins at Kegan Cove cabin and ends at the lake, where steelhead, sockeye and coho runs are internationally acclaimed. The lake has a native rainbow population and excellent fishing, which has been featured in fishing magazines. Recommended season, July to September. The Kegan Cove and Kegan Creek Forest Service cabins are so popular that they are on a lottery system and must be reserved well in advance. The trail is an easy, pleasant walk through an old-growth forest with very little undergrowth. Related USGS Topographic map: Craig A-1.

One Duck Trail. This more difficult 1-mile trail begins 1.5 miles south of Harris River bridge on Hydaburg Road and climbs 700 feet to a large alpine area with easy walking, good hunting for deer and bear and good cross-country skiing in winter and early spring. Although the trail is unfinished, it is passable and easy to find. It has been brushed and basic treadwork has been done. Related USGS Topographic map: Craig B-3.

Haines Area Trails

Trails here are found on USGS Topographic maps Skagway A-1, A-2 and B-2. Only the Mount Riley and Seduction Point trails are maintained by state parks on a regular basis. The others receive periodic volunteer maintenance, so check locally before you hike.

Battery Point Trail. The trail starts 1 mile east of Port Chilkoot and 0.25 mile beyond Portage Cove. This is a fairly level shoreline walk of about 2.4 miles with a primitive campsite and toilet behind Kelgaya Point. The last 0.75 mile of the trail is along pebble beaches and across Kelgaya Point with excellent views of Lynn Canal. Allow 2 hours for a round-trip.

Mount Riley Trails. There are 3 routes to the 1,760-foot summit of Mount Riley: Mud Bay Road, via Port Chilkoot and from Portage Cove.

Mud Bay Road: This route is the steepest and most direct. Take the Mud Bay Road from Port Chilkoot, heading southward on the west side of the Chilkat Peninsula, to the top of the second steep hill a few yards short of the Mile 3 marker. The marked path starts on the left side of the road and heads for the ridge in a southeasterly direction. Distance to the summit is 2.1 miles. Estimated round-trip time is 3.5 hours.

Via Port Chilkoot: This route connects with the Mud Bay Road trail. Take the FAA Road behind Officers Row in Port Chilkoot and follow it to its end, about 1 mile. Walk along the city of Haines water supply access route about 2 miles then take the spur trail which branches to the right to connect with the route from Mud Bay Road. Estimated round-trip time, 4.5 hours.

From Portage Cove: This route is recommended for snowshoe travel in winter. Follow the Battery Point trail almost 2 miles to a junction then take the right fork which climbs steeply at first through thick undergrowth and tall spruce forests. The trail becomes less steep and continues through small muskeg meadows over Half Dome before the final climb to the summit.

It is also possible to traverse Mount Riley from Portage Cove to the Mud Bay Road. This trip is about 7.6 miles and takes about 4 hours.

Seduction Point. Drive the Mud Bay Road to the Chilkat State Park and park at the bend of the steep hill or go to the picnic area on the beach. The trail alternates between inland forest trail and beach walking with excellent views of the Davidson Glacier. Estimated round-trip time for the 13.5-mile hike is 9 to 10 hours. Seasonal water supplies at Twin and David's coves. Campsites along the way and at the cove east of Seduction Point. Hikers should check the tides before leaving and plan to do the last long beach stretch after David's Cove at low or mid-tide.

Mount Ripinsky Summit. The trail starts north of Haines toward Lutak Inlet at the top of Young Street and along the pipeline right-of-way. The pipeline trail rises gradually, through wooded hillslope, then descends steeply after about a mile. At this point, the tank farm is visible. The trail takes off to the left a few yards down the hill and ascends through hemlock and spruce forest to alpine meadows above Johnson Creek, elevation 2,500 feet. From the ridge on clear days, you can see snowcapped mountain peaks from Haines all the way to Admiralty Island. At the summit there are views of Lutak Inlet, Taiya Inlet and a panorama of peaks and ice fields. This is a strenuous, all-day hike or overnight camp. It is possible to descend the summit and continue west, northwest along a ridge to Peak 3,920 and down to 7 Mile Saddle to the Haines Highway. This traverse is about 10 miles and overall elevation gain is about 5,100 feet. The trail is steep in places and easily lost. Until late June, water or snowmelt is found on the ridge. After that it is necessary to carry water beyond Johnson Creek where the last water is found. Related USGS Topographic maps: Skagway A-2, B-2.

7 Mile Saddle. The trailhead is located 0.2 mile east of Milepost 7. The trail climbs steeply at first through small pine forest then more gradually through spruce and hemlock until open slopes are reached at about 2,000 feet. Water is available all year in streams found in the forested sections but water should be carried after passing through those areas. It is possible to continue east toward Mount Ripinsky and reverse the traverse described above.

Juneau Area Trails

Amalga (Eagle Glacier) Trail. Trailhead is in the parking lot on the left at Mile 28.4 from Juneau on the Glacier Highway. Trail extends 4 miles to the old Amalga mine site and another 1.5 miles to the lake in front of Eagle Glacier. Usable spring, summer and fall. Rated easy, although there are some steep boardwalks and creeks to cross, and trail is overgrown with willows and alder near the end. Elevation gain 200 feet. Estimated round-trip time 7 to 8 hours. Rubber boots recommended. Bring mosquito repellent in summer. Amalga was a settlement between 1902 and 1927; the mine site is now difficult to find. Wildlife includes bears, beavers, occasional wolverines, geese and mountain goats on surrounding mountains. Impressive views of Eagle Glacier. Related USGS Topographic map: Juneau C-3.

Auke Nu Trail. This Forest Service trail is reached from the Spaulding trail, which begins at a parking area just off the Glacier Highway at Mile 12.3 (just past the post office.) The Auke Nu trailhead is 0.5 mile up the Spaulding trail, on the left. Trail then extends 2.5 mile to the John Muir Cabin. Usable all year; cross-country skiing in winter. Rated moderate. Elevation gain 1,552 feet. Estimated round-trip time 5 to 6 hours.

Trail conditions were improved in 1987 when planks were installed through the muddiest areas. First part of trail runs through forested area and contains some sections of an old corduroy road. Middle part also is forested. The last section of trail goes through muskeg meadows, most of which are planked to protect the fragile plants. Rubber boots are recommended. Blueberries and huckleberries are found in season. Be alert for bears. This trail features views of the Chilkat Mountains, Admiralty Island, Gastineau Channel and Mounts Stroller White and McGinnis. Related

USGS Topographic map: Juneau B-3.

Bessie Creek Trail. Turn left off the Glacier Highway at a road sign just 500 yards north of Milepost 34 and park on Forest Service property. Trailhead is on the northwest side of the creek at the top of a cut bank on the uphill side of the road. Go through the woods and skirt the base of the hill to the right (south) until you find the trail. Forest Service trail extends 1 mile to muskeg meadow at 900-foot elevation. Usable all year. Rated more difficult. Estimated round-trip time 3 hours. Trail named for the Bessie Mine, which was active in the 1900s. Trail ends about halfway to the old mine. Related USGS Topographic map: Juneau B-3.

Blackerby Ridge Trail. From Egan Drive, take the Salmon Creek exit and drive about 0.1 mile. Walk up short road to the right. Trail begins to the left just before the end of the road and extends 3.6 miles to Cairn Peak. Trail crosses state, private and Forest Service lands. Usable summer and fall. Rated most difficult; it's steep and strenuous. The trail is not maintained and reportedly in poor condition. Elevation gain 3,200 feet. No switchbacks. Estimated round-trip time 8 to 10 hours. Waterproof hiking boots recommended; carry your own water. Above timberline carpets of alpine flowers bloom in season. Salmonberries and blueberries are found in season. Views of Salmon Creek Reservoir and Stephens Passage from the ridge; views of Lemon and Ptarmigan glaciers from Cairn Peak. Related USGS Topographic map: Juneau B-2.

Cropley Lake Trail. Located on Douglas Island. From downtown Juneau take Egan Drive to the Juneau-Douglas bridge, cross bridge, turn right on North Douglas Highway and drive 6.7 miles to Eaglecrest Road. Turn left and follow Eaglecrest Road to the end. Trail begins to the right, a short distance past Eaglecrest Ski Lodge, in a gully by a large spruce tree. Trail extends 1.5 miles to Cropley Lake. Usable summer and winter. Rated moderate. Elevation gain 800 feet; estimated round-trip time 3 hours. Trail developed primarily as a cross-country ski trail (check in at Eaglecrest Lodge before using) but is also suitable for summer hiking (waterproof footwear recommended.) Route offers good scenery, lake fishing and views from Cropley Lake of Fish Creek Valley and mainland. Related USGS Topographic map: Juneau B-2.

Dan Moller Trail. Located on Douglas Island. Cross Juneau-Douglas bridge, turn left on Douglas Highway and take first right on Cordova Street. Turn left on Pioneer Avenue, and the trail starts past the fifth or sixth house on the right. Trailhead is marked and there is a small parking area. This Forest Service trail extends 3 miles to the Dan Moller cabin in an alpine meadow. (This is a public warming cabin from 10 a.m. to 5 p.m., but can be rented for overnight use through the Forest Service.) Usable all year. Open to snowmobiles (12 inches of snow required) and cross-country skiing in winter. Rated moderate. Boardwalk section over muskeg may be slippery when wet or frosty. Elevation gain 1,600 feet. Waterproof hiking boots recommended. Estimated round-trip time 5 to 6 hours. Trail offers excellent wildflowers in season, wildlife and scenery. Climb from bowl to ridge for view of Stephens Passage and Admiralty Island. This area is avalanche prone; cross former snowslide paths quickly. Contact the Weather Service at 586-SNOW for avalanche conditions before skiing or hiking this trail. Related USGS Topographic map: Juneau B-2.

Heintzleman Ridge Route. Trailhead is off Mendenhall Loop Road behind Glacier Valley Elementary School on Hayes Way. This undeveloped Forest Service trail extends 9.5 miles to the top of Heintzleman Ridge. Usable in summer only. Extreme avalanche danger in winter or early spring. Rated most difficult. Should be attempted only by those in excellent physical condition. Estimated round-trip time 10 to 12 hours, so start early in the morning or plan to camp overnight. Trail is sparsely marked and extremely steep with no switchbacks and many false side trails. Elevation gain 3,000 to 4,000 feet. Mountain goats may be seen; many alpine wildflowers in season. The top of Steep Creek Bowl offers an excellent view of Mendenhall Glacier. Ridge continues toward Nugget Glacier and Nugget Mountain. It is possible to hike to the Mendenhall Glacier visitor center on the Nugget Creek trail from the ridge. Related USGS Topographic map: Juneau B-2.

Herbert Glacier Trail. Trailhead is just past the Herbert River bridge, 28 miles from Juneau on the Glacier Highway. A small gravel parking lot is located to the right of the trailhead. Trail extends 4.6 miles to the moraine about 0.5 mile from Herbert Glacier. Usable all year. Rated easy. Elevation gain 300 feet. Estimated round-trip time is 4 to 5 hours. Trail relatively flat, but wet in places. Trail offers opportunity to view wildflowers in season, wildlife and a good view of the glacier. Cross-country skiing possible in winter. Do not cross the branching streams to approach the glacier. It is possible to climb over the rocks to the left of the glacier for a good view

of the glacier and a spectacular waterfall. *CAUTION: Do not approach the face of the glacier. Ice falls are dangerous. Also, this is bear country; keep a clean camp and make noise while hiking.* Related USGS Topographic map: Juneau C-3.

Lemon Creek Trail. From northbound Egan Drive, take the Lemon Creek exit. The trail begins down an unmarked road across from the shopping center; take the first right past the church. Trail extends 6 miles to the vicinity of Lemon Creek Glacier and crosses state, private and Forest Service land. Usable spring, summer and fall. Rated moderate. Elevation gain 700 feet. Estimated round-trip time 8 to 10 hours. Waterproof boots and leather gloves to handle devil's club and other brush are recommended. Trail starts as dirt road, then branches to the left. May be muddy in spots. Past Canyon Creek a poorly marked trail to the right leads to Camp No. 17, one of the research stations on the Juneau Icefield. Long stretches of log sections may be slippery. Washouts may require detours. From the end of the trail near a gaging station it is a rough trek to the ice field and should be attempted only by experienced climbers with proper gear. Related USGS Topographic map: Juneau B-2.

Montana Creek Trail. From Mendenhall Loop Road, take the Montana Creek Road about 3 miles to the end at the rifle range. Forest Service trail leads northwest 9.5 miles to Windfall Lake, where it connects with the Windfall Lake trail. This is part of a trail system established in 1907-09 by the Territory of Alaska to serve mining sites. Trail usable for hiking from late spring through fall and for cross-country skiing in winter. Rated moderate. Elevation gain 800 feet. Estimated round-trip time 8 to 10 hours. There are high concentrations of bears on this trail. Related USGS Topographic maps: Juneau B-2 and B-3.

Mount Bradley (Mount Jumbo) Trail. Trail begins in Douglas at a vacant lot behind the 300 section of 5th Street. The trail extends 2.6 miles to the summit of Mount Bradley and crosses state and private lands. Usable spring, summer and fall. Rated most difficult. Elevation gain 3,337 feet. Estimated round-trip time 10 to 12 hours. Both rubber boots and hiking boots recommended. Mountain was originally named after the Jumbo Mine at its base, but was renamed in 1939 to honor a former president of the American Mining Institute. Trail is muddy with windblown trees and is not maintained. Trail crosses Paris Creek, then the Treadwell Ditch. It is clearly defined until it reaches muskeg meadows, then is difficult to follow so observe your route to the summit carefully. There are dangerous dropoffs near the top and the trail becomes quite slippery when wet. An ice ax will be helpful during ascents in late spring. The trail offers scenery, wildflowers in season and spectacular views of Gastineau Channel and Juneau from the summit. Related USGS Topographic maps: Juneau A-2 and B-2.

Mount McGinnis Trail. Trailhead is at the end of the West Glacier trail (see below), but is difficult to find. This unmaintained Forest Service trail extends 2 miles to the summit of Mount McGinnis. Usable in summer and fall. Rated most difficult. Elevation gain 4,228 feet. Estimated round-trip time 8 hours. Trail steep and sparsely marked. It should be attempted only by those in excellent physical condition who have a good sense of direction and are carrying a map and compass. Lower section of trail passes through thick brush and hikers should watch for markers. Trail ascends through dense forest and seems to end in a small basin. One way to the summit is to follow the stream up the steep slope, then continue to the top above timberline. The top part is generally covered with snow and an ice ax should be carried. Avalanche danger may continue until late spring. From the summit there is a remarkable view of Auke Bay and Mendenhall Valley. Wildlife that may be seen includes bears and mountain goats. Alpine wildflowers in season. Related USGS Topographic map: Juneau B-2.

Perserverance Trail. This easy, 3.5-mile trail to the ruins of the old Perserverance Mine is the most popular in the Juneau area. The mine, located in Silverbow Basin, operated between 1885 and 1895, when a snowslide destroyed the mill and camp buildings. From downtown Juneau take Gold Street to Basin Road past the slide on the left above the city's main water supply lines. After crossing Gold Creek, take the lefthand fork. The trail follows a gentle grade around the horn of Mount Juneau. There is extreme danger of snowslide during winter and early spring. Near the end, a side trail to the right leads to the large, steep-sided Glory Hole; use caution when approaching the dropoff. Athletic shoes or light boots are recommended. Estimated round-trip time is 4 to 5 hours; elevation gain 1,000 feet. Related USGS Topographic maps: Juneau B-2.

Peterson Lake Trail. Trailhead is about 20 feet before the 24-mile marker on the Glacier Highway. Parking is limited; be sure not to park on private property. Forest Service trail extends 4.3 miles to Peterson Lake cabin. (This is a public warming cabin from 10 a.m. to 5 p.m., but can be rented for overnight use through the Forest Service.) Trail usable all year. Rated moderate, but it is extremely muddy in some places. Waterproof footwear recommended. Elevation gain 700 feet. Estimated round-trip time 5 to 6 hours. Trail named for John Peterson, a prospector who had a claim in the area during 1899. Trail starts out through brush but soon joins an old tramway. Narrow rails are still in place in some sections; planks have been placed alongside the old rails. About 0.7 mile from the trailhead, a spur trail to the left leads to a good fishing spot below some steep waterfalls. Keep right on this spur to avoid a portion of the lower trail that is subject to landslides. Main trail continues through forest and muskeg areas. (All of the muskeg areas in the first 3 miles have been planked.) Trail turns right in the last muskeg and continues through dense forest to Peterson Lake, which has good Dolly Varden fishing. Related USGS Topographic map: Juneau B-3.

Point Bishop/Dupont Trail. Trailhead is at the end of Thane Road, 5.5 miles south of downtown Juneau. This is a Forest Service trail except for the start, which passes over state and private lands. It's 1.5 miles to the Dupont dock and 8 miles to Point Bishop. Usable spring, summer and fall. Rated easy, but tiring due to many roots and other obstacles. Elevation gain 200 feet. Estimated round-trip time to Dupont is 2 hours; 12 hours to Point Bishop. Point Bishop was named in 1794 by Capt. George Vancouver for the Bishop of Salisbury. Dupont was named after the Dupont Powder Co., which built the powder magazine there in 1914 to supply local mines. Trail is fairly level, but quite muddy. Waterproof boots recommended. About 1 mile from the trailhead a branch to the right leads to Dupont, where there is good saltwater Dolly Varden fishing in the spring. Main trail runs above Dupont to Point Salisbury then to Point Bishop. There are many windfall trees past Dupont. Related USGS Topographic maps: Juneau A-1 and B-1.

Salmon Creek Trail. Drive north from Juneau, then turn right just past the cement abutment at mile 2.5 of Egan Drive. Turnoff is located just before the Salmon Creek exit. Trail begins behind the new Salmon Creek powerhouse. It extends 3.5 miles to Salmon Creek dam. Usable spring, summer and early fall. Rated moderate. Condition good; trail was replaced with a road in 1984. Elevation gain 1,100 feet. Estimated round-trip time 5 to 6 hours. Hiking boots recommended. The first part of the trail follows the route of the old tramline and consists of a roadbed up a long, steep slope. (Many berries along the road in season.) At the top, the trail continues to the right and eventually branches. The right branch leads to a dam (a sign marks the intersection). The dam was built in 1914 by the Alaska-Gastineau Mining Co. It is the world's first true constant-angle arch dam and still is the largest of its kind. Just before the dam, the trail goes up a steep slope to the reservoir. There is fishing for eastern brook trout in the reservoir. The trail is on BLM lands and is maintained by Alaska Electric Light & Power Co.; watch for occasional AEL&P vehicles using the road. Related USGS Topographic map: Juneau B-2.

Sheep Creek Trail. Trailhead is located on Thane Road, 4 miles south of downtown Juneau. Trail extends 3 miles to alpine ridge. Usable late spring, summer and fall. Winter travel not recommended due to avalanche danger. Rated moderate. Elevation gain 700 in valley, 3,500 feet to ridge. Estimated round-trip time 5 to 6 hours. Waterproof hiking or rubber boots recommended. Joe Juneau and Richard Harris named Sheep Creek in 1880 after mistaking mountain goats for sheep. Gold mining in the valley began in 1881. This is a scenic trail with historical mining ruins. Slope is switch-backed and brushy. Trail begins through moss-covered forest with dense brush, then rises abruptly and drops into Sheep Creek valley. Old mining buildings at Portal Camp are barely standing and should not be disturbed. Trail is relatively level through the valley, then scrambles up a forested hillside until it reaches the alpine zone. If trail is hard to find above timberline, follow the power line, but stay a safe distance from the lines. Carry an ice ax; snow sometimes persists on the ridge through the summer. Related USGS Topographic map: Juneau B-1.

Spaulding Trail. Trailhead located at Milepost 12.6 from Juneau on the Glacier Highway, just past the Auke Bay post office. Trail extends 3 miles to Spaulding Meadows. Usable all year. Rated moderate. Elevation gain 1,800 feet. Estimated round-trip time 5 to 6 hours. This trail is extremely muddy during the warm seasons (waterproof footwear is a must), but is an important cross-country ski route in winter. Trail starts on an old road that leads to the first muskeg meadow, then continues about 1 mile through a wooded area to a second meadow. After another stand of trees, the trail ends in the last muskeg meadow. In winter, the rolling hills of Auke Mountain and Spaulding Meadows offer excellent cross-country skiing, with views of

the Chilkat Mountains, upper Mendenhall Glacier, Lynn Canal and Auke Bay. The trail provides access to the John Muir Forest Service recreation cabin. Related USGS Topographic map: Juneau B-2 and B-3.

Treadwell Ditch Trail. Trail may be reached by hiking about 1 mile from the beginning of the Dan Moller trail (see above), or from the Eaglecrest ski area on North Douglas Island. Trail extends 12 miles from Eaglecrest to the Dan Moller trail. Usable all year. Rated easy. Elevation gain/drop 700 feet. Estimated time 10 hours one way. The 18-mile-long Treadwell Ditch once carried water from Cropley Lake and Fish Creek to the Treadwell Mine and other mines at the south end of Douglas. The ditch was built between 1882 and 1889. Remains of the ditch project are historic artifacts and should not be disturbed. Trail features porcupines, deer, muskeg meadows and a view of Gastineau Channel. The trail was developed as a hiking and cross-country ski trail, but skiing is often marginal because heavy forest prevents sufficient snow cover in some areas. The trail was brushed from Eaglecrest all the way to Douglas in 1981; the section between the Dan Moller trail and downtown Douglas (accessible just above D Street in Douglas) is on City and Borough of Juneau land and is not maintained. Trail is flat and wide, but slopes in some places. Stay on the trail during the warmer months; delicate muskeg vegetation deteriorates rapidly with constant foot traffic. Related USGS Topographic map: Juneau B-2.

West Glacier Trail. Turn off the Mendenhall Loop Road onto Montana Creek Road and take the first right. Follow this road past the campground entrance and the remains of Skaters Cabin to the parking area at the end of the road. This Forest Service trail begins on the north side of the parking lot. It extends 3.4 miles to a rock outcrop above Mendenhall Glacier. Usable in spring and summer. Rated moderate. Elevation gain 1,300 feet. Estimated round-trip time 5 to 6 hours. Athletic shoes or waterproof hiking boots recommended, depending on the weather. Most of this trail is below the glacier trimline and passes through willow and alder trees. In a few places the trail skirts spruce and hemlock forest which the glacier did not reach on its most recent advances. The trail seems to end at a scenic overlook and then curves back toward the glacier; be alert for cairns that mark the route. The trail ends at the top of a rock outcrop and offers spectacular views of Mendenhall Glacier, ice falls and other glacial features. This trail also is used for access onto the glacier by experienced and properly equipped climbers; this is not recommended for inexperienced hikers. Related USGS Topographic map: Juneau B-2.

Windfall Lake Trail. Turn right off the Glacier Highway at Milepost 27 from Juneau, just before the Herbert River. This 0.2-mile road ends in a parking lot; trailhead is to the right. Forest Service trail extends 3.5 miles to Windfall Lake. Usable all year. Rated easy. Elevation gain 100 feet. Estimated round-trip time 4 hours. Waterproof boots recommended in summer. Used for cross-country skiing in winter. Trail follows the Herbert River through Sitka spruce and western hemlock forest. Trail muddy in summer, but some of the worst spots have been planked over. A spur trail once led to Herbert Glacier, but flooding from beaver dams has made this impassable. When the river is safely frozen, many people ski 5 miles from the parking lot to the glacier. The Windfall Lake trail connects with the Montana Creek trail at Windfall Lake. There is a small rowboat for fishing at the lake; fishing is good for searun cutthroat trout and Dolly Varden. Pink, chum, red and silver salmon spawn in the area. Other features are highbush cranberries, blue heron, swans and geese. Bears frequent the area. Related USGS Topographic map: Juneau C-3.

Yankee Basin Trail. Take the Amalga trail at Mile 28.4 from Juneau on the Glacier Highway (see above); 1.3 miles up the Amalga trail, turn left at the junction onto the Yankee Basin trail. This unmaintained Forest Service trail extends 6 miles to Yankee Basin, named by miners in 1902. Trail usable summer and fall. Rated moderate. Elevation gain 1,500 feet. Estimated round-trip hiking time is 8 to 9 hours. High concentrations of brown bears in this area. Trail is in very poor condition and is nearly impossible to follow in places. It follows an old mining tramway. Bridges are in poor condition; logs that were placed over muddy areas are now rotten. A side trail to the left leads to Eagle Beach. The main trail continues straight ahead into Yankee Basin, a very scenic area. This trail also connects with the Bessie Creek trail (see above) but the route has not been maintained for years. Related USGS Topographic map: Juneau B-3.

Ketchikan Area Trails

Bakewell Lake Trail. Trailhead located on the east side of Bakewell Creek, south side of Bakewell Arm about 40 miles east of Ketchikan in Misty Fiords National Monument. This Forest Service trail extends 1 mile to Bakewell Lake; does not provide access to Bakewell Lake

Forest Service recreation cabin. Accessible by boat or floatplane. Rated moderate. Elevation gain 200 feet. Estimated round-trip time 2 hours. Rubber boots recommended. The first half mile of this trail follows an overgrown, abandoned road. At the midpoint there is a waterfall and fish ladder overlook. The remaining half mile leads through timber, wet muskeg. Fishing in Bakewell Lake for Dolly Varden, cutthroat trout; fishing near the lake outlet for red, pink, chum and silver salmon and some steelhead. (See Sportfishing, Ketchikan Area, in this section.) Related USGS Topographic map: Ketchikan B-2.

Black Mountain Trail. Trailhead is in Ice House Cove off Carroll Point 7 miles southeast of Ketchikan. Forest Service trail extends 2.5 miles to Snag and Hidden lakes. Accessible by boat, but watch for submerged rocks. The first 0.5-mile traverses moderate slopes with grades of more than 20 percent. The rest of the trail is on rolling muskeg and scrub timberland. The tread is in poor shape with many wet spots and rough stretches. Primarily used for hiking and fishing access to the lakes. No developed facilities on this trail system. Related USGS Topographic map: Ketchikan B-5.

Checats Cove Trail. Trailhead is on the east side of Checats Creek in Checats Cove, about 35 miles northeast of Ketchikan in Misty Fiords National Monument. Forest Service trail extends 1.1 miles to Lower Checats Lake. Does not provide access to Forest Service recreation cabin on Upper Checats Lake. Trail accessible by boat or floatplane; cove large enough for safe anchorage. Trail usable late spring through early fall. Rated moderate; elevation gain 100 feet. Estimated round-trip time is 2-1/2 hours. The trail begins in spruce-hemlock forest; tread is level but low boggy areas will be encountered. At the 0.5-mile mark the trail enters a large blowdown area. The point where the lake becomes visible is a good camping spot. After this point, the trail has a steep incline then levels off when it returns to the creek's edge. At the logjam there is another good camping spot. The trail continues along the lake for another quarter mile, then ends by a small rock island. No developed facilities. Brown bears frequent this area. Good fishing in the lake. Related USGS Topographic map: Ketchikan B-3.

Deer Mountain/John Mountain Trail. This most difficult 9.9-mile trails begins at the junction of Granite Basin and Ketchikan Dump roads and gains 3,000 feet before ending at Lower Silvis Lake. Spectacular views of Ketchikan and Tongass Narrows make the long climb worthwhile. Experienced hikers can continue past the summit. There are free-use A-frame shelters, one just below and north of the summit and one 2.3 miles farther above timberline at Blue Lake. The shelters are not maintained and may be in poor repair. Related USGS Topographic map: Ketchikan B-5.

Ella Lake Trail. Trailhead is at the mouth of Ella Creek on Ella Bay on East Behm Canal, 24 miles northeast of Ketchikan in Misty Fiords National Monument. Access is by boat or floatplane. Forest Service trail extends 2.5 miles to Lower Ella Lake. Trail does not reach Forest Service recreation cabin at Ella Narrows. Trail usable spring to fall. Rated moderate. Elevation gain 250 feet. Estimated round-trip time 5-1/2 hours. Rubber boots recommended. There is a beach marker sign at the trailhead which is visible from Ella Bay. The first quarter-mile runs through old second-growth timber. The next 1.5 miles cross wet muskeg and marsh with tall grass. The last 0.8 mile leads through timber with a slight incline that levels off at the lake outlet. There is excellent trout and salmon fishing in Ella Creek. The area also features beaver, wildflowers and berries. Near the trailhead are soda springs ringed with concrete foundations built by the Civilian Conservation Corps in the 1930s. Related USGS Topographic maps: Ketchikan B-3, B-4 and C-4.

Humpback Lake Trail. Trailhead at the mouth of Humpback Creek in Mink Bay off Boca de Quadra, about 60 miles southeast of Ketchikan. Forest Service trail extends 3 miles to Humpback Lake. Accessible by boat or floatplane; Forest Service buoy in Mink Bay. Usable late spring through fall. Rated moderate. Elevation gain 270 feet. Rubber boots recommended. Trail is in fair condition. Fairly level for the first 2 miles. After passing small waterfall on the right, the trail begins a steep climb for approximately 500 feet with a grade increase of 50 to 70 percent. At the top of the ridge the trail levels off and leads through muskeg for 0.5 mile. No boardwalk. Trail is hard to follow. After the muskeg, the trail enters timber area where recent slides have buried the trail. Trail ends where a 3-sided shelter stood until it was demolished by a landslide. Excellent trout fishing at the outlet of Humpback Lake. Brown bear very abundant on this trail. Related USGS Topographic maps: Ketchikan A-2 and A-3, Prince Rupert D-2 and D-3.

Low Lake Trail. Trailhead located at mouth of Fish Creek in the northeast corner of Thorne Arm on Revillagigedo Island, in Misty Fiords National Monument. Accessible by floatplane

or boat; Forest Service buoy in Fish Creek Cove for small boat moorage. Forest Service trail extends 2.1 miles to Big Lake. Usable late spring through fall. Rated moderate. Elevation gain 290 feet. Estimated round-trip time 3-1/2 hours. The first half-mile of the trail is partly boardwalk with split log and drainage structures in wet areas. The trail proceeds without tread improvement to the lake. Short stretches traverse sections of steep, rocky ground, some with a 20 percent grade. Fish Creek supports a run of steelhead, Dolly Varden, salmon and cutthroat trout. (See Sportfishing, Ketchikan Area, in this section.) Also, black bears, wildflowers and berries in the area. Related USGS Topographic map: Ketchikan A-4.

Manzanita Lake Trail. Trailhead located on the west side of Manzanita Bay on East Behm Canal about 28 miles northeast of Ketchikan in Misty Fiords National Monument. Forest Service trail extends 3.5 miles to Manzanita Lake; does not provide access to the 2 Forest Service recreation cabins on the lake. Accessible by floatplane or boat. Usable late spring through fall. Rated moderate. Elevation gain 250 feet. Estimated round-trip time 9 hours. There is a floating dock and mooring buoy within sight of the trailhead sign. The first mile of trail is largely muskeg, after which it closely parallels the creek, eventually climbing away from the creek. The trail crosses the creek on a puncheon bridge in the last half mile and ends at the lake. There are no developed facilities on the trail. The tread is mostly natural, with wet and muddy footing in places. Large rocks and steep dropoffs along the last third of the trail may be hazardous. Trail's primary use is hiking, sightseeing and access to fishing in Manzanita Lake. (See Sportfishing, Ketchikan Area, in this section.) Related USGS Topographic maps: Ketchikan C-3 and C-4.

Naha River Trail. From Naha Bay (accessible by boat or floatplane) this 5.4-mile trail ends at Heckman Lake. The trail features excellent salmon and trout fishing, one of the best steelhead runs in Southeast, and the scenic, interesting salt chuck at the outlet of Roosevelt Lagoon. Jordan Lake and Heckman Lake cabins are located on this trail. Small boat tram at outlet to Roosevelt Lagoon. Picnic shelters at outlet of Roosevelt Lagoon and on Naha River. Beginning on boardwalk, the trail does have some wet and muddy spot farther in, but is generally in good condition. Allow 5 hours one-way walking time. Related USGS Topographic map: Ketchikan C-5.

Nooya Lake Trail. Trailhead located in a

small bight on the west shore of the North Arm of Rudyerd Bay, in Misty Fiords National Monument. Forest Service trail extends 1.1 miles to Nooya Lake. Access is by boat or floatplane. Usable late spring through fall. Rated moderate. Elevation gain 400 feet. Estimated round-trip time 2 to 3 hours. Access to the trail is fair; anchorage at the mouth of Nooya Creek is poor. The first quarter-mile leads through wet, boggy areas, the next half-mile gently increases in grade and wet areas are less common. At the 0.8-mile point, the trail turns left away from the creek and starts a steep, 35 to 45 percent grade. The trail is wet but solid. There is a 3-sided Civilian Conservation Corps shelter at the outlet of Nooya Lake. Black and brown bears are common along this trail. Related USGS Topographic map: Ketchikan C-3.

Punchbowl Lake Trail. Trailhead located at the south end of Punchbowl Cove in the Rudyerd Bay area of Misty Fiords National Monument. Forest Service trail extends 0.7 mile to Punchbowl Lake. Accessible by floatplane or boat; moorage buoy in cove. Trail usable late spring through fall. Rated moderate. Elevation gain 600 feet. Estimated round-trip time 3-1/2 hours. This is a fairly steep trail with switchbacks, but its condition is good. Trail is very scenic. At the 0.5-mile point there is an overlook of Punchbowl Creek waterfall. Within 500 feet of this point is another vista overlooking Punchbowl Cove. Here the trail runs along a 2-foot-wide rock ledge with a 300-foot drop. Near the lake, the trail runs along Punchbowl Creek where rock walls rise approximately 250 feet. Trail ends at a new 3-sided shelter on Punchbowl Lake. Activities include fishing in the lake. (See Sportfishing, Ketchikan Area, in this section.) Related USGS Topographic map: Ketchikan C-3.

Shelokum Lake Trail. Trailhead is approximately 90 miles north of Ketchikan on Bailey Bay, 0.5 mile south of Shelokum Creek. The trail climbs 2.2 miles to Shelokum Lake at an elevation of 348 feet. Rated most difficult. Estimated round-trip hiking time 4 hours. This trail is perhaps the most scenic trail in the Ketchikan area. Special features include the largest waterfall in the area, an undeveloped hot springs, views of extremely scenic mountains and cliffs and developed boat access. Hikers must ford Maude Creek before reaching Shelokum Lake. It is impassable during high water. A 3-sided shelter is located at the inlet of Lake Shelokum, near Shelokum Hot Springs. Related USGS Topographic map: Ketchikan D-5.

Winstanley Lake Trail. Trailhead located in Misty Fiords National Monument on the south side of Winstanley Creek, across from the southern tip of Winstanley Island in East Behm Canal. Forest Service trail extends 2.3 miles to Winstanley Lake. Accessible by floatplane or boat. Usable late spring through fall. Rated moderate. Elevation gain 400 feet. Estimated round-trip time 4 to 5 hours.

The trail begins 30 feet to the right of the south bank of Winstanley Creek. There is a beach marker and mooring buoy. The first mile of trail leads through dense spruce and hemlock forest. The trail crosses over to the north side of the creek at the 1-mile marker. There is a scenic view of Winstanley Creek and falls. The trail continues on the north side of Lower Winstanley Lake, crossing over to the south side of Winstanley Creek at the lake's inlet. The remaining 0.5-mile of trail goes through 2 small muskegs before it ends at a 3-sided Civilian Conservation Corps shelter on Winstanley Lake. There are no other facilities on the trail. Related USGS Topographic map: Ketchikan B-3.

Wolf Lake Trail. This more difficult 2.6-mile trail leads from salt water in Moser Bay, 19 miles from Ketchikan, through muskegs and river bottomland and past 2 small unnamed ponds and Lower Wolf Lake, terminating at the Upper Wolf Lake shelter. Rubber boots are a must because of the wet tread. There are deer, black bears, and a large population of wolves, especially evident in winter. Cutthroats can be caught in Upper Wolf Lake. This is a year-round trail, good for skiing or snowshoeing in winter. Related USGS Topographic map: Ketchikan C-5.

Petersburg Area Trails

Affleck Canal Portage Trail. Trail begins on the beach at the north end of Affleck Canal and extends 1.5 miles to the beach at Petrof Bay. Usable June to September. Rated difficult due to blown down trees along trail. Elevation gain 50 feet. Estimated time across 1-1/2 hours. This trail was developed primarily as a portage trail for canoers and kayakers and provides access to Tebenkof Bay Wilderness Area. The trailhead is reached by water from Kake, a ferry stop on the Alaska Marine Highway System. The trail can be incorporated with 1 or more of the 3 other Tebenkof Bay kayak portage trails. Trailheads are marked with large red-and-white portage diamonds; trail is marked with blue diamond markers. Canoers and kayakers are advised to pay attention to changing weather and water conditions for their safety. Trail offers spectacular views and access to beach-combing. Shore and land birds, wolves and black bear may be seen. Bears are especially common in summer along the creek that parallels the trail as they feed on spawning salmon. Make plenty of noise to avoid an encounter with a bear and hang food in a tree at night. Related USGS Topographic map: Port Alexander B-1.

Alecks Creek Portage Trail. Trail begins on the beach at the very head of No Name Bay and extends 4 miles to the mouth of Alecks Creek in Elena Bay. Usable June to September. Rated difficult due to blown down trees along trail. Elevation gain 45 feet. Estimated time across 2-1/2 hours. This trail was developed primarily as a portage trail for canoers and kayakers and provides access to Tebenkof Bay Wilderness Area. The trailhead is reached by water from the town of Kake, a ferry stop on the Alaska Marine Highway System, and the trail can be incorporated with 1 or more of the 3 other Tebenkof Bay kayak portage trails. Trailheads are marked with large red-and-white portage diamonds; trail is marked with blue diamond markers. Portagers on this trail can put in at a small lake just to the south of Alecks Lake, then paddle across Alecks Lake and through the narrow finger lakes that are the headwaters of Alecks Creek. Once the shallower waters of the creek are reached, it is best to line the kayak down the stream to avoid grounding or running into downed logs. The easiest trail through the braided channel of Alecks Creek is marked. This trail offers spectacular views, as well as excellent fishing in Alecks Creek for steelhead in April to May, red salmon in July and silver, pink, and chum salmon mid-August to October. During the summer the tide flat at the mouth of Alecks Creek is often covered with black bears, which also range upstream in search of fish. Make plenty of noise to avoid any unexpected encounters; always hang food in a tree at night. Related USGS Topographic maps: Petersburg B-6, C-6; Port Alexander B-1, C-1.

Bay of Pillars Portage Trail. Trail begins on the beach at the east end of Bay of Pillars on Kuiu Island and extends 1.2 miles to the beach at Port Camden. Usable June to September. Rated moderate. Elevation gain 100 feet. Estimated time across 1-1/2 hours. This trail was developed primarily as a portage trail for canoers and kayakers and provides access to Tebenkof Bay Wilderness Area. The trailhead is reached by water from the town of Kake, a ferry stop on the Alaska Marine Highway System, and the trail can be incorporated with 1 or more of the 3 other Tebenkof Bay kayak portage trails. Trailheads are marked with large red-and-white portage diamonds; trail is marked with blue diamond markers. Canoers and kayakers are advised to pay attention to changing weather and water conditions for their safety. This portage passes through a beaver pond and follows a Forest Road for a short distance. During the summer black bears will be on or near the portage trail; make plenty of noise to let them know you're coming. Always hang food in a tree at night. Related USGS Topographic map: Port Alexander C-1.

Big John Bay Trail. Trail extends 2.2 miles from Forest Road 6314, 16 miles from Kake, to the Big John Bay recreation cabin. Trailhead accessible by auto from Kake. No access to cabin by trail at high tide. Rated moderate. Elevation gain 100 feet. Estimated round-trip time 2 hours. Usable spring, summer and fall. Trail marked with blue diamonds with blazes, and pink flagging. Provides access to excellent waterfowl, grouse and black bear hunting. Related USGS Topographic maps: Petersburg D-5, D-6.

Cascade Creek Trail. Trail extends 4.5 miles to Swan Lake from the Forest Service recreation cabin at Cascade Creek, 14 air miles northeast of Petersburg on Thomas Bay. Accessible by floatplane or boat. Rated most difficult. The upper portion of the trail is currently closed due to safety hazards. Major trail maintenance is scheduled for 1990. Requires good hiking skills; use caution. Elevation gain 1,514 feet. Provides access to mouth of Cascade Creek at 1 mile, Falls Lake at 3 miles and Swan Lake at 5 miles. Follows edge of Thomas Bay and north side of creek. There is fishing in Falls Lake and outstanding scenery and photo opportunities. There is exit from Swan Lake to salt water. Hikers cannot reach the Swan Lake Forest Service cabin by this trail. Related USGS Topographic maps: Petersburg D-3, Sumdum A-3.

Cathedral Falls Trail. Trail extends 0.3 mile to Cathedral Falls from Forest Road 6312, about 9 miles from Kake. Usable spring, summer and fall. Rated moderate. Elevation loss 100 feet. Estimated round-trip time 30 minutes. Provides access to trout and salmon fishing and photo opportunities at the falls. Related USGS Topographic map: Petersburg D-5, D-6.

Colp Lake Trail. Trail extends 2.3 miles from the mouth of Five Mile Creek on Frederick Sound to Colp Lake, 5 miles northwest of Petersburg. Accessible by boat or floatplane. Usable spring, summer and fall.

Rated moderate. Elevation gain 588 feet. Estimated round-trip time 2-1/2 hours. Provides access to fishing, hiking, swimming and cross-country skiing. Excellent view of Del Monte Peak and surrounding alpine terrain.

Petersburg Lake Trail. This trail extends 6.8 miles from Petersburg Creek to Petersburg Lake cabin, 9 miles northwest of Petersburg. Rated easy. Tide of 15 feet is best for reaching trailhead, which is approximately 3 miles up Petersburg Creek from Wrangell Narrows. (Or hikers can walk 10 miles on a partial boardwalk from the public dock at just across Wrangell Narrows from Petersburg.) The trail follows Petersburg Creek most of the way. There is fishing for salmon and trout, wildflower meadows and photo opportunities. Related USGS Topographic maps: Petersburg D-3 and D-4.

Petersburg Mountain Trail. Trail extends 2.5 miles from Wrangell Narrows to the top of Petersburg Mountain. Located within Petersburg Creek-Duncan Salt Chuck Wilderness. Primarily accessible by boat. Trail rated difficult. High tide access is behind Sasby Island. Low tide access is from the Kupreanof public dock. Trail offers outstanding views and photo opportunities of Petersburg, coastal mountains and glaciers, Wrangell Narrows and part of the wilderness area. Related USGS Topographic map: Petersburg D-3.

Portage Mountain Loop Trail. Trail begins at the junction of the Petersburg Creek trail and the spur trail to Petersburg Lake recreation cabin and extends 10.5 miles to the Salt Chuck East recreation cabin. Usable summer and fall for hiking; winter for cross-country skiing and snowshoeing. Rated moderately difficult. Elevation gain 150 feet. Round-trip hiking time 12 hours. Trailhead accessible by floatplane via the Petersburg Lake cabin drop-off point, or by boat and foot to the Petersburg Creek trail. Portions of this trail were blazed by the Civilian Conservation Corps in the 1930s. Efforts to re-establish the trail began in 1978. When completed, the trail will extend from near the Petersburg Lake cabin to Goose Cove, to Salt Chuck East cabin, loop around the base of Portage Mountain and then connect back to the existing trail at Petersburg Lake. Trail passes through areas of muskeg and heavy timber and crosses numerous streams. Trail offers spectacular views of Portage Mountain and the Duncan Canal Salt Chuck. Moose, deer, black bear, waterfowl and other birds may be seen. Related USGS Topographic map: Petersburg D-4.

Raven Trail. Trail extends 3.9 miles from behind the Petersburg airport to Ravens Roost Forest Service recreational cabin. Drive to end of the airport road past the red-and-white water tower and watch for trail marker. Trail rated moderate. About half the trail is boardwalk, but some very steep (70 percent slope) sections require good hiking skills. Trail offers outstanding views of Petersburg, Frederick Sound and Wrangell Narrows, as well as access to upland bird hunting and winter cross-country skiing and snowshoeing. Related USGS Topographic map: Petersburg D-3.

Spurt Lake Trail. Trail extends 1.1 miles from Thomas Bay to Spurt Lake. Trailhead on bay south of Wind Point. Accessible by boat or floatplane. Trail usable spring, summer and fall. Rated easy, elevation gain 450 feet. Estimated round-trip time 1-1/2 hours. This trail provides access to Spurt Lake, which was the original location of the Spurt Cove cabin. Lake has fair fishing for cutthroat trout; small boat provided. Related USGS Topographic maps: Sumdum A-3.

Threemile Arm Portage Trail. Trail begins on the beach at the northwest end of Threemile Arm on Kuiu Island and extends 1.1 miles to the beach at the southeast end of Port Camden. Usable June to September. Rated difficult; elevation gain 100 feet. Estimated time across 1 hour. This trail was developed primarily as a portage trail for canoers and kayakers and provides access to Tebenkof Bay Wilderness Area. The trailhead is reached by water from Kake, a ferry stop on the Alaska Marine Highway System. The trail can be incorporated with 1 or more of the 3 other Tebenkof Bay kayak portage trails. Trailheads are marked with large red-and-white portage diamonds; trail is marked with blue diamond markers. Canoers and kayakers watch for changing weather and water conditions. This trail follows a creek for the first 1,500 feet; the portager can put in and paddle the deeper sections and line the shallower areas. A beaver pond also can be paddled for about 1,300 feet. This trail offers spectacular views and fishing. During the summer there are plenty of black bears on or near the trail; make noise to let them know you are there. Always hang food in a tree at night. Related USGS Topographic map: Petersburg C-6.

Twin Ridge Ski Trail. Trail begins at Milepost 3.4 on Twin Creeks Road and extends 4.9 miles to Ravens Roost cabin. Usable October to June for cross-country skiing; June to October for hiking. Rated moderately difficult. Elevation gain 1,200 feet. Estimated round-trip time 8 hours. Trailhead at Raven's Roost cabin can be reached via the 3.8-mile

Raven Trail from town. Intermediate skiing skills required at this end. Trailhead on Twin Creeks Road can be reached by driving or skiing 3.4 miles up the road, which is very steep and narrow. Road is dangerous when it is covered with snow; at those times, park at beginning of road and ski to trailhead in a small muskeg clearing on the left-hand side of the road. Trail marked with pink flagging and blue diamond markers, which may become covered with snow at times. Trail follows ridge. Advanced skiing skills or snow-shoes required to traverse the steeper slopes. Trail offers spectacular views of Wrangell Narrows, LeConte Bay and the mainland. Moose, deer and black bear may be seen. Related USGS Topographic maps: Petersburg C-3, D-3.

Upper Twin Ski Trail. This 3.2-mile loop trail connects to Twin Creeks Road at Miles 3.3 and 4. Usable October to June for intermediate and advanced cross-country skiing; June to October for hiking. Rated moderately difficult. Elevation gain 600 feet. Estimated loop time 3 hours. Trailhead on Twin Creeks Road can be reached by driving or skiing up the road, which is very steep and narrow. Road is very dangerous when it is covered with snow; at those times, park at beginning of road and ski to trailheads on the right-hand side of the road. Trail marked with pink flagging and blue diamond markers, which may become covered with snow at times. Entire length of trail is good for intermediate skiers, except for one steep 0.3-mile slope about 0.5 mile in from the western trailhead. Skiers of intermediate skill may want to start from the eastern trailhead, then walk down the steep slope. Advanced skiers should have no trouble. This trail offers spectacular views of the mainland. Moose, deer and black bear may be seen. Related USGS Topographic map: Petersburg C-3.

Sitka Area Trails

Beaver Lake Trail. Begins at Sawmill Creek Recreation area about 5 air miles east of Sitka. Trail extends 0.8 mile to Beaver Lake. From Sawmill Creek Road, then turn left onto the uphill dirt road which leads 1.5 miles to the Sawmill Creek Recreation area. Usable all year. Rated moderate. Elevation gain, 250 feet. Round-trip hiking time between 1 and 2 hours. This is a popular trail suited to family outings and was cleared and brushed in 1987. It offers good views of nearby mountains and a nice walk over muskeges, along marshes and through stunted forests. The trail begins across the bridge over Sawmill Creek on the south side of a small clearing. At the beginning, a series of switchbacks leads through forest of hemlock, Sitka spruce and yellow cedar up 200 feet. After the climb, the planked board-walk portion of the trail begins as it breaks out onto sloping stunted forests. The trail ends in a small muskeg at the western edge of Beaver Lake which was stocked with grayling in 1986, 1987 and 1988. Bears may be present. Use Caution. Related USGC Topographic map: Sitka A-4

Blue Lake River Trail. Trailhead is 9 miles east of Sitka at the inlet stream on the east end of Blue Lake. Access by floatplane, canoe or kayak or car via Sawmill Creek Road and Blue Lake. This unmaintained Forest Service trail extends 2.5 miles to the south end of Glacier Lake. Usable spring through fall. Rated difficult. Elevation gain 1,200 feet. Estimated round-trip time 4 to 6 hours. Rubber boots recommended. This trail was built in 1898 as a mining road. Trail begins on the north side of Blue Lake's inlet stream, runs through forest on the north side of the stream for about 0.5 mile, then crosses a stretch of open brushy areas. About a mile from the trailhead it begins to climb through spruce-hemlock forest and gains 700 feet in 0.3 mile. The last half mile to Glacier Lake is a difficult up-and-down scramble through rocky, brushy and finally subalpine terrain. Wildlife includes deer around Blue Lake and mountain goats higher up. Rainbow trout are found in Blue Lake. Related USGS Topographic map: Sitka A-4.

Gavan Hill Trail. Trail starts just past the house at 508 Baranof Street, whithin walking distance of downtown Sitka. Trail extends 3 miles to the 2,505-foot summit of Gavan Hill and connects with the Harbor Mountain Trail.(see below) Rated moderate. Elevation gain 2,500 feet. Estimated roundtrip time 6 to 8 hours. Trail usable midspring to late fall. First built in 1937 to provide access to recreationists and hunters. The trail was rebuilt in 1986 and continues to offer access to alpine country for exploring and camping. The first .5 mile of the trail follows the path of an old pipeline and heads northeast across gently sloping muskegs and scrubby forests before entering the forests and beginning the climb up Gavan Hill. About 0.75 mile up the hill the Cross Trail, which skirts Sitka, branches off to the left while the Gavan Hill Trail continues looping up east and north along a low ridge. Once on the Gavan Hill Ridge, about elevation 500 feet, the trail runs through a forest of stunted trees which gives way to subalpine meadows after a .25 mile. The first peak at

2,100 feet is reached after 0.5 mile and includes a steep 200-foot climb. The trail continues another .25 mile northwest along the ridge to the second, higher peak. Bears may be present. Related USGS Topographic map: Sitka A-4.

Goulding Lake Trail. Trailhead is located at the head of Goulding Harbor on West Chichagof Island about 65 miles northwest of Sitka. Accessible by floatplane. Trail extends 1 mile to the outlet of the lowest Goulding Lake. Trail is located within West Chichagof-Yakobi Wilderness Area; it does not extend to the Forest Service's Goulding Lakes recreation cabin. Trail usable all year. Rated moderate. Elevation gain 200 feet. This trail is wet and muddy; rubber boots highly recommended. Estimated round-trip time 2 hours. Trail generally follows the lower part of an abandoned mining tramway. Some of the old mining machinery, structures and a railroad engine remain. Do not disturb them. The trail begins on the north side of the inlet stream at the head of the harbor. Sections of the trail pass through spruce-hemlock forest, muskeg and marsh. At the point where the trail meets the Goulding River is a good viewpoint for a large waterfall just upstream. Above the viewpoint, the trail crosses a tributary and continues a short distance to the lowest Goulding Lake. Fishing is good for steelhead and small cutthroat trout. Related USGS Topographic map: Sitka D-7.

Harbor Mountain Ridge Trail. Trailhead is 9 miles from Sitka at the end of the Harbor Mountain Road. The trail extends 2 miles where it joins the Gavan Hill Trail at ta peak with an elevation of 2,505 feet. Usable spring through fall. Rated moderate. Elevation gain 500 feet. This is the only subalpine area in southeastern Alaska that is accessible by road. It offers wonderful views of Sitka Sound, Sitka Mount Edgecombe and numerous other mountains and islands. The trailhead is marked by a bulletin board and handrailings. It proceeds 300 feet up the hillside in a series of switchbacks. At the ridge, a short spur trail leads to the left to an overlook. The main trail turns to the right and follows the ridge toward the summit of a knob where WWII lookout ruins are located. As the trail continues along the ridge toward the peaks, it forks to the right and skirts the hillside, circling around to join the Gavin Hill Trail. The last section of the trail is little more than a deer path and is difficult to locate at times. The other fork of the trail continues up the steep shoulder slope of the peaks and ends as it reaches the steep rocky alpine at about 2,500 feet. Related USGS

Topographic maps: Sitka A-4, A-5.

Indian River Trail. Trailhead is located within walking distance from Sitka. Trail extends 4.3 miles to the base of Indian River Falls, usable year-round. Rated easy. Elevation gain 700 feet. Estimated round-trip time 8 hours. The trail offers views of the Sisters Mountains and is a relaxing walk through northwest coastal rain forest. To find the trailhead, follow Sawmill Creek road a short distance to Indian River Road, an unmarked road east of the Troopers Academy driveway. Walk around the gate and follow the road east about 0.5 mile to the pumphouse. The trail follows Indian River up a wide valley, meandering from the trailhead. Good picnic spots can be found in numerous places along the trail. Birds and animals are common in the forest and along the river. Deer are seen frequently and bears may be present. Related USGS Topographic map: Sitka A-4.

Lake Eva-Hanus Bay Trail. Trailhead is at Hanus Bay on the northeast coast of Baranof Island about 27 miles northeast of Sitka. Accessible by floatplane or boat. Trail extends 2.9 miles to an old Civilian Conservation Corps shelter on the southwest shore of Lake Eva. Usable all year. Rated moderate. Elevation gain 50 feet. Estimated round-trip time 4 to 8 hours. Rubber boots recommended. Trail begins on the west side of the bay, on the east side of the Lake Eva outlet stream. Trail heads west along the south side of the estuary, then winds along the south side of the Lake Eva outlet stream through dense spruce-hemlock forest that offers fine vistas and good fishing for spring-run steelhead, fall coho salmon and year-round cutthroat trout and Dolly Varden. (See Sportfishing, Sitka Area, in this section.) Lake is accessed at Mile 1.1 from salt water. The trail follows the south shore of Lake Eva through old-growth forest and ends at the shelter, which is in poor condition. The last half-mile of the trail is difficult due to windfall and landslides. The trail does not lead to the Forest Service Lake Eva recreation cabin, which is on the northwest side of the lake. Related USGS Topographic map: Sitka B-4.

Mount Edgecumbe Trail. Trailhead is behind the Freds Creek recreation cabin on the southeast shore of Kruzof Island about 10 miles west of Sitka. Accessible by floatplane or 1/2-hour boat ride from Sitka. Trail extends 6.4 miles to the summit crater of Mount Edgecumbe, an inactive volcano. Usable spring through late fall. Rated moderate. Elevation gain 3,000 feet. Estimated round-trip time 8 to 12 hours. Rubber boots recommended. The trail starts on flat, forested land then gradually rises while running through several miles of muskeg alternating with forest. About 3 miles up the trail at an elevation of 700 feet, a spur leads to a trail shelter. About 1 mile beyond the shelter turnoff, the trail steepens considerably. Timberline is at about 2,000 feet, where the trail ends. Above this the ground is covered with red volcanic ash. To reach the crater rim, continue straight up the mountain. The summit offers spectacular views on clear days. If you use any flagging or marking, be sure to remove it all. Also, pack out all garbage. Related USGS Topographic map: Sitka A-5 and A-6.

Mount Verstovia Trail. Trail begins a miles east of Sitka along Sawmill Creek Road, near the Kiksadi Club and extends 2.5 miles to the summit of Mount Verstovia. Usable mid-spring to mid-fail. Rated difficult. Elevation gain 2,550 feet to Verstoviaand 3,300 feet to Arrowhead. Estimated round-trip hiking time 6 hours. The lower hillside was logged by the Russians in 1860 and charcoal pits are still somewhat visable about 0.25 mile up the trail. The trail was built in the 1930s for recreational purpose. The view from Verstovia is spectacular and the trail progresses through thickets of salmonberry and alder to western hemlockspruce forest into brushy meadows, across snowfields, through grassy meadows and finally into a rocky alpine area with stunted, twisted plants. The trail is not well maintained and it is possible to lose track of the switchbacks which begin about 0.35 mile up the trail. At about 2,000 feet the trail reaches a gentle ridge which it follows east to the summit of Verstovia. Arrowhead Peak can be climbed by heading northeast along the rocky alpine ridge. The last part of the climb is quite steep and exposed. Bears may be present. Related USGS Topographic map: Sitka A-4

Salmon Lake-Redoubt Lake Trail. Trailhead located at the southwest end of Silver Bay about 10 miles southeast of Sitka. Accessible by boat or floatplane. Trail extends 5.9 miles to the Forest Service's recreation cabin on Redoubt Lake. Usable all year. Rated moderate. Elevation gain 600 feet. Estimated round-trip time 8 to 10 hours. Rubber boots recommended. Trail begins on the east side of the mouth of the Salmon Lake stream, which is the westernmost inlet stream at the head of Silver Bay. Trail passes through Sitka spruce, hemlock and cedar forest for the first 3 miles and follows the eastern shore of Salmon Lake for about a mile. The trail crosses several creeks and streams that must be forded. At about 3 miles, the trail travels through muskegs and meadows. There are trail forks in this area; stay on the main (southwestern) trail as the forks are unmaintained trails leading up to the Lucky Chance Mountain mining areas. The trail then reenters the forest and climbs 500 feet up a narrow saddle to the pass that separates the Salmon Lake and Redoubt Lake drainages. The tread is rough in areas, planking is often slick and there are muddy areas. The pass is about 1 mile from Redoubt Lake; the downhill slope can be slippery and muddy. The trail follows the lakeshore for about half a mile, then turns southwest a short distance to the cabin. Along this trail there is fishing for cutthroat and rainbow trout and Dolly Varden. Related USGS Topographic map: Port Alexander D-4.

Sashin Lake Trail. Trailhead is at the head of Little Port Walter on the eastern side of Baranof Island about 55 miles southeast of Sitka. Accessible by boat or floatplane. Trail extends 1.7 miles to Sashin Lake. Usable all year. Rated moderate. Elevation gain 400 feet. Rubber boots recommended. Trail was built and planked by the Civilian Conservation Corps in the 1930s. Go ashore at the dock in front of the fisheries research station (a large white brick house) in Little Port Walter. The trail heads southwest along the western shore of Little Port Walter for a quarter-mile, past various research station buildings and then past the king salmon holding pens, which are quite interesting. The bridge is out above the fish weir and the Forest Service recommends using hip-boots to make the crossing. The trail then meanders southwest up Sashin Creek through open forests and meadows. Just northeast of Sashin Lake, the trail goes over a low shoulder and enters a heavy forest; stay on the north side of the lake. The trail ends at a Civilian Conservation Corps shelter. About 1.3 miles from the trailhead another branch leads north to Round Lake. Round Lake trail is not maintained and difficult to follow. There is good trout fishing in Sashin Lake. This is bear country, so exercise caution. Related USGS Topographic maps: Port Alexander B-2, B-3 and B-4.

Sea Lion Cove Trail. Trailhead at Kalinin Bay on the north side of Kruzof Island, about 25 miles northwest of Sitka. Access is by boat or floatplane. Trail extends 2.5 miles to Sea Lion Cove, a beautiful mile-long white sand beach. Usable all year. Rated moderate. Elevation gain 250 feet. Estimated round-trip time 4 hours. Rubber boots recommended; trail is muddy and rough in places although new planking and clearing was completed in 1984.

Hikers should be aware that bears frequent this area. Trail begins at the southern end of Kalinin Bay on the upper beach just west of the high-water island where there is a red, diamond-shaped trail marker on a tree. The trail runs south along the western side of the estuary for about half a mile. This stretch is inundated during high tides. The trail then turns west up into the forest at the next trail sign. At the top of the hill it cuts through muskeg, re-enters the forest and follows the north shore of an unnamed lake. The trail becomes rougher and begins to drop into the Sea Lion Cove drainage just past the lake. For the last mile it winds west on low flat ground through forest and muskeg. The trail breaks out on the northern end of Sea Lion Cove. This beach is wonderful for beachcombing, exploring, camping, watching sea lions and viewing surf and the open Pacific Ocean. Camping also is possible at Kalinin Bay. During the summer, there usually is a fish-buying scow anchored in the bay from which groceries and showers may be purchased. Related USGS Topographic map: Sitka B-6.

Sitkoh Lake Trail. Trailhead at Sitkoh Bay on the southeast part of Chichagof Island about 35 miles northeast of Sitka. Accessible by floatplane and boat. Trail extends 4.3 miles to the Forest Service recreation cabin on Sitkoh Lake. Trail usable spring through fall. Rated moderate. Elevation gain 200 feet. Estimated round-trip time 6 to 8 hours. Rubber boots recommended. Trail begins on the north side of the mouth of Sitkoh Creek (about 0.5 mile northwest of the abandoned Chatham Cannery, which is on the western shore of Sitkoh Bay). The trail marker is just above the beach. The trail is easy to follow and was cleared in 1987. Some sections are planked and some have stairs. Near the lake the trail crosses some muskeg and in some areas it is muddy and/or under water. At the cabin a spur trail leads northwest about 0.5 mile to an old logging road. Bears are numerous in the area. There is good fishing in Sitkoh Creek and Lake. The creek has a good run of pink salmon from July to mid-August; red salmon from mid-July to mid-August; and silver salmon from late August through September. The creek reportedly has the best spring steel head run in the Sitka Ranger District, generally starting in late April. The lake has an over-wintering population of cutthroat trout and Dolly Varden. (See Sportfishing, Sitka Area, in this section.) Deer hunting is good in the area. Related USGS Topographic maps: Sitka C-3 and C-4.

Warm Springs Bay Trail. Located 20 miles east of Sitka on the east shore of Baranof Island. Trail extends 0.5 mile from Baranof Warm Springs to Baranof Lake where a Forest Service cabin is located (see Tongass National Forest Cabins, this section). Rated easy with no elevation gain. Round-trip hiking time 1 hour. Usable all year. A privately operated hot spring bath is located at the Warm Springs end of the trail, which is on salt water. Hot springs, pools and streamlets are common interruption of the mossy forest floor. Generally the trail is on boardwalk over areas with hot springs. The trail terminates by fading out near the north side of the lake's outlet. Several short, unmaintained spur trails radiate from this area; these go along the lakeshore, along the river, into the muskeg and one leads to Sadie Lake. Related USGS Topographic map: Sitka A-3.

Wrangell Area Trails

Aaron Creek Trail. Trail extends 4 miles from the Berg Bay recreation cabin, located 15 miles southeast of Wrangell, to the mouth of Berg Creek. Accessible by floatplane or boat. Rated easy. The Berg Creek trail continues 5 miles up Berg Creek into the mountains. Former mining activity in this area. Trail provides access to waterfowl, moose and bear hunting on tideflats; goat hunting in the mountains.

Anan Creek Trail. Trail extends 1 mile from the mouth of Anan Creek to Anan Fishpass and Bear Observatory, a wood-frame shelter. Accessible by floatplane or boat 34 miles south of Wrangell on the mainland. Rated easy; elevation gain 100 feet. Estimated round-trip time 1-1/2 hours. Trail begins at marker just above beach adjacent to Anan Bay cabin. Most of trail follows easy grade through spruce-hemlock forest. Trail is unsurfaced except for occasional staircases and bridges used for abrupt elevation changes or wet spots. Provides access to fishpass and bear viewing station at falls. Wildlife viewing/photography and pink salmon fishing available. Bears also use this trail heavily, so make your presence known. Related USGS Topographic map: Bradfield A-6.

Kunk Lake Trail. Trail extends 1.3 miles from Zimovia Strait to Kunk Lake on the northeast coast of Etolin Island about 13 miles south of Wrangell. Accessible by boat or floatplane. Rated difficult, estimated round-trip time about 2 hours. Trail covers varied terrain with grades ranging from easy to steep and with much wet ground. Waterproof boots highly recommended. Provides access to trout fishing and picnicking areas. Related

USGS Topographic map: Petersburg B-2.

Mill Creek Trail. Trail extends 0.8 mile from Eastern Passage to the Virginia Lake outlet about 10 miles east of Wrangell. Accessible by boat or floatplane. Rated easy. Elevation gain 100 feet. Estimated round-trip time 1-1/2 hours. Provides portage from salt water to the lake. Abandoned sawmill site at the head of the trail. A portion of the trail lies atop an old corduroy truck road. Evidence of old mining activity in the area. Activities include trout fishing and picnicking. The trail also provides snowmobile access to ice fishing in winter. Related USGS Topographic map: Petersburg B-1.

Rainbow Falls and Institute Creek trails. Rainbow Falls Trail begins at Mile 4.6 Zimovia Highway directly across from the Shoemaker Bay Recreation Area and Boat Harbor. It extends 0.8 mile to Rainbow Falls and leads to picnicking and scenic views at 2 modest observation sites. Midway between the 2 sites is the junction with Institute Creek Trail, which leads 3.5 miles (1,100-foot elevation gain) to Shoemaker Overlook Recreation Site. Here are excellent vistas and cross-country skiing opportunities, also access to grouse and deer hunting in season. At trail's end are 3-sided shelter, picnic table, fire grill, and outdoor privy. Surfacing of trail was continuing in 1989, though conditions can range from excellent to poor. Allow 1-1/2 hours round-trip hiking time for the Rainbow Falls portion and 6 hours (round-trip) for the Institute Creek hike. These 2 trails are the most popular on Wrangell Island. Related Topographic map: Petersburg B-2.

Wildlife Refuges

Alaska Maritime National Wildlife Refuge

This wildlife refuge includes more than 2,400 parcels of land on islands, islets, rocks, spires, reefs and headlands of Alaska coastal waters from Point Franklin in the Arctic Ocean to Forrester Island in southern Southeast Alaska. The refuge totals about 3.5 million acres.

Most of this refuge is managed to protect wildlife and the coastal ecosystem. The refuge has the most diverse wildlife species of all the refuges in Alaska, including thousands of sea lions, seals, walrus and sea otters. Alaska Maritime is synonymous with seabirds — millions of them. About 75 percent of Alaska's marine birds (40 million to 60 million birds of 38 species) use the refuge. They congregate in colonies along the coast. Each species has a specialized nesting site, be it rock ledge, crevice, boulder rubble, pinnacle or burrow. This adaptation allows many birds to use a small area of land.

Most refuge lands are wild and lonely, extremely rugged and virtually inaccessible. Some portions are classified as wilderness. Swift tides, rough seas, high winds, rocky shorelines and poor anchorages hamper efforts to view wildlife. Several islands of southeastern Alaska are part of this refuge.

St. Lazaria Island, located at the entrance to Sitka Sound, approximately 15 miles southwest of Sitka, is host to one of the largest seabird colonies in Southeast. This 65-acre, volcanic island has been set aside as a wildlife refuge since 1909. A half million seabirds of 11 different species breed here. Burrowing seabirds include tufted puffins; rhinoceros auklets; ancient murrelets; and storm-petrels, both Leach's and fork-tailed. Common and thick-billed murres, pelagic cormorants, glaucous-winged gulls, pigeon guillemots and others inhabit the sea cliffs, while song and fox sparrows and hermit thrushes flit through the lush growth. A nearly impenetrable mass of salmonberry bushes, growing up to 6 feet high, hinders foot travel on the island. St. Lazaria was uninhabited and apparently seldom visited until a military outpost was established there during WWII. Remains of the outpost are overgrown and difficult to find; the metal is corroding and the wood is rotting rapidly in the mild, wet climate.

Since seabirds are sensitive to disturbance and the closely spaced burrows of ground nesting birds are crushed by foot traffic, one should not land on the island. Small boats can land on the island only at high tide and then only with great difficulty because of constant swells from the open ocean. The seabirds can be seen easily from boats which can circle the island. Binoculars and spotting scopes are recommended to view wildlife from a distance. The best time to visit is May through June. Visitors should be prepared for wet and windy weather. Charter boats, lodging and campgrounds are available in Sitka.

Other Southeast islands included in the refuge are 5-mile-long Forrester Island, located 10 miles west of Dall Island, and the Hazy Islands, a group of small islands extending 2.7 miles in Christian Sound, 9 miles west of Coronation Island.

For more information contact: Refuge Manager, Alaska Maritime National Wildlife Refuge, 202 Pioneer Ave., Homer, AK 99603; phone 235-6546.

Mendenhall Wetlands State Game Refuge

This 3,600-acre refuge located along the coastline north of Juneau provides excellent opportunities to view a variety of migrating birds, including geese, ducks, swans and shorebirds. This is one of the few areas in the state where visitors may see redheads, ring-necked ducks and blue-winged and cinnamon teals. The refuge encompasses estuaries created by numerous streams which flow into Gastineau Channel from the surrounding mountains. As the tides ebb and flow, much of the refuge becomes alternately a pasture, then a shallow sea. During the year the wetlands host more than 140 species of birds, nearly a dozen species of mammals, 8 fish species and a variety of other marine life.

Spring bird migrations peak in April and May and by June most of the waterfowl and shorebirds have moved on to breeding grounds farther north. Relatively few species of birds nest in the Mendenhall Refuge, but it remains important through the summer as a feeding station. After the breeding season, birds traveling south to wintering grounds stop at the refuge. Shorebirds arrive first, feeding on mollusks and other invertebrates in late July. Waterfowl begin arriving in late August and September, feeding on the seeds of sedges, grasses and other plants. Species of waterfowl and shorebirds found along the edge of the sedge meadow include mallards, pintails, green-winged teals, northern shovelers, American wigeons and several species of sandpipers.

Beach ryegrass, which grows in sandy soils beyond the reach of most high tides, provides shelter for American kestrels, marsh hawks, semipalmated sandpipers, western sandpipers, least sandpipers, arctic terns, short-eared owls and savannah sparrows. A spruce-hemlock forest rims most of the refuge, providing a home for bald eagles, common ravens and northwestern crows, as well as songbirds, including American robins, hermit thrush, ruby-crowned kinglet and warblers.

In the tidal mudflats and open salt water of the channel may be found goldeneye, bufflehead, scoters, pigeon guillemots, loons, grebes, scaup, mergansers and marbled murrelets.

The most visible waterfowl in the refuge are Vancouver Canada geese, 400 to 600 of whom form a resident population that over-winters on open water near the mouth of the Mendenhall River and some creeks. Other geese found in the refuge include cackling Canada geese, lesser Canada geese, white-fronted geese and snow geese.

Mammals found in the refuge include harbor seals, Sitka black-tailed deer, black bears, muskrats, land otter, mink, short-tailed weasels, snowshoe hares, porcupines, little brown bats and long-tailed voles.

Recreational activities allowed in the refuge include hiking, wildlife viewing and photography, boating, fishing, sightseeing and waterfowl hunting in season. Boats are the only motorized vehicles permitted. Visitors walking in the refuge should wear waterproof footwear. Always consult a tide book; much of the land is submerged at high tide. Interpretive signs, walkways and trails aid visitors on foot.

The refuge is accessible by road from 6 locations.

For more information or a list of birds that occur in the refuge contact: Alaska Dept. of Fish and Game, Game Division, P.O. Box 20, Douglas, AK 99824; phone 465-4265. Or, the Juneau Audubon Society, P.O. Box 1725, Juneau, AK 99802.

The Rivers

Alsek-Tatshenshini rivers. These 2 spectacular rivers join together in Canada and flow (as the Alsek) to the Gulf of Alaska at Dry Bay, about 50 miles east of Yakutat and 110 miles northwest of Gustavus. Part of the river flows through Glacier Bay National Park.

Portions of the upper Alsek are considered dangerous, even for seasoned river runners. The entire Alsek River has been traveled by only a few parties. There is a 10-mile portage of Tweedsmuir Glacier, which crosses the river, approximately 140 miles downstream from the access point on the Dezedeash River near Haines Junction, YT. The entire Alsek River is 230 miles in length.

The section above Tweedsmuir Glacier is difficult Class IV white water, with high water volume and velocity. High winds and brown bears are other hazards. After the long, difficult portage the river still demands respect, but becomes broader and moves more slowly. This trip is a major undertaking not to be embarked upon lightly.

The Tatshenshini is floated each year by numerous raft and kayak parties, including many commercial groups. The best months are July and August. Access to the Tatshenshini is at the abandoned Dalton Post (turnoff at Milepost 104.2 from Haines on the Haines Highway), which once served as a way point on the famed Dalton Trail. Those running the river should have advanced to expert river skills and also be well versed in wilderness and survival skills, as the distances from the nearest communities are considerable. For pickup, arrangements should be made in advance with charter plane operators from Yakutat, Gustavus or Juneau, since communication from Dry Bay is limited.

The Tatshenshini route winds through 120 miles of rugged wilderness, judged by many to be some of the best in Alaska. The trip can take 11 to 12 days. Allow time for exploring the river-level glaciers and pristine country. Use caution as this is bear country.

Below Dalton Cache, there are several rapids rated Class III and IV. From there to near the confluence with the Alsek, the Tatshenshini winds through numerous valleys where high winds can sometimes stall boat movement. There are some Class IV rapids in the lower reaches and a section near Tree Ash Corner that may need to be portaged. In the lower river, standing waves of 4 to 12 feet may be encountered. *CAUTION: At Gateway Knob, boaters should scout downriver for icebergs floating at the entrance of Alsek Lake. The bergs can prohibit boat passage.* The Tatshenshini joins the Alsek below Tweedsmuir Glacier. This area is used by many river runners in the summer and campers should be courteous. Leave campsites in their primitive state.

Chickamin-LeDuc-South Fork rivers. This river system, which offers excellent scenery, is located 45 miles northeast of Ketchikan within Misty Fiords National Monument. The Chickamin River heads at Chickamin Glacier and flows southwest 40 miles to Behm Canal. The LeDuc heads at a glacier in British Columbia and flows southwest 30 miles to the Chickamin. The South Fork Chickamin River heads at a glacier and flows west 18 miles to the Chickamin. Since these rivers are fed by alpine glaciers they are silty. Boaters should be alert for sweepers, logs and high water.

Brown bears inhabit this drainage. Fish include rainbow trout and several species of salmon.

Access is by riverboat, floatplane or helicopter from Ketchikan.

Chilkat-Klehini-Tsirku rivers. The 42-mile-long Klehini and the 25-mile-long Tsirku are tributaries to the Chilkat River, which enters salt water near Haines. These are swift rivers, but have no white water. Season of use is June to September. Rafts are recommended. The trip down the Klehini-Chilkat takes 4 to 6 hours. The trip down the Tsirku-Chilkat takes 1 to 2 days, allowing time to explore glaciers.

The Chilkat and Tsirku rivers flow through the Chilkat Bald Eagle Preserve. Many Haines residents use airboats on the rivers in summer.

Access to the Chilkat River is by car to Milepost 19 from Haines on the Haines Highway. Access to the Klehini River is by car to Milepost 26 on the Haines Highway. Access to the lower Tsirku is from a turnoff at Milepost 25 on the Haines Highway. Access to the Tsirku headwaters is by plane to LeBlondeau Glacier.

Stikine River. The Stikine, a national wild and scenic river, has headwaters in British Columbia and flows 400 miles — through 2 Provincial parks and the Coast Range — to salt water near Wrangell. The lower 130 miles of the river, from Telegraph Creek, BC, to Alaska tidewater, are used by many canoeists, kayakers and rafters. A 60-mile section above Telegraph Creek flows through the Grand Canyon of the Stikine and is considered unnavigable and dangerous.

The Stikine is multichanneled in the lower reaches and is heavily laden with silt throughout. Glaciers cover the mountains along the route and descend down to river level in some points along the side channels. Fish available in the Stikine include several species of trout and salmon.

The river's name is derived from a Tlingit name meaning "Great River." For centuries the river has been a highway for the coastal Indians to travel inland to fish or trade. Sternwheel steamers ferried gold seekers to and from Alaska and Canada until 1916 along this route. Only one town, Telegraph Creek, is found along the entire river.

Access is from Wrangell, Petersburg or Telegraph Creek. Boaters can drive to Telegraph Creek via the all-weather Cassiar Highway, then the 75-mile Telegraph Creek Road. (The latter is not designed for large vehicles, has many hairpin turns and steep slopes, but offers spectacular scenery.) Other boaters use air charter services from Wrangell, Petersburg or Telegraph Creek for transportation to upstream put-in sites. Charter boats from Wrangell also deliver some river runners. The river also can be accessed from Petersburg (Mile 35.5 of the Mitkof Highway) or from the Wrangell waterfront. Many rafters arrange for pickup from the Stikine flats by boat or plane.

The water level can change considerably in the Stikine, varying from 10 to 25 feet. The river can rise several feet in 1 day, so camping areas should be planned carefully. The river is runnable from May through October. Usually snow is off the ground by mid-May. The mosquitoes do not usually become bothersome until mid-June.

From Telegraph Creek the river can be floated or paddled in a few days. However, a trip of 7 to 10 days will allow river enthusiasts time to explore the sloughs, many of which lead to glaciers or fine fishing areas, and to soak in Chief Shakes Hot Springs. Several Forest Service recreation cabins along the river are available on a reservation basis (see Tongass National Forest Cabins in this section). No public-use cabins are located on the Canadian side.

Although the river flow is swift at various points, it is considered easy Class I or II. The Stikine drops 8 feet per mile. Boaters should, however, be alert for logjams along some of the side routes and sweepers and floating logs throughout. The water is extremely cold. Black and brown bears are common along the river. Deer, moose, wolves, beavers, mountain goats and bald eagles also may be seen.

The U.S. Forest Service has a $1 booklet, *Stikine River Canoe-Kayak Trails,* which shows the main and secondary river routes in the lower river where it divides into numerous channels. It shows tent spots, logjams and which routes are best at the varying water stages. The guide shows 3 routes for canoers and kayakers who wish to go upstream following eddies, tides and side sloughs to the Canadian border, about 35 miles from tide-water. But the guide also points out that lining will be necessary (for those going upriver) in several places where the water is too shallow or too swift. The booklet is available from the Forest Service in Wrangell (P.O. Box 51, Wrangell, AK 99929) or Petersburg (P.O. Box 1328, Petersburg, AK 99833).

For more information on this area, see *The Stikine River,* Vol. 6, No. 4 of *ALASKA GEOGRAPHIC®.* To order, see the ALASKA NORTHWEST LIBRARY section at the back of the book.

Taku River. This river heads in Canada and flows southwest 54 miles into Taku Inlet, 20 miles northeast of Juneau. This silty river is rated moderately difficult. Usable in summer. Rafts and canoes used most often. Access is by boat or small plane from Juneau. Most float trips start at Canoe Corner in Canada.

Floaters should be alert for numerous jet and motorboats and numerous sweepers. This river offers excellent wildlife viewing, fishing, hunting and climbing areas.

Unuk River. This silty river heads in Canada on the east side of Mount Stoeckl and flows southwest 28 miles to the head of Burroughs Bay, 50 miles northeast of Ketchikan. The river is located within Misty Fiords National Monument. It can be floated in 1 to 2 days. Many old mining claims line

the river and its small tributaries.

Access is by riverboat upriver or by floatplane to Border Lake in Canada or to other points on the river itself. One turn about one-third of the way down the river from the Canadian border may need to be portaged. The Unuk becomes braided near its outlet. Floaters should be alert for sweepers and logs. Huge and numerous brown bears inhabit this area. Fish in the river include rainbow, cutthroat and steelhead trout and pink, king, silver and chum salmon.

Sea Kayaking

The sheltered waterways of southeastern Alaska are ideal for sea kayaking. Whether one spends a weekend or an entire summer exploring Southeast's channels and fjords, it is possible to encounter whales, sea otters, seabirds, and view tide water glaciers without significant human contact.

The solitude, rich wildlife and breathtaking scenery help compensate for the discomfort and inconvenience of wet, rainy weather that is as characteristic of the area as the solitude and beauty. However, the weather can be more than just an inconvenience. Stormy weather combined with the remoteness of the area demand that kayakers be skilled, well equipped and prepared to wait out hazardous conditions. (For more information about general kayaking conditions and safety, see Boating in GENERAL INFORMATION section.)

Boats can be carried aboard the Alaska Ferry System. Tour operators offer drop-off service for kayakers, boats may be chartered especially for this service and folding boats can be flown into remote spots.

Among the places popular with sea kayakers are the following:

Glacier Bay National Park and Preserve. Attractions include tidewater glaciers, icebergs and abundant wildlife. Access is by air or tour boat from Juneau; the ferries do not serve Glacier Bay. (Getting to Glacier Bay by kayak is not a trip for novices because of the hazards of Icy Strait, but the waters of the bay itself are sheltered.) Kayaks can be rented at Bartlett Cove. Sightseeing vessels from Bartlett Cove will drop off and/or pick up kayakers near the glaciers at the head of the bay. (Details on these areas are provided in sections on Tongass National Forest and Marine Parks.)

Kuiu Island and Tebenkof Bay Wilderness. Attractions within the 65,000-acre wilderness include a complex system of bays, small islands and coves and a wide variety of wildlife. Several kayak/canoe routes have been established and portage trails are marked throughout this area. Access is by Alaska State ferry to Kake.

Tracy Arm and Ford's Terror Wilderness. Attractions include glaciers, icebergs, scenic fjords, dramatic tide rips. Access is by paddle (50 miles) or via the tour boat from Juneau which offers drop-offs and pickups for kayakers. An extension of the route could include Seymour Canal, Admiralty Island and a portage into the chain of lakes across that island to Angoon (where the state ferry docks).

Pelican to Sitka. Attractions include the exposed outer coast and a natural hot spring. Access: Alaska State ferries serve both Pelican and Sitka; check schedule, as service to Pelican is limited. Many other attractions for kayakers in and around Sitka Sound.

Misty Fiords National Monument. Attractions include scenic fjords, hot spring, and a sheltered route. Access: Alaska State ferries to Ketchikan. Drop-offs, pickups and support services can be arranged.

Hoonah to Tenakee Springs. Attractions include historic portage, natural hot spring, village of Tenakee Springs, sheltered route. Access via Alaska State ferries, which serve both Hoonah and Tenakee Springs.

Sportfishing

The great majority of southeastern Alaska's best fishing locations are accessible only by plane or boat. (For good fishing spots along the few highways in this region consult *The MILEPOST®*.)

Southeast offers a variety of fishing experiences, from angling in wilderness lakes and streams to ocean trolling. A variety of species are available. Salmon are the most popular sport fish in Southeast; during the summer several communities sponsor derbies that offer prizes for the largest salmon caught.

The sheltered marine waters of Southeast are perhaps the best place in Alaska to fish for king salmon. These fish range from 10 to 50 pounds, which is trophy size, and can reach 90 to 100 pounds. Kings are present in southeastern Alaska marine waters all year. The best period for big fish, however, is from mid-April to mid-June when mature fish are moving through. "Feeders" or smaller kings up to 25 pounds are available throughout the remainder of the year. Preferred bait is trolled or drifted herring. Try the edges of reefs where they drop off into deep water.

Silver (coho) salmon are available from July through September; best month is August. Herring or large spoons are used for bait and flashers often are used for attraction.

These flashy fighters usually run shallow, but do not necessarily follow shorelines. Silvers average 12 pounds, but can exceed 20 pounds.

Fishing for pink salmon is good during July and August. Pinks often follow the beach in schools as they swim toward their spawning streams. These fish are best if caught fresh from the sea. Use small, bright spoons — most fishermen use spinning gear — and keep the spoon or spinner moving and lively. These salmon average 3 or 4 pounds, but occasionally reach 10 pounds.

Chum and red (sockeye) salmon do not take bait in salt water nearly as well as other species of salmon. In freshwater streams, reds can be taken on small flies drifted slowly or on small spinning lures. Chum salmon are available in Southeast waters from July to September. They range from 2 to 15 pounds, but commercially caught chums have weighed in at 35 pounds. Red salmon are available in June and July. These are small salmon, commonly weighing 2 to 7 pounds (trophy size is anything over 10 pounds).

Other fish found in Southeast include halibut, which can weigh more than 300 pounds; rainbow trout and steelhead, which may tip the scales at 10 pounds and occasionally reach 20 pounds; Dolly Varden, which usually weigh 1 to 3 pounds (world's record is 8.07 pounds); cutthroat trout from 1 to 3 pounds, may reach 7 pounds; arctic grayling up to 2 pounds; and brook trout from 1 to 5 pounds. An isolated population of northern pike is found in the Pike Lakes system near Yakutat.

Access to most sportfishing in Southeast is by private or charter boat from most communities or via small planes — usually chartered in the larger communities such as Sitka, Juneau, Petersburg, Ketchikan and Wrangell. A charter flight can range in cost from $180 to $450 an hour, depending on the size of the plane. Fishing licenses are available in most communities and at some lodges.

For those traveling in the wilderness, a general rule from the Alaska Dept. of Fish and Game is to "plan for the worst." Travelers should take extra food and other supplies and allow for a flexible schedule in the event the weather turns bad and prevents pickup from remote sites.

For more information about fishing in Southeast consult the current sportfishing regulations or contact Alaska Dept. of Fish and Game, Sport Fish Division, P.O. Box 20, Douglas, AK 99824; phone 465-4270.

For Juneau-Yakutat Area (including

Admiralty Island, Haines and Skagway): Area Management Biologist, Sport Fish Division, P.O. Box 20, Douglas, AK 99824; phone 465-4270.

For Ketchikan Area: Area Management Biologist, Sport Fish Division, 2030 Sea Level Dr., Suite 205, Ketchikan, AK 99901; phone 225-2859.

For Petersburg-Wrangell Area: Alaska Dept. of Fish and Game, Sport Fish Division, P.O. Box 667, Petersburg, AK 99833-0667; phone 772-3801.

For Sitka Area: Area Management Biologist, Sport Fish Division, P.O. Box 510, Sitka, AK 99835-0510; phone 747-5355.

Admiralty Island Fishing

Barlow Cove. A 4-mile-long cove located on the north end of the Mansfield Peninsula, 19 miles northwest of Juneau. Accessible by boat. Fish available: king salmon — available all year but best for large fish May to June, use herring or spoons; silver salmon — best in August, use herring or spoons; pink salmon — July to August, use small spoons; chum salmon — July to September, use spoons; Dolly Varden — May to October, use bait, spinners, flies; cutthroat trout — best mid- to late summer, use bait, spinners, flies; halibut — available all year but season closed in January, best in summer, use bait or jigs; rockfish — all year, best May to September, use smaller bait or jigs.

Chatham Strait. Located on the west side of Admiralty Island. Accessible by boat. Fish available: king salmon — available all year but best for large fish May to June, use herring or spoons; silver salmon — best in August, use herring or spoons; pink salmon — July to August, use small spoons; Dolly Varden — May to October, use bait, spinners, flies; cutthroat trout — best mid- to late summer, use bait, spinners or flies; halibut — available all year, season closed in January, best in summer, use bait; rockfish — all year, best May to September, use smaller baits or jigs.

Doty Cove. Located on the northeast coast of the Glass Peninsula on the east side of Admiralty Island, 16 miles southeast of Juneau. Accessible by boat. Fish available: king salmon — available all year but best for large fish May to June, use herring or spoons; silver salmon — best in August, use herring or spoons; pink salmon — July to August, use small spoons; chum salmon — July to September, use spoons; Dolly Varden — May to October, use bait, spinners, flies; halibut — available all year but season closed in January, best in summer, use bait; rockfish

— all year, best May to September, use smaller baits or jigs.

Gambier Bay. Located on the southeast coast of Admiralty Island, 70 boat miles south of Juneau, 57 miles east of Sitka. Forest Service cabin available. Fish available: king salmon — available all year but best for large fish May to June, use herring or spoons; silver salmon — best in August, use herring or spoons; pink salmon — July to August, use small spoons; Dolly Varden — May to October, use bait, spinners, flies; halibut — all year, season closed in January, best in summer, use bait.

Hasselborg Lake. An 8.5-mile-long lake located on central Admiralty Island, 17 miles northeast of Angoon, 37 air miles south of Juneau. Forest Service cabin and boat available. Accessible by floatplane. Fish available: cutthroat trout — best May to September, use bait, spinners, flies; Dolly Varden — best May to October, use bait, spinners, flies; kokanee — best May to September, use spinners, eggs.

Jims, Davidson, Distin and Guerin lakes. Group of small lakes located on central Admiralty Island, 45 air miles south of Juneau. Forest Service cabins and boats available. Accessible by floatplane. Fish available: cutthroat trout — best May to September, use bait, spinners, flies; Dolly Varden — best May to October, use bait, spinners, flies; kokanee — best May to September, use spinners, eggs.

Lake Florence. A 4-mile-long lake located on the west coast of Admiralty Island, 21 miles north of Angoon, 33 air miles southwest of Juneau. Forest Service cabin and boat available. Accessible by floatplane. Fish available: cutthroat trout — best May to September, use bait, spinners, flies; Dolly Varden — best May to October, use bait, spinners, flies.

Lake Kathleen. A 1.7-mile-long lake located on the west coast of Admiralty Island, 28 miles north of Angoon, 28 air miles southwest of Juneau. Forest Service cabin and boat available. Accessible by floatplane. Fish available: cutthroat trout — best May to September, use bait, spinners, flies; Dolly Varden — best May to October, use bait, spinners, flies.

Mitchell Bay. A 3.5-mile-wide bay located on west central Admiralty Island, 7 miles northeast of Angoon, 49 air miles south of Juneau. Accessible by floatplane from Juneau or boat from Angoon. Excellent spring sea-run cutthroat trout fishing, use bait, spinners, flies. Other fish: Dolly Varden — May to

October, use bait, spinners; king salmon —
available all year but best for large fish May
to June, use herring or spoons; silver salmon
— best in August, use herring or spoons; pink
salmon — July to August, use small spoons.

Mole Harbor. A 1.3-mile-wide bay located
on Seymour Canal on the southeast side of
Admiralty Island, 24 air miles northeast of
Angoon, and 45 air miles or 70 boat miles
south of Juneau. Accessible by floatplane or
boat. Fish available: king salmon — available
all year but best for large fish May to June,
use herring or spoons; silver salmon — best in
August, use herring or spoons; pink salmon —
July to August, use small spoons; chum salmon
— July to September, use spoons; Dolly Varden
— May to October, use bait, spinners, flies;
cutthroat trout — best mid- to late summer,
use bait, spinners or flies; steelhead — April to
June, use spoons, eggs.

Piling Point. Located on Stephens Passage
on the northeast coast of the Mansfield Peninsula on Admiralty Island, 14 miles west of
Juneau. Accessible by boat. Fish available:
king salmon — available all year but best for
large fish May to June, use herring or spoons;
silver salmon — best in August, use herring or
spoons; pink salmon — July to August, use
small spoons; chum salmon — July to September, use spoons; red salmon — best in June, use
spoons; Dolly Varden — May to October, use
bait, spinners, flies; halibut — all year, season
closed in January, best in summer, use bait or
jigs; rockfish — all year, best May to September, use smaller baits or jigs.

Pleasant Bay Creek. Located on Admiralty Island on the west shore of Seymour
Canal, 2 miles southeast of Mole Harbor, 50
air miles and 65 boat miles south of Juneau.
Popular for steelhead, April to June, use spoons,
eggs. Other fish: silver salmon — best in August,
use herring or spoons; pink salmon — July to
August, use small spoons; Dolly Varden —
May to October, use bait, spinners, flies; cutthroat trout — best mid- to late summer, use
bait, spinners or flies.

Point Arden. Located on Admiralty Island
in Stephens Passage on the north coast of
Glass Peninsula, 13 miles southeast of Juneau.
Accessible by boat. Fish available: king salmon
— available all year but best for large fish May
to June, use herring or spoons; silver salmon
— best in August, use herring or spoons; pink
salmon — July to August, use small spoons;
chum salmon — July to September, use spoons;
Dolly Varden — May to October, use bait,
spinners, flies; halibut — all year, season closed
in January, best in summer, use bait or jigs;
rockfish — all year, best May to September, use

smaller baits or jigs.

Point Retreat. Located on the north tip of
the Mansfield Peninsula on Admiralty Island,
20 miles northwest of Juneau. Accessible by
boat. Lighthouse on point. Fish available:
king salmon — available all year but best for
large fish May to June, use herring or spoons;
silver salmon — best in August, use herring or
spoons; pink salmon — July to August, use
small spoons; chum salmon — July to September, use spoons; red salmon — best in June, use
spoons; Dolly Varden — May to October, use
bait, spinners, flies; halibut — all year, season
closed in January, best in summer, use bait;
rockfish — all year, best May to September, use
smaller baits or jigs.

Pybus Bay. A 4-mile-wide bay located on
the east coast of Admiralty Island, 53 miles
east of Sitka, 80 boat miles south of Juneau.
Accessible by boat. Good summer fishing for
large king salmon (smaller kings available all
year), use herring or spoons. Other fish: silver
salmon — best in August, use herring or spoons;
pink salmon — July to August, use small
spoons; Dolly Varden — May to October, use
bait, spinners, flies; halibut — all year, season
closed in January, best in summer, use bait.

Thayer Lake. A 7-mile-long lake located
on west central Admiralty Island, 10 miles
northeast of Angoon, 42 air miles south of
Juneau. Lodge with all facilities on lake. Fish
available: cutthroat trout and kokanee — best
May to September, use bait, spinners, flies;
Dolly Varden — best May to October, use bait,
spinners, flies.

Youngs Lake. A 6-mile-long lake located
on the northeast end of Admiralty Island, 15
miles south of Juneau by boat or plane. Forest
Service cabins with boats available. Fish available: rainbow trout — all year, best May to
September, use flies, lures, bait; steelhead —
April to June, use spoons, eggs; cutthroat trout
— best May to September, use bait, spinners,
flies; Dolly Varden — best May to October, use
bait, spinners, flies; silver salmon — use spoons.

Haines-Skagway Area Fishing

Chilkat Inlet. Inlet extends 16 miles south
from the mouth of the Chilkat River, 1 mile
southwest of Haines, to Lynn Canal. Accessible by boat; beach access from Mud Bay Road
(get directions locally.) Chilkat State Park
provides camping sites, picnic areas, boat
launch, small dock and trails and is a good
access point for the inlet. Fish available: king
salmon — best early summer, use herring or
spoons; silver salmon — September to October, use herring or spoons; pink salmon — July
to August, use small spoons; Dolly Varden —

May to October, use bait, spinners, flies; cut-throat trout — best mid- to late summer, use bait, spinners, flies; halibut — all year, season closed in January, best in summer particularly between Kochu Island and Lehunua Island, use bait; rockfish — all year, best May to September, use smaller baits or jigs. Also shrimp and crab (July through November; 2 to 5 pounds) in Kalhagu Cove.

Chilkat Lake. A 6-mile-long lake located 3 miles south of Klukwan and about 15 miles northwest of Haines. Accessible by boat or air from Haines or Skagway. Fish available: cut-throat trout — best May to September, use flies; Dolly Varden — May to October, use bait, spinners, flies; silver salmon — September to October, use spoons; red salmon — June, use spoons or flies.

Chilkat River. Flows into Chilkat Inlet 1 mile southwest of Haines. Accessible by boat from Haines or from the Haines Highway, which parallels the river at intervals. Fish available: king salmon — best in the inlet in June, use herring or spoons; silver salmon — September to October, use herring or spoons; chum salmon — September to October, use spoons; red salmon — best in June, use spoons or flies; Dolly Varden — May to October, use bait, spinners, flies; cutthroat trout — best mid- to late summer, use bait, spinners, flies.

Chilkoot Inlet. Extends 20 miles to Lynn Canal about 5 miles north of Haines, 32 miles south of Skagway. Accessible by boat from Haines or Skagway; beach access from Lutak Road from Haines. Fish available: king salmon — best early summer; use herring or spoons; silver salmon — September to October, use herring or spoons; pink salmon — July to August, use small spoons; Dolly Varden — May to October, use bait, spinners, flies; cutthroat trout — best mid- to late summer, use bait, spinners, flies; halibut — all year, season closed in January, best in summer, use bait; rockfish — all year, best May to September, use smaller baits or jigs.

Chilkoot Lake. A 3.6-mile-long lake near the mouth of the Chilkoot River, 12 miles southwest of Skagway. Accessible by boat or from the end of Lutak Road north of Haines. Fish available: silver salmon — September to October, use spoons or flies; pink salmon — best July to August, use small spoons; chum salmon — September to October, use spoons; red salmon — best in June, use spoons or flies; Dolly Varden — May to October, use bait, spinners, flies; cutthroat trout — best mid- to late summer, use bait, spinners, flies. A 32-unit camping site, located on the southern shore of the lake, is part of the Chilkoot Lake State Recreation Area.

Chilkoot River. Flows into Lutak Inlet at the head of Chilkoot Inlet, 12 miles southwest of Skagway. Accessible by boat from Haines or Skagway or from the end of Lutak Road from Haines. Fish available: silver salmon — September to October, spoons or flies; pink salmon — best July to August, use small spoons; chum salmon — September to October, use spoons; red salmon — best in June, use spoons or flies; Dolly Varden — May to October, use bait, spinners, flies; cutthroat trout — best mid- to late summer, use bait, spinners, flies.

Dewey Lakes. Lower Dewey Lake 0.8 mile long, located 2 miles southeast of Skagway. Upper Dewey Lake 0.4 mile long, located 1.4 mile east of Lower Dewey Lake. Lower lake accessible by 0.8-mile trail from the end of 4th Street in Skagway; trail continues to upper lake. Fish available: brook trout — 8 to 14 inches, June to September, use salmon eggs, small spinners and flies; Dolly Varden — May to October, use bait, spinners, flies.

Herman Lake. A 0.3-mile-long lake located on Herman Creek, southwest of Haines. Accessible via trail from Porcupine Road (get directions locally.) Fish available: grayling — best July to September, use flies.

Letnikof Cove. Located on the southwest coast of the Chilkat Peninsula in Chilkat Inlet south of Haines. Accessible by boat or from Mile 5 Mud Bay Road (get directions locally). Fish available: king salmon — best early summer, use herring or spoons; silver salmon — September to October, use herring or spoons; pink salmon — July to August, use small spoons; chum salmon — 8 to 17 pounds, September to early November, fish from banks with flashing lures; Dolly Varden — May to October, use bait, spinners, flies; cut-throat trout — best mid- to late summer, use bait, spinners, flies; halibut — all year, season closed in January, best in summer, use bait; rockfish — all year, best May to September, use smaller baits or jigs.

Lost Lake. Located 10 miles from Skagway by road at head of Taiya Inlet, then a strenuous 2-mile hike westerly to lake. Rainbow trout present, use flies, lures, bait. Use of guide recommended; information available locally.

Lutak Inlet. Located north of Haines on Lutak Road. Chilkoot River empties into head of Lutak Inlet. Accessible by boat or from Lutak Road, which parallels the inlet. Fish available: pink salmon — July and early August, use small spoons; red salmon — June to August, use spoons or flies; ocean run Dolly Varden — June through November, use bait, spinners, flies; king salmon — best early summer, use herring or spoons; silver salmon — September to October, use herring or spoons; cutthroat trout — best mid- to late summer, use bait, spinners, flies; halibut — all year, season closed in January, best in summer, use bait; rockfish — all year, best May to September, use smaller baits or jigs.

Lynn Canal. A 60-mile-long channel that extends south from Chilkat Island near Haines to Chatham Strait, 22 miles west of Juneau. Accessible by boat. Weather and water conditions should be watched closely in this large open waterway. Fish available: king salmon — best early summer, use herring or spoons; silver salmon — September to October, use herring or spoons; pink salmon — July to August, use small spoons; Dolly Varden — June to November, use bait, spinners; cutthroat trout — best mid- to late summer, use bait, spinners or flies; halibut — all year, season closed in January, best in summer, use bait or jigs; rockfish — all year, best May to September, use smaller baits or jigs.

Skagway Harbor. Located in front of the city of Skagway. Accessible from shore or by boat. Fish available: Dolly Varden — 18 to 20 inches, May to June, use Dardevles and other spoons, good fishing from shore; king salmon — 8 to 30 pounds all summer, use herring. Windy weather often dangerous for small boats.

Taiya Inlet. Extends 13 miles south from the mouth of the Taiya River to Chilkoot Inlet, 12 miles south of Skagway. Accessible by boat or from shore in Skagway. Fish available: king salmon — best early summer, use herring or spoons; silver salmon — September to October, use herring or spoons; pink salmon — July to August, use small spoons; Dolly Varden — 18 to 20 inches, May to June, use Dardevles and other spoons, good fishing from shore; cutthroat trout — best mid- to late summer, use bait, spinners, flies; halibut — all year, season closed in January, best in summer, use bait; rockfish — all year, best May to September, use smaller baits or jigs.

Taiya River. Enters Taiya Inlet 1 mile north of Dyea Point, 2 miles northwest of Skagway. Accessible by boat or from the bridge on Dyea Road. Fish available: silver salmon — September to October, use spoons; pink salmon — July to August, use small spoons; chum salmon — September to October, use spoons; Dolly Varden — 18 to 20 inches, May to June, use Dardevles and other spoons.

Walker Lake. A 1-mile-long lake located southwest of Haines. Accessible by floatplane or by trail off Porcupine River Road (ask directions locally). Fish available: grayling — best July to September, use flies.

Juneau Area Fishing

Aaron Island. A 0.4-mile-long island located in Favorite Channel, 17 miles northwest of Juneau. Accessible by boat. Fish available: king salmon — best May to June, use herring or spoons; silver salmon — best in August, use herring or spoons; pink salmon — July to August, use small spoons; chum salmon — July to September, use spoons; Dolly Varden — May to October, use bait, spinners; halibut — all year, season closed in January, best May to September, use smaller baits or jigs.

Antler Lake. Located on the mainland 11 miles east of Berners Bay and 39 air miles northwest of Juneau. Accessible by floatplane. No facilities. Grayling to 18 inches, best July to September, use flies.

Auke Bay. Located 11.8 miles north of Juneau on the Glacier Highway. Fishing primarily accessible by boat. Fish available: king salmon — available all year but best for large fish May to June, use herring or spoons; silver salmon — best in August, use herring or spoons; pink salmon — July to August, use small spoons; chum salmon — July to September, use spoons; Dolly Varden — May to October, use bait, spinners, flies; halibut — available all year, season closed in January, best in summer, use bait or jigs; rockfish — all year, best May to September, use smaller baits or jigs.

Benjamin Island. A 1.5-mile-long island located on the east shore of Favorite Channel, 25 miles northwest of Juneau. Accessible by boat. Fish available: king salmon — available all year but best for large fish May to June, use herring or spoons; silver salmon — best in August, use herring or spoons; pink salmon — July to August, use small spoons; Dolly Varden — May to October, use bait, spinners, flies; halibut — available all year, season closed in January, best in summer, use bait or jigs; rockfish — all year, best May to September, use smaller baits or jigs.

Berners Bay. A 3-mile-wide bay located on the east shore of Lynn Canal, 34 miles northwest of Juneau. Accessible by boat or from the end of the Glacier Highway (39.6 miles north of Juneau). Fish available: king salmon — available all year but best for large fish May to June, use herring or spoons; silver salmon — best in August, use herring or spoons; pink salmon — July to August, use small spoons; chum salmon — July to September, use spoons; Dolly Varden — May to October, use bait, spinners, flies; cutthroat trout — best mid- to late summer, use bait, spinners or flies; halibut — available all year, season closed in January, best in summer, use bait; rockfish — all year, best May to September, use smaller baits or jigs.

The Breadline. A 1.2-mile-long stretch of cliffs on the east shore of Favorite Channel, just north of Tee Harbor, 17 miles northwest of Juneau. Accessible by boat. Fish available: king salmon — available all year but best for large fish May to June, use herring or spoons; silver salmon — best in August, use herring or spoons; pink salmon — July to August, use small spoons; chum salmon — July to September, use spoons; Dolly Varden — May to October, use bait, spinners, flies; cutthroa trout — best mid- to late summer, use bait, spinners or flies; halibut — available all year, season closed in January, best in summer, use bait; rockfish — all year, best May to September, use smaller baits or jigs.

Dupont. Located on the northeast shore of Gastineau Channel, 7.5 miles southeast of Juneau. Accessible by boat or by trail 1.5 miles from the end of Thane Road. Fish available: king salmon — available all year but best for large fish May to June, use herring or spoons; silver salmon — best in August, use herring or spoons; pink salmon — July to August, use small spoons; chum salmon — July to September, use spoons; Dolly Varden — May to October, use bait, spinners, flies; halibut — available all year, season closed in January, best in summer, use bait or jigs; rockfish — all year, best May to September, use smaller baits or jigs.

Echo Cove. A 1.8-mile-long cove located on the south shore of Berners Bay, 34 miles northwest of Juneau. Accessible by boat or from the end of the Glacier Highway (39.6 miles north of Juneau). Fish available: king salmon — available all year but best for large fish May to June, use herring or spoons; silver salmon — best in August, use herring or spoons; pink salmon — July to August, use small spoons; chum salmon — July to September, use spoons; Dolly Varden — May to October, use bait, spinners, flies; cutthroat trout — best mid- to late summer, use bait, spinners or flies; halibut — available all year, season closed in January, best in summer, use bait or jigs; rockfish — all year, best May to September, use smaller baits or jigs.

Favorite Reef. Located off the southwest coast of Shelter Island, about 28 miles north of Juneau. Accessible by boat. Fish available: king salmon — available all year but best

for large fish May to June, use herring or spoons; silver salmon — best in August, use herring or spoons; pink salmon — July to August, use small spoons; chum salmon — July to September, use spoons; Dolly Varden — May to October, use bait, spinners, flies; halibut — available all year, season closed in January, best in summer, use bait or jigs; rockfish — all year, best May to September, use smaller baits or jigs.

Gastineau Channel. A 19-mile-long channel that lies between Juneau on the mainland and Douglas Island. Accessible by boat from Juneau or Douglas or from access points along area roads to shorelines. Fish available: king salmon — available all year but best for large fish May to June, use herring or spoons; silver salmon — best in August, use herring or spoons; pink salmon — July to August, use small spoons; chum salmon — July to September, use spoons; Dolly Varden — May to October, use bait, spinners, flies; halibut — available all year, season closed in January, best in summer, use bait or jigs; rockfish — all year, best May to September, use smaller baits or jigs.

Hand Trollers Cove. Located on the northeast side of Shelter Island north of Juneau. Accessible by boat. Fish available: king salmon — available all year but best for large fish May to June, use herring or spoons; silver salmon — best in August, use herring or spoons; pink salmon — July to August, use small spoons; Dolly Varden — May to October, use bait, spinners, flies; cutthroat trout — best mid- to late summer, use bait, spinners, flies; halibut — available all year, season closed in January, best in summer, use bait or jigs; rockfish — all year, best May to September, use smaller baits or jigs.

Icy Point. Located on the south shore of Douglas Island, 9 miles south-southwest of Juneau. Accessible by boat. Fish available: king salmon — available all year but best for large fish May to June, use herring or spoons; silver salmon — best in August, use herring or spoons; pink salmon — July to August, use small spoons; chum salmon — July to September, use spoons; Dolly Varden — May to October, use bait, spinners, flies; halibut — available all year, season closed in January, best in summer, use bait; rockfish — all year, best May to September, use smaller baits or jigs.

Lena Point. Located at the south entrance to Lena Cove on Favorite Channel, 14 miles northwest of Juneau. Accessible by boat. Wreck of *Princess Kathleen* down below. Fish available: king salmon — available all year but best for large fish May to June, use herring or spoons; silver salmon — best in August, use herring or spoons; pink salmon — July to August, use small spoons; chum salmon — July to September, use spoons; Dolly Varden — May to October, use bait, spinners, flies; halibut — available all year, season closed in January, best in summer, use bait or jigs; rockfish — all year, best May to September, use smaller baits or jigs.

Lincoln Island. A 4.7-mile-long island located in Lynn Canal, 24 miles northwest of Juneau. Accessible by boat. Fish available: king salmon — available all year but best for large fish May to June, use herring or spoons; silver salmon — best in August, use herring or spoons; pink salmon — July to August, use small spoons; Dolly Varden — May to October, use bait, spinners, flies; cutthroat trout — best mid- to late summer, use bait, spinners or flies; halibut — available all year, season closed in January, best in summer, use bait or jigs; rockfish — all year, best May to September, use smaller baits or jigs.

Marmion Island. A 0.2-mile-wide island located southeast of Douglas Island at the south end of Gastineau Channel, 9 miles southeast of Juneau. Accessible by boat. Fish available: king salmon — available all year but best for large fish May to June, use herring or spoons; silver salmon — best in August, use herring or spoons; pink salmon — July to August, use small spoons; chum salmon — July to September, use spoons; Dolly Varden — May to October, use bait, spinners, flies; halibut — available all year, season closed in January, best in summer, use bait or jigs; rockfish — all year, best May to September, use smaller baits or jigs.

Middle Point. Located in Stephens Passage on the west coast of Douglas Island, 9 miles southwest of Juneau. Accessible by boat. Fish available: king salmon — available all year but best for large fish May to June, use herring or spoons; silver salmon — best in August, use herring or spoons; pink salmon — July to August, use small spoons; chum salmon — July to September, use spoons; Dolly Varden — May to October, use bait, spinners, flies; halibut — available all year, season closed in January, best in summer, use bait or jigs; rockfish — all year, best May to September, use smaller baits or jigs.

North Pass. A passage between Lincoln Island and the north end of Shelter Island, 22 miles northwest of Juneau. Accessible by boat. Fish available: king salmon — available all year but best for large fish May to June, use herring or spoons; silver salmon — best

in August, use herring or spoons; pink salmon — July to August, use small spoons; chum salmon — July to September, use spoons; Dolly Varden — May to October, use bait, spinners, flies; halibut — available all year, season closed in January, best in summer, use bait or jigs; rockfish — all year, best May to September, use smaller baits or jigs.

Outer Point. Located on the west tip of Douglas Island in Stephens Passage, 4 miles northwest of Middle Point and 10 miles west of Juneau. Accessible by boat or by trail from end of North Douglas Highway. Fish available: king salmon — available all year but best for large fish May to June, use herring or spoons; silver salmon — best in August, use herring or spoons; pink salmon — July to August, use small spoons; chum salmon — July to September, use spoons; Dolly Varden — May to October, use bait, spinners, flies; halibut — available all year, season closed in January, best in summer, use bait or jigs; rockfish — all year, best May to September, use smaller baits or jigs.

Peterson Lake. A 0.9-mile-long lake located 17 miles northwest of Juneau. Accessible by 4.5-mile trail beginning at Mile 24.4 on the Glacier Highway north of Juneau. Fish available: Dolly Varden — best May to October, use bait, spinners, flies; rainbow trout, best May to September, use flies, lures, bait.

Point Bishop. Located at the south end of Taku Inlet on Stephens Passage, 4.8 miles southeast of Dupont and 12 miles southeast of Juneau. Accessible by boat or by trail 8 miles from the end of Thane Road. Fish available: king salmon — available all year but best for large fish May to June, use herring or spoons; silver salmon — best in August, use herring or spoons; pink salmon — July to August, use small spoons; chum salmon — July to September, use spoons; Dolly Varden May to October, use bait, spinners, flies; halibut — available all year, season closed in January, best in summer, use bait or jigs; rockfish — all year, best May to September, use smaller baits or jigs.

Point Hilda. Located in Stephens Passage on the south shore of Douglas Island, 7 miles southwest of Juneau. Accessible by boat. Fish available: king salmon — available all year but best for large fish May to June, use herring or spoons; silver salmon — best in August, use herring or spoons; pink salmon — July to August, use small spoons; chum salmon — July to September, use spoons; Dolly Varden — May to October, use bait, spinners, flies; halibut — available all year, season closed in

January, best in summer, use bait or jigs; rockfish — all year, best May to September, use smaller baits or jigs.

Point Louisa. Located on the east shore of Stephens Passage, west of Auke Bay, 12 miles northwest of Juneau. Accessible by boat or short trail from Forest Service campground. This is a favorite spot to fish from shore. Fish available: king salmon — available all year but best for large fish May to June, use herring or spoons; silver salmon — best in August, use herring or spoons; pink salmon — July to August, use small spoons; chum salmon — July to September, use spoons; Dolly Varden — May to October, use bait, spinners, flies; halibut — available all year, season closed in January, best in summer, use bait; rockfish — all year, best May to September.

Point Salisbury. Located on Stephens Passage at the south end of Gastineau Channel, 2.5 miles west of Point Bishop, 10 miles southwest of Juneau. Accessible by boat or the Dupont-Point Bishop trail from the end of Thane Road. Fish available: king salmon — available all year but best for large fish May to June, use herring or spoons; silver salmon — best in August, use herring or spoons; pink salmon — July to August, use small spoons; chum salmon — July to September, use spoons; Dolly Varden — May to October, use bait, spinners, flies; halibut — available all year, season closed in January, best in summer, use bait or jigs; rockfish — all year, best May to September, use smaller baits or jigs.

Salmon Creek and Reservoir. Reservoir located 3 miles up trail beginning at Mile 2.3 on the Old Glacier Highway north of Juneau. Trail follows creek. Fish available in creek: pink and chum salmon — July to August, use small spoons; Dolly Varden — May to October, use bait, spinners, flies. Fish available in reservoir: eastern brook trout — May to September, use eggs, spinners or flies.

Shrine of St. Therese. Located on Favorite Channel, 18 miles north of Juneau. Accessible by boat or from Mile 23.3 on the Glacier Highway. This is a favorite spot to fish from shore. Fish available: king salmon — available all year but best for large fish May to June, use herring or spoons; silver salmon — best in August, use herring or spoons; pink salmon — July to August, use small spoons; Dolly Varden — May to October, use bait, spinners, flies; cutthroat trout — best mid- to late summer, use bait, spinners or flies.

South Shelter Island. South end of 9-mile-long island located between Favorite and Saginaw Channels, 15 miles northwest of Juneau. Accessible by boat. Fish available: king salmon — available all year but best for large fish May to June, use herring or spoons; silver salmon — best in August, use herring or spoons; pink salmon — July to August, use small spoons; chum salmon — July to September, use spoons; Dolly Varden — May to October, use bait, spinners, flies; halibut — available all year, season closed in January, best in summer, use bait or jigs; rockfish — all year, best May to September, use smaller baits or jigs.

Stephens Passage. Located along the west side of Douglas Island, about 11 miles west of Juneau. Accessible by boat. Fish available: king salmon — available all year but season is closed April 15 through June 14 in Stephens Passage and Taku Inlet, use herring or spoons; silver salmon — best in August, use herring or spoons; pink salmon — July to August, use small spoons; Dolly Varden — May to October, use bait, spinners, flies; halibut — available all year, season closed in January, best in summer, use bait or jigs; rockfish — all year, best May to September, use smaller baits or jigs.

Tee Harbor. A 1.5-mile-long T-shaped bay on the east shore of Favorite Channel, 0.4 mile north of Lena Cove and 15 miles northwest of Juneau. Accessible by boat or from 18.5 Mile Glacier Highway north of Juneau. Fish available: king salmon — available all year but best for large fish May to June, use herring or spoons; silver salmon — best in August, use herring or spoons; pink salmon — July to August, use small spoons; Dolly Varden — May to October, use bait, spinners, flies; cutthroat trout — best mid- to late summer, use bait, spinners or flies; halibut — available all year, season closed in January, best in summer, use bait or jigs.

Turner Lake. A 9-mile-long lake located 1 mile east of Taku Inlet, 25 air miles east of Juneau. Accessible by boat and trail from saltwater or by floatplane. Two Forest Service cabins and boats available. Fish available: cutthroat trout — May to September, use bait, spinners, flies; Dolly Varden — May to October, use bait, spinners, flies; kokanee, May to September, use spinners, eggs.

White Marker. Located on the west coast of Douglas Island, south of Middle Point. Accessible by boat. Fish available: king salmon — available all year but best for large fish May to June, use herring or spoons; silver salmon — best in August, use herring or spoons; pink salmon — July to August, use small spoons; chum salmon — July to September, use spoons; Dolly Varden — May to October, use bait, spinners, flies; halibut — available all year, season closed in January, best in summer, use bait or jigs; rockfish — all year, best May to September, use smaller baits or jigs.

Windfall Lake. A 0.8-mile-long lake located south of the terminus of Herbert Glacier, 18 miles northwest of Juneau. Accessible by 4-mile trail from the end of Windfall Lake Road (no sign) at Mile 27.4 of the Glacier Highway north of Juneau. No facilities. Fish available: silver salmon — September to October, use spoons; red salmon — June to July, use flies; Dolly Varden — May to October, use bait, spinners, flies; cutthroat trout — May to September, use bait, spinners, flies.

Ketchikan Area Fishing

Bakewell Lake. A 4.3-mile-long lake located on the mainland east of East Behm Canal, 39 air miles southeast of Ketchikan. Accessible by floatplane or by boat to Smeaton Bay, then a 0.8-mile hike to the lake. Fish available: silver salmon — late August to early September, use flies, spoons or spinners; cutthroat trout — best May to September, use bait, spinners, flies; Dolly Varden — best May to October, use bait, spinners, flies.

Bell Island. An 8.7-mile-long island located north of Revillagigedo Island in North Behm Canal, 45 miles north of Ketchikan. Accessible by boat or floatplane. Private resort (not open to the public) at hot springs on southwest end of island. Area considered a "hot spot" for king salmon, best mid-May to mid-June, use herring or spoons. Other fish: silver salmon — best in August, use herring or spoons; pink salmon — July to August, use small spoons; chum salmon — July to September, use spoons; Dolly Varden — May to October, use bait, spinners, flies; cutthroat trout — best mid- to late summer, use bait, spinners, flies; steelhead — April to June and October to November, use spoons, eggs; halibut — available all year, season closed in January, best in summer, use bait; rockfish — all year, best May to September, use smaller baits or jigs.

Big Goat Lake. A 2.4-mile-long lake located 38 air miles northeast of Ketchikan. Accessible by floatplane. Recreation cabin and skiff available. Fish available: grayling — up to 2 pounds, use small flies, shrimp or spinners.

Blank Inlet. Extends northwest 3.3 miles off Nichols Passage on the east coast of Gravina Island, 7 miles south of Ketchikan

by boat. Fish available: king salmon — best May to June, use herring or spoons; silver salmon — best in August, use herring or spoons; pink salmon — July to August, use small spoons; chum salmon — July to September, use spoons; halibut — available all year, season closed in January, best in summer, use bait; rockfish — all year, best May to September, use smaller baits or jigs; lingcod — all year, best in summer, use herring.

Caamano Point. Located at the south tip of the Cleveland Peninsula between Behm Canal and Clarence Strait, 18 miles northwest of Ketchikan by boat. Use of guide recommended. Fish available: king salmon — best May to June, use herring or spoons; silver salmon — best in August, use herring or spoons; pink salmon — July to August, use small spoons; chum salmon — July to September, use spoons; halibut — available all year, season closed in January, best in summer, use bait; rockfish — all year, best May to September, use smaller baits or jigs; lingcod — all year, best in summer, use herring.

Chasina Point. Located on the east coast of Prince of Wales Island between Cholmondeley Sound and Clarence Strait, 22 miles southwest of Ketchikan by boat. Use of guide recommended. Fish available: king salmon — best May to June, use herring or spoons; silver salmon — best in August, use herring or spoons; pink salmon — July to August, use small spoons; chum salmon — July to September, use spoons; halibut — available all year, season closed in January, best in summer, use bait; rockfish — all year, best May to September, use smaller baits or jigs; lingcod — all year, best in summer, use herring.

Clover Pass. Located at Potter Point on Revillagigedo Island, 11 miles northwest of Ketchikan by road or boat. Commercial lodges and marina available. Fish available: king salmon — best May to June, use herring or spoons; silver salmon — best in August, use herring or spoons; pink salmon — July to August, use small spoons; chum salmon — July to September, use spoons; halibut — available all year, season closed in January, best in summer, use bait; rockfish — all year, best May to September, use smaller baits or jigs; lingcod — all year, best in summer, use herring.

Ella Lake. A 5-mile-long lake located on Revillagigedo Island, 24 air miles northeast of Ketchikan. Floatplane access. Forest Service cabin and skiff on lake. Fishing for cutthroat trout May to September and Dolly Varden May to October, use bait, spinners, flies.

Fish Creek. Located at the head of Thorne Arm, 21 miles east of Ketchikan by boat, or 18 miles by floatplane. Forest Service cabin available. Fish available: silver salmon — best in August, use herring or spoons; pink salmon — July to August, use small spoons; red salmon — June, use spoons; Dolly Varden — May to October, use bait, spinners, flies; cutthroat trout — best mid- to late summer, use bait, spinners, flies; steelhead — April to June and October to November, use spoons, eggs; rainbow trout — May to September, use flies, lures, bait.

Grace Lake. Located inland from the east coast of Revillagigedo Island, 30 air miles from Ketchikan. Accessible by floatplane. Fishing for eastern brook trout, May to September, use eggs, spinners.

Grindall Island. A 1.5-mile-long island located between Clarence Strait and Kasaan Bay on the east coast of Prince of Wales Island, 20 miles northwest of Ketchikan by boat. Use of guide recommended. Fish available: king salmon — best May to June, use herring or spoons; silver salmon — best in August, use herring or spoons; pink salmon — July to August, use small spoons; chum salmon — July to September, use spoons; halibut — available all year, season closed in January, best in summer, use bait; rockfish — all year, best May to September, use smaller baits or jigs; lingcod — all year, best in summer, use herring.

Humpback Lake. A 6.3-mile long lake located above Mink Bay in Boca de Quadra, 48 miles southeast of Ketchikan. Forest Service cabin and skiff and commercial lodge available. Fish available: cutthroat trout — best May to September, use bait, spinners, flies; Dolly Varden — best May to October, use bait, spinners, flies; grayling — use small flies, shrimp or spinners.

Karta River. Located above Karta Bay on Prince of Wales Island, 42 air miles northwest of Ketchikan. Accessible by boat or floatplane. Forest Service cabins available. Fish available: silver salmon — best in July and August, use flies or spoons; pink salmon — July to August, use small spoons; red salmon — in June and July, use spoons; chum salmon — July to September, use spoons; Dolly Varden May to October, use bait, spinners, flies; cutthroat trout — best mid- to late summer, use bait, spinners, flies; excellent for steelhead — April to June, use spoons, eggs; rainbow trout — May to September, use flies, lures, bait.

Klawock Creek. Heads in Klawock Lake on the west coast of Prince of Wales Island.

Accessible by boat, state ferry or floatplane. Excellent spring run of steelhead — use spoons or eggs, also good October to November. Excellent silver salmon — late August to September, use flies, spinners or spoons. Closed to red salmon fishing.

LeDuc Lake. A 2.5-mile-long lake located above the Chickamin River, 49 air miles northeast of Ketchikan. Accessible by floatplane. Fishing for rainbow trout — May to September, use flies, lures, bait.

Manzanita Lake. Located above Manzanita Bay, 28 air miles northeast of Ketchikan. Forest Service cabin and skiff available. Fish available: cutthroat trout — best May to September, use bait, spinners, flies; Dolly Varden — best May to October, use bait, spinners, flies; kokanee — best May to September, use spinners or eggs.

Manzoni Lake. A 2.4-mile-long lake located on the mainland, south of Walker Cove at the head of Granite Creek. Accessible by floatplane. Fishing for grayling — up to 2 pounds, use small flies, shrimp or spinners.

McDonald Lake. Located 45 air miles north of Ketchikan above Yes Bay. Accessible by floatplane or boat and trail. Forest Service cabin and skiff available. Fish available: silver salmon — best in September, use flies or spoons; red salmon — August, use flies or spoons; Dolly Varden — May to October, use bait, spinners, flies; cutthroat trout — best mid- to late summer, use bait, spinners, flies; excellent for steelhead — April to June, use spoons, eggs; rainbow trout — May to September, use flies, lures, bait.

Naha River. Located on Revillagigedo Island, 21 miles north of Ketchikan by boat. Also accessible by floatplane. Forest Service cabins and skiffs available; trail follows river. Fish available: silver salmon — best in September, use flies or spoons; pink salmon — July to August, use small spoons; red salmon — June, use flies or spoons; chum salmon — July to September, use spoons; Dolly Varden — May to October, use bait, spinners, flies; cutthroat trout — best mid- to late summer, use bait, spinners, flies; steelhead — April to June and October to November, use spoons, eggs; rainbow trout — May to September, use flies, lures, bait.

Orchard Lake. A 3.5-mile-long lake located on the northwest coast of Revillagigedo Island above Shrimp Bay, 32 air miles north of Ketchikan. Forest Service cabin available. Fish available: cutthroat trout — best May to September, use bait, spinners, flies; Dolly Varden — best May to October, use bait, spinners, flies.

Patching Lake. A 3.3-mile-long lake located in the course of the Naha River, 6 miles east of Loring, 19 air miles north of Ketchikan. Accessible by floatplane. Forest Service cabin available. Fish available: cutthroat trout — best May to September, use bait, spinners, flies; Dolly Varden — best May to October, use bait, spinners, flies.

Point Alava. Located on the south tip of Revillagigedo Island, 20 miles southeast of Ketchikan. Accessible by boat. Fish available: king salmon — best May to June, use herring or spoons; silver salmon — best in August, use herring or spoons; pink salmon — July to August, use small spoons; chum salmon — July to September, use spoons; halibut — season closed in January, best in summer, use bait; rockfish — all year, best May to September, use smaller baits or jigs; lingcod — all year, best in summer, use herring.

Point Sykes. Located at the east point of the entrance to Behm Canal, 25 miles southeast of Ketchikan. Accessible by boat. Use of a guide is recommended. Fish available: king salmon — best May to June, use herring or spoons; silver salmon — best in August, use herring or spoons; pink salmon — July to August, use small spoons; chum salmon — July to September, use spoons; halibut — season closed in January, best in summer, use bait; rockfish — all year, best May to September, use smaller baits or jigs; lingcod — all year, best in summer, use herring.

Reflection Lake. A 4.5-mile-long lake located above Short Bay on the Cleveland Peninsula, 46 air miles north of Ketchikan. Forest Service cabin and skiff available. Fish available: silver salmon — best in July and August, use flies or spoons; cutthroat trout — best mid- to late summer, use bait, spinners, flies.

Salt Lagoon Creek. Located at the head of George Inlet, 22 miles north of Ketchikan. Accessible by boat. Fish available: silver salmon — best in July and August, use flies or spoons; pink salmon — July to August, use small spoons; Dolly Varden — May to October, use bait, spinners, flies; cutthroat trout — best mid- to late summer, use bait, spinners, flies.

Silvis Lake. Located 1.5 miles from the end of the Tongass Highway, north of Ketchikan. Accessible by trail. Fish available: rainbow trout — May to September, use flies, lures, bait.

Snow Lake. A 0.9-mile-long lake located on Revillagigedo Island near the head of the Naha River, 7 miles northeast of Loring. Accessible by floatplane. Fish available: grayling— up to 2 pounds, use small flies, shrimp or spinners.

Unuk River. Located at the head of Burroughs Bay, 50 miles north of Ketchikan. Accessible by floatplane or boat. Fish available: silver salmon — best in August and September, use flies or spoons; pink salmon — July to August, use small spoons; chum salmon — July to September, use spoons; Dolly Varden — May to October, use bait, spinners, flies; cutthroat trout — best mid- to late summer, use bait, spinners, flies.

Vallenar Point. Located at the north tip of Gravina Island, 11 miles northwest of Ketchikan. Accessible by boat. Fish available: king salmon — best May to June, use herring or spoons; silver salmon — best in August, use herring or spoons; pink salmon — July to August, use small spoons; chum salmon—July to September, use spoons; halibut — season closed in January, best in summer, use bait; rockfish—all year, best May to September, use smaller baits or jigs; lingcod — all year, best in summer, use herring.

Walker Lake. Located on the mainland 3.5 miles east of Walker Cove in Misty Fiords National Monument; drains southwest into Rudyerd Bay. Accessible by floatplane. Fishing for rainbow trout — May to September, use flies, lures, bait.

Wilson Lake. A 5-mile-long lake located on the mainland; drained by the Wilson River into Wilson Arm. Accessible by floatplane. Has 2 Forest Service cabins and skiffs. Fishing for Dolly Varden — May to October, use bait, spinners, flies; cutthroat trout — best mid- to late summer, use bait, spinners, flies.

Yes Bay. Located in North Behm Canal, 44 miles north of Ketchikan by boat. Also accessible by floatplane. Commercial resort available. Fish available: king salmon — best May to June, use herring or spoons; silver salmon — best in August and September, use herring or spoons; pink salmon — July to August, use small spoons; chum salmon — July to September, use spoons; halibut — season closed in January, best in summer, use bait; rockfish — all year, best May to September, use smaller baits or jigs; lingcod — all year, best in summer, use herring.

Petersburg Area Fishing

Alecks Creek. Located on Kuiu Island on the east side of Elena Bay in Tebenkof Bay Wilderness Area. Accessible by boat or floatplane. The creek is part of the Alecks Creek Portage Trail. Fish available: steelhead — April to May; red salmon—July; silver, pink and chum salmon — mid-August to October.

Cape Strait. Located off the Kupreanof Island shoreline, 12 miles north of Petersburg. Accessible by boat. Fish available: king salmon — best May to June, use herring or spoons; silver salmon — best in August, use herring or spoons; halibut — season closed in January, best in summer, use bait; rockfish — all year, best May to September, use smaller baits or jigs.

Castle River. Located on the west shore of Duncan Canal, 22 miles southwest of Petersburg. Accessible by floatplane or boat. Fish available: silver salmon — best in August, use flies, bait or spoons; pink salmon — July to August, use small spoons; chum salmon — July to September, use spoons; Dolly Varden — May to October, use bait, spinners, flies; cutthroat trout — best mid- to late summer, use bait, spinners, flies; steelhead — April to June and October to November, use spoons, eggs; rainbow trout — May to September, use flies, lures, bait.

DeBoer Lake. A 1.5-mile-long lake located 20 air miles north of Petersburg. Accessible by floatplane. Fishing for rainbow trout — midsummer to September, use flies, lures, bait.

Duncan Salt Chuck. Located at the head of Duncan Canal, 28 miles by boat west of Petersburg. Fish available: silver salmon — best in August, use bait, flies or spoons; Dolly Varden — May to October, use bait, spinners, flies; cutthroat trout — best mid- to late summer, use bait, spinners, flies; steelhead — April to June and October to November, use spoons, eggs; rainbow trout — May to September, use flies, lures, bait.

Frederick Sound. Located northeast of Petersburg. Accessible by boat. Fish available: king salmon — best May to June, use herring or spoons; silver salmon — best in August, use herring or spoons; halibut — season closed in January, use bait; rockfish — all year.

Kadake Creek. Located on Kuiu Island, 60 miles by boat or 20 minutes by floatplane west of Petersburg. Forest Service cabin available. Excellent spring cutthroat trout fishery. Other fish: silver salmon — best in August, use bait, flies or spoons; pink salmon — July to August, use small spoons; chum salmon — July to September, use spoons; Dolly Varden — May to October, use bait, spinners, flies; steelhead — April to June and October to November, use spoons, eggs; rainbow trout — May to September, use flies, lures, bait.

Kah Sheets Creek. Located on Kupreanof Island 21 miles southwest of Petersburg by boat. Also accessible by floatplane. Forest

Service cabin on Kah Sheets Lake and on the bay. Fish available: silver salmon — best in August, use bait, flies or spoons; pink salmon — July to August, use small spoons; chum salmon — July to September, use spoons; red salmon — best in July, use flies and small spoons; Dolly Varden — May to October, use bait, spinners, flies; steelhead — April to June, use spoons, eggs; cutthroat trout — best mid- to late summer, use bait, spinners, flies.

Petersburg Creek. Located across Wrangell Narrows from Petersburg by boat. Boats and accommodations available in Petersburg. Fish available: silver salmon — best in August, use bait, flies or spoons; pink salmon — July to August, use small spoons; chum salmon — July to September, use spoons; red salmon — best in June and July, use flies and small spoons; Dolly Varden — May to October, use bait, spinners, flies; steelhead — April to June and October to November, use spoons, eggs; cutthroat trout — best mid- to late summer, use bait, spinners, flies; rainbow trout — May to September, use flies, lures, bait.

Petersburg Lake. Located 4.5 miles by trail

Hiker pauses to enjoy the view of Settler Creek near Ketchikan. Southeast has hundreds of fast, clear streams. (Rollo Pool, staff)

up Petersburg Creek (see above). Forest Service cabin and boat available. Fish available: silver salmon — best in August, use bait, flies or spoons; Dolly Varden — May to October, use bait, spinners, flies; cutthroat trout — best mid- to late summer, use bait, spinners, flies.

Security Bay. Located on the north coast of Kuiu Island, 60 miles west of Petersburg by boat. Fish available: king salmon — best May to June, use herring or spoons; silver salmon — best in August, use herring or spoons; halibut — season closed in January, best in summer, use bait; rockfish — all year, best May to September, use smaller baits or jigs; lingcod — all year, best in summer, use herring.

Swan Lake. Located on the mainland above Thomas Bay, 18 air miles north of Petersburg. Forest Service cabin and boat available. Excellent fall fishery for rainbow trout — use flies, lures, bait.

Thomas Bay. Located 15 miles north of Petersburg on mainland. Two Forest Service cabins. Accessible by boat or plane. Fish available: king salmon — best May to June, use herring or spoons; halibut — season closed in January, best in summer, use bait.

Towers Lake. Located on Kupreanof Island 20 air miles west of Petersburg. Accessible by floatplane. Fish available: Dolly Varden — May to October, use bait, spinners, flies; cutthroat trout — best mid- to late summer, use bait, spinners, flies.

Sitka Area Fishing

Avoss Lake. A 1.7-mile-long lake located on central Baranof Island 29 air miles southeast of Sitka. Accessible by floatplane. Forest Service cabin available. Excellent fishery for rainbow trout — May to September, use flies, lures, bait.

Baranof Lake. A 2.5-mile-long lake located on the east coast of Baranof Island, 18 miles west of Sitka. Accessible by floatplane and road. Forest Service cabin available. Fishing for cutthroat trout — best mid- to late summer, use bait, spinners, flies.

Davidof Lake. A 1.7-mile-long lake located on southcentral Baranof Island, 35 air miles southeast of Sitka. Accessible by floatplane. Forest Service cabin available. Good fishery for rainbow trout — May to September, use flies, lures, bait.

Gar Lake. Located on Baranof Island, 39 air miles southeast of Sitka. Accessible by floatplane. Good fishing for rainbow trout — May to September, use flies, lures, bait.

Goulding Lakes. Located on Chichagof Island, 61.3 air miles north of Sitka. Accessible by floatplane. Forest Service cabin available. Fish available: Dolly Varden — May to October, use bait, spinners, flies; cutthroat trout — best mid- to late summer, use bait, spinners, flies.

Green Lake. A 1-mile-long lake located near the head of Silver Bay, 10 miles southeast of Sitka. Accessible by floatplane or boat and short hike. Fish available: brook trout — best May to September, use eggs or spinners.

Heart Lake. A 0.1-mile-wide lake located 3.5 miles east of Sitka. Accessible by trail from Blue Lake Road. Fishing for brook trout — best May to September, use eggs or spinners.

Katlian River. Located on the west coast of Baranof Island, 11 miles northeast of Sitka. Accessible by boat. Fish available: silver salmon — best in August, use herring or spoons; pink salmon — July to August, use small spoons; chum salmon — July to September, use spoons; Dolly Varden — May to October, use bait, spinners, flies; cutthroat trout — best mid- to late summer, use bait, spinners, flies.

Khvostof Lake. A 1.4-mile-long lake located on southcentral Baranof Island, 39 air miles southeast of Sitka. Accessible by floatplane. Fishing for rainbow trout — May to September, use flies, lures, bait.

Lake Eva. A 1.7-mile-long lake located on the north coast of Baranof Island, 20 air miles northeast of Sitka. Forest Service cabin and boat available; cabin equipped for the handicapped. Accessible by floatplane. Excellent fishing for Dolly Varden — May to October, use bait, spinners, flies; cutthroat trout — best mid- to late summer, use bait, spinners, flies. Lake also has silver and red salmon and steelhead.

Lake Plotnikof. A 4-mile-long lake located on southcentral Baranof Island, 38 air miles southeast of Sitka. Accessible by floatplane. Forest Service cabin and boat available. Good fishing for rainbow trout — May to September, use flies, lures, bait.

Little Lake Eva. Located on the north coast of Baranof Island, 20 air miles northeast of Sitka. Accessible by trail from Lake Eva. Excellent fishing for cutthroat trout — best mid- to late summer, use bait, spinners, flies.

Nakwasina River. Located 15 miles north of Sitka. Accessible by boat. Excellent sea-run Dolly Varden fishing in July and August. Other fish: silver salmon — best in August, use herring or spoons; pink salmon — July to August, use small spoons; chum salmon — July to September, use spoons.

Pass Lake. Located on southeastern

Baranof Island, 33 air miles southeast of Sitka. Accessible by floatplane. Fishing for rainbow trout — May to September, use flies, lures, bait.

Port Banks. Located on the west coast of Baranof Island, 35 air miles southeast of Sitka. Accessible by boat or floatplane. No facilities. Excellent fishery for silver salmon — late July and August, use herring or spoons.

Redoubt Lake. A 9.5-mile-long lake located at the head of Redoubt Bay on the west coast of Baranof Island, 12 miles south of Sitka. Accessible by floatplane or boat. Forest Service cabin available. Fish available: silver salmon — best in August, use herring or spoons; pink salmon — July to August, use small spoons; chum salmon — July to September, use spoons; red salmon — best in June, use spoons; Dolly Varden — May to October, use bait, spinners, flies.

Rezanof Lake. A 3-mile-long lake located on southcentral Baranof Island, 40 air miles southeast of Sitka. Accessible by floatplane. Forest Service cabins and skiff available. Fishing for rainbow trout — May to September, use flies, lures, bait.

Salmon Lake. A 1-mile-long lake located at the southeast end of Silver Bay, 11 miles by boat south of Sitka. Accessible by boat and 1-mile hike to lake. Skiff available. Fish available: silver salmon — best in August, use herring or spoons; pink salmon — July to August, use small spoons; chum salmon — July to September, use spoons; red salmon — best in June, use spoons; Dolly Varden — May to October, use bait, spinners, flies; steelhead — April to June, use spoons, eggs; cutthroat trout — best mid- to late summer, use bait, spinners, flies.

Sitka Sound. Located in front of the city of Sitka. Accessible by boat. Boats, tackle and guides available in Sitka. Good fishing for king salmon — best May to June, use herring or spoons; silver salmon — best in September, use herring or spoons; pink salmon — July to August, use small spoons; Dolly Varden — May to October, use bait, spinners, flies; halibut— all year except January when the fishery is closed, best in summer, use bait; rockfish — all year, best May to September, use smaller baits or jigs; lingcod — all year, best in summer, use herring.

Sitkoh Lake Creek. Located on the southeast end of Chichagof Island. Accessible by floatplane to lake (see below). Good steelhead fishing in April and May. Other fish: silver salmon—best in August, use herring or spoons; red salmon — best in June, use spoons; Dolly Varden — May to October, use bait, spinners,

flies; cutthroat trout — best mid- to late summer, use bait, spinners, flies.

Sitkoh Lake. A 2.5-mile-long lake located on the southeast tip of Chichagof Island, 30 air miles northeast of Sitka. Forest Service cabin and boat available. Excellent fishery for silver salmon — best in August, use herring or spoons; cutthroat trout — best mid- to late summer, use bait, spinners, flies; cutthroat trout and Dolly Varden — year-round.

Thimbleberry Lake. A 0.2-mile-wide lake located 3 miles east of Sitka. Accessible by trail from Blue Lake Road. Fishing for brook trout — best May to September, use eggs or spinners.

Wrangell Area Fishing

Anan Creek. Located 40 miles south of Wrangell by boat or floatplane. Forest Service cabin available. Fish available: silver salmon — best in August, use bait, flies or spoons; pink salmon — July to August, use small spoons; chum salmon — July to September, use spoons; Dolly Varden — May to October, use bait, spinners, flies; steelhead — April to June, use spoons, eggs; cutthroat trout — best mid- to late summer, use bait, spinners, flies; rainbow trout — May to September, use flies, lures, bait.

Anan Lake. A 2.5-mile-long lake located 30 air miles southeast of Wrangell. Accessible by floatplane. Forest Service cabin available. Fishing for silver and pink salmon, rainbow trout and Dolly Varden.

Greys Pass. Located 8 miles northwest of Wrangell by boat. Fish available: king salmon — best before April 15, use herring or spoons, closed to salmon fishing from April 16 to June 15; halibut — available all year but season closed in January, best in summer, use bait.

Harding River. Located in Bradfield Canal 35 air miles southeast of Wrangell. Accessible by boat or plane. Forest Service cabin available. Fish available: silver salmon — best in August; chum salmon — (possible record-size chum in this system), best in late June and July; Dolly Varden — May to October; steelhead trout — in spring; cutthroat trout — mid- to late summer.

Kunk Lake. A 1.5-mile-long lake located on the northeast coast of Etolin Island, 14 miles south of Wrangell. Accessible by boat and short hike or by floatplane. Forest Service cabin and boat available. Fish available: silver salmon — best in August, use bait, flies or spoons; Dolly Varden — May to October, use bait, spinners, flies; steelhead — April to June, use spoons, eggs; cutthroat trout — best mid- to late summer, use bait, spinners, flies.

Luck Lake. Located inland from Luck Point on Prince of Wales Island, 35 miles south west of Wrangell. Accessible by floatplane or road from Coffman Cove. Fish available: silver salmon — best in August, use bait, flies or spoons; pink salmon — July to August, use small spoons; chum salmon — July to September, use spoons; red salmon — best in June and July, use flies and small spoons; Dolly Varden — May to October, use bait, spinners, flies; steelhead — April to June and October to November, use spoons, eggs; cutthroat trout — best mid- to late summer, use bait, spinners, flies; rainbow trout — May to September, use flies, lures, bait.

Marten Lake. Located 2 miles north of Bradfield Canal, 25 air miles southeast of Wrangell. Accessible by floatplane. Forest Service cabin and boat available. Fish available: Dolly Varden — May to October, use bait, spinners, flies; cutthroat trout — best mid- to late summer, use bait, spinners, flies; kokanee — May to September, use spinners, eggs; steelhead — available below lake toward mouth of Martin River, April to late May; coho — available below lake toward mouth of Martin River, August and September.

Salmon Bay Lake. A 3-mile-long lake located on the north coast of Prince of Wales Island, 40 miles west of Wrangell. Accessible by floatplane. Forest Service cabin available. Fish available: silver salmon — best in August, use bait, flies or spoons; pink salmon — July to August, use small spoons; chum salmon — July to September, use spoons; red salmon — best in June, use spoons and flies; Dolly Varden — May to October, use bait, spinners, flies; steelhead — April to June and October to November, use spoons, eggs; cutthroat trout — best mid- to late summer, use bait, spinners, flies; rainbow trout — May to September, use flies, lures, bait.

Stikine River. Located north of Wrangell. Accessible by boat or floatplane. Guide recommended. Forest Service cabins available. Excellent fishery. Fish available: silver salmon — best in August, use bait, flies or spoons; pink salmon — July to August, use small spoons; chum salmon — July to September, use spoons; Dolly Varden — May to October, use bait, spinners, flies; steelhead — April to June and October to November, use spoons, eggs; cutthroat trout — best mid- to late summer, use bait, spinners, flies; whitefish — all year, use flies or eggs. Fishery is closed to king salmon all year

Thoms Lake. A 1.5-mile-long lake located on the southwest coast of Wrangell Island, 18 miles south-southeast of Wrangell. Accessible by boat and 2-mile hike, road and 0.5-mile hike, or by floatplane. Forest Service cabin available. Fish available: silver salmon — best in August, use bait, flies or spoons; red salmon — best in June, use flies or spoons; steelhead — April to June, use spoons, eggs; cutthroat trout — best mid- to late summer, use bait, spinners, flies.

Virginia Lake. A 2-mile-long lake located 8 miles east of Wrangell. Accessible by boat and short hike or floatplane. Forest Service cabin and boat available. Fish available: red salmon — best in June, use spoons or flies; Dolly Varden — May to October, use bait, spinners, flies; cutthroat trout — best mid- to late summer, use bait, spinners, flies.

Wrangell Harbor. Located in front of the city of Wrangell. Accessible by skiff. Fish available: king salmon — best April to June, use herring or spoons; silver salmon — best in August, use herring or spoons; halibut — available all year but season closed in January, best in summer, use bait; rockfish — all year, best May to September, use smaller baits or jigs.

Zimovia Strait. Located west of Wrangell; separates Wrangell Island from Etolin and Woronkofski islands. A "hot spot" for king salmon — best mid-May to mid-June, use trolled or drifted herring or spoons.

Yakutat Area Fishing

Akwe River. Heads at Akwe Lake and flows southwest 20 miles to the Gulf of Alaska, 32 air miles southeast of Yakutat. Private airstrip. Excellent fishing at fork with Ustay River in fall. Fish available: king salmon — best early summer, use spoons or flies; silver salmon — mid-August, use spoons; red salmon — best in June, use small spoons; Dolly Varden — May to October, use bait, spinners, flies; cutthroat trout — best mid- to late summer, use bait, spinners, flies.

Ankau Lagoon. An estuary system located 2.6 miles west of Yakutat. Accessible by boat or from bridge at Mile 4 White Alice Road. Fish available: silver salmon — September to October, use spoons; red salmon — best in June, use small spoons; Dolly Varden — May to October, use bait, spinners, flies; cutthroat trout — best mid- to late summer, use bait, spinners, flies.

Coast Guard Lake. Located about 4 miles southwest of Yakutat. Accessible from Beach Road or by canoe or trail from Kardy Lake (see below). Fish available: silver salmon — September to October, use spoons; pink salmon — July to August, use small spoons; red salmon — best in June, use small spoons;

Dolly Varden — May to October, use bait, spinners, flies; cutthroat trout — best mid- to late summer, use bait, spinners, flies.

Gulf of Alaska. Coastline located southeast of Yakutat. Accessible by boat, plane to beaches or via White Alice, Cannon Beach and Lost River roads. Fish available: king salmon — available all year but best for large fish in early summer, use herring or spoons; silver salmon — best August to September, use herring or spoons; pink salmon — July to August, use small spoons; Dolly Varden — May to October, use bait, spinners, flies; cutthroat trout — best mid- to late summer, use bait, spinners, flies; halibut — available all year, season closed in January, best in summer, use bait or jigs; rockfish — all year, best May to September, use smaller baits or jigs.

Italio River. Heads 3 miles southeast of Harlequin Lake and flows west 20 miles to the Gulf of Alaska, 28 miles southeast of Yakutat. Accessible by boat or floatplane. Fish available: silver salmon — September to October, use lures; Dolly Varden — May to October, use bait, spinners, flies; cutthroat trout — best mid- to late summer, use bait, spinners, flies. Smelt run in this river.

Kardy Lake. A 1-mile-long lake located on the Phipps Peninsula, 1.1 miles southeast of Ocean Cape and 3.4 miles southwest of Yakutat. Accessible by boat through the Ankau Lagoon system. Fish available: silver salmon — September to October, use spoons; red salmon — best in June, use small spoons; Dolly Varden — May to October, use bait, spinners, flies; cutthroat trout — best mid- to late summer, use bait, spinners, flies.

Monti Bay. A 3.5-mile-long bay located on the southeast shore of Yakutat Bay west of Yakutat. Accessible primarily by boat or from shorelines. Fish available: king salmon — available all year but best for large fish in early summer, use herring or spoons; silver salmon — best September to October, use herring or spoons; pink salmon — July to August, use small spoons; Dolly Varden — May to October, use bait, spinners, flies; cutthroat trout — best mid- to late summer, use bait, spinners, flies; halibut — available all year, season closed in January, best in summer, use bait or jigs; rockfish — all year, best May to September, use smaller baits or jigs.

Ocean Cape. Located on the Gulf of Alaska at the west end of Phipps Peninsula, 4.6 miles west of Yakutat. Accessible by boat or White Alice Road. Fish available: king salmon — available all year but best for large fish in early summer, use herring or spoons; silver salmon — best September to October, use herring or spoons; pink salmon — July to August, use small spoons; Dolly Varden — May to October, use bait, spinners, flies; cutthroat trout — best mid- to late summer, use bait, spinners, flies; halibut — available all year, season closed in January, best in summer, use bait; rockfish — all year, best May to September, use smaller baits or jigs.

Situk River. Heads at Situk Lake and flows southwest 18 miles to the Gulf of Alaska, 11 miles southeast of Yakutat. Accessible by boat, floatplane or Situk Road. One of the top fishing spots in Alaska, spring and fall. Fish available: king salmon — best early summer, use spoons; outstanding for silver salmon — mid-August to October, use spoons; pink salmon — July to August, use small spoons; red salmon — late June through August, use spoons or flies; Dolly Varden — May to October, use bait, spinners, flies; cutthroat trout — best mid- to late summer, use bait, spinners, flies; excellent runs of steelhead — April to May and October to November, use spoons, eggs. Smelt run in this river.

Summit Lake. A 0.8-mile-long lake located on the Phipps Peninsula, 2.8 miles southwest of Yakutat. Accessible by canoe or trail from Kardy Lake (see above). Fish available: silver salmon — September to October, use spoons; red salmon — best in June, use small spoons; pink salmon — July to August, use small spoons; Dolly Varden — May to October, use bait, spinners, flies; cutthroat trout — best mid- to late summer, use bait, spinners, flies.

Yakutat Bay. Located west of Yakutat. Accessible primarily by boat. Fish available: king salmon — available all year but best for large fish in early summer, use herring or spoons; silver salmon — late August through September, use herring or spoons; pink salmon — August, use small spoons; Dolly Varden — May to October, use bait, spinners, flies; cutthroat trout — best mid- to late summer, use bait, spinners, flies; halibut — available all year, season closed in January, best in summer, use bait or jigs; rockfish — all year, best May-September, use smaller baits or jigs.

RIVERS

River difficulty ratings may change drastically between morning and evening. Exercise good judgment.

SPECIAL FEATURES

Basket Bay

Located on Chichagof Island on the west side of Chatham Strait northwest of Angoon, 8 miles south of the mouth of Tenakee Inlet. The bay is exposed to the southeast, has a rocky bottom and depths of 12 to 40 fathoms. According to the *United States Coast Pilot,* it is not recommended as an anchorage. The midchannel course up the bay is clear. This is a scenic spot for sightseeing or fishing. Lots of silver salmon enter this bay in August; use herring or spoons. A flat extends about 400 yards into the head of the bay from the mouth of Kook Creek, a large stream that enters the bay through a limestone cliff. The stream goes underground 3 times between the bay and Kook Lake, which has fishing for cutthroat and Dolly Varden trout. There is an old, unmaintained trail between Basket Bay and Kook Lake; the trail does not extend to the Forest Service cabin at the west end of the lake. Related USGS Topographic map: Sitka C-4.

Hot Springs

Hot springs are scattered throughout Southeast Alaska. The soothing springs often are a destination for wilderness travelers but in many cases, they are simply an added treat forties can be found at several hot springs, ranging from a simple hot tub to more developed resorts. The town of Tenakee Springs actually grew up around the hot springs which is still a major attraction for this community. (See Communities, this section.) Listed below are a few of the springs found

Baranof Warm Springs. Located 20 miles east of Sitka on the east shore of Baranof Island. A privately operated hot springs bath is located on Warm Springs Bay. Accessible by boat or floatplane. A Forest Service trail extends a half mile from the hot springs to Baranof Lake where a cabin is located.

Chief Shakes Hot Springs. Located off Ketili River, a slouth of the Stikine River, approximately 12 miles upriver. The Hot Springs Slough Route is one of several established Canoe/Kayak Routes along the Stikine. Two hot tubs, 1 enclosed in a screened structure, provide a good place to soak. The open-air tub has a wooden deck around it, and both tubs have changing areas. There are also a picnic table, fire ring, benches, and an outdoor privy. The area is used heavily during evenings and weekends, according to the Forest Service. Paddlers should also be aware that use of the Stikine and the slough by powerboats is especially high during evenings and weekends. The Forest Service maintains 2 cabins just up river.

Goddard Hot Springs. Located on the outer coast of Baranof Island on Hot Springs Bay off of Sitka Sound, 16 miles south of Sitka. This may have been the earliest Alaska mineral springs known to the Europeans, and before their arrival Indians came from many miles away to benefit from the healing waters. In the mid-1800s there were 3 cottages at Goddard that were used to house invalids from Sitka. In the late 1880s, a Sitka company erected frame buildings for the use of people seeking the water's benefits. By the 1920s a 3-story hotel was built to provide more sophisticated accommodations The building was purchased in 1939 by the Territorial Legislature as an overflow home for the Sitka Pioneers' Home. After 1946 the building fell into disuse and was torn down. Today, the city of Sitka owns the property and maintains 2 modern cedar bathhouses for recreational use. A few people live year-round on nearby private land.

There are open shelters over the hot tubs, which feature natural hot springs water and cold water. The springs are very popular with area residents. The area has outhouses. Boardwalks provide easy walking. Boaters can anchor in the bay and go ashore in skiffs. This is not a place to take a boat without a chart; there are lots of rocks and shoals, especially around the hot springs. There are protected routes to Sitka and a fascinating series of coves and channels just north of the hot springs. At the springs there are camp sites in a grassy meadowlike area and on higher ground. Biting black flies (whitesox) are plentiful in the summer months.

Shelokum Hot Springs. Located approximately 90 miles north of Ketchikan in the Tongass National Forest on the Cleveland Peninsula. A 2.2-mile trail begins at Bailey Bay just south of Shelokum Creek and leads to Lake Shelokum. At the inlet to the lake is a 3-sided shelter. The hot springs are completely undisturbed and support a healthy population of unique algal plant life.

Trocadero Soda Springs. This seldom-visited carbonated "soda" springs is located on the west coast of Prince of Wales Island about 12 miles southeast of Craig. Access is by boat. Rubber boots are advised for this hike. This is bear country; exercise caution, particularly when salmon are spawning. The springs are reached by walking up an unnamed creek that has its outlet in a small inlet on the south shore of the bay. The springs flow into the creek about a mile upstream. The first sign of the springs are 2 giant golden steps. These are banks of yellow tufa formed by the constant runoff from the springs. Tufa is a geological term

referring to a concretionary sediment of silica or calcium carbonate deposited near the mouth of a mineral spring or geyser. The 4- to 5-acre area around the bubbling, hissing springs features lunarlike mounds and craters, splashed with colors ranging from subtle yellow to iron red. The springs originate in muskeg, then the mineralized water meanders about 100 feet, forming a deep crust of tufa in which there are hundreds of small vents with escaping gas and bubbling water. The highly carbonated water is described as having "a sharp, pleasant taste" and has no unpleasant odors. Although water from other carbonated springs in Southeast has been bottled and sold in the past, Trocadero water has never been commercially marketed.

White Sulphur Hot Springs. Located within the West Chichagof-Yakobi Wilderness area, some 65 miles northwest of Sitka. Many visitors fly-in to a small lake nearby and hike to the cabin or boat to Mirror Harbor and walk the easy, year-round 0.8-mile trail to the hot springs. Various log bathhouses have been built over the principal springs and in earlier years occasional hunters and trappers camped here. At that time the pools

Tents pitched at the edge of Reid Glacier in Glacier Bay National Park and Preserve are dwarfed by walls of blue ice. The 3.3-million-acre park and preserve offers excellent kayaking, canoeing, hiking, and camping. (Rollo Pool, staff)

were called Hoonah Warm Springs, but years ago they were renamed for a dentist, Dr. White. In 1916 the U.S. Forest Service built its first cabin and bathhouse here. This cabin has been modernized in recent years so bathers can pull back a translucent fiberglass screen and admire the view of the often turbulent Pacific Ocean while soaking in the hot water.

Juneau Icefield

This is the world's largest glacial accumulation outside of Greenland and Antarctica. The ice cap is 15 miles wide and 70 miles long and covers 1,500 square miles. Located in the Coast Mountains 25 miles north of Juneau, it extends over the border into Canada and north nearly to Skagway. The glaciers of southeastern Alaska are born in the high mountains that rise out of the sea and tower more than 13,000 feet within a few miles of the coast. The Juneau Icefield's annual snowfall of more than 100 feet does not melt during the summer and thus accumulates over the years until the weight of the snow compacts it into ice which then deforms and begins to flow down the valleys and into the sea. When the rate of ice buildup is greater than the amount lost annually to melting or calving of icebergs at the terminus, the glacier will gain ground or advance. If the reverse happens and the ice melts faster than new ice accumulates, the glacier will lose ground or retreat.

More than 30 glaciers, including the most visited glacier in Alaska — the Mendenhall — begin in this ice field. Mendenhall Glacier is about 12 miles long and 1.5 miles across at its face. It is retreating slowly, fewer than 100 feet per year. The glacier has melted back more than 2 miles in the last 200 years. The Mendenhall is only 13 miles from downtown Juneau by road and there's an excellent view of it even from the parking lot. The Forest Service maintains a visitor center and several trails in the area.

CAUTION: Do not approach the face of this or any glacier. The glacier can "calve" (break off) at any time and crush anyone too close under tons of ice.

Other glaciers emanating from the Juneau Icefield that can be seen from the highway north of Juneau or from the water include Lemon Creek Glacier, Herbert Glacier and Eagle Glacier. None of these descend to tidewater; all are retreating. One glacier that is definitely advancing at a steady rate is the Taku Glacier on the north side of Taku Inlet, 13 miles southeast of Juneau. Extending about 30 miles, this glacier is the largest from

the Juneau Icefield. If it keeps advancing, perhaps one day ice bergs will float again in Juneau Harbor as they did in the 1890s. Today, the bergs melt before they reach Juneau.

Since 1946, scientists have been studying the ice field each summer, searching for secrets about weather patterns, the ice age and about the plants and wildlife that survive some of the world's worst weather. The Coast Range is located in the path of storms that sweep eastward from the Pacific Ocean. Studying dust and other deposits laid down by storms going back hundreds of years can help scientists predict weather patterns of the future as well as the behavior of glaciers. There are at least 6 main camps and 20 or so lesser camps on the ice field, where winds frequently reach 80 mph and the summer temperature drops into the 20s.

Several companies in Juneau and Skagway offer tours to the ice cap by small plane or helicopter that may include the opportunity to walk on the ice field.

Lighthouses

Southeastern Alaska is the location of 12 historic lighthouses that are part of a chain of navigational beacons operated by the U.S. Coast Guard. Nearly all aides to navigation in Alaska are being modified to add solar-powered battery assists. Within the next year, all Alaskan lighthouses will include solar-assist panels. Many are visible from the waterways near the lighthouses. Familiar sights to those who navigate the Inside Passage, no lighthouses are staffed today and some no longer operate. From south to north, they are:

Tree Point Light Station. This is the first light seafarers sight when traveling to Alaska from the south. It is located on a point extending to the southwest from the east shore of Revillagigedo Channel and marks the entrance to the channel near the U.S.-Canada border. It was built on a 1,207-acre lighthouse reservation. The light began operation April 30, 1904, and was disestablished in 1969.

Mary Island Light Station. This is the second lighthouse encountered by mariners entering Alaska's Inside Passage from the south. It is located on a 198-acre lighthouse reservation on a 5-mile-long island located between Felice Strait and Revillagigedo Channel, 30 miles southeast of Ketchikan. The light began service July 15, 1903. It was reduced to a minor light and unmanned in 1968.

Guard Island Light Station. Located about 8 miles from downtown Ketchikan, this light marks the easterly entrance to Tongass Narrows. It went into service in September 1904. The early station also featured a fog bell. In 1969, because of rising costs of maintenance and new technology, the Coast Guard automated the station.

Lincoln Rock Light Station. Located on the westerly end of Clarence Strait adjacent to Etolin Island, this lighthouse proved to be one of the most difficult to build. The only bidder on the project began work in May 1902 after losing a load of lumber, his small steamer and a barge enroute to the job. Storms halted construction in August that year. The Lighthouse Board hired its own laborers and completed the project in December 1903. The station was disestablished and unmanned in 1968.

Cape Decision Light Station. Located at the south tip of Kuiu Island between Sumner and Chatham straits, 26 miles southeast of Port Alexander. This was the last lighthouse to be completed in Alaska, constructed at a cost of $158,000. It began operation March 15, 1932, and was automated in 1974.

Five Finger Islands Light Station. Located in the south entrance to Stephens Passage, 5 miles northwest of Whitney Island, 67 miles east of Sitka and 45 miles northwest of Petersburg. This light shares importance with Sentinel Island as one of the earliest lighthouses in Alaska, beginning operation March 1, 1902. It also was the last manned lighthouse in Alaska, being automated in 1984.

Fairway Island Light Station. Located just inside the easterly entrance to Peril Strait, 15 miles west of Angoon. This lighthouse was constructed during the summer of 1904 as a minor light marking a turning point for boats in Peril Strait. It was disestablished by 1925 after an effective system of unmanned stake lights was erected.

Cape Spencer Light Station. Located at the north side of the entrance to Cross Sound, 30 miles west of Gustavus, 45 miles north west of Hoonah. It was first lighted in 1913 with a small, unwatched acetylene beacon placed 90 feet above the water. Federal funds allowed construction of the light station, which began service Dec. 11, 1925, with a 200-mile range radio beacon, the first in Alaska. Unmanned since 1974, it is now on the National Register of Historic Places.

Point Retreat Light Station. Located on the northerly tip of the Mansfield Peninsula on Admiralty Island, 20 miles northwest of Juneau. This was one of 4 minor light stations constructed in 1904. It was unmanned

in 1917, upgraded and remanned in 1924, and again unmanned in 1973. The station now contains a foghorn that requires only periodic service.

Sentinel Island Light Station. Located on a small island in the center of the northerly end of Favorite Channel, 25 miles northwest of Juneau. It marks the entrance to Lynn Canal. This is one of the earliest lighthouses in Alaska. Constructed by George James of Juneau at a cost of $21,000, the station began operation on March 1, 1902. The station was unmanned and automated in 1966.

Point Sherman Light Station. Located on the east shore of Lynn Canal, 46 miles northwest of Juneau. Constructed during the summer of 1904, this station began service on Oct. 18, 1904. The station was disestablished and reduced to a minor light sometime before 1917. The light itself was abandoned by 1932.

Eldred Rock Light Station. Located in Lynn Canal, 55 miles northwest of Juneau and 20 miles southeast of Haines. This was the last major station commissioned in Alaska during the surge of lighthouse construction from 1902-06. Contractors completed con-

Warm sunshine and dead calm offer a rare opportunity for hot weather clothes in Misty Fiords National Monument. (Rollo Pool, staff)

struction June 1, 1906. The Coast Guard unmanned the station in 1973.

New Eddystone Rock

A spectacular, picturesque landmark located east of Revillgigedo Island in East Behm Canal, 35 miles northeast of Ketchikan and 3 miles north of Winstanley Island. It is within Misty Fiords National Monument. This 234-foot shaft of rock, called a "stack" by geologists, was named in 1793 by Capt. George Vancouver of the Royal Navy because of its resemblance to the lighthouse rock off Plymouth, England. A popular subject for photographers, the rock rises from a low, sandy island in the middle of the canal, with deep water surrounding it. It may be passed on either side, keeping at least 0.5-mile away to avoid the sand shoal.

Pack Creek

This excellent location for viewing and photographing brown bears is on the east side of Admiralty Island within Admiralty Island National Monument. Pack Creek flows east 8 miles to Seymour Canal at the mouth of Windfall Harbor, 28 air miles south of Juneau. Visitors may see brown bears fishing for spawning pink, chum and silver salmon. The photography is especially good during the summer and fall salmon runs. The best time for bear viewing is mid-July to late August. Seymour Canal is also known for its numerous humpback whales. Bald eagles, deer, and gulls also are numerous in the area. Access is by charter floatplane or boat from Sitka or Juneau.

Visitors must obtain a permit from the U.S. Forest Serivce or the Alaska Dept. of Fish and Game in Juneau before departing for Pack Creek. Regulations restrict access to limited portions of the area, when visitors may go and prohibit possession of food in the area. Camping is not allowed within the bear viewing area but is allowed in areas adjacent to the Pack Creek watershed. Hunting of brown bears is not allowed. For additional information contact: U.S. Forest Service, Admiralty National Monument, 8465 Old Dairy Road, Juneau, AK 99801; phone

789-3111; or the Alaska Dept. of Fish and Game, Game Division, P.O. Box 20, Douglas, AK 99824; phone 465-4265.

Stikine Icefield

Naturalist-explorer John Muir ventured up one of the glaciers of the Stikine Icefield in 1879 and wrote with awe about what he saw. Adventurers today ski and climb and hike this icy wilderness, braving crevasses, avalanches, rock slides and the notoriously harsh weather.

The Stikine Icefield lies in Southeast's Coast Range along the British Columbia border. It covers 2,900 square miles and encompasses at least 4 peaks higher than 10,000 feet — quite spectacular when sea level is only a few miles away. Much of the ice field lies within the Stikine-LeConte Wilderness. Mountain climbers are attracted by the 9,077-foot Devil's Thumb, and glacier ski touring and hiking parties are drawn by the area's spectacular scenery.

The weather, however, does its best to keep human incursions to a mimimum. Wet and windy, it can pin parties in their tents for days. The unprepared or inexperienced had best stay home.

Petersburg or Wrangell serve as staging areas for ice field trips. Generally, Wrangell is used to enter the ice field via the Stikine River drainage. Petersburg is the better choice for access via the Thomas Bay drainages. If you plan to hire a helicopter, you'll have to be dropped off outside the wilderness boundaries, for no helicopters are allowed to operate within, except under emergency circumstances.

Good cross-country skiing opportunities abound for either day touring or extended excursions into the heart of the ice field. The most popular practice for day skiers is to wait for good weather then helicopter onto the Horn Mountain-Thunder Mountain ridgeline. A variety of terrain for touring and telemarking awaits skiers there. Day touring season lasts from January into June. Even on short outings, the party should carry safety and survival equipment in case the weather makes a return pickup impossible.

Extended ski touring is best between April and late June. Dozens of sites are suitable for base camps. Waxless skis best suit the variable snow conditions. Absolute necessities include *very* good rain gear and a completely waterproof domed tent. Plan to pack out everything you pack in, and bring plenty of extra food in case you get weathered in for several days.

PETS

Leave your dog at home. When hard pressed, it may run to you and bring a bear or an angry moose along too.

TOTEMS

Unique to the Northwest Coast region, totem poles reflect the rich culture of the Tlingit, Haida and Tsimshian Indians of Southeast Alaska and British Columbia.

The tall wooden sculptures were carved as clan histories or memorials to the dead and were generally clustered along the village shore in front of clan houses, but were also placed directly on house fronts or erected in cemeteries. The advent of metal tools facilitated the creation of the taller poles. The predecessors of the tall poles were house posts and smaller mortuary columns carved with traditional tools.

The uppermost figure on a pole is nearly always the animals represented on the most important family crest. Of all the crests, the frog appears most frequently, then the bear, eagle, raven, thunderbird, wolf, owl, grouse, starfish, finback whale and halibut. Also represented are figures from Indian mythology: monsters with animal features, humanlike spirits and semihistorical ancestors. Occasionally depicted are objects, devices, masks and charms, and most rarely, art illustration, plants and sky phenomena.

Yellow cedar typically is used for the poles, however, some tribes had to make do with timber that was smaller and scarce. To make a pole, the center of a tree was generally hollowed out so that when the bark was removed a narrow cylinder of wood remained for carving. The poles were traditionally painted with pigments made from soil of yellow, brown and red hues, coal, cinnabar, berry juice and spruce sap. Fungus found on hemlock produces various colors: yellow when decayed, red when roasted and black when charred. Before modern paints became available, salmon eggs chewed with cedar bark formed the case or glue, for the paint.

Poles were left to stand as long as nature would permit, usually no more than 50 to 60 years. Once a pole became so rotten that it fell, it was pushed aside, left to decay naturally or used for firewood. Most totem poles still standing in parks today are 40 to 50 years old. In 1938, the Civilian Conservation Corps working with the U.S. Forest Service, began a program to salvage and restore poles. A process that continues today.

Several Southeast communities have created totem parks and the art of wood carving has been revived through local carving centers. Ketchikan's Totem Heritage Cultural Center houses 33 poles and fragments gathered during a 1970 survey and retrieval project to preserve the art. In addition to the display and restoration work, the Center offers classes in Native arts and crafts, including carving. Outside of Ketchikan, Totem Bight State Park protects another collection of poles and a clan house in a natural setting. Also near Ketchikan, Saxman Totem Park contains 24 totem poles, some restored and some newly carved, a tribal house and a carving shed where visitors can watch carvers at work. The Chilkat Center for the Arts in Haines is also a place carvers can work. The Raven Tribal House in Haines is a popular attraction. Sitka National Historic Park, a spruce forest setting, contains 14 poles and 4 house poles. In Wrangell, the house posts on Chief Shakes Tribal House are among the oldest in Alaska.

NOTE: This information was excerpted in part from Alaska Native Arts and Crafts, *published by The Alaska Geographic Society, and* THE ALASKA ALMANAC®. *For information on ordering see the ALASKA NORTHWEST LIBRARY at the back of this book.*

Digging clams from the beach at minus tides along Southcentral and Gulf Coast beaches requires perseverence and a willingness to endure wet and cold in pursuit of the wily mollusks. (Nelda J. Osgood)

SOUTHCENTRAL/ GULF COAST

The Region

Southcentral, the 49th state's most populated region, also encompasses millions of acres of untouched wilderness. Happily, much of that wilderness is readily accessible. Yet, there is no lack of solitude for the wanderer willing to seek out the splendid isolation that lies just off the well beaten path.

Rimmed by mountains, washed by the sea, Southcentral challenges the adventuresome to a variety of the most rugged outdoor experiences. Hiking, camping, river running, wildlife viewing, hunting and fishing opportunities are never far away. For the less hardy, the edge of wilderness can be found just out the door of many a comfortable lodge and many a cozy cabin.

Location: The Southcentral/Gulf Coast region curves 650 miles north and west of Yakutat in southeastern Alaska to Kodiak Island.

Subregions: Major subregions include Anchorage and the Mat-Su Valley; Copper River/Wrangell-St. Elias; Prince William Sound; Kenai Peninsula; Kodiak; and Western Cook Inlet. The text on specific communities and attractions has been divided according to these subregions.

Physical Description: Southcentral's mainland has a roller coaster topography of high mountains and broad river valleys. Great glaciers carve icy pathways from vast ice fields to tidewater along the Gulf Coast, in Prince William Sound, in the Kenai Fjords and in Kachemak Bay.

At the eastern edge of the region lies 13.2-million-acre Wrangell-St. Elias National Park and Preserve, largest unit in the national park system. The area is famous for trophy Dall sheep hunting. The coast from Icy Bay to the

Copper River Delta is primarily flatlands flanked by the Robinson Mountains and the large glaciers that flow from the Bagley Icefield in the Chugach Mountains. (See also Katalla, Kennicott, McCarthy, May Creek.)

The Copper River, historic gateway to rich copper deposits in the Wrangell Mountains, drains into the Gulf of Alaska east of Cordova. The mud flats of the Copper River Delta are a major landfall for migrating shorebirds and waterfowl. River rafting, bird-watching (trumpeter swans nest here) and watching icebergs calve from Childs Glacier are favored activities.

At Hinchinbrook Entrance, the Gulf of Alaska merges with Prince William Sound, a 15,000-square-mile maze of water, ice and islands. The Sound is the site of important salmon, crab and shrimp fisheries. Columbia Glacier is a major visitor attraction. Tour boats and charter flightseeing services from Valdez and Whittier take visitors to view the glacier. Sportfishing, boating and blue water kayaking rate the top Prince William Sound recreation choices. (See also Marine Parks: Prince William Sound.)

A high plateau separates the eastern and western river systems of Southcentral. The Nelchina caribou herd winters in the Lake Louise area and Dall sheep are readily observed on Sheep Mountain. The Matanuska River flows between the Chugach and Talkeetna mountains near Alaska's agricultural heartland. A 120-day growing season, with up to 19 hours of summer sunlight, nourishes the giant vegetables for which the Matanuska Valley is noted. River rafting, hunting, fishing, hiking and winter sports are popular activities.

Chugach
National
Forest

Prince William
Sound

Map continues next page

Hinchinbrook
Island

Katalla

Chenega
Bay

Cape Hinchinbrook
Light Station

Kayak
Island

Montegue
Island

Cape St. Elias
Light Station

Blying Sound

A l a s k a

◊ Middleton Island

SOUTHCENTRAL
▼▼▼
GULF COAST

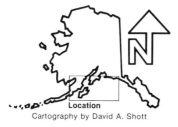

Location

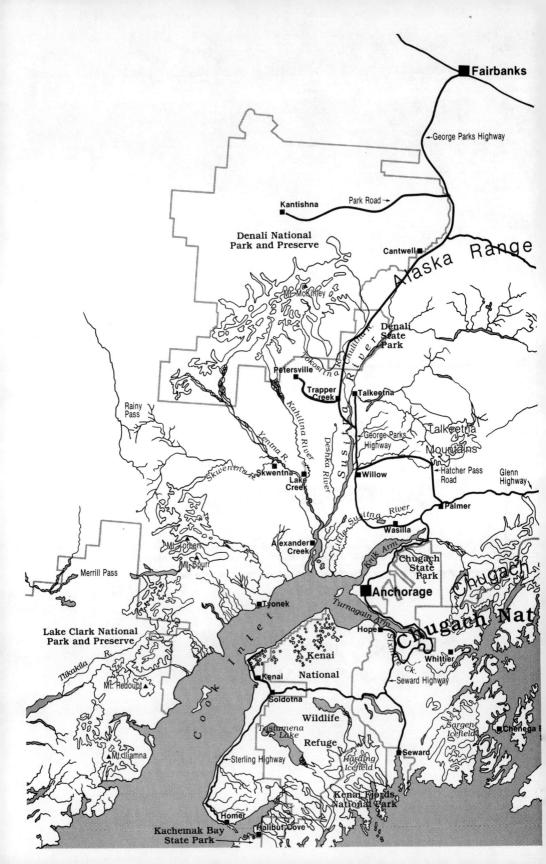

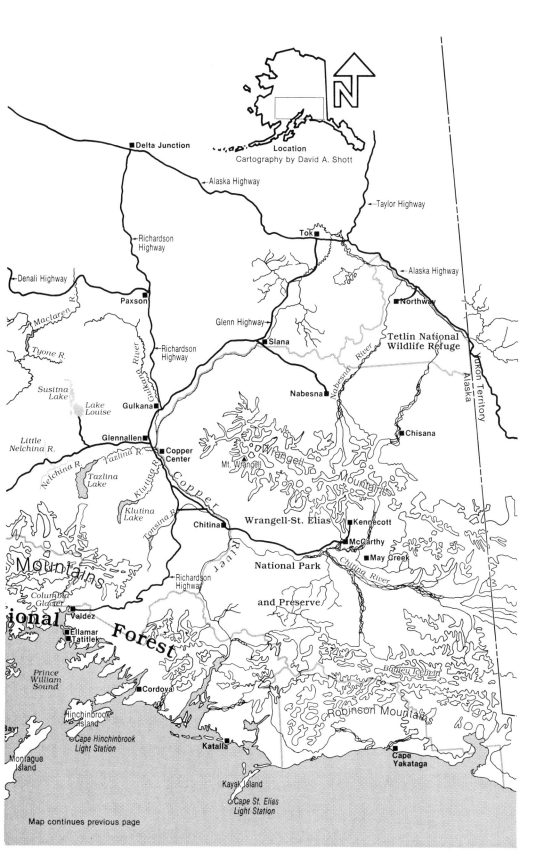

Delta Junction

Alaska Highway

Taylor Highway

Richardson
Highway

Tok

Denali Highway

Alaska Highway

Paxson

Northway

Glenn Highway

Maclaren R.

Tyone R.

Slana

Tetlin National
Wildlife Refuge

Richardson
Highway

Gulkana River

Yukon Territory

Alaska

Susitna
Lake

Nabesna

Nabesna River

Lake
Louise

Gulkana

Glennallen

Chisana

Little
Nelchina R.

Copper
Center

Tazlina R.

Wrangell

Nelchina R.

Tazlina
Lake

Mt. Wrangell

Mountains

Copper

Klutina R.

Klutina
Lake

Chitina

Wrangell-St. Elias

Kennecott

Tonsina R.

McCarthy

Mountains

May Creek

Chitina River

National Park

Richardson
Highway

River

and Preserve

Columbia
Glacier

Valdez

Forest

Bagley Icefield

Ellamar
Tatitlek

Prince
William
Sound

Cordova

Robinson Mountains

Bay

Hinchinbrook
Island

Montague
Island

Cape Hinchinbrook
Light Station

Katalla

Cape
Yakataga

Kayak Island

Cape St. Elias
Light Station

Location
Cartography by David A. Shott

Map continues previous page

To the west, the Susitna River flows from the south slopes of the Alaska Range through a valley with the Talkeetna Mountains on the south. The river winds through prime moose habitat into the silty upper reaches of Cook Inlet. The Iditarod Trail follows portions of an old mail and freight route from the Cook Inlet area to Nome. The state's major long-distance sled dog race, from Anchorage to Nome, runs along much of the trail. Anchorage, home to nearly half of Alaska's population, stands at the head of 220-mile-long Cook Inlet, which extends between the Kenai Peninsula and the Aleutian Range. Sportfishing, jet boating, flightseeing and hunting are popular here. (See also Chugach State Park.)

The Kenai Peninsula, famous for its sportfishing, is heavily used along portions of its road system, but sees little visitation in more remote areas. Kenai Fjords National Park, Chugach National Forest, Kenai National Wildlife Refuge and both Kachemak Bay State Park and Kachemak Bay State Wilderness Park offer a wide range of recreational opportunities. The Kenai Peninsula and Resurrection Pass trail systems and the Swan Lake and Swanson River canoe trails should not be overlooked. Major access points include Seward, Kenai, Soldotna, Homer and Seldovia. Offshore, halibut fishing is particularly attractive. Homer and Kenai are major access points for flights across Cook Inlet, especially to McNeil River State Game Sanctuary.

The Kodiak Archipelago extends southwest from the Kenai Peninsula and shields the western flank of the mainland, to some extent, from Gulf of Alaska storms. At 3,588 square miles, Kodiak ranks at the state's largest island; it has long been famous for its brown/grizzly bears and for its fishing. (See also Kodiak and Alaska Maritime national wildlife refuges, Shuyak Island State Park and McNeil River State Game Sanctuary.)

Western Cook Inlet, just a short plane ride from Anchorage, Kenai or Homer, offers true wilderness dominated by a spine of mountains (part of the Aleutian and Alaska ranges) and 2 large lakes, Clark and Iliamna, which offer some of the best sportfishing in the world. There are rivers to float, gorgeous country to explore on foot and a coastline to poke around on from a boat. At McNeil River the spectacle of huge brown bears fishing the river for salmon is almost rivaled by the photographers photographing those bears.

Climate

The region's climate is primarily maritime, with rain and fog and mild temperature fluctuations. Nearer the mountains, the climate becomes transitional; temperature changes are greater and the climate is generally harsher. In Anchorage, January temperatures average 13°F and July temperatures average 57°F. Protected by the Chugach and Kenai mountains from the moisture-laden clouds from the gulf, Anchorage averages only about 15 inches of precipitation annually. However, at Whittier, on the coast side, average annual precipitation is 174 inches.

Vegetation

Variable terrain and climate provide suitable habitat for an assortment of plants. The moisture-demanding vegetation of Southeast continues along the coast to the Kenai Peninsula and Kodiak. Sitka spruce and western hemlock dominate coastal forests. Inland, birch, alder and aspen are the primary species. At higher elevations, forests give way to subalpine brush thickets, fields of wildflowers, berries and alpine meadows. Major river valleys have stands of black cottonwood. Chugach National Forest, second largest in the nation, encompasses 5.8 million acres of Southcentral.

Wildlife

Big Game. Variety also characterizes Southcentral's animal populations. Brown/grizzly bears, the only large mammal native to Kodiak Island, are equally at home in the coastal forests of Prince William Sound, portions of the Matanuska and Susitna valleys and on the flats on the west side of Cook Inlet. Sitka black-tailed deer, mountain goats and Dall sheep have been introduced to Kodiak and elk to nearby Afognak Island. Mountain goats roam the sheer cliffs of the Chugach and Wrangell mountains. Moose thrive on the Kenai Peninsula, where the nearly 2- million-acre Kenai National Wildlife Refuge provides habitat for these giants. Moose occur throughout the rest of Southcentral, except on the islands of Prince William Sound and the Kodiak group. Dall sheep are found in the Talkeetna, Wrangell and Chugach mountains, on the slopes of the Alaska Range and on inland peaks of the Kenai Mountains. Sitka black-tailed deer inhabit the coastal forests of Prince William Sound. Wolves live on the Kenai Peninsula, in the Nelchina basin, the Copper River valley, the Eagle River valley near Anchorage and in the rolling country northwest of Cook Inlet.

Furbearers and Nongame Species. Smaller mammals include lynx, pine martens, weasels, beavers, muskrats, minks, red foxes, land otters, porcupines, wolverines, snow-shoe hares, shrews, voles and lemmings.

Birds. Southcentral has congregations of bald and golden eagles, hawks and falcons and an overwhelming number of shorebirds and waterfowl. The world's population of dusky Canada geese summers on the Copper River flats, and rare trumpeter swans nest on the Kenai Peninsula and near the Copper River. The mud flats of the river's delta are a major landfall for migrating shorebirds and waterfowl.

Marine Life. Rich Gulf Coast waters support crab, shrimp and clams. Salmon, herring, cod, Dolly Varden and cutthroat trout abound and nourish, in turn, harbor and Dall porpoises, sea lions, sea otters and killer whales. Largest marine mammals in the area are the baleen whales — humpbacks, fins and minkes — which feed on krill and other marine invertebrates that thrive in the nutrient-rich waters.

Transportation

Anchorage began as a railroad construction camp and the Alaska Railroad still carries passengers and freight between Anchorage and Fairbanks. The route extends to Seward and a spur line transports passengers and vehicles to Whittier, where the state ferry MV *Bartlett* connects Whittier with Valdez and Cordova. Another ferry, the MV *Tustumena*, serves Seward, Homer, Seldovia, Kodiak, Port Lions, Valdez and Cordova, and King Cove and Sand Point on the Alaska Peninsula. Cruise ship traffic is slowly increasing, but most Southcentral ports — such as Valdez, Anchorage, Kodiak and Seward — are busy with containership and tanker traffic.

Public Lands

National Parks and Preserves. The 13.2-million-acre Wrangell-St. Elias National Park and Preserve, largest unit in the national park system, lies at the eastern edge of the Southcentral/Gulf Coast region. (See Attractions, Copper River/Wrangell-St. Elias subregion.) Harding Icefield caps 580,000-acre Kenai Fjords National Park, on the southeastern side of the Kenai Peninsula, (see Kenai Peninsula subregion.) And on the west side of Cook Inlet, Lake Clark National Park and Preserve encompasses 3.6 million acres, (see Western Cook Inlet subregion).

National Wildlife Refuges. Part of Alaska Maritime National Wildlife Refuge and all of Kenai National Wildlife Refuge are found on the Kenai Peninsula (see Attractions that subregion). Kodiak National Wildlife Refuge, 1.9 million acres on the islands of Kodiak Archipelago, offers hunting, fishing, wilderness camping and also recreational cabins (see Kodiak subregion).

State Parks and Recreation Areas. Chugach State Park, Kachemak Bay State Park, Kachemak Bay Wilderness Park and Shuyak Island State Park all offer significant wilderness opportunities, as do the 7 undeveloped state marine parks in Prince William Sound. State recreation areas with wilderness or near-wilderness appeal include Nancy Lake, Kepler-Bradley Lakes, Lake Louise, Caines Head, Captain Cook and Johnson Lake. Kenai Keys is undeveloped and Morgan's Landing offers mainly Kenai River access. Clam Gulch, Ninilchik, Deep Creek and Anchor River state recreation areas are on the highway.

State Game Sanctuary, Refuges and Critical Habitat Areas. The intense usage and potential for land use conflicts led to the establishment of 15 state game refuges and critical habitat areas in the Southcentral/Gulf Coast region. Trading Bay, Susitna Flats, Palmer Bay Flats and Goose Bay game refuges protect important spring and fall migratory stopovers for millions of waterfowl; and the Anchorage Coastal Wildlife Refuge supports the greatest numbers and diversity of birds in the metropolitan area. Part of this refuge, the easily accessible Potter Marsh, is one of the state's most popular bird-watching areas.

McNeil River State Game Sanctuary protects the large numbers of brown bears that congregate near the river mouth to feed on spawning chum salmon in western Cook Inlet.

The Copper River Delta, world famous for its migratory waterfowl and the richness and diversity of its marine and mammal populations, is a state critical habitat area. Kalgin Island in Cook Inlet, and Clam Gulch, Anchor River/Fritz Creek, Kachemak Bay and Fox River Flats on the Kenai Peninsula have also received that protective designation.

Tugidak Island Critical Habitat Area, encompassing an island of the Kodiak Archipelago, protects one of the largest harbor seal pupping and haul-out areas in the world. The island is uninhabited and remarkably free of mammalian predators and supports large populations of geese, ducks and shorebirds during spring and fall migration and high concentrations of ground nesting birds.

Willow Mountain Critical Habitat Area, in the Mat-Su Valley, and Redoubt Bay Critical Habitat Area, in Western Cook Inlet, are the newest areas set aside, the former to protect important moose wintering habitat and the latter for its waterfowl nesting areas, including nests of the Tule goose, a subspecies of the white-fronted goose.

Many of these refuges and critical habitat areas are heavily used by recreationists. Hunting, fishing, trapping, wildlife viewing and photography are allowed according to state regulations. Each year thousands of clam diggers descend on Clam Gulch Critical Habitat Area, attracted by the razor clam beds at low tide. Less accessible and less heavily used is the Fox River Flats Critical Habitat Area at the head of Kachemak Bay. A primitive switchback trail leads down to the flats from East End Road out of Homer. There are no public-use facilities in this area.

Chugach National Forest

Because Chugach National Forest overlaps 3 of SOUTHCENTRAL/GULF COAST's subregions, it is included here in the introduction. For specifics about the Forest Service cabins in Prince William Sound, the Kenai Peninsula and the Copper River/Wrangell-St. Elias areas, see those subregions.

This national forest ranks second in size only to Tongass National Forest in southeastern Alaska. Chugach totals 5.8 million acres — about the size of the state of New Hampshire. It is a beautiful land of majestic mountains, free-flowing streams, frigid mountain lakes and productive waterfowl wetlands. It encompasses 3 geographic regions: the northeastern Kenai Peninsula, the arc of Prince William Sound and the Copper River Delta/Bering River area east of Cordova. Special features of Chugach National Forest are Kayak Island, site of the first documented landing of Europeans in Alaska; Columbia Glacier, one of the largest tidewater glaciers in the world; the wetlands of the Copper River Delta, which serve as nesting, staging and feeding habitat for millions of birds each year; and Portage Glacier and the Begich, Boggs Visitor Center, one of the most visited recreational facilities in Alaska.

The Begich, Boggs Visitor Center at Portage Glacier offers sightseeing, photography and nature studies. The center contains an orientation area, enclosed observatory, exhibit room and a 196-seat theater with spaces for wheelchairs. The center is open 7 days a week during the summer; winter hours are intermittent. Beginning in 1989 a 200-seat tour boat operating under a Forest Service Special Use Permit began offering close-up views of the face of the glacier. For further information, call the center at 783-2326.

This national forest is accessible by road from Anchorage, and by boat and small plane from many neighboring communities including Seward, Cordova and Valdez and Whittier.

Summer visitors to Chugach National Forest should bring warm clothing, rain gear, adequate footwear and insect repellent. Much of the area is remote and emergency assistance may be far away. The Forest Service cautions that proper equipment and knowledge are essential for safe hiking and boating. Avoid traveling alone; always inform a responsible person of your itinerary and check in with them on your return. In the winter, when temperatures may fall below zero, visitors should wear layered clothing topped by goosedown, fiberfill or wool garments. Carry emergency equipment, especially on long trips. Unless you are experienced, stay away from glaciers. Also avoid avalanche hazard areas such as gullies or open slopes, particularly after a fresh snowfall. Travel in wide flat valleys or on ridges.

Wildlife. Chugach National Forest is home to a wide variety of birds, mammals and fish. Black and brown bear inhabit most of the forest, foraging on open tundra slopes and in intertidal zones. In late summer bears may be seen feeding on spawned-out salmon along streams and rivers. Black bear occur in most areas, with the exception of some of the islands. Brown bears are found along the eastern shore of Prince William Sound, on the Copper River Delta and occasionally on the Kenai Peninsula.

Record-size moose — some with antler spreads of more than 6 feet — inhabit the Kenai Peninsula; moose have been transplanted to the Copper River Delta. Sitka black-tailed deer have been transplanted to many islands in Prince William Sound and caribou have been transplanted to the Kenai Peninsula. Dall sheep can be seen on Kenai Peninsula mountainsides; mountain goats are found on steep hillsides along Prince William Sound, the Copper River Delta and occasionally above Portage Valley. Smaller mammals found within the Chugach include coyotes, lynx, red foxes, wolverines, wolves, porcupines, red squirrels, beavers, land otters, parka squirrels, pikas and hoary marmots.

Boaters in Prince William Sound may see Dall porpoises, harbor seals, sea otters, sea lions and killer and humpback whales.

More than 214 species of resident and migratory birds occur in Chugach. Seabirds, such as black-legged kittiwakes, nest in sea-cliff colonies by the thousands. Ptarmigan scurry over alpine tundra, bald eagles perch on shoreline snags and tangled rain forest undergrowth hosts Steller's jays, named in 1741 by naturalist Georg Wilhelm Steller, the first European to set foot on Alaskan soil. The Copper River Delta protects one of the larger known concentrations of nesting trumpeter swans in North America. The total population of dusky Canada geese on the delta ranges from 7,500 to 13,500; the delta is the only nesting area of this subspecies. Nesting waterfowl are joined in spring and fall by thousands of migrating shorebirds. Checklists of the birds found in the Chugach are available from Forest Service offices.

Saltwater fish available include halibut, red snapper and 5 species of salmon. Razor clams can be dug near Cordova and shrimp and 3 species of crab may be harvested. Lakes on the Kenai Peninsula contain landlocked Dolly Varden and many larger lakes and streams are migratory routes for Dolly Varden, rainbow trout and salmon. Other freshwater fish include arctic grayling, hooligan, burbot, lake trout and cutthroat trout.

Activities and Accommodations: Chugach National Forest has 16 campgrounds that are generally open from Memorial Day through Labor Day on a first-come basis (some campground gates remain open until the first snow, but water and trash services are discontinued after Labor Day). Facilities include restrooms, picnic tables, fire grates, garbage cans and water. No RV hookups; 14-day limit. A camping fee is charged.

Water recreational opportunities abound in the Chugach National Forest. Boating, fishing and kayaking are popular. Parts of streams on the Kenai Peninsula which are suitable for kayaking and canoeing include Kenai, Portage, Quartz and Sixmile creeks. Part of Sixmile is not suitable for canoeing and should be considered only by experienced boaters. Private concessionaires under permit from the Forest Service offer river-running trips on several rivers and creeks within the national forest.

Hunting is permitted within Chugach National Forest, subject to Alaska Dept. of Fish and Game regulations. Recreational gold panning also is permitted in several areas. NOTE: Be sure to avoid trespassing on private mining claims. A leaflet containing open locations and guidelines is available from Forest Service offices.

The Summit Lake/Manitoba Mountain area offers cross-country skiing, alpine mountaineering, snowshoeing and snow machine recreational opportunities. Accessible from Milepost 48 on the Seward Highway.

Turnagain Pass, 60 miles southeast of Anchorage, is open for winter use from Dec. 1 to Feb. 15 and later if snow cover is adequate. There is a snow machine area on the west side of the highway and snowshoeing and cross-country skiing on the east side of the highway. There are summer and winter rest areas with restrooms.

Some 200 miles of hiking trails lead to backcountry cabins, ski areas and popular fishing spots within the Chugach National Forest. For more on the hiking trails, see the Kenai Peninsula subregion.

Forest Service Cabins. The 39 Chugach National Forest recreational cabins are one of the best lodging bargains in the state. Cost is $15 (increases to $20, July 1, 1990) per night per party for these rustic but comfortable cabins which are accessible by foot, boat or small plane. Local Forest Service office can provide information about fees and can reserve any cabin managed by the Forest Service in Alaska. There is a 3-day limit for hike-in cabins from May 15 through Aug. 31; for other cabins the limit is 7 nights year-round. (Cabin charts appear in the subregions.)

Obtain additional information or make cabin reservations through any Chugach National Forest office: Cordova Ranger District, P.O. Box 280, Cordova, AK 99574-0280; Seward Ranger District, P.O. Box 390, Seward, AK 99664-0390; Glacier Ranger District, Monarch Mine Road, P.O. Box 129, Girdwood, AK 99587; or, 201 E. 9th Ave., Anchorage, AK 99501; phone 271-2500. Payment must accompany the cabin application. For details on how to apply for a cabin and other cabin information, see Cabins in GENERAL INFORMATION section.

The Rivers

Once highways into the unknown for explorers and prospectors, today the rivers serve a similar function for adventurers seeking the beauty and solitude of Southcentral's backcountry. Whether your preference is a slow meander down a clear stream where the fishing is good, or a hair-raising trip through white-water rapids, the rivers here will meet your needs.

Many of them are glacier-fed, and all are very cold. Life vest should be worn at all times. (For more on river floating safety, see Boating, Canoeing and Kayaking in the GENERAL INFORMATION section.) For the inexperienced, guides offer float trips down many of the rivers. (See the BUYERS GUIDE.) Specific rivers are detailed in the subregions.

Sea Kayaking

One could spend a lifetime exploring southcentral Alaska's Gulf Coast by kayak. Indeed there has been a virtual explosion in the number of kayakers paddling South-central waters in recent years. Ease of access from Anchorage, Alaska's largest city, has drawn many paddlers to the Gulf Coast's scenic sounds and fjords where whales breech and sea otters are so abundant some fishermen have come to view them as nuisances.

The same safety precautions given to kayakers in southeastern Alaska apply to Southcentral kayakers. The weather in some areas can change abruptly, stranding kayakers. Changing wind direction and tidal currents can make paddling a tricky business at best. (See Boating in the GENERAL INFOR-MATION section for more information on kayaking safety.) For popular places to sea kayak in Prince William Sound, Kodiak and the Kenai Peninsula, see those sections.

Sportfishing

There is easy access to good sportfishing in the Southcentral/Gulf Coast region by car, but

Angler proudly displays his handsome king salmon at Port Alsworth, gateway to Lake Clark National Park and Preserve. (Mark Lang)

the majority of the best fishing locations are reached only by plane or boat. (For good fishing spots along highways in this region consult *The MILEPOST®*; to order, see the ALASKA NORTHWEST LIBRARY section at the back of the book.)

Southcentral and the Gulf Coast offer a wide range of fishing experiences, from lakes and streams to ocean trolling, and a variety of species.

King salmon, the most-prized species in Alaska, are found throughout this region. Record king salmon have been taken from road-accessible Kenai River. These fish are not uncommon at 30 pounds and up and can reach 90 to 100 pounds. The best catches of kings in Prince William Sound are near Valdez and Cordova in late winter and early spring and near Whittier in early summer. Saltwater fishing for kings is available in lower Cook Inlet from mid-May through late July and in upper Cook Inlet waters in late May. On Kodiak Island, kings start arriving in the Karluk River in early June.

Silver salmon arrive in Prince William Sound in late July and remain through mid-September; they also occur in rivers in the Cordova area in the fall. Silvers can be found off the lower Kenai Peninsula in July and August; in rivers draining into upper Cook Inlet from mid-July to September; and in Kodiak waters in late August and early September. Silvers range from 8 to 20 pounds, and can attain 25 pounds.

Fishing for pink salmon is excellent in Prince William Sound from mid-June through mid-August. In the Cook Inlet area, fishing for pinks in odd-numbered years ranges from poor to fair from mid-July through mid-August. In waters of the Kenai Peninsula, fishing for pinks is best during even-numbered years from mid-July to mid-August. These small salmon, which average 3 or 4 pounds, but occasionally attain 10 pounds, start arriving in Kodiak waters in late June and appear in streams in July and early August.

Chum salmon, which commonly weigh about 10 pounds, but occasionally reach 30 pounds, are available in Prince William Sound during July and August and often are caught while fishing for silvers or pinks. These fish are scattered sparingly throughout Cook Inlet streams from mid-July through mid-August and they usually arrive in Kodiak waters in late July and early August.

Ruby-fleshed red salmon are much prized for food; they commonly weigh 6 to 10 pounds, but occasionally reach 15 pounds. Some runs in some rivers apparently will not hit a lure, but there is excellent fly-fishing for reds in the Gulkana and Klutina rivers in the Copper River area in late June and July, and in the Russian River on the Kenai Peninsula from early June to late August and in the Kenai River from mid-July through early August. These rivers are all accessible by road. Reds are also available in several rivers in the Kodiak area from June to the first of September.

Other fish encountered in this region are: halibut, ranging up to 300 pounds; rainbow trout, which may tip the scales at 10 pounds and occasionally reach 20 pounds; arctic char and Dolly Varden, which usually weigh 1 to 3 pounds, but sometimes reach 9 to 12 pounds; lake trout, which can reach 30 pounds; burbot (also called lush or lingcod), which average 2 to 5 pounds, but can attain 20 pounds; and the wide-ranging arctic grayling. Grayling like clear, cold water and are found throughout much of the state; any grayling weighing more than 3 pounds is considered trophy size.

Access to most off-the-road sportfishing in the Southcentral/Gulf Coast region is by private or charter boat from such communities as Homer, Seward, Whittier or Valdez, or via small planes — usually chartered in the larger communities such as Anchorage, Talkeetna, Glennallen, Cordova or Homer. Fishing licenses are available in most communities and at some lodges.

For those traveling in the wilderness, a general rule from the Alaska Dept. of Fish and Game is to "plan for the worst." Travelers should take extra food and other necessary supplies and allow for a flexible schedule in the event the weather turns bad and prevents pickup from remote sites.

For more information about fishing in the Southcentral/Gulf Coast region consult the current sportfishing regulations or contact the following: Alaska Dept. of Fish and Game, Sport Fish Division, 333 Raspberry Road, Anchorage, AK 99518; phone 267-2218. Alaska Dept. of Fish and Game, 211 Mission Road, Kodiak, AK 99615; phone 486-4791. Alaska Dept. of Fish and Game, P.O. Box 234, Homer, AK 99603; phone 235-8191. Alaska Dept. of Fish and Game, Sport Fish Division, P.O. Box 47, Glennallen, AK 99588; phone 822-3309.

Listings of specific fishing areas are included in each subregion.

SOUTHCENTRAL/ GULF COAST WATERS STILL BECKON

In the early morning hours of March 24, 1989, the *Exxon Valdez* wandered off course, ran aground and dumped 11 million gallons of crude oil into the cold, clear waters of Prince William Sound. Winds and strong currents soon carried the oil south and west through the sound along the eastern shores of the Kenai Peninsula into the lower reaches of Cook Inlet then across to the Alaska Peninsula and Kodiak. It was the nation's worst oil spill.

But terrible as the accident was, it *did not* ruin all of Southcentral/Gulf Coast's beaches, or even most of them. There are still thousands of miles of unspoiled coastline waiting to be explored. And the sportfishing is still terrific. In the summer of 1989 the overwhelming majority of visitors traveling out of Homer, Seward, Valdez, Whittier and Kodiak reported seeing no evidence of the spill other than the hustle and bustle of the clean-up crews in port.

Marine adventurers in the summer of 1990 can avoid the oiled beaches by consulting a map published by the Prince William Sound Users Assoc. (3111 C St., Suite 200, Anchorage, AK 99503; phone 561-1622). These frequently updated maps are available in public lands offices, resource libraries, visitor centers and some recreational equipment sale and rental outlets. It is also wise to check locally in the gateway communities and/or consult the public land management agency for the area you'll be exploring. Park rangers at Kenai Fjords National Park and Katmai National Park and Preserve have incorporated educational information on the spill into their regular talks.

ANCHORAGE/MAT-SU VALLEY

Introduction

Anchorage is well located — only 20 minutes from Alaska. Sooner or later everyone hears this old saw about the state's largest city. What newcomers and visitors may not realize is that Anchorage also boasts a respectable amount of . . . well, wilderness. Chugach State Park lies in Anchorage's back yard, and wild animals pay no heed to municipal boundaries. The city's extensive parks and trails allow easy access for people heading into the backcountry and animals wandering into the city. Downtown residents wake up to see moose in their yard — as often as not snacking on their shrubbery. A wolf has been spotted on Delaney Park Strip downtown. And in 1989 early spring bicyclers on the Tony M. Knowles Coastal Trail almost cycled into a grizzly bear.

A city of almost 220,000 people is clearly not a wilderness in the traditional sense of the word. But every year more than one day hiker or cross-country skier gets into trouble and has to be rescued within the city limits. Several good guide books offer information about the city's parks and trails, and the municipality also has brochures with maps. But for the purposes of this book Anchorage serves principally as a gateway into Alaska's wilderness.

The Mat-Su Valley, a shortened name for the lands demarcated by the Matanuska and Susitna rivers, lies just north of Anchorage. It is a beautiful place where snowcapped mountains tower over neatly kept farms. Where ancient glaciers have spawned 2 huge river systems, one famous for its fishing, the other, a rafter's delight. Where a historic gold mine perches high among forbidding peaks in a state park that offers some of the best (and most accessible) hiking and cross-country skiing in the state. Where skiing, dog mushing and snowmobiling are a way of life in the winter. Where hunters routinely come back with their Dall sheep, or moose or caribou. And where urban, fly-in duck hunters congregate each Sept. 1 to celebrate the beginning of the season.

Located just a few minutes from downtown Anchorage, Chugach State Park offers numerous trails for day and overnight hiking trips, wildlife viewing and berry-picking. (J.H. Juday)

Alexander Creek

Located near the mouth of Alexander Creek in the Susitna River delta 27 miles northwest of Anchorage. **Transportation:** Boats; charter floatplane service from Anchorage. **Population:** 17. **Zip code:** 99695. **Emergency Services:** Alaska State Troopers, Anchorage; hospitals and clinics in Anchorage.

Visitor Facilities: Accommodations and meals available. No public laundry facilities. No stores; supplies are obtained from Anchorage. Marine engine and boat repair available. Boats and motors available for rent and river taxi service available. Guide services available. Hunting/fishing licenses and public moorage facilities available. Fuel available: regular gasoline.

Alexander Creek is a scattered, unincorporated community located on or near the former site of a small Indian village reported by U.S. Geological Survey geologist George Homans Eldridge in 1898.

Some residents of the area are commercial fishermen; others are retired.

Sportfishing is excellent for king salmon from May 20 to July 6; silver, pink, red and chum salmon from July 16 to September; rainbow trout in May and September; and grayling from July to September.

Hunting in the area is for moose, black bear and ducks.

Communications include mail plane, commercial radio and TV. There are no schools or churches. Electricity is from individual generators; water is from wells. Sewage system is flush toilets. Freight arrives by charter plane. Village corporation address: Alexander Creek Inc., 8126 Wisteria, Anchorage, AK 99502.

Anchorage

Located on Knik Arm, Cook Inlet, 1,445 air miles north of Seattle, 578 miles northwest of Juneau, 263 miles south of Fairbanks. **Transportation:** Daily jet service by domestic and international airlines; automobile and scheduled bus service via the state highway system; Alaska Railroad from Fairbanks, Whittier or Seward. **Population:** 218,979. **Emergency Services:** Police, Fire Department, Ambulance and Search & Rescue, emergencies only, phone 911. Police, nonemergency, phone 786-8900. Alaska State Troopers, phone 269-5511. Hospitals: Humana Hospital, phone 276-1131; Alaska Native Medical Center, phone 279-6661; Providence Hospital, phone 562-2211; Elmendorf Air Force, phone 331-4544.

Elevation: 38 to 120 feet.

Private Aircraft: Anchorage airports provide facilities and services to accommodate all types of aircraft. See the *Alaska Supplement,* the U.S. government's flight information publication, for the following airports: Anchorage International, Merrill Field, Birchwood, Campbell airstrip, Providence Hospital heliport, Elmendorf Hospital heliport; Elmendorf AFB, Bryant Field (Fort Richardson) and Lake Hood seaplane base.

Visitor Facilities: Anchorage is the staging and supply point for travel to wilderness areas throughout Alaska and offers a variety of visitor attractions and special events year-round. Virtually all services are available, including more than 60 hotels and motels, nearly as many homes with bed-and-breakfast accommodations and more than 300 restaurants. Clothing, food and other supplies for backcountry travel are available in local stores. There are 2 public campgrounds (open from May to October). Chugach State Park also has public campgrounds located near Anchorage, and there are several private campgrounds in the area.

Today, Anchorage is the main center of commerce and distribution for the rest of Alaska. Mainstays of the economy are federal, state and local government agencies, the oil industry, military bases and transportation facilities, including an expanding port and international airport.

Attractions readily accessible from

Anchorage include Chugach State Park, Prince William Sound and Portage Glacier. There are many air taxi operators based in Anchorage who can take you flightseeing or out on hunting, fishing, backpacking and photography excursions.

Wilderness experiences are available for all visitors with or without their own equipment. There are many guide services specializing in hiking, mountaineering, ski touring, float trips, and backpacking — equipment can be rented.

A good first stop for visitors planning to head into the backcountry is the Alaska Public Lands Information Center, 605 W. 4th Ave., Anchorage, AK 99501; phone 271-2737. Films, brochures and knowledgeable staffers provide information on every kind of outdoor activity and will help you plan your trip. The center is open 7 days a week in summer. Backcountry travel information for Chugach State Park is available at park headquarters, Frontier Bldg., 3601 C St., phone 561-2020. (Phone 694-6391 for a recorded message on current conditions.) The park also offers a trip planning service for overnight backpackers.

For information on backcountry travel in Chugach National Forest, contact the U.S. Forest Service, 201 E. 9th Ave., Suite 206, Anchorage, AK 99501; phone 271-2500. For information on specific areas, contact the district rangers: for Girdwood to Summit Lake and Hope area, phone the Girdwood ranger district at 783-3242; for Seward to the Russian River area, phone the Seward district at 224-3374; for Prince William Sound and the Copper River area, phone the Cordova district, 424-7661.

For Denali National Park and for areas in other regions of Alaska, such as Katmai and Glacier Bay national parks and the Chilkoot Trail in Klondike Gold Rush National Historic Park, contact the Alaska Public Lands Information Center (address above). The Bureau of Land Management, 701 C St. (P.O. Box 13, Anchorage, AK 99513), phone 271-5555, has information on hiking trails and canoe trails in many areas of Alaska. Other information may be obtained from the Anchorage Convention and Visitors Bureau, 1600 A St., Anchorage, AK 99501, phone 276-4118.

Anchorage, a unified home-rule municipality first incorporated in 1920, has all the amenities of big-city life, 2 daily newspapers and several radio and TV stations. Government address: Municipality of Anchorage, Pouch 6-650, Anchorage, AK 99502-0650; phone 264-4431 or 4432.

For more information see *The MILEPOST®,*

a complete guide to communities on Alaska's road and marine highway systems and *Anchorage* and *The Cook Inlet Basin* from The Alaska Geographic Society. To order, see the ALASKA NORTHWEST LIBRARY section at the back of the book.

Glennallen

Located on the eastern edge of the Anchorage and Mat-Su Valley area, near the junction of the Glenn and Richardson highways, Glennallen serves as supply center and jumping-off point for many trips into the eastern reaches of the area. For more on Glennallen, see Communities in the Copper River/ Wrangell-St. Elias subregion this section.

Lake Creek

Located on the Yentna River at Lake Creek, 70 miles northwest of Anchorage, 18 miles east of Skwentna. **Transportation:** Boat; charter air service or private plane. **Population:** 15 year-round. **Zip code:** 99667 (Skwentna). **Emergency Services:** Alaska State Troopers, Anchorage; Anchorage clinics and hospitals; Riversong Lodge is the first responder station with 5 emergency medical technicians on staff.

Climate: Summer temperatures can reach as high as 70° to 80°F, according to one resident, while -50°F for periods of time during the winter is not uncommon.

Private Aircraft: No airstrip. Planes land on the river or on a gravel bar. A winter ski plane landing strip is maintained by a local lodge.

Visitor Facilities: Accommodations and meals are available at several area lodges, 2 open year-round. No stores; most supplies are obtained from Anchorage, although a few grocery items, film and sporting goods may be purchased at the lodges. Raw furs may be purchased from local trappers. Native furs and crafts from the Kuskokwim Delta area are available at Riversong Lodge. Fishing/hunting licenses available at lodges. Boats may be rented. Marine engine repair services and moorage facilities available. Guide services can be arranged, as well as natural history tours. No Fuel available.

At the turn of the century a trading post was established across the Yentna River from Lake Creek to serve the trappers and gold miners in the area, writes one resident. Ruined cabins remain, as does the hulk of a paddle-wheeled steamboat once used for transportation.

Today, 3 families live year-round in the area. Residents guide fishermen and hunters

ANCHORAGE AIRPORTS: GATEWAY TO ALASKA

Travel to the Bush almost always means a trip in a small plane, and Anchorage is home to two of the busiest small plane bases in the nation and half of the licensed pilots in the state.

Merrill Field

Flying in Alaska is not without risk, and many bush pilots have rightfully earned legendary status. Anchorage's Merrill Field was known as Aviation Field until 1932 when it was renamed in honor of pioneer commercial pilot Russell Hyde Merrill completed a number of firsts in Alaska aviation before he disappeared without a trace in September 1929, on a flight from Anchorage to Sleetmute and Bethel. He was the first to fly a single-engine plane across the Gulf of Alaska, the first to fly a commercial flight west of Juneau and the first to attempt a night landing in Anchorage. In 1927 he discovered a key pass in the Alaska Range which opened a new and shorter route to the Kuskokwim. The pass also bears his name.

Merrill Field has ranked among the busiest airports in the nation for several years. Activity peaked in 1984 when the field was ranked 15th in the nation. In 1988, Merrill Field was the 46th busiest airport in the nation with a total of 246,853 take-offs and landings. Those operations represent 24 percent of the total aircraft activity in Alaska that year. Located just 1 mile east of downtown Anchorage on 415 acres, Merrill Field has tiedowns for 1,385 planes. The number of planes leasing space varies but as of January 1989, 950 planes were located at Merrill Field, nearly one-half of the 2,400 small aircraft in Anchorage.

Lake Hood

Most of the rest of the planes in Anchorage are based at Lake Hood, the busiest and largest seaplane base in the nation with an average of 225 planes taking off or landing each day.

Located just north of the Anchorage International Airport, the Lake Hood Seaplane Facility has seen the number of planes using its facilities double in the last 10 years. The growth is due, in large part, to the fact that more and more people want to visit Alaska's backcountry, and lakes and rivers provide the only landing sites in many of these areas.

Pilots most likely first used Lake Hood in the 1920s, and it didn't take them long to realize the true value of the area. Expansion has been ongoing in the area since the 1940s when the first channel connecting Lake Hood and Lake Spenard was built. Through the mid-1970s nearby lakes were deepened, a second channel was cut between Lake Hood and Lake Spenard, 5 fingerlike waterways constructed and a gravel airstrip was built to satisfy the growing demand. Plans are under way to add 300 additional parking spaces for floatplanes and construction of a new gravel runway as well as a paved runway to accommodate wheel planes using the area.

Located on the south shore of Lake Hood is the Alaska Aviation Heritage Museum which opened in June 1988. The museum includes exhibit galleries featuring the history and development of aviation in Alaska, a theater where films are shown continuously throughout the day, a library and archives, and space for restoring aircraft.

Waterfowl use the calmer corners of the lakes and picnickers can watch floatplane traffic from a park on the east shore.

and provide lodging for recreationists. Residents travel 18 miles to Skwentna to pick up mail and some children attend school there, traveling by snow machine in winter.

Mount McKinley and Mount Foraker can be seen from Lake Creek, which is a checkpoint for the 335-kilometer Iditaski cross-country ski race, longest such race in the world as well as the Iditabike and the Iditarod Trail Sled Dog Race.

Locally there is excellent fishing for 5 species of salmon, some up to 65 pounds, as well as for trout, northern pike and grayling. Wildlife that may be seen in the area includes eagles, ducks, moose, bears and beavers.

Lake Creek is a clear stream that flows about 50 miles south from near Mount McKinley through scenic countryside. It provides white-water excitement for river floaters, as well as good fishing. Guided raft trips are available, and in winter cross-country ski trails.

Radio is the main form of communications at unincorporated Lake Creek, which does have private telephones. There is no church or school. Electricity is from individual generators; water is from private wells. Sewage system is either septic tanks or honey buckets. Freight arrives by barge or charter plane.

Skwentna

Located in the Yentna River valley on the Skwentna River at its junction with Eightmile Creek, 62 miles north of Tyonek, 70 miles northwest of Anchorage. **Transportation:** Riverboat; daily commuter service or air

charter service from Anchorage. **Population:** About 20 locally; 200 more in the surrounding area. **Zip code:** 99667. **Emergency Services:** Alaska State Troopers, Talkeetna; Anchorage clinics and hospitals.

Climate: Mean temperature for July, the warmest month, is 58°F; mean temperature for January, the coldest month, is 5°F. Mean annual precipitation is 28 inches, including 119 inches of snow.

Private Aircraft: Airstrip adjacent northwest; elev. 148 feet; length 2,900 feet; gravel; fuel 80, 100 (available from Skwentna Roadhouse in 5-gallon cans only); unattended. Runway condition not monitored, visual inspection recommended prior to using. Runway soft during spring thaw. Ski strip west of west threshold.

Visitor Facilities: Accommodations and meals at several local lodges. Groceries and laundry facilities available. Snow machines, boats, outboard motors, all-terrain vehicles, generators and parts are available locally. Arts and crafts available for purchase include carved wood burl spoons, fur mitts and hats, raw furs. Fishing/hunting licenses, guided and unguided fishing and hunting trips available locally. Snow machines, off-road vehicles and boats may be rented. Snow machine, marine engine, boat and aircraft repair services available. Fuel available: marine gas, diesel, unleaded and regular gasoline. Moorage facilities available.

Skwentna was founded in 1923 when Max and Belle Shellabarger homesteaded and started a guide service, and later a flying

Floatplanes like the one shown here at Summit Lake on the Kenai Peninsula drop off backpackers, kayakers, fishermen and hunters at remote sites throughout Alaska. (Jerrianne Lowther, staff)

service and weather station. After WWII Morrison-Knudson built an airstrip and in 1950 the Army established a radar station at Skwentna and a recreation camp at Shell Lake, 15 air miles from Skwentna. The Shell Lake area remains a popular year-round outdoor recreation site. The airfield was turned over to the Federal Aviation Administration, who maintained it until the early 1970s when it was abandoned. The community grew up around the airstrip, which the state started maintaining in 1981.

Only a few families live in this unincorporated community; many more people receive their mail at the post office, but live up to 30 miles away. There are several fishing lodges in the area, most located on the Talachulitna River, Lake Creek and Fish Creek.

According to one resident, "There is no work and not everybody can live off of trapping as people will think they can when they show up." Most area residents make their living in Anchorage, on the North Slope or through their own fishing lodges.

Skwentna is an official checkpoint on the annual Iditarod Trail Sled Dog Race from Anchorage to Nome each March, as well as a gas stop for the Anchorage-to-Nome Gold Rush Classic snow machine race in February. It also is the turnaround point for the 200-mile Iditaski cross-country ski race, which starts in Knik. The area is a popular spot for weekend snowmobilers and cross-country skiers.

Hunting is good along area rivers for moose and grizzly and black bear. Fly-out hunts for Dall sheep and caribou are available. There also is hunting in the area for grouse and ptarmigan.

The area drained by the Skwentna and Yentna rivers has many lakes and small streams. Five species of salmon are found here in season, as well as rainbow trout, Dolly Varden, grayling, whitefish and pike.

Communications in Skwentna include bush phone service, twice-weekly mail plane, radio and satellite TV. The community has a school with grades 1 through 12 depending on demand, but no church. Electricity is from private generators; water from the river or wells. Sewage systems vary from flush toilets to outhouses. Freight arrives via periodic barge service or plane.

Talkeetna

Located 14 miles out on a paved spur road that turns off the George Parks Highway 98 miles north of Anchorage; accessible also by boat, plane or the Alaska Railroad.

While not technically in the Bush, Talkeetna is the jumping-off point for river and air travel into roadless areas of Southcentral and is the staging area for climbing assaults on Mount McKinley and other peaks of the central Alaska Range. Numerous air taxis take visitors to Kahiltna Glacier Base Camp. Several river-running services also operate out of Talkeetna for Chulitna, Tokositna and other rivers flowing from southern slopes of the Alaska Range. The community offers complete visitor facilities.

Talkeetna, established as a mining and trapping community about 1901, still has many reminders of its heritage. Visitors strolling through downtown can enjoy the sight of historic clapboard buildings and rustic log cabins in everyday use. In summer there is often the exotic sight of deeply tanned, fit-looking men and women wearing knickers, many of them speaking a foreign language — climbing parties heading to and from Mount McKinley.

As in the early years, Talkeetna's prime location near the junction of the Talkeetna, Chulitna and Susitna rivers acts as a magnet for adventurers. In winter when the rivers freeze over, Talkeetnans can use snow machines and dogsleds to get together with their "neighbors" in Trapper Creek, which in summer is 40 road miles away.

This is a community which takes its fun seriously. In addition to the Miner's Day Celebration, a family-oriented festival held in May, there is the Moose Dropping Festival held the second Saturday in July. The festival is a fund-raiser for the Talkeetna Museum, an old schoolhouse built in 1936. The museum houses local art, mountain climbing displays, and includes background on the late Ray Genet, world-renowned McKinley climber and the late Don Sheldon, famous Alaskan bush pilot.

For more information see *The MILEPOST®*, a complete guide to communities on Alaska's road and marine highways systems. To order, see the ALASKA NORTHWEST LIBRARY section at the back of the book.

SKIING

Be careful when skiing in extreme cold weather: batteries die, stoves refuse to light and equipment grows brittle and breaks.

▼ A T T R A C T I O N S ▼

National and State Parks, Forests, Etc.

Chugach State Park

Although located on the doorstep of Anchorage, Alaska's largest city, this mountainous park offers excellent wilderness experiences, summer or winter. Chugach State Park is one of the nation's largest state parks, with nearly 495,000 acres.

Several thousand years ago massive glaciers covered this area. This park's beautiful mountain lakes, sharp ridges and broad U-shaped valleys all were glacially carved. Ice fields and glaciers still remain in the park, and a few such as Eklutna Glacier can be viewed on a day's hike.

Although the spectacular alpine scenery is the park's predominant feature, it offers other natural phenomena such as the bore tide in Turnagain Arm. Twice each day, a wall of water up to 6 feet high races up the channel as the tide comes in.

Wildlife: Chugach State Park's abundant wildlife ranges from the popular bald eagles and whales to the less popular mosquitoes (27 varieties inhabit the park). Viewing areas at Eklutna Lake and Eagle River valley afford excellent opportunities to see Dall sheep and moose. The adventurous can see more elusive species, such as mountain goats, wolves and sharp-shinned hawks, that live in remote areas of the park. Brown/grizzly and black bears roam throughout the park. Do not leave open food around campsites and make noise while hiking through the bush to avoid an encounter with one of these large beasts.

The elevation change in the park, from sea level to 8,000 feet, supports a variety of vegetation, from dense forests to alpine tundra. Warm summer months provide a wealth of wildflowers (ranging from common fireweed to orchids), mosses, mushrooms, trees, berries and lichens.

Activities: Chugach Park provides a variety of recreational possibilities for young and old. Day and backcountry hiking, camping, boating, hunting and fishing are popular. Favorite hikes include the Old Johnson Trail, a historic settler's route above Turnagain Arm; the alpine tundra trails of Arctic Valley; the Eklutna Lake region; and the Hillside trail system.

Considerably more challenging and a real wilderness experience is the Crow Pass Trail, which stretches from Girdwood to Eagle River. During the 1989 running of the Crow Pass Crossing (a foot race for the truly adventurous), the lead woman runner was harassed by a black bear.

Crow Pass Trail. This trail is about 27 miles long — 4 miles are within Chugach National Forest, the rest of the trail is in Chugach State Park. This trail is steep in places; 2,000 feet in altitude is gained between trailhead and the public-use cabin at Mile 3. Trail offers outstanding alpine scenery and access to several glaciers and peaks. It is part of an old mail route that connected Portage and Knik; there are mining ruins at Mile 1.7. The Crow Pass trailhead is 5 miles up Crow Creek Road, the road that turns north at the bend in the Alyeska Access Road, which connects with the Seward Highway at Girdwood, 38 miles south of Anchorage. Trail closed to motorized vehicles; horses prohibited during April, May and June due to soft trail conditions. Winter travel not recommended due to extreme avalanche danger. Trail usually free of snow by mid-June. Cabin located in alpine area with little firewood; camp stove recommended. Water available from glacial stream. Related USGS Topographic map: Anchorage A-6.

There is wilderness camping throughout the park as well as developed campgrounds at Eklutna Lake, $5 per night; Eagle River, $10 per night; and Bird Creek, $5 per night. Use of all state campgrounds is on a first-come basis. Fires are permitted only in developed fireplaces or camp stoves.

There are canoe trailheads at Miles 7.5 and 9 of the Eagle River Road. The river offers a challenging Class II white-water trip for canoeists, rafters and kayakers; be sure to read the information posted at the trailhead before heading downriver. Mirror Lake has a public access boat ramp that can handle small boats; nonmotorized watercraft only are permitted. Eklutna Lake is open to all watercraft; no boat ramp.

Chugach State Park is not noted for fishing, but its waters do contain Dolly Varden and pink, king, chum and silver salmon. Good fishing spots are Mirror Lake and Bird Creek. A few Dolly Varden may be found in tributary streams.

This park is used widely during the winter. Many trails lead to the most remote reaches of the park; large sections lie above tree line and provide easy traveling. All of the park is open to nonmotorized winter travel, such as skis, dogsleds and snowshoes. Also, 4 large areas within the park are open to snowmobiles when there is adequate snow cover.

Winter visitors should come prepared with a good map, extra food and clothing, a first-aid kit and snow machine or ski repair supplies. For long outings, a tent, sleeping bag and small stove are strongly recommended. Never travel alone. Dress warmly, preferably in wool clothing, and in layers.

Popular winter recreation areas include the following:

Eklutna Valley, reached from the Glenn Highway via the Eklutna Road, which begins opposite Eklutna Village at Milepost 26.5 from Anchorage. Eklutna Road leads to a parking area on Eklutna Lake. Skiers and snow machines can travel along the north edge of the lake or use the frozen lake surface. The Eklutna River valley downstream from the lake is closed to snow machines. Travel toward Eklutna Glacier from the glacier trailhead is very hazardous due to avalanche danger.

The **Thunderbird Creek** area is popular for its spectacular canyon. A good day tour is up the Eklutna River from the Glenn Highway bridge, beyond the confluence of Thunderbird Creek to an old dam site. This area is open to nonmotorized activities only. Beware of thin ice and open water. Land southwest of the Eklutna River to the confluence of Thunderbird Creek, and along Thunderbird Creek for 0.8 mile is private property.

Ship Creek and the **Arctic Valley Ski Area**

are reached by turning east toward the mountains on Arctic Valley Road at Milepost 6.9 northbound on the Glenn Highway. The 8-mile trip to Arctic Valley passes through the Fort Richardson Military Reservation; military authorities may require studded snow tires or chains. The ski area has chair, poma, T-bar and rope tow lifts, as well as a lodge with food service and restrooms, but no overnight accommodations. Several cross-country routes begin at the parking lot.

Peters Creek and **Little Peters Creek** (Ptarmigan Valley), reached via the Glenn Highway, are not maintained but offer excellent snowmobiling and skiing. Parts of the Peters Creek area are privately owned.

Eagle River valley is reached via Eagle River Road, which leaves the Old Glenn Highway at Eagle River Elementary School and continues 12 miles up the valley to the Eagle River Visitor Center. Cross-country and snow machine trails leave from the parking lot. Travel on the Iditarod Trail is restricted to nonmotorized use.

Hillside Trail System and **Campbell Creek** include most of the developed and maintained cross-country ski trails. A corridor leads through the Hillside area's nonmotorized zone from the Upper Huffman park entrance to the snow machine area along the upper south fork of Campbell Creek. Parking areas are maintained at the Prospect Heights, Upper Huffman and Glen Alps park entrances.

Bird Creek valley offers good snowmobiling as well as cross-country skiing on miles of old logging roads. The area is reached via the Seward Highway at Milepost 26.5 from Anchorage; turn toward the mountains on a gravel road adjacent to the Bird House Bar and continue about 1 mile to a parking area.

For maps and other information about summer or winter activities contact: Chugach State Park, Pouch 107001, Anchorage, AK 99510; phone 561-2020. Related USGS Topographic maps: Anchorage A-5, 6, 7 and 8; B-5, 6 and 7; and Seward D-6, 7 and 8.

Hatcher Pass/Independence Mine State Historical Park

Located 60 miles from Anchorage and 22 miles from Palmer, the Hatcher Pass area overlooks the Matanuska and Susitna valleys. Bounded by the Talkeetna Mountains to the north, Wasilla and Palmer to the west and south, and the Matanuska Valley Moose Range to the east, the area has been a popular recreational destination for many years.

While use of the area has grown dramatically in recent years, it is still relatively undeveloped. In an effort to manage the increasing use, minimize conflicts and establish guidelines for future use, the state developed the Hatcher Pass Management Plan. The plan was approved in October 1986 and covers 215,820 acres, including designated Hatcher Pass Public-Use Area in the Little Susitna Valley. A Japanese firm, Mitsui, has plans to build a large, year-round resort here on land leased from the state.

The 760-acre Independence Mine State Historical Park was established in 1980, 6 years after Independence Mine was added to the National Register of Historic Places. The park includes 2 former lode gold mining sites which were active from 1909 to 1924 and again from about 1937 to 1941. Activity peaked in 1941 when 48,194 ounces of gold worth $1,686,790 were produced. But WWII put a stop to gold mining and efforts to restart mining after the war were short-lived. By 1951 the mines were closed and by 1958 the owners had sold the equipment and machinery. Only the buildings remained. The mess hall/bunk house was used for a time for biathlon training in the 1960s, and as Independence Lodge in more recent years, but the complex was virtually abandoned.

Since establishing the park, the state has restored the manager's house, which now serves as a visitor center and features interpretive exhibits and displays. Other buildings in the complex, including bunk houses, timber shed, warehouse, mess halls and collapsed mill, have been preserved, though not totally restored. The assay office has been restored and contains a hard rock mining museum.

Today, the historical park preserves evidence of the once-booming mining operations while much of the surrounding area has been set aside to protect its value as a public recreation area and important wildlife habitat.

Wildlife: Moose populations in the forested western and southern portions of the Hatcher Pass area are said to be among the largest in Southcentral. Other wildlife includes caribou, sheep, black and brown bear, wolf, wolverine, coyote, beaver, fox, marten, mink, weasel, lynx, hare, marmots and other small animals.

Nesting tundra birds occur within the area as well as bald and golden eagles, sharp-shinned hawks, red-tailed hawks, merlins, kestrels, gyrfalcons, peregrine falcons, boreal owls and great horned owls. Three resident ptarmigan species are found in the area as well as spruce grouse and a variety of songbirds.

Fish found in area streams include king, coho, red, chum and pink salmon, rainbow trout, Dolly Varden, grayling, whitefish, burbot, stickleback and long-nose suckers.

Climate: Elevations in the area range from less than 1,200 feet to more than 6,000 feet. Generally it is warmer and drier at lower elevations. The average maximum accumulation of snow at Independence Mine (3,300 feet) is 55 inches while along the Little Susitna River, at 1,700 feet, it is 42 inches. The average temperature in January ranges from 11.5° to 24.7°F. Temperatures rise above 40°F only during the summer months. Temperature inversions are common on calm clear nights, and as the cold air drains down valley floors it can create winds up to 15 mph.

Access: The 49-mile Hatcher Pass Road, a narrow, steep, rough and winding road, provides access to the area. The mostly gravel road leads north, then west over 3,886-foot Hatcher Pass from Milepost 49.5 on the Glenn Highway to Milepost 71.2 on the George Parks Highway. The road is open year-round from the Glenn Highway to the park visitor center at Mile 18, but is closed between the pass and the Parks Highway from the first snow in September until late June.

Hikers, skiers and snow machine users also take advantage of a number of former mining roads and trails to reach the more remote recreation areas.

Accommodations: A lodge located on private property just 200 feet below Independence Mine State Historical Park offers meals and lodging year-round and maintains several miles of groomed cross-country ski trails in the winter. There are no developed campgrounds in the area. Public restrooms are located at the park visitors center.

Activities: The area surrounding Independence Mine State Historical Park is a favorite for winter recreation. While other places in Southcentral may suffer from lack of snow, winter recreation enthusiasts ususally can count on good snow conditions at Hatcher Pass. Several telemarking classes are held here as well as avalanche training. Other winter activities include dog mushing, sledding, riding snow machines and some ptarmigan and bear hunting.

During the summer and fall, visitors can enjoy photography, hiking, camping, mountaineering, fishing, horseback riding, picnicking, wildflower and wildlife viewing, moose hunting, berry-picking and a number of other activities.

While the area is road accessible, it is still relatively remote and visitors should take standard precautions for backcountry travel. Winter visitors should dress in warm layers and bring additional dry clothing. Sunglasses are essential on sunny days to block ultraviolet rays and protect against snowblindness. Visitors planning travel away from the more accessible areas should be self-sufficient and knowlegdeable in winter survival techniques. Summer visitors should be prepared for cool weather, also dressing in layers with a layer to protect against wind and rain. Insect repellent will be useful at lower elevations and in river valleys. Also be aware that pockets of private land and active mining claims are located within the area and should be respected.

For more information contact: Alaska Division of Parks and Outdoor Recreation, Southcentral Region, P.O. Box 107001, Anchorage, AK 99510; phone 561-2020 or, the Mat-Su Area Office, HC32, Box 6706, Wasilla, AK 99687; phone 745-3975. Related USGS Topographic maps: Anchorage C-6, C-7, D-6, D-7 and D-8.

Nancy Lake
State Recreation Area

Located just 67 miles north of Anchorage via the Glenn and Parks highways between the Susitna River and the Talkeetna Mountains, this 22,685-acre state recreation area provides easily accessible wilderness experiences all year.

Set aside in 1966, the area is dominated by lakes, streams, and swamps which drain into the Susitna River or Cook Inlet. Mature spruce, birch and poplar forests surround the lake. Blueberry, raspberry and crowberry plants are plentiful and provide good berry-picking in late summer and early fall.

Once covered by huge glaciers, the area has been free of ice for at least 9,000 years and state archaeologists believe that the area was heavily used by early Natives. Nancy Lake's Indian Bay is the site of an Indian village that was established near the turn of the century and a few descendants of the village residents still live in the area. In 1917 the Alaska Railroad was built on the east side of the lower Susitna Valley bringing with it homesteaders and fueling the growth of the towns of Wasilla, Houston and Willow. The Nancy Lake area was avoided by settlers because it was too wet.

Climate: Summer temperatures range from lows between 40°F and 50°F and highs in the 70s and 80s reflecting the warmer and sunnier weather patterns of interior Alaska. Winter temperatures can fall to -40°F or colder and rarely rise above freezing before mid-

March. The lakes freeze in late October, about the same time as the first snow falls, and are free of ice by early June. Average snow accumulation is about 48 inches.

Wildlife: Beavers are found on numerous lakes thoughout and are important in maintaining water levels in the area. Moose and black bears are common. Lynx, coyote, wolves and brown bears may be seen in more remote areas.

Loons, grebes, ducks, geese and shorebirds use the lakes and ponds in the area during their migrations and many stay to nest in the area. Sandhill cranes can be seen exhibiting their courtship dance on the Nancy Lake Parkway during their spring migration. Arctic terns, hawks, owls, kingfishers, woodpeckers and numerous songbirds are also seen in the area.

Lake trout, rainbow trout, whitefish and Dolly Varden are found in Red Shirt, Butterfly, Lynx and Nancy lakes. Big and Little Noluck lakes were restocked with trout and silver salmon in 1975 by the Alaska Dept. of Fish and Game. Northern pike are found in Red Shirt, Lynx and Tanaina lakes.

Activities: The area's summertime attraction is its canoe trail system. Visitors can spend an afternoon or a long weekend canoeing through the various chains of lakes and streams that dot the area. Canoes can be rented at a local marina and at South Rolly campground. Other summer activities include hiking, camping and fishing. South Rolly campground at the end of the Nancy Lake Parkway has 100 units.

The summer canoe and hiking trails are transformed in winter for cross-country skiing, dog mushing, snowshoeing and snowmobiling. Most of the 40 miles of trails are open for motorized snow vehicles. Ten miles of trails are set aside for cross-country skiers only. Ice fishing is also a popular winter activity. Nancy Lake, Lynx Lake and Red Shirt offer the best opportunities for catching winter rainbow trout. Burbot and pike are found in Red Shirt.

For additional information and detailed maps of the canoe and hiking trails and information on established campgrounds contact the Division of Parks and Outdoor Recreation, Southcentral Region, P.O. Box 107001, Anchorage, AK 99510; phone 561-2020. Or, the Mat-Su Area Office, HC32, Box 6706, Wasilla, AK 99687; phone 745-3975.

Nancy Lake State
Recreation Area Cabins

The number of cabins available for public

use at the Nancy Lake State Recreation Area has been expanded by the Division of Parks and Outdoor Recreation. By the end of 1988, 12 cabins were available for rental.

Cabins may be rented for up to 3 nights. Rates are $20 to $25 per night depending on the size of the cabin. Most cabins accommodate 6, while a few larger cabins can sleep 10. Cabins may be reserved up to 180 days in advance and fees must be paid when the reservation is submitted. If more than one request is received for the same days, a lottery is held.

Cabins are furnished with plywood sleeping platforms, wood stove, window screens, kitchen counter, table and chairs or benches and an outdoor firepit and grill. A pit latrine is nearby. Bring sleeping pad and bag, food, cooking stove, fuel and other personal items. Firewood can be hard to find in winter so bring firewood or presto logs for the first night.

Four cabins are located on Nancy Lake. Three are accessible by trail from the Nancy Lake Parkway. The fourth is surrounded by private property and is accessible only by boat via Nancy Lake or by foot or snowmobile when the lake is frozen.

Four cabins are located on Red Shirt Lake, 3 on Lynx Lake and 1 on James Lake. To reach the cabins on Red Shirt Lake it is necessary to hike 3 miles and canoe a short distance in the summer. Canoe rentals are available. The cabins on Lynx and James lakes are on the canoe trail system. All cabins are accessible in winter by snowmachine or dog team. It is also possible to ski to most of the cabins but most access requires a full-day ski.

To reserve a cabin or obtain more information contact the Division of Parks and Outdoor Recreation, P.O. Box 107001, Anchorage, AK 99510; phone 561-2020.

The Rivers

Chutlitna and Tokositna rivers. (See Rivers in INTERIOR section.)

Gulkana River. (See Rivers in INTERIOR section.)

Kahiltna River. This river heads at Kahiltna Glacier, 35 miles northeast of Talkeetna between Mount Foraker and Mount Hunter in the Alaska Range, and flows southeast to the Yentna River, 53 miles northwest of Anchorage.

This Class II braided river flows through an immense valley. The gradient in the first 28 miles is 8 feet per mile. Just above the Peters Creek confluence the pace quickens appreciably, the gradient increases to 15 feet per mile for the last 46 miles and huge boulders create numerous rapids. Silty and ice cold, this is considered a challenging river. Decked canoes, kayaks or rafts are suitable.

The Kahiltna is accessible by air charter from Talkeetna or Anchorage, landing just a few miles from where it emerges from the glacier. Exit is by small plane from the Yentna River, or voyagers may continue down the Yentna to the Susitna River and Cook Inlet. Related USGS Topographic maps: Talkeetna B-3, B-2, A2; Tyonek D-2, D-3.

Klutina River. This river heads at Stevenson Glacier in the Chugach Mountains and flows 63 miles northeast to the Copper River at Copper Center on the Richardson Highway, 66 miles northeast of Valdez.

This Class III river offers excellent whitewater paddling at low water volume. It is more dangerous at high water, which is usually in mid-July to August. The usual put-in point is at 16-mile-long Klutina Lake. The first 10 miles of the river from the lake have a gradient of 17 feet per mile. The pace quickens for the last 16 miles, where the gradient increases to 23 feet per mile. Kayaks or rafts are suitable for this river; canoes and riverboats only for the very experienced. The trip takes 1 day.

The river offers excellent mountain scenery and fishing for king and red salmon in June and July. Dolly Varden and grayling are available in Klutina Lake.

Access to the Klutina River is possible by 4-wheel-drive vehicle over a bad road through private land from Copper Center bridge to the outlet of Klutina Lake. Access also is by floatplane to the lake. Exit at Copper Center, or continue on the Copper River to Chitina or the Gulf of Alaska.

Related USGS Topographic maps: Valdez C-5, C-6, D-4 and D-5.

Lake Creek. This clear-water stream heads in Chelatna Lake and flows southeast 56 river miles to the Yentna River, 58 miles northwest of Anchorage.

Lake Creek is rated Class I to IV for the first 48 miles. About half-way downriver is a severe Class IV canyon with huge boulders which should be scouted or portaged. It is possible to line the boat along the right bank. Portage is only 150 to 200 yards. It is possible to depart the river near this point via 2 portage trails. One well-marked trail leads to Shovel Lake where there is floatplane access. The other trail, marked with black ink on gray rock, leads to Martana Lake. From the canyon the river is a rocky and challenging Class III. The last 8 miles are rated Class I. Kayaks or rafts are suitable for this river. The trip takes 3 to 4 days, depending on conditions.

This river offers spectacular views of the Alaska Range and Mount McKinley to the northeast, and excellent Dolly Varden, grayling and rainbow trout fishing.

Access is by floatplane from Anchorage or Talkeetna to Chelatna Lake. Exit via floatplane or riverboat from the Yentna River.

Related USGS Topographic maps: Talkeetna A-2, A-3, B-3; Tyonek D-3.

Little Susitna River. The "Little Su" heads at Mint Glacier in the Talkeetna Mountains and flows southwest 110 miles to Cook Inlet, 13 miles west of Anchorage.

This is a fairly small river, ranging in width from 20 to 40 feet. Except for the upstream stretch, where the gradient is 20 feet per mile, it's also a slow river (2 to 4 mph) and meanders considerably as it makes its way through spruce, birch and willow forest. Be alert for sweepers, shallows, logjams and air and jet boats.

There are 2 common put-in points: At the Schrock Road bridge about 7 miles north of the Parks Highway and at the Parks Highway bridge at Milepost 57 from Anchorage. From the first put-in, the river is rated Class III for 26 miles, after which it is flat water for about 106 river miles. Canoes, kayaks or rafts are suitable. The trip takes 1 to 3 days.

Fishing in the Little Susitna is excellent for king salmon from late May through June and for silver salmon in July and August. There also are red salmon to 10 pounds in mid-July. Other fish available include Dolly Varden and rainbow trout.

Exit from this river may be by prearranged charter flight or take out at Burma Road, which starts 0.2 mile west of the Lake Marion turnoff on Big Lake Road.

Related USGS Topographic maps: Anchorage C-7 and C-8; Tyonek B-1 and C-1.

Maclaren River. (See Rivers in INTERIOR section.)

Skwentna River. This river heads at South Twin Glacier below Mount Spurr and flows north and east 100 miles to the Yentna River near the settlement of Skwentna, 70 miles northwest of Anchorage.

The Skwentna is considered one of the most difficult and remote, but spectacular, wilderness rivers in Alaska. *CAUTION: This river is recommended only for expert paddlers who are experienced in wilderness travel.*

The Skwentna is extremely fast. It has many difficult rapids and steep-walled canyons. From its headwaters the gradient is 40 feet per mile. The first 24 miles are rated

Class IV. The next 40 miles, also with a gradient of 40 feet per mile, is rated Class II and IV. Then the gradient changes to 17 feet per mile for 50 miles, rated Class II and III. The final 55-mile stretch is rated Class II; the gradient is 10 feet per mile. Decked 2-man canoes or kayaks are recommended for this river.

Moose, bear and an occasional wolf may be encountered along this river.

The Skwentna is not easy to get to. It is possible to reach the headwaters via a portage from Chakachamna Lake, but this route is difficult and takes at least a week. The primary means of access is by helicopter to the headwaters. Exit is at Skwentna, which has accommodations and scheduled air service. Related USGS Topographic maps: Tyonek B-8, C-8, D-8, D-7, D-6, D-5, D-4.

Susitna River. This large river heads at Susitna Glacier in the Alaska Range and flows southwest 260 miles to Cook Inlet, 24 miles west of Anchorage. The river's Tanaina Indian name, said to mean "sandy river," first appeared in 1847 on a Russian chart.

The Susitna offers 2 very different trips on its upper and lower sections.

A few miles from its origin the river emerges from the eastern Alaska Range. The mountains provide a magnificent backdrop to the swift, silty water. Wildlife that may be observed includes moose, bear, caribou, wolf and beaver. The best access is at the Susitna River bridge on the Denali Highway at Milepost 79.5 from Paxson. From this point the river has a gradient of 7 feet per mile and is rated Class III for 55 miles. Braided gravel flats alternate with a single river channel; some difficult rapids are in this section. Sparse forest growth clings to the shores along the river. Approximately 30 miles downriver from the bridge, the beautiful Maclaren River joins from the east. Then after 10 miles of braided gravel flats, the Tyone River comes in from the east.

The Tyone River connects Lake Louise and the Susitna. The slow, meandering Tyone can be used as a connecting waterway to leave the Susitna Valley for the extensive Lake Louise plains. A small outboard motor on a canoe speeds an otherwise slow upriver paddle; it takes about a day to get to Tyone Lake with a motor.

Below the Tyone River confluence, the Susitna has several huge oxbow bends and approximately 20 miles of swift water and rapids rated Class II. Gradient increases to 20 feet per mile.

After this stretch, the river slows for the next 70 miles, rated Class I to II. Gradient is 10 feet per mile. This tame section ends at treacherous Devil Canyon, which should not be attempted. Look for Log Creek on the left, shortly after a sharp right bend. Pick-up may be made by floatplane at this point or it is possible to portage 5 miles to Stephan Lake, for a prearranged pickup by floatplane.

The Upper Susitna trip should be attempted only by experienced wilderness travelers. Decked canoes, kayaks, rafts or riverboats are suitable for this river.

The Lower Susitna is a Class I river that poses no technical difficulties, although its many channels do test water-judging abilities. There are no rapids, but there are boils and upwellings. Some branches and sloughs may be blocked by logjams and may be hazardous. Access points are the Alaska Railroad station at Gold Creek; Talkeetna; and the Susitna River bridge on the Parks Highway at Milepost 104.3 from Anchorage. Exit at Talkeetna, the Parks Highway bridge or via floatplane pickup at the river mouth. Distance from Gold Creek to Cook Inlet is about 120 river miles. Trip takes 1 to 3 days, depending on put-in point. Canoes, kayaks, rafts or riverboats are suitable. Related USGS Topographic maps: Healy A-1, A-2; Talkeetna Mountains D-1, D-2, D-3, D-4, D-5, D-6, C-1, C-2, C-6; Talkeetna C-1, B-1, A-1; Tyonek D-1, C-1, C-2, B-2.

Talachulitna River. This river heads on Beluga Mountain and flows south and northwest to the Skwentna River, 14 miles upriver from the settlement of Skwentna, which is 70 miles northwest of Anchorage.

The upper reaches of Talachulitna Creek, which drains Judd Lake, may be shallow and have logjams. The upper river is slow and rated Class I to II. The river flows faster through a section of canyons in the lower 20 miles, rated Class II to III. Just below the Hiline Lake put-in near the midpoint of the river there is a short drop rated Class II to III. Kayaks or rafts are suitable for this river. The trip takes 3 to 5 days depending on put-in point.

The Talachulitna offers excellent views of Beluga Mountain and the Alaska Range. Moose and black bear may be seen. Fishing is good for 5 species of salmon, Dolly Varden, grayling and rainbow trout (catch and release only).

Access is by floatplane to Judd Lake or to the Talachulitna River at midpoint just south of Hiline Lake. Exit is by floatplane from the confluence with the Skwentna River, or continue down the Skwentna River and exit via scheduled air service at Skwentna or floatplane pickup from the Yentna River at its confluence with the Skwentna.

Related USGS Topographic maps: Tyonek C-4, C-5 and D-4.

Tazlina, Nelchina and Little Nelchina rivers. These rivers offer a variety of water conditions and trip alternatives. The Tazlina River drains Tazlina Lake and flows east 30 miles to the Copper River, 7 miles southeast of Glennallen and about 140 miles east of Anchorage. The Nelchina River heads at Nelchina Glacier and flows north and southeast 28 miles into Tazlina Lake. The Little Nelchina is a 48-mile-long tributary to the Nelchina.

Access is from the Glenn Highway via the Little Nelchina River at Milepost 137.5 from Anchorage. Access is also by floatplane to Tazlina Lake.

From the Glenn Highway put-in, the Little Nelchina is a fast, narrow and rocky clearwater stream. It is shallow during low-water times. It flows 4 river miles rated Class IV and drops 50 feet per mile, before joining the Nelchina River. The glacial Nelchina flows 22 river miles rated Class I to II to Tazlina Lake. This section drops 20 feet per mile.

It's an 8-mile paddle on Tazlina Lake to the Tazlina River. Be alert for a whirlpool at the lake outlet. The Tazlina flows about 50 river miles to the Copper River. This stretch, with a gradient of 15 feet per mile, is rated Class II to III. Exit at the Tazlina River Bridge on the Richardson Highway at Milepost 110.7 from Valdez or continue down the Copper River.

Water volume on these rivers should be judged carefully. The rivers are generally least difficult before spring runoff in May and June, late in a dry summer or after cold weather slows glacial runoff. The Little Nelchina may have logjams. Kayaks or rafts are suitable, or canoes for the experienced. This trip takes 2 to 3 days to the Richardson Highway, depending on put-in point.

Related USGS Topographic maps: Gulkana A-3, A-4, A-5 and A-6; Valdez D-7 and D-8.

Tyone River. This river heads at Tyone Lake and flows northwest 30 miles to the Susitna River, 68 miles northwest of Gulkana. This trip combines lake paddling with an easy river journey. About half the distance is across 3 adjoining lakes: Louise, Susitna and Tyone. The flat-water river flows slowly and meanders. This route is suitable for riverboats and canoes with small motors, as well as for kayaks and paddled canoes. The river can be run upstream from the Susitna by strong paddlers. This is considered a good trip for less experienced paddlers who are experienced in the wilderness.

Access is by floatplane to Lake Louise or via the 19.3-mile-long Lake Louise Road, which leaves the Glenn Highway at Milepost 159.8 from Anchorage. Exit is by floatplane from the Susitna River.

Lake Louise and Susitna Lake have excellent fishing for grayling, lake trout and lingcod. Related USGS Topographic maps: Gulkana C-6; Talkeetna Mountains C-1.

Yentna River. This river is formed by its east and west forks and flows southeast 75 miles to the Susitna River, 30 miles northwest of Anchorage.

This flat-water glacial river winds in graceful sweeps through the basin south of Mount McKinley. It has a large volume; white-water problems are minimal, but boaters should be alert for sweepers, logjams and floating trees. Canoes, kayaks, rafts and riverboats are all suitable.

Moose and bear may be seen; there is good fishing on clear-water tributary streams and creeks. There are several homesteads on the Yentna and riverboats may be encountered.

Access is by small plane to the headwaters. Exit is by prearranged floatplane pickup from the Susitna, or continue floating down the Susitna. Related Topographic maps: Talkeetna B-4, A-4, A-3; Tyonek D-4, D-3, D-2, C-2, B-2.

Sportfishing

The long list below covers only the highlights of the sportfishing opportunities in the Anchorage and Mat-Su Valley area. A wealth of rivers, streams and lakes offers anglers an impressive variety of choices in catch, season and wilderness experience.

Alexander Creek. Heads in Alexander Lake and flows southeast 35 miles to the Susitna River, 27 miles northwest of Anchorage. One of the best fishing streams in southcentral Alaska. Numerous lodges in the area. Primary access by floatplane from Anchorage. Fish available: king salmon — excellent from late May through June, use egg clusters, spinners or spoons; silver salmon — mid-July to September, use spinners or cluster eggs; pink salmon — in even-numbered years, mid-July through mid-August, use small spoons; rainbow trout — excellent late May through Sept. 1, use flies and spinning-type lures; grayling — late May and early June, use flies and small spinners.

Bull Lake. Fly-in lake located 20 minutes by small plane from Chulitna River Lodge, George Parks Highway, Milepost 156.2 from

Alaska's backcountry lodges are favored by those outdoor enthusiasts who look for a bit more luxury. Riversong Lodge at Lake Creek is one of many lodges in a popular Southcentral Alaska sportfishing area. (Alissa Crandall)

Anchorage. Fish available: lake trout — to 5 pounds July and August, use spoons or spinners; grayling — use flies.

Chulitna Lake. Fly-in lake located 20 minutes by small plane from Chulitna River Lodge, Parks Highway, Milepost 156.2 from Anchorage. Fish available: rainbow trout — to 4 pounds, July, August and September, use flies, lures and bait.

Crosswind Lake. An 8-mile-long fly-in lake located northwest of Lake Louise, 23 miles northwest of Glennallen. Accessible by floatplane from Glennallen. Deep, clear lake offers excellent fishing. Open water from early June through October. Best fishing early June to early July. Fish available: lake trout — use spoons or plugs; whitefish — use flies or eggs; grayling — use flies.

Deshka River. Located about 60 miles northwest of Anchorage. One of the best fishing streams in southcentral Alaska. Primary access by floatplane from Anchorage and riverboat from Susitna Landing. Numerous lodges in the area. Fish available: king salmon — excellent fishing, 20 to 25 pounds and up, late May to early July, use egg clusters, spinners or spoons; silver salmon — 4 to 6 pounds, mid-July through September, use spinners or cluster eggs; pink salmon — in even-numbered years, mid-July to mid-August, use small spoons; rainbow trout — excellent late May through September, use flies and spinning-type lures; grayling — 10 to 16 inches, best late May and early June, use flies and small spinners; northern pike — June through September, use bait.

Donut Lake. Fly-in lake located 20 minutes by small plane from Chulitna River Lodge, Parks Highway, Milepost 156.2 from Anchorage. Dolly Varden — to 2 pounds, available July and August, use spinners, spoons and flies.

Gulkana River. (See Sportfishing in INTERIOR section.)

High Lake. A 1-mile-wide lake at the 3,006-foot elevation in the Chugach Mountains southwest of Glennallen, 5.2 miles southeast of Tazlina Lake. Accessible by floatplane from Glennallen. Lake trout — to 22 inches, June and early July with small spoons; some rainbow fly-fishing. Cabins, boats and motors available.

Jan Lakes. Fly-in lakes located 5 miles from Lake Louise or 12 miles from Tolsona Lake at Milepost 160 on the Glenn Highway. Accessible by floatplane from Lake Louise, Lee's Lake or Tolsona Lake. North Jan Lake has good rainbow trout fishery. South Jan Lake has landlocked silver salmon and king salmon.

Judd Lake. Lake 0.9 mile across located on the Talachulitna River, about 65 miles northwest of Anchorage. Primary access by floatplane from Anchorage. Lodge on lake. Fish available: silver salmon — average 6 to 8 pounds, best in August; red salmon — average 7 to 8 pounds, best mid-July to early August; chum salmon — average 10 to 12 pounds, best mid-July to early August; pink salmon — in even-numbered years, average 3 to 4 pounds, best mid- to late July; grayling and Dolly Varden — mid-June through September, best early and late.

Klutina Lake. A 16-mile-long lake, 27 miles from the Copper Center bridge via extremely bad road. Excellent grayling and Dolly Varden fishing.

Klutina River. Located at Milepost 100.7 from Valdez on the Richardson Highway. Foot and vehicle access; river guides available for float fishing. King salmon — available in June and July, with peak in August, use bright lures and/or salmon eggs; red salmon — use streamer flies; Dolly Varden also available.

Lake Creek. Flows from the foothills of Mount McKinley, about 70 miles northwest of Anchorage. One of the best fishing streams in southcentral Alaska. Primary access by floatplane from Anchorage. Numerous lodges in the area. Fish available: king salmon — excellent fishing late May through early July, use egg clusters, spinners and spoons; silver and chum salmon — mid-July through August, use spinners or cluster eggs; pink salmon — in even-numbered years, mid-July through mid-August, use small spoons; rainbow trout and grayling — excellent just after breakup and just before freezeup, use flies and spinning-type lures for rainbows, flies for grayling.

Lake Louise. An 8.5-mile-long lake located in the Copper River Basin, 32 miles northwest of Glennallen. Accessible by floatplane or skiplane from Anchorage, Glennallen and other communities. Access also via the 19.3-mile Lake Louise Road from the Glenn Highway at Milepost 159.8 from Anchorage. Lodges on lake. Excellent grayling and lake trout fishing. Lake trout — average 10 pounds, up to 20 to 30 pounds, good year-round, best spring through July, late September, early season use herring or whitefish bait, cast from boat, later (warmer water) troll with #16 red-and-white spoon, silver Alaskan plug or large silver flatfish; grayling — 10 to 12 inches, cast flies or small spinners, June, July and August; burbot (freshwater lingcod) — average 5 pounds, still fish from boat using hook with herring, dangle on bottom, in winter set lines with herring-baited hook through ice holes or jig for lake trout. Lake can be rough; small, underpowered boats not recommended.

Lewis River. Heads on Mount Susitna and flows 30 miles to Cook Inlet, 30 miles west of Anchorage. Accessible by small wheel plane from Anchorage. Fish available: king salmon — late May through June, use egg clusters, spinners or spoons; silver salmon — July to September, use egg clusters, spinners or spoons; pink salmon — July and August, use small spoons; rainbow trout — year-round, use flies or lures.

Lucy Lake. (See Sportfishing in INTERIOR section.)

Portage Creek. A 1.5-mile-long tributary to the Susitna River, located 2.5 miles southwest of Curry and 18 miles northeast of Talkeetna. Access by small plane from Talkeetna or Chulitna River Lodge, Parks Highway, Milepost 156.2 from Anchorage. Fish available: rainbow trout, grayling, salmon — July, August and September, use spoons, spinners or flies.

Shell Lake. A 5-mile-long lake located 85 miles northwest of Anchorage, 15 miles from Skwentna. Primary access by floatplane in summer, skiplane in winter. Shell Lake Lodge located on lake. Fish available: red and silver salmon — late July through September; large lake and rainbow trout; some grayling. Winter ice fishing for burbot. Also wildlife-watching and photography, cross-country skiing and dog mushing.

Spink Lake. (See Sportfishing in INTERIOR section.)

Susitna Lake. A 10-mile-long lake located just northwest of Lake Louise in the Copper River Basin, 42 miles northwest of Glennallen. Accessible by boat across Lake Louise or by small floatplane or skiplane from Anchorage, Glennallen or other communities. Excellent fishing for lake trout — use spoons or plugs; grayling — use flies. Lake can be rough; underpowered boat not recommended.

Talachulitna River. Located about 65 miles northwest of Anchorage. Primary access by floatplane from Anchorage. One of the best fishing streams in southcentral Alaska. Lodges in the area. Fish available: king salmon — 25 to 50 pounds, best mid-June through early July, use big spoons and spinners; silver salmon — average 6 to 8 pounds, best August through early September, use flies or lures; red salmon — average 7 to 8 pounds, best mid-July to mid-August; chum salmon — average 10 to 12 pounds, best mid-June through mid-July; pink salmon — in even-numbered years averaging 3 to 4 pounds, best mid- to late July; rainbow trout — average 1 to 3 pounds; grayling — average 1 to 2 pounds; Dolly Varden — average 2 to 4 pounds, mid-June through September, best early and late. *NOTE: This river is restricted to single hook, artificial lures only, with no retention of rainbow trout.*

Yentna River. Located about 50 miles (35 minutes by small plane) northwest of Anchorage. Primary access by floatplane from Anchorage. Excellent fishery. Lodges on river. Fish available: king salmon — late May to early July, use spoons; red salmon — mid-June to late July, use spoons or flies; silver, chum and pink salmon — mid-July through August, use spoons; rainbow trout and grayling — year-round in season, best late August through September.

COPPER RIVER/WRANGELL-ST. ELIAS

Introduction

A swift, wide glacial river, the Copper winds its way past spectacular scenery and some of the most easily viewed wildlife in Alaska. Rafters and other floaters drift by snow-covered mountains, glaciers, tributary rivers and, near Chitina, a traditional salmon fishery that includes fish wheels and dip nets.

Where it meets the Gulf of Alaska, the Copper River and other rivers nearby braid and spread out to form a huge marshland that plays host to millions of waterfowl and shorebirds. The Copper River Delta attracts birders from all over the world to catch the spring and to a lesser extent the fall migrations of such species as trumpeter swans and dusky Canada geese.

But the delta is home to other wildlife as well — moose, brown and black bear, mountain goats (on the ridges nearby), and beaver. Outdoors lovers can hunt, fish, hike, canoe, camp, pick berries and watch glaciers calve (from a safe distance!). (For information about access to the Copper River Delta, see Cordova in the Prince William Sound subregion.)

Though most traffic on the Copper River these days flows south, in earlier times the Copper served as a gateway for explorers heading north into Alaska's unknown Interior. What they found was a beautiful, rugged wilderness of mountains and glaciers that supported large populations of trophy animals for hunters and enticing virgin peaks for mountaineers. An Italian, the Duke of Abruzzi, was first up Mount St. Elias in 1897; and a woman, Dora Keen, was first up Mount Blackburn, in 1912.

Hunters and mountain climbers were not the only ones venturing over the steep passes of the Wrangell and St. Elias mountains. Prospectors came too, and found gold that produced a few small stampedes but no major settlements. It was copper which put the Wrangells on the map as far as the world's bankers and financiers were concerned. A huge deposit some 60 miles east of the Copper River prompted construction (1907-11) of the Copper River & Northwestern Railway up the river valley to a company town named Kennicott. For 27 years the mines at Kennicott produced tons of the valuable ore before the operation was shut down suddenly in 1938.

Today visitors to Kennicott can browse among the abandoned company buildings, all of them except the infirmary painted a uniform red which has weathered well to this day. Kennicott and neighboring McCarthy, also serve as fine jumping-off points for adventurers in this beautiful, historic region.

Trumpeter swan, photographed near the Copper River Delta, has a wingspan of 6 to 8 feet. The best places to see swans in the summer, besides the delta, are the Kenai National Wildlife Refuge and Minto Flats neat Fairbanks. (Jerrianne Lowther, staff)

▼ C O M M U N I T I E S ▼

Cape Yakataga

Located on the Gulf of Alaska, 35 miles west of Icy Bay, 140 miles southeast of Cordova, 265 miles southeast of Anchorage. **Transportation:** Scheduled or charter air service from Cordova. **Population:** 4 to 8. **Zip code:** 99560. **Emergency Services:** Alaska State Troopers, Cordova.

Elevation: 12 feet at airport. **Climate:** Mild in the summer with temperatures in the 60s and rainy in the winter, with temperatures dropping to the middle teens to 35°F, according to one resident. Mean annual precipitation is 102 inches.

Private Aircraft: Airstrip 2 miles from homes; elev. 12 feet; length 4,900 feet; gravel; no fuel; unattended. Mountains north through northeast to east-southeast; 2,258-foot hill 3 nautical miles east. Runway not maintained. Contact Cordova radio for latest field conditions. Water stands on runway; soft spots rutted when dry. No transportation into town.

Visitor Facilities: No meals or accommodations available. No laundromat. No stores; supplies obtained from Cordova. Off-road vehicles available for rent. Fishing/hunting licenses not available. No guide services, fuel, moorage facilities or repair services.

The Indian name Yakataga is said to mean "canoe road," referring to 2 reefs which form a canoe passage to the village. The name was reported in 1904 by C.G. Martin of the U.S. Geological Survey. At that time there was placer mining in the area. Cape Yakataga is the site of a Federal Aviation Administration aero-beacon. Some residents mine and also trap.

Activities in the area include beachcombing and hunting for moose, mountain goat, black bear and brown bear, according to one resident. Also, a large number of birds pass through the area during migrations.

Chisana

(shoe-SHAN-na) Located in the Wrangell Mountains on the Chisana River near its headwaters, 30 miles southeast of Nabesna and about 60 miles south of Northway. **Transportation:** Charter air service from Northway, Glennallen or Tok. **Population:** 6 to 20, depending on the season. **Zip code:** 99780. **Emergency Services:** Alaska State Troopers, Glennallen, phone 822-3263; Tok Clinic or Faith Hospital, Glennallen.

Elevation: 3,170 feet. **Climate:** Mean temperature in July 51°F; mean temperature in January -14°F. Mean annual precipitation 11.4 inches, with 61 inches of snow.

Private Aircraft: Airstrip adjacent north; elev. 3,318 feet; length 4,200 feet; turf and gravel; unattended. Runway has loose rocks up to 3 inches. Airport active for hunting from the end of August to mid-September.

Visitor Facilities: Accommodations and meals available by advance reservation at 2 local lodges. There are no other facilities. Guide services are available locally.

This community, located within Wrangell-St. Elias National Park and Preserve, was settled during the Chisana gold rush of 1913. At one time the area had a population of more than 1,000. The gold rush was short-lived and Chisana quickly became a ghost town. It now serves as the base of operations for a few hunting guides and recreationists.

Anthony Dimond, Alaska's territorial delegate to Congress from 1932-45, was the town's U.S. Commissioner. His courtroom, cabin, women's jail and several other historic structures, built of logs during the town's peak years (1913 to 1920), were restored by the National Park Service in 1988.

Hunting, horseback trips, hiking and history are the primary visitor attractions.

A regular mail plane serves Chisana, which is unincorporated. There are no phones, schools or churches. Electricity is from individual generators, water is from wells or the river. There is no community sewage system. Freight arrives by plane.

Chitina

(CHIT-na) Located on the Edgerton Highway

at the confluence of the Copper and Chitina rivers, 116 miles northeast of Valdez. **Transportation:** Edgerton Highway, 33 miles from its junction with the Richardson Highway; air charter service from Gulkana. **Population:** 40. **Zip code:** 99566. **Emergency Services:** Copper River EMS, phone 822-3203; Alaska State Troopers at Glennalen, phone 822-3263.

Elevation: 556 feet. **Climate:** Summers warm (by Alaska standards) and sunny; winters cold, dark and snowy.

Private Aircraft: Airstrip adjacent; elev. 556 feet; length 3,000 feet; gravel; unattended. Runway conditions not monitored; visual inspection recommended prior to use. Aircraft at one end cannot see aircraft at other end because of downward slopes. Brush first 1,000 feet.

Visitor Facilities: Chitina has a post office, store, gas station, bar, motel, restaurant, campground, arts and crafts shop, tire repair service, public phone and National Park Service ranger station. A big attraction in Chitina is the seasonal run of Copper River salmon, which draws hundreds of dip-netters and spectators. The fishery is open June through September (depending on harvest levels), and it's a fine opportunity to see fish wheels and dip nets in action. (The fishery is open only to Alaska residents with personal use and subsistence permits.)

A bridge crossing the Copper River at Chitina gives access to the 58-mile McCarthy Road, which leads deep into the Wrangell-St. Elias National Park and Preserve. Chitina, as one of the gateway communities to the Wrangell-St. Elias, serves as jumping-off point for a number of wilderness trips that originate along the McCarthy Road. For more about Chitina, see *The MILEPOST®*, a complete guide to communities on Alaska's road and marine highway systems. To order, see the ALASKA NORTHWEST LIBRARY at the back of the book.

Copper Center

Located on the Klutina River, 1 mile west of its junction with the Copper River, 100 miles northeast of Valdez. **Transportation:** Automobile via the Richardson Highway; charter air service. **Population:** 275. **Zip code:** 99573. **Emergency Services:** State Troopers and hospital in Glennallen.

Elevation: 1,000 feet.

Kennecott Concentration Mill received ore from 2 tramways and processed up to 1,200 tons of copper ore per day from 2 mines in 14-story building. (Jerrianne Lowther)

Private Aircraft: Airstrip NR 1 adjacent west; elev. 1,033 feet; length 1,800 feet; turf; unattended. Ball field in summer; snowmobiles in winter. Airstrip NR 2, 0.9 miles south; elev. 1,150 feet; length 2,600 feet; gravel; unattended. Runway also used as a road.

Visitor Facilities: Meals, lodging, groceries, gas, general merchandise and other supplies available. A museum operated by the Copper Valley Historical Society is open June through September and features early mining, church and Native artifacts.

For more information see *The MILEPOST®*, a complete guide to communities of Alaska's road and marine highway systems. To order, see the ALASKA NORTHWEST LIBRARY section at the back of the book.

Cordova

Located near the southeastern end of Prince William Sound, Cordova was the tidewater terminus of the Copper River & Northwestern Railway and today serves as the gateway city to the Copper River Delta and to many wilderness trips into the surrounding area. For more about Cordova, see Communities in the Prince William Sound subregion.

Glennallen

Located on the Glenn Highway, near the junction of the Glenn and Richardson highways. **Transportation:** Road via the Glenn and Richardson highways. **Population:** 929. **Zip code:** 99588. **Emergency Services:** Alaska State Troopers, phone 822-3263; Fire Department emergency, phone 911; Hospital, phone 822-3203.

Elevation: 1,460 feet.

Private Aircraft: Gulkana Airstrip, 4.3 miles northeast of Glennallen; elev. 1,578 feet; length 4,200 feet; asphalt; fuel 80, 100, jet B.

Visitor Facilities: Accommodations and meals are available, as are automobile parts, groceries, gifts, clothing, sporting goods and other supplies. Fuel and major car repairs are available.

Glennallen is a convenient staging area for trips into the Wrangell-St. Elias National Park and for trips into the Copper River Delta. Several air taxis and guides and outfitters for wilderness trips are based here.

For more information see *The MILEPOST®*, a complete guide to communities on Alaska's road and marine highway systems. To order, see the ALASKA NORTHWEST LIBRARY section at the back of the book.

May Creek

Located on the Nizina River, 12 miles from McCarthy, 65 miles from Chitina. **Transportation:** Mail plane on Wednesdays from Gulkana; charter air service from Gulkana, McCarthy. **Population:** Less than 12. **Zip code:** 99588. **Emergency Services:** Alaska State Troopers, Glennallen; Cross Road Medical Center, Glennallen.

Private Aircraft: Airstrip 1 mile south; elev. 1,650 feet; length 4,000 feet; gravel and dirt; no fuel; unattended. Runway condition not monitored, visual inspection recommended prior to using. Wind cone in 30-foot trees. Road adjacent to east side of runway.

Visitor Facilities: No hotel, restaurant, store or other facilities.

The May Creek area had a roadhouse during the early 1900s gold rush when the Nizina District was booming, according to one resident. Mining was the main reason for development in the area, and likewise its decline also spelled the decline of the entire area. The May Creek airstrip was developed by the Alaska Road Commission in territorial days and was used by the entire region from McCarthy to Dan Creek before local strips were built. May Creek is located within Wrangell-St. Elias National Park and Preserve. A National Park Service Operations Center in May Creek is staffed only during the summer.

Area residents rely primarily on subsistence hunting, fishing and gathering, although there is some gold panning.

The biggest attraction in the area is superb hiking and beautiful scenery. Hiking opportunities range from easy rambles in meadows to more strenuous mountain and glacier treks. Roads and trails remaining from the early mining days make it fairly easy to get around, although many areas are wet. There are many beaver dams and swampy areas across or near the roads.

The area is rich in wildlife, particularly black and grizzly bears, beavers and other water mammals. Trumpeter swans migrate to this area in summer and nest in the lakes.

May Creek, which is unincorporated, has no phones or TV; KCAM radio from Glennallen is received. There are no churches, schools or community electricity, water or sewer systems. Freight arrives on the weekly mail plane.

McCarthy/Kennicott

Located across the Kennicott River from the end of the Edgerton Highway and the McCarthy Road, a mostly gravel route approximately 110 miles from Copper

Center. The 59-mile McCarthy Road follows the roadbed of the old Copper River and Northwestern Railway.

Transportation: To reach McCarthy from the end of the road one must cross 2 legs of the Kennicott River via 2 hand-pulled cable trams. The legs are separated by an island that visitors can walk across. There is public bus service as far as the trams. Also, charter air service from Gulkana. **Population:** 15-20. **Zip code:** 99588. **Emergency Services:** Copper River EMS at Glennallen, phone 822-3203; Alaska State Troopers at Glennallen, phone 822-3263.

Elevation: 1,531 feet at McCarthy; Kennicott considerably higher. **Climate:** Summers bring cool, cloudy, often rainy weather, though hot, sunny days are not uncommon. Winters are cold, dark and usually clear, with temperatures dropping well below zero for long periods.

Private Aircraft: Airstrip adjacent; elev. 1,531 feet; length 3,500 feet; turf and gravel; no fuel; unattended. Runway conditions not monitored; visual inspection recommended prior to using. No public transportation to lodging, though visitors can often catch a ride with a local.

Visitor Facilities: Accommodations, meals at 1 lodge, 1 bed-and-breakfast in McCarthy, 1 lodge in Kennicott. No groceries, fuel, laundromat, bank, major repairs, or rental transportation. Gift shop in McCarthy offers candy, T-shirts, minimal first-aid supplies, and film. No hunting/fishing licenses sold. Arts and crafts available for purchase include silver jewelry, T-shirts, and other locally made goods. A campground, organized tours and guides available.

McCarthy and neighboring Kennicott lie in a beautiful area of glaciers and mountains in the heart of the Wrangell-St. Elias Park and Preserve. The Kennicott River flows by the west side of town and joins the Nizina River which flows into the Chitina River. *(WARNING: Do not attempt to wade across this glacial river; strong currents and cold water make*

it extremely treacherous. The trams are small open platforms and should be attempted only by travelers strong enough to pull themselves across several hundred feet, part of the distance uphill. It is easier if a friend pulls on the return cable from the riverbank. Wear gloves.)

McCarthy's museum, located in the railway depot, has historical photos and artifacts from the early mining days. Kennicott, which lies 4.5 miles up the mountain from McCarthy, is itself a museum. The town was built by Kennecott Copper Corp. between 1910 and 1920 at the site of the richest copper mine in the world. (An early day misspelling made the mining company Kennecott, while the region, river and settlement are Kennicott.) When economic conditions forced the mine to shut down abruptly in 1938, the town was left virtually intact: eating utensils still in kitchen drawers; maps, charts and records still in offices; surgical instruments in the infirmary. The distinctive red buildings perched on the side of the mountain were locked up and left as they were. And to a large extent they remain just as the workers left them, bar the toll taken by weather, aging, and a small amount of vandalism. Kennicott is no longer owned by the copper company, but it remains in private hands, and property rights should be respected.

Besides poking around these historic communities (with or without a knowledgeable local guide), visitors to Kennicott and McCarthy have their choice of river rafting, mountaineering/glacier travel, backpacking, day hiking, bicycling, flightseeing, horseback riding, grayling fishing, taking nature walks, or simply relaxing in the rustic, historic accommodations. Cross-country skiing here in spring is becoming increasingly popular.

McCarthy and Kennicott have no phones, no running water or indoor plumbing, no radio, TV, or school. A mail plane comes in once a week. July 4 festivities include a parade, pie eating, log toss, 3-legged races, barbecues; on Labor Day there is a dance and barbecues. The communities are unincorporated.

▼ **A T T R A C T I O N S** ▼

National and State Parks, Forests, Etc.

Wrangell-St. Elias National Park and Preserve

Located northwest of Yakutat and northeast of Cordova and Valdez, Wrangell-St. Elias is the largest unit in the national park system, encompassing 13.2 million acres of superlative scenery, abundant wildlife and fascinating history. In conjunction with adjacent Kluane National Park in Canada, the 2 areas make up the largest parkland in North America. Here the Wrangell, St. Elias and Chugach mountain ranges converge, forming a mountain wilderness unsurpassed in North America and comparable to all other major mountain groups in the world. The region contains the largest concentration of peaks exceeding 14,500 feet in North America; Wrangell-St. Elias park contains 9 of the 16 highest peaks in the United States. Mount St. Elias, at 18,008 feet, is the second-tallest peak in the United States; Mount Logan, across the border in Kluane park, soars to a height of 19,850 feet, second only to Mount McKinley in North American summits.

This park has been shaped by both volcanoes and ice. Mount Wrangell (14,163 feet) erupted as recently as 1930. Dormant volcanoes include Mount Blackburn (16,390 feet), Mount Sanford (16,237 feet) and Mount Drum (12,010 feet). On the western flank of Mount Drum are 3 large thermal springs known as mud volcanoes.

The area also contains the largest concentration of glaciers on the continent. One of these, Malaspina Glacier, is North America's largest piedmont glacier, a type formed when 2 or more glaciers flow from confined valleys to form a broad fan- or lobe-shaped ice mass. Malaspina Glacier covers an area of about 1,500 square miles — larger than the state of Rhode Island. It has been designated a national natural landmark. Hubbard Glacier, which flows out of the St. Elias Mountains

into Disenchantment Bay, is one of the largest and most active glaciers in North America. In 1986, the glacier made national headlines when it surged forward, sealing off adjacent Russell Fiord. Within 2 months, the ice dam had broken, but Hubbard Glacier continues to advance and scientists agree the glacier will eventually close off the fjord permanently.

The Park Service says Chitistone and Nizina canyons "far exceed the scale of Yosemite Valley in California" and include an even greater variety of geological wonders. There is a spectacular 300-foot waterfall in upper Chitistone Canyon and the lower canyon has sheer walls rising 4,000 feet above the river.

Wrangell-St. Elias contains many prehistoric and historic sites, including ancient Eskimo and Indian villages and camps, sites of Russian fur-trading posts, gold rush relics and industrial complexes of the early 20th century — such as the Kennecott mine, the most famous and richest copper mine in Alaska until market conditions led to its abandonment in 1938. *NOTE: The Kennecott mine buildings are private property.*

Tree line in the park's interior is about 3,000 to 4,000 feet. Below this the forest cover is composed of white spruce and balsam poplar at lower elevations and a mixture of aspen, birch and balsam poplar higher on the slopes. Streambeds contain thick underbrush, usually alder, which also grows well on steep south-facing hillsides. Labrador tea and dwarf birch are major shrubs. Above 3,000 feet, moist sedges and grasses form open tundra meadows interlaced with blueberries and Labrador tea. The Bremner and Copper river valleys have typical coastal vegetation near their mouths: western and mountain hemlock and Sitka spruce rain forest with devil's club, blueberries and salmonberries.

Wildlife: These diverse habitats support varied wildlife. On higher slopes range Dall sheep and mountain goats — sheep in the Wrangell Mountains and northern slopes of the Chugach Range, goats in the coastal mountains. Caribou from 3 herds forage on parklands. Moose browse throughout the lowlands and river bottoms and 2 herds of introduced bison range along the Copper and Chitina rivers. Brown/grizzly and black bears share lower elevations with wolves, wolverines, coyotes, red foxes and a variety of small furbearers.

Marine mammals which can be observed in Yakutat Bay, where the park touches the sea, include seals, sea lions, sea otters, 2 species of dolphin and killer whales.

Sport fish, such as arctic grayling, lingcod and trout thrive in lakes adjacent to the Chitina River valley and on the northern slopes of the Wrangells, while the Copper River supports a major salmon run utilized by both commercial and subsistence fishermen.

Bird life is not outstanding within the park/preserve, although trumpeter swans, bald and golden eagles, 3 species of ptarmigan and ruffed and spruce grouse can be seen. Just to the south of the park the Copper River Delta is a major nesting area.

Climate: Weather in most of the area is typical of interior Alaska. Summer brings cool, often cloudy and rainy weather, which can interfere with scheduled air pickups and prolong trips. Clear, hot days are not uncommon, particularly in July, which has the warmest weather. August is cooler and wetter, but generally has less mosquitoes. Fall is excellent, but doesn't last long. Winters are cold and dark, with temperatures dropping to -50°F, but clear weather is common. Average snow cover is about 2 feet. In coastal areas precipitation is higher — 130 inches in some areas — and temperatures are relatively moderate with winter lows around 0°F and summer highs in the 70s.

The Park Service cautions that visitors to the Wrangell-St. Elias backcountry must be self-sufficient, carry enough food to cover unexpected delays and be prepared for the Alaskan wilderness. Rain gear, or synthetic pile, and wool clothing are essential. Animals are wild and should be respected. Travelers should know their gear and have wilderness travel and survival skills; sources of assistance are frequently many miles away. Always leave an itinerary with the Park Service or with a friend and contact that person after returning.

A Park Service ranger station is open year-round in Glennallen and during the summers at Slana, Chitina and Yakutat. Also, some of the land within the park/preserve is privately owned and local residents carry on subsistence lifestyles; respect their property and privacy.

Accommodations: Privately operated lodges, cabins and camps are scattered throughout the park and preserve, in nearby McCarthy/Kennicott area and along the Nabesna and McCarthy roads. These include fishing camps, guide cabins, full-service lodges, commercial campgrounds and air taxi services. A list of these facilities and services is available from park headquarters. Several campgrounds are operated by the Bureau of Land Management and the state of Alaska along the Richardson Highway, Tok Cutoff and Edgerton Highway. There are no designated campgrounds within the park/preserve; wilderness camping only. No permits are necessary for camping or backpacking although voluntary registration is requested. All water obtained from streams or lakes should be boiled or treated. The park's visitor center is located at Milepost 105.1 from Valdez on the Richardson Highway; rangers there provide briefings on the park and trip planning assistance. Ranger stations also are maintained at Yakutat, Slana and Chitina.

Access: Wrangell-St. Elias is one of the more accessible national parks in Alaska; 2 roads lead into the area. Major access is by road along the Richardson Highway and Edgerton Highway from Glennallen to Chitina. The unpaved Chitina-McCarthy Road extends some 61 miles up the Chitina River valley from Chitina to the Kennicott River just west of McCarthy. The road follows the abandoned railroad bed of the Copper River and Northwestern Railway. During the summer it is generally passable by 2-wheel-drive vehicles. Inquire in Chitina about road conditions before proceeding to McCarthy. The trip to the Kennicott River can easily take 3 to 4 hours. The road ends about 1 mile west of McCarthy at the 2 forks of the Kennicott River. Crossing the river to reach McCarthy currently is by 2 hand-pulled cable trams. (*DO NOT* attempt to wade across this glacial river except at very low water.) The trams are small open platforms and should be attempted only by travelers strong enough to pull themselves across several hundred feet — part of the distance is uphill. Wear gloves. Crossing is easier if someone standing on the bank does the pulling. Once across the river, follow the road to the McCarthy Museum then take the right fork of the road to McCarthy. The abandoned Kennecott Copper Mine is 4 miles beyond the McCarthy Museum. Regularly scheduled bus service is available from Glennallen and Chitina to McCarthy.

Road access to the northern section of the park/preserve is from Slana (on the Tok Cutoff) along a 43-mile unpaved state-maintained road to the privately owned mining community of Nabesna. This road is plowed intermittently in winter. All other access to the park/preserve is by boat or air. There are 4,000-foot gravel airstrips at Chisana, McCarthy and May Creek. Floatplanes can land on lakes within the park/preserve. Charter air service is available in Anchorage, Fairbanks, Northway, Glennallen, McCarthy, Cordova, Valdez and Yakutat. Several guides and outfitters offer a variety of trips in the park and preserve.

Activities: Recreational opportunities in Wrangell-St. Elias include hunting, fishing, expedition mountaineering, backpacking, photography, cross-country skiing, rafting/kayaking and wildlife observation. The Park Service offers a trip synopsis list to help in trip planning. None of the hikes listed are on marked or maintained trails; rather, they follow unimproved "backcountry" routes consisting of mining trails, historic routes, streambeds, shorelines, game trails, and open country.

For additional information contact: Superintendent, Wrangell-St. Elias National Park and Preserve, P.O. Box 29, Glennallen, AK 99588; phone 822-5235. Related USGS Topographic maps: Mount St. Elias, Yakutat, Icy Bay, Bering Glacier, McCarthy, Nabesna, Gulkana and Valdez. (See also Mountain Climbing, in the GENERAL INFORMATION section.)

For an in-depth look at this area, see *Wrangell-Saint Elias International Mountain Wilderness*. Vol. 8 No. 1 of *ALASKA GEOGRAPHIC*®. To order, see the ALASKA NORTHWEST LIBRARY section at the back of the book.

Chugach National Forest

The 5.8-million-acre national forest stretches from the Kenai Peninsula east across Prince William Sound to encompass the Gulf Coast surrounding the Copper River Delta then east from there as far as the Bering Glacier. The easternmost reaches of the forest abut the Wrangell-St. Elias National Park and Preserve. For more about Chugach National Forest, see the Introduction to this section and for a list of Forest Service cabins in the Cordova area, see Attractions in the

Prince William Sound Subregion.

The Rivers

Chitina River. This silty glacial river is located in the Chugach Mountains in Wrangell-St. Elias National Park and Preserve. The river heads at Chitina Glacier and flows west-northwest 112 miles to the Copper River, 1.2 miles east of Chitina and 66 miles northeast of Valdez.

This river is considered Class I to Class II from its headwaters and has a gradient of 10 feet per mile. It is a fast but not technically difficult river. At about its midpoint, the Chitina is joined by the Nizina River, which should be run only by experienced paddlers. It flows through a steep canyon and is considered Class II, fairly fast with difficult rapids.

Another alternative is to put in on the Kennicott River at McCarthy. The Kennicott to the Nizina is Class II, swift and braided. It is also shallow and may need to be lined or portaged. From where the Nizina joins it, the Chitina is braided with many gravel bars. Kayaks or rafts are recommended for these rivers.

The Chitina runs through wild mountain country with nearby peaks over 10,000 feet. Paddlers may see moose, brown bears and Dall sheep.

Access to the Chitina's glacial headwaters is by chartered wheel plane. The Kennicott River is accessed by the Chitina-McCarthy Road, which is usually passable by 2-wheel-drive vehicles. Check in Chitina for road conditions. Exit is at Chitina, below the highway bridge.

Related USGS Topographic maps: McCarthy A-6, B-6, B-7 and B-8; Valdez B-1, C-1 and C-2.

Copper River. This major glacial river heads on the north side of the Wrangell Mountains and flows south 250 miles through a gap in the Chugach Mountains to the Gulf of Alaska, just east of Cordova. Although the Richardson and Glenn highways parallel the river, they are rarely within sight or sound. This braided river passes through true wilderness country and features silty, but always

---

MOUNTAIN CLIMBING

For climbers wanting to escape the crowds on Mount McKinley, there are hundreds of other peaks that offer every type of climbing variety and degree of difficulty.

swift water. The Copper forms the western boundary of Wrangell-St. Elias National Park and Preserve and flows by glacier-clad peaks ranging up to 16,000 feet, including Mount Sanford, Mount Drum, Mount Wrangell and Mount Blackburn. The lower portion passes through Chugach National Forest.

This is considered a Class II river. No difficult white water is encountered except at the end of Miles Lake, where the ice of Childs Glacier forms the western bank of the river. The river narrows here and the glacier calves directly into it. The powerful current frequently creates eddies and whirlpools of frightening dimensions. There also are some holes to avoid in Abercrombie Rapids above Miles Lake. This river's gradient is 7 feet per mile for about 150 river miles from Slana to Copper Center; 6 feet per mile for the next 60 miles to Chitina; and 5 feet per mile from Chitina to the gulf. The trip takes 7 to 9 days, depending on put-in and take-out points. Canoes, rafts or kayaks are suitable.

Paddlers will be treated to outstanding scenery including mountains, glaciers, canyons and the river delta. Eagles, bears, seals and an abundance of waterfowl may be seen.

Access is from a bridge over the Gakona River, 1.8 miles from the Gakona junction on the Tok Cutoff (Glenn Highway), and a short distance from the confluence of the Gakona and Copper rivers. Access also at Copper Center on the Richardson Highway and Chitina on the Edgerton Highway. Once past Chitina, the next exit is more than 100 river miles away near the head of the Copper River Delta at a bridge on the Copper River Highway at Milepost 27 from Cordova. Or it is possible to paddle west into Cordova along the shoreline.

Related USGS Topographic maps: Gulkana A-3, B-3; Valdez A-3, B-2, B-3, C-2, C-3, D-3 and D-4; Cordova B-3, C-2, C-3, D-2 and D-3.

Nabesna River. (See Rivers in INTERIOR section.)

Sportfishing

Though the Wrangells are more noted for hunting than for fishing, there are a number of fly-in lakes which offer excellent fishing for species such as trout, grayling and burbot. The Copper River itself supports a huge salmon run. For more information consult the current sportfishing regulations or contact the following: Alaska Dept. of Fish and Game, Sport Fish Division, 333 Raspberry Road,

Anchorage, AK 99518; phone 267-2218, or the same office in Glennallen at P.O. Box 47, Glennallen, Ak 99588; phone 822-3309.

Copper Lake. A 5.5-mile-long fly-in lake located west of Tanada Lake within Wrangell-St. Elias National Park and Preserve. Accessible via Nabesna Road, which leaves the Glenn Highway (Tok Cutoff) at Milepost 65.2 from Tok. Turn off Nabesna Road at Milepost 23 for flying service at Long Lake or at Milepost 26.1 for 2-mile drive to Jack Lake and flying service. Cabins, boats and motors available. Fish available: lake trout — 10 to 12 pounds, mid-June to September, use red-and-white spoons; kokanee — 10 to 12 inches, mid-June to July, use small spinner; grayling — 12 to 20 inches, July through September, use flies; burbot — use bait.

Deep Lake. A 1.8-mile-long fly-in lake at the head of Dog Creek in the Copper River Basin, 30 miles north-northwest of Glennallen. Accessible by floatplane from Glennallen. Good fishing all summer for lake trout to 30 inches.

Hanagita Lake. A 1-mile-long fly-in lake located in the Chugach Mountains, 32 miles southwest of McCarthy. Accessible by small plane from Glennallen. Excellent grayling fishing all summer; lake trout and steelhead in September.

Tanada Lake. A 5.7-mile-long, 1-mile-wide fly-in lake located within Wrangell-St. Elias National Park and Preserve, 11 miles west of Nabesna. Accessible via Nabesna Road, which leaves the Glenn Highway (Tok Cutoff) at Milepost 65.2 from Tok. Turn off Nabesna Road at Milepost 23 for flying service at Long Lake or Milepost 26.1 for 2-mile drive to Jack Lake. Lodge on Tanada Lake. Considered one of the top lake trout fisheries in the state. Fish available: lake trout — 3 to 10 pounds, occasionally up to 30 pounds, excellent last week of June and first 2 weeks of July, use large lures; grayling — 14 to 16 inches, best last of June and first 2 weeks of July, use flies; whitefish and burbot available.

Tebay Lakes. Located in a line 7 miles long trending northeast in the Chugach Mountains, southwest of McCarthy and 68 miles east of Valdez. Accessible by small plane from Glennallen. Excellent fishing for rainbow trout — 12 to 15 inches, all summer, use small spinners. Cabin, boat and motor rentals.

SPECIAL FEATURES

Cape St. Elias Light Station

This light, 85 feet above the water, is located on the southernmost tip of Kayak Island on Cape St. Elias. The cape was named by Captain Commander Vitus Bering on July 20, 1741, for the saint whose day it was according to the Russian Orthodox Church calendar. This 1,665-foot-high cape forms an unmistakable landmark for mariners. The waters south of the cape were regarded as "one of the most dangerous points along the entire coast." Congress appropriated money for the project in 1913 and construction of the lighthouse was completed on Sept. 16, 1916, at a cost of $115,000. It was equipped with the most modern equipment available. At one time there were 3 lighthouse keepers in residence; the light was automated by the U.S. Coast Guard in 1974. It is listed on the National Register of Historic Places and is considered the best existing 1916 architectural example of a major Alaska lighthouse. The original fresnel lense, approximately 5 feet high, is now on display at the museum in Cordova.

Copper River Delta

The 400-square-mile delta of this major glacier-fed river is noted for its spectacular waterfowl and shorebird migrations each spring and, to a lesser extent, each fall. Visitors will have the opportunity to view thousands to millions of birds.

The habitats of the region range from hemlock and spruce forest, to thickets of tall shrubs, lakes, rivers and coastal wetlands,

to remote islands and marine waters.

The largest and most conspicuous of the waterfowl is the trumpeter swan, which has a wingspan of 6 to 8 feet. At one time this was an endangered species; now the greatest concentration of these swans in North America is along the Copper River and its tributaries. The Copper-Bering river deltas and adjacent areas also provide nesting grounds for dusky Canada geese.

The most abundant duck is the pintail. Hundreds of thousands pass through in the spring and many remain to breed and nest. Other species of ducks and geese found in the delta are white-fronted geese, snow geese, teals, wigeons, shovellers, scaups and goldeneyes.

Many thousands of sandhill cranes stop to rest and feed on the flats on their way north to nest. Flocks of western and dunlin sandpipers occur in late April and early May. Densities of more than 250,000 shorebirds per square mile have been observed feeding on the delta. Other bird species seen on or near the delta include arctic tern, red-throated loons, mergansers, parasitic jaegers, Bonaparte's gulls, short-eared owls, northern harriers, bald eagles, great blue herons, black-legged kittiwakes, common murres, tufted puffins, American black oystercatchers and double-crested, pelagic and red-faced cormorants.

Black and brown bears may be seen in the spring as they leave their dens to feed on grasses and in late summer and fall when they return to feed on spawning salmon. Other mammals that may be seen include black-tailed deer, moose, beaver, muskrat, mink and otter.

The Cordova Ranger District of the Chugach National Forest is developing a series of recreation and interpretative facilities on the Copper River Delta to explain the features and management of the area. Facilities will include day-use picnic site, trails, viewing platforms and displays.

Visitors are cautioned not to approach bears or moose and not to disturb nesting birds. Calving glaciers can produce waves 6 feet high, so don't get too close. When traveling on the mudflats, use great caution and pay attention to tide tables; tidewaters come in quickly and it's easy to become stranded by tidal sloughs and softening mud.

Access to the delta is by floatplane or boat from Cordova (see Communities, Prince William Sound Subregion this section) or by the Copper River Highway. Cordova is accessible by commercial jet service and the

Alaska Marine Highway System, and has all visitor facilities. The delta is part of Chugach National Forest, which has a few public-use cabins in the area. Also, there is a campground at Cabin Lake, accessible by a 3-mile road that leaves the Copper River Highway at Milepost 12.1 from Cordova. Camping permits are available from the Eyak Corp., P.O. Box 340, Cordova, AK 99574; phone 424-7161.

For additional information contact: Chugach National Forest, Cordova Ranger District, P.O. Box 280, Cordova, AK 99574; phone 424-7661.

Katalla

Although a ghost town today, Katalla *(ka-TELL-a)* once was an oil and coal boom town. Katalla, located near the mouth of the Katalla River on Katalla Bay 50 miles southeast of Cordova, is near the site of one of the first oil discoveries in Alaska, made in 1896, and the state's first oil well, drilled in 1902. The town was established about 1903 as a supply point for the oil field, 3.5 miles to the east. The Bering River coalfields are about 15 miles to the northeast and once were connected to

Katalla by a railroad. The boom town's population may have been as high as 10,000 at one time, but had dwindled to 188 by 1910 and 23 by 1940. Today, a caretaker and his family are the only residents of Katalla. The town's post office, opened in 1904, was closed in 1943.

Around 1910, the government restricted coal mining and other mineral development in Alaska and Katalla lost much of its population practically overnight. From 1902 to 1931 a total of 36 wells were drilled in the Katalla oil field, 18 were successful. A small refinery built in 1911 produced gasoline and heating oil for local markets until part of the plant burned in 1933 and the entire operation was abandoned.

Katalla also is noteworthy as the location where the coastal steamer *Portland,* which ran from Seattle to St. Michael at the mouth of the Yukon River, was wrecked in 1910. The *Portland* gained fame when it arrived in Seattle on July 17, 1897, with a ton and a half of gold from the Klondike on board and helped set off one of the biggest gold rushes in history.

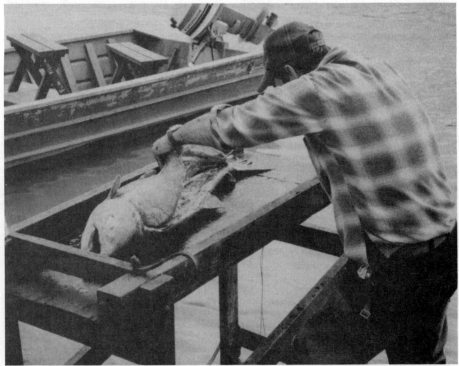

A fishing guide cleans a client's salmon. (Staff)

Much of the land surrounding Katalla is part of Chugach National Forest and is pristine wilderness. However, 500 acres at the old refinery site are privately owned and new exploration is under way by the Alaska Crude Corp. About 11,000 acres are owned by the federal government, but subject to selection by Chugach Alaska Native regional corporation and likely will be developed. Another 30,000 acres at the coalfield is privately owned and development is planned by a Chugach Alaska joint venture. A road connecting Katalla with the Copper River Highway and Cordova is proposed and if built would mean the old boom town may see some new development.

The only way to get to Katalla is by charter plane or helicopter from Cordova, the nearest major community. (For information on service and facilities in Cordova, see Prince William Sound this section.) It is possible to get to Katalla by boat, but not usually feasible. Katalla is exposed to the full force of North Pacific storms, and waters in the area are often extremely rough.

Kayak Island

Located 200 miles east-southeast of Anchorage and 62 miles southeast of Cordova, this remote, narrow island is the location of the first documented landing of Europeans on North America's northwest coast. Naturalist George Wilhelm Steller and other members of an expedition led by Captain Commander Vitus Bering landed near the mouth of a creek on the leeward (west) shore of Kayak Island on July 20, 1741. Although the party was ashore just a few hours to replenish water supplies, Steller sketched and named many plants and animals in the area, including the Steller's jay. No trace of their landing remains today, but the site is on the National Register of Historic Places. The 22-mile-long, 1.5-mile-wide island also is the location of another historic site, the Cape St. Elias Light Station.

This wild, uninhabited island offers excellent opportunities for beachcombing, hiking, camping, photography, berry-picking, fishing, hunting and exploring.

Wildlife on the island includes foxes, harbor seals, sea lions and a variety of birds including peregrine falcons. An occasional whale may be seen offshore. Brown bears inhabit the island. Avoid potentially dangerous bear encounters by keeping a clean camp; store food at least 100 to 200 yards away, preferably in a high tree. Make noise while hiking. There are no established trails on the island, so if you find one, it's probably a bear trail and should be avoided. There are no facilities on the island. The light station is totally automated and unstaffed. The buildings are U.S. Coast Guard property; do not enter them. Firewood and fresh water are available. Use only dead or downed wood (driftwood on the beach is easily accessible). Drinking water should be boiled to eliminate giardiasis, an intestinal parasite. Pack out all unburnable trash.

The U.S. Forest Service recommends that visitors bring extra food and other supplies since bad weather can prolong your stay for days at a time. Also, take a tide table with the Sitka-area tide data; some beaches are impassable at higher tides. Pinnacle Rock, 494 feet high, is connected to the southernmost tip of the island (Cape St. Elias) by a low, 0.2-mile ribbon of land and may not be accessible at higher tides. It's not a pleasant place to be stranded.

Kayak Island is not easy to get to because of its remoteness and frequent rainy, windy weather. A single-engine charter plane can get there from Cordova in less than an hour under normal conditions. Wheel planes can land only on certain sandy beaches at lower tides; floatplanes can land in the ocean on the west side of the island if the seas are calm enough. A boat trip from Cordova usually takes 12 to 16 hours, one way, depending on conditions, which in this area are often extremely rough. Helicopters are the most dependable, but most expensive, means of access. (For more information on Cordova, see Communities in the Prince William Sound subregion.)

For additional information contact: Chugach National Forest, Cordova Ranger District, P.O. Box 280, Cordova, AK 99574; phone 424-7661.

SITKA SPRUCE

Sitka spruce, *Picea sitchensis*, the largest and one of the most valuable trees in Alaska. Sitka spruce grows to 160 feet in height and 3 to 5 feet in diameter. Its long, dark green needles surround twigs that bear cones. It is found throughout Southeast, along the gulf coast of Cook Inlet and the Kenai Peninsula. Adopted in 1962 as the state tree.
– *The ALASKA ALMANAC®*

PRINCE WILLIAM SOUND

Introduction

A spectacularly beautiful coastal wilderness of secluded bays and uninhabited islands, Prince William Sound just begs to be explored. The sound is home and playground to sea otters, sea lions, whales, harbor seals, bald eagles and other birds, Dall sheep, mountain goats, brown and black bear, and Sitka black-tailed deer. Its waters carry all 5 species of Pacific salmon, halibut, rockfish, and Dungeness, king and tanner crab.

This rich ocean environment, allied with breathtaking scenery and proximity to population centers makes Prince William Sound a deservedly popular destination. Many Anchorage and Kenai Peninsula residents keep a boat moored at Whittier for weekend excursions. Out-of-state residents are often introduced to the sound via a tour boat or the state ferry between Valdez and Whittier — then come back for the more intimate exploration that the sound deserves. Kayakers, fishermen, bird-watchers, glacier watchers, marine mammal enthusiasts, hunters, pleasure boaters, fishermen — all find what they are looking for in Prince William Sound. Columbia Glacier, magnificent at tidewater, seems to make it a point to calve (break off) for the benefit of over-awed spectators. Sea otters groom themselves, whales surface, goats pose on rocky ledges. Hunting and fishing charters are available from Cordova, Valdez and Whittier, and a few adventure cruises aboard smallish vessels are also available. (See BUYERS GUIDE.)

For those who venture out on their own, the Prince William Sound Users Assoc. (311 C St., Suite 200, Anchorage, AK 99503; phone 561-1622) has produced a brochure entitled *Prince William SOUND CAMPING*. Among its suggestions: prepare for rain with rain gear, warm clothing and a waterproof shelter; obtain tide tables and charts; check short- and long-range weather forecasts; understand the dangers of hypothermia; bring extra garbage bags to carry out all trash; file travel plans with family, friends and/or the harbormaster; bring extra food in case your trip is extended by storms.

One final note: Those who know and love Prince William Sound were especially sick at heart when the *Exxon Valdez* ran aground in March of 1989 and spilled 11 million barrels of crude oil into the sound's pristine waters. Devastating as the spill was, it did *not* contaminate all of Prince William Sound. There are still hundreds of coves and beaches, inlets and passages that escaped unscathed. Strong ocean currents carried the oil southwest out of the sound. It may take a decade or longer for some of the hardest hit beaches to recover, but the sound is so large and nature itself such a powerful healer that Prince William Sound will continue to be a prime destination for marine adventurers.

Last summer the Prince William Sound Assoc. (address above) helped recreational users avoid oiled beaches by publishing a weekly map that provided oiled-shoreline updates not only for the sound but Resurrection and Kachemak bays, Lower Cook Inlet and the Kenai Peninsula's southern coast as well. The updated maps were distributed free to visitor centers, public lands offices, recreational businesses, harbormasters and libraries in nearby communities. Anyone who visited remote areas near the spill was asked to report their observations. The association was planning to produce the maps again in 1990.

GLACIERS

Prince William Sound contains the greatest concentration of tidewater glaciers anywhere in Alaska.

The fjords with active glaciers are located on the west and northwest sides of Prince William Sound, many areas which remained untouched by the oil spilled from the *Exxon Valdez* in March of 1989.

College Fjord, Harriman Fjord, Columbia Bay, Blackstone Bay, Barry Arm, Unakwik Inlet, Port Bainbridge, Port Nellie Juan, Icy Bay and Nassau Fjord, about one-third of the sound's fjords, contain 20 active tidewater glaciers. Harriman Fjord contains more than 12 glaciers.

For more information on these and other glaciers in Alaska, see *Alaska's Glaciers* by The Alaska Geographic Society. To order, see the ALASKA NORTHWEST LIBRARY at the back of the book.

Chenega Bay

Located at Crab Bay on Evans Island, 50 miles southeast of Seward. **Transportation:** Boat or charter floatplane from Anchorage, Cordova, Seward or Valdez. **Population:** 70. **Zip code:** 99574. **Emergency Services:** Village Public Safety Officer; Alaska State Troopers, Seward, phone 224-3346; Clinic.

Climate: Moderately rainy, with daytime temperatures in the mid-50s, according to one resident. Winters mild with average snowfall accumulation of 4 to 5 feet. Daytime winter temperatures from the mid-20s to the 30s.

Private Aircraft: No airstrip. Floatplane landings only.

Visitor Facilities: Two separate quarters with cooking facilities available in the community building. Laundry facilities available; no banking services. Limited supplies available. No arts and crafts available for purchase at present. Fishing/hunting licenses available; no guide services. Fuel available: marine gas, diesel and regular gasoline. The community has a dock and a floatplane landing area.

The original community of Chenega, located on the south tip of Chenega Island north of Evans Island, was destroyed by the tidal wave that followed the 1964 Good Friday earthquake. Chenega Bay was dedicated on the 20th anniversary of that quake, the culmination of years of effort to provide a new village for former residents of Chenega.

Most of the buildings were constructed in the summer of 1984. The new village consists of 21 homes, an office building, school and community store, a church, community hall and 2 school faculty houses.

The primary occupations in Chenega Bay are subsistence and commercial fishing and other seasonal employment.

Chenega Bay is built on the site of the former Crab Bay herring saltery. At nearby Sawmill Bay between Chenega Bay and Port San Juan are the ruins of Port Ashton, another abandoned herring saltery, which is acces-

sible by boat, floatplane or by foot along the beach at low tide.

The Port San Juan Hatchery, operated by the Prince William Sound Aquaculture Assoc., is located about 2 miles across Sawmill Bay by boat from Chenega Bay. The hatchery, which is open to visitors, grows pink and chum salmon and reportedly is one of the largest of its kind in the world in terms of number of fry released.

Latouche Island, site of an abandoned copper mining community, is located about 4 miles from Chenega Bay across Elrington Passage. Today there is a private airstrip on the island and a few homes.

The historic site of old Chenega is accessible by private air or boat charter.

Recreational activities at Chenega Bay include bottle collecting, rockhounding, beachcombing, hiking or backpacking. Cross-country skiing is good in winter. Whales and sea lions may be seen nearby. Bird-watching is possible year-round. Fishing in nearby waters is good in season for salmon, trout, halibut and rockfish. Hunting is primarily for deer and black bear on Evans and neighboring islands.

NOTE: Some lands near Chenega Bay are owned by the local village corporation, which should be contacted regarding the location of its lands and authorization for use.

Communications at Chenega Bay, which is unincorporated, include phones, twice-weekly mail plane, radio and TV. There are community electricity, water and sewer systems. Freight arrives by barge or mail plane. Village corporation address: Chenega Corp., General Delivery, Chenega Bay, AK 99574.

Cordova

Located on Orca Inlet on the southeast shore of Prince William Sound at the entrance to the Copper River valley, 147 miles southeast of Anchorage. **Transportation:** Daily jet service from Anchorage; Alaska Marine Highway System from Valdez, Whittier and Seward. **Population:** 2,585. **Zip code:** 99574. **Emergency Services:** Alaska State Troopers, phone 424-6100, emergency phone 911; Police, Fire Department, Ambulance, phone 424-6100, emergency phone 911; Hospital, phone 427-8000.

Elevation: Sea level to 400 feet. **Climate:** Average temperature in July 54°F, in January 21°F. Average annual precipitation 167 inches. Prevailing winds easterly at about 5 mph.

Private Aircraft: Two state-owned airports; Cordova Municipal, 0.9 mile east; elev. 12 feet; length 1,900 feet; gravel; unattended. Cordova, Mile 13, 11.3 miles east-southeast; elev. 42 feet; length 7,500 feet; asphalt. Eyak Lake seaplane base, 0.9 mile east.

Visitor Facilities: Cordova has 2 hotels, 2 motels, 9 restaurants, 2 laundromats and a variety of shopping facilities. Banking and all major repair services are available. The town has several air taxi operators. Boats also may be chartered. Cordova has a large small-boat harbor with facilities for transient boats. For additional information contact Cordova Chamber of Commerce, P.O. Box 99, Cordova, AK 99574, phone 424-7260. There also is a visitor information center at the museum.

The name Cordova probably is derived from the original Spanish name Puerto Cordova (Port Cordova), given to the area by the Spanish naval explorer Fidalgo, who sailed into Orca Inlet in 1790. Modern-day Cordova owes its origins to Michael J. Heney, builder of the Copper River & Northwestern Railway. The town was the railroad terminus and ocean shipping port for copper ore from the Kennecott mines near Kennicott and McCarthy, 112 air miles northeast of Cordova in the Wrangell Mountains. The railroad and the town prospered until 1938 when the mine was closed. Following the end of copper mining, fishing became the area's major economic base. One of the first producing oil fields in Alaska was located in Katalla, some 47 miles southeast of Cordova on the Gulf of Alaska. The discovery was made in 1902 and the field produced small amounts of oil until 1933 when part of the plant burned. (For more about McCarthy, Kennicott, Katalla, and the Copper River Delta, see the Copper River/Wrangell-St. Elias subregion.)

As a result of the 1964 Good Friday earthquake, Cordova's land mass rose 6 to 7 feet, leaving part of its harbor high and dry. In the process of deepening the harbor, the Army Corps of Engineers reclaimed 15 acres of tide-land by building a bulkhead, which served to corral the sand and mud dredged from the harbor basin. The earthquake also damaged the bridge over the Copper River known as the Million Dollar Bridge, but it has been repaired and motorists can drive 2 miles beyond the bridge. The Forest Service is building a viewing area near Childs Glacier. The drive from Cordova to the bridge is 52 miles of beautiful scenery and excellent opportunities to view wildlife.

Supporting the area's economy are the Prince William Sound fishery and fish processing plants. The fishing and canning season for salmon runs from about May to September, with red, king and silver salmon taken from the Copper River area, and chum, king and pink salmon from Prince William Sound. The season for Dungeness crab is March to June and August to December; tanner crab is caught in January; king crab opens in October and continues until the quota is caught.

Government services for the surrounding area also contribute significantly to the job base. The Coast Guard cutter *Sweetbriar* is based at Cordova.

Surrounded by Chugach National Forest and the waters of Prince William Sound, Cordova is a prime staging area for wilderness adventures such as ocean kayaking, hiking, fishing, canoeing, rafting, bird-watching and sightseeing. Numerous guides and outfitters operate from Cordova.

The Forest Service maintains 21 miles of hiking trails in the Cordova area, including trails to Sheridan Glacier, McKinley Lake and Crater Lake. For more information on the hiking trails and other Forest Service facilities, contact the U.S. Forest Service, P.O. Box 280, Cordova, AK 99574, phone 424-7661.

Cordova Historical Society and City of Cordova operate Cordova Museum featuring art, history, geology and marine exhibits. Write Box 391, Cordova, AK 99574; phone 424-6665. In addition to its museum, Cordova has a library and Olympic-sized public swimming pool. There also is skiing from December to May on 3,500-foot Eyak Mountain, which has a chair lift and 2 rope tows. Celebrations during the year include the Silver Salmon Derby from mid-August to the first of September, which offers a $5,000 prize for the heaviest sport-caught silver salmon, and the Iceworm Festival in February, with a parade, arts and crafts shows, dances, ski events and more. Highlight is the 100-foot-long "iceworm" that winds its way through the streets of Cordova.

Cordova, a home-rule city, has all the amenities of a medium-sized city, including a radio station (KLAM-AM), cable TV and a weekly newspaper, *The Cordova Times*. City government address: City of Cordova, P.O. Box 1210, Cordova, AK 99574; phone 424-6200.

Ellamar

Located on the east shore of Virgin Bay in Tatitlek Narrows on Prince William Sound, 180 miles east-southeast of Anchorage, 40 miles northwest of Cordova, 24 miles southwest of Valdez, 2 miles northeast of Tatitlek. **Transportation:** Boat; charter air service from Anchorage or Valdez direct or via Tatitlek. **Population:** About 10 year-round. **Zip code:** 99695. **Emergency Services:** Alaska State Troopers, Valdez; Health aide, Tatitlek; Valdez Hospital.

Private Aircraft: Floatplane landings only at Ellamar. Airstrip located at Tatitlek.

Visitor Facilities: Arrangements for cabin rental may be made through Ellamar Properties based in Anchorage. No laundromat. No stores or supplies available. Boat, aircraft may be chartered. Guide services available. No major repair services or fuel. Fishing/

hunting licenses not available. Roads and dock facilities have been developed for those who purchase lots. Load and off-load dock was completed in 1988. Anchorage and moorings available.

Ellamar, a historic copper mining town, is in the process of being redeveloped as a summer and weekend recreational community by Ellamar Properties Inc. in Anchorage.

Copper was discovered at Ellamar in 1897. By 1902 Ellamar was a bustling town of 700 residents, complete with stores, shops, 3 bars and an opera house. Mines throughout Prince William Sound started closing in 1919 and by the end of the 1920s Ellamar Mining was closed.

The economy was revitalized for a time when 2 cannery operations located at Ellamar, attracted by the dock and labor force from Tatitlek. The first cannery burned down in the 1940s; the second quit operating in the 1950s.

Recreational activities in the area include fishing for salmon and halibut, boating, hunting, cross-country skiing and photography. Whales, sea otters and sea lions frequent the area. Behind Ellamar, 3,051-foot Ellamar Mountain offers good views of waterfalls.

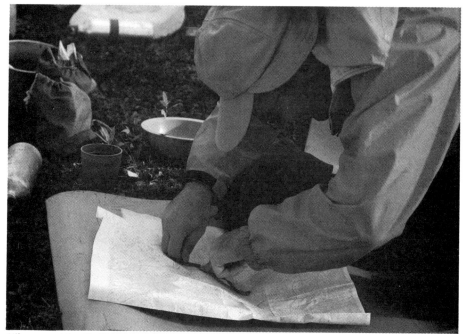

Hiker uses string tied to a compass to measure distance traveled. A map and compass are required gear for all travel in Alaska's backcountry. (Neil O'Donnell)

Columbia Glacier is 12 miles to the northwest.

Communications at Ellamar include a weekly mail plane and a public phone located at Tatitlek. There are no community electricity, sewer or water systems. Water is available from 3 creeks. The nearest church and school are at Tatitlek. Freight arrives at Ellamar by barge or floatplane.

Tatitlek

Located on the northeast shore of Tatitlek Narrows on Prince William Sound, 2 miles southeast of Ellamar, 25 miles south-southwest of Valdez, 40 miles northwest of Cordova. **Transportation:** Boat; scheduled and charter air service from Valdez. **Population: 105. Zip code: 99677. Emergency Services:** Village Public Safety Officer, phone 325-2248; Health Clinic, phone 325-2235; Fire Department, phone 325-2336 or 325-2311.

Climate: Rain frequent summer and winter. High winds possible in winter. January temperatures in Prince William Sound average 16° to 30°F; July temperatures range from 48° to 62°F. Temperatures are seldom below zero or above 75°F.

Private Aircraft: Airstrip adjacent northwest; elev. 25 feet; length 2,200 feet; gravel; no fuel; unattended. Runway condition not monitored, visual inspection recommended prior to using. Use caution, dogs and children on runway at times. No turnaround.

Visitor Facilities: Accommodations and meals at boarding house operated by Tatitlek Village IRA Council, or arrangements may be made to stay at private homes. Laundry facilities available. No banking services or hunting/fishing licenses. Groceries not available. No guide or major repair services. Air charter service available; boats may be available for rent. Fuel available: diesel. Moorage facilities available.

An Indian village in Gladhaugh Bay was reported as "Tatikhlek" by Ivan Petroff in the 1880 census. Around the turn of the century the village was moved to its present location in the shadow of 3,858-foot Copper Mountain.

Many residents of the ruined village of Chenega moved to Tatitlek following the 1964 Good Friday earthquake and tsunami.

The dominent feature in Tatitlek is the blue-domed Russian Orthodox church.

Residents of this Native village make their living primarily by fishing. Tatitlek's traditional subsistence lifestyle was severely disrupted by the oil spill in Prince William Sound in the spring of 1989. (For more on the spill see the Introduction to the SOUTH-CENTRAL/GULF COAST section.) In response to Tatitlek's plight, several Native villages on the shores of nearby Cook Inlet shared their own catch, which volunteers airlifted into Tatitlek.

Bird-watching and wildlife viewing opportunities in the area are good. Seabirds, bald eagles, sea otters, bears and mountain goats are seen frequently.

Communications in unincorporated Tatitle include phones, mail plane, radio and TV. The community is served by 3 churches and a school with grades kindergarten through 12 depending on demand as well as a community college extension program. There are community electricity, water and sewer systems. The village prohibits the sale and importation of alcoholic beverages. Freight arrives by boat and cargo plane. Government address: Village of Tatitlek, General Delivery, Tatitlek, AK 99677; phone 325-2311. Village corporation address: Tatitlek Corp., P.O. Box 1270, Valdez, AK 99686.

Valdez

(val-DEEZ) Located in southcentral Alaska near the east end of Port Valdez on Valdez Arm in Prince William Sound. **Transportation:** Daily scheduled jet service; Alaska Marine Highway Service to Cordova, Whittier and Seward; auto or bus via the Richardson Highway. **Population:** 3,686. **Zip code:** 99686. **Emergency Services:** Alaska State Troopers, phone 835-4359 or 835-4350; City Police, Fire Department and Ambulance, emergency only, phone 911; Valdez Community Hospital, phone 835-2249. To report oil spills to Dept. of Environmental Conservation, dial operator and ask for Zenith 9300, toll free. For Coast Guard Search and Rescue, dial operator and ask for Zenith 5555, toll free.

Elevation: Sea level. **Climate:** Normal daily maximum in January 30°F; daily minimum 21°F. Normal daily maximum in July 61°F; daily minimum 46°F. Snow from October to April. Winds up to 40 mph common in late fall.

Private Aircraft: Valdez, 3 miles east; elev. 120 feet; length 6,500 feet; asphalt; fuel 80, 100, jet B.

Visitor Facilities: Valdez has 6 hotel/motel facilities. Other services include several restaurants and bars, grocery stores, sporting goods stores, drugstore, gift shops, hardware store, hair stylists, public library, museum, post office, and numerous churches. There are several charter boat operators at the small-boat harbor that offer tours to Columbia Glacier and Prince William Sound as well as fishing trips for pink, silver and king salmon and halibut. Several air charter operators offer flightseeing tours.

With its port the most northerly ice-free port in the Western Hemisphere and the Richardson Highway connecting it to the Alaska highway system, Valdez has evolved into a shipping center. This was one reason the city was chosen as the terminus of the trans-Alaska oil pipeline, which stretches 800 miles from Prudhoe Bay on the Arctic Ocean to Valdez.

Valdez's economy depends on the oil industry, the Prince William Sound fishery and tourism.

Raft and kayak trips of Prince William Sound, Keystone Canyon and surrounding rivers are available from local outfitters.

Valdez, a home rule city incorporated in 1901, has all the amenities of a medium-sized city, including 2 radio stations, TV and a weekly newspaper, the *Valdez Vanguard*. City government address: City of Valdez, P.O. Box 307, Valdez, AK 99686; phone 835-4313. For visitor information: Valdez Convention and Visitors Bureau, Box 1603, Valdez, AK 99686; phone 835-2984.

For more information see *The MILEPOST®*, a complete guide to communities on Alaska's road and marine highway systems, and *Where Mountains Meet the Sea*, Vol. 13, No. 1 of *ALASKA GEOGRAPHIC®*. To order, see the ALASKA NORTHWEST LIBRARY section at the back of the book.

Whittier

Located on the Kenai Peninsula at the head of Passage Canal on Prince William Sound, 75 miles southeast of Anchorage. **Transportation:** Chartered air service from Anchorage; Alaska Railroad shuttle from Portage and Anchorage; Alaska Marine Highway System from Valdez and Cordova. **Population:** 333. **Zip code:** 99693. **Emergency Services:** Police, Fire and Medical emergencies, phone 472-2340; Clinic, phone 472-2303; Fire Department, phone 472-2560.

Elevation: 30 feet. **Climate:** Moderate; normal daily temperature for July 56°F; for January, 25°F. Recorded maximum 88°F; minimum -29°F. Mean annual precipitation 174 inches, with 263.5 inches of snow. Winter winds can reach 85 mph.

Private Aircraft: Airstrip adjacent northwest; elev. 30 feet; length 1,500 feet; gravel; no fuel; unattended. Birds in airport area. Runway condition not monitored, visual inspection recommended prior to landing. No winter maintenance; closed from first snowfall until after breakup.

Visitor Facilities: Accommodations and meals available at 2 local hotels. There are several other restaurants in town, along with 2 bars, gift shops, laundry facilities, 4 general stores, a visitors center and a camper park. No banking services. As the gateway to western Prince William Sound, the small-boat harbor is a busy place; marine supplies, charter boats, boat rentals and tours are available. Marine engine, boat and auto repair services available. Hunting/fishing licenses available. A list of guides, outfitters and charter services is available from the city office (address follows). Fuel available: diesel, unleaded, regular and supreme gasoline and marine gas.

One of the town's main attractions is the Whittier Historical and Fine Arts Museum. This museum, operated by a nonprofit organization, is located on the first floor of the Begich Towers. Exhibits include baleen, ivory carvings, Whittier's original communications system, a display showing earthquake damage, Prince William Sound marine life and St. Lawrence Island artifacts. Hours are 2-6 p.m. daily except Tuesday and Thursday.

Whittier, named after the poet John Greenleaf Whittier, is nestled at the base of mountains that line Passage Canal, a fjord that extends eastward into Prince William Sound. The surrounding peaks are snowcapped much of the year and a glacier hangs above the town to the west.

Whittier was created by the U.S. government during WWII as a port and petroleum delivery center tied to bases farther north by the Alaska Railroad and later a pipeline. The railroad spur from Portage was completed in 1943 and Whittier became the primary debarkation point for cargo, troops and dependents of the Alaska Command. No roads lead to this community. Construction of the huge buildings that dominate Whittier began in 1948 and the Port of Whittier, strategically valuable for its ice-free deep-water port, remained activated until 1960, at which time the population was 1,200. The government tank farm is still located here.

The 14-story Begich Towers, formerly the Hodge Building, contains 198 apartments and houses more than half Whittier's population. Now a condominium, the building was used by the U.S. Army for family housing and civilian bachelor quarters. The building was renamed in honor of U.S. Rep. Nick Begich of Alaska who, along with Rep. Hale Boggs of Louisiana, disappeared in a small plane near here in 1972 while on a campaign tour.

The Buckner Building, completed in 1953, was once the largest building in Alaska and was called a "city under one roof." It contained 1,000 apartments, a hospital, bowling alley, theater, library, shops, gymnasium and swimming pool for the use of Army personnel serving at this isolated post. The building is now privately owned and is to be renovated.

Whittier Manor was built in the early 1950s by private developers as rental units for civilian employees and soldiers who were ineligible for family housing elsewhere. In early 1964, the building was bought by another group of developers and became a condominium, which now houses the remainder of Whittier's population.

Since military and government activities ceased, the economy of Whittier rests largely on the fishing industry, tourism and the port.

Recreational activities at Whittier include hiking Shotgun Cove trail; climbing the path to Whittier Glacier; berry-picking; scuba diving; fishing for salmon, halibut, red snapper, cutthroat trout, Dolly Varden, crab or shrimp; sailing, sea kayaking and other water sports; and photography.

Wildlife in the area includes whales, porpoises, sea lions and sea otters. Just across Passage Canal is Kittiwake Rookery, largest of its kind in the world. Whittier is also a berry-picker's paradise: blueberries and salmonberries grow in abundance at the edge of town.

Communications at Whittier, a second-class city incorporated in 1969, include phones, radio (CB Channel 11 and Channel 16 VHF) and TV. The community has a school with grades preschool through 12. There are no churches, but services are held locally. There are community electricity, water and sewer systems. Freight arrives by barge or rail. Government address: City of Whittier, P.O. Box 608, Whittier, AK 99693; phone 472-2327.

Kayakers dry out gear before breaking camp in Prince William Sound's Harriman Fjord. The fjord was named by members of the Harriman Alaska Expedition for Edward Henry Harriman, 1848-1909, organizer and sponsor of the 1899 expedition. (Neil O'Donnell)

▼ A T T R A C T I O N S ▼

National and State Parks, Forests, etc.

Chugach National Forest Cabins

Virtually all of Prince William Sound is encompassed within the 5.8-million-acre Chugach National Forest, and the Forest Service's 22 recreation cabins in the sound rank among the best lodging bargains in the state. (For more on Chugach National Forest, see the Introduction to the SOUTHCENTRAL/GULF COAST section.)

Cost of the cabins is $15 per night per party (increases to $20 July 1, 1990), with access by foot, boat or small plane. For details about cabin rentals, see Cabins in the GENERAL INFORMATION section. You may obtain additional information or make reservations through any Chugach National Forest office: Cordova Ranger District, P.O. Box 280, Cordova, AK 99574-0280; or 201 E. 9th Ave., Anchorage, AK 99501; phone 271-2500. Payment must accompany the cabin application. Special drawings are held for the popular Nellie Martin River cabin during high-use periods. Drawing times and rules are available from the Forest Service office.

Marine Parks

The state of Alaska has established 12 marine parks as part of an international system of shoreline parks and recreation areas stretching from near Olympia, WA, up through British Columbia, and as far north as Prince William Sound. Eventually there may be more than 150 of these parks, most a 1-day boat trip from each other. Following is a list of the 7 marine parks located in Prince William Sound. For more information, contact the Alaska Division of Parks, P.O. Box 107001, Anchorage, AK 99510; phone 561-2020.

Western Prince William Sound

Surprise Cove. Located at the entrance to Cochrane Bay approximately 15 miles east of Whittier along a major route for pleasure boats between Whittier and western Prince William Sound. The park includes 2 small embayments off Cochrane Bay and 2 fresh-water lakes, and offers a well-protected anchorage. Mountain goats are found on nearby peaks; porpoises often are observed at Point Cochrane. A small beach near the entrance to the cove is used as a campsite by kayakers.

Zeigler Cove. Located on the northern shore of the entrance to Pigot Bay on the west side of Port Wells, approximately 14 miles east of Whittier. The cove is on a low, forested point extending into both Pigot Bay and Port Wells. It offers a small, but very well-protected anchorage. There is good hiking in the uplands, and good fishing nearby for red snapper, halibut, pink, chum and king salmon, as well as Dungeness crab.

Bettles Bay. Located on the western shore of Port Wells, approximately 20 miles from Whittier. This large, well-protected bay is a favorite of boaters exploring the Port Wells area, as it is considered one of the most scenic on the west shore. Wildlife in the area includes black bears, sea lions, whales, seals and waterfowl. Fish include halibut, pink and chum salmon and Dungeness crab. An abandoned mine is located approximately 0.5 mile southwest of the park.

South Esther Island. Located at the confluence of Wells Passage and Port Wells in upper Prince William Sound, approximately 20 miles due east of Whittier. This is a popular base of operations for excursions in the Port Wells, Port Nellie Juan and Culross Passage areas. Anchorages are found in both Lake and Quillian bays. Esther Island is very scenic, with a number of 2,000-foot granite peaks. Whales may be observed in Port Wells; sea lions frequently haul out on nearby islands and rocks. Seabirds nest in the area and seals

CHUGACH NATIONAL FOREST CABINS

	SLEEPS	AIR ACCESS	BOAT ACCESS	TRAIL ACCESS	HUNTING	FISHING	BEACHCOMB	SKIFF	STOVE
CORDOVA AREA									
Beach River *(Wheelplane access only at low tide)*	6	•			•	•	•		O&W
Double Bay *(Boat approach difficult at low tide)*	6	•	•		•	•			O
Green Island *(Boaters use caution; uncharted rocks in area)*	6	•	•		•	•			O
Hook Point *(Salmon stream 1 mile east of cabin)*	10	•				•	•		O&W
Jack Bay	6	•	•		•	•			O
Log Jam Bay	4	•			•	•	•		O&W
Martin Lake	4	•			•	•			O
McKinley Lake *(Boat access limited to high water periods)*	6	•	•	•	•	•			W
McKinley Trail *(Road access at Mile 22, Copper River Highway)*	6			•	•	•			G
Nellie Martin River	6	•	•		•	•	•		O&W
Peter Dahl	6	•	•						O
Port Chalmers *(Carry water)*	6	•	•			•			O&W
San Juan Bay	4	•	•		•	•	•		O&W
Softuk Bar *(Wheelplane access only at low tide)*	6	•					•		O&W
Stump Lake *(Wheelplane access only at low tide)*	6	•			•	•	•		O&W
Tiedeman Slough	6	•	•						O
WEST PRINCE WILLIAMS SOUND									
Coghill Lake *(Fishermen bring inflatable boat)*	10	•				•			W
Harrison Lagoon *(No drinking water on site)*	5		•			•			W
Paulson Bay	6	•	•			•			W
Pigot Bay	10	•	•			•			W
Shrode Lake *(Bring stove; wood scarce)*	10	•	•	•		•		•	OH
South Culross Pass *(Anchor in outer bay)*	6	•	•			•			W

The chart above lists cabins alphabetically within each of the 2 major areas of Prince William Sound. The chart shows how many people the cabin sleeps; if the cabin is accessible by air, boat or trail; if hunting, fishing or beachcombing are available; and if the cabin has a skiff or stove. Type of stove provided is indicated as follows; O=oil stove, W=wood stove, G=outdoor grill, OH=oil heater. (The Forest Service does not provide the fuel.) Special features or restrictions are also noted on the chart.

and sea otters also may be seen.

Horseshoe Bay. Located on Latouche Island in southwestern Prince William Sound, approximately halfway between Seward and Whittier. Although somewhat exposed to southwesterly winds, Horseshoe Bay offers the most protected anchorage along the island's shoreline. The bay and island are very scenic, with nearby peaks rising to 2,000 feet. The old gold mining town of Latouche is located 2 miles to the northeast. There is excellent hiking and climbing at nearby Broon Buttes. Whales, seals and sea lions frequent Latouche Passage. Except for recreational lots at the old town of Latouche and an area south of the park, Chugach Natives

Ltd. owns most of the island. Private property should be respected; observe any No Trespassing signs.

Eastern Prince William Sound

Sawmill Bay. Located on the north shore of Port Valdez, approximately 14 miles west and south of Valdez. This large, well-protected bay offers several good anchorages for pleasure boaters and receives considerable use by boaters from Valdez. There is fishing for silver salmon and halibut; crab and clams also available. A U.S. Forest Service cabin is located in the south branch of Sawmill Bay. There is good hiking along Twin Falls Creek and near Devish Lake.

Shoup Bay. Located on the north shore of Port Valdez, 7.5 miles west of Valdez. A well-protected anchorage does not exist in the bay, but short-term or fair-weather anchorages can be found in several areas depending on wind directio n. Shoup Bay is very scenic; 17-mile-long Shoup Glacier extends almost to the bay from the northwest and a large sand spit extends across the mouth of the bay. Mountain goats can be seen on the slopes above the bay, and ducks feed on the tidal flats. Shoup

Glacier is the main tributary of the huge glacier that carved Valdez Arm thousands of years ago. During the 1964 earthquake, an undersea slide from its submerged moraine created a 170-foot-high wave (listed in the *Guinness Book of World Records*). Reportedly the bay emptied and refilled 3 times.

Sea Kayaking

Ease of access from Anchorage, Alaska's largest city, has drawn many paddlers to Prince William Sound, and in recent years the numbers of ocean kayakers there has virtually exploded. But precautions must be taken. The weather can change abruptly; changing wind direction and tidal currents can make paddling a tricky business at best. (For more on kayaking safety, see Boating, Canoeing and Kayaking in the GENERAL INFORMATION section.)

Attractions include tidewater glaciers and abundant wildlife. Most enter the western Sound from Whittier. The Alaska Railroad provides a shuttle service from Portage, approximately 1 hour south of Anchorage by highway, to Whittier. For kayakers with their own equipment, the railroad

Kayakers pause at the face of Columbia Glacier to take photos of this massive tidewater glacier on a sunny day. Icebergs require cautious paddling. (J.H. Juday)

does charge for transporting hard-shell kayaks. The eastern section of Prince William Sound is accessible by air or from Valdez and Cordova.

Kayaks may be rented in Whittier, Cordova or in Anchorage. While many kayakers paddle from Whittier through Passage Canal to other more remote areas of the Sound, it is possible to charter boats for kayak drop-off and pick-up service. Camping sites along Passage Canal during peak holiday weekends are often full and many kayakers are seeking charter boat service to more remote areas. The trip from Valdez to Whittier, a 7-hour ferry ride, is growing in popularity. The trip averages about 140 miles, depending on how closely one hugs the coast and explores the fjords and bays. (See Marine Parks this section for more information on state recreation areas in Prince William Sound.) Further information on boating conditions in Prince William Sound may be found in *Cruising Guide to Prince William Sound, Vol. 1, Western Part and Vol. 2, Eastern Part,* by Jim and Nancy Lethcoe.

Sportfishing

Air charter operators in Prince William Sound know some of the best fishing locations, and several even have cabins and tents near hot spots. Winter fishing for king salmon (up to 30 pounds) from Cordova can prove to be the fishing trip of a lifetime. Other species available from the sound are halibut, pollock, Dolly Varden, cutthroat trout, and pink, sockeye and chum salmon.

For more information consult the current sportfishing regulations or contact the following: Alaska Dept. of Fish and Game, Sport Fish Division, 333 Raspberry Road, Anchorage, AK 99518; phone 267-2218.

Cordova Area. Cordova has all facilities for fishermen, including marine supplies, fuel, guides, charter boats and a small-boat harbor. Inquire locally for good fishing locations. Fish available in nearby waters include the following: silver salmon — late July through mid-September, best in August and September, use herring or spoons (Silver Salmon Derby with top prize of $5,000 takes place mid-August to Sept. 1); pink and chum salmon — good in July and August, use large red spinner or small spoons; halibut and other bottom fish — best fishing in small bays, jig with large lures and bait. Dungeness, king and tanner crab available in nearby bays or coves. Steamer clams common on gravel-mud beaches, razor clams in Orca Inlet

and south of the Copper River Delta. (See listing under Communities.)

Valdez Area. Valdez has all facilities for fishermen, including marine supplies, fuel, guides, charter boats and a small-boat harbor. Inquire locally for good fishing locations. Fish available in area waters include the following: silver salmon — late July through mid-September, excellent in August, use herring, spoons (Silver Salmon Derby with $10,000 top prize takes place the entire month of August); pink salmon — during the summer, use large red spinner or small spoons; king salmon — best late winter and early spring, use herring or large trolling lures; halibut, red snapper and shrimp — available all summer, generally in small bays, jig with large lures and bait. Littleneck clams on most gravel-mud beaches in protected bays at half-tide level in Valdez Arm. Tanner, king and Dungeness crab also available in bays or coves. (See listing under Communities.)

Whittier Area. Whittier has all facilities for fishermen, including marine supplies, fuel, guides, charter boats and a small-boat harbor. Inquire locally for good fishing locations. Fish available in area waters include the following: silver salmon — August, use large red spinner and spoons, herring and large trolling spoons; pink and chum salmon — late summer, use large red spinner and spoons; king salmon — June and early July, use herring, large trolling lures, spoons and spinners; red snapper in Passage Canal and Dungeness crab in Shotgun Cove. (See listing under Communities.)

GIARDIASIS

That crystal clear river or stream may contain a hidden hazard — *Giardia lamblia*. Purify all surface water that is to be used for drinking or cooking to avoid the intestinal disorder Giardiasis, characterized by diarrhea, gas, loss of appetite, abdominal cramps and bloating. Symptoms may appear from a few days to a few weeks after ingestion of the organism.

SPECIAL FEATURES

Cape Hinchinbrook Light Station

This light, which stands 235 feet above the water, marks Hinchinbrook Entrance, main entrance to Prince William Sound from the east. Cape Hinchinbrook, named on May 12, 1778, by the English explorer Capt. James Cook for Viscount Hinchinbroke, is located on the south tip of Hinchinbrook Island, 35 miles southwest of Cordova. Construction of the station was completed on Nov. 15, 1910, at a cost of about $100,000. It was rebuilt after earthquakes in 1927 and 1928 for $91,000. The U.S. Coast Guard automated the station in 1974. The original fresnel lense, approximately 5 feet high, is now on display at the museum in Valdez.

Columbia Glacier

Star attraction of Prince William Sound is Columbia Glacier, one of the largest and most magnificent of the tidewater glaciers along the Alaska coast. Part of Chugach National Forest, the glacier, named by the Harriman Alaska expedition in 1899 for Columbia University in New York City, spreads over about 440 square miles. It is more than 40 miles long with a tidewater terminus more than 6 miles across. The glacier has receded almost a mile in recent years. Scientists are studying its retreat and increased iceberg production, which could pose a hazard to oil tankers from Valdez, about 25 miles to the east. Columbia is expected to recede about 22 miles in the next 20 to 50 years, leaving behind a deep fjord.

The face of the glacier, visible from Colum-

bia Bay, varies in height above sea level from 164 to 262 feet. The glacier extends below sea level as much as 2,300 feet in some places. The bay teems with life at the face of the glacier. An abundance of plankton (microscopic water plants and animals) thrives here, attracting great numbers of fish, which in turn attract bald eagles, kittiwakes, gulls and harbor seals. Seals usually can be seen resting on ice floes or swimming in the frigid water.

The glacier heads in the perpetual snows of Mount Einstein (elev. 11,522 feet), in the Chugach Mountains. Near the glacier's source is Mount Witherspoon (elev. 12,012 feet). Both peaks are visible from the face of the glacier in clear weather.

Boaters can enjoy close-up views of the glacier face and watch giant icebergs calve (break off) from the ice wall. Don't get too close; calving bergs create high waves that can swamp a boat. There are daily and weekly charters by yacht and sailboat from Whittier, Valdez and Cordova as well as several tour boat operations departing from these ports too. Flightseeing tours over the glacier also are available from these communities or Anchorage. And, the glacier may be seen from the Alaska Marine Highway System ferries MV *Tustumena* and MV *Bartlett*, which sometimes approach as close as half a mile from the face of the glacier. Forest Service interpreters staff the weekend runs of these ferries during the summer to point out features of the glacier and the national forest.

ICEWORMS

Although generally regarded as a hoax, iceworms actually exist. These small, thin segmented black worms, usually less than one inch long, thrive at temperatures just above freezing. Observers as far back as the 1880s report that at dawn, dusk or on overcast days, the tiny worms, all belonging to the genus *Mesenchytraeus*, may literally carpet the surface of glaciers. When sunlight strikes them, they burrow back down into the ice.

The town of Cordova commemorates its own version of the iceworm each February in the Iceworm Festival, when a 150-foot-long, multi-legged "iceworm" marches in a parade down Main Street.

—The ALASKA ALMANAC®

KENAI PENINSULA

Introduction

User friendly and easy to reach are 2 phrases that first come to mind when describing Alaska's Kenai Peninsula. The region lies within easy weekend driving distance of Anchorage, and despite its popularity offers delightful backcountry experiences. "The Kenai" is an enticing mixture of mountains and flatlands, sandy beaches and rugged, rocky shoreline, ice fields and glaciers, 2 large, dangerous lakes, and a salmon-choked river that is colored a brilliant turquoise. Adventurous spirits can take their pick of terrain and activity.

Fishing on the Kenai is superb. Huge runs of salmon draw anglers from all over the world. (Chances are, that picture you've seen of the happy fisherman holding up a trophy-sized king salmon was taken on the Kenai.) In the marine waters halibut can weigh more than 300 pounds, and freshwater lakes boast Dolly Varden, rainbow trout and other fine species. Minus tides bring out clammers in droves. Kachemak Bay, besides being rich in fish and other marine life, may be one of the most beautiful places on earth.

The Kenai has well developed hiking and skiing trails, 2 canoe trails, numerous Forest Service cabins to rent, and any number of guides to help you achieve your desired wilderness experience. There are even outdoor equipment rental businesses to be found in the population centers. All of this makes for eminently "do-able" backcountry adventures.

Editor's note: *The disastrous Prince William Sound tanker spill in the spring of 1989 also impacted some beaches in Resurrection Bay and Cook Inlet. Check locally for any areas to avoid or contact the Prince William Sound Users Assoc. 3111 C St., Anchorage, AK 99503; phone 561-1622.*

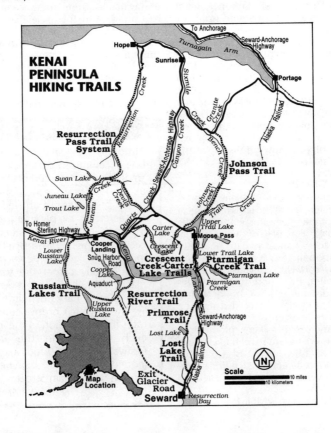

▼ C O M M U N I T I E S ▼

English Bay

Located at the south entrance to Port Graham on the Kenai Peninsula, 10 miles southwest of Seldovia, 3 miles from Port Graham. **Transportation:** Boat; scheduled and charter air service from Homer. **Population:** 172. **Zip code:** 99603 (via Homer). **Emergency Services:** Village Public Safety Officer, phone 281-2218; Alaska State Troopers, Homer, phone 235-8573; Clinic, phone 281-2227.

Private Aircraft: Airstrip adjacent southwest; elev. 27 feet; length 1,800 feet; fuel jet A-1; unattended. Runway not regularly maintained, visual inspection recommended prior to using. Approach to one end of runway restricted by village on hillside; approach to other end restricted by abrupt mountain face.

Visitor Facilities: Visitors with official business may be able to sleep on the floor of the school (281-2210) or in private homes. Village leaders ask that other visitors request permission from the village council (address and phone number below) before coming to English Bay. Store (281-2238) sells limited groceries; no fuel, no hunting/fishing licenses. No bank or laundromat.

The Russians originally applied the name *Bukhta Anglitskaya* (English Bay) to what is now called Port Graham, probably because the area was mapped by the English explorer Nathaniel Portlock in 1789. Portlock, however, called the bay "Grahams Harbour," or Port Graham, and English Bay later was reapplied to a small cove in the bay.

This Native community is unincorporated. Its Russian Orthodox church, built about 1930 to replace the original 1870 structure, is a national historic site.

English Bay has community electricity, water and sewer systems. Communications include phones, TV and CB radios. The village has a school with grades kindergarten through 12. Freight arrives by commercial air service and barge. Government address: English Bay Village Council, General Delivery, English Bay via Homer, AK 99603; home phone of village leader 281-2226. Village corporation address; English Bay Corp., General Delivery, English Bay via Homer, AK 99603.

Halibut Cove

Located on the Kenai Peninsula on Halibut Cove on the south shore of Kachemak Bay, 6 miles southeast of Homer, 125 miles south of Anchorage. **Transportation:** Boat; ferry service from Homer. **Population:** 52. **Zip code:** 99603. **Emergency Services:** Alaska State Troopers, Homer, phone 235-8209; South Peninsula Hospital, Homer, phone 235-8101.

Elevation: 10 feet. **Climate:** Average daily temperature in July, the warmest month, is 54°F; average daily temperature in January, the coldest month, is 19°F. Mean annual precipitation is 18 inches, including 26 inches of snow.

Private Aircraft: No airstrip.

Visitor Facilities: Accommodations are available and there is 1 restaurant. No banking services or laundromat. There are no grocery stores. Supplies are obtained from Homer. Arts and crafts available for purchase at several galleries include octopus ink paintings, oil paintings, fish prints, pottery, batiks and silkscreen prints. Fishing/hunting licenses not available. Guide service available. Boats available for charter; public moorage available. No major repair services or fuel available.

Between 1911 and 1928 Halibut Cove had 42 herring salteries and a population of about 1,000, according to one resident. From 1928 to 1975 the population stayed around 40, most of whom were fishermen. Since 1975 the community has steadily grown and now has a summer population of about 160, including several artists and many fishermen.

Bird-watching in the area is excellent and there are good hiking trails. Kachemak Bay is one of Alaska's most popular spots for halibut fishing, with catches often weighing 100 to 200 pounds. Halibut up to 350 pounds are fished from June through September. Inquire locally or in Homer about fishing guides.

There is a community information office located in Homer at 4390 Homer Spit Road; phone 235-8110.

Communications in unincorporated Halibut Cove include phones, mail plane, radio and TV. There is a community electricity system; water is from creeks or wells. Sewage system is septic tanks or honey buckets. Freight arrives by charter or private boat.

Homer

Located on the southwestern Kenai Peninsula on the north shore of Kachemak Bay at the easterly side of the mouth of Cook Inlet, about 173 miles southwest of Seward and 225 miles via the Sterling Highway from Anchorage (40 minutes by jet aircraft). **Transportation:** Auto-mobile or scheduled air service from Anchorage; Alaska State Ferry System connecting Seldovia, Kodiak, Seward, Port Lions, Valdez and Cordova. **Population:** 4,020. **Zip code:** 99603. **Emergency Services:** Phone 911 for all emergency services. City Police, phone 235-3150; Alaska State Troopers, phone 235-8239; Fire Department and Ambulance, phone 235-3155; Coast Guard, phone Zenith 5555; South Peninsula Hospital, phone 235-8101; Veterinary Clinic, phone 235-8960.

Private Aircraft: Airport 1.7 miles east; elev. 78 feet; length 7,400 feet; asphalt; fuel 80, 100, jet A, B. Attended irregularly. Prior visual inspection recommended.

Visitor Facilities: Homer has many hotels and motels, more than 30 restaurants, a post office, library, museum, laundromats, gas stations with propane and dump stations, many churches, 2 banks and a hospital. There are many boat and aircraft charter operators, boat repair and storage facilities, marine fuel at Homer marina, bait, tackle and sporting goods stores, and grocery stores. Several art galleries and gift shops are found in Homer, as well as a summer theater located on the Homer Spit. For visitor information contact the Homer Chamber of Commerce, P.O. Box 541, Homer, AK 99603. The Pratt Museum and visitor information center, 3779 Bartlett St., is open daily during the summer from 10 a.m. to 5 p.m. Winter hours are noon to 5 p.m., Saturday and Sunday. Admission is $3 for adults, children under 12 free. The museum is closed in January. The U.S. Fish and Wildlife Alaska Maritime National Wildlife Refuge, 202 Pioneer Ave., is open 8 a.m. to 5 p.m. Monday through Friday.

Homer's picturesque setting, mild climate and great fishing (especially for halibut) attract thousands of visitors each year. The more adventurous of these make Homer their jumping-off point for excursions onto beautiful Kachemak Bay or across the bay to Kachemak Bay State Park and State Wilderness Park. Ocean kayaking, beachcombing, nature study, hiking, camping, clamming, fishing and mountain climbing are among the area's activities. Several wilderness guides operate out of Homer. (See BUYERS GUIDE.)

Homer is a first-class city (incorporated in 1964) with a mayor, city manager and city council. It has all modern amenities. Communications include radio stations, TV and a weekly newspaper, *The Homer News*. City government address: City of Homer, 491 E. Pioneer Ave., Homer, AK 99603; phone 235-8121.

For more information see *The MILEPOST®*, a complete guide to communities on Alaska's road and marine highway systems. To order, see the ALASKA NORTHWEST LIBRARY section at the back of the book.

Port Graham

Located on the south side of Port Graham Bay at the southern end of the Kenai Peninsula, 4 miles from English Bay and 28 air miles from Homer. **Transportation:** Boat, and air charter service from Homer and Anchorage; 4-mile trail from English Bay. **Population:** 190. **Zip code:** 99603 (via Homer). **Emergency Services:** Village Public Safety Officer, phone 284-2234; Alaska State Troopers, Homer, phone 235-8573; Clinic, phone 284-2241; Ambulance, phone 284-2227; Fire Department, phone 284-2224.

Private Aircraft: Airstrip adjacent west; elev. 93 feet; length 2,245 feet; gravel; maintained. Visual inspection recommended before landing. Orange highway cones mark the runway.

Visitor Facilities: Accommodations may be available in private homes, on the school floor and at the cannery. Supplies available at 2 stores, 1 operates a snack bar. One bed-and-breakfast. Gas and diesel fuel available. Visitors may anchor boats (under 25 feet) in Port Graham Bay for short periods of time and fly home to avoid long hours on the road and possible rough conditions in Kachemak Bay. A limited number of skiffs available for use by visitors.

The earliest known settlers in Port Graham were Russians who had established a trading post at English Bay. In 1850 the Russian-American Co. established a coal mine at Port Graham but this operation only lasted a few years because it was not economic.

The Aleuts who make up the majority of

the current population came from English Bay and settled in Port Graham in 1911. The Fidalgo Island Packing Co. established a cannery in 1911 which provided the economic base of the community until it burned in 1960. Whitney/Fidalgo rebuilt the cannery in 1968 and sold it to the village corporation in 1983. The cannery continues to be the main economic force in the community. Most of the workers in the cannery are from Port Graham and English Bay. Residents also rely on local fish and game for food.

Communications in Port Graham include phones, radio and TV. The community is served by 2 churches, a school with grades kindergarten through 12 and a preschool. There are community electricity, water and sewage systems. Government address: Port Graham Traditional Village Council, General Delivery, Port Graham, AK 99603; phone 284-2227.

Seldovia

Located on the east shore of Seldovia Bay on the Kenai Peninsula across Kachemak Bay 20 miles south of Homer, 130 miles south of Anchorage. **Transportation:** Boat; scheduled and charter air service from Anchorage or Homer; Alaska Marine Highway System from Homer or Kodiak. **Population:** 565. **Zip code:** 99663. **Emergency Services:** Police, phone 234-7640; Alaska State Troopers, Homer, phone 235-8573; Clinic, phone 234-7825; Fire Department and Ambulance, phone 234-7812 or 911 for emergencies.

Elevation: Sea level to 300 feet. **Climate:** Average daytime temperatures from 21°F in January to 57°F in July. Average annual precipitation 34.5 inches. Prevailing wind is from the north at 10 to 15 mph.

Private Aircraft: Airport 1 mile east; elev. 29 feet; length 2,145 feet; gravel; no fuel; unattended. Runway condition not monitored, visual inspection recommended prior to using. Turbulence southeast and southwest due to winds. Wind shear on approach to runway 16. Taxi service into town available. Seldovia seaplane base, adjacent south; unattended.

Visitor Facilities: Accommodations at 1 hotel, 3 lodges and 3 bed-and-breakfasts. Meals at lodging facilities (except the hotel), or at 3 restaurants. Groceries, clothing, first-aid supplies, hardware, film and sporting goods available. Arts and crafts available for purchase include grass and pine needle baskets, sculpture, batik and other handcrafted items, oil paintings, watercolors, and octopus ink drawings. Fishing/hunting licenses and fishing guide services available. Fuel available:

marine gas, diesel, propane, unleaded and regular gasoline. Public moorage.

Because Seldovia is not connected to the road system, it has retained much of its old Alaska charm. Among activities enjoyed by residents and visitors are halibut, trout and salmon fishing, clam digging at low tides, kayaking and kayaking lessons, picnicking, hiking, cross-country skiing, bicycling (rentals available) and berry-picking. These attractions, along with its proximity to population centers, make Seldovia a convenient, relaxing getaway destination.

Local special events include the Annual Fuzz Ball held in midwinter, a Fourth of July salmon bake and a 10K race on Labor Day.

Seldovia has phones, regular mail service, commercial radio reception from Anchorage and Homer and TV. The community is served by 5 churches and a school with grades kindergarten through 12. There are community electricity, water and sewer systems. Freight arrives by barge, airlines and ferry. Government address: City of Seldovia, P.O. Drawer B, Seldovia, AK 99663; phone 234-7643 or 7878. Village corporation address: Seldovia Native Assoc., P.O. Drawer L, Seldovia, AK 99663; phone 234-7625 or 7890.

For more information see *The MILEPOST®*, a complete guide to communities on Alaska's road and marine highway systems. To order, see the ALASKA NORTHWEST LIBRARY section at the back of the book.

Seward

Located on Resurrection Bay on the east coast of the Kenai Peninsula, 127 miles south of Anchorage by road. **Transportation:** Auto or bus via the Seward Highway from Anchorage; scheduled or charter air service; Alaska Marine Highway System from Kodiak, Homer, Cordova or Valdez; Alaska Railroad from Anchorage (passenger service Thursday-Monday in summer). **Population:** 2,400. **Zip code:** 99664. **Emergency Services:** Police, Fire Department and Ambulance, emergency only, phone 911; Alaska State Troopers, phone 224-3033; Seward General Hospital, phone 224-5205; Coast Guard Search and Rescue, dial operator and ask for Zenith 5555.

Elevation: Sea level. **Climate:** Average daily maximum temperature in July 63°F; average daily minimum in January, 18°F. Average annual precipitation 60 inches; average snowfall 80 inches.

Private Aircraft: Seward airport 2 miles northeast; elev. 22 feet; length 4,500 feet; asphalt; fuel 80, 100, jet A, B. Taxi service available.

Visitor Facilities: Seward has all visitor facilities, including 2 hotels, 3 motels, 7 bed-and-breakfasts, many cafes and restaurants, post office, grocery stores, drugstore, travel agencies, gift shops, gas stations, bars, laundromats, churches, bowling alley and theater. Space for transients at the small-boat harbor. Several charter boat operators, who offer fishing trips, drop-off service and tours of Resurrection Bay, are based at the harbor. Air taxi operators offer flightseeing tours of the area.

Resurrection Bay is a year-round ice-free harbor, making Seward an important cargo and fishing port. Seward's economic base includes shipping, fisheries and government offices; the U.S. Coast Guard cutter *Mustang* is stationed here.

Seward is the gateway to Kenai Fjords National Park, which includes coastal mountains on the southeastern side of the Kenai Peninsula, the 300-square-mile Harding Icefield, glaciers, fjords and substantial populations of marine mammals and seabirds.

Caines Head State Recreation Area, 6 miles south of Seward, is accessible by boat. An undeveloped parkland, it has several WWII bunkers and gun emplacements that once guarded the entrance to Resurrection Bay. (See Attractions this section.)

Seward, a home rule city, has all the amenities of a medium-sized city, including radio stations, TV and a weekly newspaper, the *Seward Phoenix Log*. City government address: City of Seward, P.O. Box 167, Seward, AK 99664-0167; phone 224-3331.

For more information see *The MILEPOST®*, a complete guide to communities on Alaska's road and marine highway systems. To order, see the ALASKA NORTHWEST LIBRARY section at the back of the book.

Tutka Bay

Located on Tutka Bay 9 miles across Kachemak Bay south of Homer. **Transportation:** 45-minute boat ride or 10-minute floatplane or helicopter trip from Homer. **Population:** About 30 year-round. **Zip code:** 99603 (via Homer). **Emergency Services:** Alaska State Troopers, Homer; South Peninsula Hospital, Homer.

Climate: Weather similar to Homer's. Winter temperatures occasionally fall below zero, but seldom colder. Highest temperature recorded in the area 81°F; average annual precipitation 28 inches.

Private Aircraft: No airstrip; helicopter or floatplane landings only.

Visitor Facilities: Accommodations and meals at a local lodge. Water taxi service and fishing and hunting licenses are available at the lodge. There are no stores or other visitor facilities.

This tiny community is scattered about the coves, bights and lagoons of Tutka Bay, the largest bay adjoining Kachemak Bay. Much of the bay is within Kachemak Bay State Park and there is a state fish hatchery in Tutka Lagoon.

Residents earn their livings by boat building, fishing, working for the Alaska Dept. of Fish and Game and producing cottage crafts. One resident reports that what she likes best about Tutka Bay is living close to nature, scheduling activities according to the tides, weather and seasonal abundance of fish, crab, clams, berries and mushrooms.

Tutka Bay has secluded bays, virgin forests and tidepools teeming with marine life. Wildlife that may be seen includes orca and minke whales, sea lions, sea otters, land otters, black bear, seals, porpoises, bald eagles and a wide variety of birds including puffins, cormorants, mallards, oldsquaws, pintails, mergansers, buffleheads, goldeneyes, loons and common murres.

Recreational activities include fishing for salmon, halibut and Dolly Varden, harvesting shrimp and crab, clam digging, photography, berry-picking, beachcombing, sea kayaking, hiking and hunting for bear and ducks.

Communications is by VHF Channel 16, CB Channel 13 or Tutka Bay Lodge, phone 235-3905.

FISHING

Catch-and-release fishing is practiced widely — for the simple reason that anglers in Alaska catch so many fish. Sportfishing licenses are required for both residents and nonresidents. Remember, no matter how far from civilization you may be, a Fish and Game warden is probably nearby, so make sure you have a current fishing license and are acquainted with the latest regulations.

National and State Parks, Forests, Etc.

Caines Head State Recreation Area

This 5,961-acre park is located on Caines Head, a headland that juts into the west side of Resurrection Bay 8 miles south of Seward. To the west the terrain rises sharply to an elevation of 3,200 feet, from which Harding Icefield in Kenai Fjords National Park can be seen to the west and Bear Glacier is visible to the south. To the southeast, across Resurrection Bay, lie Renard (Fox) Island and others that form the gateway to Blying Sound and the Pacific Ocean.

This area has several WWII ammunition storage bunkers and gun emplacements that were used to guard the entrance to Resurrection Bay. Facilities include a latrine, fireplaces, campsites and a picnic shelter at North Beach. Campsites and a latrine are also located at South Beach. Approximately 4.5 miles of trail allow hikers to explore the WWII fort and the area's natural attractions including scenic views of the mountains, glaciers and the bay. A nonresident ranger is on duty.

Access is primarily by boat from Seward, which has all visitor facilities and is served by the Alaska Marine Highway System and a state highway. Adventurous hikers may hike the 4.5 miles from Lowell Point near Seward to Caines Head during periods of low tide.

For more information contact: Alaska Division of Parks and Outdoor Recreation, Southcentral Region, P.O. Box 107001, Anchorage, AK 99510; phone 561-2020. Or, Kenai Area, Division of Parks and Outdoor Recreation, P.O. Box 1247, Soldotna, AK 99669; phone 262-5581.

Chugach National Forest

Much of the eastern half of the Kenai Peninsula lies within this 5.8-million-acre national forest. Most of the forests's devel-oped hiking trails are on the Kenai (see map page 182). For more about Chugach National Forest, see the Introduction to this section.

Almost 200 miles of trails lead to backcountry cabins, ski areas and popular fishing spots on the Kenai Peninsula. Trails include the following:

Chugach National Forest Trails

Resurrection Pass Trail System. This National Recreation Trail — most popular in the Chugach — follows a route originally established in the late 1800s by miners along gold-bearing Resurrection Creek. Eight public-use cabins are located along the 39-mile-long trail, which offers beautiful scenery, fairly easy backpacking and good fishing. The trail follows Resurrection Creek from Hope (on the Hope Highway, which joins the Seward Highway at Milepost 70.3 from Anchorage) to 2,600-foot-high Resurrection Pass, then down Juneau Creek to the Sterling Highway near Cooper Landing at Milepost 53.1 from Seward. To reach the north trailhead, turn left at the Resurrection Pass trail sign at Milepost 16.1 on the Hope Highway and follow Resurrection Creek Road about 4 miles to the beginning of the trail. Road not maintained in winter. The south trailhead (near Cooper Landing) is marked with a large sign at a parking area. Devils Pass trail is a 10-mile trail connecting a trailhead at Milepost 39.4 on the Seward Highway with the Resurrection Pass trail at the Devils Pass cabin at the 2,400-foot elevation. Hiking time for this trail is about 5-1/2 hours. These trails are closed to motorized vehicles Feb. 15 to Nov. 30; and closed to horses during April, May and June due to soft trail conditions. Winter travel is not recommended on the Devils Pass Trail due to extreme avalanche danger. Dead and down wood may be scarce; carry a camp stove. No wood at Devils Pass cabin, which is above tree line. Related USGS Topographic maps: Seward D-7, D-8, C-8 and B-8.

Crow Pass Trail. This 27-mile trail begins within Chugach National Forest, but most of its length lies within Chugach State Park. For information on hiking this trail, see Chugach State Park in the Anchorage/Mat-Su Valley subregion.

Johnson Pass Trail. This 23-mile trail follows a portion of the historic Iditarod Trail, which once extended from Seward to Nome. The trail was an important route for supplies and mail to gold mining camps in the area. Trail is fairly level. It offers spectacular views and emerges in alpine country. Black bears may be encountered along this trail. Fishing for grayling in Bench Lake and rainbow trout in Johnson Lake. Johnson Pass trail has 2 trailheads on the Seward Highway. North trailhead is at Milepost 63.8 from Anchorage; look for Forest Service trail sign on the highway. Turn on a gravel road and drive about 0.3 mile to the trailhead. South trailhead at Milepost 32.6 from Seward in a turnout area marked with a Forest Service sign. This trail is closed to motorized vehicles May 1 to Nov. 30 and is closed to horses during April, May and June. Avalanche danger high in winter, travel not recommended between Mile 2 from the north trailhead and Mile 10.6 at Johnson Lake. No cabins along this trail. Bench and Johnson lakes are above tree line; some dead wood may be found for campfires, but a portable stove is recommended. Related USGS Topographic maps: Seward C-6 and C-7.

Russian Lakes Trail. This 21-mile trail offers Dolly Varden, rainbow trout and salmon in the Russian River at one trailhead, rainbow trout at Lower Lake, Aspen Flats and Upper Lake and Dolly Varden at Cooper Lake. Black and brown bears may be encountered. Three public-use cabins are located along the trail. Trail closed to motorized vehicles May 1 to Nov. 30; closed to horses in April, May and June. Trailhead at parking lot near Russian River campground on the Sterling Highway at Milepost 52.8 from Seward; trailhead also at Mile 12 on the Snug Harbor Road, Cooper Landing. Related USGS Topographic maps: Seward B8, Kenai B1.

Resurrection River Trail. This 16-mile trail connects with the Russian Lakes and Resurrection Pass trails to allow hikers to complete a 72-mile trek from Seward to Hope. The trail parallels the Resurrection River through spruce and hardwood forests. Black and brown bear may be encountered. A public-use cabin is located 6.5 miles from the trailhead. (See Chugach National Forest Cabins this section.) Trail is closed to motorized vehicles May 1 to Nov. 30 and is closed to horses April through June. Trailhead at Mile 7 of the Exit Glacier Road. To find the access, turn west onto Exit Glacier Road from Milepost 3.7 of the Seward Highway. Related USGS Topographic maps: Seward A7, A8, B8.

Lost Lake Trail. This 7-mile trail offers spectacular views and access to alpine country with an elevation gain of 1,800 feet. This trail connects with the Primrose Trail at Lost Lake. The upper trail is not free of snow until mid-July. Brown bear seldom seen, but you might see a black bear in the spring. Salmonberries near Miles 4 and 5 in August. Fishing for rainbow trout at Lost Lake at the end of the trail. Lake is above tree line; little wood for fires, so campers should carry a stove and tent. This is an excellent area for snowmobiling in winter. A snow machine trail leaves the summer trail at Mile 1.5. Access is from a parking area at Milepost 5.2 from Seward on the Seward Highway. Anyone who wishes to use this trail must contact Harbor View Partnership, 1343 G St., Suite #1, Anchorage, AK 99501; phone 274-2634, for permission.

Primrose Trail. This 7.5-mile trail is accessible from Primrose Campground, 1 mile north off the Seward Highway at Milepost 17.2. The Primrose Trail is closed to motorized vehicles May 1 to Nov. 30 and is closed to horses April through June.

This trail now provides the only public access to Lost Lake which was formerly reached from a 7-mile trail which started at Mile 5 of the Seward Highway. The Forest Service was unable to obtain a right-of-way for the Lost Lake trailhead and the first 2/3-mile of the trail in 1988 and until the right-of-way is obtained, access to Lost Lake is limited to the Primrose Trail. Related USGS Topographic maps: Seward A7, B7.

Ptarmigan Creek Trail. This 3.5-mile trail offers a good chance of seeing sheep and goats on mountain slopes. The lake outlet is at Mile 3.5 but the trail continues along the shore for another 3 miles. Popular summer and fall fisheries in the outlet of Ptarmigan Lake and a stream about 1 mile below the outlet. Insect repellent a must in summer. Trail closed to motorized vehicles May 1 to Nov. 30; closed to horses April, May and June. Winter use not recommended due to avalanche hazard. Access from Ptarmigan Creek campground on the Seward Highway at Milepost 23.1 from Seward. Related USGS Topographic maps: Seward B6, B7.

Crescent Lake Trail. This 6.2-mile trail ends at Crescent Lake; public-use cabin at lake outlet. Lake has grayling. The trail, which has a gain of 864 feet, is in excellent condition. Trail closed to motorized vehicles April 1 to Nov. 30; closed to horses April, May and June. Winter use hazardous because of avalanche danger. Access from parking area at Mile 3.5 Quartz Creek Road, off the Sterling Highway at Milepost 45 from Seward. Trailhead about 1 mile beyond Quartz Creek campground. Related USGS Topographic maps: Seward B7, B8, C7, C8.

Carter Lake Trail. This fairly short trail with a 986-foot elevation gain provides access to alpine country. Dall sheep and goats may be seen. Trail steep in places. Rainbow trout fishing at Carter Lake at Mile 2; grayling in Crescent Lake at Mile 3. Trail closed to motorized vehicles May 1 to Nov. 30 and to horses April, May and June. Trail leads to excellent winter recreational area. Access from trailhead on Seward Highway at Milepost 32 from Seward. Related USGS Topographic maps: Seward B7, C7.

For additional information contact any of the following: Chugach National Forest, 201 E. 9th Ave., Suite 206, Anchorage, AK 99501; phone 271-2500 (271-2599 for cabin and general recreation information). USDA Forest Service, Cordova Office, P.O. Box 280, Cordova, AK 99574. USDA Forest Service, Seward Office, P.O. Box 390, Seward, AK 99664. U.S. Forest Service, Glacier Ranger District, P.O. Box 129, Girdwood, AK 99587.

Chugach National Forest Cabins

The 17 Chugach National Forest recreational cabins on the Kenai Peninsula offer a wide variety of terrains and backcountry experiences. Cost is $15 per night per party for these cabins, which are accessible primarily by foot, boat or small plane. Cost increases to $20 July 1, 1990. For details about cabin rentals/furnishings, see Cabins in the GENERAL INFORMATION section.

You may obtain additional information or make reservations through any Chugach National Forest office: Seward Ranger District, P.O. Box 390, Seward, AK 99664-0390; Glacier Ranger District, Monarch Mine Road, P.O. Box 129, Girdwood, AK 99587; or 201 E. 9th Ave., Anchorage, AK 99501; phone 271-2500. Payment must accompany the cabin application. Special drawings are held for the popular Swan Lake, Trout Lake and West Swan Lake cabins during high-use periods. Drawing times and rules are available from the Forest Service office.

Kachemak Bay State Park and State Wilderness Park

Located across Kachemak Bay from Homer, this is one of the largest and most scenic parks in the state system. The state park encompasses 120,000 acres; the adjoining wilderness park 280,000 acres. This largely undeveloped park offers wilderness experiences combining ocean, forest, mountains and glaciers and a variety of wildlife. The waters of Kachemak Bay, reputedly among the most productive in the world, teem with marine life. Shifting weather patterns highlight the spectacular landscape. Twisted rock formations attest to the powerful forces produced by movement of the earth's crust. Scenic highlights and other attractions include Grewingk Glacier, Poot Peak, Gull Island, China Poot Bay, Humpy Creek, Halibut Cove Lagoon and Tutka Lagoon hatchery.

Wildlife: This park offers excellent opportunities for observation and study of wildlife, including seabirds, seals, sea otters, whales, eagles and bears. Field guides to the bay's animals and plant life are available in Homer.

Climate: Kachemak Bay is an arm of the north Pacific Ocean and is subject to severe and unpredictable weather. On clear summer days, seas are usually calm until midmorning, when breezes begin, bringing southwest winds of 15 to 20 knots and seas of 3 to 6 feet. Conditions are often calm again in the evening.

Kachemak Bay's tides, among the largest in the world, are a primary factor affecting boating in the area. The average vertical difference between high and low tides is about 15 feet; the extreme, on large tide cycles, is 28 feet. Tidal currents are substantial and whitewater rapids are frequently created in narrow passages. A tide book, available at local sporting goods stores, is essential. Use the tables for Seldovia and be aware of local variations. For weather and tide information, contact the Homer harbormaster, phone 235-8959.

Since the bay can be extremely rough, visitors should know the capabilities of their boats and themselves. Do not rush; wait for poor boating conditions to improve as they often do in the evenings. Fjords, bays and coves of Kachemak Bay contain navigational hazards; marine charts are available at sporting goods stores in Homer. Also, boaters should stay away from fishermen's buoys as their lines can damage outboard motors and propellers if run over, or the line may be cut. In July and August commercial salmon seiners operate in the area, particularly at Tutka Bay. Seine nets often stretch long distances across

KENAI PENINSULA CABINS

	SLEEPS	AIR ACCESS	BOAT ACCESS	TRAIL ACCESS	HUNTING	FISHING	BEACHCOMB	SKIFF	STOVE
SOUTH KENAI PENINSULA									
Aspen Flats *(On Russian Lakes Trail)*	6			•	•	•			W
Barber *(Handicap access at Lower Russian Lake)*	5	•		•	•	•		•	W
Crescent Lake	6	•		•	•	•			W
Devils Pass *(On Resurrection Pass Trail)*	10			•	•	•			OH
Juneau Lake *(Snowmobile access)*	6	•		•	•	•		•	W
Lower Paradise Lake	6	•			•			•	W
Resurrection River *(On Resurrection River Trail)*	6			•	•	•			W
Romig *(On Resurrection Pass Trail)*	6	•		•	•	•		•	W
Swan Lake *(On Resurrection Pass Trail)*	6	•		•	•	•		•	W
Trout Lake *(On Resurrection Pass Trail)*	6	•		•	•	•		•	W
Upper Paradise Lake	6	•			•	•		•	W
Upper Russian Lake *(On Russian Lakes Trail)*	4	•		•	•	•		•	W
West Swan Lake	6	•			•	•		•	W
NORTH KENAI PENINSULA									
Carbou *(Snowmobile access)*	6			•	•				W
Crow Pass *(Bring stove; no firewood)*	10			•					
East Creek *(Snowmobile access)*	6			•	•				W
Fox Creek *(On Resurrection Pass Trail)*	6			•	•				W

The above chart lists cabins alphabetically within each of the 2 major areas of the Kenai Peninsula. The chart shows how many people the cabin sleeps; if the cabin is accessible by air, boat or trail; if hunting, fishing or beachcombing are available; and if the cabin has a skiff or stove. Type of stove provided is indicated as follows: O=oil stove, W=wood stove, G=outdoor grill, OH=oil heater. (The Forest Service does not provide the fuel.) Special features or restrictions are also noted on the chart.

the water and recreational boaters must carefully maneuver around them.

Activities: Park visitors have many opportunities for boating, beachcombing, camping, hiking and mountain climbing. Protected waters of the park can be visited by large and small craft. Intertidal zones provide an excellent setting for marine studies. Above tree line, climbers and skiers will find glaciers and snowfields stretching for miles. The park is open to hunting and fishing in accordance with state regulations.

Hiking Trails: Several hiking trails, most of them accessible from Halibut Cove, wind through the park. The state Division of Parks and Outdoor Recreation cautions that these trails receive little maintenance and often climb over steep, rugged terrain. Routes may be difficult to find and difficult to hike. Glacial streams cut across several trails and can be dangerous to cross. For the trails listed below the hiking times given are the minimum needed by a person in good physical condition without a pack to hike the trail one way. For more information, contact a state park ranger in Homer or Halibut Cove Lagoon.

Grewingk Glacier Trail. This 3.5-mile trail, rated easy, covers flat terrain through stands of spruce and cottonwood and across the outwash of Grewingk Glacier. It offers superb views of the glacier and surrounding area. There is a small campground about 10 minutes from the trailhead and another at Right Beach, a favorite water taxi drop-off point. Rock cairns mark the trail across the outwash of the glacier. Access to the glacial ice is difficult and hazardous. There is a stream near the junction of this trail and the Saddle Trail. Hiking time is 1 hour, 20 minutes.

Saddle Trail. This 1-mile hike leads over the saddle between Halibut Cove and Grewingk Glacier and is steep on the Halibut Cove side. The trail, rated moderate, accesses the Alpine Ridge and Lagoon trails as well as the Grewingk Glacier Trail. There is no transportation available from the trailhead to Glacier Spit or Halibut Cove unless you've made prior arrangements. Hiking the beach from the trailhead to Right Beach isn't possible because of steep cliffs. The Saddle Trail trailhead is a popular spot to land boats during bad weather. Please respect private property near this trail. Hiking times is 25 minutes.

Alpine Ridge Trail. This steep hike of 2 miles, rated moderate to difficult, begins at the high point on the Saddle Trail and follows a ridge up through spruce and alder to alpine tundra and its many wildflowers. Views of Grewingk Glacier on one side and a deep glacial valley on the other are spectacular. Pick out some landmarks to help find the end of the trail for the trip back down. Hiking time is 1 hour, 40 minues to get above timberline.

Lagoon Trail. This 5.5-mile trail, rated moderate to difficult, winds along Halibut Cove and passes through a boggy area to Halibut Creek Trailhead and delta. Continue on by walking upstream on the south side about 200 yards or walk around the delta on the tide flats. A series of steep switchbacks then leads through a spruce forest up to where the trail intersects Goat Rope Spur Trail at 1,200 feet. The trail continus downhill and south, across Falls Creek and on to the end of the lagoon and the ranger station. Here you may take the stairs down to the stream where a sign directs hikers to the China Poot Lake Trail. Hiking time for Lagoon Trail is 5 hours.

Goat Rope Spur Trail. This short, steep trail, extending 0.5 mile and rated difficult, begins at the highest point on Lagoon Trail. It leads hikers up through a "notch" to alpine areas, where the trail ends. Be sure to bring along your camera to record the views. Hiking time is 1 hour.

China Poot Lake Trail. This 2.5-mile trail, rated easy to moderate, begins at Halibut Cove Lagoon and passes 3 lakes beneath China Poot Peak. About 15 minutes of hiking uphill brings you to the first lake. The trail crosses the lake outlet stream and continues though forest and bog for 30 minutes to Two Loon Lake. China Poot Lake is another 30 minutes away through more spruce and muskeg. Hiking time is 1 hour, 15 minutes.

Poot Peak Trail. This steep, slick, unmaintained 2-mile route, rated difficult, begins across the China Poot Lake inlet stream bridge and heads up to timberline. Climbing the 2,100-foot peak is hazardous because of shifting scree and rotten rock. The trail affords superb views of Wosnesenski Glacier and Kachemak Bay. Hiking time is 1 hour, 30 minutes to 2 hours.

Wosnesenski Trail. This 2-mile trail, rated easy to moderate, begins from the China Poot Peak Trail, about 10 minutes after crossing the inlet stream bridge at China Poot Lake. It winds along the shoreline of 3 lakes formed by a geologic fault. After about 25 minutes on the trail, you will find a good camping area in a stand of cottonwoods by the lake. After another 25 minutes of hiking, the trail climbs over a low saddle and drops down into the valley. Crossing the glacial rivers in the valley can be hazardous. Hiking time is 1 hour, 15 minutes.

Accommodations: While there are few visitor facilities, rough trails lead to various points of interest. A map is available from the park office. There are a few campsites in the Halibut Cove area. Campgrounds are located north of Rusty's Lagoon and on the south portion of Glacier Spit; restrooms, picnic tables and firepits are available. Fresh water is available from streams or springs; all drinking water obtained in the park should be boiled or treated. Open campfires are permitted only on beaches or gravel bars; portable stoves must be used elsewhere. Trash containers are not provided in the park; all litter must be packed out and human waste buried well away from sources of drinking water or trails.

It is recommended that visitors to the park be equipped with high quality outdoor clothing and equipment including rain gear, waterproof boots, gloves and hats, extra clothing, matches, maps, tide book, compass, tent or tarp, sleeping bag, camp stove and extra food. Boaters should be equipped with life jackets, flares, extra line, anchor gear, nautical charts, oars, fire extinguishers and adequate fuel since none is available in the park or at Halibut Cove.

A ranger station is located at the end of Halibut Cove Lagoon, but it is staffed seasonally and the ranger is not always available for assistance. Park visitors should be self-sufficient. Emergency assistance can be obtained through the U.S. Coast Guard Auxiliary (CB Channel 9, VHF Channel 16); Homer harbormaster (CB Channel 17 call number KCN 7188 Base 3, VHF Channel 16 call number WAB 958); or Alaska State Troopers, phone 235-8239.

Access: This park is reached only by plane or boat. Air and water taxi services are available in Homer. Charter boats are available in Halibut Cove. Accommodations and meals are available at Homer, Seldovia and Halibut Cove.

Many of the most attractive beaches and camping sites in the park are privately owned. Respect No Trespassing signs. Much of China Poot Bay is owned by the Seldovia Native Assoc.; contact the association, phone 234-7625, if you wish to use its land. The location of private lands can be obtained from the park office.

For additional information contact: Alaska Dept. of Natural Resources, Division of Parks and Outdoor Recreation, Pouch 107001, Anchorage, AK 99510; phone 561-2020. Or, Kenai District, Division of Parks and Outdoor Recreation, P.O. Box 1247, Soldotna, AK 99669; phone 262-5581.

Kenai Fjords National Park

This park of approximately 580,000 acres encompasses a coastal mountain-fjord system on the southeastern side of the Kenai Peninsula. The park is capped by the 300-square-mile Harding Icefield almost a mile above the Gulf of Alaska. It is believed to be a remnant of the last ice age, when ice masses covered half of the state of Alaska. The ice field's skyline is marked by nunataks, the tips of mountains whose lower slopes are submerged in ice.

Moist marine air from the Gulf of Alaska dumps 700 to 1,000 inches of snow on the ice field each year. The pull of gravity and weight of the overlying new snow causes the ice to spread until it is shaped into glaciers that flow downward, carving the landscape into spectacular shapes. There are 33 named glaciers that radiate from the ice field; along the coast, tidewater glaciers calve directly into salt water.

The park was named after the long valleys once filled with glacial ice that are now deep, ocean-filled fjords. The seaward ends of mountain ridges are dipping into the water, being dragged under by the collision of 2 tectonic plates. As the land sinks into the sea, mountain peaks become wave-beaten islands, sea stacks and jagged shorelines. Glacier-carved cirques become half-moon bays.

Wildlife: Bald eagles nest in spruce and hemlock treetops along the shoreline and mountain goats inhabit rocky slopes. Moose, black and brown bears, wolves and Dall sheep are found in the park. Raucous Steller sea lions live on rocky islands at the entrance to Aialik and Nuka bays; centuries of hauling out have worn the granite rocks smooth. Harbor seals can be seen resting on icebergs. Killer whales, Dall porpoise and sea otters, as well as minke, gray, fin and humpback whales also are found. Thousands of seabirds, including horned and tufted puffins, auklets, petrels, common murres and black-legged kittiwakes rear their young on steep cliffs.

Dolly Varden and 5 species of salmon spawn in clear-water drainages within the park. Shrimp, crabs and other shellfish are found off the coast. Sportfishing for salmon and bottom fish is popular in Resurrection and Aialik bays.

Climate: A maritime climate prevails in Kenai Fjords. Spring is usually the driest time of the year; fall and early winter are wettest. Storms are most common in winter, when waves up to 30 feet have been reported. Mean annual rainfall for nearby Seward is 67 inches. June normally begins the travel season, as spring storms cease and daytime temperatures climb into the 50s and 60s. Mean winter low temperatures range from 0° to 20°F. Warm, sunny days do occur, but they are the exception rather than the rule. Visitors should be prepared for the usual overcast and/or cool days by bringing comfortable wool clothing and good rain gear.

The Park Service cautions that the coastal fjords are rugged, remote and exposed to the stormy Gulf of Alaska. Strong currents flow past them and few landing sites exist. Those entering the fjords without a guide should seek information from the National Park Service headquarters or the U.S. Coast Guard in Seward on mooring areas, navigational hazards and weather. Also, crevasses and foul weather pose hazards on the Harding Icefield and its glaciers. The Park Service says anyone venturing to that area should have experience, good equipment and stamina. It also is recommended that you leave an itinerary with the Park Service or a friend, and contact that office or person upon completion of your trip.

Accommodations: There are overnight accommodations in Seward and Homer. The only overnight facility in the park is a public-use cabin in Aialik Bay. The cabin has no conveniences. Fee for use is $15 per party per night, with a limit of 3 nights per party per year. Reservations may be made up to 180 days in advance and will be confirmed upon receipt of fee. For information or to reserve the cabin, contact the park headquarters. Camping is permitted in the park; no fees or permits are required. The park visitor center is located at 1212 4th Ave., in Seward next to the small-boat harbor.

Access: The park can be reached from the Seward Highway. The unimproved Exit Glacier Road turnoff is at Milepost 3.7 from Seward. This 9-mile dirt road ends at a parking lot next to the Exit Glacier ranger station. The road is open from May to mid-October. Access to the fjords is from the Seward boat harbor.

Activities: A 0.7-mile trail leads to the base of the glacier. Exit Glacier is active; ice may fall at any time so approach the glacier with extreme caution. Ranger-led hikes and evening programs are available during the summer. Schedules are available at the Exit Glacier ranger station or at the visitor center in Seward. A strenuous 3.5-mile trail leads alongside the glacier and up to the Harding Icefield; this is an all-day hike.

The Exit Glacier area is open in winter for skiing, snowshoeing, snowmobiling and dog mushing. Popular summer recreational activities in the park are boating, fishing, wildlife viewing, kayaking the fjords, backpacking and bird-watching.

Boat tours and flightseeing trips within the park may be arranged with several charter boat operators in Seward and air taxi services in Seward or Homer.

Kayaks may be rented in Seward for use in the park and guided kayak trips may be arranged.

For additional information contact: Superintendent, Kenai Fjords National Park, P.O. Box 1727, Seward, AK 99664; phone 224-3175. Related USGS Topographic maps: Seward, Blying Sound, Seldovia.

Wildlife Refuges

Alaska Maritime National Wildlife Refuge

This wildlife refuge includes more than 2,400 parcels of land on islands, islets, rocks, spires, reefs and headlands of Alaska coastal waters from Point Franklin in the Arctic Ocean to Forrester Island in southeastern Alaska. The refuge totals about 3.5 million acres.

Most of this refuge is managed to protect wildlife and the coastal ecosystem. The refuge has the most diverse wildlife species of all the refuges in Alaska, including thousands of sea lions, seals, walrus and sea otters, and millions of seabirds. About 75 percent of Alaska's marine birds (40 million to 60 million birds among 38 species) use the refuge, congregating in colonies along the coast. Each species has a specialized nesting site, be it rock ledge, crevice, boulder rubble, pinnacle or burrow. This adaptation allows many birds to use a small area of land.

Access: Many islands of southcentral Alaska are part of this refuge. Accessible by charter boat from Seward are the Chiswell Islands, 35 miles southwest of Seward, and the Pye Islands, 30 miles west of the Chiswells. On the west side of Cook Inlet, Chisik and Duck islands, 55 miles southwest of Kenai, can be reached by charter boat from Kenai or Homer. The Barren Islands, located between the Kenai Peninsula and the Kodiak Island group, are accessible by boat or air charter from Homer.

Visitors who boat near most of the islands may easily view seabirds and marine mammals. Although permits for landing on the islands are required only for commercial activities, visitors are urged to view wildlife from boats whenever possible to reduce disturbance. Binoculars and spotting scopes are recommended to view wildlife from a distance. Visitors should be prepared for wet and windy weather.

Wildlife: It is estimated that nearly 60 percent of the 105,000 nesting seabirds on the south side of the Kenai Peninsula use the dozen islands of the Chiswell group. Reportedly the largest seabird colony in Cook Inlet — some 80,000 birds, mostly black-legged kittiwakes and common murres — is on 5,700-acre Chisik Island and tiny nearby Duck Island. Other birds that may be seen throughout this area include cormorants, puffins, parakeet and rhinoceros auklets, pigeon guillemots, gulls, kittiwakes, and fork-tailed storm petrels. The arrival of an occasional bald eagle or peregrine falcon will send an explosion of smaller birds from the cliffs in a chorus of cries.

The Chiswells and the Pye Island group harbor Steller sea lion rookeries. Other marine mammals that may be seen in this area are sea otters, seals, porpoises and several species of whales. Land mammals in some areas include black bears and land otters.

The Barren Islands — so-named by Capt. James Cook in May 1778 because of "their very naked appearance" — are anything but barren when seabirds and sea mammals by the thousands arrive annually to give birth and rear their young. The 7 named islands, totaling more than 10,000 acres, are geologic remnants of the Kenai Mountains on the Kenai Peninsula. Some 18 bird species with an estimated population of 500,000 feed in the productive waters around the islands, as do sea lions, harbor seals and whales. Most lands of the refuge are wild and lonely, extremely rugged and virtually inaccessible. Some portions are classified as wilderness. Swift tides, rough seas, high winds, rocky shorelines and poor anchorages hamper efforts to view wildlife.

For more information contact: Refuge Manager, Alaska Maritime National Wildlife Refuge, 202 Pioneer Ave., Homer, AK 99603; phone 235-6546.

Kenai National Wildlife Refuge

This refuge was originally established in 1941 as the Kenai National Moose Range to protect habitat of these huge animals. In 1980 the refuge was renamed and expanded to encompass 2 million acres — 1.35 million of which are wilderness lands. Kenai Refuge is bounded to the northeast by Chugach National Forest, to the southeast by Kenai Fjords National Park and to the south by Kachemak Bay State Park.

The refuge encompasses much of the total land area of the Kenai Peninsula. It includes the western slopes of the Kenai Mountains and forested lowlands along Cook Inlet. These lowlands feature spruce and birch forests intermingled with hundreds of lakes. The Kenai Mountains with their glaciers rise more than 6,000 feet to the southeast. The refuge includes a variety of Alaskan habitats: tundra, mountains, wetlands and forests.

Special features of the refuge include a portion of the Harding Icefield — 1 of 4 major ice caps in the United States — to the southeast. Numerous lakes in the northern lowland region combine to form the only nationally designated trails in the Alaska refuge system: the Swanson River and Swan Lake canoe trails, enjoyed annually by hundreds of visitors.

Other special features are the Tustumena-Skilak benchlands, a unique ecological area of mountain and glacial formations, Dall sheep and mountain goat ranges and brown bear and timberline moose habitat; the Kenai River and its tributaries, which provide vital spawning and rearing habitat for millions of salmon; the Chickaloon watershed and estuary, the major waterfowl and shorebird staging area on the peninsula; and the Skilak Lake area, a road-accessible region with abundant wildlife and scenic vistas.

Climate: Summer temperatures on the Kenai Peninsula generally range in the 60s and 70s and rarely rise above 80°F. The region receives up to 19 hours of daylight in the summer. Winter's extreme low is about -30°F, but extended periods of below 0°F are rare. Late summer and fall weather is wet; rain gear is recommended for hiking and hunting. Annual precipitation on the western side of the peninsula ranges from 19 inches at Kenai to 23 inches at Homer. On the mountainous eastern section, precipitation exceeds 40 inches annually. The first snow normally falls in October; by November the ground is usually snow-covered. Spring breakup on low lakes occurs in May, on high lakes in July.

Wildlife: Nearly 200 species of amphibians, birds and mammals live in or seasonally use the refuge. Mammals include moose, brown and black bear, caribou, Dall sheep, mountain goat, wolverine, wolf, coyote, river otter, beaver, muskrat, lemming, marten, red squirrel, shrew, lynx, porcupine, snowshoe hare, weasel, red fox and hoary marmot.

Birds found on the refuge include trumpeter swan, bald and golden eagles, peregrine falcon, northern pintail, sandhill crane, arctic tern, gulls, lesser Canada geese, mallard, green-winged teal, woodpeckers, ptarmigan, spruce grouse, cormorant, great horned owl, snow geese, junco, Swainson's thrush, common redpoll and many more.

The Kenai River king salmon fishery is world renowned. The river is reputed to support the largest genetic strain of king salmon anywhere. The world's record sport-caught king salmon, weighing 97-1/4 pounds, was caught here in 1985. Other fish occurring in refuge waters include red, pink and silver salmon, lake trout, Dolly Varden, rainbow trout, steelhead, kokanee, grayling and arctic char.

Access: The Kenai Refuge is bisected by the Sterling Highway. Secondary access roads are Skilak Lake Loop Road, Swanson River Road, Swan Lake Road and Funny River Road. The northern refuge boundary is 20 air miles from Anchorage. Airports are located at Kenai, Soldotna and Homer. The refuge also is accessible along river trails and by float- and skiplane to many lakes. However, some lakes are closed to aircraft to protect wildlife. Be sure to check with the refuge office regarding which lakes are open to aircraft landings. To reach refuge headquarters, drive south on the Sterling Highway to Soldotna and turn left after crossing the Kenai River bridge. Follow the signs to the office.

Accommodations: The refuge has 15 road-accessible public campgrounds with tables, fireplaces, parking spurs, boat ramp, water and restrooms. Several developed areas require visitors to take their trash with them. Camping is restricted to 3 consecutive days at Kenai-Russian River campground, 7 days at Hidden Lake campground and 14 days elsewhere. Camping along refuge roads is permitted only at improved sites. Backcountry camping opportunities vary from fly-in and boat-in locations to sites accessible only by trail. Use minimum-impact techniques in all backcountry areas. Build fires in established fire rings if possible; use only dead and downed timber and camp stoves where firewood is scarce. Pack out all trash.

Activities: Fishing, canoeing, hiking, hunting, bird-watching and photography are all popular activies in the refuge. More than 200 miles of trails are found in the refuge, several of which provide access to alpine benchland open to off-trail hiking.

Hiking Trails: There are 9 trails in the Skilak Lake area with trailheads on the Sterling Highway or the Skilak Lake Loop Road:

Fuller Lakes Trail: 4.8 miles to the lakes; elevation range 300 to 2,000 feet; rated strenuous. Grayling in South Fuller Lake. This is bear country. Trailhead at Milepost 110.2 from Anchorage on the Sterling Highway.

Skyline Trail: 3 miles round-trip; elevation gain 1,800 feet; rated very strenuous. Trail begins about 0.5 mile west of Lower Jean Lake Campground, 2.5 miles east of Mystery Creek Road along the Sterling Highway. Provides quick access to mountains, beginning in forest and emerging above treeline in about 0.75 mile; it gradually disappears about 1.25 mile from the trailhead in a beautiful alpine area. Spectacular views; berry-picking. Winter travel not recommended because of avalanche hazard. Related USGS Topographic map: Kenai C-1.

From the Skilak Lake Loop Road junction at Milepost 110.8 from Anchorage the trails are as follows:

Surprise Creek Trail: 4.2 miles; elevation range 300 to 2,500 feet; steep, rated strenuous; minimum maintenance. A river crossing is

---

MOSQUITOES

To avoid mosquitoes, hike above timberline in June and July and save those woodsy trails for early spring or the fall.

---

necessary to reach the trailhead.

Kenai River Trail: 6.3 miles to Skilak Lake and beyond; elevation range 400 to 1,000 feet; rated moderate.

Hidden Creek Trail: 1.4 miles to Skilak Lake; elevation range 450 to 200 feet; rated easy. Large driftwood on shore make for interesting photos.

Skilak Lookout Trail: 2.6 miles; elevation range 700 to 1,450 feet; rated moderate. Trail offers glimpses of Skilak Lake and climbs to a knob that provides panoramic view of the lake and surrounding area. Round-trip is 4 to 5 hours.

Bear Mountain Trail: 1 mile; elevation range 900 to 1,400 feet; rated moderate.

Seven Lakes Trail: 7 miles; relatively level; wet in some places; rated easy. Starts at Engineer Lake campground parking lot and links Engineer Lake with Hidden, Kelly, Petersen and other smaller lakes.

Cottonwood Creek Trail; 3.1 miles; elevation range 200 to 2,200 feet; steep, rated strenuous; minimum maintenance. Trailhead on the south side of Skilak Lake. No road access to trail; boat ramps at campgrounds on lake.

The **Funny River Horse Trail** is reached via the Funny River Road, which branches off the Soldotna Airport Road near the airport. Also for hiking. Trail is 20.8 miles long; elevation range 250 to 2,200 feet; rated moderate. Provides access to alpine benchlands. Minimum maintenance.

On the northern shore of Tustumena Lake there are 3 trailheads. None of these trails is accessible by road, although there is a road-accessible campground with a boat ramp at the outlet of Tustumena Lake to the west. These trails are:

Bear Creek Trail: 16.5 miles; elevation range 100 to 3,200 feet; rated moderate; minimum maintenance.

Moose Creek Trail: 7.7 miles; elevation range 100 to 3,200 feet; rated moderate; minimum maintenance.

Lake Emma Trail: 4.6 miles; elevation range 100 to 2,500 feet; rated strenuous; minimum maintenance.

Two short, level, easy trails leave the Swanson River Road, which joins the Sterling Highway at Milepost 136.5 from Anchorage. Trailhead for the 1-mile **Silver Lake Trail** is at Milepost 9.1 from the junction on the Swanson River Road and the 1.3-mile **Drake-Skookum Lakes Trail** begins at Milepost 13.3.

Canoe Trails: The Swanson River Road also provides access to popular canoe trails. Both trails provide excellent opportunities to see many kinds of wildlife in their natural habitat. Cow moose visit this area to give birth in late May or early June. Many species of songbirds, shorebirds and waterfowl nest along the lakeshores, marshlands and surrounding forests. Beaver inhabit many lakes and streams. Keep your distance from wildlife. Remember that cow moose and sow bears are very protective of their young and it is dangerous to approach them, especially in spring and summer. Also, do not disturb nesting birds by approaching their nests.

Canoe or kayak parties are limited to 15 people or less; register at the entrance to each trail. All trails and portages are well marked. Minimum-impact camping is encouraged. A camp stove is recommended; if you must build a fire, use established fire rings. Use only dead or downed wood, do not cut living trees or brush for bedding or any other purpose. Wash dishes away from lakes or streams; boil or treat all drinking water. Bury human waste 100 yards from campsites and water sources, and pack out all trash. Life preservers must be carried; rain gear and waterproof footwear are recommended. *NOTE: Lakes can become dangerous during high winds. Stay close to shore and watch the weather.* Canoe rentals and shuttle service available in Sterling and Soldotna.

Swanson River Canoe Trail. This 80-mile route links more than 40 lakes with 46 miles of the Swanson River. The entire route can be traveled in less than a week. Portages between lakes are generally short and cross level or slightly hilly terrain. Longest portage is about 1 mile. Rainbow trout, Dolly Varden and some red and silver salmon are found in most of the lakes, except Berry, Redpoll, Twig, Eider, Birchtree and Olsjold lakes. The first trailhead is on the Swanson River Road at Milepost 14.9 from the junction with the Sterling Highway. Enter the Swanson River at a campground here and float downstream 1 or 2 days to Captain Cook State Recreation Area. To make the entire 80-mile trip, take Swan Lake Road, which turns off to the right from Swanson River Road. Drive about 12 miles to near the end; take a branch to the left and drive a bit farther to a parking area. Carry your canoe or kayak down to Paddle Lake. Refer to the Fish and Wildlife Service

pamphlet *Canoeing in the Kenai National Wildlife Refuge* for a map of all the routes and other details. Related USGS Topographic maps: Kenai C-2 and C-3, D-2 and D-3.

Swan Lake Canoe Trail. Separate from and south of the Swanson River canoe trail, this 60-mile route connects 30 lakes with forks of the Moose River. Terminus of the trip is the confluence of the Moose and Kenai rivers at the Moose River bridge on the Sterling Highway. This route can be traveled in less than a week. Longest portage is about 1 mile. Rainbow trout, Dolly Varden and silver salmon are found in most lakes, except for Birch, Teal, Mallard, Raven, Otter and Big Mink lakes. The west entrance is off the Swan Lake Road at the end of a short trail to Canoe Lake. The east entrance is farther along the Swan Lake Road at Portage Lake. The west and east entrances are only about 6 miles apart.

Consult the canoeing pamphlet described above for details. Related USGS Topographic map: Kenai C-2.

For additional information contact: Refuge Manager, Kenai National Wildlife Refuge, P.O. Box 2139, Soldotna, AK 99669; phone 262-7021.

The Rivers

Kenai River. This river heads at Kenai Lake on the Kenai Peninsula and flows west 75 miles to Cook Inlet at Kenai. Much of this river is located in the Kenai National Wildlife Refuge. It ranges from Class II to III and features an exciting white-water canyon for the experienced paddler. This trip is suitable for kayak, raft or experienced canoeists.

Access this river at turnouts near the Kenai River bridge on the Sterling Highway at Milepost 100.8 from Anchorage for the 17-mile stretch to Skilak Lake. Or put in at the bridge at Milepost 106. Be alert for the Class III rapids at Schooner Bend below the second put-in point; stay close to the right bank. The most exciting rapids on this river are just downstream from Jean Creek; the 2-mile-long canyon is rated Class IV. This stretch should be run by experienced paddlers only; vertical walls prevent lining. The river braids before it enters Skilak Lake and there may be sweepers or logjams.

Paddle 6 miles on the lake to the Upper Skilak Lake campground. Strong winds on the lake may be hazardous, so stay close to shore. There are several miles of rock bluffs along this stretch, which means there is no place to take out if the winds suddenly whip up. From the upper campground, it's 7 miles of paddling to Lower Skilak Lake campground

---

BACKPACKING

If you pack it in, pack it out. Practice minimum-impact camping.

---

and 2 miles farther to the Kenai River outlet. There are Class III rapids 12 miles downriver from the outlet.

Fish available on this trip include Dolly Varden, rainbow trout and pink, silver, red and king salmon. (Also see Sportfishing this section.)

Exit the river at Soldotna or Kenai or at numerous other points in between.

Related USGS Topographic maps: Seward B-8, Kenai B-1, B-2, B-3, C-2, C-3, and C-4.

Sea Kayaking

Ease of access from Anchorage, Alaska's largest city, has drawn many paddlers to the Kenai Peninsula's enticing ocean waters. But precautions are necessary. The weather can change abruptly, stranding kayakers. Changing wind direction and tidal currents can make paddling a tricky business at best. For more information on kayaking safety, see Boating, Canoeing and Kayaking in the GENERAL INFORMATION section. Among the Kenai Peninsula's most popular places for kayakers are:

Kachemak Bay. Attractions include abundant wildlife. Since one can drive to Homer and enter Kachemak Bay, this is one of the most easily accessed kayaking destinations. There is a lot of private property within Kachemak Bay State Park so kayakers should take care to obtain permission before camping in these areas. Because of a prevailing southwesterly wind on sunny summer days one should plan to return to Homer before 11 a.m. or after 7 p.m. (See Kachemak Bay State Park this section for more information.)

Kenai Fjords National Park. Attractions include tidewater glaciers and abundant wildlife. Access is by air or boat charter from Seward. Kayaks can be rented in Seward or Anchorage. A number of guides and outfitters offer trips in this area. (See Kenai Fjords National Park this section for more information about attractions and access.)

Resurrection Bay. Attractions include abundant wildlife and challenging conditions. Seasoned Alaskan kayakers find paddling conditions in Resurrection Bay unpredictable. Seward is the access point which can be reached by highway or train. Kayaks can be rented in Seward. (See Seward under Communities, this section for more information.)

Sportfishing

The Kenai Peninsula is a sportfishing paradise. And if many of the finest lakes and rivers are accessible by road, there are any number of out-of-the-way spots where angling is still a solitary sport. Whether your choice is a placid lake, a swift running river, or saltwater swells, the fishing is first class.

For more information about fishing on the Kenai Peninsula, consult the current sportfishing regulations or contact the following: Alaska Dept. of Fish and Game, Sport Fish Division, 333 Raspberry Road, Anchorage, AK 99518; phone 267-2218, or Alaska Dept. of Fish and Game, P.O. Box 234, Homer, AK 99603; phone 235-8191.

Below are some of the favorite fishing destinations on the Kenai:

Bench Lake. A 1-mile-long lake located on the Kenai Peninsula in Chugach National Forest at the head of Bench Creek, 0.5 mile from Johnson Lake and 22 miles southeast of Sunrise. Lake is about halfway in on the 23-mile-long Johnson Pass trail. Arctic grayling available, best June to September, use flies or small spinners. No cabin on trail; lake above tree line.

Crescent Lake. A 6-mile-long lake on the west side of Madson Mountain on the Kenai Peninsula in Chugach National Forest. Fish available: grayling — best July to September, use flies or small spinners. Check ADF&G regulations for restrictive seasons and bag limits. Accessible by 15-minute floatplane flight from Moose Pass or via the 6.2-mile Crescent Lake trail. See Chugach National Forest Trails this section. Public-use cabin at lake outlet.

English Bay. Located at community of English Bay on the Kenai Peninsula 10 miles southwest of Seldovia. Fly-in fishing for red salmon during June, fly-fishing only upstream to lower lake. *NOTE: Some land in area belongs to English Bay Native Corp. Check at village for location.* (See listing under Communities.)

Fuller Lakes. Located in Kenai National Wildlife Refuge. Accessible by the 4.8-mile-long Fuller Lakes trail from the Sterling High-way. Spring, summer and fall fishery for grayling in South Fuller Lake, use flies; Dolly Varden — available year-round in North Fuller Lake, use bait, spinners, flies. This is bear country.

Grayling Lake. This 0.3-mile-long lake is located on the Kenai Peninsula 4.5 miles south of Kenai Lake and 10 miles north of Seward. Accessible by the Forest Service's 1.6-mile-long Grayling Lake trail, which leaves the Seward Highway at Milepost 13.2 from Seward. Fish available: 10- to 20-inch grayling — May to October, use flies. Watch for moose in the area.

Johnson Lake. A 0.8-mile-long lake

located within Chugach National Forest on the Kenai Peninsula, at the head of Johnson Creek, 0.5 mile from Bench Lake, 22 miles southeast of Sunrise. Lake is about halfway in on the 23-mile-long Johnson Pass trail. Fish available: rainbow trout — use flies, lures or bait. No cabin on trail; lake above tree line. (See Chugach National Forest Trails this section.)

Juneau Lake. A 1-mile-long lake located within Chugach National Forest on the Kenai Peninsula, 25 miles southwest of Hope. Accessible via the Resurrection Pass trail from the Sterling Highway at Milepost 53.1 from Seward. (See Chugach National Forest Trails this section.) Lake located 6 miles up trail. Fish available: summer fishery for rainbow trout — use flies, lures or bait; lake trout — use spoons or plugs; whitefish — use flies or eggs. Campground at lake.

Kachemak Bay. Kachemak Bay and Cook Inlet are popular locations for halibut fishing, with catches often weighing 100 to 200 pounds. Halibut, up to 350 pounds, from June through October. Other fish: bottom fish — use herring or clams; king salmon — up to 70 pounds, troll with herring or large lures, June and July; pink salmon — 4 to 5 pounds, July and August, use small spoons; silver salmon — to 15 pounds, August and September, use small weighted spoons, eggs and herring; red salmon — to 4 pounds, July and August, use small weighted spoons, wet flies and coho streamers; Dolly Varden — June through September, use small weighted spoons, eggs, or shrimp; rainbow trout — taken from nearby streams from April to October, try candlefish (eulachon) for bait. Fishing guides available in Homer. Dungeness crab can be caught in the bay in early spring and late fall. Several varieties of clams can be dug on nearby beaches from February to May and September to December. Shrimp also are available.

Lost Lake. A 1.5-mile-long lake located at the head of Lost Creek on the Kenai Peninsula within Chugach National Forest, 10 miles north of Seward. Accessible via the 7-mile-long Lost Lake trail from the Seward Highway at Milepost 5.2 from Seward. Obtain permission from landowner to hike-in from the south or hike from the north via Primrose Trail. (See Chugach National Forest Trails this section.) Rainbow trout available — use flies, lures or bait. Trail not free of snow until July. No cabins. Lake above tree line; little wood for fires, campers should carry stove and tent.

Russian Lakes. Located on the Kenai Peninsula within Chugach National Forest about 25 miles northwest of Seward. Accessible via the 21-mile-long Russian Lakes trail from the Sterling Highway at Milepost 52.8 from Seward. Rainbow trout — available at Lower Russian Lake (Mile 2.6) and at Upper Russian Lake (Mile 12), use flies, lures or bait. Dolly Varden — available at Cooper Lake (Mile 21), use bait, spinners or flies. Black and brown bears may be encountered. Public-use cabins available. (See Chugach National Forest Trails this section.)

Seldovia. Located on the Kenai Peninsula 20 miles across Kachemak Bay south of Homer, 130 miles south of Anchorage. Accessible by boat, scheduled and charter air service from Homer and Alaska Marine Highway System from Homer or Kodiak. Area fishing includes the following: Seldovia Bay, king, silver and red salmon — June 20 through September, use small spinners; halibut — average size, June 20 to September, use herring. Excellent bottom fishing. Fishing guides and skiffs available in Seldovia, which has food and lodging facilities. Outside Beach, 1.9 miles from Seldovia, has great fishing, casting from beach into surf for silver salmon — July 1 to 30, use any shiny lure. Silver and chum salmon and trout fishing available in Rocky River, 17 miles southeast of Seldovia, during August, use red spinning lures. NOTE: Rocky River is on Native-owned lands and a fee for fishing is required. Contact Port Graham Corporation, Port Graham, via Homer, AK 99603, for details. (See listing under Communities.)

Seward Area. Seward has all facilities for fishermen, including marine supplies, fuel, guides, charter boats and a small-boat harbor. Inquire locally for best fishing locations. Fish available in Resurrection Bay include the following: silver salmon — to 20 pounds, use herring, troll or cast, July to October (Silver Salmon Derby with more than $100,000 in prizes takes place in August); bottom fish — flounder, halibut to 200 pounds, and cod, year-round, jig with large lures and bait. (See listing under Communities.)

Swan Lake. A 2-mile-long lake near the head of the Chickaloon River on the Kenai Peninsula within Chugach National Forest, 22 miles southwest of Hope. Accessible via the Resurrection Pass trail from the Sterling Highway at Milepost 53.1 from Seward. Lake located 9 miles up trail. Summer fishery for rainbow trout — use flies, lures or bait; lake trout — use spoons or plugs; Dolly Varden — use bait, spinners or flies; and red salmon — use spoons or flies. Campground at lake.

KODIAK

Introduction

A lush green island rich in Russian history, huge brown bears, bald eagles, salmon and magnificent scenery, Kodiak lies in the Gulf of Alaska less than an hour's flight from Anchorage. The 100-mile-long island is the largest in Alaska and the second largest in the United States. It is one of some 200 islands which make up the Kodiak Archipelago.

A turbulent history of foreign conquest and natural disasters sets Kodiak apart. A brutal occupation by Russian fur traders beginning the late 1700s almost succeeded in destroying the thriving, sophisticated Kodiak Native culture. Overhunting, meanwhile, came near to wiping out the sea otters whose fur pelts had brought the Russians in the first place. The 1867 sale of Alaska to the U.S. brought an end to Russian rule, but Kodiak's Russian past remains alive today in its place names, the names of its people, and in the striking onion-domed Russian Orthodox church in the city of Kodiak.

Two natural disasters shaped Kodiak's history. In June 1912 a volcano on the mainland across Shelikof Strait erupted, blanketing Kodiak in a choking, poisonous cloud of ash. Everything was smothered under a food and a half of Novarupta's volcanic debris. It took years for the islands and the fish and wildlife to recover. Then in 1964 disaster struck again. Tidal waves from the Good Friday earthquake that also devastated Anchorage, Seward, Valdez and other communities wiped out downtown Kodiak, the fishing fleet, processing plants, canneries, and 158 homes. Again, slowly, Kodiak recovered to become today a bustling community whose economic mainstay is commercial fishing.

Hunters from all over the world come to Kodiak for its trophy-class brown bear. Two thirds of Kodiak is given over to wildlife refuge, and here these big creatures roam freely. In summertime human anglers challenge the bears for salmon. The Karluk River sees especially strong runs of kings, and it is no accident that the river and Karluk Lake are also prime brown bear country. Fishermen beware!

Kodiak calls itself the Emerald Island, and summers bring lush, tall green grass and a rainbow of wildflowers dotting every meadow. Just off the rugged coastline gray, humpback and minke whales spout and breach. Sea otters and sea lions frolic near the surface, while the saltwater depths hold halibut just waiting to snap at a fisherman's lure.

The Alaska Dept. of Fish and Game offers advise to hunters that also holds true for kayakers, hikers, campers, and other adventurers. Prepare for bad weather with high quality rain gear and a tent with a separate rainfly designed to withstand heavy winds. Given Kodiak's stormy maritime climate, rain, snow and high winds can be expected at any season. Hypothermia is a constant threat. Waterproof matches and enough food for several extra days are also recommended. (Source: "Information for Non-Resident Hunters Intending to Hunt with Registered Guides," photocopied pages provided by ADF&G, P.O. Box 3-2000, Juneau, AK 99802.)

Editor's note: *Oil from the disastrous Prince William Sound tanker spill in the spring of 1989 drifted out of the sound and made its way to some of Kodiak's beaches. Check locally for any areas to avoid or contact the Prince William Sound Users Assoc., 3111 C St., Anchorage, AK 99503; phone 561-1622.*

Floatplanes and boats are the only access to islands in the Kodiak archipelago. (USFS)

Akhiok

(AH-ke-awk) Located at Alitak Bay on the south side of Kodiak Island 80 miles southwest of the city of Kodiak, 340 miles south-southwest of Anchorage. **Transportation:** Boat; scheduled or charter air service from Kodiak. **Population:** 109. **Zip code:** 99615. **Emergency Services:** Village Public Safety Officer, phone 836-2203; Alaska State Troopers, Kodiak, phone 486-4121; Health aide; Volunteer Fire Department.

Elevation: 50 feet at airport. **Climate:** Strong marine influence, characterized by moderately heavy precipitation, cool temperatures, high clouds and frequent fog. Humidity generally high, temperature variation small. Little or no freezing weather. Average temperatures from 25° to 54°F. Annual precipitation 35 inches.

Private Aircraft: Airstrip 1 mile southwest, elev. 50 feet; length 3,100 feet; gravel; no fuel; unattended. Runway surface has many sharp rocks. Runway condition not monitored, visual inspection recommended prior to using. No public transportation to village.

Visitor Facilities: No hotel; arrangements may be made to stay in private homes. No restaurant, banking services or laundromat. Limited groceries may be purchased. No arts or crafts available for purchase. Fishing/hunting licenses not available. No guide services, rental transportation, major repair services or public moorage facilities. Fuel available: marine gas, diesel, regular.

The name Akhiok was reported in the 1880 census. The village was renamed Alitak during WWI to avoid confusion with a village near Bethel called Akiak. The name later was changed back to Akhiok. Residents of Kaguyak relocated to Akhiok after the 1964 earthquake and tsunami washed out their village. The community was incorporated as a second-class city in 1972.

No roads connect Akhiok to any other town on Kodiak Island; a foot trail leads to the cannery.

The village is located adjacent to Kodiak National Wildlife Refuge. The community's Russian Orthodox church, Protection of the Theotokos Chapel, which was built around 1900 on the site of an earlier structure, is on the National Register of Historic Places.

The community originally was a sea otter hunting settlement. With the decline of the sea otter industry, however, the village became oriented toward fishing, which today forms the basis of its economy. Many of the residents are commercial fishermen. Other employers include the cannery, school, health services, the city and occasional construction jobs. Almost all of Akhiok's residents depend on subsistence fishing and hunting for various food sources. Species harvested include salmon, crab, shrimp, scallop, clam, duck, seal, deer, rabbit and bear.

Communications in Akhiok include phones, shortwave radio, mail plane and TV. The community has a school with grades kindergarten through 12. There are community electricity, water and sewage systems. Freight arrives by barge or plane. Village government address: City of Akhiok, P.O. Box 5050, Akhiok, AK 99615; phone 836-2229. Village corporation address: Akhiok/Kaguyak Inc., Akhiok Rural Station, Akhiok, AK 99615.

Danger Bay

Located at Kazakof (Danger) Bay on Afognak Island, approximately 20 miles north of Kodiak. **Transportation:** Boat or charter air service. **Population:** Private logging camp; size varies. **Zip code:** 99615. **Emergency Services:** Alaska State Troopers, Kodiak; Kodiak Hospital, phone 486-3281; Coast Guard, call operator and ask for Zenith 5555.

Climate: Summers moist and cool, with highs occasionally up to 75°F. Winters windy, wet and gray, with low temperatures reaching 0°F. Average temperature from November to the first of March is 20°F.

Private Aircraft: No airstrip. Floatplane landings only.
Visitor Facilities: No restaurant, laundromat or banking services. No stores; supplies are obtained from Kodiak. No rental transportation; public moorage facilities available. Rustic recreation cabins may be rented.

Alaska's only elk herds live on Afognak and nearby Raspberry Island. Other wildlife includes Sitka black-tailed deer and Kodiak brown bear, as well as otter, fox and marten. Fishing is active from late May to mid-September for pink, red, chum and coho salmon, Dolly Varden and rainbow trout. Halibut also are available. Waters around Afognak are fished commercially for salmon; tanner and Dungeness crab; halibut; and herring. Photography, hiking and kayaking are also favorite pastimes.

Air and boat charters are available in Kodiak for the 15-minute flight or 1-1/2- to 3-hour boat trip to Kazakof Bay. Communications at the camp include occasional mail planes and 2-way radio. The camp has its own electricity, water and sewer services. Freight arrives by plane, barge or charter boats.

Much of Afognak Island is owned by the Afognak Native Corp., Box 1277, Kodiak, AK 99615; phone 486-6014. Contact the corporation to reserve cabins or to use private lands.

Karluk

Located on Karluk Lagoon on the west coast of Kodiak Island 75 air miles from Kodiak. **Transportation:** Boat, scheduled and charter air service from Kodiak. **Population:** 107. **Zip code:** 99608. **Emergency Services:** Village Public Safety Officer, phone 241-2230; Alaska State Troopers, Kodiak, phone 486-4761; Health aide; Kodiak Hospital; Volunteer Fire Department.
Elevation: 137 feet at airport. **Climate:** Kodiak Island has a strong marine influence, characterized by moderately heavy precipitation, cool temperatures and frequent clouds and fog, with little or no freezing weather. Humidity is generally high and the temperature variation is small. Temperature at Karluk ranges from 31° to 54°F.
Private Aircraft: Airstrip 1 mile east; elev. 137 feet; length 2,000 feet; gravel; no fuel; unattended. Runway condition not monitored, visual inspection recommended prior to using.
Visitor Facilities: No overnight accommodations or restaurant available at the village. Accommodations in summer at a private fishing lodge located across Karluk Lagoon from the village. No banking services

or laundromat. Limited groceries, first-aid supplies and hardware available at small store operated by tribal council; most supplies obtained from Kodiak. No arts and crafts available for purchase. Fishing/hunting licenses and guide services available. No rental transportation, major repair services, moorage facilities or fuel available.

Prior to 1979, the village was located on both sides of the Karluk River at Karluk Lagoon. A spit and foot bridge connected Old Karluk on the northeast side of the lagoon with Karluk on the southwest side. On January 7 and 8, 1978, waves driven by northeasterly winds reaching 100 mph breached the spit at the mouth of the river. Travel between the 2 settlements was disrupted and the residents decided to relocate to an entirely new site about 0.75 mile upstream on the south side of the lagoon.

Russian hunters established a trading post in Karluk in 1786; however, the mouth of the Karluk River is thought to have been populated several hundred years before the Russians' arrival. In 1805, Capt. U.T. Lisianski of the Imperial Russian Navy reported the name of the settlement as "Carlook" or "Karloock." Between 1790 and 1850 many tanneries, salteries and canneries were established in the area. In 1890, Karluk was renowned for having the largest salmon cannery in the world and the river was known as the greatest red salmon stream in the world.

In the early 1900s, canneries were constructed by the Alaska Packers Assoc. Overfishing of the area forced the canneries to close in the 1930s, and today the buildings stand vacant and deteriorating.

Karluk is located adjacent to the Kodiak National Wildlife Refuge. The community's Ascension of Our Lord Russian Orthodox chapel, built in 1888, is a national historic site.

Fishing is the primary source of livelihood for Karluk residents; there are a few year-round, part-time positions. Almost all residents depend on fishing and hunting as a food source. Species found in the area include salmon, trout, steelhead, flounder, duck, seal, deer, reindeer, rabbit and ptarmigan.

NOTE: Land along the Karluk River as well as the riverbed is owned by Koniag Inc. and the village corporations of Karluk and Larsen Bay. There is a $50 per person per day fee for fishing or camping on the Karluk River. Permits may be obtained from Koniag Inc., 201 Kashevarof, Suite 6, Kodiak, AK 99615; phone 486-4147.

Communications in unincorporated Karluk include phones, daily mail plane, commercial radio from Kodiak and satellite TV. The community has a school with grades kindergarten through 10. There are community electricity, water and sewage systems. Freight arrives by mail plane and charter planes, fishing boats and occasional barges. Government address: Karluk Tribal Council, General Delivery, Karluk, AK 99608; phone 241-2224. Village corporation address: Koniag Inc., 201 Kashevarof, Suite 6, Kodiak, AK 99615; phone 486-4147.

Kodiak

Located at the north end of Chiniak Bay near the eastern tip of Kodiak Island. **Transportation:** Commercial jet service from Anchorage or Seattle; commuter air service from Anchorage or the Kenai Peninsula; Alaska State Ferry System from Seward and Homer. **Population:** 6,774, city; 15,575, borough. **Zip code:** 99615. **Emergency Services:** Dial 911 for emergencies. Alaska State Troopers, phone 486-4121; Fire Department, phone 486-5728; Kodiak Island Hospital, phone 486-3281; Coast Guard emergency, dial operator and ask for Zenith 5555.

Elevation: Sea level. **Climate:** Average daily temperature in July 54°F; in January 32°F. Average annual precipitation 74 inches. September, October and May are the wettest months, each averaging more than 6 inches of rain.

Private Aircraft: Kodiak state airport, 3 miles southwest; elev. 73 feet; length 7,500 feet; asphalt; fuel 80, 100, jet A-1. Kodiak Municipal Airport, 2 miles northeast; elev. 139 feet; length 2,800 feet; gravel; attended daylight hours. Kodiak (Lily Lake) seaplane base, 1 mile northeast; elev. 130 feet. Inner Harbor seaplane base, adjacent north; unattended; docks; watch for boat traffic; no fuel.

Visitor Facilities: There are several hotels/motels at Kodiak, and many restaurants, general merchandise, sporting goods and 1 gift shop. There are 3 state campgrounds and a city campground; several remote fly-in hunting and fishing lodges in the Kodiak area and recreation cabins available in the Kodiak National Wildlife Refuge, Shuyak Island State Park and on Afognak from Afognak Native Corp., Box 1277, Kodiak, AK 99615; phone 486-6014. There are several air charter services in Kodiak for flightseeing trips, fly-in hunting and fishing or side trips to nearby points of interest. Boats can be chartered for fishing and hunting trips, sightseeing and photography. There are 5 car rental agencies, an airport bus service, taxi cabs, a year-round van touring service and seasonal sightseeing bus

tours. (Kodiak has about 100 miles of roads which offer beautiful scenery and access to tidewater but not to the Kodiak National Wildlife Refuge. Kodiak's world famous brown bears are rarely seen from the roads.)

Kodiak Island, home of the oldest permanent European settlement in Alaska, is about 100 miles long. Kodiak is the largest island in Alaska, with an area of 3,670 square miles. The Kodiak Borough includes some 200 islands, the largest being Kodiak.

Commercial fishing is the backbone of Kodiak's economy. Kodiak was the largest commercial fishing port in the U.S. in 1988 for product landed. Some 2,000 commercial fishing vessels use the harbor each year delivering salmon, shrimp, herring, halibut and whitefish, plus king, tanner and Dungeness crab to the 15 seafood processing companies in Kodiak.

Kodiak also is an important cargo port and transshipment center. Container ships stop here to transfer goods to smaller vessels bound for the Aleutians, the Alaska Peninsula and other destinations.

Kodiak, a home rule city incorporated in 1940, has all the amenities of a medium-sized city, including radio stations, TV via cable and satellite and a daily newspaper, *The Kodiak Daily Mirror*. City government address: City of Kodiak, P.O. Box 1397, Kodiak, AK 99615; phone 486-3224. Borough address: Kodiak Island Borough, 710 Mill Bay Road, Kodiak, AK 99615; phone 486-5736. Kodiak Island Convention and Visitors Bureau, 100 Marine Way, Kodiak, AK 99615; phone 486-4782. Native corporation address: Koniag Inc., 203 Marine Way, Kodiak, AK 99615; phone 486-4147.

For more information see *The MILEPOST®*, a complete guide to communities on Alaska's road and marine highway systems, and *Where Mountains Meet the Sea*, Vol. 13, No. 1 of *ALASKA GEOGRAPHIC®*. To order, see the ALASKA NORTHWEST LIBRARY section at the back of the book.

Larsen Bay

Located near the mouth of Larsen Bay on the west shore of Uyak Bay on the northwest coast of Kodiak Island, 62 miles westsouthwest of Kodiak. **Transportation:** Boat; scheduled and charter air service from Kodiak. **Population:** 169. **Zip code:** 99624. **Emergency Services:** Village Public Safety Officer, phone 847-2262; Alaska State Troopers, Kodiak, phone 486-4761; Clinic, phone 847-2208; Volunteer Fire Department.

Elevation: 20 feet. **Climate:** Kodiak

Island's climate is dominated by a strong marine influence, characterized by moderately heavy precipitation, cool temperatures and frequent high clouds and fog. There is little freezing weather. Humidity is generally high and temperature variation is small. Mean maximum temperatures range from 32° to 62°F. Larsen Bay gets approximately 23 inches of precipitation a year, with 23 inches of snow.

Private Aircraft: Airstrip adjacent southwest; elev. 77 feet; length 2,400 feet; gravel; no fuel; unattended. Runway condition not monitored, visual inspection recommended prior to using. No public transportation to town.

Visitor Facilities: No hotel or restaurant. Arrangements may be made for accommodations in private homes. No laundromat or banking services. Groceries, clothing, first-aid supplies, hardware, film and sporting goods may be purchased. No arts and crafts available for purchase. Fishing/hunting licenses available. No guide or major repair services. Private boats may be rented; charter aircraft available locally. No public moorage facilities. Fuel available: marine gas, diesel, propane, regular gasoline.

Larsen Bay was named for Peter Larsen, an Unga Island furrier, hunter and guide. The Native name for the town is Uyak. The area is thought to have been inhabited for 2,000 years by the Aleut people. In the early 1800s there was a tannery in Uyak Bay. The Alaska Packers Assoc. built a cannery in the village of Larsen Bay in 1911. The cannery is now owned by Kodiak Island Seafoods Inc.

Larsen Bay is a second-class city, incorporated in 1974. It is located adjacent to Kodiak National Wildlife Refuge.

The economy is primarily based on fishing and cannery work. A large majority of the residents depend on subsistence activities for their livelihood. Species found in the area include seals, sea lions, salmon, halibut, codfish, ducks, clams, sea urchins, gumboots (chitons), crab, deer and various types of berries. There are a few local jobs with the city, the tribal council, school, post office and stores.

The main attraction in the area is the Karluk River, which is located 2 to 3 miles from the head of Larsen Bay. This river is known for its excellent king salmon, silver salmon and steelhead fishing. Raft trips from Karluk Lake to Karluk Lagoon also are popular.

NOTE: Land along the Karluk River as well as the riverbed is owned by Koniag Inc. and the village corporations of Karluk and Larsen Bay. There is a $50 per person per day fee for fishing or camping on the Karluk River. Permits may be obtained from Koniag Inc., 203 Marine Way, Kodiak, AK 99615; phone 486-4147.

Hunting in the area is good for Sitka black-tailed deer. Other wildlife include Kodiak brown bear, fox, rabbit, ermine, otter, seal, whale, sea lion and porpoise. Bird-watchers may see eagles, gulls, petrels, kittiwakes, mallards, green-winged teals, wigeons, pintails, lesser Canada geese, puffins, loons, cormorants and more. (Approximately 120 species of birds have been recorded in the Kodiak area, although most are migratory.)

Communications in Larsen Bay include phones, mail plane, commercial and single sideband radio and satellite TV. The community is served by 2 churches and a school with grades kindergarten through 12. There are community electricity, water and sewer systems. Freight arrives by cargo plane, barge, ship and charter plane. Government address: City of Larsen Bay, P.O. Box 8, Larsen Bay, AK 99624; phone 847-2221. Village corporation address: Larsen Bay Tribal Council, General Delivery, Larsen Bay, AK 99624; phone 847-2207.

Old Harbor

Located on the southeast shore of Kodiak Island on the west shore of Sitkalidak Strait across from Sitkalidak Island, 54 miles from Kodiak. **Transportation:** Fishing and charter boat; scheduled and charter air service from Kodiak. **Population:** 380. **Zip code:** 99643. **Emergency Services:** Village Public Safety Officer, phone 286-2295; Alaska State Troopers, Kodiak, 486-4761; Clinic, phone 286-2205; Volunteer Fire Department.

Elevation: 20 feet. **Climate:** Kodiak Island's climate is dominated by a strong marine influence, characterized by moderately heavy precipitation, cool temperatures, frequent high clouds and fog. Humidity is generally high and temperature variation small. Average temperature at Old Harbor 24° to 60°F. Precipitation averages 48 inches per year, with 18.5 inches of snow.

Private Aircraft: Airstrip adjacent northeast; elev. 15 feet; length 2,200 feet; gravel; no fuel; unattended. Runway condition not monitored, visual inspection recommended prior to using. Vehicles may be on runway. Severe erosion adjacent to runway; usable runway width is 70 feet. No public transportation into town.

Visitor Facilities: No hotel; arrangements for accommodations in private homes may be made. No laundromat or banking services. Some groceries, clothing, first-aid supplies, hardware and film may be purchased at 2 stores; most supplies are obtained from Kodiak. No arts and crafts available for purchase. Fishing/hunting licenses not available. Guide services can be arranged locally. No major repair services. Private boats may occasionally be chartered. Moorage facilities available. Diesel and regular gasoline available.

The area around Old Harbor is thought to have been inhabited for nearly 2,000 years. Grigori Shelikov, considered to be the founder of the Russian-American colonies, entered a harbor on the south coast of Kodiak Island in 1784. His flagship, the *Three Saints,* is the namesake for the harbor as well as the first Russian settlement in Alaska, Three Saints Bay. In 1788, a tsunami destroyed the settlement; it was hit by 2 more devastating earthquakes before 1792. In 1793, Alexander Baranov, who replaced Shelikov, relocated the town to Saint Paul Harbor, now known as Kodiak. A settlement at Three Saints Harbor was re-established in 1884. The census of 1890 designated the settlement in that area as Staruigavan, meaning "old harbor" in Russian. The town was nearly destroyed by a tidal wave from the 1964 Good Friday earthquake; only 2 homes and the church remained standing. Old Harbor has since been rebuilt in the same location.

Many of Old Harbor's residents are commercial fishermen; however, most of the residents depend to some extent on subsistence activities for some food sources. Species harvested for subsistence use includes salmon, halibut, cod, Dolly Varden, crab, herring, shrimp, clams, duck, seal, deer, rabbit and bear. Berries are also harvested. There are a few jobs locally with the stores, school, city and post office.

Old Harbor is a second-class city, incorporated in 1966. It is located adjacent to the Kodiak National Wildlife Refuge.

Marine wildlife includes sea lions, harbor seals, fur seals, sea otters, porpoises and gray and humpback whales. Land mammals include Kodiak brown bear, Sitka black-tailed deer, weasels, land otters, ground squirrels, marten, beaver, muskrats and arctic foxes. Some 120 species of birds, most migratory, have been reported on Kodiak.

Communications in Old Harbor include phones, mail plane, commercial radio reception from Kodiak and satellite TV. The community is served by a Russian Orthodox church and a school with grades kindergarten through 12. There are community electricity, water and sewer systems. Freight arrives by barge, mail plane or charter boat. Government address: City of Old Harbor, P.O. Box 109, Old Harbor, AK 99643; phone 286-2204 or 9219. Village corporation address: Old Harbor Native Corp., General Delivery, Old Harbor, AK 99643.

Ouzinkie

(you-ZENK-e) Located on the west coast of Spruce Island on Narrow Strait across from Kodiak Island, 10 miles north of the city of Kodiak. **Transportation:** Boat; scheduled or charter air service from Kodiak. **Population:** 204. **Zip code:** 99644. **Emergency Services:** Village Public Safety Officer, phone 680-2259; Alaska State Troopers, Kodiak, phone 486-4761; Clinic, phone 680-2265; Volunteer Fire Department.

Elevation: 55 feet at airport. **Climate:** Maritime, with moderately heavy precipitation (approximately 60 inches per year), predominantly cool temperatures with little variation and frequent clouds and fog. Mean maximum temperatures 62°F in July and August, 32°F December to February. Snowfall occurs from December through March and averages 87 inches per year. Winds can become quite strong.

Private Aircraft: Airstrip adjacent north; elev. 55 feet; length 2,300 feet; gravel; no fuel; unattended. Runway condition not monitored, visual inspection recommended prior to landing. *CAUTION: Large red-and-white board markers identify end of 2,500-by-100-foot safety area and are 195 feet before runway landing threshold.*

Visitor Facilities: No hotel; arrangements may be made to stay in private homes. No restaurant, laundromat or banking services. Groceries available at Ouzinkie Community Store. No arts or crafts available for purchase. Fishing/hunting licenses not available. No guide or major repair services, rental transportation or public moorage facilities. Fuel available: marine gas, diesel, regular gasoline.

Ouzinkie is one of the oldest settlements of the Kodiak Island group. The village is nestled in a small cove among tall stands of

HYPOTHERMIA

Hypothermia, the number one killer of outdoor recreationists, most often occurs when temperatures range between 30° and 50°F.

spruce and hemlock. Spruce Island is separated from Kodiak Island by a strait named Uskiy, meaning "very narrow" in Russian. The village name is a transliteration of Uzenkiy which is derived from Uskiy.

The town was originally settled as a retirement community for the Russian-American Co. In 1889, the Royal Packing Co. constructed a cannery at Ouzinkie. Shortly afterward, the Russian-American Packing Co. built another. In the mid-1800s, a Russian Orthodox church was built. In the early 1900s, almost all Ouzinkie residents owned cattle. Through the years, however, ranching became less popular and finally disappeared altogether.

Ouzinkie is a second-class city, incorporated in 1967. The Russian Orthodox Nativity of Our Lord Chapel, built in 1906 next to the older church, is a national historic site.

The fishing industry flourished through the years with new canneries replacing those that were destroyed by fire. In 1964, a tidal wave resulting from the Good Friday earthquake destroyed the Ouzinkie Packing Co. cannery. Following that disaster, Columbia Ward bought the remains and rebuilt the store and dock, but not the cannery. In the late 1960s, the Ouzinkie Seafoods cannery was constructed. The operation, sold to Glacier Bay, burned down in 1976 shortly after the sale.

Ouzinkie's economic base is commercial fishing. Since 1976 there have been no local fish processing facilities and Ouzinkie fishermen use those in Kodiak or floating processors. There are a few other jobs locally with the store, city government, clinic and schools.

Almost all the residents depend to some extent on subsistence activities for various food sources. Species harvested locally include salmon, king crab, tanner crab, Dungeness crab, herring, halibut, shrimp, scallops, clams, ducks, deer and rabbits.

Communications in Ouzinkie include phones, mail plane, commercial radio from Kodiak, satellite and cable TV. The community is served by Russian Orthodox and Baptist churches and a school with grades kindergarten through 12. There are community electricity, water and sewer. Freight arrives by barge or mail plane. Government address: City of Ouzinkie, P.O. Box 109, Ouzinkie, AK 99644; phone 680-2209. Village corporation address: Ouzinkie Native Corp., P.O. Box 89, Ouzinkie, AK 99644; phone 680-2208.

Pleasant Harbor

Located on Spruce Island, 3 miles east of Ouzinkie, 12 miles north of Kodiak. **Transportation:** Boat; charter air service. **Population:** 26. **Zip code:** 99644. **Emergency Services:** Village Public Safety Officer, Ouzinkie; Alaska State Troopers, Kodiak; Ouzinkie Clinic.

Climate: Winters are usually mild with very little snow, but it can snow 3 feet when you least expect it, says one resident. Winter temperatures range from 25° to 40°F. Summers are usually sunny with occasional rain showers. Temperatures range between 60° and 70°F.

Private Aircraft: Airstrip at Ouzinkie. Floatplane landings at Pleasant Harbor.

Visitor Facilities: Accommodations and meals available at a local lodge. (See advertisement, this section.) Laundry facilities available. No banking services. No store; supplies obtained from Kodiak. No arts or crafts available for purchase. Fishing/hunting licenses available. Marine engine and boat repair services available. No guide services, rental transportation or fuel. Public moorage facilities available.

Pleasant Harbor was founded in 1923 when Chris Opheim homesteaded a piece of land which included Sunny Cove and Pleasant Harbor. He and his family operated a cod saltery in Sunny Cove. Son Ed Opheim inherited the homestead and in 1947 moved his family to Pleasant Harbor where the family earned a living salting and smoking salmon. Ed Opheim later built and operated a sawmill.

The tidal wave generated by the 1964 Good Friday earthquake washed away both the old house at Sunny Cove and the Pleasant Harbor home. The Opheims have since rebuilt on higher ground. The family has been selling homesites and there are now 13 homes in the community.

Most residents earn their living by fishing. Others take seasonal jobs in Kodiak and a few work for the lodge.

Attractions include Monks Lagoon, about an hour's walk from Pleasant Harbor, where St. Herman lived and worked during the early days of Russian America. It is now a Russian Orthodox sanctuary. The chapel built over St. Herman's grave is a national historic site.

New Valaam Monastery is located at Pleasant Harbor and the monks who live there are more than willing to share their knowledge of the history of the church in Alaska with visitors.

Salmon fishing is particularly good in July and August. Halibut and Dolly Varden can be caught in May and June. There are clams nearby and tide pools where a variety of marine creatures hide. Dolphins, harbor seals and sea lions are plentiful. Deer and rabbits venture near the homes; eagles soar overhead and nest on a point overlooking the ocean. On a tiny island nearby many sea and land birds, their nests and young can be seen. This island is covered with wildflowers in season. Elk and deer hunting can be done on Kodiak and Afognak islands, about 2 hours by boat from Pleasant Harbor.

Kathy Opheim writes that her father-in-law Ed Opheim is also a tourist attraction: "He's the builder of the world famous Opheim dories, author of the book *Old Mike of Monk's Lagoon,* plus many very popular stories. . . ."

Communications in unincorporated Pleasant Harbor include radio and TV. Freight arrives by plane or ship.

Port Lions

Located on Settler's Cove near the mouth of Kizhuyak Bay on the north coast of Kodiak Island, 21 miles from Kodiak. **Transportation:** Boat; scheduled and charter air service from Kodiak; Alaska Marine Highway System from Homer and Seward via Kodiak. **Population:** 296. **Zip code:** 99550. **Emergency Services:** Village Public Safety Officer, phone 454-2330; Alaska State Troopers, Kodiak, phone 486-4761; Clinic, phone 454-2275.

Elevation: 52 feet at airport. **Climate:** Relatively cool summers and warm winters, moderately heavy precipitation and frequent high clouds and fog. Temperatures from 20° to 60°F. Approximately 60 inches of precipitation per year.

Private Aircraft: Airport 2 miles northeast; elev. 52 feet; length 2,600 feet; crushed rock runway and apron; no fuel; unattended. Runway equipped with marker lights, beacon and wind direction indicator. Subject to downdrafts during northeast winds. Runway width 100 feet between edge markers.

Visitor Facilities: Accommodations and meals at 2 lodges. There is also 1 cafe. No public laundry facilities or banking services. Groceries, clothing, hardware and film available. Some arts and crafts available for purchase. Fishing/hunting licenses and guide services available locally. Marine engine repair available. Boats and off-road vehicles may be rented. Fuel available: diesel, regular gasoline. Public moorage facilities available.

Port Lions was founded in 1964 by Lions International, the Bureau of Indian Affairs

and the Public Health Service for the displaced residents of Afognak. The village of Afognak was partially destroyed by tidal waves in the aftermath of the March 27, 1964 earthquake. Afognak was 1 of 10 permanent settlements founded by Russian-American Co. employees between 1770 and 1799.

For many years, Port Lions was the site of the large Wakefield Cannery on Peregrebni Point. The cannery burned down in March 1975. Floating crab processors have operated there in recent years.

Port Lions has become one of the fastest growing communities on Kodiak Island; it incorporated as a second-class city in 1966.

The economy of Port Lions is based primarily on commercial fishing. There are a few other jobs with the lodges, cafe, stores, boat harbor, oil company, school, city and health clinic. All residents depend to some extent on subsistence activities. Food harvested includes salmon, halibut, crab, shrimp, scallops, clams, ducks, seals, deer, rabbits, berries and plants.

Port Lions has excellent recreational opportunities. Boating and riding all-terrain vehicles are very popular. The surrounding area offers good hunting and fishing. There is an abundance of wildlife for the photographer.

Communications in Port Lions include phones, mail plane, radio and TV. The community is served by a Russian Orthodox church and Hillside Bible Chapel, a library, and a school with grades kindergarten through 12. Electricity is provided by Kodiak Electric Assoc. Utilities include a community water supply, sewer and refuse collection. Freight arrives by air, ship and state ferry. Government address: City of Port Lions, P.O. Box 278, Port Lions, AK 99550; phone 454-2332. Village corporation address: Afognak Native Corp., 413 E. Rezanof Dr., Kodiak, AK 99615; phone 486-6014.

Port William

Located on the south shore of Shuyak Island, 65 miles north of Kodiak. **Transportation:** Boat, scheduled and charter air service. **Population:** 9. **Zip code:** 99697. **Emergency Services:** Alaska State Troopers, Kodiak; Kodiak Island Hospital, Kodiak.

Climate: According to one resident, summer weather varies. Some are rainy, others are sunny; temperatures are usually in the 60s and low 70s. Winters are normally mild; the temperature ranges from the upper teens to the 30s and seldom drops to zero.

Private Aircraft: No airstrip; seaplane landings only.

Visitor Facilities: None.

Port William originally was a cannery. For years it was the only ice and cold storage plant in the Kodiak area, according to a resident. Now privately owned, the cannery facilities are no longer operating. Residents of Port William are commercial fishermen.

Most of Shuyak Island is a wilderness. The northern end of the island is the new Shuyak Island State Park, while a section along the east side has been proposed for a state game sanctuary. The middle of the island is part of the Kodiak Island Borough.

There is fishing for Dolly Varden in the spring, and for silver and pink salmon in the fall. There are many birds, including bald eagles and puffins. Poor grade jade and jasper can be found on some beaches. There is hunting for deer, bear and elk (on Afognak Island just to the south). Other wildlife includes sea lions (on the Latax Rocks to the north), sea otters, land otters, beavers and whales.

Communications at Port William include mail plane and radio. There is no church or school. Supplies are obtained from Kodiak. Freight arrives by mail plane.

Uganik Bay

(you-GAN-ik) Located on Uganik Bay on the northwest side of Kodiak Island, 40 miles west of Kodiak, 270 miles south-southwest of Anchorage. Transportation: Boat; scheduled and charter air service from Kodiak. Population: 15. Zip code: 99615 (via Kodiak). Emergency Services: Alaska State Troopers, Kodiak; Kodiak Island Hospital.

Elevation: 50 feet. Climate: Mean daily maximum temperature in July 64°F; mean daily maximum in January 36°F. Mean annual precipitation 44 inches, with 51 inches of snow.

Private Aircraft: No airstrip; seaplane landings only.

Visitor Facilities: No lodging, meals or laundry facilities. Fishing/hunting licenses not available. No major repair services, rental transportation or public moorage facilities.

Village Islands in Uganik Bay was the location of an Eskimo village in the 1800s. There are a few homes at West Point and another in Mush Bay in the east arm of Uganik Bay. Fishing is the only industry, according to one resident. There were 3 canneries operating in the bay in the 1920s. Today all canneries are closed.

Uganik Bay is located within the Kodiak

Island National Wildlife Refuge. Most visitors to the area are deer or bear hunters who fly in with air charter operators from Kodiak.

Steelhead, rainbow trout and silver salmon are available at Lake Uganik.

Communications in unincorporated Uganik Bay include mail plane and shortwave radio. Electricity is from individual generators; water is from streams. Sewage systems vary from flush toilets to pit toilets. There is no school or church. Freight arrives by mail plane, barge or ship.

Woody Island

Located 2.6 miles east of the city of Kodiak. Transportation: Private boat; charter air service. Population: 1 to 4 in winter; 1 to 6 in summer. Zip code: 99615 (via Kodiak). Emergency Services: Alaska State Troopers, Kodiak; Kodiak Island Hospital.

Climate: Similar to Kodiak.

Private Aircraft: No airstrip; floatplane or helicopter landings only.

Visitor Facilities: Available in nearby Kodiak.

The island was named by the Russian explorer U.T. Lisianski in 1804. Woody Island figured in the early history of Alaska as a boat-building center and a port from which the Russian American Ice Co. and Kodiak Ice Co. shipped ice to California in the early and middle 1800s. It is believed the first horses in Alaska were brought to Woody Island in 1867, and that the first road built in Alaska — 2.7 miles long — was built around this island. Boat building flourished at both Kodiak and Woody Island during the late 1880s. The settlement of Woody Island gradually diminished as the population settled more and more at Kodiak.

Woody Island has few residents; a Baptist youth camp operates here in the summer.

Communications at Woody Island include radio and satellite TV. A public electricity system is available; water is from wells and a lake; residents have flush toilets. Freight arrives by private boat. Village corporation address: Leisnoi Inc., 4300 B St., Suite 407, Anchorage, AK 99503.

MOUNTAINS

Of the 20 highest mountains in the United States, 17 are in Alaska, which has 19 mountains measuring more than 14,000 feet.

– The ALASKA ALMANAC®

▼ A T T R A C T I O N S ▼

National and State Parks, Forests, etc.

Shuyak Island State Park

This 11,000-acre wilderness park created in 1984 is one of the newest in the state system. The park is located on the northern end of Shuyak Island, northernmost sizable island of the Kodiak archipelago, and includes a number of smaller islands, rocks, passages and beaches. A section along the east side of the island has been proposed for a state game sanctuary. The middle of the island is Kodiak Island Borough land.

Shuyak Island is low — highest point is 700 feet — and mostly covered with a virgin forest of Sitka spruce, although there are open tundra areas. On clear days the volcanic peaks of the Alaska Peninsula across 30-mile-wide Shelikof Strait can be seen from the park.

Climate: Shuyak's climate is similar to Kodiak, where the average daily temperature in July is 54°F; in January, 30°F. Average annual precipitation at Kodiak is 54.52 inches. September, October and May are the wettest months, with each month averaging more than 6 inches of rain.

Wildlife: Seals, sea lions, brown bears, Sitka black-tailed deer, land otters, beavers and large numbers of sea otters may be seen on Shuyak Island. Birds, too, are abundant. Species that may be seen include a large number of bald eagles, gulls, cormorants, oystercatchers, guillemots, red-breasted mergansers, harlequin ducks, common and red-throated loons, horned and tufted puffins, eider ducks, terns, kittiwakes and scoters.

Pink and silver salmon spawn in the island's many streams; fishing for silvers is particularly good in August. Other sport fish are steelhead and Dolly Varden. Halibut, crabs and clams also are available.

Activities: Hiking is good on the open tundra on the north and west sides of the island, where the ground cover is grass, lichens and low heath plants, such as crow-berry, bearberry and blueberry. Flowers are everywhere during spring and summer. Small ponds and a few isolated spruce dot the tundra. Jaegers fly overhead searching for voles; deer browse on the heath and ducks raise their young in the ponds.

The virgin forest on Shuyak may be the last stand of pure Sitka spruce in Alaska; other coastal forests are generally a mixture of spruce, hemlock and sometimes cedar. The forested area is thick with devil's club, sometimes growing head high; hikers may find it easier to follow the deer and bear trails that lace the island.

Shuyak Island's convoluted coastline of protected bays, channels and lagoons offers safe cruising by canoe or kayak. Many of the bays are separated by short portages. Skiff Passage, a long, narrow channel, completely cuts through Shuyak park from north to south.

Accommodations: Four cabins are located in the park and are available for $15 per night per person through the Division of Parks and Outdoor Recreation. (See Shuyak Island State Park Cabins section for details.) Camping is permitted. Minimum-impact camping should be practiced; all trash should be packed out. Boil or treat all drinking water.

Access: The park is easily reached by charter plane from either Kodiak or Homer, both of which have daily air service. From Kodiak it's a 45-minute flight; Homer is a little farther away. A suggested landing spot is Big Bay.

For more information or to reserve cabins contact: Alaska Dept. of Natural Resources, Division of Parks and Outdoor Recreation, Southcentral Region, P.O. Box 107001, Anchorage, AK 99510; phone 561-2020. Or, Division of Parks and Outdoor Recreation, Kodiak District, SR Box 3800, Kodiak, AK 99615; phone 486-6339.

Shuyak Island
State Park Cabins

Alaska State Parks maintains 4 recreational public-use cabins on Shuyak Island, 2 on Big Bay, 1 on Carry Inlet and 1 on Neketa Bay. All are accessible by floatplane or boat, although floatplane is usually more practical.

The cabins can be rented for up to 7 days at a time for $15 per night per person (up to a maximum of 8). The fee is waived for children 15 years or younger if the child's name and date of birth are listed on the application.

Anyone who is at least 18 years of age may apply for a cabin permit. Applications may be made in writing up to 180 days before the requested time. Reservations are accepted on a first-come basis and must be accompanied by a check.

The cabins are 12 feet by 20 feet and are equipped with wood stoves, propane lights and hot plate, 4 full-sized bunks with pads, manual shower and wash area, stainless steel sink, cooking utensils, and pit toilets.

Bring maps of the island, compass, first-aid kit, matches, rope, rain gear, garbage bags for packing out all garbage, sleeping bag, individual eating utensils and extra clothes and food in case bad weather prolongs your stay.

Obtain additional information or make cabin reservations through the Division of Parks and Outdoor Recreation, Kodiak District, S.R. Box 3800, Kodiak, AK 99615, phone (907) 486-6339; or Southcentral Region, Pouch 7001, Anchorage, AK 99510, phone (907) 762-4532.

Wildlife Refuges

Kodiak National
Wildlife Refuge

This refuge encompasses 1.9 million acres on Kodiak, Uganik, Afognak and Ban islands — all part of the Kodiak Archipelago. The city of Kodiak is some 250 air miles from Anchorage and about 21 miles northeast of the refuge boundary. Kodiak is accessible by commercial jet and the Alaska Marine Highway System. The refuge is larger than the state of Delaware, but because of its convoluted coastline, no place on the island is more than 15 miles from the sea.

The refuge's varied landscapes include glacially carved valleys, tundra uplands, lakes, wetlands, sand and gravel beaches, salt flats, meadows and rugged mountains to 4,000 feet. Spruce forests dominate the northern part of Kodiak Island and all of the Afognak Island portion of the refuge. The interior of the refuge is covered with dense vegetation in summer. Sedges and fireweed to 6 feet are often mixed with salmonberry, blueberry and rose bushes. Dense thickets of willow, alder and elderberry abound. Devil's club, with thorns that can penetrate leather, grow up to 6 feet high in the woods and on the slopes. The heathland in the southwest portion of the refuge is covered with hummocks — small knolls of grass and soil that make walking difficult.

Climate: The climate is mild and wet. Winter temperatures average between 24° and 36°F and rarely fall below zero. Summer days average between 48° and 60°F. The island has an average annual precipitation of 54 inches, including 75 inches of snow. The sky is completely overcast about half the time. Despite mild temperatures, the weather and winds are unpredictable and change abruptly. Climatic conditions change within short distances because of the varied terrain. The weather can make flying conditions hazardous and flights often are delayed for days.

Visitors should be equipped with plenty of warm clothes, rain gear and appropriate footwear. Bring extra food and other supplies in case weather prolongs your stay. Use only dead or downed wood, and carry a camp stove. Trash must be burned or packed out. Take precautions against unwanted encounters with bears, especially along salmon-spawning streams in midsummer. Do not leave food uncovered in camp; make noise while hiking to alert bears of your presence.

Wildlife: This refuge was originally established in 1941 to protect the habitat of the huge Kodiak brown bear and other wildlife. The brown bear remains the refuge's most well-known feature, attracting visitors from all over the world. The refuge supports the highest density of brown bears in the world. The 3 largest brown bears ever taken and 33 of the 50 largest in the Boone and Crockett North American records are from Kodiak Island. Females weigh about 650 pounds; larger males up to 1,500 pounds.

Besides the bears, there are only 5 other native land mammals in Kodiak refuge: red fox, river otter, short-tailed weasel, little brown bat and tundra vole. Several other species, including Sitka black-tailed deer, elk and beaver, have been introduced. Whales, porpoises, sea otters and sea lions are found in bays.

More than 210 species of birds have been seen on the archipelago. At least 200 pairs of bald eagles nest in the refuge. An estimated 2 million seabirds winter in the refuge's bays and inlets, and at least 200,000 waterfowl also winter along shorelines.

The refuge's 11 large lakes and many rivers are major spawning grounds for king, red, silver, pink and chum salmon. The various species spawn from June through August and begin to decrease in numbers in September, although a few silver salmon continue to spawn until December. Steelhead, rainbow trout and Dolly Varden also are found in refuge waters.

Access: Kodiak Refuge is roadless and reached most easily by chartered floatplane or boat from the city of Kodiak. Hovercraft and off-road vehicles are not permitted on refuge lands. Helicopter access is restricted to special use permit holders and is not permitted for recreational users. Recreational jet boats and airboats are not permitted.

Accommodations: There are motels and campgrounds at Kodiak. Wilderness camping is allowed throughout the refuge without advance reservations, permits or fees. There are 9 public-use cabins in the refuge which may be reserved in advance (see chart, next page). A visitor center located in Kodiak pro-

vides orientation for anyone traveling to the refuge.

Activities: Predominant activities in the refuge are hunting, fishing, photography and trapping. Other activities are hiking, wildlife viewing, beachcombing, berry picking and clamming.

For additional information contact: Refuge Manager, Kodiak National Wildlife Refuge, 1390 Buskin River Road, Kodiak, AK 99615; phone 487-2600. A visitor center is open year-round 8 a.m. to 4:30 p.m. Monday to Friday and noon to 4:30 p.m. Saturday and Sunday. The center features exhibits and provides visitor orientation.

Kodiak National Wildlife Refuge Cabins

Kodiak National Wildlife Refuge maintains 9 recreational cabins available to the public by advance reservation. Cabins may be reserved for up to 7 days per year. Drawings for reservations take place Jan. 2 for April, May and June; April 1 for July, August and September; July 1 for October, November and December; and Oct. 1 for January, February and March. Cabins not reserved during the drawing are avail-

Protected waters of Kodiak's Shuyak Island attract ocean kayakers, who can hike the open tundra rich with wildflowers or explore a virgin forest of pure Sitka spruce. Four cabins provide shelter to adventurers in this remote state wilderness park. (Bill Sherwonit)

KODIAK ISLAND CABINS

	SLEEPS	AIR ACCESS	BOAT ACCESS	TRAIL ACCESS	HUNTING	FISHING	BEACHCOMB	SKIFF	STOVE
NORTHWEST KODIAK ISLAND									
Chief Cove	4	•	•		•	•	•		O
Little River *(Use discouraged after Oct. 1)*	4	•			•	•			O
Uganik Lake *(Use discouraged after Oct. 1)*	3	•			•	•	•		O
Viekoda Bay *(Clamming at minus tide)*	4	•	•		•	•	•		O
Uganik Island	4	•	•		•	•	•		O
SOUTHWEST KODIAK ISLAND									
North Frazer Lake *(Use discouraged after Nov. 1)*	4	•			•	•			O
O'Malley *(Notable concentration of brown bears mid to late summer; access may be different after Nov. 1)*	4	•			•	•			O
Red Lake *(Access may be difficult after Nov.1)*	4	•			•	•			W
South Frazer Lake *(Access may be difficult after Nov. 1)*	4	•			•	•			W

The above chart gives a brief description of each cabin. Type of stove provided is indicated as follows: O=oil stove, W=wood stove, G=outdoor grill, OH=oil heater.

able on a first-come basis. Mail applications with choice of dates (including second choices if desired) to the refuge office. Fee for the cabins is $10 per night, due only after successful applicants have been notified.

All cabins have wood or oil heating stoves. Collect only dead or downed wood for stoves; leave caches of wood that are stored at the cabins for emergency use only. You must provide oil or kerosene for oil stoves; 5 gallons is usually sufficient for 1 week in mild weather. All cabins have pit toilets. No utensils or cook stoves are provided.

For a cabin pamphlet or reservation application contact: Refuge Manager, Kodiak National Wildlife Refuge, 1390 Buskin River Road, Kodiak, AK 99615; phone 487-2600.

The Rivers

NOTE: The river described below is also included in the Sportfishing section where additional information on species, seasons and bait suggestions is provided.

Karluk River. This river heads in Karluk Lake on the west coast of Kodiak Island and flows north and west 24 miles through Karluk Lagoon to Shelikof Strait at the village of Karluk. This is a Class I river, but a portage is necessary around a fish weir about 1 mile up from Karluk Lagoon.

This is a very popular river for king, red and silver salmon, Dolly Varden and rainbow trout in season. *NOTE: Land along the Karluk River as well as the riverbed is owned by Koniag Inc., and the village corporations of Karluk and Larsen Bay.* There is a $50 per person per day fee for fishing or camping on the Karluk River. Permits may be obtained from Koniag Inc., 201 Kashevarof, Suite 6, Kodiak, AK 99615; phone 486-4147. Canoes, kayaks, or rafts are suitable for this river. The trip takes 2 to 5 days.

Access is by floatplane from Kodiak to Karluk Lake or to Larsen Bay, from where a 2-mile trail leads to the river. Access also by scheduled air service to Larsen Bay village. Exit is via the portage trail to Larsen Bay, or from Karluk village via charter or scheduled air service.

Related USGS Topographic maps: Karluk B-1, C-1 and C-2.

Sea Kayaking

Kodiak's rocky, irregular coastline makes for miles and miles of fine sea kayaking opportunities. But precautions must be taken. The weather can change abruptly, and changing wind direction and tidal currents can make paddling a tricky business at best. For more information on kayaking safety, see Boating, Canoeing and Kayaking in GENERAL INFOR-

MATION section. Perhaps the prime area for ocean kayaking on Kodiak is:

Shuyak Island State Park. Attractions include abundant wildlife and spectacular coastlines. The inner coast, a maze of narrow, interconnected bays, inlets and passages offer protected paddling for kayakers. Access is by air charter from Homer or Kodiak. (See Shuyak Island State Park, this section for more information.)

Sportfishing

King salmon weighing more than 60 pounds find their way back to the Karluk River every summer, and both brown bears and human anglers lie in wait along the banks. The strength of the run makes the Karluk one of the best king salmon rivers in the world. But this is only one of the excellent fishing opportunities on Kodiak.

For more information consult the current sportfishing regulations or contact the following: Alaska Dept. of Fish and Game, Sport Fish Division, 333 Raspberry Road, Anchorage, AK 99518; phone 267-2218, or Alaska Dept. of Fish and Game, 211 Mission Road, Kodiak, AK 99615; phone 486-4791.

Among the best fishing spots on Kodiak are:

Afognak Island. Afognak Island and adjacent Raspberry Island, both approximately 30 air miles northeast of Kodiak, offer excellent remote fishing. There is a lodge on Afognak Island. This is brown bear country; try to avoid bears, make noise when traveling and carry a .30-06, or larger, rifle. Part of Afognak Island is within Kodiak National Wildlife Refuge and part is owned by Koniag Native Corp.

On Afognak Island, **Afognak River** and **Afognak Lake** provide good fishing for Dolly Varden — 10 to 20 inches, abundant most of the summer; red salmon — peak runs in early June; silver salmon — September best; pink salmon — July and August; steelhead — October and November; rainbow trout — 10 to 16 inches, in the upper river June 15 to September. Steelhead and rainbow trout fishery is closed April 1 to June 14. This 6-mile-long lake is 32 air miles from Kodiak. **Waterfall Lake**, 40 air miles from Kodiak, offers excellent fishing for Dolly Varden to 20 inches. **Pillar Lake** has small Dolly Varden. **Portage Lake**, 35 air miles north of Kodiak, **Malina Lake**, 36 air miles northwest of Kodiak, and **Laura and Pauls lakes**, 40 air miles northeast of Kodiak, all yield red salmon, silver salmon, Dolly Varden and rainbow trout. Portage, Malina and Laura lakes also yield

pink salmon and steelhead.

Akalura Lake. Measures 2.5 miles across, located in the Kodiak Island National Wildlife Refuge approximately 80 air miles southwest of Kodiak, 3 miles north of Olga Bay. Access by floatplane from Kodiak. Fish available: rainbow trout — best June 15 to September, use flies, lures or bait, closed April 1 to June 14; small numbers of steelhead — September to November, use spoons or eggs, closed April 1 to June 14; Dolly Varden — May to October, best May and September, use bait, spinners or flies; silver salmon — good mid-August through September, use herring or spoons; red salmon — June to July, use spoons or flies; pink salmon — July to August, use small spoons.

Barabara Lake. Located 21 air miles west of Kodiak within Kodiak Island National Wildlife Refuge. Access by floatplane from Kodiak. Fish available: small numbers of rainbow trout — best after June 15, use flies, lures or bait, closed April 1 to June 14; Dolly Varden — May to October, use bait, spinners or flies; red salmon — June to July, use spoons or flies; silver salmon — September through October, use herring or spoons.

Karluk Lake, River and Lagoon. Located approximately 75 air miles southwest of Kodiak. Fish available: rainbow trout — season closed April 1 to June 14, use flies, lures or bait; steelhead — from 25 to 35 inches, best in October, use spoons or eggs, closed April 1 to June 14; Dolly Varden — best in May and September, use bait, spinners or flies; 2 runs of red salmon — running strong in June and August and tapering off by mid-September, use spoons or flies; pink salmon — best in July and early August, use small spoons; silver salmon — plentiful late August through October, use herring or spoons; excellent for king salmon — 10 to 40 pounds, peak runs mid-June to the end of June, use herring or spoons. *NOTE: Land along the Karluk River as well as the riverbed is owned by Koniag Inc., and the village corporations of Karluk and Larsen Bay.* Permits for fishing or camping on the Karluk River. may be obtained from Koniag Inc., 201 Kashevarof, Suite 6, Kodiak, AK 99615; phone 486-4147.

Lake Miam. A 1-mile-long lake on the east coast of Kodiak Island, a 15- to 20-minute flight by small plane from Kodiak. Fish available: small numbers of rainbow trout — season closed April 1 to June 14, use flies, lures or bait; small numbers of steelhead — September to November, use spoons or eggs; Dolly Varden — May to October, best May and September, use bait, spinners or flies; silver salmon —

September through October, use herring or spoons; red salmon — June to July, use spoons or flies; pink salmon — July to August, use small spoons.

Offshore Waters. In Kodiak Archipelago waters halibut, rockfish, flounder and other marine fish are caught throughout the year, although offshore fishing is best in summer. Most halibut are taken off Long and Woody islands. Other fish: Dolly Varden — along rocky beaches from June through July, use herring strips and small- to medium-sized lures; pink salmon — late June to mid-August, best from mid-July on, use small spoons; chum salmon — arrive late July through early August, use spoons; silver salmon — mid-August to November, use herring or spoons.

Red (Ayakulik) Lake and River. Located in Kodiak National Wildlife Refuge approximately 85 air miles southwest of Kodiak. Fish available: rainbow trout — season closed April 1 to June 14, best after June 15, use flies, lures or bait; steelhead — good at lake outlet in late September and early October, use spoons or eggs; Dolly Varden — May to October, best May and September, use bait, spinners or flies; king salmon — best mid-June to mid-July, use herring or spoons; silver salmon — September through October, use herring or spoons; red salmon — June to July, use spoons or flies; pink salmon — July to August, use small spoons.

Saltery Lake and River. Located 36 miles southwest of Kodiak via a 15- to 20-minute air charter from Kodiak. Fish available: rainbow trout — 9 to 14 inches, present in small numbers most of the summer, use flies, lures or bait; small numbers of steelhead — closed April 1 to June 14, October through November, use spoons or eggs; Dolly Varden — 10 to 18 inches abundant in May, August and September, use bait, spinners or flies; silver salmon — excellent late August through mid-October, use spoons; red salmon — abundant in July, use spoons or flies; pink salmon — abundant in mid-July to August, use small spoons.

Uganik Lake and River. Located 36 air miles southwest of Kodiak in Kodiak National Wildlife Refuge. Fish available: rainbow trout — season closed April 1 to June 14, best after June 15, use flies, lures or bait; steelhead — September to November, use spoons or eggs; Dolly Varden — May to October, best May and September, use bait, spinners or flies; silver salmon — September through October, use herring or spoons; red salmon — June to July, use spoons or flies; pink salmon — July to August, use small spoons.

Upper Station lakes. Located approximately 90 air miles southwest of Kodiak in Kodiak National Wildlife Refuge. Fish available: rainbow trout — season closed April 1 to June 14, best after June 15, use flies, lures or bait; small numbers of steelhead — September to November, use spoons or eggs; Dolly Varden — May to October, best May and September, use bait, spinners or flies; silver salmon — September through October, use herring or spoons; red salmon — June to July, use spoons or flies; pink salmon — July to August, use small spoons.

Woody and Long Island lakes. Located 2 to 4 miles east of Kodiak. Accessible by small plane or boat. Good camping, hiking, picnicking and beachcombing. Fish available: rainbow trout — year-round, best after June 15 and October, use flies, lures or bait; Dolly Varden — May to October, best May and September, use bait, spinners or flies; silver salmon — September through October, use spoons; grayling — in Long Lake year-round, use flies.

POTLATCH

These Native gatherings, primarily an Indian custom, are held to commemorate just about any kind of event. Traditional Native foods are served and gifts are distributed to everyone who attends. A funeral potlatch might result in the giving away of the deceased's possessions to relatives or to persons who had done favors for the deceased during his or her lifetime. Before the federal government imposed legal constraints in the nineteenth century, potlatches could take years of preparation. The host family might give away all its possessions in an attempt to demonstrate its wealth to the guests. Each guest in turn would feel an obligation to hold an even bigger potlatch.
— *The ALASKA ALMANAC®*

WESTERN COOK INLET

Introduction

Just across Cook Inlet from metropolitan Anchorage and its heavily used playground, the Kenai Peninsula, lies a land where wilderness rules. Almost roadless, sparsely populated and dotted with active volcanoes, the western side of Cook Inlet is a wilderness lover's dream.

A few traditional Native villages break up the mountainous expanses, and Lakes Clark and Iliamna sport a number of lodges that cater to hunters and fishermen. But outside these centers of human activity lie miles and miles of spectacular country begging to be explored. There are rivers to be run — the lyrically named Chilikadrotna, Mulchatna and Tlikakila have been designated by Congress as wild and scenic. There is also high tundra country to be hiked, big game to be photographed or hunted; and fishing that ranks among the best in the word. The long expanses of beach bordering Cook Inlet play host to thousands of shorebirds such as kittiwakes and cormorants, and just offshore come walrus, sea otters, salmon fishermen, and, at extreme low tides, clammers.

One of the most spectacular attractions on Cook Inlet's west side, and indeed in the entire state, is the bear show at McNeil River. A strong run of chum salmon lures as many as 3 dozen brown bears a day to a falls on that river, and photogaphers by the dozen congregate nearby under the watchful eye of Alaska Dept. of Fish and Game biologists. (Visitors are strictly limited, and a lottery system decides who gets to go.) Many of the most astonishing bear photos in the world are taken here; a sow teaching her cubs how to fish; a young bear doing a belly flop "dive" into the water; a triumphant bruin with a huge salmon still struggling between its teeth.

A brown bear, still wet from fishing, tears into a salmon caught at McNeil River falls. A state game sanctuary at McNeil River protects a spectacular gathering of bears and salmon — and photographers — at the falls. (Bill Sherwonit)

▼ C O M M U N I T I E S ▼

Igiugig

(ig-ee-AH-gig) Located on the south shore of the Kvichak River at the southwest end of Lake Iliamna, 50 miles southwest of Iliamna and 50 miles northeast of King Salmon. **Transportation:** Scheduled air service from King Salmon. **Population:** 32. **Zip code:** 99613. **Emergency Services:** Health aide.

Climate: Average summer temperatures from 42° to 62°F; average winter temperatures from 6° to 30°F. Total precipitation averages 26 inches annually, with an average snowfall of 64 inches.

Private Aircraft: Airstrip adjacent south; elev. 110 feet; length 2,700 feet; dirt and gravel; unattended. No airport facilities.

Visitor Facilities: Some supplies are available in the community. Accommodations available at several area lodges. Guide service for fishing; tackle is available for purchase. No other services available.

Igiugig began as a fishing village. Kiatagmuit Eskimos populated the village at the turn of the century. St. Nicholas Chapel, a Russian Orthodox church located in the village, is on the National Register of Historic Places. Igiugig is unincorporated.

Salmon fishing is the mainstay of Igiugig's economy. Some residents are employed in the community. During the red salmon season in late June and July, many leave the village to fish in Bristol Bay. In summer, sportfishing is popular in the Kvichak River-Lake Iliamna area. *NOTE: Contact Igiugig Native Corp. regarding land use fees before hunting, fishing or cutting wood.*

Communications include phones, mail plane, radio and TV. The community is served by old and new Russian Orthodox churches, and a school with grades 1 through 12. There are community electric and water systems. Residents use privies and honey buckets. Freight arrives in the village by air transport or barge. Native corporation address: Igiugig Natives Corp., P.O. Box 4009, Igiugig, AK 99613. Village council address: Igiugig Village Council, P.O. Box 4008, Igiugig, AK 99613.

Iliamna

(ill-ee-YAHM-nuh) Located on the north side of Lake Iliamna, 17 miles from Nondalton, 187 miles east-northeast of Dillingham, 225 miles southwest of Anchorage. **Transportation:** Boat; scheduled or charter air service from King Salmon, Dillingham and Anchorage. **Population:** 119. **Zip code:** 99606. **Emergency Services:** Alaska State Troopers, phone 571-1236; Health aide, phone 571-1386; Clinic, phone 571-1383; Volunteer Fire Department, phone 571-1246 or 1376.

Elevation: 190 feet. **Climate:** Transitional zone, with strong maritime influences. Average summer temperatures from 42° to 62°F; average winter temperatures from 6° to 30°F. Mean annual precipitation 26 inches; mean annual snowfall 61 inches.

Private Aircraft: Airport 3 miles west; elev. 207 feet; length 4,800 feet; gravel; fuel 100, jet A; attended on request. Runway soft when wet. Airport facilities include ticket counter, rest rooms and traffic control tower. Public transportation to town.

Visitor Facilities: Accommodations and meals available. There is a laundromat. No banking services. Groceries, clothing, first-aid supplies, hardware, camera film and sporting goods available in the community. Arts and crafts available for purchase include grass baskets. Fishing/hunting licenses available, as well as guide service. Aircraft mechanic available. Rental transportation includes autos, boats, trucks and charter aircraft. Fuel available includes diesel, propane, marine gas, white gas, kerosene and regular and unleaded gasoline. No public moorage facilities.

"Old Iliamna" was located near the mouth of the Iliamna River. Around 1935, the Indian village moved to its present location, approximately 40 miles from the old site. The first of several hunting and fishing lodges opened in Iliamna in the 1930s. A few lodges stay open year-round for those interested in ice fishing and winter hiking. An 8-mile gravel road connects Iliamna to Newhalen and there is an overland crossing from Old Iliamna to Iliamna Bay on Cook Inlet, still used for delivering freight and fishing boats.

Commercial fishing, sportfishing and hunting lodges are the major sources of income for the community. The majority of lodge employees, however, are hired from outside the village. There are several other jobs in the village with government agencies and local businesses.

Most Natives and an increasing number of non-Natives depend to varying degrees on subsistence hunting and fishing. Red and chum salmon are caught in summer. Freshwater fish, rabbit and porcupine are taken year-round. Moose, caribou, bear, ptarmigan, ducks and geese are hunted in season. Seals are taken occasionally from Lake Iliamna. In the fall, residents pick blackberries, blueberries, cranberries, salmonberries and raspberries. Wild celery, spinach and onions are gathered in spring.

Iliamna is a major gateway to the world-class fishing and hunting in the Kvichak River drainage. The system, with headwaters in Lake Iliamna and Lake Clark, is historically the most important spawning and rearing habitat for sockeye or red salmon in the world and the largest contributor to the Bristol Bay fishery. King, coho, chum and humpback salmon also are present, although in fewer numbers. State sportfishing regulations designate the Kvichak River system as a trophy fish area. Some of the largest rainbow trout in the world can be found in these waters.

Lake Iliamna , 75 miles long and 20 miles wide, is the largest lake in Alaska. It reputedly is the home of a "sea monster." Residents from villages around the lake claim to have seen the creature on several occasions.

Visitors planning to hike or canoe in the area should contact the National Park Service in Anchorage; much of the land is privately owned or owned by Native corporations. NOTE: Iliamna Natives Ltd. charges fees for camping on corporation land: $25 per person per night for 1 or 2 people; $50 per night for a group of 3 or more people. Fees are payable in advance and are nonrefundable. Hiking, berry picking and fishing also are permitted on corporation lands; hunting in general is not. Wood cutting is not permitted. These and other land-use regulations are available from the corporation office, P.O. Box 245, Iliamna, AK 99606.

Communications in Iliamna, which is incorporated, include phones, mail plane, radio and TV. The community is served by 2 churches and a school with grades preschool through 12. There are community electricity, water and sewer systems. Freight arrives by cargo plane. The sale of alcoholic beverages is prohibited. Government address: Iliamna Village Council, General Delivery, Iliamna, AK 99606, phone 571-1246. Village corporation address: Iliamna Natives Ltd., P.O. Box 245, Iliamna, AK 99606, phone 571-1256.

Kokhanok

(KOKE-a-nok) Located on the south shore of Lake Iliamna, 25 miles south of Iliamna and 210 miles west of Anchorage. **Transportation:** Charter and air taxi service from Iliamna. **Population:** 132. **Zip code:** 99606. **Emergency Services:** Clinic, phone 282-2203; Volunteer Fire Department.

Elevation: 50 feet. **Climate:** Average summer temperatures from 40° to 64°F; average winter temperatures from 3° to 30°F. Total precipitation about 32 inches annually; average annual snowfall 89.4 inches. Fierce windstorms are characteristic of the area.

Private Aircraft: Airstrip 2 miles west; elev. 100 feet; length 3,400 feet; gravel; attended irregularly.

Visitor Facilities: No accommodations, except for cots in the community hall. Two stores are located in private homes. The population of Kokhanok, also commonly called Kokhanok Bay, is primarily Aleut. Residents rely heavily on subsistence hunting and fishing for their survival. NOTE: Hiking, berry-picking, camping and fishing are permitted on lands owned by the Alaska Peninsula Corp. upon payment of a $20 per person/per day fee. Hunting and woodcutting on corporation lands is not permitted. Contact the corporation for more information. (See address below.)

Community employment is available for some residents. The community is accessible only by air and water. In winter snow machines and trucks are used to cross the frozen lake to Iliamna and other villages. Village festivals take place in winter and sled dog racing is a popular pastime.

Communications include phones, mail plane, radio and TV. The community is served by the Saints Peter and Paul Russian Orthodox Church, which is on the National Register of Historic Places, and by a school with grades preschool through 12. Electricity is provided by private generators. Water is hauled from Lake Iliamna, and residents have privies or honey buckets. Freight is brought in by air transport or by barge. The village bans the sale and importation of alcoholic beverages. Village corporation address: Alaska Peninsula Corp., P.O. Box 104360, Anchorage, AK 99510. Government address: Kokhanok Traditional Council, P.O. Box 1007, Kokhanok, AK 99606; phone 282-2202.

Newhalen

Located on the north shore of Iliamna Lake at the mouth of the Newhalen River, 4.5 miles southwest of Iliamna and 320 miles south-southwest of Anchorage. **Transportation:** Scheduled air service to Iliamna, then by road to Newhalen. **Population:** 172. **Zip code:** 99606. **Emergency Services:** Village Public Safety Officer, phone 571-1403; Clinic; Volunteer Fire Department, phone 571-1231.

Elevation: 190 feet. **Climate:** Transitional zone. Average summer temperatures from 42° to 62°F; average winter temperatures from 6° to 30°F. Annual precipitation averages 26 inches, with 64 inches of snow.

Private Aircraft: There is an old airstrip at Newhalen, but it has been out of use for years. Residents use the Iliamna airport.

Visitor Facilities: Accommodations, visitor services available in nearby Iliamna. There is a washeteria with showers and a store. Fishing/ hunting licenses available in Iliamna. No information on guide or repair services, rental transportation, fuel or moorage. *NOTE: Hiking, berry-picking, camping and fishing are permitted on lands owned by the Alaska Peninsula Corp. upon payment of a $20 per person/per day fee. Hunting and woodcutting on corporation lands is not permitted. Contact the corporation for more information. (See address below.)*

The 1890 census listed the Eskimo name of Noghelingamiut, meaning "people of Noghelin," at this location. The present name is an anglicized version of the original. The village was established in the late 1800s to take advantage of the plentiful fish and game in the area. Today, it remains a fishing village. Newhalen was incorporated as a second-class city in 1971. It is connected by a 9-mile-long road to Iliamna and the airport.

During the red salmon season most residents leave Newhalen to fish in Bristol Bay; many return at the end of the red season, although a few stay to fish the smaller pink and silver salmon runs later in the summer and fall. Other employment is in the public sector, such as with the school district or seasonal firefighting for the Bureau of Land Management.

Income from these enterprises is supplemented by subsistence hunting and fishing.

Freshwater fish, rabbit and porcupine are taken year-round. Moose, caribou, bear, ptarmigan, ducks and geese are hunted in season and seals are occasionally taken from Lake Iliamna. In the summer and fall, residents pick blackberries, blueberries, cranberries, salmonberries and raspberries. Wild celery and spinach are gathered in early spring.

Communications in Newhalen include phones, radio and TV. The community is served by a Russian Orthodox church and 2 schools with grades preschool through 12. There is a community electricity system. Most homes now have wells and bathrooms, and there are 15 new HUD homes. Freight arrives primarily by air cargo. Government address: City of Newhalen, P.O. Box 165, Iliamna, AK 99606; phone 571-1226. Village corporation address: Alaska Peninsula Corp., P.O. Box 104360, Anchorage, AK 99510.

Nondalton

Located on the west shore of Six Mile Lake, 15 miles north of Iliamna and 200 miles southwest of Anchorage. **Transportation:** Scheduled and charter air service from Anchorage and Iliamna. **Population:** 247. **Zip code:** 99640. **Emergency Services:** Police, phone 294-2262; Clinic, phone 294-2238; Volunteer Fire Department, phone 294-2262.

Elevation: 250 feet. **Climate:** Transitional zone. Weather information from Iliamna indicates average summer temperatures in Nondalton from 42° to 62°F and average winter temperatures from 6° to 30°F. Annual precipitation averages 26 inches, with 64 inches of snow.

Private Aircraft: Airstrip 1 mile northwest; elev. 250 feet; length 2,700 feet; gravel; fuel unavailable; unattended. Runway condition not monitored, visual inspection recommended prior to using. Transport to town available.

Visitor Facilities: Accommodations available at 3 lodges, 2 bed-and-breakfasts. Restaurant. No bank or public showers, but laundromat available. Groceries, first-aid supplies, hardware, film, sporting goods and Nondalton hats and T-shirts available. Fuel includes marine gas, regular and unleaded gasoline, diesel, propane, white gas and kerosene. Arts and crafts available for purchase include birch-bark baskets and dolls from the local doll factory. Fishing/hunting licenses, guides and repairs to marine engines, boats and autos all available. Rental transportation includes automobiles, boats, aircraft and off-road vehicles.

Nondalton is a Tanaina Indian name, first

recorded in 1909 by D.C. Witherspoon of the U.S. Geological Survey. The village originally was located on the north shore of Six Mile Lake. In 1940, firewood supplies were depleted and growing mudflats made it increasingly difficult to reach the lake, so the village relocated to the west shore. Nondalton was incorporated as a second-class city in 1971.

Nondalton's St. Nicholas Russian Orthodox Chapel, originally constructed in 1896 and moved with the rest of the village, is on the National Register of Historic Places.

Nondalton residents work seasonally in the commercial salmon fishery or firefighting for BLM. A few other jobs are with governmental agencies and the village Native corporation.

Residents depend heavily on subsistence hunting and fishing for food. Red salmon are caught in the summer and freshwater fish, rabbit and porcupine are taken year-round. Moose, caribou, bear, ptarmigan, ducks and geese are hunted in season. In late summer and fall, residents pick blueberries, blackberries and cranberries. Wild onions are gathered in the summer.

Communications include phones, TV via satellite and radio. The community is served by a school with grades preschool through 12. Nondalton has a new Russian Orthodox church. There are community electricity, water and sewer systems. Freight arrives by barge or small plane. The sale of alcoholic beverages is prohibited. Government address: City of Nondalton, General Delivery, Nondalton, AK 99640; phone 294-2235. Village corporation address: Kijik Corp, 4153 Tudor Centre Drive, Suite 104, Anchorage, AK 99508; phone 561-4487.

Pedro Bay

Located at the head of Pedro Bay in Lake Iliamna, 180 miles southwest of Anchorage. **Transportation:** Scheduled or charter air service from Iliamna. **Population:** 67. **Zip code:** 99647. **Emergency Services:** Village Public Safety Officer, phone 850-2236; Health aide, phone 850-2229; Volunteer Fire Department.

Climate: Transitional zone, with strong maritime influences. Weather data for Iliamna, 25 miles away, generally reflect conditions at Pedro Bay. Average summer temperatures from 42° to 62°F; average winter temperatures from 6° to 30°F.

Private Aircraft: Airstrip 1 mile west; elev. 45 feet; length 2,600 feet; crushed gravel topping; no fuel; unattended. Runway condition not monitored, visual inspection recommended prior to using. No transportation into village.

Visitor Facilities: Accommodations at a local lodge and in private homes. No laundromat or banking services. Groceries and first-aid supplies available in the community. Some beadwork and skin sewing available for purchase. Fishing/hunting licenses available, as well as guide service. No repair services. Boats may be rented. No public moorage facilities.

The Denaina Indians have occupied this area for hundreds of years. A Denaina village was once located at the west entrance to Pedro Bay and the Denaina warred with Russian fur traders over trade practices in the early 20th century. Denaina Indians still live in the area. Much of the "old way of life" has changed, but some folklore still remains. Pedro Bay is unincorporated.

Most Pedro Bay residents depend on subsistence hunting and fishing. Red salmon are caught in the summer and freshwater fish are taken year-round. Moose, rabbit, bear, ptarmigan and ducks are hunted in season. In early summer, residents gather wild celery and onions. In the fall, they pick blueberries, cranberries, blackberries and salmonberries.

Some residents obtain short-term government jobs and a few are fishermen. Others must leave the area to earn enough money to support themselves.

St. Nicholas Russian Orthodox Chapel, built in 1890, is on the National Register of Historic Places.

During spring and summer, brown bears gather along the salmon streams near Pedro Bay. Black bears are numerous and can be a nuisance because they often wander into the village. Moose concentrate year-round in the area surrounding the village.

Pedro Bay is located within the Kvichak River system, with headwaters in Lake Clark and Lake Iliamna. This is historically the most important spawning and rearing habitat for sockeye salmon in the world. Sportfishing for rainbow trout, arctic char and Dolly Varden also is excellent. A winter carnival in March features shooting matches, team games and food.

Communications in Pedro Bay include phones, mail plane, radio and TV. The community is served by 1 church and a school with grades kindergarten through 9. There is a community electricity system. Water is from private wells. Sewage system is septic tanks. Freight arrives by barge and air taxi. Government address: Pedro Bay Village Council, P.O.

Box 470020, Pedro Bay, AK 99647, phone 850-2225. Village corporation address: Pedro Bay Native Corp., P.O. Box 47015, Pedro Bay, AK 99647, phone 850-2232.

Pope & Vannoy Landing

Located on Intricate Bay on Lake Iliamna, 25 miles from Iliamna. **Transportation:** Boat; air taxi from Iliamna. **Population:** 14. **Zip code:** Via Iliamna 99606. **Emergency Services:** Alaska State Troopers, Iliamna; Health aide, Kokhanok.

Private Aircraft: No airstrip. Float or ski landings only.

Visitor Facilities: Lodging available 1 mile from the Copper River on Lake Iliamna. Guide services available.

Pope & Vannoy Landing is a settlement primarily of Pope family members. Art Pope writes that his son bought a cabin and moved here in 1955. He was followed by Pope's brother-in-law in 1957, Pope and his wife in 1965, and a granddaughter, Marlene DeNeut, in 1980. Another couple from Iliamna moved over in 1983.

All residents of the area obtain their supplies from Anchorage. Art Pope and his wife, both in their 70s, set net for salmon in the summer and tend an 11,000-square-foot garden.

Electricity is from individual generators. Water is hauled from the lake or a spring. Sewage system is outhouses.

Port Alsworth

Located on Lake Clark, 22 miles northeast of Nondalton, 180 miles from Anchorage. **Transportation:** Boat; scheduled and charter air service from Iliamna. **Population:** 30. **Zip code:** 99653. **Emergency Services:** Alaska State Troopers, phone 571-1236; Health aide, Iliamna, phone 781-2218.

Elevation: 230 feet. **Climate:** Summers are mild, according to one resident. Temperatures from 45°F to 80°F. Winters are usually mild, with temperatures from -30° to 40°F. Mean annual precipitation 17 inches; mean annual snowfall 68 inches.

Private Aircraft: There are 2 private airstrips in the center of the community. Aviation fuel 80, 100 available from The Farm Lodge for emergencies only. Airstrip use is by prior permission only from Glen or Wayne Alsworth, phone 781-2212 or 2204.

Visitor Facilities: Accommodations at several lodges and 1 bed-and-breakfast on Lake Clark. Meals available in the community. No banking services or laundry facilities. There are no stores; all supplies are obtained from Anchorage or Soldotna. Arts and crafts available for purchase include Indian and Eskimo hats, dolls, yo-yos, wood articles and local paintings. Fishing/hunting licenses available, as well as guide service. No major repairs available. Rental transportation includes boats and charter aircraft. No public moorage facilities.

Early Port Alsworth was a weather reporting station and stopover for airline flights to the Bristol Bay area, according to local residents. Pioneer bush pilot "Babe" Alsworth and his wife Mary, the settlement's first postmistress, were among the early settlers in the 1940s. They homesteaded on 160 acres and developed an airstrip and flying service. They also were involved in developing the Tanalian Bible Church and Camp. Port Alsworth now has several fishing lodges and is the local headquarters for Lake Clark National Park and Preserve. One resident describes it as "one of the finest places to live and visit in rural Alaska."

Most residents make their living either directly or indirectly from tourism. Employment is through the lodges, flying service, school, commercial fishing and a few local businesses.

Local attractions include 40-mile-long Lake Clark, one of the spawning grounds for the Bristol Bay red salmon run; the ruins of historic Kijik village, listed on the National Register of Historic Places; and picturesque Tanalian Falls. Activities include hiking, wildlife photography, bird-watching, river rafting, fishing, cross-country skiing, sledding, snowmobiling and hunting for moose, caribou, bear and small game.

From Anchorage, air access to Port Alsworth is by way of 1,000-foot Lake Clark Pass through the Aleutian Range.

Lake Clark National Park and Preserve offers a prime wilderness experience. The area boasts steaming volcanoes, rugged mountains, craggy peaks, alpine valleys, blue-green glaciers, free-flowing rivers and sparkling lakes. Its wildlife includes eagles, hawks, waterfowl and seabirds; grayling, northern pike, trout and salmon; bear, moose, caribou and Dall sheep. For more information write: Superintendent, Lake Clark National Park and Preserve, 701 C St., Box 61, Anchorage, AK 99513.

Communications at Port Alsworth, which is unincorporated, include phones, mail plane, radio and TV. The community is served by Tanalian Bible Church and a school with grades 1 through 12. Electricity is from individual generators, water from private wells. Sewage system is septic tanks.

Freight arrives by cargo plane and an occasional small barge.

Tyonek

Located on the northwest shore of Cook Inlet on the Cook Inlet Lowland, 43 miles southwest of Anchorage. **Transportation:** Boat; scheduled and charter air service from Anchorage. **Population:** 280. **Zip code:** 99682. **Emergency Services:** Village Public Safety Officer; Clinic, phone 583-2461; Volunteer Fire Department; Rescue Squad.

Elevation: 80 feet. **Climate:** Maritime climate characterized by moderate precipitation, generally cool summers and warm winters. Lowest recorded temperature -27°F; recorded high 91°F. Average annual precipitation 23 inches.

Private Aircraft: Airstrip 0.3 mile northeast; elev. 110 feet; length 3,350 feet; gravel; no fuel. Pilots must obtain prior permission from the village before landing. Unicom radio is manned from 8 a.m. to 5 p.m. Monday through Friday. Pilots report turbulence when the wind blows from the east.

Visitor Facilities: Accommodations at guest house. No laundry facilities. Groceries available. No major repair services or rental transportation. Fuel available: regular gasoline. No public moorage facilities. Fishing/hunting licenses and fishing guide service available. Half-day tour of Tyonek available from Anchorage. *NOTE: Much of the land along the Chuitna River is owned by the Tyonek Native Corp. and fishermen must have a guide from Tyonek.* Land on the north side of the Chuitna River mouth is public land.

Accessible by road from Tyonek is Trading Bay State Game Refuge, established to protect waterfowl nesting, feeding and migration; moose calving areas; salmon spawning and rearing habitats; public use of fish and wild life habitat (waterfowl, moose and bear hunting); viewing photography; and general public recreation. This is a popular waterfowl and moose hunting area in the fall. Fly-in sportfishing and commercial set-net fishing occur in the refuge. There are no developed public-use facilities in the refuge.

Prehistory of the upper Cook Inlet region is practically unknown. Earliest written descriptions of the Cook Inlet Athabascans are found in Captain Cook's journal. Cook explored the inlet which bears his name some 37 years after Vitus Bering discovered Alaska in 1741. Cook found that the Natives had iron knives and glass beads, which led him to conclude they were trading indirectly with the Russians. Russian fur-trading posts proliferated in Alaska and trading settlements were established at Tuiunuk (one of the various past spellings of Tyonek) and Iliamna. These 2 outposts were destroyed in the 1790s due to dissension between the Natives and Russians. After the sale of Alaska to the United States in 1867, the American Alaska Commercial Co. (ACC) replaced the Russian-American Co. as the dominant trading company in Alaska.

ACC's major outpost in upper Cook Inlet was Tyonek. Records show that this post operated from at least 1875. Following the discovery of gold at Resurrection Creek near Turnagain Arm in the 1880s, Tyonek became a major disembarking point for goods and people. The population of Tyonek decreased when Anchorage was founded but it still is the main settlement on the western shore of Cook Inlet.

In 1965 the Tyonek Indians won a landmark decision when the federal court ruled that the Bureau of Indian Affairs had no right to lease Tyonek Reservation land for oil development without permission of the Indians themselves. The tribe subsequently sold rights to drill for oil and gas beneath the reservation to a group of oil companies for $12.9 million, which has been invested for the benefit of Tyonek residents.

Employment opportunities at Tyonek are limited. Many residents are commercial fishermen or have jobs with the school, store, post office, village administration and other government agencies.

Tyonek residents continue to follow a subsistence lifestyle resembling that of their ancestors. They fish for king, pink and red salmon, hooligan, rainbow trout, Dolly Varden and whitefish. Hunting is for moose, ducks, geese, spruce hens, porcupines, beluga whales and seals. There is some trapping for marten, mink, red fox and beaver. Blueberries, raspberries, highbush and lowbush cranberries and salmonberries are gathered in late summer and early fall.

Communications at Tyonek include phones, daily mail service, radio and TV. The community is served by a Russian Orthodox church and a school with grades kindergarten through 12. There are community electricity and water systems. Sewage system is septic tanks. Freight arrives by cargo plane and barge. Government address: Native Village of Tyonek, P.O. Box 82009, Tyonek, AK 99682; phone 583-2201. Village corporation address: Tyonek Native Corp., 4433 Lake Otis Parkway, Anchorage, AK 99507; phone 563-0707.

▼ A T T R A C T I O N S ▼

National & State Parks, Forests, Etc.

Lake Clark National Park and Preserve

This 3.6-million-acre park and preserve is located north of Lake Iliamna, 150 miles southwest of Anchorage. The park and preserve boasts an array of features including a jumble of glacier-carved peaks ranging up to 10,000 feet; 2 steaming volcanoes; countless glaciers; many lakes, ranging from 40-mile-long Lake Clark to shallow tundra ponds; deep U-shaped valleys with rushing streams; open, lichen-covered uplands where streams meander languidly; 3 wild and scenic rivers — the Mulchatna, Tlikakila and Chilikadrotna; and a coastline along Cook Inlet full of tidal bays and rocky inlets. Lake Clark is fed by hundreds of mountain waterfalls and is part of an important red salmon spawning ground. Some 56 archaeological sites have been located within the park and preserve, including the Kijik village site which is on the National Register of Historic Places.

Climate: The climate on the eastern Cook Inlet side of Lake Clark differs markedly from that on the northwestern slopes and plains. A maritime climate influences the former; drier, continental patterns dominate the latter. In summer the temperature ranges between 45° and 65°F in the eastern portion and reaches into the 80s in the western part. Precipitation along the coast reaches 60 inches annually, while the interior gets only 20 inches. March and early April are best for cross-country skiing. From mid-April to late May thawing streams and lakes make all travel difficult. Strong winds — severe in and near mountain passes — can occur at any time.

Wildlife: The Mulchatna caribou herd, moose, brown and black bear, wolf, wolverine, marten, mink, land otter, weasel, beaver, lynx and red fox are found in the park and preserve. Dall sheep reach the southern limit of their range in the Lake Clark mountains.

Whales and seals swim offshore along the coast. Waterfowl are abundant along Tuxedni Bay and in the ponds and marshes of the tundra plains. Bald eagles, peregrine falcons and numerous other birds nest in the park and preserve.

Sportfishing is good in the area. Grayling, northern pike, and several trout and salmon species can be caught throughout most of the season of open water. Sport hunting is allowed in the preserve under Alaska Dept. of Fish and Game regulations.

Activities: Backpacking, river running and fishing are the primary activities in this predominantly wilderness area. Wildlife nature viewing and photography are excellent.

Access: The region is accessible by air from Anchorage or the Kenai Peninsula. There is daily commercial air service to Iliamna, linked by road to Nondalton at the west end of Lake Clark. In addition, there are many air charter operators in Anchorage, the Kenai Peninsula, Iliamna and other communities who fly to the park or preserve. There are no roads or trails in the park or preserve. Helicopter landings are prohibited on park and preserve lands except by permit from the park superintendent.

Accommodations: Several private lodges on Lake Clark offer accommodations and services by advance reservation and stores in Iliamna and Nondalton have limited supplies. Many attractions, however, are far from modern conveniences.

The Park Service advises visitors to arrive self-sufficient and carry extra supplies in the event weather delays air or boat pickup. Warm clothing, good-quality camping and rain gear, and insect repellent or a head net are essential. The Park Service further cautions that this is a vast and sometimes hostile region; the animals are wild and must be respected. Also, local residents carry on subsistence hunting, fishing and other activities, and their camps and equipment are critical to their livelihood and should be left undisturbed.

Additional information about the park and preserve, as well as guides, outfitters and lodges in the area are available from: Superintendent, Lake Clark National Park and Preserve, 222 W. 7th Ave., #61, Anchorage, AK 99513-7539; phone 271-3751. Related USGS Topographic Series maps: Lime Hills, Lake Clark, Iliamna, Kenai, Seldovia, Tyonek.

McNeil River State Game Sanctuary

McNeil River is located approximately 200 air miles southwest of Anchorage and 100 air miles west of Homer. The river drains into Kamishak Bay in the shadow of Augustine Island, an active volcano with a history of violent eruptions, the most recent in March of 1986. McNeil River is bordered to the south by Katmai National Park and Preserve.

The McNeil River State Game Sanctuary draws photographers from all over the world, attracted by the large numbers of brown bears that congregate in the summer to feast on spawning chum salmon. The greatest numbers may be seen at the McNeil River falls, about 1 mile up from the river mouth. Nowhere else can groups of up to 20 wild brown bears or 60 or so individual bears coming and going be seen.

In order to reduce disturbance of the bears and minimize the risk of human-bear encounters, the Alaska Dept. of Fish and Game allows visitors to the sanctuary by permit only during the peak season July 1 through Aug. 25. A Fish and Game employee is stationed at the camp to escort visitors to the falls each day. No more than 10 permit holders per day are allowed to visit the falls during peak season; permittees are selected by a lottery drawing held May 15. Return a completed application and $50 fee per applicant by April 1 to be eligible for the drawing. Ten dollars of the fee is nonrefundable. Unsuccessful applicants automatically receive a $40 refund after the drawing.

Other wildlife that may be observed at McNeil River includes red fox year-round, spawning salmon in July and August, bald eagles May to September and common murres and double-crested cormorants May to August.

Access to the sanctuary is usually by private or charter floatplane from Anchorage,

Kenai or Homer, landing at high tide.

Visitors to McNeil River must be self-sufficient and prepared for a wilderness experience. There are no visitor facilities. Equipment and clothing must be adequate to withstand cold, wind and rain. Bring camping gear, rain gear, hip boots (you have to wade through water over knee-deep to reach the falls) and lots of film. Carry extra food in case bad weather prolongs your stay for several days. It also is recommended that photographers bring a packboard or packsack to carry camera equipment.

Additional information and permit applications may be obtained from the Alaska Dept. of Fish and Game, Game Division, P.O. Box 37, King Salmon, AK 99613; phone 246-3340. Or contact: Alaska Dept. of Fish and Game, Game Division, 333 Raspberry Road, Anchorage, AK 99502; phone 267-2179.

The Rivers

Chilikadrotna River. This wild and scenic river heads in Twin Lakes in Lake Clark National Park and Preserve and flows 60 miles to join the Mulchatna River 46 miles northwest of Nondalton on Lake Clark. The first 11 miles of the river are within the park and preserve. This swift (usually 5 mph) river flows through the forest west of the Alaska Range. It offers an excellent, but demanding, white-water experience with many stretches of fast water and rapids for the intermediate boater. The first 4 miles are Class II, followed by about 4 miles of flat water. Then it's 31 miles of Class II; there are many sweepers, which combined with the swift current and twisting course require constant alertness. About midway along this stretch — approximately 5 miles below the Little Mulchatna River — there is one Class III rapids. Rafts or kayaks are recommended; canoes should be used only by very experienced paddlers. The trip generally takes 4 days from Twin Lakes to the first Mulchatna River takeout.

This trip offers fishing for grayling, rainbow trout, Dolly Varden and pike. There also is lake trout fishing at Twin Lakes. Hiking is good throughout the course of the river and there is mountain scenery around Twin Lakes.

Access is by floatplane from Anchorage or the Lake Clark area to Twin Lakes. Exit is from the Mulchatna River 12 miles or more below the Chilikadrotna confluence, or from villages farther down on the Nushagak River. Related USGS Topographic Series maps: Lake Clark C-2 through C-7. (The Chilikadrotna River is shown on our map of the Bering Sea Coast.)

Copper (Iliamna) River. This fast, clear-water river heads in Meadow Lake and flows 40 river miles southwest into Intricate Bay on Lake Iliamna. The river connects Upper and Lower Copper lakes, and Upper and Lower Pike lakes. From Upper Pike Lake, the river offers a 1-1/2-day-long trip with possible short portages suitable for relatively inexperienced boaters. This stretch features 6 miles of Class II consisting of 4 miles of Class I separating several larger rapids, some of which border on Class III. Boaters should be alert for right-angle turns. For white-water enthusiasts, the upper river offers a 2-mile stretch of Class III-IV between Upper and Lower Copper lakes, then 3 miles of Class III before 3 falls, which must be portaged on the left bank. From Upper or Lower Copper Lake the trip takes approximately 3 to 3-1/2 days. Rafts are recommended.

The Copper River flows through a scenic forest and offers seasonally good fishing downstream from the falls for salmon and rainbow trout. Pike can be caught in side sloughs and lakes. Wildlife that may be seen includes bears, moose, eagles and beavers.

Access is by floatplane from Iliamna to Upper Pike Lake or to Upper or Lower Copper Lake. Exit is by floatplane from Intricate Bay or Lower Pike Lake. Related USGS Topographic Series maps: Iliamna C-3 through C-5.

Mulchatna River. This wild and scenic river heads in Turquoise Lake in the foothills of the Chigmit Mountains in Lake Clark National Park and Preserve and flows 220 river miles to join the Nushagak River, 65 miles northeast of Dillingham. The first 24 miles of the Mulchatna are within the park and preserve. Above Bonanza Hills for the first 22 miles the Mulchatna is shallow Class II to Class III, rocky and fast. The alpine tundra around Turquoise Lake changes to spruce and hardwood forest downriver. Below the Bonanza Hills, the Mulchatna is an easy, leisurely float, wandering through a forest, although there is a 2- to 3-foot ledge drop about midway from the Bonanza Hills to the confluence of the Chilikadrotna River. Floaters also should be alert for numerous sweepers or logjams in the many channels of this section. Above Keefer Creek the river passes through low hills; below Keefer Creek it meanders across the tundra of the Nushagak lowlands. Rafts are recommended above Bonanza

Bush planes provide access to Lake Clark National Park and Preserve through Port Alsworth, just 22 miles from Nondalton and 180 miles from Anchorage via the 1,000-foot Lake Clark Pass through the Aleutian Range. (Alissa Crandall)

Hills; rafts, canoes or kayaks are suitable for the rest of the river. This trip usually takes 2 days from Turquoise Lake to the end of the Bonanza Hills, then 4 days to the first takeout point. Thereafter, boaters average 12 to 18 miles per day.

Portions of the river valley are swampy, but many high places provide good campsites. Fishing varies from poor to good for grayling, rainbow trout, Dolly Varden and salmon, depending on water conditions and the time of year. There is beautiful scenery and good hiking around the Turquoise Lake area. Wildlife along the river includes a large beaver population.

Access is by floatplane from Anchorage or Lake Clark area communities to Turquoise Lake or to small lakes along the Mulchatna below Bonanza Hills. Exit is by floatplane from the Mulchatna 12 miles or more below the Chilikadrotna River confluence, or from villages on the Nushagak served by scheduled air service. Related USGS Topographic Series maps: Lake Clark D-3 through D-6, C-6 through C-8, B-7 and B-8; Taylor Mountains B-1, A-1 and A-2; Dillingham D-1 through D-3, C-3. (The Mulchatna River is shown on our map of the Bering Sea Coast.)

Newhalen River. This large, clear white-water river heads in Sixmile Lake, then flows south 22 miles to Lake Iliamna. This beautiful turquoise-colored river has flat water for 8 miles from Sixmile Lake to an area called Upper Landing reached by road from Iliamna airport. Then there is 9 miles of Class I, with a few Class II riffles. Serious white water begins about 7 miles from the mouth of the river where there is a difficult Class V rapid, followed by 7 more Class IV rapids. The Class V rapid is signaled by a ledge extending nearly the width of the river at a right-hand bend. This ledge should be run on the left. Then there is a series of narrower ledges on a long, straight stretch, which should be run midstream. Boaters then reach a left-hand bend, below which an island divides the river into 2 chutes, with a rock pillar in the left chute. There are dangerous falls in the right chute, so run the left chute or portage on the left side. Portage can start from an eddy just above the island. This route requires a sure crossover from the midstream route around the series of ledges. A longer, safer portage begins at the wide ledge at the previous right-hand bend.

This river offers very good fishing in season for all salmon, grayling, arctic char, rainbow and lake trout.

Boaters should be aware that all of the land bordering the Newhalen has been selected by Native corporations. Contact BLM, 4700 E. 72nd Ave., Anchorage, AK 99507 for the location of public easements.

Access is by floatplane from Iliamna, by commercial air service, to Sixmile Lake. Or put in at Upper Landing via taxi. Exit is via a trail to Iliamna airport below a series of ledges called "The Falls" or float to the village of Newhalen. Related USGS Topographic Series maps: Newhalen dam site map or Iliamna C-6, D-5 and D-6.

Telaquana and Necons rivers. These rivers are semiclear-water tributaries to the silt-laden Stony River. The Necons heads in Two Lakes in Lake Clark National Park and Preserve and flows 16 miles to the Stony. It offers a relatively easy float on moderately swift water through an upland forest. There are 2 short (100 to 250 yards) stretches of Class II rapids on the Necons — a set near its outlet and another close to its confluence with the Stony River. Both may be lined or portaged. The Necons provides easier access to the Stony than does the Telaquana with the trip taking a day from Two Lakes to Stony River.

The Telaquana heads in Telaquana Lake, also located in Lake Clark National Park and Preserve, and flows 29 miles to the Stony. It offers more white water and better fishing for salmon than the Necons. There are 2 small falls on the Telaquana. The first is about 11 miles from its outlet and drops about 8 feet in 2 steps; the second drops 4 to 5 feet in several steps. Both may be portaged or the second drop may be lined or run. This trip generally takes 2 days from Telaquana Lake to Stony River.

Rafts, kayaks and canoes all are suitable for these rivers, although canoeists on the Telaquana should be experienced.

Telaquana and Two Lakes are scenic, offer good hiking and seasonally good hunting or viewing opportunities for moose, caribou, bear and waterfowl. Fishing is fair for Dolly Varden and grayling in both rivers and seasonally good for red salmon in the Telaquana River. Reportedly there are no good campsites at the outlet of Two Lakes.

Access is by floatplane to Telaquana or Two Lakes. Exit is by floatplane from the Stony River or lower Telaquana River, by mail plane from Lime Village or by scheduled air service from Stony River village, which has limited accommodations. Related USGS Topographic Series maps: For the Necons, Lime Hills A-3; for the Telaquana, Lake Clark D-3, D-4 and Lime Hills A-4.

Tlikakila River. *(ta-lick-a-KEEL-a)* This designated wild and scenic river heads in

Summit Lake and flows 51 miles to Lake Clark. This is an extremely fast but small glacial river that flows through a narrow, deep valley in the Alaska Range. A short portage may be necessary from Summit Lake to the river. Most of the river is Class I, but there are several hundred yards of Class III just below the North Fork confluence which can be portaged on the left side. This trip takes about 3 days from Summit Lake to Lake Clark. Rafts or kayaks are recommended for this river, although canoes are suitable for experienced paddlers.

Access to the Tlikakila is by floatplane from Iliamna or Port Alsworth to Summit Lake. Exit is by floatplane from a small bay west of the river's mouth. Or boaters can paddle to Port Alsworth or farther down Lake Clark. Related USGS Topographic Series maps: Lake Clark B-2, B-3, C-1, C-2 and Kenai C-8 and D-8.

Sportfishing

Except for a few roads around Iliamna, access to good fishing in Western Cook Inlet is primarily by airplane. If you have the time, however, you can sometimes hike or go by boat to a hot fishing spot. Boats occasionally can be rented or chartered at villages along the waterways. There are daily commercial flights to Iliamna and from there to Port Alsworth or charters to more remote destinations.

The Alaska Dept. of Fish and Game recommends that anyone traveling here should plan for the worst. Take a few days' extra food and fuel if necessary, and allow for flexible scheduling since weather can delay travel. Although many villages and lodges have fishing licenses for sale, officials recommend that you buy yours before you head into the backcountry.

More information about fishing in Western Cook Inlet may be obtained from: Alaska Dept. of Fish and Game, Sport Fish Division, 333 Raspberry Road, Anchorage, AK 99518; phone 267-2220.

Bristol Bay Wild Trout Area. This special designation encompasses the Kvichak-Alagnak watershed, except Lake Clark and its tributaries above Six-Mile Lake. For additional information, see Lake Iliamna under Special Features this subregion, and Sportfishing in the Bristol Bay subregion of the BERING SEA COAST section.

Chuitna River. Flows southeast 37 miles to Cook Inlet, 2 miles north of Tyonek. Fish available: king salmon — June through early July, use cluster eggs, spinners or spoons; silver salmon — July and August, use cluster eggs, spinners or spoons; pink salmon — July and August, use small spoons or spinners; rainbow trout — use flies, lures or bait. Accessible by wheel plane (30 minutes flying time from Anchorage). *NOTE: Much of the land along the Chuitna River is owned by the Tyonek Native Corp. and fishermen must have a guide from Tyonek.* Land on the north side of the Chuitna River mouth is public land.

Lake Clark Area. Located approximately 30 miles north of Iliamna in Lake Clark National Park and Preserve. Excellent fishery. Fish available: lake trout, burbot, whitefish and northern pike year-round; red salmon June to August; arctic char, best June to September; grayling, best May to September. Accessible by small plane from Iliamna and Port Alsworth. Several private lodges in area require advance reservations. Other accommodations limited.

Lake Iliamna. Located approximately 200 miles southwest of Anchorage, 30 miles south of Lake Clark, the state's largest lake, lies outside any park or refuge boundary. Peak months for fish: rainbow trout — first 3 weeks June, 2nd week August through mid-October; king salmon — late June through late July; sockeye salmon — late June through July; pink salmon — first 3 weeks August; chum salmon — last 3 weeks July; arctic char — June through early August; grayling — June through August; lake trout — first 2 weeks June; northern pike — late June through August.

Nushagak-Mulchatna River System. Though most of this river system lies farther west in the Bristol Bay area, the headwaters lie in Lake Clark National Park and Preserve in Western Cook Inlet. For details on sportfishing these hundreds of miles of rivers, see Sportfishing in the Bristol Bay subregion in BERING SEA COAST section.

Theodore River. This river flows southeast 35 miles to Cook Inlet, 32 miles west of Anchorage. Accessible by small wheel plane from Anchorage. Fish available: king salmon — late May through June, use egg clusters, spinners or spoons; silver salmon — July to September, use egg clusters, spinners or spoons; pink salmon — July and August, use small spoons; rainbow trout — year-round, use flies or lures.

STATE FLOWER

The Alaska State flower is the Forget-Me-Not.   — *The ALASKA ALMANAC*®

SPECIAL FEATURES

Lake Iliamna

A huge inland lake covering 1,000 square miles; strewn with islands on its east and south sides; surrounding by wild, beautiful country; and dotted here and there with settlements, villages and wilderness fishing lodges. This is Lake Iliamna.

Alaska's largest lake helps support the largest sockeye (red) salmon run in the world. Iliamna, along with Lake Clark and tributary rivers, provides spawning grounds for the salmon, which grow to maturity in Bristol Bay then find their way back up the Kvichak River to lay their eggs, fertilize them and die. (For more on Bristol Bay and the Kvichak River, see the Bristol Bay subregion of the BERING SEA COAST section.) But sockeyes are only one of the salmon species that anglers go after in Iliamna Lake. There are also fine runs of kings, silvers, pinks and chums. Other fish include Dolly Varden, arctic char, lake trout and grayling.

The Alaska Board of Fisheries has designated the Kvichak-Alagnak watershed, which includes all of Lake Iliamna, as a Wild Trout Area. Regulations are conservative, designed to perpetuate the high quality wild rainbow trout fisheries while providing anglers a variety of fishing experiences. Large rainbow trout, probably the most sought-after sport fish in southwest Alaska, are available all season long, but most of the big ones (up to 18 pounds) are taken in late summer and early fall. During September the rainbows will leave the lake and enter clearwater streams to feast on salmon eggs and insects feeding on decaying salmon.

Besides the world-class fishing, anglers are treated to beautiful fall colors. Catch-and-release is practiced here, except for the occasional mortally hooked fish (kept for dinner) and the once-in-a-lifetime trophy saved for mounting. (For more on catch-and-release, see Fishing in GENERAL INFORMATION section.)

Summers at Lake Iliamna tend to be cool and rainy, especially in August and September. When storms brew up, winds can whip the waters of the lake into high, dangerous waves. One wilderness lodge advises its vistiors to bring down vests and jackets, wool shirts and good rain gear. Binoculars and, of course, a camera are also recommended.

Accommodations range from basic shelter to luxurious, first-class world renowned lodges. There are no established campgrounds around the lake. Some anglers prefer to stay in Iliamna itself (see Communities this section) and take day trips out via floatplane and hire a guide with a boat. Reservations at lodges should be made well in advance, but air taxi operators can usually accommodate the day fisherman.

The Alaska Dept. of Fish and Game reminds visitors that timing is critical, particularly for anglers targeting one or two species of fish. The department's *Recreational Fishing Guide* (available for $5 from Alaska Dept. of Fish and Game, Box 3-2000, Juneau, AK 99802-2000) provides preliminary information, and local guides and lodges can also help you plan your trip. Air taxi operators in Anchorage, Kenai and Homer can put you in contact with many of the sportfishing experts. The lake and its excellent fishing are accessible by scheduled and charter flights from Anchorage, Dillingham and King Salmon.

Lake Iliamna does not lie within any established park or refuge boundaries. Much of the land is owned by Native corporations. *NOTE: Iliamna Natives Ltd. charges fees for camping on corporation land; $25 per person per night for 1 or 2 people; $50 per night for a group of 3 or more. Fees are payable in advance and are nonrefundable.* Hiking, berry-picking and fishing also are permitted on corporation lands; hunting in general is not. Wood cutting is not permitted. These and other land-use regulations are available from the corporation office, P.O. Box 245, Iliamna, AK 99606.

VOLCANOES

Alaska contains some 70 potentially active volcanoes. Three of the tallest and one of the most active volcanoes are located on the west coast of Cook Inlet. Part of the "Ring of Fire" that surrounds the Pacific Ocean, these Western Cook Inlet volcanoes have all erupted within the past 50 years, one as recently as 1986.

Mounts Spurr (11,070 feet), Redoubt (10,197 feet), and Iliamna (10,016 feet) are 3 of the 4 tallest volcanoes in Alaska. Only Mount Wrangell in eastern Alaska at 14,163 feet is taller.

Mount Augustine, while much smaller at 4,025 feet, is the most active volcano in the Cook Inlet region. Since written records have been kept, the most significant eruptions on Mount Augustine have occurred in 1812, 1883, 1902, 1935, 1963-64, 1976 and most recently in 1986.

Located on a small uninhabited island in lower Cook Inlet, Mount Augustine rises above the sea in a symmetrical cone-shape that seems more illusion than reality from Homer on hazy days. Not much has been writtten about the mountain or the island and as far as anyone knows, no one has lived on the island, although pumice was mined on its southwest flank from 1946 to 1949. Few seek out the island for recreation although air services from Homer fly out campers and hikers for occasional visits. Foxes are the largest land mammals found on the island. Alders and low brush are the primary vegatation, although a few spruces are scattered on the southwest side of the island. The island can be a good spot for viewing marine mammals and seabirds.

Mount Augustine's most recent eruption on March 27, 1986 sent ash 8 miles high and disrupted air traffic in southcentral Alaska for several days. After the 1976 eruption, prevailing winds dumped ash on the Kenai Peninsula and a mixture of snow and ash fell on Anchorage, 180 miles northwest, the morning after the eruption. Prevailing winds took ash from that eruption as far as Sitka in Southeast Alaska, some 680 miles away.

The taller volcanoes have been less active. Mount Iliamna spouts steam frequently from a vent near its summit but there are no documented reports of eruptions, according to the USGS. Redoubt Volcano, just north of Iliamna, awakened Dec. 14, 1989, dumping varying amounts of ash primarily north and west of the volcano and lightly dusting Anchorage and Kenai. Periodic eruptions continued through the week before Christmas, disrupting holiday air traffic. Until 1989, Redoubt had not erupted since 1966.

Mount Spurr, the northernmost in the Aleutian Chain-Alaska Peninsula volcano line, last erupted the morning of July 9, 1953. That spectacular explosion sent a cloud of ash up 70,000 feet in just 40 minutes according to U.S. Air Force pilots who were flying in the area when the eruption occurred. Ash dropped on Anchorage, only 80 miles east, just before noon and continued to fall until 3 p.m. with a total accumulation of 1/8 to 1/4 inch.

Mountaineers have tackled both Mounts Spurr and Redoubt. As with all Alaska mountaineering, weather is a major factor in the successful climbs.

NOTE: Information was gathered from *Alaska's Volcanoes,* published in 1976 by The Alaska Geographic Society, from *The ALASKA ALMANAC®, Mount Augustine* by Jan O'Meara and from an interview with Tom Miller, USGS.

Kayaker in Katmai National Park and Preserve displays sockeye salmon catch. Abundant fishing opportunities in the park provide a welcome change from traditional camp food. (George Wuerthner)

ALASKA PENINSULA/ ALEUTIANS

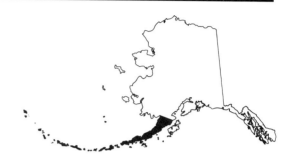

The Region

Active volcanoes, fish-clogged rivers, huge brown bears, and storm-washed islands characterize this remote, beautiful region full of critical wildlife habitat that draws fishermen, hunters, and bird-watchers from all over the world.

Location: This region takes in the Alaska Peninsula which curves about 500 miles southwest from Naknek Lake to the first of the Aleutians. The more than 124 islands of the Aleutian chain and the Pribilof group to the north in the Bering Sea make up the rest of the region. The Aleutians, extending more than 1,000 miles from Unimak to remote Attu, separate the Bering Sea from the North Pacific in a divide known as the "birthplace of winds."

Physical Description: The Aleutians and Pribilofs are treeless tops of submerged mountains. The Aleutians sit atop the "Ring of Fire," a necklace of volcanoes around much of the Pacific Rim. Shishaldin Volcano on Unimak Island, highest point in the Aleutians, rises 9,372 feet above sea level and 32,472 feet from the ocean floor. Off the Pacific side of the region lies the Aleutian Trench, 2,000 miles long, 50 to 100 miles wide, and up to 25,000 feet deep, where continental plates meet and the Pacific plate is carried down into the earth. To the north, the Bering Sea slopes downward in a shallow underwater valley, 249 miles long and up to 10,677 feet deep.

The Alaska Peninsula is a slender spine, steep sloped and topped with volcanoes on the Pacific side and tapered on the Bering Sea side to a rich, coastal wetland.

Few rivers etch the steep slopes of the Aleutians; the Alaska Peninsula has abundant rivers, many offering some of the world's finest fishing.

Climate

Aleutian weather has been called the worst in the world. Storm fronts generally move from west to east here. But, climatic conditions on the Pacific side often differ vastly from those on the Bering side placing the islands in the middle of a continual weather conflict.

Measurable precipitation occurs more than 200 days each year. Annual average is 33.44 inches at Cold Bay near the tip of the peninsula and 28.85 inches at Shemya in the western Aleutians.

Aleutian temperatures usually are milder than elsewhere in Alaska because of the chain's southern location and the moderating influence of surrounding waters. At Shemya summer temperatures range from 39° to 53°F, with 28° to 39°F in winter. Summer temperatures at Dutch Harbor in the eastern Aleutians range from 40° to 60°F in summer and 27° to 37°F in winter.

Vegetation

In summer the Aleutians and Pribilofs are covered with a carpet of lush grass and decorated with abundant wildflowers. The islands are treeless except for a few stands transplanted from other regions which have survived in sheltered nooks.

The peninsula is forested in its northern reaches, carpeted with upland tundra, and on the Bering Sea side covered with valuable wetlands.

Wildlife

Big Game: Brown/grizzly bears inhabit Unimak, easternmost of the Aleutians, but are absent from the rest of the chain and

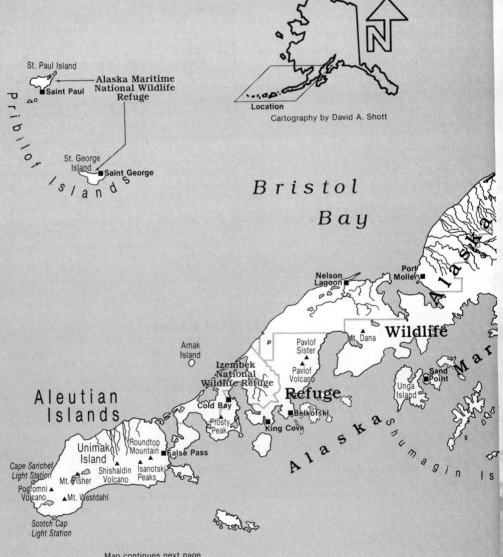

ALASKA PENINSULA
▼▼▼
ALEUTIANS

Location

Cartography by David A. Shott

St. Paul Island

■Saint Paul

Alaska Maritime
National Wildlife
Refuge

Pribilof

St. George
Island ■Saint George

Islands

Bristol

Bay

Nelson
Lagoon ■

Port
Moller ■

Alaska

Wildlife

Mt. Dana ▲

Pavlof
Sister ▲

Refuge

Amak
Island ○

Izembek
National
Wildlife Refuge

Pavlof
Volcano ▲

Sand
Point ■

Unga
Island

Mar

**Aleutian
Islands**

Cold Bay ■

Belkofski ■

Alaska

Shumagin

Frosty
Peak ▲

King Cove ■

Roundtop
Mountain ▲

False Pass ■

Unimak
Island

Cape Sarichef
Light Station

Shishaldin
Volcano ▲

Isanotski
Peaks ▲

Mt. Fisher ▲

Pogromni ▲
Volcano

▲Mt. Westdahl

Is

Scotch Cap
Light Station

Map continues next page

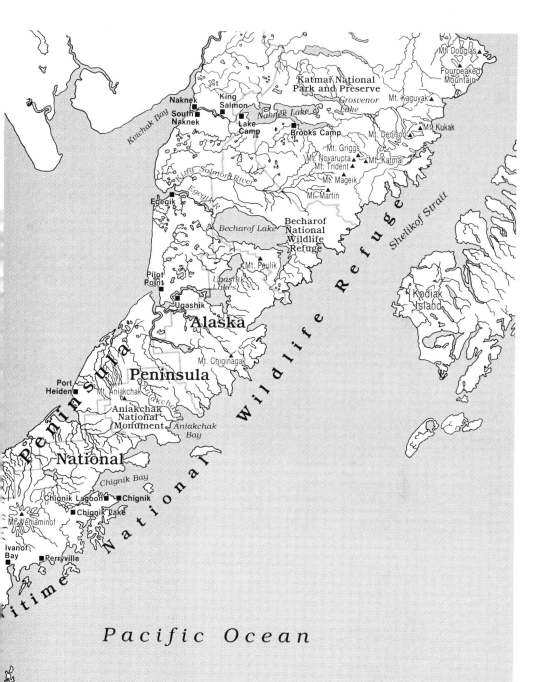

Mt Douglas ▲

Fourpeaked
Mountain ▲

Katmai National
Park and Preserve

*Grosvenor
Lake*

Mt. Kaguyak ▲

Naknek
King
Salmon
South
Naknek

Kvichak Bay

Naknek Lake

Lake
Camp

Brooks Camp

Mt. Denison ▲

▲Mt. Kukak

Mt. Griggs ▲

Mt. Novarupta ▲
Mt. Trident ▲

▲Mt. Katmai

Mt. Mageik ▲

King Salmon River

Egegik R.

Egegik

Mt. Martin ▲

Becharof
National
Wildlife
Refuge

Becharof Lake

Shelikof Strait

Pilot
Point

Mt. Peulik ▲

*Ugashik
Lakes*

Ugashik

Alaska

N
a
t
i
o
n
a
l

W
i
l
d
l
i
f
e

R
e
f
u
g
e

Kodiak
Island

Mt. Chiginagak ▲

Peninsula

Port
Heiden ■
Mt. Aniakchak ▲

Aniakchak

Aniakchak
National
Monument

*Aniakchak
Bay*

National

Chignik Bay

Chignik Lagoon ■ ■ Chignik
■ Chignik Lake

▲ Mt. Veniaminof

Ivanof
Bay ■
■ Perryville

P
e
n
i
n
s
u
l
a

N
a
t
i
o
n
a
l

itime

lands

Pacific   Ocean

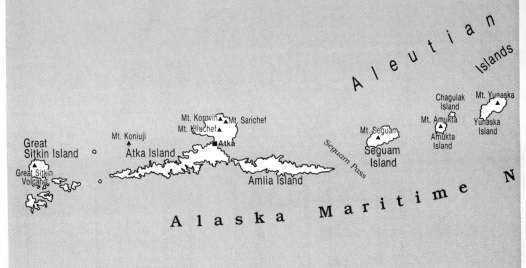

Bering Sea

A l e u t i a n

Islands

Chagulak
Island

Mt. Yunaska

Great
Sitkin Island

Mt. Koniuji

Mt. Korovin
Mt. Kliuchef

Mt. Sarichef

Mt. Amukta

Yunaska
Island

Great Sitkin
Volcano

Atka Island

Atka

Mt. Seguam

Amukta
Island

Seguam
Island

Seguam Pass

Amlia Island

A l a s k a   M a r i t i m e   N

Map continues below

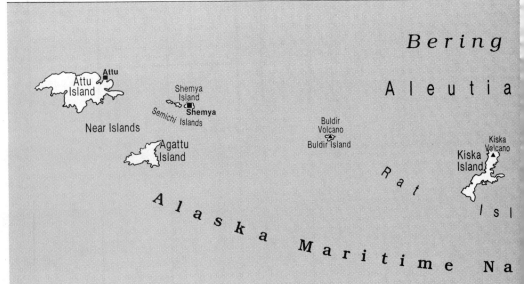

Bering

Attu
Island

Attu

Shemya
Island

A l e u t i a

Semichi Islands

Shemya

Buldir
Volcano

Kiska
Volcano

Near Islands

Buldir Island

Kiska
Island

Agattu
Island

R a t

I s l

A l a s k a   M a r i t i m e   N a

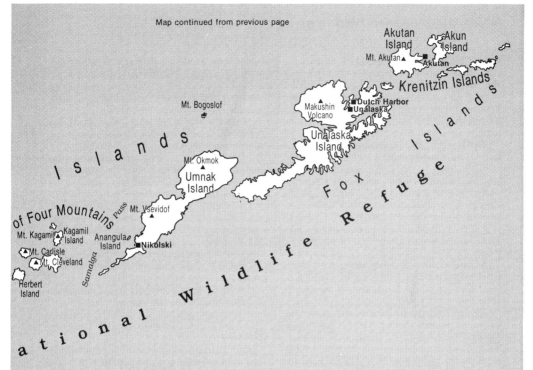

Akutan
Island

Akun
Island

Mt. Akutan ▲ ■ Akutan

Krenitzin Islands

Mt. Bogoslof

Makushin
Volcano ▲ ■ Dutch Harbor
■ Unalaska

I s l a n d s

Mt. Okmok ▲

Umnak
Island

Unalaska
Island

Fox   Islands   Refuge

of Four Mountains

Samalga Pass

Mt. Vsevidof ▲

Mt. Kagamil ▲ Kagamil
Island

Anangula●
Island

■ Nikolski

▲ Mt. Carlisle

▲ Mt. Cleveland

Herbert
Island

a t i o n a l   W i l d l i f e   R e f u g e

Pacific Ocean

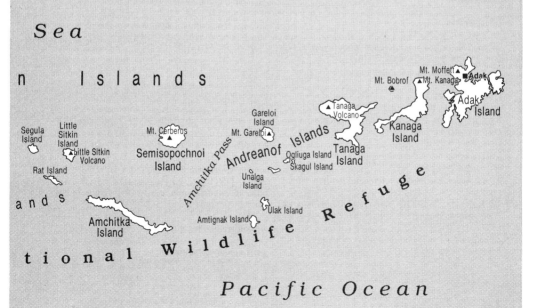

Sea

n   I s l a n d s

Mt. Moffett ▲ ● Adak

Mt. Bobrof ▲ Mt. Kanaga ■ Adak
●

Adak
Island

Segula
Island

Little
Sitkin
Island

Mt. Cerberus ▲

Gareloi
Island

▲ Tanaga
Volcano

Kanaga
Island

Little Sitkin
Volcano ▲

Semisopochnoi
Island

Mt. Gareloi ▲

Andreanof Islands

Tanaga
Island

Rat Island

Ogliuga Island ●
● Skagul Island

Amchitka Pass

Unalga
Island

a n d s

Amchitka
Island

Amtignak Island ●

Ulak Island ●

W i l d l i f e   R e f u g e

t i o n a l

Pacific Ocean

the Pribilofs. They are abundant on the peninsula, and Katmai rangers claim to have the largest unhunted brown/grizzly population in Alaska within their park's boundary. Reindeer have been introduced to a few islands in the Aleutians and on the Pribilofs; caribou thrive on the Alaska Peninsula.

Furbearers and Nongame Species: The natural range of wolves, wolverine and most small mammals does not extend beyond Unimak Island. Only introduced mammal species inhabit the rest of the Aleutians with the possible exception of the arctic fox population in the western islands. Norway rats arrived aboard sailing ships in the mid-1800s and the Rat Islands were named for them.

Marine mammals from the great baleen whales to sea lions, northern fur seals, true seals and sea otters are found in numerous colonies.

Birds: Seabirds, shorebirds and waterfowl by the millions throng to the peninsula, Aleutians and Pribilofs. More than 230 species have been recorded in the region, whose western reaches sit astride the flyway for oriental species moving from the South Pacific and southern Asia to breeding grounds in the high Arctic.

Fish: Sockeye salmon clog the rivers of the peninsula in season; other species of salmon, grayling, arctic char, Dolly Varden and trout also fill the streams in this fishermen's paradise.

Offshore, commercial fishermen seek salmon, halibut, bottom fish, crab and shrimp.

Minerals

Except for the Apollo Mine on Unga Island in the Shumagins, which has produced gold, silver and other metals, minerals have not played a major role in this region.

Public Lands

National Parks and Preserves: Katmai National Park and Preserve is home to volcanoes and large congregations of bears and fish. Access is by plane to campgrounds and lodges with excellent fishing.

Aniakchak National Monument protects a volcanic moonscape in one of the most remote areas in Alaska.

National Wildlife Refuges: Much of the Aleutians and portions of the Pribilofs are part of Alaska Maritime National Wildlife Refuge. Alaska Peninsula National Wildlife Refuge takes in the bulk of the peninsula. At its western tip Izembek National Wildlife Refuge shelters critical waterfowl habitat, while Becharof National Wildlife Refuge at its northern end protects critical brown/grizzly bear habitat.

State Game Refuge and Critical Habitat Areas: To protect hundreds of thousands of migrating birds, the state has established a string of 6 areas in coastal wetlands along the Bristol Bay side of the Aleutian Peninsula. Izembek Game Refuge; and Port Moller, Port Heiden, Cinder River, Pilot Point and Egegik critical habitat areas. These coastal wetlands serve as important feeding and resting stops during spring and fall migrations. Ducks, geese and shorebirds stop over here. Cinder River and Pilot Point are particularly important to the world's population of cackling Canada geese.

Access to these protected areas is by small plane or boat from the nearby community. There are no public-use facilities.

History

Abundant marine mammal populations with their valuable furs drew the first Russians to the Aleutians. The fur traders eventually formed companies which competed with one another for domination. This competition severely disrupted the Aleut culture of the indigenous people and decimated the wildlife populations.

As the Russians moved on, first to Kodiak and then to Southeast, the Aleuts were left to rebuild their villages and continue their fishing and marine-mammal-hunting lifestyle.

After 1867, when the United States took control of Alaska, the marine mammal populations were again hunted to near extinction. Later fox farming and fishing stirred the region's economy.

The Aleutians bore the brunt of WWII activities on Alaskan soil when the Japanese invaded Attu and Kiska islands and bombed Dutch Harbor. American forces retook the islands, but not without substantial casualties and total disruption of Aleut life. The U.S. government moved the islanders to southeastern Alaska during the war, and many never returned.

Today most residents live by fishing or seafood processing or are in the military. The federal government maintains bases in the Aleutians and on the Alaska Peninsula.

Access to the region is usually by air, although a state ferry makes the run down the peninsula to the Aleutians about 4 times annually.

▼ C O M M U N I T I E S ▼

Adak

Located on Kuluk Bay on Adak Island in the Aleutians, 1,200 miles southwest of Anchorage. Adak is a restricted military installation not open to casual visitors or tourists. **Transportation:** Military or scheduled airline from Anchorage. **Population:** More than 5,000, all military service members and their dependents, civil service employees and their dependents, and civilian contractors. **Zip code:** FPO Seattle, WA 98791. **Emergency Services:** Navy Security, phone 592-8051; Navy Branch Hospital.

Elevation: 20 feet. **Climate:** The average relative humidity is 83 percent. Precipitation occurs throughout the year, including an average of 102 inches of snow during the winter months (November through March). Rain in the summer and occasional blizzards during the winter are common. Drizzle, ice, snow and fog occur at various times of the year. Adak is occasionally buffeted by intense storms which migrate east-north-eastward. Average wind velocity throughout the Aleutian chain is 16 knots; however, winds in excess of 40 knots are not uncommon. The highest recorded gust is 109 knots in March 1954. Hence, Adak's well-known nickname, "birthplace of the winds."

Private Aircraft: Mitchell Field 1 mile from town; elev. 18 feet; length 7,880 and 7,600 feet; asphalt. No public transportation to town. Prior approval from the Navy required for all civilian aircraft.

Visitor Facilities: There is no tourist or unsponsored casual visitation to Adak. All requests to visit Adak are denied, except bonafide official visitors or temporary guests of island residents. There is no private civilian sector or community on the island of Adak. Except for one McDonald's and a Baskin-Robbins, all dining facilities are operated by the military. Banking, laundromat/dry cleaning, barber/beauty shop and recreational services are available. Navy exchange and commissary are the only sources for supplies

and commodities. Fishing/hunting licenses available; no guide services. Repair services available for autos. Rental cars available for island residents and authorized visitors. Available fuel limited to unleaded gasoline and JP5 (substitute for diesel). Moorage facilities available only for U.S. Navy or other military vessels, and vessels under government contract.

The U.S. Navy base on 28-mile-long Adak Island, in the Andreanof group, is the westernmost city in the United States. It is Alaska's largest naval base and is "home" for the Naval Air Station, Naval Security Group Activity, Naval Facility, Marine Barracks and several other associated tenant commands and activities.

There is archaeological evidence of earlier habitation, but Adak was unoccupied in 1942 when the military arrived after the outbreak of WWII. The installations on Adak are significant in the history of the Aleutian campaign because they allowed U.S. forces to mount a successful offensive against the Japanese-held islands of Kiska and Attu. Facilities from the old Adak Army base and Adak naval operating base have been nominated to the National Register of Historic Places. The Adak Community Museum, P.O. Box 5244, Naval Air Station, Adak, FPO Seattle, WA 98791, houses WWII memorabilia, wildlife displays and Native artifacts.

The southern part of the island is part of Alaska Maritime National Wildlife Refuge. The U.S. Fish and Wildlife Service maintains a headquarters and visitors center on the island.

Like the rest of the Aleutians, Adak is noted for its unpredictable weather. Fishing at Adak is good for halibut and cod. Game includes caribou and ptarmigan.

Communications at Adak include phones, radio and TV. The base is served by 2 chapels and 2 schools with grades preschool through 12. College courses are offered through the University of Alaska Extension Service. All utilities and services are provided by the military.

Akutan

Located on the north shore of Akutan Harbor on the east coast of Akutan Island, one of the Krenitzin Islands of the Fox Island group in the mid-Aleutian chain, 45 miles east of Unalaska, 750 miles southwest of Anchorage. **Transportation:** Boats; scheduled and charter amphibious aircraft from Cold Bay or Dutch Harbor. **Population:** 103 plus 300 temporary processor workers. **Zip code:** 99553. **Emergency Services:** Police, Clinic, Volunteer Fire Department, phone 698-2208, 698-2227.

Climate: Maritime, characterized by mild winters and cool summers. High winds with gusts up to 100 mph are common in winter. There is frequent cloudy weather and there is fog 64 percent of the days in July. The warmest month of the year is August; the coldest is February. Precipitation averages 28 inches per year.

Private Aircraft: Akutan has no airstrip; amphibious or floatplane only. New landing ramp completed in 1987.

Visitor Facilities: Accommodations available. No restaurant or banking services.

There is a laundromat. Groceries, clothing, first-aid supplies, hardware, camera film and sporting goods are available in the community. Arts and crafts available for purchase include fox traps and carvings. No fishing/hunting licenses available; no guide service. Repair service for marine engines and boats may be available. Arrangements may be made to rent boats. Fuel available includes diesel and regular gasoline. Moorage facilities available.

The village was established in 1878 as a fur storage and trading port by the Western Fur and Trading Co. The company's first resident agent helped establish a commercial cod fishing and processing business. Residents of nearby villages moved to Akutan and a church and school were built in 1878. The community was incorporated as a second-class city in 1979.

After the Japanese attacked Dutch Harbor and seized Attu and Kiska in June 1942, the U.S. government evacuated Akutan residents to the Ketchikan area. They were allowed to return in 1944, but many chose not to. The exposure to the outside world brought about many changes in the traditional lifestyle of the community, but the Aleut language is still spoken in most homes.

Akutan on the east coast of Akutan Island. (Bureau of Land Management)

Commercial fishing and fish processing dominate Akutan's economy. Trident Seafoods has one of the largest onshore fish processing plants in Alaska. There is also employment at the school, post office, store, tavern and clinic.subsistence hunting and fishing also is important. Game includes seals, wild cattle, ducks and geese. Fish include salmon, pogies, black bass, cod, herring, halibut, flounder and trout. Shellfish include clams, sea urchins and "bidarkies" (chitons).

Alexander Nevsky Chapel, a Russian Orthodox church built in 1918 to replace the 1878 structure, is listed on the National Register of Historic Places.

Akutan Island is mountainous and rugged, and 4,275-foot Akutan Volcano is considered active, belching fire and smoke throughout fall 1978. Lava flows occasionally run into the sea on a distant side of the peak. Akutan village also is within an area affected by tsunamis. In 1946 a tsunami run-up reached 115 feet and destroyed Scotch Cap Lighthouse on the west side of Unimak Island facing Unimak Pass, less than 30 miles east of Akutan.

Communications in Akutan include phones, CB radios, FAX, mail plane and TV. The community has a school with grades kindergarten through 12. There are community electricity, water and sewer systems. Freight arrives by ship. Government address: City of Akutan, General Delivery, Akutan, AK 99553. Village corporation address: Akutan Corp., General Delivery, Akutan, AK 99553. Aleutians East Borough, P.O. Box 349, Sand Point, AK 99661; phone 383-2699.

Atka

Located on Atka Island in the Andreanof Island group, 90 miles east of Adak, 1,100 miles southwest of Anchorage. **Transportation:** Boat; scheduled and charter aircraft from Cold Bay and Adak. **Population:** 83. **Zip code:** 99502. **Emergency Services:** Village Public Safety Officer, phone 839-2202 or 2224; Clinic, phone 839-2232; Volunteer Fire Department.

Elevation: 40 feet. **Climate:** Atka's maritime climate is characterized by mild winters and cool summers. The wind is calm only 2.5 percent of the time. The warmest month is August; the coldest is February. Mean annual precipitation is 60 inches, including 61 inches of snow.

Private Aircraft: Airstrip 1 mile north; elev. 33 feet; length 3,100 feet; asphalt; unattended. Runway condition not monitored; visual inspection recommended prior to

using. A small supply of AV gas and jet 100 fuel is kept by Peninsula Airways.

Visitor Facilities: Atka Village Council has 2 rooms with kitchen facilities for rent. No banking services or laundromat. Groceries, first-aid supplies, hardware and camera film are available for purchase, as well as grass baskets. Fishing/hunting licenses available. No guide or repair services. Fuel available includes marine gas, diesel and regular gasoline. No moorage facilities.

Atka is the most western and most isolated Native village on the Aleutian chain. The island has been occupied for at least 2,000 years and recent archaeological evidence suggests that the present village site may have had human use even earlier. The town was settled in the 1860s.

Atka residents were evacuated to the Ketchikan area after the Japanese attack on Dutch Harbor and seizure of Attu and Kiska in June 1942. The community was almost completely burned during the war by the Navy to keep the Japanese from using it. The Navy rebuilt it after the war. Many Attuans who had been held captive in Japan resettled in Atka after their release in 1945.

The community has persisted through the decades despite a lack of local jobs. After the end of the sea otter hunting era in the late 1800s, Atka had no cash economy, although it became relatively affluent during the fox farming boom in the 1920s. The economy today is based primarily on subsistence hunting and fishing and wages earned from seasonal employment in the crab and salmon fisheries elsewhere in the Aleutians.

The village is located within Alaska Maritime National Wildlife Refuge. Fish include halibut, salmon, black cod, Pacific Ocean perch and king crab. Reindeer introduced in 1914 have multiplied to 2,500 to 3,500 head and provide meat for the villagers. Foxes, seals and sea lions are also common.

Forming the northern end of the island is 4,852-foot Korovin Volcano, which has been active in recent years.

Communications in Atka, which incorporated in 1988 as a second-class city, include phones, FAX, and mail plane. The community is served by St. Nicholas Russian Orthodox Church and a school with grades kindergarten through 12. Sale and importation of alcohol are prohibited. Freight arrives at the community by ship once a year. Government address: Atka Village Council, Atka Rural Branch, Atka, AK 99502; phone 839-2233.

Village corporation address: Atxam Corp., Atka Rural Branch, Atka, AK 99502.

Attu

Located on Attu Island in the Aleutian chain, 1,700 miles west of Anchorage, 500 miles east of the USSR mainland. **Transportation:** Air charter or U.S. Coast Guard aircraft. **Population:** 29. **Zip code:** 99502.

Elevation: 60 feet. **Climate:** Storms and dense fog are common. Mean annual precipitation is 54 inches, including 86 inches of snow.

Private Aircraft: Airport at southeast end of island; elev. 40 feet; length 6,300 feet; asphalt. Civilian authorization other than emergency must be obtained from U.S. Coast Guard District 17, Juneau. No transient service or maintenance available.

Visitor Facilities: No accommodations; camping only.

Attu Island is farthest west of the Aleutian chain and westernmost of the Near Islands. A Coast Guard loran station is located at Massacre Bay on the southeast coast of the island.

A granite memorial was dedicated at Attu in 1981 to honor American soldiers who fought and died in the Aleutians during WWII. Attu was the site of a brutal 19-day battle during May 1943 between American forces and Japanese entrenched on the island, second only to the Pacific theater's Iwo Jima in terms of troops involved. U.S. forces suffered 2,300 casualties, including 549 killed. While only 29 Japanese were captured on Attu, Americans counted 1,851 bodies and estimated 650 others had been buried in the hills. The Japanese have erected several monuments to their dead since the war. Much evidence of the battle still remains on the east end of the island. The Attu battlefield and old Army and Navy airfields have been named national historic landmarks; listed on the National Register of Historic Places is the wreckage of a P-38 fighter aircraft on the east bank of the Temnac River a mile from its mouth.

The entire island is part of Alaska Maritime National Wildlife Refuge, administered by the U.S. Fish and Wildlife Service. For information about the refuge contact Refuge Manager, Aleutian Islands Unit, Alaska Maritime National Wildlife Refuge, Box 5251, NAS, FPO Seattle, WA 98791. Arctic fox, sea otters, whales and a variety of North American and Asiatic birds can be seen on the island. Although remote, the island is popular for spring birding expeditions.

Belkofski

(See **King Cove.**)

Chignik

Located on the south shore of the Alaska Peninsula at the head of Anchorage Bay, 5 miles southeast of Chignik Lagoon, 450 miles southwest of Anchorage. **Transportation:** Boat; scheduled airline and air charter from King Salmon; occasional state ferry service from Kodiak. **Population:** 120. **Zip code:** 99564. **Emergency Services:** Alaska State Troopers, King Salmon, phone 246-3346; Subregional Clinic with Nurse Practitioner on staff, services include x-ray, ambulance and trained squad, phone 749-2282; Village Public Safety Officer/Fire Chief, phone 749-2273.

Elevation: 30 feet. **Climate:** Chignik's maritime climate is characterized by cool summers, relatively warm winters and rainy weather. Mean precipitation is 83 inches, including 50 inches of snow.

Private Aircraft: Airstrip 2 miles from village; elev. 50 feet; length 2,400 feet; gravel; no fuel, unattended. Runway condition not monitored, visual inspection recommended prior to using. Birds on and in vicinity of airfield. No airport facilities or public transportation to village.

Visitor Facilities: No hotel. Restaurant operates in summer. Laundromat available. No banking services. Groceries, first-aid supplies, hardware and camera film may be purchased in the community. Two novelty shops are open for business during the summer months, as well as a bakery. Fishing/hunting licenses available; no guide service. No major repair service. Rental transportation includes boats and charter aircraft. Fuel available includes marine gas, diesel, propane and regular gasoline. Moorage facilities operated by fish processors.

Chignik, also called Chignik Bay, is an Aleut village established as a fishing village and cannery in the second half of the 19th century. Chignik is a second-class city, incorporated in 1983.

Most people in Chignik depend on subsistence hunting and fishing, but commercial fishing for salmon and crab provides seasonal employment. Salmon are caught year-round. Other fish caught are rainbow trout and Dolly Varden. Dungeness, king and tanner crab, clams and octopus also are taken. Game includes moose, caribou, ptarmigan, ducks and geese.

The village is located within 3.5-million-acre Alaska Peninsula National Wildlife Refuge. During the winter, warm ocean currents keep much of the water relatively ice free and thousands of Steller's, common and king eiders, scoters, harlequins, oldsquaws and loons winter there. Brant and Canada geese fly over Chignik in the spring and fall. There are many seabird colonies along the coast and cormorants, puffins, murres, black-legged kittiwakes, gulls, terns and jaegers are occasional visitors at Chignik. Bald eagles, common along the coast, concentrate along streams during the salmon runs and along lagoons and bays in the winter. Peregrine falcons nest in the area, usually near seabird colonies.

A variety of marine mammals are present near Chignik, including harbor seals, sea otters, Steller sea lions, Dall porpoises and several species of whales.

Communications in Chignik include phones, mail plane and TV. The community is served by a church and a school with grades preschool to 12. There are public water, sewer and electricity systems. Freight arrives by barge once a month. Government address: City of Chignik, General Delivery, Chignik,

AK 99564. Village corporation address: Far West Inc., General Delivery, Chignik, AK 99564.

Chignik Lagoon

Located on the south shore of the Alaska Peninsula 5 miles west of Chignik, 450 miles southwest of Anchorage. **Transportation:** Boat; charter plane from King Salmon, Dillingham or Kodiak. **Population:** 46. **Zip code:** 99565. **Emergency Services:** Alaska State Troopers, King Salmon, phone 246-3346; Health aide, phone 840-2214; Volunteer Fire Department.

Elevation: 50 feet. **Climate:** Maritime climate characterized by cool summers, relatively warm winters and rainy weather. Total precipitation averages 127 inches annually, with an average of 58 inches of snow. Summer temperatures range from 39° to 60°F; winter temperatures range from 21° to 36°F.

Private Aircraft: Airstrip adjacent southwest; elev. 50 feet; length 1,700 feet; gravel; unattended. Runway condition not monitored; visual inspection recommended prior to using. Seabirds on and near airfield.

American flag flying out front marks the post office at Chignik Lagoon. The small Native fishing community lies in the shadow of Veniaminof Volcano which last erupted in 1983. (Jack Dodge)

No airport facilities or transportation to village. Public domain seaplane base.

Visitor Facilities: No accommodations, laundromat or banking services. Restaurant in summer only. Groceries, clothing, first-aid supplies, hardware, some camera film and ammunition may be purchased in the community. Boots, rain gear, limited fishing gear available. No arts and crafts available for purchase. Fishing/hunting license available, as well as guide service. Marine engine and boat repair at cannery in summer only, and at a local Johnson dealer which provides outboard maintenance and warranty work, plus other fishing essentials. Fuel available at the cannery includes marine gas, diesel, propane and regular gasoline. No public moorage facilities.

Chignik Lagoon took its name from its proximity to Chignik. The area was originally populated by Kaniagmiut Eskimos. After the Russian occupation, the intermarriage of the Kaniags and Aleuts produced the Koniags who now reside in Chignik Lagoon. The village was a fishing village and now serves, along with Chignik, as a regional fishing center. The community is not incorporated.

Subsistence hunting and fishing are the mainstay of the local economy, with commercial fishing providing seasonal employment. Fish include pink, chum and silver salmon, cod, black bass, halibut, rainbow trout and Dolly Varden. Also taken are Dungeness, king and tanner crab, clams and octopus. Game includes moose, caribou, ptarmigan, ducks and geese. In the fall, residents pick blueberries, cranberries, raspberries and salmonberries.

Veniaminof Volcano, which last erupted in 1983, dominates the horizon to the west, sending up occasional puffs of steam. Wildflowers abound along the beaches and there is fossil hunting along the north side of the lagoon. The nearby valley provides hiking opportunities, although care must be taken not to surprise brown bears. Many eagles can be observed nesting and hunting in the area. There is beach recreation along Ocean Spit, which protects the lagoon from the open sea.

Communications in Chignik Lagoon include phones, mail plane, post office, radio and TV. There are church services in the summer. One school has grades kindergarten through 8. No community electricity, but there are water and sewer systems. Freight arrives by plane, barge and ship. Government address: Chignik Lagoon Village Council, General Delivery, Chignik Lagoon, AK 99565.

Village corporation address: Chignik Lagoon Native Corp., General Delivery, Chignik Lagoon, AK 99565.

Chignik Lake

Located on Chignik Lake on the Alaska Peninsula, 15 miles southwest of Chignik, 265 miles southwest of Kodiak. **Transportation:** Scheduled airline and air charter from Anchorage. **Population:** 153. **Zip code:** 99564. **Emergency Services:** Clinic, phone 845-2236; Volunteer Fire Department.

Climate: Cool summers, warm winters. Summer temperatures range from 39° to 60°F. Average winter temperatures range from 21° to 50°F.

Private Aircraft: Airstrip adjacent southwest; elev. 50 feet; length 2,600 feet; gravel; unattended. Runway condition not monitored, visual inspection recommended prior to using. No airport facilities or transportation to village.

Visitor Facilities: None. Groceries can be purchased in Chignik Lagoon.

Established in the 1950s, the village has developed as a fishing village. During the summer, most residents move to a fish camp near the village of Chignik Lagoon; some to work in the cannery at Chignik Bay. Chignik Bay is unincorporated.

Communications include phone, mail plane, radio and TV. There is a washeteria and community well. Electricity is from individual generators. Sewage system is private septic tanks, privies and honey buckets. The community has an old and a new Russian Orthodox church. School offers preschool through grade 12. Freight arrives by air transport and barge. Village corporation address: Chignik River Limited, P.O. Box 4, Chignik Lake, AK 99564. Government address: Chignik Lake Village Council, General Delivery, Chignik Lake, AK 99564, phone 845-2212.

Cold Bay

Located on the west shore of Cold Bay, 40 miles from the extreme westerly tip of the Alaska Peninsula, 630 miles southwest of Anchorage. **Transportation:** Boat; scheduled direct jet service from Anchorage; limited state ferry access in summer. **Population:** 250. **Zip code:** 99571. **Emergency Services:** Alaska State Troopers, Sand Point, phone 383-2552; Clinic, phone 532-9989; Volunteer Fire Department, phone 532-2416.

Elevation: 100 feet. **Climate:** The area has frequent but light rains, cool temperatures, high clouds and fog. Measurable precipitation occurs approximately 200 days per year. Mean annual precipitation is 35 inches, including 55 inches of snow.

Private Aircraft: Airport adjacent north; elev. 98 feet; length 10,400 feet; asphalt; fuel 100, jet A; attended. The paved, crosswind runway is one of the largest in the state. All facilities at airport; no public transportation to town.

Visitor Facilities: Hotel accommodations available (See advertisement, this section). There is a restaurant and a laundromat. No banking services. Limited groceries, first-aid supplies, hardware, camera film and sporting goods available in the community. Aleut grass baskets may be purchased. Fishing/hunting licenses available, as well as fishing guide service. Truck rental available. Fuel available includes white gas, kerosene, diesel and regular gasoline. No moorage facilities.

Cold Bay was near the southern edge of the Bering Land Bridge and probably played an important role in the migration of Asiatic peoples to North America. Although not yet excavated, the presence of numerous middens in the area suggests that it was inhabited by a relatively large population of Native people. Russian ships wintered nearby during the first coastal explorations by Europeans. The name Izembek was bestowed on the region in 1827 by Count Feodor Lutke when he named Izembek Lagoon after Karl Izembek, surgeon aboard the sloop *Moller.*

After the onset of WWII a large air base was built at Cold Bay; bulldozed roads and decaying Quonset huts still mark the landscape. The airstrip is the third longest in Alaska and the airport now serves as the transportation and communications hub for the entire Aleutian-Pribilof islands region.

Cold Bay is the gateway to 320,893-acre Izembek National Wildlife Refuge and the southwestern portion of 3.5-million-acre Alaska Peninsula National Wildlife Refuge. Izembek refuge attracts 142 species of birds, but was established in 1960 primarily to benefit the brant. Izembek Lagoon has the world's largest eelgrass beds on which up to 150,000 brant, the North American continent's entire population, feed during spring and fall migrations. For more information, contact the Refuge Manager, Izembek National Wildlife Refuge, Pouch 2, Cold Bay, AK 99571. (See also Wildlife Refuges in Attractions.)

The west side of the Izembek Lagoon also is the site of the wreck of the 3-masted schooner *Courtney Ford* in 1902. It is a good example of commercial ships used in the late 19th century and is the oldest intact hull in the state.

The land surrounding Cold Bay is rolling and treeless. Mount Frosty, a 5,785-foot-high volcano, is located 9 miles southwest of town. Two active volcanoes, Pavlof (35 miles east) and Shishaldin (60 miles west), are visible from Cold Bay when weather permits. The weather in this broad, exposed area is among the worst along the Alaska Peninsula and probably has contributed more to limiting development than any other factor.

There is good fishing in the area for Dolly Varden, salmon, arctic char, Pacific cod, flounder and halibut. Contact the Alaska Dept. of Fish and Game, Box 127, Cold Bay, AK 99571, for more information.

Communications in Cold Bay, a second-class city incorporated in 1982, include phones, FAX, mail plane and radio. The community is served by a church and a school with grades kindergarten through 12. Community water, sewer, electricity available. Freight arrives in the community by cargo plane and barge. Government address: City of Cold Bay, P.O. Box 10, Cold Bay, AK 99571. Aleutians East Borough, P.O. Box 349, Sand Point, AK 99661; phone 383-2699.

Dutch Harbor

(See **Unalaska.**)

Egegik

(EEG-gah-gik) Located on the northwest coast of the Alaska Peninsula near the mouth of the Egegik River, 50 miles south of King Salmon and 340 miles west of Anchorage. **Transportation:** Boat; scheduled and charter plane. **Population:** 100 in winter; 1,000 to 3,000 in summer. **Zip code:** 99579. **Emergency Services:** Public Safety Officer, phone 233-2241; Clinic, phone 233-2229; village office, phone 233-2235.

Elevation: 50 feet. **Climate:** The predominantly maritime climate is characterized by cool, humid and windy weather. Average summer temperatures range from 42° to 63°F; average winter temperatures range from -29° to 40°F. Total precipitation averages 20 inches annually; average annual snowfall is 45 inches.

Private Aircraft: Airstrip adjacent northeast; elev. 100 feet; length 2,100 feet; gravel; fuel limited 80, 100; unattended. Runway condition not monitored, visual inspection recommended prior to using. Tie-down chain available. Transportation to village with air carrier agent.

Visitor Facilities: Accommodations in private homes, a commercial lodge located on the north side of the river. A community-owned facility has a few rooms with showers available. Meals at lodge or at restaurants in town during summer. Laundromat available; no banking services. Groceries, some clothing, hardware, camera film and sporting goods may be purchased in the community. Arts and crafts available for purchase include carved ivory and fur hats. Fishing/hunting licenses available, as well as guide service. Marine engine and boat repair available in summer. No rental transportation. Fuel available includes marine gas, diesel, propane and regular gasoline. No moorage facilities.

This village was first reported as a fish camp called Igagik during the early U.S. administration of 1867 to 1890. In 1895, the Alaska Packers Assoc. established a salmon saltery at the mouth of the river. The town developed around a cannery in the early 1900s, that also was established at the river's mouth. Egegik is unincorporated.

The economy in Egegik is based on commercial fishing, and residents there claim one of the largest red salmon runs in the world. Several canneries in the area provide seasonal employment from May to August. Residents supplement their income with subsistence hunting and fishing.

Becharof National Wildlife Refuge is accessible by plane or skiff up the Egegik River. There is sportfishing for salmon and trout and hunting for caribou and bear. (See also Wildlife Refuges in Attractions.)

Communications in Egegik include phones, mail plane, radio and TV. The community is served by the Egegik Bible Church and a school with grades kindergarten through 8. There is a community electricity system and public water and sewer. Freight arrives by cargo plane and barge. Government address: Egegik Improvement Corp., P.O. Box 189, Egegik, AK 99579. Village corporation address: Becharof Corp., P.O. Box 145, Egegik, AK 99579; phone 233-2235.

False Pass

Located on the east end of Unimak Island on Isanotski Strait which separates Unimak Island from the Alaska Peninsula, 35 miles southwest of Cold Bay, 670 miles southwest of Anchorage. **Transportation:** Boat; scheduled and charter airline from Cold Bay. **Population:** 81, plus 300 temporary processor workers. **Zip code:** 99583. **Emergency Services:** Village Public Safety Officer; Clinic; Village Health Aide; Fire Department.

Elevation: 20 feet. **Climate:** Mild winters and cool summers. The warmest month is August; the coldest is February. Average annual precipitation at Cold Bay is 33 inches, including 56 inches of snow.

Private Aircraft: Airstrip adjacent south; elev. 20 feet; length 2,630 feet; gravel; fuel 80, 100; unattended. Runway condition not monitored, visual inspection recommended prior to using. Surface may be soft during spring thaw and heavy rains.

Visitor Facilities: Limited accommodations available through Peter Pan Seafoods. No restaurants, laundromat or banking services. The cannery store is open year-round. Fishing/hunting licenses available. No guide service. Rental transportation includes boats, charter aircraft. Fuel available includes marine gas, diesel, propane and regular gas. Moorage facilities available.

Isanotski is the Russianized Aleut word "Issanak" which means The Pass. Americans whose large ships could not navigate through the narrow Isanotski Strait into the Bering Sea from the Gulf of Alaska called it False Pass. The name stuck for the village although the strait is used extensively by vessels under 150 feet and the U.S. Coast Guard has buoyed the entrance to guide the vessels. False Pass originated with the establishment of a cannery in 1918 by P.E. Harris Co. (now Peter Pan Seafoods owned by the Nichiro Corp. of Japan). False Pass is unincorporated.

The economy of False Pass has always been tied to salmon fishing and processing. It suffered a blow in March 1981 when the cannery and central power facility burned down. The store, fuel dock and other support facilities were unharmed. Despite the loss, the village is thriving. Most crab and salmon boats passing through the strait continue to stop at False Pass.

Subsistence hunting and fishing also play an important role in the local economy. The area has abundant geese, ducks, caribou, bear, seals, octopus, cod, halibut, salmon and a variety of berries.

The village is located within Alaska Maritime National Wildlife Refuge. Bears are often seen near the village. During migrations, spectacular concentrations of waterfowl rest and feed in the freshwater and saltwater wetlands, lagoons and shoals bordering the Bering Sea side of the pass. Shorebirds frequent the beaches, tidal flats and shallow areas. Harbor seals are abundant; sea lions are present; an occasional walrus also is observed. The once-rare sea otter reestablished itself in the area and is now abundant.

Communications in False Pass include

phones, FAX, mail plane, radio and TV. There are no churches. The community has a school with grades kindergarten through 12. Freight arrives by cargo plane, barge and ship. Government address: False Pass Village Council, General Delivery, False Pass, AK 99583. Village corporation address: Isanotski Corp., General Delivery, False Pass, AK 99583. Aleutians East Borough, P.O. Box 349, Sand Point, AK 99661; phone 383-2699.

Ivanof Bay

Located on the Alaska Peninsula at the north end of Ivanof Bay on the northeast end of the Kupreanof Peninsula, 200 miles from Sand Point, 510 miles southwest of Anchorage. **Transportation:** Charter plane from Sand Point. **Population:** 45. **Zip code:** 99502. **Emergency Services:** Alaska State Troopers, Sand Point; Clinic, phone 669-2213.

Climate: Maritime climate characterized by cool summers, relatively warm winters and rainy weather. Total precipitation at Chignik, the nearest weather station 50 miles away, averages 127 inches annually. Average annual snowfall is 58 inches.

Private Aircraft: Airstrip 0.3 mile from village; length 1,200 feet; gravel; no airport facilities; no transportation to village. Approximately 10,000 feet of open water used for seaplane landing. High winds occasionally create violent turbulence.

Visitor Facilities: No accommodations, restaurant, laundromat or banking services. Groceries may be purchased in the community. No arts and crafts available. Fishing/hunting licenses not available. No guides, major repair service, rental transportation or moorage facilities. Fuel may be available.

The bay on which this predominantly Aleut village is located was named by Lieutenant Dall of the U.S. Coast and Geodetic Survey in 1880. The village occupies the site of a former salmon cannery which operated from the 1930s to the early 1950s.

Almost all residents of Ivanof Bay fish for a living. Most families move to cabins in Chignik for the summer salmon fishing season. A few residents work for the store, school and village, and most of the men run traplines in the winter for mink, otter, red fox, wolverine, ermine and lynx. Subsistence hunting and fishing also play a big role in the economy of Ivanof Bay.

Fish include salmon, cod, black bass and halibut. Also taken are king and Dungeness crab, cockles and clams. Game includes moose, caribou, bear, ptarmigan, ducks, geese, seals, porcupine and rabbits.

Communications include phones, mail plane once a week, radio and TV. There is no church. A school has grades kindergarten through 8. There are community electricity and water systems. Freight arrives once a year by barge, or by parcel post. Government address: Ivanof Bay Village Council, General Delivery, Ivanof Bay, AK 99502. Village corporation address: Bay View Inc., P.O. Box 2738, Kodiak, AK 99615.

King Cove

Located on the Pacific Ocean side of the Alaska Peninsula, 18 miles southeast of Cold Bay, 630 miles southwest of Anchorage. **Transportation:** Boat; scheduled and charter aircraft from Cold Bay or Sand Point. **Population:** 790, plus almost double that number during fishing season. **Zip code:** 99612. **Emergency Services:** Police, phone 497-2211; Clinic, phone 497-2311; Volunteer Fire Department, phone 497-2211.

Climate: King Cove's maritime climate is characterized by mild winters and cool summers. The warmest month is August; the coldest is February. Precipitation averages 33 inches per year at Cold Bay.

Private Aircraft: Airstrip 4.8 miles northeast; elev. 148 feet; length 4,300 feet; gravel; no fuel; unattended. No airport facilities. Public transportation available to town. Runway condition not monitored, visual inspection recommended prior to using.

Visitor Facilities: Accommodations at 1 hotel. There are 2 restaurants. A laundromat is available at the hotel for guests. No banking services. Groceries, clothing, first-aid supplies, hardware, camera film and sporting goods may be purchased in the community. No arts and crafts available. Fishing/hunting licenses available. No guide service. Auto repair service available and arrangements may be made to rent autos. Fuel available includes marine gas, diesel, propane and regular gas. Moorage facilities available.

King Cove, one of the larger communities in the Aleutian region, was founded in 1911 when Pacific American Fisheries built a salmon cannery. It is a first-class city, incorporated in 1947. Although the cannery burned down in 1976, it was immediately rebuilt and is now the largest cannery operation under one roof in Alaska.

The community has a fairly stable economy, dependent almost entirely on fishing and seafood processing. Other employment locally is with the store, school and city government. Subsistence activities add salmon, halibut, caribou, waterfowl, eggs of marine birds, ptarmigan and berries to local diets.

King Cove is located near the Alaska Peninsula National Wildlife Refuge. The Alaska Peninsula has long been a major big game hunting area, especially for huge brown/grizzly bears. Other mammals found in the refuge are caribou, wolves and wolverine.

King Cove is 20 miles east of 5,784-foot Frosty Peak, a dormant volcano. The active Pavlof Volcano complex and Cathedral Ledge are 40 miles east of King Cove.

Twelve miles southeast of King Cove lies the ghost town of Belkofski, which was settled in 1823 by Russians. They came to harvest sea otters in the Sandmand Reefs and other nearshore banks. During the height of this exploitation, Belkofski was one of the most affluent villages in the area. The near extinction of the sea otter forced residents to seek subsistence elsewhere.

An imposing Holy Resurrection Russian Orthodox Church was built in Belkofski in the 1880s, and the village became an administrative center for the church. The structure is on the National Register of Historic Places. When the last of the Belkofski residents moved to King Cove in the early 1980s, they took the church's bell and icons with them and built a new Orthodox church at King Cove. A seldom-used trail connects the former village to King Cove.

King Cove goes all out for the Fourth of July, with a fishing derby, games, contests, a community barbecue and a fireworks display.

Communications at King Cove include phones, mail plane and TV. Radio reception is occasional. The community has 2 churches and a school with grades kindergarten through 12. There are community electricity, water and sewer systems. Freight arrives by cargo plane, barge and ship. Government address: City of King Cove, P.O. Box 37, King Cove, AK 99612; phone 497-2340. Village corporation address: King Cove Corp., General Delivery, King Cove, AK 99612. Aleutians East Borough, P.O. Box 349, Sand Point, AK 99661; phone 383-2699.

King Salmon

Located on the Alaska Peninsula on the Naknek River, 15 miles east of Naknek, 290 miles southwest of Anchorage. **Transportation:** Scheduled airline from Anchorage. **Population:** 434. **Zip code:** 99613. **Emergency Services:** Police, phone 246-4222; Alaska State Troopers, phone 246-3346; Camai Clinic, Naknek, phone 246-6155; Volunteer Fire Department.

Elevation: 50 feet. **Climate:** Cool, humid and windy weather. Average summer temperatures range from 42° to 63°F; average winter temperatures range from 29° to 44°F. Total precipitation averages 20 inches annually, including an average snowfall of 48 inches. Cloud cover is present an average of 76 percent of the time year-round. Naknek River is ice free between May and October.

Private Aircraft: Airport adjacent southeast; elev. 57 feet; length 8,500 feet; asphalt; fuel 100, jet A; attended. *CAUTION: Air Defense aircraft may scramble at any time.* Passenger and freight terminals, ticket counter, restrooms, traffic control tower at airport. Transportation available.

Visitor Facilities: Accommodations at several local lodges and hotels. There are 3 restaurants. No laundromat available. Banking services available. Groceries, clothing, first-aid supplies, hardware, camera film and sporting goods may be purchased in the community. Arts and crafts available for purchase include carved ivory, baskets and masks. Fishing/hunting licenses available, as well as guide service. Major repair service for marine engines, boats and aircraft. Rental transportation includes autos in summer, boats and charter aircraft. Fuel available includes marine gas and regular gas. Moorage facilities available.

In the 1930s, an air navigation silo was built at the present site of King Salmon. At the onset of WWII an Air Force base was constructed that continues today as the major military installation in western Alaska. In 1949, the U.S. Army Corps of Engineers built the road connecting King Salmon to Naknek. The community has continued to develop as a government, transportation and service center.

King Salmon is the gateway to several large lakes (Naknek, Iliamna, Becharof, Ugashik) and to Katmai National Park and Preserve. A 10-mile unimproved road leads from King Salmon to the park's western boundary and there are floatplane connections from King Salmon to the lodge at Brooks River, the National Park Service ranger station and public campground on Naknek Lake. There are 2 other lodges in the park. Independent travelers must make their own arrangements for visiting Katmai, including air service to King Salmon and Brooks River. Campers can purchase meals and scenic bus tour tickets at the lodge.

Communications in King Salmon include phones, mail plane, radio and TV. The community is served by a church. Children are bused to school in Naknek. There is a community electricity system; water is from individual wells. Sewage system is septic tanks. Freight arrives by air cargo or by barge to Naknek then is trucked to King Salmon. Government address: Bristol Bay Borough, Box 189, Naknek, AK 99633; phone 246-4224. Village corporation address: Alaska Peninsula Corp., Box 104360, Anchorage, AK 99510.

Naknek

(See Bristol Bay subregion in BERING SEA COAST section.)

Nelson Lagoon/ Port Moller

Located on a narrow spit that separates Nelson Lagoon and low-lying north coastalareas of the western Alaska Peninsula from the Bering Sea, 30 miles west of Port Moller, 550 miles southwest of Anchorage. **Transportation:** Air charter from Cold Bay. **Population:** 60. **Zip code:** 99571. **Emergency Services:** Clinic, Volunteer Fire Department.

Climate: The area's maritime climate features mild winters and cool summers. The warmest month is August; the coldest is February. Precipitation averages 37 inches per year at Port Moller, including 99 inches of snow.

Private Aircraft: Airstrip 1 mile east; elev. 13 feet; length 3,300 feet; gravel; unattended. Runway condition not monitored; visual inspection recommended prior to using. Large seabirds feed along beach adjacent to runway.

Visitor Facilities: Accommodations available. One store. No banking facilities or arts and crafts. Fishing/hunting licenses are available. Guides, repair service and rental transportation may be available, but arrangements must be made in advance. In a pinch, fuel might be available, but most supplies are kept for transient fishermen.

The community derived its name from the lagoon, which was named in 1882 for Edward William Nelson of the U.S. Signal Corps, an explorer in the Yukon delta region between 1877 and 1920. The area was settled in 1906 when a salmon saltery was built there. A cannery operated between 1915 and 1917, but there has been no local plant since. For many years Nelson Lagoon was a seasonal camp, but families began to settle there and a school was established in 1965. Nelson Lagoon is part of the Aleutians East Borough.

Commercial fishing is the basis for the local economy. Subsistence hunting and fishing is done for caribou, fox, wolverine, mink, geese and seal.

The area supports hundreds of thousands of waterfowl and shorebirds during migration. Whales and birds can be observed from the village spit.

Nelson Lagoon has phones and mail service. There is a school. Water is from individual wells or hauled from lakes; sewage system is flush toilets and seepage pits. There is a community electricity system. Freight arrives by ship once a year or by barge via Port Moller. Government address: Nelson Lagoon Village Council, General Delivery, Nelson Lagoon, AK 99571. Village corporation address: Nelson Lagoon Corp., General Delivery, Nelson Lagoon, AK 99571. Aleutians East Borough, P.O. Box 349, Sand Point, AK 99661; phone 383-2699.

Nikolski

Located on Nikolski Bay on Umnak Island, one of the Fox Island group in the mid-Aleutian chain, 116 miles from Dutch Harbor, 880 miles southwest of Anchorage. **Transportation:** Scheduled or charter flights from Dutch Harbor. **Population:** 54. **Zip code:** 99638. **Emergency Services:** Alaska State Troopers, Unalaska; Clinic.

Elevation: 73 feet. **Climate:** Mild winters and cool summers characterize the climate. The warmest month is August; the coldest is February. Precipitation is 21 inches annually; snowfall averages 41 inches annually.

Visitor Facilities: Supplies available in the community. Availability of all other visitor facilities and services is unknown.

Nikolski was actively involved in sea otter hunting during the Russian period. A sheep ranch that is still operating today was established in Nikolski in 1926 as part of the Aleutian Livestock Co.

After the Japanese attacked Dutch Harbor and seized Attu and Kiska in June 1942, Nikolski residents were evacuated to the Ketchikan area until 1944. In the mid-1950s, the Air Force built a White Alice site which was later operated by RCA Alascom. It was abandoned in 1977.

Most residents work outside the village at crab canneries and processing ships during the fall season, fishing in the summer or seasonal jobs in Cold Bay or St. Paul. Subsistence hunting and fishing provide a substantial part of the villagers' diets. Most families catch Dolly Varden and halibut in the bay. They also hunt ducks and seals. Octopus, fish and sea urchins can be gathered from the reef.

Ananiuliak (Anangula) Island on the

north side of Nikolski Bay is the site of the earliest presently documented evidence of human habitation in the Aleutian Islands. Radiocarbon dating indicates occupation as far back as 8,000 years.

The Chaluka site in the village of Nikolski exhibits 4,000 years of virtually continuous occupation and is listed on the National Register of Historic Places. Also on the register is Nikolski's St. Nicholas Russian Orthodox Church, built in 1930.

Communications include phones and mail plane. The community has a school with grades kindergarten through 12. There are community electricity and water systems. The sewage system is septic tanks. Freight arrives by ship once or twice a year. Nikolski is unincorporated under state law, but is incorporated as an IRA village under the Indian Reorganization Act. Government address: Nikolski Village Council, General Delivery, Nikolski, AK 99638. Village corporation address: Chaluka Corp., General Delivery, Nikolski, AK 99638.

Perryville

Located on the south coast of the Alaska Peninsula, 215 miles south-southwest of Dillingham and 285 miles southwest of Kodiak. **Transportation:** Scheduled airline, air charter from Dillingham or King Salmon. **Population:** 107. **Zip code:** 99648. **Emergency Services:** Alaska State Troopers, Sand Point or King Salmon; Clinic, phone 853-2236; Fire Department, phone 853-2206.

Elevation: 25 feet. **Climate:** Cool summers, with a fair amount of rain. Winters are relatively warm. The average snowfall is 58.5 inches. Total precipitation at Chignik, the nearest weather station (40 miles away), averages 127 inches annually.

Private Aircraft: Airstrip adjacent south; elev. 25 feet; length 2,500 feet; gravel; unattended. Runway condition not monitored, visual inspection recommended prior to use. No airport facilities or transportation to village, though private vehicles may be available.

Visitor Facilities: Limited accommodations. No restaurant, laundromat or banking services. Clothing (few), first-aid supplies, hardware, camera film and sporting goods may be purchased in the community. No arts and crafts available. Fishing/hunting licenses not available. No guide service, major repair service, rental transportation or public moorage facilities.

Perryville was founded in 1912 as a refuge for Native people driven away from their villages by the eruption of Mount Katmai. It was named after Captain Perry, who rescued the people with his boat and took them to Ivanof Bay, and later to the location of Perryville.

St. John the Theologian Church, a Russian Orthodox church built sometime after the 1912 founding of Perryville is on the National Register of Historic Places.

Nearby rivers and the ocean in front of the village are used for sportfishing, and most of the residents fish commercially. There is berry-picking in season and hunting for bear, moose and caribou. The village is unincorporated. *NOTE: Much of the land around Perryville is owned by the local village firm, Oceanside Corp. You will need to contact the corporation in advance (address below) for permission to enter.*

Communications include phones, mail plane, radio and TV. Public electricity and water are available. Sewage system is individual septic tanks. The community is served by the Russian Orthodox church, and a school with grades preschool through 12. Freight arrives by cargo and mail plane. Government address: Perryville IRA Council, General Delivery, Perryville, AK 99648. Village corporation address: Oceanside Corp., P.O. Box 84, Perryville, AK 99648.

Pilot Point

Located on the east shore of Ugashik Bay on the Alaska Peninsula, 90 miles south of King Salmon, 380 miles southwest of Anchorage. **Transportation:** Scheduled and charter air service from King Salmon. **Population:** 67. **Zip code:** 99649. **Emergency Services:** Alaska State Troopers, King Salmon, phone 246-3346; Clinic, phone 797-2212; Volunteer Fire Department.

Elevation: 50 feet. **Climate:** Cool, humid and windy. Temperature and precipitation data were collected at Pilot Point from 1939 to 1945 only. Low cloud cover and fog frequently limit travel into Pilot Point.

Private Aircraft: Airstrip adjacent east; elev. 75 feet; length 3,500 feet; gravel; fuel; some A.V. gas available from the store; unattended. Runway condition not monitored, visual inspection recommended prior to using. Runway soft when wet. No airport facilities; summer taxi service to village.

Visitor Facilities: Accommodations available at 2 cabins. No banking services. A restaurant and gift shop are open only in summer. A new laundromat opened in 1987. Groceries, clothing, first-aid supplies, hardware, camera film and sporting goods may be purchased in the community. Arts and crafts available. Fishing/hunting licenses available; no guide service. No major repair service. Charter flights available. Fuel available includes diesel, propane and regular gasoline. Bulkhead dock at Dago Creek available for temporary tie-up, load and off-load only.

This predominantly Aleut village, which had a fish saltery in 1900, originally was known as Pilot Station, for the Ugashik River pilots who were stationed there and took boats up the river to a larger cannery at Ugashik. By 1918 the saltery had developed into a large cannery, and was forced to close in 1958 because of deterioration of the harbor. In 1933, the name of the village changed to Pilot Point. The community is unincorporated.

Residents depend on commercial salmon fishing for the majority of their cash income. Other jobs are found with the store, school and government. Subsistence hunting and fishing play a major role in the economy, based primarily on salmon and caribou.

Record-sized grayling have been taken from Ugashik Lakes. Other sportfishing is for salmon and trout. Hunting is for moose, caribou and brown bear. The Kvichak River is a major migration corridor for the sandhill crane and whistling swans that nest near the village. White-fronted and emperor geese, Canada geese and loons rest in the area in the spring and fall; some stay to nest and molt. Ugashik Bay and the Ugashik, Dog Salmon and King Salmon rivers are important bald eagle feeding areas.

NOTE: The majority of the land surrounding the village, as well as the Ugashik One Airfield, is owned by the Pilot Point Native Corp. Use of this land for hunting, fishing, or recreation is forbidden without the express permission of the Pilot Point Native Corp. Board of Directors.

Communications at Pilot Point include phones, mail plane, radio and TV. The community is served by St. Nicholas Russian Orthodox Church, which was built circa 1912 and is on the National Register of Historic Places. There also is a school with grades kindergarten through 12. Community electricity system is available; public water or sewage systems. Freight arrives by cargo plane and barge. Government address: Pilot Point Village Council, P.O. Box 449, Pilot Point, AK 99649. Village corporation address: Pilot Point Native Corp., P.O. Box 487, Pilot Point, AK 99649.

Port Heiden

Located on the Alaska Peninsula on the north shore of Port Heiden, 150 miles from King Salmon; 435 miles southwest of Anchorage. **Transportation:** Boat; scheduled airline from King Salmon. **Population:** 114. **Zip code:** 99549. **Emergency Services:** Village Public Safety Officer, phone 837-2223; Clinic, phone 837-2208; Volunteer Fire Department, phone 837-2238.

Elevation: 90 feet. **Climate:** Mean annual precipitation is 15 inches, including 53 inches of snow.

Private Aircraft: Airstrip 6 miles northeast; elev. 86 feet; length 6,100 feet; gravel; fuel jet A and 100. Airport has passenger and freight terminal, ticket counter, restrooms. Taxi service to village.

Visitor Facilities: Accommodations at a boarding house. Meals at lodging facility. No laundromat or banking services. Groceries, first-aid supplies, hardware and camera film may be purchased in the community. Arts and crafts which may be purchased include carved ivory. Fishing/hunting licenses and guide service available. Everyone does their own marine engine, boat and auto repairs. Make arrangements with private owners to rent autos or boats. Charter aircraft available. Fuel available includes marine gas, diesel and regular gasoline. No moorage facilities.

Port Heiden was founded by a Norwegian who came to the area in the 1920s and married a Native woman. Other families moved in later. Prior to that time many Native people lived in the area, but many died during an influenza epidemic in the 1900s. Port Heiden is a second-class city, incorporated in 1972.

NOTE: Hiking, berry-picking, camping and fishing are permitted on lands owned by the Alaska Peninsula Corp. upon payment of a $20 per person/per day fee. Hunting and woodcutting on corporation lands is not permitted. Contact the corporation for more information. (See address below.)

The community is the gateway to 514,000-acre Aniakchak National Monument and Preserve. Access by floatplane from King Salmon or Port Heiden to Surprise Lake inside the caldera. By foot, it's 10 miles from Port Heiden to the park boundary on a very difficult trail.

Communications in Port Heiden include phones, mail plane, radio and TV. The community is served by 2 churches and a school with grades kindergarten through 12. There are community electricity, water and sewage systems. Freight arrives in the community by cargo plane, air taxi and barge. Government address: City of Port Heiden, P.O. Box 49050, Port Heiden, AK

99549. Village corporation address: Alaska Peninsula Corp., P.O. Box 104360, Anchorage, AK 99510.

Port Moller

(See **Nelson Lagoon**.)

Sand Point

Located on the north coast of Popof Island in the Shumagin Islands off the south coast of the Alaska Peninsula. **Transportation:** Scheduled air service from Anchorage; state ferry service in summer. **Population:** 993. **Zip code:** 99661. **Emergency Services:** Police, fire, medical, phone 911.

Private Aircraft: Airport 2 miles southwest; elev. 22 feet; length 3,800 feet; gravel; no fuel available; unattended. *CAUTION: 80- to 120-foot cliff on east side of runway.*

Visitor Facilities: Accommodations at 1 hotel. There are 4 restaurants, 2 bars, and a laundry facility. Cab service available. Supplies available in the community. Fishing licenses available at the city office. Guide service available, also major repairs. Charter air service available, as well as diesel fuel and gasoline. Moorage facilities available. Shower facilities, 2 gyms, a teen center, and an indoor swimming pool.

One of the most prosperous and modern Aleut communities, Sand Point has a cannery and a locally owned fishing fleet for crab, bottom fish and salmon. The community was founded by the Russians in the 1870s. The town became a supply center for the surrounding area after a cod-fishing station was built by the McCollam Fishing and Trading Co. In 1946, the first cold storage plant in Alaska was built there. Sand Point is a first-class city, incorporated in 1966.

Two major exploratory gold mining operations are ongoing, one within the city limits of Sand Point and one 20 minutes away at Squaw Harbor on Unga Island.

Sand Point's St. Nicholas Russian Orthodox Church, constructed in 1936, is on the National Register of Historic Places.

The community has churches and a school with grades kindergarten through 12. There are community electricity, water and sewer systems. Freight arrives by air cargo, ship and barge. Government address: City of Sand Point, P.O. Box 249, Sand Point, AK 99661, phone 383-2696. Village corporation address: Shumagin Corp., P.O. Box 174, Sand Point, AK 99661, phone 383-3525. Aleutians East Borough, P.O. Box 349, Sand Point, AK 99661; phone 383-2699.

Shemya

(SHEM-ee-a) Shemya Island is located near the west end of the Aleutian Chain, 1,500 miles southwest of Anchorage. **Access:** Shemya is a private military base with access strictly controlled by the U.S. Air Force. Visitors must be on official military business to go to Shemya. The contact point for visit requests is AAC/LGX, Elmendorf AFB, AK 99506; phone 552-5202. Private aircraft are not authorized access to Shemya. **Transportation:** U.S. Air Force plane or military charter plane only. **Population:** Approximately 576. **Zip code:** 98736. **Emergency Services:** Air Force Security; Air Force Medical Aid Station, phone 392-3552.

Elevation: 90 feet. **Climate:** Generally winters are cloudy, windy and cold. Snow showers are numerous, but short. Considerable fog is experienced during the summer. Clear, calm days are rare. Temperatures range from an average high of 51°F in August to an average low of 28°F in February. Mean annual precipitation is 30 inches, including 65 inches of snow.

Private Aircraft: Airport adjacent south; elev. 90 feet; length 10,000 feet; asphalt. Official business only. Civilians must obtain prior permission to land; contact HQ USAF/PRPJ, Washington, D.C. 20330, phone (202) 697-5967.

Visitor Facilities: Military transient lodging and dining facilities only.

Shemya, largest in the Semichi Islands group, measures 4.5 miles long by 2.3 miles wide. The island is entirely controlled by the U.S. Air Force, which conducts operations at Shemya Air Force Base.

Black volcanic sand on the island inspired Shemya's nickname of "The Black Pearl of the Aleutians." The island also is referred to as "The Rock" because of its steep cliffs and rocky terrain. Summer brings a profusion of wildflowers, some unique to the Aleutians. Driftwood, various types of rocks and shells, and many WWII relics and ruins abound on Shemya, making for interesting beachcombing and hiking.

Shemya's involvement in the war began in May 1943, when 2,500 Army troops landed on the island to construct runways. The plan was to use Shemya as a secret air base for the bombardment of Japan. The first bombing mission flew from Shemya on March 16, 1944; the last on Aug. 13, 1945.

Communications at Shemya include phones, mail plane, radio and TV. All utilities are provided on base.

South Naknek

(See Bristol Bay subregion in BERING SEA COAST section.)

St. George

Located on St. George Island, southernmost of the Pribilof Island group, 780 miles west-southwest of Anchorage. **Transportation:** Scheduled airline from Anchorage via St. Paul and twice weekly flights from Anchorage. **Population:** 216. **Zip code:** 99591-0929. **Emergency Services:** Village Public Safety Officer, phone 859-2268 or 859-2206; Alaska State Troopers in Dutch Harbor; Clinic, Volunteer Fire Department.

Elevation: 100 feet. **Climate:** The climate is controlled by the cold waters of the Bering Sea; there is cool weather year-round. Temperatures ranging from a high of 63°F in summer to a low of -7°F in winter have been recorded. The warmest month is July; the coldest is March. Heavy fog is frequent from May through August. Mean annual precipitation is 30 inches, including 47 inches of snow.

Private Aircraft: Airstrip adjacent west; elev. 90 feet; length 3,100 feet; gravel; fuel 100; unattended; contact City of St. George. Avoid flying over seal rookeries on northwest end of island May through October. Airport facilities in Tanaq building. Cab service available into town.

Visitor Facilities: Accommodations at the St. George Hotel (recently designated a national historic landmark). Hotel may close during winter months. Meals available at hotel. There is a laundromat. No banking services. Groceries, clothing, first-aid supplies, hardware and camera film are available in the community. Arts and crafts available for purchase include seal pelts, model bidarkas (skin boats), model seals and baskets. Fishing/hunting licenses not available. Tour guide service available in summer. Repair service for marine engines, boats and autos available. Arrangements can be made to rent private autos. Fuel available includes marine gas, diesel, propane, unleaded and regular gasoline. Moorage facilities available.

St. George Island has perhaps the largest seabird colony in the northern hemisphere: 2.5 million seabirds nest on the cliffs each summer. In addition, an estimated 250,000 seals congregate in 6 rookeries on the island. Because of scientific research on the island,

Common murres on St. Paul Island. (National Marine Fisheries Service)

camping is not permitted. The St. George Tanaq Corp. offers guided tour programs in the summer, which include transportation, lodging and meals. Travelers should leave itineraries loose in case weather delays flights; keep baggage to a minimum.

The treeless uplands around St. George are inhabited by a diverse population of songbirds, blue foxes, lemmings and a few reindeer that are descendants of 3 bucks and 12 does introduced in 1911.

Communications in St. George, a second-class city incorporated in 1983, include phones, mail plane, radio and TV. The community's St. George the Great Martyr Russian Orthodox Church, built circa 1932-35, is on the National Register of Historic Places. There is a school with grades kindergarten through 8. There are community electricity, water and sewer systems. Freight arrives by cargo plane, barge, ship and mail. Government address: City of St. George, P.O. Box 929, St. George, AK 99591; phone 859-2263 or City of St. George, 1689 C St., Anchorage, AK 99501; phone 276-2700. Village corporation address: St. George Tanaq Corp., P.O. Box 939, St. George, AK 99591 or One Aleut Plaza, 4000 Old Seward Hwy.,

Suite 302, Anchorage, AK 99503.

For more information on the area, see also Pribilof Islands this section and *Islands Of The Seals, The Pribilofs*, Vol. 9, No. 3 *ALASKA GEOGRAPHIC*®. To order see the ALASKA NORTHWEST LIBRARY at the back of the book.

St. Paul

Located on St. Paul Island, northernmost of the Pribilof Island group. **Transportation:** Ship; scheduled and charter plane from Anchorage via Cold Bay or Dutch Harbor. **Population:** 600. **Zip code:** 99660. **Emergency Services:** Village Public Safety Officer, phone 546-2333 or 546-2331; Chief of Police, Clinic, phone 546-2310; Volunteer Fire Department, EMTs, VHF Channel 16.

Elevation: 20 feet. **Climate:** Cool year-round. Heavy fog is frequent May through August. Mean annual precipitation is 23 inches, including 56 inches of snow.

Private Aircraft: Airstrip 3 miles northeast; elev. 44 feet; length 5,100 feet; gravel; fuel 100 and jet; unattended. For runway lights contact the National Weather Service on 123.6 or phone 546-2215. No airport

Angler tries his luck at shallow edge of Katmai's Lake Grosvenor, named for Gilbert Hovey Grosvenor, 1875-1966, of the National Geographic Society. (George Wuerthner)

facilities. Public transportation to town available.

Visitor Facilities: Accommodations at local hotel which may operate only in summer. There are 2 restaurants. Laundry and shower facilities available. No banking services. Groceries, clothing, first-aid supplies, hardware, camera film and sporting goods available in the community. Arts and crafts including ivory jewelry, photographs of local flora and fauna, dried wildflowers and fur seal garments are available at 4 gift shops. Guide service available, as well as local tours. Repair service available for marine engines, boats and autos. Off-road vehicles available for rent. Fuel available includes diesel, propane, and unleaded gasoline. Breakwater to 800; completion to 1,800 feet expected in 1989.

Each summer more than a million northern fur seals gather in rookeries on the shores of the Pribilof Islands and can be observed from 2 blinds. Access is by permit or with a tour group.

St. Paul Island also is the breeding ground for 211 species of birds that nest every year on the coastal cliffs west and south of the village. The U.S. Fish and Wildlife Service acquired 1,000 acres of nesting area on St. Paul and 2,000 acres on St. George as additions to Alaska Maritime National Wildlife Refuge.

The uplands around St. Paul have a diverse population of songbirds, white and blue foxes and about 500 reindeer, descendents of 4 bucks and 21 does introduced in 1911.

Tourists are encouraged to visit Black Diamond Hill, where they may find shiny crystals of augite. Crystals of olivine and rutile found on the island may reach semiprecious gem size and quality.

Communications in St. Paul, a second-class city incorporated in 1971, include phones, mail plane, radio and TV. There are community electricity, water and sewage systems. The community is served by Saints Peter and Paul Russian Orthodox Church, which is on the National Register of Historic Places, an Assembly of God church and a school with grades kindergarten through 10. Freight arrives by cargo plane, ship and barge. Government address: City of St. Paul, Pouch 1, St. Paul Island, AK 99660; phone 546-2331 or 2332. Village corporation address: Tanadgusix Corp., P.O. Box 88, St. Paul Island, AK 99660; phone 546-2312. IRA Council, P.O. Box 86, St. Paul Island, AK 99660; phone 546-2211.

Ugashik

(Yoo-GA-shik) Located on the Ugashik River on the Alaska Peninsula, 90 miles south of King Salmon, 370 miles southwest of Anchorage. **Transportation:** Boat; scheduled and charter air service from King Salmon. **Population:** 17. **Zip code:** 99683. **Emergency Services:** Alaska State Troopers, King Salmon, phone 246-3346; Health aide, Pilot Point, Camai Clinic, Naknek; Kanakanak Hospital, Dillingham.

Elevation: 25 feet. **Climate:** Cool, humid and windy. Temperature and precipitation data were collected at Pilot Point from 1939 to 1945. Average summer temperatures ranged from 41° to 60°F. Average winter temperatures ranged from 12° to 37°F. Total precipitation averaged 19 inches annually, with an average snowfall of 38 inches.

Private Aircraft: Airstrip 1 mile north; elev. 25 feet; length 3,500 feet; gravel. No airport facilities or public transportation to village.

Visitor Facilities: No visitor facilities or services available. Supplies obtained from Pilot Point.

Ivan Petroff recorded the Eskimo village of Oogashik in 1880. It was one of the largest villages in the region until the influenza epidemic of 1919 decimated the population. The village has since remained small. A cannery in the village has operated under several owners, the most recent being the Briggs-Way Cannery. This predominantly Aleut village is unincorporated.

Fishing is the basis of Ugashik's economy. Usually about 10 residents fish commercially for salmon each season. Subsistence hunting and fishing supplements this income.

Recreational opportunities include sport-fishing at Ugashik Lakes, accessible by air taxi or boat.

NOTE: Hiking, berry-picking, camping and fishing are permitted on lands owned by the Alaska Peninsula Corp. upon payment of a $20 per person/per day fee. Hunting and woodcutting on corporation lands is not permitted. Contact the corporation for more information. (See address below.)

Communications in Ugashik are mail plane, radio and TV. It is the only community in the region without phones. Electricity is from individual generators; water from private wells. Sewage system is pit privies. There is no church. Children are flown to Pilot Point to attend school. Freight arrives by cargo plane or barge. Government address: Ugashik Village Council, General Delivery,

Ugashik, AK 99683. Village corporation address: Alaska Peninsula Corp., P.O. Box 104360, Anchorage, AK 99510.

Unalaska/Dutch Harbor

Unalaska is located on the northern end of Unalaska Island, second island in the Aleutian Chain, 800 miles southwest of Anchorage; Dutch Harbor is located across a bridge from Unalaska on Amaknak Island. **Transportation:** Boat; scheduled and charter airline from Anchorage; state ferry April to October. **Population:** 1,630. **Zip code:** Unalaska 99685; Dutch Harbor 99692. **Emergency Services:** For all emergencies, phone 911; Iliuliuk Family Health Clinic, phone 581-1202; Volunteer Fire Department, phone 581-1233; Volunteer Ambulance Service, phone 581-1233.

Elevation: 20 feet. **Climate:** This is the "Cradle of the Storms," where the warm Japan Current from the south meets the colder air and water currents of the Bering Sea. This mingling creates storm centers which sweep westward, influencing weather systems over most of North America. While the temperature is moderate, there can be tremendous winds and days of almost constant rain. Mean annual precipitation is 64.5 inches.

Private Aircraft: Airport 1 mile north; elev. 22 feet; length 3,900 feet; gravel; fuel 100, jet A; attended. Passenger terminal, ticket counters, restrooms, taxi.

Visitor Facilities: Hotel accommodations at Dutch Harbor and Unalaska; bunkhouses, several operated by several seafood canneries, 7 restaurants, 1 take-out, 2 laundromats and banking services available. Groceries, clothing, first-aid supplies, hardware, camera film and sporting goods may be purchased in the community. Arts and crafts for purchase include Aleut grass baskets, wood block prints, paintings, and wood and ivory carvings. Fishing/hunting licenses available; no guide service. Major repair service available for ships and marine engines and equipment; limited repairs for autos; check with air carriers for aircraft mechanic or go to Cold Bay. Vehicle and boat rental available. Air and fishing boat charters available. Moorage facilities available, contact the Port Director, phone 581-1254. Several other commercial enterprises are located in the community.

Ounalashka, or Unalaska, was the early headquarters of the Russian-American Co. and a key port for the sea otter fur trade in the 1700s. After the U.S. purchased Alaska, the North American Commercial Co. became manager of the seal harvest in the Pribilofs and built a station at Dutch Harbor. Unalaska became a major stop for ships heading to and from the Nome goldfields in the early part of this century. In 1939 the U.S. Army and Navy began building installations at Unalaska and Dutch Harbor. In June 1942, the area was bombed by the Japanese and almost all of the local Aleut people were evacuated to southeastern Alaska. Military relics still dot the hillsides, although there has been a major cleanup program in recent years. The Dutch Harbor Naval Base and Fort Mears on Amaknak Island have been designated national historic landmarks.

Unalaska is the major civilian port west of Kodiak and north of Hawaii and is the gateway to the Bering Sea region. It is one of the most productive seafood processing ports in the U.S and remains ice free year-round. There are 4 large canneries which form the basis for the local economy.

Two local attractions are on the National Register of Historic Places. They are the Russian Orthodox Church of the Holy Ascension in Unalaska, which was built in 1825, and the Sitka Spruce Plantation in Dutch Harbor — 6 trees which were planted by the Russians in 1805 and have survived in the harsh climate of the naturally treeless Aleutians.

At the entrance of the airport is a memorial to those killed in the Aleutians in WWII; a special tribute to the Aleuts who died during their relocation to southeastern Alaska also is planned.

Hiking in the area is easy and there is no need for trails. There are no bears on Unalaska Island; however, hikers should watch out for cliffs. Dress appropriately and be prepared for the weather to change for the worst.

Fish include halibut; red, pink and silver salmon; Dolly Varden and greenling. Shrimp, crab, "bidarkies" (chitons) and clams are taken, but there is no guarantee that shellfish are free of paralytic shellfish poisoning. There is no big game on Unalaska; local hunting is for ptarmigan, ducks or red fox. Contact the Alaska Dept. of Fish and Game office, phone 581-1239, for more information.

Unalaska is a first-class city, incorporated in 1942, which encompasses Amaknak Island and Dutch Harbor, and a portion of Unalaska Island.

National and State Parks, Etc.

Aniakchak National Monument and Preserve

This 580,000-acre monument and preserve is located on the Alaska Peninsula 10 miles east of Port Heiden and 150 miles southwest of King Salmon. Its centerpiece is 6-mile-wide, 2,000-foot-deep Aniakchak caldera, which was created by the collapse of a 7,000-foot volcano some 3,500 years ago. Later activity built a 2,200-foot cone, Vent Mountain, inside the caldera.

The caldera remained hidden from the outside world until 1922, when a government geologist noticed that the taller peaks in the area formed a circle on the map he was making. Even today, few people have seen the crater; fewer still have walked upon its floor.

It is believed that the caldera at one time contained a deep lake. Eventually the lake waters began to spill over the caldera wall and through time the fast-flowing Aniakchak River has gouged a spectacular 1,500-foot-deep gap in the wall called The Gates. The wild and scenic Aniakchak River heads in Surprise Lake inside the caldera, which is fed by hot springs. The river then flows 32 miles southeastward to the Pacific Ocean.

Aniakchak last erupted in 1931, adding a "small, but impressive," explosion pit to the pocked caldera floor and scouring the caldera of vegetation. The caldera today chronicles a history of volcanic activity in its lava flows, cinder cones and explosion pits, as well as the beginnings of revegetation bringing life to the barren landscape.

Climate: Aniakchak is remote, difficult to reach and has "notoriously bad weather," says the National Park Service. Temperatures vary greatly. Winter's maximum may range from the low 30s to -30°F. Summer temperatures range from the mid- and upper 40s to a high of 70°F. Violent windstorms in the caldera — even when the weather is calm outside — can

make camping there difficult. In June and July 1973, a man's camp was destroyed twice in 6 weeks and his boat blown away. Local pilots have reported strong turbulent winds in the caldera, particularly through the narrow Gates, which make flying conditions extremely hazardous.

Wildlife: Occasional caribou, grizzly bears and eagles are found in the area. Red salmon spawn up the Aniakchak River all the way to Surprise Lake (fish from here are recognizable by the flavor of soda and iron from the mineral-laden water).

Access: Getting to Aniakchak isn't easy. Reeve Aleutian Airways has a flight between Anchorage and Port Heiden 2 or 3 days per week. From Port Heiden you can charter a small floatplane to Surprise Lake or walk the 10 miles to the monument and preserve, a difficult day- to day-and-a-half-long hike through tundra meadows interspersed with thickets of willow, alder and birch. There is no trail and few people have attempted this route. There are daily commercial flights from Anchorage to King Salmon, where you also can charter a small airplane to Aniakchak. Seasonal ferry service from Kodiak serves a few villages in the region, some of which have air charter services. Charter costs are high, ranging from $150 to $400 an hour depending on the size of the plane. Aniakchak is about 1-1/2 hours flying time from King Salmon and a half hour from Port Heiden.

Accommodations: There are accommodations at Port Heiden through Reeve Aleutian Airways or in King Salmon, which has several lodges. In the monument and preserve, there is primitive camping only in most areas, although, there is a shelter cabin on the north side of the mouth of the Aniakchak River.

Activities: Recreation in Aniakchak includes hiking, camping, fishing, photography, natural history study, rafting the Aniakchak National Wild and Scenic River (whose upper reaches are termed "challenging") and beach walking. The Park Service recommends that anyone spending time in Aniakchak be equipped with wool clothing, rubber boots and good rain gear. Bring your own food if camping and be sure your tent can withstand strong winds. The Park Service further cautions that a number of dangers may confront the inexperienced and for safety a copy of your itinerary should be left at park headquarters in King Salmon. For more information contact: Superintendent, Aniakchak National Monument and Preserve, P.O. Box 7, King Salmon, AK 99613; phone 246-3305. Related USGS Topographic maps: Sutwick Island, Chignik, Bristol Bay, Ugashik.

Katmai National Park and Preserve

The original Katmai National Monument at the top of the Alaska Peninsula was created in 1918 to preserve the volcanic wonders of the Valley of the Ten Thousand Smokes, formed by a cataclysmic eruption just 6 years earlier. In the intervening years, the thousands of fumaroles have dwindled to a few active vents and the park has been enlarged several times to its present 4 million acres.

The June 6, 1912, eruption of Novarupta Volcano, in which Mount Katmai also collapsed, was one of the most violent ever recorded and it darkened the sky over much of the northern hemisphere for several days. At nearby Kodiak, for 2 days a person could not see a lantern held at arm's length. Acid rain caused clothes to disintegrate on clotheslines as far away as Vancouver, B.C. Novarupta spewed 7 cubic miles of incandescent ash and pumice which buried the 40-square-mile Ukak River valley as much as 700 feet deep. The valley remains one of the prime attractions of the park where streams have cut dramatic gorges through the volcanic debris.

For anyone interested in volcanoes and brown bears, Katmai is the place to go. This huge, diverse wilderness encompasses 15 active volcanoes and the largest unhunted population of brown bears in the world.

In some of Katmai's streams the salmon are so thick that you could almost walk across their backs and never get your feet wet. Both humans and bears come to fish for these salmon, and the resulting *close* interaction makes for an experience unique in all the world. At Brooks Camp, where the rangers know some of the bears by name, there are strict rules to minimize the danger. For example, never give a bear the fish you've caught, even if you have to throw it back into the water. If a bear learns that a bluff charge will get it a free meal, it will endanger not only humans but itself as well.

Besides the salmon, Katmai's waters boast grayling, Dolly Varden, northern pike and trophy-sized rainbow trout — all of which make the fishing here world renowned. Catch-and-release fishing is encouraged, and Brooks River is for fly-fishing only.

Climate: Visitors to Katmai should be prepared for stormy weather as well as some sunshine. Summer daytime temperatures range from the mid-50s to the mid-60s; the average low is 44°F. Strong winds and sudden gusts called williwaws frequently sweep the area. Skies are clear about 20 percent of the summer. Light rain can last for days. Bring a warm sweater, windbreaker or lightweight fiberfill jacket, footgear that provides good support, wool socks and a wool hat. Rain gear should include raincoat and pants, parka and hat. You will need insect repellent.

Wildlife: In addition to bears, other wildlife that may be seen are moose, river otter, marten, weasel, mink, lynx, muskrat, beaver and an occasional caribou. Seals, sea lions, sea otters and beluga and gray whales can be found in the coastal waters of Shelikof Strait. There also is excellent fishing for Dolly Varden, grayling, lake trout and salmon. A variety of birds, including bald eagles, osprey, ptarmigan, spruce grouse, swans and game ducks, can be readily observed.

Access: King Salmon is the transportation gateway to the park and preserve. There is daily jet service from Anchorage to King Salmon and a commercial amphibious plane flies daily to Brooks Camp in the park from June to September. Air charter service is available in King Salmon or Iliamna for access to other areas in the park from May to October. The park and preserve also is accessible by a 10-mile road from King Salmon to Lake Camp on the western side of Naknek Lake, which has a boat dock and ramp.

Accommodations: There are hotels and restaurants in King Salmon and nearby Naknek. Within the park and preserve there are 4 lodges, 2 privately operated camps and a public campground at Brooks Camp. Reservations are needed for the campground. Backcountry camping is by permit. Park headquarters is located in King Salmon and a ranger station is located at Brooks Camp.

Activities: A wide range of recreational opportunities includes comfortable lodge accommodations, tour buses into the Valley of 10,000 Smokes, flightseeing, extensive canoeing and rafting, sportfishing, wildlife viewing, day hiking, backpacking, wilderness camping, and ocean kayaking. The rangers conduct guided nature walks and evening programs at Brooks Camp from Memorial Day to Labor Day week. Information, maps, and other publications are available at the Brooks Camp Visitor Center and at park headquarters in King Salmon (address below).

From Brooks Camp a 4-mile trail leads up Dumpling Mountain with its commanding view of Naknek Lake, and a 1-mile trail goes to a bear-viewing platform at Brooks Falls. There are also 50 identified major prehistoric archaeological sites/districts, and pit houses offer the chance to learn about Katmai's earliest human occupants.

Limited camping and food supplies, including white gas, and some fishing tackle are sold at Brooks Lodge. Several commercial operators are authorized to provide air taxi, flightseeing, backpacking, canoe, and fishing guide service. Write the park for a list. Katmai's rugged wilderness offers rewarding experiences — providing reasonable precautions are taken. Cold winds and icy waters pose great hazards. Carry extra dry clothing. Read up on hypothermia and its treatment. (See Hypothermia in GENERAL INFORMATION section.) Be prepared to wait out storms: carry matches, first-aid kit, and emergency food. Rains or melting glaciers can make stream crossings impossible. You need sneakers *and* hiking boots. Be extremely cautious when crossing muddy waters. The Park Service also warns that firewood is limited and asks that campers use stoves. At Brooks Camp you can arrange in advance for meals at the lodge. Otherwise, bring all food with you.

The serene Grosvenor River, the swifter Savonoski River and a series of large lakes connected by a portage form a circular waterway of almost 100 miles for canoeists and kayakers. The wild and scenic Alagnak and Nonvianuk rivers offer a good float trip to the Kvichak River, which empties into Bristol Bay. (See also The Rivers.)

For hikes down into the Valley of 10,000 Smokes, take the bus to the end of the 23-mile dirt road. From an overlook a 2-mile trail winds down to the valley floor. For overnight valley hikes you can arrange a van drop-off and pickup. (The concessionaire's daily van tours to the valley cost about $50.)

For a copy of the free *Traveling the Katmai Backcountry* brochure, the bear safety leaflet, and other information contact: Superintendent, Katmai National Park and Preserve, P.O. Box 7, King Salmon, AK 99615; phone 246-3305. Related USGS Topographic maps: Katmai, Naknek, Iliamna.

Wildlife Refuges

Alaska Maritime National Wildlife Refuge

This refuge consists of more than 2,400 parcels of land on islands, islets, rock spires, reefs and headlands of Alaska coastal water from Port Franklin on the Chukchi Sea to Forrester Island in southeastern Alaska. The refuge totals about 35 million acres, most of which is in the Aleutian Islands Unit.

Nearly all of the more than 124 named islands in the Aleutians are included in the refuge. The Alaska Peninsula Unit includes Simeonof and Semidi islands, the Shumagin Islands, Sutwik Island, islands and headlands of Puale Bay, and other lands south of the peninsula from Katmai National Park and Preserve to False Pass.

Wildlife: Alaska Maritime is synonymous with seabirds — millions of them. About 75 percent of Alaska's marine birds (40 million to 60 million birds among 38 species) use the refuge. The refuge has the most diverse wildlife species of all the refuges in Alaska, including thousands of sea lions, seals, walruses and sea otters.

Activities: Visitor activities in the refuge include wildlife observation, backpacking and photography. Bird-watching is popular on Attu Island, far out in the Aleutians, where Asian birds stop on their migrations.

Access: Most of the refuge is wild and lonely, extremely rugged and virtually inaccessible. Some portions are classified as wilderness. Swift tides, rough seas, high winds, rocky shorelines and poor anchorages hamper efforts to view wildlife. Some islands within the refuge have restricted access to protect wildlife. There is scheduled air service to Dutch Harbor and Cold Bay, which have hotels, restaurants and air charter operations. Military clearance is required to visit Adak, Shemya and Attu islands. In the Pribilof Islands, St. Paul and St. George have scheduled air service from Anchorage and locally guided tours of seabird rookeries and fur seal haul-out sites.

For more information contact: Refuge Manager, Alaska Maritime National Wildlife Refuge, 202 Pioneer Ave., Homer, AK 99603;

phone 235-6546; or Alaska Maritime National Wildlife Refuge, Aleutian Islands Unit, Box 5251, Naval Air Station, Adak, FPO Seattle, WA 98791; phone 592-2406.

Alaska Peninsula National Wildlife Refuge

This 4.3-million-acre refuge on the Pacific side of the Alaska Peninsula extends southwest from Becharof National Wildlife Refuge to False Pass. Aniakchak National Monument and Preserve splits the refuge into 2 parts.

The refuge is one of the most scenically diverse, featuring active volcanoes, lakes, rivers, tundra and a beautiful stretch of rugged, rocky Pacific Ocean coastline. The Alaska Peninsula is dominated by the rugged Aleutian Range, part of a chain of volcanoes known as the "Ring of Fire" that encircles the Pacific Rim. Mount Veniaminof (elev. 8,224 feet) in the refuge is one of Alaska's active volcanoes, last erupting in June 1983. Other special features of the refuge are the Ugashik lakes, renowned for trophy grayling fishing; Black Lake-Chignik Lake area, which has one of the densest concentrations of brown bears in North America; Castle Cape Fjords, a famous landmark to ships with its distinctive light and dark rock layers; and the needle-pointed Aghileen Pinnacles and vertical buttresses of Cathedral Valley near recently active Pavlof Volcano.

Climate: This area is characterized by high winds, mild temperatures, cloud cover and frequent precipitation. Fog and drizzle are common in summer. Severe storms can occur year-round, often with intense winds, known as williwaws. Fall usually is the wettest season. July is the warmest month, with temperatures averaging 54°F. December is the coldest month, with temperatures averaging 12°F.

Wildlife: Besides bears, large mammals found in the refuge include moose, caribou, wolves and wolverines. The bears are especially attracted to the productive salmon streams. Large populations of sea lions, seals, sea otters and migratory whales inhabit the coastline and offshore waters. The population of sea otters on the Pacific side of the peninsula numbers at least 30,000. The entire refuge provides habitat for millions of birds — especially waterfowl — that use the area as a staging ground on their way to and from nesting grounds in the Arctic.

Access: The refuge is accessible by air or by boat. There is scheduled air service from Anchorage to King Salmon, Kodiak, Sand Point and Cold Bay, where small planes may be chartered to the refuge. There are no commercial facilities, roads or trails in the refuge; wilderness camping only.

Activities: This refuge is renowned for big game hunting, especially for moose, caribou and brown bear. Fishing is outstanding for king and silver salmon, arctic char, lake trout, northern pike and grayling. A list of commercial guides holding permits to operate in the refuge is available from the refuge manager. For additional information contact: Refuge Manager, Alaska Peninsula/Becharof National Wildlife Refuges, P.O. Box 277, King Salmon, AK 99613; phone 246-3339.

Becharof National Wildlife Refuge

This 1.2-million-acre refuge is located on the Alaska Peninsula, sandwiched between Katmai National Park and Preserve and the Alaska Peninsula National Wildlife Refuge. It is dominated by Becharof Lake, second-largest lake in Alaska, which covers a quarter of the refuge and is surrounded by low rolling hills, tundra wetlands in the northwest and volcanic peaks to the southeast. The lake area also includes abandoned Kanatak village and the Kanatak Portage trail that allowed people to traverse the Alaska Peninsula.

Climate: Becharof skies are usually cloudy. Less than 20 inches of precipitation falls annually in the western lowlands, while as much as 160 inches falls on the eastern side of the Aleutian Range. October is the wettest month. Temperatures in December, the coldest month, average 12°F. In July, the warmest month, they average 54°F. Vegetation does not begin growing until late May or early June and the first frost usually occurs in late September.

Wildlife: The salmon spawning streams attract a large concentration of brown bears, many of which make their dens on islands in Becharof Lake. Moose inhabit the refuge in moderate numbers and about 10,000 caribou migrate through and winter in the refuge. Other mammals include wolves, wolverines, river otters, red fox and beaver. In addition, thousands of sea mammals such as sea otters, sea lions, harbor seals and migratory whales inhabit the Pacific coastline. Waterfowl are common in the wetlands and coastal estuaries, while nesting eagles, peregrine falcons and thousands of seabirds inhabit the sea cliffs and islands. About 20 species of seabirds nest in 13 colonies in the refuge; 2 colonies in Puale Bay are among the largest on the Alaska Peninsula.

Access: The refuge is accessible by air or by boat. There is scheduled air service from

Anchorage to King Salmon, Kodiak, Sand Point and Cold Bay, where small planes may be chartered to the refuge. There are no commercial facilities or roads in the refuge; wilderness camping only.

Activities: Becharof offers outstanding bear and caribou hunting. Sportfishing in the refuge so far has been light, although trophy-sized rainbow trout, arctic char, grayling and salmon exist. Write the refuge manager for a list of commercial guides holding permits for the refuge. For additional information contact: Refuge Manager, Alaska Peninsula/ Becharof National Wildlife Refuges, P.O. Box 277, King Salmon, AK 99613; phone 246-3339.

Izembek National Wildlife Refuge

One of the older national refuges in the state, 315,000-acre Izembek is located at the tip of the Alaska Peninsula just across False Pass from Unimak Island, first in the Aleutian chain. It faces the Bering Sea and abuts the Alaska Peninsula National Wildlife Refuge.

Izembek's landscape includes volcanoes with glacier caps, valleys and tundra uplands that slope into lagoons adjoining the Bering Sea, pristine streams, and sand dunes. The main feature of the refuge is Izembek Lagoon, protected by barrier islands from the Bering Sea. The lagoon falls under state ownership and is itself a state game refuge.

Wildlife: This lagoon, along with several smaller lagoons, hosts up to 300,000 geese, 150,000 ducks and nearly all of the world's population of black brant — 120,000 to 150,000 birds — during the fall migration. These birds feed on Izembek Lagoon's 84,000-acre eelgrass bed, one of the largest in the world. Most waterfowl arrive in the refuge in late August or early September. By early November a second wave of northern waterfowl (primarily sea ducks) arrives to winter at Izembek. The colorful Steller's eider, which nests on the Arctic coast of Alaska and Siberia, is the most common wintering duck. In addition, thousands of shorebirds feed on the bay shore at low tide. At high tide they gather in such large flocks that in flight they look like smoke clouds.

Other wildlife includes brown bear, caribou, ptarmigan and furbearers. Fish in the refuge include 4 species of salmon, Dolly Varden, arctic char and steelhead trout. Sea lions, sea otters, harbor seals and gray, killer and minke whales are seen in bays and lagoons.

Climate: Izembek summers are charac-terized by fog, drizzle and cloud cover, but they can vary from year to year. Severe storms may occur year-round, often accompanied by intense winds. The average annual precipitation is about 35 inches, with most occurring in fall. Temperatures range from an average of 28°F in February to 51°F in August. Vegetation usually starts growing in late May or early June; the first frost usually occurs in October or November.

Access: The refuge boundary is less than a mile from refuge headquarters in Cold Bay and is accessible by a road system. Vehicles may be rented in Cold Bay. Motorized travel off the roads in the refuge is prohibited. Cold Bay is reached by scheduled air service from Anchorage and has food and lodging facilities. Aircraft are not permitted to land in the refuge; however, they can land adjacent to the refuge below the mean high tide line. The area around Moffet Point, at the north end of the refuge is popular for landing aircraft. The 42 miles of roads in the Cold Bay area lead to Frosty Peak, a 5,820-foot volcano on the refuge's eastern boundary; Grant Point, which provides an excellent overlook on Izembek Lagoon; and to the lagoon itself, which also is the location of the wreck of the wooden brig, *Courtney Ford*, under consideration for nomination to the National Register of Historic Places.

Activities: Hunting is excellent for waterfowl, ptarmigan, caribou and brown bear. Write the refuge manager for the names of authorized commercial guides. Sportfishing for salmon and Dolly Varden also is popular, although no commercial fishing guides currently operate in the refuge. For additional information contact: Refuge Manager, Izembek National Wildlife Refuge, P.O. Box 127, Cold Bay, AK 99571; phone 532-2445.

The Rivers

NOTE: Some of the rivers described below are also included in the Sportfishing section where additional information on species, seasons and bait suggestions is provided.

Alagnak and Nonvianuk rivers. (Part of the Kvichak watershed, Bristol Bay Wild Trout Area.) The 80-mile-long Alagnak River and its 11-mile tributary, the Nonvianuk, both originate within Katmai National Preserve. The Nonvianuk and the first 67 miles of the Alagnak were included in the National Wild and Scenic River System in 1980. The Alagnak originates in Kukaklek Lake, then flows west-southwest to join the Kvichak River, which empties into Bristol Bay. Either the main branch or the Nonvianuk, which heads in Nonvianuk Lake, offers excellent boating.

The Alagnak leaves Kukaklek Lake at a moderate speed (3 to 4 mph), but quickly picks up speed (7 to 8 mph) as it drops through a canyon where there are 2 sets of Class III rapids, neither of which can be easily portaged because of extremely steep canyon walls. Below the canyon the river slows, braids and then becomes a broad channel (2 to 3 mph) as it empties into the Kvichak.

The Nonvianuk offers a leisurely float in its entirety, with some Class II rapids possible 4 to 5 miles from its origin during low water periods. High water season is during May, June and the first part of July. Inflatable rafts are recommended for the main branch; on the Nonvianuk rafts, kayaks and canoes are all suitable. The average trip takes approximately 4 to 5 days if just floating, 5 to 6 days if floating and fishing.

These rivers offer good fishing seasonally for all 5 species of salmon (especially sockeye), Dolly Varden, rainbow and lake trout, grayling and pike in side sloughs and lakes. Floaters also have a good chance of seeing brown bear, moose, wolf, red fox, wolverine, beaver, river otter and lynx. A variety of birds including bald eagles, osprey, ptarmigan, spruce grouse, swans and game ducks are readily observed. Hunting is allowed in the preserve in season.

Access to the river system is by scheduled air service from Anchorage to King Salmon, then by chartered floatplane to Kukaklek or Nonvianuk Lake, about 60 miles to the northeast. Exit is usually by floatplane from the lower 30 miles of the Kvichak, before the tidal influence in the last 10 miles. Related USGS Topographic maps: Iliamna A-7, A-8; Dillingham A-1, A-2 and A-3.

Aniakchak River. The 32-mile-long Aniakchak River is unique in that it heads in a freshwater lake inside the caldera of an active volcano, which last erupted in 1931. The river, located entirely within Aniakchak National Monument, was included in the National Wild and Scenic River System in 1980.

The river starts slowly from Surprise Lake and speeds up as it flows through a narrow 1,500-foot-high opening in the caldera wall called The Gates. The river is shallow and rocky, Class III to IV, and has low falls as it drops 70 feet per mile for the first 13 miles. Then the river meanders slowly, Class II to I, through flatlands to Aniakchak Bay on the Pacific Ocean side of the Alaska Peninsula. Inflatable rafts are recommended because of numerous, closely-spaced boulders. The trip from Surprise Lake to Aniakchak Bay generally takes 3 days.

The number of groups on the river is increasing and 15 operators hold commercial use licenses for services in Aniakchak.

The caldera is scenic, featuring 2,000-foot walls, cinder cones and other volcanic wonders. There is good hiking in the monument. Fish available in the river include salmon, arctic char, Dolly Varden and rainbow trout. Wildlife that may be observed includes caribou, moose, brown bears, wolves, river otters, wolverines, sea otters, harbor seals, sea lions, bald eagles, waterfowl and shorebirds.

Weather in this area is generally miserable, with much rain, cold temperatures and high winds, especially through The Gates. (See cautionary notes in the section on Aniakchak National Monument.) Bad weather may delay put-in or take-out; floaters should be equipped with extra food and supplies. There is a shelter cabin on the north side of the mouth of the Aniakchak River where parties can wait for pickup.

Access to Aniakchak River is by chartered floatplane from King Salmon or Port Heiden to Surprise Lake. Exit is generally by floatplane from Aniakchak Bay; the bay often is too rough for floatplanes, but small, wheeled planes can land on the beach. Related USGS Topographic maps: Chignik D-1, Sutwik Island D-5, D-6.

Katmai lakes. Several lakes and a river in Katmai National Park afford a circular trip of nearly 100 miles for kayakers and canoeists in a scenic setting among low mountains. This trip generally starts at Brooks Camp on Naknek Lake, then skirts the shore of Naknek Lake to the Bay of Islands, where there is a 1-mile portage to Grosvenor Lake. The portage begins at an old log cabin (available for public use on a first-come basis), then leads to a small lake which can either be paddled across or walked around on its eastern shore (do not take an obvious trail to the right as it will take you back to the Bay of Islands). After paddling the length of Lake Grosvenor, you'll enter the 3-mile, flat-water Grosvenor River which joins the Savonoski River, a braided, fairly slow glacial stream which will take you 12 miles to Iliuk Arm. Stay on the south shore of Iliuk Arm as the north shore is steep with few places to pull out in case of bad weather. Iliuk Arm joins Naknek Lake just a few miles from Brooks Camp.

These are very large lakes and easterly or westerly winds can quickly cause choppy water. Staying close to shore is highly recommended. Also, be aware that this is prime brown bear country; camping along the Savonoski River from mid-July to September is not recommended because large numbers of bears will be feeding on spawning salmon. A backcountry permit is required for this trip and can be obtained from the National Park Service in King Salmon or Brooks Camp. The trip, starting and finishing at Brooks Camp, generally takes 5 to 7 days.

This trip offers good fishing for sockeye salmon, rainbow and lake trout. Brush makes hiking difficult, except along the lake shores. Bear, moose, red fox, wolf, lynx, wolverine, river otter, mink, marten, weasel and beaver may be seen. Lake edges and marshes are nesting sites for whistling swans, ducks, loons, grebes and arctic terns.

Access to the lakes is by scheduled air service from Anchorage to King Salmon, then a scheduled flight or charter floatplane to Brooks Camp or Grosvenor Camp. Also, there is a road from King Salmon to Lake Camp at the west end of Naknek Lake. Related USGS Topographic maps: Mount Katmai B-5, C-4 through C-6.

Hiker in Katmai National Park's Valley of 10,000 Smokes makes his way over a snow bridge. (George Wuerthner)

King Salmon River. This is a slow (1 to 2 mph), silty river flowing westward about 60 miles across a soggy, tundra-covered coastal plain to Egegik Bay. (Not to be confused with the King Salmon River farther south which flows into Ugashik Bay.) This river's headwaters are in Katmai National Park and it flows partially through Becharof National Wildlife Refuge. Raft, kayak and canoe are all suitable for this river. There can be strong upstream winds and tidal influences on the lower river. Stay in the far left channel of the King Salmon and Egegik rivers to reach the village of Egegik on Egegik Bay at low tide.

There is good scenery at the headwaters and observation of wildlife is good in season. King, sockeye and chum salmon are plentiful and rainbow trout, Dolly Varden and grayling also are present. Brown bears and Canada geese are abundant, caribou and moose also may be seen. The area is popular for big game sport hunting.

Access is by wheel or floatplane from King Salmon to a lake near the head of Gertrude Creek or to headwater gravel bars outside Katmai National Park. Exit is generally from the village of Egegik, which is served by commercial air service from King Salmon. Related USGS Topographic maps: Katmai A-6, Naknek A-1, A-2, A-4, A-5, B-2 to B-4.

Sportfishing

Except for a few miles of road out of King Salmon and Dillingham, access to lakes and rivers on the Alaska Peninsula is almost solely by airplane, although you can take a boat or walk to some spots if you have enough time. There are daily commercial flights from Anchorage to King Salmon, Dillingham and Iliamna, where you can charter a plane for $150 to $400 an hour, depending on plane size. The charter operators usually do not supply camping gear, boats or tackle. You can rent a boat in King Salmon, however. There are many lodges in the area and their guides will take care of logistics if you are fishing with them.

This region offers some of the finest sportfishing in the world. Probably the most prized sport fish are the trophy-sized rainbow trout. Rainbows in this area regularly attain 10 pounds. The Kvichak and Alagnak watersheds are within the state's Bristol Bay Wild Trout Area. Special regulations printed in the Sport Fish Regulations, designed to perpetuate the original wild rainbow trout stocks, apply here.

Tackle-breaking king salmon are at their best from mid-June through July. These fish are not uncommon at 30 pounds and up. Chums and reds show up by July 1, pinks by mid-July (in even-numbered years) and silvers by mid-August. Salmon fishing is concentrated in the river systems.

Arctic char and Dolly Varden are found throughout the peninsula region and are most abundant either in spring when some migrate to the sea, or in midsummer when large schools concentrate at river mouths to feed on outmigrating juvenile salmon. These fish usually weigh 1 to 3 pounds, but occasional 9- to 12-pound lunkers have been reported. Grayling can be caught most of the summer, but larger ones are more plentiful August through October, with record-breakers found in the outlet of lower Ugashik Lake. Grayling measuring 18 inches are not uncommon and they can reach 23 inches.

Throughout this region, the philosophy of catch and release is encouraged by everyone associated with the fishery, says the Alaska Dept. of Fish and Game.

Cloudy skies and light rain are common here. Bring warm clothing, rain gear and hip boots. Also be sure to bring lots of insect repellent. It's recommended that you purchase your fishing license in Anchorage or another large Alaska city. They can be purchased in Bristol Bay communities, but sometimes the vendors themselves have "gone fishing." The Dept. of Fish and Game does not sell licenses.

For more information about fishing on the Alaska Peninsula contact: Area Management Biologist, Alaska Dept. of Fish and Game, P.O. Box 230, Dillingham, AK 99516; phone 842-5227.

Alagnak River System. Located at the top of the Alaska Peninsula partially in Katmai National Preserve. Also within the state's Bristol Bay Wild Trout Area; check the regulation book for special rules. The Alagnak River drains Battle and Kukaklek lakes and flows into Kvichak Bay. The Nonvianuk River, a tributary of the Alagnak, drains Kulik and Nonvianuk lakes. This drainage offers good fishing for 5 species of salmon. Excellent rainbow trout fishery; use unbaited, single-hook artificial flies June 8 through Oct. 31. Also available are grayling; arctic char — use spoons; northern pike — use spoons and spinners; and lake trout — use spoons and plugs. Air charter service available from Anchorage,

Kenai, Homer, King Salmon, Dillingham and Iliamna.

Egegik River System. Located approximately 40 miles south of King Salmon, partially within Becharof National Wildlife Refuge. Egegik River drains Becharof Lake and empties into Egegik Bay, as does one of the King Salmon rivers (the other one is in the Ugashik system farther south). Five species of salmon are found in this drainage; sockeyes spawn in Becharof Lake. Other fish present are grayling — use flies; arctic char — use spoons and eggs; northern pike — use spoons and spinners; and lake trout — use spoons and plugs. Air charter service available in King Salmon. Commercial fishing lodge at Egegik.

Naknek River System. The Naknek system extends from the town of Naknek, adjacent to King Salmon, upstream approximately 75 miles to the east. Much of the system is in Katmai National Park and is subject to additional federal regulations. The Naknek River drains Naknek Lake, Brooks Lake, Lake Colville and Lake Grosvenor; its outlet is Kvichak Bay, a good fishing location for those operating on a restricted budget. King salmon fishing excellent on the Naknek River at King Salmon, where boats can be rented. Naknek Lake accessible by road from King Salmon. This drainage offers good fishing for 5 species of salmon. Excellent rainbow trout fishery. Also available are grayling, arctic char, northern pike, lake trout and whitefish. Smelt are available in winter. Outlying lakes served by air charter planes from King Salmon. Several commercial fishing lodges in the area.

Ugashik System. Located approximately 80 miles south of King Salmon; Ugashik lakes are within Alaska Peninsula National Wildlife Refuge. The Ugashik River drains Upper and Lower Ugashik lakes and flows into Ugashik Bay, as does the King Salmon River, which drains Mother Goose Lake and the glacier-fed Dog Salmon River. Five species of salmon found in this drainage; sockeyes spawn in the Ugashik lakes. No rainbow trout here, but the lakes are world renowned for trophy-sized grayling — use flies. Other fish present are arctic char — use spoons and eggs; northern pike — use spoons and spinners; and lake trout — use spoons and plugs. Air charter service available in King Salmon or Pilot Point.

SPECIAL FEATURES

Anangula

Dating back at least 8,000 years, Anangula is the oldest known settlement in the Aleut world. This site is located on now-uninhabited Anangula (Ananiuliak) Island at the northern end of Samalga Pass off Nikolski village. Thousands of stone artifacts have been found at Anangula that link this culture to those of northern and central Asia, particularly the Kamchatka Peninsula. The fate of those who lived at Anangula is in question, however, as the site appears to have been occupied less than a century when a heavy cover of volcanic ash rained down from Okmok Volcano, probably killing local plants and animals on which the people depended. The 4,000-year gap between settlement here and evidence man again lived in the area appears to correspond to a period of volcanism.

Lighthouses

Cape Sarichef Light Station. This is the most westerly lighthouse in North America, located in the Aleutian Chain on the northwest side of Unimak Island overlooking Unimak Pass. Cape Sarichef began operating July 1, 1904. Construction crews reinforced the structures and the station was relighted in 1950. Now automated, the station serves as a National Weather Service forecasting center.

Scotch Cap Light Station. The first to be built on the outside coast of Alaska, Scotch Cap Light Station is the second most-westerly lighthouse in North America and the most southerly in Alaska. The station is a monument also to many ship disasters, before and

after its establishment. It was automated in 1971. The station began operation July 18, 1903. Partly because of the hazardous duty, each of Scotch Cap's 3 keepers received a year's vacation every 4 years. On April 1, 1946, an earthquake that registered 7.4 on the Richter Scale occurred southwest of Unimak Island, generating a 100-foot tsunami that swamped Scotch Cap and killed all 5 Coast Guardsmen at the station. The wave crossed the Pacific Ocean and hit the north side of the Hawaiian Islands, killing 159 people. It then continued to Chile, rebounded and hit the southern side of Hawaii, causing what is rated as Hawaii's worst natural disaster ever because it hit with no warning.

Pribilof Islands

In 1786, when Russians searching for fur seals first encountered this isolated island group 200 miles out in the Bering Sea, they stumbled upon some of the continent's grandest wildlife spectacles. St. Paul and St. George islands claim North America's largest northern fur seal and seabird colonies, a wildlife extravaganza that still draws visitors to this remote corner of Alaska.

Archaeological records reveal no signs of habitation of the Pribilofs prior to their occupancy by Russian fur hunters who imported Aleuts from Unalaska and Atka and founded the island group's 2 communities, St. Paul and St. George. From 1867, when the U.S. purchased Alaska, to 1909 the government contracted with private companies to harvest the fur seals. From 1910 federal officials managed the sealing operations, and the residents of the Pribilof Islands were treated as wards of the government. During WWII, the entire population of the Pribilof Islands was evacuated and restricted to an abandoned cannery and mining camp at Funter Bay in southeastern Alaska. In 1983 the Pribilof people were given full control of their islands, and in 1987 they celebrated their bicentennial.

Although the fur seal industry has dominated the islands' economy in the past, it has been replaced by a growing fisheries industry and tourism. Subsistence centers around fur seal harvesting and fishing, especially for halibut.

(For more details on St. George and St. Paul, see Communities in this section.)

Unga Island Petrified Forest

Although the Aleutians are one of the most extensive treeless zones in the world, there is much evidence that trees thrived here before the ice ages. Some 150 acres of beach on the northwest coast of Unga Island, located west of Sand Point, contain black, yellow and gray petrified stumps measuring 2 to 4 feet in diameter. Petrified wood also is found on Amchitka and Atka islands. Unga's forest, experts claim, rivals those of national parks in the Lower 48. The rock stumps are the remains of metasequoia trees, thought to be an ancestor of the redwood trees of the western United States. Scientists estimate they lived 11 million to 25 million years ago, encouraged by the warm humidity of the Miocene period. These are angiosperms rather than gymnosperms (cone-bearing evergreens), which are the trees that do well today in the Aleutians, having been transplanted to sheltered areas at Unalaska, Atka, Adak, Unga, Akutan and Squaw Harbor. Access to the Unga Island petrified forest is via charter plane or boat from Sand Point.

World War II
Military Sites

Several sites in the Aleutians relating to WWII have been designated national historic landmarks including the following:

Adak Island, Adak Army Base and Adak Naval Operating Base. The bases have been nominated to the National Register of Historic Places. Adak, one of the Andreanof Islands in the Aleutian chain, is about 1,400 air miles southwest of Anchorage.

The island was unoccupied at the outbreak of WWII. Alaska's largest and most expensive wartime base of operations was established after the Japanese bombings of Unalaska and Dutch Harbor and the invasion of Attu and Kiska islands in June 1942. The need for an advance base farther west than Unalaska and Umnak islands became urgent and Adak was selected because of its all weather harbor. The first airstrip was built on Adak in 12 days and on Sept. 14, 1942, the first Liberators flew from Adak to bomb Japanese forces on Kiska. Permanent airfields later were built and Adak served as the command post for the invasions of Attu and Kiska in 1943. Adak continued to serve as an active base throughout the war. In 1950, the Army Air Force turned it over to the Navy. Today, Adak Naval Air Station, located on the WWII site, occupies the northern half of the island; the southern half is part of the Alaska Maritime National Wildlife Refuge. As with many of the other islands that played a major role in WWII, Adak is littered with military Quonset huts and other buildings and relics.

World War II relics litter Kiska island. This is a Japanese mini-sub. (Staff)

Permission to visit Adak must be obtained by writing Commanding Officer, U.S. Naval Air Station, Adak, FPO Seattle, WA 98791.

Amaknak Island, Dutch Harbor Naval Operating Base and Fort Mears. At the time of the Dec. 7, 1941, Japanese attack on Pearl Harbor in Hawaii, these, along with top-secret Fort Glenn on nearby Umnak Island, were the only U.S. defense facilities in the Aleutians. Shortly after Pearl Harbor, a naval base was constructed at Unalaska. Some 60,000 men were stationed at Dutch Harbor/Unalaska, which was the target of Japanese bombing on June 3 and 4, 1942, in conjunction with the Battle of Midway. Much of the military installations remained at Dutch Harbor and Unalaska until June 1985, when a clean-up program began. Many of the old buildings are now gone, although old machine gun nests, barbed wire, trenches and bomb shelters will remain for years to come. The remains of the bombed-out ship, *Northwestern*, which had been used for barracks, still lie partially submerged at the head of Captain's Bay, a short drive from town. Unalaska is accessible by commercial air service from Anchorage.

Attu Island, Attu Battlefield and the U.S. Army and Navy airfields. Site of the only WWII battle fought on the North American continent, Attu Island is at the western end of the Aleutian chain, 1,500 air miles southwest of Anchorage, 500 miles east of the USSR mainland.

The Japanese occupation of Attu and Kiska took place in June 1942, coordinated with the Battle of Midway. Attu was held for nearly a year before American troops invaded. During the bitterly fought, 19-day battle, most of the 2,500 Japanese troops were killed, many during a *banzai* attack out of the hills. Only 29 Japanese survived. U.S. casualties were heavy, too. Of 15,000 troops, 550 were killed, 1,500 wounded and another 1,200 disabled by Attu's harsh climate. During the remaining years of the war, the U.S. flew bombing raids on Japan from Attu. Today, there is much evidence of the desperate battle on Attu's eastern end; thousands of shell and bomb craters in the tundra,

Japanese trenches, foxholes and gun emplacements. American ammunition magazines and dumps and spent cartridges, shrapnel and shells are found at the scenes of heavy fighting. The steel-matted runways at Alexai Field and the asphalt runways at the U.S. Naval Air Station exist, the latter still operational. Portions of deteriorating piers still stand at Massacre Bay. Roads may still be traced, but only 5 miles are maintained.

The only occupants today are a few U.S. Coast Guardsmen who operate a long-range navigation (loran) station. The Aleut village of Attu, whose residents had been captured and taken to Japan, was destroyed during the battle and no trace remains. The entire island is part of the Alaska Maritime National Wildlife Refuge, administered by the U.S. Fish and Wildlife Service. For information about Attu contact: Refuge Manager, Aleutian Islands Unit, Alaska Maritime National Wildlife Refuge, Box 5251, Naval Air Station, Adak, FPO Seattle, WA 98791; phone 592-2406.

Kiska Island, Japanese Occupation Site. The Japanese withdrew from Kiska after the U.S. reclaimed Attu. Kiska, one of the Rat Islands group near the western end of the Aleutian chain, is 165 miles southeast of Attu.

On June 7, 1942, a Japanese task force invaded Attu and Kiska, overrunning a U.S. weather station on Kiska and constructing coastal and antiaircraft defenses, camps, roads, an airfield, submarine base, seaplane base and other installations. The occupation marked the peak of Japan's military expansion in the Pacific and caused great alarm in North America that a Japanese invasion would be mounted through Alaska. As Allied forces prepared to invade Kiska, 5,183 Japanese were secretly evacuated in less than an hour under cover of fog on July 28, 1943. On Aug. 15, 34,000 U.S. and Canadian troops invaded a deserted island. The Allies subsequently established their own camps. Kiska was abandoned after the war, but relics from Japanese and U.S. camps still litter the countryside.

Today Kiska is unoccupied and is part of Alaska Maritime National Wildlife Refuge. For information about access restrictions contact: Refuge Manager, Alaska Maritime National Wildlife Refuge, 202 Pioneer Ave., Homer, AK 99603; phone 235-6546. Or contact: Alaska Maritime National Wildlife Refuge, Aleutian Islands Unit, Box 5251, Naval Air Station, Adak, FPO Seattle, WA 98791; phone 592-2406.

WILDLIFE

When viewing or photographing wildlife, keep your distance. If an animal shows signs of being crowded or disturbed, sit quietly or move away slowly.

Angler on the Unalakleet River prepares to land a Dolly Varden. This wild and scenic river offers excellent fishing. (George Wuerthner)

BERING SEA COAST

The Region

A fish-rich bay and immense river delta bordered by rugged mountains describe the Bering Sea Coast region of western Alaska. Fishing and gold mining have lured outsiders to this Yup'ik Eskimo world where many of the traditional ways are still followed.

Location: The region extends from the Arctic Circle south to where the Alaska Peninsula joins the mainland near Katmai National Park.

Subregions: This huge area is divided into 3 subregions, Bristol Bay, Yukon-Kuskokwim Delta and Seward Peninsula/Norton Sound. The text on specific communities and attractions is divided according to these subregions. The Bering Sea Coast area also includes St. Lawrence Island, home of the Siberian Yup'iks; uninhabited St. Matthew and Hall islands; and Nunivak Island, across Etolin Strait from the delta.

Physical Description: South of the Arctic Circle, the Seward Peninsula reaches 200 miles west toward Asia. Cape Prince of Wales at the peninsula's tip points toward Little Diomede Island, about 25 miles offshore and 3 miles from the Soviet Union's Big Diomede Island. The international boundary and dateline run between the islands. Norton Sound, a 125-mile finger of the Bering Sea, separates Seward Peninsula from the Yukon-Kuskokwim delta, a wetland that stretches 250 miles south to Kuskokwim Bay and 200 miles inland.

The Ahklun Mountains border the delta's flatlands on the south and separate them from Bristol Bay. The bay is renowned for its fishing, particularly the world's largest sockeye salmon run. The bay spans 200 miles from its base at Port Moller on the Alaska Peninsula to its northwest boundary at Cape Newenham and stretches northeastward nearly the same distance to the mouths of the Nushagak and Kvichak rivers which drain its inland reaches.

Rivers: Several major rivers cross the region, the most important of which are the Yukon, Alaska's longest river, Kuskokwim, Unalakleet, Nushagak and Kvichak. The rivers provide access for fish heading for spawning grounds and are the traditional route for inland travel.

Climate

Climate varies throughout the region, with temperatures ranging from the low 40s to low 60s in summer, and from -5°F to the low 20s in winter in the north. Farther south the weather moderates a bit. Highs in the 30s and lows around 0°F occur in winter; summers average from the mid-30s to mid-60s. Wind chill is an important factor in this region where few topographical features break its sweep across the land. Total annual precipitation is about 20 inches. The northern regions are drier than southern ones. North of Bristol Bay rain and snow fall more frequently on the coast than farther inland. Near the bay the opposite is true.

Vegetation

Tundra carpets much of the region where grasses, sedges, mosses, lichens and wildflowers grow beneath scrub willow and alder. Forests which cover eastern Seward Peninsula and Norton Sound, give way to wetland tundra on the delta, then pick up again near Bristol Bay.

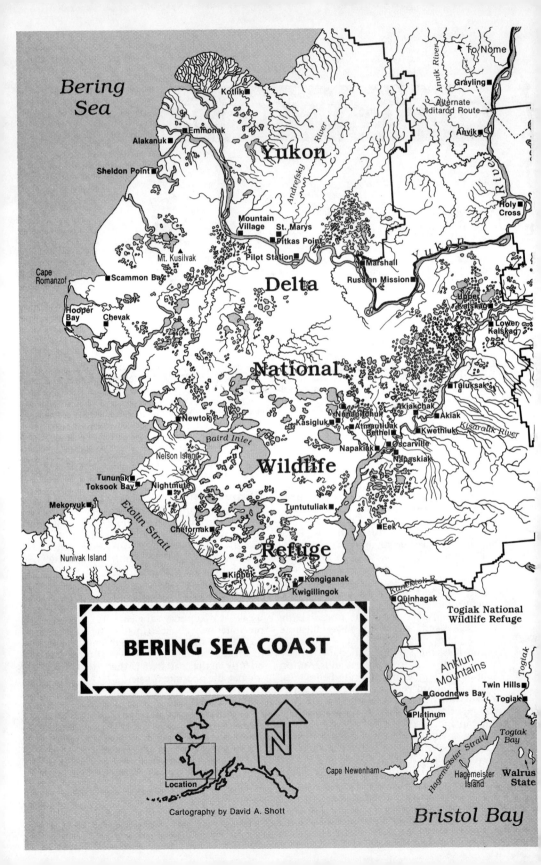

Bering
Sea

to Nome

Kotlik

Grayling

Alternate
Iditarod Route

Emmonak

Alakanuk

Anvik

Yukon

Sheldon Point

Andrefsky River

Yukon River

Holy
Cross

Mt. Kusilvak

Mountain
Village
St. Marys

Pitkas Point

Pilot Station

Marshall

Cape
Romanzof

Scammon Bay

Delta

Russian Mission

Upper
Kalskag

Hooper
Bay

Chevak

Lower
Kalskag

National

Tuluksak

Newtok

Kasigluk

Nunapitchuk

Akiakchak

Akiak

Kwethluk

Kisaralik River

Baird Inlet

Atmautluak
Bethel

Nelson Island

Wildlife

Napakiak

Oscarville

Napaskiak

Tununak
Toksook Bay

Nightmute

Tuntutuliak

Eek

Mekoryuk

Etolin Strait

Chefornak

Refuge

Nunivak Island

Kipnuk

Kongiganak

Kwigillingok

Kanektok R.

Quinhagak

Togiak National
Wildlife Refuge

BERING SEA COAST

Ahklun
Mountains

Togiak

Twin Hills
Goodnews Bay

Togiak

Platinum

Togiak
Bay

Location

Cape Newenham

Hagemeister Strait

Hagemeister
Island

Walrus
State

Cartography by David A. Shott

Bristol Bay

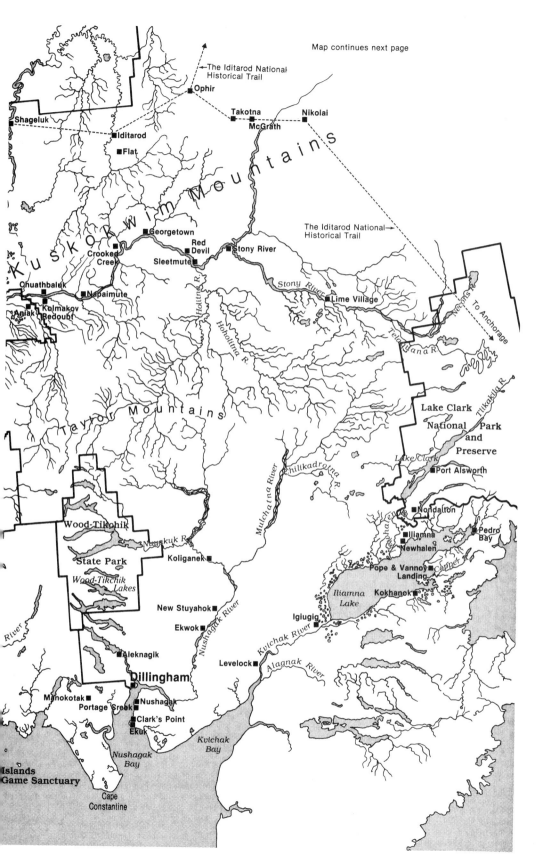

Map continues next page

→The Iditarod National
Historical Trail

■Ophir

Shageluk■

Takotna■ Nikolai■
■ McGrath

■Iditarod

■Flat

K u s k o k w i m   M o u n t a i n s

The Iditarod National→
Historical Trail

■Georgetown
Red
Devil■ ■Stony River
Crooked■
Creek Sleetmute■

Ohuathbaluk■
■Napaimute

Holitna R.

Stony River

■ Lime Village

Aniak■
Kolmakov
Redoubt

Hoholitna R.

T a y l o r   M o u n t a i n s

Mulchatna River

Chilikadrotna R.

Telaquana R.

Tlikakila R.

Welcome To Anchorage

Lake Clark

National   Park
and
Preserve

Lake Clark

■Port Alsworth

Wood-Tikchik

Mulakuk R.

State Park

Koliganek■

Wood-Tikchik
Lakes

Chulitna R.

■Nondalton

■Iliamna
■Newhalen

■Pedro
Bay

New Stuyahok■

Nushagak River

Pope & Vannoy■
Landing

Copper R.

Ekwok■

Igiugig■

Iliamna
Lake

Kokhanok■

River

Kvichak River

Aleknagik■

Levelock■

Alagnak River

Dillingham

Manokotak■
Portage Creek

■Nushagak

Clark's Point

Ekuk

Kvichak
Bay

Nushagak
Bay

Islands
Game Sanctuary

Cape
Constantine

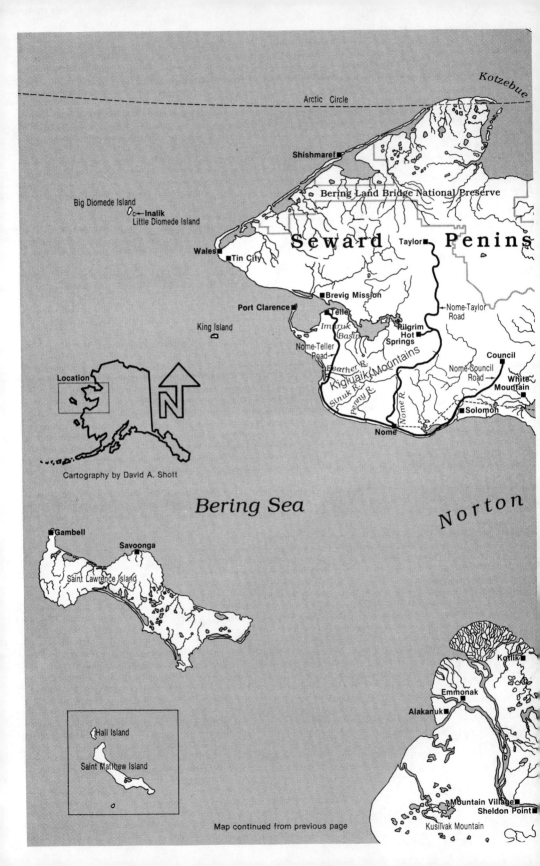

Kotzebue

Arctic Circle

Shishmaref ■

Big Diomede Island
○○—Inalik
Little Diomede Island

Bering Land Bridge National Preserve

S e w a r d   Taylor ■   P e n i n s

Wales ■
■ Tin City

Brevig Mission ■
Port Clarence ■   ■ Teller
Imuruk Basin
Pilgrim Hot Springs ■

King Island

Location
Nome-Taylor Road

Nome-Teller Road

Nome-Council Road
Council ■
White Mountain ■

Feather R.
Kigluaik Mountains
Sinuk R.
Penny R.
Nome R.

N

Cartography by David A. Shott

Solomon ■

Nome ■

Bering Sea

N o r t o n

■ Gambell
Savoonga ■
Saint Lawrence Island

Kotlik ■

Emmonak ■
Alakanuk ■

Hall Island
Saint Matthew Island

Mountain Village ■
Sheldon Point ■
Kusilvak Mountain

Map continued from previous page

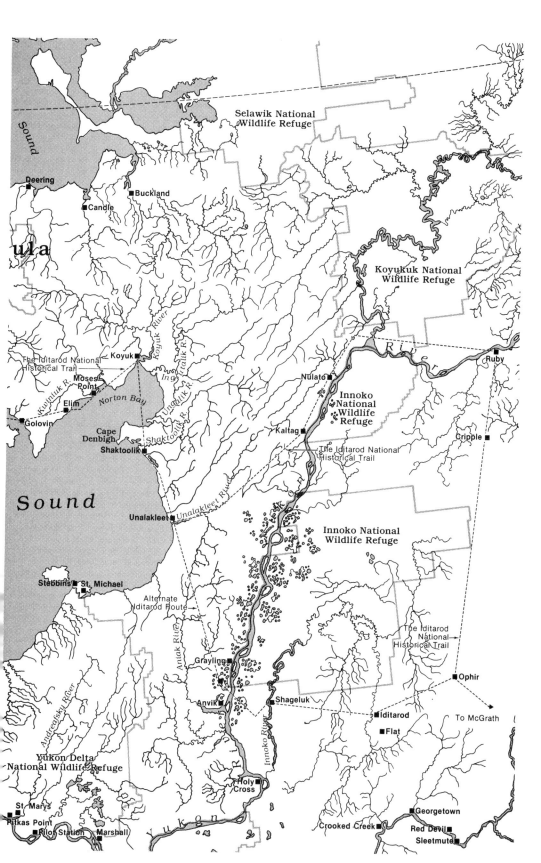

Wildlife

Big Game: Numerous big species make their home in mountainous areas of the region including bears, moose, caribou, wolves and Dall sheep. Musk-ox, once hunted to near extinction in Alaska, were reintroduced to Nunivak Island in the 1930s and now thrive there and on the Seward Peninsula. Reindeer, introduced from Siberia just before the 20th century, roamed much of the Bering Sea Coast region but are now confined to the Seward Peninsula and Nunivak Island.

Furbearers and Nongame Species: The delta lacks suitable shelter for large mammals, but small furbearers such as foxes, muskrats, beaver, otters and weasels find the area a haven. Offshore pass bowhead, gray, killer and beluga whales, sea lions, fur seals, and several species of true seals.

Birds: Millions of shorebirds and waterfowl breed on the delta, while a host of seabirds crowd cliffs along the mainland coast and on offshore islands.

Fish: Residents of the region depend on salmon, including the great Bristol Bay sockeye run and a substantial fishery in the Yukon and Kuskokwim rivers; grayling, trout, Dolly Varden, pike, arctic char, burbot and several species of whitefish. In the Bering Sea, several species of shellfish and bottom fish feed a commercial and subsistence market.

Eskimo doll is one example of the traditional crafts of this region. (Marion Stirrup)

Minerals

Minerals have greatly influenced the region's economy. A gold rush led to the founding of Nome, and prospectors were some of the earliest settlers on the Seward Peninsula. Near Goodnews Bay south of Kuskokwim Bay lies an important platinum deposit. The western Seward Peninsula has substantial tin deposits, while the Red Devil area near the delta contains mercury deposits.

Public Lands

National Parks and Preserves: Bering Land Bridge National Preserve protects portions of the original pathway of prehistoric man from Asia to North America.

Wildlife Refuges and Sanctuaries: The region's rich habitat is protected in a number of refuges from Togiak on Bristol Bay's north shore to giant Yukon Delta, largest wildlife refuge in the country. Cape Newenham State Game Refuge, at the mouth of the Kinegnak River, encompasses Chagvan Bay, a large shallow estaurine embayment known for its vast eelgrass beds. The bay is especially critical to black brant which stop in spring to feed on eelgrass. Many important coastal seabird rookeries and those on offshore islands are within the umbrella of Alaska Maritime National Wildlife Refuge. Walrus Islands State Game Sanctuary, off Togiak in northern Bristol Bay, was set aside primarily to protect a major hauling ground for male walrus.

State Parks: Wood-Tikchik State Park north of Dillingham encompasses a series of lakes and excellent wildlife habitat.

History

Russians were the first visitors to enter the Eskimo world of the Bering Sea coast in the early 1800s. They explored along the coasts and established trading posts. Late in the century, after the U.S. purchased Alaska, missionaries, prospectors, traders and fishermen came to the region. The prospecting paid off in the discovery of gold near Nome and the rush to the Seward Peninsula. Reindeer husbandry proved a viable industry for some years, and in recent times has become again important in the economy of several areas.

Today, mining and fishing stir the region's economy with commercial and transportation centers at Nome, Bethel, Naknek and Dillingham.

Access is primarily by jet or smaller plane, with local travel by bush plane and boat. In winter, residents travel by plane, snow machine or sled dog teams.

BRISTOL BAY

Introduction

World-class fishing and beautiful, remote rivers, perfect for floating, lure visitors from all over the world to Bristol Bay. A host of private lodges which range from spartan to luxurious accommodate anglers drawn by trophy fishing in the rivers that feed into the bay. At the east end are the Kvichak River (which drains Lake Iliamna) and the Nushagak; while farther west are the Yuyukuk, Tikchik, Wood and Togiak rivers. All offer fine floating and excellent fishing. (For more on Lake Iliamna, see Western Cook Inlet subregion in SOUTHCENTRAL/GULF COAST section.)

Just to stand on a riverbank and watch salmon swim by can be the experience of a lifetime. Each summer millions of salmon enter the drainages on the way to their spawning grounds. Anglers wanting to catch a particular species of salmon should time their trip carefully to coincide with the height of the run. In general, king salmon arrive first, in June, followed by red and chum, then pink and finally silvers, which can be fished in some areas through late September.

Freshwater fish include rainbow trout, grayling, char, Dolly Varden , lake trout and northern pike. These are available throughout the season, though timing and location are again important. (See Sportfishing, this section.)

The Kvichak-Alagnak watershed, except Lake Clark and its tributaries above Six-Mile Lake, have been designated a Wild Trout Area with fishing restrictions established to protect and perpetuate the high quality wild rainbow trout fisheries and provide anglers a variety of fishing experiences. Anglers looking for arctic char might try the Wood River lakes chain in late May and June. The Nushagak is a favorite king salmon river, while the Togiak is known for its silvers. Information provided by the lodges and wilderness guides will help dedicated anglers plan their trip, and the Alaska Dept. of Fish and Game is also a helpful source of information. (See Fishing in GENERAL INFORMATION section.)

Bristol Bay is bear country, and anglers should take special precautions. The very rivers, lakes and streams best for fishing are also the likeliest places to encounter bears, who also come to search for salmon. Make noise when traveling through tall brush: clap your hands, talk loudly, bang pots together, wear a bear bell on your day pack. Keep a clean camp; and Alaska Dept. of Fish and Game advises that you consider carrying a suitable firearm.

Beach grass, braided and hung on a clothesline to dry, is a frequent sight in western Alaska where grass is woven into beautiful baskets. (William Adams)

▼ C O M M U N I T I E S ▼

Aleknagik

(a-LECK-nuh-gik) Located where Wood River flows out of Lake Aleknagik, 25 miles north of Dillingham, 330 miles west of Anchorage. **Transportation:** Scheduled air service, car or taxi from Dillingham. **Population:** 182. **Zip code:** 99555. **Emergency Services:** Police, phone 842-5953; Clinic, phone 842-5512; Volunteer Fire Department.

Elevation: 70 feet. **Climate:** Cloudy skies, mild temperatures and moderately heavy precipitation. Annual precipitation ranges from 20 to 35 inches, with most occurring during the summer. Two-foot snowpack on ground in winter.

Private Aircraft: Airport 1 mile east; elev. 66 feet; length 2,100 feet; gravel; unattended. Fuel 80, 100 available. Condition not monitored, visual inspection recommended prior to use. Aleknagik Mission Lodge airstrip, private, adjacent northeast; elev. 150 feet; length 1,200 feet; silt and gravel; unattended. Unusable during winter months.

Visitor Facilities: Accommodations and meals available at 2 lodges on Lake Aleknagik. Groceries and hardware may be purchased locally. Arts and crafts for sale at Aleknagik Native Store. Hunting and fishing licenses not available. Guide service available. New laundromat available. Marine engine, boat and car repair service available. Fuel available; marine gas, diesel and regular.

The few early settlers in Aleknagik nearly all died in the influenza epidemic of 1918-19. Resettlement occurred around 1928, when a small Seventh Day Adventist colony was established on the shores of Lake Aleknagik near the area now known as Mosquito Point. The settlement grew as former residents who survived the epidemic started drifting back and a school, churches and a small sawmill were established. There is an influx of people during summer when families return to summer homes for the fishing season.

A scenic, 25-mile dirt road connects Aleknagik with Dillingham. The community is also the gateway to Wood-Tikchik State Park. Fishing in the park and surrounding watersheds is excellent with 5 species of salmon, char, grayling, northern pike and Dolly Varden available. The trip from Lake Kulik to Aleknagik is about 140 miles of big lakes and short, fast rivers, suitable for canoeing and kayaking.

Residents live by subsistence hunting and commercial fishing, mainly for salmon. Grayling and Dolly Varden are among some of the other fish harvested. Moose, caribou and many varieties of berries are found in the area. Many of the residents are still practicing traditional arts and crafts, such as basket weaving and snowshoe making.

Aleknagic is a second class city, incorporated in 1973. Communications include phones, mail plane, radio and TV. The community is served by Seventh-Day Adventist, Russian Orthodox and Moravian churches, and a school with grades kindergarten through 12. Public electricity is available. Water is obtained from private wells or hauled from Aleknagik Lake. Residents have privies and honey buckets. Freight arrives by air transport, barge or truck. Government address: City of Aleknagik, P.O. Box 33, Aleknagik, AK 99555, phone 842-5953. Village corporation address: Aleknagik Natives Ltd., P.O. Box 14, Aleknagik, AK 99555.

Clark's Point

Located on a spit on the northeastern shore of Nushagak Bay, 15 miles south of Dillingham and 350 miles southwest of Anchorage. **Transportation:** Scheduled air service from Dillingham. **Population:** 83. **Zip code:** 99569. **Emergency Services:** Police, phone 842-5943; Clinic; Volunteer Fire Department.

Climate: Cloudy skies, mild temperatures and moderately heavy precipitation, with frequent strong surface winds. Average summer temperatures from 37° to 66°F; winter temperatures from 4° to 30°F. Annual precipitation from 20 to 26 inches, with most of the precipitation occurring in July and August.

Private Aircraft: Airstrip adjacent north; elev. 10 feet; length 2,700 feet; gravel; unattended. Runway condition not monitored, visual inspection recommended prior to landing. Watch for birds on runway and pedestrians and vehicles on west end. No fuel or airport facilities.

Visitor Facilities: None. Community store available with limited selection of items.

Settled in 1888, when Nushagak Packing Co. established a cannery there, the village was named for John W. Clark. He was manager of the Alaska Commercial Co. store at Nushagak, and was reputed to have operated a saltery on the spit prior to establishment of the cannery. The cannery closed and reopened several times during the years and shut down permanently in 1952. Since that time Alaska Packers Assoc. has operated the facility as a headquarters for its fishing fleet. A major flood occurred in 1929. Plagued by erosion and threat of floods, the village has since been relocated to higher ground.

The village, incorporated in 1971 as a second-class city, is a "designated anchorage" for scows, floaters and fishing boats working the bay during the summer fishing season. Commercial fishing is the primary base of the economy, and residents depend largely on subsistence activities for food sources.

Communications include phones, mail plane, radio and TV. The community has a Catholic church and a school with grades kindergarten through 12. Community water, sewer, electricity. Freight is transported by air transport and skiffs from Dillingham. Government address: Clark's Point, P.O. Box 7, Clark's Point, AK 99569; phone 842-5943. Village corporation address: Saguyak Inc., General Delivery, Clark's Point, AK 99569.

Dillingham

Located on the south side of Snag Point at the confluence of the Wood and Nushagak rivers at the north end of Nushagak Bay, 175 miles southeast of Bethel, 320 miles west of Anchorage. **Transportation:** Scheduled airline from Anchorage. **Population:** 2,153. **Zip code:** 99576. **Emergency Services:** Police and fire, emergency only, phone 911; Alaska State Troopers, phone 842-5641; Kanakanak Hospital, phone 842-5201; Fire Department, phone 842-2288.

Elevation: 80 feet. **Climate:** Transitional climate zone, affected primarily by the waters

Whalebone sculpture by Willie Wassillie is displayed at Dillingham Heritage Museum, which features contemporary and traditional art. (Marion Stirrup)

of Bristol Bay, but also by the arctic climate of the Interior. Cloudy skies, mild temperatures and fairly heavy precipitation. There are often strong winds. Heavy fog occurs often in July and August. Mean annual precipitation 25 inches, with 71 inches of snow.

Private Aircraft: Airport 2 miles west; elev. 85 feet; length 6,400 feet; asphalt, grooved; fuel 80, 100 and jet A; attended Monday to Friday. Airport has passenger and freight terminals, ticket counters, restrooms and traffic control tower. Public transportation to town available.

Visitor Facilities: Accommodations available. Visitor center, open summers. Meals available at lodging facilities and at several restaurants. Laundromat, dry cleaners (alterations), and banking services available. Supplies available at several grocery and general mercantile stores, as well as specialty shops. Arts and crafts available for purchase include grass baskets, carved ivory, Eskimo dolls, masks, skin sewing and Eskimo yo-yos. Fishing/hunting licenses available, as well as guide services. Repair services available for marine engines, boats, autos and aircraft. Autos can be rented. Fuel available includes marine gas, diesel, propane, unleaded and regular gasoline. Moorage facilities available.

The area around Dillingham was long inhabited by various Eskimo and Indian groups. In 1818, Alexander Baranof, first governor of Russian America, ordered construction of a permanent post at the mouth of the Nushagak River. The post came to be known as Alexandrovski Redoubt and drew people from the Kuskokwim region, Cook Inlet and the Alaska Peninsula. The community was called Nushagak by 1837 when a Russian Orthodox mission was established there. In 1881 the U.S. Signal Corps established a meteorological station at Nushagak and in 1884 the first salmon cannery in the Bristol Bay region was constructed by the Arctic Packing Co. Two more canneries were established in the next 2 years, the second one at the present city of Dillingham, then known as Snag Point. In 1903, U.S. Senator William Paul Dillingham of Vermont toured through Alaska with his subcommittee. The town was named after the senator in 1904. Dillingham is a first-class city, incorporated in 1963.

Dillingham is the economic and transportation hub of the Bristol Bay region. Northbound cargo ships unload supplies for area villages at the Dillingham dock. The city-run dock handles 10,000 tons of freight and fish annually. The city also maintains a harbor serving more than 500 boats. The economy is augmented by commercial fishing, the cannery, trapping and tourism. An annual event, the Beaver Roundup, occurs each March. Bristol Bay is the world's largest producer of red salmon.

The Dillingham Heritage Museum, Pouch 202, Dillingham, AK 99576; phone 842-5610 or 842-5521, is an ethno-history museum featuring contemporary and traditional Alaskan arts, crafts and artifacts. The Yup'ik Eskimo culture of southwestern Alaska is represented in basketry, carving, skin sewing and dolls. The museum also hosts traveling exhibits from around the state. The museum shares a building with the public library. Hours are from noon to 6 p.m. Monday and Tuesday and Thursday through Saturday; 5-9 p.m. on Wednesday. No admission charge; donations accepted.

Numerous sportfishing lodges are located near Dillingham and there is a 25-mile road connecting the town with the Eskimo village of Aleknagik located on Lake Aleknagik near Wood-Tikchik State Park. The park also is accessible by floatplane from Dillingham.

In addition to salmon, trout, grayling and arctic char are the main species of fish caught in the areas. There is hunting for brown bear in the area and trapping for wolf, wolverine, fox, lynx, marten and beaver. Float trips down the Nushagak or Wood River systems are popular.

Much land in the Dillingham area is owned by the local Native corporation, Choggiung Ltd., which requires that a permit be obtained for any public use of its lands.

Communications in Dillingham include phones, radio, TV and 2 newspapers. The community is served by 8 churches, a public library, 3 public schools, a private school and a community college. There are community electricity, water and sewer. Freight arrives by cargo plane, barge and ship. Government address: City of Dillingham, P.O. Box 191, Dillingham, AK 99576; phone 842-5211. Village corporation address: Choggiung Ltd., P.O. Box 889, Dillingham, AK 99576; Chamber of Commerce, City of Dillingham, P.O. Box 294, Dillingham, AK 99576.

Ekuk

(E-kek) Located on the east shore of Nushagak Bay, 16 miles south of Dillingham and 340 miles west of Anchorage. **Transportation:** Scheduled air service from Dillingham. **Population:** 3. **Zip code:** 99576. **Emergency Services:** Police and health service at Dillingham.

Climate: Cloudy skies, mild temperatures and moderately heavy precipitation; subjected to strong surface winds, fog during winter months. Average summer temperatures from 37° to 66°F; average winter temperatures from 4° to 30°F. Annual precipitation from 20 to 26 inches, with most of the precipitation occurring in the summer months.

Private Aircraft: Private airstrip adjacent south; elev. 30 feet; length 1,200 feet; gravel and dirt; unattended. Runway not maintained during winter months; soft when wet. No fuel or airport facilities.

Visitor Facilities: None.

Ekuk, mentioned in Russian accounts of 1824 and 1828 (in the latter referred to as Village Ekouk and Seleniye Ikuk), was thought to be a major Eskimo village in prehistoric and early historic times. In Eskimo Ekuk means "the last village down," being the farthest village south on Nushagak Bay. St. Nicholas Chapel, a Russian Orthodox church dating from 1917, located in the village is on the National Register of Historic Places. A cannery was opened in 1903 which drew many people to the area. Floods, erosion and lack of a school caused residents to leave. During summer months people return to fish and work in the cannery.

Fishing includes all species of salmon, as well as freshwater fish found nearby. The area supports a large and diverse population of small mammals and an abundance of birds.

Much land in the Ekuk area is owned by the local Native corporation, Choggiung Ltd., which requires that a permit be obtained for any public use of its lands.

Communications in Ekuk, which is unincorporated, includes phones, mail plane, radio and TV. Electricity and water supplied by individual generators and wells. Sewage system is honey buckets and outhouses. Freight arrives by air transport or barge. Village corporation address: Ekuk Natives Ltd., General Delivery, Ekuk, AK 99576. Choggiung Ltd., P.O. Box 889, Dillingham, AK 99576.

Ekwok

(EK-wok) Located on the Nushagak River, 48 miles east of Dillingham, 290 miles west of Anchorage. **Transportation:** Boat, snow machine, scheduled and charter air service from Dillingham. **Population:** 110. **Zip code:** 99580. **Emergency Services:** Village Public Safety Officer, phone 464-3326; Alaska State Troopers, phone 246-3346; Clinic, phone 464-3322; Volunteer Fire Department.

Elevation: 130 feet. **Climate:** Transition zone, primarily maritime, also influenced by colder Interior weather. Cloudy skies, mild temperatures, fairly heavy precipitation and strong winds. Average summer temperatures from 30° to 66°F; average winter temperatures from 4° to 30°F. Annual precipitation from 20 to 35 inches, most of which occurs during summer. Fog and low clouds also in summer.

Private Aircraft: Airstrip adjacent south, elev. 130 feet; length 2,700 feet; gravel and dirt; no fuel; unattended. Runway condition not monitored, visual inspection recommended prior to using. Runway has 240-foot overrun at each end. No airport facilities or public transportation.

Visitor Facilities: Accommodations available during summer at a local lodge. Arrangements also can be made to stay at private homes. No restaurant, banking services or laundromat. Groceries, clothing, first-aid supplies, sporting goods can be purchased in the community. Fishing/hunting licenses available. Arts and crafts available for sale include beaver hats, mukluks and ulus. Guide services available. No repair service. Rental transportation includes boats, charter aircraft and off-road vehicles. Fuel available includes diesel, regular and unleaded gasoline. No moorage facilities.

Ekwok is the oldest continuously occupied village on Nushagak River. Approximately 100 years ago the settlement was first used in spring and summer as a fish camp, and then in the fall as a base for berry picking. The village was reputed to be the largest settlement along the river by 1923. In 1930 the Bureau of Indian Affairs established a school there. Mail service began in 1930. Ekwok is a second-class city, incorporated in 1974.

The main source of income for the village is commercial fishing, but most residents fish for subsistence purposes. A few residents trap beaver, mink, wolverine, otter, red fox and marten. Ekwok's entire population depends heavily on subsistence. Species commonly harvested include salmon, pike, Dolly Varden, char, duck, moose and caribou. Villagers pick blackberries, blueberries, salmonberries and highbush cranberries. Some of the women grow vegetable gardens. Ekwok residents exchange subsistence items with coastal communities.

A sportfishing lodge 2 miles downriver from Ekwok is owned by the village corporation and operates in summer only. It features modern accommodations and fishing for salmon, grayling, char, rainbow trout and pike. Near the lodge are the remains of several old sod houses used by previous

Native residents of the area.

Communications in Ekwok include a village phone, 464-8001; mail plane, radio and TV. The community is served by 2 churches and a school with grades kindergarten through 12. Many residents celebrate Russian Orthodox holidays. Community electricity, water and sewer are available. Ekwok prohibits the sale and importation of alcoholic beverages. Freight arrives by plane, barge and fishing boats. Government address: City of Ekwok, P.O. Box 49, Ekwok, AK 99580; phone 464-3311. Village corporation address: Ekwok Natives Ltd., P.O. Box 10064, Dillingham, AK 99576.

Igiugig

(See Western Cook Inlet subregion in SOUTHCENTRAL/GULF COAST section.)

Iliamna

(See Western Cook Inlet subregion in SOUTHCENTRAL/GULF COAST section.)

King Salmon

(See Western Cook Inlet subregion in SOUTHCENTRAL/GULF COAST section.)

Kokhanok

(See Western Cook Inlet subregion in SOUTHCENTRAL/GULF COAST section.)

Koliganek

(ko-LIG-a-neck) Located on the Nushagak River, 65 miles northeast of Dillingham, 280 miles west of Anchorage. **Transportation:** Scheduled air service from Dillingham. **Population:** 112. **Zip code:** 99576. **Emergency Services:** Alaska State Troopers, Dillingham, phone 842-5351; Volunteer Fire Department.

Private Aircraft: Airstrip adjacent south; elev. 240 feet; length 2,100 feet; gravel; fuel information unavailable; unattended. Runway condition not monitored, visual inspection recommended prior to landing. Runways unusable during breakup and after heavy rainfall.

Visitor Facilities: Information about most facilities and services unavailable; however, fishing/hunting licenses may be obtained in the community.

This Eskimo village is unincorporated. Many residents may be gone to fish camps during the summer.

The community has a school with grades kindergarten through 12. Electricity is obtained from private generators or from the school. There is a community water supply and a sewer system. Freight arrives by

mail plane and barge. Village corporation address: Koliganek Natives Ltd., General Delivery, Koliganek, AK 99576.

Levelock

(LEEV-lok) Located on the west bank of the Kvichak (KWE-jak) River, 40 miles north of Naknek, 60 miles east of Dillingham, 280 miles southwest of Anchorage. **Transportation:** Scheduled and charter air service from King Salmon. **Population:** 127. **Zip code:** 99625. **Emergency Services:** Alaska State Troopers, King Salmon; Clinic, phone 287-3011; Volunteer Fire Department.

Elevation: 60 feet. **Climate:** Transitional zone with primarily a maritime influence. However, because the village is located about 10 miles inland, the colder continental climate significantly affects local weather. Average summer temperatures from 30° to 66°F; average winter temperatures from 4° to 30°F. Annual precipitation from 20 to 35 inches. Most precipitation occurs during the summer months.

Private Aircraft: Airstrip adjacent west; elev. 60 feet; length 1,900 feet; gravel; no fuel; unattended. Runway condition not monitored, visual inspection recommended prior to using. Runway surfaces soft and muddy during spring breakup or heavy rains. Sharp dropoff at west end of runway.

Visitor Facilities: Accommodations, meals and laundry facilities are available. No banking services. Groceries available at 2 stores. Arts and crafts available for purchase include carved ivory and pen-and-ink drawings. Fishing/hunting licenses available, as well as guide service. Boat and auto repair services available. Arrangements can be made to rent autos, off-road vehicles and boats. Fuel available includes marine gas, diesel, propane and regular gasoline. Moorage facilities available.

Early Russian explorers reported the existence of Levelock, which they called Kvichak. In 1908, a survey of Russian missions in the region referred to the village as Lovelock's Mission.

Levelock was likely devastated by a smallpox epidemic in the region in 1837 and again by a combination of measles and influenza in 1900 and flu in 1918-19.

Canneries operated at Levelock in 1925-26 and again in 1928-29. In 1929-30 the first school was built. A third cannery operated here briefly in the 1950s.

Nearly all residents participate in the commercial salmon fishery, with about 75 percent of the residents going to Naknek during the fishing season. The entire community relies on subsistence hunting and fishing. Species commonly harvested include red, silver, chum, dog and king salmon, lake trout, rainbow trout and Dolly Varden; moose and caribou; and lowbush cranberries, blueberries, salmonberries and blackberries.

According to one resident the best reason to go to Levelock, besides its location in the designated sport trophy fishing area, is that Alaskan artist Ted Lambert used to live here and residents still have many of Lambert's paintings and block prints.

Communications in Levelock, which is unincorporated, include phones, mail plane, radio and TV. The community is served by Russian Orthodox and Baptist churches and a school with grades kindergarten through 12. There are public water, electricity and sewer systems. Freight arrives by cargo plane, arge and ship. Government address: Levelock Village Council, General Delivery, Levelock, AK 99625; phone 287-3030. Village corporation address: Levelock Natives Ltd., General Delivery, Levelock, AK 99625; phone 287-3040.

Manokotak

(Man-a-KOT-ak) Located on the Igushik River, 25 miles southwest of Dillingham, 370 miles west of Anchorage. **Transportation:** Air charter service from Dillingham. **Population:** 370. **Zip code:** 99628. **Emergency Services:** Village Public Safety Officer; Alaska State Troopers, Dillingham; Clinic; Volunteer Fire Department.

Climate: Transitional zone with strong maritime influence; however it also is affected by the colder continental climate. Cloudy skies, mild temperatures and moderately heavy precipitation. Average summer temperatures from 40° to 70°F; average winter temperatures from 4° to 30°F. Annual precipitation from 20 to 26 inches, with most occurring from late June through August. Rain generally is accompanied by southwest winds.

Private Aircraft: Airstrip 1 mile north; elev. 107 feet; length 2,600 feet; gravel; no fuel; unattended. Runway condition not monitored, visual inspection recommended prior to using. Runway surface soft and muddy during spring breakup or heavy rains.

Visitor Facilities: No hotel, restaurant or banking services. Laundry facilities available. Groceries, limited clothing, first-aid supplies, hardware, camera film and sporting goods available in the community. Arts and crafts available for purchase include carved ivory, grass baskets, masks, fur hats and coats.

Fishing/hunting licenses available. No guide service. No repair service or rental transportation. Fuel available includes marine gas, diesel and regular gasoline. Moorage facilities available.

Manokotak is one of the newer communities in the Bristol Bay region, having become a permanent settlement in 1946-47 when several older villages consolidated. Beginning in 1949, school was conducted in a church which now serves as a workshop for students. A school was established in the community in 1958-59.

Almost everyone in Manokotak participates in the commercial salmon fishery. About 95 percent of the residents leave the village during the fishing season and most of them fish near the mouth of the Igushik River. About 40 percent of the residents also trap fox, beaver, mink, otter, lynx, wolverine and muskrat. Furs are sold at the Beaver Roundup held annually in Dillingham or to furriers in Anchorage.

The entire community depends heavily on subsistence hunting and fishing. Besides salmon, species taken include sea lion, beluga whale, caribou, herring, smelt, clams, grayling, trout, pike, sheefish, grouse and ptarmigan. Bird eggs, wild celery and various berries also are harvested. Trade with Togiak and Twin Hills brings Manokotak residents seal oil and whitefish.

Birds are abundant in the Manokotak area. The bald eagle is a summer resident and can be found nesting in the tops of trees or preying on seabirds, ground squirrels and fish. The Igushik River and its wetlands provide excellent habitat for migrating waterfowl and shorebirds in spring and fall. Peak migrations usually occur during the first week of May.

Communications in Manokotak, a second-class city incorporated in 1970, include a village phone, 842-5978, mail plane, radio and TV. The community is served by a Moravian church and a school with grades kindergarten through 12. There are community electricity, water and sewer systems. Freight arrives by cargo plane and barge. Possession of alcoholic beverages is prohibited. Government address: City of Manokotak, P.O. Box 170, Manokotak, AK 99628; phone 289-1027. Village corporation address: Manokotak Natives Ltd., General Delivery, Manokotak, AK 99628.

Naknek

Located on the Alaska Peninsula on the Naknek River near its mouth, 15 miles west of King Salmon, 300 miles southwest of Anchorage. **Transportation:** Boat; scheduled airline and air taxi. **Population:** 405 (borough 1,297). **Zip code:** 99633. **Emergency Services:** Police, phone 246-4222; Alaska State Troopers, King Salmon, phone 246-3346; Camai Clinic, phone 246-6155; Volunteer Fire Department. **Elevation:** 50 feet. **Climate:** Cool, humid and windy weather predominate. Average summer temperatures at nearest weather station in King Salmon range from 42° to 63°F. Average winter temperatures range from 29° to 44°F. Total precipitation in King Salmon averages 20 inches annually, with an average snowfall of 48 inches. Kvichak Bay and the Naknek River freeze solid from late October to April. **Private Aircraft:** Airstrip 1 mile north; elev. 70 feet; length 2,300 feet; gravel; fuel 80, 100; attended. Runway condition not monitored, visual inspection recommended prior to using. Aircraft parking along entire length. Seaplane base adjacent north; elev. 30 feet; fuel 80, 100. **Visitor Facilities:** Accommodations at 2 hotels. There are 3 restaurants. Laundry facilities and banking services available. Groceries, clothing, first-aid supplies, hardware, camera film and sporting goods may be purchased in the community. Arts and crafts available for purchase include carved ivory, baskets and masks. Fishing/hunting licenses available, as well as guide service. Major repair service for marine engines, boats, autos and aircraft. Rental transportation includes autos, boats and aircraft. Fuel available includes marine gas, diesel and regular gasoline. Moorage facilities available.

Naknek is the seat of the 500-square-mile Bristol Bay Borough, a second-class borough incorporated in 1962. The region was settled more than 6,000 years ago by Yup'ik Eskimo and Athabascan Indians. The Russians built a fort near the village and fur trappers inhabited the area for some time prior to the U.S. purchase of Alaska.

By 1883, the first salmon cannery opened in Bristol Bay; in 1890, the first cannery opened on the Naknek River. By 1900, there were approximately 12 canneries in Bristol Bay.

The community was developed as a major center for commercial fishing and processing, which today form the base of the area's economy. There are 9 salmon processors on the Naknek side of the river and Naknek bustles during the summer as a couple of thousand people arrive in June to fish and work in the canneries. Borough government also is a significant source of employment. Many residents also depend on subsistence hunting and fishing.

Hunting, fishing, camping and photography provide most of the outdoor recreation for borough residents. The Naknek River is famous for its excellent sportfishing; caribou and bear hunting are popular. There are scores of excellent fishing streams throughout the region.

The Russian Orthodox St. John the Baptist Chapel in Naknek, reportedly constructed in 1886, is on the National Register of Historic Places. Naknek also has the Bristol Bay Historical Museum, P.O. Box 43, Naknek, AK 99633; phone 246-4432. The collections of this "living history museum" feature archaeology, history and ethnology, and document Naknek's history as one of the largest commercial salmon fishing and canning headquarters in the world. Displays show the progression from the early subsistence-oriented lifestyle of the first Bristol Bay residents to the coming of the Russian fur traders on up to the oral histories and family trees of present residents. The museum building is the original Fisherman's Hall, an early meeting place for fishermen. Facilities include a gift shop, a library and parking. Hours June to August are 1-3 p.m., Tuesday, Thursday and Saturday. Open in winter by appointment. No admission fee; donations accepted.

Communications in Naknek include phones, mail plane, radio and TV. The community is served by 4 churches and a school with grades preschool through 12. There is a community electricity and sewage system; water is from individual wells. Freight arrives in the community by cargo plane and barge. Government address: Bristol Bay Borough, Box 189, Naknek, AK 99633. Village corporation address: Paug-Vik Incorporated, Ltd., Box 61, Naknek, AK 99633; phone 246-4424.

Newhalen
(See Western Cook Inlet subregion in SOUTHCENTRAL/GULF COAST section.)

New Stuyahok
(New STU-ya-hock) Located on the Nushagak River, 51 miles northeast of Dillingham, 290 miles southwest of Anchorage. **Transportation:** Boat; snow machine; scheduled or charter air service from Dillingham. **Population:** 380. **Zip code:** 99636. **Emergency Services:** Village Public Safety Officer, phone 693-3170; Alaska State Troopers, Dillingham, phone 842-5641; Clinic, phone 693-3131; Kanakanak Hospital, Dillingham, phone 842-5101 or 5202; Health aide, phone 693-3102 or 3133. **Elevation:** 125 feet. **Climate:** Transitional

zone; primary influence maritime. Because the village is inland the continental climate significantly affects local weather. Cloudy skies, mild temperatures and moderately heavy precipitation. There often are strong winds. Average summer temperatures from 37° to 66°F; average winter temperatures from 4° to 30°F. Annual precipitation 20 to 35 inches, with most of it occurring in August and September.

Private Aircraft: Airstrip 1 mile west; elev. 325 feet; length 1,800 feet; gravel; no fuel; unattended. Runway condition not monitored, visual inspection recommended prior to landing. Access road to parking apron not maintained; takeoffs and landings on road prohibited. No facilities at airport or public transportation into town.

Visitor Facilities: There is a roadhouse. Arrangements for accommodations in private homes also may be made. There is no restaurant, laundromat or banking facility. Groceries, clothing, first-aid supplies, hardware, camera film and sporting goods available in the community. Arts and crafts available for purchase include hand-sewn fur items. Fishing/hunting licenses not available. No guide or repair services, rental transportation, or moorage facilities. Fuel available: diesel, regular gasoline.

This Eskimo village was relocated several times because of flooding and has been at its present site since 1942. Stuyahok is an Eskimo word meaning "going downriver place." New Stuyahok got its first school, a log building, in 1961, and incorporated as a second-class city in 1972.

The community's economic base is the commercial salmon fishery, although about 30 people trap commercially and several are employed full time by the government or school district.

Beaver, lynx, fox and mink are the primary species trapped for fur; and muskrat, otter, wolverine, bobcat, marten and weasel also are taken. Furs are sold to buyers who pass through the village, at the Beaver Roundup in Dillingham, or at the annual New Stuyahok Beaver Festival.

The entire community depends heavily on subsistence activities for food. Many residents go to fish camps during the summer season. Moose, caribou and rabbit are the primary game animals. Beavers also are eaten. Fishing is for salmon, pike, grayling, smelt, whitefish, sucker, rainbow trout, lingcod and Dolly Varden. In the fall, blackberries, red berries, cranberries and some blueberries are gathered.

Communications include phones and radio. The community is served by a Russian Orthodox church and a school with grades kindergarten through 12. There are community electricity, water and sewer systems. Freight generally arrives by plane. Government address: City of New Stuyahok, P.O. Box 10, New Stuyahok, AK 99636; phone 693-3111. Village corporation address: Stuyahok Ltd., P.O. Box 50, Stuyahok, AK 99636; phone 693-3122.

Nondalton
(See Western Cook Inlet subregion in SOUTHCENTRAL/GULF COAST section.)

Nushagak
(NOOSH-a-gack) Located on the east shore of Nushagak Bay, 5 air miles from Dillingham, 330 miles southwest of Anchorage. **Transportation:** Boat; charter plane from Dillingham. **Population:** Up to 100 during summer fishing season. **Zip code:** 99695. **Emergency Services:** Alaska State Troopers, Dillingham; Kanakanak Hospital, Dillingham.

Private Aircraft: No airstrip. Small planes land on the beach at low tide.

Visitor Facilities: None. Camp or sleep in one of several vacant huts (look for one with an intact roof). Supplies are airlifted from Dillingham.

Nushagak is a former Eskimo village established as a trading post about 1819. The Russians called it Aleksandrovsk. It was called Fort or Redoubt Alexander until 1899. The area is now used seasonally as a base for set-net fishermen.

The Russian Orthodox Transfiguration of Our Lord Chapel at Nushagak is on the National Register of Historic Places.

Pedro Bay
(See Western Cook Inlet subregion in SOUTHCENTRAL/GULF COAST section.)

Pope & Vannoy Landing
(See Western Cook Inlet subregion in SOUTHCENTRAL/GULF COAST section.)

Portage Creek
Located 30 miles southeast of Dillingham, 320 miles southwest of Anchorage. **Transportation:** Boat; charter air service from Dillingham. **Population:** 46. **Zip code:** 99695. **Emergency Services:** Alaska State Troopers, Dillingham; Kanakanak Hospital, Dillingham.

Climate: Transition zone, characterized by cloudy skies, mild temperatures and moderately heavy precipitation. Average summer temperatures from 30° to 66°F; average winter temperatures from 4° to 30°F. Annual precipitation from 20 to 35 inches. Most precipitation occurs during the summer months.

Private Aircraft: Airstrip east of village; elev. 137 feet; length 1,900 feet; gravel; no fuel; unattended. Runway condition not monitored, visual inspection recommended prior to landing. Runway surface soft and muddy during spring breakup or heavy rains; runway edges subject to erosion. Watch out for crosswind when landing.

Visitor Facilities: None.

This site was long used as an overnight camp. As the name implies, Portage Creek is part of a summer route from the head of Nushagak Bay to the mouth of the Kvichak River which avoided the open waters of Bristol Bay and a long trip around Etolin Point.

The first residence was built in 1961. At that time a few families had left Koliganek and other villages up the Nushagak River for settlement in Portage Creek. A school was established in 1963.

Portage Creek is an example of a phenomenon once common along the Nushagak River. Before the advent of expensive public institutions and development, villages were extremely mobile and the relocation of a few families could signal the beginning or ending of a village. Passage of the Alaska Native Claims Settlement Act and construction of schools have ended this practice except for summer fish camps.

The primary employment for Portage Creek residents is the fishing industry, but the entire population depends to some extent on subsistence hunting and fishing. Species commonly harvested include salmon, pike, whitefish, rainbow trout, moose, caribou, duck, geese, crane. There is also berry picking in season. Varieties available include salmonberries, blackberries, cranberries and blueberries.

There is superb king salmon fishing from the riverbank in front of the village in June and early July. Arrangements for guided fishing in the area are best made in Dillingham.

Much land in the Portage Creek area is owned by the local Native corporation, Choggiung Ltd., which requires that a permit be obtained for any public use of its lands.

Communications in Portage Creek, which is unincorporated, include a phone in the council house (842-5966), mail plane, radio and TV. The community is served by a Russian Orthodox church and Ohgsenakale School with grades kindergarten through 12. Electri-

city is from individual generators in summer and the school in winter. Water is hauled from wells. Sewage system is outhouses. Freight arrives by barge or charter plane. Government address: Portage Creek Village Council, General Delivery, Portage Creek, AK 99695. Village corporation address: Choggiung Ltd., P.O. Box 196, Dillingham, AK 99576.

Port Alsworth

(See Western Cook Inlet subregion in SOUTHCENTRAL/GULF COAST section.)

South Naknek

Located on the Alaska Peninsula on the Naknek River, 2 miles south of Naknek, 15 miles west of King Salmon and 300 miles southwest of Anchorage. **Transportation:** Scheduled airline and air taxi. **Population:** 185. **Zip code:** 99670. **Emergency Services:** Police, phone 246-4222; Alaska State Troopers, King Salmon, phone 246-3346; Clinic, phone 246-6546; Volunteer Fire Department.

Climate: Cool, humid and windy weather. Average summer temperatures at the nearest weather station in King Salmon range from 42° to 63°F; average winter temperatures from 4° to 29°F. Average annual precipitation 20 inches; average snowfall 45 inches.

Private Aircraft: Airstrip 1 mile southwest; elev. 130 feet; length 2,200 feet; gravel; unattended. Runway condition not monitored, visual inspection recommended prior to using.

Visitor Facilities: No hotel. There is a combined store, snackbar and bar. Fishing/hunting licenses available. Guide service available. Availability of repair service, rental transportation, fuel and moorage facilities unknown.

South Naknek, located just across the river from Naknek, is part of the Bristol Bay Borough. Hunting camps along the Naknek River date back to 3,000 to 4,000 B.C. South Naknek was settled after the turn of the century as a result of salmon cannery development.

Commercial fishing and salmon processing are the mainstays of South Naknek's economy. Three of the 5 canneries that line the south bank of the Naknek River are in operation and recruit 400 to 500 people from outside the village for the brief summer salmon season. Most other employment is in community service. About 75 percent of South Naknek's residents depend on subsistence hunting and fishing as a vital source of food.

NOTE: Hiking, berry-picking, camping and fishing are permitted on lands owned by the

Alaska Peninsula Corp. upon payment of a $20 per person/per day fee. Hunting and woodcutting on corporation lands is not permitted. Contact the corporation for more information. (See address below.)

South Naknek's Russian Orthodox Elevation of the Holy Cross Church, built in the early 1900s, is listed on the National Register of Historic Places.

Communications in South Naknek include phones, radio, mail plane and TV. The community is served by 2 churches and a school with grades preschool to 6; older students are flown to Naknek daily to attend school. There is a community electricity system; water is from individual wells or hauled from a central watering point. Sewage system is septic tanks. Freight arrives by air and barge. Government address: Bristol Bay Borough, P.O. Box 189, Naknek, AK 99663; phone 246-4224. Village corporation address: Alaska Peninsula Corp., Box 104360, Anchorage, AK 99510.

Togiak

Located at the head of Togiak Bay, 70 miles west of Dillingham, 395 miles southwest of Anchorage. **Transportation:** Scheduled and charter air service from Dillingham. **Population:** 623. **Zip code:** 99678. **Emergency Services:** Police, phone 493-5212; Alaska State Troopers, Dillingham, phone 842-5351; Clinic, phone 493-5511; Volunteer Fire Department.

Elevation: 12 feet. **Climate:** Maritime; however, the arctic climate of interior Alaska also affects the Bristol Bay coastal region. Cloudy skies, mild temperatures, moderately heavy precipitation and strong winds. Average summer temperatures from 37° to 66°F; average winter temperatures from 4° to 30°F. Annual precipitation from 20 to 26 inches, with most of the precipitation occurring in the summer, when low clouds and rain can reduce visibility. In winter, there is lots of fog.

Private Aircraft: Airstrip adjacent southwest; elev. 21 feet; length 4,400 feet; gravel; no fuel; unattended; aircraft instructed to land. Runway condition not monitored, visual inspection recommended prior to using. No airport facilities. Public transportation into village.

Visitor Facilities: Some accommodations available, along with a store, camping facilities and cannery tours. The cannery is across the bay from Togiak, phone 493-5331 or 5531. Restaurant and laundry facilities available. No banking services. Groceries available. Arts and crafts available for pur-

chase include grass baskets, some carved ivory, and fur hats and mittens. Fishing/hunting licenses available. *NOTE: Permission must be obtained from Togiak Natives Limited to hunt or fish on Native lands.* Sportfishing guide service on Togiak River and charter boat trips to Walrus Islands State Game Sanctuary. No repair services. Moorage facilities available. Regular gasoline sometimes available.

Many residents of the Yukon-Kuskokwim region migrated south to the Togiak area after a devastating influenza epidemic in 1918-19. "Old" Togiak, or Togiagamute, located across the bay from "New" Togiak where a cannery now is located, had a population of 276 in 1880 and only 94 in 1890. Heavy winter snowfalls made wood gathering difficult at "Old" Togiak, so gradually people settled at a new site on the opposite shore, where snow tended only to make deep drifts on the beach and a trail made wood gathering easier. In addition, a slough behind the new site provided good shelter for boats. Togiak was incorporated as a second-class city in 1969.

Togiak's economy is based primarily on commercial salmon fishing. Approximately 400 residents fish commercially. Two fish processing facilities are located near Togiak. The entire community also depends heavily on subsistence hunting and fishing. Species harvested include seal, sea lion, walrus, 5 species of salmon, herring, herring roe-on-kelp, smelt, clams, geese, ducks, ptarmigan and trout. Residents also gather gull and murre eggs.

The major attraction near Togiak is Round Island, one of the Walrus Islands group. This is a popular place to view and photograph the 12,000 to 15,000 male walruses that summer on the island. Transportation to Round Island is by boat from Togiak or by charter plane from Dillingham or King Salmon. A trip to Round Island is a true wilderness experience; visitors must bring all their own food, shelter and equipment. Access to the game sanctuary is only by permit from the Alaska Dept. of Fish and Game offices in Anchorage, Dillingham or King Salmon. For information about permits and other information about the sanctuary, write the Alaska Dept. of Fish and Game, Division of Game, P.O. Box 199, Dillingham, AK 99576.

Some of the other islands in the Walrus Islands group also have large populations of seabirds such as puffins, murres, cormorants, kittiwakes, terns and gulls.

Fishing in the Togiak River is excellent during July, August and September for 5 species of salmon, rainbow trout and Dolly Varden.

Togiak is located within Togiak National Wildlife Refuge, a breeding and resting area for waterfowl and shorebirds. Peak migrations usually occur the first week in May.

Communications in Togiak include phones, mail plane, radio and TV. The community is served by a Moravian church and a school with grades kindergarten through 12. There are community electricity, water and sewage systems. Togiak prohibits the possession of alcoholic beverages. Freight arrives by cargo plane and barge. Government address: City of Togiak, P.O. Box 99, Togiak, AK 99678; phone 493-5820 or 5920. Village corporation address: Togiak Natives Ltd., P.O. Box 169, Togiak, AK 99678; phone 493-5520.

Twin Hills

Located near the mouth of a branch of the Togiak River known as Twin Hills River, 2 miles north of Togiak, 395 miles southwest of Anchorage. **Transportation:** Boat from Togiak; scheduled and charter air service from Dillingham. **Population:** 67. **Zip code:** 99576. **Emergency Services:** Village Public Safety Officer, phone 525-4114; Alaska State Troopers, Dillingham, phone 842-5641; Clinic, phone 525-4115; Volunteer Fire Department.

Elevation: 20 to 30 feet. **Climate:** Transitional zone; primary influence is maritime; however, the arctic climate of interior Alaska also affects the Bristol Bay coast. Cloudy skies, mild temperatures, moderately heavy precipitation and strong winds. Average summer temperatures 37° to 66°F. Average winter temperatures 4° to 30°F. Annual precipitation 20 to 26 inches, with most of the precipitation occurring in summer. Fog occurs often in winter.

Private Aircraft: Airstrip adjacent east; elev. 82 feet; length 2,000 feet; gravel; no fuel; unattended. Runway condition not monitored, visual inspection recommended prior to using. Bluff at north end may cause some turbulence when landing to the south. Loose rock on runway and apron up to 3 inches in diameter. Passenger terminal at airport; no public transportation into village.

Visitor Facilities: Arrangements may be made to stay in private homes. No restaurant, banking services or laundromat. Groceries available at 1 store. Arts and crafts available for purchase include carved ivory, grass baskets and fur dolls. Fishing/hunting licenses not available. No guide or repair services. No rental transportation or moorage facilities. Fuel

available: diesel, propane, unleaded and regular gasoline.

Located within Togiak National Wildlife Refuge, Twin Hills is a fairly new village located at the base of 2 hills which rise to 291 feet and 427 feet, prominent features in the generally flat coastal region. The village was established in 1965 following severe flooding in the upper Togiak Bay area. Some of the current residents migrated from Quinhagak, a small community on Kuskokwim Bay. The people of Twin Hills have strong cultural ties to the Yukon-Kuskokwim region not only because they have relatives there today, but also because many of their ancestors migrated south to the Togiak area following the devastating worldwide influenza epidemic of 1918-19.

Virtually all residents of Twin Hills participate in the commercial salmon fishery. A handful of jobs are available with the school, post office, clinic and the state. The entire community depends heavily on subsistence hunting and fishing, and people range great distances to obtain subsistence items. Species harvested include seals, sea lion, whale and walrus, 5 species of salmon, herring, herring roe-on-kelp, smelt, clams, geese, ducks, seagull and murre eggs, ptarmigan, trout and whitefish. In addition, Twin Hills residents trade food items with people from Manokotak.

There is a road leading from Twin Hills to the beach of Togiak Bay. From there it is possible to drive an auto or 3-wheeler to the Togiak Fisheries cannery on the bay across from Togiak.

NOTE: Twin Hills Native Corp. lands are closed to sportfishing, hunting and hiking by nonmembers. Before traveling in the Twin Hills area, check with the corporation about the location of restricted lands.

Communications in Twin Hills includes phones, mail plane, radio and TV. There is a Moravian church and a school with grades preschool through 8; older students attend boarding school in other communities. There are community electricity, water and sewer systems. Freight arrives by cargo plane and barge. Government address: Twin Hills Traditional Council, General Delivery, Twin Hills, AK 99576. Village corporation address: Twin Hills Native Corp., General Delivery, Twin Hills, AK 99576.

AREA CODE

All of Alaska uses the Area Code 907.

▼ **A T T R A C T I O N S** ▼

National and State Parks, Etc.

Wood-Tikchik State Park

This 1.5-million-acre state park — largest in the system and in the country — is located about 30 miles north of Dillingham and 329 miles southwest of Anchorage. Wood-Tikchik is an undeveloped wilderness park containing 2 separate systems of large, interconnected pristine lakes that are spawning and rearing habitat for the Bristol Bay salmon fishery: 6 in the Tikchik River drainage and 6 in the Wood River drainage.

Rugged mountains 3,000 to 5,000 feet tall form a backdrop for some of the lakes on the western side of the park. Pinnacle peaks, high alpine valleys, hanging valleys and dramatic V-shaped incisions contribute to this area's fjordlike appearance. The eastern edge of the lakes overlooks numerous shoals and islands, gravel beaches and the broad tundra landscape of the Nushagak flats.

Climate: The area is characterized by cloudy skies, mild temperatures and fairly heavy precipitation. There are often strong winds. In the park, snow and ice cover, especially on the upper lakes, is common until mid-June. By early October, the lakes start to freeze and snow to fall.

Wildlife: The area supports brown and black bears, moose, wolf, wolverine, fox, lynx, marten and beaver. Fishing is excellent throughout the summer for arctic char, rainbow trout, northern pike, red salmon, Dolly Varden and grayling. Sportfishing and hunting are allowed in the park in season under Alaska Dept. of Fish and Game regulations. Catch-and-release fly-fishing for rainbow trout is encouraged.

Activities: The park offers excellent opportunities for boating, hiking, sightseeing and photography. There are no restrictions on camping in the park and motors on boats are allowed. The Alaska Division of Parks and Outdoor Recreation cautions that winds can quickly create rough water conditions on the lakes and white-water conditions may exist on streams, although most streams are navigable by canoe, kayak or inflatable raft. Since this is a remote wilderness, visitors are advised to leave a copy of their itinerary with a friend or the air charter operator.

Access: Wood-Tikchik is accessible by scheduled air service to Dillingham, where charter air service to the park is available at about $200 an hour, depending on size of plane, party size and number of trips. There is road access to Aleknagik village on Lake Aleknagik, which is adjacent to the southern end of the park. Much of the land around lakes Aleknagik and Nerka is private property and should be respected. Pickup can be arranged from any of the lakes. For those floating the Nuyakuk River, which heads in Tikchik Lake and joins the Nushagak River, there also is scheduled air service from the villages of Koliganek, New Stuyahok, Ekwok and Portage Creek along the Nushagak.

Accommodations: There are hotel accommodations in Dillingham, as well as supplies and services. There are several commercial lodges in or near the park which cater only to fishing/sightseeing clients on an advance reservation basis only — they are not equipped to accommodate drop-in visitors. In the park there are no developed facilities, trails, shelters, cabins, campsites, waste receptacles, sanitary facilities or emergency services. Visitors should arrive self-sufficient and the Division of Parks and Outdoor Recreation urges the pack-it-in, pack-it-out method of wilderness camping. Visitors should be prepared for cool nights, wind chill, rain — and mosquitoes.

Additional information may be obtained from: Wood-Tikchik State Park, General Delivery, Dillingham, AK 99576; phone 842-

2375. Or from Alaska Dept. of Natural Resources, Division of Parks and Outdoor Recreation, Chugach/Southwest Area, P.O. Box 107001, Anchorage, AK 99510.

Wildlife Refuges

Togiak National Wildlife Refuge

This 4.3-million-acre refuge is located about 3 miles west of Dillingham at its closest point. More than half of the refuge is an established wilderness area. The refuge, 80 percent of which is in the Ahklun Mountains, offers outstanding scenery with a wide variety of terrain, including glacial valleys, tundra uplands, wetlands, sand and gravel beaches, rugged mountains and coastal cliffs. The myriad lakes range in size from tundra potholes to 13-mile-long Togiak Lake. Togiak Valley is the site of a rare geological feature: a 2-mile-long tuya, a flat-topped, steep-sided volcano formed when lava erupted under a glacier.

Climate: Summer months are usually moist and rainy, with temperatures ranging between 45° and 75°F. Snow covers the mountains by early October. Ice forms on lakes and rivers in November and will remain until June. Winter temperatures range from -30° to 45°F. The weather is unpredictable and it is not uncommon for a warm and sunny day to turn cold, windy and wet.

Wildlife: Togiak is a haven for migrating birds. As many as 200,000 waterfowl have been counted in the bays, lagoons and lakes along the coast of the refuge, where waterfowl await spring breakup in the Arctic. About 50 percent of the world's population of brant use the refuge — up to 50,000 birds can be seen at one time in Nanvak and Chagvan bays.

Thousands of emperor geese and common and Steller's eiders migrate through the refuge, along with significant numbers of king eiders, harlequin ducks and black scoters. Bald eagles nest inland and on coastal cliffs. The refuge is home to one of the largest populations of cliff-nesting seabirds in the eastern Bering Sea. Cape Newenham, Cape Peirce, Bird Rock and Shaiak Island support an estimated population of 1 million common murres and black-legged kittiwakes.

Brown bear are the most numerous large mammal. Caribou occasionally migrate through the northeastern corner of the refuge. Smaller mammals include the hoary marmot, beaver, wolverine, otter, mink, red fox and an occasional wolf. Walrus, Steller sea lions and harbor seals haul out on the shoreline. Gray whales feed close to shore; beluga and killer whales are sometimes seen along the coast.

The refuge attracts sportfishermen from around the world with major concentrations of 5 species of salmon, grayling, rainbow trout and Dolly Varden (arctic char) in the Togiak, Kanektok and Goodnews drainages. Other fish available are lake trout, burbot and northern pike.

Activities: Sportfishing and hunting are the major recreational activities on the refuge. Other activities are river floating, hiking, sightseeing, camping and wildlife observation/photography. The refuge office suggests that drinking water be boiled or chemically purified to avoid giardiasis, an intestinal disease.

Archaeological evidence indicates that humans have occupied the area for at least 2,000 and perhaps 5,000 years. Today, the residents of 6 nearby Eskimo villages use the refuge for subsistence activities. Their camps, fish nets and other equipment are critical to their livelihood and should be left undisturbed. Also, much of the land around the villages of Quinhagak, Platinum, Goodnews Bay, Togiak, Twin Hills and Manokotak is private property and should be respected. To avoid trespassing, consult the refuge office in Dillingham about the location of private lands.

The refuge office encourages anyone planning a trip to the refuge to discuss planned itineraries with the refuge staff as a safety precaution and also to allow the Fish and Wildlife Service to assess public use of the refuge. The refuge currently is in the planning stage and may in the future require visitors to obtain permits.

Access: The refuge can be reached by scheduled airline to Dillingham or Bethel, then a scheduled flight to one of the adjacent villages or a charter flight to the refuge.

Accommodations: Hotel, food and medical services can be found in Dillingham and Bethel. There are limited facilities in Goodnews Bay, Togiak and Quinhagak. There are no campgrounds or established trail systems on the refuge. Camping on gravel bars below the high water mark is encouraged to reduce environmental impact and trespass on Native lands. Several guides and outfitters operate within the refuge. For a list, and other information, contact: Refuge Manager, Togiak National Wildlife Refuge, P.O. Box 270, Dillingham, AK 99576; phone 842-1063.

Walrus Islands State Game Sanctuary

This sanctuary in Bristol Bay offers an unsurpassed opportunity to view and photograph large numbers of bull walrus from May to September. There are 7 islands in the sanctuary, but Round Island 70 miles southwest of Dillingham is the one most used.

Wildlife: Between 5,000 and 10,000 male walruses return to the island each spring as the ice pack recedes northward. Females with young are seldom seen in Bristol Bay as they remain near the edge of the ice pack.

Hundreds of thousands of seabirds arrive on Round Island in the wake of the walruses. Murres, tufted and horned puffins, kittiwakes, auklets and others nest on the rocky cliffs until August. Steller sea lions haul out on the southern shore of the island from May to September, and gray whales pass by during April and May as they migrate north. Year-round residents of the island are red foxes.

Access: Travel to Round Island is difficult and regulated by permit from the Alaska Dept. of Fish and Game. Access is possible only by boat or airplane and is subject to weather conditions, which can quickly change for the

Ivory-tusked walrus on Round Island's rocky beaches attract photographers from around the world. (John W. Warden)

worse at any time of year. Floatplanes can be chartered in Dillingham or King Salmon, and boats may be available for charter in Togiak. A list of charter operators is available from the Fish and Game office in Dillingham.

Accommodations: Round Island provides a true wilderness experience. There are no facilities or services available to visitors. Fresh water is available in the camping area, but visitors must bring their own food, fuel, shelter and equipment. Tents should have waterproof flies and be able to withstand winds up to 60 knots. A full suit of rain gear and waterproof boots are essential. Fish and Game advises visitors to keep their schedules flexible and bring extra supplies since unpredictable weather can delay travel to or from the island.

Fifteen permits per week are issued on a first-come, first-served basis to visitors wishing to camp at Round Island. Permits are valid for 1 week beginning on a Friday and ending on a Thursday. Requests for permits should include the dates and possible alternative dates you wish to visit the island. Contact the Alaska Dept. of Fish and Game, Division of Wildlife Conservation, P.O. Box 1030, Dillingham, AK 99576; phone 842-1013.

The Rivers

NOTE: Some of the rivers described below are also included in the Sportfishing section where additional information on species, seasons and suggested bait is provided.

Chilikadrotna River. This wild and scenic river heads in Twin Lakes in Lake Clark National Park and Preserve and flows 60 miles to join the Mulchatna River 46 miles northwest of Nondalton on Lake Clark. For more on floating the Chilikadrotna, see Rivers in Western Cook Inlet subregion in the SOUTHCENTRAL/GULF COAST section.

Mulchatna River. This wild and scenic river heads in Turquoise Lake in Lake Clark National Park and Preserve and flows 220 river miles to join the Nushagak River 65 miles northeast of Dillingham. For more on floating the Mulchatna River see Rivers in the Western Cook Inlet subregion in SOUTHCENTRAL/GULF COAST section.

Nushagak River. This river heads at 60°35' N, 156°06' W and flows southwest 275 river miles to the head of Nushagak Bay, 3 miles south of Dillingham. The Nushagak was the first river in this area ascended by the Russians in the early 1800s. Much of the river is edged by scattered forests, but the tundra is never very far away. The headwaters drain the Taylor Mountains, while the major tributaries

— the Nuyakuk and Mulchatna rivers — carry drainage from the western lake country and glaciers to the east. The upper reaches of this river are very isolated. It is flat water all the way, but sweepers and logjams can be major obstacles. Canoes, kayaks and riverboats all are suitable for this river.

This river passes by the villages of Koliganek, New Stuyahok and Ekwok and boaters should be aware that there is much private property along the river corridor. Contact BLM, 4700 E. 72nd Ave., Anchorage, AK 99507 for the location of public easements.

Access is by charter plane from Dillingham to the upper reaches of the river or by scheduled air service to any of the villages. Exit can be from one of the villages or float to Dillingham. Dillingham has all facilities for visitors; there are limited accommodations in Ekwok and New Stuyahok.

Nuyakuk River. This river heads in Tikchik Lake in Wood-Tikchik State Park and flows about 50 miles to join the Nushagak. The upper 12 miles of the river are in the park. This river traverses a relatively flat valley and offers an easy float, with the exception of 2 short sets of rapids and a portage around a falls. The Class II rapids in the first 6 miles of the river can be easily portaged. The falls at the 6-mile point can be portaged by a well-used trail on the right that is clearly visible from the river. This trip generally takes 3 to 4 days from Tikchik Lake to Koliganek, the first village encountered going down the Nushagak. Rafts, canoes and kayaks are suitable for this river.

This trip offers very good fishing in season for all 5 species of salmon, arctic char, grayling, rainbow trout and pike. Moose, bear, beaver and waterfowl may be seen along the way. Campsites are adequate on the upper three-quarters of the river, but scarce on the lower quarter.

Access is by floatplane from Dillingham or King Salmon to Tikchik Lake. Exit is by scheduled air service from Koliganek, which has no visitor facilities, or one of the other villages farther down the Nushagak. Also, floatplanes can land on most of the Nuyakuk and Nushagak rivers. Related USGS topographic maps: Dillingham D-4 through D-6.

Tikchik River. This river heads in Nishlik Lake in the Ahklun Mountains and flows 65 river miles south to Tikchik Lake in Wood-Tikchik State Park. This is a clear, gravelly stream. It is fast, and has sweepers but no rapids. Water conditions range from flat water to Class I, making this an excellent river for fishermen to float. For one of the most highly recommended trips in western Alaska,

boaters can continue from Tikchik Lake down the Nuyakuk River to the Nushagak River and then to Bristol Bay. Canoes, kayaks and rubber rafts are suitable for the Tikchik.

This river has superb fishing for rainbow trout, grayling and arctic char. Along its banks boaters may see ptarmigan, migratory birds, beavers and bears.

Access is to Nishlik Lake by chartered floatplane from Dillingham. Exit is by floatplane from Tikchik Lake for those not continuing down the Nuyakuk River.

Togiak River. This river heads in 13-mile-long Togiak Lake in Togiak National Wildlife Refuge and flows 60 river miles to the village of Togiak on Togiak Bay. This river offers an easy, leisurely float ranging from flat water to Class I through tundra sparsely covered with willow, alder, cottonwood and some spruce. Low mountains flank the upper river. Boaters should use caution in crossing Togiak Bay from the mouth of the river to the village. Strong winds are possible and shallow sandbars may preclude staying close to the shoreline. It is possible to float the 12 miles between Upper Togiak Lake and Togiak Lake, but the river is small, multichanneled, meandering and obstructed in spots by logjams and many sweepers. There are riffles, but no rapids between the lakes.

The trip from Togiak Lake to the river mouth usually takes 4 days. Canoes, rafts and kayaks are suitable.

Refuge waters attract fishermen from all over the world. The Togiak River offers very good fishing for 5 species of salmon, grayling and arctic char. Moose, brown bear and eagles may be seen along the river.

There is private land along the river corridor. Check with the village of Togiak (493-5820) or contact Refuge Manager, Togiak National Wildlife Refuge, P.O. Box 270, Dillingham, AK 99576, regarding the location of private holdings.

Access is by floatplane from Bethel or Dillingham to Togiak or Upper Togiak Lake. Exit is by scheduled airline from the village of Togiak where there are some visitor facilities, or by floatplane from the lower river. Related USGS Topographic maps: Goodnews.

Wood-Tikchik Lakes. The 2 lake systems in Wood-Tikchik State Park north of Dillingham offer a combination of lake and river paddling, good fishing and beautiful mountain scenery. Many trip variations are possible. Favorite trips include floating the Tikchik River (Class I) from Nishlik Lake to Tikchik Lake; floating from Lake Kulik down the Wind River (Class II) and Peace River (flat water and

Class I) to Lake Beverly, then the short Agulukpak River (Class I) to Lake Nerka, and the 5-mile Agulowak River (Class I) to Lake Aleknagik, from which flows the Wood River (flat water) to Dillingham. *(NOTE: Nushagak Bay tides influence the lower half of the Wood River, making boating more difficult and creating tidal flats with few, if any, campsites.)* Other trip variations are exploring the fjords, enjoying the alpine setting of the Nishlik or Upnuk lakes area or floating the Nuyakuk. The Allen River connecting Chikuminuk Lake with Lake Chauekuktuli should be run only by experienced white-water boaters, according to the Alaska Division of Parks and Outdoor Recreation.

Kayaks, canoes or rafts with motors are recommended. No fuel for motors is available in the area. For lake travel, estimate 10 to 12 miles per day, paddling 5 hours per day. On the lakes the wind can quickly create white cap conditions; be sure to have survival gear and life jackets. Seasonally there is good fishing for 5 species of salmon, especially sockeye, and for rainbow and lake trout, grayling, arctic char and pike. Fishing is generally best in the rivers or at the river mouths. This area has beautiful mountain scenery. Hiking is generally hampered by dense brush separating lakes and alpine areas. Good campsites abound, but choose open, breezy spots to avoid mosquitoes and other insects.

Access is by floatplane from Dillingham to any of the lakes. Exit is by floatplane from one of the lakes or by road from Lake Aleknagik to Dillingham.

Sportfishing

Except for a few roads around Dillingham, access to good fishing in the Bering Sea Coast region is primarily by airplane. If you have the time, however, you sometimes can walk or go by boat to a hot fishing spot. Boats occasionally can be rented or chartered at villages along the waterways. There are daily commercial flights to the transportation centers of the region where you can catch a commuter flight to a smaller village or charter a plane to a lake or river. In addition, commercial outfitters will handle logistics for you on guided fishing trips.

Bristol Bay is world famous for its sportfishing, particularly for trophy-sized rainbow trout which regularly attain 10 pounds. These fish are at their best in late summer and early fall. The Kvichak and Alagnak watersheds are within the state's Bristol Bay Wild Trout Area. Special regulations (included in the Sport Fish Regulations), designed to perpetuate the original wild rainbow trout stocks, apply here.

Throughout the Bristol Bay area, the philosophy of catch-and-release is encouraged by everyone associated with the rainbow trout fishery, according to the Alaska Dept. of Fish and Game.

Tackle-breaking king salmon are at their peak from mid-June through July. These fish are not uncommon at 30 pounds and up. Chums and reds show up by July 1, pinks by mid-July (in even-numbered years) and silvers by mid-August. Salmon fishing is concentrated in the river systems.

Arctic char and Dolly Varden are found throughout this area and are most abundant in spring or in midsummer. Grayling can be caught most of the summer, but larger ones are more plentiful from August to October.

Farther west, rivers and their headwater lakes in Togiak National Wildlife Refuge provide excellent sportfishing for salmon, grayling, rainbow trout and arctic char. Lake trout are available in the lakes.

The Alaska Dept. of Fish and Game recommends that anyone traveling to remote areas should plan for the worst. Take a few days extra food, and fuel if necessary, and allow for a flexible schedule since weather can delay travel.

Although many villages have hunting and fishing license vendors, officials recommend that you purchase your license in Anchorage or another large community, since sometimes the local vendors themselves have "gone fishing." The Dept. of Fish and Game does not sell licenses.

More information about fishing in the Bristol Bay area may be obtained from:

Alaska Dept. of Fish and Game, Sport Fish Division, 333 Raspberry Road, Anchorage, AK 99518; phone 267-2220.

Alaska Dept. of Fish and Game, P.O. Box 199, Dillingham, AK 99576-0199; phone 842-5925.

Bristol Bay Wild Trout Area. This special designation includes the entire Kvichak watershed, including Lake Iliamna. It does not extend to Lake Clark and its tributaries above Sixmile Lake. Special rules included in the Alaska Sport Fishing Regulations apply here. Fish available: all salmon in season; grayling — best May to September; arctic char — best June to September; rainbow trout — best late summer and early fall; northern pike and lake trout — abundant all year. Iliamna has scheduled air service from Anchorage. Entire area served by air charter service from Anchorage, Kenai, Homer, King Salmon,

Dillingham and Iliamna. Several commercial lodges operate in the area.

Igushik River System. Located approximately 20 miles west of Dillingham. Heads in Amanka Lake in Togiak National Wildlife Refuge. Fish available include red salmon — June to August; grayling — best May to September; arctic char — best June to September; rainbow trout — best in late summer and early fall; northern pike — all year. Charter floatplanes available in Dillingham and King Salmon. No accommodations on lake or river.

Nushagak-Mulchatna River System. This river system offers hundreds of miles of river fishing from Twin and Turquoise lakes in Lake Clark National Park and Preserve downstream to Dillingham. Float trips are popular. Fish available in the system: king salmon — best in June and July; coho salmon — best Aug. 15 to September; lake trout — in headwater lakes year-round; grayling — best May to September; arctic char — best June to September; rainbow trout — best in late summer and early fall; northern pike — all year. Access by floatplane from Dillingham, King Salmon or Iliamna. Private lodges on the river.

Tikchik System. Located approximately 80 miles north of Dillingham in Wood-Tikchik State Park. Fish available: red salmon — June to August; pink salmon — July to August; grayling — best May to September; arctic char — best June to September; rainbow trout — best in late summer and early fall; lake trout and northern pike — year-round. Access by floatplane from Dillingham or King Salmon. Commercial lodge on lake requires advance reservations; no other accommodations.

Togiak System. Located approximately 60 miles west of Dillingham. Togiak River heads in Togiak Lake in Togiak National Wildlife Refuge and flows southwest 48 miles to Togiak Bay, 2 miles east of Togiak village. A popular river to float. Popular lakes in the system are Togiak Lake, Ongivinuk Lake, Gechiak Lake and Pungokepuk Lake. Fish available: all salmon in season; king salmon — best June and July; coho salmon — best Aug. 15 to September; grayling — best May to September; arctic char — best June to September; rainbow trout — best in late summer and early fall; northern pike — year-round. Access by charter floatplane from Dillingham, Bethel or King Salmon. Private accommodations on river.

Wood River System. Located 20 to 60 miles north of Dillingham. The lower lake, Lake Aleknagik, may be reached by road. Entire system navigable by riverboat or can be floated. Fishing best in rivers or at the river mouths. Fish available: all salmon in season; grayling — best May to September; arctic char — best June to September; rainbow trout — best in late summer and early fall; northern pike — year-round. Access by boat from Dillingham or Aleknagik village; or by charter floatplane from Dillingham or King Salmon. Commercial lodges located on the system require advance reservations.

Cannery employees pack salmon into cans for processing. (Marion Stirrup)

YUKON-KUSKOKWIM DELTA

Introduction

A vast, watery expanse of treeless lowland that supports millions of waterfowl and lies at the heart of the strong, traditional Yup'ik Eskimo culture — this is the Yukon-Kuskokwim delta.

Villages, some 50 of them, are sprinkled generously up and down the Yukon and Kuskokwim rivers, around the shores of the Bering Sea and — occasionally — inland. Few of these villages have more than 500 residents; and Bethel itself , the region's commercial and government hub, has fewer than 5,000.

In the delta outside Bethel life goes on much as it has for generations. Subsistence hunting, fishing and trapping provide the livelihood, supplemented by seasonal fire fighting, construction and commercial fishing and cottage industries such as basketry and skin sewing. Yup'ik is still spoken widely throughout the delta.

When Russian traders arrived early in the 19th century, their priests made converts to Russian Orthodoxy. The Moravians set off a second round of conversions in 1884 when they established a village which they renamed Bethel. But perhaps the strongest influence in the spiritual life of the Yup'iks is an older, intuitive connection to the land, the rivers, the sea and the creatures which live there. Respect for animals taken in hunting runs deep in the Yup'ik culture and traditional festivals and dances honor animal spirits.

Most of the delta is encompassed in the Yukon Delta National Wildlife Refuge, which draws visitors for hiking, boating and bird-watching. Those who do venture into this remote, hauntingly beautiful country can count themselves lucky to catch glimpses of the Yup'ik culture manifested in racks of salmon drying in the open air or in women wearing *kuspuks* weaving baskets while listening to a radio newscast from Bethel broadcast in both English and Yup'ik.

The Russian Orthodox Church in Chauthbaluk, seen behind the filled clothesline, was established in 1891 and is on the National Register of Historic Places. (Alissa Crandall)

▼ C O M M U N I T I E S ▼

Akiachak

(ACK-ee-a-chuck) Located on the Kuskokwim River, 15 miles northeast of Bethel, 390 miles west of Anchorage. **Transportation:** Scheduled air service from Bethel. **Population:** 448. **Zip code:** 99551. **Emergency Services:** Village Public Officer, phone 825-4313; Alaska State Troopers, Bethel, phone 543-3494; Clinic, phone 825-4011; Volunteer Fire Department.

Climate: Maritime; mean summer temperature 53°F; mean winter temperature 11°F. Mean annual precipitation 17 inches with 50 inches of snow.

Private Aircraft: Airstrip adjacent southeast; elev. 25 feet; length 1,900 feet; gravel and dirt; no fuel; unattended. The runway is used year-round. Runway condition not monitored; visual inspection recommended prior to using. Runway has rough, rolling soft spots.

Visitor Facilities: Lodging available at the IRA (Indian Reorganization Act) Council building; make arrangements through the school, phone 825-4013. No restaurant. There is a washeteria. Some supplies available. Fishing/hunting licenses available.

Akiachak was founded in the early 1890s by former residents of another village; a population of 43 was recorded in the 1890 census. By 1895 the Moravian Church at Bethel had stationed a helper here.

Akiachak's school was established in 1930 and an airstrip was built in 1967. Akiachak is located within Yukon Delta National Wildlife Refuge and was incorporated as a second-class city in 1974. Many village residents are likely to be gone to fish camps during the summer. This Eskimo community has a Moravian church. There is a school here which offers grades kindergarten through 12. There is a community electricity system and a community water supply at the washeteria; sewage system is privies and honey buckets. Freight arrives by barge or mail plane. Government address: Akiachak IRA Council, P.O. Box 70, Akiachak, AK 99551; phone 825-4626. Village corporation address: Akiachak Ltd., P.O. Box 100, Akiachak, AK 99551; phone 825-4328.

Akiak

(ACK-ee-ack) Located on the Kuskokwim River, 20 miles northeast of Bethel, 380 miles west of Anchorage. **Transportation:** Scheduled air service from Bethel. **Population:** 247. **Zip code:** 99552. **Emergency Services:** Village Public Safety Officer, phone 765-7527; Alaska State Troopers, Bethel, phone 543-3494; Clinic, phone 765-7527; Volunteer Fire Department.

Climate: Maritime, summers cool, winters moderate.

Private Aircraft: Airstrip adjacent southwest; elev. 22 feet; length 2,000 feet; gravel; no fuel; unattended. Runway condition not monitored, visual inspection recommended prior to using. Southwest 1,000 feet of runway subject to flooding during breakup.

Visitor Facilities: Arrangements for accommodations may be made through the village office, phone 765-7411; or at the school, phone 765-7212. No restaurant, banking or laundry facilities. Supplies available in the community. Fishing/hunting licenses available.

The name Akiak reportedly means "crossing over" and refers to a trail that connected the Kuskokwim River at Akiak with the Yukon River. The earliest census including Akiak was that of 1880 when 175 people were reported living here.

An early convert to the Moravian Church, Helper Neck, who was noted for writing a syllabary of the Eskimo language, was born in Akiak and was stationed here in 1895.

A school was established at Akiak in 1911 by John H. Kilbuck, co-founder in 1885 of the Moravian Mission at Bethel, the first Protestant mission on the Kuskokwim. Kilbuck was a Bureau of Education teacher at Akiak for several years; he died here of typhoid in 1922.

In 1907, gold was discovered along the upper Tuluksak River near present-day Nyac. Akiak was a supply point for the mining operations until an airstrip was built at Nyac. An airport was completed in 1958 and a National Guard armory in 1960. Akiak, located within Yukon Delta National Wildlife Refuge, was incorporated as a second-class city in 1970.

The community is served by 2 schools with grades kindergarten through 12. There is a community electricity system. Water is from individual wells; the sewage system is septic. Freight arrives by barge or mail plane. Government address: City of Akiak, P.O. Box 52167, Akiak, AK 99552; phone 765-7411. Village corporation address: Kokarmuit Corp., General Delivery, Akiak, AK 99552; phone 765-7228.

Alakanuk

(a-LACK-a-nuk) Located at the east entrance to Alakanuk Pass, the major southern channel of the Yukon River delta, 160 miles northwest of Bethel and 110 miles south of Nome. **Transportation:** Jet service from Bethel or Nome. **Population:** 571. **Zip code:** 99554. **Emergency Services:** Police, phone 238-3421; Clinic, phone 238-3212; Bethel Hospital, phone 543-3711; Volunteer Fire Department.

Climate: Subarctic. Temperatures from -25°F in winter to 79°F in summer. Annual average snowfall 60 inches, precipitation 19 inches.

Private Aircraft: Airport adjacent southwest; elev. 10 feet; length 2,100 feet; gravel; no fuel; unattended. 60-foot gravel turnaround midway of runway. Condition not monitored, visual inspection recommended prior to using.

Visitor Facilities: Accommodations at city lodge through the city office. Groceries, clothing, first-aid supplies, hardware, camera film and sporting goods can be purchased at 3 stores in the community. Local arts and crafts available for purchase include carved ivory, grass baskets, Eskimo boots and beading. Laundromat facilities available. No banking or major repair services. Rental transportation and taxi service available. Diesel fuel available at the Native store. Moorage facilities available at city dock with depth of 7 feet. Water available from the city.

Alakanuk is a Yup'ik word meaning "wrong way," aptly applied to a village on a maze of watercourses. The Eskimo village was first reported by G.R. Putnam of the U.S. Coast and Geodetic Survey in 1899, although it was occupied before Russians arrived in the delta region in the 1830s. It is the longest village on the lower Yukon, stretching for 3 miles along a slough. With the establishment of a school in 1959, population increased and the village became a second-class city with its incorporation in 1969.

Recreation is fishing and hunting. Fish include king, coho and chum salmon, whitefish, sheefish and lush. Traveling is done by snowmobile in winter and boat in summer. Larger boats should use caution at the entrance of the Yukon. The controlling depth is 10 feet and extreme caution is advised because of shifting sandbars. Pilot services available, phone 238-3629 or VHF16.

Communications include phones, mail plane, radio and TV. The community is served by Catholic and Assembly of God churches and a school with grades kindergarten through 12. Public water and electricity is available. Sewage system is honey buckets. Alakanuk prohibits the sale and importation of alcoholic beverages. Freight arrives by cargo plane and barge. Government address: City of Alakanuk, Box 167, Alakanuk, AK 99554, phone 238-3313. Village corporation address: Alakanuk Native Corp., P.O. Box 89, Alakanuk, AK 99554; phone 238-3117.

Andreafsky

(See **St. Marys**)

Aniak

(AN-ee-ack) Located on the south bank of the Kuskokwim River at the head of Aniak Slough, 59 miles southwest of Russian Mission, 90 miles northeast of Bethel, 325 miles west of Anchorage. **Transportation:** Scheduled or charter air service from Bethel. **Population:** 518. **Zip code:** 99557. **Emergency Services:** Village Public Safety Officer, phone 675-4326; Alaska State Trooper, phone 675-4398; Clinic, phone 675-4346; Fire Department, 911.

Elevation: 80 feet. **Climate:** Maritime in the summer and continental in the winter, thus summer temperatures are higher and winter temperatures colder than along the Bering Sea coast. Annual precipitation averages 17 inches, with 85 inches of snow. Expect snow between late September and early May. Strong winds common, especially in winter.

Private Aircraft: Airport adjacent south; elev. 88 feet; length 6,000 feet; gravel; fuel 80, 100; attended Monday to Saturday. Runway condition reports and snow and ice removal available only during duty hours. Passenger terminal, ticket counter, restrooms at airport. Transportation into village available. Seaplane landings in Aniak Slough and river in front of town.

Visitor Facilities: Accommodations available. Restaurant and laundry facilities available; no banking services. Groceries, clothing, first-aid supplies, hardware, camera film and sporting goods available in the community. Arts and crafts available for purchase include carved ivory. Fishing/hunting licenses available. Guide services available. Repair services available for marine engines, boats and airplanes. Rental transportation available. Fuel available includes marine gas, diesel, propane and regular gasoline. No moorage facilities.

Aniak is a Yup'ik Eskimo word meaning "place where it comes out," referring to the nearby mouth of the Aniak River. This river played a key role in the placer gold rush of 1900-01 when prospectors from Nome stampeded to the Kuskokwim delta after hearing of discoveries along the "Yellow River" (later identified as the Aniak River) so-called because of its discoloration from silt. A Russian-era trader called Semen Lukin is credited with the discovery of gold near Aniak in 1832, but no 20th century settlement was started until Tom L. Johnson homesteaded the long-abandoned site of the old Eskimo village in 1914 and opened a general store. A territorial school opened in 1936. Construction of an airfield in 1939 was followed by the erection of a White Alice radar-relay station in 1956. The community started to grow as people from the surrounding area moved to Aniak to find jobs. Several businesses were started to serve the increased population and Aniak became the transportation hub for the mid-Kuskokwim region. Aniak today is the headquarters of the regional school district, as well as the regional offices of several state and federal agencies. Aniak is a second-class city, incorporated in 1972.

Aniak has a mixed economy comprising income from private businesses and publicly funded programs. The community is closely knit and has several related families. The Yup'ik language is still commonly spoken among the elders. Subsistence lifestyles are still practiced.

Mail plane and charter service are provided to several area villages through a local air service and other independent carriers. Aniak also is a transfer point for the commercial fishing industry and a staging area for fire-fighting crews in the summer.

The Kuskokwim River is frozen 6 months of the year, with ice often 8 feet thick. Spring breakup is a spectacular and often disastrous event when ice moving downriver hangs up in horseshoe bends and on sandbars. These ice jams can cause flooding at Aniak.

Fish in the Aniak area include most species of salmon, trout, pike, whitefish, sheefish and lush. Game includes moose, black and brown bear, and caribou. Other wildlife common to the region are fox, rabbit, mink, eagles, ptarmigan, beaver, lynx, marten, songbirds and waterfowl.

Communications in Aniak include phones, mail plane and TV. The community is served by Catholic and Assembly of God churches and Aniak school with grades preschool through 12. Public electricity and water are available. Water is from individual wells. Community sewage system to some homes; honey buckets also used. Freight arrives by cargo plane and barge. Government address: City of Aniak, P.O. Box 43, Aniak, AK 99557; phone 675-4481. Village corporation address: The Kuskokwim Corp., 429 D St., Suite 307, Anchorage, AK 99501; phone 276-2101.

Anvik
(See INTERIOR section.)

Atmautluak
(at-MAUT-loo-ack) Located on the Petmigtalek River in the Yukon-Kuskokwim delta, 15 miles northwest of Bethel, 410 miles west of Anchorage. **Transportation:** Boat, snow machine, scheduled and charter air service from Bethel. **Population:** 234. **Zip code:** 99559. **Emergency Services:** Police, phone 553-5215; Health aide, phone 553-5114; Fire Department.

Private Aircraft: Airstrip adjacent southwest; elev. 17 feet; length 2,000 feet; gravel; no fuel; unattended. Runway condition not monitored, visual inspection recommended prior to using. Passenger terminal, transportation into village available.

Visitor Facilities: Sleeping accommodations available at the school, phone 553-5112. No restaurant, laundromat or banking services. Supplies available in the community. Carved ivory and beadwork available for purchase. Fishing/hunting licenses not available. No guide or major repair services. Arrangements can be made to rent boats. Marine gas, diesel and regular gasoline and moorage available.

Atmautluak, a second-class city incorporated in 1976, is located within the Yukon Delta National Wildlife Refuge.

Communications at Atmautluak include phones, mail plane and radio. The community has 2 churches and a school with grades preschool through 12. Community water and electricity systems available. Sewage system is honey buckets. Atmautluak prohibits the sale and importation of alcoholic beverages. Freight arrives by cargo plane and barge. Government address: City of Atmautluak, General Delivery, Atmautluak, AK 99559;

phone 553-5511 or 553-5610. Village corporation address: Atmautluak Limited, General Delivery, Atmautluak, AK 99559; phone 553-5428.

Bethel

Located on the north bank of the Kuskokwim River 90 miles from its mouth, 400 miles west of Anchorage. **Transportation:** Scheduled airline from Anchorage and all villages in the delta. **Population:** 4,462. **Zip code:** 99559. **Emergency Services:** Police, Fire Department, Ambulance, emergency only, phone 911; Alaska State Troopers, phone 543-2294; Yukon-Kuskokwim Delta Regional Hospital, phone 543-3711; Bethel Family Clinic, phone 543-3773.

Elevation: 10 feet. **Climate:** Maritime; mean summer temperature 53°F, mean winter temperature 11°F. Mean annual precipitation 17 inches, with 50 inches of snow. The last day of freezing usually is May 30 and the first freeze is usually about Sept. 9.

Private Aircraft: Airport adjacent southwest; elev. 131 feet; length 6,400 feet; asphalt; fuel 80, 100 and jet A; attended. Airport facilities include passenger and freight terminals, ticket counters, restrooms and traffic control tower. Taxi service to town available.

Visitor Facilities: Accommodations available. There are several restaurants. Public laundry facilities and banking services. Four grocery stores, 3 department stores and several specialty shops. Arts and crafts available for purchase include carved ivory, grass baskets, masks, beadwork, mukluks, kuspuks, Eskimo yo-yos, and fur coats, clothing and slippers. Fishing/hunting licenses available, as well as guide service. Repair services for marine engines, boats, autos and airplanes. Rental transportation includes autos and charter aircraft; arrangements can be made to rent boats. Also 3 taxi services in town, and bus service on weekdays. All types of fuel available. Moorage facilities at small-boat harbor.

The historic Kilbuck Building in Bethel became the city's new Visitor Center and Museum Annex. Appropriately named Yugtarvik, which means "a place for people's things," the center houses exhibits of traditional Native tools and clothing of the region, and a gift shop offers visitors information on local and regional events and services, and will host traditional Native art classes, videotapes produced jointly by KYUK-TV and the museum, photo exhibits and traveling exhibits. Yugtarvik Regional Museum first opened in 1967. Its present museum building

was constructed with a grant to commemorate the U.S. purchase of the Territory of Alaska from Russia in 1867 and its operation is supported financially by the local Chamber of Commerce and by volunteers. The museum hosts more than 10,000 visitors each year.

A visitor center for the Yukon Delta National Wildlife Refuge is located across from the Bethel Regional Hospital, on the main road to town from the airport. The center features exhibits and refuge staff present periodic programs for schools and the public.

Bethel was settled in the 1800s and originally was known as Mumtrekhlagamute, which means "smokehouse village" in the Eskimo language. The first trading post was established in the early 1870s. When the Moravian Church established a mission here in 1885, its missionaries christened the place Bethel, in obedience to a scripture verse which commanded, "Arise, go up to Bethel, and dwell there." The community celebrated its centennial in 1985.

Bethel is one of the largest towns in western Alaska. It serves as the administrative hub for the area's villages with a district court and superior court, Alaska Dept. of Fish and Game, U.S. Fish and Wildlife Service, and Bureau of Indian Affairs offices.

The area's commercial fishing industry provides a major portion of Bethel's economy and employment. Bethel is the transportation center for 57 villages in the Yukon-Kuskokwim delta. Bethel's location at the head of Kuskokwim Bay provides access to the Bering Sea. The town has the only medium-draft port in western Alaska. Bethel's flight service station is reported to be the third busiest in the state. Transportation and related industries contribute significantly to the town's economy.

While there are still many people living mainly by subsistence hunting and fishing in the surrounding villages, most of Bethel's residents work year-round in the growing private industries, Native corporations and government jobs.

The Kisaralik and Kwethluk rivers, 1 to 2 hours from Bethel by boat, offer good recreational fishing for grayling, Dolly Varden and rainbow trout, as well as silver and chum salmon. The Kisaralik also is used regularly in the summer for guided float trips sponsored by the City of Bethel Parks and Recreation Dept.

Bethel is located within 20-million-acre Yukon Delta National Wildlife Refuge, largest in the United States. Many species of water-fowl make the refuge their summer home.

There are several recreational events during the year in Bethel, including the Kuskokwim-300 Sled Dog Race, Yukon-Kuskokwim State Fair, Mink & Fox Festival, Fourth of July Fete and Eskimo dance festivals.

Communications in Bethel include phones, radio, TV and weekly newspaper, *The Tundra Drums*. The community is served by 13 churches, 3 public schools, a private school, a community college, 3 day-care centers and a prematernal home. There are community electricity, water and sewage systems. Freight arrives by cargo plane, barge and ship. For several years Bethel banned the sale of alcoholic beverages, but an election late in 1989 was scheduled to put the sale prohibition before the voters again. Government address: City of Bethel, P.O. Box 388, Bethel, AK 99559; phone 543-2097. Village corporation address: Bethel Native Corp., P.O. Box 719, Bethel, AK 99559; phone 543-2124. Chamber of Commerce address: Bethel Chamber of Commerce, P.O. Box 329, Bethel, AK 99559.

Chefornak

(sha-FOR-nack) Located at the junction of the Keguk and Kinia rivers in the Yukon-Kuskokwim delta, 100 miles southwest of Bethel, 480 miles west-southwest of Anchorage. **Transportation:** Scheduled air service from Bethel; snow machines; outboards. **Population:** 299. **Zip code:** 99561. **Emergency Services:** Village Public Safety Officer, phone 867-8712; Alaska State Troopers, Bethel, phone 543-2294; Clinic, phone 867-8919; Volunteer Fire Department, phone 867-8712.

Private Aircraft: Airstrip adjacent east; elev. 40 feet; length 2,500 feet; gravel; no fuel; unattended. Runway condition not monitored, visual inspection recommended prior to using. Gulls and birds in airport area.

Visitor Facilities: Make arrangements for lodging at the high school, phone 867-8515 or 8700. Groceries, clothing, first-aid supplies, hardware, camera film, sporting goods, vehicles and boats available. Marine engine and boat repairs available; rental boats and off-road vehicles. No bank, laundromat or fishing/hunting licenses.

This Eskimo village, located within Yukon Delta National Wildlife Refuge, was incorporated as a second-class city in 1974. Many village residents are likely to be gone to fish camps during the summer.

Local recreation includes basketball games, dancing and Eskimo dancing, bingo, Sunday night gatherings for young adults and 2 arcades.

Communications include phones, CB radio, VHF radio, radio and TV. The community is served by a Catholic church and 2 schools with grades kindergarten through 12. There is a community electricity system. Water is hauled from a community watering point or rain water or ice is collected. Sewage system is honey buckets. Chefornak prohibits the sale and importation of alcoholic beverages. Freight arrives by plane and barge. Government address: City of Chefornak, P.O. Box 29, Chefornak, AK 99561; phone 867-8528. Village corporation address: Chefornamuit Inc., General Delivery, Chefornak, AK 99561; phone 867-8211.

Chevak

(CHEE-vak) Located on the north bank of the Ninglikfak River, 17 miles east of Hooper Bay, 120 miles northwest of Bethel, 500 miles west of Anchorage. **Transportation:** Boats; snow machines; scheduled or charter air service from Bethel. **Population:** 586. **Zip code:** 99563. **Emergency Services:** Village Public Safety Officer, phone 858-7728; Alaska State Troopers, Bethel; Clinic, phone 858-7029; Volunteer Fire Department.

Climate: Maritime; temperatures range from -25°F to 79°F at nearby Cape Romanzof. Snow depth on the tundra averages between 2-1/2 and 3 feet, with an average of 60 inches of snowfall per year. Freezeup occurs at the end of October; breakup in June.

Private Aircraft: Airstrip 1 mile north; elev. 75 feet; length 2,600 feet; gravel; no fuel; unattended. Runway condition not monitored, visual inspection recommended prior to using. Strong crosswinds. No transportation to village.

Visitor Facilities: Lodging sometimes available at the school, phone 858-7713. No restaurant or banking services. Laundry facilities available. Supplies available in the community. Arts and crafts available include carved ivory, grass baskets, masks, beadwork and skin boots. Fishing/hunting licenses available. No guide service or rental transportation. Marine engine repair available. Fuel available: marine gas, regular gasoline. No moorage facilities.

Chevak is also known as New Chevak because residents inhabited another village called Chevak before 1950. "Old" Chevak, on the north bank of the Keoklevik River, 9 miles east of Hooper Bay, was abandoned because of flooding from high storm tides. The name Chevak refers to "a connecting slough" on which "old" Chevak was situated.

It was incorporated as a second-class city in 1967.

Employment in Chevak is at its peak in the summer months, with seasonal firefighting for the Bureau of Land Management and summer construction projects. The city also usually hires several people for city improvement projects. Other jobs exist with the city, village corporation, local stores and the school.

Income is supplemented by public assistance programs and local subsistence activities. Residents hunt seal, walrus, geese, swans, ducks and ptarmigan. Additionally, clams, salmon, whitefish, blackfish, needlefish, sheefish, pike and tomcod are taken. In the fall, families gather greens and harvest berries.

Local recreation includes basketball games, dancing and Eskimo dancing.

Chevak is located within Yukon Delta National Wildlife Refuge, which is the summer home for many thousands of migratory birds.

Communications include phones, mail plane, radio and TV. The community has a Catholic church and a school with grades kindergarten through 12. There is community electricity; water is hauled from central watering points. Sewage system is primarily honey buckets. Freight arrives by barge or mail plane. Goverment address: City of Chevak, P.O. Box 6083, Chevak, AK 99563; phone 858-7427. Village corporation address: Chevak Co. Corp., General Delivery, Chevak, AK 99563; phone 858-7011.

Chuathbaluk

(Chu-ATH-ba-luck) Located on the north bank of the Kuskokwim River, 10 miles east of Aniak, 100 miles east of Bethel and 310 miles west of Anchorage. **Transportation:** Charter plane from Aniak. **Population:** 131. **Zip code:** 99557. **Emergency Services:** Alaska State Troopers, Aniak, phone 675-4398; Clinic, phone 467-4114; Volunteer Fire Department.

Climate: Continental; temperatures range between -55° and 87°F. Annual snowfall 85 inches; precipitation 17 inches.

Private Aircraft: Airstrip 5 miles northeast; elev. 300 feet; length 1,800 feet; gravel; unattended. Runway condition not monitored, recommend visual inspection prior to using. No transportation to village; no airport facilities.

Visitor Facilities: Lodging at the school, phone 467-4129, or community center through the city office, phone 467-4115. Laundromat available. No banking services. Groceries and general merchandise available

in the community. Fishing/hunting licenses and guide service not available. No major repair service or rental transportation. There are moorage facilities; the only fuel available is marine gas.

The community existed as a Native settlement as early as 1833. It has been known by several names, most recently as "Little Russian Mission." However, this led to confusion between this community and a village on the lower Yukon River called Russian Mission. As a result, within the last 20 years the village was renamed Chuathbaluk, Yup'ik Eskimo for "big blueberries."

For many years the village had a small population. It grew considerably when permission to live on the property was given by the Russian Orthodox Church. It became a second-class city with its incorporation in 1975. The economy depends heavily on subsistence activities, supplemented by some construction work, and cottage industries such as skin sewing and basketry.

The community is served by a Russian Orthodox church — established in 1891 and on the National Register of Historic Places — and a school with grades preschool through 12.

Communications available are phones, radio and TV. Community electricity available. Water hauled from a community well. Sewage system is honey buckets. Freight arrives by air cargo and barge. Government address: City of Chuathbaluk, General Delivery, Chuathbaluk, AK 99557; phone 467-4115. Village corporation address: The Kuskokwim Corp., 429 D St., Suite 307, Anchorage, AK 99501, phone 276-2101.

Crooked Creek

Located on the north bank of the Kuskokwim River, at its junction with Crooked Creek, in the Kilbuck-Kuskokwim Mountains, 50 miles northeast of Aniak, 145 miles northeast of Bethel, 280 miles west of Anchorage. **Transportation:** Scheduled air service from Bethel. **Population:** 119. **Zip code:** 99575. **Emergency Services:** Alaska State Troopers, Aniak, phone 675-4398; Health aide; Volunteer Fire Department.

Elevation: 130 feet. **Climate:** Continental with low winter temperatures and high summer temperatures. Mean annual precipitation 15 inches, with 61 inches of snow.

Private Aircraft: Airstrip 2 miles south; elev. 128 feet; length 2,000 feet; gravel; fuel 100; unattended. Runway condition not monitored, visual inspection recommended prior to using. No line of sight from one end of runway to the other. Some erosion of south end of runway.

Visitor Facilities: Accommodations for 12 people at local roadhouse. No banking services. Supplies, laundry and shower facilities available. Fishing/hunting licenses not available. Information on guide and repair services, rental transportation, fuel and moorage unavailable.

The village of Crooked Creek or "Kipchapuk," was first reported in 1844 by Russian explorer L.A. Zagoskin, who noted that the site was used as a summer camp by residents of a nearby village. Crooked Creek also has been known as Portage Village. A more permanent settlement was established at the site in 1909 following a gold strike along the nearby upper Iditarod River. An influx of people to the area in 1909-10 led to the founding of the Flat and Iditarod mining camps. Crooked Creek was a supply point for those camps which were within easy access of the Kuskokwim River.

Crooked Creek village, which is spread out on both sides of Crooked Creek, is unincorporated.

There are few year-round employment opportunities at Crooked Creek. Government programs, the regional school district and a few support services provide the only permanent jobs. Subsistence activities supplement this income.

Crooked Creek residents hunt beaver, muskrat, game birds, hare, moose, caribou and waterfowl. Income also is obtained from trapping and the sale of marten, wolverine, lynx, fox and mink. In summer, the Kuskokwim River and Crooked Creek yield king, silver, red and chum salmon, as well as whitefish, pike, grayling, Dolly Varden, sheefish and eel. In the fall, cranberries, blueberries, raspberries, blackberries, salmonberries and currants are harvested.

Communications in Crooked Creek include 4 private phones; a pay phone is located at the post office. Two air/ground radios are available for planes. TV signals are relayed to Crooked Creek via statewide satellite. The community is served by a Russian Orthodox church and a school with grades preschool through 12. Electricity is provided by the Middle Kuskokwim Electric Coop, which serves 5 villages on the river. Water is hauled from the washeteria or laundromat. Sewage system is honey buckets. Freight arrives by mail plane or barge. Government address: Crooked Creek Traditional Council, General Delivery, Crooked Creek, AK 99575. Village corporation address: The Kuskokwim Corp., 429 D St., Suite 307, Anchorage, AK 99501.

Eek

Located on the Eek River near the mouth of the Kuskokwim River on Kuskokwim Bay, 45 miles south of Bethel, 420 miles west of Anchorage. **Transportation:** Boat, snow machine, scheduled and charter air service from Bethel. **Population:** 273. **Zip code:** 99578. **Emergency Services:** Village Public Safety Officer, phone 536-5129; Alaska State Troopers, Bethel, phone 543-2595; Clinic, phone 536-5314.

Climate: Summers cool and rainy, winters cold, with a brisk north wind. Winter temperatures drop to -35° to -40°F.

Private Aircraft: Airstrip 1 mile east; elev. 40 feet; length 1,300 feet; gravel; no fuel; unattended. Runway condition not monitored, visual inspection recommended prior to landing. No airport facilities or public transportation into village.

Visitor Facilities: Arrangements can be made to stay at the school by contacting the principal, phone 536-5229. No restaurants or banking services. There is a laundromat with bathing facilities. Groceries, clothing, first-aid supplies, hardware, camera film and sporting goods available in the community. Arts and crafts available for purchase include Eskimo dolls, grass baskets and fur hats. Fishing/hunting licenses available, but best to purchase before arriving in Eek. Arrangements may be made for guide service with local hunters and fishermen. No major repair service or rental transportation available. Fuel available includes marine gas, diesel, propane and regular gasoline. No moorage facilities.

Eek was founded by residents who moved from an older village affected by erosion. Most of Eek residents are commercial fishermen, but there also is subsistence hunting and fishing.

Eek is located within Yukon Delta National Wildlife Refuge. Travel up the Eek River by boat is a treat, offering a real wilderness experience, according to one resident. There are birds, beavers and an occasional bear to be seen. Fish caught locally include salmon, pike, grayling, trout and smelt. Hunting is for moose, caribou, ptarmigan, rabbits and seal.

Some prospecting for gold has been reported in the area.

The village corporation, Iqfijouaq Co., has established no user fees or other restrictions on its lands. However, check with the corporation regarding location of private lands.

Communications in Eek, a second-class city incorporated in 1970, include phones, mail plane, radio and TV. The community is served by Moravian and Russian Orthodox churches and a school with grades preschool through 12. There are community electricity and water systems. Sewage system is honey buckets. Eek prohibits the sale and importation of alcoholic beverages. Freight arrives by plane and barge. Government address: City of Eek, General Delivery, Eek, AK 99576; phone 536-5129. Village corporation address: Iqfijouaq Co., General Delivery, Eek, AK 99578; phone 536-5211.

Emmonak

(e-MON-nuk) Located at the mouth of the Yukon River on the north bank of Kwiguk Pass in the Yukon-Kuskokwim delta, 175 miles northwest of Bethel, 490 miles west-northwest of Anchorage. **Transportation:** Scheduled and charter air service from Bethel or Nome. **Population:** 660. **Zip code:** 99581. **Emergency Services:** Village Public Safety Officer, phone 949-1728; Clinic, phone 949-1511; Volunteer Fire Department.

Elevation: 10 feet. **Climate:** Maritime; mean precipitation 24.5 inches per year; mean snowfall 57 inches.

Private Aircraft: Airstrip adjacent east; elev. 10 feet; length 1,900 feet; gravel; fuel jet A. Runway unattended and not monitored. Recommend visual inspection prior to using.

Visitor Facilities: Accommodations and meals available. There is a restaurant. No banking services. Groceries, laundry, clothing, first-aid supplies, hardware, camera film and sporting goods available in the community. Arts and crafts available for purchase include carved ivory, grass baskets, fans, fur hats and spears. Fishing/hunting licenses available. No guide service. Marine engine repair available. Charter aircraft available. Fuel available includes marine gas, diesel, propane, unleaded and regular gasoline. No moorage facilities.

Emmonak was originally called Kwiguk, a Yup'ik Eskimo word meaning "big stream." Kwiguk Pass is one of the fingers of water leading from the Yukon River above its mouth to the sea. The village was first reported by G.R Putnam of the U.S. Coast and Geodetic Survey in 1899. Later, commercial fishing became a major industry and Northern Commercial Co. built a cannery, which was washed away by floods in 1964. Heavy erosion affected the rest of the village and it was relocated in 1964-65 to a site 1.4 miles north. The new location was renamed Emmonak and is becoming a center for commercial fishing and processing on the lower Yukon River. Emmonak is a second-class city, incorporated in 1964.

Emmonak has a seasonal economy, with most activity in commercial fishing taking place in June, July and August. The Native-owned Yukon Delta Fish Marketing Cooperative operates a barge with a self-contained cannery at Emmonak. Whitney-Fidalgo also operates a fish-cleaning plant. Other jobs are provided by local businesses and government. Income from employment is supplemented by public assistance programs and subsistence activities. Residents hunt moose, beluga whale, seal, ptarmigan, hare and waterfowl, and fish for salmon, whitefish, blackfish, lush (burbot), sheefish and tomcod. In the fall, families travel upriver to harvest berries. Income also is derived from trapping mink, otter, red and arctic fox and lynx.

Recreational activities at Emmonak include winter potlatches for other nearby villages, and city league and high school basketball games.

Emmonak is located within Yukon Delta National Wildlife Refuge. Winter trails connect Emmonak with Kotlik, Alakanuk and Sheldon Point.

Communications include phones, mail plane, radio and TV. Emmonak is served by Catholic and Assembly of God churches and a school with grades kindergarten through 12. There are community electricity, water systems. Emmonak prohibits the sale and importation of alcoholic beverages. Freight arrives by cargo plane and barge. Government address: City of Emmonak, P.O. Box 48, Emmonak, AK 99581; phone 949-1227. Village corporation address: Emmonak Native Corp., General Delivery, Emmonak, AK 99581; phone 949-1411.

Flat

(See INTERIOR section.)

Georgetown

Located on the north bank of the upper Kuskokwim River east of the mouth of the George River, 16 miles northwest of Red Devil, 22 miles northwest of Sleetmute. **Transportation:** Charter air service from Bethel or Red Devil; riverboat; snow machine. **Population:** 3 permanent. **Zip code:** 99656. **Emergency Services:** Alaska State Troopers, Aniak.

Climate: Continental; mean precipitation 15 inches per year, with 61 inches of snow. Greatest snowfall, according to Sleetmute data, is in January.

Private Aircraft: A private, 1,100-foot dirt airstrip adjacent to the north accommodates small planes. Heavy winds in the fall and winter often make air travel difficult or impossible for days.

Visitor Facilities: None.

When Russian explorer L.A. Zagoskin passed by the George River in 1844, he noted that there were summer houses at a nearby place called Keledzhichagat that belonged to people from Kwigiumpai-nukamiut.

Gold was found along the George River near Georgetown in 1909. An early mining settlement, located west of the mouth of the George River and the George River itself, were named for the first 3 traders at the site: George Hoffman, George Fredericks and George Morgan. By summer 1910, about 300 prospectors were living in the vicinity. About 200 log cabins had been built when a fire swept through the settlement in July 1911, destroying all but 25 cabins along the riverbank and 2 general stores. By 1953 the only large structure that remained was the 2-story log house that belonged to George Fredericks.

In the 1950s, the present settlement, also called Georgetown, began emerging on the river east of the mouth of the George River opposite the earlier community. A school was established at the new site in 1965 and operated until 1970. The present community consists of 5 homes and an airplane hangar belonging to Vanderpool Flying Service of Red Devil.

Georgetown residents must travel to other communities for seasonal employment. Otherwise they depend on subsistence hunting and fishing. Moose, caribou, bear, waterfowl, game birds, rabbit and porcupine are hunted. Fishing yields salmon, whitefish, sheefish, burbot, grayling and trout. In the fall the tundra offers blueberries, blackberries and currants. Some income is obtained from trapping and selling beaver, marten, lynx, fox and mink pelts.

Communication is by radio; there are no phones. Fresh produce and other freight is shipped air freight from Anchorage to nearby Red Devil and then flown to Georgetown. There is no school or church. Electricity is from individual generators. Water from wells or the river. Sewage system is septic tanks or outhouses. Georgetown is not incorporated. Village corporation address: The Kuskokwim Corp., 429 D St., Suite 307, Anchorage, AK 99501; phone 276-2101.

Goodnews Bay

Located on Goodnews Bay on the east shore of Kuskokwim Bay, 70 miles south of Bethel, 430 miles west of Anchorage. **Transportation:** Scheduled and charter air service from Bethel or Dillingham. **Population:** 230. **Zip code:** 99589. **Emergency Services:** Alaska State Troopers, Dillingham, phone 842-5641, or Bethel, phone 543-3781; Health aide, phone 967-8128; Volunteer Fire Department.

Private Aircraft: Airstrip adjacent southeast; elev. 15 feet; length 2,500 feet; gravel; no fuel; unattended. Runway condition not monitored, visual inspection recommended prior to using. No airport facilities or public transportation into village.

Visitor Facilities: Accommodations available through the village or the school, phone 967-8213. No restaurant, banking services or laundry facilities. Clothing, first-aid supplies, hardware, camera film and sporting goods available in the community. Arts and crafts available for purchase include grass baskets, carved ivory, beadwork, hand-sewn skin garments and knitted goods. Fishing/hunting licenses available. Fishing guide service available. No major repair service or rental transportation. Fuel available includes marine gas, diesel and propane. Moorage facilities available.

Originally known as Mumtrak, the village's present name comes from the bay on which it is located. The name comes from the Russian Port Dobrykh Vestey, which probably was named by members of a Russian expedition in 1818-19.

The community grew because of nearby gold mining activities in the 1900s, according to one resident. Goodnews Bay is a second-class city, incorporated in 1970.

Communications at Goodnews Bay include phones, mail plane, radio and TV. The community has a church and 2 schools with grades kindergarten through 12. There are community electricity and water systems. Sewage system is honey buckets. Goodnews Bay prohibits the sale and importation of alcoholic beverages. Freight arrives by cargo plane, barge and ship. Government address: City of Goodnews Bay, City Hall, P.O. Box 70, Goodnews Bay, AK 99589; phone 967-8614. Village corporation address: Kuitsarak Inc., General Delivery, Goodnews Bay, AK 99589; phone 967-8520. Also: Traditional Council, P.O. Box 56, Goodnews Bay, AK 99589.

Grayling
(See INTERIOR section.)

Holy Cross
(See INTERIOR section.)

Hooper Bay

Located on Hooper Bay, 20 miles south of Cape Romanzof in the Yukon-Kuskokwim delta, 120 miles northwest of Bethel, 540 miles west of Anchorage. **Transportation:** Scheduled and charter air service from Bethel. **Population:** 776. **Zip code:** 99604. **Emergency Services:** Police, phone 758-4615; Clinic, phone 758-4711; Volunteer Fire and Search and Rescue Department.

Elevation: 18 feet. **Climate:** Maritime. Mean annual snowfall and precipitation are 75 inches and 16 inches, respectively. Mean annual temperature is 29°F, with temperatures ranging between -25° and 79°F. Winter ice pack and strong winds often cause severe winter conditions.

Private Aircraft: Airstrip 2 miles southwest; elev. 18 feet; length 3,600 feet; asphalt; lighted; unattended. Runway condition not monitored, visual inspection recommended prior to using.

Visitor Facilities: Accommodations available. Four stores supply groceries and general merchandise. Laundromat with showers. Crafts available at most stores. Hooper Bay is famous for the grass baskets produced by village women. Other crafts include sealskin books, ivory and ulu knives. Fishing/hunting licenses available. Limited guiding services for birdwatching, contact city office. Gasoline and diesel fuel is available at Hooper Bay Native Store. Limited motor repairs available.

The population of Hooper Bay is 98 percent Yup'ik Eskimo. The Eskimo name for the community, Askinuk, refers to the mountainous area between Hooper Bay and Scammon Bay. The village was first reported in 1878 by E.W. Nelson of the U.S. Signal Service. The present-day Eskimo name, Naparyarmiut, means "stake village people".

Hooper Bay incorporated as a second-class city in 1966. The local economy depends heavily upon subsistence activities. A small commercial herring fishery at Kokechik Bay takes place each spring. Full-time employment is principally with the village corporation stores, school and local government.

Communications include telephones, cable and state satellite TV. There are Catholic and Covenant churches and a school with grades kindergarten through 12. Community has electricity and 2 public wells supply the community water. Sewage system for homes is honeybuckets. Freight arrives by air and barge. The village prohibits the importation, sale and possession of alcoholic beverages. Government address: City of Hooper Bay, P.O. Box 37, Hooper Bay, AK 99604; phone, 758-04311. Village corporation: Sea Lion Corp., P.O. Box 44, Hooper Bay, AK 99604; phone 748-4015.

Kasigluk

(ka-SEEG-luk) Located 20 miles northwest of Bethel, 425 miles west of Anchorage. **Transportation:** Boat, snow machine, scheduled and charter air service from Bethel. **Population:** 413. **Zip code:** 99609. **Emergency Services:** Alaska State Troopers, Bethel; Clinic, phone 477-6120; Volunteer Fire Department.

Climate: Average temperature in Kasigluk ranges from 65° to 70°F during a dry, warm summer and 40° to 55°F during a wet, cold summer, according to one resident.

Private Aircraft: Airstrip 2 miles south; elev. 40 feet; length 2,400 feet; gravel; fuel 80; unattended. Runway condition not monitored, visual inspection recommended prior to using. Runway badly rutted with dips and rolls. No summer or winter maintenance. Ice runway on river during winter. Watch for trucks and vehicles on runway.

Visitor Facilities: Arrangements can be made for accommodations at the school, phone 477-6615. No restaurant or banking services. Laundry facilities available. Limited groceries available in the community. Arts and crafts available for purchase include Eskimo dolls, mukluks, beaver hats, Eskimo yo-yos and fur mittens. Fishing/hunting licenses available. No guide or major repair services, rental transportation or moorage facilities. Fuel available includes marine gas and propane.

The Eskimo village of Kasigluk, located on a small river, is one of a handful of tundra villages in the Yukon-Kuskokwim delta. Most of the others are located on the sea coast or on a major river.

Kasigluk is situated within Yukon Delta National Wildlife Refuge.

Communications in Kasigluk, a second-class city incorporated in 1982, include phones, mail plane, radio and TV. There is a community electricity system. Water is hauled from a central watering point. Sewage system is honey buckets. The community is served by 2 churches and a school with grades kindergarten through 12. Kasigluk prohibits the sale and importation of alcoholic beverages. Freight arrives by cargo plane and barge. Government address: City of Kasigluk, Akula Heights, Kasigluk, AK 99609; phone 477-6929. Village corporation address: Kasigluk Inc., General Delivery, Kasigluk, AK 99609; phone 477-6026.

Kipnuk

Located on the Kugkaktlik River near the Bering Sea coast, 95 miles southwest of Bethel, 320 miles south of Nome, 500 miles west of Anchorage. **Transportation:** Scheduled air service from Bethel. **Population:** 500. **Zip code:** 99614. **Emergency Services:** Alaska State Troopers, Bethel, phone 543-3494; Clinic, phone 896-5927; Volunteer Fire Department.

Private Aircraft: Airstrip adjacent southeast; elev. 20 feet; length 2,100 feet; gravel; no fuel; unattended. Runway condition not monitored, visual inspection recommended prior to using. *CAUTION: Frequent crosswinds and heavy bird activity near runway.* Erosion in safety area outside the gravel runway surface.

Visitor Facilities: No accommodations, though visitors with an agency or organization may arrange to sleep in the local school or community building. Three general stores provide groceries, limited range of clothing, first-aid supplies, film, limited hardware. Blazo available; no propane. No fishing/hunting licenses. Arts and crafts not available for purchase in stores, though they may be available from individual artisans. Local craftspeople usually sell their goods through the gift shop at the Alaska Native Service Center hospital in Anchorage or through the Alaska Native Arts and Crafts cooperative, with an outlet in Anchorage.

Kipnuk, which is not incorporated, is located within Yukon Delta National Wildlife Refuge.

The community is served by a Moravian church and 2 schools with grades kindergarten through 12. There is a community electricity system. Water is hauled from a central watering point. Sewage system is honey buckets. Kipnuk prohibits the sale and importation of alcoholic beverages. Freight arrives by mail plane and barge. Government address: Kipnuk Village Council, General Delivery, Kipnuk, AK 99614; phone 896-5515. Village corporation address: Kugkaktlik Limited Corp., General Delivery, Kipnuk, AK 99614; phone 896-5415.

Kongiganak

(kon-GIG-a-nuck) Located on the west shore of Kuskokwim Bay, 70 miles west of Bethel, 460 miles west of Anchorage. **Transportation:** Scheduled air service from Bethel. **Population:** 166. **Zip code:** 99559. **Emergency Services:** Alaska State Troopers, Bethel, phone 543-3494; Volunteer Fire Department.

Private Aircraft: Airstrip 8 miles northeast; elev. 25 feet; length 2,000 feet; gravel; no fuel; unattended. Runway condition not monitored, visual inspection recommended prior to using. Runway rough its full length.

Visitor Facilities: Lodging available at the school, phone 557-5126. There is a washeteria with bathing facilities. Supplies available in the community. Arts and crafts available for purchase. Fishing/hunting licenses not available. Information on other visitor services and facilities unavailable.

This Eskimo village, located within Yukon Delta National Wildlife Refuge, is unincorporated. Many residents work seasonally in the summer commercial fishery or go to their own fish camps.

The community has a school with grades kindergarten through 12. There is a community electricity system. Water is hauled from the washeteria. Sewage system is honey buckets. Kongiganak prohibits the sale and importation of alcoholic beverages. Freight arrives by plane and barge. Village corporation address: Qemirtalik Coast Corp., General Delivery, Kongiganak, AK 99559; phone 557-5428.

Kotlik

(KOT-lick) Located on the east bank of Kotlik Slough, 35 miles northeast of Emmonak in the Yukon-Kuskokwim delta. **Transportation:** Scheduled and charter plane service from Nome or Bethel. **Population:** 446. **Zip code:** 99620. **Emergency Services:** Police, phone 899-4626; Alaska State Troopers, St. Marys, phone 438-2018; Clinic, phone 899-4511; Volunteer Fire Department.

Climate: Subarctic. Temperatures range between -50° and 87°F. Snowfall averages 60 inches annually; annual precipitation averages 16 inches.

Private Aircraft: Airstrip located adjacent southwest; elev. 5 feet; length 2,200 feet; gravel; no fuel; unattended. Runway condition not monitored, visual inspection recommended prior to using. No airport facilities or public transportation into village. *CAUTION: Cleared strip east of town unusable.*

Visitor Facilities: No hotel. Arrangements may be made to sleep at the day care center (899-4326) or the local school (899-4415). No restaurant. Supplies available in the community. Arts and crafts available for purchase include grass baskets, parkas and mukluks, and carved ivory. Fishing/hunting licenses available. Information on guide and repair services, rental transportation, fuel and moorage facilities unavailable.

Prior to 1960, only 5 or 6 families lived at Kotlik. Early in the 1960s, people from surrounding villages moved there because a school had been built and accessibility was easier to the oil and freight barges serving the delta. By 1965, Kotlik emerged as one of the larger ports and commercial centers of the lower Yukon River, a status that it retains today.

Kotlik was incorporated in October 1970 as a second-class city. It has a seasonal economy which peaks in the June through August fishing season. Most families leave for their fish camps up the Yukon River where they set their nets for king, silver and chum salmon. People also hunt for seals, ducks and geese. During the winter months, families ice fish, trap, hunt and hold potlatches. Traditional dances are celebrated on Christmas and Easter and other special days. February brings a village potlatch. Dog races are held each March.

Communications include phones, mail plane, radios and TV. Assembly of God and Catholic churches serve the community, as well as a school with grades kindergarten through 12. There is a community electricity system and a community water supply at the washeteria. Sewage system is outdoor pit privies and honey buckets. Freight is transported by air and barge. The village has banned the possession of alcoholic beverages. Government address: City of Kotlik, P.O. Box 20268, Kotlik, AK 99620; phone 899-4313. Village corporation address: Kotlik Yup'ik Corp., Kotlik, AK 99620; phone 899-4014.

Kwethluk

Located on the Kwethluk River near its junction with the Kuskokwim River, 10 miles east of Bethel, 385 miles west of Anchorage. **Transportation:** Boat; snow machine; dog team; scheduled or charter air service from Bethel. **Population:** 541. **Zip code:** 99621. **Emergency Services:** Village Public Safety Officer, phone 757-6928; Alaska State Troopers, Bethel, phone 534-2294; Clinic, phone 757-6715; Volunteer Fire Department, phone 757-6928.

Private Aircraft: Airstrip adjacent south; elev. 28 feet; length 1,700 feet; gravel; no fuel; unattended. Runway condition not monitored, visual inspection recommended prior to using. Freight terminal at airport. There is no public transportation to the village.

Visitor Facilities: No hotel. Arrangements can be made to stay in private homes or the high school through the city office, phone 757-6614 or the village corporation, phone 757-6612. No restaurant or banking services. Laundry facility may be available. Groceries, clothing, first-aid supplies, hardware, camera film and sporting goods available in the community. Arts and crafts available for purchase include carved ivory, Eskimo dolls, ulus, baskets, model dogsleds, beadwork and fur garments. Fishing/hunting licenses not available. No guide services. No rental transportation or repairs. Fuel available includes marine gas, diesel and regular gasoline. Moorage facilities available.

The name Kwethluk means "bad river" in the Yup'ik Eskimo language. There is evidence that Kwethluk was occupied by Native people in prehistoric times.

Kwethluk apparently was the only place along the Kuskokwim River where a Moravian church worker was killed while doing missionary work. An Eskimo helper of missionary J.H. Kilbuck was assigned to Kwethluk in 1889. The following spring Kilbuck went to Kwethluk because he was told the helper might have gone insane. The men of Kwethluk became hostile and forced Kilbuck to leave a few days before they took the lay missionary out of the village, killed him and left his body to be eaten by dogs. Another helper was later assigned to the village and in 1895 a Moravian chapel was built.

Gold prospectors worked the Kwethluk River after discoveries were made on the George River and Crooked Creek in 1909. Most efforts were unsuccessful, but at Canyon Creek on the upper Kwethluk River a small placer deposit was found and mined until WWII.

A Russian Orthodox church was built in Kwethluk in 1912 and a school was built in 1924. An airfield was constructed in 1956 and the community became a second-class city in 1975.

Communications in Kwethluk include phones, mail plane, radio and TV. There are 2 churches and 2 schools with grades kindergarten through 12. Community electricity and water; sewage system serves some homes, though many residents still use honey buckets. Kwethluk prohibits the sale and importation of alcoholic beverages. Freight arrives by cargo plane and barge. Government address: City of Kwethluk, P.O. Box 63, Kwethluk, AK 99621; phone 757-6614 or 6711. Village corporation address: Kwethluk Inc., General Delivery, Kwethluk, AK 99621; phone 757-6613 or 6612.

Kwigillingok

(kwi-GILL-in-gock) Located on the west side of Kuskokwim Bay, 85 miles south-southwest of Bethel, 465 miles west of Anchorage. **Transportation:** Scheduled air service from Bethel. **Population:** 246. **Zip code:** 99622. **Emergency Services:** Village Public Safety Officer; Alaska State Troopers, Bethel, phone

543-3494; Health Clinic, phone 588-8526; Volunteer Fire Department.

Private Aircraft: Airstrip 1 mile northwest; elev. 20 feet; length 2,600 feet; gravel; no fuel; unattended. Runway condition not monitored, visual inspection recommended prior to using. Erosion in safety area on fill outside the gravel runway surface.

Visitor Facilities: Arrangements may be made to stay in private homes through the IRA Council, phone 588-8114. Limited groceries, other supplies available. Fuel includes marine gas, regular gasoline, diesel and kerosene. Fishing/hunting licenses available. Arts and crafts available for purchase include carved ivory and grass baskets.

This Eskimo village, located within Yukon Delta National Wildlife Refuge, is unincorporated. Many residents work seasonally in the summer commercial fishery or go to their own fish camps.

Communications include phones, mail plane, radio and TV. The community has 2 schools with grades kindergarten through 12. Community electric system. Water is hauled from a central watering point. Sewage system is honey buckets. Kwigillingok prohibits the sale and importation of alcoholic beverages. Freight arrives by plane and barge. Government address: Kwigillingok IRA Council, General Delivery, Kwigillingok, AK 99622; phone 588-8114. Village corporation address: Kwik Inc., General Delivery, Kwigillingok, AK 99622; phone 588-8112.

Lime Village

Located on the Stony River, 90 miles south of McGrath, 85 miles northwest of Lake Clark and 190 miles west of Anchorage. **Transportation:** Scheduled or charter air service from McGrath or Aniak. **Population:** 33. **Zip code:** 99627. **Emergency Services:** Alaska State Troopers, McGrath, phone 524-3222, or Aniak, phone 675-4352; Clinic; Volunteer Fire Department.

Elevation: 552 feet. **Climate:** Continental. Temperatures range from -47°F to 82°F. Precipitation averages 22 inches per year, with 85 inches of snowfall.

Private Aircraft: Airstrip adjacent north; elev. 552 feet; length 1,500 feet; gravel; no fuel; unattended. Runway condition not monitored, visual inspection recommended prior to using. Heavy winds in the fall and winter can limit air travel to the village for days at a time.

Visitor Facilities: None.

Lime Village is named for the nearby Lime Hills, composed almost entirely of limestone.

The earliest recorded settlement at the site was in 1907 when Paul, Evan and Zacar Constantinoff were year-round residents. The community was first cited in the 1939 census when it was called Hungry Village, a name that was reportedly coined by prospectors after they starved along nearby Hungry Creek.

A Russian Orthodox chapel, Saints Constantine and Helen, was constructed in 1923 and is on the National Register of Historic Places. A state school was established in 1974.

Income in Lime Village is primarily from government programs, supplemented by subsistence activities. Lime Village residents hunt black and brown bear, moose, caribou, waterfowl and ptarmigan. Seasonal fishing is for red, king, silver and chum salmon; whitefish, pike and grayling. Additional income comes from trapping and selling the pelts of beaver, muskrat, marten, mink, fox, lynx and wolverine. In the fall, blueberries, raspberries, highbush and lowbush cranberries and salmonberries are harvested.

Communication is by single-sideband radio. AM/FM radio reception is good, but TV signals are not received. Lime Village has 1 phone, 648-8001, located in the clinic. The community has a school that offers grades preschool through 12 based on demand. Electricity is from private generators. Water is hauled from the school well. Sewage system is honey buckets. Freight arrives by mail plane. Government address: Lime Village Traditional Council, General Delivery, Lime Village, AK 99627. Village corporation address: Lime Village Co., General Delivery, Lime Village, AK 99627.

Lower Kalskag

Located on the Kuskokwim River, 65 miles north of Bethel and 350 miles west of Anchorage. **Transportation:** Scheduled air service from Bethel. **Population:** 273. **Zip code:** 99626. **Emergency Services:** Village Public Safety Officer; Clinic; Volunteer Fire Department.

Climate: Semiarctic with maritime influences from the Bering Sea. Annual precipitation 19 inches with 60 inches of snow.

Private Aircraft: Kalskag airport 2 miles upriver; elev. 49 feet; length 3,200 feet; gravel; no fuel; runway condition not monitored; visual inspection recommended prior to using. Runway is maintained by the state. Kalskag also has a grader to service the runway and main road between Upper and Lower Kalskag. Airport serves both Upper and Lower Kalskag. Transportation into village available.

Visitor Facilities: Arrangements may be

made to stay at the school, phone 471-2318. Restaurant located in the community. No laundromat or banking services. Supplies available at a general store. Fishing/hunting licenses available. No guide or repair services. No rental transportation or moorage facilities. Fuel available: marine gas, diesel.

The site of this Eskimo village originally was used as a fish camp for families from Upper Kalskag. It wasn't until 1930 that people began living in Lower Kalskag year-round. The upper village was a Roman Catholic center and because of religious differences many of its residents moved to Lower Kalskag after the Russian Orthodox Chapel of St. Seraphim (now on the National Register of Historic Places) was built in 1940. Lower Kalskag was incorporated as a second-class city in 1969. It is located within Yukon Delta National Wildlife Refuge.

Lower Kalskag's economy is based primarily on subsistence activities. Employment is largely limited to public programs. Hunting is for moose, black bear, rabbit, game birds, porcupine and waterfowl; fishing for salmon, pike, whitefish, blackfish and eel; and trapping for muskrat, beaver, lynx, otter, wolverine and mink. In addition, the tundra yields raspberries, cranberries, blackberries, blueberries, strawberries and currants.

Communications include phones, mail plane, radio and TV. The community is served by 2 Russian Orthodox churches and 2 schools with grades 1 through 12. There are community electricity, water and sewer systems. Freight is transported by plane and barge. Government address: City of Lower Kalskag, P.O. Box 81, Lower Kalskag, AK 99626; phone 471-2228. Village corporation address: The Kuskokwim Corp., 429 D St., Suite 307, Anchorage, AK 99501; phone 276-2101.

Marshall

(Also known as Fortuna Ledge.) Located on Poltes Slough, north of Arbor Island on the east bank of the Yukon River in the Yukon-Kuskokwim delta, 75 miles north of Bethel, 400 miles west-northwest of Anchorage. **Transportation:** Boat; scheduled or charter air service from Bethel. **Population:** 270. **Zip code:** 99585. **Emergency Services:** Village Public Safety Officer; Alaska State Troopers, Bethel; Health aide, phone 679-6226; Volunteer Fire Department.

Climate: Temperatures range between -54° and 86°F. Rainfall measures 16 inches a year; the growing season lasts 100 days.

Private Aircraft: Airstrip 1 mile southeast; elev. 90 feet; length 1,700 feet; gravel; no fuel; unattended. Runway condition not monitored, visual inspection recommended prior to using. No airport facilities. Transportation to town for scheduled flights.

Visitor Facilities: Accommodations available. No restaurant, banking services or laundromat. Groceries, clothing, first-aid supplies, hardware, camera film and sporting goods available in the community. Arts and crafts available for purchase include fur and beadwork. Fishing/hunting licenses available. No guide service. Marine engine repair available. Arrangements can be made to rent boats or off-road vehicles. Fuel available includes marine gas, diesel, propane and regular gasoline. No moorage facilities.

This community has been known by several names since it was first recorded in 1880. After gold was discovered on a nearby creek in 1913, the settlement quickly became a placer mining camp and riverboat landing known as Fortuna Ledge, named after Fortuna Hunter, the first child born in the camp. Later the village was named for Thomas Riley Marshall, vice president of the United States under Woodrow Wilson from 1913-21; at that time the village was known as Marshall's Landing. It was incorporated as a second-class city named Fortuna Ledge in 1970, but also was commonly referred to as Marshall. The community officially became Marshall in 1984.

Marshall residents work primarily during the summer salmon season, either in fishing or processing. Other seasonal employment includes firefighting for the Bureau of Land Management. A few year-round jobs are available through the local government, school, village corporation and businesses. Income is supplemented by subsistence activities. Residents hunt black and brown bear, moose, rabbit, waterfowl and ptarmigan, and fish for salmon, whitefish, blackfish, sheefish, lush (burbot) and pike. In the fall, families harvest blueberries, blackberries, cranberries and salmonberries. Some residents also trap beaver, lynx, mink, otter and red fox.

Marshall is located at the northeastern boundary of Yukon Delta National Wildlife Refuge.

There are 2 gold mines in the area, which are reached by all-terrain vehicles.

Communications include phones, mail plane, radio and TV. The community is served by Russian Orthodox and Catholic churches. There are community electricity, water and sewer systems. Marshall prohibits the possession of alcoholic beverages. Freight arrives by cargo plane and barge. Government address: City of Marshall, General Delivery, Marshall,

AK 99585; phone 679-6415. Village corporation address: Maserculiq Inc., General Delivery, Marshall, AK 99585; phone 679-6512.

Mekoryuk

(ma-KOR-ee-yuk) Located in the Bering Sea on Nunivak Island, 210 miles west of Bethel, 600 miles west of Anchorage. **Transportation:** Scheduled and charter air service from Bethel. **Population:** 173. **Zip code:** 99630. **Emergency Services:** Village Public Safety Officer, phone 827-8315; Alaska State Troopers, Bethel; Clinic, phone 827-8111; Volunteer Fire Department.

Elevation: 40 feet. **Climate:** Summer weather cool and rainy, with temperatures averaging 50° to 60°F. Winters average temperature around 0°F, but gets down to -30°F. Wind chill can force the temperature to -100°F. Mean annual precipitation 15 inches; mean annual snowfall 57 inches.

Private Aircraft: Airstrip 3 miles west; elev. 48 feet; length 3,000 feet; gravel; no fuel; unattended. Runway condition not monitored, visual inspection recommended prior to using. Runway soft during heavy rains or spring breakup. Animals occasionally on runway. No airport facilities. Public transportation into village available.

Visitor Facilities: Accommodations in private homes or at the high school for $10 per night, phone 827-8415. No restaurant, banking services or laundromat. Groceries, clothing, first-aid supplies, hardware, camera film and sporting goods available in the community. During school days lunches available at the school. Arts and crafts available for purchase include carved ivory, grass baskets, masks and fur garments. Fishing/hunting licenses available. Guide services, including lodging and meals, available. No repair service. Private boats available for charter. Fuel available includes marine gas, propane, unleaded and regular gasoline. No moorage facilities.

Mekoryuk is the only community on Nunivak Island which is part of Yukon Delta National Wildlife Refuge. Approximately half the island is classified as wilderness. Nunivak, third-largest island in Alaska, measures 60 miles long by 40 miles wide. The federal government built a school at Mekoryuk because its well-protected bay made it easy to unload goods.

The people here live mostly off the land and sea, although there are a few federal government jobs. A 21-unit housing project was completed in late 1988. Many of the residents go to fish camps around the island

during the summer. According to one resident, villagers hunt birds, walrus, seal, and red and arctic fox. The island has many rivers offering excellent fishing for salmon, trout, char and grayling, including the Mekoryuk River which runs by the village. Halibut and cod are caught in the Bering Sea. Many of the people also are involved in reindeer herding and the roundups that take place usually in July. Approximately 3,000 head of reindeer roam the island, along with 400 head of musk-ox, which were introduced in the 1930s. People come from all over the world to hunt musk-ox during annual permit hunts.

Some of the finest ivory carving in the world is done here. Villagers also make unique wooden masks and knit *qiviut* wool from musk-ox into lacy garments which are sold in Anchorage.

The island supports many species of birds, including ducks, geese, swans, murres, puffins, cormorants, several varieties of loon, ptarmigan and arctic tern.

Attractions for visitors include wilderness trips to see and photograph musk-ox, reindeer, seal, walrus and birds. Advance arrangements should be made for lodging and meals.

Communications in Mekoryuk, a second-class city incorporated in 1969, include phones, mail plane, radio and TV. The community is served by a Covenant church and 2 schools with grades preschool through 12. There are community electricity and water. Sewage system is honey buckets. Mekoryuk prohibits the possession of alcoholic beverages. Freight arrives in the community by cargo plane and barge. Government address: City of Mekoryuk, P.O. Box 29, Mekoryuk, AK 99630; phone 827-8314. Village corporation address: Nima Corp., General Delivery, Mekoryuk, AK 99630; phone 827-8313.

Mountain Village

Located on the Yukon River, 20 miles west of St. Marys, 470 miles west-northwest of Anchorage. **Transportation:** Scheduled or charter air service from Nome or Bethel, and direct air service from Anchorage. **Population:** 665. **Zip code:** 99632. **Emergency Services:** Village Public Safety Officer; Village Public Officer; Alaska State Troopers, St. Marys, phone 438-2018; Area Clinic, phone 591-2926; Volunteer Fire Department.

Elevation: 40 feet. **Climate:** Both maritime and continental influences. Winters long and cold; summers short and cool, often cloudy but with little rainfall. Mean annual precipitation 17 inches; mean annual snowfall 45 inches.

Private Aircraft: Airstrip adjacent north-east; elev. 165 feet; length 2,200 feet; gravel; no fuel; unattended. Runway condition not monitored, visual inspection recommended prior to using. No airport facilities or public transportation into village.

Visitor Facilities: Accommodations available through the city of Mountain Village, phone 591-2929. There is a restaurant, but no laundromat or banking services. Groceries, clothing, first-aid supplies, hardware, camera film and sporting goods available in the community. Arts and crafts available for purchase include grass baskets and Eskimo clothing. Fishing/hunting licenses available. No guide service. Marine engine repair available. Autos and charter aircraft can be rented. Fuel available includes marine gas, propane and regular gasoline. There is a village marina.

Mountain Village was named because of its location at the foot of the first "mountain" encountered by those traveling up the Yukon River. Mountain Village was a summer fish camp site until the opening of a general store in the village in 1908 prompted immigration by the residents of 2 small upriver settlements. A salmon saltery was built in 1956 and a cannery in 1964. Mountain Village became a regional educational center after it was selected as headquarters for the Lower Yukon School District in 1976. It is a second-class city, incorporated in 1967.

The town's economy is expanding due to its relative accessibility, growing fishing industry and its function as a regional education center. The school district, village corporation, government and local business provide year-round employment for about 70 people. This income is supplemented by subsistence hunting and fishing for moose, swan, geese, ducks, salmon, blackfish, sheefish, whitefish, burbot, grayling and pike. Income also is obtained from trapping beaver, muskrat, otter, mink and fox.

Mountain Village is located within Yukon Delta National Wildlife Refuge. A 17.7-mile road links Mountain Village with the communities of Pitka's Point, St. Marys and Andreafsky.

Communications at Mountain Village include phones, mail plane, radio and TV. The community is served by 3 churches and a school with grades kindergarten through 12. There are community electricity, water and sewer systems. Mountain Village prohibits the sale and importation of alcoholic beverages. Freight arrives by cargo plane and barge. Government address: City of Mountain

Village, P.O. Box 32085, Mountain Village, AK 99632; phone 591-2929. Village corporation address: Azachorak Inc., P.O. Box 213, Mountain Village, AK 99632; phone 591-2026 or 2027.

Napaimute

(na-PAI-mute) Located on the Kuskokwim River in the Kilbuck-Kuskokwim Mountains, 28 miles east of Aniak, 120 miles northeast of Bethel and 285 miles west of Anchorage. **Transportation:** Charter air service from Aniak or Bethel, riverboats, snow machines or dogsleds. **Population:** 2 permanent; 30 part time. **Zip code:** 99557. **Emergency Services:** Alaska State Troopers, Aniak.

Elevation: 200 feet. **Climate:** Napaimute's climate is continental. Annual precipitation averages 20 inches, with 85 inches of snow.

Private Aircraft: No airstrip; floatplanes land on river.

Visitor Facilities: None.

Napaimute, which reportedly means "forest people," was once called Hoffmans after George W. Hoffman, an Englishman who established a trading post at the site in 1906. The modern-day village grew around the trading post and was primarily occupied by non-Natives, although a significant number of Eskimo residents also lived here. Hoffman built a territorial school in the village in 1920. In 1942 the village had 47 residents. By the early 1950s, most residents had moved to nearby settlements, particularly Aniak. Reportedly there are only 2 permanent residents at Napaimute, although there are a few other permanent residents a few miles upriver and as many as 30 part-time residents arrive during the summer fishing season. Napaimute is unincorporated.

Communication is by a single-sideband radio; there are no phones. There is no school. Electricity is provided by private generators; rain water is collected or river water is hauled; sewage system is honey buckets or the community privy. Village corporation address: The Kuskokwim Corp., 429 D St., Anchorage, AK 99501; phone 276-2101.

Napakiak

(na-PAK-ee-ack) Located at the head of Kuskokwim Bay, 10 miles southwest of Bethel, 410 miles west of Anchorage. **Transportation:** Scheduled air service from Bethel. **Population:** 353. **Zip code:** 99634. **Emergency Services:** Police, phone 589-2920; Clinic, phone 589-2711; Volunteer Fire Department.

Private Aircraft: Airstrip adjacent west;

elev. 20 feet; length 2,100 feet; gravel; fuel information unavailable; unattended. Runway condition not monitored, visual inspection recommended prior to using. Unmarked poles located 200 feet west and 260 feet east of approach for runway 16.

Visitor Facilities: Arrangements may be made for accommodations at the school, phone 589-2420. There is a washeteria. Supplies available in the community. Fishing/hunting licenses available. Boats may be rented. Information on guide and repair service and fuel unavailable.

This Eskimo community reportedly was established around 1890 by residents of an older village that had been located at the mouth of the Johnson River and also was known as Napakiak. A Moravian Church chapel was dedicated in 1930, a Bureau of Indian Affairs school opened in 1939 and an airport was completed in 1973. Napakiak was incorporated as a second-class city in 1970. It is located within Yukon Delta National Wildlife Refuge. Many residents may be gone to fish camps during the summer.

Napakiak's school has grades kindergarten through 12. There are community electricity and water systems. Sewage system is honey buckets. Napakiak prohibits the possession of alcoholic beverages. Freight arrives by plane and barge. Government address: City of Napakiak, General Delivery, Napakiak, AK 99634; phone 589-2611. Village corporation address: Napakiak Corp., General Delivery, Napakiak, AK 99634; phone 589-2227.

Napaskiak

(na-PASS-key-ack) Located on the Kuskokwim River 8 miles southwest of Bethel, 400 miles west of Anchorage. **Transportation:** Scheduled air service from Bethel and winter air and river taxi service. **Population:** 311. **Zip code:** 99559. **Emergency Services:** Police; Alaska State Troopers, Bethel, phone 543-3494; Clinic, phone 737-7329; Volunteer Fire Department.

Private Aircraft: Airstrip adjacent south; elev. 24 feet; length 2,400 feet; gravel; no fuel; unattended. Runway condition not monitored, visual inspection recommended prior to using. Center of runway is 20 feet of gravel. Runway rough due to dips and ruts, and it floods in spring.

Visitor Facilities: Accommodations at city building, phone 737-7626. Supplies available in the community. Fishing/hunting licenses not available. Fuel available for snow machines, boat motors, and 3- and 4-wheelers. Information on other visitor

services and facilities unavailable.

This Eskimo community may have been established around 1800 by residents of another village forced to move because of erosion. The population in 1880 was 196. Many people died in the influenza and measles epidemics of 1900 and the village was abandoned for a time.

In 1905 the first Russian Orthodox priest arrived and baptized the entire village. St. Jacob's Chapel, listed on the National Register of Historic Places, was built in 1931; a new church was constructed in 1978.

A Bureau of Indian Affairs school opened in 1939 and an airport was completed in 1974. Napaskiak, which is located within Yukon Delta National Wildlife Refuge, was incorporated as a second-class city in 1971. Many residents leave town during the summer season to go to fish camps.

The community is served by 2 schools with grades kindergarten through 12. There is a community electricity system and water supply. Sewage system is honey buckets. Napaskiak prohibits the sale and importation of alcoholic beverages. Freight arrives by plane and barge. Government address: City of Napaskiak, General Delivery, Napaskiak, AK 99559; phone 737-7626. Village corporation address: Napaskiak Inc., General Delivery, Napaskiak, AK 99559; phone 737-7413.

Newtok

Located north of Nelson Island on the Kealavik River, 90 miles west-northwest of Bethel, 500 miles west of Anchorage. **Transportation:** Scheduled air service from Bethel. **Population:** 213. **Zip code:** 99559. **Emergency Services:** Alaska State Troopers, Bethel, phone 543-3494; Clinic, phone 237-2111; Volunteer Fire Department.

Private Aircraft: Airstrip 1 mile west; elev. 25 feet; length 2,100 feet; gravel; no fuel; unattended. Runway condition not monitored, visual inspection recommended prior to using.

Visitor Facilities: Supplies available in the community. Fishing/hunting licenses not available. Information on other visitor services and facilities unavailable.

Newtok, located within Yukon Delta National Wildlife Refuge, is a relatively new village established around 1949. It was incorporated as a second-class city in 1976. Many residents go to fish camps during the summer.

Newtok has a Catholic church and 2 schools with grades 1 through 12. There is a community electricity system. Water is hauled from a central watering point or ponds and rain water is collected. Sewage system is honey buckets. Newtok prohibits the sale and importation of alcoholic beverages. Freight arrives by mail plane and barge. Government address: City of Newtok, General Delivery, Newtok, AK 99559; phone 237-2315. Village corporation address: Newtok Corp., General Delivery, Newtok, AK 99559; phone 237-2320.

Nightmute

Located on the Toksook River on Nelson Island in the Bering Sea, 105 miles west of Bethel, 510 miles west of Anchorage. **Transportation:** Scheduled and charter air service from Bethel. **Population:** 153. **Zip code:** 99690. **Emergency Services:** Village Public Safety Officer, Toksook Bay; Alaska State Troopers, Bethel; Health aide, phone 647-6312; Volunteer Fire Department.

Private Aircraft: Airstrip 2 miles north; elev. 14 feet; length 1,600 feet; gravel; no fuel; unattended. Runway condition not monitored, visual inspection recommended prior to using.

Visitor Facilities: Arrangements may be made for accommodations in private homes; contact the city of Nightmute, phone 647-6426. Lodging also may be available at the school, phone 647-6313. Meals available at the high school in winter. No banking services or laundromat. Groceries, clothing, first-aid supplies, hardware and camera film available in the community. Arts and crafts available for purchase include carved ivory, grass baskets and fur garments. Fishing/hunting licenses not available. Guide service available. No repair services or rental transportation. Fuel available includes marine gas, diesel and regular gasoline. Moorage facilities available.

According to local residents, the village grew as Native people gradually moved to Nelson Island. The Bureau of Indian Affairs established a school in the 1950s. Nightmute lost population in 1964 when many residents moved to Toksook Bay, 15 miles to the northwest, but the community was incorporated as a second-class city in 1974.

Nightmute is located within Yukon Delta National Wildlife Refuge.

Residents work at seasonal jobs and engage in subsistence hunting for geese, ducks, rabbits, cranes, swans, ptarmigan, fox, beaver, muskrat, otter and mink. Fishing is for herring, king, silver, red and pink salmon, halibut, devil fish and pike.

Most of the residents go to fish camp at Umkumute, 18 miles from Nightmute during the summer.

Communications at Nightmute include phones, mail plane and TV. The community is served by a church and 2 schools with grades kindergarten through 12. There is a community electricity system. Water is hauled from a central watering point. Sewage system is honey buckets. Freight arrives by cargo plane and barge. Government address: City of Nightmute, Nelson Island, Nightmute, AK 99690; phone 647-6426. Village corporation address: NGTA Ltd., General Delivery, Nightmute, AK 99690; phone 647-6115.

Nunapitchuk

(nu-NA-pit-CHUCK) Located on Johnson River 30 miles northwest of Bethel and 425 miles west of Anchorage. **Transportation:** Scheduled air service from Bethel. **Population:** 365. **Zip code:** 99641. **Emergency Services:** Police, phone 527-5718; Clinic, phone 527-5329; Volunteer Fire Department.

Climate: Transitional zone. Mean July maximum temperature 62°F; mean January minimum temperature 13°F. The village endures lots of wind and blowing snow in the winter, according to one resident.

Private Aircraft: Airstrip east of village; elev. 12 feet; length 2,000 feet; gravel; unattended. Runway condition not monitored, recommend visual inspection prior to using. There is a freight terminal and public transportation from airport. Seaplane base with small float on the river.

Visitor Facilities: Three rooms with kitchen area available at IRA Council building; contact the city office, phone 527-5327, to make arrangements. No restaurant or banking services. Washeteria available. Groceries, clothing, first-aid supplies, hardware, camera film and sporting goods available in the community. Arts and crafts available for purchase include otter parkas, beaver hats, mukluks, knitted gloves and earrings. Fishing/hunting licenses available at the city office. Marine engine repair available. No guide service. Private off-road vehicles and boats may be rented. Fuel available: propane, regular gasoline. No moorage facilities.

In the 1930s, there were 5 or 6 families in the settlement. More families moved to the area after the federal government built a school in the 1940s. Nunapitchuk has an IRA (Indian Reorganization Act) Council that was established in the 1940s. It also had a second-class city government that was incorporated with Kasigluk in 1969 as the city of Akolmiut. In October 1982 they split and went back to their individual status as second-class cities.

Residents depend on commercial fishing and subsistence activities. They hunt for moose, caribou and small game and fish for salmon and pike. They also trap for mink, muskrat, fox and land otters.

Communications include phones, mail plane, radio and TV. The community is served by Russian Orthodox, Moravian and Pentacostal churches, and a school with grades preschool through 12. There is an AVEC electricity system. Water is hauled from wells or the washeteria, or rain water is collected. Sewage system is honey buckets. Freight arrives by air transport and barge. The village bans the possession of alcoholic beverages. Government address: City of Nunapitchuk, c/o City Clerk, P.O. Box 190, Nunapitchuk, AK 99641; phone 527-5327. Village corporation address: Nunapitchuk Limited, P.O. Box 129, Nunapitchuk, AK 99641; phone 527-5717.

Oscarville

Located on the north shore of the Kuskokwim River across from Napaskiak, 5 miles south of Bethel, 400 miles west of Anchorage. **Transportation:** Boat, snow machine and float-plane service from Bethel. **Population:** 39. **Zip code:** 99695. **Emergency Services:** Alaska State Troopers, Bethel, phone 543-3949; Clinic.

Visitor Facilities: Arrangements for accommodations may be made by contacting the school, phone 737-7214. Supplies may be available at a general store. Fishing/hunting licenses are not available. Information on other facilities not available.

In about 1906, a man named Oscar Samuelson, born in Norway in 1876, and his Eskimo wife moved to Napaskiak and opened a small store. Samuelson became a mail carrier and in 1908 the Samuelsons moved across the river to what became known as Oscarville. Samuelson opened another small store that he ran until his death in 1953. His daughter and subsequent owners have operated the store. The first school opened in 1964. Oscarville is unincorporated.

Oscarville is served by a 2-teacher school with grades kindergarten through 12 depending on demand. Electricity is from individual generators. Water is hauled from the school well and ponds or rain water is collected. Sewage system is honey buckets. Freight arrives by plane or barge. Village corporation address: Oscarville Native Corp., General Delivery, Oscarville, AK 99695; phone 543-2066.

Pilot Station

Located on the Yukon River, 11 miles east of St. Marys and 26 miles west of Marshall in the Yukon-Kuskokwim Delta, 430 miles west of Anchorage. **Transportation:** Scheduled and charter air service from Bethel. **Population:** 455. **Zip code:** 99650. **Emergency Services:** Village Public Safety Officer, phone 549-3213; Alaska State Troopers, St. Marys, phone 438-2019; Clinic, phone 549-3728; Volunteer Fire Department.

Climate: More maritime than continental, averaging 60 inches of snowfall and 16 inches of precipitation per year.

Private Aircraft: Airstrip 1 mile southwest; elev. 275 feet; length 3,000 feet; gravel; no fuel; unattended. Runway condition not monitored, visual inspection recommended prior to using. Heavy winds in fall and winter and crosswinds up to 50 mph year-round often limit access. No airport facilities. Transportation usually available for arriving passengers.

Visitor Facilities: Accommodations available. No restaurant, banking services or laundromat. Groceries, clothing, first-aid supplies and camera film available in the community. Arts and crafts available for purchase include carved ivory, wood carvings, grass and birch-bark baskets and masks. Fishing/hunting licenses available. No guide or major repair services. Rental transportation includes boats, off-road vehicles and charter aircraft. Fuel available includes propane, kerosene, marine gas and regular gasoline. No moorage facilities.

This Eskimo village was first called Ankachak, but later moved 0.3 mile upstream to another site called Potiliuk. R.H. Sargent of the U.S. Geological Survey noted that the village name was Pilot Station in 1916. Local riverboat pilots who used the village as a checkpoint were responsible for the name change.

Employment in Pilot Station is primarily related to the summer fishing season, supplemented with year-round enterprises and subsistence activities. There also is summer firefighting work with BLM.

Residents hunt black bear, moose, ptarmigan, waterfowl and porcupine, and fish for salmon, whitefish, blackfish, sheefish and pike. Berries are harvested in the fall. Income also is earned from trapping beaver, muskrat, marten, fox, lynx and wolverine.

Near Pilot Station is the old village site of Kurgpallermuit, designated by the Calista Regional Corp. as a historic place because it was occupied during bow and arrow wars between the Yukon and Coastal Eskimos.

Pilot Station is located within Yukon Delta National Wildlife Refuge. Favorite leisure activites include Eskimo dancing, square dancing, otlatches, and dog and snow machine racing.

Communications at Pilot Station, a second-class city incorporated in 1969, include phones, mail plane, radio and TV. The community is served by 2 churches and a school with grades kindergarten through 12. There are community electricity, water and sewer systems. Pilot Station prohibits the sale and importation of alcoholic beverages. Freight arrives by cargo plane and barge. Government address: City of Pilot Station, P.O. Box 5040, Pilot Station, AK 99650; phone 549-3211. Village corporation address: Pilot Station Native Corp., General Delivery, Pilot Station, AK 99650; phone 549-3512.

Pitkas Point

Located near the junction of the Yukon and Andreafsky rivers, 5 miles northwest of St. Marys and Andreafsky, 445 miles west of Anchorage. **Transportation:** Scheduled airline from Bethel to St. Marys airport. **Population:** 67. **Zip code:** 99658. **Emergency Services:** Alaska State Troopers, St. Marys, phone 438-2019; Pitkas Point Clinic, phone 438-2546.

Climate: Both maritime and continental. Temperatures range from -44°F to 83°F at St. Marys. Annual precipitation 16 inches, with 60 inches of snow.

Private Aircraft: See St. Marys airport.

Visitor Facilities: Accommodations and supplies available in St. Marys. No accommodations, restaurant or banking services in Pitkas Point. There is a laundromat with showers. No arts and crafts available for purchase. Fishing/hunting licenses available at St. Marys. No guide service available. Repair service available for marine engines and boats in St. Marys. Autos may be rented for $70 a day. Fuel available includes marine gas, diesel, propane and regular gasoline. No moorage facilities.

Eskimos who first settled here called the village Nigiklik, a Yup'ik word meaning "to the north." The settlement was first reported by the U.S. Geological Survey in 1898. It was later renamed for a trader who opened a general store there, which was a branch of the Northern Commercial Co. station at nearby Andreafsky. Pitkas Point is unincorporated.

The village economy peaks during the summer fishing season when most residents are involved in commercial salmon fishing. Summer also provides work in construction and firefighting for BLM. There also are a few full-time jobs held by local people.

Public assistance payments and subsistence activities supplement this income. Residents of the area hunt moose, bear, hare, duck, geese, swan and ptarmigan. In the fall, berries are harvested from the surrounding tundra. Some income also is derived from trapping beaver, fox and otter.

Pitkas Point is surrounded by Yukon Delta National Wildlife Refuge.

The village is connected by a 17.7-mile road to St. Marys and Mountain Village. In winter, snow machines often are used for intervillage travel.

Communications in Pitkas Point include phones, mail plane and TV. The community is served by a Russian Orthodox church and a school with grades kindergarten through 12. There is a community electricity system. Water is hauled from the laundromat building. Sewage system is honey buckets. Freight arrives by cargo plane and barge. Government address: Pitkas Point Village Council, General Delivery, Pitkas Point, AK 99658; phone 438-2012. Village corporation address: Pitkas Point Native Corp., General Delivery, Pitkas Point, AK 99658; phone 438-2232.

Platinum

Located on Goodnews Bay, 11 miles southwest of Goodnews Bay village, 135 miles south of Bethel, 445 miles southwest of Anchorage. **Transportation:** Scheduled air service from Bethel. **Population:** 62. **Zip code:** 99651. **Emergency Services:** Volunteer Fire Department.

Elevation: 20 feet. **Climate:** Summers are mild, with cool winds and some rain, according to one resident. Mean annual precipitation 22 inches; mean annual snowfall 43 inches.

Private Aircraft: Airstrip adjacent west; elev. 9 feet; length 3,800 feet; gravel; no fuel; unattended. Runway condition not monitored, visual inspection recommended prior to using. Runway soft when wet.

Visitor Facilities: Arrangements may be made for accommodations at the school, phone 979-9111. No restaurant, banking services or laundromat. Supplies available in the community. Fishing/hunting licenses available. No guide services or rental transportation. Fuel available includes diesel, propane and regular gasoline. No moorage facilities.

Platinum got its name from an important lode of platinum that was discovered nearby in 1926 by an Eskimo named Walter Smith. The community was described as a boom town with 50 residents in 1937. The population reached a high of 72 in 1950. Platinum is a second-class city, incorporated in 1975.

People in Platinum work seasonally in commercial fishing, and also in the stores, post office, school and other odd jobs. Subsistence hunting and fishing are also important.

Residents fish in Goodnews Bay or up the Goodnews River for king, red and chum salmon and Dolly Varden. Hunting is for seal, sea lion, walrus, fox, rabbit, squirrel, otters, beaver, mink, muskrat, ptarmigan, geese, ducks and sandpipers.

A long beach at Platinum offers good beachcombing, and the community is located within Togiak National Wildlife Refuge.

Communications at Platinum include phones and mail plane. The community is served by a church and a school with grades preschool through 12. There is a community electricity system. Water is hauled from a central watering point. Sewage system is honey buckets. Platinum prohibits the sale and importation of alcoholic beverages. Freight arrives by barge or mail plane. Government address: City of Platinum, P.O. Box 28, Platinum, AK 99651; phone 979-8114. Village corporation address: Arviq Inc., General Delivery, Platinum, AK 99651; phone 979-8113.

Quinhagak

(QUIN-a-hock) Located on the southeast shore of Kuskokwim Bay, 70 miles south of Bethel, 425 miles west of Anchorage. **Transportation:** Boat; scheduled and charter air service from Bethel. **Population:** 493. **Zip code:** 99655. **Emergency Services:** Police, phone 556-8314; Clinic, phone 556-8320; Volunteer Fire Department.

Private Aircraft: Airstrip 1 mile northeast; elev. 10 feet; length 2,700 feet; gravel; no fuel; unattended. Runway condition not monitored, visual inspection recommended prior to using. Potholes entire length of runway. Equipment occasionally on runway. No airport facilities or public transportation into village.

Visitor Facilities: No hotel, restaurant or banking services. Laundry and shower facilities available. Groceries, clothing, first-aid supplies, hardware, camera film and sporting goods available in the community. Arts and crafts available include carved ivory, grass baskets and Eskimo yo-yos. Fishing/hunting licenses available, as well as guide service. Marine engine repair available, also air charter

service. No rental transportation. Fuel available: marine gas, diesel, propane, regular gasoline. No moorage facilities.

Private sportfishing is prohibited on all property owned by the village corporation. All sportfishing must be from a boat, on state-owned land or with a guide.

This Eskimo village was reported by Lieutenant Sarichev in 1826. In 1975, Quinhagak was incorporated as a second-class city.

The village is located within Togiak National Wildlife Refuge.

Communications in Quinhagak include phones, mail plane, radio and TV. There is a community electricity system. Water is hauled from the washeteria. Sewage system is honey buckets. The village prohibits the possession of alcoholic beverages. Freight arrives by barge. Government address: City of Quinhagak, P.O. Box 58, Quinhagak, AK 99655; phone 556-8315. Village corporation address: Quanirtuuq Inc., General Delivery, Quinhagak, AK 99655; phone 556-8211.

Red Devil

Located on the upper Kuskokwim River at the mouth of Red Devil Creek, 8 miles west of Sleetmute, 73 miles east of Aniak, 250 miles west of Anchorage. **Transportation:** Boat; scheduled and charter air service from Bethel or Aniak. **Population:** 27. **Zip code:** 99656. **Emergency Services:** Alaska State Troopers, Aniak; Health aide; Volunteer Fire Department.

Climate: Continental. At nearby Sleetmute, temperatures range between -58° and 90°F. Annual precipitation is 20 inches, with 85 inches of snow.

Private Aircraft: Airstrip 1 mile northwest; elev. 210 feet; length 5,200 feet; gravel; no fuel; unattended. Runway condition not monitored, visual inspection recommended prior to using. No airport facilities or public transportation.

Visitor Facilities: Accommodations and meals available. No banking services or laundromat available. Groceries available at combination roadhouse/bar/store. Hand-sewn fur items available for purchase. Fishing/hunting licenses available. No guide or repair services. Rental transportation includes boats and charter aircraft through local air service. Fuel available: marine gas, diesel and regular gasoline. No moorage facilities.

The village was named after the Red Devil Mine, which was established in 1933 by Hans Halverson after numerous quicksilver deposits were discovered earlier in the surrounding Kilbuck-Kuskokwim Mountains. The mine operated from 1939 to 1946 as the Kuskokwim Mining Co. and was reopened in 1952 as the DeCourcy Mountain Mining Co. Inc. The mine was last worked in 1971 when the mercury, cinnabar and antimony reserves were depleted. By that year the mine had produced some 2.7 million pounds of mercury — Alaska's total output. By 1971 a community had developed at the mining site. A school was established in 1958. The population was 152 in 1960, but declined when mine closed.

In the summer of 1989 access to the inactive mine was closed because of a chemical hazard. An investigation revealed stored quantities of copper sulfate, potash and sodium hydroxide. In 1988, the federal Bureau of Land Management posted signs warning of potential health hazards and later removed 2 transformers containing polychlorinated byphenyls, or PCBs.

Employment opportunities in Red Devil today are limited. A few residents work for the school district, post office, clinic, store and flying service. There also is employment through the BLM's summer firefighting program. This income is supplemented by public assistance payments and subsistence activities. Local residents hunt bear, moose, caribou, rabbit, ptarmigan and waterfowl, and fish for king, chum, red and silver salmon, sheefish and whitefish. Trapping for marten, beaver, mink, wolverine, fox, otter and lynx also provides income.

Communications in Red Devil, which is unincorporated, include a phone (447-9901), mail plane, radio and TV. The community has a school with grades preschool through 12, but no church. Electricity is supplied by Middle Kuskokwim Electric Corp.; water is from private wells or the river. Sewage system is septic tanks or privies. Freight arrives by cargo plane and barge. Village corporation address: The Kuskokwim Corp., 429 D St., Suite 307, Anchorage, AK 99501; phone 276-2101.

Russian Mission

Located on the Yukon River, 70 miles north of Bethel, 225 miles west-northwest of Anchorage. **Transportation:** Scheduled and charter air service from Bethel. **Population:** 231. **Zip code:** 99657. **Emergency Services:** Village Public Safety Officer; Alaska State Troopers, St. Marys; Volunteer Fire Department.

Elevation: 50 feet. **Climate:** Both maritime and continental, with a greater maritime influence. Annual precipitation 16 inches; annual snowfall 60 inches.

Private Aircraft: Airstrip adjacent south;

elev. 70 feet; length 2,700 feet; gravel; unattended. Runway condition not monitored, visual inspection recommended prior to using. Airport has lighting system. No public transportation to village.

Visitor Facilities: Arrangements can be made for accommodations in private homes. Lodging also may be available at the school, phone 584-5126. No restaurant, laundromat or banking services. Groceries, limited clothing, hardware and sporting goods available in the community. Arts and crafts available for purchase include birch-bark baskets and masks. Fishing/hunting licenses available. No guide services or rental transportation. Marine engine and boat repairs available. Fuel available: diesel, propane and regular gasoline. No moorage facilities.

The first Russian-American Co. fur-trading post was established at this village in 1837, but the Eskimos held the outsiders responsible for the smallpox epidemic that followed in 1838-39 and massacred the post's inhabitants. The first Russian Orthodox mission in the interior of Alaska was established here in 1851 by a Russian-Aleut priest, Jacob Netzuetov. Originally called Pokrovskaya Mission, the title Russian Mission replaced the previous name in 1900. The village was incorporated as a second-class city in 1970.

Employment opportunities in Russian Mission are concentrated in commercial fishing and public employment programs. Most residents of the community are directly or indirectly involved in commercial fishing from June through September. There are a few full-time jobs at the 2 local stores, the post office and the clinic. Summer work also includes firefighting for BLM. This income is supplemented by subsistence activities. Residents hunt moose, black bear, ptarmigan, waterfowl, porcupine and rabbit. They fish for salmon, blackfish, whitefish, sheefish, pike and lush (burbot). Berries are harvested in the fall. Income also comes from trapping beaver, mink, lynx, marten and fox.

Communications include phones, mail plane, radio and TV. The community is served by Russian Orthodox and Catholic churches and a school with grades kindergarten through 12. There are community electricity, water and sewage systems. Freight arrives by cargo plane and barge. Sale and importation of alcoholic beverages are banned. Government address: City of Russian Mission, P.O. Box 49, Russian Mission, AK 99657; phone 584-5111. Village corporation address: Russian Mission Native Corp., General Delivery, Russian Mission, AK 99657; phone 584-5411.

St. Marys

Located on the Andreafsky River near its confluence with the Yukon River, 37 miles northwest of Marshall, 450 miles west-northwest of Anchorage. **Transportation:** Boat up and down lower Yukon; scheduled and charter air service from Bethel; road from Mountain Village. **Population:** 437. **Zip code:** 99658. **Emergency Services:** Police, phone 438-2212; Alaska State Troopers, phone 438-2019; Clinic, phone 438-2347; Health Aide, phone 438-2313; Volunteer Fire Department, phone 438-2911.

Elevation: 30 feet. **Climate:** St. Marys' climate is both maritime and continental, with a greater maritime influence. Mean annual precipitation is 17 inches. Mean annual snowfall is 69 inches.

Private Aircraft: Airport 4 miles west; elev. 311 feet; length 6,000 feet; gravel; no fuel; attended variable hours. Runway conditions reported only during duty hours. Airport has passenger and freight terminals, ticket counter and restrooms; no traffic control tower. Taxi service to town.

Visitor Facilities: Accommodations, meals and laundry facilities available. No banking services. Groceries, clothing, first-aid supplies, hardware, camera film and sporting goods available in the community. Arts and crafts available for purchase include carved ivory, grass baskets, beaded jewelry and hand-sewn skin garments. Fishing/hunting licenses available. No guide service. Marine engine, boat and aircraft repair available. Charter aircraft available. Fuel available: marine gas, propane, regular gasoline. Public moorage facilities available.

St. Marys' history actually begins some 90 miles downriver at Akulurak. In 1903, Jesuit missionaries set up a mission at Akulurak to educate and care for children orphaned by a flu epidemic in 1900-01. Akulurak is an Eskimo word meaning "in between place," aptly describing the settlement on an island in a slough connecting 2 arms of the Yukon River. The mission school flourished and by 1915 there were 70 full-time students. During the years, though, the slough surrounding Akulurak silted in so severely that in 1948 the mission and village moved to higher ground.

Present-day St. Marys was chosen as the new mission site. Materials from an abandoned hotel built during the gold rush were used to construct the new mission and several village homes. The mission closed in 1987.

The names St. Marys and Andreafsky are sometimes confused. Andreafsky was established in 1899 as a supply depot and winter quarters for Northern Commercial Co.'s riverboat fleet. The village took its name from the Andrea family which settled on the river, originally called Clear River. The family built a Russian Orthodox church in the village. When St. Marys was incorporated as a first-class city in 1967, Andreafsky was not included within the new city's boundaries and remained a separate, unincorporated community until 1980.

Employment in St. Marys peaks during the summer fishing season when 70 percent of the residents are involved in some form of commercial fishing activity. Other seasonal employment includes construction projects and firefighting for BLM. Other jobs are with the school district, the city, airlines, state government and Native corporations. Cash income is supplemented by subsistence activities. Residents hunt for moose, bear, duck, geese, swan and ptarmigan; and fish for salmon, sheefish, blackfish, whitefish, grayling and trout. In the fall berries are harvested. Income also is earned from trapping beaver, fox, mink, otter and muskrat.

St. Marys has become a subregional center for air transportation. Its airport is capable of handling aircraft as large as a Boeing 727. St. Marys also is linked by a 17.7-mile road to Mountain Village.

St. Marys is surrounded by Yukon Delta National Wildlife Refuge. Locally, birdwatchers can see jaegers, falcons and numerous smaller passerines. There is good fishing on the Andreafsky River for Dolly Varden, grayling, pike and salmon. Favorite activities include annual potlatches and the Andreafsky 90 Sled Dog Race, held in mid-March.

In the slough opposite the dock is a burial ground for old river steamers. Rusting boilers can be seen above the water.

Communications in St. Marys include phones, mail plane, radios and TV. The community has 2 Catholic churches, public schools with grades kindergarten through 12 and a Catholic high school. There are community electricity, water and sewer systems. St. Marys prohibits the sale and importation of alcoholic beverages. Freight arrives in the community by cargo plane and barge. Government address: City of St. Marys, P.O. Box 163, St. Marys, AK 99658; phone 438-2515. Village corporation address: St. Marys Native Corp., P.O. Box 162, St. Marys, AK 99658; phone 438-2315. Nerklikmute Native Corp., General Delivery, Andreafsky, AK 99658; phone 438-2332.

Scammon Bay

Located on the Kun River 1 mile from the Bering Sea in the Yukon-Kuskokwim Delta, 145 miles northwest of Bethel, 525 miles west of Anchorage. **Transportation:** Scheduled and charter air service from Bethel. **Population:** 326. **Zip code:** 99662. **Emergency Services:** Police, phone 558-5529; Alaska State Troopers, Bethel, phone 543-2294; Clinic, phone 558-5511; Volunteer Fire Department.

Elevation: 22 feet. **Climate:** Maritime. Mean January temperature 9°F; mean July temperature 49°F. Temperatures range between -25° and 79°F. Annual precipitation 14 inches; annual snowfall 65 inches. Easterly winds during the winter cause severe wind chill.

Private Aircraft: Airstrip adjacent north; elev. 22 feet; length 2,800 feet; gravel and dirt; no fuel; unattended. Runway condition not monitored, visual inspection recommended prior to using. Road crosses runway to river. Runway soft during breakup, after rains and during extreme high tides. No airport facilities or public transportation into village.

Visitor Facilities: Arrangements may be made for accommodations at the school, phone 558-5312. No restaurant, laundromat or banking services. Groceries, clothing, first-aid supplies, hardware, camera film and sporting goods available in the community. Arts and crafts available for purchase include carved ivory, grass baskets and masks. Fishing/hunting licenses available. No guide services. Marine engine repair available. Arrangements may be made to rent autos. Fuel available: marine gas, diesel, propane, unleaded and regular gasoline. No moorage facilities.

The Eskimo name for this village is Mariak. The site is believed to have been settled in the 1700s because it had high ground and good water. The village was named after the nearby bay which honors Capt. Charles M. Scammon, who served as marine chief of the Western Union Telegraph expedition in Alaska in 1865-67. Scammon Bay was incorporated as a second-class city in 1967.

Peak economic activity in Scammon Bay occurs during the summer fishing season when most residents are involved in commercial fishing. Other employment opportunities in the summer include firefighting for BLM and various construction projects. There are a few year-round jobs with the city, stores, school and village corporation. This income is supplemented by subsistence activities. Residents hunt beluga whale, walrus, seal, geese, swans, cranes, ducks, loons and ptarmigan. Fishing yields salmon, whitefish, blackfish, needle-fish, herring, smelt and tomcod. Berries are harvested in the fall.

Scammon Bay is located within Yukon Delta National Wildlife Refuge. A winter trail connects Scammon Bay with nearby Hooper Bay.

Communications in Scammon Bay include phones and mail plane. The community is served by Catholic and Covenant churches and a school with grades kindergarten through 12. There are community electricity, water and sewer systems. The village prohibits the possession of alcoholic beverages. Freight arrives by cargo plane and barge. Government address: City of Scammon Bay, P.O. Box 90, Scammon Bay, AK 99662; phone 558-5529 or 5626. Village corporation address: Askinuk Corp., General Delivery, Scammon Bay, AK 99662; phone 558-5311.

Shageluk

(See INTERIOR section.)

Sheldon Point

Located on a south fork of the Yukon River, 18 miles southwest of Emmonak, 500 miles west-northwest of Anchorage. **Transportation:** Boat; scheduled or charter airline from Emmonak; snow machine. **Population:** 134. **Zip code:** 99666. **Emergency Services:** Village Public Safety Office; Alaska State Troopers, St. Marys; Clinic, phone 498-4228.

Climate: Climate is maritime, averaging 60 inches of snowfall and 18 inches of precipitation per year. Temperatures range from between -25° and 79°F.

Private Aircraft: Airstrip adjacent northeast of village; length 2,200 feet; gravel; unattended. No airport facilities or public transportation into village.

Visitor Facilities: Arrangements may be made for accommodations and meals in private homes; or at the school, phone 498-4112. No banking services. Groceries, clothing, first aid supplies, hardware, camera film and sporting goods available in the community. Arts and crafts available include Native jewelry, ivory, beadwork and Eskimo clothing. Fishing/hunting licenses not available. Arrangements may be made with local residents for guide services and to rent off-road vehicles and boats. No repair services. Fuel available: diesel, propane, regular gasoline. No moorage facilities.

A relatively new Eskimo village, established in the 1940s, the community is named for a man called Sheldon, who owned and operated a fish saltery at the site. It is a second-class city, incorporated in 1974.

Commercial fishing supports the economy. Fish-buying companies from the lower Yukon, Bering Sea, Fort Yukon and the Yukon Delta Fish Marketing Co-op come here to buy fish. A few other employment opportunities exist with the store, post office, clinic, airlines and schools. Income is supplemented by public assistance payments and subsistence activities. Residents hunt beluga whale, seal, moose, geese, ducks and hare; and fish for salmon, whitefish, blackfish, sheefish, lush (burbot) and smelt. Additional income is gained from trapping fox and mink.

Sheldon Point is surrounded by Yukon Delta National Wildlife Refuge.

Communications in Sheldon Point include phones, mail plane, radio and sometimes TV. The community is served by a Catholic church and a school with grades kindergarten through 12. There is a community electricity system. Water is collected in summer or melted from ice in winter. Sewage system is primarily honey buckets. Freight arrives by cargo plane, barge, small boat and snow machine. Sale and importation of alcoholic beverages is prohibited. Government address: City of Sheldon Point, General Delivery, Sheldon Point, AK 99666; phone, 498-4226. Village corporation address: Swan Lake Corp., General Delivery, Sheldon Point, AK 99666; phone 498-4227.

Sleetmute

Located on the Kuskokwim River, 1.5 miles north of its junction with the Holitna River, 78 miles east of Aniak, 240 miles west of Anchorage. **Transportation:** Boat; scheduled and charter air service from Bethel or Aniak. **Population:** 74. **Zip code:** 99668. **Emergency Services:** Alaska State Troopers, Bethel, phone 675-4398; Clinic, phone 449-9901; Volunteer Fire Department.

Elevation: 290 feet. **Climate:** Continental with temperatures ranging between -58° and 90°F. Mean annual precipitation 21.5 inches; mean annual snowfall 77 inches.

Private Aircraft: Airstrip adjacent east; elev. 178 feet; length 3,100 feet; gravel; no fuel; unattended. Runway condition not monitored, visual inspection recommended prior to using. No airport facilities or public transportation into village. High winds in the fall and winter can prevent planes from landing for days at a time.

Visitor Facilities: Accommodations may be arranged on floor of city offices, phone 449-9901. A store carries groceries, first-aid supplies and sporting goods. Laundry facilities and public showers available. No banking

services. Fishing/hunting licenses available. Guide services available. No repair services, rental transportation or moorage facilities. Fuel available: marine gas, diesel and propane.

The Native village of Sleetmute, which means "whetstone people" was named for nearby slate deposits. The village was founded by Ingalik Indians. In the early 1830s, the Russians developed a trading post near the present village site. By 1841, however, this post had been moved from Sleetmute to another site approximately 100 miles down the Kuskokwim River. Frederick Bishop established a trading post at Sleetmute's present location in 1906. A school was opened in 1921. Saints Peter and Paul Russian Orthodox Chapel was built in 1931. Sleetmute is unincorporated.

Most income in Sleetmute is from public employment programs, the school district and summer firefighting jobs with BLM. Other residents work in canneries in other villages during the fishing season. Residents rely on subsistence hunting for moose, bear, ptarmigan, waterfowl, porcupine and rabbit; fishing for salmon, whitefish, sheefish, trout, pike, grayling, lush (burbot), char and Dolly Varden.

Communications in Sleetmute include a phone (449-9901), radio, mail plane and TV. (Private phones were scheduled for installation late in 1989.) The community is served by a Russian Orthodox church and a school with grades preschool through 12. There are community electricity and water; sewage system is outhouses. The village prohibits the sale and importation of alcoholic beverages. Freight arrives by cargo plane and barge. Government address: Sleetmute Village, Box 9, New Road, Sleetmute, AK 99668; phone 449-9901. Village corporation address: The Kuskokwim Corp., 429 D St., Suite 307, Anchorage, AK 99501; phone 276-2101.

Stony River

Located on Stony River Island in the Kuskokwim River near its junction with Stony River, 185 miles northeast of Bethel, 245 miles west-northwest of Anchorage. **Transportation:** Boat; snow machine; scheduled and charter air service from Aniak. **Population:** 73. **Zip code:** 99673. **Emergency Services:** Alaska State Troopers, Aniak, phone 675-4398; Clinic, phone 537-3228; Volunteer Fire Department.

Elevation: 220 feet. **Climate:** Continental. Record high was 85°F in July 1967; record low was -57°F in January 1951. Mean annual precipitation 23 inches; mean annual snowfall 93 inches.

Private Aircraft: Airstrip adjacent north; elev. 230 feet; length 2,900 feet; gravel; no fuel; unattended. Runway condition not monitored, visual inspection recommended prior to using. No airport facilities or public transportation into village.

Visitor Facilities: Arrangements may be made for accommodations in private homes; or in the IRA Council building by contacting the Traditional Council. No restaurant, banking services or laundry facilities. Staple items, cigarettes and snacks available at local stores; most supplies are obtained from Sleetmute, Red Devil, Aniak or Anchorage. Arts and crafts available for purchase include birch-bark baskets, wooden bowls, moccasins, mukluks, beaver mittens and beaver-and-marten hats. Fishing/hunting licenses and guide service not available. Residents repair their own marine engines. No rental transportation or moorage facilities. Fuel available: marine gas, regular gasoline.

This unincorporated Eskimo and Indian village, which has been known as Moose Village and Moose Creek, began as a trading post and riverboat landing used to supply mining operations to the north. The first trading post was opened in 1930, followed by a post office in 1935. These facilities were used primarily by people who lived in one-family settlements nearby. In the early 1960s, villagers built cabins near the store. A state school opened in 1961 and work began on the airstrip the next year.

Most income in Stony River comes from public employment programs, including seasonal firefighting work with BLM. This income is supplemented by subsistence activities. Residents hunt for moose, caribou, bear, waterfowl, ptarmigan, rabbit and porcupine. They fish for salmon, whitefish, sheefish, burbot, grayling and trout. Income also is obtained from trapping beaver, marten, lynx, fox and mink.

Communications in Stony River include phones, mail plane, radio and TV. There is a community electricity system. Water is pumped from individual wells. Sewage system is honey buckets or outhouses. Freight arrives by barge or chartered plane. Government address: Stony River Traditional Council, General Delivery, Stony River, AK 99673. Village corporation address: The Kuskokwim Corp., 429 D St., Suite 307, Anchorage, AK 99501; phone 276-2101.

Toksook Bay

(TOOK-sook) Located on Nelson Island 5 miles southeast of Tununak, 100 miles west of Bethel and 505 miles west of Anchorage. **Transportation:** Scheduled and charter air service from Bethel. **Population:** 396. **Zip code:** 99637. **Emergency Services:** Alaska State Troopers, Bethel, phone 543-3494; Clinic, phone 427-7712; Volunteer Fire Department.

Private Aircraft: Airstrip adjacent west; elev. 95 feet; length 1,800 feet; gravel and dirt; no fuel; unattended. Runway condition not monitored, visual inspection recommended prior to using. Runway grade uneven. Deep dip at one end.

Visitor Facilities: Arrangements for accommodations may be made at the school, phone 427-7815. Supplies available in the community. Fishing/hunting licenses available. Information on other visitor services and facilities unavailable.

Toksook Bay was established in 1964 when most of the population of Nightmute moved to what was considered a better village site. Toksook Bay, which is located within Yukon Delta National Wildlife Refuge, was incorporated as a second-class city in 1972. Many residents may be gone to fish camps during the summer.

Toksook Bay is served by a Catholic church and 2 schools with grades kindergarten through 12. There are community electricity, water and sewer systems. Toksook Bay prohibits the sale and importation of alcoholic beverages. Freight arrives by barge and plane. Government address: City of Toksook Bay, Nelson Island, Toksook Bay, AK 99637; phone 427-7613. Village corporation address: Ninakaviak Yup'ik Corp., General Delivery, Toksook Bay, AK 99637; phone 427-7929.

Tuluksak

(TOO-luck-sack) Located on the south bank of the Kuskokwim River near the mouth of the Tuluksak River, 45 miles northeast of Bethel and 375 miles west of Anchorage. **Transportation:** Scheduled and charter air service from Bethel. **Population:** 302. **Zip code:** 99679. **Emergency Services:** Village Public Safety Officer; Alaska State Troopers, Bethel, phone 543-3494; Clinic, phone 695-6115; Volunteer Fire Department.

Private Aircraft: Airstrip adjacent southwest; elev. 30 feet; length 2,500 feet; gravel; no fuel; unattended. Runway condition not monitored, visual inspection recommended prior to using. Loose gravel to 2 inches in diameter on the northeast 1,000 feet of the runway. Potholes and ruts in runway.

Visitor Facilities: Arrangements for accommodations may be made through the city office, phone 695-6212. There is a washeteria. Supplies available at 2 general stores. Fishing/hunting licenses not available.

This Eskimo village reportedly was named after a species of loon called "tulik" in the Eskimo language. It has been occupied continuously since early historic times and the Moravian missionaries had an Eskimo helper stationed there in 1895. Outside interest in the area was generated in 1907 when gold was found along Bear Creek on the upper Tuluksak River. The first Moravian chapel was built in 1912; a new chapel was completed in 1925. A Bureau of Education school opened in 1930.

Tuluksak, which is located within Yukon Delta National Wildlife Refuge, was incorporated as a second-class city in 1970. Many residents may be gone to fish camps during the summer season.

The community has 2 schools with grades kindergarten through 12. There is a community electricity system. Water is hauled from the washeteria. Sewage system is honey buckets. Tuluksak prohibits the sale and importation of alcoholic beverages. Freight arrives by mail plane and barge. Government address: City of Tuluksak, General Delivery, Tuluksak, AK 99679; phone 695-6212. Village corporation address: Tulkisarmute Inc., General Delivery, Tuluksak, AK 99679.

Tuntutuliak

(TOON-too-TOO-lee-ack) Located on the north bank of the Kuskokwim River, 45 miles southwest of Bethel, 440 miles west of Anchorage. **Transportation:** Scheduled and charter air service from Bethel. **Population:** 203. **Zip code:** 99680. **Emergency Services:** Village Public Safety Officer, phone 256-2512; Alaska State Troopers, Bethel, phone 543-3494; Clinic, phone 256-2129; Volunteer Fire Department.

BE PREPARED

Always carry in your pocket: waterproof wooden matches, a pocket knife and toilet tissue to use as fire-starter.

Emergency shelters can be built of brush or snow.

Private Aircraft: Airstrip 1 mile south; elev. 16 feet; length 1,900 feet; gravel; no fuel; unattended. Runway condition not monitored, visual inspection recommended prior to using. Runway has 40-foot gravel strip down the center; gravel edges may be soft.

Visitor Facilities: Arrangements for accommodations may be made with the school, phone 256-2415. There is a washeteria. Supplies available in the community. Fishing/hunting licenses available.

Unincorporated Tuntutuliak is located within Yukon Delta National Wildlife Refuge. Many residents may leave for fish camps in the summer.

The community has a church and 2 schools with grades kindergarten through 12. There is a community electricity system. Water is hauled from the washeteria. Sewage system is honey buckets. Tuntutuliak prohibits the possession of alcoholic beverages. Freight arrives by mail plane and barge. Government address: Tuntutuliak City Office, General Delivery, Tuntutuliak, AK 99680; phone 256-2112. Village corporation address: Tuntutuliak Land Ltd., General Delivery, Tuntutuliak, AK 99680; phone 256-2315.

Tununak

(tu-NOO-nak) Located at Tununak Bay on the northwest coast of Nelson Island, 120 miles west of Bethel, 520 miles west of Anchorage. **Transportation:** Scheduled and charter air service from Bethel. **Population:** 337. **Zip code:** 99681. **Emergency Services:** Village Public Safety Officer, phone 652-6812; Alaska State Troopers, Bethel; Clinic, phone 652-6829; Volunteer Fire Department.

Private Aircraft: Airstrip adjacent southwest; elev. 17 feet; length 2,000 feet; gravel; no fuel; unattended. Runway condition not monitored, visual inspection recommended prior to using. Passenger terminal at airport; public transportation into village.

Visitor Facilities: For sleeping accommodations in the school or clinic, contact the school, phone 652-6827, or the city office, phone 652-6626. No restaurant or banking services. Washeteria available. Groceries, clothing, first-aid supplies, hardware, camera film and sporting goods available in the community. Arts and crafts available for purchase include carved ivory, baskets and earrings. Fishing/hunting licenses available. No guide or repair services. Arrangements may be made to rent autos and off-road vehicles. Fuel available: marine gas, propane and regular gasoline. No moorage facilities.

This Eskimo village was visited in December 1878 by E.W. Nelson of the U.S. Signal Service and reported as Tununuk, population 6. A Roman Catholic mission was established here in 1891. Tununak was incorporated as a second-class city in 1975.

Tununak residents go to fish camps in the summer and also work on seasonal firefighting crews for BLM.

Communications in Tununak include phones and mail plane. The community is served by a Roman Catholic church and 2 schools with grades kindergarten through 12. There is a community electricity system. Water is hauled from the washeteria. Sewage system is honey buckets. Tununak prohibits the sale and importation of alcoholic beverages. Freight is hauled by cargo plane and barge. Government address: City of Tununak, P.O. Box 69, Tununak, AK 99681; phone 652-6626. Village corporation address: Tununrmuit Rinit Corp., General Delivery, Tununak, AK 99681; phone 562-6311.

Upper Kalskag

(Also known as Kalskag) Located on the north bank of the Kuskokwim River, about 24 miles west of Aniak. **Transportation:** Scheduled and charter air service from Aniak or Bethel. **Population:** 165. **Zip code:** 99607. **Emergency Services:** Village Public Safety Officer; Clinic; Volunteer Fire Department.

Elevation: 49 feet. **Climate:** Semiarctic with maritime influences from the Bering Sea. Snowfall and precipitation are 60 inches and 19 inches, respectively. Weather records at nearby Aniak indicate that temperatures at Upper Kalskag range from a low of -55°F to a high of 87°F.

Private Aircraft: Kalskag airport adjacent west; elev. 49 feet; length 3,200 feet; gravel; no fuel. Runway is maintained by the state. Kalskag also has a grader to service the runway and main road between Upper and Lower Kalskag. Runway conditions not monitored; visual inspection recommended prior to using. Airport serves both Upper and Lower Kalskag. Transportation into village available.

Visitor Facilities: Arrangements for accommodations may be made at the school, phone 471-2288. No laundromat or banking services. Groceries, clothing, first-aid supplies, hardware and sporting goods available in the community, along with a restaurant. Fishing/hunting licenses available in Lower Kalskag. No guide or repair services. No rental transportation or moorage facilities. Fuel available: marine gas, diesel.

Most of the inhabitants of Upper Kalskag were originally residents of the Eskimo village of Kaltkhagamute, located on a slough 4 miles southwest of Upper Kalskag. At the turn of the century, the people moved to the present site of Upper Kalskag. Paul Kameroff, Sr. is credited with founding the village of Upper Kalskag. He operated the only general store which was established in the 1930's and transported freight, groceries and fuel from Bethel on a barge he named for his daughter Pauline. A federal Bureau of Education school was built in 1931. At that time the community owned a herd of 2,100 reindeer. Throughout the years, residents of Ohagamiut, Crow Village and the Yukon River communities of Russian Mission and Paimute moved to Upper Kalskag. The community of Lower Kalskag, 2 miles to the southwest, was established during this same period. Upper Kalskag was incorporated as a second-class city in 1975.

Most income in Upper Kalskag comes from public employment programs. Subsistence activities account for about 70 percent of the total livelihood in the village. Some residents still go to fish camps, but most fish at or near the village. Seasonal fish catches include king, dog, silver and red salmon; grayling, whitefish, sheefish, blackfish, pike, burbot and eel. Moose are the most important meat source, supplemented by rabbit, waterfowl and game birds. Some income also is obtained from trapping and the sale of lynx, fox, wolf, otter, muskrat, mink, marten, beaver and wolverine pelts. Berries are harvested in the fall and some residents cultivate gardens.

Upper Kalskag is located within Yukon Delta National Wildlife Refuge.

Communications in Upper Kalskag include phones, mail plane, radio and TV. The community is served by 2 churches and 2 schools with grades 1 through 12. There are community electricity, water and sewer systems. Freight is transported by plane and barge. Government address: City of Upper Kalskag, General Delivery, Upper Kalskag, AK 99607; phone 471-2220. Village corporation address: The Kuskokwim Corp., 429 D St., Suite 307, Anchorage, AK 99501; phone 276-2101.

BEARS

Never camp on a bear trail — that's just asking for trouble!

▼ A T T R A C T I O N S ▼

Wildlife Refuges

Yukon Delta National Wildlife Refuge

At 19.6 million acres, this is the nation's largest wildlife refuge and encompasses the great deltas of the Yukon and Kuskokwim rivers, the 2 longest rivers in Alaska. It also includes 1.1-million-acre Nunivak Island, 20 miles off the coast. On Nunivak the terrain includes volcanic craters, sand dunes, sea cliffs and rolling tundra. This region is treeless and apart from the Andreafsky and Kilbuck hills is a seemingly limitless expanse of wetlands. The Andreafsky River in the northern section of the refuge above St. Marys is a designated wild river within an established wilderness area.

Wildlife: This refuge is one of the most significant waterfowl breeding areas in North America. A total of 170 species have been observed and upwards of 136 species nest here, including more than 750,000 swans and geese, 2 million ducks and 100 million shore and water birds. More than half the continent's black brant population hatches in the refuge coast and all of North America's cackling Canada geese are produced in the coastal lowlands. Large populations of emperor geese, Pacific white-fronted geese and tundra swans nest near the coast and on the inland tundra.

Nunivak Island shelters herds of reindeer and musk-ox. Musk-ox vanished from Alaska in 1865 because of overhunting. The Nunivak herd, introduced from Greenland in 1935, has provided breeding stock for establishing herds elsewhere in Alaska and the Soviet Union. The reindeer herd is a major source of food and income for residents of Mekoryuk, the only village on the island.

Other wildlife in the refuge includes moose, caribou, grizzly and black bear, and wolves, found primarily in the northern hills and eastern mountains. Smaller mammals include beaver, muskrat, mink, land otter and fox. On Nunivak, native land animals include only red and arctic foxes, weasel, mink, shrews, voles and lemmings. Coastal waters support harbor, ribbon, ringed and bearded seals, walrus, and many species of whales during migrations.

Fish found in refuge waters include trout, arctic char and grayling in the mountain streams and pike, sheefish, whitefish and burbot in lowland waters. Great numbers of king, silver, red, pink and chum salmon migrate through the delta rivers during the summer on their way to spawning grounds.

Climate: Weather in the refuge is unpredictable at best. January temperatures average near 0°F, although high winds often cause a wind chill factor exceeding -60°F. Winter in the delta region begins early in October. Annual snowfall may exceed 50 inches, but winter thaws prevent much accumulation. Ice breakup usually occurs in late May or early June. Summer temperatures in Bethel on the Kuskokwim River and St. Marys on the Yukon River average in the mid-50s, with occasional highs in the 70s and 80s.

Activities: Major recreational activities in the refuge include wildlife observation, photography and boating. Other activities include hiking, camping, sled dog racing, snowmobiling and cross-country skiing. Hunting and fishing are allowed in accordance with state and federal regulations. Because of the refuge's remoteness and fickle weather, careful planning is necessary to ensure a safe trip. Top quality equipment and a good insect repellent are essential, according to the Fish and Wildlife Service.

For many centuries, the abundance of wildlife has made the delta the heart of Yup'ik Eskimo culture. Residents of at least 56 villages depend on this region for subsistence purposes. Their equipment and camps are essential to their livelihood and should be left undisturbed. Also, ownership of large areas within the refuge has been conveyed to Native regional and village corporations and this private property should be respected. Anyone planning a trip to the region should consult about the location of private lands with the Assoc. of Village Council Presidents, P.O. Box 219, Bethel, AK 99559, or with individual village corporations.

Access: The refuge is accessible only by boat or airplane. There is scheduled airline service from Anchorage to Bethel, St. Marys and Aniak, where flights to other villages or remote areas can be arranged.

Accommodations: Lodging may be available in some villages, but should be arranged in advance. In general, travelers to the refuge should be self-sufficient. Wilderness camping is permitted in the refuge, but there are no established campgrounds or trails.

A visitor center for the Yukon Delta National Wildlife Refuge is located across from the Bethel Regional Hospital on the main road from the airport to Bethel. The center features exhibits on the refuge, its wildlife and how the resources have been and are used by Eskimos in the region. Refuge staff present periodic wildlife programs for schools and the public.

For more information, contact: Refuge Manager, Yukon Delta National Wildlife Refuge, P.O. Box 346, Bethel, AK 99559; phone 543-3151.

The Rivers

NOTE: *Some of the rivers described below are also included in the Sportfishing section where additional information on species, seasons and suggested bait is provided.*

Andreafsky River. The Andreafsky is located within Andreafsky Wilderness, which is in the northern portion of Yukon Delta National Wildlife Refuge. The wild river consists of the Main Fork and the East Fork Andreafsky, which join together approximately 5 miles north of the village of St. Marys.

The river flows southwest 120 miles to the Yukon River at Pitkas Point. Both forks of the Andreafsky are scenic, and wildlife along the river includes black and brown bears, fox, caribou, beaver, otter, bald and golden eagles, peregrine falcons, a variety of hawks, gulls and ducks, Canada geese and tundra swans. Fish include chum, king and silver salmon, grayling, Dolly Varden and rainbow trout.

Access to the Andreafsky River is difficult and expensive. The easiest method is to fly commercially to St. Marys. From there, arrange to have a raft towed up river by jetboat or charter a floatplane to take you up the river to a convenient dropoff point. A major problem is that there are no lakes along the rivers that a larger floatplane can land on. A small floatplane is required to land along the river. A further problem is that charter and guide service either do not exist in the area, or are quite limited. A potential visitor will need to research extensively in order to set up a float trip. Related USGS Topographic maps: Kwiglik A-2, A-3, B-1, B-2, C-1, C-2, D-1; St. Michael A-1; Unalakleet A-6; Holy Cross C-6, D-6.

Aniak River. The Aniak flows 140 river miles to the Kuskokwim River, 1 mile east of Aniak.

This river has 3 distinct phases. It is clear, fast flat water over a gravel bed from its headwaters at Aniak Lake. It drops at 10 feet per mile for 40 miles through the forest and into the tundra. In its second phase, the course disintegrates into numerous channels filled with many sweepers, logjams and uprooted trees. It continues dropping at 10 feet per mile for 20 miles to where the Salmon River joins the Aniak. Below this very difficult stretch of Class II, the water becomes tame, flat water for the remaining 80 miles to Aniak. It is recommended that this isolated river be attempted only by the most experienced wilderness travelers. Decked canoes and kayaks are recommended.

Fishing on the Aniak is excellent for king, chum and coho salmon, pike, sheefish and grayling. Aniak Lake has lake trout and grayling.

Access is by chartered floatplane from Bethel or Aniak. Exit is from Aniak, where there are overnight accommodations and other facilities. Related USGS Topographic maps: Bethel B-1, C-1, D-1; Russian Mission A-1, B-1, C-2.

Holitna River. This is a slow taiga river that was the Russians' first route into the Interior from Bristol Bay. Although it once saw much activity, today it is seldom visited. The Holitna flows northeast 200 river miles from its source at the confluence of Kogrukluk River and Shotgun Creek to the Kuskokwim River across from Sleetmute village. The Holitna poses few technical problems for the boater; it is flat water all the way. However, boaters must be alert for sweepers and logjams. The Holitna is isolated and recommended only for travelers with wilderness experience. Canoes, kayaks and riverboats all are suitable.

Five species of salmon are available in this river, but especially kings, chums and cohos, along with pike and sheefish. Also grayling and arctic char upstream.

Access is by floatplane from Bethel. Exit is from Sleetmute, which has scheduled air service, but no overnight facilities. Related USGS Topographic maps: Taylor Mts. D-5; Sleetmute A-5, A-4, B-4, B-3, C-3.

Kanektok River. This river heads at scenic Kagati Lake in the Ahklun Mountains in Togiak National Wildlife Refuge and flows 85 miles to Kuskokwim Bay near the village of Quinhagak. The upper river flows through a mountain valley, while the lower portion wanders through flat tundra. There are numerous gravel bars and islands along the length of the river, particularly on the coastal plain. The first 25 miles are Class I, followed by 30 miles of Class I-II and then another 30 miles of flat water. There are no rapids in the middle 30 miles, but sweepers, combined with a moderately swift current and a winding course, require frequent maneuvering. Traveling the length of this river usually takes 5 to 7 days. Canoe, raft or kayak all are suitable.

Seasonally there is very good fishing for 5 species of salmon, arctic char, grayling and rainbow trout. The number of large fish in this river qualifies it as one of the premier sportfishing rivers on the North American continent, according to the Fish and Wildlife Service.

Access is by floatplane to Kagati Lake from Bethel or Dillingham. Exit is by scheduled commercial air service from Quinhagak, which has no overnight facilities. Related USGS Topographic maps: Goodnews C-5, C-6, D-3, D-4, D-5, D-6, D-7, D-8.

Kisaralik River. This river heads in Kisaralik Lake in the Kilbuck Mountains and flows northwest 100 miles to the Kuskokwim River, 20 miles northeast of Bethel. This is considered an exciting white-water float for boaters with intermediate skills. The river is swift, with long stretches of small rocky rapids. The upper half of the river flows through a tundra-covered valley bracketed by mountains rising to 2,000 to 3,000 feet. Low bluffs parallel the river. Crossing the Kuskokwim lowlands, the river meanders slowly through paper birch, aspen and spruce forest. There are 4 short (50 yards or less) Class III rapids and then 20-yard-long Upper Falls (Class IV), which can be portaged easily on either side of the river. The left side is an easier portage but the right side has a better campsite. Quicksilver Creek, 3 miles downriver, and then the ridge through which the river cuts to form the falls are recognizable landmarks. Upper Falls is followed by 12 miles of Class II, then the Class II Lower Falls, 4 miles of Class I-II and then Class III Golden Gate. The lower portion of the river consists of 35 miles of Class I and 25 miles of flatwater. This trip generally takes 6 days. Rafts or kayaks are recommended; canoes for experienced paddlers.

There is superb mountain scenery and good hiking throughout the upper portion of the river. Downstream, boaters can take a break and explore tundra-covered ridges. Seasonally there is good fishing for all varieties of salmon, rainbow trout, grayling and arctic char. Lake trout are available in Kisaralik Lake.

Access is by floatplane from Bethel to Kisaralik Lake. Exit is by floatplane from the lower portion of the Kisaralik or pickup by riverboat can be arranged at Bethel. There are accommodations and meals at Bethel. Related USGS Topographic maps: Bethel.

Kuskokwim River. This 540-mile-long river is Alaska's fourth-longest. Its North Fork reaches far north to the Tanana basin and once served as a watercourse for Natives and later prospectors and trappers. Lake Minchumina is connected by a long, once well-trodden portage to the North Fork. There are few travelers today, so boaters must be prepared to rely on their own resources. The first village reached is Medfra, located where the East Fork merges with the North Fork. From that point, the Kuskokwim is a wide river, flowing slowly through mountains southwest to the broad coastal plain and Kuskokwim Bay. The largest settlements are McGrath, Sleetmute, Chuathbaluk, Aniak and Bethel. This river is flat water all the way. Canoes, kayaks, rafts and riverboats all are suitable. Access is by portage from Lake Minchumina or more easily by floatplane from Anchorage, Fairbanks or McGrath. Exit is by floatplane from any point on the river or by scheduled air service from most of the communities on the river. Related USGS Topographic maps: Kantishna River B-5, A-5, A-6; Mount McKinley D-6; Meafra D-1, C-1, C-2, B-2, B-3, A-3, A-4, A-5; McGrath D-5, D-6, C-6, B-6; Iditarod B-1, A-1; Sleetmute D-1, D-2, C-3, C-4, D-4, D-5, D-6, C-6, C-7, C-8; Russian Mission C-1, C-2, C-3, C-4, B-4, B-5, A-5, A-6; Bethel D-6, D-7, D-8, C-8; Baird Inlet C-1, B-1, B-2, A-2.

Stony River. This river heads at Stony Glacier in the Alaska Range and flows southwest and northwest 190 miles to the Kuskokwim about 1 mile from Stony River village. This is a swift (averaging 5 mph), silty river flowing through a forest. Below its confluence with the Necons River, it flows through foothills then passes into lowlands. Below its confluence with the Telaquana River, the Stony flows through a series of small, scenic canyons for 19 miles of Class II. Here there are short (100 yards or less) stretches of rapids, alternating with 1 to 4 miles of swift flat water. The remaining 90 miles of the river is flat water or Class I. The trip from the Telaquana confluence takes approximately 5 to 6 days. Rafts, kayaks and canoes all are suitable.

This river offers good grayling fishing in the clear-water tributaries; the river itself is too silty for sportfishing. There are numerous gravel bars for campsites. Mountain scenery upstream from the Necons River is good. This trip is popular with hunters; travelers who only want to sightsee should plan their trips before hunting season.

Access is by wheel plane or floatplane to the upper reaches of Stony River; or floatplane to Telaquana Lake, headwaters of the Telaquana River; or Two Lakes, headwaters of the Necons River. Exit is by mail plane from Lime Village on the Stony River; scheduled air service from Stony River village; or floatplane pickup from the lower river. Lime Village has no visitor facilities; Stony River has limited accommodations. Boaters also may continue down the Kuskokwim River to a larger village. Related USGS Topographic maps: Lime Hills A-4 through A-6, B-5 through B-8; Sleetmute B-1, C-1, C-2 and D-2.

Telaquana and Necons rivers. These 2 rivers are semiclear tributaries to the silt-laden Stony River, and both head in Lake Clark National Park and Preserve. For information see Rivers in Western Cook Inlet subregion in SOUTHCENTRAL/GULF COAST section.

Sportfishing

Access to good fishing in the Yukon-Kuskokwim area is primarily by air. If you have the time, however, you sometimes can walk or go by boat to a hot fishing spot. Boats occasionally can be rented or chartered at villages along the waterways. There are daily commercial flights to the transportation centers of the region — Bethel, Aniak or St. Marys — where you can catch a commuter flight to a smaller village or charter a plane to a lake or river. In addition, commercial outfitters will handle logistics for you on guided fishing trips.

Tackle-breaking king salmon are at their peak from mid-June through July. These fish are not uncommon at 30 pounds and up. Chums and reds show up by July 1, pinks by mid-July (in even-numbered years) and silvers by mid-August. Salmon fishing is concentrated in the river systems.

Arctic char and Dolly Varden are found throughout this area and are most abundant in late summer. These usually weigh 1 to 3 pounds, but an occasional 9- to 12-pounder has been reported. Grayling can be caught most of the summer, but larger ones are more plentiful from August to October. Grayling measuring 16 inches are not uncommon and they reach 23 inches.

Other species that may be encountered are whitefish, which can reach 5 pounds; burbot (also called lush or lingcod) which can weigh in at 10 to 12 pounds; and northern pike, which average 5 to 8 pounds but can attain 30 pounds. Pike have very sharp teeth, so beware.

The Alaska Dept. of Fish and Game recommends that anyone traveling to remote areas should plan for the worst. Take a few days extra food, and fuel if necessary, and allow for a flexible schedule since fickle weather can delay travel for days.

Although many villages have hunting and fishing license vendors, it is recommended that you purchase your license in Anchorage or another large community, since sometimes the local vendors themselves have "gone fishing." The Dept. of Fish and Game does not sell licenses.

More information about fishing in the Yukon-Kuskokwim area may be obtained from the following:

Alaska Dept. of Fish and Game, Sport Fish Division, 1300 College Road, Fairbanks, AK 99701-1599; phone 456-8819. Alaska Dept. of Fish and Game, P.O. Box 90, Bethel, AK 99559-0090; phone 543-2433.

Andreafsky River. This is a wild and scenic river located in the northeast corner of Yukon Delta National Wildlife Refuge. It joins the Yukon River just east of St. Marys. Excellent fishery. Fish available: king, chum, coho and pink salmon — use spoons; grayling — year-round, best in late summer, use flies; arctic char — best June to September, use spoons, eggs. Charter air service and accommodations available in St. Marys.

Aniak River. Joins the Kuskokwim River 1 mile east of Aniak village. Excellent fishery. Fish available: king, chum and coho salmon — use spoons; rainbow trout — use flies, lures or bait; arctic char — best in fall, use spoons, eggs; grayling — year-round, best in late summer, use flies; northern pike — year-round, use spoons, spinners; sheefish — best May to September, use spoons; lake trout in Aniak Lake — use spoons, plugs. Accommodations, guides and air charter service at Aniak.

Anvik River. This 140-mile-long river joins the Yukon 1.5 miles south of the village of Anvik (see INTERIOR section). Fish available: chum salmon in season — use spoons; arctic char — best in fall, use spoons, eggs; grayling — year-round, best in late summer, use flies; northern pike — year-round, use spoons, spinners. Access by scheduled air service to Anvik or air charter to river from Grayling or St. Marys. Some accommodations in Anvik.

Goodnews River. Heads in Goodnews Lake in the Togiak National Wildlife Refuge and flows southwest 60 miles to Goodnews Bay at the village of Goodnews Bay. Excellent fishing. Fish available: 5 species of salmon, grayling, rainbow trout and Dolly Varden. Lake trout in Goodnews Lake. Access by air charter from Bethel or Dillingham.

Hoholitna River. Heads in Whitefish Lake and flows northwest 165 miles to the Holitna River, 13 miles southeast of its junction with the Kuskokwim River near Sleetmute. Fish available: northern pike — year-round, use spoons, spinners; sheefish — best late June to August, use spoons; grayling — best in late summer, use flies; arctic char — best June to September, use spoons, eggs. Access by air charter from Bethel or Aniak.

Holitna River. Joins the Kuskokwim River 1.5 miles south of Sleetmute. Fish available: 5 species of salmon in season, but especially kings, chums and coho. Other fish upstream are: northern pike — year-round, use spoons, spinners; sheefish — best late June to August, use spoons; grayling — year-round, best in late summer, use flies; arctic char — best in fall, use spoons. Commercial lodge on river. Access by boat from Sleetmute, or air charter from Aniak or Bethel.

Kanektok River. Heads at Kagati Lake in the Togiak National Wildlife Refuge and flows southwest 75 miles to Kuskokwim Bay, 1.5 miles west of Quinhagak. Excellent fishery. Fish available: salmon in season; rainbow trout — best in late summer and early fall; arctic char — best July to September; grayling — year-round, best May to September; and lake trout. Access by charter floatplane from Bethel or Dillingham. No accommodations on lake or river, but several outfitters have commercial camps in the area. No overnight accommodations at Quinhagak.

Kisaralik River. Flows into the Kuskokwim River 20 miles northeast of Bethel. Fish available: 5 species of salmon in season; rainbow trout — best in late summer and early fall, use flies, lures or bait; grayling — year-round, best late summer, use flies; arctic char — best in fall, use spoons, eggs. Rental boats and charter planes available in Bethel.

Kwethluk River. Flows into the Kuskokwim River 10 miles east of Bethel. Located in Yukon Delta National Wildlife Refuge. Fish available: 5 varieties of salmon in season; rainbow trout — best in late summer and early fall, use flies, lures or bait; grayling — year-round, best in late summer, use flies; arctic char — best in fall, use spoons, eggs. Rental boats available in Bethel.

Owhat River. Joins the Kuskokwim River 4.5 miles upriver from Aniak. Fishing best at its mouth. Fish available: sheefish — best late June to August, use spoons; grayling — year-round, best in late summer, use flies; whitefish — use flies, eggs. Access by boat from Aniak.

STATE BIRD

The willow ptarmigan, commonly found from southwestern Alaska into the Arctic is Alaska's state bird. Its plumage changes from brown in the summer to white in the winter.

The willow ptarmigan is one of 427 species of birds confirmed in Alaska by authorities at the University of Alaska. Thousands of ducks, geese and swans come to breeding grounds in Alaska from many corners of the world. Millions of seabirds congregate in nesting colonies on exposed cliffs along Alaska's coastline.

The Yukon-Kuskokwim Delta is a key waterfowl habitat and a large portion of this area has been set aside in the Yukon Delta National Wildlife Refuge which is described in more detail on page 318.

SEWARD PENINSULA/NORTON SOUND

Introduction

Successive waves of prehistoric migrations brought the first peoples to Alaska's Seward Peninsula. These nomads came across the ancient Bering Land Bridge from Asia, leaving evidence of their culture which archaeologists are still piecing together today.

Yup'ik and Inupiat Eskimos, descendants of these wanderers, continue the hunting, fishing and trapping which have supported them from time immemorial. In coastal and island villages marine mammals — whales, seals and walrus — are the mainstays. More easterly villages rely on moose and caribou and salmon runs up the rivers.

Russian explorer Vitus Bering made the first documented sighting of the Diomede Islands in 1728, but it would be another century before the Russian-American Co. established a permanent settlement on the mainland, at St. Michael in 1833. European and American whaling crews had considerable contact with Eskimos along the coast. Pioneer missionary Sheldon Jackson introduced reindeer as a new source of protein. But not until the gold strike near Nome in 1898 did the Seward Peninsula receive another major wave of migration — this time of gold seekers.

As miners spread their search for gold throughout the peninsula, new towns emerged and Western ways were introduced. These new traditions, however, by no means supplanted the Eskimo way of life.

Visitors to the Seward Peninsula and Norton Sound today enjoy seeing relics from the area's exciting gold rush past. Hiking, fishing, beachcombing, camping and watching birds are favorite activities. Serious birders can add checks to their life list with sightings of rare Asiatic species. Though much of the tundra is too boggy for hiking, the gentle mountains and alpine tundra make for excellent cross-country traveling, both winter and summer. Many visitors are especially drawn to the Norton Sound villages in March, when Iditarod Trail sled dog race teams pass through Unalakleet, Shaktoolik, Koyuk, Elim, Golovin and Solomon on their way to the finish line at Nome. That city overflows with visitors during the exciting late winter event.

A visit to St. Lawrence Island, home of the Siberian Yup'iks, is a step back in time, where skin boats and drums made of walrus stomachs are taken for granted and family ties are much closer to the mainland of Siberia than that of Alaska.

Walrus range along the entire Bering Sea coast and are an important resource for many of the region's Eskimo villages. (Alissa Crandall)

▼ C O M M U N I T I E S ▼

Brevig Mission

Located at the mouth of Shelman Creek on the north shore of Port Clarence on the Seward Peninsula, 6 miles northwest of Teller, 60 miles northwest of Nome, 481 miles west of Fairbanks. **Transportation:** Scheduled or charter air service from Nome. **Population:** 172. **Zip code:** 99785. **Emergency Services:** Village Public Safety Officer, phone 642-4341; Alaska State Troopers, Nome, phone 443-2835; Clinic, phone 642-4311; Volunteer Fire Department.

Elevation: 25 feet. **Climate:** Maritime climate, cool and damp, when the Bering Sea is ice free from early June to mid-November. Freezing of the sea causes a change to a more continental climate, with less precipitation and colder temperatures. Annual precipitation is 11.5 inches, with an average of 50 inches of snowfall. Average winter temperatures are between -9° and 8°F. During the summer, temperatures average between 44° and 57°F.

Private Aircraft: Airstrip adjacent east; elev. 25 feet; length 2,400 feet; gravel; unattended; runway condition not monitored, recommend visual inspection prior to using. Airport has lights and freight terminal. Transportation into village sometimes available.

Visitor Facilities: No hotel accommodations; arrangements can be made to stay in private homes. No restaurants or banking services. Laundry facilities available. Groceries, clothing, first-aid supplies, hardware, camera film and sporting goods available. Arts and crafts available for purchase include carved ivory, fur slippers, mukluks, beadwork, crocheted and knitted items. Fishing/hunting licenses available. No guide service. Marine engine and boat repair available. Arrangements can be made to rent boats. Fuel available includes white gas, propane and regular gasoline. No moorage facilities.

The "Teller Reindeer Station" was established nearby in 1892 by Sheldon Jackson, who named it after Henry Moore Teller, U.S.

senator and secretary of the Interior. The reindeer station was operated by the U.S. government from 1892 to 1900. The Norwegian Evangelical Lutheran Mission was established in 1900 at the present site of Brevig Mission and the settlement became known as Teller Mission. By 1906, the government role in reindeer herding had diminished and the mission became dominant. Brevig Mission is a second-class city, incorporated in 1969.

The Natives living around Port Clarence were Kauwerak Eskimos with no permanent settlement prior to 1892. They lived in migratory communities, pursuing fish and game. They traded furs with Siberia, Little Diomede and King Island and alliances were formed with Wales, Little Diomede and others for protection.

Reindeer were the economic base of this community from 1892 to 1974, but their importance is now declining. Skin sewing for arts and crafts and jobs on seasonal construction projects bring in some cash income.

The people of Brevig Mission depend on both sea mammals and fishing for subsistence, going to seasonal hunting and fishing camps. Seal, oogruk and beluga whale are the most important subsistence mammals. Fish staples include salmon, whitefish, herring, tomcod, flounder, sculpin and smelt. Residents also rely on waterfowl, game birds, eggs, rabbits, squirrels, moose, berries and an occasional polar bear.

There is a winter trail to Teller used by snow machines and dogsleds.

Communications in Brevig Mission include phones, mail plane, radio and TV. The community is served by a Lutheran church and a school with grades preschool through 12. There are community electricity and water systems; sewage system is honey buckets. Brevig Mission prohibits the sale and importation of alcoholic beverages. Freight arrives by cargo plane and barge. Government address: City of Brevig Mission, P.O. Box 85021, Brevig

Mission, AK 99785; phone 642-3851. Village corporation address: Brevig Mission Native Corp., General Delivery, Brevig Mission, AK 99785; phone 642-3951.

Buckland

Located on the west bank of the Buckland River on the Seward Peninsula, 75 miles southeast of Kotzebue, 400 miles west of Fairbanks. **Transportation:** Boats; snow machine; scheduled air service from Kotzebue. **Population:** 312. **Zip code:** 99727. **Emergency Services:** Village Public Safety Officer, phone 494-2145; Alaska State Troopers, Kotzebue; Clinic, phone 494-2122; Volunteer Fire Department.

Climate: Transitional zone characterized by long, cold winters and cool summers. Temperatures in July and August average 60°F. Precipitation is light, less than 9 inches annually, with 35 to 40 inches of snow.

Private Aircraft: Airstrip 1 mile southwest from village; elev. 30 feet; length 2,200 feet; gravel. No airport facilities. Runway condition not monitored, recommend visual inspection prior to using; subject to turbulent crosswinds during summer months. Public transportation into village available.

Visitor Facilities: No hotel, restaurant, banking services or laundry facilities. Groceries, clothing, first-aid supplies, hardware, camera film and sporting goods available at 3 stores. Fishing/hunting licenses available. No guide or major repair services. No rental transportation. Fuel available includes marine gas, propane and regular gasoline. No moorage facilities.

This village has existed at several other locations under various names in the past, including Elephant Point, so named because fossil mammoth or mastodon bones were found at the site in 1826. The presence of the fossil finds show that this site was used by prehistoric man.

Buckland people moved repeatedly as conditions changed and the people depended at various times on reindeer or beluga whale or seal for survival. In the 1920s, they moved with their reindeer herd from Old Buckland, 1 mile downriver, to the present area. The townsite, however, was later relocated. Today, Buckland is a second-class city, incorporated in 1966.

Buckland has a primarily subsistence economy. In the fall and winter, residents hunt caribou; in spring they hunt beluga whale and seal off Elephant Point.

Some employment is provided with a locally owned reindeer herd, numbering 2,000 head. Herring, salmon, smelt, grayling, white-fish, rabbit, ptarmigan, berries and waterfowl and their eggs supplement the local diet.

Communications in Buckland include phones, mail plane and radio. The community is served by a church and 2 schools with grades preschool through 12. There is a community electricity system. Water is hauled from the river in summer and melted from lake ice in winter. Sewage system is honey buckets. Buckland prohibits the sale and importation of alcoholic beverages. Freight arrives by barge. Government address: City of Buckland, P.O. Box 49, Buckland, AK 99727; phone 494-2121. Village corporation address: NANA Regional Corp., P.O. Box 49, Kotzebue, AK 99752.

Candle

Located on the Kewalik River, 90 miles southeast of Kotzebue. **Transportation:** Scheduled air service; charter plane; boat. **Population:** 4 year-round, 35 during summer mining season. **Zip code:** 99728. **Emergency Services:** Public Health Service Hospital in Kotzebue, phone 442-3321; Alaska State Troopers in Kotzebue, phone 442-3911.

Climate: June clear and cool, July hot and dry. In August, expect rain, then usually 2 or 3 weeks of Indian summer in September. Winters are cold, similar to Kotzebue.

Private Aircraft: Airstrip adjacent northeast; elev. 15 feet; length 5,200 feet; gravel; no fuel; unattended.

Visitor Facilities: None. Supplies are obtained from Kotzebue and Anchorage.

Candle is a mining community which started in 1904. Most of the town burned down approximately 20 years ago; just a few houses were left standing. There are 4 year-round residents, with the population increasing from May until freezeup or Oct. 1. Because the mining season is so short, July 4 is the only summer holiday, and residents hold a town picnic with horseshoes and a softball game.

There is an old deserted dredge about 6 miles from town. Fishing is good in the Kewalik River from July through September for salmon, grayling and trout. There are moose, caribou, reindeer and occasionally bear. Two mining operations in Candle are available for people to walk through and watch, as well as an old cemetery to view.

Council

Located on the left bank of the Niukluk River on the Seward Peninsula, 33 miles northeast of Solomon, 74 miles northeast of Nome, 470 miles west of Fairbanks. **Transportation:**

Boat, charter plane or auto from Nome. **Population:** 11 year-round, up to 50 in summer. **Zip code:** 99790. **Emergency Services:** Alaska State Troopers, Nome; Health aide, phone 665-8001.

Elevation: 100 feet. **Climate:** Continental, with long, cold winters and short, mild summers. Average annual precipitation is 14 inches, with 46 inches of snowfall. Temperatures range between -9° and 64°F.

Private Aircraft: Melsing Creek airstrip adjacent northeast; elev. 95 feet; length 2,000 feet; gravel; no fuel; unattended. Runway subject to crosswinds, not maintained in winter; unattended; recommend visual inspection prior to using. Runway connected to section of the road, which has been widened to serve as part of the airstrip. No airport facilities. Transportation into village sometimes available. Pederson airstrip adjacent east of mining camp; elev. 95 feet; length 2,100 feet; gravel; no fuel; unattended. Prior permission for use required in writing from owner. South end of runway rough. Runway doglegs, use east side runway by road. Grass on strip, use caution.

Visitor Facilities: Accommodations and meals available in summer at a fishing lodge. No public laundry facilities or banking services. Limited groceries and sporting goods available at a small store in a local residence; most visitors bring their own supplies. No arts and crafts available for purchase. Fishing/hunting licenses not available. Guide services available. No repair service or rental transportation. Fuel available includes propane and regular gasoline. No moorage facilities.

Council, once one of the largest communities in Alaska, was founded in 1897 by Daniel B. Libby and his party. Libby had been 1 of 3 members of the Van Bendeleben expedition of 1896 who discovered gold in the area. Council became the site of the recording office and center of the Council Gold Mining District. By October 1897, it was a city of approximately 50 log houses and 300 people. The gold strikes at Council Creek predate major strikes at Nome, and a single claim on Ophir Creek was said to be the second richest claim in the world, second only to a claim in Klondike. During the summers of 1897-99, Council's population was estimated to be as high as 15,000 people and was said to be bigger than Nome although the actual population was never documented. "Council City" was a genuine boom town with a hotel, wooden boardwalks, a post office, a 20-bed hospital and numerous bars. At one time 13 dredges worked streams and rivers between

Solomon and Council and the town was the southern terminus of a railroad that climbed a 600-foot ridge into Ophir Creek. Many of the boomers left Council in 1900 for the gold beaches of Nome, but a sizable community remained. Council, which still had a population of 686 in 1910, was for many years the second-largest community in western Alaska. The influenza epidemic of 1918, the Great Depression and WWII contributed to its decline, and by 1950 only 9 people remained. The post office was closed in 1953.

Council is one of the few villages in the region connected to Nome by a road, which originated as a trail during the gold rush. The road was constructed in 1906-07. The road terminates across from Council at the river, which can be forded at low water periods. Three roads branch out from Council: to Ophir Creek, to Melsing Creek and the airstrip, and a third over a hill northeast to Mystery. Except for the Ophir Road, 4-wheel-drive vehicles are necessary.

The movie *North to Alaska* starring John Wayne was filmed in this area. Remnants of gold mining activity are everywhere. The countryside is dotted with old cabins, roads, a railroad, mines and dredges, including an operating dredge at Ophir Creek. The old post office, school, hotel and numerous other buildings in various stages of deterioration still stand among newer buildings in the settlement.

All permanent residents of Council, and many of the seasonal residents, rely in part on local hunting and fishing for food. The Niukluk River provides some of the finest fishing on the Seward Peninsula. Arctic char, grayling, pike, whitefish, and chum, pink and king salmon abound. Rabbits, ptarmigan, moose, grizzly bears and wolves all inhabit the area. Some placer gold mining currently takes place in the area, primarily at Ophir Creek.

Communications in Council include a phone in the community building (665-8001) and radios. There is a community electricity system. Water is hauled from a central watering point. The sewage system is honey buckets. Freight is hauled over the Nome-Council Road for $500 per truckload. Council is unincorporated. Village corporation address: Council Native Corp., P.O. Box 727, Nome, AK 99762.

Deering

Located at the mouth of the Inmachuck River on Kotzebue Sound, 57 miles southwest of Kotzebue, 150 miles north of Nome, 440 miles west-northwest of Fairbanks. **Transportation:** Scheduled and charter air service from Kotzebue; boat; snow machine. **Population:** 165. **Zip code:** 99736. **Emergency Services:** Village Public Safety Officer; Alaska State Troopers, Kotzebue, phone 442-3911; Health aide, phone 363-2137; Volunteer Fire Department.

Climate: Transitional zone; long cold winters and cool summers. Precipitation is light and averages less than 9 inches per year, with 36 inches of snow.

Private Aircraft: Airstrip 2 miles southwest; elev. 15 feet; length 2,200 feet; gravel; no fuel; unattended. Runway condition not monitored, visual inspection recommended prior to landing. No airport facilities; no public transportation to village.

Visitor Facilities: No hotel, restaurant or banking services. Laundromat available. Groceries, clothing, first-aid supplies and camera film available in the community. Some carved ivory available for purchase. Fishing/hunting licenses available. No guide service, major repair service or rental transportation. Fuel available includes diesel, propane, regular gasoline. No moorage facilities.

Deering, described as a beautiful oceanside community by one local resident, is built on a spit approximately 300 feet wide and 0.5 mile long. The village was established in 1901 as a supply station for Seward Peninsula gold mines and located near the historic Malemiut Eskimo village of Inmachukmiut. The village name probably was taken from the 90-ton schooner *Abbey Deering*, which was in the nearby waters in 1900. Deering is a second-class city, incorporated in 1970.

The economy is based on subsistence hunting and fishing. Main sources of meat are moose, seal and beluga whale; residents go to hunting camps in the spring and fall. A local reindeer herd provides some employment.

A 20-mile road connects Deering with the mining area of Utica to the south. Also, many trails along major streams and across the tundra are used year-round for traveling to other villages, hunting and fishing.

Communications in Deering include phones, mail plane, radio and TV. The community has a church and a school with grades preschool through 12. There is community electricity. Water comes from a Public Health Service tank in summer; ice is hauled for water in winter. Sewage system is honey buckets. Deering prohibits the sale and importation of alcoholic beverages. Freight arrives by cargo plane and barge. Government address: City of Deering, P.O. Box 36049, Deering, AK 99736;

phone 363-2136. Village corporation address: NANA Regional Corp., P.O. Box 49, Kotzebue, AK 99752.

Diomede

Located on the west coast of Little Diomede Island in Bering Strait, 80 miles northwest of Teller, 130 miles northwest of Nome, 650 miles west of Fairbanks. **Transportation:** Scheduled (in winter) and charter airplane service from Nome; helicopter. **Population:** 184. **Zip code:** 99762. **Emergency Services:** Alaska State Troopers, Nome, phone 443-2835; Health Clinic, phone 686-3311; Health aide, phone 686-3071 Volunteer Fire Department, phone 686-3071.

Climate: Maritime climate when the strait is ice free June through November. When the strait and the Bering and Chukchi seas freeze, there is an abrupt change to a cold continental climate. Winters cold and windy, with average of 35 inches of snowfall. Annual precipitation, recorded at nearby Wales, 10 inches. Thick fog covers the island in May and June. Winter temperatures average between -10° and 6°F. Summer temperatures average between 40° and 50°F.

Private Aircraft: No airstrip. Helicopter landing pad. Floatplane access in summer; ski-equipped planes can land on the frozen strait in winter.

Visitor Facilities: No hotel. Arrangements for accommodations can be made at the school or in private homes through the Inalik Village Corp. No restaurant or banking services. Laundromat with showers available. Limited groceries and sporting goods available in the community. Arts and crafts available for purchase include carved ivory and hand-sewn skin slippers and other garments. Fishing/hunting licenses not available. No guide or major repair services. Arrangements can be made to rent boats. Fuel available includes marine gas, diesel, propane and Blazo. No moorage facilities.

Diomede is only 2.5 miles from the Soviet Union's Big Diomede. The international boundary between the U.S. and USSR lies between the islands. Early Eskimos on the island were great travelers to both Siberia and the Alaska mainland, conducting trade with both continents. The present village site, age unknown, was originally a spring hunting site. It gradually became a permanent settlement. The Native name for the village is Inalik, meaning "the other one" or "the one over there"; the village is commonly known as Diomede.

On Aug. 16, 1728, Captain Commander

Vitus Bering named the islands in honor of St. Diomede. Explorers discovered that the Diomeders had an advanced culture with elaborate whale hunting ceremonies.

After WWII, the Soviet Union established the Iron Curtain and Big Diomede became a Russian military base. All Native residents were moved to mainland Russia and the residents of Little Diomede never saw their relatives again. During the post-WWII cold war, Little Diomede residents who strayed into Soviet waters were taken captive and held as prisoners in Siberia for a whole summer. The villagers are very cautious about straying into Soviet waters today.

Diomeders depend almost entirely on a subsistence economy. Blue cod, bullhead, flounder and tanner crab are harvested during the summer, and walrus, whale, seal and bear during spring and fall when these animals migrate through the area. Seal hides are used for mukluks, rope, harpoon lines and mittens, and walrus hides are used for boat hulls. Salmonberries, greens and some roots are found on the island. Migratory birds and their eggs supplement the subsistence diet.

The Diomede people are excellent ivory carvers. Many villagers market their crafts in Anchorage, Teller, Kotzebue and Nome.

Communications in Diomede, a second-class city incorporated in 1970, include phones, mail plane, radio and TV. The community has a church and a school with grades preschool through 12. There are community electricity and water. Sewage system is honey buckets, except in the clinic and laundromat, which have flush toilets. Diomede prohibits the sale and importation of alcoholic beverages. Freight arrives by plane in winter, barge in summer. Delivery of freight can be hampered by ice or weather conditions. Government address: City of Diomede, General Delivery, Diomede, AK 99762; phone 686-3071. Village corporation address: Inalik Native Corp., General Delivery, Diomede, AK 99762; phone 686-3221.

Elim

Located on the northwest shore of Norton Bay on the Seward Peninsula, 65 miles east of Solomon and 96 miles east of Nome. **Transportation:** Scheduled or charter air service from Nome. **Population:** 294. **Zip code:** 99739. **Emergency Services:** Police, phone 890-3081; Clinic, phone 890-3311; Volunteer Fire Department, phone 890-3441.

Climate: Subarctic, but changes to a more continental climate with the freezing of Norton Sound. Winter cold and relatively dry,

average 40 inches of snowfall. Average annual precipitation 18.9 inches.

Private Aircraft: Airstrip adjacent southwest; elev. 130 feet; length 3,000 feet; gravel; no fuel; unattended; recommend visual inspection prior to using. Cliff south, runway rutted but usable. No line of sight between runway ends. Use caution.

Visitor Facilities: Accommodations available at city building, phone 890-3441. Groceries, clothing and sundry items can be purchased. No restaurant. Fishing/hunting licenses available. Carved ivory available. No banking facilities or guide services. Boat, auto, aircraft repairs available; boats, autos and off-road vehicles available for rent. Fuel includes marine gas, diesel, propane, kerosene and regular gasoline.

Formerly the Malemiut Eskimo village of Nuviakchak, Elim is located on a former federal reindeer reserve, established in 1911, but dissolved with the Alaska Native Claims Settlement Act. A mission and school, opened in the early 1900s, increased the population. The village incorporated as a second-class city in 1970. Its economy is subsistence based, supplemented by seasonal employment in construction, fish processing and timber.

The Iditarod Trail passes through Elim, serving as a trail to Nome to the west and Unalakleet to the south.

Communications include phones, mail plane, radio and TV. The community has a church and a school with grades 9 through 12. Public electricity, water and sewage systems available. Freight arrives by air transport and barge. The village bans the sale and importation of alcoholic beverages. Government address: City of Elim, P.O. Box 39009, Elim, AK 99739; phone 890-3441. Village corporation address: Elim Native Corp., General Delivery, Elim, AK 99739; phone 890-3281.

Gambell

Located on Northwest Cape on St. Lawrence Island in the Bering Sea, 200 miles west of Nome, 675 miles west of Fairbanks. **Transportation:** Scheduled or charter air service from Nome. **Population:** 522. **Zip code:** 99742. **Emergency Services:** Police, phone 985-5333; Alaska State Troopers, Nome, phone 443-2835; Clinic, phone 985-5012; Volunteer Fire Department.

Elevation: 30 feet. **Climate:** Cool, moist maritime climate with some continental characteristics in the winter when much of the Bering Sea freezes. Winds and fog are common and precipitation occurs 300 days per year. Precipitation is usually very light rain, mist or snow, and total annual precipitation is only 15 inches. Average snowfall 80 inches, distributed evenly from November to May. Winter temperatures -2° and 10°F. Summer temperatures 34° and 48°F.

Private Aircraft: Airstrip adjacent south; elev. 27 feet; length 4,500 feet; asphalt; no fuel; unattended. No airport facilities or transportation into village.

Visitor Facilities: Accommodations and meals available at 1 lodge. Laundry facilities available; no banking services. Groceries, clothing, first-aid supplies, hardware, camera film and sporting goods available in the community. Arts and crafts available for purchase include carved ivory, baleen boats and Eskimo artifacts. Fishing/hunting licenses available. Contact the city of Gambell regarding guide service. No major repair service available. Arrangements can be made to rent off-road vehicles or boats. Fuel available includes diesel, propane and regular gasoline. No moorage facilities. Group tours available from Anchorage or Nome. *NOTE: Visitors to Gambell and Savoonga who wish to leave the city limits are required to pay a one-time fee of $25. The entire island is private property; the fee helps monitor use and serves as a registration system to make sure people don't get lost. The corporation also requires that any stories or photographs involving areas outside the townsite be submitted for prepublication approval.*

St. Lawrence Island has been inhabited for several thousand years. The island sits astride one of the great prehistoric migration routes — the Bering Land Bridge which linked Asia with the Americas. Evidence of Eskimo culture at Gambell dates back to 1700. Sivuqaq (Sivokak) is the Siberian Yup'ik name for the village and for St. Lawrence Island. The city was named in 1898 for Presbyterian missionaries and teachers Mr. and Mrs. Vene C. Gambell, who were lost in the schooner *Jane Grey* on their return from a leave of absence. The name was proposed by the new teacher William F. Doty. The village was established under the Indian Reorganization Act of 1934 as the Native village of Gambell in 1939. It was incorporated as a second-class city under state law in 1963.

The economy in Gambell is largely based on subsistence hunting. Residents hunt walrus and bowhead and gray whales in spring and fall. During summer the people fish, crab, hunt birds, gather eggs and harvest seafoods, greens and berries. Seal, fish and crab are harvested throughout the winter. Arctic fox are trapped as a secondary source of cash income. Some reindeer roam the island, but most harvest activities take place out of Savoonga.

The Native people of Gambell still hunt from walrus-hide boats and follow many old customs. A whaling festival takes place in Gambell each spring when a whale is taken.

There are 5 prehistoric village sites at Gambell which had been on the National Register of Historic Places. That designation was recently stripped from the sites because of extensive looting by the villagers. For half a century artifacts have been dug up and sold to supplement meager village incomes on this harsh island where unemployment stays about 25 percent.

Ivory carvings are a popular retail item and the St. Lawrence Islanders are famous for their beautiful work.

Numerous species of birds, some of them rare Asiatic species, populate the island during summer.

Communications at Gambell include phones, mail plane, radio and TV. The community is served by Presbyterian and Seventh Day Adventist churches and a school with grades kindergarten through 12. There is a community electricity system. Water is hauled from the laundromat. Sewage system is honey buckets. Gambell prohibits the possession of alcoholic beverages. Freight arrives by cargo plane and barge. Government address: City of Gambell, P.O. Box 189, Gambell, AK 99742; phone 985-5112. Village corporation address: Gambell Native Corp., General Delivery, Gambell, AK 99742; phone 985-5826.

Golovin

Located on a point between Golovnin Bay and Golovnin Inlet on the Seward Peninsula, 42 miles east of Solomon, 90 miles east of Nome and 450 miles west of Fairbanks. **Transportation:** Snow machine; scheduled and charter air service from Nome. **Population:** 158. **Zip code:** 99762. **Emergency Services:** Village Public Safety Officer, phone 779-3911; Health clinic, phone 779-3311; Volunteer Fire Department.

Elevation: 25 feet. **Climate:** Marine climate when the sea is ice free. Average annual precipitation 19 inches; average annual snowfall 40 inches. Average winter temperatures between -2° and 19°F; average summer temperatures between 40° and 60°F.

Private Aircraft: Airstrip adjacent north; elev. 25 feet; length 2,000 feet; gravel; no fuel; unattended; runway condition not monitored, recommend visual inspection prior to using. Road crosses 300 feet from the end of runway. Apron and runway floods. No airport facilities or public transportation into village.

Visitor Facilities: No hotel, restaurant or banking services. Laundromat available. Supplies available in the community. Arts and crafts available for purchase include fur hats, some ivory and woven wool mittens. Fishing/hunting licenses available. No guide service. Aircraft mechanic available, as well as charter aircraft. Fuel available includes diesel, propane and regular gasoline.

The Eskimo village of Chinik, located at the present site of Golovin, was originally settled by the Kauweramiut Eskimos who later mixed with Unaligmiut Eskimos. Lieutenant L.A. Zagoskin of the Imperial Russian Navy, reported the village as Ikalikguigmyut in 1842. The name Golovin was derived from the name of Golovnin Lagoon, which was named after Captain Vasili Mikkailovich Golovnin of the Russian Navy.

Around 1890, John Dexter established a trading post at Golovin that became the center for prospecting information for the entire Seward Peninsula. Gold was discovered in 1898 and Golovin became the supply point for the Council goldfields to the northwest. Golovin incorporated as a second-class city in 1971.

Golovin's economy is based on subsistence food harvest, reindeer herding, fish processing and commercial fishing. Local businesses, government and construction work provide additional employment. Residents go to summer fish camps to catch salmon, whitefish, trout, grayling, pike and herring. Subsistence hunting includes seal, beluga whale, moose, ducks, geese and ptarmigan. Bird eggs and berries are gathered from the tundra.

The Iditarod Trail passes through Golovin and is used as a winter trail.

A privately owned herd of 520 reindeer is managed from Golovin. Butchering takes place in February and June.

Communications in Golovin include phones, mail plane, radio and TV. The community has a Covenant church and a school with grades kindergarten through 12. Community electricity and water systems. Sewer system is honey buckets. Golovin prohibits the sale and importation of alcoholic beverages. Freight arrives in the community by cargo plane and barge. Government address: City of Golovin, P.O. Box 62059, Golovin, AK 99762; phone 779-3211. Village corporation address: Golovin Native Corp., General Delivery, Golovin, AK 99762; phone 779-3251.

Koyuk

Located at the mouth of the Koyuk River, at the northeastern end of Norton Bay on the Seward Peninsula, 132 miles east of Nome and 75 miles north of Unalakleet. **Transportation:** Scheduled air service to Nome. **Population:** 216. **Zip code:** 99753. **Emergency Services:** Police, phone 963-3541; Clinic, phone 963-3311; Volunteer Fire Department.

Climate: Winters cold and relatively dry, with an average of 40 inches of snowfall. Summers cool, with most rainfall in July, August and September. Average annual precipitation 18.9 inches. Average winter temperatures -8° and 8°F. Summer temperatures 46° to 62°F.

Private Aircraft: Airstrip adjacent northeast; elev. 130 feet; length 2,400 feet; gravel; unattended. No line of sight from runway ends. Runway condition not monitored, recommend visual inspection prior to using. Turbulence on approach when wind from northwest. Caution advised.

Visitor Facilities: No hotel or restaurant. Washeteria available. Groceries, clothing, first-aid supplies, hardware, camera film and sporting goods available in the community. Pay phone (963-9991) available. No arts and crafts available. Fishing/hunting licenses available, as well as guide service. No banking or major repair service; no moorage facilities or rental transportation. Fuel available includes marine gas, propane and unleaded gasoline.

The village known as Kuynkhak-muit was first recorded by Lt. L.A. Zagoskin of the Imperial Russian Navy in the 1840s. Prior to 1900, the village was nomadic, gradually settling around the present site where supplies could easily be lightered to shore. Located 40 miles downriver from the Norton Bay Station trading center and near a coal mine which supplied steamships and the city of Nome, Koyuk became a natural transfer point for goods and services.

The archaeological site of Iyatayak, with traces of early man 6,000 to 8,000 years old, is located south of Koyuk on Cape Denbigh.

The village was incorporated in 1970 as a second-class city. The economy is based on subsistence supplemented by part-time wage earnings. Some income is derived from reindeer herding, with hides and antlers being sold on the commercial market. Salmon, herring, grayling, beluga, seal, caribou, wildfowl, moose and berries are harvested.

Communications include phones, mail plane, radio and TV. The community has a Covenant church and a school with grades preschool to 12. Community electricity system is available. Sewage system is honey buckets. Water from a community well is hauled from the washeteria. Freight arrives by air transport and barge. The village bans the sale and importation of alcoholic beverages. Government address: City of Koyuk, P.O. Box 29, Koyuk, AK 99753; phone 963-3441. Village corporation address: Koyuk Native Corp., Koyuk, AK 99753; phone 963-3551.

Nome

Located on the south coast of the Seward Peninsula, 550 air miles west of Anchorage. **Transportation:** Daily jet service from Anchorage available year-round. Charter air service to and from villages; in winter, snow machines, dogsleds. **Population:** 3,876. **Zip code:** 99762. **Emergency Services:** Norton Sound Regional Hospital; Police, Fire and Ambulance, phone 911.

Elevation: 13 to 44 feet. **Climate:** Average temperature in January from -3° to 12°F; average temperature in July from 45° to 60°F. Mean annual precipitation 15.5 inches; mean annual snowfall 55 inches. Snow usually starts falling in early October; last snowfall in late April.

Private Aircraft: Nome airport 2 miles west; elev. 36 feet; length 6,000 feet; asphalt; fuel 80, 100, jet A, A1. Three cab companies available for transportation to town. Nome city aerodrome 0.9 mile north; elev. 59 feet; length 3,200 feet; gravel.

Visitor Facilities: Accommodations at 2 hotels and 2 bed-and-breakfast homes. For additional information, contact the Nome Convention and Visitors Bureau. There are a number of restaurants, 1 bank, laundry and shower facilities. Groceries, clothing, first-aid supplies, hardware, camera film and sporting goods available at local stores. Native arts and crafts available at several excellent gift shops. Fishing/hunting licenses available, as well as guide service. Public moorage facilities available. Truck and van rentals available.

Nome owes its name to a misinterpretation of "? name" annotated on a manuscript chart prepared aboard the HMS *Herald* about 1850. The question mark was taken as a C (for cape) and the A in "name" was read as O. However, Nome residents generally dispute this. Local tradition holds that the word Nome was derived from the Eskimo phrase *Kn-no-me*, meaning, "I don't know," probably the Eskimo reply when asked the name of the area.

Gold was found in the Nome area in September 1898 and the town got its start that winter when 6 miners met at the mouth of Snake River and formed the Cape Nome

Mining District. Originally the settlement was called Anvil City, after Anvil Creek where the first major gold strike was found. During the following summer gold was found on the beaches of Nome. News of the gold strike set off a major rush in the summer of 1900 when the news reached Seattle. By August 1900, there were some 20,000 people in Nome. The entire Seward Peninsula is believed to hold 100 gold dredges from bygone days; 44 dredges, some complete and others in pieces, lie in the immediate Nome area.

Incorporated in 1901, Nome is the oldest first-class city in Alaska and has the state's oldest first-class school district.

Nome is the transportation and commerce center for northwestern Alaska. Alaska's reindeer industry is centered in the Nome vicinity and the area has rich mineral potential. Nome also is a major stopover on arctic tours and a jumping-off point for tours to surrounding Eskimo villages.

Nome is the location of Northwest College. The city has 1 parking meter in front of the newspaper office.

The Bering Sea is only a stone's throw from Front Street. The granite sea wall protecting Nome from the sea was built between 1949 and 1951 by the U.S. Army Corps of Engineers. The 3,350-foot-long seawall is 65 feet wide at its base, 16 feet wide at its top, and stands 18 feet above mean low water.

Carrie McLain Memorial Museum, P.O. Box 53, Nome, AK 99762, phone 443-2566, is located in the basement of the building containing the Kegoayah Kozga Library on Front Street. This history museum has a fascinating collection of some 6,000 photographs of the gold rush and early Eskimo life. Copies of the photographs can be purchased on request. Permanent exhibits include the Bering Land Bridge; natural history; Eskimo lifestyles and art; contemporary art; the Nome gold rush; and dog mushing history. Special exhibitions and demonstrations take place throughout the year. Hours vary according to season. No admission charge; donations accepted.

Nome's city hall, with turn-of-the-century decor, is on Front Street. A massive wood-burl arch sits in the lot next to city hall until March each year, when it is raised over Front Street for the Month of Iditarod festival celebrating the 1,049-mile Iditarod Trail Sled Dog Race from Anchorage to Nome. Hundreds of visitors come to Nome to take part in the various activities that include a statewide basketball tournament, the 200-mile Nome to Golovin snowmobile race, a snowshoe softball tournament, Eskimo blanket toss, Eskimo dancing and dog weight-pulling contest. Another event that attracts national attention and participants is the Bering Sea Ice Golf Classic, a golf tournament played on the frozen Bering Sea in March. The highlight of the month comes with completion of the Iditarod Trail Sled Dog Race. All the townspeople turn out to welcome each tired musher and team at the finish line.

In June Nome celebrations include the annual Midnight Sun Festival, sponsored by the chamber of commerce. The highlight of the festival is a raft race on the Nome River, in which many strange craft take part. Winner of the raft race is traditionally awarded a fur-lined honey bucket.

The Anvil Mountain Run is scheduled for the Fourth of July. This 12.5-mile race follows a very rugged course from city hall to the top of 1,977-foot Anvil Mountain, so named because of the anvil-shaped rock on its peak, and down again via the face of the mountain.

Other events in the community are the Memorial Day Polar Bear Swim and the Labor Day Bathtub Race.

Reactivated gold dredges operate near the north end of the main Nome airport and 2 miles north of town. Nome is home to the 14-story offshore dredge, the BIMA. It is the largest dredge of its kind in the world and pulls more than 36,000 ounces of gold from the floor of Norton Sound each season.

Three roads, maintained only in summer, extend east, north and west from the city: the 72-mile Nome-Teller Road, the 72-mile Nome-Council Road, and the 86-mile Nome-Taylor Road. Check snow conditions with the Dept. of Transportation or the Alaska State Troopers, phone 443-2835. Travelers can spot many varieties of wildflowers and birds along these roads. More than 184 species of birds have been identified in the Nome area, many of which are unique to the area. Blueberries, salmonberries and cranberries ripen all over the Seward Peninsula around August.

For more information about attractions in Nome, contact the Nome Convention and Visitors Bureau, Box 251, Nome, AK 99762; phone 443-5535.

Communications in Nome include phones, 2 radio stations, TV and the weekly *Nome Nugget* newspaper. There are community electricity, water and sewer systems. The community is served by 15 churches, elementary and high schools, a 26-bed hospital and port facilities for vessels up to 22 feet of draft in 30-foot depth. Government address: City of Nome, P.O. Box 281, Nome, AK 99762; phone 443-5242.

For more information, see *Nome: City of the Golden Beaches*, Vol. 11, No. 1, *ALASKA GEOGRAPHIC®*. To order, see ALASKA NORTHWEST LIBRARY section at the back of the book.

Port Clarence

Located on Point Spencer on the Bering Sea coast, 80 miles northwest of Nome, 560 miles west of Fairbanks. **Transportation:** U.S. Coast Guard aircraft or charter air service from Nome. **Population:** 30. **Zip code:** 99762. **Emergency Services:** Alaska State Troopers, Nome; U.S. Coast Guard corpsman.

Elevation: 10 feet. **Climate:** Mean annual precipitation 10 inches; mean annual snowfall 47 inches. Snow starts falling in late October; last snowfall usually in late May.

Private Aircraft: Airstrip 1 mile northeast; elev. 10 feet; length 4,500 feet; asphalt; no fuel. Closed to the public. Available to private aircraft only in emergencies (contact 122.8 MMZ), unless prior permission obtained from Coast Guard District 17 headquarters in Juneau, phone 586-7705.

Visitor Facilities: None.

Port Clarence is a U.S. Coast Guard loran station with no public facilities. The airfield originally was constructed for bombers in WWII. In 1961 the Coast Guard station was built to aid in navigation for ships in the Bering Sea.

Residents of nearby communities use the Point Spencer spit during the summer fishing season.

St. Michael

Located on St. Michael Island, 48 miles southwest of Unalakleet, 125 miles southwest of Nome and 420 miles northwest of Anchorage. **Transportation:** Boat, snow machine, scheduled and charter air service from Unalakleet and Nome. **Population:** 305. **Zip code:** 99659. **Emergency Services:** Village Public Safety Officer; Alaska State Troopers, Unalakleet, phone 624-3646; Clinic, phone 923-3311; Volunteer Fire Department.

Elevation: 30 feet. **Climate:** Subarctic with maritime influence in summer, when Norton Sound is ice free (usually June to November), and a cold continental influence during the winter. Summers are moist, with clouds and fog common, but annual precipitation is only 12 inches, much of which occurs in July, August and September. Annual snowfall averages 38 inches, with most of it during October and February. Winter temperatures average -4° to 16°F; summer temperatures average 40° to 60°F.

Private Aircraft: Airstrip adjacent north; elev. 30 feet; length 2,300 feet; gravel; no fuel; unattended; runway condition not monitored, visual inspection recommended prior to using.

Visitor Facilities: No hotel or restaurant. Arrangements for accommodations at the school or private homes can sometimes be made by contacting the school principal, phone 923-3041, or the city office, phone 923-3211. There is a washeteria. Supplies available in the community. Fishing/hunting licenses available. Information on other visitor services and facilities unavailable.

The Russians established a stockade post there in 1833, named after a governor of the Russian-American colony. Its name soon became Michaelovski or Redoubt St. Michael, and the post was the northernmost Russian settlement in Alaska. The Eskimo village of Tachik was located to the northeast.

During the gold rush era at the end of the century, St. Michael became the major gateway to the Interior via the Yukon River. A U.S. military post, Fort St. Michael, was established in 1897, but was closed in 1922. As many as 10,000 people were said to live in St. Michael during the Nome gold rush. The village remained an important transshipment point until the Alaska Railroad was built. St. Michael also was a popular trading post for Eskimos trading for Western goods.

Remnants of St. Michael's historic past can still be seen. Three Russian-built houses, the hulks of steamboats and several old cemeteries remain. The old Russian church and most military buildings have been torn down, and an old cannon and other Russian artifacts were moved to Sitka. The sites of the old U.S. fort and the Russian redoubt are on the National Register of Historic Places.

St. Michael is the closest deep-water port to the Yukon and Kuskokwim rivers. It remains a transfer point for freight hauled from Seattle on large ocean-going barges to be placed on smaller river barges or shipped to other Norton Sound villages. St. Michael incorporated in 1969 as a second-class city.

St. Michael's economy is based on subsistence food harvest supplemented by part-time jobs. Residents harvest sea mammals, including seal and beluga whale. Moose and caribou are important winter staples. Summer fishing provides salmon, whitefish, tomcod and herring. Waterfowl, particularly ducks and geese are hunted in nearby marshes. The tundra yields salmonberries, blackberries, blueberries, raspberries and cranberries.

St. Michael is served by Catholic and Assembly of God churches, as well as a school with grades preschool through 12. There is a community electricity system. Water is hauled from a central watering point. Sewage system is honey buckets. St. Michael prohibits the sale and importation of alcoholic beverages. Freight arrives by barge and plane. Government address: City of St. Michael, P.O. Box 70, St. Michael, AK 99659; phone 923-3211. Village corporation address: St. Michael Native Corp., P.O. Box 70, St. Michael, AK 99659; phone 923-3231.

Savoonga

(suh-VOON-guh) Located on St. Lawrence Island in the Bering Sea, 39 miles southeast of Gambell, 164 miles west of Nome and 700 miles west of Fairbanks. **Transportation:** Scheduled and charter air service from Nome. **Population:** 509. **Zip code:** 99769. **Emergency Services:** Police, phone 984-6011; Clinic, phone 984-6513; Volunteer Fire Department, phone 984-6234.

Climate: Cool, moist, subarctic maritime with some continental influences during winter, when the Bering Sea freezes. Mean annual precipitation 11 inches; mean annual snowfall 58 inches. Winter temperatures average -7° to 11°F; summer temperatures average 40° to 51°F.

Private Aircraft: Airstrip 2 miles south; elev. 53 feet; length 4,600 feet; gravel; no fuel, unattended. Passenger terminal at airport. There is usually transportation into the village with local people.

Visitor Facilities: Accommodations at a local bed-and-breakfast. Washeteria with showers available. No banking services. Groceries, clothing, first-aid supplies, hardware, camera film and sporting goods available in the community. Arts and crafts available for purchase include carved ivory, baleen baskets, hand-sewn skin garments and Eskimo artifacts. No repair services. Arrangements may be made to rent off-road vehicles. Fuel available: marine gas, diesel, kerosene, propane, unleaded and regular gasoline. Moorage on beach. *NOTE: Visitors to Gambell and Savoonga who wish to leave the city limits are required to pay a one-time fee of $25. The entire island is private property; the fee helps monitor use and serves as a registration system to make sure people don't get lost. The corporation also requires that any stories or photographs involving areas outside the townsite be submitted for prepublication approval on some occasions.*

St. Lawrence Island has been inhabited for several thousand years. The Siberian Yup'ik Eskimos lived by subsistence for many years and had little contact with the rest of the world until European traders began to frequent the area.

A herd of 70 reindeer was introduced to the island in 1900. The herd grew during the next 40 years, increasing to a peak of 10,000 animals. The reindeer tended to remain on the eastern side of the island and managing them from Gambell became impossible. A reindeer camp was established at Savoonga, 4 miles west of the abandoned village of Kookoolik, in 1916. Good hunting and trapping in the area attracted more residents. The population of Savoonga steadily increased and in the 1980 census it surpassed that of Gambell. The community is built on wet, soft tundra and boardwalks crisscross the village providing dry routes to all buildings. In 1969 Savoonga was incorporated as a second-class city.

The economy of Savoonga is based largely on subsistence hunting, with some cash income. Savoonga is hailed as the "Walrus Capital of the World," and residents hunt these animals, as well as bowhead and gray whales, in spring and fall. During summer, the people fish, crab, hunt birds, gather eggs and harvest various seafoods, greens and berries. Seal, fish and crab are harvested through the winter. Arctic fox is trapped as a source of income, but there is no other commercial hunting or fishing. Reindeer roam free on the island, but the herd is not really managed. There are a few jobs in the village with the city, Native corporation, school and store.

St. Lawrence Islanders are famous for their ivory carvings which are a popular retail item. Artifacts found at some of the 35 older village sites on the island also are sold for income. These older villages were occupied in the 18th and 19th centuries when St. Lawrence Island supported a population of about 4,000 people. A tragic famine from 1878 to 1880 decimated the population and in 1903 only 261 people were reported on the entire island.

Bird-watching also is popular with visitors, who come to view and photograph the 2.7 million seabirds that nest on the island.

Communications in Savoonga include phones, mail plane, radio and TV. There is a community electricity system. Water is hauled from 3 watering points. Sewage system is honey buckets. The community is served by Presbyterian and Seventh Day Adventist churches and 2 schools with grades kindergarten through 12. The village prohibits the sale and importation of alcoholic beverages. Freight arrives by plane, barge and ship.

Government address: City of Savoonga, P.O. Box 87, Savoonga, AK 99769; phone 984-6614. Village corporation address: Savoonga Native Corp., P.O. Box 142, Savoonga, AK 99769; phone 984-6613.

Shaktoolik

(shack-TOO-lick) Located on the east shore of Norton Sound, 33 miles north of Unalakleet, 180 miles east of Nome, 410 miles northwest of Fairbanks. **Transportation:** Boat; scheduled and charter air service from Nome or Unalakleet. **Population:** 197. **Zip code:** 99771. **Emergency Services:** Village Public Safety Officer; Alaska State Troopers, Unalakleet, phone 624-3646; Clinic, Health Aide, phone 955-3511; Volunteer Fire Department, phone 955-3661.

Climate: Subarctic with considerable maritime influence when Norton Sound is ice free, usually from May to October. Winters cold and relatively dry, with an average of 43 inches of snowfall. Winds from the east and northeast predominate. Summers cool, with most precipitation occurring in July, August and September. Average annual precipitation is 14 inches. Winter temperatures average between -4° and 11°F. Summer temperatures average between 47° and 62°F.

Private Aircraft: Airstrip 3 miles northwest; elev. 15 feet; length 2,200 feet; gravel; no fuel; unattended. Runway condition not monitored, visual inspection recommended prior to using. No airport facilities. Public transportation available to village.

Visitor Facilities: No hotel, restaurant or banking services. Arrangements may be made to stay at 1 bed-and-breakfast, in private homes, or on the school floor. Laundromat with showers available. Groceries, clothing, first-aid supplies, hardware, camera film and sporting goods available in the community. Arts and crafts available for purchase include carved ivory, wooden berry-picking buckets, wooden masks, Eskimo dolls, parkas, mukluks and beadwork. Fishing/hunting licenses available. No guide services. Residents do their own marine engine, boat and auto repairs. Arrangements may be made to rent private off-road vehicles and boats. Fuel available: diesel, white gas, propane and regular gasoline. No moorage facilities.

Shaktoolik was first mapped in 1842-44 by Lt. L.A. Zagoskin of the Imperial Russian Navy, who called it Tshaktogmyut. The village moved from a site 6 miles up the Shaktoolik River to the river mouth in 1933, but was subject to erosion and wind damage at that location. In 1967 the village moved again to a more sheltered location 2.5 miles to the north. Shaktoolik is a second-class city, incorporated in 1969.

The economy is subsistence, supplemented by part-time earnings from jobs with the city, school, construction, store, airlines and Native corporation. About 1,500 privately owned reindeer provide meat, hides and additional income. Residents harvest moose, caribou, whale, seal, squirrel, rabbit, waterfowl and ptarmigan. They fish for salmon, arctic char, tomcod, flounder, sculpin, herring and smelt. In fall they pick berries.

The Iditarod Trail passes through Shaktoolik and links the village to Unalakleet and coastal villages to the west along Norton Sound.

Cape Denbigh, 12 miles to the northeast, is the site of Iyatayat, a national historic landmark 6,000 to 8,000 years old. Another attraction is Besboro Island off the coast, site of a major seabird colony.

Communications in Shaktoolik include phones, mail plane, radio and TV. The community is served by Covenant and Assembly of God churches and a school with grades preschool through 12. There are community electricity and water systems. Sewage system is flush toilets and seepage pits. The village prohibits the sale and importation of alcoholic beverages. Freight arrives by cargo plane. Government address: City of Shaktoolik, P.O. Box 10, Shaktoolik, AK 99771; phone 955-3441. Village corporation address: Shaktoolik Native Corp., General Delivery, Shaktoolik, AK 99771; phone 955-3451.

Shishmaref

Located on Sarichef Island between the Chukchi Sea and Shishmaref Inlet, 5 miles from the mainland, 100 miles southwest of Kotzebue, 120 miles north of Nome, 550 miles west of Fairbanks. **Transportation:** Scheduled and charter air service from Nome. **Population:** 444. **Zip code:** 99772. **Emergency Services:** Police, phone 649-3411; Alaska State Troopers, Nome, phone 443-2835; Clinic, phone 649-3311; Volunteer Fire Department. **Elevation:** 20 feet. **Climate:** Transitional zone; winters windy, cold and dry, and snowfall averages only 33 inches. Winter temperatures average -12° to 2°F. Summers can be foggy, with west winds prevailing and temperatures averaging 47° to 54°F. Average annual precipitation is 8 inches.

Private Aircraft: Airstrip 1 mile northeast; elev. 8 feet; length 2,000 feet; asphalt; no fuel; unattended; runway condition not monitored, visual inspection recommended prior to using. Beach sand on ocean side is solid enough to permit landing, used when airstrip is subject to crosswinds. All air travel is "weather permitting," says one resident.

Visitor Facilities: Accommodations available in trailer owned by Nayokpuk General Store, in private homes, on school floor and at the Shishmaref city hall. One restaurant. No banking services. Washeteria available. Groceries, clothing, first-aid supplies, hardware, camera film and sporting goods available in the community. Arts and crafts available for purchase include carved and etched ivory, fur slippers and mukluks, horn dolls and bone carvings. Fishing/hunting licenses available. No guide or repair services; no rental transportation. Fuel available: diesel, propane, white gas, kerosene, regular gasoline. No moorage facilities.

Shishmaref is just 20 miles south of the Arctic Circle and only 100 miles east of Siberia. The original Eskimo name for the island is Kigiktaq. Lieutenant Otto Von Kotzebue named the inlet Shishmarev in 1816 after Capt. Lt. Glieb Semenovich Shishmarev, who accompanied him on his exploration. Archaeologists excavated some of the sites at Kigiktaq around 1821 and found evidence of Eskimo habitation going back several centuries. After 1900, when a supply center was established to serve gold mines in the interior of the Seward Peninsula, the village was renamed after the inlet. The site offered a fairly good harbor and proximity to mining operations. Shishmaref was incorporated as a second-class city in 1969.

The Shishmaref economy is based on subsistence and part-time employment at local stores, the school district, city and Native corporations. In spring residents harvest *oogruk,* walrus, seal, rabbit, squirrel, ptarmigan, waterfowl, eggs, various greens and plants. Summer brings the harvest of herring, smelt, salmon, whitefish, trout, grayling, greens and plants. In fall berries, waterfowl, squirrel, moose, *oogruk,* seal, herring, grayling and lingcod are taken. In winter residents hunt for seal, polar bear, rabbit and ptarmigan; and fish for tomcod, flounder, sculpin and smelt. Two reindeer herds totaling 7,000 head are managed from Shishmaref and reindeer meat and skins are sometimes available at a local store.

Shishmaref is the home of Eskimo artist Melvin Olanna and Iditarod Trail dog musher Herbie Nayokpuk.

Each year, the Shishmaref Spring Carnival, highlighted by the Seward Peninsula Open-Class Championship Sled Dog Races, takes place on the third weekend in April.

Shishmaref is surrounded by 2.6-million-acre Bering Land Bridge National Preserve, considered to be part of the land bridge over which prehistoric hunters traveled from Asia to North America. It offers a variety of arctic wildlife and plants, hot springs, lava beds and other volcanic phenomena, and archaeological sites. For more information write: Superintendent, Bering Land Bridge National Preserve, P.O. Box 220, Nome, AK 99762.

Winter travel in Shishmaref consists mainly of snow machines, dogsleds and snowshoes. There are winter trails to the mainland and along the coastline.

Communications in Shishmaref include phones, mail plane and radio. There is a community electricity system. The community is served by a Lutheran church and a school with grades preschool through 12. Water is hauled from the washeteria, collected from rain water or melted from ice hauled from the mainland. Sewage system is primarily honey buckets. The village prohibits the sale and importation of alcoholic beverages. Freight arrives by cargo plane and barge. Government address: City of Shishmaref, General Delivery, Shishmaref, AK 99772; phone 649-3781 or 4811. Village corporation address: Shishmaref Native Corp., General Delivery, Shishmaref, AK 99772; phone 649-3751.

Solomon

Located on the west bank of the Solomon River, 1 mile north of Norton Sound, 32 miles east of Nome, 500 miles west of Fairbanks. **Transportation:** By auto on the Nome-Council Road; charter air service from Nome. **Population:** 8. **Zip code:** 99762. **Emergency Services:** Alaska State Troopers and Norton Sound Regional Hospital in Nome.

Climate: Solomon's climate is both maritime and continental. Summers are short, wet and mild. Winters are cold and windy. Weather data from Nome shows annual precipitation is 16.4 inches, with 54 inches of snowfall. Temperatures range from -30° to 56°F.

Private Aircraft: Lee's (mining) Camp is a private strip, 5 miles north of Solomon. Permission necessary from owner to use this 1,000-foot unpaved runway.

Visitor Facilities: None.

This location was called Erok on a 1900 Map of Nome Peninsula by Davidson and Blakeslee. Originally established as a mining camp in 1900 on a spit between the Solomon and Bonanza rivers, the townsite was destroyed by a 1913 storm. Townspeople decided to move Solomon east across the

Solomon River to the site of the abandoned southern terminus of the Council City and Solomon River railroad, which had been known as Dickson. Flooding continued to threaten the low-lying town, and in the 1930s the townsite was moved once again to the base of Jerusalem Hill on the west side of the river.

During summer 1900, a thousand or more people lived in Solomon. The community had 7 saloons, a post office, a ferry dock, and by 1904 was the terminus of a standard gauge railroad that ran north.

The town's boom was short-lived. Few held productive mining claims and several disasters befell the community. Besides the 1913 storm, the 1918 worldwide influenza epidemic devastated the population. Mining picked up a bit between the wars, but people moved out again during WWII to find work. In 1956 the Bureau of Indian Affairs school closed.

Rusting railroad equipment, the old school and the river ferry today offer reminders of Solomon's historic past. The Solomon Roadhouse, built in 1904 in Dickson, was nominated to the National Register of Historic Places in 1979.

The unpaved Nome-Council Road, which originated as a trail during the gold rush, runs through town. The road, maintained only in summer, brings many visitors to the area, including bird-watchers, fishermen, hunters and tourists. A section of the road is part of the Iditarod Trail from Seward to Nome and a spur extends up the Solomon River into the Casadepaga River valley.

Communication is by radio. There is no public electricity system. Water is hauled from the Solomon River or Jerusalem Creek. The sewage system is honey buckets or outhouses.

Four families live in Solomon year-round. Many Nome residents, including members of Solomon Native Corp., P.O. Box 243, Nome, AK 99762; phone 443-2844, have seasonal homes or camps there.

Stebbins

Located on the northwest coast of St. Michael Island on Norton Sound, 53 miles southwest of Unalakleet, 120 miles southeast of Nome, 300 miles northwest of Anchorage. **Transportation:** Scheduled and charter air service from Unalakleet. **Population:** 384. **Zip code:** 99671. **Emergency Services:** Village Public Safety Officer, phone 934-3451; Clinic, phone 934-3311; Volunteer Fire Department.

Elevation: 26 feet. **Climate:** Subarctic with a maritime influence June to November when

Norton Sound is ice free and a cold continental influence in winter. Clouds and fog common in summer. Weather data for St. Michael indicates annual precipitation at Stebbins is 12 inches, with 38 inches of snow. Winter temperatures between -1° and 16°F, summer temperatures between 40° and 60°F, with a record high of 77°F.

Private Aircraft: Airstrip adjacent northwest; elev. 26 feet; length 3,200 feet; gravel; no fuel; unattended; runway condition not monitored, visual inspection recommended prior to using. No airport facilities; public transportation to village available.

Visitor Facilities: Arrangements for lodging at small inn or in private homes may be made. No restaurant or banking services. Laundry facilities and showers available. Groceries, clothing, first-aid supplies, hardware, camera film and sporting goods available in the community. Arts and crafts available for purchase include carved ivory, masks and grass baskets. Fishing/hunting licenses available. For guide services, contact city office. No repair services. Arrangements may be made to rent off-road vehicles and boats. Fuel available includes marine gas, propane, diesel and regular gasoline. Moorage facilities available.

The Eskimo village of Atroik or Atowak was first recorded in 1898 by the U.S. Coast and Geodetic Survey at a site on the hillside north of Stebbins. The Native name for the village is Tapraq; the name Stebbins was first published on a USCGS map in 1900. In 1950, Stebbins was described as a village of Eskimos who made their livelihood by hunting, fishing and herding reindeer. Stebbins was incorporated as a second-class city in 1969.

The Stebbins economy is still based on subsistence hunting and fishing, supplemented by part-time wage earnings. There is presently an unmaintained herd of reindeer on Stuart Island just off the coast. Subsistence harvest includes bearded, ring and spotted seal; salmon, tomcod, walrus, flounder, sculpin, herring, beluga whales, smelt; wildfowl, ptarmigan, rabbit; and berries. Commercial fishing in the area is on the increase.

Stebbins is located at the northern tip of Yukon Delta National Wildlife Refuge. Bird-watching is for peregrine falcons and a myriad of migratory wildfowl.

Recreational activities in Stebbins include basketball, bingo, Eskimo dances and an annual potlatch.

Overland travel is by snow machine in the winter. A number of trails link Stebbins with St. Michael.

Communications in Stebbins include phones, mail plane, radio and TV. The community is served by a church and a school with grades kindergarten through 12. There are community electricity and water. Sewage system is honey buckets. Stebbins prohibits the sale and importation of alcoholic beverages. Freight is hauled by cargo plane, barge and ship. Government address: City of Stebbins, P.O. Box 22, Stebbins, AK 99671; phone 934-3451 or 4561. Village corporation address: Stebbins Native Corp., General Delivery, Stebbins, AK 99671.

Teller

Located on a spit between Port Clarence and Grantley Harbor on the Seward Peninsula, 72 miles north of Nome, 540 miles west of Fairbanks. **Transportation:** By auto on the Nome-Teller Road; scheduled and charter air service from Nome. **Population:** 244. **Zip code:** 99778. **Emergency Services:** Village Public Safety Officer, phone 642-4291; Alaska State Troopers, Nome, phone 443-2441; Clinic, phone 642-3693.

Elevation: 10 feet. **Climate:** Maritime when the Bering Sea is ice free, usually early June to mid-November. Freezing of the sea causes a change to a more continental climate with less precipitation and colder temperatures. Mean annual precipitation 11 inches; mean annual snowfall 50 inches. Winter temperatures average -9° to 8°F; summer temperatures average 44° to 57°F.

Private Aircraft: Airstrip 2 miles south; elev. 293 feet; length 2,300 feet; gravel; no fuel; unattended; unlighted; runway condition not monitored, visual inspection recommended prior to using. No airport facilities. Public transportation into town available.

Visitor Facilities: No hotel, restaurant or banking services. Washeteria available. Groceries, clothing, first-aid supplies, hardware, camera film and sporting goods available in the community. Arts and crafts available include carved walrus and mastodon ivory, hand-sewn seal skin items, and Eskimo dolls. Fishing/hunting licenses available. No guide or repair services. No rental transportation or moorage facilities. Fuel available: diesel and regular gasoline.

Captain Daniel B. Libby and his party from the Western Union Telegraph expedition wintered here in 1866 and 1867; the site was then called Libbyville or Libby Station. The first permanent settlement, named for U.S. Sen. H.M. Teller, was established around 1900 after the Bluestone Placer discovery 15 miles to the south. During those boom years at the turn of the century, Teller had a population estimated at 5,000 and was a major regional trading center. Although Teller's population had dropped to 125 by 1910 and continued to decrease through 1930, the number of residents since has increased gradually. The community was incorporated as a second-class city in 1963.

The economy of Teller is based on subsistence food harvest supplemented by part-time wage earnings. Some foxes are trapped in the area and reindeer herding has been practiced since Teller's founding. Residents hunt for seal, beluga whale, moose, squirrel, rabbit, ptarmigan, wildfowl and their eggs. They fish for salmon, herring, smelt, whitefish, sculpin, tomcod and flounder.

Teller was the landing site of the *Norge,* the first dirigible to be flown over the North Pole. The craft, piloted by Roald Amundson, flew 71 hours from Spitzbergen, Norway. Its intended landing site was Nome, but bad weather forced it to land May 13, 1926, on the beach at Teller instead. Near the landing site, a plaque commemorating the event has been placed on an old 2-story false-front building in which some of the disassembled segments and gear from the *Norge* were stored. The storage site is on the National Register of Historic Places.

Teller also is the home of Libby Riddles, 1985 winner of the Iditarod Sled Dog Race. Riddles, first woman to win the grueling 1,049-mile race from Anchorage to Nome, raises and trains her dogs in Teller.

From May through October a 72-mile gravel road is open from Teller to Nome. Taxis will make the trip for $150 each way, according to one Teller resident. Air taxis also operate between the 2 communities, charging $40 per person one way in 1985.

Winter trails, traveled primarily by snow machines and a few dogsled teams, radiate from Teller to Brevig Mission, Marys Igloo and Nome.

Communications in Teller include phones, mail plane, radio and TV. The community has Lutheran and Catholic churches served by itinerant pastors. It also has a school with grades preschool through 12. There are community electricity and water systems; sewage system is primarily honey buckets. Teller prohibits the sale and importation of alcoholic beverages. Freight arrives by cargo plane and barge. Government address: City of Teller, P.O. Box 548, Teller, AK 99778; phone 642-3401. Village corporation address: Teller Native Corp., P.O. Box 509, Teller, AK 99778; phone 642-4011.

Tin City

Located at the mouth of Cape Creek, 7 miles southeast of Wales, 100 miles northwest of Nome, 600 miles west-northwest of Fairbanks. **Transportation:** Boat; scheduled and charter air service from Wales. **Population:** 10 to 20. **Zip code:** 99762. **Emergency Services:** Village Public Safety Officer, Wales; Alaska State Troopers, Nome; Tin City Air Force Station Medic.

Elevation: 270 feet. **Climate:** Mean annual precipitation 12 inches; mean annual snowfall 45.5 inches. Snowfall usually starts in late September or early October; last snow in late May or early June. Temperatures in winter -10° to 7°F. A record high of 84°F was reached in early July 1987.

Private Aircraft: Tin City Air Force Station airport 1 mile east; elev. 269 feet; length 4,700 feet; gravel. Closed to the public. Aircraft on official business may land only with 24-hour advance permission from airstrip supervisor, phone 552-3793. *CAUTION:* Turbulence on approach due to high winds. Field on high bluff.

Visitor Facilities: For accommodations contact Richard Lee, owner of the trading post and Tin City's sole resident not connected with the military. (General Delivery, Tin City, AK 99762; phone 664-3141.) Reservations should be made in advance. There is no food or lodging available to the public at the military site. No restaurant, banking services or laundry facilities available. Groceries, clothing, first-aid supplies, hardware, camera film and sporting goods available. Arts and crafts available for purchase include carved ivory, moccasins and other hand-sewn skin items from Diomede, Wales, Shishmaref, Brevig Mission and other villages. Fishing/hunting licenses not available. No guide or repair services. No rental transportation or moorage facilities. Fuel available includes marine gas and propane.

Tin City was established as a mining camp at the base of Cape Mountain in 1903 after tin ore was discovered on the mountain in 1902. Tin City Air Force Station was constructed in the early 1950s; military personnel have now been replaced by GE Government Services employees. The military site is closed to the public. An abandoned White Alice communications site is located on a nearby hill.

Tin is still mined in the area. Lee Mining Camp operated in the 1960s, but was sold to Lost River Mining Co. in the 1970s. Tin is mined from breakup to fall.

There are several privately owned cabins

facing the beach. Tin ore, along with jade and other minerals, can be found on the beach, according to a Wales resident. Trout and salmon can be caught with rod and reel from the beach.

Communications in Tin City include mail plane, radio and TV. There is no church or school. There are community electricity and water systems and flush toilets on the Air Force site. Freight arrives by cargo plane and barge.

Unalakleet

(YOU-na-la-kleet) Located on the east shore of Norton Sound at the mouth of the Unalakleet River, 145 miles southeast of Nome, 395 miles west-northwest of Anchorage. **Transportation:** Scheduled and charter air service from Nome. **Population:** 802. **Zip code:** 99684. **Emergency Services:** Police, phone 624-3700; Alaska State Troopers, phone 624-3646; Clinic, phone 624-3535; Medical emergencies, phone 624-3700; Volunteer Fire Department.

Elevation: 8 to 12 feet. **Climate:** Subarctic with considerable maritime influence when Norton Sound is ice free, usually from May to October. Freezing of the sound causes a change to a colder, more continental climate. Winters cold and relatively dry, with an average of 41 inches of snowfall. Summers cool with most rainfall occurring in July, August and September. Average annual precipitation is 14 inches. Winter temperatures average -4° to 11°F; summer temperatures average 47° to 62°F.

Private Aircraft: Airport 1 mile north; elev. 21 feet; length 6,000 feet; gravel; fuel 80, 100; attended Monday to Friday. Airport facilities include passenger and freight terminals, ticket counter and restrooms. Public transportation to town available.

Visitor Facilities: Accommodations at 1 lodge. Meals available in the community. No banking services or laundromat. Groceries, clothing, first-aid supplies, hardware, camera film and sporting goods available. Arts and crafts available for purchase include carved ivory, birch-bark baskets, grass baskets, masks, ulus, beadwork, mukluks and slippers, fur hats and other clothing. Fishing/hunting licenses available, as well as guide service. Marine engine, boat, auto and aircraft repair services available. Arrangements can be made to rent autos and boats, and charter aircraft. Fuel available includes marine gas, propane, diesel and regular gasoline. Moorage facilities available.

NOTE: Land surrounding Unalakleet is owned by the Unalakleet Native Corp. Trespassing laws are strictly enforced, but permits can be obtained from the corporation office in Unalakleet for camping, hunting, fishing, bird-watching, boating, sledding and photography.

The Unalakleet area has been occupied for centuries. Archaeologists have dated house pits along the old beach ridge at 200 B.C. to 300 A.D. More than 100 of these pits extend for a quarter mile near the Unalakleet airport. The name Unalakleet means "place where the east wind blows." The Eskimo name Ounakalik was recorded by Lt. L.A. Zagoskin of the Imperial Russian Navy on an 1850 map. A village site inhabited before the smallpox epidemic of 1838-39 exists along the south side of the Unalakleet River. Reindeer herders brought to Alaska from Lapland in 1898 settled at Unalakleet and quickly established sound herding practices. Descendants of a few of them still live in Unalakleet. The community was incorporated as a second-class city in 1974.

Commercial fishing and subsistence hunting and fishing form the basis of Unalakleet's economy. A fish processing plant employs up to 50 persons from May through August. Other jobs are with the Bering Strait School District, airlines, local stores, Native corporation, city and schools. For subsistence, several species of salmon, char, grayling and herring are fished and seal, caribou, moose, bear, birds and waterfowl are hunted.

Unalakleet is the takeoff point for sportfishing in Norton Sound and the Unalakleet and North rivers.

The Unalakleet River, above its junction with the Chiroskey River, has been designated a wild and scenic river and is popular for float trips. The area is administered by BLM and additional information can be obtained from BLM, Anchorage District Office, 4700 E. 72nd Ave., Anchorage, AK 99507.

Unalakleet is the terminus of a long-used winter trail from Anvik, on the Yukon River, that forms a leg of the Iditarod Trail. Unalakleet is a checkpoint each March for the Iditarod Trail Sled Dog Race from Anchorage to Nome.

Communications in Unalakleet include phones, mail plane, radio and TV. The community is served by Covenant, Mormon and Catholic churches. There are 3 schools: public elementary and high schools and a boarding high school run by the Covenant church. There are community electricity, water and sewer systems. Freight arrives by cargo plane, barge and ship. Government address: City of Unalakleet, P.O. Box 28, Unalakleet, AK 99684; phone 624-3531 or 3474. Village corporation address: Unalakleet Native Corp., P.O. Box

100, Unalakleet, AK 99684; phone 624-3020 or 3411.

Wales

Located on the western tip of the Seward Peninsula, on the coast of Cape Prince of Wales, 7 miles west of Tin City, 111 miles northwest of Nome, 595 miles west of Fairbanks. **Transportation:** Scheduled and charter air service from Nome. **Population:** 159. **Zip code:** 99783. **Emergency Services:** Village Public Safety Officer, phone 664-3671; Alaska State Troopers, Nome; Clinic, phone 664-3691; Volunteer Fire Department.

Elevation: 25 feet. **Climate:** Maritime when Bering Sea is ice free, usually June through November. Freezing of the sea causes abrupt change to a cold continental climate. Winters cold and windy; temperatures average -10° to 6°F. One resident says the wind chill factor pushes the temperature as low as -100°F. Summer temperatures average 40° to 50°F. Mean annual precipitation 11 inches; mean annual snowfall 41 inches.

Private Aircraft: Airstrip 1 mile northwest; elev. 25 feet; length 4,000 feet; gravel; unattended. Easterly winds may cause severe turbulence in the vicinity of the runway. Frequent fog, wind and occasional blizzards limit access to Wales. No airport facilities; transportation available to village.

Visitor Facilities: Accommodations in 1 room of the Wales Native Corp. building available through the corporation, phone 664-3641. Arrangements also may be made for accommodations in private homes. No restaurant or banking services. Laundromat and showers available. Groceries, first-aid supplies, hardware and camera film available in the community. Arts and crafts available for purchase include carved walrus ivory, moccasins, Eskimo dolls, fur mukluks and knitted caps, gloves and socks. Fishing/hunting licenses available. Informal guide service may be available. No repair service. Arrangements may be made to rent private off-road vehicles and boats. Fuel available: marine gas, diesel, propane. Moorage on beach.

Cape Prince of Wales is the farthest west point of mainland Alaska; 2,289-foot Cape Mountain which rises above Wales is the terminus of the Continental Divide separating the Arctic and Pacific watersheds. The Wales area has been inhabited for centuries; archaeological evidence dates back to 500 A.D. A burial mound of the Birnirk culture (500 A.D. to 900 A.D.) was discovered behind the present village and is now a national historic landmark.

In historical times, the villages of Eidamoo near the coast and King-a-ghe farther inland were noted in 1827 by Captain Beechy of the Imperial Russian Navy. In 1880, Capt. E.E. Smith of the U.S. Revenue Cutter Service reported Kingigamute, meaning "the high place," with a population of 400. In 1890, the American Missionary Assoc. established a mission here and in 1894 a reindeer station was organized. Wales was incorporated as a second-class city in 1964.

Wales was a major center for whale hunting due to its strategic location on the animals' migratory route until the 1918-19 worldwide influenza epidemic claimed the lives of many of Wales' finest whalers. The village retains a strong Eskimo culture; ancient songs and dances are still performed and customs practiced.

The economy of Wales is based on subsistence hunting and fishing, trapping, some mining and Native arts and crafts. Wales artisans make excellent ivory carvings, especially birds, which are sold locally or marketed in Nome, Anchorage or Fairbanks. Other crafts such as skin sewing bring additional income to the community. There is some trapping of fox and wolverine. A private reindeer herd of about 1,500 head is managed out of Wales and local residents are employed during roundup. A few jobs are provided by the city, store, clinic, airlines, school and Native corporation.

The mining potential is great in the area. Tin placers located nearby have estimated reserves of 2,000 tons of tin. Gold also is plentiful in the region.

Vast herds of walrus and whales migrate through Bering Strait and villagers hunt them from early April to the end of June. Ice cellars are used to store and preserve the meat. Polar bear, moose, waterfowl, salmon, ptarmigan, tomcod and flounder supplement local diets, along with berries and various greens.

In Wales, the visitor will get a glimpse of Eskimo life relatively unaffected by Outside contact. During the summer, Wales is a base for residents of Little Diomede Island and these Eskimos often can be seen traveling to and from their island in the large traditional skin boats. Air service and tours to Wales are available out of Nome.

The city has established the George Otenna Museum in the community center, City of Wales, Wales, AK 99783, phone 664-3671. This local history museum features contemporary arts and crafts, as well as Eskimo artifacts and the history of Wales and the surrounding area.

Activities in Wales include the annual Fourth of July celebration with games for all ages, community feasts on Thanksgiving and Christmas, and competitive indoor games for men's and women's teams from Dec. 26 to Dec. 31 each year. The city also plans to initiate an annual celebration on its incorporation date, April 16.

Winter trails connect Wales to Tin City and the interior of the Seward Peninsula. A tractor trail also runs to Tin City.

Communications in Wales include phones, mail plane, radio and TV. The community is served by a Lutheran church and the Wales-Kingikme School with grades kindergarten through 9; older students go to boarding schools in other communities. There is a community electricity system. Water is hauled from Village and Gilbert creeks in summer and ice blocks are cut in winter. Sewage system is honey buckets. Wales prohibits the sale and importation of alcoholic beverages. Freight arrives by ship, barge and plane. Government address: City of Wales, P.O. Box 489, Wales, AK 99783; phone 664-3671. Village corporation address: Wales Native Corp., General Delivery, Wales, AK 99783; phone 664-3641.

White Mountain

Located on the west bank of the Fish River near the head of Golovin Lagoon on the Seward Peninsula, 15 miles northwest of Golovin, 65 miles east of Nome, 490 miles west of Fairbanks. **Transportation:** Boat; snow machine; scheduled and charter air service from Nome; Nome-Council Road open late June, early July. **Population:** 189. **Zip code:** 99784. **Emergency Services:** Village Public Safety Officer, phone 638-3411 or 3351; Alaska State Troopers, Nome; Clinic, phone 638-3311; Volunteer Fire Department, phone 638-3411.

Elevation: 50 feet. **Climate:** Transitional, with less extreme temperature variations than interior Alaska. Colder continental weather during the icebound winter. Mean annual precipitation 16 inches, with 57 inches of snow. Winter temperatures average -7° to 15°F; summer temperatures average 43° to 80°F.

Private Aircraft: Airport 1 mile north; elev. 262 feet; length 2,100 feet; runway condition not monitored, gravel; no fuel; unattended; runway condition not monitored, visual inspection recommended prior to using. Runway slopes at both ends. Passenger terminal at airport; no public transportation into village.

Visitor Facilities: Accommodations available at 1 local lodge (open summers and for Iditarod Trail Sled Dog Race in March) or arrangements may be made for lodging in private homes. No restaurant or banking services. Washeteria with showers available. Groceries, clothing and sporting goods available in the community. Arts and crafts available for purchase include knitted gloves and caps, porcupine quill, beaded and ivory earrings. Fishing/hunting licenses available, as well as sportfishing guide service. Boat repair available. Fuel available: diesel, marine gas, propane, white gas, kerosene and regular and unleaded gasoline. Moorage on beach.

The Eskimo village of Nutchirviq was located here prior to the influx of white settlers during the turn-of-the-century gold rush. Bountiful fish populations in both the Fish and Niukluk rivers supported the Native populations. In 1899 C.D. Lane erected a log warehouse as supply headquarters for his numerous gold claims in the Council district. The name White Mountain was derived from the color of the mountain located next to the village. White Mountain was incorporated as a second-class city in 1969.

White Mountain residents rely both on subsistence hunting and fishing and on wages from seasonal work in commercial fishing, construction, firefighting, woodcutting, trapping, some cannery work and reindeer herding. There are a few jobs locally with the school, city, store and airlines. Residents spend much of the summer at fish camps. The year-round diet includes lingcod, pike, whitefish, grayling, trout and skipjack. Assorted greens and roots, berries, wildfowl and squirrel are harvested in the fall; seal, moose, brown bear, reindeer, flounder, sculpin, rabbit and ptarmigan in the winter; rabbit, ptarmigan, *oogruk*, seal, wildfowl and eggs, and assorted roots and greens in the spring; and herring, smelt, salmon and beluga whale in the summer.

White Mountain serves as a checkpoint on the Iditarod Trail.

Communications include phones, mail plane, radio and TV. The community is served by a Covenant church and a school with grades kindergarten through 12 and a village library. Community electricity and water. Sewage system is honey buckets. Freight arrives by barge and cargo plane. Government address: City of White Mountain, P.O. Box 66, White Mountain, AK 99784; phone 638-3411. Village corporation address: White Mountain Native Corp., General Delivery, White Mountain, AK 99784; phone 638-3411.

▼ A T T R A C T I O N S ▼

National and State Parks, Etc.

Bering Land Bridge National Preserve

This 2.8-million-acre preserve is located just below the Arctic Circle on the Seward Peninsula, 50 miles south of Kotzebue and 90 miles north of Nome. It is a remnant of the land bridge that once connected Asia and North America 14,000 to 25,000 years ago. More than just a narrow strip across the Bering Strait, the land bridge at times was up to 1,000 miles wide. It rose as the formation of massive glaciers during the ice ages caused the water levels of the Bering and Chukchi seas to fall. Across this bridge people, animals and plants migrated to the New World and the preserve is considered one of the most likely regions where these prehistoric hunters crossed over. An archaeological site at Trail Creek caves has yielded evidence of human occupation 10,000 years old.

Other interesting features of the preserve are several lava flows around Imuruk Lake, some as recent as 1,000 years ago; low-rimmed volcanoes called maar craters, which have become lakes, in the northern lowlands around Devil Mountain; and Serpentine Hot Springs, long recognized by Natives for its spiritual and medicinal values. The springs' Inupiat Eskimo name is Iyat, which means "cooking pot." Hillsides in the preserve are dotted with the remains of ancient stone cairns, their original purpose lost in the misty past. Also of interest are the more recent historical sites from early explorations and mining activities.

Today, Eskimos from neighboring villages pursue their subsistence lifestyles and manage reindeer herds in and around the preserve. Their camps, fish nets and other equipment are critical to their livelihood and should be left undisturbed.

Climate: Temperatures in the preserve vary. On the coast, January temperatures are -10° to -20°F, while inland they may reach -60°F. Maximum July temperatures on the coast are in the lower 50s, while inland they are in the mid-60s. Summer is the wettest time, receiving 3 to 4 inches of the annual 10 inches of precipitation. Snowfall averages 50 to 60 inches per year. Insects are most bothersome from mid-June to early August.

During the short summer the preserve bursts into life and many of the 245 species of plants bloom with bright colors.

Wildlife: The preserve includes 112 species of migratory birds; marine mammals such as bearded, hair and ribbon seals, walrus, and humpback, fin and bowhead whales; grizzly bears, some wolves, caribou to the north and east, some musk-ox from transplanted herds, moose, red and arctic foxes, weasels and wolverines. Fish in preserve waters include salmon, grayling and arctic char.

Access: Commercial jet to Nome or Kotzebue, which have connecting flights to Deering and Shishmaref provide access to the preserve. Visitors to the preserve usually arrive by charter plane from Nome or Kotzebue, landing on lakes, gravel bars, beaches or private mining camp airstrips just outside the preserve. There also is an airstrip at Serpentine Hot Springs, location of a public-use cabin. That strip is 1,100 feet long and 50 feet wide, the runway slopes, crosswinds are common and the surface is muddy when wet. Access also is possible by driving from Nome on the 86-mile-long Taylor Highway to the Kougarok River, about 20 miles from the preserve, and then hiking in. You also can travel a road from Deering 25 miles along the Inmachuk River to within 5 or 10 miles of the preserve. Or it's possible to go by boat from Shishmaref to the preserve.

Accommodations: Aside from the cabin

at the hot springs, there are no accommodations or campgrounds in the preserve. There are hotel and restaurant facilities in Nome and Kotzebue (although during the summer most of the rooms are booked by tour groups), and limited accommodations in Shishmaref. Visitors to the preserve must arrive self-sufficient, with food, clothing, shelter, and in some cases fuel. There is driftwood on beaches, but wood is scarce inland. The Park Service further advises that visitors to the preserve should have good outdoor skills — including hiking, backpacking and camping experience — and the stamina to survive difficult conditions.

Activities: Recreational opportunities in the preserve include hiking, camping, fishing, sightseeing, wildlife observation and photography.

For more information contact: Superintendent, Bering Land Bridge National Preserve, P.O. Box 220, Nome, AK 99762; phone 443-2522. Related USGS Topographic Series maps: Kotzebue, Shishmaref, Bendeleben, Teller.

The Rivers

Unalakleet River. This designated wild and scenic river flows southwest through the low, rugged Nulato Hills to the village of Unalakleet where it drains into Norton Sound. This clear-water river is approximately 105 miles long, but only the lower 76 miles is deep enough to float; often the river is floatable only from the confluence of Old Woman River. This river has a few riffles; sweepers line much of the river and its tributaries. Canoes, kayaks or rafts all are suitable for this river.

The usual put-in point is at the Unalakleet's confluence with Tenmile Creek about 29 miles from the river's source. Stream flow is relatively fast and there are many obstructions across the river. Fishing is excellent from this point to Old Woman River. The Old Woman Mountain can be seen as boaters approach Old Woman River. Many sand and gravel bars provide camping sites. The flow slows, depth increases and the river braids. About 4 miles beyond the Old Woman River confluence, the Unalakleet flows through a flat valley where marshes and oxbows can be seen. Around Mile 51, the North Fork joins the Unalakleet. A series of braided channels flow through heavy cover, making identification of the main channel difficult. In this area

Lucy Simeon uses an ulu, a traditional Eskimo woman's knife designed for scraping and chopping, to prepare this salmon for storing and eating later. (Alissa Crandall)

there are several private cabins that are used seasonally for fishing, trapping and hunting. Do not trespass. The river widens as it stretches toward the confluence with the Chiroskey River, the end of the wild river corridor. For the remaining 24 miles, the river crosses Native corporation land. There also is one commercial fishing lodge on this lower portion. The trip from Tenmile Creek to the river mouth generally takes 6 days.

Fish in the Unalakleet include king, silver, chum and pink salmon, arctic char, Dolly Varden and grayling. (See also SPORTFISHING this section.) Wildlife that may be seen include moose, black and brown bears, wolves, waterfowl, beavers and foxes.

Access is by scheduled air service to Unalakleet, then a local guide or boat operator may be hired to take parties to Tenmile Creek by riverboat. Exit is from Unalakleet, where there are visitor facilities. Related USGS Topographic Series maps: Norton Sound A-1 and A-2, Unalakleet D-2 through D-4.

Sportfishing

Except for a few roads around Nome, access to good fishing in the Seward Peninsula/Norton Sound area is primarily by airplane. If you have the time, however, you sometimes can walk or go by boat to a hot fishing spot. Boats occasionally can be rented or chartered at villages along the waterways. There are daily commercial flights to the transportation centers of the region — Nome and Unalakleet — where you can catch a commuter flight to a smaller village or charter a plane to a lake or river. In addition, commercial outfitters will handle logistics for you on guided fishing trips.

King salmon are at their peak from mid-June through mid-July. These fish are not uncommon at 30 pounds and up. Chums show up by July 1, pinks by mid-July (in even-numbered years) and silvers by mid-August. Salmon fishing is concentrated in the river systems.

Arctic char and Dolly Varden are found throughout this area and are most abundant in the fall. Grayling can be caught most of the summer, but larger ones are more plentiful in late summer. Other species that may be encountered are whitefish, burbot (also called lush or lingcod) and northern pike.

In general the best fishing throughout the northern half of the Bering Sea Coast region is in July and August.

The Alaska Dept. of Fish and Game recommends that anyone traveling to remote areas should plan for the worst. Take a few days

extra food, and fuel if necessary, and allow for a flexible schedule since fickle weather can delay travel.

Although many villages have hunting and fishing license vendors, officials recommend that you purchase your license in Anchorage or another large community, since sometimes the local vendors themselves have "gone fishing." The Dept. of Fish and Game in Nome sells licenses.

More information about fishing in the Seward Peninsula/Norton Sound area may be obtained from:

Alaska Dept. of Fish and Game, Sport Fish Division, 1300 College Road, Fairbanks, AK 99701-1599; phone 456-8819.

Alaska Dept. of Fish and Game, P.O. Box 1148, Nome, AK 99762-1148.

Agiapuk River. Heads 8 miles northeast of Black Mountain and flows southeast 60 miles to the Imuruk Basin, 21 miles southeast of Teller. Excellent fishery. Fish available: pink, chum and coho salmon — use spoons; grayling — year-round, best in late summer, use flies; arctic char — best in fall, use spoons, eggs. Access by plane from Nome or Teller.

Bluestone River. Located at Mile 58.1 on the Nome-Teller Road. Named for the color of the stones in the river. Fish available: chum, pink and coho salmon — use spoons; arctic char — best in fall, use spoons, eggs; grayling — year-round, best in late summer, use flies. Access by car from Nome or Teller.

Cripple River. Located at Mile 20.3 on the Nome-Teller Road, 9 miles beyond the Penny River. Narrow bridge crossing. Fish present include grayling — year-round, best in late summer, use flies; arctic char — best in fall, use spoons, eggs. Also available in season are chum, coho and pink salmon — use spoons. Access by car from Nome.

Feather River. Located at Mile 37.4 on the Nome-Teller Road. Fish available: chum, pink and coho salmon — use spoons; arctic char — best in fall, use spoons, eggs; grayling — year-round, best in late summer, use flies. Access by car from Nome or Teller.

Fish River. Located about 35 miles east of Solomon on the Nome-Council Road. Fish available: king, chum, pink and coho salmon — use spoons; large grayling — year-round, best in late summer, use flies; arctic char — best in fall, use spoons, eggs; northern pike — year-round, use spoons, spinners. Access by car from Nome.

Grand Central River. Located 35 miles north of Nome on the Nome-Taylor (Kougarok) Road. Very small turnoff present. Excellent canoe/small boating river. Fish available:

grayling — year-round, best in late summer, use flies; arctic char — best in fall, use spoons, eggs; whitefish — available year-round, use flies, eggs. Access by car from Nome.

Inglutalik River. Heads at Traverse Peak and flows 80 miles to Norton Bay north of Shaktoolik and south of Koyuk. Fish available: king, chum, pink and coho salmon; arctic char — best in fall, use spoons, eggs; grayling — year-round, best in late summer, use flies. Boats may be available for rental in Shaktoolik or Koyuk.

Koyuk River. Flows into Koyuk Inlet at the village of Koyuk at the head of Norton Bay off Norton Sound. Only river in immediate area with sheefish, best June to September, use spoons. Other fish available: northern pike — year-round, use spoons, spinners; chum salmon — July to August, use spoons; grayling — year-round, best in late summer, use flies. Boats may be available for rental or charter in Koyuk.

Kuzitrin River. Located at Mile 68 on the Nome-Taylor (Kougarok) Road. Fine, clear-water fishery. Fish available: chum salmon — July to August, use spoons; arctic char — best in fall, use spoons, eggs; grayling — year-round, best in late summer, use flies; northern pike — year-round, use spoons, spinners; few whitefish, use flies, eggs. Access by car from Nome.

Kwiniuk River. Flows into Norton Sound near Moses Point, northeast of Elim. Fish available: king, chum, pink and coho salmon; arctic char — best in fall, use spoons, eggs; grayling — year-round, best in late summer, use flies. Access by charter air service from Nome or Unalakleet. No accommodations in Elim. The Moses Point airport is privately owned and permission is needed to land.

Niukluk River. Nome-Council Road ends at this river (Mile 72). There is good fishing in July and August for king, chum, pink and coho salmon — use spoons; arctic char — fishing good August and September, use spoons, eggs; other fish available: grayling — year-round, best in late summer, use flies; whitefish — use flies, eggs; burbot — in the fall, use bait. Access by car, or small plane from Nome to Council airstrip.

Nome River. Fishing locations 4 miles east of Nome on Main Street extension at the junction of the river and the ocean. Also, 10 miles north of Nome on Nome-Taylor (Kouga-rok) Road where river parallels road. There are numerous turnoffs. Spring and fall fishery best here. Fish available at both locations: chum and pink salmon — July to August, use spoons; coho salmon — July to September, use

spoons; arctic char — best in fall, use spoons, eggs; grayling — available at upriver location, best in late summer, use flies.

Penny River. Located at Mile 13.2 on the Nome-Teller Road. Old gold mining area. Turnout present. Fish available: grayling — year-round, best in late summer, use flies; arctic char — best in fall, use spoons, eggs. Access by car from Nome.

Pilgrim (Kruzgamepa) River. Located north of Nome at Mile 65 on the Nome-Taylor (Kougarok) Road, 19 miles beyond Salmon Lake. Old gold mining area. Turnoffs present. No accommodations, but there are undeveloped areas suitable for camping. Excellent fishery. Fish available below bridge near Pilgrim Hot Springs: pink and chum salmon — July to August, use spoons; coho salmon — July to September, use spoons; arctic char — best in fall, use spoons, eggs; northern pike — year-round, use spoons, spinners. Above bridge, mostly grayling and char — best in late summer or early fall. Access by car from Nome.

Safety Sound. Located east of Nome at Mile 17.6 on the Nome-Council Road. Bridge crosses lagoon outlet. Boat fishing recommended. Eskimo summer fishing camps throughout the area. Fish available: pink and chum salmon — July to August, use spoons; arctic char and coho salmon — best in fall, use spoons, eggs; flounder — use cut bait; burbot — in the fall, use cut bait. Access by car from Nome.

Salmon Lake. Located at Miles 36 to 44 north of Nome on the Nome-Taylor (Kouga-rok) Road. The lake is parallel to the road, numerous side roads lead to the lake shore. Camping area with picnic sites and outhouses available. No accommodations, but there is an airstrip. Fish available: arctic char — best in fall, use spoons, eggs; grayling — year-round, best in late summer, use flies; northern pike — year-round, use spoons, spinners; whitefish — use flies, eggs. The lake is closed to all salmon sportfishing. Access by car, or small plane from Nome.

Shaktoolik River. Flows into Shaktoolik Bay on Norton Sound just north of Shaktoolik village. Fish available: king, chum, pink and coho salmon — use spoons; arctic char — best in fall, use spoons, eggs; grayling — year-round, best in late summer, use flies. Boats may be available for rental or charter in Shaktoolik.

Sinuk River. Located at Mile 26.7 on the Nome-Teller Road. Best fishing on this road. Bridge crossing. Fish available: chum and pink salmon in season — use spoons; arctic char — best in fall, use spoons, eggs; large grayling — year-round, best in late summer, use flies. Access by car from Nome.

Snake River. Bridge crossing at Mile 7.9 on the Nome-Teller Road. Turnoff present. Good fishery in spring and fall. Excellent for pink salmon in July (even numbered years), use spoons. Other fish available: chum salmon — July to August, use spoons; coho salmon — July to September, use spoons; grayling — year-round, best in late summer, use flies; arctic char — best in fall, use spoons, eggs. Access by car from Nome.

Solomon River. Located from Miles 40 to 50 on the Nome Council Road. River parallels road. Good fishing about 1 mile beyond Solomon. Fish available: pink and chum salmon — July to August, use spoons; arctic char — best in fall, use spoons, eggs; grayling — year-round, best in late summer, use flies. Access by car from Nome.

Unalakleet River. Mouth is just south of Unalakleet village on Norton Sound. Commercial fishing lodge on lower river. Accommodations in Unalakleet. Boats may be available. Good fishing for king salmon in late June; use lures. Other fish available: coho — July to September, chum and pink salmon — July to August, use spoons; arctic char — best in fall, use spoons, eggs; grayling — year-round, best in late summer, use flies. Access by boat from Unalakleet. (See also The Rivers this section.)

Ungalik River. Heads on Traverse Peak and flows southwest 90 miles to Norton Bay north of Shaktoolik and south of Koyuk. Fish available: king, chum, pink and coho salmon — use spoons; arctic char — best in fall, use spoons, eggs; grayling — year-round, best in late summer, use flies. Boats may be available for rental or charter in Shaktoolik or Koyuk.

SPECIAL FEATURES

Cape Denbigh

The Iyatayat archaeological site at Cape Denbigh, 12 miles west-northwest of the village of Shaktoolik on Norton Sound, is a national historic landmark. Cape Denbigh was named by English explorer Capt. James Cook on Sept. 11, 1778; its Eskimo name is Nuklit. This site, excavated by archaeologist J.L. Giddings from 1948-52, is the type site for the Norton culture and the Denbigh Flint complex, and was a momentous discovery because it was older than previously known sites. The site is located on an old beach ridge and represents 3 cultural periods dating back as far as 5,000 B.C. Access is by boat from Shaktoolik, which is reached by scheduled air service from Unalakleet. Check with the city government or the village corporation about the location of private lands in the area.

Cape Nome Roadhouse

Located just east of Cape Nome at Mile 14 on the Nome-Council Road, this historic roadhouse is listed on the National Register of Historic Places. The original section was built in 1900 of logs hauled 70 miles from Council by horse. In 1913, after a flood destroyed the log building, an abandoned government building from Safety reportedly was moved to the site and became the present roadhouse. From about 1910 it was a major stopover for dog teams traveling the Iditarod Trail. It was the only roadhouse still standing that was used in the famous 1925 "race to Nome"

to deliver serum during the diptheria epidemic. The building also was used as a temporary orphanage. It has been converted to a private residence.

Hot Springs

Pilgrim Hot Springs. Located on the left bank of the Pilgrim River 13 miles northeast of Salmon Lake. This site of a gold rush resort and later a Catholic mission is listed on the National Register of Historic Places. In the early days of gold mining on the Seward Peninsula about 1900, the property was known as Kruzgamepa Hot Springs and was a recreation center for miners attracted by its spa baths, saloon, dance hall and roadhouse. The roadhouse and saloon burned in 1908. It was homesteaded soon thereafter and became an important source of produce for markets in Nome. The property was given to Father Bellarmine Lafortune who turned the ranch into a mission and orphanage in 1917-18. It operated until 1941, housing up to 120 children at the orphanage. Ruins of the mission school and other church properties remain at the site, which is still owned by the Catholic Church. Access is by charter air service from Nome to a small airfield at Pilgrim Hot Springs. Or by car on a new 8-mile gravel road (completed in 1984) that joins the Nome-Taylor Road at Cottonwood.

Serpentine Hot Springs. Located within Bering Land Bridge National Preserve. The waters of Serpentine Hot Springs have long been sought for their healthful properties. Eskimo shamans gathered here in earlier times. When the influence of the shamans had passed, native healers still relied on these waters to help their followers. Likely the most visited area of Bering Land Bridge National Preserve, Serpentine still offers a soothing break from the harsh surrounding climate and the nearby granite tors create a dramatic landscape that lures hikers to explore. A public-use cabin is located at the springs. Winter trails from Shishmaref and other traditional villages lead to Hot Springs Creek near the tractor trail, traversed by snow machine and dogsled in winter reaches the springs from the end of the Nome-Taylor (Kougarok) road. A 1,100 foot airstrip at the hot springs allows wheeled plane access.

Kigluaik Mountains

These mountains are located about 50 miles north of Nome on the Seward Peninsula, 100 miles south of the Arctic Circle. The range is oriented east to west and is approximately 75 miles long and 25 miles wide. It is bordered by the Kougarok Road (Nome-Taylor Road) on the east, the Nome-Teller Road on the west, and the Imuruk Basin and Kuzitrin River on the north.

Visitors will find a wide variety of recreational opportunities: hiking, dog mushing, cross-country skiing or snow machining through the spectacular and changing panorama of mountain passes and glacial valleys. There is evidence of early day gold seekers to explore as well as plenty of fish in the clear mountain streams. Access is easy, by western Alaska standards: You can rent a car in Nome and drive to either the east or west end of the range; you can arrange for an air charter to any number of potential landing sites within the range; in the winter you can drive a snow machine from Nome. Snow machines can get into areas that are not accessible during the rest of the year.

One area of particular interest starts at glacially formed Crater Lake, a deep, still pool that discharges into the Grand Central River. The Wild Goose Pipeline starts at Crater Lake and runs down the southern side of the Grand Central Valley. Built about 1920, the pipeline carried water to early mining operations near the Nome River, 10 to 20 miles away. The 21-inch pipeline is made of redwood slats held together with iron hoops. The wood has not deteriorated and the pipe is still intact in some places. (Please respect this historical artifact and help preserve the region's heritage by taking nothing but pictures!) The pipeline's name comes from the Wild Goose Railroad which carried supplies north from Nome to the early mining camps near Shelton, located on the Kuzitrin River. Remnants of old cabins, possibly built for maintenance personnel, still remain along the pipeline.

Another point of interest is the Mosquito Pass area. A hike from Windy Creek to the Cobblestone River through Mosquito Pass provides access to some spectacular side canyons, with abrupt peaks reaching nearly 3,000 feet above sea level. Cirque lakes in some of the side canyons offer outstanding photo opportunities. During the summer you can hike into the Mosquito Pass area by leaving the Nome-Taylor Road in the vicinity of the confluence of Hudson Creek and the Nome River.

A testament to the sense of humor of residents of Bethel, this sign welcomes visitors to the Bethel National Forest which consists of one lonely tree, unfortunately not visible in this photograph. (Alissa Crandall)

In the Kigluaik Mountains, pronounced KIG-lee-uk or KIG-loo-ak, you may encounter wolves, grizzly bear, moose, red fox, ground squirrels, and hoary marmots. Reindeer that are part of domesticated herds are also present throughout the year. The varied landscape provides nesting habitat for a variety of birds during the summer. Many Asiatic species frequent this region, making it particularly interesting for ornithologists. Among the species that have long migration routes and nest here are the wheatear, the arctic warbler, bluethroat, yellow wagtail and the white wagtail. Birds of prey such as the rough-legged hawk, golden eagle and gyrfalcon may also be observed soaring overhead, taking advantage of the updrafts in this mountainous region.

Facilities in the Kigluaiks are limited. There is a campground at Salmon Lake on the eastern end of the range near Mile 40 on the Kougarok Road. There is also a public shelter cabin in the Mosquito Pass area. There are no public trails in the mountains, and the Bureau of Land Management advises that visitors should be aware of the demands of the backcountry where help may be far away. Related USGS Topographic maps: Nome D-1, D-22, D-3, Teller A-1, A-2, A-3, Bendeleben A-6, Solomon A-6.

For additional information, contact the Bureau of Land Management, Kobuk District Office, 1150 University Ave., Fairbanks, AK 99709; phone 474-2330, or the Bureau of Land Management, Nome Field Office, P.O. Box 925, Nome, AK 99762; phone 443-2177.

King Island

This rocky, 1,196-foot-high island located in the Bering Sea, 40 miles west of Cape Douglas on the Seward Peninsula, is the ancestral home of the King Island Eskimos, who now live at Nome. The island was named by Capt. James Cook of the Royal Navy on Aug. 6, 1778, for Lt. James King, a member of his party. The Eskimo name for the island, and the tiny village on stilts that clings to the hillside, is Ukivok. The island today is inhabited only by thousands of seabirds: puffins, auklets, murres, sea gulls and kittiwakes. Villagers began moving away in the 1950s, attracted by job opportunities and health facilities in Nome. The BIA closed the school in 1959. The village was last inhabited in 1966. A group of former residents organized to keep their cultural traditions alive, and today the King Island Inupiat Singers and Dancers perform widely before appreciative audiences. The 2-mile-wide island is isolated 8 months of the year and reached only by a 6-hour boat ride. King Islanders still return in late May or June each year to pick greens, gather bird eggs and hunt walrus.

Moses Point

Located on a sandspit on the north shore of Norton Bay in the northeast corner of Norton Sound 110 miles east of Nome, this is an abandoned Federal Aviation Administration Flight Service Station. Several old buildings are still standing in various states of disrepair, and some relics from the gold rush in the early part of this century can be found in the area. There is hunting for moose, grizzly bear and possibly caribou. Local streams may provide some salmon fishing. Streams thaw in early to mid-June. Grayling and Dolly Varden inhabit clear steams. After a storm, beachcombing is usually interesting. Access is by charter plane from Nome. Airstrip adjacent to the south (elev. 14 feet; length 4,600 feet) is asphalt but badly eroded in spots and not maintained in the winter. Fish disposal off end of runway attracts birds.

NOTE: Prior permission for use of Moses Point is required from Elim Native Corp., General Delivery, Elim, AK 99739; phone 890-3281. The corporation warns that trespassers will be prosecuted.

Dramatic Iniakuk Gorge confronts hiker in Gates of the Arctic. (George Wuerthner)

BROOKS RANGE AND THE ARCTIC

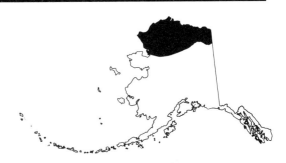

The Region

This last great wilderness of mountain range and arctic coastal plain stretches for miles across the top of Alaska, beckoning visitors with the promise of beauty and solitude and grandeur. The Brooks Range and the Arctic are true wilderness, immense and almost roadless, remote and sparsely populated. They offer endless opportunities to explore pristine country almost untouched by human endeavor.

In the Brooks Range the mountains stand like sentinels protecting the fragile ecosystem of the Arctic from casual intrusion. These mountains are themselves protected in a series of national parks and preserves that stretch from the Dalton Highway (North Slope Haul Road) west almost to the Chukchi Sea. And to the east of the highway the Arctic National Wildlife Refuge preserves both the north and south slopes of the Brooks Range all the way to the Canadian border.

Location: An irregular line drawn between the great flatlands of the Interior and the southern foothills of the remote Brooks Range delineates the southern boundary of this region. The Chukchi Sea borders to the west. The Arctic Ocean with the Beaufort Sea in the northeast are the region's northern boundaries.

Physical Description: The Brooks Range, though not as high as Alaska's coastal mountains or the Alaska Range, rises majestically between Interior's flat expanses and the Arctic's coastal plains. Lying east to west across the width of the state, it consists of endless gentler mountains interrupted by the spectacular granite spires of Arrigetch Peaks.

The treeless Arctic is interlaced with meandering rivers and dotted with thousands of shallow thaw lakes. Permafrost, beginning a few inches under the surface and extending down as far as 2,000 feet, underlies most of the Arctic. Most areas receive less than 10 inches of precipitation a year, but soggy tundra and bogs are common in summer because there is little evaporation and poor drainage.

Rivers: The Brooks Range spawns a host of rivers running north and south, east and west. Many of these rivers have been designated wild and scenic and are among the most beautiful and remote in the world.

The Kobuk River, an important highway for prehistoric and contemporary people, and the Noatak with its pristine watershed drain much of northwestern Alaska. On the arctic plain, the Colville and north-flowing streams in the eastern Arctic provide access to the region's interior.

Climate

Winters are long and cold in the Brooks Range with temperatures as low as -60°F. Summers on the south slopes are considerably warmer than on the north, and precipitation is low.

Strong winds, cold temperatures and low precipitation characterize the arctic climate. The Beaufort and Chukchi seas moderate temperatures in summer somewhat, but readings drop when ice covers the sea for 9 months each year. At Barrow, July and August temperatures average between 30° and 40°F; in January and February between -15° and -18°F.

Vegetation

A taiga forest on the south side of the Brooks Range gives way to tundra that stretches

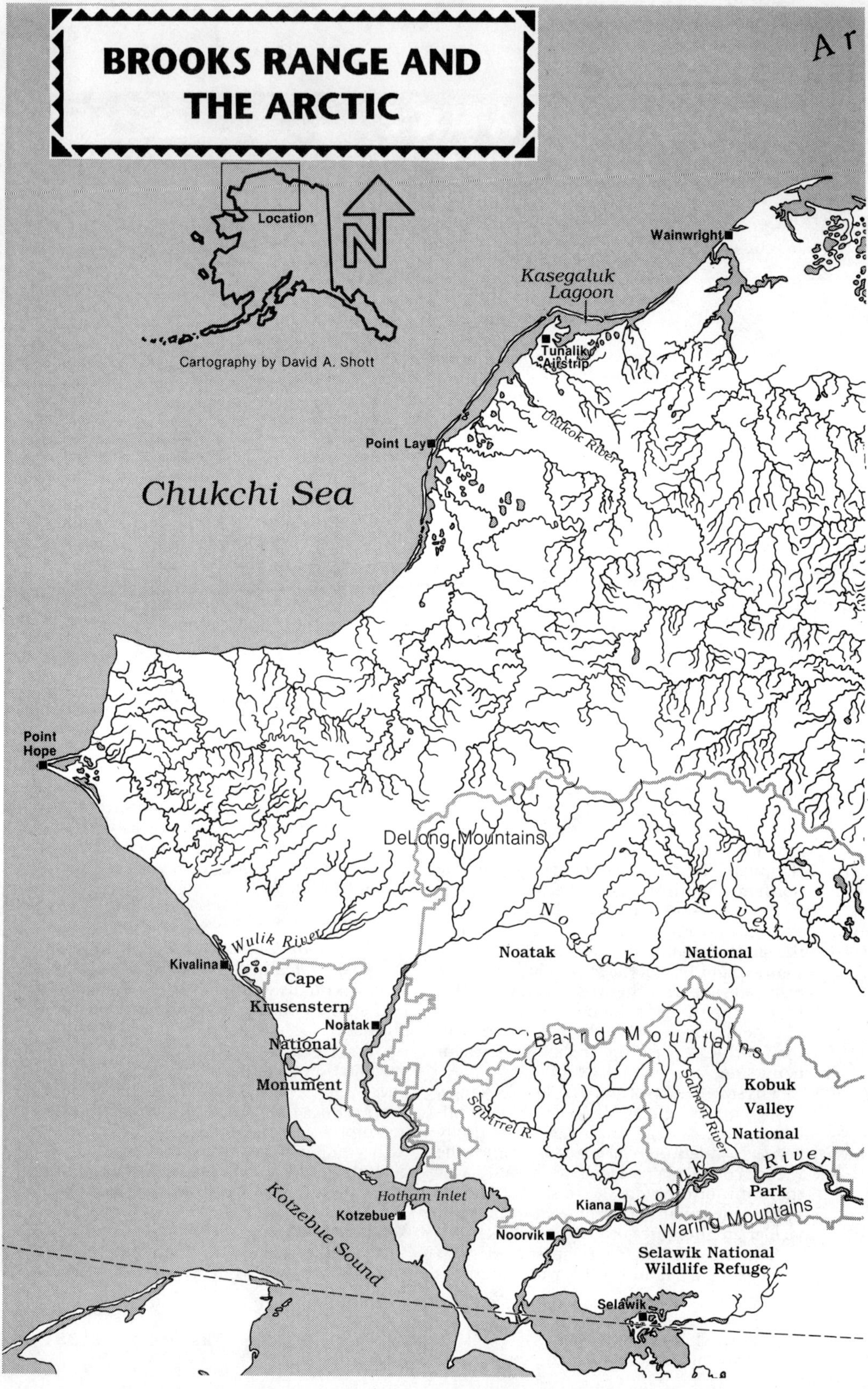

BROOKS RANGE AND THE ARCTIC

Location

N

Cartography by David A. Shott

Wainwright ■

Kasegaluk Lagoon

Tunalik ■
Airstrip

Utukok River

Point Lay ■

Chukchi Sea

Point
Hope ■

DeLong Mountains

Wulik River

N o a t a k   *River*

Noatak   National

Kivalina ■

Cape

Krusenstern
Noatak ■

National

B a i r d   M o u n t a i n s

Salmon River

Monument

Kobuk
Valley
National

Squirrel R.

Kobuk   *River*

Kiana ■   Park

Hotham Inlet   Waring Mountains

Kotzebue ■

Kotzebue Sound

Noorvik ■

Selawik National
Wildlife Refuge

Selawik ■

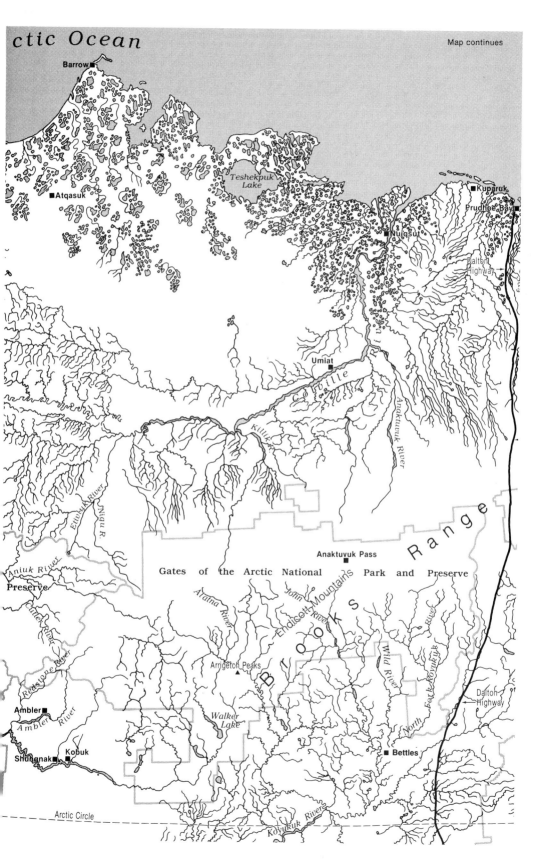

ctic Ocean

Map continues

Barrow■

Atqasuk■

■Kuparuk

Prudhoe Bay■

Teshekpuk Lake

■Nuiqsut

Dalton Highway→

Umiat■

Colville River

Anaktuvuk River

Killik R.

Etivluk River

Nigu R.

R a n g e

Aniuk River

Preserve

Anaktuvuk Pass■

Gates   of   the   Arctic   National   Park   and   Preserve

Endicott Mountains

John River

B r o o k s

Dalton →Highway

Alatna River

Ambler River

Redstone River

Kugrua River

▲ Arrigetch Peaks

Walker Lake

Wild River

North Fork Koyukuk R.

Ambler■

■Kobuk

Shungnak■

■ Bettles

- - - Arctic Circle

Koyukuk River

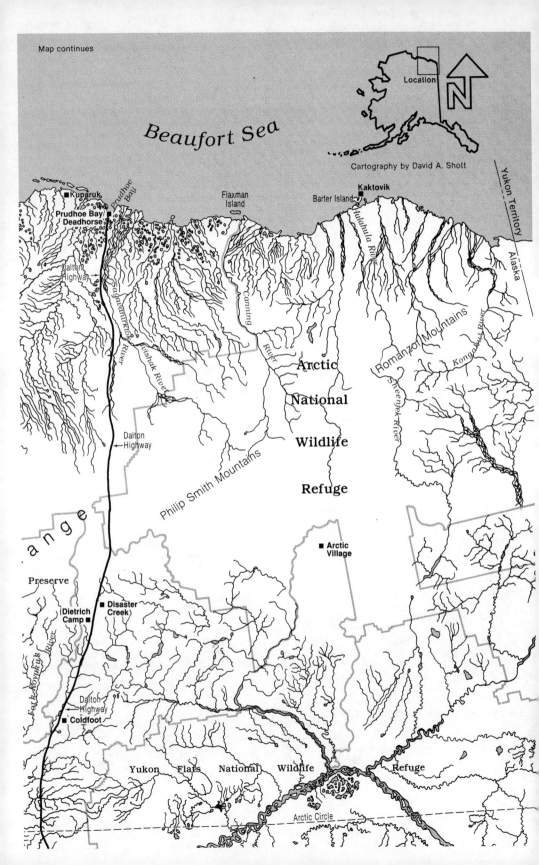

Map continues

Beaufort Sea

Location

N

Cartography by David A. Shott

Kuparuk

Prudhoe Bay

Flaxman Island

Kaktovik

Barter Island

Yukon Territory

Prudhoe Bay/ Deadhorse

Dalton Highway

Sagavanirktok River

Anishak River

Canning River

Hulahula River

Alaska

Romanzof Mountains

Kongakut River

Arctic

National

Wildlife

Refuge

Sheenjek River

Dalton Highway

Philip Smith Mountains

a n g e

Preserve

Arctic Village

Dietrich Camp

Disaster Creek

Fork Koyukuk River

Dalton Highway

Coldfoot

Yukon   Flats   National   Wildlife   Refuge

Arctic Circle

north to the Arctic Ocean. While the Arctic is covered by snow and ice for much of the year and veiled in darkness for up to 3 months, there is enough sunshine in the remaining months to transform the bleak winter tundra into a summer carpet of flowering plants.

Several varieties of tundra grow in the Arctic. Higher elevations support alpine tundra: lichens, grasses, sedges and some herbs. Moss campion grows on drier slopes. Cotton grass, mosses, lichens, dwarf birch and willows cover the foothills. Sedges, mosses, cotton grass and lousewort predominate on the boggy plain, and high brush vegetation, featuring willow and alder, grows along major rivers.

Wildlife

Big Game: Brown/grizzly bears, Dall sheep, wolves and moose roam areas of the Brooks Range and the Arctic where there is suitable habitat. Two major caribou herds, the western Arctic and Porcupine, migrate through the Brooks Range to summer calving grounds on the arctic plain.

After being hunted out of Alaska in the mid-1800s, musk-ox were successfully reintroduced to Nunivak Island in western Alaska in the 1930s. Today several herds range the Arctic.

Furbearers and Non-Game Species: Wolverines, weasels, a few river otters, snowshoe hares, lynx, arctic and red foxes, shrew, lemmings and voles roam the Brooks Range and the Arctic.

The frigid waters of the Beaufort and Chukchi seas support polar bears, walrus, bowhead and beluga whales, and bearded and ringed seals. In summer when ice retreats from the coast, harbor seals, harbor porpoises, and killer and gray whales feed here. Rarer species of great whales — fin, sei and little piked — have been reported in Chukchi waters. Even more unusual are the occasional spottings of narwhals.

Birds: Many bird species migrate to summer breeding grounds in the Arctic although few winter here. Summer visitors to tundra-covered plains can look for the conspicuous white vision of a snowy owl guarding its nest. Thousands of snow geese feed and raise their young near the arctic coast. In the mountains look for hawks, owls, ptarmigan and migrating waterfowl.

Fish: Anglers try for arctic char, lake trout, pike, whitefish, lingcod, salmon and grayling in rivers and lakes. The Kobuk River is known for its sheefish. The Kobuk also has a chum salmon run, the northernmost commercial salmon fishery in the state.

Minerals

Gold is not a big draw in the Arctic, but oil certainly is. Early Eskimos knew of oil seeps leaking from the coastal plain, but the big discovery at Prudhoe Bay was not made until 1968. Development of the Prudhoe Bay field, the largest oil field yet discovered in North America, brought about construction of a huge industrial complex on the North Slope (see Prudhoe Bay/Deadhorse) as well as the trans-Alaska pipeline to carry the oil to market.

In the western Arctic discovery of a large zinc/lead/silver deposit at Red Dog has led to construction of a 54-mile industrial road from the mine site to tidewater 12 miles south of Kivalina. The mine was in the final stages of construction in 1989 with start-up scheduled for late that year. Once production begins, Red Dog will be the largest operating zinc mine in the western world. The year-round open-pit mine will employ some 300 workers.

At the port site on the Chukchi Sea, barges will lighter the zinc to vessels during the sea's brief 90- to 100-day shipping season. A 7-acre concentrate storage building at the port (dimensions: 1,425 feet long by 225 feet wide by 110 feet high) will be one of the largest structures in the state. Plans are to paint the building's long sides with the blue of the Alaska flag and red and white stripes, the whole to represent an American flag. On clear days the building should be visible from aircraft flying 45 to 50 miles away.

CAUTION: The 30-foot-wide gravel road will carry significant volumes of oversized truck traffic and is not safe for backpackers, snowmobilers and other recreational users.

Public Lands

National Parks and Preserves: Millions of acres of land in this region have been set aside as a monument, preserve, park or refuge. Cape Krusenstern National Monument on the Chukchi coast contains ancient beachfronts created by ocean currents and storms. Artifacts dating back thousands of years have been unearthed here. East from the sea is Noatak National Preserve, Kobuk Valley National Park and Gates of the Arctic National Park and Preserve.

National Wildlife Refuges: Just south of the Kobuk valley lies Selawik National Wildlife Refuge, part of which is above the Arctic Circle. In the northeastern corner of Alaska is the 18-million-acre Arctic National Wildlife Refuge.

History

Few settlements have been established in

the Brooks Range and the Arctic. Barrow, largest Inupiat Eskimo community in the world, is the trade center for the North Slope Borough, which includes the smaller communities of Point Hope, Point Lay, Atqasuk, Nuiqsut, Anaktuvuk Pass, Umiat, Kaktovik and the oil complex at Prudhoe Bay.

Commerce among villages in the southwestern Arctic revolves around Kotzebue, center of the newly created Northwest Arctic Borough. Transportation and supplies go out from there to Kobuk, Shungnak, Ambler, Kiana, Noorvik, Noatak, Kivalina and Selawik. To the east, the old mining community of Bettles is flourishing anew as the gateway to Gates of the Arctic National Park and Preserve. Anaktuvuk Pass is settled by inland Eskimos who for generations have hunted in the Anaktuvuk River area. And farther south the Athabascan Indians hunted and fished and gathered berries along the river systems of the south slopes of the Brooks Range.

Oil and subsistence hunting and fishing provide the majority of economic support for the Arctic. The 800-mile-long oil pipeline from Prudhoe Bay to Valdez on Prince William Sound began operation in 1977. Oil field development and related construction created jobs for many arctic residents and provided the economic stimulus for new houses, schools, hospitals and civic buildings.

Residents of smaller villages rely on subsistence and temporary work, usually in construction or government. Caribou are important to inland Eskimos, while coastal villagers depend on fish and marine mammals.

Subsistence, some tourism, commercial fishing and trapping, and mining generate income for the western Arctic.

Access

Access into this remote mountain range and the arctic wilderness beyond comes via scheduled or charter flights or the Dalton Highway. Also known as the North Slope Haul Road, the 414-mile Dalton was built to serve construction and operation of the trans-Alaska pipeline from Prudhoe Bay. The road is open to the public as far as Disaster Creek. Permits for travel beyond Disaster Creek are granted only for commercial and industrial uses related to the oil, gas or mineral industries; official government business; University of Alaska-affiliated research; tour buses; and access by residents to their property. Anyone wishing to drive the Dalton beyond Disaster Creek for reasons other than these should contact the Director of Maintenance and Operations, 2301 Peger Road, Fairbanks, AK 99701; phone 451-2209.

For more about the Dalton Highway, see *The MILEPOST®*, a complete guide to Alaska's road and marine highway systems. To order, see the ALASKA NORTHWEST LIBRARY section at the back of the book.

Massive antlers of a bull caribou are silhouetted against the sky. (© John W. Warden)

▼ C O M M U N I T I E S ▼

Ambler

Located on the north bank of the Kobuk River near the confluence of the Ambler and Kobuk rivers, 125 miles east of Kotzebue, 320 miles northwest of Fairbanks. **Transportation:** Scheduled airline, air taxi from Kotzebue. **Population:** 271. **Zip code:** 99786. **Emergency Services:** Police, phone 445-2180; Clinic, phone 445-2129; Volunteer Fire Department.

Elevation: 135 feet. **Climate:** Continental climate, characterized by long, cold winters and warm summers. Average annual precipitation 16 inches, including 80 inches of snow.

Private Aircraft: Airstrip 1 mile north; elev. 289 feet; length 2,600 feet; gravel; fuel 80, 100; unattended. Runway condition not monitored, visual inspection recommended prior to using. No facilities at airport.

Visitor Facilities: Accommodations and meals available at 1 lodge. No laundromat or banking services. Groceries, some clothing, first-aid supplies, hardware, camera film and sporting goods available in the community. Local arts and crafts available for purchase include birch-bark baskets, masks, mukluks, beaver hats and yo-yos. Fishing/hunting licenses available, as well as guide service. Aircraft mechanic for major repair service only. Rental transportation available includes autos, off-road vehicles, boats and charter aircraft. Fuel available includes marine gas, diesel, propane and regular gasoline. Boat moorage on riverbank.

This Eskimo village was settled in 1958 when people from Shungnak and Kobuk moved here because of its spruce forest and the availability of game. The second-class city was incorporated in 1971. Ambler's economy is based on arts, crafts and subsistence hunting and fishing. In the summer, many residents go to Kotzebue for commercial fishing. Some local employment is provided by government, school and local businesses.

Ambler is some 20 miles from the archaeological dig at Onion Portage, where artifacts dating back 10,000 years have been found. Kobuk Valley National Park lies about 15 miles downriver and the Great Kobuk Sand Dunes are approximately 35 miles away. Visitors often charter aircraft out of Ambler to Walker Lake in the Brooks Range, then float back down the Kobuk River.

Fishing near Ambler includes salmon, sheefish, grayling, whitefish and trout. The western Arctic caribou herd migrates near Ambler; other game includes moose, grizzly and black bear. Jade can be found in some local streams. A ski track is maintained in winter. Bird-watching, especially good around breakup time, includes swans, cranes and other waterfowl.

Communications include phones, mail plane, radio and TV. The community is served by 2 churches and a school with grades preschool through 12. Public water, electricity and sewage systems available. Ambler prohibits the sale and importation of alcoholic beverages. Freight arrives in the community by cargo plane and barge. Government address: City of Ambler, P.O. Box 9, Ambler, AK 99786; phone 445-2122. Village corporation address: NANA Regional Corp., P.O. Box 49, Kotzebue, AK 99752.

Anaktuvuk Pass

(an-ak-TU-vuk) Located on a divide between the Anaktuvuk and John rivers in the central Brooks Range, 260 miles north-northwest of Fairbanks. **Transportation:** Scheduled airline, air taxi from Fairbanks. **Population:** 364. **Zip code:** 99721. **Emergency Services:** Public Safety Officer, phone 661-3911; Clinic, phone 661-3914; Fire Department, phone 661-3529.

Elevation: 2,200 feet. **Climate:** Due to high elevation, temperatures remain below freezing most of the year, with daily maximum temperature higher than freezing only 142 days of year. January is the coldest month; July is the warmest month. Mean annual precipitation is 10.3 inches. Average annual snowfall is 63 inches.

Private Aircraft: Airstrip adjacent to southeast; elev. 2,100 feet; length 5,000 feet; gravel; attended. No public transportation to village.

Visitor Facilities: Public campground (check with National Park Service ranger station or village store). No restaurant, laundromat or banking services. Groceries available. Local arts and crafts available for purchase include caribou skin masks and carvings. Fishing/hunting licenses available. No guide service. No major repair service or rental transportation. Fuel available includes propane and regular gasoline.

This Nunamiut Eskimo village in Anaktuvuk Pass, a historic caribou migration route, is the last remaining settlement of the inland northern Inupiat Eskimo, whose ancestors date back to 500 B.C. The original nomadic Nunamiut bands left the Brooks Range and scattered in the early 1900s, primarily due to the collapse of the caribou population in 1926 and 1927, but also because of cultural changes brought about by the influx of western civilization. By 1938, however, several Nunamiut families returned to the mountains at Killik River and Chandler Lake. In the late 1940s, both groups joined at broad, treeless Anaktuvuk Pass, "the place of caribou droppings," to settle permanently. The community incorporated as a second-class city in 1957.

Subsistence hunting, primarily of caribou, and some construction work, in addition to arts and crafts, form the economic base. This is perhaps the most scenic village on the North Slope as it is surrounded by tall mountains and is near rivers and lakes. Anaktuvuk Pass is located in Gates of the Arctic National Park and Preserve. There is public access to parklands across nearby regional and village Native corporation lands; check with a park ranger about planned routes.

Simon Paneak Memorial Museum, P.O. Box 21085, Anaktuvuk Pass, AK 99721, is open all year. The museum focuses on recording and preserving the history of the Nunamiut. Exhibits are on the early natural, geological and cultural history of the Anaktuvuk Pass area, including the migrations of people across the Bering Land Bridge. Exhibits also feature clothing, household goods and hunting implements used by the Nunamiut Eskimos around the time of the first contact with Westerners. No admission fee.

Communications include phones, mail plane, radio and TV. The community is served by a Presbyterian church and the Nunamiut School with grades preschool through 12.

Public electricity is available. Water is delivered by truck from the village well. Sewage system is pit privies and honey buckets. Anaktuvuk Pass prohibits the possession of alcoholic beverages. Freight arrives by air transport. Government address: City of Anaktuvuk Pass, P.O. Box 21030, Anaktukvuk Pass, AK 99721; phone 661-3612. Village corporation address: Nunamiut Corp., General Delivery, Anaktuvuk Pass, AK 99721.

Arctic Village
(See Communities in INTERIOR section.)

Atqasuk
(AT-ka-sook) Located on the west bank of Meade River near Imakrak Lake, 58 miles southwest of Barrow. **Transportation:** Scheduled airline, air taxi from Barrow. **Population:** 219. **Zip code:** 99791. **Emergency Services:** Public Safety Officer, phone 633-6911; Clinic, phone 633-6711; Fire Department, phone 633-6611.

Elevation: 65 feet. **Climate:** Temperatures remain below freezing for most of the year. July is the warmest month; February the coldest. Annual precipitation averages 5 inches, with snowfall averaging 30 inches annually.

Private Aircraft: Meade River airstrip south; elev. 95 feet; length 4,400 feet; gravel; no fuel available; unattended; runway condition not monitored, visual inspection recommended prior to using. No facilities. No public transportation to village.

Visitor Facilities: No hotel, restaurant or banking services. Groceries, clothing, first-aid supplies, camera film, laundromat and hardware are available in the community. Arts and crafts available for purchase include masks, mittens, dolls, yo-yos, ulus and parkas. Fishing/hunting licenses available. No guide service. No major repair service or rental transportation. Fuel available includes propane, regular gasoline, diesel and motor oil. No moorage facilities.

The area around this Inupiat Eskimo village has traditionally been hunted and fished by the Inupiat (northern Eskimo). During WWII, coal was mined here and freighted to Barrow. The mine was operated by residents for personal use from 1978-79 and opened again in 1987 for a trial period according to one resident. The village had a post office from 1951 to 1957 under the name Meade River. The village was reestablished in 1977 by former Barrow residents and incorporated into a second-class city in 1982. Abandoned sod houses, an old cellar and gravesite near the village provide evidence of earlier settlements in the area.

Atqasuk's economy is based on subsistence caribou and whale hunting, fishing and construction work. Residents also migrate to Barrow periodically for temporary employment. Fish in the Meade River include grayling, burbot, 3 types of whitefish and 3 species of salmon. Local hunters bag seals, walruses, ptarmigan, ducks and geese.

Communications include phones, mail plane, radio and TV. The community has a church and a school with grades preschool through 12. Public electricity is available. Lake water is hauled by truck. Most residences have honey buckets. Freight arrives in the community by air transport or sometimes by cat train from Barrow in winter. Atqasuk bans the possession of alcoholic beverages. Government address: City of Atqasuk, General Delivery, Atqasuk, AK 99791; phone 633-6811. Village corporation address: Atkasook Corp., General Delivery, Atqasuk, AK 99791.

Barrow

Located on the Chukchi Sea coast, 10 miles southwest of Point Barrow, 500 miles northwest of Fairbanks. **Transportation:** Scheduled airline from Anchorage via Fairbanks. **Population:** 3,075. **Zip code:** 99723. **Emergency Services:** Public Safety Officer, phone 852-6111; Alaska State Troopers, phone 852-3783; Hospital, phone 852-4611; Volunteer Fire Department.

Elevation: 20 feet. **Climate:** Normal daily maximum temperature in July (warmest month) is 44°F. Normal daily minimum in January (coldest month) is -24°F. The sun rises May 10 and does not set until Aug. 2. When the sun disappears at noon Nov. 18 it does not appear again until noon, Jan. 24.

Private Aircraft: Wiley Post-Will Rogers Memorial Airport adjacent southeast; elev. 44 feet; length 6,500 feet; asphalt; fuel 80, 100, jet A1; attended 4 to 10:30 p.m. or upon request; phone 852-6199.

Visitor Facilities: Accommodations at 3 hotels. There are 6 restaurants, a dry cleaners and a bank. Available in the community are groceries, clothing, first-aid supplies, hardware, camera film and sporting goods. Arts and crafts available for purchase include baleen boats, etched baleen, carved ivory, masks, parkas and fur mittens. Fishing/hunting licenses available. No guide service. Major repair services include marine engine, boat, auto and aircraft mechanics. Air taxi service available. Fuel available includes marine gas, diesel, propane, aviation fuel, unleaded, regular and supreme. No moorage.

During the summer months tour operators offer package tours of the area. For more information on what to see and do, contact the Barrow Convention and Visitors Assoc.

Barrow is one of the largest Eskimo settlements and the seat of the 88,000-square-mile North Slope Borough, the world's largest municipal government. Traditionally, Barrow is known as Ukpeagvik "place where owls are hunted." Barrow takes its name from Point Barrow, named for Sir John Barrow of the British Admiralty by Captain Beechey of the Royal Navy in 1825. Beechey had been assigned the task of plotting the Arctic coastline of North America in the HMS *Blossom*. Barrow was incorporated as a first-class city in 1959.

Across from the airport sits the Will Rogers and Wiley Post Monument, dedicated in 1982 to commemorate the 1935 airplane crash of the American humorist and the famous pilot. The accident happened 15 miles south of Barrow where the men had landed seeking directions to Barrow, a planned stop on their trip from Fairbanks to Siberia. Upon takeoff their plane rose to 50 feet, stalled and then plunged into a river below, killing both men. Two monuments, both on the National Register of Historic Places, are located where the men died. Other sites on the national register are the Cape Smythe Whaling and Trading Station in nearby Browerville and the Birnirk archaeological site approximately 2 miles north of the Barrow airfield. Cape Smythe was built as a whaling station in 1893 and is the oldest frame building in the Arctic. The Birnirk culture, which existed about 500-900 A.D., is represented by a group of 16 dwelling mounds and is considered a key link between the prehistoric cultures of Alaska and Canada.

Visitors also may view the Eskimos heading for whale camps in April and May. Despite the fact that the village is very much into the 20th century, hunting of whales, seals, walrus, caribou and ducks is still important traditionally and to the economy. It also provides a great portion of the food for the residents. If the whalers are successful, there is a festival called "Nalukataq" when whaling season ends in May.

Barrow residents work for the oil companies at Prudhoe Bay, for the borough, the Native corporation and for various other local businesses.

Barrow has all communications services, including cable TV, a public radio station, as well as community electricity, water and sewer systems. Many homes are heated by natural gas from the nearby gas fields. The community is served by 7 churches, a high school, an elementary school and a post secondary Higher Education Center affiliated with the University of Alaska in Fairbanks. There is also a recreation center that includes a new gymnasium, 2 racquetball courts, a weight room and saunas, as well as adult dances and sport tournaments, exercise classes and cross-country skiing. The high school has a swimming pool, weight room and gymnasium that is open to the community evenings and weekends.

Freight arrives by cargo plane and barge. Barrow bans the sale of alcoholic beverages. Government address: City of Barrow, Box 629, Barrow, AK 99723; phone 852-5211. Regional corporation address: Arctic Slope Regional Corp., Box 129, Barrow, AK 99723; phone 852-8633; Village corporation address: Ukpeagvik Inupiat Corp., Box 427, Barrow, AK 99723. Borough government address: North Slope Borough, Box 69, Barrow, AK 99723; phone 852-2611. Barrow Convention and Visitors Assoc., P.O. Box 1060, Barrow, AK 99723; phone 852-8687.

Bettles

(Also known as Evansville and Bettles Field.) Located on the south bank of the Upper Koyukuk River in the foothills of the Brooks Range, 180 miles northwest of Fairbanks. **Transportation:** Scheduled air service from Fairbanks and charter air service in Bettles. Also accessible by boat in summer, snow machine in winter. Connected by trail to Allakaket and Anaktuvuk Pass. **Population:** 55. **Zip code:** 99726. **Emergency Services:** Clinic, phone 692-5035; Health aide, phone 692-5141; Fish and Game Protection, phone 692-5166.

Elevation: 624 feet. **Climate:** Semiarid and subarctic. January temperatures average -9°F, with winter winds making it colder. July temperatures average 59°F, with both rain and sun. Greatest mean monthly precipitation is in August with 2.63 inches.

Private Aircraft: Bettles airstrip adjacent north; elev. 643 feet; length 5,200 feet; gravel; fuel 80, 100, A1+, B. FAA installation, runway maintained year-round. Evansville seaplane base 4.3 miles northwest of Bettles; river sometimes very low, visual inspection recommended prior to using. Fuel available at airport.

Visitor Facilities: Meals and overnight accommodations available; open all year. Campground. Groceries, clothing, hardware, camera film, sporting goods and first-aid supplies may be purchased in the community. Arts and crafts available locally include furs, gloves, hats, parkas, ivory, baskets, masks and locally crafted gold jewelry. Fishing/hunting licenses available from the Fish and Wildlife Protection officer. Brooks Range outfitters/guides are headquartered here. Major repair available for aircraft; check locally for mechanics to work on other types of engines. Residents may lease transportation such as boats and autos. Fuel available: diesel, propane, aviation and unleaded gas. Moor boats on riverbank.

Evansville, 5 miles east of "old" Bettles, was founded by Wilfred Evans, who built the Bettles Lodge. Bettles began as a trading post in 1899 and was named for the proprietor, Gordon C. Bettles. It developed into a mining town and was eventually abandoned. Bettles Field, the airstrip, was built by the U.S. Navy upriver from old Bettles in 1945. Natives relocated Evansville to the north end of the airfield. Employment here consists mainly of state and federal jobs. Bettles is incorporated.

Bettles is the gateway to Gates of the Arctic National Park and Preserve and is generally receptive to the growing number of Outside visitors. The community sees a number of hikers and river rafters in summer. Visitors are advised, however, not to pick up souvenirs. Camps, cabins and claims that appear to be abandoned may be privately owned and still in use. Also, Bettles is trying to preserve some of its local mining history. There is hunting and fishing in the area, but visitors should be aware of subsistence claims and rules governing park and preserve lands.

Communications include phones, mail plane and TV. There is a church in the community and a 2-classroom school with grades 1 through 12. There is community electricity service, but water is either hauled from the river or obtained from private wells, and the sewage system is either flush toilets and septic tanks. Freight comes in by cargo plane or via winter tractor trail. Village government address: City of Bettles, Box 26023, Bettles, AK 99726; phone 692-5191.

Coldfoot

Located at Mile 175 on the Dalton Highway in the southern slopes of the Brooks Range, 248 miles north of Fairbanks. **Transportation:** Dalton Highway from Fairbanks (no permit needed); charter air service from Fairbanks. **Population:** est. 35 summers; est. 12 winters. **Zip code:** 99701. **Emergency Services:** Alaska State Troopers, phone 678-5201 and leave message.

Climate: Subarctic winters average from 10°F above zero to -20°F or -30°F; summers, temperatures average 75°F.

Private Aircraft: State-maintained airstrip adjacent west; elev. 1,050 feet; length 3,500 feet; gravel; no fuel; unattended. No airport facilities.

Visitor Facilities: Accommodations at 1 motel. Restaurant, lounge, laundry services, mechanical repair, RV park with full hookups; automotive fuels; propane. No banking services. General store has groceries, some clothing, hardware, film, sporting goods, etc. Carved ivory, Eskimo dolls, silver jewelry available for purchase. Fishing/hunting licenses available from Fish and Wildlife officer; no guide service.

Coldfoot is the site of a historic mining camp at the mouth of Slate Creek on the east bank of the Middle Fork Koyukuk River. Originally named Slate Creek, Coldfoot reportedly got its name in 1900 when gold stampeders got as far up the Koyukuk as this point, then got cold feet, turned and departed. The old cemetery still exists. Emma Dome (elev. 5,680 feet) lies to the west.

Coldfoot's one commercial facility for visitors is owned and operated by Dick and Cathy Mackey. Dick, one of the organizers of the Iditarod Trail Sled Dog Race and 1978 champion, maintains his racing kennels at Coldfoot. The community is home of the 350-mile Coldfoot Classic Sled Dog Race. Cathy became Coldfoot's postmistress in 1985, marking the first time postal service has been provided since the early 1900s. With the increase in gold mining activities in the area, it is not unusual to find a miner bartering his gold for some cool refreshment at the local lounge.

The National Park Service, Bureau of Land Management, and U.S. Fish and Wildlife Service operate a visitor center for Gates of the Arctic National Park and Kanuti National Wildlife Refuge and provide daily presentations on related topics. The visitor center sells USGS topographical maps of the area and books of interest. A Fish and Wildlife officer is stationed at Coldfoot.

Locals report good fishing for grayling at nearby creeks and a couple of hike-in lakes. Because the trans-Alaska pipeline is adjacent, there is no hunting nearby. (North of the Yukon River, hunting is prohibited within 5 miles on either side of the pipeline.) Motorcycles and all-terrain vehicles provide summertime leisure activity, and winters are taken up with dog mushing and snow machining.

The unincorporated community has no public utilities. The 4 private phones, all located at the motel, are for collect and credit card calls only. Mail arrives by truck; TV via satellite.

Deadhorse

(See Prudhoe Bay/Deadhorse.)

Kaktovik

(Kack-TOE-vik) Located on the north coast of Barter Island on the Beaufort Sea, 390 miles north of Fairbanks. **Transportation:** Scheduled airline, air taxi via Fairbanks or Barrow. **Population:** 227. **Zip code:** 99747. **Emergency Services:** Public Safety Officer, phone 640-6911; Clinic, phone 640-6413; Fire Department, phone 640-6611.

Elevation: 40 feet. **Climate:** February is the coldest month; July the warmest. Mean annual precipitation is 6.5 inches, with 39 inches of snow.

Private Aircraft: Airstrip 1 mile from village; fuel 80, 100; control tower. Transportation to village.

Visitor Facilities: Accommodations and meals available. Laundromat may be available. No banking services. Grocery items, some clothing, first-aid supplies, hardware, camera film and sporting goods can be purchased in the community.

Local arts and crafts which can be purchased include etched baleen, carved ivory and masks. Fishing/hunting licenses available, as well as guide service. Major repair services include auto and aircraft mechanic. Charter aircraft is the only rental transportation. Fuel available includes marine gas, diesel, propane, unleaded and regular. No moorage.

This Inupiat Eskimo village is on the northern edge of the 20.3-million-acre Arctic National Wildlife Refuge, the most northerly unit of the national wildlife refuge system.

The ruins of old Kaktovik can be seen from the road into the village from the airport. Hunting in the nearby area is for Dall sheep, moose, caribou and fox.

Communications in Kaktovik, which incorporated as a second-class city in 1971, include phones, mail plane, radio and TV. The community is served by a Presbyterian church and Harold Kaveolook School with grades preschool through 12. Public water and electricity are available; sewage system is honey buckets. Freight arrives by cargo plane and barge. Government address: City of Kaktovik, P.O. Box 27, Kaktovik, AK 99747; phone 640-6313. Village corporation address: Kaktovik Inupiat Corp., Box 73, Kaktovik, AK 99747.

Kiana

(ky-AN-a) Located on the north bank of the Kobuk River, 57 miles east of Kotzebue, 390 miles west of Fairbanks. **Transportation:** Boat; snow machine; scheduled airline and air taxi from Kotzebue. **Population:** 434. **Zip code:** 99749. **Emergency Services:** Police, phone 475-2129; Clinic, phone 475-2199; Volunteer Fire Department.
Elevation: 150 feet. **Climate:** Kiana is in the transitional climate zone and has long, cold winters and warm summers. Summer temperatures average 60°F. Precipitation averages over 16 inches annually, including 60 inches of snow.

Private Aircraft: Bob Baker Memorial Airport 1 mile from village; elev. 150 feet; length 3,400 feet; gravel; no fuel available. Runway conditions monitored by airport manager. No facilities at airport. Public transportation usually available from airfield.

Visitor Facilities: No lodging facilities or banking services. A small restaurant and laundromat are available. Groceries, clothing, first-aid supplies, hardware, camera film and sporting goods can be purchased in the community. No arts and crafts available for purchase. Fishing/hunting licenses and guide service available. Outboard engine repair only. Rental transportation includes boats and charter aircraft. Fuel available includes marine gas, diesel, propane and regular gasoline. Moorage facilities available.

This Eskimo village was probably established as a seasonal camp or central village of the Kowagmiut Eskimos. Its name means "place where 3 rivers meet." It is the most modern of the villages in the Kobuk River area. It became a supply center for Squirrel River placer mines in 1909. It is a second-class city, incorporated in 1964.

Kiana has a subsistence economy based on moose, caribou, rabbits and various waterfowl. Fishing includes chum salmon, sheefish, whitefish, lingcod and grayling. In summer, many men go to Kotzebue, Red Dog mine or Prudhoe Bay to work in construction or commercial fishing.

The community is downstream from Kobuk Valley National Park, where winter's dry, cold climate still approximates that of late Pleistocene times, supporting remnant flora once common on the vast arctic steppe. From Kiana, a network of old trading trails is still used for intervillage travel, hunting and fishing. All-terrain vehicles, snow machines and, less frequently, dog sleds are used in the winter.

Communications include phones, mail plane 6 times daily, radio and TV. The community is served by 2 churches and 2 schools with grades preschool through 12. There are public electricity, water and sewer systems. Freight arrives by barge and air transport. Kiana bans the sale and importation of alcoholic beverages. Government address: City of Kiana, P.O. Box 150, Kiana, AK 99749; phone 475-2136. Village corporation address: NANA Regional Corp., P.O. Box 49, Kotzebue, AK 99752.

Kivalina

(Kiv-a-LEEN-a) Located on an 8-mile-long barrier beach between the Chukchi Sea and Kivalina Lagoon, 90 miles north of Kotzebue, 465 miles west of Fairbanks. **Transportation:** Boat; snow machine; scheduled airline, air taxi from Kotzebue. **Population:** 290. **Zip code:** 99750. **Emergency Services:** Alaska State Troopers, Kotzebue, phone 442-3222; Clinic, phone 645-2141; Volunteer Fire Department.

Elevation: 11 feet. **Climate:** Located in the transitional climate zone, Kivalina has long, cold winters and cool summers. The Chukchi Sea is ice-covered from November to June. Precipitation is light, with an annual mean of 8.6 inches, including 57 inches of snow.

Private Aircraft: Airstrip adjacent; elev. 10 feet; length 5,000 feet; no fuel. Runway condition not monitored, visual inspection recommended prior to using. Support facilities and transportation to village.

Visitor Facilities: Accommodations sometimes available in private homes. No restaurant, laundromat or banking services. Groceries, clothing, first-aid supplies, hardware, camera film and sporting goods can be purchased in the community. Arts and crafts available for purchase include model skin kayaks, model dog sleds, whale bone masks, ivory carvings and baskets. Fishing/hunting licenses not available. No guide or major repair services. Boats can sometimes be rented. Fuel available: marine gas, diesel, propane, regular and unleaded. No moorage.

This Eskimo village, built on a flat sand and gravel spit, has long been a stopping-off place for seasonal travelers between the Arctic coast and Kotzebue Sound. Lieutenant L.A. Zagoskin of the Imperial Russian Navy recorded the name "Kivualinagmut" in 1847. It is a second-class city, incorporated in 1969.

Kivalina has a subsistence economy based on bowhead and beluga whales, walruses, seals, moose and caribou. There is fishing for salmon, grayling and arctic char in 2 rivers near the village. The Chukchi Sea usually is open to boat traffic from about mid-June to the first of November. Winter travel is by snow machine and dogsled from late October through May.

Communications include phones, mail plane, radio and TV. The community is served by 2 churches and 2 schools with grades preschool through 12. There are public electricity and water supply systems. Sewage system is honey buckets. Kivalina prohibits the sale and importation of alcoholic beverages. Freight arrives in the community by plane, barge and ship. Government address: City of Kivalina, P.O. Box 50079, Kivalina, AK 99750; phone 645-2137. Village corporation address: NANA Regional Corp., P.O. Box 49, Kotzebue, AK 99752.

Kobuk

Located on the right bank of the Kobuk River, 150 miles east of Kotzebue, 300 miles west of Fairbanks. **Transportation:** Scheduled airline, charter from Kotzebue. **Population:** 86. **Zip code:** 99751. **Emergency Services:** Village Public Safety Officer; Clinic and Health aide; Volunteer Fire Department.

Elevation: 140 feet. **Climate:** Kobuk is located in the continental climate zone; winters are long and cold, summers relatively warm. Mean annual precipitation 16.7 inches, including 56 inches of snow.

Private Aircraft: Airstrip adjacent; elev. 145 feet; length 2,500 feet; gravel; no fuel; visual inspection recommended prior to using. Restroom facilities. No public transportation. Floatplane operation on lake. Also, 3,800-foot gravel airstrip at Dahl Creek, 3 miles from Kobuk.

Visitor Facilities: Accommodations at 1 hotel or arrangements can be made with private homes or clinic. Laundromat with showers available. No restaurant or banking services. Groceries, first-aid supplies, hardware, camera film and sporting goods can be purchased in the community.

Local arts and crafts available for purchase include birch-bark baskets and picture frames, mukluks, beaver hats and fur mittens. Fishing/hunting licenses available, as well as a fishing guide. No major repair services. Rental transportation includes boats and charter aircraft. Fuel available includes marine gas, diesel, propane, unleaded and regular gasoline. Moorage available.

This Eskimo community of log homes was founded in 1899 as a supply point for mining activities in the Cosmos Hills to the north and was then called Shungnak. Area residents gravitated to the trading post, school and mission. Riverbank erosion forced relocation of the village in the 1920s to present-day Shungnak, 10 miles downriver. The few people who stayed and those who returned named the old village Kobuk. The village is a second-class city, incorporated in 1973.

Kobuk has a subsistence economy largely based on fishing and hunting. Fish include sheefish (up to 60 pounds), salmon, grayling, whitefish, pike and trout. Game includes caribou, moose, black and grizzly bear, and Dall sheep. Residents also work for the local government, school district and village corporation. Firefighting provides summer work.

Kobuk is located near the headwaters of the Kobuk River. Visitors to Kobuk Valley National Park can fly into Kobuk from Nome or Kotzebue and float down the Kobuk to the national park and the Great Kobuk Sand Dunes or fly to Walker Lake in Gates of the Arctic National Park in the Brooks Range and float the river from there. Also of interest is the jade mine, 3 miles from Kobuk by jeep, owned by Oro Stewart of Stewart's photo in Anchorage. Visitors are welcome in June and July to watch jade mining and cutting. No charge for cabins; bring sleeping bags and food. NANA Regional Corp. also operates a jade mine at nearby Jade Mountain. Historic trails along the river are still used for inter-village travel, hunting and fishing.

Communications include phones, mail plane, radio and TV. The community is served by a church and a school with grades preschool through 8. There are public water supply and electricity systems. The sewage system is honey buckets. Freight arrives by plane or barge. Kobuk bans the sale and importation of alcoholic beverages. Government address: City of Kobuk, P.O. Box 20, Kobuk, AK 99751; phone 948-2217. Village corporation address: NANA Regional Corp., P.O. Box 49, Kotzebue, AK 99752.

Kotzebue

(KOT-sa-byou) Located on the northwest shore of Baldwin Peninsula in Kotzebue Sound, 26 miles above the Arctic Circle. **Transportation:** Daily jet service from Anchorage via Nome. **Population:** 3,705. **Zip code:** 99752. **Emergency Services:** For police, fire, ambulance, phone 911; Women's Crisis Project, phone 442-3969; Maniilaq Medical Center, phone 442-3321.

Elevation: 10 feet. **Climate:** In summer the temperature averages between 40° and 50°F. During winter, the average temperature is between -20° and -15°F. Mean annual precipitation is 8.6 inches, including 46 inches of snow. During summer the sun does not set for approximately 36 days.

Private Aircraft: Ralph Wien Memorial Airport, 1 mile south; elev. 11 feet; length 5,900 feet; asphalt; fuel 80, 100, jet A. Transportation to town available. Kotzebue seaplane base within city.

Visitor Facilities: Accommodations at 1 hotel and 1 lodge. There are restaurants and banking services, several stores carrying all supplies, beauty salons, a library and taxis. Among the many Eskimo arts and crafts items that can be purchased are jade items made at a local factory as well as parkas and mukluks made locally. Fishing/hunting licenses and guide service available, as well as several air charter companies. All fuel is available.

Kotzebue is the commercial center for a 48,000-square-mile area of northwestern Alaska which includes 10 villages and a population of about 7,047. It is a second-class city, incorporated in 1958.

The town is on a spit that is about 3 miles long and 1,100 to 3,600 feet wide. The site has been occupied for some 600 years and centuries before Europeans arrived "Kikiktagruk" was a busy trading center. It acquired its present name from the adjacent sound named for Polish explorer Otto von Kotzebue.

The population is more than 80 percent Eskimo. The economy is based on government services, commercial fishing and subsistence hunting and fishing. The wage economy of the entire region is concentrated in Kotzebue, which contains the regional offices of several state and federal agencies.

Local attractions include the NANA Museum of the Arctic, P.O. Box 49, Kotzebue, AK 99752; phone 442-3304, which features a 2-hour program that includes a diorama show unequaled anywhere in Alaska. Shows are scheduled at 9:15 a.m. and 3 p.m. daily, tickets for the show are $20. Collections in the museum reflect the ethnology and natural history of northwestern Alaska, along with wildlife exhibits. Also included in a trip to the museum is a visit to the jade manufacturing factory, a panoramic slide show, cultural heritage demonstrations featuring skin sewing, ivory carving, Eskimo dancing and other traditional arts, and an Eskimo blanket toss. The museum is open from June to September and hours are 8:30 a.m. to 5:30 p.m. daily. Winter hours are by appointment. General admission is free. The west end of the museum building houses administrative offices of the National Park Service, phone 442-3890 or write Superintendent, Northwest Alaska Areas, National Park Service, Box 287, Kotzebue, AK 99752 for information about national parks in the area. The Park Service public information center is down the street from the museum. The excellent city museum, Ootukahkuktuvik or "Place Having Old Things," City of Kotzebue, P.O. Box 46, Kotzebue, AK 99752 requires special arrangements to view; contact the city hall. Among the items to see are a raincoat made from walrus intestine and a coat fashioned from bird feathers.

Points of interest include the large cemetery, with graves lavishly decorated with artificial flowers, and spirit houses over some of the graves.

The July 4 celebration, followed closely by the Northwest Native Trade Fair, is the biggest event of the year in Kotzebue. The fair features traditional Native games and awards for the largest beluga whales caught during the season. A muktuk eating contest, seal-hook throwing contest and an Eskimo buggy race are among the special events. People from all over the region come to trade handicrafts and participate in traditional dances and feasts.

Preliminaries to the Eskimo Olympics take place between Christmas and New Year's Day. Events include the knuckle hop, high-kicks, blanket toss, finger-pulling contest and greased pole walk.

During the summer, tour groups are entertained with Eskimo blanket tosses and often dances and skin-sewing demonstrations.

Kotzebue has all communications systems, as well as community water, sewer and electricity. The community is served by 8 churches, 2 schools, a community college and a technical center. Freight arrives by ship, barge and air cargo planes. The community bans the sale of alcoholic beverages. Government address: City of Kotzebue, P.O. Box 46, Kotzebue, AK 99752; phone 442-3401. Native corporation: NANA Regional Corp., P.O. Box 49, Kotzebue, AK 99752.

Kuparuk

(Koo-PAH-ruk) Located on the arctic coastal plain, 40 miles west of Prudhoe Bay, 400 miles north of Fairbanks. **Transportation:** Charter plane or gravel road from Prudhoe Bay. **Population:** Approximately 300 oil field workers. **Emergency Services:** North Slope Borough Police, Prudhoe Bay; ARCO security officers; ARCO medical clinic.

Climate: Summer weather usually cool,

windy and foggy, with 1 or 2 good days each month. Winter weather is cold, dark and very windy. Bugs can be ferocious during calm periods in June and July.

Private Aircraft: Airstrip 0.5 mile from camp. No facilities. No public transportation.

Visitor Facilities: The land is privately leased and there are no visitor facilities.

Kuparuk is the ARCO Alaska base camp for the second-largest oil field in the United States. Communications include phones, mail plane, radio and TV. Freight arrives by cargo plane and barge, or by truck up the Dalton Highway to Prudhoe Bay.

Noatak

(NO-a-tack) Located on the west bank of the Noatak River, 55 miles north of Kotzebue, 470 miles northwest of Fairbanks. **Transportation:** Boat; scheduled air service and air taxi from Kotzebue. **Population:** 305. **Zip code:** 99761. **Emergency Services:** Police, phone 485-2168; Alaska State Troopers, Kotzebue, phone 442-3911; Clinic, phone 485-2162; Volunteer Fire Department.

Elevation: 60 feet. **Climate:** Noatak is on the border between the transitional and continental climate zones; winters are long and cold, summers warm. Precipitation averages 10 to 13 inches annually, including 48 inches of snow.

Private Aircraft: Noatak airstrip adjacent southwest; elev. 99 feet; length 2,200 feet; gravel; fuel 80, 100. No airport facilities or transportation to village. Floatplanes can land on river usually from second week of June to first week of October.

Visitor Facilities: Arrangements can be made for sleeping at the school and in private homes. No restaurant, laundromat or banking services. Groceries, some clothing, hardware and some sporting goods available. Arts and crafts available for purchase include hand-knitted gloves, mukluks and beaver caps. Fishing/hunting licenses available. No guide or major repair services. Boats can be rented. Fuel available includes marine gas, propane and regular gasoline. No moorage facilities.

Noatak, a community of log and wood-frame homes 70 miles above the Arctic Circle, is situated on a bluff overlooking the river. It was established as a fishing and hunting camp in the 19th century and developed into a permanent settlement listed in Ivan Petroff's 1880 census as "Noatagamute," which meant "Noatak (River) people." The community is unincorporated. Its economy is based primarily on subsistence hunting and fishing. Fish include chum salmon, whitefish, gray-

ling, pike, lingcod and Dolly Varden. Game includes caribou, moose, waterfowl, rabbits and Dall sheep. There is summer employment in Kotzebue or at the nearby Red Dog zinc mine.

Noatak is the only settlement along the 396-mile-long Noatak River, eighth-longest river in Alaska. The 6.6-million-acre Noatak National Preserve encompasses the major portion of the river, except the headwaters located in Gates of the Arctic National Park and Preserve. Access to the lower river is by air charter from Kotzebue; access to the upper river for float trips is generally by air charter from Bettles to a lake along the river. Many historic trails along the Noatak are still used for intervillage travel, hunting and fishing. (See also The Rivers this section.)

Communications in Noatak include phones, TV, radio and mail plane. The community is served by a church and a school with grades preschool through 12. There are public water, electricity and sewer systems. Noatak prohibits the sale and importation of alcoholic beverages. Freight arrives by cargo plane and barge. Government address: Noatak Village Council, General Delivery, Noatak, AK 99761. Village corporation address: NANA Regional Corp., P.O. Box 49,

Noorvik

Located on right bank of the Nazuruk Channel of the Kobuk River, 45 miles east of Kotzebue, 400 miles west of Fairbanks. **Transportation:** Boat; scheduled and charter plane from Kotzebue. **Population:** 560. **Zip code:** 99763. **Emergency Services:** Police, phone 636-2173; Clinic, phone 636-2103; Volunteer Fire Department.

Elevation: 70 feet. **Climate:** Transitional, with long, cold winters and cool summers. Mean annual precipitation 16 inches, with 60 inches of snow.

Private Aircraft: Robert Curtis Memorial Airport 1 mile from village; elev. 63 feet; length 2,800 feet; gravel; no fuel; unattended; visual inspection recommended prior to using. Airport manager and freight terminal at airport. No transportation to village.

Visitor Facilities: Accommodations at 1 hotel. There is a restaurant. No banking services. Groceries, clothing, first-aid supplies, hardware, camera film and sporting goods may be purchased in the community. Fishing/hunting licenses available, as well as guide service. Repair services available for marine engines and boats. Arrangements can be made to rent autos, off-road vehicles and boats.

Available fuel includes marine gas, diesel, propane and regular gasoline.

This village was established by Kowagmiut Eskimo fishermen and hunters from the village of Deering in the early 1900s. The village was first called Oksik, but became known as Noorvik around 1914. Noorvik is a second-class city, incorporated in 1964.

The economy is based primarily on subsistence hunting and fishing. There is some full-time employment in the village with local government and businesses and seasonal employment in Kotzebue, Fairbanks, the Red Dog zinc mine or Prudhoe Bay. Noorvik is downstream from Kobuk Valley National Park. Many historic trails in the area are still used for intervillage travel, hunting and fishing.

Communications include phones, mail plane, radio and TV. The community has a church and 2 schools with grades preschool through 12. There are public water, sewer and electricity systems. Noorvik bans the sale and importation of alcoholic beverages. Freight arrives by cargo plane and barge. Government address: City of Noorvik, P.O. Box 146, Noorvik, AK 99763; phone 636-2100. Village corporation address: NANA Regional Corp., P.O. Box 49, Kotzebue, AK 99752.

Nuiqsut

(noo-IK-sut) Located on the west bank of the Nechelik Channel of the Colville River delta, about 35 miles from the Beaufort Sea coast, 60 miles west of Prudhoe Bay, 380 miles north of Fairbanks. **Transportation:** Scheduled or charter plane from Prudhoe Bay or Barrow. **Population:** 314. **Zip code:** 99789. **Emergency Services:** Public Safety Officer, phone 480-6111; Clinic, phone 480-6729; Fire Department, phone 480-6611.

Elevation: 50 feet. **Climate:** Temperatures remain below freezing most of the year, rising above freezing only 122 days per year. July is the warmest month; February the coldest month. Precipitation is light, measuring 5 to 6 inches per year. Total snowfall averages 20 inches.

Private Aircraft: Airstrip adjacent; elev. 50 feet; length 4,600 feet; gravel; no fuel; unattended; visual inspection recommended prior to use. Runway soft or flooded during late spring breakup. No facilities at airport. Transportation to village.

Visitor Facilities: No hotel or restaurant. Laundromat available. No banking services. Groceries, clothing, first-aid supplies, hard-

Backpackers prepare dinner in a single pot at camp on the Anaktuvuk River. (George Wuerthner)

ware, camera film and sporting goods may be purchased in the community. Arts and crafts available for purchase include skin masks and boats, fur mittens and parkas and carved ivory. Fishing/hunting licenses available. No guide service. No major repair services or rental transportation. Fuel available includes marine gas, diesel, propane, white gas, kerosene and regular gasoline. No moorage facilities.

The Colville River Delta has traditionally been a gathering and trading place for the Inupiat Eskimo people, and has always offered good hunting and fishing. The village was constructed in 1974 under sponsorship of Arctic Slope Regional Corp. after a winter overland move of 27 Barrow families with ties to the Colville River delta area. The new residents lived in a tent city for 18 months before permanent housing could be built. Nuiqsut, which encompasses 9 square miles, was incorporated as a second-class city in 1975.

The economy is based primarily on subsistence hunting and fishing, but many residents are employed in seasonal construction work. Fish include whitefish, burbot, arctic char and grayling. Game animals include bowhead and beluga whales, caribou, seals, moose and many species of waterfowl such as swans, geese, ducks and loons. Local recreational activities include riding snowmobiles and 3-wheelers, playing bingo, and activities at the Kisik Community Center. On the Fourth of July various outdoor games take place. Traditional dances are performed at these and other celebrations.

Communications include phones, mail plane, radio and TV. The community is served by a Presbyterian church and a school with grades preschool through 12. There is a public electricity system. Water is delivered from a freshwater lagoon. The sewage system is honey buckets. Nuiqsut prohibits the possession of alcoholic beverages. Freight arrives by barge or plane. Government address: City of Nuiqsut, P.O. Box 148, Nuiqsut, AK 99789; phone 480-6727. Village corporation address: Kuukpik Corp., P.O. Box 187, Nuiqsut, AK 99789.

Point Hope

Located on a triangular foreland which juts into the Chukchi Sea 275 miles north of Nome, 570 miles northwest of Fairbanks, 325 miles southwest of Barrow. **Transportation:** Scheduled airline, air charter from Kotzebue. **Population:** 591. **Zip code:** 99766. **Emergency Services:** Public Safety Officer, phone 368-2911; Clinic, phone 368-2234; Fire Department, phone 368-2774.

Elevation: 13 feet. **Climate:** Temperatures cool year-round but much less severe than elsewhere in the North Slope Borough. Temperatures are above freezing 162 days of the year. February is the coldest month with temperatures averaging -15°F; August is the warmest month when the mercury soars to 44°F average. Mean annual precipitation is 10 inches, including 36 inches of snow.

Private Aircraft: Airstrip 2 miles southwest; elev. 14 feet; length 4,000 feet; asphalt; emergency fuel only; unattended. Tickets and reservations through Point Hope Native Store or other agents in town. City bus available to village.

Visitor Facilities: Accommodations, restaurant and laundry facilities available. Native store will cash checks. Groceries, clothing, first-aid supplies, hardware, camera film and sporting goods available in the community. Arts and crafts available for purchase include carved ivory, baleen baskets, carved whale bone masks and animals, caribou skin masks, etched baleen, Eskimo parkas, ivory-tipped harpoons and bird spears, and oosiks. Fishing/hunting licenses available, as well as guide service. Repair services available for marine engines, boats and autos. Arrangements may be made to rent private autos, off-road vehicles or boats, including skin boats. Fuel available: marine gas, diesel, propane, unleaded, regular and supreme. Public moorage available.

The village was named in 1826 by Capt. F.W. Beechey after Englishman Sir William Johnstone Hope.

The point's favorable location for harvesting bowhead whales attracted an earlier people to settle here some 2,000 years ago after they crossed a land bridge connecting Siberia and Alaska. The Point Hope peninsula is one of the longest continually occupied areas in North America. At Point Hope are the remains of the sod houses of Old Tigara Village, a prehistoric site, and an even earlier site with about 800 house pits known as Ipiutak, occupied from about 500 B.C. to 100 A.D. Ipiutak and the surrounding archaeological district are on the National Register of Historic Places.

The Point Hope people traditionally dominated an extensive area from the Utukok River to the Kivalina River and far inland. By 1848 commercial whaling activities brought an influx of Westerners, many of whom employed Point Hope villagers. By the late 1880s, the whalers established shore-based whaling stations on the peninsula, notably at nearby Jabbertown (so-named because of the many languages spoken there). These disappeared with the demise of the whaling industry in the early 1900s.

Point Hope village was incorporated in 1966 and 6 years later became a second-class city. Erosion and a threat of storm flooding from the Chukchi Sea led to its relocation to higher ground in the mid-1970s.

Construction work is the main source of income in Point Hope, while capital improvement programs create new jobs in operations and maintenance. Other jobs are available with the city, school, Native corporation and local businesses.

Nearly every man in the village participates in the spring whale hunt, in which traditional skin boats still are used. A festival, to which visitors are welcome, takes place after the whaling season, around June 1. There also are village-wide celebrations on the Fourth of July, Thanksgiving and Christmas.

In addition to the prehistoric village sites, there are old burial grounds in the area, including a cemetery marked by large whale bones standing on end. Beachcombing and rockhounding are available in the area and the point also is home to an abundance of tiny arctic wildflowers. Other activities include boating and bird, wildlife and whale watching, cold dip swimming in the lagoon, egg gathering at Cape Thompson and Cape Lisburne, and bingo 6 nights a week.

Fish available include salmon, trout, grayling and whitefish. Hunting is for caribou, moose, bear, ptarmigan, ducks and geese.

Communications in Point Hope include phones, mail plane, radio and TV. There are community electricity and water systems. Sewage system is honey buckets. The community is served by an Episcopal church — the oldest in the region, established in 1890 — and Assembly of God and Church of Christ churches. The Tikigaq school has grades preschool through 12. Point Hope prohibits the sale and importation of alcoholic beverages. Freight arrives by cargo plane and barge. Government address: City of Point Hope, P.O. Box 169, Point Hope, AK 99766; phone 368-2537. Village corporation address: Tigara Corp., P.O. Box 9, Point Hope, AK 99766.

Point Lay

Located on the Chukchi Sea, 550 miles northwest of Fairbanks, 300 miles southwest of Barrow. **Transportation:** Scheduled airline, air charter from Barrow. **Population:** 158. **Zip code:** 99723. **Emergency Services:** Public Safety Officer, phone 833-2911; Clinic,

phone 833-2527; Fire Department, phone 833-2611.

Elevation: 10 feet. **Climate:** The temperature averages around 40°F in summer and -35°F in winter. July is the warmest month; January is the coldest month. Mean annual precipitation is 6.73 inches, including 18.5 inches of snow.

Private Aircraft: Seldom-used sand airstrip at old village site; length 700 feet. Airstrip at DEW line station; elev. 20 feet; length 3,500 feet; gravel; civilian aircraft need 5 days prior landing clearance from the U.S. Air Force.

Visitor Facilities: No hotel, restaurant, laundromat or banking services. There is a store. Arts and crafts available for purchase include baleen baskets, masks, carved ivory and fur parkas. Fishing/hunting licenses available. No guide service, major repair service, rental transportation or public moorage facilities. Fuel available includes propane and regular gasoline.

Kali, the Eskimo name for the village, means "mound" and refers to the elevated area on which it stands. It is probably the last remaining village of the so-called Kukpowruk people.

The deeply indented shoreline prevented effective bowhead whaling, and the village never fully participated in the whaling culture. People of the village engage in subsistence hunting including the harvesting of beluga whales and some construction work.

Recreational activities include snowmobiling, 3-wheeling, hunting, fishing and trapping. Point Lay is an unincorporated village within the North Slope Borough.

Communications include phones, mail plane, radio and TV. Water is delivered by truck from freshwater lakes. Sewage system is honey buckets. There are no churches. School has grades preschool through 12. Point Lay bans the sale and importation of alcoholic beverages. Freight arrives by air transport and barge. Village corporation address: Cully Corp., General Delivery, Point Lay, AK 99723.

Prudhoe Bay/Deadhorse

This industrial complex of prefabricated modules sits atop millions of barrels of oil on the flat, treeless plain of the North Slope adjacent to the Arctic Ocean, 650 miles north of Anchorage and 400 miles north of Fairbanks. **Transportation:** Scheduled jet service from Fairbanks, or (by permit only) driving up the Dalton Highway. **Population:** Between 3,500 and 8,600 oil field workers. **Zip code:** 99734. **Emergency Services:** Public Safety Dept., 659-2515; emergency medical and fire handled by oil field operators ARCO Alaska and BP Exploration Alaska.

Climate: Winter temperatures hover between -55°F and -60°F, but with wind chill factor they can fall as low as -115°F. For 56 days in midwinter, the sun never rises. But from mid-April to mid-August, daylight is continuous, and temperatures can reach as high as 70°F.

Private Aircraft: State-maintained airport adjacent at Deadhorse; elev. 57 feet; length 6,500 feet; paved, attended most days; fuel available.

Visitor Facilities: Accommodations are available at several camps, but reservations should be made well in advance as increased oil drilling activity will result in a shortage of available rooms. Motel rooms are expensive ($90 and up a night); meals are included in some prices. A general store at Deadhorse sells hunting and fishing licenses and some local handicraft items.

One of the truly amazing sights in Alaska's Arctic is a herd of caribou grazing placidly amid the hustle and bustle of oil field activity. But Prudhoe Bay is not a place for drop-in, independent visitors. Oil field workers, tour groups, and visitors on official business are accommodated. For security reasons, however, unescorted visitors are not allowed on the docks or on area roads. Some parties heading for the Arctic National Wildlife Refuge do fly to Deadhorse, where arrangements can be made for an air taxi service to fly them to the refuge.

Communications include phones, mail plane, radio and TV. Church services are held at several camps. An indoor gym, swimming pool, library, racquetball courts, exercise rooms, running track, theater, and other amenities help make life pleasant for the workers. Utilities are provided to the modular structures by each camp. Freight arrives by cargo plane, by truck up the Dalton Highway, or is shipped in from the West Coast on barges that dash to Prudhoe during the brief 6 weeks each summer when the arctic icepack moves offshore. For more information, contact ARCO Alaska, Inc., P.O. Box 100360, Anchorage, AK 99510 or BP Exploration Alaska, P.O. Box 196612, Anchorage, AK 99519-6612.

Selawik

(SELL-a-wik) Located at the mouth of the Selawik River, 90 miles southeast of Kotzebue, 375 miles west of Fairbanks. **Population:** 682. **Zip code:** 99770. **Emergency Services:** Police, phone 484-2229; Alaska State Troopers, phone 911; Clinic, phone 484-2199;

Volunteer Fire Department.

Elevation: 50 feet. **Climate:** Long, cold winters and cool summers. Precipitation is 8.7 inches annually, including 35 to 40 inches of snow.

Private Aircraft: Airstrip adjacent; elev. 25 feet; length 1,900 feet; gravel; no fuel; unattended. No facilities at airport. No transportation to village. Roland Norton Memorial Airstrip 12 miles north; elev. 360 feet; length 3,000 feet; gravel; attended upon request.

Visitor Facilities: Contact city office, phone 484-2132, to arrange for accommodations in private homes or at the school. No restaurant or banking services available. Groceries, clothing, first-aid supplies, hardware, camera film and sporting goods may be purchased in the community. Arts and crafts available for purchase include masks, baskets and caribou jawbone model dog sleds. Fishing/hunting licenses available. No guide service. Repair services available for marine engines, boats and autos. Fuel available: diesel, propane and regular gasoline. No moorage facilities.

Lieutenant L.A. Zagoskin of the Imperial Russian Navy first reported Selawik's existence in the 1840s as the settlement of "Chilivik." Some traditional sod houses are still found in this Eskimo village. Selawik is a second-class city, incorporated in 1977.

The economic base is arts and crafts, and subsistence hunting and fishing. Some residents are employed as firefighters during the summer. Fish include whitefish, sheefish, grayling, northern pike and arctic char. Caribou and moose are the most important game animals.

Selawik is located near Selawik National Wildlife Refuge. The refuge includes the delta area formed by the Kobuk and Selawik rivers, an important breeding and resting spot for migratory waterfowl. The Selawik River is classified as a wild and scenic river.

Communications in Selawik include phones, mail plane, radio and cable TV. The community is served by Seventh-Day Adventist and Baptist churches and a Friends Mission. It also has 2 schools with grades preschool through 12. There is a public electricity system, and parts of town have public water. The sewage system is honey buckets. Selawik prohibits the sale and importation of alcoholic beverages. Freight arrives by cargo plane and barge. Government address: City of Selawik, P.O. Box 49, Selawik, AK 99770; phone 484-2132. Village corporation address: NANA Regional Corp., P.O. Box 49, Kotzebue, AK 99752.

Shungnak

(*SHUNG-nak*) Located on the Kobuk River, 150 miles east of Kotzebue and 300 miles west of Fairbanks. **Transportation:** Boat; scheduled or charter airline from Kotzebue. **Population:** 245. **Zip code:** 99773. **Emergency Services:** Police, phone 437-2147; Alaska State Troopers, Kotzebue, phone 442-3222; Clinic, phone 437-2138; Volunteer Fire Department.

Elevation: 140 feet. **Climate:** Shungnak is in the continental climate zone and has long, cold winters and relatively warm summers. Mean precipitation is 16 inches, including 71 inches of snow.

Private Aircraft: Airstrip 0.5 mile from village; elev. 200 feet; length 3,300 feet; gravel; fuel 80, 100; unattended. No facilities at airport. Transportation available to village.

Visitor Facilities: Accommodations cafe and laundromat available. No banking services. Groceries, clothing, first-aid supplies, hardware, camera film and sporting goods available. Arts and crafts available for purchase include birch-bark baskets, jade, beadwork, masks, mukluks, beaver hats, mittens, parkas and bone carvings. Fishing/hunting licenses available, as well as guide service for river floating, dog mushing and other activities. Some repair service available for marine engines, boats and autos. Fuel available includes marine gas, diesel, kerosene, propane and regular and unleaded gasoline. Moorage available for boats.

Shungnak is a fractured English spelling for "Issingnak", an Inupiat word meaning jade. The original settlement of Shungnak was 10 miles upriver at the present location of Kobuk. Residents relocated in the 1920s because of riverbank erosion at the old site. Shungnak was incorporated as a second-class city in 1967.

Shungnak has a subsistence economy based on fishing and hunting. There also is seasonal employment in construction, firefighting, mining and recreation, and some year-round employment with the local government and schools. Fish include sheefish, whitefish, salmon and grayling. Game animals are caribou, moose and bear, as well as ducks and geese. There also is trapping for marten, beaver, fox, lynx, otter, wolverine and wolf.

Shungnak has a strong and active elders' council. In the summer of 1989 the Upper Kobuk Elders sponsored a 3-week camp to teach children from Ambler, Shungnak and Kobuk the traditional subsistence lifestyle. The children learned how to seine with nets, cut and hang fish to dry, pick berries and play traditional children's games. Maniilaq, the regional nonprofit corporation, provided funding for the camp.

The 347-mile-long Kobuk, a wild and scenic river and the ninth-largest in Alaska, begins in Gates of the Arctic National Park and Preserve. It has become popular for float trips to Shungnak and beyond to Kobuk Valley National Park. The upper river is excellent for bird-watching in spring and summer. The river is generally safe for boats from the last week of May to the first week in October. (See also THE RIVERS, this section).

Onion Portage Archaeological District, listed on the National Register of Historic Places, is 35 miles downriver from Shungnak. First discovered by Dr. J. Louis Giddings in 1941, this site containing 30 layers of middens and old dwellings is described as the most important ever found in the Arctic.

Other recreational activities in the area include camping, hiking, canoeing, gold panning and photography, as well as observing jade mines at Dahl Creek near Kobuk and at Jade Mountain.

Communications include phones, mail plane, radio and TV. The community is served by Friends, Baptist and Seventh-Day Adventist churches, as well as a school with grades preschool to 12. There are community water, sewage disposal and electricity systems. Shungnak prohibits the sale and importation of alcoholic beverages. Freight arrives by cargo plane and barge. Government address: City of Shungnak, General Delivery, Shungnak, AK 99773. Village corporation address: NANA Regional Corp., P.O. Box 49, Kotzebue, AK

Umiat

Located on the Colville River, 75 miles south of Harrison Bay and 340 miles north-northwest of Fairbanks. **Transportation:** Charter aircraft from Prudhoe Bay. **Population:** 15. **Zip code:** 99790. **Emergency Services:** North Slope Borough Public Safety Officer, Prudhoe Bay; Small local dispensary or Prudhoe Bay Clinic.

Elevation: 340 feet. **Climate:** Cool, fairly dry summers, but it can be windy. Extremely cold winters; Umiat frequently is the coldest reporting station in Alaska. Mean annual precipitation is 6.5 inches including 34 inches of snow.

Private Aircraft: Airstrip adjacent; elev. 266 feet; length 5,400 feet; gravel; fuel 80, 100 and jet; attended regularly; visual inspection recommended prior to using. Mountain ridges north and south. Restrooms at airport. Transportation to village available ($40 or more per trip).

Visitor Facilities: Rustic accommodations available at a lodge. Rates in excess of $100 per night, including meals. Single, family-style meals can be purchased. No laundromat, banking services or stores. No arts and crafts available. Fishing/hunting licenses not available. Fly-in hunting can be arranged. Limited aircraft repair available. Charter service is the only rental transportation. Fuel available for aircraft only. No moorage facilities.

An emergency airfield was established here and in 1945 became a supply and operations base for oil exploration. It still is a major airfield and refueling stop between Fairbanks and Barrow.

There is excellent moose and caribou hunting along the Colville River west of the village. Caribou hunting is usually best the week before moose season opens in early September. There are good landing areas for light planes on river bars and coal from the riverbank can be used for fires.

Communications at Umiat include phones, mail plane, radio and TV. There is no church or school. Also, no public water, sewage or electricity systems. Freight arrives by cargo plane. Facilities are managed by O.J. and Eleanor Smith, who staff the weather station. Their Umiat Enterprises can be contacted for fuel, sandwiches, rooms or guiding services. Address: Box 60569, Fairbanks, AK 99706; phone 488-2366 (North Pole) or 452-9158 (Umiat via Fairbanks).

Wainwright

Located on Chukchi Sea coast, 85 miles southwest of Point Barrow, 520 miles north-northwest of Fairbanks. **Transportation:** Scheduled airline or charter plane from Barrow. **Population:** 502. **Zip code:** 99782. **Emergency Services:** Public Safety Officer, phone 763-2911; Clinic, phone 763-2714; North Slope Borough Fire Department.

Elevation: 30 feet. **Climate:** Maximum daily temperature above freezing point only 123 days of the year. Mean annual precipitation is 5.85 inches.

Private Aircraft: Wainwright airstrip 0.3 mile south; elev. 30 feet; length 4,700 feet; gravel; no fuel; unattended; visual inspection recommended prior to using. No facilities at airport. Public transportation available to village.

Visitor Facilities: Accommodations available at 1 hotel. No banking services. Restaurant, laundromat, groceries, clothing, hardware, camera film and sporting goods available. Local arts and crafts available for purchase are carved ivory figurines and jewelry, baleen boats, whale bone carvings, clocks, knitted caps and gloves. Fishing/hunting licenses available, as well as guide service. No major repair service. Arrangements can be made to rent private autos, off-road vehicles and boats. Fuel available includes marine gas, diesel, propane, unleaded, regular and supreme. No moorage facilities.

For centuries villages have stood on the land between Wainwright Inlet and the sea, the most recent one being the Inupiat Eskimo village of Wainwright. Wainwright Inlet was named in 1826 by Capt. F.W. Beechey for his officer, Lt.John Wainwright. The present village was established in 1904 when the Alaska Native Service built a school. The community was incorporated as a second-class city in 1962.

Wainwright's subsistence hunting economy is based primarily on whales and caribou, but some residents work at local businesses, the borough government and seasonal construction. Villagers' lives revolve around whaling during the spring and summer months, and the taking of a bowhead or beluga whale is cause for celebration — a Nalukatak festival, which takes place usually in June. Eskimo dances also are performed occasionally by the villagers. Other recreational activities in the village include boating; riding snowmobiles and 3-wheelers; and smelt fishing on the lagoon in the spring. Bird-watching can be done anywhere on the tundra away from the village and seashells can be found on the beach.

Communications in Wainwright include phones, mail plane, radio and TV. The community is served by 3 churches and a school with grades preschool through 12. Public water and electricity is available; sewage system is primarily chemical toilets. Wainwright prohibits the sale and importation of alcoholic beverages. Freight arrives in the community by cargo plane and barge. Government address: City of Wainwright, P.O. Box 9, Wainwright, AK 99782; phone 763-2815/2726. Village corporation address: Olgoonik Corp., General Delivery, Wainwright, AK 99782.

▼ **A T T R A C T I O N S** ▼

National and State Parks, Etc.

Cape Krusenstern National Monument

This 660,000-acre monument, 10 miles northwest of Kotzebue, contains some of the most important prehistoric sites in the Arctic. The 114 beach ridges of Cape Krusenstern and nearby bluffs contain a chronological record of some 6,000 years of prehistoric and historic use, primarily by Native groups. The ridges were formed by shifting sea ice, ocean currents and waves, each new one being used in succession by Eskimos for their hunting camps. Eskimos still hunt seals along the cape's outermost beach. At shoreline campsites, the women trim and render the catch for the hides, meat and seal oil still vital to their diet.

Climate: Cloudy skies, frequent fog, westerly winds and minor fluctuations in daily temperatures are normal in the monument. Average daily summer temperatures range from 43° to 53°F, with the highest temperatures occurring in July. Coldest months are January until early March, when average daily temperatures range between -20° and 0°F. August is the wettest month, with a mean monthly precipitation of 2.26 inches.

Wildlife: The monument includes grizzly bear, Dall sheep, caribou, moose, an occasional musk-ox, wolves and lynx. Walrus, polar bear and several species of seal and whale can be seen offshore at various times of the year. Many species of waterfowl nest around the lagoons in summer. Fish in monument waters include whitefish, arctic char, 2 species of salmon (especially chums), northern pike, burbot, Dolly Varden and herring.

Access: There are daily commercial jet flights from Anchorage to Kotzebue. From Kotzebue, access to the monument is by chartered light aircraft (1 hour round-trip) or boat. When there is adequate sea ice in winter, access by snow machine and dogsled is possible. Weather is extremely variable and can curtail travel to the monument at any time of year. Airplane access is unrestricted, but planes may not be used in pursuit of subsistence hunting and fishing. Helicopter landings are not permitted unless authorized by written permit from the monument superintendent.

Accommodations: There are no accommodations or campgrounds within the monument. A hotel is located at Kotzebue. Camping is permitted throughout most of the monument, except in archaeological zones, where it would interrupt subsistence activities, or on private land holdings located primarily along river and beachfronts. There is a dilapidated shelter cabin in the monument, but no National Park Service facilities, trails or services.

Activities: Recreational activities in the monument include primitive camping, hiking, bird watching and fishing. Visitors to the monument should be self-sufficient and prepared for a variety of weather conditions. Contact the Park Service for specific information before traveling to the area; leave a copy of your planned itinerary with the regional office.

For further information visit the Park Service visitor information center in Kotzebue or contact: Superintendent, Cape Krusenstern National Monument, P.O. Box 1029, Kotzebue, AK 99752; phone 442-3890. Related USGS Topographic maps: Noatak, Kotzebue, Point Hope and DeLong Mountains.

Gates of the Arctic National Park and Preserve

The major feature of this 8-million-acre park and preserve is the Brooks Range, an extension of the Rocky Mountains which stretches across Alaska from the Canadian border almost to the Chukchi Sea. Gates of the

Arctic was the name that Robert Marshall, a forester who explored the then-unmapped areas north and west of Wiseman in the 1920s and 1930s, gave Boreal Mountain and Frigid Crags. Marshall named both and they rise like sentinels on either side of the North Fork Koyukuk River.

Climate: Long, cold winters and short, mild summers are the rule. On the Brooks Range's south slopes midsummer temperatures range from 32° to 85°F; winter temperatures range from 32° to -60°F. North of the Brooks Range, summer temperatures are much cooler; winter temperatures are somewhat milder but there is more wind. Annual precipitation of 8 to 10 inches classifies the area as semiarid, but this can be hard to believe while slogging through frequent showers and boggy tundra during the summer, particularly August. Mid-May through mid-August, the area has 18 to 24 hours of daylight. North of the Continental Divide snow may fall every month of the year and freezing temperatures occur by early September, sometimes in mid-August.

Wildlife: Thirty-six species of mammals live in the park and preserve, ranging in size from lemmings to brown/grizzly bears. Others are moose, caribou, Dall sheep, black bear, wolf, beaver, hoary marmot, wolverine, otter, marten, mink, weasel, lynx, red fox, porcupine and an assortment of small rodents. Eagles and many migratory birds occur here. Fisheries include grayling in clear streams and lakes; lake trout in larger, deep lakes; char in streams on the North Slope; and sheefish and chum salmon in the Kobuk and lower Alatna rivers. Fisheries productivity is low in the short seasons and cold waters of the Arctic.

Access: Most people get to the central Brooks Range via scheduled flights from Fairbanks to Bettles, where they charter small aircraft for flights into the park and preserve. Charter flights also can begin in Fairbanks, Kotzebue and Ambler and additional scheduled flights are available from Fairbanks to Allakaket (see Communities in INTERIOR section) and Anaktuvuk Pass. There is overland access from the Dalton Highway at Coldfoot and Wiseman at the southeast corner of Gates of the Arctic. Chandler Lake on the north slope of the Brooks Range lies within Native land and is open to float- and skiplane landings by permission of the Anaktuvuk Pass village corporation (Nunamiut Corp., General Delivery, Anaktuvuk Pass, AK 99721). Ultralights or recreational helicopters are not permitted in the park or preserve.

Accommodations: A commercial fishing lodge is located at Walker Lake. Bettles also has a lodge, general store and canoe rentals. There are no campgrounds in the park, but wilderness camp sites are available. To minimize impact, visitors are asked to camp on gravel bars or areas with hardy heath or moss. There are no established Park Service facilities, roads or trails in the area. Some cases of giardiasis, an intestinal disease, have been reported and visitors may wish to boil or purify drinking water.

Activities: Six designated wild rivers flow within and out of Gates of the Arctic: Noatak, Alatna, John, Kobuk, Tinayguk and North Fork Koyukuk. These, plus the Killik, are considered floatable by the National Park Service. (See The Rivers this section.) The Mount Igikpak and Arrigetch areas offer superb rock and mountain climbing, as well as impressive photographic opportunities. Hiking in the Arctic is made more difficult by tussocks and abundant wet areas. Hikers should plan on no more than 5 miles per day. Hikers and backpackers generally are dropped off and picked up by chartered aircraft. Winter activities include cross-country skiing, snowshoeing and dogsledding. Sport hunting is allowed in the 2 preserve areas in the northeast and southwest.

Gates of the Arctic is a remote wilderness. Animals are wild and unpredictable. Keep a clean camp and use common sense. Cook away from your camp. Local residents carry on subsistence activities within the park and preserve, and their camps, fishnets and other equipment should not be disturbed.

For further information contact: Superintendent, Gates of the Arctic National Park and Preserve, P.O. Box 74680, Fairbanks, AK 99707; phone 456-0281. Related USGS Topographic maps: Chandler Lake, Wiseman, Survey Pass, Killik River, Hughes, Ambler River, Philip Smith Mountains, Chandalar.

Kobuk Valley National Park

This 1.7-million-acre park encompasses a nearly enclosed mountain basin on the middle section of the Kobuk River in northwestern Alaska, 350 miles west-northwest of Fairbanks and 75 miles east of Kotzebue. Today's cold, dry climate approximates that of the ice age and supports similar plants. During the Pleistocene epoch, the Kobuk Valley provided an ice-free corridor joined to the land bridge that periodically formed between Alaska and Siberia. The valley contains artifacts dating 10,000 years of human occupation. At Onion Portage, near the eastern boundary of the park, Dr.J.Louis Giddings, the same archaeologist who made the discoveries at Cape Krusenstern, found what has been described as the most important archaeological site unearthed in the Arctic. The diggings are now within a designated National Register Archaeological District. Great herds of caribou still cross the Kobuk River at Onion Portage, attracting hunters today just as they did long ago.

Covering 25 square miles south of the Kobuk River are the wind-sculpted Great Kobuk Sand Dunes, some up to 100 feet high and overrunning the nearby forest. These, along with the Little Kobuk Sand Dunes near Onion Portage, and the Hunt River Dunes, are among the few dune fields found in the Arctic.

Within the park, the Salmon River has been classified a wild and scenic river. The Kobuk River is designated a wild and scenic river from where it flows out of Walker Lake to the western boundary of Gates of the Arctic National Preserve, located east of Kobuk Valley National Park.

Climate: Long cold winters and warm, brief summers characterize the park. Summer highs in the mid-80s to 92°F have been recorded, but the mean July temperature is in the mid-50s. Winter temperatures can drop to -60°F, and -20°F is common. Freezeup usually occurs from early to mid-October and breakup in mid- to late May. Mosquitoes appear in late May, are worst in June and disappear in August, when the whitesox and gnats come on the scene until the September frosts.

Wildlife: The park includes grizzly and black bear, caribou, moose, wolf, lynx, marten, wolverine and some Dall sheep. Numerous ponds and oxbows provide excellent waterfowl habitat; more than 100 species of birds have been spotted in the area. Arctic peregrine falcons may pass through the park during migrations. Fish found in park waters include 3 species of salmon, grayling, pike and sheefish.

Access: Aircraft provide the primary access to the park, although boats can be taken from Kotzebue during the ice-free season to the 5 villages on the Kobuk River. Scheduled commercial flights are available from Anchorage to Kotzebue and from Fairbanks to Ambler and Shungnak. Connecting flights are available to all the villages in the region. Aircraft may land throughout the park; recreational helicopters are not allowed. Other means of travel in the region are snow machines and dog sleds during the winter.

Accommodations: No accommodations are available in the park and none are planned. There are no established campgrounds; primitive camping is permitted throughout the park, except in archaeological zones and on private lands along the Kobuk River, without consent of the owners. There is a hotel at Kotzebue and a lodge at Ambler. Limited amounts of groceries, gasoline and other supplies can be purchased in the villages. There are no Park Service facilities, roads or trails. The only public-use facility in the park is an emergency shelter near the mouth of the Salmon River.

Activities: Most visitors float through the park on the Kobuk River. (See The Rivers this section.) Some start at the headwaters in Gates of the Arctic National Preserve, while others begin their trips in Ambler, Shungnak or Kobuk. The Great Kobuk Sand Dunes can be reached by an easy hike from the river. The lower Salmon River offers good canoeing and kayaking. Other activities include backpacking in the Baird and Waring mountains, fishing and photography. Sport hunting is prohibited.

In Kobuk Valley National Park, human settlement and use of the land is part of the area's heritage. People have hunted and fished in this region for centuries and continue to do so. Please do not interfere with local subsistence activities. Private land within the park boundaries, mostly along the Kobuk River corridor, should not be used without permission.

For more information contact: Superintendent, Kobuk Valley National Park, P.O. Box 1029, Kotzebue, AK 99752; phone 442-3890. Related USGS Topographic maps: Ambler River, Baird Mountains, Selawik.

Noatak National Preserve

This 6.6-million-acre preserve, located 350 miles northwest of Fairbanks and 16 miles northeast of Kotzebue, protects the largest untouched mountain-ringed river basin in America. Of its area, 5.8 million acres have been designated wilderness. The 396-mile-long Noatak River is contained within a broad and gently sloping valley which stretches more than 150 miles east-west. The river, from its source in Gates of the Arctic National Park to its confluence with the Kelly River in Noatak National Preserve, is part of the National Wild and Scenic Rivers System. This is one of the finest wilderness areas in the world and UNESCO has designated it an International Biosphere Reserve.

The Noatak River passes through 6 regions

on its way to the sea: headwaters at the base of Igikpak Mountain; the great Noatak Basin with its rounded mountains and plentiful wildlife; the 65-mile-long Grand Canyon of the Noatak and the much steeper, 7-mile Noatak Canyon; plains dotted with spruce, balsam and poplar; the rolling Igichuk Hills; and finally the flat coastal delta.

Climate: Long, cold winters and short, mild summers are the rule in this area. Temperatures during June, July and August range from 40° to 85°F, with average midsummer daytime temperatures in the 60s and 70s. However, subfreezing temperatures can occur on summer nights. June is generally the clearest summer month; clouds increase in July and August. Fog around Kotzebue during the summer can create transportation problems. Winter temperatures sometimes drop to -50°F, and -20°F occurs often. Strong winds produce a severe windchill. Mosquitoes appear in late May, are worst in June and disappear in August. Whitesox are present from August until September frosts. Good insect repellent and a head net are essential.

Wildlife: The western Arctic caribou herd, numbering about 200,000 animals, crosses the preserve in April and August on migrations. Other wildlife seen in the preserve are moose, Dall sheep, grizzly bear, wolf, fox, lynx, marten, beaver and muskrat. Approximately 125 species of birds have been identified in the preserve and another 31 are thought to occur, including the arctic peregrine falcon. Fish present in preserve waters include grayling, char, salmon, lake trout, burbot, pike and whitefish.

Access: Scheduled commercial flights are available from Anchorage and Fairbanks to Kotzebue and from Fairbanks to Ambler, Shungnak and Bettles. Scheduled flights also are available to Noatak village, several miles downriver from the preserve's southwestern boundary. From Kotzebue, chartered flights provide access to the lower Noatak River. Access to the upper Noatak for float trips generally begins with a scheduled flight from Fairbanks to Bettles and a charter floatplane flight to any of several lakes along the river's upper reaches. Other means of travel are by boat from Kotzebue in summer and by snow machine and dogsled in winter. All travel is dependent on the weather. There are no trails or roads in the preserve.

Accommodations: There are no accommodations or campgrounds within the preserve. Camping is permitted throughout the preserve; however, there are numerous private holdings along the lower Noatak River in

the preserve and these properties should be respected. Kotzebue has stores, a hotel and eating facilities, as does Bettles.

Activities: Recreational activities in the preserve include floating down the Noatak by raft, canoe or kayak; backpacking along the river and in the foothills; wildlife observing and photography. (For more information on floating the Noatak see The Rivers this section.) Sportfishing and hunting are allowed in season. The National Park Service cautions that the Noatak basin is one of the least traveled areas in Alaska. A passing aircraft may not even be seen for days. You are truly "on your own" here. For safety, leave a copy of your itinerary with the Park Service in Kotzebue and carry a few days extra supply of food. Also, local residents carry on subsistence activities within the preserve. Their camps, fishnets and other equipment should not be disturbed.

For additional information contact: Superintendent, Noatak National Preserve, P.O. Box 1029, Kotzebue, AK 99752; phone 442-3890. Related USGS Topographic maps: Survey Pass, Ambler River, Howard Pass, Baird Mountains, Misheguk Mountain.

Wildlife Refuges

Arctic National Wildlife Refuge

This 19.6-million-acre refuge in the northeastern corner of Alaska encompasses some of the most spectacular arctic plants, wildlife and land forms in the world. Designed to preserve a large portion of the migration routes of the great Porcupine caribou herd, numbering about 160,000 animals, the refuge also is home to musk-ox, Dall sheep, moose, packs of wolves and such solitary species as wolverines, polar bear and grizzly bear. Some 140 species of birds can be seen in the refuge. Thousands of ducks, geese, swans and loons breed on coastal tundra and birds throng coastal migration routes all summer. Snowy owls and other predators can be seen along lagoons and rivers. Peregrine falcons, gyrfalcons, rough-legged hawks and golden eagles nest inland.

The refuge extends from the Porcupine River basin near the Canadian border north through the Sheenjek River valley and across the eastern Brooks Range down to the Arctic Ocean. For the most part, this land is above tree line and offers rugged, snowcapped, glaciated peaks and countless streams and rivers, draining north into the Beaufort Sea and south into the Porcupine and Yukon drainages.

Climate: Winter in the refuge is long and severe; summer is brief and intense. Snow showers can occur at any time, but days can be warm in June and July. Mountain lakes usually are ice free by mid-July; south slope lakes usually open by mid-June. Daylight is nearly continuous in summer. Frost is not uncommon in August; by early August autumn has turned the tundra scarlet. Snow usually covers the ground at least 9 months of the year. Arctic plants survive even though permafrost is within 1-1/2 feet of the surface. Annual growth of trees and shrubs is slight. It may take 300 years for a white spruce at tree line to reach a diameter of 5 inches; small willow shrubs may be 50 to 100 years old.

Access: The only access to the refuge is by air. Commercial air service is available from Fairbanks to Fort Yukon, Arctic Village, Deadhorse and Kaktovik on Barter Island, the usual jumping-off points for refuge visitors. Charter air service is available at Kaktovik, Deadhorse and Fort Yukon and should be prearranged whenever possible. Private aircraft are permitted in the refuge; helicopter use requires a special permit from the refuge manager. Off-road vehicles are not permitted.

Accommodations: There are no lodges or other commercial facilities in the refuge. Spartan accommodations are available at Kaktovik through Ice Services and at Arctic Village (see Communities in INTERIOR section) through the city. Food and equipment should be purchased in Fairbanks. Some supplies may be available in Kaktovik, but travelers should not depend on doing last-minute shopping there. Camping is permitted throughout the refuge; use of gas or alcohol stoves is recommended because wood supplies are scarce. To avoid giardiasis, boil or purify drinking water. Mosquitoes are most numerous in June and July; a good insect repellent and a head net are recommended.

Activities: Visitors to the refuge have rapidly increased in the last few years. Recreational activities include kayaking and rafting on rivers both north and south of the Brooks Range. Plane charters out of Fort Yukon, Deadhorse, Fairbanks or Kaktovik land parties on takeoff points throughout the refuge for excellent hiking and backpacking. Mountain climbing — on 9,020-foot Mount Chamberlin and 8,855-foot Mount Michelson is possible. Coastal lagoons offer excellent wildlife observation and photography. The refuge includes 3 wild and scenic rivers: the Ivishak, Sheenjek and Wind. (See The Rivers this section for more information.)

This area, more than anywhere in America, provides the true wilderness experience; where wild has not been taken out of the wilderness. There is little information about specific hiking routes and rivers in the area. Visitors planning a trip to the Arctic National Wildlife Refuge should be prepared mentally and physically, well-equipped and understand the risks involved.

For additional information or advice on planning a trip to the refuge contact: Refuge Manager, Fish and Wildlife Service, Arctic National Wildlife Refuge, Room 266, Federal Bldg. and Courthouse, 101 12th Ave., Box 20, Fairbanks, AK 99701; phone 456-0250.

Selawik National Wildlife Refuge

This 2.15-million-acre refuge straddles the Arctic Circle in northwestern Alaska, 360 miles northwest of Fairbanks. The north eastern part of the refuge — 240,000 acres — is wilderness. The refuge's northern boundary abuts Kobuk Valley National Park and its southeastern corner joins Koyukuk National Wildlife Refuge. Its northwestern edge lies along Hotham Inlet across from Baldwin Peninsula and Kotzebue, the region's largest town. Selawik is a showcase of estuaries, lakes, river deltas and tundra slopes. Its most prominent feature is an extensive system of tundra wetlands nestled between the Waring Mountains and Selawik Hills.

The refuge is located near the Bering Land Bridge that once connected Asia and North America. Many years ago animals and humans migrated across these lands. In later years prospectors searched these lands for gold. The refuge contains relics of these ancient and recent migrations.

Climate: Temperatures in June and July reach 70° and 80°F, and there is 24-hour daylight. Insects become bothersome by mid-July. Winter comes quickly and temperatures reach the -20°F mark in October. Temperatures are coldest in January and February, when it can drop to -60°F. By the winter solstice there is only 1 hour and 43 minutes of daylight each day.

Wildlife: Selawik is a vital breeding and resting area for a multitude of migratory waterbirds. Nesting ducks number nearly 100,000. Tundra swans, sandhill cranes, Canada and white-fronted geese and several species of loons are also common in the area. Thousands of caribou winter in the refuge, feeding on lichen-covered foothills. Other common mammals include moose, grizzly bear and furbearers. Sheefish (some weighing up to 40 pounds), whitefish, grayling and northern pike inhabit lakes, ponds, streams and rivers.

Access: The refuge is accessible by boat, aircraft, snowmobile, dog team, foot and cross-country skis — depending on the season and weather. There are no roads. Scheduled air service is available to Kotzebue from Anchorage, and to Selawik, Kiana and Noorvik from Kotzebue. Charter air service to the refuge is available at Kiana, Ambler, Galena and Kotzebue. In the summer floatplane and boats are the only practical way of visiting refuge islands and waters.

Activities: Recreation in the refuge includes hiking, boating, camping, wildlife viewing and photography. Portions of the Selawik River are designated as a wild river and it provides good river rafting and sportfishing. Limited commercial guide service is available. Hunting, trapping and fishing are permitted in accordance with state and federal regulations. Main activities in the refuge are subsistence hunting, fishing and edible plant gathering by local residents. There are over 500 Native allotments in the refuge, which are private land and should not be trespassed. These allotments are mainly along the rivers, including the wild river portion of the Selawik River.

The Fish and Wildlife Service cautions that the Selawik Refuge, like most of Alaska, has changeable weather. Visitors must be self-sufficient and prepared for emergencies as well as inclement weather. For more information, and location of private inholdings, contact: Refuge Manager, Selawik National Wildlife Refuge, P.O. Box 270, Kotzebue, AK 99752; phone 442-3799.

The Rivers

NOTE: Many of the rivers listed below are also included in the Sportfishing section where additional information on species, seasons and suggested bait is provided.

Alatna River. The upper portion of this designated wild and scenic river flows in Gates of the Arctic National Park on the south slope of the Brooks Range. River trips on the Alatna start in an area famous for the dramatic granite spires of Arrigetch Peaks to the west. The Alatna then meanders through the Endicott Mountains and the Helpmejack Hills, before winding through the lowlands of the Koyukuk River.

Highly advanced paddling skills are not required on this trip, but the country is a remote wilderness. Float trips start either at the headwater alpine lakes or from Arrigetch Creek, 47 miles downstream. For the first 5 miles out of the headwater lakes lining is necessary; then there is a short stretch of Class III rapids just above Ram Creek that is easily portaged. The next 22 miles to Arrigetch Creek is fast-flowing, with sweepers present. From Arrigetch Creek the Alatna flows slowly, offering a good float for those with moderate river experience.

There are numerous hiking and backpacking opportunities, as well as fishing for grayling, whitefish, arctic char and pike.

Access is by floatplane from Bettles or Fairbanks to the headwater lakes or to lakes near Arrigetch Creek. Exit is possible from the Indian village of Allakaket (see Communities in INTERIOR section) on the Koyukuk, where there are no accommodations, but there is scheduled air service to Fairbanks. Or the floater can continue down the Koyukuk. Related USGS Topographic maps: Survey Pass, Hughes, Bettles.

Canning River. This is a fast white-water river in Arctic National Wildlife Refuge, heading in the Franklin Mountains and flowing 125 miles northward to Camden Bay on the Beaufort Sea. It flows through a scenic mountain valley and then through the arctic coastal lowlands. The clear Marsh Fork passes through a narrow valley between mountains that rise sharply on both sides of the river. The silty main stem of the Canning River leaves the mountains about halfway from its origin. Portions of the main stem below the confluence of Marsh Fork are heavily braided and the channel must be carefully selected. Strong headwinds may impede progress on the lower river. The Marsh Fork has a couple of rocky stretches up to 4 miles long that have rapids in the upper limit of Class II.

Rafts or small white-water kayaks are recommended on the Marsh Fork or the main stem, while a folding boat is suitable only on the main stem.

This trip offers good hiking, arctic scenery and wildlife viewing. There is fishing for arctic char, grayling and whitefish.

Access to the Canning is from Fairbanks, Deadhorse, Fort Yukon or Kaktovik by charter wheel plane with short landing and takeoff capability to gravel bars on the Marsh Fork or the main stem. Pickup can be arranged from gravel bars in the Canning delta.

Arctic National Wildlife Refuge is remote, weather is unpredictable and trips should be carefully planned. Information and assistance with planning trips to the refuge are available by writing Refuge Manager, Arctic National

Wildlife Refuge, Room 266, Federal Bldg. and Courthouse, 101 12th Ave., Box 20, Fairbanks, AK 99701; phone 456-0259. Related USGS Topographic maps: Arctic and Mount Michelson.

Colville River. This is Alaska's largest river north of the Continental Divide and is the seventh longest in the state at 428 miles. The Colville heads in the De Long Mountains, part of the Brooks Range, and bisects the arctic lowlands as it flows east-northeast into Harrison Bay on the Arctic Ocean.

From its headwaters to the Kiligwa River, the Colville's water levels are shallow in some sections and must be lined. From the Kiligwa confluence to Umiat, 225 miles downriver, the Colville consists of several 1- to 4-mile pools connected by shallow riffles. The Colville is not considered a difficult river to run, but this is extremely remote country and travelers should be experienced with wilderness camping.

The North Slope of the Brooks Range has much wildlife, including lots of grizzly bears. Thousands of migratory birds breed and nest here. Most notable are nesting peregrine falcons, gyrfalcons and rough-legged hawks. Dall sheep, caribou, moose and fox also may be spotted. Other activities along the river include hiking, photography and exploring the arctic environment. Fishing is so-so for whitefish, arctic char, grayling, chum salmon, pike and trout.

Access is generally by scheduled commercial air service to Bettles, Kotzebue, Barrow or Prudhoe Bay, then charter plane to the Kiligwa River confluence. Exit is at Umiat or Nuiqsut, where there is air service to Barrow, Prudhoe Bay or Fairbanks. At least 2 outfitters that offer trips on the Colville. Related USGS Topographic maps: Misheguk Mountain, Utukok River, Howard Pass, Ikpikpuk River, Killik River, Umiat, Harrison Bay.

Hulahula River. This seldom-run river in Arctic National Wildlife Refuge flows west and north 100 miles to Camden Bay on the Beaufort Sea about 20 miles from Barter Island. The trip generally takes 8 days from the headwaters.

This trip offers magnificent views of some of the highest wilderness in the Brooks Range, then continues through canyons and gorges to the lowlands of the Arctic Slope. Rapids between Class II and Class IV can be portaged or lined. Rafts and kayaks are suitable for this trip. It is recommended that anyone taking this trip be in top physical condition, as this is a fast-flowing river through continuous boulders with many drops and rapids.

There are excellent hiking and photography opportunities. Wildlife viewing includes Dall sheep in the hills and vast herds of caribou during migrations in late June.

Access to the Hulahula is generally by scheduled air service from Fairbanks to Kaktovik. Charter flights are available from Kaktovik to and from the river.

Arctic National Wildlife Refuge is remote, weather is unpredictable and trips should be carefully planned. Outfitters offer float trips on the Hulahula. Also, information and assistance with planning trips to the refuge are available by writing Refuge Manager, Arctic National Wildlife Refuge, Room 266, Federal Bldg. and Courthouse, 101 12th Ave., Box 20, Fairbanks, AK 99701; phone 456-0250. Related USGS Topographic maps: Barter Island A-5; Flaxman Island A-1; Mount Michelson B-1, C-1, D-1.

John River. This designated wild and scenic river in Gates of the Arctic National Park offers a rewarding voyage for the adventuresome traveler. It is possible to paddle the length of the river by starting at the Eskimo village of Anaktuvuk Pass. A short portage and lining on the small creek near the village is necessary. Experience is essential for safe negotiation of some fast water and easy rapids above Hunt Fork.

Most float trips, however, start at Hunt Fork and continue 100 miles to the confluence with the Koyukuk. The John, a clearwater tributary to the Koyukuk, then offers an exciting but safe trip through an extremely scenic area of the Brooks Range, which has not yet been exploited by large numbers of people. Rugged mountains along the way offer excellent hiking and are home to Dall sheep. Other wildlife that may be seen are grizzly bear, moose and wolf. Fishing is fair for grayling, whitefish, burbot, pike in the lakes, and chum salmon.

Access to the river is by floatplane from Bettles or Fairbanks to Hunt Fork Lake or Anaktuvuk Pass. It generally takes 5 days to float from Hunt Fork to the mouth of the John, then another half a day to line 5 miles up the Koyukuk to Bettles, where there are overnight accommodations and regularly scheduled air service to Fairbanks. Related USGS Topographic maps: Wiseman A-4, A-5, B-4, B-5, C-5, D-5; Bettles D-4.

Killik River. This scenic river heads in Gates of the Arctic National Park at the Continental Divide and flows northward 105 miles to the Colville River. The river passes through mountainous terrain and then into the lowlands of the Arctic Slope. The trip generally takes 10 days from the usual put-in point at Easter Creek to Umiat, on the Colville River about 70 miles downstream from the Killik River confluence.

The Killik offers Class I and Class II conditions throughout its course. About halfway to the Colville, Sunday Rapids might be Class I or Class II, depending on water levels and should be inspected before passage is attempted. A white-water kayak is recommended for this river.

There is good hiking in the mountainous region, where Dall sheep can be seen. Wildlife viewing also can be excellent in the river valley, where grizzly bear, moose, caribou, wolf, fox, lynx and wolverine may be spotted. Fossils can be seen in rock outcroppings below Sunday Rapids. Fishing is for grayling, arctic char and pike.

Access is generally by scheduled airline from Fairbanks to Bettles, then charter floatplane from Bettles to the Easter Creek area. Pickup from gravel bars on the Colville just upstream from the Killik River confluence can be arranged. Or there is air service out of Umiat to Prudhoe Bay and Fairbanks. At least 2 outfitters offer float trips on the Killik. Related USGS Topographic maps: Survey Pass, Killik River, Ikpikpuk River.

Kobuk River. This 347-mile-long river is the ninth longest in Alaska and one of the most popular for float trips. It is designated a wild and scenic river from its headwaters at Walker Lake in Gates of the Arctic National Park to the park's western boundary. Lower stretches of the Kobuk pass through Kobuk Valley National Park.

The Kobuk flows between the Baird Mountains to the north and low-lying Waring Mountains to the south, and the wide, forested valley offers sweeping views. After 2 sets of rapids, which are usually portaged, the Kobuk winds through 2 canyons, then meanders serenely to the sea. The 125-mile journey to Kobuk, where most floaters stop, can be made in about 6 days by raft, kayak or canoe. Some floaters continue on to Kiana.

River floaters can fish for sheefish, northern pike, grayling, whitefish, chum salmon and, in Walker Lake, lake trout. Wildlife that may be seen along the river includes bears, moose, caribou and wolves.

The Kobuk has for centuries been a major river highway for both coastal and inland Eskimos and still is used as such today. Recreational river travelers are cautioned not to interfere with any subsistence activities taking place along the Kobuk. Also check with the National Park Service about the location of private lands.

Access to the Kobuk River is by floatplane from Bettles or Ambler to Walker Lake. All 5 villages along the river have scheduled air service to Kotzebue or Fairbanks. There are overnight accommodations in most of the villages. It's a good idea to contact the village ahead of time if you plan to spend time there. Several outfitters offer a variety of float trips down the Kobuk. Related USGS Topographic maps: Survey Pass, Hughes, Shungnak, Ambler River, Baird Mountains, Selawik.

Kongakut River. This is a high-use river in Arctic National Wildlife Refuge that flows through country of primeval beauty and wildness on the north slope of the Brooks Range. The Kongakut flows northeast from the Davidson Mountains, ending 100 miles away at Siku Lagoon, 8 miles northwest of Demarcation Point in the far northeast corner of Alaska. The trip generally takes 11 days from the headwaters.

Rafts or folding boats are suitable for this trip, which is suggested for the intrepid explorer in good condition.

The Fish and Wildlife Service says North Slope rivers tend to be swift and rocky. They also are icy cold and life jackets should have pockets to carry waterproof matches, candles, insect repellent and other survival gear. Rivers on the North Slope usually are free-flowing by mid-June, and remain high and silty for several weeks, depending on the weather.

Wildlife viewing can be excellent in the refuge, particularly during migrations of the Porcupine caribou herd.

Access to the Kongakut is generally by scheduled air service from Fairbanks to Kaktovik on Barter Island. Charter flights are available from Kaktovik to and from the river.

Arctic National Wildlife Refuge is remote, weather is unpredictable and trips should be carefully planned. Outfitters offer float trips on the Kongakut. Also, information and assistance with planning trips to the refuge are available by writing Refuge Manager, Arctic National Wildlife Refuge, Room 266, Federal Bldg. and Courthouse, 101 12th Ave., Box 20, Fairbanks, AK 99701; phone 456-0520. Related USGS Topographic maps: Table Mountain; Demarcation Point.

Nigu-Etivluk. Both the Nigu and Etivluk rivers are small, swift and clear tributaries to the Colville River. The Nigu's headwaters are in Gates of the Arctic National Park and it tumbles for 70 miles before joining the Etivluk. Then it's another 70 miles to the Colville.

The Nigu generally has shallow Class I water, with frequent Class II rapids. The Nigu is floatable by raft only until about the third week of June or by canoe or kayak until the last week of June. The Etivluk has fast Class I water, with scattered Class II rapids. Canoes or small rafts are recommended, although kayaks also are used. This trip passes through majestic mountains, rolling hills and level coastal plain. Animals that may be seen are grizzly bear, Dall sheep, caribou, wolf and fox.

There is good hiking in the treeless valleys and on the tundra ridges and lower mountains. Fishing is good for grayling, whitefish and arctic char.

Access is by floatplane from Bettles or Fairbanks to lakes at the Nigu headwaters (be prepared to portage a mile over soggy tundra from the headwaters) or to Nigtun Lake at the Etivluk headwaters. Arrange for pickup from lakes or gravel bars along the lower Etivluk or the Colville River. Or travel down the Colville to Umiat, which has air service to Prudhoe Bay and Fairbanks. Related USGS Topographic maps: Killik River, Howard Pass.

Noatak River. This 396-mile-long designated wild and scenic river winds through Gates of the Arctic National Park and Noatak National Preserve before flowing into Kotzebue Sound. Considered by many to be the finest wilderness river in the Arctic, the Noatak flows through forest and tundra country entirely above the Arctic Circle. Highlights of this river are the mountains along the upper river, Noatak Canyon and the run to the sea below the village of Noatak. There are several stretches of Class II rapids, but the river is generally smooth flowing. The trip from the headwaters to the village of Noatak generally takes 16 days.

The Noatak features changing scenery along with a variety of animals and birds. The Noatak basin is particularly rich in migratory birds during spring and summer and the river traveler also may glimpse moose, caribou, wolves or grizzly bears. Fishing is good for grayling, whitefish, arctic char, pike and chum salmon. Wild berries are abundant in July and August.

Access to the Noatak generally begins with a commercial flight from Fairbanks to Bettles and a charter floatplane flight to any of several lakes along the upper river. There is scheduled air service from Noatak village to Kotzebue, or pickup can be arranged from scattered lakes, the river itself or gravel bars. There is no hotel in Noatak, but arrangements for overnight accommodations at the school or private homes may be made by contacting the village. Related USGS Topographic maps: Survey Pass, Ambler River, Howard Pass, Misheguk Mountains, Baird Mountains, Noatak.

North Fork Koyukuk. This is a designated wild and scenic river in Gates of the Arctic National Park that provides a good family-type wilderness boating experience.

Canoe, raft or kayak can be used. The river is not difficult, but there are some sharp turns and obstacles to watch for. The river offers good hiking and scenery — waterfalls, jagged peaks and hanging valleys. Old cabins dot the banks — silent reminders of a historic mining past. Fishing is good for grayling, pike and whitefish.

Access to the river is generally by floatplane from Bettles to Summit Lake, or to lakes near the mouth of Redstar Creek. From Redstar Creek it takes approximately 4 to 5 days to float to Bettles. Bettles is served by scheduled commercial air service from Fairbanks and has meals and lodging.

Many guide services are available for this area of Alaska. A list of those licensed to operate in Gates of the Arctic can be obtained from the National Park Service, Box 74680, Fairbanks, AK 99707; phone 456-0281. Related USGS Topographic maps: Wiseman D-1, D-2, C-2, C-3, B-2, A-2, A-3; Bettles D-3, D-4; Chandler Lake A-1.

Redstone and Cutler rivers. These rivers in northwestern Alaska offer access from the Kobuk River to the Noatak River. The traverse crosses some extremely remote country, but connects the 2 major river systems with an 8-mile portage.

Heading north from the village of Ambler to the Redstone River is recommended. The slow-flowing Redstone permits upstream paddling and easy lining.

A low valley opening shows one obvious route for the portage. A second, somewhat shorter portage is through the next valley, about 6 miles upriver. The clear and shallow Cutler River, which has a string of easy rapids, is just over the divide from the Redstone.

The traverse in the opposite direction — from the Cutler to the Redstone — is possible, but involves a longer upstream paddle and more lining.

Access to Ambler, which has overnight accommodations, is by plane from Kotzebue. Before making the traverse, it's advisable to contact the village of Ambler regarding your plans. Related USGS Topographic map: Ambler River.

Squirrel River. This is a clear water, free-flowing stream that originates in the Baird Mountains of northwestern Alaska. It flows for about 95 miles through a broad, mountain-flanked valley before entering the Kobuk River near the village of Kiana. The valley supports a variety of vegetative systems rang-ing from alpine tundra to upland spruce/hardwood and bottomland spruce/poplar forest. The Squirrel River is readily accessible by light aircraft from Kotzebue (approxi-mately 30-minutes flying time, one way). It provides a relatively safe, easy float, although there is some white water in the upper few miles of the river. Sportfishing for arctic char, chum salmon and grayling is available. There is good hiking terrain in the headwaters area. Good overnight campsites are plentiful along most of the river. Additional information is available from the BLM office located in Kotzebue, Box 1049, Kotzebue, AK 99752; phone 442-3430. Related USGS Topographic maps: Baird Mountains A-3, A-4, A-5, B-5, B-6; Selawik D-3.

Wild River. This clear, fast tributary of the Koyukuk flows from Wild Lake, where fishing is good for grayling, pike and lake trout, to the Koyukuk.

Trips on this river generally take place only in June, before water levels drop.

Floaters pass through beautiful mountain scenery, then into typical arctic taiga where the river occasionally slows on its meandering course to the Koyukuk River. Brief shallow areas may be encountered.

Access is possible by chartering a plane from Bettles to Wild Lake. The trip down the Wild River generally takes 4 to 6 days. After reaching the Koyukuk River, it's only a few miles downriver to Bettles where there are overnight accommodations and regularly scheduled flights to Fairbanks. Related USGS Topographic maps: Bettles D-3, D-4; Wiseman A-3, B-3, B-4, C-4.

Wind River. This river heads at 68°34′N, 147°18′W in the Brooks Range and flows southeast 80 miles within Arctic National Wildlife Refuge to the East Fork Chandalar River.

The Wind River at moderate to high-water stages is swift and is considered an exciting white-water river for intermediate boaters. At these water levels, the river is Class II from the vicinity of Center Mountain for 22 miles, then there's a 10-mile stretch of Class I, followed by 7 miles of Class III and 25 miles of Class II. The last 6 miles are Class III. This trip generally takes 4 days. Rafts or kayaks are recommended; canoes are suitable for advanced paddlers. Below its confluence with the Wind River, the East Fork Chandalar is Class I, with some Class II rapids at low water levels. Lining through some boulder rapids may be necessary at low water.

On the Wind there is good mountain scen-ery and hiking, particularly along the upper river. There is fishing for arctic grayling, pike and whitefish. Travelers also can hike into several lakes close to the river for good pike fishing.

Access is by charter air service from Fair-banks or Fort Yukon to a lake behind Center Mountain or lakes farther downriver. Gravel bars in this area, or farther upriver, may be suitable for wheel planes; consult local pilots. Exit is from a lake located 5 miles below the confluence with the East Fork Chandalar River, possibly from East Fork itself, or con-tinue on to Venetie, which has scheduled air service but no visitor facilities.

Related USGS Topographic maps: Chris-tian, Arctic A-5, Philip Smith Mountains A-1, B-1.

Sportfishing

Rivers and lakes in the Arctic are accessible for sportfishing primarily by air, although riverboats occasionally can be rented or char-tered at villages along the waterways. In the Far North there is virtually no sportfishing around communities such as Barrow, Kaktovik, Wainwright or Point Lay. However, there are lakes and rivers on the Arctic Slope that con-tain arctic char, which average 4 to 6 pounds, but can reach 12 to 15 pounds.

Lakes in the Brooks Range are popular for lake trout, which can reach 30 pounds. Any-one planning a trip to one of these mountain lakes should be aware that they may not be totally ice free until July. Listed in this section are some of the largest and most scenic of these lakes.

At other locations anglers can encounter sheefish, which can reach 60 pounds in the Selawik-Kobuk area. Other species present in arctic waters are whitefish, which can reach 5 pounds; burbot (also called lush or lingcod) which can weigh in at 20 pounds, northern pike, which average 4-8 pounds, but can at-tain 30 pounds; and arctic grayling, which can reach 4 pounds and which fisheries biologists say can be found "everywhere it's clear and wet."

Most sportfishing in the Arctic takes place in August and September, with anglers flying their own planes or chartering aircraft in Fairbanks, Bettles, Kaktovik or Kotzebue. A general rule from the Alaska Dept. of Fish and Game is to "plan for the worst" when travel-ing in the Arctic. Take a few days extra food and allow for a flexible schedule since fickle weather can play havoc with the best laid plans.

For more information contact the Alaska

Dept. of Fish and Game, Sport Fish Division, 1300 College Road, Fairbanks, AK 99701.

Anaktuvuk River. Located in the Brooks Range in Gates of the Arctic National Park near Anaktuvuk Pass. Good arctic char fishery — at its best in September, use spoons and eggs. Air charter available at Bettles.

Canning River. Located at the western boundary of Arctic National Wildlife Refuge. Good arctic char fishery — at its best in September, use spoons and eggs. Air charter service available in Fairbanks or Kaktovik.

Chandler Lake. Fly-in lake located on the north slope of the Brooks Range 26 miles west of Anaktuvuk Pass, about 1 hour by floatplane or small wheel plane from Bettles. Short, rough airstrip at lake. Ice may be present until July. Excellent lake trout and grayling fishing. Lake trout — fishing best as ice is leaving, good through the season, use spoons or plugs; grayling — year-round, use flies; arctic char — through the season, best in fall, use spoons, eggs; whitefish also present — use flies, eggs. Air charter available in Bettles.

Elusive Lake. Located on the north slope of the Brooks Range 80 miles northeast of Anaktuvuk Pass. A popular lake trout fishery — best just after the ice leaves, use spoons, plugs; grayling also present. Air charter available in Fairbanks or Bettles.

Fish Lake. Fly-in lake located south of the Brooks Range about 1 hour by floatplane from Bettles. Excellent lake trout, grayling and arctic char fishing. Lake trout — fishing best in spring and good through the season, use spoons or plugs; arctic char — through the season, best in fall, use spoons, eggs; grayling — year-round, use flies; whitefish — use flies, eggs. Air charter available in Bettles.

Helpmejack Lake. Fly-in lake located south of the Brooks Range west of Bettles about 35 minutes by floatplane. Lake trout — fishing best in spring and good through the season, use spoons or plugs; northern pike — year-round, best June 1 through Sept. 15, use spoons, spinners; whitefish — use flies, eggs. Air charter available in Bettles.

Iniakuk Lake. Fly-in lake located south of the Brooks Range 50 miles west of Bettles. Lake trout fishing — best in spring and good through the season, use spoons or plugs; northern pike — year-round, best June 1 through Sept. 15, use spoons, spinners; whitefish — use flies, eggs. Iniakuk Lake Lodge on lake. Air charter available in Bettles.

Itkillik Lake. Located on the north slope of the Brooks Range 60 miles northeast of Anaktuvuk Pass. A popular lake trout fishery — best in spring just after the ice leaves, use spoons, plugs; grayling also present. Air charter available in Fairbanks or Bettles.

Kobuk River (Upper and Lower). Located

Sod-roofed miner's cabin looks out toward Wild Lake in the Brooks Range. (George Wuerthner)

in northwestern Alaska — flows from Walker Lake in Gates of the Arctic National Park to Kotzebue Sound. Boats may be chartered from residents of villages along the Kobuk: Kiana, Noorvik, Ambler, Shungnak and Kobuk. The Kobuk is famous for sheefish — present in the upper and lower rivers, use spoons; northern pike — year-round, best June 1 through Sept. 15, use spoons, spinners; grayling — year-round, use flies; whitefish — present in upper river, use flies, eggs. Air charter available in Kotzebue.

Kongakut River. Located within Arctic National Wildlife Refuge. Good arctic char fishery — at its best in September, use spoons and eggs. Air charter service available in Fairbanks or Kaktovik.

Kurupa Lake. Located on the north slope of the Brooks Range 75 miles west of Anaktuvuk Pass. A popular lake trout fishery — best in spring just after the ice leaves, use spoons, plugs; arctic char and grayling also present. Air charter available in Fairbanks or Bettles.

Nanushuk Lake. Fly-in lake located on the north slope of the Brooks Range northeast of Anaktuvuk Pass, about 1 hour by floatplane from Bettles. Lake trout fishing — best as ice is leaving, good through the season, use spoons or plugs; grayling — year-round, use flies; whitefish — use flies, eggs. Air charter available in Bettles.

Noatak River. Fly-in river located in northwestern Alaska — flows through Gates of the Arctic National Park and Noatak National Preserve to Kotzebue Sound. Arctic char — fishing excellent in the fall, use spoons and eggs; grayling — use flies; chum salmon — July 15 through Sept. 30, peaking in August, use spoons; some pike also present. Arrangements may be made for accommodations at Noatak village. Commercial and charter air service available from Kotzebue.

Nutuvukti Lake. Fly-in lake located south of the Brooks Range in Gates of the Arctic National Preserve. No camps or boats available. Good summer fishery. Lake trout — through the season, use spoons or plugs; grayling — year-round, use flies; northern pike — year-round, best June 1 through Sept. 15, use spoons, spinners; burbot — throughout the season, best in fall and winter, use bait such as head or tail of lake trout. Charter floatplane available in Bettles or Kotzebue.

Round Lake. Fly-in lake located on the North Slope of the Brooks Range about 1 hour by floatplane from Bettles. Lake trout — fishing best as ice is leaving, good through the season, use spoons or plugs; grayling — good year-round, use flies; arctic char — use spoons,

eggs; whitefish — use flies, eggs. Air charter available in Bettles.

Sagavanirktok River. Also known as "The Sag." Located on the Arctic Slope with its outlet near Prudhoe Bay. Good arctic char fishery — at its best in September, use spoons and eggs. Char fishery outstanding on Ivishak River, a tributary to the Sagavanirktok. Air charter service available in Fairbanks, Prudhoe Bay or Kaktovik.

Schrader Lake. Located on the Arctic Slope 65 miles south of Barter Island. A popular lake trout fishery — best in spring just after the ice leaves, use spoons, plugs; arctic char and grayling also present. Air charter available in Kaktovik or Fairbanks.

Selawik River. Fly-in river about 70 miles southeast of Kotzebue. Fishing excellent for small- to medium-sized sheefish — in summer and fall, use spoons; northern pike — year-round, best June 1 through Sept. 15, use spoons, spinners. Air charter available in Kotzebue.

Selby Lake. Fly-in lake located south of the Brooks Range in Gates of the Arctic National Preserve. Summer fishery is excellent. Lake trout — through the season, use spoons or plugs; grayling — year-round, use flies; northern pike — year-round, best June 1 through Sept. 15, use spoons, spinners; burbot — throughout the season, best in fall and winter, use bait such as head or tail of lake trout. Charter floatplane available in Bettles or Kotzebue.

Shainin Lake. Fly-in lake located on the north slope of the Brooks Range, 22 miles northeast of Anaktuvuk Pass, about 1 hour by floatplane from Bettles. Excellent lake trout and grayling fishing. Lake trout — fishing best as ice is leaving, good through the season, use spoons or plugs; grayling — year-round, use flies; whitefish — use flies, eggs. Air charter available in Bettles.

Walker Lake. Fly-in lake located in the Brooks Range within Gates of the Arctic National Park, about 45 minutes northwest of Bettles by floatplane. Lake trout — fishing excellent through the season, use spoons or plugs; northern pike — year-round, best June 1 through Sept. 15, use spoons, spinners; arctic char — use spoons, eggs; whitefish — use flies, eggs. Walker Lake Wilderness Lodge on lake. Air charter available in Bettles.

Wulik River. Located in northwestern Alaska near Kivalina 90 miles northwest of Kotzebue. Excellent arctic char fishery — in spring and fall, use spoons and eggs; grayling — use flies. Midnight Sun Lodge located 30 miles upriver from Kivalina. Commercial and charter air service available in Kotzebue.

SPECIAL FEATURES

Leffingwell Camp

On southcentral Flaxman Island stand the remains of what is believed to be the camp established by explorer and geologist Ernest de Koven Leffingwell in 1907 to carry out important permafrost studies, mapping and other studies of arctic conditions. The camp is on the National Register of Historic Places.

Leffingwell spent 6 years between 1901 and 1914 in the Canning River region and compiled the first accurate maps of that part of the northern coast. A cabin at the campsite was built from the timbers of the expedition's ship, the *Duchess of Bedford,* which had been damaged by the ice pack. The camp is about 4.5 miles west of Brownlow Point located west of Kaktovik on Barter Island.

Kasegaluk Lagoon

Stretching southwest along the Chukchi Sea coast from just south of Wainwright to beyond Point Lay, this shallow 120-mile-long body of water is the largest barrier island-lagoon system in North America. It offers excellent wildlife viewing, as well as kayaking in shallow (3- to 6-foot) waters protected from ocean waves by the low barrier islands. During July, August and September half a million migrating eiders and thousands of terns, gulls, jaegers, loons, brants and oldsquaws can be seen. Many beluga whales move into the lagoon in late June. At other times of the year it is possible to see arctic foxes, lemmings, caribou, brown bears, various types of seals and gray whales. The lagoon (pronounced ka-SEE-ga-luk) is considered an

important and productive habitat by the Alaska Dept. of Fish and Game. South of Icy Cape, near the mouth of the Utukok River, is the abandoned village of Tolageak, marked by the remains of Eskimo sod huts.

The only access to the lagoon area is by chartered plane from Barrow or Kotzebue. There is a landing strip at an abandoned DEW line site at Icy Cape which is not maintained and may be in poor or unusable condition. Lodging is available at Barrow or Kotzebue, but it's wilderness camping only at the lagoon. Campers and kayakers should be prepared for high winds and cold weather year-round. Take a few extra days' supply of food in the event you get weathered in. Do not in any way harass nesting birds or other wildlife. And, be aware that there is considerable subsistence hunting, fishing and other activity in the area at various times of the year. The village of Wainwright owns some of the land at the north end of the lagoon. For additional information contact: Arctic District Manager, Bureau of Land Management, 1541 Gaffney St., Fairbanks, AK 99703; phone 356-5130.

Teshekpuk Lake

This large lake lies just a few miles from the Arctic Ocean in the wet, low tundra region southeast of Barrow. Teshekpuk Lake, which is 22 miles across, and smaller surrounding lakes, are considered a crucial waterfowl and caribou habitat area. Wildlife viewing and photography are excellent. The region is home to migratory brants, greater white-fronted and Canada geese, which arrive in July and August from the Alaska Peninsula, Canadian Arctic and Siberia. The lake system protects these large birds from predators while they molt and regrow their wing feathers. Other birds that nest in the region include plovers, sandpipers, phalaropes, dunlins, loons, oldsquaws, jaegers, gulls and snowy owls. Caribou, arctic foxes and lemmings also can be seen.

The only access to the area is by charter plane from Barrow or Prudhoe Bay. There is lodging in Barrow, but wilderness camping only in the lake area. Special use regulations are in effect in the summer to minimize aircraft and other disturbance of wildlife. For additional information, contact: Arctic District Manager, Bureau of Land Management, 1541 Gaffney St., Fairbanks, AK 99703; phone 356-5130.

Tunalik

This 5,000-foot airstrip is located south of Icy Cape in the vicinity of Kasegaluk Lagoon.

The Tunalik River mouth, 10 miles south of Icy Cape at 70°11'N, 161°44'W, is 5 to 10 miles downstream from the airstrip, which was built to supply oil exploration expeditions. The strip is reported to be still usable, although it is not maintained and should be inspected before a landing is attempted. There is a gravel pad on one side of the runway for camping. This open tundra region offers a real arctic tundra wilderness experience, with good opportunities for wildlife viewing and photography in the summer. There are no facilities here. You're on your own and should be prepared with adequate clothing and extra food and supplies in the event the weather changes for the worst.

Jagged Arrigetch Peaks are a familiar landmark in Gates of the Arctic National Park and Preserve. (George Wuerthner)

Paddlers enjoy a wide, swift section of the Fortymile River, which also offers rapids and a portage around the historic section known as the Kink. (George Wuerthner)

INTERIOR

The Region

Alaska's Interior is a land of superlatives. Majestic Mount McKinley crowns the region's southern border. The Yukon, Alaska's longest river, carves a swath across the entire region. The Interior encompasses almost one third of the state, most of it wilderness. Rivers were, and are, the Interior's natural highways.

Location: Encompassing the Alaska Range on the south, stretching to the southern foothills of the Brooks Range on the north and the Canadian border on the east, Alaska's Interior blends with the Bering Sea Coast region on the west. The state's geographic center is located near Lake Minchumina, about 60 miles northwest of Mount McKinley.

Physical description: Low, rolling hills, braided streams flowing into meandering rivers, stunted taiga and ground-hugging tundra dominate the central lowlands between the mountain ranges. Discontinuous permafrost occurs throughout the region.

Rivers: Great rivers have forged Alaska's Interior. The Yukon, Tanana, Porcupine, Koyukuk and many others provided avenues of exploration for the Athabascan Indians and later white explorers, trappers and miners. South of the Yukon, the Kuskokwim River rises in the hills of the western Interior before beginning its meandering course across the Bering Sea Coast region.

Climate

The climate here is largely governed by latitude. The Arctic Circle sweeps through the region. Shining almost 24 hours a day in summer, the sun is nearly absent in winter. The aurora borealis illuminates long winter nights.

Temperatures in the Interior range widely,

from winter lows of -50° to -60°F to summer highs of 80° to 90°F. Stagnant air masses typify the semiarid continental climate, which averages about 12 inches of precipitation annually.

Vegetation

Two distinct environments, forests and tundra, characterize the Interior. Below 2,000 feet and in river valleys, forests of white spruce, birch and aspen are broken by stands of balsam poplar and tamarack. Cottonwood thrive near river lowlands, and hardy black spruce grow in bogs. Willows, alders, berries, wildflowers, grasses and sedges abound, as does reindeer moss, a type of lichen which makes up a substantial portion of the diet of caribou.

In northern and western reaches of the Interior, the forests give way to slow-growing tundra. Above 2,500 feet, most mountains are bare, except for flowering plants and rock lichens.

Wildlife

Big Game: Caribou from several different herds spend all or part of the year in the Interior. Moose are common in second-growth forests, on timberline plateaus and along the rivers. Grizzly bears, black bears and wolves range throughout the region. Dall sheep are found in the high mountains. All these species may be seen at Denali National Park and Preserve. Wolverines are classed as big game but are seldom seen. An introduced bison herd ranges near Delta Junction, and a smaller, private herd grazes near Healy.

Furbearers and Nongame Species: Coyotes, red fox, lynx and snowshoe hare

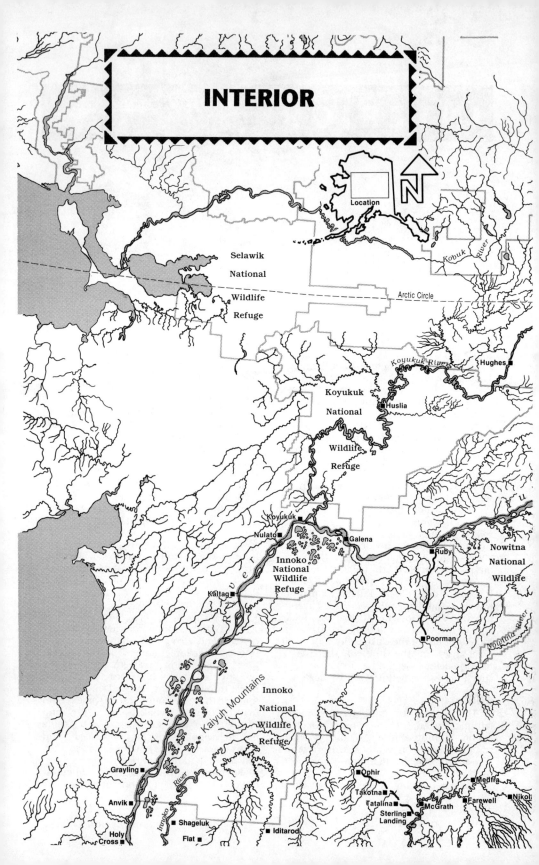

Map continues next page

Arctic
Village

Wind R.

Coldfoot

Venetie

Dalton Highway

Chandalar River

Porcupine R.

Bettles

Yukon Flats National

Fort
Yukon

Wildlife Refuge

Alatna River

Kanuti

Beaver

Birch
Creek

Alatna
Allakaket

National

Birch Creek

Wildlife

River Koyukuk

Refuge

Stevens
Village

Steese
National
Conservation
Area

Ray Mountains

White
Mountains
National
Recreation
Area

Rampart

Livengood

Beaver Creek

Tanana

Elliott Highway

Chena
Hot Springs

Tofty

Fox

Manley Hot Springs

Fairbanks

Chena River
State Recreation
Area

Refuge

Alaska
Highway

Nenana

George Parks Highway

Delta Junction

Nenana River

Richardson
Highway

Lake Minchumina

Lake
Minchumina

Healy

Telida

Denali National

Kantishna

Delta River

Park and

Cantwell

Preserve

Denali Highway

Gulkana R.

Mt. McKinley

Denali
State
Park

Cartography by David A. Shott

may be hunted or trapped. Porcupine may be hunted. Beaver, marten, mink, weasel, muskrats, land otter, flying squirrel, arctic ground squirrel, red squirrel, hoary marmot and pika are protected from hunting, though all but the pika may be trapped.

Birds: Millions of birds make their homes in this region including wigeon; pintail; green-winged teal; northern shoveler; canvasback; Canada geese; several species of scoter, scaup and swans; and many other species. Endangered peregrine falcons nest in Yukon-Charley Rivers National Preserve. (See also Minto Flats State Game Refuge.)

Fish: Five species of salmon, especially king and chum, provide excellent sportfishing opportunities and are also important subsistence species. Grayling, arctic char, burbot, northern pike, lake trout and several species of whitefish are also significant to subsistence.

Minerals

Gold discoveries of the 1880s and 1890s brought the major influx of non-Natives to the Interior. Abandoned dredges may be seen near Fairbanks, once a booming gold mining camp, now the Interior's largest community.

Angler lands northern pike along Yukon River. (George Wuerthner)

Other dredges rest near Chicken and Jack Wade camp not far from the Fortymile River, where active gold mining continues. At Healy, southwest of Fairbanks, the state's only operating coal mine produces coal used to generate electricity in the Interior. (See also The Kink.) For more information, see *ALASKA GEOGRAPHIC®*, Vol. 9, No. 4, *Alaska's Oil/Gas & Minerals Industry.* To order, see the ALASKA NORTHWEST LIBRARY section at the back of the book.

Public Lands

State and National Parks and Preserves: Mount McKinley's 20,320-foot peak, the abundant wildlife surrounding it and its relatively easy access have made Denali National Park and Preserve one of Alaska's most popular visitor attractions. Yukon-Charley Rivers National Preserve, which protects a nearly untouched wilderness, receives comparatively little visitation.

Denali State Park abuts Denali National Park and Preserve to the south and adds 324,420 largely undeveloped acres to the protected ecosystem surrounding North America's tallest mountain.

National Wildlife Refuges: Yukon Flats State and National Wildlife Refuge shelters one of the highest densities of nesting waterfowl in North America and contributes more than 2 million ducks and geese to the continent's flyways. Other crucial habitat has been set aside in the Innoko, Kanuti, Koyukuk, Nowitna, Tetlin and the newly created Minto Flats State Game Refuge.

State and National Recreation Areas: Chena River State Recreation Area, at 254,080 acres, is by far the largest in the state. Other state recreation areas include Quartz Lake, Harding Lake and Lower Chatanika. Also recognized for their recreation value are the Steese National Conservation Area and the White Mountain National Recreation Area.

GOLD PANNING

The entire process of agitating and washing, agitating and washing is what settles the gold into the bottom of your pan.

▼ C O M M U N I T I E S ▼

Alatna

Located on north bank of the Koyukuk River, 2 miles downriver from Allakaket, 182 miles northwest of Fairbanks. **Transportation:** Boat or snow machine from Allakaket. **Population:** 35. **Zip code:** 99790. **Emergency Services, Elevation, Climate** and **Private Aircraft:** See Allakaket.

The village is situated on a high open plateau where Kobuk Eskimos and the Koyukukhotana Athabascans met to trade goods. The Indians settled across the river in what is now Allakaket.

The Eskimo village of Alatna has no visitor facilities. Water is hauled from the Koyukuk River. Electric service is provided by a generator. Sewage system is outhouses. Most services and facilities are available at Allakaket.

Allakaket

(alla-KAK-it) Located on south bank of the Koyukuk River at the mouth of the Alatna River, 2 miles upriver from Alatna, 180 miles northwest of Fairbanks. **Transportation:** Scheduled air service from Fairbanks; boat or snow machine to Alatna and Hughes. **Population:** 202. **Zip code:** 99720. **Emergency Services:** Village Public Safety Officer; Clinic, phone 968-2210; Volunteer Fire Department.

Elevation: 600 feet. **Climate:** Warmest month is July with a mean temperature of 58°F and 2.06 inches of precipitation. Coldest month is January, averaging -18°F. Snow from about September through May.

Private Aircraft: Airstrip adjacent village beside river (river floods south end of runway in spring); elev. 350 feet; length 2,800 feet; gravel; unattended. Runway condition not monitored, visual inspection recommended prior to using (watch for children and dogs on runway). No facilities.

Visitor Facilities: No accommodations or meals available, though arrangements can be made to sleep on the school floor. Two stores in the community carry groceries, clothing, hardware, camera film and sporting goods. No

banking services but there is a community-owned laundromat (washeteria) which is also the village watering point. Beaded arts and crafts and fur hats available for purchase. Fishing/hunting licenses available. Diesel, white gas and gasoline are available and boats may be rented.

This area was originally a place where the Kobuk Eskimos and the Koyukukhotana Athabascans met to trade goods. The Eskimos settled on the north bank of the river (now Alatna) and the Athabascans on the south bank. The population declined with the influx of Russians in 1838. In 1906, Archdeacon Hudson Stuck established a mission here.

"A hard subsistence life" is how one Allakaket resident describes it here. Fishing in local rivers includes sheefish, grayling and whitefish. Gates of the Arctic National Park and Preserve is located to the north of the village, and Kanuti Wildlife Refuge is adjacent. The village has first priority for subsistence hunting, but caribou and moose are scarce.

Communications include phones, mail plane, CB radios, radio and TV. There is an Episcopal church (St. John's-in-the-Wilderness) and a school with grades preschool through 10. There are a municipal electric service and small private generators. Water is obtained from the river and the laundromat. Sewage system is outhouses. Freight comes in by plane. Allakaket bans the possession of alcoholic beverages. Government address: City of Allakaket, P.O. Box 30, Allakaket, AK 99720; phone 968-2241.

Anvik

Located on the Anvik River at its mouth just west of the Yukon River and east of the Nulato Hills; 34 miles north of Holy Cross, 160 miles northwest of Bethel and 350 miles west-northwest of Anchorage **Population:** 83. **Zip code:** 99558. **Emergency Services:** Police, phone 663-3644; Clinic; Volunteer Fire Department.

Elevation: 325 feet. **Climate:** In the continental climate zone. Annual average snowfall is 110 inches; total precipitation per year is 21 inches.

Private Aircraft: Airstrip 1 mile southeast; elev. 325 feet; length 2,800 feet; gravel and dirt; unattended. Runway condition not monitored, visual inspection recommended prior to using. Runway dish-shaped; severe erosion adjacent to runway shoulder 800 feet from south end.

Visitor Facilities: Accommodations available. Meals available at one local lodge. Groceries, general merchandise, gifts and novelties, local arts and crafts available. There is a laundromat. Fishing/hunting licenses may be obtained locally. Major repair services, charter aircraft available. All fuels available except premium gasoline. No banking services.

Anvik, 1 of 5 villages inhabited by the Ingalik Athabascan Indians, was incorporated as a second-class city in 1969. In 1834, Russian Andrei Glazanov reported several hundred people living here. Anvik was originally located across the Yukon River at an area called the point. Spring flooding forced people to move from the point to a higher location where, in 1887, the Episcopalians established a mission. Anvik has been known by many names throughout the years.

Anvik has a seasonal economy which shows an upswing in summer when local construction programs get under way. Most families have fish camps and rely heavily on subsistence activities such as hunting, fishing and home gardening.

The site of the Christ Church Mission with its remaining structures, founded in 1888, is on the National Register of Historic Places.

Every other year, Anvik is a checkpoint in the 1,049-mile Iditarod Trail Sled Dog Race held in March.

Communications include phones, mail plane, radio and TV. The community is served by an Episcopal church and a school with grades preschool through 12. Public electricity is available. Water is provided by a city well. Sewage system is privies and honey buckets. Freight arrives by air transport and barge. Government address: City of Anvik, General Delivery, Anvik, AK 99558, phone 663-6328. Village corporation address: Ingalik Inc., General Delivery, Anvik, AK 99558, phone 663-6330.

Arctic Village

Located in the Brooks Range on the east bank of the East Fork Chandalar River, 100 miles

north of Fort Yukon, 290 miles north of Fairbanks. **Transportation:** Scheduled air service from Fairbanks; winter trail to Venetie. **Population:** 109. **Zip code:** 99722. **Emergency Services:** Village Public Safety Officer; Clinic (with a health aide); Volunteer Fire Department.

Elevation: 2,250 feet. **Climate:** Mean temperature in July is 56°F, in January, -29°F.

Private Aircraft: Airstrip 1 mile southwest of village; elev. 2,086 feet; length 5,200 feet; gravel; unattended. Check for runway construction; watch for loose gravel on approach and vehicles on runway.

Visitor Facilities: The village council operates a bunkhouse for visitors; contact the council, phone 587-9320. No meals or banking services available. Supplies are available in the community. There is a community-owned laundromat with showers. Arctic Village is a traditional Athabascan Indian village and crafts may be available for purchase locally. Gasoline and fuel oil are available.

The Neets'ik Gwich'in Indians, a once seminomadic people known for trading *babiche* "sinew lacings" and wolverine skins for seal oil and skins from the Barter Island Eskimos, settled Arctic Village.

Arctic Village elected to retain title to the 1.8-million-acre Venetie Indian Reservation under the Alaska Native Claims Settlement Act. The reserve and Arctic Village are bounded to the north by Arctic National Wildlife Refuge, although recreational access to the refuge is primarily from Kaktovik on Barter Island. Employment in Arctic Village is limited to the National Guard Armory, post office, clinic, school, village services, trapping and crafts.

There is an Episcopal chapel in the village, which replaced the old Mission Church now on the National Register of Historic Places. Under restoration, the old church — built entirely of logs with handcrafted finish and furnishings — reflects the skill of the Native artisans under Albert Tritt, who later became its minister.

Communications include phones, mail plane, radio and TV. There is a school with grades preschool through 12. Village services include the laundromat and showers, and electric generator. Honey buckets and outhouses are used. Freight delivery by plane. Government address: Arctic Village Council, P.O. Box 22050, Arctic Village, AK 99722; phone 587-9320.

Beaver

Located on the north bank of the Yukon River, 60 miles southwest of Fort Yukon, 110 miles northwest of Fairbanks. **Transportation:** Scheduled air service from Fairbanks. **Population:** 65. **Zip code:** 99724. **Emergency Services:** Clinic, phone 628-6228; Volunteer Fire Department. **Elevation:** 365 feet.

Private Aircraft: Airstrip adjacent north; elev. 365 feet; length 3,600 feet; gravel; unattended; recommend visual inspection prior to using.

Visitor Facilities: There are no hotels, restaurants, banks or other services. There is a community laundromat with bathing facilities. Some supplies and fishing/hunting licenses are available in the community. Diesel and gasoline are available.

Beaver is an unincorporated Eskimo and Indian village. The village was founded by Frank Yasuda, whose interest in the location was two-fold. Married to an Eskimo woman, Yasuda saw Beaver as a place to relocate his Eskimo family and friends, who were facing hard times with the decline of whaling in arctic waters. Yasuda was also a partner of J.T. Marsh and Tom Carter, who had prospected for gold throughout the Arctic before settling in the Chandalar region to the north. Yasuda founded Beaver as a river landing for the Chandalar quartz mines started by Marsh and Carter in about 1909. In 1910, the Alaska Road Commission pushed through a trail from the mines south some 100 miles to Beaver, and Marsh and Carter spent the next several years trying to turn a profit from the modest amount of gold in the mines. A stamp mill was shipped in to crush the quartz for gold, although only parts of the 28-ton mill survived the rugged trail to the mines. With the Great Depression and the subsequent withdrawal of financial backing, mining ceased.

Communications include phones, mail plane, radio and TV. The 2 churches in the community are St. Matthew Episcopal and Assembly of God. The school has grades preschool through 12 and also houses both the health clinic and generator for the community. Water is available at the laundromat. The sewage system is privies. Freight service is by plane or via Yutana Barge service 4 times a year. Government address: Beaver Tribal Council, General Delivery, Beaver, AK 99724; phone 628-6126.

Bettles

(See Communities in BROOKS RANGE AND THE ARCTIC section.)

Birch Creek

Located on Lower Birch Creek, 26 miles southwest of Fort Yukon, 120 miles northeast of Fairbanks. **Transportation:** Mail and charter plane. **Population:** 53. **Zip code:** 99790. **Emergency Services:** Volunteer Fire Department; police and medical aid available from Fort Yukon or Fairbanks.

Elevation: 450 feet. **Climate:** According to a Birch Creek resident, "summers dry and warm, winters cold and lots of snow."

Private Aircraft: Airstrip 1 mile north; elev. 450 feet; length 2,500 feet; gravel; runway condition not monitored, visual inspection recommended; radio operated landing lights.

Visitor Facilities: Visitors may be able to arrange for accommodations in private homes. There are no stores. Supplies — including fuel — are obtained from Fort Yukon and Fairbanks. Birch Creek has no laundromat or banking services.

Birch Creek was an Athabascan Indian village in the 1800s and became a mining community with the discovery of gold. According to a local resident, the community got its start after a break with Fort Yukon. The people here hunt moose and bear, fish northern pike and trap furs for a living.

Communications include phones, radio, TV and a mail plane. There is a 2-classroom school with grades kindergarten through 12. There is a community power system, but honey buckets still comprise the sewage system. Water is hauled from Birch Creek Community Storage Tank. Freight comes in by cargo plane. Birch Creek bans the possession of alcoholic beverages. Village corporation address: Birch Creek Corp. Office, General Delivery, Birch Creek, AK 99790.

Chalkyitsik

(chal-KEET-sik) Located 45 miles north of Fort Yukon, 170 miles northeast of Fairbanks, on the Black River. **Transportation:** Boat; charter or scheduled air service from Fort Yukon or Fairbanks. There is a trail to Fort Yukon. **Population:** 98. **Zip code:** 99788. **Emergency Services:** Village Public Safety Officer in town or Alaska State Troopers in Fort Yukon; Clinic, phone 848-8215; Volunteer Fire Department.

Elevation: 560 feet. **Climate:** Summers are generally hot with some cool and rainy weather; mean temperature in July is 61°F. Winters are cold, with the mean monthly temperature in January -25°F.

Private Aircraft: Airstrip adjacent southwest; elev. 560 feet; length 2,600 feet; gravel. No airport facilities, fuel, navigational aids or lighting.

Visitor Facilities: There are no formal

accommodations but residents may provide a place to stay in their homes if asked. Meals are not available. The community carries groceries, camera film, hardware and sporting goods. Propane and gasoline are available, but there are no other services or facilities.

Originally an Athabascan seasonal fish camp, Chalkyitsik means "fish with a hook at the mouth of the creek." Postmistress Geraldine Nathaniel says "fishhook town is small, kind of growing yet. The town is very quiet. Nice town to live in." The people work for the school, clinic, post office, Native store and village council. There is fishing for jackfish, whitefish and dog salmon; trapping; and hunting for ducks, grouse and ptarmigan.

Communications include phones, mail plane and radio. The log community hall in the center of town houses the clinic, village council office, Native corporation office, store and post office. There is a school with grades preschool through 12 and there are 2 churches. A community utility service provides power, but water is hauled from the river (the pipes at the pump house freeze in winter) and the sewage system is honey buckets. The sale and importation of alcoholic beverages has been banned here. Freight arrives by cargo plane. No moorage facilities. Government address: Chalkyitsik Village Council, General Delivery, Chalkyitsik, AK 99788, phone 848-8227. Village corporation address: Chalkyitsik Native Corp., General Delivery, Chalkyitsik, AK 99788; phone 848-8214.

Chicken

Located on the Taylor Highway, 78 miles from Tok, 95 miles from Eagle. **Transportation:** Auto in summer (Taylor Highway closed in winter). **Population:** 37. **Zip code:** 99732. **Emergency Services:** Alaska State Troopers (Tok), phone 883-5111; Tok Community Clinic, phone 883-5855 during business hours; Tok Public Health Clinic, phone 883-4101; Tok Fire Department, phone 883-2333.

Private Aircraft: Tok airstrip; elev. 1,670 feet; length 2,700 feet; paved; unattended; fuel 80, 100.

Visitor Facilities: RV parking, 1 cafe, country store, bar, 2 gas stations offering tire changes and repairs. Gold in vials, nuggets, or gold nugget jewelry made from local gold all available for purchase; also recreational gold panning.

A mining camp and post office established in 1903, Chicken probably got its name from the plentiful ptarmigan in the area. In the North "chicken" is a common name for that bird. One story has it that the early day miners

wanted to name their camp "Ptarmigan" but were unable to spell it and settled for Chicken instead. Chicken was the home of the late Ann Purdy, whose autobiographical novel *Tisha* recounted her adventures as a young schoolteacher in the Alaska Bush.

Below the airstrip at Chicken is an access point for the South Fork Fortymile River, a route which avoids the more challenging waters of the North Fork. (See The Rivers, this section, for more information on floating the Fortymile.)

NOTE: All gold-bearing ground in the Fortymile area is claimed. Do not pan in streams.

For more information about Chicken, see *The MILEPOST®*, a complete guide to communities on Alaska's road and marine highway systems. To order, see the ALASKA NORTHWEST LIBRARY section at the back of the book.

Circle

Located on the banks of the Yukon River, at Mile 162 Steese Highway, 125 miles northeast of Fairbanks. **Transportation:** Road via the Steese Highway. **Population:** 94. **Zip Code:** 99733.

Elevation: 700 feet. **Climate:** Mean monthly temperature in July is 61°F; in January, -10°F. Snow from October through April.

Private Aircraft: Airstrip adjacent north, elev. 610 feet; length 3,500 feet; gravel; untended.

Visitor facilities: Accommodations and meals are available. Other facilities include a grocery store, gas station, post office, trading post and general store. Hunting/fishing licenses are available. A campground on the banks of the Yukon at the end of the road offers tables, toilets and a grassy parking area.

Before the Klondike gold rush of 1898, Circle was the largest gold mining town on the Yukon River. Today, Circle is a popular put-in and take-out spot for Yukon River boaters. For more information see *The MILEPOST®*, a complete guide to communities on Alaska's road and marine highway systems. To order, see the ALASKA NORTHWEST LIBRARY section at the back of the book.

Eagle

Located on the banks of the Yukon River, at mile 161 Taylor Highway, near the Alaska-Yukon Territory border, about 200 miles east of Fairbanks. **Transportation:** Scheduled and charter air service year-round; auto in summer via Taylor Highway (closed in winter); tour boat down river (100 miles) from Dawson City, YT. **Population:** 174. **Zip code:** 99738.

Emergency Services: Health aide, phone 547-2218; Village Public Safety Officer, phone 547-2246; Fire Department, phone 547-2282. **Elevation:** 820 feet. **Climate:** Mean monthly temperature in July 59.4°F, in January -13.3°F. Record high, 95°F (July 1925), record low -71°F (January 1952). Mean precipitation in July, 1.94 inches; in December, 10.1 inches.

Private Aircraft: Airstrip 2 miles east; elev. 880 feet; length 3,500 feet; gravel; no fuel; unattended. Runway condition not monitored, visual inspection recommended prior to landing.

Visitor facilities: Accommodations are available at area motels and rental cabins or the Eagle BLM campground just outside town; other services include several restaurants, gas stations, gift shops, showers, laundromat, grocery stores, hardware store and mechanic shop with tire repair. National Park Service office, headquarters for Yukon-Charley Rivers National Preserve, is located on the banks of the Yukon River at the base of Fort Egbert.

Historically an important riverboat landing, today Eagle boasts many charming and handsomely restored old buildings and is a popular jumping-off point for Yukon River travelers. For more information see *The MILEPOST®*, a complete guide to communities on Alaska's road and marine highway systems. To order, see the ALASKA NORTHWEST LIBRARY section at the back of the book.

Fairbanks

Located 263 air miles north of Anchorage and 1,519 air miles north of Seattle. **Transportation:** Several international, interstate and intrastate airlines provide scheduled service; auto and bus access via the Alaska Highway or the George Parks Highway; railroad access via the Alaska Railroad from Anchorage. **Population:** 27,141, borough 73,540. **Zip code:** 99701. **Emergency Services:** Alaska State Troopers, 1979 Peger Road, phone 452-1313 or, for nonemergencies, phone 452-2114; Fairbanks Police, 656 7th Ave., phone 911 or, for nonemergencies, the Dept. of Public Safety, phone 452-1527; Fire Department and Ambulance Service (within city limits), phone 911. Hospitals: Fairbanks Memorial, 1650 Cowles St., phone 452-8181; Bassett Army Hospital, Fort Wainwright, phone 353-5143; Eielson Clinic, Eielson AFB, phone 377-2259. Crisis Line, phone 452-4357. Civil Defense, phone 452-4761. Borough Information, phone 452-4761.

Elevation: 434 feet at Fairbanks Interna-

tional Airport. **Climate:** The weather changes dramatically here. The average temperature is 2°F in winter, 59°F in summer. In June and July, daylight lasts 21 hours. Annual precipitation is 10.4 inches, with an annual average snowfall of 68.4 inches. Ice fog forms over the city when the temperature is -25°F or lower.

Private Aircraft: Facilities for all types of aircraft. Consult the *Alaska Supplement* for information on the following airports: Eielson AFB, Fairbanks International, Fairbanks International Seaplane, Phillips Field and Wainwright AAF.

Visitor Facilities: Fairbanks has about 2 dozen major hotels and motels; reservations are a must during the busy summer season. There also are several bed-and-breakfast operations and a youth hostel. The town has at least 100 restaurants with a range of prices. Banks, laundromats and a wide variety of stores are available. All major repair services are available. Many air taxi operators, guides and outfitters are based in Fairbanks. Boats also may be rented. For additional information contact the Fairbanks Convention and Visitors Bureau, 550 1st Ave., Fairbanks, AK 99701; phone 456-5774. For information on Alaska's recreational lands, contact the Alaska Public Lands Information Center, 250 Cushman St., Suite 1A, phone 451-7352. The center offers free exhibits, films and brochures on forests, parks and refuges in Alaska.

In 1901, Capt. E.T. Barnette set out from St. Michael by steamer up the Yukon River with supplies for a trading post he planned to establish at Tanana Crossing (Tanacross), the halfway point on the Valdez to Eagle trail. But the steamer could not navigate the fast-moving, shallow Tanana River beyond the mouth of the Chena River. The captain of the steamer finally dropped off the protesting Barnette on the bank of the Chena River, near what is now 1st Avenue and Cushman Street. A year later, Felix Pedro, an Italian prospector, discovered gold about 15 miles north of Barnette's temporary trading post. The site is now marked at Mile 16 Steese Highway. The opportunistic Barnette quickly abandoned his plan to continue on to Tanana Crossing.

The ensuing gold rush in 1903-04 established the new gold mining community, which was named at the suggestion of Barnette's friend, Judge James Wickersham, for Sen. Charles Fairbanks of Indiana, who later became vice president of the United States under Theodore Roosevelt. The town became an administrative center in 1903 when Wickersham moved the headquarters of his Third Judicial District Court from Eagle to

Fairbanks. For the complete story of the founding and growth of Fairbanks, read *E.T. Barnette*. To order, see the ALASKA NORTH-WEST LIBRARY section at the back of the book.

The city's economy is linked to its role as a service and supply point for interior and arctic industrial activities, with emphasis in recent years on construction and operation of the trans-Alaska oil pipeline. Fairbanks is once again becoming a mining town. Old claims have been reopened and active mining is taking place in the Fairbanks Mining District.

Tourism also plays an important role in the Fairbanks economy. During the winter, several sled dog races are staged in Fairbanks, including the Yukon Quest International Sled Dog Race, which starts in February from Fairbanks in even-numbered years, and the Open North American Sled Dog Championship in March. During the summer, Fairbanks hosts a number of events, including the largest summertime event in Alaska, Golden Days held in July to commemorate the discovery of gold near Fairbanks in 1902. The World Eskimo-Indian Olympics attracts international attention and is held in July. Each August, Fairbanks hosts the Tanana Valley Fair and the Fairbanks Summer Arts Festival.

Creamer's Field Migratory Waterfowl Refuge, which lies about a mile north of downtown between College and Farmer's Loop roads, provides opportunities for viewing, photography and study of plants, wildlife and geological features. The refuge is best known for its spring and fall concentrations of ducks, geese and cranes that stop over on the refuge fields during migration. Visitors also enjoy a 2-mile, self-guided nature path complete with moose-viewing tower. The path passes through a variety of habitats common to Interior.

Fairbanks has all the amenities of a large city, including 11 radio stations, 4 TV channels (plus cable) and 2 newspapers — the *Fairbanks Daily News-Miner* and the *All-Alaska Weekly*. City government address: City of Fairbanks, 410 Cushman St., Fairbanks, AK 99701; phone 452-1881. Borough government address: Fairbanks North Star Borough, P.O. Box 1267, Fairbanks, AK 99707; phone 452-4761.

For more information, see *The MILEPOST®*. To order, see the ALASKA NORTHWEST LIBRARY at the back of the book.

Flat

Located on Otter Creek, 8 miles southeast of Iditarod, 59 miles northeast of Holy Cross, 85 miles southwest of McGrath, 375 miles west of Anchorage. **Transportation:** Charter plane from Anchorage or Fairbanks. **Population:** 5 in winter, 30 in summer. **Zip code:** 99584. **Emergency Services:** Alaska State Troopers, McGrath; McGrath Health Center.

Elevation: 309 feet. **Climate:** According to residents, Flat is dry during June and July. August and September are wet. Winter is cold and windy and the temperature can drop to -50°F.

Private Aircraft: Airstrip adjacent east; elev. 309 feet; length 4,100 feet; turf and gravel; no fuel; unattended. Runway condition not monitored, visual inspection recommended prior to using. Runway slick when wet. Both sides of runway used as road. Trees and tailings along runway edge.

Visitor Facilities: None.

This gold mining camp was reported in 1910 by A.G. Maddren of the U.S. Geological Survey. At that time, Flat was the leading settlement on Otter Creek with a population of about 400. Its population was 158 in 1920 and 124 in 1930. Flat is unincorporated.

The area around Flat is mostly private mining claims and owners carefully watch for trespassers, according to one resident.

Some of the buildings in Flat were moved from the ghost town of Iditarod. A padlocked store and bank gather dust, and cars and trucks from the 1930s sit rusting on the streets. A tramway once connected the 2 communities; a gravel trail now parallels the old tramway route.

Today only 1 family lives in Flat year-round, Mark and Sherri Kepler and their 3 children. Sherri teaches the children by correspondence, talking to a teacher twice a week by radio. Mark, a pilot and a wizard at making things run, is the postmaster, complete with Zip code and flag: "I fly the flag by the rules," he told a reporter for the Associated Press in 1989. "I raise it at dawn, which here in Alaska happens in April, and I take it down at sunset, in September."

The summer population swells when miners, who scatter to warm climates in winter, return to work their claims. The sluice boxes still show color, and if nobody is getting rich, Flat's isolation and simpler lifestyle still prove a draw.

Flat has no phones. There is no community electricity system. Water from springs or individual wells. Sewage system is honey buckets. Supplies are obtained by plane from McGrath or Anchorage.

Fort Yukon

Located at the confluence of the Porcupine

and Yukon rivers, 140 miles northeast of Fairbanks and about 8 miles north of the Arctic Circle. **Transportation:** 6 airlines provide scheduled service from Fairbanks; charter air service available; accessible by boat. **Population:** 708. **Zip code:** 99740. **Emergency Services:** Police, phone 662-2311; Alaska State Troopers, phone 662-2509; Clinic, phone 662-2460; Volunteer Fire Department, phone 662-2311.

Elevation: 420 feet. **Climate:** Dry and warm in summer, with a mean temperature of 61°F and mean precipitation of 0.94 inch in July. Winters are very dry and cold, with a mean temperature of -20°F and mean precipitation of 0.41 inch in January.

Private Aircraft: Airstrip 0.3 mile north of town; elev. 433 feet; length 5,800 feet; gravel; fuel 80, 100, A1+. Transportation to town via municipal transit weekday afternoons, phone 662-2567, or by taxi.

Visitor Facilities: Accommodations and meals are available. There is no bank, but there is a laundromat. Supplies are available in the community. Beaded moose skin accessories and clothing, furs and carved ivory jewelry are available for purchase in local trading posts. Fishing/hunting licenses are available and local fishing trips may be arranged. Major marine engine, boat and auto repair is available. Charter aircraft and boats may be rented. Fuel is available. Boat moorage on riverbank.

In 1847, Alexander Hunter Murray founded a Hudson's Bay Co. trading post near the present site of Fort Yukon. After the purchase of Alaska in 1867, it was determined that Fort Yukon was within U.S. territory. By 1873, the Alaska Commercial Co. was operating a steamer on the Yukon and had established a post here run by trader Moses Mercier. The gold rush of 1897 dramatically increased both river traffic and the white population of Fort Yukon, while disease reduced the population of Kutchin Athabascans. Fort Yukon remained the largest settlement on the Yukon below Dawson for many years, and was headquarters for a hospital and pioneer missionary Hudson Stuck, who is buried here. Fort Yukon was incorporated as a second-class city in 1959.

Hub of the Yukon Flats area, Fort Yukon has just about everything a big city has except it is in the Bush. Employment is in sales and service, local, state and federal government, and also the traditional subsistence fishing (salmon, pike, etc.), hunting (moose, bear, small game) and trapping (lynx, beaver, fox). Recreation includes boating and canoeing the Yukon River, camping, softball, swimming and driving 3-wheelers in summer; cross-country skiing, dog mushing, snow machining, ice skating, ice fishing and bingo in winter. The community itself is the attraction for visitors, as one resident points out. Subsistence fish wheels, traps and garden plots exist alongside utility poles and cable TV. The Old Mission House here is on the National Register of Historic Places.

Communications include phones, mail plane, radio and TV. The community is served by Assembly of God, Baptist and Episcopal churches. The sizable school here has grades preschool through 12. The city has public water, power and sewage systems. Freight is delivered by cargo plane and by Yutana Barge Service. Government address: Fort Yukon, P.O. Box 269, Fort Yukon, AK 99740; phone 662-2379 or 2479. Village corporation address: Gwitchyaa Zhee Corp., P.O. Box 57, Fort Yukon, AK 99740; phone 662-2325.

Galena

Located on the north bank of the Yukon River, 270 miles west of Fairbanks, 350 miles northwest of Anchorage. **Transportation:** Scheduled air service from Fairbanks; accessible by boat or barge service from Nenana, and over marked snow machine trails. **Population:** 998. **Zip code:** 99741. **Emergency Services:** Police, phone 656-1303; Alaska State Troopers, phone 656-1233; Clinic, phone 656-1266; Fire Department, phone 911.

Elevation: 120 feet. **Climate:** Mean monthly temperature in January is -12°F. Warm and sunny in summer with a mean monthly temperature in July of 60°F. August is the wettest month with 2.31 inches mean precipitation. Mean snow and sleet in January is 7.2 inches.

Private Aircraft: Galena airport adjacent northwest; elev. 152 feet; length 6,200 feet; asphalt/concrete; caution — work may be in progress. Galena airport is the commercial air center for 6 surrounding villages and is also the forward U.S./A/F Air Force base for F-15 jet fighters. An FAA station is located here. All facilities, including passenger terminal. Taxi service available.

Visitor Facilities: Accommodations at an inn and a lodge. No banking services. Public laundromat and showers are available. Restaurants and all supplies available in the community. Local arts and crafts available for purchase include Indian beadwork, birchbark baskets, skin moccasins, fur hats and ivory work. Fishing/hunting licenses available from the local Alaska Dept. of Fish and

Game officer and guide service. All types of fuel and repair service are available. Autos and boats may be rented in Galena. Moorage facilities are also available.

Galena was founded as a supply point for nearby galena (lead ore) prospects in 1919. The airstrip was built in 1940 by the U.S. Army. Galena was incorporated in 1971. Koyukon Athabascans comprise most of the town's population. The population increases in summer with firefighters. There is some construction and commercial fishing in summer, and year-round employment in government jobs, but traditional subsistence hunting and fishing support many residents. There is sportfishing for salmon, grayling, whitefish, sheefish, burbot and pike in nearby clear-water lakes and streams. Koyukuk National Wildlife Refuge lies to the north of Galena, and the northern portion of the Innoko refuge lies across the Yukon River to the south.

As transportation hub for several outlying villages, Galena sees many visitors in summer. In winter, when the Yukon is frozen solid, neighbors come in by dogsled or snow machine. Galena is the turnaround point for the Yukon 800 boat race from Fairbanks, held in June. The town has its own Fourth of July softball tournament, a Native arts and crafts bazaar on Thanksgiving weekend, and a Winter Carnival the last weekend in March.

Communications include phone, mail plane, radio and TV. There are 2 churches: St. John Berchman's Catholic Church and the Galena Bible Church. The community is proud of its city schools, which include an elementary school (grades kindergarten through 6), a high school (grades 7 through 12) and a branch of the University of Alaska. There are community electric, water and sewage systems, although honey buckets and a water haul system are also used. Freight arrives by air cargo plane and Yutana Barge Service. Government address: City of Galena, P.O. Box 149, Galena, AK 99741; phone 656-1301. Village corporation address: Gana-a'Yoo, Ltd., P.O. Box 38, Galena, AK 99741.

Grayling

Located on the west bank of the Yukon River east of the Nulato Hills, 21 miles north of Anvik, 350 miles west-northwest of Anchorage. **Transportation:** Scheduled and charter air service from McGrath or Bethel. **Population:** 211. **Zip code:** 99590. **Emergency Services:** Alaska State Troopers, Aniak, phone 675-4398; Health aide; Volunteer Fire Department.

Elevation: 90 feet. **Climate:** Continental; mean annual precipitation 21 inches; mean annual snowfall 110 inches.

Private Aircraft: Airstrip 1 mile south; elev. 99 feet; length 2,400 feet; gravel; unattended. Runway condition not monitored, visual inspection recommended prior to using. North end of runway and taxiway floods in spring.

Visitor Facilities: Arrangements can be made for accommodations in private homes. No restaurant or banking services. Groceries, clothing, first-aid supplies, hardware, camera film, sporting goods available in the community. Arts and crafts available for purchase include birch-bark baskets, grass baskets, skin boots, fur hats and beadwork. Fishing/hunting licenses available. No guide service. Aircraft mechanic available, as well as charter aircraft. Fuel available includes diesel, propane and regular gasoline. Moorage facilities available.

When the U.S. Revenue Service steamer *Nunivak* stopped here in 1900, Lt. J.C. Cantwell reported an Indian village of approximately 75 residents. They had a large stockpile of wood to supply fuel for steamers. When gold mining in the area diminished, the village was abandoned until 1962, when residents of Holikachuk on the Innoko River moved to the site. Grayling today is a second-class city, incorporated in 1948 under the name of Holikachuk, Territory of Alaska. The name was changed to Grayling in 1964.

Grayling's economy depends on subsistence, and employment is primarily seasonal summer work in construction, road work and commercial fishing. Most families fish for salmon, whitefish, sheefish, pike and eels, and hunt for moose, black bear, small game and waterfowl. Residents also trap marten, mink, otter, beaver, wolf, lynx and wolverine, and sell the pelts.

Grayling is located across the Yukon River from Innoko National Wildlife Refuge.

Every other year Grayling is a checkpoint on the 1,049-mile Iditarod Trail Sled Dog Race.

Communications in Grayling include phones, mail plane, radio and TV. The community is served by St. Paul's Episcopal Church and the Arctic Mission, as well as a school with grades kindergarten through 12. There are community electricity, water and sewer systems. Grayling prohibits the sale and importation of alcoholic beverages. Freight arrives by barge or mail plane. Government address: IRA Council, Village of Grayling, P.O. Box 89, Grayling, AK 99590, phone 453-5148. Village corporation address:

Hee-Yea-Lingde Corp., General Delivery, Grayling, AK 99590, phone 453-5133 or 5126.

Holy Cross

Located on the west bank of Ghost Creek Slough (on Walker Slough), off the Yukon River, 34 miles southeast of Anvik and 420 miles southwest of Fairbanks. **Population:** 296. **Zip code:** 99602. **Emergency Services:** Alaska State Troopers, phone 476-7127; Clinic, phone 476-7174; Volunteer Fire Department.

Elevation: 150 feet. **Climate:** Summer temperatures average 70° to 80°F; winter temperatures -50° to 50°F. Annual precipitation averages 18.97 inches, with snowfall averaging 79.4 inches a year.

Private Aircraft: Runway 1 mile south; elev. 61 feet; length 4,000 feet; gravel; fuel 80, 100; unattended. Runway condition not monitored, visual inspection recommended prior to use.

Visitor Facilities: Accommodation and meals available at a local lodge. Groceries, limited clothing and hardware items, first-aid supplies and camera film available in the community. Arts and crafts include beaded jewelry and skin-sewn items such as mukluks, mittens and hats. Fishing/hunting licenses available. No guide service, banking services, moorage facilities or rental transportation. Fuel available is propane and regular gasoline.

Holy Cross first had contact with Europeans in the early 1840s when Russian explorers led by Lieutenant Zagoskin sighted the village which they called Anilukhtakpak. Population increased with establishment of a Jesuit mission and school in 1886. The founder of the mission was Father Aloysius Robaut who came to Alaska across the Chilkoot Trail.

The village was incorporated in 1968 as a second-class city. The economy is seasonal with its peak in the summer fishing season. Community and construction employment is supplemented by subsistence hunting, fishing and gardening.

Communications include phones, mail plane and TV. The community has a Catholic church and a school with grades kindergarten through 12. Public electricity, water and sewage systems available. Most residents have flush toilets, some use honey buckets. Freight arrives by air transport and barge. Village bans the sale and importation of alcoholic beverages. Government address: City of Holy Cross, P.O. Box 203, Holy Cross, AK 99602; phone 476-7139. Village corporation address: Deloycheet Inc., P.O. Box 53, Holy Cross, AK 99602, phone 476-7177.

Hughes

Located on the Koyukuk River, 120 miles northeast of Galena, 215 miles northwest of Fairbanks. **Transportation:** Scheduled air service from Galena; accessible by boat; trails to Allakaket, Alatna, Huslia and Indian Mountain. **Population:** 80. **Zip code:** 99745. **Emergency Services:** Alaska State Troopers in Galena, phone 656-1233; Clinic, phone 889-2206; Volunteer Fire Department.

Elevation: 550 feet. **Climate:** Fair weather in the summer, with both hot, sunny days and rainy, cool days. It can get windy here since the community is in a valley surrounded by rolling hills and mountains. Mean temperature in July is 60°F; in January -10°F. August is the wettest month with 2.48 inches of precipitation. Mean snow and sleet in January is 6.6 inches.

Private Aircraft: Airstrip 0.9 mile southwest; elev. 289 feet; length 4,000 feet; gravel; runway condition not monitored.

Visitor Facilities: Lodging at the School ($20 per night) or visitors may arrange with local residents to stay in private homes for a fee. Meals, laundry and banking services are not available. Supplies may be purchased in the community. Native beadwork and sometimes snowshoes, baskets and baby sleds may be available for purchase. If you can catch Alfred S. Attla, Sr., in town, you can purchase a fishing/hunting license from him; if he's not around, the nearest outlet is the Alaska Dept. of Fish and Game office in Galena. No major repair services are available, but visitors can rent the town pickup or local 3-wheelers, autos or boats. Regular gasoline, diesel and propane are available. Public moorage on the riverbank.

Some of the older citizens here remember when Hughes was a riverboat landing and supply point for gold mining camps in the nearby mountains about 1910. It was named for Charles Evans Hughes (1862-1948), then governor of New York. The store remained here and Hughes became a Koyukon Indian village. The post office was re-established in 1942 and the city was incorporated in 1973. There are about 27 military personnel stationed at Indian Mountain Air Force Station, 15 miles east of Hughes. Employment in Hughes is in local services with seasonal firefighting and trapping. There is fishing for grayling, chum, sheefish and salmon.

Communications include phones, mail plane, radio and TV. An Episcopal church is here and a school with grades kindergarten through 8. There are municipal water and electric services; sewage is individual septic tanks or honey buckets. Freight arrives by cargo plane or barge. Government address: City of Hughes, P.O. Box 45010, Hughes, AK 99745; phone 889-2206.

Huslia

(HOOS-lee-a) Located on the Koyukuk River, 70 miles north of Galena, 250 miles north west of Fairbanks. **Transportation:** Scheduled air service from Galena; accessible by boat. **Population:** 258. **Zip code:** 99746. **Emergency Services:** Alaska State Troopers, phone 656-1233; Health Clinic, phone 829-2204; Volunteer Fire Department.

Elevation: 180 feet. **Climate:** Conditions at Huslia are similar to those of Galena with cold winters, hot summers and generally low precipitation. In June and July, the average maximum temperature is in the lower 70s. During the winter months below zero temperatures are common. Local residents report a record low of -65°F and a record high of above 90°F. Most precipitation occurs between July and September with a total annual precipitation of only 13 inches. Annual snowfall is about 70 inches and generally persists from October through April.

Private Aircraft: Airstrip 1 mile northeast; elev. 180 feet; length 3,000 feet; gravel. Runway condition not monitored, no facilities.

Visitor Facilities: No accommodations or meals, though arrangements can be made to stay in private homes or on the school floor. Most supplies available in the community. There is a laundromat but no bank. Beadwork, knitted gloves and other arts and crafts may be purchased. No local guides; fishing/hunting licenses not available. There is no major repair service and no rental transportation available. Diesel, propane and regular gasoline are available.

Huslia was originally settled in the late 1940s by Koyukon Indians from Cutoff trading post. The community takes its name from a nearby stream. Huslia was incorporated in 1969. Employment here includes seasonal fire-fighting, construction and trapping, along with positions at the school, church and in local government. Many local residents spend the summer at fish camps. Other summer activities include softball, berry-picking, camping and gardening.

Communications include phones, mail plane and TV. There are Catholic and Episcopal churches and a school with grades 1 through 12. The community has water, sewage and electrical systems as well as privies. Huslia bans the sale of alcoholic beverages. Freight arrives by barge and cargo plane. Government address: City of Huslia, P.O. Box 10, Huslia, AK 99746; phone 829-2256.

Kaltag

Located on the Yukon River, 90 miles southwest of Galena, 330 miles west of Fairbanks. **Transportation:** Scheduled air service from Galena; trails to Nulato and Galena; accessible by boat. **Population:** 295. **Zip code:** 99748. **Emergency Services:** Alaska State Troopers in Galena, phone 656-1233; Clinic, phone 534-2209; Volunteer Fire Department, phone 534-2254; Search and Rescue Team, phone 534-9221.

Elevation: 200 feet. **Climate:** Warm summers with high temperatures in the 70s. Rainiest months are August and September. Winters are cold with average temperatures of -20°F and lows of -60°F. A resident reports up to 6 feet of snow accumulates in winter.

Private Aircraft: Airstrip 0.25 mile from village; elev. 200 feet; length 3,200 feet; gravel; unattended. Runway condition not monitored; recommend visual inspection prior to use.

Visitor Facilities: No formal accommodations or restaurants. Some supplies available in the community. Marine gas, diesel, propane, kerosene and regular gasoline are available. No other services available.

This is an Indian village called Kaltag by the Russians. An 1880 census listed a Lower Kaltag and Upper Kaltag here. The present village is believed to be the former Upper Kaltag, while Lower Kaltag is now referred to as the Old Kaltag site. Kaltag was incorporated in 1969.

As a resident puts it: "The people still rely on subsistence for their living. They fish during the summer (for salmon and grayling) and stay out at fish camps; they sell the fish or put some away for the winter; they also go hunting for moose, bear and other animals for food. They set traps in the winter for animals such as marten, rabbits or beaver. They sell the fur or make clothing out of it for themselves. The people mostly make a living for themselves and raise their families."

There is a Catholic church and a school with grades kindergarten through 12. There is also a community water and sewer system, although some homes still haul water and have privies. A generator provides the community's power. Freight is shipped in by plane or barge. Government address: City of Kaltag, General Delivery, Kaltag, AK 99748; phone 534-2230.

Koyukuk

Located at the confluence of the Koyukuk and Yukon rivers, 30 miles northwest of Galena, 300 miles west of Fairbanks. **Transportation:** Scheduled air service from Galena; accessible by boat. **Population:** 131. **Zip code:** 99754. **Emergency Services:** Public Safety Officer, phone 927-2214; State Troopers in Galena; Clinic, Volunteer Fire Department.

Elevation: 115 feet. **Climate:** Described as typical of interior Alaska, with warm summers, and cold, dry winters, with a temperature range of -60°F to 90°F.

Private Aircraft: Airstrip adjacent west of village; elev. 115 feet; length 2,600 feet; gravel; unattended; no facilities.

Visitor Facilities: No formal accommodations or restaurants. Visitors may arrange to stay in private homes or at the school, phone 656-1201. There are showers and a laundromat at the community watering facility. Some supplies available in the community. Arts and crafts include beadwork, marten hats, moose skin gloves and sleds. Fishing/hunting licenses may be purchased in the village. Propane and gasoline are available.

Originally a Koyukukhotana Indian village, a trading post was established here in the late 1800s. The village served the growing number of miners in the area and the increasing river traffic. Today, people here make a living as trappers and fishermen; in seasonal construction or in local clerical and maintenance jobs; or they commute to larger communities for work. Fishing for salmon in the Yukon and Koyukuk rivers is done both commercially and for subsistence, and local summer fish camps are active. Local people do occasional guiding, but visitors should be well prepared with equipment and supplies since none are available locally. Moose hunting is good in the fall and black bear are prevalent.

Communications include mail plane, phones, radio and TV. Freight arrives by plane or by barge. Koyukuk has a school (grades kindergarten through 10), a public library, recreation center, a community generator and a safe-water plant. Sewage system is private privies. Government address: City of Koyukuk, Box 49, Koyukuk, AK 99754; phone 927-2215.

Lake Minchumina

(*min-CHEW-min-a*) Located on the northwest shore of Lake Minchumina, 205 miles northwest of Anchorage, 150 miles southwest of Fairbanks. **Transportation:** Scheduled air service from Fairbanks. **Population:** about 30. **Zip code:** 99757. **Emergency Services:** Alaska State Troopers in Fairbanks; trained rescue group, no phone.

Elevation: 640 feet. **Climate:** Summers are cool and wet with a monthly mean temperature in July of 59°F. June is the driest summer month with 1.7 inches of precipitation. Winters are cold with moderate snowfall; monthly mean temperature in January is -6°F, mean snow/sleet for January is 9.5 inches.

Private Aircraft: Airstrip adjacent southeast; elev. 684 feet; length 4,100 feet; gravel; unattended; no facilities.

Visitor Facilities: Accommodations at 1 lodge. Groceries available from 1 store that opens 1 day a week and upon request. Originally a Tanana Indian village until a flu epidemic wiped it out early this century, Lake Minchumina saw further settlement with construction of the airstrip in 1941. The lake yields some pike. There is no central utility or sewage system here. Water is hauled from the lake or obtained from wells. Communication is through a single public phone booth at the lodge (939-4000). Freight is delivered by small plane.

Manley Hot Springs

Located at Mile 152 Elliott Highway, 90 miles west of Fairbanks. **Transportation:** Scheduled and charter air service from Fairbanks; road via the Elliott Highway. **Population:** 88. **Zip Code:** 99756.

Elevation: 330. **Climate:** Mean monthly temperature in July is 59°F; in January, -10°F. Snow from October through April, with traces in September and May.

Private Aircraft: Airstrip adjacent southwest; elev. 270 feet; length 2,500 feet; gravel; fuel 80, 100; unattended. Runway condition not monitored, visual inspection recommended prior to using.

Visitor facilities: Meals and overnight accommodations are available, as are groceries, gas, arts and crafts, post office, laundromat, showers and boat rentals. There is a public campground; fee is $2 per night. The hot springs are a short walk from the campground. Manley Hot Springs Slough offers good pike fishing, May through September.

Once a busy trading center for nearby Eureka and Tofty mining districts, today Manley Hot Springs is a quiet settlement. For more information see *The MILEPOST®*, a complete guide to communities on Alaska's road and marine highway systems. To order, see the ALASKA NORTHWEST LIBRARY section at the back of the book.

McGrath

Located on the Upper Kuskokwim River opposite the junction with the Takotna River, 220 miles northwest of Anchorage, 250 miles northeast of Bethel, and 280 miles southwest of Fairbanks. **Transportation:** Scheduled air service from Anchorage and Yukon River communities; on-demand air charter service to outlying communities; river travel May to October. **Population:** 535. **Zip code:** 99627. **Emergency Services:** Public Safety Officer, phone 524-3075; Fish and Wildlife Protection, phone 524-3222; Clinics, phone 524-3299 or 524-3104; Emergency Fire and Medical, phone 911.

Elevation: 337 feet. **Climate:** Average daily maximum temperatures in summer in the upper 60s, with highs in the 80s; minimum winter temperatures below zero, with lows to -60°F. More than 40 percent of the normal annual precipitation occurs between July and September. Comparatively low precipitation in winter, with accumulated snowfall averaging 86 inches.

Private Aircraft: Airport adjacent west; elev. 337 feet; length 5,400 feet; asphalt; fuel 80, 100, A1+. All facilities including flight service station and passenger and freight terminals. McGrath seaplane base on the Kuskokwim River east of east/west taxiway; fuel 80, 100.

Visitor Facilities: Overnight accommodations and meals available. There are also groceries, hardware, gas and other supplies. Limited arts and crafts available for purchase include birch-bark baskets, carvings and fur items. There are no banking services here. The laundromat has shower facilities. Fishing/hunting licenses are available, as well as local guides/outfitters. All types of fuel (marine, diesel, propane, etc.) and major repair services are available, as well as charter aircraft. Boats and off-road vehicles may be rented from private individuals.

Prospecting in the upper Kuskokwim and Innoko River valleys in the late 1800s brought increasing numbers of non-Native people into the area. In the spring of 1907, Peter McGrath, U.S. Commissioner sent from Nome, established a trading post and recording office at Old McGrath (across the Kuskokwim River from current site). Strikes on Ganes Creek and other Innoko Valley streams in 1906, and on Otter Creek and adjacent streams in 1908, made McGrath's location strategic as a supply point. Today it continues to serve as a supply point for a number of active gold mines in the area. The town relocated to its current location on the left bank of the Kuskokwim River in 1938. In February 1924, McGrath became the first Alaska town to receive mail by air, delivered by pioneer aviator Carl Ben Eielson. An Army base was located in McGrath from 1942 to 1943, and the new runway was an alternate stop for fueling lend-lease aircraft during WWII. Since early days, McGrath has been a transportation and supply center for the region. The city was incorporated in 1975. The majority of employment is in government jobs, the school district and local services. Many residents also rely on subsistence activities, including fishing, hunting, vegetable gardening and harvesting berries and timber for food and fuel.

Forty homestead parcels opened by the state a few miles out of town brought a few new residents to McGrath; but largely the disposal program accorded McGrath residents the opportunity to own a tract of land (up to 40 acres) and build "get-away" cabins, increasing their own recreational opportunities.

The oldest celebration in McGrath is held on the Fourth of July with floats, a parade, a huge potluck picnic and games for all ages. The annual KSKO Music Festival is held in mid-July and the McGrath State Fair is in late August. The Iditarod Trail Sled Dog Race takes mushers through McGrath each year, and dog mushing is a major winter activity in the area. The Upper Kuskokwim Mushers Assoc. sponsors many local races for all age groups.

Communications include phone, daily mail, public radio station KSKO and cable TV. Public services include the McGrath Community Library, 4 Rivers Counseling Service, the Upper Kuskokwim Mushers Assoc., McGrath Native Village Council, Tanana Chiefs Conference subregional office, Tochak Historical Society, University of Alaska Cooperative Extension Service and the Kuskokwim Valley Rescue Squad. There are 4 churches: McGrath Christian Fellowship, St. Michael Catholic Church, McGrath Community Church and Spiritual Assembly of Baha'is. School includes grades preschool through 12 and postsecondary classes are available through the University of Alaska Rural Education Center. Homes are heated with wood or oil stoves. Most homes have individual cesspools (FAA and the Dept. of Natural Resources have their own sewage treatment plants) and a city owned/maintained piped water system is utilized by most homes. Electrical power is generated by McGrath Light and Power. Barge service from Bethel delivers fuel products, heavy equipment and building materials. Other freight arrives by air. Government address: City of

McGrath, P.O. Box 30, McGrath, AK 99627; phone 524-3825. McGrath Native Village Council address: P.O. Box 134, McGrath, AK 99627; phone 524-3024.

Medfra

Located on the Kuskokwim River 30 miles east northeast of McGrath, 210 miles northweat of Anchorage. **Transportation:** Charter air service only. **Population:** 1 year-round resident. Population doubles in summer. **Zip code:** 99627. No Emergency services.

Elevation: 435 feet. **Climate:** Weather conditions are similar to those found in McGrath with warm summers and cold winters with relatively low precipitation.

Private Aircraft: Airstrip adjacent west; elev. 435 feet; length 2,200 feet; turf; unattended. No winter maintenance or snow removal. Runway is soft during spring thaw and the north end is potholed.

Visitor facilities: None.

Perhaps a native camp site originally, modern-day Medfra began when F.C.H. Spencer operated a trading post here in the early 1900s. Travelers to the 1917 gold strike on Nixon Fork of the Takotna River found that the easier route was along the Kuskokwim River to a landing near the site of Medfra, then overland to the gold fields.

Arthur Berry bought out Spencer and for a time the site was known as Berrys Landing. By 1920 Berrys Landing had become an important transfer point for upper Kuskokwim area gold fields. In 1922 a post office was established and the settlement renamed, perhaps after an early settler. Arthur Berry operated a fur farm in the area and ran the store until 1937 when he sold it to Clint W. Winans who kept the store going until he died in 1958. Winan's widow, Bertha, operated the store until 1963 when she turned it over to Jack Smith who continued operations until sometime in the late 1970s or early 1980s when a store opened in Nikolai.

Minto

Located on the Tolovana River, 11 miles from the Elliott Highway on the Minto Road, adjacent to the newly created Minto Flats State Game Refuge, 35 miles west of Fairbanks. **Transportation:** Auto or charter air from Fairbanks. **Population:** 233. **Zip Code:** 99758.

Elevation: 460 feet. **Climate:** Temperatures range from 55° to 90°F in summer and from 32° to -50°F in winter. Snow from October through April with traces in September and May.

Private aircraft: Airstrip 1 mile east of village; elev. 460 feet; length 2,000 feet; gravel; unattended. Runway condition not monitored, recommend visual inspection prior to using. A hump is in the middle of the runway with a grade of 2 percent down in each direction.

Visitor facilities: Accommodations, meals available at 1 local lodge. Also a general store and crafts available at the senior center.

The Athabascan Indian village was moved to its present location from the east bank of the Tanana River in 1971 because of flooding. The original site, Old Minto was established in 1915. Minto is a major access point for the newly created Minto Flats State Game Refuge, a popular duck hunting area. Most residents make their living by hunting and fishing. Some local people also work making birch-bark baskets and beaded skin and fur items. Minto bans the sale and importation of alcoholic beverages. Government address: Minto Village Council, P.O. Box 26, Minto, AK 99758; phone 798-7112. For more information see *The MILEPOST®*, a complete guide to communities on Alaska's road and marine highway systems. To order, see the ALASKA NORTHWEST LIBRARY section at the back of the book.

Nikolai

Located 40 miles northeast of McGrath, 195 miles northwest of Anchorage. **Transportation:** Scheduled air service from McGrath and Anchorage; charter air service based in McGrath; winter trails to McGrath, Medfra and Telida; accessible by river (May to October). **Population:** 119. **Zip code:** 99691. **Emergency Services:** Clinic, phone 293-2328; other services in McGrath.

Elevation: 450 feet. **Climate:** Mean monthly temperature in July is 54°F; in January, -15°F. More than half of the normal annual precipitation occurs between July and September. Relatively low snowfall in winter.

Private Aircraft: Airstrip adjacent northwest; elev. 450 feet; length 2,500 feet; dirt and gravel; unattended.

Visitor Facilities: A city-owned hotel/apartment building provides limited accommodations for visitors. A coffee shop in the community center serves breakfast and lunch. A laundromat is also located in the community center. There are no banking facilities. All supplies available at the general store. Arts and crafts, such as snowshoes, moccasins, slippers and beaded items may be available for purchase locally. Fishing/hunting licenses may be purchased in the village and there is a local guide. Villagers use 3-wheelers, snow machines and dog teams for transportation. Gasoline is available; no major repair service.

Like other communities in this region, Nikolai was an Athabascan Indian village in the late 1800s and has been relocated since its original settlement. A trading post and roadhouse here served miners during the Innoko gold rush. Nikolai was incorporated as a second-class city in 1970.

Heavily dependent on subsistence, Nikolai residents rely on hunting (moose, caribou, rabbits, ptarmigan and waterfowl) and fishing (king, chum and coho salmon, whitefish, sheefish and grayling). Some residents spend the summer at Medfra at fish camps. There is also trapping and vegetable gardening. Seasonal construction and firefighting offers some employment.

Communications include phones, mail plane, TV and radio, with most residents tuned to McGrath's KSKO radio station. There is a school with grades preschool through 12, housed in a building completed in 1983. The Russian Orthodox church here was built in 1927. A large community building houses the post office, clinic, a laundromat and showers, library, poolroom, coffee shop and city offices. The city provides electricity and cable TV to Nikolai residences and home heating is with wood stoves. While some homes, the school, hotel and store have indoor plumbing and running water, most residents haul water from private wells or the community center. Sewage system is primarily outdoor privies. Fuel and heavy equipment are delivered by barge; other freight is delivered by plane. Government address: City of Nikolai, P.O. Box 25, Nikolai, AK 99691; phone 293-2113.

Northway

Located 7 miles south of the Alaska Highway within the Tetlin National Wildlife Refuge, about 100 miles west of the Canadian border. **Transportation:** Auto via side road from Alaska Highway 256 miles southeast of Fairbanks; charter air service from Fairbanks, Gulkana. **Population:** est. 360 in area. **Zip code:** 99764. **Emergency Services:** Alaska State Troopers, phone 778-2245; Emergency Medical Service, phone 778-2211; Fire Department.

Climate: Mean monthly temperature in July, 55°F; in January, -21°F.

Private Aircraft: Northway airport, adjacent south; elev. 1,716 feet; length 5,147 feet; asphalt; fuel 80, 100, jet; customs available; FAA station.

Visitor Facilities: Motels, groceries, liquor store, bar, propane, gas stations, air taxi service. Hardware, camera film, fishing/hunting

licenses available. Wide range of Athabascan Indian crafts including beadwork, birch-bark baskets, moose hide and fur items such as moccasins, mukluks, mittens and hats.

Historically occupied by Athabascan Indians, Northway was named to honor the village chief who adopted the name of a riverboat captain in the early 1900s. The rich Athabascan tradition of dancing, crafts, and hunting and trapping continue in Northway today. The community has a community hall, post office and modern school.

Northway's airport was built in the 1940s as part of the Northwest Staging Route. This cooperative project of the U.S. and Canada was a chain of air bases from Edmonton, AB, through Whitehorse, YT, to Fairbanks. This chain of air bases helped build up and supply Alaska defense during WWII and also was used during construction of the Alcan and the Canol project. Lend-lease aircraft bound for Russia were flown up this route. Northway is still an important port of entry for air traffic to Alaska, and a busy one.

For more about Northway, see *The MILE-POST®*, a complete guide to communities on Alaska's road and marine highway systems. To order, see the ALASKA NORTHWEST LIBRARY section at the back of the book.

Nulato

Located on the Yukon River, 25 miles west of Galena, 310 miles west of Fairbanks. **Transportation:** Scheduled air service; local air charter; accessible by boat. **Population:** 378. **Zip code:** 99765. **Emergency Services:** Public Safety Officer, phone 898-2240; Clinic, phone 898-2209; Volunteer Fire Department.

Elevation: 510 feet. **Climate:** Mean monthly temperature in July, 57°F; in January, -6°F. The greatest mean precipitation occurs in August, with 2.81 inches.

Private Aircraft: Airstrip 1 mile northeast; elev. 310 feet; length 2,500 feet; gravel; unattended; no facilities.

Visitor Facilities: No formal overnight accommodations or restaurants, but there is a small lodge with 3 beds, kitchenette and privy; water must be hauled. Arrangements can be made by calling 898-2205. Some supplies available in the community. There is a laundromat with showers at the safe-water facility. Fishing/hunting licenses are available, but there are no registered guides (ask local people about fishing). Diesel, propane and gasoline are available, and visitors may be able to rent boats and autos from area residents. Charter aircraft is available. There are no major repair services.

Nulato is the site of one of the most chronicled events in Alaskan history, the murder of Lt. John J. Barnard by Koyukuk Indians in 1851. Barnard came to Alaska as part of the British search party sent after Sir John Franklin. While Barnard was staying with the agent in charge of the Russian-American Co.'s post at Nulato, the Koyukon Indians attacked the Russian fort, killing both Barnard and the Russian (Darabin), and the Indian village below the fort, killing 53 inhabitants. Various reasons have been given for the Nulato massacre, among them the traditional rivalry of the Lower Koyukon and Upper Koyukon, a possible insult by the British lieutenant of the Koyukon shaman, or the assumed challenge by the British to the Koyukuk trade monopoly. Barnard's gravesite is about 0.5 mile downriver from present-day Nulato. The village was incorporated as a second-class city in 1963.

Communications include phones, mail plane and TV. The 12-classroom school has grades kindergarten through 12. There is electric service. Water is hauled from the river or available through the village safe-water facility. Sewage system is honey buckets. Freight arrives by barge or plane. Government address: Nulato City Council, P.O. Box 65009, Nulato, AK 99765; phone 898-2205.

Rampart

Located on the Yukon River, 61 miles northeast of Tanana, 85 miles northwest of Fairbanks. **Transportation:** Scheduled air service from Fairbanks; charter air service; river travel except during breakup and freezeup. **Population:** 49. **Zip code:** 99767. **Emergency Services:** Clinic, phone 358-3219; Volunteer Fire Department.

Elevation: 380 feet. **Climate:** Cold in winter and warm in summer. Mean monthly temperature in January, -11°F; in July 57°F.

Private Aircraft: Airstrip 2 miles east; elev. 275 feet; length, 3,000 feet; gravel; no fuel; unattended. Inspection recommended prior to using. Frequent crosswinds at both ends; no line of sight between runway ends.

Visitor Facilities: No accommodations or meals available. Some supplies available in the community. Local arts and crafts include marten hats and slippers. The village does not have a laundromat, banking services, rental transportation or any repair facilities. Regular gasoline, marine gas, diesel and propane are available. Fishing/hunting licenses may be purchased here, but there are no guides.

Originally an Indian village, the community grew with the influx of miners following the 1896 gold discovery on Minook Creek. Today, Rampart is an unincorporated Athabascan village where some residents trap and fish for a living. There are still gold mines in the area. Employment also includes commercial fishing and fish processing. Residents fish for salmon in the summer. Rampart's location also makes it a good stop for anyone traveling the Yukon River, although one resident warns that there are many bears in the area.

Communications include some private phones, mail plane, radio and TV. Rampart has a school with grades preschool through 12. Generators provide electrical service, but water is hauled from the Yukon River or the school well. The sewage system is outhouses. Freight arrives via cargo plane and barge. Tribal government address: Rampart Traditional Council, General Delivery, Rampart, AK 99767. Village corporation address: Baan o yeel Kon Corp., P.O. Box 74558, Fairbanks, AK 99707; phone 456-6259.

Ruby

Located on the Yukon River, 50 miles east of Galena, 220 miles west of Fairbanks. **Transportation:** Scheduled air service; river travel except during breakup and freezeup; dogsled, snow machine or skis in winter. **Population:** 248. **Zip code:** 99768. **Emergency Services:** Public Safety Officer, phone 468-4460; Fire station, phone 468-4412; Clinic, phone 468-4433.

Elevation: 710 feet. **Climate:** Fair in summer with temperatures to 80°F, lows in winter to -50°F. The mean monthly temperature in January is -2°F; in July it is 58°F.

Private Aircraft: Airstrip 1 mile southeast of community; elev. 635 feet; length, 3,000 feet; gravel. No facilities. Transportation to town available.

Visitor Facilities: Accommodations and meals at 1 roadhouse. Groceries, clothing, first-aid supplies, hardware and film available in the community. No banking services available. There is a laundromat and most types of fuel are available. Automobiles may be rented and there are charter aircraft, but no major repair services available. Fishing/hunting licenses are available as well as guide service. Public moorage available on river.

Gold was discovered on Ruby Creek near the present-day townsite in 1907, but the gold rush did not take place until 1911 with a second gold discovery on Long Creek. Part of the Ruby Roadhouse, which is on the National Register of Historic Places, dates from 1911. Today's residents make their living by commercial fishing, subsistence fishing, hunting, trapping (marten, beaver, mink, fox, wolf), logging, or working for the school, city or private businesses. There are some summer jobs in construction and at the sawmill.

Recreation for residents in summer includes swimming, waterskiing or fishing in clear pools on the Melozi River. In winter there are races by dogsled, snowshoe, snow machine or skis. Ruby is also a checkpoint for the annual Iditarod Trail Sled Dog Race in alternate years.

Communications include phones, mail plane and TV. Ruby has a Bible church and a Catholic church (St. Peter In Chains), a school with grades kindergarten through 12 and a library. There is a public electric power system and a community well. Individual residences have private wells and septic tanks or privies. Freight arrives by cargo plane and barge. Government address: City of Ruby, P.O. Box 15, Ruby, AK 99768; phone 468-4401. Village corporation address: Dineega Corp., P.O. Box 28, Ruby, AK 99768; phone 468-4405.

Shageluk

(SHAG-a-luck) Located on the Innoko River, 20 miles east of Anvik, 34 miles northeast of Holy Cross, 330 miles west of Anchorage.

Transportation: Scheduled and charter air service from Bethel, Aniak, Grayling, Anvik and McGrath. **Population:** 167. **Zip code:** 99665. **Emergency Services:** Village Public Safety Officer, phone 473-0221; Clinic; Volunteer Fire Department.

Elevation: 70 feet. **Climate:** Continental. Temperatures range from -60°F to 87°F. Average annual precipitation 21 inches, with 110 inches of snow. Snowfall usually starts in October and ends in April.

Private Aircraft: Airstrip 1 mile north; elev. 70 feet; length 2,300 feet; gravel; no fuel; unattended. Runway condition not monitored, visual inspection recommended prior to using. Floods during breakup, may be soft after heavy rain. Transportation to village available for $5 per person per ride.

Visitor Facilities: Accommodations at an apartment at the school, phone 473-8232. There is a washeteria with showers. Supplies available in the community. Fuel available: gasoline, propane. Information on other visitor services and facilities unavailable.

Shageluk is an old Ingalik Indian village first reported in 1850 as Tie 'goshshitno, by Lt. L.A. Zagoskin of the Imperial Russian Navy. In 1861, P. Tikhmenien, considered to be the

Mary Lene Esmailka hangs salmon she has skillfully cut with her ulu knife. (Alissa Crandall)

chief historian of the Russian-American Co., noted 6 villages. These were collectively called the Chageluk settlements in the 1880 census. Shageluk became one of the permanent communities in the area, however, the village was relocated to its present location in the mid-1960s because of flooding. Shageluk, which is located about 10 miles south of Innoko National Wildlife Refuge, was incorporated as a second-class city in 1970.

About half of the buildings in Shageluk are built of logs, including a 6-sided *kashim,* a structure used for traditional social gatherings.

Although many residents own snow machines, dog teams are popular in Shageluk and every other year the village is a checkpoint on the 1,049-mile Iditarod Trail Sled Dog Race from Anchorage to Nome. There also are trails connecting Shageluk with Anvik and Grayling.

There are a few full-time jobs with the school, city, clinic, post office, store or village corporation and some seasonal construction work on public projects or firefighting. This income is supplemented by subsistence activities. Residents hunt moose, black bear, small game and waterfowl; and fish for salmon, whitefish, sheefish and pike. They also trap and sell the pelts of beaver, marten, mink, fox, otter, wolverine, lynx and muskrat. Some families also grow potatoes, cabbage, onions, carrots, turnips and lettuce.

Communications in Shageluk include phones, commercial radio and TV via satellite. The community is served by St. Luke's Episcopal Church and a school with grades kindergarten through 12. There is a community electricity system. Water is hauled from the washeteria, rain water is collected in summer and fall, and ice blocks are cut in winter. Sewage system is outhouses or honey buckets. Shageluk prohibits the sale and importation of alcoholic beverages. Freight arrives by barge several times each summer or by mail plane. Government address: City of Shageluk, General Delivery, Shageluk, AK 99665; phone 473-8221. Village corporation address: Zho-Tse Inc., General Delivery, Shageluk, AK 99665.

Stevens Village

Located on the Yukon River, 90 miles north of Fairbanks. **Transportation:** Scheduled air service from Fairbanks; river travel except during breakup and freezeup. **Population:** 94. **Zip code:** 99774. **Emergency Services:** Alaska State Troopers in Fairbanks; Clinic with health aides; Volunteer Fire Department. **Elevation:** 310 feet.

Private Aircraft: Airstrip adjacent north; elev. 310 feet; length, 2,000 feet; gravel; unattended. Runway condition not monitored, visual inspection recommended prior to using. Prevailing winds from west and southwest.

Visitor Facilities: No accommodations or restaurants. Visitors may arrange with villagers to stay in private homes. There is a laundromat with showers. Supplies are available in the community. Marine gas and regular gasoline are available. Visitors may arrange to rent boats and boat repair is available. There are no banking services.

According to local tradition, this Indian village was founded by 3 brothers: Old Jacob, Gochonayeeya and Old Steven. When Old Steven was elected chief in 1902, the village was named for him.

Stevens Village is unincorporated. People here today make their living working in the post office or store, the Native corporation clinic, in maintenance, or at the school. Villagers also do some trapping and spend summers at fish camp.

There are 2 churches: Assembly of God and Episcopal. Stevens Village School has grades preschool through 12. There is a community power supply and safe-water supply. Sewage system is privies. There is a mail plane and a phone at the village school. Freight comes in by plane or barge. Stevens Village bans the sale and importation of alcoholic beverages. Government address: Stevens Village IRA Council, General Delivery, Stevens Village, AK 99774. Village corporation address: Dinyea Corp., 544 9th Ave., Suite 107, Fairbanks, AK 99701; phone 456-2871.

Takotna

Located on the Takotna River, 17 miles west of McGrath, 230 miles northwest of Anchorage. **Transportation:** Scheduled passenger and mail plane from McGrath; charter plane; river travel June through September; snow machine and dogs. Takotna has more roads than most Interior communities. About 90 miles of road connect the community with Tatalina Air Force Station; Sterling Landing, on the Kuskokwim River, where the barge docks; Ophir, an old mining community with a few occupants in summer; and other mining areas. **Population:** 67. **Zip code:** 99675. **Emergency Services:** Alaska State Troopers in Bethel; Public Safety Officer in McGrath; Clinic with health aide, phone 298-2214; Volunteer Fire Department.

Elevation: 825 feet. **Climate:** With more than 40 percent of the normal precipitation occurring between July and September, summers are "more wet than dry" as one resident puts it. Average daily maximum temperatures during summer are in the upper 60s. Winters are drier and cold, with minimum temperatures to -60°F.

Private Aircraft: Village airstrip adjacent north; elev. 825 feet; length 2,000 feet; gravel; unattended.

Visitor Facilities: There are no formal lodges, but the community hall has beds for rent. Limited groceries are available in the community. There is a laundromat with showers. Marine gas and diesel are available. Meals, banking services, rental transportation and major repair service are not available.

Takotna started as a supply town for gold mines in the upper Innoko region. The town prospered through the 1930s, when gold mining in the region declined and McGrath replaced Takotna as the supply center. Nearby Tatalina Air Force Station was established in 1949. Community capital improvement projects have employed many village residents in construction during the summer, although as these projects slow down, some residents may have to go to Anchorage for summer work. Takotna is a checkpoint for the annual Iditarod Trail Sled Dog Race.

Most residents are involved in subsistence activities. Hunting for moose, the staple red meat, is fair. There is some duck hunting and local fishing for grayling, pike and trout. Local residents also grow vegetable gardens and harvest wild berries.

Communications include phones, mail plane, radio and TV. There are no churches. The new 2-classroom schoolhouse has grades preschool through 12. There is a community electricity system. Most residents heat their homes with wood stoves. Water is hauled from the PHS building or from a nearby stream (referred to locally as Takotna Waterworks). Some residents use indoor honey buckets, but most houses have indoor plumbing with wells; the community hall and PHS building are on septic tanks and have running water. Freight arrives by plane or by barge to Sterling Landing. Takotna is unincorporated and within the unorganized borough and therefore is without a regional government. Native residents of Takotna are shareholders in MTNT Ltd., P.O. Box 104, McGrath, AK 99627; phone 524-3391.

Tanana

(TAN-a-nah) Located near the confluence of the Yukon and Tanana rivers, 135 miles northwest of Fairbanks. **Transportation:** Scheduled air service from Fairbanks and local charter; river travel in summer; snow machine and dogs. **Population:** 414. **Zip code:** 99777. **Emergency Services:** City police, phone 366-7158; Clinic, phone 366-7223; Fire Department, phone 366-7158.

Elevation: 227 feet. **Climate:** Hot and dry in June and July, cooler in August, cold October through February. One resident says September (sunny and cool) and March and April (cold and sunny) are the best months.

Private Aircraft: Ralph M. Calhoun Memorial Airport, 1 mile west; elev. 227 feet; length 4,400 feet; gravel. Runway condition not monitored; visual inspection recommended before use. Restrooms at airstrip, transportation to town available.

Visitor Facilities: Meals and accommodations available. All supplies available in the community. Beadwork, parkas, mukluks, birch-bark baskets and other crafts may be purchased. Fishing/hunting licenses available. There are no banking services, but there is a laundromat. Charter aircraft are the only rental transportation available. Diesel, propane, unleaded and regular gasoline are available. Major marine engine repair available; minor repairs also available. Charter aircraft available to rent, and other vehicles may be rented from private individuals.

Tanana is located at a historic Indian trading locality known as Nuchalawoya, meaning "place where the 2 rivers meet." A Nuchalawoya Indian festival, with potlatch and contests, is held in Tanana every June. Arthur Harper established an Alaska Commercial Co. trading post here in 1880, and in 1891 the U.S. Army built Fort Gibbon (the fort was abandoned in 1923). Tanana was incorporated as a first-class city in 1961. Under restoration today is the wood plank Mission of Our Savior Church, which overlooks the Yukon and Tanana rivers. The church was part of an Episcopal mission established here in 1891 by Rev. J.L. Prevost.

Residents cite the mission, Indian festival and Tanana's sled dog races as some of its attractions. The Yukon River sled dog championships are held in early April, and several outfitters locally offer sled dog trips or freighting on ski trips in winter. In summer, the Yukon River is swimmable ("65°F and silty in July"), and fish wheels can be seen operating, especially in August and September. Boating is good throughout the area, and boat races are held over Labor Day weekend. There is canoeing on tributary streams. Tanana's residents make their living trapping and fishing and in government jobs.

Communications include phones, mail plane, radio and TV. There are 3 churches: St. Aloysius Catholic Church, St. James Episcopal Mission and Arctic Mission Bible Church. The school has grades kindergarten through 12. Tanana Power provides electricity to the city. Water is from community wells and the sewage system is both outhouses and flush toilets. Freight comes in by cargo plane and by barge. Government address: City of Tanana, P.O. Box 181, Tanana, AK 99777; phone 366-7159 or 7202. Village corporation address: Tozitna Native Corp., P.O. Box 202, Tanana, AK 99777; phone 366-7166 or 7255.

Telida

(Ta-LIE-da) Located 80 miles northeast of McGrath, 185 miles northwest of Anchorage. **Transportation:** Scheduled mail plane; charter plane; small riverboat; winter trail to Nikolai. **Population:** 32. **Zip code:** 99627. **Emergency Services:** Alaska State Troopers in McGrath, phone 524-3222; Clinic, phone 843-8126; Volunteer Fire Department.

Elevation: 650 feet. **Climate:** Average daily maximum temperatures in summer in the 60s, with occasional highs in the 80s. Minimum temperatures in winter below zero, with lows to -60°F. More than half the normal precipitation occurs between July and September.

Private Aircraft: Airstrip adjacent south; elev. 650 feet; length 1,100 feet; turf; unattended; no facilities. Some rough spots on runway.

Visitor Facilities: No meals or accommodations available. There are no stores; supplies are obtained from McGrath and Anchorage. Some beadwork is done in the village. Gasoline is available and boats may be rented, but there are no other visitor services.

This old Indian village has had 3 locations since white explorers first camped in the village in 1899. The village's second location, 4 or 5 miles upstream from present-day Telida, was abandoned and is now referred to as Old Telida. New Telida was settled by the Carl Sesvi family. The lifestyle here is heavily subsistence. Residents hunt moose, bear, waterfowl and small game; fish for whitefish, sheefish, chum salmon, grayling, pike and Dolly Varden; and trap fox, lynx, wolverine, beaver, muskrat, marten and mink. There is some vegetable gardening and families harvest wild berries in late summer and fall.

Communications in Telida, which is unincorporated, include phones, mail plane, radio and a TV set at the school. There is a Russian Orthodox church in the village and a 1-class-room schoolhouse with grades 1 through 4. The school also supplies the community's water. Electrification of the village was under way in 1985. The school has a self-contained sewer system; each Telida home has an outhouse. Freight comes in by plane. Tribal government address: Telida Traditional Council, General Delivery, Telida, AK 99627. Village corporation address: MTNT Ltd., P.O. Box 104, McGrath, AK 99627; phone 524-3391.

Venetie

(VEEN-e-tie) Located on the Chandalar River, 140 miles north of Fairbanks. **Transportation:** Scheduled air service from Fairbanks and Fort Yukon; winter trail from Arctic Village and Fort Yukon. **Population:** 208. **Zip code:** 99781. **Emergency Services:** Alaska State Troopers in Fort Yukon, phone 662-2509; Health aides.

Elevation: 620 feet. **Climate:** Mean monthly temperature in January, -18°F. Mean monthly temperature in July, 57°F. Greatest mean monthly precipitation is in August, with 1.5 inches.

Private Aircraft: Airstrip adjacent northeast; elev. 550 feet; length 4,100 feet; dirt and gravel; unattended. Runway soft and muddy after rain. Some dips in runway. NOTE: Airstrip is privately owned and landing fees may be assessed,

Visitor Facilities: No meals or overnight accommodations available. Some supplies available in the community.

An Indian village settled in 1900, Venetie is unincorporated and is part of the 1.8-million-acre Venetie Indian Reservation. Residents are employed in seasonal trapping and firefighting. Some year-round employment in the school and store. Venetie school, established in 1938, has grades preschool through 12. There is also an Episcopal church here. Electrical power is provided by a village generator. Homes are on septic tanks. Freight comes in by plane. Venetie is a dry village; the sale and importation of alcoholic beverages is prohibited. Tribal government address: Arctic Village-Venetie IRA Council, General Delivery, Arctic Village, AK 99722; phone 587-5129.

PLAN AHEAD

Be prepared — bring extra clothes and food in the event weather delays your return.

National and State Parks, Forests, etc.

Chena River State Recreation Area

This 254,080-acre recreation area straddles the Chena River, taking in the river valley and adjoining ridges, 30 miles east of Fairbanks between Mileposts 26 and 50.6 of Chena Hot Springs Road.

Accommodations: There are 2 developed campgrounds in the state recreation area. Rosehip Campground at Milepost 27 has 38 sites; Tors Trail Campground at Milepost 39.5 has 23 sites. Both campgrounds charge $5 per night for overnight camping and offer campsites that will accommodate large RVs and have tables, fireplaces and tent pads. Potable water, latrines and visitor information displays are provided.

Wildlife: The recreation area offers opportunities to view many species, including moose, beaver, snowshoe hare, red squirrel, weasel, mink, muskrat, porcupine and marten. Wolves, wolverines and lynx are present but rarely seen. Waterfowl and shorebirds can be seen along the river. Black bears are occasionally observed along the river during salmon migrations and in berry patches on hillsides in August and September. Grizzly bears periodically wander through the area as part of their territory. Hunting in the recreation area is allowed in season, except within 0.25 mile of a developed facility.

The Chena River arctic grayling fishery is the most popular in the state. Grayling can be caught from May to October on a variety of small flies and lures. If weather conditions or turbidity make river fishing unproductive there are several man-made ponds that have been stocked with grayling at Mileposts 30, 42.8, 45.5 and 47.8. The Chena also has a small run of king and chum salmon that migrate up from the Yukon and Tanana rivers in July and August. However, fishing for salmon upstream from the Chena flood control dam (which is well below the recreation area) is prohibited.

Activities: The recreation area offers a full range of outdoor activities associated with the river, adjacent spruce and birch forests, alpine ridges and historic trails. Summer activities include fishing, camping, hiking, floating, bicycling, berry picking, target shooting, hunting, ATV use, sightseeing and horseback riding. Winter activities include dog mushing, snowmobiling, snowshoeing, trapping, hunting and cross-country skiing. Several sleddog races cross the recreation area, including the Yukon Quest, and the Hiitto, a 33-mile (55-kilometer) Scandinavian style cross-country ski race, is held each spring.

The road paralleling the clear-water Chena River offers several access points for float trips. Popular launch sites are at Mileposts 48.9. 44.1, 39.5 and 37.7. Easy take-out points are Mileposts 44.1, 39.5, 37.7 and 27. Float times vary according to stream flow, type of craft and ability of the paddlers.

There are 3 established hiking trails and many backcountry routes for summer hiking along the river and on hillsides. Weather in this area is unpredictable; take suitable clothing for a range of conditions. Mosquitoes can be a nuisance, so bring repellant. Water sources on the trails are unreliable in dry weather; carry enough drinking water for the trip. Bears inhabit this area, so act accordingly: keep food containers sealed and away from your tent, and carry out all trash.

Granite Tors Trail begins at the campground at Milepost 39.5. The tors are monoliths of jointed granite jutting skyward to 100 feet. The trail is a 15-mile loop, with the closest group of tors 5.5 miles in on the trail. The upper portion of the trail is rocky and suitable footgear should be worn. A trail guide is available at the bulletin board in the campground. Related USGS Topographic map: Big Delta D-5.

Chena Dome Trail is a 29-mile loop beginning at Milepost 50.5, encircling the Angel Creek Valley, and ending at Milepost 49.1. The trail crosses Chena Dome at its highest point (4,421 feet), and offers high alpine scenic views not seen elsewhere in the recreation area. At each end of the loop a three-mile section of trail has been cut through the forest to treeline. The rest of the trail traverses tundra ridges marked by rock cairns and blanketed with wildflowers in late May, June and July. The loop provides a good 3- to 4-day trip for backpackers. Some portions of the trail are steep; wear suitable footgear. Additional information about this hike is available on bulletin boards at the trailheads. Related USGS Topographic maps: Big Delta D-5, Circle A-5 and A-6.

Angel Rocks Trail begins at Milepost 48.9 and is a short (3.5-mile), relatively easy hike. It is less than two miles to the spectacular rock outcropping. At the top, there are three alternatives: return on the same improved trail, continue up to the end of the tor formations for beautiful views of the Alaska Range, Chena Dome and Far Mountain, or continue on the loop trail that is currently under construction. Approximate hiking time is 3 to 4 hours. Related USGS Topographic maps: Big Delta D-5 and Circle A-5.

For additional information, contact Alaska State Parks, 3700 Airport Way, Fairbanks, AK 99709; phone 451-2695.

Chena River State Recreation Area Cabins

The Division of Parks and Outdoor Recreation maintains 5 public-use recreation cabins in the state recreation area that can be rented for up to 3 consecutive nights for $15 per night. Reservations can be made up to 180 days in advance; fees must be paid when reservations are submitted.

Access to each of the cabins varies. Some are located up to 6 miles from the road and are reached by snow machine, dogsled, cross-country skiing, hiking or by boat. A detailed map of the cabin's location is provided when reservations are made.

All cabins will accommodate at least 4 people. Each cabin is furnished with plywood sleeping platforms, a woodstove, table, benches, fire extinguisher, bow saw and ax. An outhouse is located nearby.

For more information or to reserve a cabin, contact Alaska State Parks, 3700 Air-port Way, Fairbanks, AK 99709: phone 451-2695.

Denali National Park and Preserve

This national park is located 120 miles south of Fairbanks and 240 miles north of Anchorage. The main attraction is the wildlife. Grizzly bear, caribou, moose and Dall sheep are seen frequently along the park road. A looming backdrop for this wildlife preserve is in Mt. McKinley, the tallest peak on the North American continent. The north summit reaches a height of 19,470 feet; the south, 20,320 feet.

The Athabascan Indians called McKinley *Denali* meaning "the high one," and in 1980 the name of the park itself was changed to Denali. That year, too, the park was enlarged from 1.9 million acres to its present 6 million acres to protect Mount McKinley on all sides and also to preserve the habitat of the many species of animals found in the area.

Other interesting features of the park are Wonder Lake, the Savage River Canyon, the Outer Range, Sanctuary River, Muldrow Glacier and the Kantishna Hills — all of which can be seen from a 90-mile road that traverses the park.

The Outer Range is located just north of the central Alaska Range and is composed of some of Alaska's oldest rocks, called Birch Creek Schist, which can be seen clearly in the Savage River canyon. The 22.5-mile-long Sanctuary River passes through the Outer Range between Mount Wright and Primrose Ridge. Caribou calving grounds are located near its headwaters. Muldrow Glacier, largest on the north side of the Alaska Range, flows for 32 miles and descends 16,000 feet from near Mount McKinley's summit.

Wonder Lake, 4 miles long and 280 feet deep, is a summer home for loons and grebes, as well as many migrating species, and also provides a wonderful reflection of Mount McKinley from Bald Knob. The Kantishna Hills were first mined in 1906, when the town of Eureka boomed with gold seekers. The area was included in the park in 1980.

Climate: Typical summer weather in the park is cool, wet and windy. Visitors should bring clothing for temperatures that range from 40° to 80°F. Rain gear, a light coat, sturdy walking shoes or boots and insect repellent are essential. Mount McKinley is clouded more often than not. (From June through August the chances of seeing the summit on any given day run about 35 percent to 40 percent.) Winter weather is cold and clear, with temperatures sometimes dropping to -50°F at park headquarters. In the lowlands, snow seldom accumulates to more than 3 feet.

There are more than 450 species of trees, shrubs and herbs growing in the taiga and tundra of Denali National Park and Preserve. The major species of the taiga are white spruce in dry areas and black spruce where it's wet, intermingled with aspen, paper birch, balsam poplar and tamarack. Wet tundra features willow and dwarf birch, often with horsetails, sedges and grasses along pothole ponds. Dry tundra covers the upper ridges and rocky slopes above the tree line from about 3,500 feet to 7,500 feet.

Wildlife: Denali Park is most famous for the high visibility of its wildlife. In the shadow of Mount McKinley live 37 species of mammals including caribou, grizzly bear, wolf, wolverine, moose, Dall sheep, red fox, lynx, ground squirrel, snowshoe hare and voles.

About 155 species of birds occur in the park. Year-round residents include the great horned owl, raven and the white-tailed, rock and willow ptarmigan. The majority, however, visit the park only during summer. Some of these are sandhill cranes, oldsquaws, sandpipers, plovers, gulls, buffleheads and goldeneyes. Sport fish in park waters includes lake trout and grayling.

Access: Denali National Park and Preserve can be reached by auto or bus from Anchorage or Fairbanks on the George Parks Highway; by the Alaska Railroad; or by small plane to an airstrip near park headquarters or to Lake Minchumina adjacent to the northwestern boundary of the preserve. The best time to visit the park is from late May to early September; the park is open year-round, but the road into the park is not plowed in winter.

Accommodations: Denali Park Hotel is the only hotel within the park boundaries; open May 19 to Sept. 16, reservations advised. Several hotels and campgrounds are located just outside the park. Food is available at a restaurant and snack shop at the hotel and also from a grocery store. Gasoline, oil, propane and air are available at a gas station near the hotel; 225 campsites are available at several campgrounds on a first-come basis. A backcountry permit is required for hiking and camping in the wilderness areas. Register for campsites and obtain backcountry permits at the Visitor Access Center, located 1 mile west of the George Parks Highway. Private vehicles are restricted on the Park Road past Savage River, 15 miles from the park entrance. Several campgrounds are accessible only by camper shuttle buses. There is a wildlife tour

bus operated by the park concession and also a free shuttle bus service between the park entrance and Wonder Lake that will pick up and drop off visitors anywhere along the way.

Admission fees are charged for anyone who travels beyond the Savage River Check Station. Fees are collected at the Visitor Access Center where tickets for shuttle buses are obtained.

Activities: Denali abounds with hiking opportunities. There are several established trails in the "front country" — the area near the park entrance — or hikers may travel along the Park Road or across the tundra. For the latter, it is necessary to check at the Visitor Access Center for information about backcountry areas which may be closed to hikers and also to register for any overnight stays. Camping gear should include a gasoline or propane stove because firewood is limited; a tent or waterproof shelter because of frequent rains; and rain gear. Water should be boiled or treated.

Other recreational activities include ice and rock climbing, photography and wildlife viewing, nature walks, slide programs, sled dog demonstrations, cross-country skiing, and bus and flightseeing tours.

For more information, contact Superintendent, Denali National Park and Preserve, P.O. Box 9, Denali Park, AK 99755; phone 683-2294. Related USGS Topographic maps: McKinley, Talkeetna, Healy.

Denali State Park

Located adjacent to the southern border of Denali National Park, this 324,420-acre park offers a spectacular view of nearby Mount McKinley and surrounding peaks and glaciers. The park is located between the Talkeetna Mountains and the Alaska Range and straddles the George Parks Highway, the main route between Anchorage and Fairbanks. Its landscape is dominated by Curry and Kesugi ridges, which form a rugged 30-mile spine down the length of the park. Small lakes dot these rock- and tundra-covered ridges; high points up to 3,500 feet overlook the heart of the Alaska Range. Mount McKinley's 20,320-foot summit, highest in North America, rises just 40 miles from Curry Ridge. The mountain and its companions, known as the McKinley Group, are accented by a year-round mantle of snow above 8,000 feet, spectacular glaciers and deep gorges. Other prominent peaks seen from Denali State Park viewpoints are Mounts Hunter and Silverthrone, the Moose's Tooth and the spires of the Tokosha Mountains. Valley glaciers, including Ruth, Buckskin and

CLIMBING MOUNT McKINLEY

Mount McKinley, North America's tallest peak, draws climbers each year who seek the challenges of the mountain's climate, terrain and altitude.

The peak's popularity is reflected in National Park Service (NPS) records, which show the number attempting to climb Mount McKinley has doubled in the last 10 years. Of the 13,269 climbers who have made the attempt since 1913, 7,576 have done so since 1978.

About half of all climbers reach the summit. Climbing experience and physical fitness are important factors for success, but climate extremes found on Mount McKinley have rebuffed even the most experienced and fit climbers. Weather was largely to blame for the low success rate of 1987 expeditions. Only 31 percent of the climbers reached the summit compared to 61 percent in 1988. The 1989 climbing season saw 974 tackle the mountain with fewer than half (461) reaching the summit. The year brought 6 deaths, half involving a British team in May, the other half a winter party of Japanese.

Experience: Safe glacier travel and self-rescue techniques, with skills in belaying partners on steep slopes and climbing in snow and ice are requirements for anyone climbing McKinley. Knowledge of winter camping techniques and familiarity with symptoms and treatment of acute mountain sickness are necessary. Unguided climbers must be able to plan and pack meals to maintain health in the unforgiving environment.

The NPS has licensed 7 companies to guide on Mount McKinley. Guides are trained in first aid and mountain rescue, have years of experience on the mountain, know the weather patterns, handle menu planning and provide group gear. Beginning or experienced climbers who do not have local knowledge are encouraged to hire a guide.

Training: Conditioning for the climb is crucial. A training program of several months with emphasizes aerobic fitness and upper-body strength is recommended.

Weather: Temperatures well below zero, winds gusting up to 100 mph, or sudden snowstorms can keep climbers tent-bound for days. Weather days are generally planned for but extended delays can force retreat.

No one month is considered perfect for climbing Mount McKinley. Most expeditions occur between April and July; May and June see the greatest activity. Few expeditions are launched during winter months. Ray Genet, Art Davidson and Dave Johnston made the first successful winter ascent in February and March, 1967. Vern Tejas made the first complete solo winter climb in March, 1988.

History: A 1910 expedition of pioneer Alaskans was the first to reach the North Peak of Mount McKinley (elev. 19,470 feet), after leaving Fairbanks in December 1909. Two of the 4-member party reached the North Peak on April 3, where they planted a 14-foot spruce flagpole. Their route took them to Muldrow Glacier and along Karstens Ridge to the summit.

A 4-man party led by the Rev. Hudson Stuck and Harry Karstens made the first successful ascent of the South Peak in 1913. This group also climbed up Muldrow Glacier and Karstens Ridge.

During their summit ascent, expedition members spotted the flagpole on the North Peak and thereby confirmed the success of the 1910 expedition. (NOTE: *Denali*, Vol. 15, No. 3 of ALASKA GEOGRAPHIC® provides accounts of these early climbs. To order see the ALASKA NORTHWEST LIBRARY section at the back of the book.)

There was much competition to be the first to reach McKinley's summit, but once that goal had been achieved 19 years passed before anyone else made the attempt. Much of the knowledge of the mountain and its routes is due to the explorations of Bradford Washburn. His expeditions in the 1940s and 1950s included several firsts. In 1947 Washburn's wife, Barbara, became the first woman on the summit, and in 1951 Washburn led the first successful expedition up the West Buttress.

Routes: The West Buttress route is the most popular way to the summit and usually takes 18 to 20 days. In 1987, 84 percent of all climbers used this route. Each year a few groups, taking about 4 weeks, tackle traverse expeditions that approximate the route of the Sourdoughs on Muldrow Glacier and Karstens Ridge. Other summit routes include the West Rib, Cassin Ridge, South Buttress, South Face, Northwest Buttress and East Buttress.

Information: The NPS offers excellent information for climbers. To request a copy, write the National Park Service, Denali National Park and Preserve, P.O. Box 9, Denali Park, AK 99755. Also check the BUYERS GUIDE section at the back of this book for a list of air taxis and guide services.

Eldridge, flow from these high peaks and feed the wide, braided Chulitna River.

The park is a relatively untouched wilderness: wildlife undisturbed by contact with man; a summer explosion of tundra plantlife; and constantly shifting channels of wide, glacier-fed streams.

The landscape is dominated by upland spruce-hardwood forests, especially along the highway, and by fragile alpine tundra above tree line at about 2,000 feet. Moist tundra occurs in some poorly drained areas and patches of dense birch, alder and willow thickets grow on hillsides. Black spruce grows in muskeg areas and large black cottonwoods inhabit riverbanks, particularly west of the Chulitna River. In late summer and early fall, berry pickers are rewarded with blueberries, highbush and lowbush cranberries, currants, watermelon berries, crowberries and cloudberries.

This park is large and mostly undeveloped. Accidents are infrequent, but dangers do exist, cautions the Alaska State Parks Division. Proper equipment and experience are essential for safe backcountry travel. Emergency aid is often far away. The parks division recommends that USGS topographic maps be used; but travelers can avoid getting lost by remembering that all drainages in the park and surrounding areas lead to the Chulitna River near the Parks Highway or the Susitna River along the Alaska Railroad.

Travelers should use caution when crossing rivers; glacial and snowmelt streams rise drastically between morning and midday. Glaciers and avalanche terrain should be avoided unless you are experienced and properly equipped. Do not travel alone in the backcountry, especially in winter. Leave an itinerary with a friend or at the visitor information log cabin at the Byers Lake campground and notify that person or office on your return.

Climate: Weather in the park is moderated by coastal waters 100 miles to the south near Anchorage. The Alaska Range shields the park from the extreme cold of the Interior to the north. Snow accumulations, beginning in October, build to 5 or 6 feet by March. Snow usually melts during April and May, although snow patches above 2,500 feet often last into July. Summer temperatures average 44° to 68°F, with occasional highs above 80°F. Midsummer brings more than 20 hours of daylight. In winter, average temperatures range from 0° to 40°F, although extreme lows can drop to -40°F and lower.

Summer visitors should bring warm

clothing for cool evenings, rain gear, adequate footwear and insect repellent. Winter visitors should have warm clothing and carry emergency food and equipment, particularly on long trips. Hikers should plan for a variety of conditions, including gravel bars, woodland, heavy brush and soggy tundra.

Wildlife: Brown/grizzly and black bears are common throughout the park — above and below tree line. Other large mammals found in the park are moose, wolf and occasionally caribou in the northern section. Smaller mammals include red fox, wolverine, lynx, marten, mink, weasel, beaver, snowshoe hare and red squirrel. A large number of resident and migratory birds, including ravens, ptarmigan, golden and bald eagles, peregrine falcons and many songbirds can be seen in the park.

The state parks office further cautions that wildlife, particularly bears, can be dangerous. Never approach wild animals, especially their young. To avoid surprises, warn animals of your presence by making noise, whistling or carrying bells.

Fish in the Susitna and Chulitna rivers include Dolly Varden, arctic grayling, rainbow trout and chum, king, red and silver salmon. Small numbers of lake trout occur in Byers, Spink and Lucy lakes and rainbow trout, grayling and Dolly Varden are found in Byers Lake and Troublesome and Little Coal creeks.

Access: Denali State Park is accessible from the George Parks Highway or the Alaska Railroad, which forms the eastern boundary of the park. The seldom-used east side of the park offers excellent wilderness recreation opportunities. The best place to get off the train is just after the railroad crosses the Susitna River past Gold Creek. The railroad offers regular local rural service from May to September between Anchorage and Denali National Park. Check with the Alaska Railroad for current schedules.

Accommodations: The main recreational development at the park is Byers Lake campground at Milepost 147 from Anchorage on the Parks Highway. (The grizzlies seem fond of this campground too, and it is occasionally shut down because of a troublesome bear.) Overnight camping fee is $6. Byers Lake has 66 campsites, picnic areas, boating and fishing; gas-powered motors are not allowed on the lake. Fires must be confined to developed fireplaces or camp stoves. No fires are permitted in the backcountry, except in camp stoves. Minimum impact camping is encouraged; all trash should be hauled out of backcountry areas.

Trails: Several trails offer a variety of hiking experiences:

The 5-mile Byers Lake trail leaves the campground and offers an easy hike around the lake; 6 tent campsites are located on the trail across from the campground.

The scenic, 7-mile Cascade trail takes off from the Byers Lake trail at the northeast end of the lake and climbs Curry Ridge to Tarn Point, a 1,900-foot elevation change.

Trails heading at Troublesome Creek (Milepost 137.7 from Anchorage on the Parks Highway) and Little Coal Creek (Milepost 163.8) extend to tree line. Open areas of the park, dotted with alpine lakes, offer easy hiking and spectacular views. The 32-mile route above tree line from Troublesome Creek trail (which intersects Cascade trail) and Little Coal Creek trail (which leads to Indian Mountain) is marked only with rock cairns. Bears are a problem along Troublesome Creek during the salmon spawning season in July and August and park managers are considering re-routing a portion of the trail to minimize bear encounters; exercise extreme caution from the Chulitna River upstream to Ultima Poole. Salmon cannot get beyond the falls and the bear danger beyond Ultima Poole is not as great. (Ultima Poole is reached via a 500-yard-long side trail which leaves the Troublesome Creek trail at about Mile 4.5. Ultima Poole is a deep pool at the base of a small falls on the creek and a pleasant place for a rest or a bracing swim.)

Two other trips are from either trailhead to Byers Lake campground via the Cascade trail. Distance from Troublesome Creek trailhead to Byers Lake is about 15 miles; from Little Coal Creek trailhead it's about 25 miles.

A day-long hike that offers an outstanding view is from the Little Coal Creek trailhead to the summit of Indian Mountain. Round-trip is about 9 miles; elevation gain is 3,300 feet.

Cross-country skiing is outstanding during March, April and often into May. No trails are maintained in the park in winter. Snow depths may reach 6 feet, covering most brush and rocks. Skiers who travel up Curry or Indian ridges should take care to avoid potential avalanche slopes, especially above timberline. Snow machines and other off-road vehicles are permitted in the park only when the snow is deep enough to protect vegetation (about 16 inches).

For more information contact: Alaska State Parks, Mat-Su Area Office, HC32, Box 6706, Wasilla, AK 99687; phone 745-3975. Related USGS Topographic maps: Talkeetna C-1, C-2 and D-1; Talkeetna Mountains C-6 and D-6.

Gates of the Arctic National Park and Preserve

See the Attractions listing in BROOKS RANGE AND THE ARCTIC section for the main entry for Gates of the Arctic. Note, however, that visitors may reach the park by following the Dalton Highway (formerly the North Slope Haul Road) north from Fairbanks. Wiseman and Coldfoot, just off the highway, are entry points to the park. Services are available at Coldfoot.

Steese National Conservation Area

This 1.2-million-acre conservation area, administered by BLM, consists of 2 portions. One area is on the northern side of the Steese Highway, adjacent to White Mountains National Recreation Area; the other lies south and east within the drainage of Birch Creek, a wild and scenic river.

Placer gold mining occurs in and around the conservation area and has caused Birch Creek to be extremely turbid during the summer.

The only recreational development in the conservation area is the **Pinnell Mountain National Recreation Trail**. This rugged, 27-mile trail is accessible at Twelvemile Summit (Milepost 85.6) or Eagle Summit (Milepost 107.1) on the Steese Highway near Fairbanks. The hike takes 2 to 3 days.

Some of Alaska's large carnivores — wolves, grizzly bears and wolverines — are occasionally spotted from the trail by an attentive eye. More frequently seen is the hoary marmot, perched atop a lookout rock issuing its shrill call. Also living in the rocky slopes is the small pika or "rock rabbit" with its brief, high-pitched squeak. Small groups of caribou can sometimes be seen from the trail.

Birdlife includes rock ptarmigan, gyrfalcons, ravens, northern harriers, golden eagles, northern wheatears, lapland longspurs, and various surf birds. Wildflowers bloom in profusion along some sections. Look for moss campion, alpine azalea, oxytrope, frigid shooting star, arctic forget-me-not, lousewort, and mountain avens.

Some of the oldest rocks in Alaska are found along this trail. These rocks are made up from sediments first deposited over a billion years ago.

This is one of the most accessible northern alpine tundra areas in the Interior. The trail, marked by rock cairns, winds along mountain ridges and through high passes mostly above 3,500 feet; the highest point reached is 4,721 feet. Along the trail are vantage points with views of the White Mountains, Tanana Hills, Brooks Range and Alaska Range. Between June 18 and 25 hikers can see the midnight sun from many high points along the trail, including the Eagle Summit trailhead parking area.

No horses or motorized vehicles are allowed on the trail. Water is scarce; carry your own supply and boil or treat any water from streams. Backcountry camping is allowed along the trail; 8-by-12-foot shelter cabins are located at Mile 10 and Mile 18 from the Eagle Summit trailhead. Be prepared for mosquitoes and cool, windy weather. Bring a camp stove and a windscreen. Lodging is available at Fairbanks, Chatanika, Central and Circle Hot Springs; a few campgrounds are located along the Steese Highway. The state now maintains the Steese Highway during the winter, but for current road conditions call the Alaska State Dept. of Transportation and Public Facilities in Fairbanks, phone 452-1911.

For additional information contact: Yukon Resources Area Manager, Bureau of Land Management, 1541 Gaffney Road, Fairbanks, AK 99703; phone 356-5337.

Tanana Valley State Forest

Created in 1983, this 1.81 million acre state forest is located almost entirely within the Tanana River basin and includes 200 miles of the Tanana River. It extends from near the Canadian border approximately 265 miles west to Manley Hot Springs and encompasses areas as far south as Tok, and is interspersed with private and other state lands throughout the basin. The elevation varies from 275 feet along the Tanana River below its confluence with the Kantishna River to more than 5,000 feet in the Alaska Range, south of Tok. The Bonanza Creek Experimental Forest near Nenana is located within the State Forest.

Hardwood and hardwood-spruce trees dominate almost 90 percent of the forest. Seven percent is shrubland. The major tree species are paper birch, quaking aspen, balsam poplar, black spruce, white spruce and tamarack. Twenty-two percent of the forest, 392,000 acres, is suitable for harvest. Forty-four rivers, streams and lakes within the forest have significant fish, wildlife, recreation and water values and will receive additional protection. Nearly all of the land will remain open for mineral development.

Climate: The Tenana basin includes some of the warmest and coldest areas of the state. The continental climate is characterized by cold, dry winters and warm but relatively moist summers. The mean July daytime high temperature in Fairbanks is 72°F. while the mean January daytime low in Tok is -30°F. Precipitation averages about 12 inches each year for the entire region, however variations in altitude influence the amount of precipitation.

Wildlife: The Tanana River valley provides habitat for moose, caribou, bears and bison. A large population of beaver is found in the region, especially in the Chena River drainage. Other furbearers include muskrat, mink, red fox, lynx, marten, land otter, weasel and wolverine. Three species of salmon, king, chum and coho are found in the Tanana River drainage. Arctic grayling, northern pike and Dolly Varden are found throughout the clear water streams and lakes of the area. Waterfowl nest on the lakes, sloughs and ponds scattered throughout the lowlands. Spruce grouse are found in the forested regions, peregrine falcons have been reported in the bluffs along the Tanana River and bald eagles are known to overwinter in the southeastern section near the Delta-Clearwater rivers.

Access: Approximately 85 percent of the forest is located within 20 miles of a highway, making it one of the more accessible public lands in the interior. Rivers and trails throughout the river basin provide additional access to areas within the forest.

Accommodations: The Eagle Trail State Recreation Site is the only developed facility within the State Forest and has 40 campsites. Additional campgrounds, public use cabins, boat launches and waysides are planned. Eighteen communities are located near the forest, including Fairbanks, the second largest city in Alaska. Supplies, lodging, charter transportation, rentals and guides are available in Fairbanks or may be found in some of the smaller communities.

Activities: Fishing, hunting, hiking, boating, cross-country skiing, dog-mushing, snowmachining and some all-terrain vehicle use are pursued throughout the forest. Some 250 miles of trails have been identified in the forest, some of which are maintained. The Tanana Basin Trails Management Plan, which is not complete, inventories trails in the borough, several of which are located within the State Forest and will provide more detailed information on existing trails and plans for their management. Many rivers, lakes and streams within the forest offer sportfishing and boating opportunities.

For more information, contact the Regional Forester, Northcentral District, 3726 Airport Way, Fairbanks, AK 99701; phone 451-2666. Other sources of information include: Alaska Dept. of Fish and Game, 1300 College Road, Fairbanks, AK 99709, phone 452-1531; Alaska Div. of Parks and Outdoor Recreation, Northern Region, 4420 Airport Way, Fairbanks, AK 99709, phone 479-4114; or the Fairbanks North Star Borough, P.O. Box 1267, Fairbanks, AK 99707, phone 452-4761.

White Mountains National Recreation Area

The 1-million-acre White Mountains National Recreation Area, administered by BLM, is located along the north side of the Steese Highway. The recreation area includes major portions of Beaver Creek, a national wild and scenic river.

Historically there has been considerable placer gold mining in this region. There are many mining claims in the recreation area, but only 1 or 2 are actively mined during the summer.

Access is by U.S. Creek Road, which leaves the Steese Highway at Milepost 57.3, then extends 7 miles to Nome Creek. This gravel road was upgraded in 1983 and is passable by 2-wheel-drive vehicles for several miles, but there are a few mudholes around Nome Creek which may require 4-wheel drive. A trail continues across Nome Creek to Little Champion Creek, but is much rougher and not passable by wheeled vehicles.

There also is access to the recreation area via summer and winter trails from the Elliott Highway. Both trails lead to BLM's Borealis-LeFevre cabin on Beaver Creek (see BLM Cabins section).

The winter trail no longer leaves the Elliott Highway at Milepost 23.6. It now leaves at the same place as the summer trail, at Milepost 27.8. The move adds about 3 miles to the formerly 17-mile trail, which has been renamed the **Wickersham Creek Trail.** It follows the route of the old trail that once extended to Chandalar and joins the summer trail about 2 miles from Beaver Creek. Good snowpack in most years provides excellent conditions on the trail for snowmobilers, cross-country skiers and dog mushers; it is generally too wet for summer hiking. There is an emergency shelter, with a stove and firewood, approximately 8.5 miles from the highway on the west side of the trail. Related USGS Topographic maps: Livengood A-2, B-2.

The 22-mile summer hiking trail via Wickersham Dome leaves the Elliott Highway at Milepost 27.8. The dome is an easy 4-hour round-trip from the highway. It's a moderate 2-day hike from the trailhead to the cabin. The trail (now called **Summit Trail**) is marked by rock cairns or wooden posts; in low, wet areas and across streams, plank walks have been constructed. Horses and motorized vehicles are prohibited on this trail.

Grayling fishing is excellent in Beaver Creek. Hunting is allowed in season.

Two other winter trails should be noted: **Colorado Creek Trail** originates at Mile 57 of the Elliott Highway where the highway crosses the Tolovana River. There is a parking area on the west side of the highway next to the river. To get to the trail, cross over the highway or under, on the river, and turn right 50 yards beyond the highway bridge. The trail passes the turnoff to the Colorado Creek Cabin 12 miles from the highway and continues another 7 miles to its end at Beaver Creek.

In the forested areas a cleared trail has been visibly cut. In the open areas along Colorado Creek frequent high winds may blow snow across the trail, making it difficult to follow. These open areas provide good views of the White Mountains. This trail currently receives a moderate amount of use. Related USGS Topographic maps: Livengood B-2, B-3, C-2, C-3.

Trail Creek Trail originates 3 miles from the Elliott Highway on the Wickersham Creek Trail and travels east along a ridgeline that eventually parallels Trail Creek until it ends at Beaver Creek, 26 miles from the highway. It passes the Trail Creek Cabin 9 miles from its origin at the Wickersham Creek Trail. This is a clearly cut trail which receives a moderate amount of use as far as the cabin. Related USGS Topographic maps: Livengood A-2, B-1, B-2.

From May to September temperatures may range from 20° to 80°F, with snow possible at any time at higher elevations. Wind can become a problem in areas with little shelter, such as treeless ridges on the summer trail. Winter temperatures may dip as low as -70°F. Any wind will drop the chill factor to a critical level, so adequate protection from the cold and wind is necessary at all times.

Travelers should carry a portable stove — with a windscreen — since wood is not always available in this alpine setting. Also, water should be carried and any water obtained from streams or lakes should be boiled or treated. Winter travelers should carry a survival kit containing a sleeping bag, extra clothing, extra food and a heat source.

For more information contact: Steese/White Mountains District Office, Bureau of Land Management, 1541 Gaffney Road, Fairbanks, AK 99703; phone 356-5367.

Yukon-Charley Rivers National Preserve

This 2.5-million-acre preserve is located in east-central Alaska north and west of Eagle. The preserve includes a 128-mile stretch of the Yukon River, as well as the entire 106 miles of the wild and scenic Charley River.

The broad, swift Yukon flows by old cabins and relics from mining camps. The Park Service is preserving a dredge, camp buildings and equipment as a clue to the region's mining history. Gold was discovered on Coal Creek in the early 1900s by miner Frank Slaven. His claims were later sold and the company that bought them had a dredge shipped up from San Francisco. It was the first gold dredge to operate in Yukon-Charley and continued operation until the early 1960s. A roadhouse named for Slaven is on the National Register of Historic Places. It opened about 1930, taking advantage of the traffic along the Yukon River, as well as up Coal Creek. The main mining camp on Coal Creek is also part of the donation. The camp includes 10 cabins that served a variety of uses. They were built on skids so they could be moved along with the floating gold dredge. Some gold discoveries at Circle and other eastern Yukon localities preceded the Klondike gold rush.

By contrast, the Charley River watershed is virtually untouched by modern man. It flows crystal clear and is considered to be one of Alaska's finest recreational streams. The 2 rivers merge between the early-day boom towns of Eagle and Circle.

Humans have lived in the Yukon-Charley country since long before recorded time. Archaeological surveys are only beginning, but evidence found so far indicates people have been present for at least 10,000 years. Much of the preserve was unglaciated during the last ice age and there is a good chance that sites older than 10,000 years will be found. Because it was in the ice-free corridor, the area also contains a diverse cross-section of vegetation.

Climate: The preserve is located in a subarctic climate zone, characterized by exceptionally cold winters, relatively warm summers, low annual precipitation and generally light winds. Summer highs average in the low 70s and lows in the mid-40s, although freezing at night can occur any month of the year at higher elevations. Winter lows can reach -40°F and lower for extended periods. Normal winter temperatures range from -5° to -25°F. Precipitation is light, about 8 to 10 inches annually, mostly falling as rain in summer. Thunderstorms are common in summer.

Snow cover is light but continues for about 7 months of the year. Breakup of the Yukon River ice usually occurs in early May. In mid-May 24-hour daylight begins. The transition from summer to winter is rapid; peak fall colors occur in the high country in late August and by mid-September most aspens and birches at lower elevations have turned golden. Ice begins flowing in the Yukon in October, with freezeup usually by mid-November.

Wildlife: The preserve includes caribou from the Fortymile herd which migrate to Canada and back. A moderate number of moose browse along streams and lowland areas, while Dall sheep occupy heights above the Charley River. Other wildlife includes grizzly and black bears, wolves and many small mammals.

More than 200 species of birds have been reported to occur in the preserve, including bald and golden eagles, rough-legged hawks and gyrfalcons. In its cliffs and rocky peaks the preserve contains some of North America's finest habitat for the peregrine falcon, an endangered species. Yukon-Charley lies along a major flyway for waterfowl that breed on the Yukon Flats and winter in the continental United States.

Fish in preserve waters include king salmon in July and chum salmon in September or October. A few coho also are taken. Other species include sheefish, whitefish, northern pike and burbot. Sportfishing centers primarily on arctic grayling, found at the mouths of tributary streams early in the season and farther upstream as the summer progresses. Northern pike are found in the lower reaches of most tributary streams and in the backwater sloughs of the Yukon. Dolly Varden are found in one nameless tributary of the upper Charley River.

Access: The preserve is accessible primarily by small plane or boat from Eagle, 12 river miles south of the preserve on the Taylor Highway, or Circle, 14 river miles to the north on the Steese Highway. Both Eagle (pop. 198) and Circle (pop. 101) are easily accessible by auto or plane from Fairbanks. Floating the 154 miles of the Yukon River from Eagle to Circle is the most popular means of visiting the preserve. Most travelers spend about 4 days on this section. July and August are the most popular months for floaters. (See also The Rivers.)

Access to the headwaters of the Charley River for float trips is primarily by helicopter, although it is possible to fly to a bush airstrip just outside the preserve boundary and then hike 15 miles to the upper Charley River.

Charter Super Cub access can be arranged to an unimproved gravel strip above Copper Creek. Most people prefer to float the Charley River in late June to mid-July. There are no roads or maintained trails within the preserve. No fees or permits are required to use any of the rivers. Inflatable raft rentals, charter boat service and fixed-wing and helicopter charters are available in nearby communities.

Accommodations: There are no accommodations in the preserve. In the summer food service is available in Eagle and Circle, along with basic supplies, gas and limited lodging facilities. Both communities also have campgrounds and public boat landings. There are no formal campgrounds in the preserve, but camping is permitted on any federally owned land. Campsites on river bars are recommended because there is usually a breeze to keep the insects at bay. Minimum-impact camping, leaving no garbage, is encouraged. Also, land on both sides of the Yukon River from Calico Bluff near Eagle to just below the Tatonduk River mouth is owned by the Hungwitchin Native Corp. of Eagle, which requests that visitors not camp on its land.

The Park Service cautions that the preserve is a vast and sometimes hostile environment. The preserve's small staff can provide only minimal patrol or rescue services. Self-sufficiency is the rule; visitors are completely on their own once they leave the well-traveled Yukon River corridor. Weather conditions or equipment failure often can cause schedules to go awry; visitors should bring extra supplies to be prepared. As a safety precaution, visitors may leave a copy of their planned itinerary with the rangers at the Park Service office in Eagle. Also, local residents carry on subsistence activities within the preserve. Their camps and equipment are crucial to their livelihood and should be left undisturbed.

Activities: Besides river floating and camping, recreational opportunities in the preserve include hiking, fishing, wildlife observation and photography, cross-country skiing, dogsledding, snowmobiling and snowshoeing. Sport hunting is permitted in season.

For additional information contact headquarters for the Yukon-Charley Rivers National Preserve at the foot of Fort Egbert on the bank of the Yukon River in Eagle. Books and USGS maps are sold and a library of reference material is available there, or write, Superintendent, Yukon-Charley Rivers National Preserve, P.O. Box 64, Eagle, AK 99738; phone 547-2233. Related USGS Topographic maps: Eagle, Charley River, Big Delta, Circle.

Wildlife Refuges

Innoko National Wildlife Refuge

This refuge is located about 300 miles northwest of Anchorage in the central Yukon River valley. Its 2 units encompass approximately 4 million acres. The upper unit is bordered on the north and west by the Yukon River and on the east and much of the south by the Kaiyuh Mountains. The lower unit includes the middle portion of the Innoko River and its drainage. The Yukon River borders on the west and the Kuskokwim Mountains on the east.

The terrain of the upper unit consists of black spruce muskeg, bogs, marshes and wet meadows. Along the Yukon there are white spruce, birch, aspen and cottonwood, with stands of willow and alder in wetter areas. About half of the lower unit consists of black spruce muskeg, wet meadow and sedge or horsetail marsh. There are many lakes and ponds. The other half of the lower unit is mostly white spruce and birch covered hills, most of which do not exceed 1,000 feet.

Climate: Summer high temperatures may exceed 80°F although 60s and 70s are more common. Visitors should anticipate rain at any time during the spring, summer or fall and carry rain gear. Also, a surprise freeze can happen even in the summer, particularly in June or August, so visitors should prepare accordingly. During the fall, it is wise to expect cold, wet weather. Winters are cold; the temperature may drop to -60°F.

Wildlife: This refuge was established to protect waterfowl nesting and breeding habitat. More than 100,000 waterfowl and shorebirds use The Wetlands which encompass nearly 80 percent of the refuge lands. This is an important nesting area for white-fronted and lesser Canada geese, pintail, wigeon, shoveler, scaup, scoter, red-necked grebe, lesser yellowleg and hudsonian godwit.

The refuge is home to moose, black and grizzly bears and wolves. Caribou use the refuge in winter when deep snow drives them down from the mountains. This area also is renowned for its beaver population. Other furbearers include muskrat, marten, wolverine, lynx, river otter and red fox.

Fish found in refuge waters include salmon, sheefish, grayling, blackfish, whitefish and northern pike.

Access and Accommodations: Chartered aircraft from McGrath, Galena or Grayling provide access to the refuge. Some supplies are available in Grayling, but there is no commercial lodging. Food service and lodging are available in McGrath and Galena. There are no facilities in the refuge; wilderness camping only. No roads or trails exist. Campers should be prepared for a wet environment and be sure to bring waterproof boots, a tent and warm sleeping bag. Drinking water should be boiled or purified to protect against giardiasis. A first-aid kit and plenty of mosquito repellent are recommended. The Fish and Wildlife Service also recommends that anyone planning to enter the refuge check in with the refuge manager in McGrath for safety purposes.

Activities: Recreational opportunities include moose hunting, floating the Innoko River, hunting black bear, fishing, wildlife observation and photography. The refuge staff will assist in planning trips.

For additional information contact: Refuge Manager, Innoko National Wildlife Refuge, P.O. Box 69, McGrath, AK 99627; phone 524-3251. Related USGS Topographic maps: Ophir, Holy Cross, Iditarod and Unalakleet for the lower unit and Nulato for the upper unit.

Kanuti National Wildlife Refuge

This 1.6-million-acre refuge straddles the Arctic Circle approximately 150 miles northwest of Fairbanks and south of Bettles. It extends westward to the villages of Allakaket and Alatna. The refuge encompasses a portion of the Koyukuk River basin and the Kanuti flats near the southern foothills of the Brooks Range. It is characterized by lakes and marshes dotting the broad, rolling plain of the Kanuti and Koyukuk river valleys.

Climate: Kanuti's climate is typically continental. The long summer days are mild, with maximum temperatures mostly in the high 60s and low 70s. The sun does not set from June 2 through July 9. From November through March, minimum temperatures average below zero and readings of -45° to -55°F are common. Annual precipitation averages approximately 14 inches. Snow has occurred during all months but July. Winds prevail from the north 10 months of the year, but are seldom strong.

Wildlife: Some 105 species of birds have been observed on the Kanuti, which provides important nesting habitat for waterfowl, particularly white-fronted geese, Canada geese, pintail, wigeon, scaup and scoters.

Portions of the large western Arctic caribou herd winter within the refuge. Black bears and grizzly bears, wolves, wolverines and moose are found there, along with numerous smaller mammals. Fish in refuge waters include 4 species of salmon, arctic char, grayling, whitefish, sheefish, lake trout, burbot and northern pike.

Access and Accommodations: The refuge is accessible by charter air service from Bettles. Also, by boat down the Koyukuk River from Bettles to Allakaket. Commercial and charter air service is available in Fairbanks to Bettles and in Allakaket. Overnight accommodations are available in Bettles, but not Allakaket. On the refuge there are no facilities; wilderness camping only. Visitors should arrive self-sufficient. As a safety precaution, visitors should leave a copy of their itinerary with a friend.

Activities: Fishing, hunting, trapping, wildlife observation and photography, camping, boating, recreational gold panning and rockhounding are the main activities in Kanuti. Backpacking is good in only a few areas due to the terrain.

For additional information contact: Refuge Manager, Kanuti National Wildlife Refuge, Federal Bldg. and Courthouse, 101 12th Ave., Fairbanks, AK 99701; phone 456-0329.

Koyukuk National Wildlife Refuge

This 3.5-million-acre refuge is located 320 miles northwest of Fairbanks. Lying in the circular floodplain formed by the lower Koyukuk River, the refuge is heavily forested and contains much wetlands. Fourteen rivers and hundreds of creeks meander throughout the refuge providing habitat for salmon, beaver and waterfowl. More than 15,000 lakes also are found in the refuge. The topography is relatively gentle. Lowland forests gradually merge with tundra vegetation at the 3,000-foot elevation.

The refuge has a 400,000-acre wilderness area surrounding the 10,000-acre Nogahabara Sand Dunes. These, along with the Great Kobuk Sand Dunes, are the only large, active dune fields in interior Alaska. Both were formed some 10,000 years ago by windblown deposits during the mid- to late Pleistocene period.

Wildlife: Moose are abundant and are important to the subsistence economy of villages in the area. The entire region is part of the winter range of the western Arctic caribou herd. With the presence of both moose and caribou, wolves also are common. Black bears are abundant in forests and grizzly bears inhabit the open tundra at higher elevations. The refuge is productive beaver country and excellent habitat for other furbearers.

Fish available in the refuge include king and chum salmon. Whitefish and northern pike are abundant in lowlands and arctic grayling are found in colder headwater streams.

Access and Accommodations: Access to the refuge is by boat, snowmobile or charter plane from Galena or Bettles, both of which have overnight accommodations. There are no accommodations in the refuge; wilderness camping is permitted. According to the Fish and Wildlife Service, some of the villages on or adjacent to the refuge are not encouraging tourism at the present.

For additional information contact: Refuge Manager, Koyukuk National Wildlife Refuge, P.O. Box 287, Galena, AK 99741; phone 656-1231.

Minto Flats State Game Refuge

Created in 1988, this new state refuge encompasses more than 500,000 acres and is located 35 air miles west of Fairbanks. One of the highest quality waterfowl habitats in Alaska and probably in all of North America, Minto Flats is the third most popular duck hunting area in the state. The wetland is also an important year-round hunting, fishing and trapping area for local villagers and archaeological evidence suggests use of the area by Athabascan Indians predate historic contact.

Wildlife: The flats produce as many as 150,000 ducks annually and supports a breeding population averaging 213 ducks per square mile. Trumpeter swans nest on numerous lakes dotting the area and white-fronted geese, sandhill cranes, common and arctic loons nest on the flats. The flats are also an important staging area for waterfowl from the Yukon Flats and the North Slope during the fall migration. Predominate species are tundra swan, mallard, pintail, scaup, green-winged teal, redhead, bufflehead and gadwall.

Also found in the refuge are a large beaver population, river otter, lynx, wolverine, wolf, red fox, mink, muskrat and black bear. Marten are seen occasionally and the number of moose on the flats appears to be increasing.

Access: The flats can be reached by floatplane from Fairbanks; by boat from Minto, which can be reached from Fairbanks via the Elliott Highway; by boat from Nenana down the Tanana River, then up Swan Neck Slough into the flats; or by the Murphy Dome Road. In winter, snow machines and skiplanes can be used.

Activities: The Alaska Dept. of Fish and Game reports more than 5,000 hunter days are logged each year and more than 11,000 ducks and 700 geese are taken. Fishing for northern pike, sheefish, humpback whitefish, grayling, and king, silver and chum salmon is also popular.

Accommodations: A lodge with accommodations and meals and a general store is located in Minto, a village adjacent to the flats. Generally those using the flats camp on one of the islands in the flats. Fresh water should be carried and anyone headed for the area during the fall hunting season should be prepared for any type of weather, from 70°F. to rain to snow. Hip boots are a must and a boat or inflatable raft is also recommended.

For additional information contact: Alaska Dept. of Fish and Game, 1300 College Road, Fairbanks, AK 99701.

Nowitna National Wildlife Refuge

This 2.1-million-acre refuge is located approximately 200 miles west of Fairbanks in the central Yukon River valley. It protects a lowland basin bordering the Nowitna and Yukon rivers and encompasses forested lowlands, hills, lakes, marshes, ponds and streams. The dominant feature is the Nowitna River, part of which is a nationally designated wild river. This river is considered outstanding for float trips and also provides spawning grounds for northern pike and sheefish. However, the primary reason the refuge was established was to protect waterfowl and their habitat.

Nowitna is 1 of 4 refuges (the others are Innoko, Kanuti and Koyukuk) encompassed by solar basins, which are characterized by encircling hills, light winds, low rainfall, severe winters and short, warm summers.

Wildlife: The forested lowlands of Nowitna Refuge provide excellent wetland habitats that support good populations of fish and waterfowl. More than 250,000 birds, including the trumpeter swan, breed on the refuge. Other wildlife found here include black and grizzly bear and moose.

Activities: Moose and bear hunting are major activities on the refuge. Marten, mink, wolverine, beaver and muskrat are important furbearers that provide income, food and recreation for local residents. Fishing for northern pike and sheefish is excellent. Other fish found in refuge waters include salmon, whitefish and arctic grayling.

Access and Accommodations: Access to Nowitna is by boat or charter air service from Galena or Fairbanks, both of which have overnight accommodations.

For additional information contact:

Refuge Manager, Nowitna National Wildlife Refuge, P.O. Box 287, Galena, AK 99741; phone 656-1231.

Tetlin National Wildlife Refuge

This 700,000-acre refuge is located in east central Alaska. It is bordered on the north by the Alaska Highway, on the east by the Canadian border, on the south by Wrangell-St. Elias National Park and Preserve and on the west by the Tetlin Reserve (formerly the Tetlin Indian Reservation).

Tetlin Refuge is a showcase of geographic and ecological features created by wildfires, permafrost and fluctuating river channels. The refuge features an undulating plain broken by hills, forests, ponds, lakes and extensive marshes. The glacial Chisana and Nabesna rivers dominate the valley where they meander before joining to form the Tanana River. Parabolic sand dunes, formed of windblown glacial flour, are found southeast of Northway and at Big John Hill.

Tetlin's vegetation is a good example of the benefits of wildfires. These natural phenomena help create diverse plant habitats such as grasslands or birch forests. Spruce forests are usually the dominant vegetation in a subarctic environment. When fire destroys such a forest, a series of habitats follow until once again spruce trees dominate.

Wildlife: These varied habitats are home to a diverse group of animals: moose, black and brown bears, ptarmigan, wolf, coyote and red fox. Caribou winter in the refuge and Dall sheep can be seen on mountain slopes. The refuge also is a stopover for migrating birds and its wetlands provide important summer breeding habitat. Refuge wetlands are critical when drought in Canada sends birds farther north. The refuge supports a growing population of trumpeter swans, as well as the largest population of nesting osprey in Alaska. As many as 100,000 sandhill cranes pass through the refuge each fall. Other large birds found in the refuge include arctic and common loons, bald eagles and golden eagles. Birds that are rarely, if ever, seen in other parts of Alaska (because their usual range is farther south) may be seen here, including blue-winged teals, ruddy ducks, ring-necked ducks, sharp-tailed grouse, red-winged blackbirds and mountain bluebirds. The refuge also is the western or northern limit of distribution of the American coot, rail and brown-headed cowbird.

Arctic grayling, whitefish, lake trout, burbot and northern pike inhabit lakes and streams. There are no significant salmon runs, although a few chum salmon run up the Tanana and its tributaries.

Climate: Temperatures in June and July often exceed 80°F, with lows to 40°F. During these months it is light around the clock. By mid-September daytime temperatures of 45°F and nighttime of 25°F are common. Winter temperatures can drop to -70°F, and often stay below -40°F for a week or below 0°F for several months. Weather can change rapidly. Snow can occur as early as August.

Access: The Alaska Highway provides access along 65 miles of the refuge's northern border. Foot access is possible along the highway from the Canadian border to Gardiner Creek and at other points. The refuge is accessible by small boat from the Alaska Highway at Desper Creek and from the Northway Road at the Chisana River bridge. The Chisana River site will accommodate boats up to 18 feet. Charter planes are available in Tok and Northway, as well as Fairbanks and Anchorage. Riverboats also are available at Tok and Northway. There are no designated roads or trails for motorized vehicles in the refuge. The refuge has no foot trails; some appear on maps but are not identifiable on the ground. Topographic maps and a compass are necessary for cross-country trips.

Accommodations: Camping and the opportunity to view wildlife and scenic vistas are available at 2 refuge campgrounds and 6 interpretative pullouts on the Alaska Highway. Wilderness camping is allowed throughout the refuge. The best summer campsites are river bars and ridges where breezes reduce the insect problem. Choose sites carefully to avoid possible flooding from rainstorms or rising rivers. Dead or downed wood is usually available on river bars or in spruce stands. Pack out all unburnable trash and bury firepits. Human waste should be buried at least 100 yards from the water source. Camping supplies, as well as gas, food and lodging are available in Tok, and Northway and Beaver Creek, Yukon Territory.

Activities: Recreational activities popular on Tetlin refuge include fishing and hunting in accordance with state regulations, wildlife observation and photography. Fishing and hunting guide services are available in Tok; 3 big game guides operate within the refuge. The refuge office is located on the Alaska Highway in Tok directly across from the Alaska State Troopers and the Tok Information Center/Alaska Public Lands Information Center at Milepost 1314.1. The refuge sponsors wildlife movies at the center. The new Tetlin National Wildlife Refuge Center located at Alaska Highway Milepost 1229

east of Tok is open 7 a.m. to 7 p.m. from Memorial Day to Labor Day. The center offers an excellent scenic vista, interpretative displays, animal mounts and general information.

Visitors to the refuge should leave an itinerary with a friend or the refuge office in Tok and contact that person or office upon returning. Take precautions to avoid encounters with bears; make noise when hiking, keep a clean campsite and store food outside of tents out of bear's reach. Do not bury garbage; it will encourage animals to dig it up and then seek other campsites as a source of food. Boil or treat all drinking water from lakes or streams to avoid giardiasis, a water-borne intestinal disease. Be prepared for Alaska's infamous mosquitoes by bringing plenty of insect repellent and/or netting.

For additional information contact: Refuge Manager, Tetlin National Wildlife Refuge, P.O. Box 155, Tok, AK 99780; phone 883-5312.

Yukon Flats
National Wildlife Refuge

This refuge, about 100 miles north of Fairbanks, encompasses 8.6 million acres in east-central Alaska. This area is primarily a complex of wetlands of more than 30,000 lakes, ponds and sloughs.

The refuge is bisected by the Yukon River, America's fifth-largest river, which meanders for 225 miles through it. Here the river breaks free from canyon walls and spreads out through the vast floodplain. In the spring, millions of migrating birds converge on the flats before the ice moves from the river. The refuge has one of the highest nesting densities of waterfowl in North America and contributes more than 2 million ducks and geese to the continent's flyways.

The Porcupine River is the major tributary of the Yukon River within the refuge, joining the Yukon just downstream from Fort Yukon. Others include the Chandalar, Christian, Hadwenzic, Hodzana and Dall rivers and Birch and Beaver creeks. All are important for salmon spawning except the Christian River.

Climate: Yukon Flats has a continental subarctic climate characterized by great seasonal extremes of temperature and daylight. Summer temperatures regularly top 90°F and have hit 100°F, the highest ever recorded above the Arctic Circle. Winter minimums to -50°F and lows in excess of -70°F have been recorded. Precipitation is low, averaging about 6.5 inches annually at Fort Yukon. July and August are the wettest months. Freezeup usually occurs in October. Breakup occurs at Fort Yukon around May 15; larger lakes are not free of ice until later.

Wildlife: Mammals on the refuge include a substantial population of moose, as well as Dall sheep in the White Mountains, caribou, wolves, grizzly and black bear, marten, lynx, snowshoe hare, beaver, muskrat and some red fox and wolverine.

King, coho and chum salmon from the Bering Sea pass through and spawn in the flats each summer — the longest salmon run in the U.S. Other fish found in refuge waters include Dolly Varden, arctic grayling, whitefish, sheefish, cisco, burbot and northern pike.

Activities: Residents of 7 communities — Beaver, Birch Creek, Chalkyitsik, Circle, Fort Yukon, Stevens Village and Venetie — use the refuge for subsistence activities. Their camps and equipment are crucial for their survival and should be left undisturbed. Subsistence accounts for 90 percent of the public use of the refuge. The remaining uses center around sport hunting and river floating. There are considerable private holdings within the refuge, particularly along river corridors; contact the refuge office for the location of these lands to avoid trespassing.

Accommodations: There are no accommodations within the refuge. There are commercial visitor facilities at Fort Yukon and Circle, but not at the other villages in the area.

Most of the Yukon Flats Refuge is a pristine, but remote wilderness and visitors must be self-sufficient. The Fish and Wildlife Service cautions that the area's isolation, variable weather and water levels can combine to make

a dangerous experience for those who are not well prepared and equipped.

Access: Yukon Flats Refuge can be reached by air and water. Scheduled commercial air service is available to all the communities on the refuge. Charter air service to remote areas of the refuge is available in Fairbanks, Fort Yukon and Circle. A few bush airstrips, as well as numerous lakes and sand or gravel bars, make most areas of the refuge accessible by light aircraft. Local residents use riverboats and these, plus canoes, kayaks and rafts, are used for river floating and other recreational activities. There is no road access to the refuge, although the Dalton Highway runs adjacent to the refuge's southwestern boundary.

For additional information and assistance in planning a trip to the refuge contact: Refuge Manager, Yukon Flats National Wildlife Refuge, Federal Bldg. and Courthouse, P.O. Box 14, Fairbanks, AK 99701; phone 456-0407.

BLM Cabins

The Bureau of Land Management (BLM) has 6 recreational cabins (listed below) and 1 shelter cabin (on the White Mountains winter trail) available to the public in the Interior. The reservation fee for all recreational cabins is $15 per night and use is restricted to 3 consecutive nights. Reservations will be accepted 30 days in advance with payment. If reserving by phone, payment must be received within 48 hours. A receipt will be issued which should be taken along as proof of cabin reservation. No reservations are required and no fee is charged for the shelter cabin. While staying in these cabins, use only dead or downed trees for firewood and

BLM CABINS

	SLEEPS	AIR ACCESS	BOAT ACCESS	TRAIL ACCESS	HUNTING	FISHING	BEACHCOMB	SKIFF	STOVE
FAIRBANKS AREA									
Borealis-Lefevre	5	•	•		•				W
Colorado Creek	5		•						W
Cripple Creek (*Road access at Mile 60.5 Steese Highway*)	3		•	•					W
Trail Creek	3		•						W
Windy Gap (*Difficult trail*)	4		•	•					W

The above chart gives a brief description of each cabin. Type of stove provided is indicated as follows: O=oil stove, W=wood stove, G=outdoor grill, OH=oil heater.

carry out all unburnable litter.

For information contact the BLM Steese/ White Mountain District Office, phone 356-5367. Make reservations and payments in person or by mail to the BLM Fairbanks Support Center, 1541 Gaffney Road, Fairbanks, AK 99703; phone 356-2025.

The Rivers

Alatna River. See The Rivers in BROOKS RANGE AND THE ARCTIC section.

Beaver Creek. Beaver Creek, a national wild and scenic river, originates within White Mountains National Recreation Area north of Fairbanks and then flows northerly through Yukon Flats National Wildlife Refuge into the Yukon River.

This clear-water stream is classified as Class I overall by BLM. Canoes, kayaks and rafts are suitable. From its headwaters the river drops 9 feet per mile to the end of the wild river corridor below Victoria Creek 127 miles away. The trip to this point usually takes 7 to 10 days. Exit from this point is by floatplane or gravel bar landing in the Victoria Creek area. It is possible to continue on through Yukon Flats Refuge to the Yukon River and exit at the Yukon River bridge on the Dalton Highway. This segment is another 268 miles, which takes approximately 8 to 14 days.

Fish available in Beaver Creek include grayling, burbot, whitefish and northern pike.

Access is by auto from Mile 58 on the Steese Highway, via U.S. Creek Road, to Nome Creek.

For additional information about Beaver Creek, or to reserve the cabin, contact: Steese/ White Mountains District office, phone 356-5367 or Bureau of Land Management, Fairbanks Support Center, 1541 Gaffney Road, Fairbanks, AK 99703, phone 356-2025. Related USGS Topographic maps: Circle B-6, C-6, D-5 and 6; Livengood B-1 and 2, C-1 and 2, D-1.

Birch Creek. Birch Creek, a wild and scenic river, originates about 70 miles northeast of Fairbanks and flows generally east then north into the Yukon River. Most of Birch Creek is within the Steese National Conservation Area.

BLM classifies this river as Class I and II, with some Class III rapids above the confluence of Wolf Creek. From the put-in point it is generally Class I water; the upper 8 miles may be shallow and require lining through riffles. There is a stretch of Class II rapids just below the confluence of Clums Fork. Canoes, kayaks or rafts all are suitable. From the usual put-in point to the usual exit point is 126 miles; the river drops 10 feet per mile. The trip generally

takes 7 to 10 days. There is extensive mining above the put-in point and outside the river corridor which has muddied the water of this stream; it may be difficult to identify submerged rocks. *NOTE: Respect the rights of others, avoid actively mined areas.*

Grayling up to 12 inches may be caught in this stream from June to October. Northern pike and whitefish also are available.

This stream is accessible at both ends by auto from the Steese Highway. The usual put-in point is near Milepost 94, where a short road leads down to a parking area and canoe launch. The usual take-out point is the Steese Highway bridge at Milepost 147.1.

For additional information about Birch Creek contact: Steese/White Mountains District Office, phone 356-5367 or Bureau of Land Management, Fairbanks Support Center, 1541 Gaffney Road, Fairbanks, AK 99703, phone 356-2025. Related USGS Topographic maps: Circle A-3 and 4, B-1 through 4, C-1.

Black River. This slow, meandering stream flows some 200 miles to join the Porcupine River, about 17 miles northeast of Fort Yukon. Much of the river is within Yukon Flats National Wildlife Refuge. The section above the confluence of the Salmon Fork flows moderately fast (3 to 4 mph) through forested lowlands of white spruce and willow. Below the Salmon Fork confluence, the river slows to 2 to 3 mph as it widens and passes along numerous bluffs. Below Chalkyitsik the river slows further to 1 to 2 mph as the meanders increase in size.

This trip takes approximately 13 to 16 days from the vicinity of Birch Lake to Fort Yukon or 9 to 10 days from Birch Lake to Chalkyitsik. Canoes or kayaks are suitable for this trip.

Above the Salmon Fork, and again upstream from Chalkyitsik, sand or gravel bars are infrequent or not suitable for campsites. Upstream winds on the lower river can create whitecaps in a short time. There is low water after July 1 and the river usually is not floatable above Chalkyitsik. Views generally are limited to the river corridor because of high banks, although bluffs below Salmon Fork add variety.

Fishing varies from poor to fair depending on water conditions and season for grayling, Dolly Varden, northern pike, whitefish and sheefish. Moose, bear and other wildlife inhabit the area, but high vegetation limits viewing. Waterfowl are numerous.

Access is by floatplane from Fort Yukon to the river or to adjacent lakes between Salmon and Grayling forks. Exit is by floatplane from the Black or Porcupine rivers, by scheduled air service from Chalkyitsik, or float to Fort Yukon. To reach Fort Yukon, paddle 3 miles up the Sucker River from its confluence with the Porcupine River to a road-accessible landing.

Related USGS Topographic maps: Black River A-3, B-3 and 4, C-4 through 6; Fort Yukon C-1 through 3.

Chandalar River. Both main forks head in the Brooks Range and flow south to become the Chandalar River, which empties into the Yukon River south of Venetie. Below the confluence of the North and East Fork Chandalar rivers, it is quite fast and never dull. The Junjik River, which joins the east fork above Arctic Village, offers white-water challenges. The upper East Fork Chandalar is very fast, but not spiked with rapids. The more difficult North Fork flows through Chandalar Lake.

From the usual put-in on the East Fork Chandalar, there are 72 miles of fast, flat water to Arctic Village. For those trying the Junjik, it's Class II, descending at 6 feet per mile, to the East Fork Chandalar, then on to Arctic Village for a total of 40 river miles. From Arctic Village, the East Fork Chandalar is Class II, dropping at 7 feet per mile for 160 river miles, to its confluence with the North Fork. From the usual put-in at Chandalar Lake, the North Fork offers 120 miles of Class II and III, dropping at 15 feet per mile. Below the confluence of the North and East forks, the Chandalar is 90 river miles of flat water, dropping at 5 feet per mile, to the Yukon.

The East Fork Chandalar is bounded on the east by the Venetie Indian Reservation, owned by the people of Venetie and Arctic Village, and by Arctic National Wildlife Refuge to the north and west. The Chandalar River is bounded to the northeast by the reservation and to the southwest by Yukon Flats National Wildlife Refuge. Camping is permitted on wildlife refuge lands; do not use reservation lands without permission.

Access is by charter air service from Fairbanks or Fort Yukon to the rivers. Exit is by scheduled air service from Arctic Village, which has limited overnight accommodations, or Venetie, which has no visitor facilities.

Charley River. All 106 miles of this wild and scenic river flow within Yukon-Charley Rivers National Preserve. The Charley originates at the 4,000-foot level and flows northeast to join the Yukon River.

The Charley is rated Class II, or intermediate, with a few areas rated Class III, or more difficult. Paddlers should be experienced; canoes, kayaks or rafts are suitable because they are very portable and inflatable rafts

are most commonly used.

Maximum stream flow is in late May and early June. The boating season generally begins in June and there is usually sufficient flow for small boats through August, although exposed rocks and bars necessitate portaging during August. The Charley flows from its headwaters with an average gradient of 31 feet per mile and an average current of 6 to 8 mph. During high water the upper two-thirds of the river provide a good white-water experience. As the water level lowers, maneuvering becomes a constant necessity and some rapids must be scouted to determine the best channel. Rapid runoff from rainstorms during June and July, and occasionally in August, can cause the river to rise as much as several feet within hours posing a hazard for floaters. From the usual put-in point at Copper Creek, it is usually a 4-day float to the Yukon, then another 2 days to Circle.

The Charley is considered good to excellent for grayling fishing. Northern pike are found as far as 16 miles upstream. Sheefish and king, chum and coho salmon are occasionally found in the river.

Access is generally by helicopter from Tanacross to the Copper Creek area. A primitive landing strip located just above Copper Creek provides limited fixed-wing aircraft access to the Charley River. Exit is by riverboat up the Yukon River to Eagle, floating down the Yukon to Circle, or by floatplane from the Yukon. Circle is accessible by auto from Fairbanks via the Steese Highway.

Ranger patrols are infrequent and visitors should exercise caution and be prepared for any hazard.

For additional information about the Charley River contact: Yukon-Charley Rivers National Preserve, P.O. Box 64, Eagle, AK 99738; phone 547-2233. Related USGS Topographic maps: Charley River A-4 and 5, B-4 through 6; Circle D-1; Eagle C-6, D-5 and 6.

Chulitna and Tokositna rivers. The Chulitna, located along the George Parks Highway north of Talkeetna, runs partially through Denali State Park. The Middle Fork is clear water, generally shallow and rocky. The East Fork is clear, too, but fast (4 to 5 mph). Below the West Fork confluence, the Chulitna moves even faster (5 to 7 mph) and is braided in spots. Canoes, kayaks or rafts may be used on this river.

The upper section of the river drops 28 feet per mile and offers exciting white water (up to Class III). Fallen trees and sweepers are hazards. The water volume can change river conditions drastically. From the Parks Highway bridge (Milepost 132.8 from Anchorage), near the southern boundary of Denali State Park, to Talkeetna its gradient is 10 feet per mile and it is an easy river to float, although fast and very cold. Below Talkeetna, the river joins the Susitna. It is recommended that only skilled white-water paddlers with wilderness river experience test the section north of the Chulitna bridge.

Along this river boaters may see eagles, black bear and other wildlife. There also are views of the Alaska Range, including Mount McKinley. Fishing for grayling above Honolulu Creek is poor to moderate.

The Middle Fork is accessible at a bridge at Milepost 194.5 from Anchorage on the George Parks Highway just below Broad Pass. There is an undeveloped parking area southwest of the bridge below the highway. The East Fork can be reached from the same highway farther south at Milepost 185.1. From the Alaska Railroad the Chulitna can be reached at Broad Pass, Colorado, East Fork bridge, Honolulu, Hurricane and Talkeetna. The trip is 98 river miles from the bridge put-in on the Middle Fork; other alternatives are shorter. Trip length is 1 to 5 days.

Another alternative is to start on the Tokositna River, described as one of the most scenic and easy to run rivers in the area. It has glaciers along its course and Mount McKinley towers above it. The Tokositna can be reached in a few minutes by air charter from Talkeetna to Home Lake. Its flow is moderately swift, but it presents no special obstacles down to its confluence with the Chulitna River just above the bridge on the Parks Highway. Distance is about 26 river miles from the usual put in point to the Chulitna River.

Related USGS Topographic maps: Healy A-5 and 6; Talkeetna B-1, C-1; Talkeetna Mountains D-6.

Delta River. The Delta River flows north out of Tangle Lakes, near Milepost 21.5 on the Denali Highway. The upper portion of this national wild and scenic river is clear water; below Eureka Creek it is cold, silty glacial water with debris.

BLM classifies the Delta as Class I and II to Milepost 212.5 on the Richardson Highway. A falls must be portaged. From Milepost 212.5 to Black Rapids, the Delta is Class III with standing waves. From Tangle Lakes to Milepost 212.5 the trip is 35 miles or about 2 days. From that point it is 17 miles to Black Rapids, or less than a day's travel. Canoes, kayaks or rafts are suitable.

Rapids on the Fortymile challenge even the most intrepid rafters. The river, once an access route to the gold fields of the Interior, today carries adventurers of a different sort. (George Wuerthner)

Start the trip at BLM's Tangle Lakes campground on the Denali Highway, 22 miles west of Paxson. Paddle north through the lakes. There is a falls 2 miles below the last lake. A quarter-mile portage on the right bank crosses the Denali Fault, one of the longest fault zones in Alaska. Two hundred yards after reentering the river, traverse to the left bank to run a difficult rapid or line on the right bank. Class II water for the next 2 miles requires quick maneuvering around the rocks. *NOTE: Each year 5 or 6 canoes are damaged beyond repair along this stretch. It is a long walk out.* The remainder of the river to the takeout at Milepost 212.5 is mostly Class I, with some Class II. There is a view of Rainbow Mountain to the right.

From Milepost 212.5, continue in raft or kayak only. There are long stretches of rapids with high, irregular waves and hidden boulders. End the float trip at Milepost 227.4 on the Richardson Highway.

Wildlife that may be seen along the Delta River include moose, bear, Dall sheep, caribou, beaver, muskrat, golden eagles, bald eagles and many species of waterfowl. Fish available include lake trout, arctic grayling, whitefish and burbot.

For more information about the Delta River contact: Bureau of Land Management, Anchorage District Office, 4700 E. 72nd Ave., Anchorage, AK 99507; phone 267-1200. Related USGS Topographic maps: Mount Hayes A-4, B-4, C-4.

Fortymile River. This clear-water wild and scenic river is located in east-central Alaska. It is fed by numerous creeks and streams and flows eastward into the Yukon River at Fortymile in Canada.

There are 2 major options for trips on the Fortymile: via the Middle or South forks.

The Middle Fork is classified by BLM as Class I over all. However, there are several Class II rapids, a Class III and a Class V rapid known as "The Kink." In general the rapids become progressively more difficult downstream, but all can be checked out on foot first and easily portaged. In late July and August the river may be low, making for a safer if slower voyage. Mining claims cover several stretches of the Fortymile and virtually all of the bed of the South Fork is claimed. (Although the Fortymile River is a national wild and scenic river, the riverbed belongs to the state, which allows underwater mining claims.) Travelers may see some suction dredging. *NOTE: Mining claims are posted. Please avoid these areas!* There is fishing in these rivers for arctic grayling and burbot.

If floating the Fortymile to the Yukon River, travelers will cross into Canada and then back into the United States. Upon arriving in Clinton, YT, travelers must report to Canadian customs in Whitehorse, phone (403) 667-6471. After reentering the U.S. on the Yukon River, check in again with U.S. customs at Eagle.

There are numerous access points, both road and fly-in, and a number of float trips can be made on the various forks. For the Middle Fork trip, charter flights can be taken from Tok on the Alaska Highway, to the abandoned mining settlement of Joseph at the confluence of Joseph Creek and the Middle Fork Fortymile. The Joseph airstrip is unmaintained. Access to the river is by a 50-yard trail from the east end of the runway. There are takeouts at the O'Brien Creek bridge, Milepost 112.6 on the Taylor Highway, and at the Clinton Creek bridge at Clinton, YT, Canada. The 90-mile trip from Joseph to the O'Brien Creek bridge usually takes 4 to 5 days; the 182 miles from Joseph to Eagle via the Yukon River, takes about 7 to 9 days.

The Class III rapids, called "The Chute," is on the North Fork Fortymile just below its confluence with the Middle Fork. Exercise extreme care at the first right turn after the confluence. Canoes can be lined on the right bank. Rafts should stay close to the right bank. A few miles farther is "The Kink." Now on the National Register of Historic Places, The Kink was a major engineering feat in 1904 when a narrow channel was blasted 100 feet through a ridge of land forming the neck in what was a sharp bend in the river. The channel rerouted the river and left the riverbed open for mining. The Kink today is a Class V rapids and should be portaged. (For more information on The Kink, see Special Features this section.)

If leaving the river at the O'Brien Creek bridge, land 100 yards upstream from the bridge on the right bank. There is a trail to the parking lot.

A few miles downriver from O'Brien Creek is the Class III rapids known as "Deadman Riffle," which is hazardous for canoes. This area is not far from the Canadian border. Shortly before reaching Clinton there is a Class IV rapids called "The Canyon." Line from either bank depending on water level. This rapid is in 2 sections separated by a quarter mile of calm water; it is very dangerous during high water. There is road access once again at the Clinton Creek bridge, or floaters can continue on to the Yukon River and float the 57 miles to Eagle. At Eagle, there are 2 boat landings. The upstream landing is generally preferred because vehicles can be driven very close to the water. The downstream landing requires a 2-story climb up a steep stairway to reach downtown Eagle.

Floating the clear-water South Fork Fortymile will avoid The Chute and The Kink. This fork is Class I overall, with some Class II and III rapids.

There are numerous accesses from the Taylor Highway: at the BLM recreation site at Milepost 48.8; via an unmaintained 2-track trail that heads south from the airstrip at Chicken (Milepost 66.7); and at the South Fork bridge, Milepost 72.

The trip is 72 miles from Milepost 48.8 to O'Brien Creek bridge and takes 3 to 4 days; from O'Brien Creek to Eagle via the Yukon River it's 92 miles and takes 4 to 5 days. A few miles above the confluence of the South and North forks, floaters will pass by the site of Franklin, a small mining community established about 1887. It was the hub of mining activity for the southern portion of the Fortymile mining district.

For additional information about the Fortymile River system contact: Bureau of Land Management, Steese/White Mountain District Office, 1541 Gaffney Road, Fairbanks, AK 99703; phone 356-5367 or Bureau of Land Management, Field Office in Tok (behind the Alaska Public Lands Information Center), P.O. Box 307, Tok, AK 99780; phone 883-5121. Related USGS Topographic maps: Eagle B-3 through 5, C-3. Canadian Maps: 40-Mile 116-C7, Cassiar Cis. 116-C8, Shell Creek 116-C9, Mount Gladman 116-C10. Purchase Canadian maps from dealers or Canada Map Office, 615 Booth St., Ottawa, ON, Canada K1A 0E9.

Gulkana River. A river trip of nearly 300 miles is possible by using this nationally designated wild and scenic river. Start at the Denali Highway, paddle and portage through the Tangle Lakes canoe trail, then float the Middle Fork Gulkana to the very popular Gulkana River, which joins the Copper River for the final leg to the Gulf of Alaska.

The Middle Fork Gulkana is generally Class I with some Class II, according to the Bureau of Land Management, which manages this river.

Start this trip at the BLM's Upper Tangle Lakes campground at Milepost 21.7 from Paxson on the Denali Highway. Paddle south through Tangle Lakes; 300-foot portage between first lake and Upper Tangle Lake. At the southwest end of Upper Tangle Lake, a 0.3-mile portage leads to Lake 2865. A shallow wadeable portage between Lake 2865 and the

southernmost Tangle Lake is necessary, followed by a 1.3-mile portage to Dickey Lake. No trail markings, but most of the portage is low tundra brush.

The Middle Fork Gulkana flows out of Dickey Lake at the extreme southeast corner. The first 3 miles of the river are runnable, but less than 1 foot deep. The river is extremely swift, shallow and rocky for the next 3 miles; generally too swift and rocky to float. Toward the end of this stretch there is a small rock canyon with very steep gradient which requires careful lining. The next 19 miles to the main Gulkana is easy Class I and II; the river meanders a lot and has sweepers and logjams in some sections, especially between Swede Lake and Hungry Hollow Creek. The 9-mile trip from the Denali Highway to the river takes 1 to 2 days; the 25 miles to the Gulkana takes 2 to 3 days.

Paddlers floating the Gulkana also can start at Paxson Lake. Access is at Paxson Lake campground, Milepost 175 from Valdez on the Richardson Highway. Access also at Paxson Wayside, Milepost 179.4, but this requires a 5-mile longer trip on the lake. Paddle across lake to river outlet in southwest corner. (Old cabins may be seen on the lakeshore; do not trespass.)

The first 3 miles on the Gulkana River are Class II. From the confluence of the Middle Fork, the next 15 miles are Class I, followed by the Class III Canyon Rapids, which should be run by experienced paddlers only. A sign marks a quarter-mile portage around the rapids on the left bank. The following 8 miles are Class II, requiring careful maneuvering around boulders and logs. Several canoes are wrecked here each year. At the first bend after the portage there is a 1-mile side trip to Canyon Lake, which has excellent grayling fishing; trail begins on the left bank. The remainder of the trip to Sourdough is Class I. There is road access at the Sourdough campground, Milepost 147.4 from Valdez on the Richardson Highway. The remainder of the river to the take-out at Gulkana and the Gulkana River's confluence with the Copper River is Class I, with the last 8 miles ranging from Class I to Class II.

Use canoes or kayaks on Tangle Lakes; canoes, kayaks or rafts are suitable on the rivers.

Fish available include rainbow trout, whitefish, arctic grayling, red and king salmon, lake trout and burbot, depending on location and season. Wildlife that may be seen includes moose, bear, wolf, fox, caribou, muskrat, beaver, eagle, hawk and waterfowl.

For additional information contact: Bureau of Land Management, Anchorage District Office, 4700 E. 72nd Ave., Anchorage, AK 99507; phone 267-1200. Related USGS Topographic maps: Mount Hayes A-5; Gulkana B-3, B-4, C-4, D-4 and D-5.

Kantishna River. The Kantishna is an ancient route between the Tanana and the Kuskokwim (via the Lake Minchumina portage). In later years, many prospectors and trappers traveled up the river, summer and winter, to work their claims or traplines along the foothills of Mount McKinley.

This river is not difficult. It meanders and flows slowly. More skillful paddlers may wish to try an alternate route on the tributary stream, Moose Creek, which has some rapids and shallow stretches in dry seasons. Canoes, kayaks and riverboats are suitable.

Access is by air charter service from Anchorage to Lake Minchumina or by scheduled air service to the community of Lake Minchumina. Float the Muddy River, which drains Lake Minchumina, east 25 miles to Birch Creek, which joins shortly thereafter with the McKinley River to become the Kantishna. From the outlet of Lake Minchumina to the confluence of the Kantishna and the Tanana River is 220 miles of flat water. Related USGS Topographic maps: Mt. McKinley D-3, D-4, C-4, B-4, B-3, A-3; Kantishna River B-2, B-1, C-1.

Maclaren River. This river heads at Maclaren Glacier in the Clearwater Mountains and flows southwest 55 miles to the Susitna River.

The Maclaren flows from the high tundra country into the forests of the Lake Louise basin. From the usual access point on the Denali Highway, the river flows 52 miles with a gradient of 18 feet per mile. It is rated Class II and III and is rocky with many shallow rapids. Voyagers should take plenty of boat repair materials. Water volume can change rapidly. Canoes, kayaks and rafts are suitable.

Wildlife that may be seen along the way includes bear, moose and caribou.

Put-in point is at the end of a state road which leaves the Denali Highway at Milepost 43.3 from Paxson. Once on the Susitna River it is possible to exit via the Tyone River to the road at Lake Louise. Or continue down the Susitna to the portage to Stephan Lake. Related USGS Topographic maps: Mount Hayes A-5, A-6; Gulkana D-6, D-5; Talkeetna Mountains D-1.

Nabesna River. This river heads at Nabesna Glacier and flows northeast to join with the Chisana River to form the Tanana River near Northway Junction on the Alaska Highway. The river begins in Wrangell-St. Elias National Park and Preserve and flows through Tetlin National Wildlife Refuge.

This cold stream is in a wide graveled valley and is braided and quite fast at the start. Eventually it slows to meander through the foothills and taiga forest east of the Wrangell Mountains. The first 10 miles from the put-in point are rated Class I to II, with a gradient of 20 feet per mile. The gradient for the next 15 miles of flat water is 13 feet per mile and the gradient for the last 40 miles is 5 feet per mile. Canoes, kayaks or rafts are suitable.

The river can be reached from the 45-mile-long Nabesna Road, which leaves the Glenn Highway (Tok Cutoff) at Milepost 65.2 from Tok. This gravel road becomes very rough after Milepost 28.5; check on road conditions at Sportsman's Paradise Lodge at this point. There are several creeks that must be forded. A trail approximately 5 miles long leads to the Nabesna River from Milepost 41. Exit the river at Northway or at the Alaska Highway at the confluence of the Chisana River. Related USGS Topographic maps: Nabesna B-4, C-4, C-3, D-3, D-2; Tanacross A-2.

Nenana River. The Nenana River heads at Nenana Glacier in the Alaska Range and flows north 140 miles to the Tanana River at the town of Nenana. This river is easily accessible at several locations on the Denali and George Parks highways and the Alaska Railroad.

A popular put-in is 18 miles from Cantwell where the Denali Highway closely parallels the Nenana River. The trip from this point to the Tanana usually takes 5 days. Put-ins on the Parks Highway: McKinley Village, Milepost 231; the Riley Creek bridge Milepost 237; Nenana River bridge Milepost 238; Healy, Milepost 248.8; Rex Bridge over Nenana Milepost 275.8. Put-ins along the Alaska Railroad: Windy Station; Denali Park Station; Riley Creek bridge; Healy; and Nenana.

From the Denali Highway put-in, the Nenana River is Class I to Class II for the 38 miles to McKinley Village. From this point for the next 32 miles to below Healy, heavy water and very difficult rapids rated at Class IV to Class V through a narrow canyon make the river suitable only for expert paddlers. Others should skirt this section via the Parks Highway. (Organized raft tours are offered down this part of the river by outfitters based near the entrance to Denali National Park and Preserve.) Below this canyon area, the Nenana's course to the Tanana has braided channels, but no difficult rapids. Canoes, kayaks and rafts are suitable for the upper and lower river.

Kayaks or rafts only on the middle river.

Related USGS Topographic maps: Fairbanks A-5, B-5, C-5; Healy B-3 and 4, C-4, D-4 and 5.

Porcupine River. This river heads in Canada at 65°28'N, 139°32'W and flows 460 miles to the Yukon River, 2 miles north of Fort Yukon. Difficulties along the river are minor, so the trip is considered suitable for families with older children. Canoes or kayaks are recommended for the trip; rafts also are suitable, but progress may be slower due to upstream midafternoon winds.

The Porcupine is generally slow moving (2 to 4 mph) flat water to Class I with somewhat swifter current (4 to 6 mph) through multihued, steep-walled canyons beginning a few miles upstream from New Rampart House, in Yukon Territory. From the border to Fort Yukon the river flows within the Yukon Flats National Wildlife Refuge. Downstream from Canyon Village, AK, the canyons give way to low rolling hills on either side of the river. Farther downstream, the river meanders across the wetlands of the Yukon Flats. To reach Fort Yukon, paddle 3 miles up the Sucker River from its confluence with the Porcupine River to a road-accessible landing.

The most common put-in is at Old Crow, YT. From there it generally takes 6 to 10 days to float the 250 miles to Fort Yukon. It also is possible to charter a plane to the upper Porcupine or to Summit Lake on the Bell River, a tributary to the Porcupine, and extend the trip some 250 additional miles. For a description of the trip from Summit Lake, send for a Parks Canada booklet titled *Wild Rivers: Yukon Territory* available for a nominal fee from Printing and Publishing, Supply and Services Canada, Ottawa, ON, Canada K1A 0E9.

Grayling, whitefish, northern pike, sheefish and burbot are present in the Porcupine. Coho, king and chum salmon from the Bering Sea migrate up this system, one of the longest fish migrations in North America.

Old Crow is served by scheduled commercial air service from Whitehorse or Dawson, YT. Fort Yukon, where travelers can clear customs upon reentering the United States, is served by scheduled commercial air service from Fairbanks.

Related USGS Topographic maps: Coleen A-1 through 4, B-1 through 2; Black River D-4 through 6; Fort Yukon C-1 through 3; D-1. Canadian maps may be purchased from Canada Map Office, 615 Booth St., Ottawa, ON, Canada K1A 0E9.

Yukon River. The Yukon River originates in the coastal mountains of Canada and flows 2,300 miles in a great, wide arc to the Bering Sea.

Historically, travelers on the Yukon have used all manner of watercraft from log rafts to stern-wheelers. Today, most visitors use canoes, kayaks, inflatable rafts or outboard-powered riverboats. Freight-loaded barges are also seen on this major transportation corridor.

If starting your float trip in Canada, be sure to check in with U.S. customs upon arrival at Eagle. Between Eagle and Circle, the Yukon flows for 128 miles through Yukon-Charley Rivers National Preserve and then, shortly after Circle, into Yukon Flats National Wildlife Refuge for 300 miles.

According to the National Park Service "The segment of the Yukon beginning at Dawson and continuing downstream through (Yukon-Charley) preserve comprises one of the most scenic yet safely traversable stretches of any large river in North America."

Floaters generally take 4 to 10 days to travel from Eagle to Circle, depending on whether they take any side trips up tributaries or day hikes. Most camp on open beaches or river bars where winds keep down the insects.

Downriver from Eagle, the vivid black-and-white limestones of Calico Bluff form one of the most striking attractions on the river. *NOTE: Land on both sides of the Yukon River from Calico Bluff to just below the Tatonduk River mouth is owned by the Hungwitchin Native Corp. of Eagle, which requests that visitors not camp on its land.*

As the river enters Yukon-Charley Preserve 12 miles north of Eagle, it flows across a narrow floodplain flanked by high bluffs and heavily forested hills. The bluffs become less prominent as the river leaves the preserve near Circle, 14 miles north of the preserve, and enters Yukon Flats.

Through the preserve the river drops 230 feet for an average gradient of 1.5 feet per mile, producing a 6- to 8-mph current. Flows of 10 to 11 mph occur during and just after breakup, which usually takes place in early May. Width of the river along this stretch varies from less than half mile to several miles near Circle, where the stream becomes braided, making it difficult to pick out the main channel. There are no rapids on this section, but reef-formed riffles may be encountered in the low water of late summer and debris may be encountered in early summer. Beware of the occasional whirlpool. In any season strong winds may develop, building waves of 2 or 3 feet over exposed stretches; small boats should head for shore at such times.

There are numerous cabins in this area to explore that date back to the last century. *NOTE: Respect private property. Take only photographs!*

The Yukon River enters Yukon Flats National Wildlife Refuge along its southern boundary approximately 10 miles downstream from Circle. Then it flows northwesterly in a braided channel for some 60 miles to Fort Yukon, where it bends and flows southwest for another 240 miles in a meandering course with many sloughs before leaving the refuge in a narrow valley between the Ray and White mountains.

Fort Yukon is the primary community along this stretch of the river. Floaters generally take 4 to 7 days to pass through the refuge.

Downstream from the wildlife refuge is the Ramparts section, from the Dalton Highway to Tanana. This 128-mile section of the river — classified as Class I — has broad vistas, mile-wide river channels, high rock bluffs and hills covered with spruce and paper birch.

From the Dalton Highway, it generally takes 5 days to float to Tanana.

After the village of Rampart, the river passes between the high walls of Rampart Canyon.

Popular put-ins for the Yukon River are at Dawson, YT, Canada; Eagle, located at the end of the Taylor Highway; Circle at the end of the Steese Highway; and about a half mile upstream from the Yukon River bridge on the Dalton Highway (Milepost 56). Exit can be at Eagle, Circle, Fort Yukon, the Dalton Highway or Tanana, all of which have scheduled air service. Or pickup by charter air service can be arranged from the river. Floaters also can continue from Tanana down the broad, flat-water Yukon to the Bering Sea. Some communities along the way have overnight accommodations, and most of the larger ones have scheduled air service.

Related USGS Topographic maps: From Eagle to Circle — Charley River A-1 and 2, B-2 through 6, C-6, D-6, Circle C-1, D-1, Eagle C-1, D-1

From Circle to Dalton Highway — Fort Yukon, Beaver.

From Dalton Highway to Tanana — Livengood C-6, D-6. Tanana A-3 through 5, B-1 through 3, C-1, D-1.

Sportfishing

Access to sportfishing in Alaska's Interior can be as simple as climbing in your car and heading down one of several highways in the region. But the majority of the lakes and rivers of the Interior are reached only by plane or boat. (For good fishing locations along Interior highways consult *The MILE-POST®.*)

Northern pike live throughout the Interior. These fish average 2 to 5 pounds and occasionally attain trophy status of 15 pounds. Some lucky anglers have even caught 25- to 30-pound pike. Watch out for their sharp teeth! Use a wire leader and carry pliers for unhooking your catch.

Another enthusiastic fighter commonly found in Interior waters — particularly Yukon River tributaries, the Minto Flats and the lower Chena River — is the sheefish. Sheefish average 7 to 12 pounds in these waters, but occasionally attain 30 pounds.

Other fish found in the Interior are whitefish, which average 1 to 2 pounds; burbot (also called lush or lingcod) which average 2 to 5 pounds, but can attain 20 pounds; and arctic grayling. Grayling like clear, cold water and are found throughout much of the state; any grayling over 3 pounds is considered trophy size.

Access to most off-the-road sportfishing in the Interior is via small planes — usually chartered in Fairbanks — which can land on lakes or rivers, or on bush airstrips or gravel bars. However, boats occasionally can be rented in villages along the waterways. Fishing and hunting licenses can often be purchased from village vendors, but it is recommended that licenses be purchased in Fairbanks or another large community since rural vendors may be out hunting or fishing themselves.

For those traveling in the wilderness, a general rule from the Alaska Dept. of Fish and Game is to "plan for the worst." Travelers should take a few days extra food and other necessary supplies and allow for a flexible schedule in the event the weather turns bad and prevents pickup from remote sites.

For more information about fishing in the Interior, contact the Alaska Dept. of Fish and Game, Sport Fish Division, 1300 College Road, Fairbanks, AK 99701.

Delta Clearwater River. A spring-fed stream located near Delta Junction. Access from the Alaska Highway at Milepost 1414.8. Boat needed for best fishing. Tops for grayling — May 1 to Sept. 30, use flies or lures; whitefish — in spring and summer, use flies; burbot — also available; silver salmon — spawn here in October. Buffalo sometimes seen along rivers in this area.

East Twin Lake. Fly-in lake located in the Tanana Lowlands approximately 85 air miles southwest of Fairbanks, 40 miles east of the Bitzshtini Mountains. Trophy-sized pike — use spoons, spinners. Air charter service available in Fairbanks.

Goodpaster River. Located northeast of Delta Junction. Accessible by boat via the Delta Clearwater and Tanana rivers. Excellent grayling — fishing April 1 to Sept. 30, use flies, lures or bait.

Gulkana River. Located near the community of Gulkana. Foot and vehicle access at various points between Milepost 123 and 148 from Valdez on the Richardson Highway. Excellent king salmon fishery. Fly-fishing only below highway bridge. Above bridge, use bright lures and/or salmon eggs. Also good fly-fishing for red salmon. River guides for float fishing available. (See The Rivers this section.)

Koyukuk River. Joins the Yukon River 22 miles northeast of Nulato. Boats may be available for rental at communities on the river. Pike and sheefish available at Huslia. Sheefish in late September and pike year-round at Hughes. Sheefish — in September; grayling and pike — year-round at Allakaket.

Lake Minchumina. Fly-in lake located 66 miles northwest of Mount McKinley, 150 miles southwest of Fairbanks, 205 miles northwest of Anchorage. Pike — averaging 5 to 15 pounds, use spoons or spinners. Lodge on lake. Scheduled air service from Fairbanks to Lake Minchumina village. Charter air service available in Fairbanks or Anchorage.

Lucy Lake. Fly-in lake 1.6 miles long located within Denali State Park near Eldridge Glacier terminus, 40 miles north of Talkeetna. Access by small plane from Talkeetna or Chulitna River Lodge, Parks Highway, Milepost 156.2 from Anchorage. Fish available: lake trout — to 20 pounds, June and July, use spinner and spoons; grayling — use flies.

Mansfield Lake. Fly-in lake located 7 miles north of Tanacross on the Alaska Highway. Fish available: northern pike — year-round, use spoons or spinners; burbot — year-round, use bait. Air charter service available in Tanacross or Tok.

Melozitna River. Tributary of the Yukon River; mouth located 2 miles upstream from Ruby. Good sheefish — fishery upriver in July, use spoons. Boat accessible from Ruby.

Roped climber makes his way up the West Buttress route on Mount McKinley. (Bill Sherwonit)

Minto Lakes. Located in Minto Flats about 40 miles northwest of Fairbanks and southeast of the village of Minto. Good spring, summer and fall fisheries. The Fish and Game Dept. says this area has some of the best pike fishing in Alaska; pike — up to 20 to 25 pounds can be caught here. Pike fishing expected to be fair as they rebound from a year of low water and low numbers caught. Other fish available: sheefish — in midsummer, use spoons; whitefish — year-round, use flies or eggs; burbot — year-round, use bait. Accessible by small plane from Fairbanks; boat from Minto village, which is reached via the Elliott Highway, or via the Murphy Dome Extension Road from the top of Murphy Dome down to the Chatanika River.

Mystic Lake. Located in the foothills of the Alaska Range near the upper Tonzona River, 48 miles west of Mount McKinley, 158 miles northwest of Anchorage. Fish available: lake trout — to 4 to 5 pounds, use spoons or plugs; northern pike — to 4 feet, use spoons or spinners. Access by floatplane from Anchorage.

Nowitna River. Flows into the Yukon River 38 miles northeast of Ruby. Fish available: northern pike — year-round, use spoons or spinners; sheefish — in late summer, use spoons; grayling — in abundance, use flies. Salmon also spawn in this river.

Nulato River. Flows into the Yukon River 1 mile southwest of Nulato. Fish available: arctic char — in late summer, use spoons and eggs; grayling — May to October, use flies, lures or bait; king and chum salmon — arrive in July, use spoons. Access by boat from Nulato.

Porcupine River. Heads in Canada at 65°28'N, 139°32'W and flows 460 miles west to join the Yukon River 2 miles northwest of Fort Yukon. Fish available: arctic grayling — May to October, use flies; sheefish — July to October, use spoons; northern pike — year-round, use spoons. Access by boat or air charter service from Fort Yukon.

Quartz Lake. Excellent fishing for rainbow and silver salmon — near Delta Junction. Developed campsites on a loop road, with firepits, water, tables, toilet and boat launch. A trail connects Lost Lake and Quartz Lake camping areas. Commercial lodge located on lake.

Rainbow Lake. Located approximately 8 air miles across the Tanana River from Big Delta. Excellent rainbow trout — fishing, use flies or lures. Access by floatplane during summer or by winter trail.

Spink Lake. A 1.3-mile-long fly-in lake located in Denali State Park, 31 miles north of Talkeetna, 15 minutes by air west of Chulitna River Lodge, Parks Highway, Milepost 156.2 from Anchorage. Fish available: rainbow trout — to 8 pounds; a few Dolly Varden — July, August and September, use spinners and spoons.

Tetlin Lake. Located 16 miles southeast of Tok. Excellent northern pike — fishery, use spoons or spinners. Access by riverboat up the Tetlin River from the Tanana River, or by floatplane from Tok, Tanacross, Northway or Fortymile on the Alaska Highway.

Tozitna River. Flows into the Yukon River 6 miles downstream from Tanana. Fish available: northern pike — year-round, use spoons, spinners; sheefish — July to October, use spoons. Access by boat or small plane from Tanana.

Wien Lake. Fly-in lake located 60 miles south of the Yukon River between the Nowitna and Kantishna rivers. Good fishing for northern pike up to 18 pounds. Lodge on lake. Access by floatplane from Fairbanks.

GOLD FACTS

Gold was first discovered in Alaska in 1848 at the Russian River on the Kenai Peninsula.

The largest gold nugget ever found in Alaska was discovered at Anvil Creek, Nome District on Sept. 29, 1903. The nugget weighed 107 ounces, 2 pennyweight and measured 7 inches long, 4 inches wide and 2 inches thick.

Four other large nuggets have been found in Alaska. One, also from Anvil Creek found in 1899, was 6 inches long, 3 inches wide, 1 3/8 inches thick at one end and 1 inch thick at the other. Other large nuggets were found on Hammond River in 1914, Lower Glacier Creek in 1984, and Ganes Creek in 1986.
— *The ALASKA ALMANAC®*

SPECIAL FEATURES

Ghost Towns

Gold seekers came to the Interior before the turn of the century and built their towns and camps along its rivers. Some — like Fairbanks — flourished. Others died when the miners' luck ran out. Their picturesque remains still can be seen today — although sometimes they are overgrown with brush and difficult to find. We've listed a few of the old camps here. *NOTE: Respect private property. State and federal laws prohibit removing or destroying relics. Take only photographs.*

Caro. Located on the north bank of the Chandalar River at the mouth of Flat Creek, 26 miles south southeast of Chandalar, 45 miles north of the Arctic Circle. The cluster of log cabins on a slight, brush-covered rise is not visible from the river. This settlement was named for Caro Kingsland Clum, the daughter of Fairbanks postmaster John P. Clum, in 1907 when the Caro post office opened. The post office was discontinued in 1912. A wagon trail known as the Government Road, now overgrown with brush, once led to Caro from Beaver on the Yukon River.

Chandalar. Located on the east shore of Chandalar Lake at Rosalie Creek about 75 miles north of the Arctic Circle. This mining camp was established in 1906-07 and named after John Chandalar, who operated a Hudson's Bay Co. trading post there. Chandalar had a post office from 1908 to 1944.

Diamond (or Diamond City). Located at the junction of Moose Creek and Bearpaw River, which flows out of Denali National Park and Preserve into the Kantishna River. This

mining camp was the head of small-boat navigation on the Bearpaw and probably was a supply point for miners working farther upriver. Several buildings are still standing; a trapper may be using one during the winter. Check with the Park Service about any restrictions.

Fortymile. Located at the junction of Bullion Creek and North Fork Fortymile River, 37 miles southwest of Eagle. The U.S. Army Signal Corps established a telegraph station called North Fork here in 1903. Prospectors later called the place Fortymile. A few cabins remain standing.

Franklin (or Franklin Gulch). Located at the junction of Franklin Creek and the South Fork Fortymile River, 48 miles southwest of Eagle. A post office was established at this mining camp in 1902; it was discontinued in 1945. A few buildings remain.

Glacier (or Glacier City). Located at the junction of Glacier Creek and Bearpaw River within Denali National Park and Preserve. Dozens of old homes, warehouses and the like remain from this mining community that thrived from about 1908 until the 1920s, when it was abandoned. This ghost town is virtually invisible from the air when leaves are on the trees; it's easiest to visit in winter when overland access is possible. Check with the Park Service about any restrictions.

Kemperville (also known as Buckholtz Roadhouse). Located on the right bank of the Tanana River at the mouth of Hot Springs Slough, approximately 6 miles downstream from Manley Hot Springs. A trading post was established here in 1909 in one of the log cabins still standing. The camp, reportedly named for prospector George Kemper, was active until 1911.

Mastodon. Located on Mastodon Creek, south of the Yukon River, 40 miles southwest of Circle. The first gold strike was made in this area in 1894. The creek, and subsequently the camp, were named by miners after they found mastodon bones and tusks at their diggings. This camp was active from 1902 to 1906.

Nation (or Nation City). Located on the south bank of the Yukon River, 2.2 miles below the mouth of the Nation River. This was a mining camp and supply point for the Fourth of July placer mining area from 1908 to 1924. Only 2 cabins remain standing; 13 more are in ruins.

Rooseveldt (or Roosevelt). Located on the Kantishna River near the confluence of the Bearpaw River. This town was a regular stop for stern-wheelers in the early days. Cargo was unloaded here and placed in smaller craft for shipment to Diamond, Glacier and points farther upriver. The river has washed most of the buildings away, but a few still stand. There are many old sod doghouses behind the existing buildings; at least one cache has been used in recent years.

Woodchopper Creek. Located on Woodchopper Creek at the mouth of Iron Creek, 19 miles west of the junction of the Charley and Yukon rivers. This mining camp was established about 1907 and was active between 1919 and 1936.

Hot Springs

Chena Hot Springs: Located about 50 air miles northeast of Fairbanks, this popular private resort can be reached via the Steese Highway and Chena Hot Springs Road. The road cuts through Chena River State Recreation Area (see pages 411-412), an exceptional area offering picnic sites, campgrounds and easy access to the Chena Rivers excellent grayling fishery.

Chena Hot Springs were first reported in 1907 by U.S. Geological Survey field teams. The resort offers food, lodging and swimming

With tent set up, hiker relaxes on his pack in Denali National Park and Preserve. (George Wuerthner)

in the mineral springs. There is also an airstrip at the lodge. Overnight camping is available for a fee in the parking area at the end of the road.

Circle Hot Springs: About 100 miles northeast of Fairbanks, the springs are 8 miles off mile 127.8 Steese Highway. Ketchum Creek BLM Campground is located at Mile 5.7 of the Circle Hot Springs Road, offering 12 campsites with toilets, tables and firepits. At the hot springs, year-round swimming, lodging, food, groceries, bakery, gas and camper parking are available.

Circle Hot Springs was discovered in 1893 by prospector William Greats. In 1905, Franklin Leach homesteaded around the springs. Tents were used as the first bathhouses. Many miners wintered over at the springs when they could not work on the creeks.

The springs provide warm water for irrigating the resort's garden, which produces vegetables of great variety and size. Many buildings have been extensively renovated.

Melozi Hot Springs: Located on Hot Springs Creek, 30 miles northeast of Ruby. There is a group of 20 or so springs along the creek. A 1911 U.S. Geological Survey team reported finding a 2-room cabin and 2 small bathhouses on the springs. Today Melozi Hot Springs is the site of a private fly-in in wilderness lodge.

The Kink

Originally the name of a sharp bend in the North Fork Fortymile River, it came to mean the 15-foot-wide channel (eroded to 50 feet by the 1970s) that was blasted 100 feet through a ridge that formed the neck in the bend.

The channel was blasted through in 1904 by miners to divert the flow of the river and leave an approximately 2.8-mile area of riverbed open for mining. It was abandoned in 1905 when prospects turned out to be unprofitable. Now on the National Register of Historic Places, The Kink was a major engineering feat at its time and place and is considered a permanent monument to man's undertakings in the pursuit of gold at the turn of the century.

The Kink is located 40 miles southwest of Eagle on the east side of the North Fork Fortymile River, about 1 mile south of the confluence of Hutchinson Creek.

ALASKA NORTHWEST LIBRARY

- ALASKA: A PICTORIAL GEOGRAPHY, $4.95
- ALASKA AIRLINES STORY, THE, $12.95
- ALASKA ALMANAC, THE, 1990 Edition, $6.95
- ALASKA BEAR TALES, $12.95
- ALASKA BLUES: A Fisherman's Journal, $14.95
- ALASKA JOURNAL, Limited Edition, $24.95
- ALASKA SOURDOUGH, $7.95
- ALASKA WILD BERRY GUIDE AND COOKBOOK, $14.95
- ALASKA WILDERNESS MILEPOST®, THE, 1990 Edition, $14.95
- ALASKAN BIRD SKETCHES OF OLAUS MURIE, $11.95
- ALASKAN CAMP COOK, $4.95
- ALASKAN IGLOO TALES, $12.95
- ALASKAN MUSHROOM HUNTER'S GUIDE, $19.95
- ALASKA'S SALTWATER FISHES, $19.95
- ALASKA'S WILDERNESS MEDICINES, $9.95
- ALASKA-YUKON WILD FLOWERS GUIDE, $16.95
- ANTARCTIC, RICHARD HARRINGTONS, $8.95
- BAIDARKA, $19.95
- BITS AND PIECES OF ALASKAN HISTORY, Vol. I, $14.95
- BITS AND PIECES OF ALASKAN HISTORY, Vol. II, $14.95
- BUILDING THE ALASKA LOG HOME, $19.95
- CANADIAN BUSH PILOT: ERNIE BOFFA, $7.95
- CAPTURE OF ATTU, THE, $6.95
- CHILKOOT PASS: The Most Famous Trail in the North, $9.95

- COAST OF BRITISH COLUMBIA, THE, $34.95
- COOKING ALASKAN, $16.95
- DALE DE ARMOND: A First Book Collection of Her Prints, $14.95
- DESTINATION WASHINGTON, $4.95
- DISCOVERING WILD PLANTS (cloth), $34.95
- E.T. BARNETTE, $7.95
- EXPEDITION TO THE COPPER, TANANA AND KOYUKUK RIVERS IN 1885, $7.95
- EYE OF THE CHANGER, $9.95
- FISHERIES OF THE NORTH PACIFIC, $24.95
- FRANK BARR: Bush Pilot in Alaska and the Yukon, $7.95
- FRUITS & BERRIES OF THE PACIFIC NORTHWEST, $24.95
- GOLD HUSTLERS, THE, $7.95
- GUIDE TO THE BIRDS OF ALASKA, Revised Edition, $19.95
- GUIDE TO THE QUEEN CHARLOTTE ISLANDS, 1989-1990 Edition, $9.95
- HEROES AND HEROINES IN TLINGIT-HAIDA LEGEND, $14.95
- HIBROW COW, $9.95
- HOW TO BUILD AN OIL BARREL STOVE, $1.95
- I AM ESKIMO, $12.95
- I MARRIED A FISHERMAN, $7.95
- ICEBOUND IN THE SIBERIAN ARCTIC, $4.95
- ISLAND, $9.95
- ISLANDS OF HAWAII: E KOMO MAI!, THE, $4.95
- JUNEAU: A BOOK OF WOODCUTS, $12.95
- KENDLERS': The Story of a Pioneer Alaska Juneau Dairy, $7.95
- KOOTENAY COUNTRY, $9.95

BUYER'S GUIDE

This is a listing of those offering services to travelers in areas off Alaska's road system. The guide is divided initially by the service offered and then subdivided by region.

Please note that businesses are listed in the region where the service is offered. Many businesses serving remote areas maintain their headquarters in the city nearest their service area. One should not assume that an address represents the location of the lodge or air taxi service. In cases where a business serves more than one region, the business is listed in the region which appears to be the primary region served.

Readers also should be aware that many lodges and air taxi services offer guide services and some guides and outfitters may offer both fishing and hunting guide services but may be listed only under the category which represents their primary service.

Many communities along the road system also offer services to adventure travelers and readers should refer to *The MILEPOST®* for the most complete listing of those businesses. To order see the ALASKA NORTH-WEST LIBRARY.

Services listed by category are:
Airline/Air Taxi Operators
Adventure Guides & Outfitters
Boats—Charter & Scheduled
Fishing Guides & Outfitters
Hunting Guides & Outfitters
Lodging
Outdoor Equipment Rental & Sales
Services—Other
Winter Sports

AIRLINE/AIR TAXI OPERATORS

STATEWIDE

Alaska Airlines, 4750 W. International Airport Rd., Dept. WM, Anchorage, AK 99502. (800) 426-0333 or (907) 243-3300.

Alaska Bush Carrier, 4801 Aircraft Dr., Dept. WM, Anchorage, AK 99512. (907) 243-3127. *See display ad, page 443.*

ERA Aviation, 6160 S. Airpark Dr., Dept. WM, Anchorage, AK 99502. (907) 243-6633.

Ketchum Air Service, Inc., P.O. Box 190588, Dept. WM, Anchorage, AK 99519-0588. (907) 243-5525 or (800) 433-9114. 25-year family business located on Lake Hood International Airport. Seaplane. Fishing. Flightseeing. Hunting. Cabins. Lodges. Fly-in by floatplane to remote locations. Call or write for information. *See display ad, page 443.*

MarkAir, Inc., Box 196767, Dept. WM, Anchorage, AK 99519. (907) 243-6275 or (800) 478-0800.

Merrill Field Municipal Airport, 800 Merrill Field Dr., Dept. WM, Anchorage, AK 99501. (907) 276-4044. *See display ad, page 442.*

North Star Air Cargo, Inc., 1704 E. 5th Ave., Dept. WM, Anchorage, AK 99501. (907) 276-1244. *See display ad, this page.*

Rust's Flying Service, Box 190325, Dept. WM, Anchorage, AK 99519. (800) 544-2299 or (907) 243-1595.

SOUTHEAST REGION

Channel Flying, Inc., 8595 Yandukin Dr., Dept. WM, Juneau, AK 99801. (907) 789-3331. (800) 478-3331.

Ketchikan Air Service, Inc., 1600 International Airport, Dept. WM, Ketchikan, AK 99901. (907) 225-6608.

L.A.B. Flying Service, Box 272, Dept. WM, Haines, AK 99827. (907) 766-2222.

Misty Fjords Air and Outfitting, Box 3047, Dept. WM, Ketchikan, AK 99901. (907) 225-5155.

Temsco Helicopters, Inc., 1650 Maplesden Way, Dept. WM, Juneau, AK 99801. (907) 789-9501.

Wings of Alaska, 1873 Shell Simmons Dr., Dept. WM, Juneau, AK 99801. (907) 789-0790. *See display ad, this page.*

SOUTHCENTRAL/GULF COAST REGION

Aero Tech Flight Service, Inc., 1100 Merrill Field Dr., Dept. WM, Anchorage, AK 99501. (907) 279-6558.

Air Adventures, Island Lake, North Kenai, Box 22, Dept. WM, Kenai, AK 99611. (907) 776-5444.

Alaska Air Guides, Box 190989, Dept. WM, Anchorage, AK 99519. (907) 243-3969.

Alaska Air Tours, Box 671188, Dept. WM, Chugiak, AK 99567. (907) 276-5422.

Alaska West Air, Box 8553, Dept. WM, Nikiski, AK 99635. (907) 776-5147.

Alaskan Airventures, HC 03, Box 8758-WM, Palmer, AK 99645. (907) 822-3905. *See display ad, page 445.*

Anchorage Air Center, Inc., 2301 Merrill Field Dr., Dept. WM, Anchorage, AK 99501. (907) 278-9752.

Bush Pilots Air Service, Inc., Box 190389, Dept. WM, Anchorage, AK 99519. (907) 248-0149.

Chitina Air, Box 720, Dept. WM, Cordova, AK 99574. (907) 424-3534.

Cook Inlet Aviation, 2214 Kachemak Dr., Box 175, Dept. WM, Homer, AK 99603. (907) 235-8163.

Cordova Air Service, Inc., Box 528-WM, Cordova, AK 99574. (907) 424-3289. *See display ad, page 444.*

Gulkana Air Service, P.O. Box 31-WM, Glennallen, AK 99588. (907) 822-5532. Gulkana Airport, Mile 118.2 Richardson Hwy. Air tours in Wrangell St. Elias National Park. Catering to wilderness hiking groups, mountain climbers, hunters and fishermen. Guided fishing and hunting trips arranged. Floatplane service available. Write for brochure.

Harbor Air Service, P.O. Box 269-WM, Seward, AK 99664. (907) 224-3133. *See display ad, page 444.*

Iliamna Air Taxi, Tim and Nancy LaPorte, P.O. Box 109-WM, Iliamna, AK 99606. (907) 571-1248. Charter service for unguided hunting, fishing, river float trips, flightseeing and wilderness backpacking. Scheduled service to the lake villages. Comfortable lodging available with excellent family-style meals for the "do-it-yourself" fisherman. *See*

display ad, page 444.

Kachemak Air Service, Inc., Box 1769, Dept. WM, Homer, AK 99603. (907) 235-8924.

Kenai Lake Air Services, Box 830, Dept. WM, Cooper Landing, AK 99572. (907) 595-1363.

McCarthy Air, via Glennallen, Dept. WM, McCarthy, AK 99588.

Raven Air, Inc., 3541 Amber Bay Loop, Dept. WM, Anchorage, AK 99515. (907) 243-5586.

Regal Air, Box 190573, Dept. WM, Anchorage, AK 99519. (907) 243-8535.

Willow Air Service, Box 42-WM, Willow, AK 99688. (907) 495-6370. *See display ad, page 444.*

BERING SEA COAST REGION

Bering Air, Inc., Box 1650, Dept. WM, Nome, AK 99762. (907) 443-5464.

Branch River Air Service, 4540 Edinburgh Dr., Dept. WM, Anchorage, AK 99515. (907) 248-3539.

Herman's/MarkAir Express, Box 7010, Dept. WM, Bethel, AK 99559. (907) 543-4220.

Olson Air Service, Box 142, Dept. WM, Nome, AK 99762. (907) 443-2229.

ARCTIC REGION

Alaska Air Outfitters, Box 81897, Dept.

WM, Fairbanks, AK 99708. (800) 262-5769. (summer) or Box 270168, Dept. WM, San Diego, CA 92128. (619) 748-5796. (winter)

Arctic Air Guides, Box 187, Dept. WM, Kotzebue, AK 99752. (907) 442-3030.

Golden Plover Air, Colville Village via Pouch 340109-WM, Prudhoe Bay, AK 99734. (907) 659-3991. *See display ad, page 445.*

Wright Air Service, Box 60142-WM, Fairbanks, AK 99706. (907) 474-0502. Statewide charter plus scheduled service to Anaktuvuk, Fort Yukon, Allakaket, Arctic Village, Bettles and Venetie. Licensed in Gates of the Arctic and Kobuk Valley national parks, Noatak National Preserve. Cabins, boats, at Minto Flats for northern pike, bird-watching.

Yukon Air Service, Roger Dowding, Box 111, Dept. WM, Fort Yukon, AK 99740. (907) 662-2445.

Frontier Flying Service, Inc. & Frontier Expeditions, 3820 University Ave., Dept. A, Fairbanks, AK 99701. (907) 474-0014. Statewide and Canadian charter plus scheduled service to Kotzebue, Barter Island, Bettles, Anaktuvuk Pass, Fort Yukon, Allakaket, Coldfoot and other Yukon River villages. Information available on backpacking, hunting, rafting, flightseeing, museums in Eskimo & Indian villages. *See display ad, this page.*

INTERIOR REGION

Denali Air, Box 82, Dept. WM, Denali National Park, AK 99755. (907) 683-2261.

Doug Geeting Aviation, Box 42, Dept. WM, Talkeetna, AK 99676. (907) 733-2366.

Hudson Air Service, Box 82, Dept. WM, Talkeetna, AK 99676. (907) 733-2321.

K2 Aviation, Box 545, Dept. WM, Talkeetna, AK 99676. (907) 733-2291.

Talkeetna Air Taxi, P.O. Box 73-WM, Talkeetna, AK 99676. (907) 733-2218. Scenic flights, glacier landings, photographers, hunters, fishermen, rafting and climbing expedition support. Serving McKinley, Alaska Range, Lake Clark. Charters to and from Anchorage and Denali National Park. David J. Lee, Owner and Chief Pilot.

Tatonduk Flying, Dept. WM, Eagle, AK 99738. (907) 547-2221.

Tundra Air, General Delivery, Dept. WM, Manley Hot Springs., AK 99756. (907) 672-3692. *See display ad, this page.*

ADVENTURE GUIDES & OUTFITTERS

STATEWIDE

Adventures & Delights, 300 W. 36th St., Dept. WM, Anchorage, AK 99503. (907) 276-8282. *See display ad, page 447.*

Alaska Bush Adventures, 610 W. 91st Ave., Dept. WM, Anchorage, AK 99515. (907) 522-1712.

Alaska River Adventures, George Heim, 1831 Kuskokwim St., Dept. WM, Anchorage, AK 99508. (907) 276-3418.

Alaska Treks 'n Voyages, P.O. Box 625W, Seward, AK 99664. (907) 224-3960. Custom mountain adventure, wild and scenic river trips, dogsled tours and packdog trips throughout Alaska's parklands. Also sea kayak rentals/instruction/tours out of Seward and Kenai Fjords. *See display ad, page 447.*

Alaska Wilderness Guides Association, Box 141061-W, Anchorage, AK 99514. (907) 276-6634.

Alaskan Wilderness Outfitting Company, Box 1516, Dept. WM, Cordova, AK 99574. (907) 424-5552.

Back-Trails Tours, 2316 Galewood, Dept. WM, Anchorage, AK 99508. (907) 276-5528.

Canoe Alaska, Box 81750, Dept. WM, Fairbanks, AK 99708. (907) 479-5183.

Denali Raft Adventures, Drawer 190-WM, Denali National Park, AK 99755. (907) 683-2234. Come with the original Nenana River rafters! Alaska-owned and operated. Paddle-boats, too! All ages welcome. Five departures daily. Wildwater or scenic floats. Get away to untouched wilderness! 2-hour, 4-hour and multi-day trips.

Eruk's Wilderness Float Trips, 12720 Lupine Rd., Dept. WM, Anchorage, AK 99516. (907) 345-7678.

Hugh Glass Backpacking Co., Chuck Ash, P.O. Box 110796-M, Anchorage, AK 99511. (907) 344-1340. Treks, raft and canoe trips, sea kayaking, trophy fishing and photographic

trips statewide since 1975. Guided and outfitted. Brooks Range, Wrangell-St. Elias, Lake Clark, A.N.W.R., Katmai, Kenai Fjords, Prince William Sound and Bristol Bay.

National Outdoor Leadership School, Box 981, Dept. WM, Palmer, AK 99645. (907) 745-4047.

Nature Alaska Tours, Box 10224, Dept.

WM, Fairbanks, AK 99710. (907) 488-3746.

North to Alaska! Expeditions and Adventures, 200 W. 34th Ave., Suite 300-WM, Anchorage, AK 99503. (907) 696-2696.

Nova River Runners, Inc., HC 03, Box 8337, Dept. WM, Palmer, AK 99645. (907) 745-5753.

Osprey Expeditions, Aaron Underwood or Juliette Boselli, Box 209, Denali National Park, AK 99755. (907) 683-2734. 2- to 12-day wilderness raft trips throughout Alaska. Custom expeditions, small groups, paddle raft or oar power, exploratories, kayak support, white water and/or scenic. Everything provided. Come see us at Denali National Park, Mile 224 Parks Highway.

Ouzel Expeditions, 7540 E. 20th Ave., Dept. WM, Anchorage, AK 99504. (907) 338-0620.

St. Elias Alpine Guides, Box 111241, Dept. WM, Anchorage, AK 99511. (907) 277-6867.

Weber-Alyeska Wilderness Guides, Box 111663, Dept. WM, Anchorage, AK 99511. (907) 345-2081.

Wilderness Alaska, 6710 Potter Heights Dr., Dept. WM, Anchorage, AK 99516. (907) 345-3366.

Women of the Wilderness, Box 775226, Dept. WM, Eagle River, AK 99577. (907) 688-2226.

SOUTHEAST REGION

Admiralty Island Wilderness Charters, Box 020295, Dept. WM, Juneau, AK 99802. (907) 586-3822.

Alaska Cross Country Guiding, Box 124, Dept. WM, Haines, AK 99827.

Alaska Discovery, 369 S. Franklin St., Dept.

WM, Juneau, AK 99801. (907) 586-1911.

Alaska Nature Institute, Box 68, Dept. WM, Gustavus, AK 99826. (907) 697-2302.

Alaska Nature Tours, Box 491, Dept. WM, Haines, AK 99827. (907) 766-2876.

Alaska Rainforest Treks, Box 210845, Dept. WM, Auke Bay, AK 99821. (907) 463-3466.

Alaska Sea Adventures, Box 101, Coleman Dr., Dept. WM, Juneau, AK 99801. (907) 586-4792.

Alaska Travel Adventures, 9085 Glacier Highway, Suite 204W, Juneau, AK 99801. (907) 789-0052.

Alaska Wyldewind Charters, 617 Katlian, B-33, Dept. WM, Sitka, AK 99835. (907) 747-3287.

Brownie's Budget Charters, 2038 Halibut Point Highway., Dept. WM, Sitka, AK 99835. (907) 747-5402.

Chichagof Charters, Dept. WM, Elfin Cove, AK 99825. (907) 239-2211.

Chilkat Guides, Box 170, Dept. WM, Haines, AK 99827. (907) 766-2409.

Glacier Bay Alaska Tours & Charters, Box 60, Dept. WM, Gustavus, AK 99826. (907) 697-2254.

Glacier Bay Sea Kayaks, Box 26, Dept. WM, Gustavus, AK 99826. (907) 697-2257.

Grand Pacific Charters, Box 5, Dept. WM, Gustavus, AK 99826. (907) 697-2288.

Harding's Old Sourdough Charters, Box 1062, Dept. WM, Wrangell, AK 99929. (907) 874-3455.

Misty Fjords Air & Outfitting, Box 3407, Dept. WM, Ketchikan, AK 99901. (907) 225-5155.

Myriad Adventures, 203 Lincoln St., Dept. WM, Sitka, AK 99835. (907) 747-8279.

Outdoor Alaska, Dale Pihlman, Box 7814-WM, Ketchikan, AK 99901. (907) 225-6044. *See display ad, this page.*

Seahorse Riding Adventures, Box 122, Dept. WM, Gustavus, AK 99826. (907) 697-2266.

Southeast Exposure, Box 9143, Dept. WM, Ketchikan, AK 99901. (907) 225-8829.

Spirit Walker Expeditions, Inc., Box 122-W, Gustavus, AK 99826. (907) 694-2266.

SOUTHCENTRAL/GULF COAST REGION

Adventure North, 1040 W. 4th Ave., Dept. WM, Anchorage, AK 99501. (907) 276-0713.

Ageya Kayak Tours, 2517 Foraker St., Dept. WM, Anchorage, AK 99517. (907) 248-7140.

Alaska Sea Kayaking, Box 1386, Dept. WM, Palmer, AK 99645. (907) 745-3487.

Alaska Seacoast Charters, Box 319, Dept.

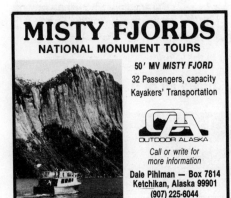

WM, Cordova, AK 99574. (907) 424-7742.

Alaska Treks 'n Voyages, P.O. Box 625W, Seward, AK 99664. (907) 224-3960. Sea kayak rentals, instruction, tours in Resurrection Bay and Kenai Fjords highlight our Seward-based operations. Also guided mountain hikes, backpacking, and glacier skiing trips on Harding Icefield and in Kenai Mountains. *See display ad, page 447.*

Alaska Waterways, Box 1881, Dept. WM, Valdez, AK 99686. (907) 835-5151.

Alaska Wilderness Explorations, Box 2074, Dept. WM, Homer, AK 99603. (907) 235-6094.

Alaska Wildland Adventures, HC 64, Box 26-WM, Cooper Landing, AK 99572. (907) 595-1279.

Alaskan Sojourns Wilderness Guides, P.O. Box 87-1410, Dept. WM, Wasilla, AK 99687. (907) 376-2913. *See display ad, this page.*

Alpine Sports Unlimited, Box 1502-WM, Valdez, AK 99686., (907) 835-4817.

Bicycle Tours, Box 90375, Dept. WM, Anchorage, AK 99509. (907) 563-0706.

Chuitna River Guides, Box 82051, Dept. WM, Tyonek, AK 99682. (907) 583-2302.

Distant Shores, 421 W. 88th Ave., Dept. WM, Anchorage, AK 99515. (907) 344-8849.

Great Alaska Fish Camp, The, HC 01, Box 218-WM, Sterling, AK 99672. (800) 544-2261 or (907) 262-4515. Fly-in hunting/ fishing camps. Float fish wild rivers. Canoe safaris in wilderness refuge. Natural history treks. Deluxe lodge, cabins and fishing pro- gram or economy packages.

Hatcher Pass Trail Rides, HC 01, Box 6871, Dept. WM, Palmer, AK 99645. (907) 745- 2789.

High Adventure, Box 486, Dept. WM, Soldotna, AK 99669. (907) 262-5237.

Kachemak Bay Horse Trips, HCR 58335

East End Rd., Dept. WM, Homer, AK 99603. (907) 235-7850.

Keitl-Daan Outfitters, Box 315, Dept. WM, Tok, AK 99780. (907) 883-5603.

Kenai Guide Service, Box 40, Dept. WM, Kasilof, AK 99610. (907) 262-5496.

Keystone Raft and Kayak Adventures, Box 1486, Dept. WM, Valdez, AK 99686. (907) 835-2606.

Kichatna Guide Service, Box 670790, Dept. WM, Chugiak, AK 99567. (907) 696-3256.

Kodiak Adventures, Box 285, Dept. WM, Kodiak, AK 99615. (907) 345-1160 (summer) or (907) 373-2285 (winter).

Nabesna Whitewater Rafting, Star Route A, Box 1420, Dept. WM, Slana, AK 99586. (907) 822-3426.

Naturalist Hiking with Donna Larson, Mile 111.5 Glenn Highway., HC 03, Box 8488A, Palmer, AK 99645. (907) 745-5143. Guided hikes for all interests and ages from mountain to marsh. Fossil/rock hunting, birding, plant identification, wildlife viewing and photography. 2- 3- 4-day hiking packages

including room and board. Rustic bunk 'n breakfast. Need sleeping bag. $10/person plus 5% bed tax, $5 breakfast.

Northsport, Box 40, Dept. WM, Talkeetna, AK 99676. (907) 733-2411.

Personal Alaskan Adventures, 12900 Norak Place, Dept. WM, Anchorage, AK 99516. (907) 345-4493.

Prince William Sound Recreation Assoc., 3111 C. St., Suite 200-WM, Anchorage, AK 99503. (907) 561-1622.

Rafter T Ranch, Box 1493, Dept. WM, Palmer, AK 99645. (907) 745-2894. (Horse rentals)

Sam Barber's Coastal Adventures of Alaska, 6458 Citadel Lane, Dept. WM, Anchorage, AK 99504. (907) 337-0313.

Silver Bullet Ranch, HC 02, Box 7347-A2 Hutoka Circle, Dept. WM, Palmer, AK 99645. (907) 745-8646. (Horse rentals)

South Fork Outfitters, HC 03, Box 8485, Dept. WM, Palmer, AK 99645. (907) 745-6323.

Talkeetna Mountain Trail Rides, Box 322, Dept. WM, Talkeetna, AK 99676. (907) 733-2475.

Talkeetna Rafting Adventures, Box 470, Dept. WM, Talkeetna, AK 99676. (907) 733-2281.

Tyonek Village Tour, 1577-MP, C St., Suite 304, Anchorage, AK 99501. *See display ad, page 449.*

Ultima Thule Outfitters, Box 109-WM, Chitina, AK 99566. (907) 344-1892 (FAX also).

Water Wilderness Guides & Outfitters, Box 1386, Dept. WM, Palmer, AK 99645. (907) 745-3487.

Wrangell-St. Elias Mountaineering, Box 111816, Dept. WM, Anchorage, AK 99511. (907) 344-3986.

BERING SEA COAST REGION

Bethel Village Tour, 1577-MP, C St., Suite 304, Anchorage, AK 99501. *See display ad, this page.*

Gambell Village Tour, 1577-MP, C St., Suite 304, Anchorage, AK 99501. *See display ad, this page.*

Idita-Tours, Box 723, Dept. WM, Nome, AK 99762. (907) 443-2636.

St. George Pribilof Island Tours, 4000 Old Seward Highway., Dept. WM, Anchorage, AK 99503. (907) 562-3100.

ARCTIC REGION

A.B.E.C's Wilderness-Alaska/Mexico: Ramona Finnoff & Ron Yarnell, Dept. AWM, 1304 Westwick Dr., Fairbanks, AK 99712. (907) 457-8907. Guided backpack, kayak and raft trips in Alaska's Brooks Range since 1971 including the Gates of the Arctic, Arrigetch Peaks, Noatak River and the Arctic National Wildlife Refuge. Wildlife Observation–Fishing – Nature Study. Custom trips available.

Alatna Guide Service, Box 80424, Dept. WM, Fairbanks, AK 99708. (907) 479-6354.

Arctic Treks, Jim Campbell & Carol Kasza, Box 73452M, Fairbanks, AK 99707. (907) 455-6502. Arctic adventure at its grandest! Backpack and raft in an untamed arctic expanse so vast and complete you'll redefine your whole notion of wildness — and yourself. Arctic National Wildlife Refuge and Gates of the Arctic National Park.

Bettles Lodge, P.O. Box 27-WM, Bettles, AK 99726. (907) 692-5111. Your gateway to the Gates of the Arctic National Park. Wilderness rafting and hiking excursions or enjoy a night in this landmark lodge providing traveler services since 1950. Open year-round. AV gas, restaurant, lodging, liquor.

Brooks Range Expeditions, Box 7, Dept. WM, Bettles, AK 99726. (907) 692-5333.

Brooks Range Wilderness Trips, Box 48, Dept. WM, Bettles, AK 99726. (907) 692-5312.

Gates of the Arctic Lodge, Nick or Susan Jennings, 1677 Souhrada Rd., Dept. WM, Delta Junction, AK 99737. (907) 895-4065. The ultimate Wilderness . . . Arctic Alaska. Fully guided adventures. Over 15 years experience. River float trips, flightseeing, wildlife photography, cross-country skiing, backpacking, fishing, hunting. Specializing in custom trips and service throughout Alaska's Brooks Range. March-September.

Isuma Guideworks, Box 55235, Dept. WM, North Pole, AK 99705. (907) 488-8943.

Nichols Expeditions, Chuck & Judy Nichols, 590 North 500 West, Dept. WMP, Moab, UT 84532. (800) 635-1792 or (801) 259-7882. We offer 7-14 day guided rafting and backpacking expeditions in the Brooks Range and Copper River. Spectacular scenery, remote wilderness. No experience necessary. Write or call for our free catalogue.

Peregrine Expedition, Dept. WM, Shungnak, AK 99773. (907) 437-2159.

Quest Expeditions, 28909 N. Cedar, Dept. WM, Deer Park, WA 99006. (509) 276-5621. *See display ad, this page.*

Sourdough Outfitters, Box 90-WM, Bettles, AK 99726. (907) 692-5252.

Tour Arctic, Box 49-W, Kotzebue, AK 99752. (907) 442-3301. *See display ad, this page.*

Wilderness Alaska, Box 83044, Dept. WM, Fairbanks, AK 99708.

INTERIOR REGION

Alaska-Denali Guiding, Inc., Box 566-WM, Talkeetna, AK 99676. (907) 733-2649.

Alaska Rafting Adventures, Box 295, Dept. WM, Talkeetna, AK 99676. (907) 733-2681.

Alaska Wilderness Expeditions, Box 73297, Dept. WM, Fairbanks, AK 99707. (907) 479-5496.

Alaskan Back Country Guides Cooperative, Box 81533, Dept. WM, College, AK 99708. (907) 479-2754.

Charley River Canoe, 875 Ensley Rd., Dept. WM, North Pole, AK 99705. (907) 488-6990.

Circle North River Outfitters, Box 111-WM, Fort Yukon, AK 99740. (907) 662-2445.

Denali Floats, Box 330, Dept. WM, Talkeetna, AK 99676.

Four Season River Runner Andy Bassich, Box 11-WM, Eagle, AK 99738. (907) 547-2291. Yukon River jetboat charter service. Guided day trips, drop-off/pick-up, hunter transport, canoe rentals. Customized trips. Winter dog mushing adventures. Eagle-Dawson City; Eagle-Circle Hot Springs; backcountry trips. Brochures available or call for details.

Genet Expedition, Dept. WM, Talkeetna, AK 99676. (907) 376-5120.

McKinley Raft Tours, Box 138, Dept. WM, Denali National Park, AK 99755. (907) 683-2392.

Mt. McKinley Alaska Glacier Tours, Box

102315, Dept. WM, Anchorage, AK 99510. (800) 327-7651. (907) 272-7958.

Mystic Pass Treks and Floats, 12 Toklat Dr., Dept. WM, Lake Minchumina, AK 99757. (907) 733-2630 (summer) or Box 110481, Dept. WM, Anchorage, AK 99511. (907) 344-2644 (winter).

Owl Rafting, Inc., Box 612, Dept. WM, Denali National Park, AK 99755. (907) 683-2215 (summer) or 7822 175th SW, Dept. WM, Edmonds, WA 98020. (206) 775-6409 (winter).

Rainbow Riverrunners, Box 81149, Dept. WM, Fairbanks, AK 99708. (907) 479-5859.

Teklanika Tours, Box 10367, Dept. WM, Fairbanks, AK 99710. (907) 457-7194.

BOATS—CHARTER & SCHEDULED

SOUTHEAST REGION

A.A.A. Charters, 167 S. Franklin, Dept. WM, Juneau, AK 99801. (907) 586-1000.

58 Degrees 22 Minutes North Sailing Charters, Box 32391, Dept. WM, Juneau, AK 99803. (907) 789-7301.

Ken's Charters, Box 9609, Dept. WM, Ketchikan, AK 99901. (907) 225-7290 (summer) or Box 19329, Dept. WM, Thorne Bay, AK 99919. (907) 828-3387 (winter).

Knudson Cove Marina, Route 1, Box 965, Dept. WM, Ketchikan, AK 99901. (907) 247-8500.

Marine Adventure Sailing Tours, 2765 Fritz Cove Rd., Dept. WM, Juneau, AK 99801. (907) 789-0919.

Masterson Charters, 8127 Poplar, Ave., Dept. WM, Juneau, AK 99801.

Nine Lives Charters, Box 32563, Dept. WM, Juneau, AK 99803. (907) 780-4468.

Stellar Charters, 319 Peterson, Dept. WM, Sitka, AK 99835. (907) 747-6711.

SOUTHCENTRAL/GULF COAST REGION

Alaska Island Adventure, Box 101004, Dept. WM, Anchorage, AK 99510. (907) 892-6503. (Seward)

Alaskan Wilderness Sailing Safaris, Box 1313, Dept. WM, Valdez, AK 99686. (907) 338-2134. (summer) or Box 701, Dept. WM, Whittier, AK 99693. (907) 835-5175 (winter).

Bountiful Ventures, Box 77-1688, Dept. WM, Eagle River, AK 99577. (907) 696-2628. (Whittier)

Choice Marine Charters, Box 200592, Dept. WM, Anchorage, AK 99520. (907)

243-0069. (Whittier)

Gail Sea Marine Charters, 6426 Blackberry, Dept. WM, Anchorage, AK 99502. (907) 248-4305. (Whittier)

Jackpot Charters, 3015 Nugget Lane, Dept. WM, Anchorage, AK 99516. (907) 345-4109. (Whittier)

Kachemak Bay Ferry, *Danny J,* P.O. Box 6410-WM, Halibut Cove, AK 99603. (907) 296-2223 or (907) 235-7847. Noon starting time from the picturesque Kenai Peninsula town of Homer, a visit to Gull Island, on to Halibut Cove. Stroll the 12 blocks of boardwalk. Enjoy a bite to eat at the Saltry Restaurant. *See display ad, page 454.*

Pop-Eye Boat Charters, 5028 Mills Dr., Dept. WM, Anchorage, AK 99508. (907) 338-2322. (Whittier)

Port Lions Charters, Box 251, Dept. WM, Port Lions, AK 99550. (907) 454-2264.

Prince William Sound Charters, Box 91227, Dept. WM, Anchorage, AK 99509. (800) 247-0003. (Whittier)

Rainbow Charters, Box 1526, Dept. WM, Homer, AK 99603. (907) 235-7272.

St. Augustine's Sailing Charters and Water Taxi, Box 2412, Dept. WM, Homer, AK 99603. (907) 235-7972.

Sinbad Charters, Box 77-1003, Dept. WM, Eagle River, AK 99577. (907) 694-2224. (Whittier)

South Central Sports Water Taxi, 1411 Lakeshore Dr., Dept. WM, Homer, AK 99603. (907) 235-5403.

Sound Water Taxi, 3001 E. 42nd, #107, Dept. WM, Anchorage, AK 99508. (907) 563-2976 or (907) 472-2455. (Whittier)

Stan Stephens Charters, P.O. Box 1297, Dept. WM, Valdez, AK 99686. (907) 835-4731. *See display ad, page 453.*

BERING SEA COAST REGION

Don's Round Island Boat Charters, P.O. Box 68-WM, Togiak, AK 99678. (907) 493-5127. *See display ad, page 453.*

INTERIOR REGION

Yukon Explorer, 3330 Riverside Dr., Dept. WM, Fairbanks, AK 99709. (907) 479-8817.

FISHING GUIDES & OUTFITTERS

STATEWIDE

Alaska Dept. of Fish and Game, P.O. Box 3-2000, Juneau, AK 99802-2000. (907) 465-4112.

Custom Alaska Fishing Packages, 321 E. 5th Ave., Dept. WM, Anchorage, AK 99501. (907) 276-1151.

Devito-Fishing Guide, Box 317, Dept. WM, Soldotna, AK 99669. (907) 283-7437.

Sportfishing Alaska, 1401 Shore Dr., Dept. WM, Anchorage, AK 99515. (907) 344-8674.

Klawock Bay Charters and Lodging, Box 145, Dept. WM, Klawock, AK 99925. (907) 755-2329.

Leviathan Charters, Box 787, Dept. WM, Petersburg, AK 99833. (907) 772-3818 or (800) 327-2571.

SOUTHEAST REGION

Alaska Adventure Charters, Box 7236, Dept. WM, Ketchikan, AK 99901. (907) 225-2792.

Alaska Fishing Adventures, 326 Front St., Dept. WM, Ketchikan, AK 99901. (907) 225-9423.

Alaska Wilderness Steelhead Safaris, Box 101, Dept. WM, Angoon, AK 99820. (907) 788-3123.

Anderson Charters, Box 7118, Dept. WM, Ketchikan, AK 99901. (907) 225-2456.

Beartrack Charters, 800 F St., Suite A-2, Dept. WM, Juneau, AK 99801. (907) 586-6945.

Bluewater Outfitters, Box 3107, Dept. WM, Sitka, AK 99835. (907) 747-3934.

Chan IV Charters, Box 624, Dept. WM, Petersburg, AK 99833. (907) 772-4859.

Elfin Cove Charters, Box 69, Dept. WM, Elfin Cove, AK 99825. (907) 239-2207 (summer) or 7504 NE Par Lane, Dept. WM, Vancouver, WA 98662. (800) 323-5346. (winter).

Floyd's Icy Straits Highliner, Box 245, Dept. WM, Hoonah, AK 99829. (907) 945-3327.

Glacier Guides, Inc., Box 66, Dept. WM, Gustavus, AK 99826. (907) 697-2252 (summer) or Box 460, Dept. WM, Santa Clara, UT 84765. (801) 628-0973.

Grafin Marine Services, Box 6081, Dept. WM, Ketchikan, AK 99901. (907) 225-3747.

High Hook Charters, 110 Bayview, Dept. WM, Coffman Cove, AK 99950. (907) 329-2249.

Islander Charters, Box 020927, Dept. WM, Juneau, AK 99802. (907) 780-4419.

Ken & Toni's Angling Adventures, Box 2027, Dept. WM, Wrangell, AK 99929. (907) 874-3084.

Mike Nigro's Gustavus Marine Charters, Box 81, Dept. WM, Gustavus, AK 99826. (907) 697-2233.

Ocean Chinook Charters, Box 210483, Dept. WM, Auke Bay, AK 99821. (907) 789-1771.

Ramblin' Marine Charters, Box 1068, Dept. WM, Petersburg, AK 99833. (907) 772-3039.

Seabreeze Charters, 1033 Millar St., Dept. WM, Ketchikan, AK 99901. (907) 225-5317.

Seawind Charters, Box 126, Dept. WM, Douglas, AK 99824. (907) 364-3341.

Southeast Charters, Box 211, Dept. WM, Haines, AK 99827. (907) 766-2968.

Sportsman Charters, 821 Pherson St., Dept. WM, Sitka, AK 99835. (907) 747-8756.

Steamboat Bay, Inc., Box 132, Dept. WM, Craig, AK 99921. (907) 826-3227.

W.T. Fugarwe Inc., P.O. Box 27-WM, Gustavus, AK 99826. (907) 697-2244 (summer). P.O. Box 459, Georgetown, CO 80444. (303) 623-7108 or 569-2255 (winter). *See display ad, page 455.*

Wings of Alaska, 1873 Shell Simmons Dr., Dept. WM, Juneau, AK 99801. (907) 789-0790. Year-round operation offers scheduled commuter flights in northern southeast Alaska and charter flights throughout southeast Alaska and western Canada. Charter flights for fishing and hunting, Glacier Bay, Juneau Icefield and Tracy Arm Fjord. *See display ad, page 443.*

Wrangell Charter Boat Assoc., Box 1078, Dept. WM, Wrangell, AK 99929. (907) 874-3800.

SOUTHCENTRAL/GULF COAST REGION

Alaska Float Camps, 4505 Spenard Rd., #660-WM, Anchorage, AK 99517. (800) 826-7541.

Beluga River Camp, Box 141884, Dept. WM, Anchorage, AK 99514. (907) 268-9533.

Brightwater Alaska, Chuck Ash, P.O. Box 110796-M, Anchorage, AK 99511. (907) 344-1340. Fishing float trips in Bristol Bay and Cook Inlet. Guided and outfitted on Alaska's finest waters since 1975. World-class fishing for all 5 species of salmon, rainbow trout, grayling, Dolly Varden, and arctic char.

Dodge Outfitters, SR Box 880, Dept. WM, Kodiak, AK 99615.

Eagle Adventures, Box 2898, Dept. WM, Kodiak, AK 99615. (907) 486-3445.

Iliamna Lake Resort, P.O. Box 103984-WM, Anchorage, AK 99510. (907) 276-5595. *See display ad, page 457.*

Moonliter II Charters, 528 N St., Dept. WM, Anchorage, AK 99501. (907) 279-0703. (Whittier)

Seldovia Fishing Adventures, Box 121, Dept. WM, Seldovia, AK 99663. (907) 234-7417.

Winter King Charters, Box 14, Dept. WM, Cordova, AK 99574. (907) 424-7170.

ALASKA PENINSULA/ALEUTIANS REGION

Alaska Trophy Fishing Safaris, Box 670071, Dept. WM, Chugiak, AK 99567. (907) 696-2484.

Freebird Charters, Box 418, Dept. WM, King Salmon, AK 99613. (907) 246-3000. (summer) or 6682 Fairweather Dr., Dept. WM, Anchorage, AK 99518. (907) 561-2310 (winter).

Katmai Lodge, 2825 90th SE, Dept. WM, Everett, WA 98204. (206) 337-0326. *See display ad, page 458.*

Katmailand, Inc., 4700 Aircraft Dr., Dept. WM, Anchorage, AK 99502. (907) 243-5448. *See display ad, page 458.*

Ugashik Narrows Lodge, P.O. Box 101068-WM, Anchorage, AK 99510. (907) 272-9401. Fax: (907) 272-0251. *See display ad, page 466.*

BERING SEA COAST REGION

Nunivak Island Guide Service, Box 31, Dept. WM, Mekoryuk, AK 99630. (907) 827-8213.

Russian Mountain Lodge, Box 116, Dept. WM, Aniak, AK 99557. (907) 675-4376.

Western Alaska Sport Fishing, Inc. Box 274, Dept. WM, Dillingham, AK 99576. (907) 842-5480. (summer) or Box 206, St. Dept. WM, Xavier, MT 59075. (406) 666-2340 (winter).

ARCTIC REGION

Minakokosa Lake Fish Camp, Box 27, Dept. WM, Bettles, AK 99726. (907) 692-5111.

INTERIOR REGION

Alaska Backcountry Angling, Box 81483, Dept. WM, Fairbanks, AK 99708. (907) 457-2281.

Alaska Fish and Trails Unlimited Outfitters, 1177 Shypoke Dr., Dept. WM, Fairbanks, AK 99709. (907) 479-7630.

Alaska River Charters, Box 81516, Dept. WM, Fairbanks, AK 99708. (907) 455-6827.

Arctic Grayling Guide Service, Box 83707,

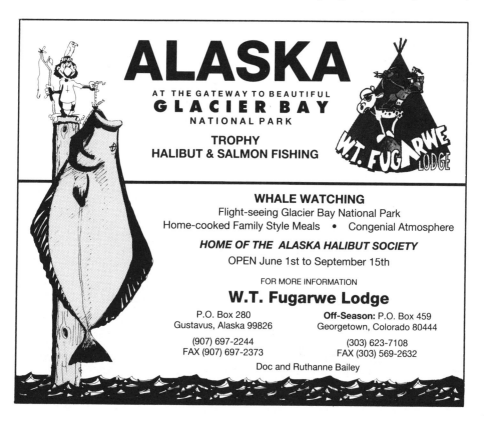

ALASKA

AT THE GATEWAY TO BEAUTIFUL

GLACIER BAY

NATIONAL PARK

TROPHY HALIBUT & SALMON FISHING

W.T. FUGARWE LODGE

WHALE WATCHING

Flight-seeing Glacier Bay National Park

Home-cooked Family Style Meals • Congenial Atmosphere

HOME OF THE ALASKA HALIBUT SOCIETY

OPEN June 1st to September 15th

FOR MORE INFORMATION

W.T. Fugarwe Lodge

P.O. Box 280
Gustavus, Alaska 99826

Off-Season: P.O. Box 459
Georgetown, Colorado 80444

(907) 697-2244
FAX (907) 697-2373

(303) 623-7108
FAX (303) 569-2632

Doc and Ruthanne Bailey

Dept. WM, Fairbanks, AK 99708. (907) 452-5201.

Marina Air, Inc., 1219 Shypoke, Dept. WM, Fairbanks, AK 99709. (907) 479-5684.

Midnight Sun Adventures, 1306 E. 26th Ave., Dept. WM, Anchorage, AK 99508. (907) 277-8829.

Rainbow Riverrunners, Box 81149, Dept. WM, Fairbanks, AK 99708. (907) 470-5859.

HUNTING GUIDES & OUTFITTERS

STATEWIDE

Alaska Professional Hunters Association, Inc., Box 451-W, Talkeetna, AK 99676. (907) 733-2688.

Master Guides and Registered Guides, Alaska Department of Commerce, 3601 C St., Anchorage, AK 99503. (907) 562-2728.

SOUTHEAST REGION

Alaska Fair Chase, Box 443, Dept. WM, Thorne Bay, AK 99919 (summer) or 439 Sudden Valley, Dept. WM, Bellingham, WA 98226. (206) 676-9351 (winter).

SOUTHCENTRAL/GULF COAST REGION

Alaska Wilderness Outfitters, Gary Pahl, HC 03, Box 8422-WM, Palmer, AK 99645. (907) 745-7610.

Dick Gunlogson, Master Guide, Box 193-WM, Willow, AK 99688. (907) 495-6434.

Ellis Big Game Guides & Outfitters, Star Route A, Box 1455-WM, Slana, AK 99586. (907) 822-3426.

Exclusive Alaskan Hunts, Andy Runyan, Master Guide, HC 01, Box 1702-WM, Glennallen, AK 99588-9602. Radiophone: (907) 822-3335. Exclusive Alaskan hunts. Brown bear, blacktail deer, caribou. All hunts fair chase on Kodiak or Alaska Peninsula. Both camps are in

game refuges, Units 8 and 9.

Gary Larose Game Guide Service & Charters, Box 345, Dept. WM, Palmer, AK 99645. (907) 745-3775.

North American Outfitters, Jim Metheny, Master Guide, Box 40015-WM, Clear, AK 99704. (907) 582-2354. Big game hunting for moose, brown bear, black bear and mountain goat from camps on the North Gulf Coast at Katalla. Caribou hunting on North Slope from Aug. 5-20.

Running W Outfitters, Dennis Wade, Registered Guide, Box 1848, Dept. WM, Homer, AK 99603. (907) 235-6168.

Sugak Bush Camp, Box 32, Dept. WM, Karluk, AK 99608. (907) 241-2230.

ARCTIC REGION

Alatna Guide Service, Box 80424, Dept. WM, Fairbanks, AK 99708. (907) 479-6354.

Brooks Range Arctic Hunts, Parks Highway, Mile 329, Rt. 1, Dept. WM, Nenana, AK 99760. (907) 452-8751.

Chandalar River Outfitters, Box 74877, Fairbanks, AK 99707. (907) 488-8402.

Gates of the Arctic Lodge, Nick or Susan Jennings, 1677 Souhrada Rd., Dept. W., Delta Junction, AK 99737. (907) 895-4065. The ultimate Wilderness . . . Arctic Alaska. Fully guided adventures. Over 15 years experience. Hunting, fishing, backpacking, river float trips, wildlife photography, flightseeing, cross-country skiing. Specializing in custom trips and service throughout Alaska's Brooks Range. March-September.

INTERIOR REGION

Alaska Trophy Hunts/Mystic Lake Lodge, Box 887, Dept. WM, Palmer, AK 99645. (907) 745-3168.

Denali Hunting Adventures, Box 295, Dept. WM, Talkeetna, AK 99676. (907) 733-2681.

Kichatna Guide Service, Box 670790, Dept. WM, Chugiak, AK 99567. (907) 696-3256.

Lambert Guide Service, 1419 2nd Ave., Dept. WM, Fairbanks, AK 99701. (907) 456-6472.

LODGING

In instances where the location of a lodge is not the same as the address or cannot be determined by the name of the lodge (i.e. Shell Lake Lodge is located on Shell Lake), the general location of the lodge is given in parentheses after the phone number.

SOUTHEAST REGION

AMC-Colver Bay Floating Fishing Lodge, Box 8944, Dept. WM, Ketchikan, AK 99901. (907) 247-8555 or (907) 247-2282. (Prince of Wales Island)

Admiralty Inn, Box 32239, Dept. WM,

Juneau, AK 99803. (907) 789-3263.

Alaskan Home Fishing, Route 1, Box 807, Dept. WM, Ketchikan, AK 99901. (907) 225-6919.

Aldersheim Lodge, Box 210447, Dept. WM, Juneau, AK 99821. (907) 780-4778.

Anchor Point Lodge, Box 210064, Dept. WM, Auke Bay, AK 99821. (907) 789-4664 (summer) or 1315 S. King St., #4, Dept. WM, Honolulu, HI 96814. (808) 537-9312 (winter).

Baranof Wilderness Lodge, Box 210022, Dept. WM, Auke Bay, AK 99821. (907) 586-8110.

Bear Creek Camp and Hostel, Box 1158, Dept. WM, Haines, AK 99827. (907) 766-2259.

Beyond Goode River, Box 37, Dept. WM, Gustavus, AK 99826. (907) 697-2241.

Blueberry Lodge, 9436 N. Douglas Highway, Dept. WM, Juneau, AK 99801. (907) 463-5886 or (907) 789-0716.

Chinook Wilderness Lodge, Box 239, Dept. WM, Gustavus, AK 99826. (907) 697-2314.

Coffman Cove Bunkhouse & Skiff Rental, 306 Harbor Ave., Dept. WM, Coffman Cove, AK 99950. (907) 329-2219 or (907) 329-2247. (Prince of Wales Island)

Don's Fish Camp, Box 74, Dept. WM, Haines, AK 99827. (907) 766-2303.

Elfin Cove Sportfishing Lodge, Box 44, Dept. WM, Elfin Cove, AK 99825. (907) 239-2212 (summer) or Box 4007, Dept. WM, Renton, WA 98057. (800) 422-2824.

Fishin' Lodge, Box 205, Dept. WM, Haines, AK 99827. (907) 766-2375.

Fort Seward Lodge and Restaurant, Box 307, Dept. WM, Haines, AK 99827. (907) 766-2009.

Glacier Bay Country Inn, Box 5WMP, Gustavus, AK 99826. (907) 697-2288. Secluded retreat offers the chance to really experience Alaskan country living — away from the crowds and in a wilderness setting. Enjoy home-baked breads, garden-fresh produce, local seafoods. Private baths. Glacier Bay boat/plane tours, fishing charters.

Glacier Bay Lodge, 523 Pine St., Suite 203-WM, Seattle, WA 98101. (800) 622-2042.

Gold Coast Lodge, Box 9629, Dept. WM, Ketchikan, AK 99901. (907) 225-8375. (Prince of Wales Island)

Gustavus Inn, Box 60, Dept. WM, Gustavus, AK 99826. (907) 697-2254.

Harris River Wilderness Cabins, Box 153, Dept. WM, Craig, AK 99921.

Hidden Inlet Lodge, Box 3047, Dept. WM, Ketchikan, AK 99901. (907) 225-4656 or (907) 225-5155. (Misty Fjords)

Hotel Halsingland, P.O. Box 1589-WM,

Haines, AK 99827. (907) 766-2000. *See display ad, page 460.*

Karta Inn, Box 71, Dept. WM, Craig, AK 99921.

Leonard's Landing Lodge, Leonard Wittwer, Box 282, Dept. WM, Yakutat, AK 99689. (907) 784-3245.

Lisianski Lodge, Box 776, Dept. WM, Pelican, AK 99832. (907) 735-2266.

Louie's Place, Box 020704, Dept. WM, Juneau, AK 99802. (907) 586-2032 or (907) 230-2222. (Elfin Cove)

McFarland's Floatel, Box 159, Dept. WM, Thorne Bay, AK 99919. (907) 828-3335.

Meyers Chuck Lodge, Box 6141-WMP, Ketchikan, AK 99901. (907) 225-4608. Beachfront lodge in one of Southeast's best-known fishing hot spots. Accommodates up to 8 guests. Private rooms with baths. Restaurant and bar. Fishing package includes all meals and saltwater fishing gear.

Misty Fjords Resort, 1600 International Airport, Dept. WM, Ketchikan, AK 99901. (907) 225-6608 or (907) 225-6600.

Prince of Wales Lodge, Box 72-AWM, Klawock, AK 99925. (907) 755-2227. Fishing lodge, hotel and restaurant in a friendly village 80 air miles from Ketchikan. Car and boat rentals, guided fishing packages. Credit cards accepted. Brochure available upon request.

Puffin, The, Box 3-WM, Gustavus, AK 99826. (907) 697-2260. *See display ad, page 460.*

Rockwell Lighthouse, Box 277, Dept. WM, Sitka, AK 99835. (907) 747-3056.

Salmon Falls Resort, Box 5420, Dept. WM, Ketchikan, AK 99901. (907) 225-2752 or (800) 247-9059.

Salmon River Rentals, Box 13, Dept. WM, Gustavus, AK 99826. (907) 697-2245.

Silverking Lodge, Box 8331, Dept. WM, Ketchikan, AK 99901. (907) 225-1900 or (907) 225-3655.

Sitka Total Vacations, Box 2487, Dept. WM, Sitka, AK 99835. (907) 747-6562 or (907) 747-5460.

Snyder Mercantile Company, Box 505, Dept. WM, Tenakee Springs, AK 99841. (907) 736-2205.

Tanaku Lodge, Box 49, Dept. WM, Elfin Cove, AK 99825. (907) 239-2205 (summer) or 1060 Old Salem Rd., NE, Dept. WM, Albany, OR 97321. (503) 928-4868. (winter).

Unuk River Post, Box 5065, Dept. WM, Ketchikan, AK 99901. (907) 225-5054.

W.T. Fugarwe Inc., P.O. Box 27-WM, Gustavus, AK 99826. (907) 697-2244. (winter)

459

P.O. Box 459, Georgetown, CO 80444. (303) 623-7108 or 569-2255. Located at the gateway to Glacier Bay National Park. Offering flightseeing, trophy fishing, home-cooked family meals. Open June 1 to Sept. 15. *See display ad, page 455.*

Warm Springs Lodge, 9720 Trappers Lane, Dept. WM, Juneau, AK 99801. (907) 789-5070.

Waterfall Resort, Waterfall Communications, Dept. WM, Santa Barbara, CA 93101. (907) 225-9461 or (800) 544-5125.

Yes Bay Lodge, Dept. WM, Yes Bay via Ketchikan, AK 99950. (907) 247-1575.

SOUTHCENTRAL/GULF COAST REGION

ANCHORAGE/MAT-SU

Alaska's Little Susitna Lodge, Box 6783, Dept. WM, Anchorage, AK 99502. (907) 243-

3556. (Little Susitna River)

Anchorage Eagle Nest Hotel, 4110 Spenard Road, Dept. WM, Anchorage, AK 99517. (907) 243-3433. Fax (907) 248-9258. *See display ad, page 462.*

Barony Lodge, 7400 Upper DeArmoun Rd., Dept. WM, Anchorage, AK 99516. (907) 345-7291. (Skwentna)

Deshka Silver-King Lodge, Box 1037, Dept. WM, Willow, AK 99688. (907) 733-2055.

King Point Lodge, Box 241604, Dept. WM, Anchorage, AK 99524. (907) 248-7447 or 1-800-327-2570. (Lake Creek)

Lake Creek Lodge, Box 92696, Dept. WM, Anchorage, AK 99509. (907) 248-3530.

Lake Shore Motel, 3009 Lakeshore Dr., Dept. WM, Anchorage, AK 99517 or P.O. Box 92696, Anchorage, AK 99509. (907) 248-3485. Anchorage's newest motel. Located near the shores of Lake Hood. Free airport shuttle, economy rates. Overnight units; kitchenettes; deluxe suites with full kitchens; fish freezers. MC/VISA/Diners.

Martana Enterprises, Box 141345, Dept. WM, Anchorage, AK 99514. (907) 333-7692. (65 miles NW of Anchorage)

Mother Goose Lodge, Donkey Lake East, Dept. WM, Skwentna, AK 99667. (907) 268-1168.

Northwoods Lodge, Box 770722, Dept. WM, Eagle River, AK 99577. (907) 694-9734. (Lake Creek)

Riversong Lodge, 2463 Cottonwood St., Dept. WM, Anchorage, AK 99508. (907) 274-2710 or General Delivery, Dept. WM, Skwentna, AK 99667. (907) 733-2931. Fly-in lodge 60 miles NW of Anchorage. Open year-

round. Family-style meals, fresh breads and pastries baked daily. Excellent fishing, cross-country skiing. *See display ad, page 462.*

Salmon-Run Lodge, General Delivery, Dept. WM, Skwentna, AK 99667. (907) 733-2816. (Yentna River)

Sheep Mountain Lodge, SRC Box 8490, Dept. WM, Palmer, AK 99645. (907) 745-5121. Home-cooked meals, bar, liquor store, Alaskan gifts, cozy log cabins and camp-sites, showers, RV hookups, hot tub, sauna, gasoline. Telescope to view Dall sheep. Good hiking, rock and fossil hunting. Cross-country ski trails. Airstrip available. Open year-round. *See display ad, page 462.*

Shell Lake Lodge, P.O. Box 28-WM, Skwentna, AK 99667. (907) 733-2817. *See display ad, page 462.*

Silvertip Lodges, Box 190389, Dept. WM, Anchorage, AK 99519. (907) 248-0149. (Talachulitna River)

Skwentna Roadhouse, 100 Happiness Lane, Dept. WM, Skwentna, AK 99667. (907) 733-2722.

Talachulitna River Lodge, Box 220144, Dept. WM, Anchorage, AK 99522. (907) 243-2971.

Talaview Lodge, Box 49, Dept. WM, Skwentna, AK 99667. (907) 345-3215 or (907) 268-1720. (Talachulitna River)

Wilderness Place Lodge, Box 190711, Dept. WM, Anchorage, AK 99511. (907) 248-4337. (Lake Creek)

COPPER RIVER/WRANGELL-ST. ELIAS

Chistochina Lodges & Trading Post, Dept. WM, Mile 32.8 Tok-Slana Highway via Gakona, AK 99586. (907) 822-3366. *See display ad, page 463.*

Copper Lake Fish Camp, SRA Box 1320-WM, Slana, AK 99586. (907) 822-3313. Wilderness cabins located on Copper Lake in Wrangell mountains. Year-round service; bring sleeping bags and food. Offers photography, excellent lake trout, grayling and Kokanee salmon. Winter snowmobiling, ice fishing. Air taxi, boats, motors available.

Evergreen Lodge at Lake Louise, Ed and Shelley Peck; Jack and Jan Hansen. HC 01, Box 1709-WMP, Glennallen, AK 99588. (907) 822-3250. Private log cabins or rooms with private bath. Home-cooked, family-style meals. Fishing, cross-country skiing, snowmobiling. Aviation gas. A comfortable, relaxing place for a weekend getaway or a stopover en route. Year-round. *See display ad, page 472.*

Lake Louise—Wolverine Lodge, HC 01, Box 1704-WM, Glennallen, AK 99588. (907) 822-3988. Lake trout, burbot fishing. Family-

owned and operated lodge on beautiful Lake Louise. A great place to bring family and friends. Open year-round. Cocktail lounge, restaurant, rooms, gas, repair shop, fishing charters, boat rentals.

Kennicott Glacier Lodge, Box 103940, Dept. WM, Anchorage, AK 99510. (907) 258-2350. (Wrangell St. Elias National Park)

McCarthy Lodge, Dept. WM, McCarthy, AK 99588. (907) 333-5402 or (907) 376-2992.

Sportsmen's Paradise Lodge, Star Route A, Box 1320-WM, Slana, AK 99586. (907) 822-3888.

Tanada Lake Lodge, Box 258, Dept. WM, Fairbanks, AK 99707. (907) 452-1247.

Wrangell R Ranch, Dept. WM, Chisana via Tok, AK 99780. (907) 345-1160 (radiophone).

PRINCE WILLIAM SOUND

Alaska Wild Wings, Goose Cove Lodge, Belle and Pete Mickelson, P.O. Box 325-WM, Cordova, AK 99574. (907) 424-5111. Goose Cove Lodge is a wonderful place to: watch birds; study natural history; photograph wildflowers, fish, birds and mammals; fish for salmon, halibut, and trout; explore pristine beaches; and view spectacular scenery.

Anchor Inn, Box 746, Dept. WM, Whittier, AK 99693. (907) 472-2354.

Ellamar Properties, Inc., 1577 C St., Suite 236-WM, Anchorage, AK (907) 278-1311. *See display ad, page 463.*

Sportsman's Inn, Box 698, Dept. WM, Whittier, AK 99693. (907) 472-2352.

Stan Stephens Charters, Growler Island Wilderness Camp, P.O. Box 1297-WM, Valdez, AK 99686. (907) 835-4731. A true Alaskan experience as you stay in a fully set up tent camp overlooking Columbia Glacier. Fishing, hiking, rafting, canoeing. Everything furnished. *See display ad, page 453.*

KENAI PENINSULA

Fedora's Bed & Breakfast, Dept. WM, Port Graham, AK 99683. (907) 284-2239. *See display ad, page 464.*

Halibut Cove Cabins, P.O. Box 1990-WM, Homer, AK 99603. (907) 296-2214. *See display ad, page 464.*

Harmony Point Wilderness Lodge, Box 110, Dept. WM, Seldovia, AK 99663. (907) 234-7858.

Ishmalof Island Lodge, Box 6430, Dept. WM, Halibut Cove, AK 99603. (907) 296-2217.

Kachemak Bay Wilderness Lodge, P.O. Box 956-WM, China Poot Bay, Homer, AK 99603. (907) 235-8910. Deluxe log wilderness lodge, sauna, hot tub, modern bathrooms.

Private cabins. Accessible by boat. Meals include fresh local seafood. Salmon, trout and halibut fishing; wildlife viewing, photography, bird-watching, clamming, exploring, beachcombing. Guided by naturalists. $1750/5 nights. 12 guests.

Loonsong Mountain Lake Camp, Box 956, Dept. WM, Homer, AK 99603. (907) 235-8910.

Tutka Bay Lodge, via P.O. Box 960-W, Homer, AK 99603. (907) 235-3905. Outdoor enthusiasts will enjoy friendly, personalized service, beautiful accommodations, mouth-watering fresh breads and seafood, wildlife viewing, birding, hiking, fishing charters, helicopter adventures with year-round residents. Recommended by managing editor, *Gourmet Magazine*. $200 per day.

Willard's Moose Lodge, SRA Box 28, Dept. WM, Homer, AK 99603. (907) 235-8830.

KODIAK

Afognak Wilderness Lodge, Dept. WM, Seal Bay, AK 99697, (907) 486-6442. *See display ad, this page.*

Munsey's Bear Camp, Dept. WM, Amook Pass, Kodiak, AK 99615. (907) 847-2203.

Olga Bay Lodge, Inc., 321 Maple, Dept. WM, Kodiak, AK 99615. (907) 486-5373.

Pleasant Harbor Lodge, Box 8049, Dept. WM, Kodiak, AK 99615. (907) 486-6526.

Shuyak Island State Park, SR Box 3800-WM, Kodiak, AK 99615. (907) 486-6339. *See display ad, page 465.*

Silver Salmon Lodge, Box 378, Dept. WM, Kodiak, AK 99615. (907) 486-5563.

WESTERN COOK INLET

Alaska's Wilderness Lodge, 1 Lang Rd, Dept. WM, Port Alsworth, AK 99653. (907) 781-2223. (Lake Clark)

Big Mountain Lodge, 14940 Longbow Dr., Dept. WM, Anchorage, AK 99516. (907) 345-2459. (Kvichak River)

Chenik Wilderness Camp, Box 956, Dept. WM, Homer, AK 99603. (907) 235-8910. (McNeil River)

Copper River Lodge, Box 200831, Dept. WM, Anchorage, AK 99520. (907) 346-2924.

Haeg's Wilderness Home, Chinitna Bay, Box 338, Dept. WM, Soldotna, AK 99669. (Lake Clark)

Iliamna Lake Resort, P.O. Box 103984-WM, Anchorage, AK 99510. (907) 276-5595. Finest trophy fishing resort. Rainbows, sheefish, 5 kinds of salmon and total 12 kinds of fish during June 15-Sept. 30 season. Fly-in boat fishing. Newest, largest, luxurious, 24 guests. Lounge, dining room, tackle shop. Telex: 26413. *See display ad, page 457.*

Koksetna Lodge, Dept. WM, Port Alsworth, AK 99653. (907) 781-2227. Located in Lake Clark National Park and Preserve for a wilderness experience you will always treasure. Hiking, boating, wildlife and bird observation, photography and quiet. *See display ad, page 465.*

Lake Clark Air Service, The Farm Lodge, Dept. WM, Port Alsworth, AK 99563. (907) 781-2211. *See display ad, page 445.*

Lake Country Lodge, HC-2, Box 852, Soldotna, AK 99669 (907) 283-9432. (Lake Clark)

Lakeside Lodge, 5 Airstrip Dr., Dept. WM, Port Alsworth, AK 99653. (907) 781-2202 (summer) or Box 1047-WM, Soldotna, AK 99669. (907) 262-5245 (winter).

Newhalen Lodge, Box 009-WM, Nondalton, AK 99640. (907) 294-2233 (summer) or Box 102521-WM, Anchorage, AK 99510. (907) 279-4236 (winter).

Pedro Bay Lodge and Halibut Camp, Box 47015-WM, Pedro Bay, AK 99647. (907) 850-2232. *See display ad, page 456.*

Silver Salmon Creek Lodge, Box 3234, Dept. WM, Soldotna, AK 99669. (907) 262-4839. (Lake Clark National Park)

Todd's Igiugig Lodge, P.O. Box 871395-WM, Wasilla, AK 99687. (907) 376-2859. *See display ad, page 458.*

Valhalla Lodge, Box 190583, Dept. WM, Anchorage, AK 99519. (907) 276-3569.

ALASKA PENINSULA/ALEUTIANS REGION

Alaska Rainbow Lodge, Box 190166, Dept. WM, Anchorage, AK 99510. (907) 287-3059 (summer) or Box 10459, Dept. WM, Fort Worth, TX 76114. (817) 236-1002 (winter).

"Angler's Paradise" Lodges, Katmailand, Inc., 4700 Aircraft Dr., WM, Anchorage, AK 99502. (907) 243-5448 or 1-800-544-0551. Kulik Lodge, Alaska's premier fly-out sportfishing lodge. Grosvenor Lodge, superb sportfishing and rustic comfort. Brooks Lodge, fishing and sightseeing in Katmai National Park, Katmai-Bristol Bay float trips from Nonvianuk Camp. *See display ad, page 458.*

Chernofski Fishing Lodge, 3400 Kvichak Circle, Dept. WM, Anchorage, AK 99515. (907) 522-1323. (Unalaska)

David River Lodge, Box 193, Dept. WM, Willow, AK 99688. (907) 495-6434 or (907) 495-6625.

Katmai Lodge, Tony Sarp, Box 421-WM, King Salmon, AK 99613. Oct.-June: 2825 90th SE, Dept. WM, Everett, WA 98204. 206-337-0326. Fly-in fishing lodge located on the Alagnak River in Bristol Bay Wild Trout Area. Offers guided fishing trips for trophy rainbow and lunker salmon. Float trips. Fly-out

fishing. Accommodates 21 guests. Seminar facilities available. *See display ad, page 458.*

Painter Creek Lodge, Box 1350, Dept. WM, Palmer, AK 99645. (907) 745-3772 or (907) 745-6944.

Pavlof Services, Box 111-WM, Cold Bay, AK 99571. (907) 532-2437. *See display ad, page 467.*

Prestage's Sportfishing Lodge, Box 213, Dept. WM, King Salmon, AK 99613. (907) 246-3320.

Quinnat Landing Hotel, P.O. Box 418-WM, King Salmon, AK 99613. (907) 246-3000. *See display ad, page 458.*

Ugashik Narrows Lodge, Kay Sugimoto, P.O. Box 103984-WM, Anchorage, AK 99510.

(907) 276-5595. Most famous trophy-sized arctic grayling in Alaska. Fly or spinning, fly-out or boat fishing. Lodge is old hunting cabin. Salmon, char, trout. June 20-Sept. 30 season. Combination fishing available with Iliamna Lake Resort. Telex 26413 AFR ILR. *See display ad, page 466.*

Wildman Lake Lodge, 3646 Point Dr., Dept. WM, Anchorage, AK 99515. (907) 243-5087 or (907) 243-0535.

Wood-Z Lodge, Box 196, Dept. WM, King Salmon, AK 99613. (907) 246-3449.

BERING SEA COAST REGION

Aleknagik Mission Lodge, Box 165, Dept. WM, Aleknagik, AK 99555. (907) 842-2250. (summer) or 200 W. 34th St., Suite 908-WM, Anchorage, AK 99503. (907) 349-2753. (winter)

Bristol Bay Lodge, P.O. Box 1509-M, Dillingham, AK 99576. (907) 842-2500. (June-Sept.) Rt. 1, Box 580-M, Ellensburg, WA 98926. (509) 964-2094. (Oct.-May). One of Alaska's oldest fly-out lodges located in the Wood-Tikchik region overlooking Lake Aleknagik. Fishing for trout, grayling, Dolly Varden, pike and salmon. Open June 1 to Sept. 30.

Bristol Inn, The, P.O. Box 330-M, Dillingham, AK 99576. (907) 842-2240. Gateway to the world-class Bristol Bay fishery. 30 rooms with private baths, cable TV and in-room phones. Also features restaurant and lounge with banquet facilities. *See display ad, page 467.*

Camp Bendeleben, Box 1045, Dept. WM, Nome, AK 99762. (907) 443-2880.

Crystal Creek Lodge, Box 3049, Dept. WM, Dillingham, AK 99576. (907) 842-2646 (summer) or 3819 E. LaSalle, Dept. WM, Phoenix, AZ 85040. (602) 8780 (winter).

Maurice's Floating Lodge, Box 1261, Dept.

WM, Dillingham, AK 99576. (907) 235-8885 (summer) or 35-25 Crescent St., Dept. WM, Queens, NY 11106. (718) 361-0326 (winter).

Royal Coachman Lodge, Box 1887, Dept. WM, Anchorage, AK 99510. (907) 346-2595.

Tikchik Narrows Lodge, Box 220248, Dept. WM, Anchorage, AK 99522. (907) 243-8450. (Wood River-Tikchik Lakes State Park)

Wood River Lodge, 4437 Stanford Dr., Dept. WM, Fairbanks, AK 99709. (907) 479-0308.

ARCTIC REGION

Coldfoot Services & Arctic Acres Inn, Mile 175 Dalton Highway, Dept. WM, Coldfoot, AK 99701. (907) 678-5201. Fax 678-5202. Complete highway accessible facilities close to Gates of the Arctic National Park and Preserve. Meals, lodging, lounge, fuels, RV hookups. Aviation gas. State maintains 3,500-foot airstrip 1 mile west. Hosts: Dick and Cathy Mackey. *See display ad, page 468.*

Golden Plover Guiding, Colville Village, Pouch 340109-WM, Prudhoe Bay, AK 99734. (907) 659-3503. *See display ad, page 445.*

Iniakuk Lake Lodge, P.O. Box 80424-WM, Fairbanks, AK 99708. (907) 479-6354. Near the Gates of the Arctic and Arrigetch Peaks. Open June through September. Complete guiding and outfitting services. Excellent cuisine. Fully equipped conference room. Remote lodge and cabins available inside the Gates. *See display ad, page 468.*

Midnight Sun Lodge, 1306 E. 26th Ave., Dept. WM, Anchorage, AK 99508. (907) 277-8829. (Wulik River)

Nullagvik Hotel, P.O. Box 336-WM, Kotzebue, AK 99752. (907) 442-3331. *See display ad, page 468.*

Peace of Selby Cabins, Box 46, Dept. WM, Manley Hot Springs, AK 99756. (907) 672-3206. (Gates of the Arctic National Park)

Takahula Lake Bed and Breakfast, 4683 Chena Small Tracks Rd., Dept. WM, Fairbanks, AK 99709. (907) 479-4737. (Gates of the Arctic National Park)

INTERIOR REGION

Alaska's 7 Gables Bed & Breakfast, P.O. Box 80488-WM, Fairbanks, AK 99708. (907) 479-0751. *See display ad, page 469.*

Black Spruce Lodge, 2740 Old Richardson Highway, Dept. WM, Delta Junction, AK 99737. (907) 895-4668. (Quartz Lake)

Camp Denali, Box 67, Dept. WM, Denali National Park, AK 99755. (907) 683-2290 (summer) or Box 216-WM, Cornish, NH 03746. (603) 675-2248 (winter).

Commack Lodge & Store, Box 195, Dept. WM, Fort Yukon, AK 99740.

Denali Mountain Lodge, Box 229, Denali National Park, AK 99755. (907) 683-2643 (summer) or 200 W. 34th Ave., #362-WM, Anchorage, AK 99503. (907) 258-0134 (winter).

Denali West Lodge, Dept. WM, Lake Minchumina, AK 99757. (907) 733-2630.

Kantishna Roadhouse, Box 130, Dept. WM, Denali National Park, AK 99755. (907) 733-2535 or (907) 683-2710.

Lost Creek Ranch, Box 84334, Dept. WM, Fairbanks, AK 99708.

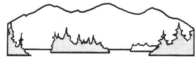

Alaska's
Ugashik Narrows Lodge

Alaska Frontier Resorts, Inc., now offers, in addition to Iliamna Lake Resort, **Ugashik Narrows Lodge,** the home of trophy grayling and arctic char fishing. Arrangements can be made for a portion of your stay to be at this rustic lodge which is in the center of the Alaska Peninsula Wildlife Refuge.

The fishing is truly on the back porch, as five species of salmon and resident grayling, arctic char and lake trout pass from Lower to Upper Ugashik Lakes.

Ugashik Narrows has been the gathering place of hunters and fishermen for over 1,000 years. Traces of this are located on the land adjoining the lodge. Indians, Aleuts, and Eskimos gathered here in times past, but now only the sounds of the fish jumping and the wildlife calling break the serenity of the Narrows.

Fishing Guide

Species	June 1 2 3 4	July 1 2 3 4	August 1 2 3 4	September 1 2 3 4	October 1 2 3 4
*Rainbow Trout	● ● ✱	✱ ✱ ✱ ✱	✱ ✱ ✱ ✱	✱ ● ● ●	● ●
Arctic Grayling	● ● ●	✱ ✱ ✱ ✱	✱ ✱ ✱ ✱	✱ ● ● ●	● ●
Arctic Char	✱ ✱ ✱	✱ ✱ ✱ ✱	✱ ✱ ✱ ✱	✱ ● ● ●	● ● ●
Lake Trout	✱ ✱ ✱	✱ ✱ ✱ ✱	✱ ✱ ✱ ✱	✱ ✱ ✱ ✱	✱ ✱
*Northern Pike	✱ ✱ ✱	✱ ● ●	● ✱ ✱ ✱	✱ ✱ ✱ ✱	✱ ✱
*King Salmon	✱ ✱	● ● ● ✱	✱		
Sockeye Salmon		✱ ● ●	● ● ● ●	✱ ✱ ✱	
Pink Salmon		✱ ✱	✱ ● ● ✱	✱ ✱	
*Chum Salmon	✱ ✱	✱ ✱ ✱ ✱	✱ ✱ ✱		
Silver Salmon			✱ ✱	● ● ● ✱	✱

● PEAK SEASON   ✱ AVAILABLE

* Rainbow, King Salmon, Northern Pike and Chum Salmon are available by fly-out only.

Come join us for the real Alaskan experience with rustic accommodations; catch fish before breakfast, and enjoy the seclusion offered by our location.

Let your booking agent know that you would like to spend a couple of days at Ugashik during your **Alaskan Fishing Experience.** Air fare between Iliamna and Ugashik will be arranged at additional cost.

For reservations or information write or call:
P.O. Box 101068, Anchorage, Alaska 99510 U.S.A.
Telephone: (907) 272-9401
Telex: 090 26413 AFR ILR AHG   **Fax: (907) 272-0251**

Manley Hot Springs Resort, Box 28-WM, Manley Hot Springs, AK 99756. (907) 672-3611. Open year-round. Natural hot mineral pool. Rooms with bath, log cabins, restaurant, bar, laundromat, showers, gas, diesel, canoe rentals. River tours, gold mine tours (summer) or Iditarod Kennel tours. Cross-country dogsled rides (winter). *See display ad, page 470.*

Manley Roadhouse/Manley Trading Post, Dept. WM, Manley Hot Springs, AK 99756. (907) 672-3161/672-3221. *See display ad, page 469.*

Melozi Hot Springs Lodge, Box 520801, Dept. WM, Big Lake, AK 99652. (907) 892-8381

New Sourdough Hotel, Arnold and Corky Stewart, P.O. Box 109-WM, Fort Yukon, AK 99740. (907) 662-2402. *See display ad, page 470.*

R & L's Anvik River Lodge, General Delivery, Dept. WM, Anvik, AK 99668. (907) 262-6324 or (907) 462-3307.

Ruby Roadhouse, Box 149, Dept. WM, Ruby, AK 99768. (907) 468-4463.

Takusko House, Tom Sheets, P.O. Box 11-WM, McGrath, AK 99627. (907) 524-3198. *See display ad, page 469.*

Tolovana Lodge, Box 281, Dept. WM, Nenana, AK 99760. (907) 832-5569. (Minto Flats/Tanana River)

OUTDOOR EQUIPMENT RENTAL & SALES

SOUTHEAST REGION

Alaska Discovery Kayak Rentals, Box 26, Dept. WM, Gustavus, AK 99826. (907) 697-2257.

Baidarka Boats, Box 6001, Dept. WM, Sitka, AK 99835. (907) 747-8996.

Glacier Bay Sea Kayaks, Box 26, Dept. WM, Gustavus, AK 99826. (907) 697-2257.

People Power Bicycle/Sports, 1719 Tongass, Dept. WM, Ketchikan, AK 99901. (907) 225-2488.

Thomas Basin Boat Rentals & Fishing Excursions, Box 6413, Dept. WM, Ketchikan, AK 99901. (907) 225-1989.

SOUTHCENTRAL/GULF COAST REGION

Alaska Mountaineering & Hiking, 2633 Spenard Rd., Dept. WM, Anchorage, AK 99503. (907) 272-1811.

Alaska Sports Rental, 300 W. 36th Ave., Dept. WM, Anchorage, AK 99503. (907) 562-2208.

Alaska Treks 'n Voyages, Box 625-WM,

Seward, AK 99664. (907) 224-3960.

Alaska Wildwaters, 12640 Saunders Rd., Dept. WM, Anchorage, AK 99516. (907) 345-4308.

Backcountry Sports, 1314 Mill Bay Rd., Dept. WM, Kodiak, AK 99615. (907) 486-3771.

Quiet Sports, 144 W. Pioneer, Box 874-WM, Homer, AK 99603. (907) 235-8620.

Recreational Equipment Inc. (REI), 1200 W. Northern Lights, Dept. WM, Anchorage, AK 99503. (907) 272-4565.

Rental Room, The, 5905 Lake Otis Pkwy., Dept. WM, Anchorage, AK 99507. (907) 563-4034 or (907) 472-2452 in Whittier.

Rent A Raft, Recreational Services, Box

PAVLOF SERVICES
AT
COLD BAY, ALASKA

Hunting
Fishing
Restaurant
Bar
Hotel
Groceries

Open Year-Round

Box 111
Cold Bay,
Alaska 99571

(907) 532-2437

THE BRISTOL INN
Dillingham's Finest Hotel

Featuring: 30 Rooms — Private Baths
Cable TV • In-room Phones

... and the services of

The CANNERY
Restaurant and Lounge
Banquet Facilities

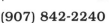

(907) 842-2240
Box 330, Dillingham, Alaska 99576

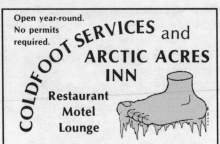

1112, Dept. WM, Palmer, AK 99645. (907) 745-2447.

Sound Inflatables, 4530 E. 7th Ave., Dept. WM, Anchorage, AK 99508. (907) 333-9043.

South Central Sports, 1411 Lakeshore Dr., Dept. WM, Homer, AK 99603. (907) 235-5403.

Tippecanoe Rentals, Box 1175, Dept. WM, Willow, AK 99688. (907) 495-6688.

Whisky Ridge Trading Company, Box 911, Dept. WM, Cordova, AK 99574. (907) 424-3354.

Wilderness Way, Box 298, Dept. WM, Soldotna, AK 99669. (907) 262-3880.

INTERIOR REGION

Backcountry Logistical Services, Box 82265, Dept. WM, Fairbanks, AK 99708. (907) 457-7606.

Canoe Alaska, 1738 Hilton Ave., Dept. WM, Fairbanks, AK 99708. (907) 479-5183.

Independent Rentals, Inc. 2020 S. Cushman, Dept. WM, Fairbanks, AK 99701. (907) 456-6595. *See display ad, page 471.*

Quartz Lake Boat Rentals, 2740 Old Richardson Highway, Dept. WM, Delta Junction, AK 99737. (907) 895-4668.

SERVICES—OTHER

STATEWIDE

Alaska Division of Tourism, Box E, Juneau, AK 99811. (907) 465-2010.

Alaska Grocery Shippers, P.O. Box 200246-WM, Anchorage, AK 99520. (907) 276-1656. *See display ad, page 471.*

All Ways Travel, 302 G St., Dept. WM, Anchorage, AK 99501. (907) 276-3644. *See display ad, page 471.*

Sanctuary Travel Services, Inc., 3701 E. Tudor Rd., Dept. WM, Anchorage, AK 99507. (800) 247-3149 or (907) 561-1212. A full service, professional agency. We donate most of our profits to nonprofit organizations chosen by our clients. Support a specific environmental group or project at no extra cost. Help us keep Alaska beautiful!

SOUTHEAST REGION

Haines Visitor Center, Box 518-WM, Haines, AK 99827. (907) 766-2202.

Juneau Visitor Center, 134 3rd St., Dept. WM, Juneau, AK 99801. (907) 586-2201.

Ketchikan Information Center, 131 Front St., Dept. WM, Ketchikan, AK 99901. (907) 225-6166.

Petersburg Visitor Center, Box 649, Dept. WM, Petersburg, AK 99833.

Sitka Convention & Visitors Bureau, Box 1226, Dept. WM, Sitka, AK 99835. (907) 747-5940.

Skagway Visitor Bureau, Box 415, Dept. WM, Skagway, AK 99840. (907) 983-2854.

Southeast Alaska Tourism Council, Box 20710, Dept. WM, Juneau, AK 99802. (907) 586-4777.

Wrangell Visitor Bureau, Box 1078, Dept. WM, Wrangell, AK 99929. (907) 874-3800.

SOUTHCENTRAL/GULF COAST REGION

Alaska Public Lands Info Center, 605 W. 4th Ave., Suite 105-WM, Anchorage, AK 99501. (907) 271-2737.

Anchorage Convention & Visitors Bureau, 1600 A St., Dept. WM, Anchorage, AK 99501. (907) 276-4118.

Cordova Visitor Center, Box 99, Dept. WM, Cordova, AK 99574. (907) 424-7260.

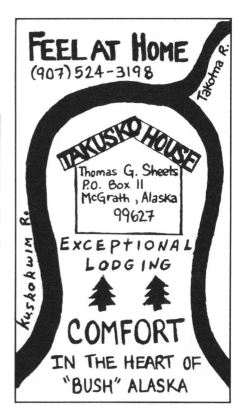

Homer Visitor Center, Box 541, Dept. WM, Homer, AK 99603. (907) 235-7740.

Kodiak Island Convention & Visitors Bureau, 100 Marine Way, Dept. WM, Kodiak, AK 99615. (907) 486-4782. *See display ad, page 472.*

Matanuska-Susitna Visitors Bureau, HC 01, Box 6616J21-WM, Palmer, AK 99645. (907) 746-5000 or 746-5002.

Prince William Sound Tourism Coalition, Box 1477, Dept. WM, Valdez, AK 99686. (907) 424-7260, (907) 835-2984 or (907) 472-2379.

Seldovia Visitor Center, Drawer M, Dept. WM, Seldovia, AK 99663. (907) 234-7816.

Seward Visitor Center, Box 749, Dept. WM, Seward, AK 99664. (907) 224-3094.

Valdez Convention & Visitors Bureau, Box 1603, Dept. WM, Valdez, AK 99686. (907) 835-2984.

Whittier Visitor Center, Box 608, Dept. WM, Whittier, AK 99693.

BERING SEA COAST REGION

Bethel Visitor Center, Box 388, Dept. WM, Bethel, AK 99559. (907) 543-2798.

Nome Convention & Visitors Bureau, Box 251, Dept. WM, Nome, AK 99762. (907) 443-5535.

ARCTIC REGION

Coldfoot Services and Arctic Acres Inn, Mile 175 Dalton Highway, Dept. WM, Coldfoot, AK 99601. (907) 678-5201. *See display ad, page 468.*

INTERIOR REGION

Alaska Public Lands Info Center, 250 Cushman, Suite 1A, Fairbanks, AK 99701. (907) 451-7352.

Alaska Public Lands Info Center, Box 359, Tok, AK 99780. (907) 883-5666.

All Star Rent-A-Car, P.O. Box 83970-WM, Fairbanks, AK 99708. (907) 479-4229. *See display ad, page 472.*

Clem's Backpacking Sports, 315 Wendell, Fairbanks, AK 99701. (907) 456-6314.

Fairbanks Visitors Center, 550 1st Ave., Fairbanks, AK 99701. (907) 456-5774.

H.C. Company Store, P.O. Box 1-WM, Circle, AK 99733. (907) 773-1222. *See display ad, page 472.*

Yukon Trading Post, Dan & Virginia Pearson, Dept. WM, Circle, AK 99733. (907) 773-1217. Free campground, good water, rooms with showers, laundromat, cafe with good home cooking, saloon, ice, liquor store, general store, post office, Chevron gas and oil, aviation gas, propane, tire repair, hunting and fishing licenses, gifts and souvenirs. Open year-round.

WINTER SPORTS

SOUTHEAST REGION

Eaglecrest Ski Area, 155 S. Seward St., Dept. WM, Juneau, AK 99801. (907) 586-5284.

Telemark Line, The, Box 491, Dept. WM, Haines, AK 99827. (907) 766-2876.

SOUTHCENTRAL/GULF COAST REGION

Alpenglow at Arctic Valley, Box 112311, Dept. WM, Anchorage, AK 99511. (907) 522-3645.

Alyeska Ski Resort, Box 249, Dept. WM, Girdwood, AK 99587. (907) 783-2222.

Chugach Express Dog Sled Tours, Box 261, Dept. WM, Girdwood, AK 99587. (907) 783-2266.

Evergreen Lodge at Lake Louise, Ed and Shelley Peck; Jack and Jan Hansen. HC 01, Box 1709-WMP, Glennallen, AK 99588. (907) 822-3250. Private log cabins or rooms with private bath. Home-cooked, family-style meals. Fishing, cross-country skiing, snowmobiling. Aviation gas. A comfortable, relaxing place for a weekend getaway or a stopover en route. Year-round. *See display ad, page 472.*

Forks Roadhouse, The, P.O. Box 13109-WM, Trapper Creek, AK 99683. (907) 268-1851. Some of the best snow machining in Alaska. Cross-country skiing. Fantastic scenery in foothills of Mt. McKinley. Lodging, home-cooked meals, bar, poolroom in historic roadhouse. Relaxed, friendly atmosphere. Mile 18.7 Petersville Road. Your hostess: Ginger Jones.

Hatcher Pass Lodge, Box 280, Dept. WM, Palmer, AK 99645. (907) 745-5897.

Mush Alaska, Box 871752, Dept. WM, Wasilla, AK 99687. (907) 376-4743.

Sheep Mountain Lodge, SRC Box 8490, Dept. WM, Palmer, AK 99645. (907) 745-5121. Excellent cross-country skiing on 20 km of groomed trails. Lighted ice skating rink, sauna, hot tub with jacuzzi. Cozy cabins, delicious home-cooked meals, well-stocked bar (featuring a wide variety of imported beers). Open year-round. *See display ad, page 462.*

Shell Lake Lodge, P.O. Box 28-WM, Skwentna, AK 99667. (907) 733-2817. *See display ad, page 462.*

Tokosha Treks, Box 13188, Dept. WM, Trapper Creek, AK 99683. (907) 733-2821.

INTERIOR

Alaska Trek Dogsledding, Box 82655, Dept. WM, Fairbanks, AK 99708. (907) 455-6326.

Real Alaska Mushing Company, The, Box 84627, Dept. WM, Fairbanks, AK 99708. (907) 455-6895.

Red Mountain Enterprises, 2175 Penrose Lane, Dept. WM, Fairbanks, AK 99709. (907) 455-6985.

INDEX

FIELD EDITOR REPORT

Some of the best travel information comes from readers — all of you who do the traveling.

If, during your travels, you find changes such as the opening of new lodging facilities or the closure of a store or other changes that will be helpful to future travelers, please give us details on the form below (or on a separate sheet of paper) and mail it to The Editor, *The ALASKA WILDERNESS MILEPOST®*, 137 East 7th Ave., Anchorage, AK 99501. We'll take note of your report when we prepare the next edition of *The ALASKA WILDERNESS MILEPOST®*.

Please feel free to elaborate — we're always anxious to hear about your travel experiences in the North Country (favorite attractions, areas that might deserve more editorial coverage, or whatever).

Have a good trip . . . and let us know how it goes!   —The Editor

On page_____ of *The ALASKA WILDERNESS MILEPOST®*, in column _____(1 or 2), we suggest that you make the following change(s):

_____

_____

_____

_____

_____

On page_____ of *The ALASKA WILDERNESS MILEPOST®*, in column _____(1 or 2), we suggest that you make the following change(s):

_____

_____

_____

_____